PUBLIC LAW

By

John F. McEldowney, LL.B., Ph.D.
Reader in Law at the University of Warwick

LONDON ● SWEET & MAXWELL ●1998

Published in 1998 by
Sweet & Maxwell Limited of
100 Avenue Road
London NW3 3PF
(http://www.smlawpub.co.uk)

First Edition 1994
Reprinted in 1995

Phototypeset by
LBJ Typesetting Ltd
of Kingsclere
Printed in England by
Clays Ltd, St. Ives plc.

A catalogue reference for this book is
available from The British Library.

ISBN 0-421-604204

To the memory of my parents

Acknowledgements

In the task of revising this edition the author is grateful to a number of people. First thanks are due to Sweet and Maxwell for their courtesy and understanding in the preparation of the second edition. At the University of Warwick, particular mention should be made to Gavin Anderson, Upendra Baxi, Hugh Beale, Lee Bridges, Roger Burridge, Chris Marsden, Judith Masson, George Mésaros, Mike McConville, Ann Stewart and Geoffrey Wilson. Also to Dominic Glover for help with the proofs. The Library staff and the staff of the Official Publications section of the Library also deserve mention for their help and kindness. Members of the Study of Parliament Group are also due my thanks. Thank you to Professor Spencer for permitting the reproduction of the court diagrams from *Jackson's Machinery of Justice* (CUP). Finally thanks to Emma and Sharron for their practical help and support during the writing of the new edition.

Preface to the Second Edition

Public law has continued to change and evolve since the publication of the first edition of this book. First, the pace of developments in domestic legislation and case law has continued with major changes to the law on public order, emergency powers, police powers, the security services and in the law on asylum and immigration, and additional privatisation legislation. Changes to local government continue, through local government re-organisation and contracting out. Judicial review has developed with significant decisions in the areas of natural justice, *locus standi* and procedure, in the law on remedies and on discretion. The rights of the citizen and the role of pressure groups have been the subject of a number of important cases. Judicial self-confidence has grown considerably and the judges have continued to develop the common law to meet new challenges—no doubt in part influenced by access to the European Court of Justice of the European Community and the European Convention on Human Rights.

Secondly, in the area of public administration important changes have taken place especially the growth in the implementation of the Next Steps agencies currently amounting to over 71 per cent of the civil service. The number of civil servants has fallen below 500,000, its lowest level since the Second World War. There is a new Civil Service Code, in effect from January 1, 1996 and a new Government Code of Practice on Access to Government Information. Deregulation legislation and the creation of a Deregulation Unit to reduce the burden of regulation on industry and commerce have important implications for administration. The functions and role of public inquiries has been highlighted, amidst much publicity by Sir Richard Scott's report on *The Export of Defence and Dual-use Goods to Iraq and Related Prosecutions* (H.C. 115 1995/6).

Thirdly, in the area of Parliament and its procedures, the Jopling Report on parliamentary procedure published in 1992 has taken effect in the day to day business of the House of Commons. Concerns about parliamentary standards are a recurring theme reflected in a number of new developments. The setting up of the Nolan Committee on *Standards in Public Life* and the newly formed House of Commons Public Service Committee (H.C. 313 1995/6) are important events in the development of structures setting parliamentary standards. There is also the newly created Parliamentary Commissioner for Standards answerable to the House of Commons Committee on Standards and

Privileges. Changes to the budgetary process through proposals for the introduction of resource accounting have important implications for Parliament. The Private Finance Initiative is an important innovation in capital spending between public and private sectors.

Fourthly, in the European Union through the development of the single market since 1993 and post Maastricht, there are controversial proposals for the introduction of a single currency from 1999.

The significance of all these developments has led to some modifications to the text since the first edition. There has also been some updating and revision of the text with the inclusion of new material. The introduction of diagrams on the structure of the courts and the re-organisation of some of the chapters is to assist with clarity.

The aims of the second edition remain the same as the first edition. The absence of a written constitution for the United Kingdom makes the task of explanation a formidable one. However, it remains the objective of the book to provide an explanation of the complex nature of public law in the United Kingdom. The changing pace of practices and ideas that public law encompasses remains a considerable challenge. The student of public law in Britain is requried to understand the wider social, political and cultural context of public law. The book is written in the belief that the study of not only the main institutions, the courts, Parliament and executive, but also the working practices and understandings, the informal, the explicit and implicit is essential to the study of public law. There are often contradictory and confusing principles that the law student must confront and a wide range of disciplines must be examined to understand how the values and constraints of law apply. It is important to see the ebbs and flows in the nature of public law, particularly in relation to the government and politics of this country. The trends are clear: the transformation of the public sector into various contractual relationships; the development of regulatory structures for the privatised utilities; the growth in the stakeholder economy; and increasing centralisation including increasing central government controls over local government, all impact on law, the citizen and democracy.

The law is as stated on May 2, 1997.

John McEldowney
May 2, 1997

CONTENTS

Part I: An Introduction to Public Law

CHAPTER 1

AN INTRODUCTION TO THE CONSTITUTION OF THE UNITED KINGDOM

Part II: Public Law, Politics, Ideas and Influences

CHAPTER 6
THE ELECTORATE, POLITICS AND THE CONSTITUTION

CHAPTER 7
PUBLIC LAW AND LEGAL THOUGHT

Part III
The Public Law of the United Kingdom

CHAPTER 11

PUBLIC FINANCE

CHAPTER 12

LOCAL GOVERNMENT

CHAPTER 21
CONSTITUTIONAL REFORM

TABLE OF CASES

xix

TABLE OF STATUTES

TABLE OF STATUTORY INSTRUMENTS

Part I:
An Introduction to Public Law

Chapter 1

An Introduction to the Constitution of the United Kingdom

1. Introduction

The public law of the United Kingdom is defined by the prevailing **1–01** constitutional order, the Government and the various institutions of the State, the rights of the citizen and membership of the European Union. Local Government exists under a unitary state. Administrative law exerts a dominant influence. There is a vast array of administrative agencies. The newly privatised utilities have their own statutory framework including a regulatory structure specific to each industry. A wide plethora of administrative tribunals and inquiries provide administrative procedures and redress for the citizen. The role of the courts is important as the growth in judicial review has maintained the courts pre-eminence in the development of constitutional principles.[1] Judicial self-confidence is marked by an interventionist style of review.

The inheritance of a common law tradition with an unwritten constitution provides a system of public law that is ad hoc in its development. Over the past decade the public law of the United Kingdom has come of age. Public law has its own technical rules and procedures and techniques of analysis. There is a widely drawn academic discourse from lawyers, economists and political scientists. Constitutional reform is an important theme, including reform of the composition of the House of Lords, the enactment of a modern Bill of Rights and the introduction of a written constitution. Devolution in Scotland and Wales and perhaps to the English regions is also proposed. Amidst the calls for change there is respect given to the continuity of many existing practices and institutions.

---

[1] Graham Zellick, "Government Beyond Law" (1985) *Public Law* 283.

1–02   A country's constitutional arrangements may assist in explaining the relationship between the citizen and the State.[2] A constitution helps determine how the State may exercise its powers and duties, how duties may be enforced and how the citizen may exercise rights. A constitution defines and sets out the relationship between the main organs of government which in the British context means the Crown, Cabinet, Parliament and the courts. A constitution may also influence how government may govern and may provide for accountability over government activities. A country's constitution may reflect the character of its people, their beliefs, "norms," prejudices and preferences. It may also in turn help to shape and inform attitudes to government, law and relations with other countries.

1–03   In 1993 the transitional Constitution of South Africa allowed for a five-year period to permit the drafting of a constitutional text. This is a good example of constitutional law building institutions and systems to lay the foundations of a new state. The constitution reflects on the culture of society and sets the standards to which constitutional government may aspire. The aims of these arrangements are to allow time for negotiation and reconciliation of the various political differences in South Africa. The 1993 Constitution reflected the difficulties of developing a multi-national society in the aftermath of apartheid. Such constitutional evolution is intended to avoid disruption and bloodshed. At the heart of this process is the role of the establishment of a constitutional court with jurisdiction to enforce the rights protected in the Constitution, to test the constitutionality of laws and administrative decisions and to settle disputes between the different parts of government including the power to advise on the constitutionality of any Bill and to ensure that any new constitutional text complies with the Constitutional principles enshrined under the Constitution.[3]

In modern times there is the example of the United States drafted Japanese Constitution of 1946 which has introduced into Japan western democratic principles, rights and duties which look beyond the national characteristics of the Japanese themselves. Although imposed on Japan when it was first introduced, the 1946 Constitution has been gradually accepted and generally supported.

1–04   Professor Wheare in his book, *Modern Constitutions*[4] wrote that in defining a constitution, there may exist six points of classification:

---

[2] Useful textbooks include: de Smith (Rodney Brazier, ed.), *Constitutional and Administrative Law* (6th ed., Penguin, 1989); E. C. S. Wade and A. W. Bradley, *Constitutional and Administrative Law* (11th ed., Longman, 1993). Also see generally; W. Cornish, *Law and Society in England and Wales 1750-1950* (London, 1989).

[3] See Hugh Corder, "South Africa's Transitional Constitution: Its Design and Implementation" (1996) *Public Law* 291.

[4] K. C. Wheare, *Modern Constitution* (1966), pp. 4–8. Generally on Japan as an example of a modern written constitution see Percy R. Luney, "The Constitution of Japan—the Fifth Decade" (Winter and Spring 1990) 53 *Law and Contemporary Problems* 1–201. M. Dean, *Japanese Legal System: Text and Materials* (Cavendish, 1977).

written and unwritten; rigid and flexible; supreme and subordinate; federal and unitary; separated powers and fused powers; republican and monarchical. Adopting Wheare's classifications it is at once apparent that the United Kingdom has a unitary, flexible, monarchical constitution whose powers are fused. There is some doubt about the question as to the extent to which, within fused powers, the doctrine of separation of powers may apply. Doubts exist as to how the different organs of government may operate. The most distinctive feature of the Constitution however, is that the United Kingdom, unlike other European countries, does not have in a single document, a written constitution with overriding legal force and authority.

In this chapter it is intended to explain the main principles which **1–05** define the United Kingdom's Constitution and how those principles evolved over time. The influence of Albert Venn Dicey (1835-1922),[5] the major constitutional lawyer in the nineteenth century who has informed and shaped our views of the Constitution is considered. At the outset a number of questions may be posed. In the absence of a written constitution, in the sense of a single codified document, how may the United Kingdom Constitution be defined? How does government derive its legal authority to carry out its functions? How compatible is the British view of its Constitution with membership of the European Community?

Our starting point is to examine the constitutional order within the United Kingdom and the nature of constitutional values. It is necessary to explain what a constitution is intended to achieve and how the United Kingdom's constitution may best be defined and explained. Inevitably, given the historical nature of developments it is necessary to explain how the United Kingdom was formed. So much of present-day constitutional thinking and the way our legal culture has evolved is drawn from the past. We begin by first considering some of the historical developments[6] which have helped shape our present arrangements in the Union treaties involving England, Scotland, Wales and Ireland to form the United Kingdom of Great Britain and Northern Ireland. We next consider how the creation of colonies and dominions set new legislative requirements for the British Parliament and finally how accession into the European Community has ultimately challenged some of our traditional ideas about the United Kingdom Constitution.

---

[5] A. V. Dicey, *Introduction to the Study of the Law of the Constitution* (Macmillan, 1885).
[6] See C. Munro, *Studies in Constitutional Law* (1987), p. 3; J. Jowell and D. Oliver (eds.), *The Changing Constitution* (OUP, 1994).

2. The United Kingdom: An Historical Explanation

(a) The unwritten constitution

1–06 The absence of a written constitution which sets out in a single document all the main rules which determine how the United Kingdom is governed, is the first obstacle to the study of a subject which many find elusive and perplexing. The starting point for the study of public law is to consider how the Constitution of the United Kingdom may be defined.

Constitutional lawyers approach the Constitution by pointing out that whereas there is no written constitution in the formal sense, there are a large number of written documents, statutes, cases and unwritten rules and understandings, commonly called conventions, which comprise the Constitution of the United Kingdom.

1–07 This approach provides a practical solution to the question of where the historical sources of the United Kingdom's Constitution may be found. This serves to highlight a distinctive feature of constitutional law that in the absence of a written constitution no special pre-eminence is afforded to constitutional law. Unlike countries where there is a written constitution and the term "unconstitutional" carries with it a legal meaning which may imply enforcement or consideration by some higher authority or by the courts, British lawyers do not strictly speaking define "unconstitutional" in that legal sense. The term "unconstitutional" frequently appears in common usage and may, in a parliamentary sense, imply the breach of a convention, parliamentary process, or failure to comply with the etiquette of the House of Commons. "Unconstitutional" may be contrasted with the term "illegal" which lawyers may use to denote a judgment by a court on the lawfulness of a particular activity.

1–08 In the absence of a formal written constitution, constitutional lawyers provide an historical explanation of the development of constitutional law in the United Kingdom. This historical explanation of why the United Kingdom has developed its Constitution in the way it has, does not fully address the question of why the United Kingdom uniquely among other European countries, did not enact its own written constitution in the sense explained above. This question becomes a recurring one throughout this textbook. Indeed there is a broader and more fundamental question posed and examined in detail in Chapter 7, namely the contribution of academic writing to the intellectual developments and discussion of constitutional and administrative law. This question involves discussion of what Loughlin has termed "the traditions of public law thought." Loughlin's view is that: "Unless those who work in the field are able to explain the distinctive nature of the study of public law, there seems little hope of attracting and maintaining a student's interest.'[7] There is a need therefore to provide students with sufficient discussion of the social, political and economic context of the society in which they live for them to achieve a better understanding of the nature of constitutional and administrative law.

At the outset, the absence of a written constitution may be **1–09** examined. Some reasons may be advanced such as, historically there was no revolutionary break which necessitated the writing down of a completely new basis for the authority and legitimacy of government and law.[8] A reluctance to codify, a characteristic of the common law approach to legal problems, may be detected in the eighteenth and nineteenth centuries which may have been linked to the question of drafting a written constitution. Constitutional reform may have had little support as a political demand and consequently may not have been much considered. The English common law tradition encouraged a pragmatic approach to legal change and any constitutional amendment may have been accommodated through the Parliamentary process of statutory reform, rather than major constitutional revision. Characteristically as no great discontent or dissatisfaction may have been evidenced over the years, constitution-drafting was a low priority compared to economic, social and political reforms. A preference for tinkering rather than a complete rethink favoured leaving the United Kingdom's Constitution to evolve. Finally, in the nineteenth century a sense of complacency mixed with a reverence for what appeared as ancient and historically consistent with medieval beginnings, left a sense of self-satisfaction with the distinctive attributes of the common law system which had progressed without a formal written constitution. At the beginning of the present century parliamentary government was seen as a triumph of democracy over the despotism of absolute power. No single explanation seems satisfactory, the United Kingdom's unwritten constitution remains as a legacy of the past which endures today. Our starting point is to briefly outline the legislative history of the United Kingdom of Great Britain and Northern Ireland.

(b) England

It is possible to point to a number of fundamental statutes which **1–10** created important legal principles in the early medieval relationship between the Crown, the courts and Parliament, such as the Magna

---

[7] M. Loughlin, *Public Law and Political Theory* (Oxford, 1992), pp. 1–2. Also see: Eric Evans, *The Forging of the Modern State 1783–1870* (2nd ed., Longman, 1996).

[8] See P. Craig, *Public Law and Democracy in the United Kingdom and the U.S.A.* (Oxford, 1990).

Carta 1215. Earlier history records that under William the Conqueror, England was a feudal state; all land was held of the King; the King's subjects owed allegiance; law-making was in the power of the King. Early historical records show that Parliament had its early origin in the National or Great Council, representing advisers to the King. Parliament's growth in importance began in the thirteenth century and evolved slowly. In the late seventeenth and early eighteenth centuries, statutes such as the Bill of Rights 1689 and the Act of Settlement 1700 are recognisable as having created the institutions of government which have modern day significance. We have already mentioned that no revolution occurred in Britain which necessitated a complete severance from the past causing a major rethink of how government should govern. The fact that the Civil War led to the execution of Charles I and the experiment of republican government through Parliament, created change in the position of Parliament *vis-à-vis* the Crown, but continuity prevailed, in that the institutions of government survived albeit in a different form. As Munro explained[9]:

> "The balance between Crown and Parliament which had existed at the commencement of the Long Parliament in 1640 was the same as that struck in 1660 when the new monarch came to the throne, and it was as if the last twenty years had never been."

1–11   The Bill of Rights 1689 laid the foundations of the modern constitution, because in England both the House of Lords and the last vestiges of Charles II's Parliament approved and thereby confirmed Parliament's, that is, the House of Commons' authority. The grant of various freedoms contained in the Bill of Rights is accompanied by a sanction, that of "illegality," a term which connotes both the statutory authority of the Bill of Rights and the interpretation of that authority when applied by the courts.

In Scotland, the Scottish Parliament enacted the Claim of Rights in 1689 following the English model with certain variations. In common with the English Bill of Rights, the use of proclamations to exercise powers was "declared illegal."

1–12   Equally important in constitutional history is the Act of Settlement 1700. This complemented the Bill of Rights by enacting that the Church of England was to be established by law, ensuring the independence of the Judiciary and further regulating the King's authority, such as the power to grant pardons.

No historical understanding of how the British constitution developed in its present form would be complete without an explanation of the fact that the United Kingdom was formed through a series

---

[9] Munro, *op. cit.* p. 3.

of legislative enactments. The Acts of Union with Wales, Scotland and Ireland helped to form a single entity.

(c) Wales

In the case of Wales,[10] absorption with England may be said to owe **1–13** its origins to the period of Edward I and the English domination of Wales by conquest. One of the earliest statutory enactments was the Statute of Wales 1284 which applied to only part of what is today, modern Wales. It did however settle the independence of Wales by asserting the possession of the King of England over Llewellyn the Great's principality of Wales, leaving the feudal territories of the Lords of the Marches unaffected. In 1471 a Council of Wales and the Marches was set up as an agency of the Privy Council and later in 1535 the Laws in Wales Act[11] was passed which stated that the "Lawes and Justice [were] to be ministered in Wales in like fourme as it is in this Realme." The result was an effective integration between England and Wales, with Wales divided into shires and hundreds comparable to the English equivalent. For a time Wales was administered by a separate system of courts with specific representation for Wales in Parliament. However, the Council of Wales, which survived the early changes, had an expanded role to include some English border counties, but it was abolished in 1689. In 1830 Welsh circuits were absorbed into the English Court system and the judicial system of Wales was thereby assimilated into the English system.[12]

Since 1964, there has been a Secretary of State for Wales, a position of responsibility in the Cabinet. The Welsh language is protected under the Welsh Language Act 1993. This Act provides for the appointment of a Board to encourage the use of the Welsh language in government and the courts.

(d) Scotland

In the case of Scotland, there was a distinct entity we know today as **1–14** Scotland, formed out of four kingdoms between the fifth and ninth centuries. Scotland stands apart from Wales and Northern Ireland as maintaining its own distinct independence.[13]

---

[10] Generally see Munro, *op. cit.* p. 11. Also J.A. Andrews (ed.), *Welsh Studies in Public Law* (1970).

[11] (27 Hen. 8 c. 26).

[12] For a general account of early Welsh constitutional history, see S. Keel, *Council in the Marches of Wales.* J. F. Rees, *Studies in Welsh History* (Cardiff, 1947).

[13] See *MacCormick v. Lord Advocate* [1953] S.C. 396.

The attempts by Henry VII to stabilise relations between England and Scotland through marriage of his daughter to Scotland's King James IV in 1503, came to little. Conquest was tried and failed by Henry VIII's union in 1544 and 1545, but in 1603 when Elizabeth I died, James VI of Scotland became James I of England which signified a personal, rather than a completely administrative or consitutional union. Administratively Scotland remained under a separate government from England. In 1707 the Treaty and Acts of Union formed the United Kingdom of Great Britain. Turpin explains how this union was unitary rather than federal[14]:

"In terms of these instruments the two Parliaments were superseded by a Parliament of Great Britain – 'a new Parliament for a new State' (Scottish Law Commission, Memorandum No. 32, 1975, p. 16). This was to be a unitary, not a federal state; as K. C. Wheare observes [*Federal Government* (4th ed. 1963) p. 43] there was no model of federal government in existence which might have been urged against the unitary scheme then proposed and adopted. Scottish arguments for retention of the Scottish Parliament did not prevail."

1–15   The constitutional significance of these[15] various Acts of Parliament may be clearly appreciated, but no hierarchy of Acts of Parliament exists in British constitutional law. Such examples serve to show the scope and extent of legislative intervention. Through the Acts of Union the United Kingdom was created as a legal entity. Similarly, the granting of independence to various colonies, illustrates the authority of Parliament to confer independent status on particular countries, while appearing to exercise self-restraint over future legislative enactments. This self-denying aspect of Parliament's powers

---

[14] C. Turpin, *British Government and the Constitution* (2nd ed., 1990), pp. 222–223. See A. V. Dicey and R. S. Rait, *Thoughts on the Union between England and Scotland* (1920). An excellent account may be found in C. Munro, *op. cit.* pp. 12–16. Also see D. L. Keir, *The Constitutional History of Modern Britain 1485–1937* (London, 1938); S. B. Chrimes, *English Constitutional Ideas in the 15th Century* (Blackwell, 1966).

[15] There are also a number of significant constitutional cases worthy of study: *The Case of Monopolies* (1602) 11 Co. Rep. 84b prohibited the King from dispensing with an Act of Parliament in matters of personal gain. Also see *Bates case, Att.-Gen. v. Bates* (1606) 2 State Tr. 371, and *The Case of Prohibition del Roy* (1607) 12 Co. Rep. 63 and *The Case of Proclamations* (1610) 12 Co. Rep. 74 where the judges refused the King authority to create new offences by proclamation. In the case of *Ship Money, R. v. Hampden* (1637) 3 State Tr. 825, the courts by a majority upheld the King's power to levy money *re the case of Ship Money* for funds to pay for ships to defend the realm under prerogative powers.

Also useful to examine for constitutional purposes see *Thomas v. Sorrell* (1674) Vaugh 330; *Godden v. Hales* (1686) 11 State Tr. 1166; the *Seven Bishops' Case* (1688) 12 State Tr. 371.

becomes an important convention for the future intentions of a future Parliament. Strict constitutional theory forbids Parliament to bind its successors in legal terms. In practical terms Parliament may accept the political and economic limitations on its powers, without conceding any limit on its legal powers to legislate.

Thus, although the Acts of Union created the Parliament of the **1–16** United Kingdom, English constitutional lawyers do not ascribe any significant status to those Acts, which are treated in the same way as any other Act of Parliament. We shall see that this assumption may be questioned in the context of British membership of the European Community. Turpin points out that: ". . . [i]t would seem to follow from the doctrine of Parliamentary sovereignty that an Act of Parliament is valid even if it violates fundamental provisions of the Union legislation."[16] Some support for this view may be found in the decided cases, but the courts may appear equivocal on the issue. Some support for Turpin's view over the legal status of the Scottish Union[17] can be found in the case of *MacCormick v. Lord Advocate*.[18] In that case the Scottish courts were asked to consider the significance of the Act of Union. The Rector of Glasgow University in Scotland challenged the Queen's title as "Elizabeth the Second" on the grounds that this contravened article 1 of the Treaty of Union 1707.

The Royal Titles Act 1953 authorised the use of the numeral "II" **1–17** and the challenge made by the Rector brought into issue the constitutional status of an Act of Parliament.[19] At first instance the justiciability of a challenge to the validity of an Act of Parliament was doubted and the challenge dismissed. On appeal to the First Division of the Inner House of Court of Session, Lord Cooper accepted the reasoning adopted in the lower court, but doubted if the 1953 Act had any bearing on the matter, as that Act had been enacted after the proclamation of the Queen as Elizabeth II. His opinion on the status of the Act of Union between Scotland and England is therefore *obiter dicta*, but nevertheless Lord Cooper questioned the English view of unlimited sovereignty of Parliament "which has no counterpart in Scottish Constitutional law."[20] Instead his view was emphatically, that the Union Treaty did contain some fundamental and unalterable elements which made their status distinct and separate from any other Act of Parliament. However, in strict English Constitutional theory Lord Cooper's view does not find favour. The English view is

---

[16] Turpin, *op. cit.* p. 223.
[17] N. MacCormick, "Does the United Kingdom have a Constitution? Reflections on *MacCormick v. Lord Advocate*" (1979) 28 N.I.L.Q. 1. A useful historical account is provided in Maitland, *Constitutional History of England* (Cambridge, 1959).
[18] [1953] S.C. 396.
[19] Munro, *op. cit.* pp. 12–15; D. M. Walker, *The Scottish Legal System* (5th ed., 1981).
[20] Lord Guthrie in *MacCormick v. Lord Advocate* [1953] S.C. 396.

that there is no hierarchy of laws. No Scottish court has held a public Act of Parliament to be void since the Act of Union. When considering the Acts of Union Dicey admitted "the possibility of creating an absolutely sovereign Legislature which should yet be bound by unalterable laws"[21]; but this is insufficient to create "unalterable statutes."

We shall return to consider the question of Parliamentary sovereignty later in the following chapter, but it will become apparent that however attractive the notion of fundamental law is in a constitutional sense, this has been resisted by English constitutional lawyers. Lord Cooper's opinion merely confirmed that a Scottish view of the British Constitution differs markedly from that of an English view!

(e) Ireland

1–18 In the case of Ireland[22] its early history was rooted in the law of the early Irish chiefs. These Brehon laws, as they were known, represent some of the earliest forms of law, contained in the form of law tracts which are complex in style and language and riddled with different forms of old and middle Irish. The administrations of England and Ireland before the Norman invasions of 1066 and 1171, shared a common characteristic namely that they were both regionally administrated. Ireland, unlike England was relatively free from significant foreign intervention which allowed secular custom and native common law to take hold. England, from the eleventh century developed its own system of local courts, but under the influence of central administration and Royal power. Ireland, however did not share the centralising effect of a single or unifying kingship. Instead, in Ireland, tribal loyalties formed the predominant influence and from the sixth to the eighth century there is documentary evidence of at least eight significant law tracts, the most notable being *Senchas Mar* or Patrick's law. One feature of these early laws was the division of the society into two groups one free, the other unfree.

1–19   The English invasion of Ireland, carried out by Henry II, established an English administration in the area around Dublin known as

---

[21] Dicey and Rait, *op. cit.*
[22] See J. McEldowney and P. O'Higgins, *The Common Law Tradition Essays in Irish Legal History* (Irish Academic Press, 1990); C. Palley, "The Evolution, Disintegration and Possible Reconstitution of the Northern Ireland Constitution" (1972) *Anglo-Am. Law Journal*, 368; Anson, "The Government of Ireland Bill and the Sovereignty of Parliament" (1886) 2 L.Q.R. 427; H. Calvert *Constitutional Law in Northern Ireland: A Study in Regional Government* (Belfast, 1968); N. Mansergh, *The Government of Northern Ireland: A Study in Devolution* (1936).

the Pale, circa 1171. There had previously been attempts to establish an Irish Lord in Leinster in return for allegiance to Henry II as feudal Lord, but these efforts had limited success. Once conquest had secured influence, Henry II left the Irish Kings to continue to rule, but owing strict allegiance to Henry. The early records show that in 1226 a justiciar called De Mansio was appointed to act as the Royal representative in Ireland. The success of the English monarchy in Ireland was such that the English common law was gradually introduced.

The adoption of the common law in Ireland endured for many centuries to come. Under the English system of land law, tracts of land were granted and subinfeudation was widespread. Dublin was the administrative centre where the major Royal Courts carried out the King's justice under the *King's Writ* or *Breve*. Brehon laws, although referred to in records as late as 1558, were gradually superseded by the English common law. The assumption, often offered as an explanation for the continued preservation of Brehon law, is that Norman law was personal rather than territorial. Gradually Brehon law gave way to common law principles enforceable in the courts.

The common law taking root in Ireland eventually led to profound **1–20** constitutional changes. *Poynings law* 1494 provided that statutes in force in England had legal force in Ireland. The approval of the King in English Council was required for Irish Bills. The existing Lord of Ireland became King of Ireland in 1541. Religious differences ensured that Ireland was governed according to English law but not that English law was accepted in Ireland. The Battle of the Boyne in 1690 assured Protestant ascendancy with the victory of William of Orange over James II.

The Act of Union between England and Ireland[23] was passed in **1–21** 1800 and had the unusual characteristic of being enacted by both the English and Irish Parliaments. The latter succumbed to a degree of English influence and persuasion that tainted the propriety of the entire episode. The Act proclaimed that both pre- and post-Union legislation was subject to the "Parliament of the United Kingdom." It simultaneously ended the life of the Irish Parliament, united the Anglican Churches of England and Ireland and established the Union as "for ever after." Dicey freely admitted that the Union was not

---

[23] Generally see Christopher Harvie, "Ideology and Home Rule"; James Bryce, "A. V. Dicey and Ireland 1880–1887" (1976) *English Historical Review* 91; *English Historical Review* 298–314; A. V. Dicey, "How is the Law to be enforced in Ireland?" (November 1881) 36 *Fortnightly Review* 539–552; J. F. McEldowney, "Dicey in Historical Perspective – A Review Essay" in McAuslan and McEldowney, *Law, Legitimacy and the Constitution* (Sweet and Maxwell, 1985), pp. 39–61.

"voluntary"[24] and was, therefore, tainted with suspicion from its inception.

At the time of the union, the majority of the population were Catholic tenants and excluded from the franchise and land ownership. After considerable pressure Catholic emancipation was granted in 1829 but this only served to make the Irish Land question a dominant issue for the remainder of the century. Protestant resistance and Orange Lodges feared the end to Protestant ascendancy and land ownership. The unsettled state of affairs in Ireland led to calls for constitutional reform, most notably Home Rule. Although a number of Home Rule Bills were presented during the 1880s, these failed to find sufficient Parliamentary support. A failed uprising in Dublin in 1916 eventually advanced the cause of independence for Ireland.

1–22   In constitutional terms the Union endured until 1921–22 when the Irish Free State was formed. This necessitated a change to the Act of Union under subsequent legislation namely: the Irish Free State (Agreement) Act 1922; the Irish Free State Constitution Act 1922 and the Irish Free State (Consequential Provisions) Act 1922. While the Irish Free State became a dominion, Northern Ireland comprising six counties of the North East of Ireland, remained within the United Kingdom. The Government of Ireland Act 1920 provided for a separate Parliament and Government in Belfast but ultimate sovereignty resided within the competence of the United Kingdom Parliament. This form of devolved government under its terms of grant under the 1920 Act allowed the Northern Ireland Parliament, powers "to make laws for the peace order and good government of Northern Ireland." Northern Ireland became unique within the United Kingdom in having a written Constitution. Effectively the Northern Ireland Parliament was, within its own legislative competence, unrestrained by the sovereign power who had overriding legal powers under section 75 of the 1920 Act, to govern Northern Ireland. A constitutional convention became established that the United Kingdom Parliament would not legislate on matters which were within the "transferred" powers of the Northern Ireland Parliament. Representation in the United Kingdom Parliament was set at 13 seats until 1948, and thereafter 12, until 1979 when the number was increased to 17.

1–23   The experiment in devolved government was overshadowed by the early historical problem of Ireland's post-Union relationship with

---

[24] A. V. Dicey, "Two Acts of Union – A Contrast" 30 (1881) *The Fortnightly Review* 168–78. Also see his views on the disestablishment of the Church of England: "The Church of England: The Legal Aspects of Disestablishment" 39 (1890) *The Fortnightly Review* 822–840; and see "The Defence of the Union." 61 (1892) *Contemporary Review* 314–331; Grimes and Morgan, *Introduction to Law: Ireland* (Dublin, 1981).

England. Catholics comprise about 40 per cent of its population and live under a Nationalist identity which rejected the Union with England. Civil liberties, although theoretically protected under the 1920 Government of Ireland Act, were often ignored. From 1921-72 Northern Ireland was ruled by a single majority party, the Unionists, who dominated the Government of Northern Ireland. Religious and political differences were endemic and resulted in civil unrest. From 1968–72 attempts at constitutional reform by the Northern Ireland Government were too late to avert a constitutional crisis which resulted in March 1972, with the arrival of British troops and the prorogation and eventual abolition of the Northern Ireland Parliament. The functions of the Parliament and Government of Northern Ireland were vested in the Secretary of State for Northern Ireland.

Direct rule was imposed from Westminster. The first period, from **1–24** 1972–74, resulted in considerable parliamentary time at Westminster being devoted to Northern Ireland's affairs. A new written Constitution for Northern Ireland in 1973 provided for a system of power sharing, whereby the two communities in Northern Ireland might form a legislative assembly through proportional representation and an executive broadly representative of the community. The attempt to introduce power sharing failed after a general strike of loyalist workers forced the resignation of a newly-formed power sharing executive in 1974. "Interim" direct rule for a period of five years was resumed under the Northern Ireland Act 1974. A second attempt in 1982 to achieve a new form of power sharing under the Northern Ireland Act 1982, failed and resulted in the return to direct rule. Currently Northern Ireland is governed by direct rule. Direct rule provides that the Government of Northern Ireland is the responsibility of a Secretary of State together with a Minister of State and up to four parliamentary Under-Secretaries of State. The bulk of legislation for Northern Ireland is made through Orders in Council under the Northern Ireland Act 1974. Most Orders are subject to affirmative resolution of both Houses of Parliament but are not subject to amendment in debate. These procedures are heavily criticised for not allowing the same degree of debate and scrutiny as an ordinary Bill.

Northern Ireland's formal written Constitution was created in **1–25** order to achieve a greater consensus in its Government. Yet the status of its Constitution is formally that of an Act of Parliament. It may be modified, amended or repealed at a later date. Attempts to address the concerns of Unionists over the status of the Union with the United Kingdom may be seen in the various protections built into the constitutional status of Northern Ireland; for example, the Ireland Act 1949 simultaneously recognised the secession of Southern Ireland and its republican status while declaring that Northern Ireland would not cease to remain part of the "United Kingdom without the consent of the Parliament of Northern Ireland." After the abolition of the

Northern Ireland Parliament in 1973, this guarantee was replaced by a new form of protection namely that Northern Ireland would not cease to remain part of the United Kingdom without "the consent of the majority of the people of Northern Ireland voting in a poll held for the purposes of this section." It is questionable whether such a "guarantee" constitutes a fundamental protection which would prevent amendment by a subsequent Act of Parliament. This issue may be examined in more detail as an example of the difficulty of "entrenching" any fundamental rule by Act of Parliament.

1-26   The modern form of protecting the status of Northern Ireland owes its origins to Article 1 of the Act of Union with England in 1800, which stated that the Kingdoms of Great Britain and Ireland shall "for ever after, be united in one kingdom." In common with Scottish and Welsh Acts of Union already noted above, might not the Union with Ireland appear to be a constituent treaty of such fundamental importance that its status absolves it from modification or repeal?

English lawyers addressed this issue in 1868 when the Irish Church Bill was debated in the House of Commons. The Bill set out to disestablish the Church of Ireland and thereby dissolve its union with the Church of England – a union guaranteed in the Act of Union 1800. Lord Claud Hamilton explained in the debate over the constitutional protection afforded by the Act of Union that[25] "by solemn compact they [the Parliament which passed the Act of Union] refused to future Parliaments the power to rescind the Act of Union, and they explicitly and solemnly declared no such power should exist."

Hamilton certainly expressed an accurate record of the *intentions* of Parliament in 1800, but the 1868 Church Bill disestablishing the Church of Ireland, was passed. Parliament may not legally bind future Parliaments. We have already seen how subsequent legislation has successfully amended the Act of Union.

1-27   Since August 31, 1994 and a cease-fire by the Irish Republican Army, attempts have continued to provide a peace process in Northern Ireland and some initiatives have involved constitutional innovation. The Northern Ireland (Entry to Negotiations, etc.) Act 1996 provided for elections in Northern Ireland to allow all-party negotiations. The decommissioning of arms has been the subject of a report under the United States Senator George Mitchell on January 22, 1996 and the Northern Ireland Arms Decommissioning Act 1997 provides a statutory framework for arms decommissioning.

---

[25] See Turpin, *op. cit.* p. 239. See D. G. T. Williams, "The Constitution of the United Kingdom" [1972] C.L.J. 266.

(f) The Commonwealth

The legal view of the British Constitution which appears from the **1–28**
above review of the legislation which encompasses the various
geographical areas which make up the United Kingdom of Great
Britain and Northern Ireland, illustrates how the laws which created
the United Kingdom are themselves subject to change or modification. Parliament, when granting independence to former colonies,
also considered their new constitutional status and relationship with
Britain.[26] Thus Parliament's authority and jurisdiction was altered by
the Colonial Laws Validity Act 1865 and the Statute of Westminster
1931.

The Colonial Laws Validity Act 1865 changed what had once been **1–29**
a vague common law rule that colonial constitutions enacted before
1865 and possessing a legislative assembly could not pass laws
repugnant to the law of England. The 1865 Act assumed that colonies
were subject to Parliamentary regulation by the "Imperial Parliament" but added the *caveat* that a colonial legislature was required to
observe only those Acts of Parliament which expressly or impliedly
applied to the colonies. This marked a gradual shift in the development of constitutional relations between the colonies and the United
Kingdom. Colonies such as Canada, Australia and New Zealand
emerged as enjoying greater freedoms in the actual exercise of their
powers. Gradually this gave rise to the creation of a new legal status
of dominion. Various colonial conferences[27] recognised the governance of these countries as having a "dominion status" rather than
being in a colonial relationship. In 1907 the term "dominion status"
was first used and after the First World War, it signified a country's
greater status and independence from the Imperial power. In 1926 the
famous Balfour Declaration[28] accepted that "status, equality and
autonomy" should be given to dominions within the British Empire.

Many dominion governments still experienced great dissatis- **1–30**
faction[29] with the Colonial Laws Validity Act 1865. This centred on
the practical restrictions and limitations experienced by dominion
legislatures. In particular: restrictions on passing laws which might
have extra-territorial effect; the convention that Bills would be

---

[26] See K. C. Wheare, *The Statute of Westminster and Dominion Status* (5th ed.); O. Hood
Phillips, "Statute of Westminster in the Courts" (1983) 99 L.Q.R. 342; H. R. Gray,
"The Sovereignty of the Imperial Parliament" (1960) 23 M.L.R. 647.
[27] See G. Marshall, *Parliamentary Sovereignty and the Commonwealth* (1957). There was a
conference in 1926, the Balfour Declaration, Cmnd. 1768 (1926).
[28] *ibid.*
[29] Y. Ghai and J. McAuslan, *Public Law and Political Change in Kenya* (1970). Also D. P.
O'Connell and A. Riordan, *Opinions on Imperial Constitutional Law* (1971); K. C.
Wheare, *The Constitutional Structure of the Commonwealth* (1960).

reserved for the views of the United Kingdom Government; and the application of United Kingdom Acts of Parliament expressly or impliedly relevant to the dominion legislation rendering the latter void if inconsistent or repugnant to a United Kingdom Act. These restrictions contributed to the unease that the United Kingdom's influence remained too powerful. The right of appeal to the Judicial Committee of the Privy Council was also seen as an indication of the lack of independence enjoyed by dominions.

1-31   In 1931 the Statute of Westminster put into legal effect the various resolutions made over the period of the preceding few years. For the first time, the dominions were defined to include Canada, Australia, New Zealand, South Africa, the Irish Free State and Newfoundland. The Colonial Laws Validity Act 1865 ceased to apply to dominions, thus granting a dominion Parliament power to amend or repeal Acts of the United Kingdom Parliament. A dominion parliament was also given power to make laws having extra-territorial operation. Included in the Statute of Westminster was the power for dominion parliaments to abolish the right of appeal to the Judicial Committee of the Privy Council.

1-32   The effect of the 1931 Act still left a number of matters unresolved. It was unclear, for example, whether independence statutes such as the British North America Acts 1867–1930 which formed the basis of the Canadian Constitution required legal authority from the United Kingdom Parliament to be amended. The view which prevailed, was that the United Kingdom Parliament had to give assent if the Acts were to be changed and this was duly given by the Canada Act 1982. That Act thereby placed sole responsibility in Canada for the amendment and modification of the Constitution of Canada.

In the cases of Australia and New Zealand, the effect of the 1931 Act was withheld in respect of the power to alter or amend their constitution (see sections 8 and 9(1)). This resulted in both countries lacking the power to legislate in ways repugnant to United Kingdom law, to abolish on their own initiative, appeals to the Privy Council, or to legislate extra-territorially. Eventually in 1986 the Australia Act abolished such limitations and ended the power of the United Kingdom Parliament to legislate for Australia. New Zealand had received complete constitutional powers under the New Zealand Constitution (Amendment) Act 1947.

1-33   Constitutional supervision of colonial states by the United Kingdom Parliament has led to constitutional difficulties. One example is illustrative of the problem. In the case of Southern Rhodesia[30] a

---

[30] A penetrating analysis is provided by C. Palley, *The Constitutional History and Law of Southern Rhodesia 1888–1965* (Oxford, 1979). Also see: Peter Hogg, *Constitutional Law of Canada* (3rd ed., Carswell, 1992).

colony since 1923, which today is the independent republican State of Zimbabwe and enjoys Commonwealth membership, the United Kingdom faced a direct challenge to its constitutional authority. In 1965 an illegal Unilateral Declaration of Independence (UDI) led to the passage of the Southern Rhodesia Act 1965, a United Kingdom Act of Parliament asserting sovereignty over Rhodesia. The 1965 Act declared that Rhodesia remained part of Her Majesty's dominions and the power to make laws by Order in Council was maintained under the Act. The UDI purported to establish independent legislative powers for the Rhodesian legislature, originally set up under the 1961 Constitution with a large measure of self-government granted thereunder by the United Kingdom. The terms of the UDI declared that Southern Rhodesia was to cease to be a colony and conferred full legislative powers on the Rhodesian legislature, including the abolition of appeals to the Judicial Committee of the Privy Council. It also sought to protect the status of independence by removing the jurisdiction of the courts to question its validity.

The constitutional crisis, whereby the government in Rhodesia **1–34** continued unrecognised in law and enacted rules expressly repugnant to an Act of the United Kingdom Parliament, tested the authority of Parliament against the self-proclaimed independence of a newly formed state. This matter was raised as an issue in *Madzimbamuto v. Lardner-Burke*[31] which the Privy Council heard in a special application made by Madzimbamuto who challenged his detention under Rhodesian emergency laws made in 1966. Lord Reid in the Privy Council made some useful observations as to the extent of the legal powers of the United Kingdom's Parliament, including the case where even if the United Kingdom Parliament acted "unconstitutionally" it would not render the Act of Parliament invalid. The decision of the Privy Council declared the UDI illegal and sought to enforce the Rhodesia Act 1965. It also declared Madzimbamuto's detention illegal. Lord Reid's *dicta* included the following:

> "It is often said that it would be unconstitutional for the United Kingdom Parliament to do certain things, meaning that the moral, political and other reasons against doing them are so strong that most people would regard it as highly improper if Parliament did these things. But this does not mean that it is beyond the power of Parliament to do such things. If Parliament chose to do any of them the courts could not hold the Act of Parliament invalid."

The decision in the *Madzimbamuto* case, while observed under **1–35** United Kingdom law, was not given effect in Rhodesia. Attempts to

---

[31] [1969] 1 A.C. 645, 723. Also see *The State v. Dosso* [1958] S.C. 533 and *Uganda v. Commission of Prisons, ex p. Matovu* [1966] E.A. 514.

solve the constitutional impasse were long and difficult. Economic sanctions were applied by the United Kingdom Government. After protracted discussions in 1980, following the passage of the Southern Rhodesia Act 1979, the Zimbabwe Act 1979 and various statutory instruments under that authority, enabling legislation permitted the setting up of Zimbabwe.[32] Zimbabwe became an independent state recognising black majority rule.

1–36   The above examples serve to show how the unwritten United Kingdom Constitution, has coped with a wide variety of diverse changes, stresses and innovations. As we have seen, this includes: the definition of the constitutional status of other countries; the conditions for the granting of independence to newly formed states; as well as the supervision of legislative changes brought about by newly independent legislatures. In defining the shape of the political union which makes up the United Kingdom of Great Britain and Northern Ireland, we have seen that change has come about through gradual adaptation rather than a radical reform of the constitution. Flexibility and a certain pragmatism characterise the ability of the United Kingdom's constitutional arrangements to be reformed and changed without seeming to alter any fundamental constitutional principle. This characteristic of evolutionary change is also present when it comes to explain political and social developments within the United Kingdom such as the broadening of the franchise in 1832, 1867 and 1880 which changed the nature of many political institutions, but similarly did not cause a reform of the constitutional arrangements. The South Africa Act 1995 marked a significant change to take account of re-admission of South Africa as a member of the Commonwealth on June 1, 1994.

3. Government and the Constitution

(a) Political Science and the Constitution

1–37 A legal perspective of Britain's constitutional arrangements may be said to be too narrowly defined and to focus only on a narrow legal and technical explanation of parliamentary sovereignty, which Dicey attributed in 1885 as Parliament's "right to make or unmake any law whatever."[33] In the sense that Dicey ascribed such wide powers to

---

[32] See Cmnd. 7758 (1979) and Cmnd. 7800 (1980); see also Southern Rhodesia Act 1979, Zimbabwe Act 1979; S.I. 1979 No. 1600. Particularly useful on the aftermath of U.D.I. is C. Palley (1967) 30 M.L.R. 263; [1968] P.L. 293.

[33] See McEldowney, op. cit.; Paul Craig, op. cit. pp. 20–25.

Parliament, it might be asked whether the United Kingdom in fact possesses a constitution. Thomas Paine's analysis of the *Rights of Man*[34] which was influential in the drafting of the present American Constitution noted the characteristics which defined a constitution.

"A Constitution is not the act of a government, but of a people constituting a government, and a government without a constitution is power without right . . .".

Paines' analysis causes us to consider the question of where power and authority lies. There is no legal definition of government in the United Kingdom's constitutional arrangements and no supreme or fundamental constitutional law. De Tocqueville, writing about the relationship between parliament and the constitution in the nineteenth century observed that, "In England Parliament has the right to modify the Constitution." The relevance of this point has been elaborated upon by a number of political scientists. F. F. Ridley argues[35] that Britain "does not really have a constitution at all, merely a system of government, even if some parts of it are more important to our democratic order than others . . . ."

1–38 Ridley calls in aid the views of James Bryce in the latter part of the nineteenth century when he argued that " . . . there is no text to discriminate between constitutional and less than constitutional elements since labelling has no defined consequence, unlike countries where constitutions are a higher form of law." The idea of confronting government power with some superior rule of obligation is commonly accepted in written constitutions.[36] The degree to which constitutions limit government, as K. C. Wheare observed, depends on the provisions which the framers of those constitutions wish to safeguard.

1–39 Written constitutions may also settle the relationship between local and central government, the role of the courts and the separation of powers within the framework of the constitution. Ridley identifies

---

[34] T. Paine, *Rights of Man* in *The Complete Works of Thomas Paine* (1791–92) pp. 302–303. Also see the discussion in C. H. McIlwain, *Constitutionalism Ancient and Modern* (1947) pp. 8–10; Rousseau, *Le Contract Social* (1762).

[35] F. F. Ridley, "There is no British Constitution: A Dangerous Case of the Emperors' Clothes" (1881) 41 *Parliamentary Affairs* 340–345; Samuel H. Beer, *Modern British Politics* Faber and Faber (3rd ed), 1982; Max Beloff and Gillian Peele, *The Government of the U.K.: Political Authority in a Changing Society* (2nd ed., Weidenfeld and Nicolson, 1985); Nevil Johnson, *In Search of the Constitution: Reflections on State and Society in Britain* (1977); Bogdanor (ed.), *Introduction to Constitutions in Democratic Politics* (1988); J. M. Schaar, "Legitimacy in the Modern State" in Connolly *et. al., Legitimacy and the State* (1984).

[36] M. Loughlin, *Public Law and Political Theory*, pp. 16–17. Loughlin notes the Diceyan legacy, namely, that constitutional law is too formalistically defined by lawyers.

four characteristics which he suggests are important and without which it is impossible to say a country has a constitution "in the current international sense of the word." He explained that the four characteristics are as follows:

(a) The constitution establishes the system of government. This is taken to mean that the system of government depends on the constitution for its rules and is not independent from the constitution.

(b) The constitution sets the authority outside the order it establishes. The meaning intended is that the constitution should provide the *legitimacy* for law and the governmental system. Common to modern constitutions like the Japanese or Irish, there is some reference to "the people" in whom ultimate authority is derived for the constitution to gain legitimacy.

(c) The constitution is a form of law superior to other laws. This authority is partly due to the point made above, but also the principle of hierarchy admits the possibility of judicial review of ordinary legislation to test its constitutional validity.

(d) The constitution is entrenched which thereby admits its general purpose which is to limit the power of government and because of its higher form of authority, this makes the constitution safe from political intervention. It is usual that only special procedures may be used to seek amendment and in such cases protection is afforded by requiring some form of popular consultation.

1–40   Ridley's analysis has some force when it is considered that in the absence of a written constitution in the United Kingdom, there is an omission in our present arrangements which fails to address Ridley's four characteristics. One answer might be that this is not a surprising omission, as Ridley has in mind the formula for written constitutions which he is unfairly applying to our "unwritten arrangements." There remains, however, the question of what is fundamental in the United Kingdom's constitution and how might government be made to conform to fundamental principles?

1–41   Turpin addresses[37] much the same question and provides a number of possible solutions. First, the courts provide an important role in maintaining legal rules against the excesses of administrators. This

---

[37] Turpin, *loc. cit.* note 9.

raises a question of how the courts might be said to be themselves accountable and to whom? Still further limitations on the courts' power to interpret legislation are that the courts are ultimately subject to parliamentary sovereignty and their decisions may be reversed by Acts of Parliament. Principles of judicial review, exercised by the courts, are restrained by the political decisions of Ministers who are ultimately answerable to Parliament for their decisions. While the courts have been active in developing principles of judicial review, especially in the last decade, they are as de Smith[38] has admitted, "inevitably sporadic and peripheral." Not every decision of a public authority is reviewable and the possibility of legal redress through the courts cannot always be available to every aggrieved citizen.

Secondly, the institutions of government may provide their own **1–42** internal "checks and balances." Civil servants and ministers operate within important conventions, principles and understandings. Occasionally these procedures have a legal framework such as the processes and procedures used by government to account for public money. Often the procedures come in the form of minutes, letters, circulars and public statements. Inevitably there are restraints which are never made public but exist beneath the surface – personal promotion, professional standards and ultimately self-advancement all serve to provide standards in the machinery of government decision taking.

None of these arrangements, however, will *guarantee* that government conforms to the acceptable and high standards which should reasonably be expected. Occasionally civil servants and ministers may be subject to scrutiny such as before a select committee or in a parliamentary debate. Even here the ultimate sanction may not be found in resignation or judicial rebuke, but in the day to day political life of the nation. Newspapers and the news media have a contribution to make through investigative journalism in providing information and critical analysis of government activities.

Counterbalancing any likely effect this combination of factors may **1–43** have, is the secrecy which surrounds government in Britain. It begins with the need for collective Cabinet decision-taking and the anonymity of civil servants. Supported by both the civil and criminal law, Britain's secrecy laws have penetrated deeply inside the very culture of the machinery of government. Commercial confidentiality between government and business or industry in their contractual relationships also provides a reason for secrecy in many government activities.

The third, and final, check on government may be found in the use **1–44** of elections which ultimately determine the fate of government

---

[38] de Smith, *Judicial Review of Administrative Action* (3rd ed., Stevens, 1973), p. 3.

policies. Political parties, individual politicians and pressure groups all promote the political agenda of the nation. In a constitutional sense political parties look to the electorate for a mandate to govern. Local as well as central government has to account to electoral choices determined by popular support.

The weakness about elections[39] serving as a mainstay of fundamental principles is that the results are not necessarily representative of public opinion. There is a sizeable number, estimated in 1981 at 2.5 million, of eligible electors who are not registered to vote. The turnout at central government elections fluctuates from 70 per cent to 85 per cent of the electorate. More significantly the British electoral system does not favour fairness between the number of votes cast at the election in favour of one particular party and the number of seats held in Parliament by that party. The statistical returns of all the general elections since the franchise was reformed in the nineteenth century show how "the first past the post system" may distort electoral preferences. For example, at the general election in 1992, the Conservative and Labour parties respectively won 42 per cent and 34 per cent of the votes, each winning 336 and 271 seats. The Liberal Democrats won 18 per cent of the vote but only 20 seats. These results are used to support the claim that the plurality system (as it is known) or two-party system may discriminate against a third party or minority parties. More importantly, while the present electoral system may favour strong government, *i.e.* a government which holds a majority overall in the House of Commons, this *may* be at the expense of *representative* government. To the extent that this is true it may considerably weaken the case for relying on electoral choice as a mainstay of constitutional protection of fundamental principles.

1–45   The electoral system[40] is, however, responsive to the shifting changes in public opinion. The relationship between public opinion and voting preferences is hard to predict and is capable of producing quite dramatic change. In 1997 the Labour party ended four consecutive election victories by the Conservative party since 1979. The 1997 election result showed that the Labour and Conservative parties respectively won 44 per cent and 31 per cent of the vote, winning 419 and 165 seats. The Liberal Democrats won 17 per cent of the vote and obtained 46 seats. This result shows the significance of tactical voting, whereby in a number of marginal constituencies, voters were encouraged to vote for the opposition candidate that was most likely to win

---

[39] On electoral returns and their interpretation see J. Lively, *Democracy* (1975); David Butler, "Electoral Reform" in Jowell and Oliver, *op. cit.* Vernon Bogdanor, *The People and the Party System* (1981) and J. A. Chandler, "The Plurality Vote: A Reappraisal" (1982) 30 *Political Studies* 87; S. E. Finer, "Adversary Politics and the Eighties" (1982) 1 *Electoral Studies* 221; Turpin, *op. cit.* pp. 494–520.

[40] See Robert Blackburn, *The Electoral System in Britain* (Macmillan, 1995).

the seat to prevent the Conservative candidate winning. Tactical voting is capable of providing a government with a large majority and diminishing even the most powerful political parties.

The conclusion which may be drawn from the above analysis is **1–46** that while there are many important and *disparate* elements containing fundamental principles in the working of the United Kingdom's Constitution, political scientists have been correct to point out to constitutional lawyers, that the Constitution does not fit easily within the ideas of constitutionalism resulting from the experience of modern written constitutions. It may seem surprising that British constitutional lawyers who have written many constitutions throughout the world should be reluctant to adopt a written constitution for Britain.

In recent years there has been intense debate over whether Britain should adopt a Bill of Rights and/or a written constitution, but there is a marked reluctance to adopt such changes. This reluctance may be partly attributed to the strong legal tradition surrounding the United Kingdom's constitution which owes its origins mainly to the work of Albert Venn Dicey.

(b) Dicey's influence

We have already seen from the above discussion, the centrality of **1–47** parliamentary sovereignty to Dicey's view of the constitution. Recently Paul Craig has assessed Dicey's influence in his book *Public Law and Democracy in the United Kingdom and the United States of America*.[41] Craig makes a number of points about Dicey's influence and importance. First, that Dicey believed in legislative monopoly partly because he assumed that the House of Commons did control the executive with significant and important government power directed through Parliament, which was duly elected. Secondly, that Dicey supported what he articulated as the "rule of law," a term which Craig explains had both a descriptive and a normative content[42]:

> "In descriptive terms it was assumed that the regular law predominated, that exercise of broad discretionary power was absent, and that all people were subject to the ordinary law of the realm. Public power resided with Parliament. In normative terms it was assumed that this was indeed a better system than that which existed in France, where special rules and a distinctive regime existed for public law matters."

[41] (OUP, 1990): Craig's analysis is used throughout this section as further clarification of some of the views already noted in McEldowney *op. cit.*.
[42] Craig, *op. cit.* p. 21.

1–48   Thirdly, that in asserting the pre-eminence of ordinary law which he assumed applied to all aspects of government, Dicey rejected for England any coherent or separate body of administrative law which resembled the French *Droit Administratif*.[43] The courts in Britain were at first reluctant to develop administrative law. They were concerned as to the level of intervention in decision-making which could be justified through judicial review. Craig describes the courts' role in terms of "non-constitutional review." This means that the role of the courts is limited by the fact of Parliamentary sovereignty. Although Dicey later recanted his objections to *Droit Administratif* and admitted that English law had developed through the courts, a body of administrative law rules, Dicey's ideas had taken root so firmly, that the growth and development of administrative law in Britain has been one of restrained growth until relatively recently when judicial intervention has become more widespread. The hallmark of judicial development has been to reserve a large measure of discretion for the courts in setting the conditions where they might choose to intervene.

1–49   Fourthly and finally, Craig notes that Dicey perceptively shifted his views about the constitution. Particular changes such as the increase in the power of Cabinet government, the rise of the party system, the use of referendum to curtail the dangers of democratic government and the growth of administrative discretion, were all recognised by Dicey but they did not cause him to re-think his basic evaluation of the constitution centred in his original text in *Law of the Constitution*. As Craig points out not only did Dicey's major text remain unaltered but also constitutional writers who were Dicey's immediate predecessors, failed to understand the changing social, political and economic influences which overtook the principles Dicey espoused. This point we will return to, when considering the process of elections and the value of democracy[44] and in the influence of Dicey's successors on generations of constitutional lawyers.[45]

1–50   The reality of constitutional power, beginning in the latter part of the nineteenth century in Britain contains lessons for the concerns of the constitutional lawyer today. Government had expanded its role from its traditional preserve of raising revenue, entering foreign relations and maintaining peace throughout the realm. Legislation, including the redefinition of Parliament's powers[46] in the Parliament Acts of 1911 and 1949, expanded to cover a wide range of social issues such as health, education, local government, factories, railways

---

[43] The decision of *Local Government Board v. Arlidge* [1915] A.C. 120 caused Dicey to re-think his ideas on administrative law.

[44] See Chap. 6.

[45] McEldowney, *op. cit.*.

[46] See Trowbridge Ford, *Albert Venn Dicey Victorian Jurist* (Barry Rose, 1986).

explain the fact that Cabinet Government operates with a parliamentary Executive; that the Law Lords may act as both legislators as well as judges, although in practice the Law Lords abstain from party political matters in debates in the House of Lords.

The doctrine of the separation of powers is based on the theory that **2–06** the separation of the legislative, executive and judicial functions provide the best means to restrain or prevent any abuse of governmental power. This theory was explained in the seventeenth and eighteenth centuries by Locke and Montesquieu.[6] It was adopted in countries with written constitutions, most notably in America in the Federal Constitution in 1798. As a theory of government in the United Kingdom, it has been influential but not as an absolute and rigid rule. As the Donoughmore Committee[7] commented, within the United Kingdom's constitutional arrangements "there is no such thing as the absolute separation of powers." Opposition to the theory in England came from the view that a balanced constitution controlled by checks and balances affords the best protection against abuse. On this view all the different elements within the constitutional arrangements may be held in equilibrium. Reliance on a balanced constitution emerged in the context of the development of parliamentary democracy.

Some support for the theory of the separation of powers came from **2–07** William Blackstone in his influential *Commentaries on the Laws of England*.[8] Blackstone's influence did not succeed to elevate the separation of powers into a fundamental[9] design for the constitution. In modern Britain the doctrine is deficient as an accurate description of present day constitutional arrangements. The doctrine does retain important value as a descripion of how the different elements of our constitution should operate independent from each other. The result is that the doctrine of the separation of powers is an important element in the protection of the judiciary.[10] As Lord Templeman explained in *In Re M*[11]:

". . . Parliament makes the law, the executive carry the law into effect and the judiciary enforce the law."

---

[6] Locke, *Second Treatise of Civil Government* (1690) and Montesquieu, *The Spirit of Laws* (1748) T. R. S. Allan, *Law, Liberty and Justice* (Oxford, 1993), pp. 48–64. M. J. C. Vile, *Constitutionalism and the Separation of Powers* (Oxford, 1967).

[7] *Report of the Committee on Ministers' Powers*, Cmd. 4060 (1932), pp. 4–5.

[8] William Blackstone, *Commentaries on the Laws of England* (1765).

[9] See Lord Diplock in *Duport Steels Ltd v. Sirs* [1980] 1 W.L.R. 142.

[10] See Sir John Donaldson in *R. v. HM Treasury, ex p. Smedley* [1985] 1 All E.R. 589 and also in *M. v. Home Office* [1992] 2 W.L.R. 73.

[11] *In Re M* [1993] 3 W.L.R. 433.

(b)   Parliament's role

2–08   Walter Bagehot in *The English Constitution*[12] identified the role and function of Parliament to provide an expression of the will of the people, to provide information and to perform an educative value. These roles are in addition to the functions of providing legislation and finance. A brief historical overview allows us to see all these roles emerge as part of the evolution of Parliamentary democracy.

Parliament's legal and political authority developed historically, and explains the close relationship between government and legislature as part of the history of Parliament's evolution.

2–09   The early medieval meaning given to Parliament was that of "any meeting for speech or conference."[13] In its law-making function Parliament shared judicial and legislative business. In the thirteenth century a common practice was to use parliamentary power to redress specific grievances contained in petitions presented to Parliament. Earlier kings asserted a wide power to redress grievances to individuals and a system of petitions was well established by 1280. Edward I was able to exploit the granting of petitions to extend his influence over even the most powerful of his subjects via the King's Council in his Parliament.

During the reign of Edward III (1327-77), the use of regular petitions being presented to the Commons was established. The Crown made law through parliamentary legislation as a means to expedite petitions in a similar way that Government Bills may be introduced in Parliament today.

2–10   During the fourteenth century Parliament gained influence through a variety of practices which assisted in the development of parliamentary power. Taxation required the consent of both Houses of Parliament and hence also required regular meetings. Parliaments, by the statutes of 1330 and 1362, were required to be held frequently. Although this was not always followed, Parliament began to meet regularly and developed a constitutional basis of "making law." By the end of the fifteenth century the institution of Parliament had replaced the Great Council of the King.[14]

2–11   In the seventeenth century Parliament's powers grew in importance and influence as its constitutional status developed. The Petition of Right 1627 established that taxation was not to be levied without the

---

[12] Walter Bagehot, *The English Constitution* with an introduction by R. Crossman (1963).

[13] *ibid.* See McIlwain, *The High Court of Parliament* (1910) and O. Hood Philips, *Constitutional and Administrative Law* (1987). Parliament's origins were in the *Curia Regis*, where judicial, executive and legislative powers were fused. The medieval Constitution permitted the King to decide whether or not there was a parliament and the extent of parliament's authority in respect of legislation.

[14] *ibid.*

consent of Parliament. The events of the seventeenth century of constitutional significance included: the English Civil War (1642-49); the defeat of the King and his execution; and the operation by Cromwell of a protectorate (1653). These events resembled a revolution. In 1661, however, the "convention Parliament of Lords and Commons" restored the monarchy by inviting Charles II to take the throne.[15] The restoration settlement legitimated the convention Parliament under Cromwell but also asserted the King's authority in Parliament under the Constitution. Parliament's authority ensured its continued supremacy. An uneasy settlement between King and Parliament led to the Bill of Rights 1688 which curtailed royal power under Parliament's authority. James II (1685-88) abdicated and fled, but constitutional change was accomplished by Parliament's acceptance of the Bill of Rights and under William and Mary, by Royal Assent to Parliament's authority.

The term "Queen in Parliament"[16] has the technical significance of **2–12** the power to make laws vested in the Queen, Lords and Commons and may be found in the enacting words of an Act of Parliament.[17] In common usage "Parliament" is often used as a term to denote that authority.

The eighteenth and nineteenth centuries saw the continued **2–13** development of Parliament's legislative activities. It had an important role in the life of the nation even though the franchise was narrow and unrepresentative of popular support, because few were allowed to vote. The Septennial Act 1715 provided for an election every seven years. During the eighteenth century the principal advisers of the King formed a cabinet and by *convention* were members of one or other House of Parliament. Support for policies was irratic, often obtained through corrupt practices and seldom through popularity. The offices of state, such as Prime Minister, emerged as royal influence replaced royal power. In more modern times monarchy has endured even after the abdication crisis in 1936 when Edward VIII abdicated the throne.[18]

The nineteenth century with the two major Reform Acts of 1832 **2–14** and 1867 gave the franchise to a wider section of the population than ever before, and allowed all male urban householders to vote. Similarly, in 1880 county householders were granted the vote.

Parliament's legislative activities[19] were greatly altered and change brought about by various political, economic and social factors rather

[15] D. Pollard and D. Hughes, *Constitutional and Administrative Law Text and Materials* (1990), pp. 3–13.
[16] An alternative version of this is the Crown in Parliament.
[17] A discussion of the electoral procedures may be found in Chap. 6.
[18] See David Lieberman, *The Province of Legislation Determined: Legal Theory in 18th century Britain* (Cambridge, 1989).
[19] C. Turpin, *British Government and the Constitution* (2nd ed., 1990), p. 424.

than constitutional reform.[20] It is noteworthy that no general review
of the Constitution occurred. Change was organic and often unpredictable. Constitutional arrangements preserved what was needed
and discarded the unnecessary.

2–15   The style and content of legislation deserves mention. Up until the
end of the nineteenth century, legislation was narrow in scope and
covered matters of local and even temporary significance. Watson[21]
observes that there was "a paucity of general statutes covering what
we would term private law or mercantile law." Subjects covered
included such matters as divorce through Acts of Parliament, patents,
and the incorporation of companies with limited liability. Rarely were
general statutes passed and as codification was resisted in the
common law tradition, there were only a few statutes which "consolidated" rather than codified the law, such as the Offences Against the
Person Act 1861.

2–16   Dicey observed that Parliament had become the repository of all
public power with Parliament overseeing a unitary state and legislating on particular issues no matter how local or specific. On this view
Parliament exercised all public power. Craig refers to Dicey's
analysis[22] as "parliamentary monopoly"; a belief that Parliament's
legislative power in all matters was accompanied by the equally
important view that the Commons could and should control the
Executive. This has given rise to a strong tradition setting out "the
order of things" which has been influential in the study of the
Constitution.[23]

2–17   The period of transformation from Parliament acting through
legislation to deal with individual problems and grievances into a
more collective action on social, economic and political problems may
be said to begin in the mid-nineteenth century. Precise dates are
difficult to provide but it is generally agreed that between 1830 and
1850 central government expanded its functions to include railways,
factories, poor law, public health and licensing. Legislation concerning these areas may be identified to indicate the growth in government activities and administration. Government policies were
proactive in providing the impetus for change in society in the
industrial and agrarian revolution of the period.[24]

---

[20] Alan Watson, *Failures of the Legal Imagination* (Edinburgh, 1988), pp. 39–40.
[21] A. Watson, *Society and Legal Change* (Edinburgh, 1977); Milsom, *Historical Foundations of the English Common Law* (2nd ed., 1981); F. Pollock and F. W. Maitland, *The History of English Law* (Cambridge, 1968); A. Watson, *The Evolution of Law* (John Hopkins, 1985).
[22] P. S. Atiyah and R. S. Sumners, *Form and Substance in Anglo-American Law* (Oxford, 1987). M. Lobban, *The Common Law and English Jurisprudence 1760–1850 (Oxford, 1991)*.
[23] M. Loughlin, *Public Law and Legal Theory* (1992), pp. 158–9; T. R. S. Allan, *Law, Liberty and Justice* (Oxford, 1993), pp. 264–90.
[24] P. Craig, *Administrative Law* (2nd ed., 1989), pp. 34–51.

Simultaneously with the growth of central government[25] activities, **2–18** local and municipal government also changed. The Reform Act 1832, broadening the franchise for central government after a Royal Commission reported on municipal corporations and their defects led to the Municipal Corporations Act 1835, which extended the franchise for local government. The result was that after 1835 the franchise included a wider range of people than before, bringing urban middle class interests into the activities of local government. Local government was further reformed, after the 1867 and 1884 central government franchise was expanded; the Local Government Act 1888 instituted a two-tier system of government in the metropolis.

Craig points out that the local government system developed in the **2–19** nineteenth century, survived virtually unchanged until 1972[26]:

"The metropolis had a two-tier system with the London County Council at the top and metropolitan boroughs providing the second tier. County boroughs, the larger towns, were single purpose authorities. The counties were slightly more complex. The County Council was the main authority for the area. Beneath it existed three types of institution: non County boroughs; urban districts; and rural districts. The last of these could have parish councils within its area, thereby providing a third tier of authority."

Local government is a good example of the extensive legislative powers granted by Parliament,[27] to enable local authorities to expand their activities and diversify their interests.

Changes also occurred in parliamentary procedures for legislation, reflecting a change in the policies and directions of the government. Private Bill procedures and private Members' Bills gave way to Public General Acts of Parliament.

Craig notes two further trends in the centralisation of legislative **2–20** power. The first is that the use of standing committees of the whole House, favoured discussion by the Government of policy in detail and helped expedite busy legislative programmes. Added to this was the increase in Cabinet Committees to discuss and debate any legislative proposals, thus preparing the way for the safe passage of proposals knowing that agreement and party political support would most likely be given.

The second is the growth of delegated legislation which considerably broadened the scope of government powers and ministerial discretion; this is discussed in more detail in Chapter 9.

---

[25] *ibid.*

[26] Brebner, "Laissez-faire and State Intervention in nineteenth century Britain" (1948) 8 *Journal of Economic History* 61.

[27] Craig, *op. cit.*

2-21   The growth of party politics is also significant in the development of Parliament's political authority. The extension of the franchise broadened Parliament's appeal and rooted its legitimacy in its responsiveness to the popular vote. This could easily detract from the power and authority of Parliament itself, if voting patterns were not focused on group activity and electoral manifestos. Successive governments responded by tightening control over party political policies and discipline which included the use of guillotine procedures, the whip system of party voting and the selection of members of Parliament to sit in committees. Electoral choices through elections replaced appointments through patronage, but patronage returned in a different guise as a means of operating party politics effectively.[28]

The development of the parliamentary system of government is an important part of the discussion of administrative law. It also provides a perspective on the constitutional arrangements for the United Kingdom in its relations within the European Community.[29]

(c)   The Forms of Legislation

2-22 So far we have discussed the output of Parliament using the general term "legislation." The term legislation may be used in three senses. First, it refers to "Acts of Parliament" these are primary rules contained in government legislation and called "Public General Acts." Erskine May[30] defined such an Act as "a law affecting the whole public, one which belongs to the *jus generale publician*": generally today we would recognise such Acts as forming the bulk of Government policy and as reflecting a major part of the *legislative* role of Parliament. Second, it may refer to private Acts of Parliament. Erskine May referred to such Acts as being "in the form of an Act of Parliament, some special rule affecting only a special section of the nation, what may be called *jus particulor*." Private Acts of Parliament were once an important device to promote specific interests – local authorities, railways, companies and even to circumvent the existing law on planning matters. Since 1987 criticism of the use of private Bill procedures in the planning system led to a recommendation that private legislation should[31] be available only as a last resort and not

---

[28] See Chap. 5.

[29] This point is partly made by Wilson, *Cases and Materials on Constitutional and Administrative Law* (2nd ed., 1976). *Twenty Eighth Report: The Role of National Parliaments in the European Union* (1995/6; H.C. 51–XXVIII).

[30] May, *Parliamentary Practice*. Also see David Miers and Alan Page, *Legislation* (2nd ed., 1990).

[31] Report of the Joint Committee on Private Bill Procedure 1987–88 (1988; H.C. 625; H.L. 97).

as an alternative to established statutory procedures. In fact, the increase in public general Acts has reduced the quantity of private Bills. A specialised procedure is required for the introduction and debate of private Bills which is expensive and time consuming.

Private Bills may be introduced by members of Parliament and are **2–23** usually termed "private Member's Bills." There are primarily two methods or procedures which may be used. The first is a ballot of Members of Parliament held each session giving 20 members the opportunity to introduce a private Bill in the limited time available.[32] Since 1972 the Government has allocated annually £200 towards drafting expenses but even this modest change has little impact. In 1982 Norman St. John Stevas M.P. successfully introduced his private Member's Bill, Parliamentary Control of Expenditure (Reform Bill). This Bill was later adopted by the Government of the day in return for a number of changes which were duly made. The new revised Bill successfully became law as the National Audit Act 1983. Nevertheless the experience was far from satisfactory, illustrating the dependence of the success of a private Members' Bill on government assistance and drafting.[33]

The second procedure is under "the Ten Minute Rule." Members of **2–24** Parliament unsuccessful in the ballot may set down a motion for leave to introduce a Bill on Tuesdays and Wednesdays. Three weeks' notice is usually required and the majority of such Bills have been allowed to lapse and were unsuccessful. It is estimated that only 10 to 12 private Members' Bills became law each session. The ballot procedure is usually the best chance of a private Member's Bill becoming law.[34]

In constitutional terms there is no *legal* distinction between the **2–25** authority of a private Act and a public general Act. The courts are unwilling to allow a challenge to the validity of either a public or private Act as explained in 1974 in *Pickin v. British Railways Board.*[35] This marks out the limits of judicial scrutiny under the United Kingdom's constitutional arrangements.[36] This does not, however, prevent the Courts from taking account of E.C. law and whenever

---

[32] In Scotland see Private Legislation Procedure (Scotland) Act 1936. Also see "Private Bill Procedure: A Case for Reform" [1981] P.L. 206.

[33] On the background to the Bill see Gavin Drewry [1983] P.L. 531.

[34] Bills under the 10-minute rule are limited to one per day. An M.P. is limited to one within 15 sittings days.

[35] [1974] A.C. 765. Also see Wade, "The Basis of Legal Sovereignty" [1955] C.L.J. 172.

[36] Northern Ireland has a written constitution, first under the Government of Ireland Act 1920, now repealed, and presently under the Northern Ireland Constitution Act 1973 as amended. The courts have considerable powers to hold "measures of the Northern Ireland Assembly" as unconstitutional. Under the Government of Ireland Act 1920 the courts could review legislation passed by the old Stormont Parliament. See *R. v. Londonderry JJ., ex p. Hume and others* [1972] N.I. 91.

there is a conflict between a United Kingdom Act of Parliament and E.C. law, resolving the conflict in favour of the latter. This includes the recent *Factortame*[37] case illustrating the overriding of a United Kingdom Act of Parliament in subservience to E.C. law.

2–26   The term legislation may also apply to a third category of Bill known as a "Hybrid Bill."[38] It is difficult to provide an exact definition of a hybrid Bill. Erskine May defines it as legislation which[39] "affects a particular private interest in a manner different from the private interests of other persons or bodies of the same category or class."

One *caveat* to introducing a private Bill whether or not it is a hybrid Bill, is *Standing Order No. 48* of the House of Commons, namely that the main object of such a Bill *may not create a charge on public funds,* as this lies within the allocation of ministerial power only. In the case of a dispute over the exact procedure for a Bill, the matter may be adjudicated by the Clerk of Public Bills and the Members concerned.[40]

2–27   The legislative output of the Government also includes a vast number of statutory instruments which are loosely described by the phrase "delegated legislation." Generally the average number of public general Acts in any one year is 63; a corresponding assessment of the number of statutory instruments comes to over 6,000. Since 1900 the growth in legislation has been a remarkable feature of Parliament's activities. Griffith and Ryle conclude[41]: "In our opinion the growth of work and activity is the most noteworthy change in the functioning of the House of Commons in this century."

As we shall see in Chapter 9 the growth in legislation has had an effect on the procedures, character and nature of the House of Commons and this includes the use of select committees. Back-bench Members of Parliament have been given a greater role through the formation of the numerous select committees to expedite legislation.

2–28   A distinctive feature of English law has been the formal structures and procedures adopted. Atiyah and Summers identified the heavy reliance on statute law[42]:

---

[37] [1991] 1 A.C. 603; Case C–213/89, [1990] E.C.R. I–2433; [1990] 3 C.M.L.R. 375.

[38] Erskine May, *Parliamentary Practice* (20th ed., 1983), p. 896. See D. Miers and Alan Page, *Legislation* (London, 1990), p. 10; Griffith and Ryle, *Parliament* (1989), pp. 229, 312.

[39] May, *op. cit.* p. 896.

[40] One of the most controversial in recent years was the Channel Tunnel Bill, criticised because the Government used a hybrid Bill procedure which effectively blocked the usual planning procedures such as inquiries, to permit the building of the tunnel. An undertaking that "no public funds" be used in the project has caused subsequent embarrassment to the government. See the Channel Tunnel Act 1987.

[41] Griffith and Ryle, *op. cit.* p. 288.

[42] Atiyah and Summers, *op. cit.* p. 298. See N. J. Ornstein (ed.), *The Role of the Legislature in Western Democracies* (American Enterprise Institute for Public Policy Research, Washington, 1981).

" . . . the English political – legal system relies more heavily than the American on statute law and less on case-law, and that, because statute law is more formal than case-law, this is one factor which makes English law more formal."

The authors conclude that to a large extent the wide use of **2-29** legislation in the United Kingdom is a reflection of the constitutional arrangements present under the parliamentary system of government. The characteristics of the parliamentary system may be enumerated as follows: strong centralised political institutions; the English judiciary has a relatively weak role as compared with the centralised executive – legislative machinery; strong ministerial influence has a powerful control over the legislative; the United Kingdom parliamentary system combines executive and legislative powers; party political influence may strengthen cabinet government and this in turn strengthens the ministerial *fiat*; Ministers are effectively in control of making most delegated legislation and it is uncommon for government-supported legislation not to be successfully passed through Parliament.[43]

Concern about delegated legislation[44] led to the Donoughmore **2-30** Committee on Ministers Powers in 1932 which recognised the problem of scrutiny over delegated legislation. Many of these problems remain. S. A. Walkland noted[45]:

"Much of the suspicion of delegated legislation is aroused by the fact that civil servants are intimately associated with its procedures, and that the opportunities for participation in the process by representative and politically responsible members of the House of Commons are necessarily limited."

Finally, it is necessary to consider European Community legisla- **2-31** tion. Since 1972 the United Kingdom's accession into the E.C. has committed her to adopting a variety of E.C. legislation. In 1972 both the House of Commons and the House of Lords provided new committees to scrutinise proposals for Community legislation and consider how best they might be adopted. The role of the United Kingdom Parliament with such legislation is to ensure that the

---

[43] A. H. Birch, "The theory and Practice of Modern British Democracy" in J. Jowell and D. Oliver, *The Changing Constitution* (2nd ed., 1990); P. Norton, *Parliament in the 1980s* (Blackwells, Oxford, 1985); J. A. G. Griffith, *Parliamentary Scrutiny of Government Bills* (Allen and Unwin, London, 1974); N. Johnson, *In Search of the Constitution, Reflections on State and Society in Britain* (1977).

[44] *Machinery of Government Committee* Cd. 9230 (1918); Hewart, *New Despotism* (London, 1929); Report of the Committee on Ministers' Powers, Cmd. 4060 (1932).

[45] S. A. Walkland, *The Legislative Process in Great Britain* (1968), pp. 16–17.

domestic law is made consistent with E.C. Law. Thus, the committee does not consider the substantive *merits* of legislative proposals or other E.C. documents. Its role does not include any formal input into the Community's own law-making processes. United Kingdom ministries participate in legislation through the Council of Ministers. Thus there is no direct means for the United Kingdom *Parliament* to adopt a formal role in the law-making process of the E.C.

2–32   It is noticeable that the remit of the House of Lords Scrutiny Committee over E.C. legislation is wider than the House of Commons committee, the former's terms of reference allow for a limited inquiry into "the merits of community proposals." More time is devoted in the House of Lords committee than in the Commons committee and the Lords reports are generally accepted as authoritative.

(d)   Drafting and interpreting legislation

2–33   An important but often neglected subject is the question of how legislation is drafted. The existence of the Parliamentary Counsel Office is all too often ignored. The office came into existence in 1869 during Gladstone's first administration.[46] Previously Acts of Parliament were drafted either by the judges or by practising lawyers or by Members of Parliament. The creation of the Parliamentary Counsel Office regularised the drafting of Bills.

Today Parliamentary Counsel are responsible for the drafting of Government Bills with the exception of those relating exclusively to Scotland. Counsel are involved in advising government departments on aspects of Parliamentary procedure and in the drafting of amendments. The staff of the Office of Parliamentary Counsel in Whitehall in London comprise over 30 members including the First Parliamentary Counsel. The Finance Bill 1996 was subjected to external drafting through a contract awarded outside the Office of the Parliamentary Counsel.

2–34   The Law Commission provides important input into the drafting of new legislation through its work on law reform and its duty to keep the statute book under review. It publishes consultation papers and its reports contain draft Bills containing details of law reform proposals. There is a Common Law and Public team within the Law Commission engaged in an overview of public law matters.[47]

---

[46] Treasury Minute February 8, 1869. See: "The Parliamentary Counsel Office" *The House Magazine* March 20, 1981, pp. 20–1. I am very grateful to Mr Jenkins, First Parliamentary Counsel and the staff of his office for this information.

[47] See *Administrative Law: Judicial Review and Statutory Appeals, Law Commission* No. 226 (1994) The draft Bill provides an important model for administrative reform.

Although there is a special parliamentary procedure for Law Commission Bills there is no special status attached to such Bills to ensure that they are taken into the parliamentary timetable or to ensure that they become law.

Increasingly important in the techniques of drafting Bills are the **2–35** rules of statutory interpretation. It is more common than in the past for the courts to look at reports of Parliamentary debates in *Hansard* as an aid to interpretation. The use of *Hansard* in certain circumstances as an aid to interpretation[48] has been recently approved by the House of Lords in *Pepper v. Hart.*[49] The discussion and analysis contained in the reports of Parliamentary Select Committees is also very helpful.

There are various aids in the interpretation of statutes. These **2–36** consist of rules or presumptions about how words in a statute may be interpreted. Taken together they form what are called principles of statutory interpretation that are generally applied in English law. Different rules apply in the interpretation of European Community law. The continental style of drafting only sets out general broad principles. This leaves the exact details to be filled in by the judges, who are expected to promote the general legislative purpose of the law.

In English law the principles of statutory interpretation consist of rules and presumptions and at the discretion of the judge may be applied when seeking to understand the meaning of a statute. The following are the main rules to aid interpretation.

(i) **The literal rule.** The literal rule refers to the method of **2–37** interpretation of words in a statute by giving words their plain, ordinary or literal meaning. Courts attempt to find the parliamentary intention behind the statute. As an aid to interpretation the dictionary meaning of words may be used.

(ii) **The golden rule.** The golden rule when applied is used to **2–38** modify the literal rule by seeking to avoid any absurdity. If the words used in legislation are ambiguous, the golden rule allows the court to avoid the absurdity and adopt a meaning that is suitable for the purpose intended rather than permit some absurd outcome. The application of the golden rule is at the discretion of the court. It may be used in preference to the literal rule. Where the courts decide that public policy requires an interpretation beyond the literal interpretation of the words, the golden rule may ensure effect is given to public policy. In public law cases the golden rule is frequently used to understand the nature of the legislation.

---

[48] See Lord Lester, "Pepper v. Hart Revisited" (1992) 15 (1) *Statutory Law Review* (1994) 10.

[49] *Pepper v. Hart* [1993] 1 All E.R. 42.

2–39   (iii) **The mischief rule.** The mischief rule, otherwise referred to as the rule in *Heydon's Case*[50] allows the courts to examine the law before the statute was made in order to ascertain the nature of the *mischief* which the statute was intended to remedy. The mischief rule allows the courts some discretion in finding the construction of the statute that best applies to the facts of the case. In public law cases the mischief rule provides the courts with the means to look behind the policy and objectives of the legislation.

2–40   (iv) *Ejusdem generis* **rule.** In applying the rules of interpretation the court may read the statute as a whole to understand the overall context of the law. Normally the courts give attention to the *ejusdem generis* rule, meaning that general words which follow particular words are limited in meaning to those of the particular words. The courts may follow certain presumptions when interpreting a statute. Property rights or private rights are not implicitly interfered with unless there are very clear words. The individual's liberty is presumed not to be interfered with unless Parliament has provided clear words.[51] Parliament is assumed not to have altered the common law unless the statute expressly makes this clear. There are also presumptions that for a criminal offence there must be proof of the requisite intention or guilty mind before the accused may be convicted. Statutes are generally presumed not to have retrospective effect. The courts presume that crimes are not to be created by Parliament retrospectively because it would be oppressive or abhorrent to do so.[52]

2–41   As already mentioned there is no hard and fast rule as to the rule of interpretation or presumption the courts may wish to follow. Courts exercise a discretion according to the context of the law and the facts of the case. Statutory interpretation is aided in the way the statute is drafted. The preamble to the Act sets forth the need for the legislation and sometimes the effect the legislation is intended to have. The long title of an Act may assist the court in cases of ambiguity. It explains the purpose behind the legislation. The short title to an Act provides a general description of the Act but rarely is a guide to interpretation. Modern Acts of Parliament may have headings delineating particular sections or parts of the Act. There are marginal notes and side-notes. These are not part of the Act and are not discussed in Parliament. They may provide some help in finding the sense of a difficult section but are not normally used by the

---

[50] (1584) 3 Co. Rep. 7a.

[51] See *R. v. Secretary of State for the Home Department, ex p. Leech* [1993] 4 All E.R. 539 upholding the citizen's right to the free flow of communication between a solicitor and client.

[52] See *R. v. Lord Chancellor, ex p. Witham* [1997] 2 All E.R. 779.

courts. Finally there are schedules to many modern Acts. There is an increasing tendency to use the schedules to contain more detail than is possible in the main part of the Act. This is to avoid the main part of the Act becoming unduly cluttered. This has the disadvantage that often reference must be made to the schedules of the Act to understand the main content of each of the sections.

Attempts to simplify legislation may fall under the new procedures **2–42** under the Deregulation and Contracting Out Act 1994. This allows for ministerial Order by affirmative resolution to amend or repeal existing primary legislation. The draft of the proposed Order must be scrutinised by the Deregulation Committee in the House of Commons and by the Delegated Powers Scrutiny Committee in the House of Lords.

There is a Deregulation Task Force. Its remit is to identify regulatory burdens on industry[53] and make recommendations for their removal. In its first report, the Task Force identifies some of the areas where business is carrying a heavy regulatory burden. There are over 600 proposals for reducing the legislative burden of regulation.

(e) Debate and Scrutiny

Parliament's role is not confined to the passage of legislation. It **2–43** performs a number of other functions – it informs, debates, scrutinises and approves. It is widely accepted that as the Commons has limited influence over the substance of legislation[54] since most governments can almost always ensure that their legislation becomes law, these other functions may be of questionable significance. Even though the government with a large working majority will nearly always ensure that its legislation is passed, the House of Commons provides, through its procedures and processes, legitimation for legislation. Debates, votes and censure are the life blood of party politics and the House of Commons provides the opposition with a forum to censure the Government of the day. Opposition M.P.s may introduce Bills, ask questions, introduce amendments, table motions and attend as members of select committees to oversee the activities of government departments.

---

[53] See *Lifting the Burden* Cmnd. 9571 (1985).
[54] A novel example of how debate and scrutiny may be given to M.P.s is over Sunday trading. At the start of the 1993–94 session, the White Paper on Sunday trading Cm. 2300, (1993) (July 13) included the text of a draft Bill and policy considerations. Four different options were considered in Clause 1. In the event three options for Sunday trading were considered on a free vote of the House of Commons. The House of Commons agreed to large shops opening on Sunday subject to a six-hour limitation by 333 votes to 258. See the Sunday Trading Act 1994. Also see: Licensing (Sunday Hours) Act 1995.

2–44 The development of Select Committees has been piece-meal. The most prestigious is the Public Accounts Committee (PAC) established in 1861 to ensure the financial scrutiny of Government activities. Uniquely placed among the other select committees because the Comptroller and Auditor General may give evidence to that Committee, prepare reports and assist the Committee in its work. Once the Auditor General makes a report, there is an opportunity for the PAC to respond in the form of a report followed by the Treasury, on behalf of the Government Department setting out in a Treasury minute its own findings. Parliamentary scrutiny of government finance is a specialised area of activity, and one that emphasises Parliament's authority to approve expenditure. Public finance is examined in detail in Chapter 11.

2–45 Since 1979 "new select committees"[55] were introduced in a reform of existing committee procedures. The new committees are intended to scrutinise the departments of government, covering all aspects of the departments' roles and adopting investigative techniques as a means of control. It was expected that the select committee system would help the House of Commons to exercise some control over government activities. A major sanction comes from an adverse report which might later be reported to the House of Commons and lead to ministerial embarrassment.[56]

The number of Select Committees may change over time. In the last Parliament before the general election held on May 1, 1997, there were 18 House of Commons select committees covering all the main departments of government. In addition there were 25 other committees including the Committee on Standards and Privileges, the Committee of Public Accounts, the Joint Committee on Consolidation, etc. Bills, and the Select Committee on European Legislation.

2–46 The composition of select committees allows back-bench M.P.s the opportunity to take an active role in the scrutiny of government. There is an all-party Committee of Selection which makes nominations for appointment, having regard to the balance of parties in the House. However, the fear of domination by party politics and the system of Whips is a real one. This ensures that party policy may be represented in the selection of M.P.s for the committees. Outspoken or too independently minded M.P.s may be persuaded not to stand for election. This is seen as an inevitable weakness in the present arrangements.

Technically, a select committee has power "to send for persons, papers and records" but this power is subject to practical restraints.

---

[55] G. Drewry, *The New Select Committees* (1985) (2nd ed., 1989); also see Griffith and Ryle, *op. cit.* Chap. 11.

[56] Fourth Report from the Defence Committee (1985–86); H.C. 519, paras. 225–238; Griffith and Ryle, *op. cit.* pp. 423–451.

The private citizen may choose to claim his right to silence, especially if there is a possibility of criminal proceedings pending. Although attendance may be made compulsory, replies to questions are largely left to the citizen's discretion.

In the case of civil servants, negotiation is required between the **2–47** minister responsible for the Department and the Committee, if a civil servant is to be allowed to give evidence. Questions asked of civil servants by the committee are constrained by the embargo Ministers may place on civil servants over matters of confidentiality, policy questions or the individual conduct of an official. The attendance of a particular civil servant, even though requested by the committee, is ultimately decided by Ministers. In the recent Westland affair,[57] which raised issues relating to the leaking of a confidential letter of the Solicitor General, the Defence Committee was refused the attendance of five civil servants. The Westland company supplied helicopters and required re-organisation in the light of new market conditions. Rival financial packages from U.S. and European companies caused intense debate within the Government and the Cabinet. The leaking of the confidential letter of the Solicitor General involved certain civil servants, allegedly acting under the direction of a Cabinet Minister.

Since then directions issued to civil servants, reminding them of **2–48** their duty of loyalty to Ministers[58] and the government of the day raises doubts about the ability of select committees to penetrate the relationship between civil servants and Ministers. In strict constitutional theory, this relationship supports the doctrine of ministerial responsibility whereby *Ministers* and not civil servants, are accountable directly to Parliament.

In addition to the new select committees there are a plethora of other committees of the House of Commons. Amazingly these come to 30 select committees in total (including the new committees) dealing with a variety of matters such as the Committee of Privileges, and the Select Committee on the Parliamentary Commissioner.

The assessment of the impact of select committees on government **2–49** behaviour is difficult and is considered in further detail in Chapter 9.[59] On the one hand in favour of their role, there is a fact-finding and information contribution which undoubtedly exists because of the

---

[57] Michael Heseltine, then Secretary of State for Defence resigned over his allegation that he had been excluded from various Cabinet committees. See *The Observer*, January 12, 1986. Also see Marshall, [1986] P.L. 184. Discussion of the affair may be found in the Defence Select Committee (1985–86; H.C. 519); Cm. 9916 (1986) and Cm. 9841 (1986).

[58] Memorandum of Guidance for Officials Appearing before Select Committees, Cm. 78 (1987).

[59] Anne Davies, *Reformed Select Committees : The First Years* (1981). See Chap. 9 for a fuller discussion of the role of select committees.

select committee system. We know more and have more information about government as a result. On the other hand there is a lack of success in bringing measurable differences in the way that government is conducted. Ministers and civil servants may, through careful briefing, actually second guess the committee's work. Often committees are *ex post facto* inquiries and they depend on the enthusiasm and skill of the individual M.P.s for their success. A lot may depend on the tenacity of the chairman and his skill in avoiding the division of opinion on the committee along party political lines. This system may be too random and haphazard to be relied upon. Ultimately political issues may intervene in the work of the committees, as when back-bench M.P.s attempt to use committee's findings in debates in the House of Commons to criticise or defend Government policy. There is the added concern that strengthening select committees moves the *locus* of power away from the House of Commons to back room committees. Reassurance on this point has come from the televised proceedings of select committee hearings, which have done much to publicise their work and gain recognition for their important role. Finally, it may be conceded that select committees in this country look less impressive than the U.S. Congressional Committees with which they are commonly compared. This seems an unfair comparison given the difference in the constitutional role of each.

2–50   Select committees have a further function, that is they provide a scrutiny over the financial affairs of the government. We have already discussed the PAC, but the role of each select committee includes within their respective remit, scrutiny of departmental expenditures. Flegmann and others have noted[60] that only limited interest has been shown in the select committees' development of financial scrutiny over departments.

2–51   Parliamentary debate is often party political and adversarial in style whereas select committees are intended to be bi-partisan and inquisitorial. Craig observes[61]:

"Select committees run counter to both of these tenets: they seek to strengthen the power of Parliament as against the executive, and to proceed by a more non-partisan approach."

The essence of committees, however, is that they are "committees of the whole House." Any weakening of that fundamental link might leave committees untrusted as an unrepresentative intrusion into government decision-taking and even a usurpation of parliamentary

[60] V. Flegman, "The Public Accounts Committee; A Successful Select Committee?" XXXIII *Parliamentary Affairs* (1980).
[61] Craig, *Administrative Law* (2nd ed., 1989), pp. 68–69.

control. The tightrope existence between committees as "independent" scrutineers of government activities and the application of party politics, is difficult to explain. The further committees expand their independent scrutiny, the more tension may arise between their role and the government of the day. This may expose the constitutional limitations which surround their role.

(f) Parliament, the Crown and Prerogative

In a constitutional sense the Government's law-making powers are **2–52** exercised by the Crown in Parliament. Today, legislation in its various forms, is the most common source of the Government's legal powers. The powers of government may also exist by virtue[62] of custom and derived from the common law. These provide the sources for the Crown's discretionary powers vested in the government of the day and known as the royal prerogative.

The significance[63] of the royal prerogative, as a source of governmental powers is examined in detail in Chapter 3 in the discussion of the powers and practices of government. It is sufficient here to mention how Parliament's legislative authority was established through limiting, by law, the authority of the Crown, but maintaining the continuity of the royal prerogative.

Munro has defined the royal prerogative as "those attributes **2–53** peculiar to the Crown which are derived from common law, not statute, and which still survive".[64] In origin they appear in custom and in the recognition given to them by the common law. The prerogative had an external use in waging war, but also a domestic application in Royal patronage. Attempts to extend their scope in the fourteenth and fifteenth centuries were largely successful, even if resisted. A variety of Royal powers were appended to the use of the prerogative, including the controversial one of levying different forms of taxation. Such powers were occasionally upheld by the courts but the matter was never finally[65] settled until the Bill of Rights 1688. By abolishing a number of prerogatives and amending others, the Crown's powers were curtailed but at the same time maintained. Parliamentary control once asserted has remained intact; but as Munro observes:

---

[62] Anson, *Law and Custom of the Constitution* (3rd ed., 1907), pp. 1–16.
[63] See Munro, *Studies in Constitutional Law* (1987), p. 159.
[64] *ibid.* p. 159.
[65] See K. L. Keir, *The Constitutional History of Modern Britain since 1485* (1966); *Prohibitions del Roy* (1607) 12 Co. Rep. 63; *Case of Proclamations* (1610) 12 Co. Rep. 74; *The Five Knights' case* (1627) 3 State Tr. 1.

"It is not surprising that modern governments have found it useful to retain such broad discretionary powers to act, which enable action to be taken without the necessity of prior parliamentary approval."

Gap-filling and residual powers are apt descriptions of how the prerogative may be perceived by modern government. Parliament, moreover has condoned the use of the prerogative in this way and has sometimes replaced prerogative powers with statute.[66]

2–54 Parliament has the power to regulate succession to the throne as it thinks fit. Title to the throne is determined under the Act of Settlement 1700 upholding the right of primogeniture; males are preferred over females. The right of succession to the Crown is restricted to being Protestant. The Act of Settlement disqualifies Roman Catholics and those who marry Roman Catholics. The Sovereign must swear to uphold allegiance and maintain the Churches of England and Scotland. Parliament has regulated succession to the throne, as in 1936 under His Majesty's Declaration of Abdication Act 1936 permitting Edward VIII's brother becoming King George VI.

2–55 Parliament has also made special provision under the Regency Acts 1937–53 for the Sovereign's minority, incapacity or absence from the Realm. In recent years public controversy has surrounded the modern Monarchy. The provisions by Parliament of a Civil List of public money for the upkeep of the Royal Family has attracted attention to the role and function of the modern Monarchy. The Civil List Act 1952 provides that a sum of money was annually voted to the Monarch. This sum was amended by the Civil List Act 1972 increasing the sum allocated and requiring an annual report from the Royal Trustees on the current state of the royal finances. The Civil List Act 1975 built into the sum allocated a Treasury power to increase the sum to take account of inflation. In 1991 the Government agreed a 10-year arrangement whereby an annual sum, approximately £8 million, would be paid from the Consolidated Fund. The Queen's personal wealth and income is distinguished from official income and expenditure. Estimates of the Queen's personal wealth appear unreliable as private wealth is not officially disclosed to the public. Since 1992 the Queen undertook responsibility to make provision for certain members of the Royal family out of private wealth. With effect from 1993 the Queen undertook to pay income tax on her private income. This is a voluntary agreement as the Crown is not liable to pay taxes unless Parliament has expressly provided.

[66] The Crown Proceedings Act 1947 partly places the Crown in the same status as the ordinary citizen in connection with legal proceedings.

3. The House of Lords

Historical developments outlined in Chapter 1 explain how relations **2–56** between the Commons and Lords were acrimonious. Even in the late-nineteenth century, the Lords attempted to assert its authority against the will of the elected and newly enfranchised House of Commons. The right to veto Money Bills was the main issue in 1860 when a measure for the repeal of paper duty was accepted in the Commons, but rejected by the Lords. Gladstone, as Chancellor of the Exchequer, had embarked on a major re-organisation of taxes, simplifying and clarifying their collection. Rejection by the Lords according to Gladstone's *Political Memorandum* (May 26, 1860)[67]:

> "amounted to the establishment of a revising power over the House of Commons in its most vital function long declared exclusively its own, and to a divided responsibility in fixing the revenue and charge of the country for the year."

The outcome of the Lords rejection was for the Commons to pass a resolution containing the assertion of principle, namely that: "in its own hands [the House of Commons] had the power to remit and impose taxes and that the right to frame Bills of supply in its own measure, manner and time is a right to be kept inviolable."[68]

The solution came in the form of presenting a single Bill to the **2–57** Lords containing the various financial proposals, and thereby forcing the Lords to accept or reject the whole Bill. This procedure did not prevent debate of the content of the Bill, but it made rejection difficult.

The House of Lords[69] opposed Gladstone's Church Bill in 1869, but the Bill was eventually passed. Irish Home Rule was similarly resisted in 1886 and 1893. Eventually the Commons acted to curtail the powers of the House of Lords by passing the Parliament Acts 1911 and 1949. This was achieved after some resistance from the Lords. In 1909 the Lords rejected the Finance Bill, but agreed to pass it on return of the Liberals after the election. After the second general election in 1910, the passage of certain Bills was achieved only when the Government threatened to swamp the Lords with newly created peers. The Lords finally agreed to pass the Parliament Bill curtailing their powers.

---

[67] Quoted and discussed in John Morley, *Life of Gladstone* (London, 1903), Vol. II, p. 33.
[68] *ibid.*
[69] Note the early origins of the House of Lords may be found in the *Curia Regis*. See R. Brazier, *Constitutional Practice* (1988), Chap. 10; D. Shell, *The House of Lords* (1988), (2nd ed., 1992).

2–58   Both Parliament Acts are relevant to the powers of the House of Lords today. The 1911 Act achieved three major alterations in the law. The Lords' powers to veto or delay Money Bills was abolished. In the case of other public Bills, the Lords' absolute veto was abolished, and a power to delay legislation for two years was substituted. Finally, the life of Parliament was reduced from seven to five years.

The two-year-period of delay still permitted the Lords an influence over the political policy of the government of the day. In certain circumstances this might become crucial and amount to an effective veto if the delay was timed to coincide with the period before a general election.

2–59   Further reforms of the Lords were considered and resulted in the Parliament Act 1949. The results of the 1949 legislation may be outlined as follows: Together, the Parliament Acts 1911–49, provide that Bills may receive the Royal Assent if only approved by the Commons.[70] This may occur either if the Lords fail within one month to pass a Bill which has passed the Commons and been endorsed by the Speaker as a Money Bill, or where the Lords refuse in two successive sessions to pass a Public Bill other than a Bill certified as a Money Bill. This last situation includes a Bill to extend the maximum duration of Parliament beyond five years which has been passed by the Commons in those two sessions provided that one year has elapsed between the date of the Bill's second reading in the Commons, in the first of those sessions, and the date of its third reading in that House, in the second of those sessions.[71]

2–60   The definition of a Money Bill is contained in the Acts[72], Section 1 of the 1911 Act, as amended by the 1949 Act, and by the National Loans Act 1968, refers to a Public Bill which the Speaker certifies covers:

> "the important, repeal, remission, alteration or regulation of taxation; the imposition of charges on the Consolidated Fund or the National Loans Fund or on money provided by Parliament for the payment of debt or other financial purposes or the variation or repeal of such charges, supply, the appropriation, receipt custody, issue or audit of public accounts or the raising or guarantee or repayment of loans."

A strict interpretation applies and rarely are certificates issued; even the Finance Bill presented annually does not often meet the above criteria.

---

[70] D. R. Shell, "The House of Lords and the Thatcher Government" *Parliamentary Affairs* XXXVIII, pp. 16–32; Janet Morgan, *The House of Lords and the Labour Government 1964–1970* (1975).

[71] *ibid.*

[72] P. Norton (ed.), *Parliament in the 1980s* (1985).

The restrictions set out above on the Lords' powers seldom apply **2–61** in practice and thus, the basic principle that "the Crown demands money, the Commons grant it, and the Lords assent to the grant" remains true today. The fact that the Speaker's certificate, once issued, is conclusive proof of the status of the Bill, means that it may not be questioned in any court of law. The Poll Tax legislation, the Local Government Finance Bill 1988, did not qualify as a Money Bill. It was debated and amended in the Lords but passed after the Government defeated an amendment that the Bill should take account of Poll Tax payers' incomes.

In fact, few Bills[73] have been introduced invoking the 1911 Act procedure. The examples often cited include the Government of Ireland Act 1914, the Welsh Church Act 1914 and the Parliament Act 1949 itself.

In 1990–91 the War Crimes Bill, retrospecively authorising prosecu- **2–62** tions in Britain in respect of war crimes in Germany or German occupied territory during the Second World War, resulted in sufficient controversy for the Government to invoke the Parliament Acts. The Bill was passed after being twice defeated in the Lords but agreed in the Commons on a free vote.[74] This example clearly illustrates the use of the Parliament Acts to ensure the ultimate authority of the Commons over the Lords.

Ironically there is a dispute over the question of whether the 1911 Act procedure was capable of allowing the change introduced by the 1949 Act. The principle objection to using the 1911 Act is that a power conferred for one purpose should not be used for another purpose.[75] Given the fact that the 1949 Act consolidated and amended the 1911 Act this may be seen as a step in the direction originally taken by the 1911 Act and therefore the 1949 Act is consistent with the 1911 Act.

Attempts to reform the House of Lords have continued since 1949. **2–63** Discussion of the aims and objectives of the Lords have been included in a *White Paper on House of Lords Reform*[76] in 1968. The functions performed by the Lords may be summarised as follows: (i) debate and discussion; (ii) the consideration of delegated legislation; (iii) the initiation of pubic legislation including both Government and private Members' Bills; (iv) the revision of public Bills received from

---

[73] Hood Phillips, *Constitutional and Administrative Law*, p. 193:
  " . . . The Parliaments Acts do not apply to Bills which seek to extend the maximum duration of Parliament beyond five years, nor to local and private legislation, nor to Public Bills, which confirm Provisional Orders. Nor do they apply to delegated legislation; here the formal powers of the Lords will depend on whether the parent Act expressly empowers the Lords to approve or disapprove of the delegated legislation in question."

[74] G. Ganz (1992) 55 M.L.R. 87.

[75] P. Norton (ed.), *op. cit.*

[76] Cmnd. 3799 (1968).

the Commons; (v) the general scrutiny of Government and of private legislation; (vi) the work of select committees such as the European Communities and, finally; (vii) in its judicial capacity as the Supreme Court of Appeal in domestic matters, excluding the law of the European Community.

Taken together, such functions contribute to the process of legislation and in the general debate about government and its powers. The Lords were the first to allow radio and television to broadcast their debates. Generally it is accepted that the quality and standard of debate is high. This is partly attributable to the fact that many of their Lordships hold or have held prominent positions[77] in life, and partly to the individual expertise the Lords may bring to the discussion.

2–64   The fact that the Lords is unelected and does not have equal political legitimacy to the Commons, leaves the question of the function and role of the Lords difficult to justify in terms of democratic accountability. Most reform proposals for the House of Lords provide some means to replace the appointment process with some form of elections. This would considerably alter the Lords' role and function.

2–65   Norton[78] offers the analysis that many of Parliament's functions may be formulated within six categories: (i) legislative scrutiny; (ii) latent legitimisation; (iii) scrutiny and influence; (iv) tension release; (v) support mobilisation and (vi) providing the personnel of government.

Taking each of the six categories, their relevance to the House of Lords may be seen as follows. Legislative scrutiny includes similar procedures in the Lords as in the Commons for the reading of Bills, debate and scrutiny. It is said that the less crowded political agenda and the absence of party political divisions, favours a more constructive role for the Lords in terms of scrutiny of the Executive, because of the greater influence of ideas and learned opinion from eminent experts in their field. All this may seem to add up to a "constitutional safeguard" provided by the Lords.

2–66   Latent legitimisation[79] is of more doubtful relevance to the Lords. The fact that it meets regularly and without interruption may provide a source of legitimacy; but the Commons undoubtedly is seen to offer legitimacy to government because it has claims to electoral support. In recent years the Lords has adopted a robust approach to the policies of the government of the day.

2–67   Griffith and Ryle note that, recently, opportunities for the Lords to contribute to debates, come through the introduction of substantial

---

[77] Griffith and Ryle, op. cit. p. 481.
[78] Norton, "The House of Lords and Parliamentary Reform" in Jones et al., Politics U.K. (1991) p. 365.
[79] ibid. p. 365.

Bills into the Lords to avoid over-burdening the parliamentary time in the Commons.[80]

In addition to Bills introduced into the Lords, the opportunity for revision comes in the form of amendments to Bills. One estimate[81] is that:

> "... the number of amendments made has increased from an average per session of 511 under the 1964-5 Labour adminstration to 788 per session from 1970-74, 645 per session for 1976-79 and 1,061 per session in 1979-86."

The Lords may be said to fit into Norton's category of scrutiny and **2–68** influence.[82] In that connection because the Lords are largely independent of party politics, they may have "a limited tension release function." Particular causes may be debated and pressure groups given a voice which may not be easily accommodated within the agenda of the House of Commons. This does not go so far as to provide "support mobilisation" in Norton's terminology meaning popular support, because of the Lords' lack of political legitimacy.

The last remaining function identified by Norton, is the role of the Lords in contributing to the personnel of government through providing junior ministers (normally about 10). It is also customary that some peers have a seat in the Cabinet (normally about two).

Finally, the House of Lords, by supplying a judicial function through the Law Lords, contributes to the judicial function under the Constitution.

The potential for acrimony between the Lords and Commons rose **2–69** throughout the period when Mrs Thatcher was Prime Minister. Norton notes[83]:

> "The Thatcher administration was defeated more than one hundred times, several of the defeats taking place on contentious political issues including the 1980 Education (No. 2) Bill and the 1984 Paving Bill for the abolition of the Greater London Council."

A number of explanations may be offered: (i) a growing criticism of the style and management of Mrs Thatcher's government found support in the Lords, especially as a number of ex-Cabinet ministers were given seats in the Lords; (ii) an influx of new life peers more

---

[80] Griffith and Ryle, *op. cit.* pp. 480–481.
[81] *ibid.*
[82] N. Baldwin, "The House of Lords: Behaviour Changes" in P. Norton (ed.), *Parliament in the 1980s* (Blackwell, 1985).
[83] *ibid.*

willing to adopt an active role in the criticism of government; and (iii)
the unlikelihood of the introduction of any reform of the House of
Lords may have added to its need to find a more robust and publicly
acknowledged role.

A recurring theme in discussing the current role of the House of
Lords is its unelected status. This raises questions about its
composition.[84]

(a) Composition

2–70   Entitlement to membership of the House of Lords reflects its historic
past. Five categories of membership exist. First the Church of
England, including the 26 Lords Spiritual who are the Archbishops of
Canterbury and York, plus the Bishops of London, Durham and
Winchester together with 21 Senior Bishops of the Church of
England. Other ecclesiastical groupings may be represented through
the nomination of Life Peers. The Roman Catholic Archbishop of
Westminster is not included and only recently the Chief Rabbi, head
of the Jewish faith, has been made a Life Peer.

2–71   The second category of membership includes hereditary peers.
Discrimination against women has been reduced since the Sex
Disqualification (Removal) Act 1919 and in 1958 this was extended to
life peers. Hereditary peers include the holders of peerages created in
England before 1707, in Great Britain (1707-1800) and the United
Kingdom from 1801.

The third category of membership covers hereditary peers of
Scotland created before the Union with Scotland. After 1903 the
Peerage Act 1903 removed the restriction of 16 members. The fourth
category is numerically more significant, namely life peers under the
Life Peerages Act 1958. The final category of membership are the
Lords of Appeal in Ordinary.

2–72   The Peerage Act 1963 was passed to permit hereditary peers to
disclaim their title. Instances occur when the peerage may be dis-
claimed such as Tony Benn and the Stansgate Peerage. Peers are paid
a small emolument for attendance, parliamentary business travel, and
subsistence, which includes payment of secretarial and research
expenses.

Membership of the House of Lords may, in theory, run to over
1,000. However, regular attendance in the 1970s fluctuated between
250 to 275 members reaching a peak in 1976. In the 1980s general
attendance increased[85] to an average of 300 daily, with regular
meetings and sittings late into the night.

---

[84] Report by the Group on the Working of the House (1988; H.L. Paper 9).
[85] Griffith and Ryle, *op. cit.* pp. 472–474. See *Viscountess Rhondda's Claim* [1992] 2 A.C.
339 held that the Sex Disqualification (Removal) Act 1919 did not enable a peeress in
her own right to receive a writ of summons to Parliament.

The political outlook of the House of Lords mainly supports the **2–73** Conservative Party, but diverse representation in the Lords ensures that opinions voiced in debates may cross party political boundaries. One estimate of the actual party allegiance[86] is estimated on figures for 1992 to be 475 Conservative, 119 Labour, 58 Liberal and 263 Crossbench.[87] The power to move amendments may call government to rethink its strategy. In 1972, over 600 Lords amendments were made to the Local Government Bill after it was passed in the House of Commons. The majority of the amendments came from the Government.

As noted above, Mrs Thatcher's Government received over 100 **2–74** legislative defeats in the House of Lords, which was on a par with previous governments even though the Lords were sympathetic to the Conservative Party.[88] Ewing and Gearty note how the Lords may be susceptible to the politics of the day[89]:

> "Thus, in May 1988, one of the highest turn-outs of Lords this century saw the Government home on the introduction of a flat-rate poll tax, a measure which had caused great concern amongst regular attendants. In July 1988 the Lords voted by 120 to 94 to reject the imposition of charges for eye tests. The Government's response was to call on its country support [normally absent peers] and put the matter before the Lords again. This time, they won by 257 to 207 votes."

Prime Minister, Mrs Thatcher caused some controversy[90] by re-introducing the use of hereditary peers; none had been created between 1964 and 1983.

(b)   Select Committees

An active role for the Lords may be found in the business of the **2–75** Lords Select Committees in areas of specialisation such as E.C. law and practice, where the Lords have established a good reputation for the authority of their reports.

The use of select committees in the House of Lords is noteworthy in its role as scrutineer of the Executive. Unlike the House of

---

[86] See I. Loveland, *Constitutional Law: A Critical Introduction* (Butterworths, 1966) p. 201.

[87] See Donald Shell and David Beamish, *The House of Lords at Work* (Oxford, 1993).

[88] D. Shell, "The House of Lords and the Thatcher Government" (1985) *Parliamentary Affairs* pp. 16–30. See D. Shell, *The House of Lords* (1992).

[89] *Freedom under Thatcher* (1990), p. 6.

[90] Controversy with government measures also include defeat on various provisions in 1985 in the Prosecution of Offences Bill 1985.

Commons, which has departmental select committees, the Lords has developed only three types of committee. Before 1970, these consisted of investigative committees on general matters, committees on public Bills and public committees. Investigative committees covered a wide range of public affairs, but the practice of setting up such committees has gradually fallen into disuse.

2–76 Since 1970, the role of specific committees identified with particular bills was rarely used and there is a tendency to make use of investigative committees of the old style to cover a variety of ad hoc matters; examples include committees on unemployment (1979-82), overseas trade (1984-85), and on private Members' Bills. These illustrate the variety and type of activities which come under scrutiny. In fact new life has been rekindled into the use of investigative committees, as a form of technique which adds stature to the Lords. Especially important in the public's perception of the House of Lords at work are the televised hearings of such committees.

2–77 In December 1972, the Lords set up an investigation into how best to carry out scrutiny of E.C. legislation. The result was the European Communities Committee, first appointed in 1974, and since then appointed every session. In addition a number of sub-committees have been appointed to carry out a review in specialist areas of activity connected with the work of the main committee. The authority of the European Select Committee has been established, and it has been described as performing "an essential role" and making "a unique contribution to the process of European scrutiny by national Parliaments."[91]

(c) House of Lords Reform

2–78 Proposals for reform of the House of Lords in modern times have been discussed since the passage of the Parliament Act 1911. The debate on Gladstone's paper duty in 1866, produced an objection to the right of the Lords to interfere with the activities of the Commons. John Bright complained that the House of Lords[92] "have not behaved even with fair honour towards the House of Commons." That sentiment may appear to be at the heart of the objections to an unelected chamber having a legislative role alongside an elected chamber. The most recent proposals for reform have come from the Institute for Public Policy Research (IPPR), in their written constitution for the United Kingdom. They recommend that the Lords be

---

[91] Report from the Select Committee on the Committee work of the House (Sess. 1991–92 (1992) H.L. Paper 35–1).

[92] (6 July, 1860; H.C. Debs.); see John Bright, *Speeches* (1868).

replaced by an elected second chamber for a term of four years, "but at a two-year interval from the elections to the Commons."[93] Under such proposals the existing arrangements under the Parliament Acts 1911 and 1949, restricting the Lords powers over Money Bills would be retained. However, the terms of the present delaying powers of the Lords might be amended in line with the proposals contained in a 1969 Labour Government Bill, reducing the period of delay over Bills to 60 parliamentary days from the date of disagreement between the two Houses.

At the heart of any reform proposals, and there are wide variations **2–79** on the IPPR proposals, is the idea of creating a more representative House of Lords, in line with general reforms of the electoral system in the United Kingdom. Electoral reform is intended to replace the current "first past the post" electoral system with some form of proportional representation.[94] This might suggest that reform of the Lords on its own is merely "tinkering with the system", when a more radical rethink might be desired.[95]

Norton, in his analysis of the prospects for reform of the House of **2–80** Lords, distinguishes between external and internal reform. External reform is discussed in terms of the proposals such as those advanced in the IPPR's paper *A Written Constitution for the United Kingdom* (1991). Internal reforms may refer to improvements in the scrutiny and effectiveness of the Lords in strengthening existing committees and the Lords' contribution to making Parliament a more effective body. This might mean adopting some of the proposals outlined above, for improvements in the investigative committees of the Lords and accepted in the recent report on the Committee Work of the House of Lords.[96]

The movement for reform within the European community, since **2–81** the Single European Act 1986, favours reconsideration of the role of the House of Lords, as part of a general inquiry into the effectiveness of national parliaments.[97]

The newly elected Government on May 1, 1997 is sympathetic to reform of the House of Lords.[98] One possibility is an elected second chamber which would be granted powers to delay legislation that affected fundamental rights for the life of a single Parliament.

[93] "A Written Constitution for the United Kingdom" (IPPR, 1991), Article 68.
[94] See Chap. 6.
[95] See S. E. Finer, *Adversary Politics and Electoral Reform* (1975) also N. Johnson, *In Search of the Constitution: Reflections on State and Society in Britain* (1977).
[96] (H.L. Paper 35–1.)
[97] Proposals for reform of the Lords were included in the Parliament (No. 2) Bill 1969 but this failed to receive Parliamentary acceptance.
[98] See Donald Shell, "The House of Lords: Time for a Change" (1994) 47(4) *Parliamentary Affairs* 721.

However, if such a reform were introduced might there not be a claim of equal legitimacy if the second chamber was elected from the same electorate as the House of Commons?[99] It is likely that considerable more thought, and detail will be required before any viable reform of the House of Lords can be attempted.

4. Parliamentary Privileges

(a)   The nature of privileges

2–82   In considering the function and role of Parliament, account must be taken of the individual Members of Parliament. The medieval history of the House of Commons and House of Lords is reflected in the retention of ancient privileges.[1] As the title "the High Court of Parliament" reminds us, laws and customs of Parliament developed historically. Parliament was and still is a court. As the highest court in the land many of Parliaments' procedures remain from its historical origins. Hood Phillips links parliamentary privileges with the royal prerogative as part of the common law. Parliamentary privileges are the rights that are[2] "recognised by the courts and are deemed necessary to maintain the dignity and proper function of Parliament." In 1967 the House of Commons Report from the Committee of Privileges suggested that the term "privileges" should be replaced by "rights and immunities."[3] This suggestion appears attractive because it expresses more clearly the reality of the various "privileges" today.

2–83   The important privileges of the House of Commons, may be divided into two: first, freedom of speech and debate, and second, freedom from arrest. In the case of freedom of speech this may be traced back to medieval times and accepted by the courts. The Bill of Rights 1688, asserted the freedom of speech of Members of Parliament by providing that "debates or proceedings in Parliament ought not to be impeached or queried in any court or place out of Parliament."

2–84   Freedom of speech is interpreted to mean that Members of Parliament are free from civil suits for defamation and are granted

---

[99] Brigid Hadfield, "Whither or Whether the House of Lords" (1994) 35(4) *Northern Ireland Legal Quarterly* 320.
[1] Erskine May, *op. cit.* p. 70. May defined privileges as "the sum of peculiar rights enjoyed by each House collectively and by Members of each House individually."
[2] Hood Phillips, *op. cit.* pp. 234–235.
[3] Third Report from the Committee of Privileges: recommendations of the Select Committee on Parliamentary Privilege (1976–77; H.C. 417).

immunity in criminal law for words spoken in the course of parliamentary proceedings. Any threat of prosecution would itself be viewed as a contempt of the House. The House has its own internal rules and procedures and the office of the Speaker, on behalf of the House, can control debate within the House. Freedom of speech is, therefore, subject to adjudication by the House itself.

The term "proceedings in Parliament" is open to a variety of **2–85** interpretations. Does the term refer only to debates as proceedings within the Chamber? The Committee of Privileges in 1938 accepted that immunity applied to the asking of questions or the giving of notice of questions. However in 1957, a letter from a constituent[4] to his Member of Parliament was held not to be a proceeding in Parliament. An attempt to show a film about security matters in a committee room of the House of Commons that was banned by an interim injunction obtained by the Attorney-General, was considered not to be immune. The Speaker intervened to issue an order to ban the film, when a judge in chambers declined to issue an injunction applying to the Member of Parliament[5] or the House Committee.

Uncertainty may surround the operation of the immunities permitting free speech, but the procedure of referring doubtful or hotly disputed cases to the Committee of Privileges allows an important element of debate and discussion to take place. The strength of the system is therefore to be found in the autonomy of Parliament in these matters. On average at least a dozen cases appear to require the views of the Committee each year, which may or may not be adopted on report to the full House of Commons.

The Defamation Act 1996 provides the right for M.P.s and others to **2–86** waive parliamentary privilege in order to pursue actions for defamation in the courts. Section 13 of the 1996 Act provides[6] that the protection of parliamentary privilege afforded by Article 9 of the Bill of Rights 1688 might be waived. This important amendment was prompted by the case taken by Neil Hamilton, then an M.P., who wished to pursue an action against the *Guardian* newspaper over allegations that he had received cash for asking parliamentary questions, an allegation he has strongly denied. In the course of legal proceedings the newspaper argued that it could not offer an adequate defence when it was unable to examine parliamentary proceedings in court.[7] Subsequently, Mr Hamilton withdrew his action but continued

---

[4] (1957/58 H.C. Deb. 227), George Strauss M.P.
[5] Griffith and Ryle, *op. cit.* pp.103–104. The security matter on film was code-named "Zircon."
[6] See *Hansard*, H.L. Vol. 575, col. 52.
[7] *Prebble v. Television New Zealand* [1994] 3 W.L.R. 970 a Privy Council discussion of what constitutes activity outside and inside Parliament. Also see *Rost v. Edwards* [1990] 2 Q.B. 460.

to claim his innocence. The Commons appointed Sir Gordon Downey to act as the first Parliamentary Commissioner for Standards[8] to examine the conduct of M.P.s. The allegations against Mr Hamilton came under investigation. The calling of the general election for May 1, 1997 took place before Sir Gordon could produce his final report.

2–87   The second freedom claimed is that of arrest. This used to refer to arrest for civil cases, but this is of little effect as this procedure is rarely used today. Members of Parliament cannot claim immunity from criminal charges, arrest or imprisonment. It appears that arrest may even occur within the House itself, provided the House has given leave when it is a "sitting day."[9]

It may be concluded that freedoms enjoyed by Members of Parliament, may be greater than those itemised above as falling within the classification of the "proceedings of Parliament." Redlich in 1908 noted that[10]:

"Parliamentary government as a system of law is intimately connected with parliamentary government as a political system determined by history and by national and social characteristics."

(b)   Regulating financial and other interests

2–88   The disclosure of M.P.s' interests in the matters that they may vote has become a matter of considerable importance. A House of Commons resolution on May 25, 1974 refers to the disclosure of "any relevant pecuniary interest or benefit." Members of Parliament from June 1975 are expected to register any such interest in a register of members' interests maintained by a senior clerk of the House who acts as Registrar. A Select Committee on Members' Interests may examine any matter arising from a failure to disclose an interest. The scope of the registration is all-embracing to include any pecuniary interest or benefit which a member may receive which[11] "might be thought to affect his conduct as a member or influence his actions, speeches or vote in Parliament. Financial sponsorship, directorships, ownership of land, payments from clients, occupational or professional conduct or consultancies" should be included. Registration of an interest does not absolve the member from stating in debate whenever he has a relevant interest in the matter. Sanctions against

---

[8] For the Standing Orders see *Hansard*, H.C. Debs November 1995, cols. 610–12.
[9] Griffith and Ryle, *op. cit.* pp. 86–104.
[10] Quoted in Wilson, *op. cit.* p. 286. See Redlich, *The Procedure of the House of Commons* (1908).
[11] See Griffith and Ryle, *op. cit.* pp. 55–68.

any member in default are rare and limited. In serious cases it may be regarded as a contempt. In 1990 John Browne M.P. failed to register his financial interests in a company. The select committee found the case proven and the House of Commons suspended Browne for 20 days.[12] Browne did not seek re-election in 1992. While this example illustrates the serious nature of a breach of the duty on members to disclose their interest, the policing of the register is left too often to the good faith of members. The influence of professional lobbyists is so all—embracing that the register and its operation should be re-examined in the light of modern practice.

Allegations[13] of political corruption and sleaze[14] have centred on **2–89** the question of whether M.P.s have been willing to table questions in Parliament in return for financial rewards. The outcome was the setting up of the Nolan Committee under the chairmanship of Lord Nolan, a Law Lord. The Select Committee on Standards and Privileges set up after the Nolan report recommended a Parliamentary Code of Conduct.[15]

It may be concluded that modern parliamentary government in the **2–90** United Kingdom has continued to develop, albeit alongside Parliament's medieval inheritance. Preserving the balance of the constitution, whereby in Blackstone's analysis[16] "the executive power should be a branch, though not the whole of the legislature" remains a perplexing and constant challenge to the institution of Parliament.

---

[12] H.C. Deb. Vol. 506, Col. 108 (1989–90) and H.C. Deb., Col. 213 (June 23, 1992).
[13] *The Times*, July 10, 1994.
[14] See David Leigh and Ed. Vulliamy, *Sleaze* (Fourth Estate, 1997). Also see: D. Oliver, "Standards of Conduct in Public Life — What Standards?" (1995) *Public Law* 497.
[15] See H.C. 604, 1995/96.
[16] W. Blackstone, *Commentaries on the Laws of England* (1830) (Book 1) pp. 153–154.

Chapter 3

Government

1. Introduction

3–01 Government is carried out through Ministers of the Crown answerable to Parliament. Under the United Kingdom's constitutional arrangements, with the Queen as Head of State, government is carried on in her name as is fitting for a country with a constitutional monarchy.

The system of government in the United Kingdom is often referred to as responsible government. In that sense there is a degree of self-limitation in how government may operate its legal authority. This is partly attributable to party politics but also to the theoretical possibility at least that the government may lose the confidence of the House of Commons. The government requires the authority of Parliament for the passage of legislation and the expenditure of money. Government in the United Kingdom is highly centralised and although local government is an elected tier below central government, its practical autonomy has been greatly eroded in recent times. There is decentralisation of administration to Scotland, Wales and Northern Ireland. Devolution of legislative authority and tax-raising powers to a regional assembly in Scotland and administrative devolution to an assembly in Wales is currently being considered after the election victory of the Labour Government in May 1997.

Government in the United Kingdom must also take account of the changes in membership of the European Union which comprises 15 Member States and 370 million people and is considered in detail in Chapter 8. Many government decisions are made in alliance with other Member States and are implemented more formally through community law.

3–02 Consideration of the powers and role of government involved explaining how it is carried out. Discussion of government is divided between this chapter and the next. In this chapter, first consideration is given to the prerogative powers of government which are a source of governmental power in addition to the extensive reliance on legislation already discussed in Chapter 2. Secondly, the role of the Cabinet and Prime Minister and the administration of the government through the civil service is discussed. The institutions of government also include a wide variety of bodies connected with administrative decision-taking and these are discussed more fully in Chapter 5.

Government is carried out according to the conventions of the **3–03** Constitution and the rule of law, which prescribe how government ought to exercise power. Consideration is given to the importance of conventions and the rule of law in Chapter 4.

2. Government

(a) Central and Local

No special status is accorded to government within the United **3–04** Kingdom's constitutional arrangements. The term "government" is not given a precise legal meaning and not accorded any special pre-eminence. It may occasionally be found in a statute but rarely does the legal status or significance of government receive specific judicial evaluation. An example of reference to the word "minister" and the word "state" in the context of government, may be found in the House of Commons Disqualification Act 1975 and in the Ministers of the Crown Act 1975. Both Acts contain technical rules applicable to government ministers, without explaining the powers, duties and responsibilities of ministers or the role of government.

Government[1] may be defined in a variety of ways. Some definitions **3–05** express the significance of the State, the way the State is governed or other definitions may more generally refer to the executive powers enjoyed by the Cabinet and Prime Minister. Government carries out a wide range of activities with its own policies and ideas developed to administer public money or implement its election promises.

Government enjoys a wide range of powers of patronage or **3–06** influence. Legal powers may be derived from statute, the prerogative or from the legal obligations derived from the European Community. External affairs such as foreign relations and signing treaties, or

---

[1] Bagehot explained the operation of the United Kingdom's constitution when he drew a distinction between the "dignified," that is, those parts of the Constitution which excite and preserve the reverence of the population and the "efficient," that is "those by which it in fact rules." The dignified parts permit government to acquire and maintain its authority, while the efficient parts allow government to exercise power. See W. Bagehot, *The English Constitution (1867)* (R. M. S. Crossman ed., London, 1963).

maintaining diplomatic relations, may be carried out through the Crown's prerogative in foreign affairs.

3–07 Government is also capable of forming contractual relations. Given the Governments vast economic power it can wield considerable influence as an economic contractor.[2] Statutory authority is not normally required for the Crown to enter into contracts. Though prior statutory authority is often necessary for the approval of expenditure. In the case of departments making contracts, this is achieved through the authority of a civil servant acting on behalf of the Crown and no statutory authority is needed. As Turpin noted:

> "Nor does there appear to be any reason to doubt that the Crown's capacity extends to ordinary commercial contracts whether or not closely connected with the traditional activities of government."

Increasingly central government has viewed itself as a commercial enterprise, freely entering into contracts, or as a regulator overseeing contract activities.

3–08 Government is amenable to the jurisdiction of the courts. Lord Templeman has observed[3]: "Parliament makes the law, the executive carry the law into effect and the judiciary enforce the law." A finding of contempt may be made against a government department or a Minister of the Crown. In *M. v. Home Office*[4] the House of Lords upheld a finding of contempt against a Minister of the Crown for not complying with an injunction. The injunction was granted ordering M to be returned to this country after the Home Office rejected his claim for asylum. Lord Templeman concluded[5]:

> "To enforce the law the courts have power to grant remedies including injunctions against a minister in his official capacity. . . . For the purpose of enforcing the law against all persons and institutions, including ministers in their official capacity and in their personal capacity, the courts are armed with coercive powers exercisable in proceedings for contempt of court."

Lord Woolf in the House of Lords considered that it would rarely be justified to make use of injunctions against government departments in judicial review proceedings.

3–09 The generic term "government" requires further clarification. It is important to distinguish between central and local government. All

---

[2] T. Daintith, "Legal Analysis of Economic Policy" (1982) 9 *Journal of Law and Society* 191; Birks, "Restitution from Public Authorities" [1980] C.L.P. 191.

[3] *M. v. Home Office* [1993] 3 W.L.R. 433 at p. 437.

[4] [1993] 3 W.L.R. 433.

[5] *ibid.* at p. 437F.

the powers discussed above refer to central government. Local government has no special status under the United Kingdom's constitutional arrangements, even though it is elected and provides an enormous variety of services and activities for the community. Since the nineteenth century, local government has gained considerable statutory powers, which have been granted by central government enabling local government to carry out tasks and responsibilities in the provision of public health, education, planning, policing and other services.

Local government is perceived to be an agent of central government carrying out its tasks as a unique administrative agency. Each local authority has its own distinct legal personality from other local authorities. In law, local authority status as a body corporate gives it considerable financial autonomy within the framework of its legal powers. Local authority elections offer the local community an opportunity to participate in a different tier of government distinct from central government. Councillors, as local authority representatives, may carry out their policies subject to the legal controls set by central government. **3–10**

Compared to central government local authorities do not operate as an emanation of the Crown. As statutory corporations, local authorities must act within their powers according to law. Local authorities do not all conform to a single model of government as central government may appear to. The role, function and organisation of local government is examined in more detail in Chapter 12.

(b) Devolution

The United Kingdom is described as unitary. The arrangements for the government of Scotland[6] and Wales comprise[7] decentralisation of a large range of administrative tasks which are described as "administrative devolution". In the case of Scotland there are under the Secretary of State for Scotland five main departments with a wide range of statutory responsibilities and duties. The five departments are the Scottish Office, Agriculture, Environment and Fisheries Department, The Scottish Office Education and Industry Department, The Scottish Office Home Department and the Scottish Office Department of Health. There are also the Scottish Courts Administration, the department of the Registrar General for Scotland, the Scottish Record Office and the department of Registers for Scotland. The administration of the government of Scotland allows the Secretary of State some **3–11**

---

[6] T. StJ. N. Bates, *Devolution to Scotland: The Legal Aspects* (Edinburgh, 1997).
[7] Northern Ireland is considered separately in Chapter 19.

freedom in the development of matters of particular significance for Scotland. The Lord Advocate and the Solicitor-General for Scotland advise the Government on Scottish questions. Criminal justice, courts and prosecution matters under the Crown Office provide Scotland with its own distinct legal system from England and Wales.[8]

3–12   In Wales the degree of administrative devolution is markedly less than for Scotland. There is a Secretary of State for Wales who has responsibility in Wales for ministerial functions relating to a whole host of different areas such as health, education, personal social services, the environment, local government, the European Regional Development Fund and with oversight of economic and regional planning responsibilities for Wales.

In Northern Ireland following the introduction of direct rule in 1972, administrative devolution is a hotchpotch of functions but without any locally elected Northern Ireland Assembly. What was intended as an interim arrangement of direct rule appears to have become permanent.[9] There is a Secretary of State for Northern Ireland who is the minister responsible for the government of Northern Ireland. In addition there are two Ministers of State with shared responsibilities for a number of key Northern Ireland departments such as the Departments of Agriculture, Economic Development, Education, Environment, Finance and Personnel and Health and Social Services. There is the Northern Ireland Office which is the United Kingdom government department for Northern Ireland.

3–13   The system of devolution, described above, maintains the sovereignty of the United Kingdom Parliament and the principle of collective decision making by the cabinet is taken for the whole of the United Kingdom. Devolution is seen as avoiding the introduction of any form of federalism into the United Kingdom by maintaining the ultimate sovereignty of the United Kingdom Parliament.

3–14   There are efforts to introduce legislative devolution with locally elected assemblies. The idea of some form of legislative devolution for Scotland and Wales may be traced back to the 1960s. The centralisation of governmental power in the United Kingdom and the growth of nationalism in Scotland and Wales put the issue of "legislative devolution" on the political agenda. This would entail hiving off to separate assemblies in Scotland and Wales legislative and most likely fiscal powers. This would entail adopting the model of the Government of Ireland Act 1920 which from 1920 until 1972 was the constitution of Northern Ireland and established a Parliament for Northern Ireland with extensive legislative powers. There were powers transferred to the Northern Ireland Parliament and matters

---

[8] Northern Ireland has its own distinctive legal system.
[9] See Chap. 19 on Northern Ireland.

retained at Westminster. After 1972 the Northern Ireland Constitution Act 1973 was passed followed by a Northern Ireland Assembly Act 1973. Although overtaken by events in Northern Ireland both Acts remain useful models that might be adopted for some form of regional government in Scotland and Wales. The strength of the argument in favour of devolution came from the analysis offered by the report of the Royal Commission on the Constitution known as the Kilbrandon Report[10] published in 1973. The Kilbrandon report identified dissatisfaction with the centralised Westminster model of government. The Kilbrandon Report was greatly influenced by the Northern Ireland[11] form of devolution introduced under the Government of Ireland Act 1920 which it regarded as having worked well in providing legislation particular to the needs of Northern Ireland. One strength of the system was the opportunity to judge whether United Kingdom Acts of Parliament ought to be applied in Northern Ireland after a period when the legislation was "tested" in England and Wales.

The Government's response to the Kilbrandon report was to **3–15** attempt to establish assemblies in Scotland and Wales. The Government ruled out devolution for England but undertook consideration of executive devolution to new English regional authorities. The matter of English devolution was finally dropped after the Government found a lack of consensus on the issue. In the case of Scotland and Wales separate Scotland and Wales Acts passed in 1978 failed to receive the support of necessary 40 per cent of the electorate necessary for the Acts to come into force. While a majority voted in Scotland in support of devolution, this only amounted to 32.9 per cent of the electorate and not the 40 per cent required. In Wales only 20.2 per cent of the vote favoured devolution representing 11.9 per cent of the electorate, well below the 40 per cent required. After the referendum results, devolution lapsed as a major issue for some time. It was conceded by some that the vote may have reflected what was on offer rather than a rejection of devolution in principle.

Pressure for some form of devolved government, or outright **3–16** independence has grown in recent years. Opposition parties unsuccessfully introduced a Devolution Bill in November 1987. The Campaign for a Scottish Assembly has lobbied for devolution in the late 1980s. In July 1988. A Claim of Right for Scotland was launched and recommended a Constitutional Convention and this held its first meeting in Edinburgh on March 30, 1989.

The left of centre Institute for Public Policy Research published its draft Constitution in 1991 which included a devolved assembly for

---

[10] Cmnd. 5460.
[11] The influence of the late Professor Francis Newark was important in understanding the model the Northern Ireland Parliament offered.

Scotland, Wales and the English regions. More recently the Constitution Unit has studied the question of devolution and considered a Scottish Parliament with legislative and tax-varying powers. Similar proposals have been discussed for Wales.

3–17   The election of the new government on May 1, 1997 has firmly established constitutional reforms as a central element in the government's agenda. The Queen's Speech promised a devolution Bill within the present Parliament and, with the Government's overall majority, legislative devolution is at long last likely to become a reality. In terms of legislative drafting the model of the Northern Ireland Constitution Act 1973 is a valuable one to produce a workable system.

(c) Crown and Prerogative

3–18   (i) **Definition and review.** In addition to the various forms of legislation outlined in the previous chapter on Parliament, an important source of governmental powers may arise from the use of prerogative powers. Various definitions are applied to the prerogative. Dicey defined the royal prerogative[12] as "the residue of discretionary or arbitrary authority which at any given time is legally left in the hands of the Crown"; de Smith attributed to the Crown "inherent legal attributes" which belong to the Queen as a person, and to the institution called the Crown. The latter may be defined to include Her Majesty's Government or the State. Defining the prerogative in legal terms is always difficult. This is largely because of the complexities of its historical evolution and uncertainties about its present usage. Dicey's description of the prerogative as a "residue" of powers should be confined to powers or privileges that are unique to the Crown. A wider description of the prerogative meaning all the powers of the Crown that have their source in the common law is inaccurate. Powers or privileges enjoyed by private persons are not strictly speaking part of the prerogative. Some writers find it convenient to classify power under the prerogative as "personal" and distinguish this from "political" prerogatives. The former are exercised by the Queen as a person, the latter apply as Head of State. Personal prerogatives refer to such of the immunities and property rights of the Sovereign which survive today, such as a right not to be sued or prosecuted in the courts. Personal estates such as the Crown's Private Estates are vested in the Sovereign.

3–19   Political prerogatives are arrogated to the Crown whereby the Queen may act in her personal capacity, such as in the choice of the

---

[12] Dicey, *Law of the Constitution*, p. 424. Lord Reid in *Burmah Oil v. Lord Advocate* [1965] A.C. 75, 99. See also, *Laker Airways Ltd v. Department of Trade* [1977] Q.B. 643.

Prime Minister. Today the prerogative powers of the Crown are largely exercised by ministers reponsible to Parliament who in theory act on behalf of the Crown. The Courts have recognised prerogative powers as early as the *Case of Proclamations*[13] (1610), but have from time to time restricted their scope and attempted to define their meaning

The royal prerogative is regarded as part of the common law powers of the Crown. It consists mainly of executive government powers such as the conduct of foreign affairs, the making of war and peace, the appointment of Ministers, the dissolution of Parliament and the assent to Bills. The difficulty of exact legal definition may have prompted Dicey to define the prerogative in very broad terms:

"Every act which the executive government can lawfully do without the authority of the Act of Parliament is done in virtue of the prerogative . . ."[14]

The difficulty of precise legal definition and the breadth of Dicey's **3–20** vision of the extent of prerogative powers has not been helped by any clarity to be found in legal cases. The history of prerogative powers is the history of relations between the King and Parliament and the attempts by the courts to mediate.

The historical origins of the prerogative may be traced back to medieval times. The inherent powers of the King to govern the realm rested on the prerogative. Legal definitions appeared unhelpful as they may have attempted to expand or limit the powers of the King. Advice sought was usually influenced by the expected outcome in terms of defining the King's powers. Blackstone[15] identified the pre-eminence accorded to the prerogative in English law":

" . . . [i]t signified in its etymology (from prae and rogo) something that is required or demanded before, or in preference to, all others."

Maitland[16] cautions us about the "often great uncertainty as to the **3–21** exact limits of the royal prerogative." His suggestion that there is "no such doctrine as that a prerogative may cease to exist because it is not used," may not easily fit within modern representative government with extensive statutory powers.

Keir and Lawson make the important distinction between the powers enjoyed by the King at common law and those powers

---

[13] (1610) 2 State Tr. 723.
[14] Dicey, *op. cit.* p. 424.
[15] Blackstone, *Commentaries*, Bk. 1, p. 239.
[16] Maitland, *Constitutional History of England* (Cambridge, 1908), p. 418; Keir and Lawson, *Cases in Constitutional Law* (Oxford, 1967), pp. 72–80.

conferred by statute. Statutes have restricted prerogative powers and in some cases statutes either repeal the prerogative completely or overlap with prerogative powers. An example where statutory authority has *replaced* prerogative powers are the powers of the sovereign to spend money or raise taxation prior to the seventeenth century. Such powers are today ceded to Parliament and statutory authority. Another example is the Crown Proceedings Act 1947 which abolished the Crown's absolute immunity from legal suit in contract and tort.

3–22   In adapting to changing circumstances the courts may be required to give further thought to long accepted principles. It was until recently commonly assumed that injunctions were not available against the Crown. In *M v. Home office*[17] the House of Lords clarified the position regarding the availability of injunctions against the Crown. Lord Woolf, giving the views of the House, held that injunctions including interim injunctions were available against Ministers of the Crown. A Minister could be personally liable for wrongs done by the Minister when acting in an official capacity. The importance of the case lies in the clarification over the use of injunctions against the Crown. The current law lays emphasis on the limited circumstances where it is considered appropriate to grant an injunction against the Crown.

3–23   How relevant is the prerogative to modern government when it is of such ancient origin? Present day prerogative[18] powers may be found in: the Executive's power to conclude treaties with Sovereign States; the power to declare war; to provide for the security of the Realm; to grant pardons to convicted criminals or reprieve sentence; to mint the currency and to appoint Commissions by Royal Warrant. Some prerogative powers remain in the personal control of the Sovereign such as power to dismiss and appoint a Prime Minister and the power of dissolution of Parliament. Undoubtedly the prerogative is a "residual" power as it can be removed, altered or amended by an Act of Parliament. No new prerogatives may be created but surprisingly old prerogatives have an "elastic quality" which allows their adaption into modern government.

3–24   A prerogative power was claimed as the basis for setting up a scheme for compensation payable to victims of violent crime. The Criminal Injuries Compensation Board has recently received statutory authority and recognition under the Criminal Justice Act 1988, s.108; but in 1964, it was set up by prerogative powers subject to express statutory approval by Parliament of the necessary government expenditure under the Appropriation Act.

---

[17] [1993] 3 All E.R. 537.
[18] Hood Phillips, *Constitutional and Administrative Law* (1987), pp. 262–290.

In *Secretary of State for the Home Department, ex p. Fire Brigades Union*[19], despite the existence of the statutory scheme under the Criminal Justice Act 1988, the Home Secretary attempted to introduce a tariff scheme[20] under the prerogative. The tariff scheme was different than the statutory one and the Home Secretary purported to exercise powers under section 171 of the Criminal Justice Act 1988 which gave the Home Secretary discretion when to bring the statutory scheme into operation. It was accepted by Lord Browne-Wilkinson that the tariff scheme was inconsistent with the statutory scheme. In effect it might involve the winding up of the old Criminal Injuries Compensation Board and the creation of a new body, the Criminal Injuries Compensation Authority. The House of Lords by a majority held that such a tariff scheme introduced under the prerogative was unlawful. The tariff scheme under the prerogative was inconsistent with parliamentary intent established under Part VII of the Criminal Justice Act 1988. The case is important because it establishes the important relationship between statute and prerogative. Lord Browne-Wilkinson stated that[21] "the existence of legislation basically affects the mode in which such prerogative powers can be lawfully exercised". The case restored the validity of the scheme under the Criminal Injuries Compensation Board.[22] As a result of the House of Lords decision, the Home Secretary introduced new legislation providing for the introduction of a new scheme of compensation under the Criminal Injuries Compensation Act 1995. In the final analysis the government won the day but the entire episode illustrates the pre-eminence of statutory powers over the prerogative.

The civil service falls under prerogative influence[22a] in the sense **3–25** that the Crown has historically the power to appoint or dismiss its servants at pleasure. This power may be identified as a prerogative power. The civil service is regulated not by statute, though statutes may apply to civil servants, but by Orders in Council made under the royal prerogative, notably the Civil Service Order in Council 1982 which determines a code of regulations in pay and conditions of service. The Order in Council also empowers the Minister for the Civil Service and the Treasury to make regulations for the conduct of the civil service.

The prerogative power in the Crown to establish courts to administer the common law has fallen into disuse as new courts are created

---

[19] [1995] 2 All E.R. 244.

[20] See *Compensating Victims of Violent Crime. Changes to the Criminal Injuries Compensation Scheme* (Cm. 2434 (December 1993).

[21] at p. 255.

[22] *R. v. Criminal Injuries Compensation Board, ex p. P.* [1995] 1 All E.R. 870.

[22a] See the case law analysis offered in *CCSU v. Minister for the Civil Service* [1985] A.C. 374, known as the *GCHQ* case. Also see the precise status of a civil servant discussed in *R. v. Civil Service Appeal Board, ex p. Bruce* [1989] 2 All E.R. 907.

by statute. The Crown may pardon convicted prisoners. The Attorney General may enter a *nolle prosequi* in prosecutions on indictment. However under section 23 of the Prosecution of Offences Act 1985 the Crown Prosecution Service has statutory powers to discontinue cases without the leave of the court.

3–26　　The versatility of the prerogative is demonstrated by Turpin's[23] reference to such orders in council as the 1982 Order, as "prerogative legislation." This is an apt but perhaps misleading phrase. It is the case that during the two world wars many prerogative Orders in Council were adopted without statutory authority. The Reprisals Orders in Council of 1915 and 1917, more recently in 1982 the requisitioning of ships on account of the Falklands war was achieved through the prerogative. The misleading part of the phrase is the word "legislation" when used alongside the word prerogative. This may imply parliamentary approval and scrutiny which may be misleading, because no such detailed scrutiny is undertaken. However, in the general sense legislation may mean the power to make rules for others. In that meaning it is clear that the prerogative may be defined.

3–27　　Prerogative powers that apply in relation to Parliament, include the power to summon, to dissolve or to prorogue Parliament. The Royal Assent to Bills is also a prerogative power. Prerogative powers are not subject to the processes of scrutiny of the House of Commons nor is it always clear whether a prerogative power exists. Such doubts can give rise to questions about the relationship between prerogative powers and statute. Wade suggests somewhat tentatively[24] that:

> "Prerogative powers may also, it seems, be atrophied by mere disuse"

As to the exact nature or remit of the prerogative Lord Justice Nourse explained[25]:

> "It is not at any stage in our history been practicable to identify all the prerogative powers of the Crown. It is only by a process of piecemeal decision over a period of centuries that particular powers are seen to exist or not to exist, as the case may be. From time to time a need for more exact definition arises. The present need arose from a difference of view between the Secretary of State and a police authority over what is necessary to maintain public

---

[23] Turpin, *British Government and the Constitution*, p. 382.
[24] William Wade, *Constitutional Fundamentals* (1989), pp. 58–64.
[25] *R. v. Secretary of State for the Home Department, ex p. Northumbria Police Authority* [1989] Q.B. 26.

order, a phenomenon which has been observed only in recent times. There has probably never been a comparable occasion for investigating a prerogative of keeping the peace within the realm."

This sets the potential scope for future development of the prerogative to be largely discretionary, save for the fact that "no new prerogative" may be created.

Some doubts may be advanced as to the desirability of such a wide **3–28** discretion. Does the Executive have a choice as to when it may rely on prerogative powers or require statute? Does the prerogative overlap with statute or co-exist with statutory authority? Conventional wisdom has drawn back from the creation of new prerogative powers to revive an existing statute or create new prerogatives. It is settled law that in the *Case of Proclamations*[26] the Crown has no prerogative to create new wrongs; but in *Malone v. MPC,*[27] Megarry V.-C. accepted that the limited power to authorise telephone tapping under the prerogative was devised from the extension of the power to open articles sent through the post. Today such powers have a firmer statutory foundation under the Interception of Communications Act 1985 which followed the decision in *Malone* after a decision of the European Court of Human Rights[28] which held that the absence of legal controls over the circumstances in which phone tap warrants could be issued was incompatible with Article 8 of the Convention.

It might be suggested that statutory authority is preferable to **3–29** reliance on prerogative powers thus enabling debate and parliamentary scrutiny to take place. This form of democratic check on the Executive provides a *visible* and public forum for discussion. In the GCHQ case[29] in 1985, the House of Lords held that in legal principle the prerogative could be subject to judicial review in much the same way as an Act of Parliament or delegated legislation made under the Act. The Prime Minister relied on an Order in Council *made under the prerogative* to ban trade union membership by staff at the Government Communications Headquarters. Reliance on the Order in Council was claimed on the basis of national security. In the past prerogative powers had not always been amenable to judicial review and GCHQ has settled the question of justiciability. However, the judges have shown reluctance to offer a fundamental reconsideration of how such review might operate. The wide discretion given to the Executive in their use of prerogative powers in the *Northumbria Police Authority* case may indicate a judicial willingness to support executive powers.

[26] (1610) 2 State Tr. 723.
[27] [1979] Ch. 344.
[28] (1985) 7 E.H.R.R. 14.
[29] [1985] A.C. 374.

The supply of CS gas and baton rounds to the Northumbria Police Authority was open to the Home Secretary as a prerogative power "to supply equipment reasonably required by police forces to discharge their functions." The provision of equipment was authorised by the Police Act 1964 but also by the prerogative. Such a prerogative may be found in the Crown's right to prevent crime and maintain justice. This is an example of a prerogative being updated with modern society.

3–30   In the *GCHQ* case the power of the courts to review the prerogative was confined to "justiciable acts" performed under the prerogative. Excluded from review under the term "justiciable" were matters described by Lord Roskill to be decided "on the subject matter of the prerogative powers which are being exercised." Examples included[30]: the making of treaties; the defence of the realm; the prerogative of mercy; the grant of honours; the dissolution of Parliament and the appointment of Ministers. There were others which Lord Roskill described as not reviewable:

> "because their nature and subject matter is such as not to be amenable to the judicial process. The courts are not the place wherein to determine whether a treaty should be concluded or the armed forces disposed in a particular manner or Parliament dissolved on one date rather than another."

Therefore it is misleading, to regard the entire prerogative as following entirely under judicial scrutiny.

In *Secretary of State for the Home Department, ex p. Fire Brigades Union*[31] the House of Lords acknowledged the importance of statutory authority over the prerogative. The case concerned the attempt by the Home Secretary to introduce a tariff system of compensation under prerogative powers in preference to the system of compensation established under the Criminal Justice Act 1988. The House of Lords held that this was an abuse of prerogative powers and unlawful.

3–31   Prerogative powers may appear to sit uneasily with the legislative functions provided by a democratically elected Parliament. Nevertheless the importance of the prerogative is undiminished. Consider, for example, the prerogative of mercy, one of the personal prerogatives of the Crown which is exercised theoretically by the Sovereign on advice of the Home Secretary. A pardon so granted may be free or conditional. It may be regarded as an essential power, a necessary part of the criminal process to remedy mistakes either at trials or

---

[20] [1985] A.C. 374.
[31] [1995] 2 All E.R. 244.

appeal. At present such a power appears as a final determination made by the Home Secretary and to date the courts have been reluctant to provide review of how it is exercised. Arguments for and against such a review may be made but the question is should such a power of pardon remain a prerogative and not a statutory power?[32]

The preference for a legislative rather than a prerogative power is **3–32** intended to regularise and bring up-to-date ancient practice and provide clarification of a vague and uncertain area of the law.

The courts have been willing to define the existence of the prerogative and its applicability. But in the *GCHQ* case the House of Lords were reluctant to extend judicial scrutiny to the question of whether or not prerogative powers should or should not be exercised. This leaves potentially a wide discretion as to whether statutory or prerogative powers should be used, which apparently does not fall within the remit of judicial scrutiny.

The example of the *Northumbria*[33] case has shown the use of the **3–33** prerogative to secure a particularly broad discretion to preserve the peace. Since the Second World War, legislation such as the Emergency Powers (Defence) Acts and various Public Order Acts such as the consolidation in the Public Order Act 1986 and the Prevention of Terrorism (Temporary Provisions) Act 1984 on terrorism in the United Kingdom has shown the wide powers required for the maintenance of peace. But despite the width of these wide statutory powers, they do not preclude the future use of the prerogative.

An alternative perspective offers a more restrictive use of preroga- **3–34** tive powers. On this perspective if statutory powers exist which apply to the same activities as a prerogative power, the statutory powers should be used. In *Attorney-General v. De Keysers Royal Hotel Ltd*[34] the House of Lords preferred a statutory basis for possession of a London hotel for Staff officers during the First World War, as opposed to the use of prerogative powers. Lord Moulton explained:

> "There can be no excuse for reverting to prerogative powers simpliciter – if indeed they even did exist in such a form as would cover the proposed acquisition, a matter which is far from clear in such a case as the present – when the legislative has given to the Crown statutory powers which are wider than anyone pretends that it possessed under the prerogative . . . "

In *Burmah Oil Co. v. Lord Advocate*[35] the House of Lords accepted that the use of the prerogative did not prevent a claim for compensation

[32] [1989] Q.B. 26.
[33] [1989] Q.B. 26.
[34] [1920] A.C. 508.
[35] [1965] A.C. 75.

even where the destruction of oil installations was required to prevent the enemy from using a valuable resource. After the decision of the House of Lords, the War Damage Act 1965 retroactively removed the subjects' rights to compensation.

3–35   Prerogative powers allow the Crown the power of incorporation, such as the incorporation of universities, professional societies and even the British Broadcasting Corporation. Additional powers required are usually statutory and the prerogative is confined to the power to hold property, enter contracts and engage in the terms of the activities contained in the Royal Charter. In most cases today, statutory authority is provided in the relevant legislation which is adapted to ensure the corporate entity has sufficient legal powers. Historically this "incorporation" of local authorities such as Parish, District and County Councils provided the early basis of local government.

3–36   (ii) **The prerogative in foreign affairs.** Foreign relations often involve international agreements and are primarily conducted under prerogative powers. International agreements cover a wide range of activities contained in treaties, conventions, agreements, protocols or charters. While often binding in international law, their application as part of the United Kingdom's domestic law requires an Act of Parliament. While the Crown has no prerogative powers to enforce treaties as part of English law, the Crown possesses wide prerogative powers in foreign affairs where the Crown in an action for tort liability may plead the defence of "Act of State" for acts performed abroad. This defence is strictly confined to acts done "abroad" and not within domestic jurisdiction.

3–37   The term "Act of State" is itself a complex expression which does not facilitate easy definition in constitutional law. Hood Phillips explains that[36]:

> " . . . the expression is generally used for an act done by the Crown as a matter of policy in relation to another state, or in relation to an individual who is not within the allegiance to the Crown."

It is clear that Acts of State in relation to foreign states includes such matters as the declaration of war and making peace. The making of treaties and associated diplomatic relations including the recognition of foreign governments.

3–38   In *Laker Airways v. Dept. of Trade*[37] Lord Denning considered the use of the prerogative in connection with the designation of an airline.

[36] Hood Phillips, *Constitutional and Administrative Law* (1987), pp. 278–279.
[37] [1977] Q.B. 643.

The Bermuda Agreement 1946, a Treaty between the United States and the United Kingdom, stated that designated carriers would be able to obtain a foreign air carrier permit from the United States Civil Aeronautical Board which was subject to Presidential signature. On the part of the United Kingdom, the Civil Aviation Act 1971 permitted the Civil Aviation Authority (CAA) to issue an air transport licence to provide a designated carrier permission. The case arose when Laker airlines who had been granted a licence for its low-cost transatlantic air service, found that a change of government resulted in the Secretary of State issuing the CAA guidelines effectively withdrawing the licence designation from Laker. The Secretary of State claimed *both* statutory and prerogative powers. Lord Denning in an *obiter dicta* rejected the use of prerogative powers "to deprive the subject of a right conferred on him by statute." Once a licence had been granted under the 1971 Act it could not be removed by prerogative powers.

Where an Act of State[38] is more directly relevant is where the **3–39** Crown may use its authority to protect itself from action at the suit of a private individual. Here the courts may examine the facts to decide whether an Act of State may be pleaded and whether done within the limits of the discretion. It has been held that a wrong committed by a Crown servant against a British citizen in a British territory has no defence of Act of State.[39] However this view is not always accepted by the courts and each case would seem to depend on its own particular facts. Particularly confusing is the question of the definition of "British citizen" under the British Nationality Act 1981; does it mean the same as British subject or those "who owe allegiance to the Crown?"

In defining the limits of the prerogative and its reviewability, the **3–40** courts have broadened their review to the issuing of passports which are Crown property issued at the discretion of the Secretary of State. In *R. v. Secretary of State for Foreign and Commonwealth Affairs, ex p. Everett*[40] the Court of Appeal reviewed the Secretary of State's refusal to issue a passport under the prerogative. Lord Justice Taylor explained that:

> "the grant or refusal of a passport is . . . a matter of administrative decision, affecting the rights of individuals and their freedom of

---

[38] The limits of this protection are recognised in *Walker v. Baird* [1892] A.C. 491, but see the leading authority of *Johnstone v. Pedlar* [1921] 2 A.C. 262. An Act of State could not be pleaded in defence of a tort committed under the authority of the Crown.

[39] *Buron v. Denman* (1848) 2 Ex. 167. See the confusing discussion in *Nissan v. Att.-Gen.* [1970] A.C. 179. The House of Lords appeared to uphold the view of the Court of Appeal that the acts of British forces in occupying an hotel in Cyprus were not non-justiciable as Acts of State.

[40] [1989] Q.B. 811.

travel. It raises issues which are just as justiciable as, for example, the issues arising in immigration cases."

This view rejected the argument that the issuing of passports fell within the category of foreign affairs involving executive functions and therefore outside the power of the courts to review.

The prerogative in foreign affairs developed historically and continues to exist as an important "residuary" power of the Crown.

3–41　Some general conclusions might be made about the prerogative. Although the existence and precise limits of the prerogative are at times vague and unchartered, it is subject to judicial review and the remit of its use may be subject to judicial control. Many of the conventions, characteristic of the United Kingdom's Constitution, owe their origins to ancient prerogative powers. The principal convention, for example, is that the Queen shall exercise her formal legal powers only in accordance with the advice of Ministers.[41] However, there are some prerogative powers such as choice of Prime Minister in the event of a hung Parliament, which leave the Sovereign a degree of discretion when deciding who is likely to command the support of the House of Commons.

3–42　Total abolition of the prerogative and its replacement with statutory powers, would out of necessity, require codification of rules covering many of the areas it currently regulates. This may prove difficult and more challenging than might appear at first glance. Especially so, if it is intended to retain in a newly codified arrangement, some degree of discretion.

A major advantage is the inherent flexibility and versatility of the prerogative. For example the prerogative of mercy may remove "all pains, penalties and punishment." In foreign affairs diplomatic relations and representation have their source in prerogative and not statutory powers. Democratic accountability is argued in favour of statutory powers over the prerogative because statutory authority is more visible, clearly defined and subject to the parliamentary process.

3.　The Crown and the Government

3–43　The Monarch as Head of State performs many ceremonial functions.[42] The money to finance the Royal Family is separate from the expenses of maintaining the Government. Since George III's time, in return for

---

[41] For a full discussion see G. Marshall, *Constitutional Conventions* (Oxford, 1984), pp. 19–53. Also useful is Bagehot, *The English Constitution, op. cit.* p. 30 note 2.

[42] See Vernon Bogdanor, *The Monarchy and the Constitution* (Oxford, 1995).

the surrender to Parliament of the ancient hereditary revenues of the Crown and any income from Crown land, Parliament has made provision for the salaries and other expenses of the Royal Family. The Civil List Act 1952 provided for a fixed annual sum but the Civil List Act 1972 provided that the sum may be varied by Treasury Order. In 1975 the effects of inflation caused the Civil List Act 1975 to be passed allowing supplements to be paid. This remains the case today although from 1991 it was agreed that a fixed annual payment of about £8 million per annum would be made. The result it was hoped would avoid any incremental increases and that royal finances would fall into line with the principles of ordinary departmental expenditure. Increasingly the Royal Family is being treated like any other government department. Indeed some expenses such as the royal yacht are paid out of departmental expenses. In 1992 the Queen agreed to pay for certain members of the Royal Family out of her own funds. The Prince of Wales has never received any money from the Civil List as provision is made for income out of the Duchy of Cornwall. Also in 1992 the Queen agreed for the first time to pay income tax in respect of her private income.

While some favour abolition of the monarchy claiming that it is **3–44** unrepresentative or out of touch with ordinary people, the trend is more in favour of incremental modernisation. How to make the monarchy compatible with a modern and vibrant democracy is less easy to achieve. Hereditary office appears inconsistent with elected and open competition. Today there is less tolerance of the ancient relics of the Constitution[43] and it is generally accepted that the Monarchy's survival depends on the wish of the British people to maintain a Monarchy.[44] This debate should not undervalue the importance of the Monarchy in the terms of Walter Bagehot's defined roles[45] "the right to be consulted, the right to encourage and the right to warn". In these matters the Monarch is ruled by convention.

(a) The Personal Powers of the Sovereign

Some of the personal powers of the Queen[46] have been touched upon **3–45** above. Three require some special mention. First the appointment of the Prime Minister, secondly the dismissal of Ministers and finally the dissolution of Parliament. In the case of the appointment of the Prime

---

[43] *The Economist* opinion poll October 22, 1994.
[44] See: *The Guardian*–ICM poll January 1995. 28% of British people wished the Monarchy to be abolished.
[45] Walter Bagehot, *The English Consitution* (Fontana, 1963), p. 111.
[46] See Rodney Brazier (ed.), *Constitutional texts* (1990), pp. 127–8.

Minister, the Monarch's choice is governed by the convention that the person appointed must have the confidence of the House of Commons. The judgment as to who fulfils this criteria is usually straightforward. The party leader with the majority of seats is appointed as the Prime Minister. Where a party leader resigns or dies in office then the election of the leader falls to the rules of the political party in power. The resignation of Mrs Thatcher as Prime Minister in 1990 resulted in the Conservative Party's election of Mr Major as the leader of the Conservative Party, the party with the largest number of seats and therefore Prime Minister.

3–46   If there is an election which results in a "hung Parliament" that is, where no one party is in the majority the choice of the Monarch as to who should be asked to form a Government may become the crucial issue. There is a general convention that the Monarch will seek a wide canvass of views but there is in the final analysis a personal choice to be made within the boundaries of the question of who is most likely to be able to form a government. This residual discretion may in practice be delegated to political leaders as to their advice or to the Queen's personal advisers. A more transparent system of decision making may appear more appropriate.[47]

3–47   The second prerogative power relates to the dismissal of Ministers. This undertaken on the advice of the Prime Minister. This in turn must rest on the political reality of most government power, the ability to command the support of the political party in power. It is unlikely that today the Queen could exercise a personal choice over the dismissal of the Prime Minister or Ministers. What is clear is that here the reality of public opinion must caution any interference with democratic choices made by the electorate.

3–48   Finally, there is the question of the prerogative of dissolution. The advice of the Prime Minister is normally accepted in these matters. A Cabinet decision is unnecessary before any request is made and it is accepted convention that the request for a dissolution should not be refused nor has one been refused over the past century.

The question of whether the Monarch's prerogative powers should be codified in a written constitution or provided for in a statute has been raised in several reform proposals. In the case of dissolution there is an additional argument in favour of fixed term Parliaments.[48]

---

[47] The Institute of Public Policy research favours the role of the Speaker of the House of Commons. *Draft Constitution* (IPPR, 1991).
[48] See Robert Blackburn, *The Meeting of Parliament* (1990).

4. Cabinet and Prime Minister

(a) Powers and functions

Executive powers in the United Kingdom are carried out by the **3–49** Cabinet and Prime Minister. Crick, writing in 1964,[49] commented:

> "Of all Governments of countries with free political institutions, British government exhibits the greatest concentration of power and authority. Nowhere else is a Government normally so free to act decisively, so unfettered by formal restraints of constitutional law"

Crick's analysis appears equally valid in recent times. The Government enjoys considerable powers and rights over the citizen through a wide variety of sources. Statutory, prerogative or E.C. Directives or Regulations may permit the Government or its agents to carry out different tasks and functions. Such extensive powers are said to be exercised according to the law. In this respect it may be noted that the courts' role in overseeing ministerial decision-taking, becomes important when ministerial decisions are challenged in the courts. The function of judicial review in the oversight of government, involves the broader question of how government is made accountable and the different techniques both legal and political involved in the scrutiny[50] of government.

The executive powers of government in the United Kingdom are **3–50** exercised by or on behalf of Ministers of the Crown who are members of the Cabinet. The Cabinet has its origins in the seventeenth and eighteenth centuries.[51] No exact date for its beginning may be given as it evolved around confidential advisers to the Monarch. The Cabinet's independence from royal influence was gradual and probably due to the incapacity of various Monarchs rather than a revolutionary break with tradition.

Historical traces of the exact form the eighteenth-century Cabinet **3–51** may have taken are obscure. References in 1740 as to the existence[52] of the inner Cabinet bear similarities to the modern Cabinet system of

---

[49] B. Crick, *The Reform of Parliament* (1964), p. 16, (2nd ed., 1968).
[50] See Chap. 9.
[51] The cabinet is fully discussed in J. P. Mackintosh, *The British Cabinet* (1977); Ivor Jennings, *Cabinet Government* (1959); Patrick Gordon Walker, *The Cabinet* (1972); Douglas Wass, *Government and the Governed* (1984).
[52] Turner, *The Cabinet Council, 1622–1784*; Keir, *A Constitutional History of Modern Britain* (1938), pp. 381–382; Atiyah, *The Rise and Fall of the Freedom of Contract* (Oxford, 1988), pp. 17–20.

today. As the role of domestic government expanded beyond the collection of finance, the regulation of the State became a shared enterprise not solely within royal power. Various departments of State may be identified with specific[53] responsibilities such as the Lords Commissioners of the Treasury. Hennessy[54] identifies the Privy Council as the model of how the earliest Cabinet took shape. Some writers are reluctant[55] to link the modern Cabinet with any particular committee such as the Foreign Committee or Intelligence Committee of the Privy Council in the 1660s and 1670s.

3–52   Blackstone[56] linked the Monarch with exclusive executive powers. Advice taken by the Monarch came from the Privy Council. Cornish notes[57] that:

> "Queen Ann had held regular "Cabinets" and the idea persisted, dividing at some stages into inner and outer works, but still contributing to a process in which the monarch would play a decisive personal role. The Chief among these Ministers, forerunner of the modern Prime Minister, remained so long as he kept the royal confidence, though it was already part of that favour that he should also enjoy the support of the Commons on most issues."

Bagehot,[58] writing of the English Constitution in 1867, identified the principal characteristics which linked the legislature and executive elements of the Constitution. He acknowledged "the efficient secret of the English Constitution" as the close union and complete fusion between the executive and legislative powers. The Prime Minister was at the head of the "efficient" part of the Constitution. Bagehot distinguished the "efficient" from the "dignified." The Queen was head of the "dignified" part of the Constitution. The "efficient" were the parts of the constitution "by which it, in fact works and rules." The "dignified" parts were those which "executed and preserved the reverence of the population."

3–53   Bagehot's classification that the Cabinet and Prime Minister performed the "efficient" elements of the Constitution, endures today as a classic explanation of the theory of Cabinet government.[59]

> "A Cabinet is a combining committee – a *hyphen* which joins, a buckle which fosters, the legislative part of the State to the

---

[53] R. R. Sedgwick, "The Inner Cabinet from 1732 to 1741" 34 *English Historical Review* pp. 290–302.

[54] P. Hennessy, *Cabinet* (1986), pp. 100–103.

[55] I. Jennings, *Cabinet Government* (3rd ed., 1959), p. 86.

[56] Blackstone Commentaries, Bk I., Chap. 6.

[57] W. R. Cornish and G. de Clark, *Law and Society in England 1750-1950*, pp. 10–14.

[58] Bagehot, *The English Constitution* (1867).

[59] *ibid.*

executive part of the State. In its origin it belongs to the one, in its functions it belongs to the other."

Cabinet government has continued to develop, conforming to the theory of Bagehot's definition, but in recent times evolving modern characteristics.

Cabinet size and the allocation of seats within Cabinet does not **3–54** conform to a rigid convention but the choice exercised by the Prime Minister of the day. Since the Second World War the size of the Cabinet has varied. The smallest modern Cabinet of 16 members was achieved by Churchill by excluding Ministers of Education and Agriculture and Fisheries. The recent experience of Cabinet Government suggests between 22 and 24 members. Mrs Thatcher's Cabinet had 22 members. Mr Wilson's had 24.

However, the House of Commons Disqualification Act 1975 and the Ministerial and other Salaries Act 1975 allows no more than 95 holders of ministerial office to sit and vote in the Commons. In addition the Prime Minister may appoint between 20 to 30 parliamentary private secretaries. Such appointments are largely held by supporters of the Government in the Commons.

The working of the Cabinet, as distinct from its membership has **3–55** always been cloaked with secrecy. Gladstone, when Prime Minister, sent copies of Cabinet discussions to the Queen with personal notes and suggestions added. Glimpses of the Cabinet at work in recent times have emerged from the published diaries of ex-Cabinet Ministers, most notably Richard Crossman's Diaries.[60] Often such diaries reveal more about individual ministers than the exact functioning of the Cabinet which remains secret. The 30 year rule allows the disclosure of Cabinet documents, but this is subject to "weeding" out those that remain sensitive or too confidential to be made available to the public. Some of the more confidential papers may be withheld for a longer period than the 30 year rule may provide.

The Haldane Report[61] (1918) described the functions of Cabinet **3–56** government in a classic formulation of the theory and practice of Cabinet government. The Cabinet's functions include the determination of policy to be submitted to Parliament, the control of the national Executive in accordance with policy presented by Parliament and "the continuous co-ordination and delineation of the activities of several Department of State." A noticeable part of Haldane's description of the Cabinet function is the parliamentary aspect of the Cabinet's role, thus acknowledging Parliament's ultimate authority.

Since the Haldane Report, the Cabinet has continued to change **3–57** reflecting the party political aspects of its development. In 1986 Peter

---

[60] *Att.-Gen. v. Jonathan Cape Ltd* [1976] Q.B. 752.
[61] *Report of the Machinery of Government Committee*, Cd. 9230 (1918).

Hennessy published a confidential government memorandum[62] which reveals how the modern Cabinet has developed. In *Questions on Procedure for Ministers, A Guide for Cabinet Ministers* (1986, as amended in 1994) the business of the Cabinet is identified as:

"(a) questions which engage the collective responsibility of the Government, either because they raise major issues of policy or because they are likely to occasion public comment or criticism:

(b) questions on which there is an unresolved conflict of interest between departments."

In addition, financial proposals are submitted to the Cabinet and Ministers may set out their views on general issues of policy before the Cabinet. Advice may be given by the Secretary to the Cabinet, who is also the Head of the Civil Service, as to the question of when matters which may be suitable for the discussion of the whole Cabinet may be raised. The Prime Minister's consent must be sought if an individual Minister wishes to raise a matter at Cabinet.

3–58   A noticeable distinction is drawn between the individual work of Ministers in departments and *general policy* issues to be put before Cabinet. Defining such a distinction is clearly problematic but leaves the setting of the tone, culture and overall policy of the Cabinet within the Prime Minister's ambit.

The evolution of the modern Cabinet through incremental change from the nineteenth century to the modern style of management, is a remarkable demonstration of the inherent flexibility in constitutional arrangements. Constitutional innovation may take place without any general reconsideration.

3–59   One innovation of modern Cabinets has been the gradual increase in the Prime Minister's influence. Crossman[63] believed that the era of Prime Ministerial government was the reality of modern government. The outcome, he feared, was to relegate the Cabinet from the "efficient" to the "dignified" according to the Bagehot classification.

Examples cited of the so-called "decline" in the decision-making role of the Cabinet include the announcement that the first British A-bomb was tested without the Cabinet having made a formal decision on the matter, when the Atlee Government commissioned its development with only the Prime Minister and a number of close Cabinet colleagues[64] consulted.

---

[62] Hennessy, *Cabinet* (1986), pp. 8-13. Also published in *The New Statesman*, February 14, 18, 21, 1986.

[63] R. H. S. Crossman, *Memoirs of a Cabinet Minister* (London, 1976), 3 Vols.

[64] Turpin, *British Government and the Constitution* (1990), pp. 168-70. See G. W. Jones, "Development of the Cabinet" in W. Thornhill (ed.), *The Modernisation of British Government* (1975).

In 1984 the decision of the Government to ban trade union **3–60** membership at GCHQ Cheltenham was made by a small group[65] of Cabinet Ministers rather than the Cabinet as a whole. In 1986 Mr Heseltine, the Secretary of State for Defence, complained and later resigned because the Cabinet had not discussed a key policy issue over the future of Westland plc, a major defence supplier of helicopters. His resignation came at a Cabinet meeting, when it was decided that Ministers' statements on the affair should first be submitted to the Cabinet Office for clearance as to their consistency with Government policy.[66]

In the final analysis, Westland may be seen as the assertion of Cabinet decision-making. However in the initial stages the problem may have arisen because of the use of Cabinet committees, the restricted membership of each committee preventing a full debate of the issues before the full Cabinet. Mrs Thatcher's resignation in 1990, may have underlined the importance of Cabinet support, even when the Prime Minister appears popular and successful.

Committees of the Cabinet are of nineteenth century origin. Their **3–61** use has evolved over time in an ad hoc way. Some committees are chaired by the Prime Minister, others by senior Ministers. Some are referred to as standing committees which are permanent for the duration of the Prime Minister's period in office. Others are called ad hoc committees because they have specific and particular issues to exercise. One good example of this is the "Star Chamber", well known because it met each Autumn to reconcile the competing claims made by the various spending departments. Membership of the Star Chamber included the Chief Secretary to the Treasury and the Chancellor of the Exchequer. In recent years since 1992 the Star Chamber has not met.[67] There is a third category known as ministerial committees which are composed of only civil servants.

The existence of such committees has been, until recently, kept within the inner workings of No. 10 Downing Street. However, the committees and their operation are now more openly publicised and acknowledged.

Such committees have added to the debate on the question of **3–62** Cabinet or Prime Ministerial government. The influence of the Prime Minister is seen as a key element in their functioning, appointment and operation. In theory, Ministers have access to the full Cabinet should they require approval against the wishes of the Committee but only where the Committee chairman gives approval. Mrs Thatcher when Prime Minister continued the procedure of her predecessors by

---

[65] *ibid.*
[66] Heseltine, Resignation statement, *The Times,* January 10, 1986.
[67] For a fuller discussion of public finance see Chap. 12.

using committees to make key decisions. In 1980, the decision to
replace Polaris with Trident was taken by an ad hoc committee with
the Defence Secretary, Foreign Secretary, Chancellor of the Exchequer
and Home Secretary present.[68]

3–63   In addition to the above committees, there is conclusive evidence
that Prime Ministers in recent times have developed the habit of
summoning an "inner Cabinet" of key Ministers. Clement Atlee,
Chamberlain, Churchill, Eden and Wilson throughout their premier-
ships made use of a small group of close friends or allies drawn from
the Cabinet. In a constitutional sense the existence of such an inner
Cabinet is not recognised in our formal constitutional arrangements.
However its existence is a political fact, reflecting the way in which
Prime Ministers may wish to function. During periods of crisis such
as the Falklands or Gulf Wars, small war cabinets exist containing key
Ministers[69] relevant to the success of wartime operations.

The question arises as to whether such "inner cabinets" are
consistent with Prime Ministerial government which may conform to
a Presidential style or should be compared to collective decision-
taking through Cabinet government. The existence of the inner
Cabinet and various committees of the Cabinet, such as the defence
and overseas policy committee; the economic strategy committee; the
legislation committee and a home and social offices committee is used
as evidence to strengthen the view that Prime Ministerial influence is
paramount.

3–64   Crossman wrote in 1972,[70] that Prime Ministerial government arose
because the Prime Minister decides the membership of the Cabinet,
sets the agenda of Cabinet discussion and organises Cabinet committees. An opposing view to Crossman is provided by Jones,[71] who
doubts that the evidence against Cabinet government is conclusive.
Jones offers the analysis that trends in favour of Prime Ministerial
government may just as easily be interpreted to show that the
Cabinet's survival depends on effective delegation to cope with a
growing bureaucracy in government. In recent years, Mrs Thatcher's
style and method dominated the work of the Cabinet. Her years as
Prime Minister seemed to support the view that "collective decision-
making in Cabinet" had suffered a decline[72] and a shift[73] to a
Presidential style.

3–65   Another dimension to the debate is the party political nature of
government's decision-taking. Prime Ministers are simultaneously

[68] Turpin, *op. cit.*
[69] Seymour-Ure, "British 'War Cabinets' in Limited Wars: Korea, Suez and the
Falklands" (1984) 62 *Public Administration* 181.
[70] Crossman, *Inside View* (1972), pp. 62–67.
[71] Jones, *op. cit.* pp. 31–32.
[72] K. Minogue and M. Biddiss, *Thatcherism: Personality and Politics* (1987).
[73] Peter Kellner "The War that started a Revolution," *The Independent*, August 28, 1989.

leaders of their party. At a party political level, the choices exercised by the Prime Minister must ensure electoral success. The timing of the election and the decision to dissolve Parliament are at the discretion of the Prime Minister and choosing wrongly has the penalty of losing the election and political power.

The ebb and flow of Prime Ministerial[74] influence through Cabinet reshuffles and policy decision-making is often constrained by the realities of political life. In the case of Mrs Thatcher, the epitome of the shift to a Presidential style Prime Minister, her demise as Prime Minister[75] was the signal of ultimate Cabinet and therefore party control.

It may be concluded that in recent years the shifts in style and management techniques between the Cabinet and Prime Minister do not necessarily signal *institutional* change in the role of the Cabinet. The Prime Minister remains *primus inter pares* with considerable powers to influence the Cabinet and ultimately the success or failure of the Government.

The Cabinet Office provides the Cabinet and Prime Minister with **3–66** the administrative services necessary for the circulation of the Cabinet's agenda reports and recording the Cabinet's conclusion. It is headed by the Secretary to the Cabinet who serves as a Principal Private Secretary to the Prime Minister and is Head of the Civil Service. Contained within the Cabinet office from 1970 to 1983, was the Cabinet "think-tank" as it was known or more precisely the *Central Policy Review Staff* (CPRS) to cross departmental activities and take a long term view of the policies and strategies to be recommended. It was staffed by non-civil servants and abolished by Mrs Thatcher in 1983. It was replaced by a Downing Street Policy Unit which operates as part of the Prime Minister's Office.

Also within the working of No. 10, there are various political staff attached to the Prime Minister, including a Principal Private Secretary, press agent and various advisers. Political advisers have in recent years had an increasingly important role within government departments as well as within the Prime Minister's office.

5. Collective and Individual Ministerial Responsibility

Individual ministerial responsibility is the cornerstone of our consti- **3–67** tutional arrangements. The responsibility arises from convention and is defined to mean that Ministers are responsible, *i.e.* accountable,[76] or

[74] Marshall [1991] *Public Law* 1–6.
[75] B. Jones, "Thatcher and After" in Jones *et al.*, *Politics U.K.* (1991), pp. 588–597.
[76] Generally, see P. Norton, "The House of Commons and the Constitution: The Challenges of the 1970s" (1981) 34 *Parliamentary Affairs* 253.

answerable to Parliament. In modern times it has been interpreted to mean that Ministers take responsibility for their departments and for the consequences of what has been decided as a matter of policy. Turpin has identified the meaning of responsibility and the question of how sanctions might apply to uphold responsibility.[77]

"The obligations to answer, to submit to scrutiny, and to redress grievances may seem in practice to lack the support of any coercive rule or sanction. Undoubtedly these obligations are imperfect, resting as they do upon conventions, practices, and procedures which are liable to change and to be variously interpreted and applied, and which depend ultimately upon the political culture."[78]

3–68 Ministerial responsibility has been acknowledged by the courts as a guiding principle of the constitution. It provides constitutional principles as the basis for the Parliamentary scrutiny of the Executive. Ministers may appear before Select Committees to answer questions or before the whole House of Commons. It has been invoked as the basis of ministerial resignation, for example, Lord Carrington over the Falklands invasion by Argentina in 1982, and the resignation of Mr Leon Brittan in 1986, after he authorised the improper release of the confidential letter written by the Solicitor-General to the Secretary of State for Defence.

In the classic case of resignation that of Sir Thomas Dugdale in 1954 over the sale of land[79] in Devon compulsorily acquired during the war, resignation is seen as not an automatic or inevitable sanction,[80] but as the basis of what the Prime Minister regards as the interests of the Government.

3–69 Ministerial resignation may follow from serious policy misjudgments, from errors within a government department or may come from personal error arising from a Minister's private life. Instances, where some degree of fault is perceived to lie with the Minister in the period 1982–94 have been unusually high. A number of resignations include[81]:

---

[77] C. Turpin, "Ministerial Responsibility: Myth or Reality?" in J. Jowell and D. Oliver (eds.), *The Changing Constitution* (2nd ed., 1989), pp. 55–60. See D. Woodhouse, "Ministerial Responsibility in the 1990's: When Do Ministers Resign?" [1993] 46 *Parliamentary Affairs* 277. See Chap. 4 for a fuller discussion of conventions.

[78] See the House of Lords in *Local Government Board* v. *Arlidge* [1915] A.C. 120.

[79] *Report of the Public Inquiry into the Disposal of Land at Crichel Down*, Cmd. 9176 (1954). See. I. F. Nicolson, *The Mystery of Crichel Down* (1986).

[80] Resignation does not invariably follow from mistakes: When it does the reasons are couched in the political language of the government of the day: Westland, 1985–86, *The Times*, January 24, 1986; the Falklands see Carrington's resignation statement, April 5, 1982; Turpin, *British Government and the Constitution*, p. 433.

[81] See D. Woodhouse, "Ministerial Responsibility in the 1990s: When Do Ministers Resign?" [1993] 46 *Parliamentary Affairs* 277 at 279.

" . . . Lord Carrington, Richard Luce and Humphrey Atkins (1982), Cecil Parkinson (1983), Leon Brittan (1986), Edwina Currie (1988), Patrick Nicholls (1990), Nicholas Ridley (1990), and David Mellor (1992) . . .."

Resignation arising out of personal indiscretion has become more common in recent years. David Mellor and Cecil Parkinson are in that category while Patrick Nicholls resigned after being arrested for drunk driving. Tim Yeo (1994) resigned for personal reasons during a period when public opinion became critical of the personal morality of Ministers and Members of Parliament.

(a) The Scott report

In November 1992 the trial of three former executives of the machine tool manufacturer Matrix Churchill[82] for the illegal export of arms to Iraq, collapsed after a former Minister Alan Clark gave testimony. Clark's testimony revealed that government departments had been aware of the nature of the equipment when export licences were granted. Despite this fact four Ministers had signed public interest immunity certificates intended to prevent confidential documents from being revealed to the defence at the trial. It was also revealed that one of the defendants had provided information to the secret service over a number of years. Signing the certificates also prevented full Parliamentary disclosure of the reality of government policy.

3–70

Public disquiet forced the Prime Minister to set up an inquiry under Sir Richard Scott. The Scott report into the arms to Iraq affair consists of five volumes and index amounting to over 1,800 pages in length and was published in February 1996 as a House of Commons paper.[83] The conclusions reached in the Scott report go to the heart of government accountability.

3–71

Trade and its regulation fall under the provisions of the Export and Customs Powers (Defence) Act 1939 which, until the Scott report was published, was a little known but vital piece of legislation that was passed on the outbreak of the Second World War. The 1939 Act has remained unrepealed ever since. Successive Governments enjoyed the benefits of the legislation without having to confront the need to amend or reform its basic provisions to keep pace with modern developments and practice. Keeping quiet about legislation that in

---

[82] See M. Phythian and W. Little, "Parliament and Arms Sales: Lessons of the Matrix Churchill Affair" [1993] 46 *Parliamentary Affairs* 293.

[83] Thus securing protection for the report under the Parliamentary Papers Act 1840 against defamation proceedings.

modern times ought to have been revised is a serious flaw in the system of internal checks and balances. At the heart of the problem was the fear that amending legislation would draw public attention to existing practice and lead to contentious debate. This fact alone drawn from the Scott report confronts one of the basic assumptions made about parliamentary democracy – that when in doubt the government of the day will seek parliamentary authority for its actions. More important is the point that when legislation lies dormant it should be updated to take account of changing circumstances.

3–72 The Scott report leads to the conclusion that the operating assumptions within the inner workings of government are that government assumes that it has the necessary legal powers until specifically and categorically prohibited by legislation. This assumption or working practice is seriously called into question and challenged by the Scott report. It is a fundamental weakness of existing systems of parliamentary scrutiny that such internal checks and balances very often fail to alert Parliament to the necessity for law reform.

More immediately, the facts leading up to the Matrix Churchill trial[84] in November 1992 that precipitated the Scott inquiry go back to the circumstances surrounding the outbreak of war between Iran and Iraq in 1980. The outbreak of war resulted in a speedy assurance from the government that no lethal weapons would be supplied through licensed sales to either side. This trade embargo was applied on the basis of the 1939 legislation and a government statement which made public the nature of the restrictions on sales to Iran and Iraq. Though ambiguously worded these restrictions were added to by the Government in 1981 with the view that every opportunity should be taken to exploit Iraq's potential as a promising sale of defence equipment with the exception of lethal weapons interpreted in the narrowest sense.

3–73 In 1984 what has become known as the Howe guidelines were promulgated and made public. The guidelines contained four restrictions namely: that the consistent refusal to supply lethal weapons to either side should be maintained; that existing contracts and obligations should be fulfilled; no new orders should be sanctioned for any defence equipment which might significantly enhance the capability of either side to the conflict; all applications for export licences should be scrutinised with great care for the supply of defence equipment to Iran or Iraq.

3–74 The Howe guidelines were certainly intended to tighten up, and strengthen existing practice. However, they left considerable doubt as

[84] Details of this trial may be found in: D. Leigh, *Betrayed, The Real Story of the Matrix Churchill Trial* (London, 1993), and a background analysis is provided in: J. Sweeney, *Trading with the Enemy* (Pan, 1993).

to the actual restrictions to be observed. The restriction on lethal weapons was vaguely expressed, the acceptance that defence equipment might be provided was equally unclear and the juxtaposition of both concepts appeared contradictory. Defence equipment might indeed include lethal weapons and lethal weapons might be required for defence purposes. Government policy as represented in the Howe guidelines appeared sufficiently ambiguous and flexible to provide very little difficulty in their observance. According to the Scott report up until August 1988 they appeared to be an accurate reflection of government policy.

The cessation of the Gulf war in 1988 brought to an end the apparent mischief that the Howe guidelines were intended to deal with. The signal given by the Government including Lord Howe himself was that the end of the war and the cease-fire could allow economic opportunities to be exploited to the full.

With the benefit of hindsight what was required was a full scale 3–75 review of the guidelines, the applicable law and how arms sales are regulated. What occurred instead was incremental change through stealth rather than a fundamental review. A more flexible approach over arms sales appeared to be necessary and the Government exploited the ambiguous nature of the guidelines to that end. A number of key government departments had responsibilities over arms sales.

The Foreign Office appeared reluctant to allow fundamental 3–76 changes to the guidelines themselves. The system of licensing required formal approval from the Department of Trade and Industry (DTI) of exports and the DTI appeared willing to embrace a more open policy of trade. Pressure from British companies intensified for a share in the arms trade and the economic opportunities of trade amidst intense competition from foreign companies. The Ministry of Defence broadly favoured a more market-based approach and supported the DTI in a more flexible interpretation of the Howe guidelines. The guidelines were subtly amended. The original Howe guidelines contained the following:

> "we should not in future approve or sanction new orders for any defence equipment which in our view would significantly enhance the capability of either side to prolong or exacerbate the conflict . . ."

The revised guidelines included:

> "we should not in future **approve new orders for any defence equipment which in our view would be of direct and significant assistance to either country in the conduct of offensive operations in breach of the ceasefire**" (author's emphasis).

3–77   Interpretation of the revised guidelines appeared to offer more flexibility than the original guidelines. Given the sensitive nature of the arms trade the revised guidelines were not published or announced in Parliament. Incongruous though it sounds, it was naively believed that shifts in policy would probably be detected by the public at large and so the revised guidelines would receive tacit public approval once they were operative. It was tacitly assumed that the Government was prepared to withstand robust questioning on its policy both inside and outside Parliament. On the other hand it was assumed that if the Government made the guidelines public it was assumed that great public debate would ensue with the implication that political embarrassment might follow. This might force the Government into an unwelcome review of the entire arms licensing system.

3–78   Scott considered that the guidelines on arms sales appeared as a statement of policy and that as a result of revising the guidelines this reflected the *actualité* that policy had been changed. Government statements made in 1989 and 1990 about policy on arms exports "consistently failed to discharge the obligations imposed by the constitutional principle of Ministerial responsibility."[85]

Sir Richard Scott also found that the Attorney-General was at fault in not making clear to the court at the trial of the Matrix Churchill directors that Mr Heseltine, then President of the Board of Trade was reluctant to agree signing the certificate claiming public interest immunity.[86] A second criticism was that the Attorney-General had mistakenly interpreted the law on public interest certificates when he claimed that Ministers were bound to sign such certificates when requested to do so. Criticism was also made of a number of Ministers for the reasons they gave for signing certificates.[87]

3–79   Aside from such criticisms Sir Richard considers that Ministers were, albeit perhaps mistakenly, engaged in acting in what they took to be the national and therefore the public interest. Ministers gained no direct benefits from the arms sales and had been influenced by the need to operate within the competitive conditions of the market. The information then available to Ministers at the time was less than the information which is now available with the benefit of hindsight. Ministers and civil servants are to be judged by what they then knew and on the basis of what they believed at that time. At the heart of the ministerial defence on arms exports was the claim that ministers had applied the spirit of the guidelines out of necessity. In short, ministers

---

[85] See the Scott report D4.63. Also see: Ian Leigh and Laurence Lustgarten, "Five volumes in search of accountability: The Scott Report" [1996] *Modern Law Review* 695.
[86] See the Scott report para. G13.6 9–72.
[87] See the Scott report paras. G117, 125, 54, 67 and 106.

could rely only their subjective defence. They may now appear to have been mistaken but at the time they acted in good faith and with the public interest in mind.

In effect Parliament and the public were left at best confused and at **3–80** worst misled about the Government's true policy on arms sales by parliamentary answers. The question of whether Ministers were to blame for this state of affairs was a central issue of importance for the Scott report. Scott approaches this issue with some degree of dexterity. The approach adopted is to provide throughout the report an elaborate and detailed analysis of the facts and evidence that justifies the main conclusions reached in the main report. In so doing he read, digested and had access to more secret information than possibly any single individual in recent times. Far from being captivated by the ethos of secrecy Scott adopts a highly critical stance of the conduct of Government.

Scott[88] provides detailed and systematic evidence about government indifference to Parliament and the public. Three Ministers deliberately failed to inform Parliament about sales to Iraq for fear of the public outcry that might result. The policy on exports as explained to Parliament and M.P.s was according to Scott "designedly led to believe that a stricter policy was applied than was the case". Scott does not accept that the Attorney-General was not personally at fault. The Department's attitude to disclosure of information was consistently grudging. The letters on exports to Iraq conveyed the idea that no military equipment had been sold to Iraq during the Gulf conflict. This assertion could not truthfully be made.

Following publication of the Scott report the report was considered **3–81** in debate in the House of Commons.[89] No minister resigned and by a majority of one, ministerial censure or resignation was avoided. The Scott report provides an important summary of ministerial accountability[90] where the focus is not on resignation but the requirement to give information to Parliament. In this respect Scott has supported a Freedom of Information Act to underline the importance attached to information. It is expected that Ministers should not knowingly mislead Parliament and should be as open as possible in the giving of information. This omits any obligation to volunteer information when not specifically requested. This may result in the current responsibilities upon Ministers appearing to be too weak and inadequate when faced with others who are prepared to be economical in their answers. There is a more worrying legacy left behind after the Scott report, if Ministers can rely on their subjective defence. If at the time

---

[88] See Richard Norton Taylor, *Truth is a Difficult Concept: Inside the Scott Inquiry* (1995).
[89] H.C. Deb. February 26, 1996, cols. 589 and 663–9.
[90] Scott report K8. 1–16.

Ministers were questioned they may have been mistaken in their answers, but so long as they acted in good faith and with the public interest in mind they should not be held at fault. This leaves a remarkable void. Very often at the time it is only Ministers who will know whether their answers may have misled. Without an obligation to provide a full answer, full ministerial responsibility may remain elusive.

(b) Collective responsibility

3–82 Historically ministerial responsibility has been formulated to include the whole Ministry responsible for all official acts of the individual Ministers. This carries the implication of collective responsibility when a Minister is acting on behalf of the Government[91] as a whole. Jennings noted[92] that this link between individual Minister and Government did not require the Cabinet to approve the policy in question. Undoubtedly collective responsibility means collective resignation, should there be a no confidence vote in the House of Commons in the government of the day. Such votes are rare. This leaves unanswered the precise formulation of collective responsibility, as inevitably different views within the Cabinet may lead to lack of unanimity over the precise nature of government policy.

Collective responsibility may have a different aspect other than explaining how the Cabinet is responsible to Parliament. It may explain the *process* which ties the Cabinet to confidentiality in its decision-making. Thus dissenting voices are silenced once a decision has been agreed in Cabinet.

3–83   The confidentiality aspect of Cabinet deliberations was acknowledged in the *Crossman Diaries* case, *Attorney-General v. Jonathan Cape Ltd*[93] when the Attorney-General attempted unsuccessfully to prevent the posthumous publication of Crossman's Diaries compiled while he was a Cabinet Minister. The view of Lord Widgery C.J., was that opinions by Cabinet Ministers in the course of Cabinet discussions were protected by confidentiality, and in the public interest, publication could be prohibited by the courts. On the facts of the Crossman case a period of 10 years had elapsed and it was considered unlikely that publication would damage the doctrine of joint Cabinet responsibility. Lord Widgery C.J., rejected the view that the Diaries should

---

[91] Turpin, *op. cit.* "Symposium on Ministerial Responsibility" (1987) 65 *Public Administration*, 61–91. See D. Woodhouse, "Ministerial Responsibility: the Abdication of Responsibility through the Receipt of Legal Advice" [1993] P.L. 412.
[92] I. Jennings, *Cabinet Government* (3rd ed., 1959).
[93] [1976] Q.B. 752.

not be published because they disclosed advice given by senior civil servants.

The *Crossman* case should not be interpreted to mean that in every **3–84** case publication of diaries would be accepted by the courts. Instead, the case lays the foundation for protecting Cabinet discussion on the basis of confidentiality and therefore the law of confidence. Thus, a claim that disclosure would not be in the public interest is usually sufficient to maintain confidentiality.

In 1976, after the *Crossman* case, Lord Radcliffe considered the publication of ministerial memoirs as Chairman of a Committee of Privy Counsellors on Ministerial Memoirs.[94] The Report identified working principles as to "the public interest" especially matters which in the international sphere might be detrimental to relations with other nations, or in the domestic sphere, information which would destroy the trust between Ministers or between Minister or advisers or private bodies.

Since publication of the *Crossman Diaries*, the diaries of other ex- **3–85** Cabinet Ministers, notably Barbara Castle and Tony Benn have been successfully published in what might be regarded as against the spirit of the Radcliffe rules. Recent publications have also included diaries of ex-civil servants and advisers.[95] Retired Prime Ministers find a lucrative market among publishers willing to provide large cash advances for publication of diaries or reflections made during the period of office. Nevertheless the confidentiality of the Cabinet has been used to prevent publication, by civil servants and others, of Cabinet discussion. The conclusion must be that stemming from the doctrine of collective Cabinet responsibility, the secrecy of the system of government emanates from the principles of Cabinet government. Mr Justice McCowan in *R. v. Ponting*[96] directed the jury that Clive Ponting, an Assistant Secretary of the Ministry of Defence, could not rely on his belief that the government deliberately misled Parliament over the sinking of the Argentine warship, the *General Belgrano*, during the Falklands war, to leak documents to Tam Dalyell M.P., a critic[97] of government policy.

The case illustrates how government may be conceived as both a **3–86** political entity and a constitutional institution. In that sense collective Cabinet decision-making is an effective means of allowing political debate and discussion to take place, whilst the inner workings of the Cabinet are protected from external scrutiny and accountability.

---

[94] Cmnd. 6386 (1976).
[95] Nicholas Ridley, Norman Lamont, Margaret Thatcher, Alan Clark are all examples of the genre "ministerial memoir contained in published diaries."
[96] [1985] Crim.L.R. 318.
[97] *Falkland Islands Review*, Cmnd. 8787 (1983).

6. The Civil Service

3–87 There are currently less than 500,000 civil servants and over two-thirds work in executive agencies. It is expected by the end of the century over 90 per cent of the civil service will be found in executive agencies. In this introductory part an overview of the role and function of the civil service is considered. In Chapter 10 executive agencies are explained and defined in some detail.

(a) *Definition*

3–88 The civil service is permanent and appointed on merit. Described[98] as "the ultimate monster to stop governments changing things," the civil service provides the main administration for the activities of the government of the day. Civil servants may be defined in general terms as servants of the Crown employed in government departments. The Fulton Committee[99] in 1968 added certain exclusions: "servants of the Crown, other than holders of political or judicial officers, who are employed in a civil capacity and whose remuneration is paid wholly and directly out of monies voted by Parliament."

In most discussions about civil servants; the judiciary, Ministers of the Crown, the army, police, officials in local government or National Health Service, are excluded. Commonly used terms to describe civil servants are: "public officials"; public servants; administrators or crown servants. The latter term has found acceptance in law, as describing the employment relationship and sometimes status of civil servants.

3–89   Civil servants are regulated by many different Acts of Parliament such as the Official Secrets Acts 1911-89 and the Superannuation Act 1972. This is piece-meal[1] legislation; none of the Acts clarifies the legal status, duties, obligations or rights of civil servants. In addition, there are numerous memoranda such as instructions to civil servants when appearing before select committees or when acting under the Royal prerogative. There are also regulations and instructions made by the Treasury and the Minister for the Civil Service under the Civil Service Order in Council 1982. Civil servants receive a code containing details of their service and pay, entitled[2]: "The Civil Service Pay and Conditions of Service Code." The Code is supplemented by regulations made by each government department for their staff.

[98] Quoted in the preface in P. Hennessy, *Whitehall* (1989), p. xiii.
[99] Cmnd. 3638 (1968).
[1] P. Kellner and Lord Crowther-Hunt, *The Civil Servants* (1980).
[2] Turpin, *op. cit.* p. 209.

There has always been difficulty in precisely categorising the legal **3–90**
status of civil servants in their employment situation. Modern
employment legislation has been applied to civil servants granting
rights in common with other employees regarding unfair dismissal.
At common law, service as a civil servant was at the pleasure of the
Crown. The exact basis of this rule is a mixture of constitutional law
and public policy. The latter has always been difficult to estimate and
predict. This is partly due to the fact that as "there is in law no
universally applicable definition of civil servant or civil service. The
most important distinguishing characteristic is service on behalf of
the Crown."[3] There is difficulty in expressing a legal implication for
such service.

In addition to the 1978 Employment Protection Consolidation Act, **3–91**
Pt. V and section 138 on unfair dismissal, numerous other recent
employment legislation also applies. The Equal Pay Act 1970, the Sex
Discrimination Act 1975 and the Race Relations Act 1976, all apply to
civil servants.

Civil servants are also regulated by a wide variety of regulations,
rules, codes of practice, disciplinary codes and Orders in Council.
Specifically the Civil Service Order in Council 1982 made under the
royal prerogative. Wide powers are granted under the 1982 Order
namely Article 4, entitles the Minister for the Civil Service "to give
instructions . . . for controlling the Conduct of the Service, and
providing for . . . the conditions of service."

Pay and conditions of civil servants are negotiated through the **3–92**
Civil Service National Whitley Council, dating from 1919. National
pay bargaining has gradually broken up and individual negotiations
with trade unions are not uncommon. Employment conditions are
likely to be further delegated to departments and agencies after the
setting up of "Agencies under The Next Steps" in 1988. The Civil
Service (Management of Functions) Act 1992 facilitates this system of
delegation.

Some doubt has been expressed about whether there is a contractual relationship between the civil servant and the employer, the
Crown. It seemed to be accepted in the GCHQ[4] case that a contractual
relationship did not exist, or at any rate, in arguing for or against
retraction of trade union membership, this issue of contract was not
relied upon.

Mr Justice Otton considered the issue in R. v. Civil Service Appeal **3–93**
Board, ex p. Cunningham.[5] A prison officer because of his status as a

---

[3] Cmd. 7117, (1976–77 H.C. 535 I–III), para. 107. See Mulvenna v. The Admiralty 1926
S.C. 842.
[4] [1984] 3 All E.R. 935.
[5] [1991] 4 All E.R. 310.

civil servant and constable had forfeited his rights by not appearing before an industrial tribunal but had been given an assurance in the Civil Service Pay and Conditions of Service that he would not be "less favourably" treated as a result. Whether contractual rights existed was unclear. This matter of contract rights becomes important because of the present law on how an aggrieved citizen may seek remedies in the courts, through the procedure known as judicial review. Such a procedure must relate to public law matters and normally disciplinary procedures of a purely domestic nature were not amenable to judicial review. A civil servant may have private contractual rights but also as a public official, rights under the civil service Pay and Conditions of Service Code. Do such rights fall into the category of public law rights or are they entirely private law rights based on contract? The case law has not provided a clear answer to this question.

3-94   There is in existence a Civil Service Appeal Board (CSAB) set up under the prerogative which may hear appeals against disciplinary action. In *R. v. Civil Service Appeal Board, ex p. Bruce,*[6] Bruce, a civil servant, was an Inland Revenue employee who appealed to the CSAB against his dismissal. The Court of Appeal and the Divisional Court accepted that the CSAB was amenable to judicial review even though in that particular case an alternative remedy could have been sought. There was some doubt as to whether a contract might exist, as no intention to create legal relations existed. This point was *obiter dictum* and *Bruce* did not decide whether civil servants had contracts of employment. Earlier in *McClaren v. Home Office,*[7] again *obiter dictum* Woolf L.J. stated that "an employee of a public body is normally in the same position as other employees." The *McClaren* case concerned the appointment of prison officers, appointed under the Prison Act 1952, rather than the prerogative so the case may be unhelpful when it is applied to civil servants normally appointed under the prerogative.

The uncertainty in the law leaves unanswered the fundamental question of whether civil servants have contractual rights. The answer to this question may prove elusive, in the absence of any legislative intervention.

(b)   Role and Function of the Civil Service

3-95 The convention of ministerial responsibility applies not only to the relationship between Ministers and the House of Commons but also to that between Ministers and civil servants. The formulation of this principle may take a number of forms.

---

[6] *The Times*, March 14, 1990; [1988] 3 All E.R. 686.
[7] [1990] I.C.R. 824; [1990] I.R.L.R. 338.

First, civil servants owe a duty to Ministers. Here there is no distinction between the Government of the day and the role of the civil service. The civil servant is answerable to the Minister and through the Minister, to Parliament.

Secondly, Ministers do not normally reveal the role played by civil servants in formulating policy. Even when advice is problematic, rarely do Ministers reveal the identity of civil servants.

Thirdly, civil servants may advise Ministers on policy but in theory **3–96** they are not called upon to act politically. Where a civil servant has doubts or misgivings about the instructions received from Ministers, the Armstrong Memorandum[8] in 1987, provides guidelines as to how civil servants should behave. Especially when questions of constitutional propriety or legality are involved or even politically embarrassing decisions are made, civil servants should seek redress or resolution of such doubts within the civil servants' own Department. This may be achieved through appeal to the senior officer in the Department or to the legal adviser to the Department in question.

Criticism[9] of the Armstrong guidelines points to doubts over the **3–97** effectiveness of such arrangements especially after the Westland affair. Differences between Government Ministers were being resolved by the disclosure of a confidential letter, between the Solicitor General and the then Secretary of State for Defence (Mr Heseltine), by the civil servants acting with the authority of the Secretary of State for Trade and Industry (Mr Britton). This disclosure broke the convention of strict confidentiality over the letters and advice of[10] law officers. Civil servants did not seem able to prevent such disclosure and there may have been no option in the circumstances but to have complied with the instructions of the Minister. Civil servants in this matter, were prohibited from appearing before select committees or giving interviews to the press.

Ministers may claim to know what is in the best interests of the public as well as in the interests of the Government. Ministers are self-authorising over the publication of confidential information. Leaks may be authorised by a Minister. Oddly, what appears to be a means of holding Ministers to account, the doctrine of ministerial accountability, may allow a wide exercise of ministerial discretion.

The *Crichel Down* affair in 1954 raised the possibility that ministerial **3–98** resignation might follow the acts of civil servants. Since 1984 the papers, official and private on the affair, have cast doubts over whether the facts in 1954 support ministerial resignation over the

---

[8] *The Duties and Responsibilities of Civil Servants in Relation to Ministers (Note by the Head of the Home Civil Service*, revised in 1987). Cm. 9841 (1986).
[9] R. Rose, *Loyalty, Voice or Exit? Margaret Thatcher's Challenge to the Civil Service* (1988).
[10] Westland Affair. See Turpin, *op. cit.* pp. 185–186, 208–209, 436–437.

alleged failure of civil servants to act correctly over the application of Commander Marten to buy or rent land originally compulsorily acquired by the Air Ministry in 1938. It seems that the civil servants had not been negligent, rather that they acted according to the wishes of the Minister. In both the Westland affair and in Crichel Down ministerial resignation came about because of political embarrassment caused in both cases by revelations about ministerial impropriety in supervising the conduct of their respective departments.

3–99   The role and function of the modern civil service is undergoing considerable change. A useful contrast may be drawn between the Victorian legacy of the civil service and the modern tendency to transfer civil servant activities to Next Step agencies, discussed below.

Johnson has[11] identified four features of the civil service, inherited from the nineteenth century Victorian reforms which placed the civil service at the centre of administering the Welfare State and the managed economy of the post-1945 period.

3–100   First, since 1853 following the Northcote-Trevelyan Report, the civil service has been selected by fair and open competition rather than patronage. Selection on merit is intended to achieve high standards and efficiency. Secondly, the civil service has attempted to encourage the ethos of public service. Non-party political in outlook, it espouses neutrality and service. Neutrality, in its adaptation to any incoming government which adopts even a radically different political agenda from the outgoing government. Service, through its desire to set high standards, professionalism, confidentiality and competence in all its activities whether between departments within central government or in working alongside industry or business, the civil service in theory has developed institutional structures designed to encourage the practical work of administration. A theoretical perspective is not required to undertake such a role. No single specialism is favoured as a recruitment[12] policy.

"The civil service has few lawyers or accountants employed as civil servants. Generalist in recruitment, the civil service is accused of favouring 'the cult of the amateur.' Training in business, accountancy, law or management was not seen as advantageous. Internal professional training was seen as a substitute for outside expertise."

Finally, the civil service operates in terms of "adjustment and negotiation, advice and support." This characteristic makes the civil servant adopt compromise rather than confrontation.

[11] N. Johnson "Change in the Civil Service; Retrospect and Prospects" (1985) 63 *Public Administration* 415–434.
[12] *ibid.*

Johnson's four characteristics also include the protection afforded **3–101**
to the civil service, of permanence. In particular, civil servants have
traditionally enjoyed job protection, index-linked pensions and the
security which comes from such protection. However in recent years
the civil service has undergone change.

First, the size of the civil service has been consistently reduced.
Between 1979 and 1984 this reduction amounted to one-fifth of the
total, *i.e.* 1,000,000 civil servants. The reduction was achieved through
the transfer of a number of civil servant functions to non-civil service
or private sector departments. Efficiency studies and cost-benefit
analysis contributed to other reductions. The most significant change
has come through the transfer of civil servant functions to departmental agencies. One example is the Property Services Agency
responsible for accommodation and services for government bodies
and set up in the Department of the Environment. As an agency it has
a director or chief executive responsible to the permanent secretary of
the parent department or directly to the Minister. The use of such an
agency system is intended to give greater flexibility to the management of the day-to-day activities without ministerial intervention.

Secondly, in 1988 the Government published a report written by **3–102**
members of the Efficiency Unit (Cabinet Office, Efficiency Unit 1988)
entitled Improving Management in Central Government: the Next
Steps.[13] This report called the Next Steps envisages further expansion
in the range of activities placed inside Next Step agencies. The
emphasis in the Next Steps Agencies is to shift focus from service
provision to regulating and providing responses to customers' needs.

There has been no detailed inquiry into the civil service since the **3–103**
Fulton Report in 1969 which created the Civil Service Department
soon after. In 1981 the Civil Service Department was abolished and its
responsibility for civil service manpower, pay and superannuation
reverted to Treasury control. The Next Steps Agencies provide the
most radical changes to the civil service since Fulton and possibly this
century. Such agencies raise questions about accountability. Recently
ministers have agreed that written answers from Chief Executives
should be published daily in Hansard,[14] a major change brought
about through pressure to bring more open government to the fore
and a commitment to a more open style of government in the
Citizens' Charter.[15]

Thirdly, the political neutrality of the civil service has come under **3–104**
question as to the political nature of advice tendered by civil servants

---

[13] HMSO (1988). R. Butler, "The Evolution of the Civil Service – A Progress Report"
(1993) 71 *Public Administration,* 395–406.

[14] *The Independent,* July 27, 1992.

[15] Cm. 1599 (1991). See Chap. 10 for more details of the civil service, its organisation
and functions.

to Ministers. Ministers have increasingly sought advice from outside the civil service[16] through the appointment of advisers sympathetic to the policies of the Government. This is a trend which was noticeable in the Wilson Government in 1974. The trend has continued and prompted a former retired civil servant[17] to suggest that "a large number of senior civil servants" might be replaced with politically appointed officials on contracts.

Political neutrality, permanence, independence and professionalism are seen as advantages in the recruitment and ethos of public service. Such an ethos is under detailed scrutiny[18] today.

---

[16] R. Baldwin, "The Next Steps" (1988) 51 M.L.R. 622; Gavin Drewry [1988] P.L. 505.
[17] John Hoskyns, "Whitehall and Westminster: An Outsider's View" (1983) 36 *Parliamentary Affairs*, 137–147.
[18] Greenwood and Wilson, *Public Administration in Britain Today* (1989). R. Butler, "The Evolution of the Civil Service – A Progress Report" (1993) 71 *Public Administration*, 395–406.

Chapter 4

Conventions and the Rule of Law

1. Introduction

Constitutional conventions[1] are an important part of the United **4–01**
Kingdom's constitutional arrangements. Conventions may explain the
common practices and workings of government and how the United
Kingdom's unwritten Constitution accommodates change.

Dicey's influence has led constitutional lawyers to regard conventions as a means for past practices to be examined in order to
determine future conduct. In that sense conventions appear to link
the ancient, medieval Constitution with the modern and present day
Constitution. Conventions may provide some order to practices
which are, by their nature forms of political behaviour, and therefore
difficult to categorise in any strictly legal or constitutional sense.
Conventions are usually descriptive of a particular practice.

Conventions have been likened to rules or laws in many of their **4–02**
characteristics, with the exception that conventions are not enforceable by the courts. There is however some ambiguity about the
meaning of enforceable, because the courts acknowledge the existence
of conventions as aids to interpretation.[2] Frequently, conventions may
appear to be objective or neutral in the exposition of a rule or
understanding. This may be misleading as conventions often contain
value judgements prescribing how certain conduct of government or
officials should take place. Conventions often recognise the political
facts of life and help explain the political workings of the
Constitution.

---

[1] The most useful account may be found in G. Marshall, *Constitutional Conventions*
(1984). See Hood Phillips, *Constitutional and Administrative Law* (London, 1987), Chap.
6; C. R. Munro, *Studies in Constitutional Law* (Butterworths, 1987).
[2] See the Crossman Diaries case: *Att.-Gen. v. Jonathan Cape Ltd* [1976] Q.B. 752.
Discussion of conventions may be found in *ex p. Notts C.C.* [1988] A.C. 240. The
Canadian Courts have discussed conventions see: *Reference; Re Amendment of the
Constitution of Canada* (1982) 125 D.L.R. (3d) 1.

4-03   Conventions have grown historically as unwritten rules, and may adapt to the changing methods of modern government. That is their enduring quality. They are not the product of either judicial or legislative intervention, but rather custom, usage, habit and common practice. The most formative period for their development was probably in the eighteenth and towards the end of the nineteenth century. Conventions have the shortcoming that they reflect the values of mid-Victorian Government and perhaps, fail to take account of modern party political realities. The growth in the complexity of the machinery of government may make accountability through conventions more of a myth[3] than a reality. Many important practices are part of the *internal* working of government and it is difficult[4] to give internal working practices special value or elevation to the status of convention.

4-04   In this chapter the value and significance of conventions is examined. This is followed by an account of the influence of Dicey in defining and explaining the rule of law. The United Kingdom's constitutional arrangements provide that government is subject to law and may only exercise its powers according to law. The discussion on the rule of law leads into the question of the role of the courts, preparatory to the discussion on administrative law in Chapter 5.

2. Conventions

4-05 Dicey defined conventions[5] to mean "the rules which make up constitutional law" that made the United Kingdom distinctive. The use of the term "rules" is deliberate. In Dicey's definition he distinguished "laws" from "conventions." The former, he defined as comprising in the strictest sense, laws such as statute, judge-made law and common law doctrines which are enforceable by the courts.[6] The latter, conventions,[7] are "understandings, habits and practices

---

[3] C. Turpin, "Ministerial Responsibilty: Myth or Reality?" in J. Jowell and D. Oliver (eds.), *The Changing Constitution* (2nd ed., 1989), pp. 55-57.

[4] See "Improving Management in Government: The Next Steps" (1988) The Ibbs Report.

[5] A. V. Dicey, *Law of the Constitution*, Chaps. 14 and 15. Dicey tends to provide general principles in the early part of his text which he then re-capitulates later on as he reflects more deeply on their meaning. This may give rise to problems of interpretation. See pp. 24, 28–32. Generally, see R. A. Cosgrove, *The Rule of Law, Albert Venn Dicey Victorian Jurist* (1981), pp. 87–90.

[6] Prerogative powers, discussed above may today be added to the list as coming under judicial scrutiny.

[7] C. R. Munro, *Studies in Constitutional Law* (1987), Chap. 3, pp. 35–52. Also Munro, "Laws and Conventions Distinguished" (1975) 91 L.Q.R. 218; Munro, "Dicey on Constitutional Conventions" [1985] P.L. 637.

which are not enforced by the courts but which regulate the conduct of members of the sovereign power."

Dicey's emphasis on the "non-enforcement" of conventions by the courts is suitably ambiguous to create controversy over whether in principle there is any real distinction between laws and conventions. Since not all laws are enforceable by the court, as some are enforceable by tribunals, and some through discretion bestowed upon Ministers after inquiries, the distinction may seem a curious one today. Despite this reservation it is possible to see the usefulness of the distinction that laws *are* given effect to, or are recognised by the courts whereas conventions *may* not be recognised.

Dicey's views about conventions appear to have been influenced[8] **4–06** by John Austin (1790–1859), who distinguished non-legal rules from legal rules and believed in the general value of rules made for the guidance of man. Austin pioneered the analytical form of jurisprudence which was influential in Dicey's analysis of the Constitution. Conventions are regarded in Austin's analysis as part of "positive morality." But conventions do not appear to fit within Austin's definition of law as no clear sanction or enforcement accompanies any breach of a convention, they do however fit in with the idea of morality. Dicey followed this[9] analysis when describing conventions as "the morality of the constitution."

However, taking a different perspective from Dicey, Jennings **4–07** doubted[10] whether the distinction between laws and convention was of any "substance or nature." This might appear to place conventions in a diminished role in the constitution. Perhaps Jennings doubted the validity of the distinction between laws and conventions to be determined by the courts alone.

Jennings' views however would seem to ignore the working practices of most courts who appear to follow Dicey's distinction that conventions may be recognised but not enforced. Rarely have the courts in the United Kingdom used a convention as an enforceable rule. Some leading cases illustrate how the courts are reluctant to treat conventions as enforceable. This does not prevent the courts from recognising the *existence* of a convention and such acknowledgement may at times appear to be similar to enforcement.

In *Madzimbamuto v. Lardner-Burke*,[11] the Privy Council had to **4–08** consider a convention contained in a 1961 declaration that the Westminster Parliament was not to legislate for Southern Rhodesia. Lord Reid commented that the convention, although important, had no legal effect "in limiting the legal power of Parliament."

[8] J. Austin, *The Province of Jurisprudence Determined* (1832).
[9] G. Marshall, *Constitutional Conventions* (1984).
[10] Jennings, *The Law and the Constitution* (5th ed., 1959).
[11] [1969] 1 A.C. 645.

4–09   A similar convention of legislative self-restraint was said to have developed historically over Northern Ireland affairs. The Government of Ireland Act 1920 provided for a Parliament for Northern Ireland. Over the years a practice developed, that in the House of Commons at Westminster ministerial responsibility excluded any discussion of Northern Ireland transferred matters, that is discussion of matters which[12] were transferred to the competence of the Northern Ireland Parliament. Calvert explains.[13]

> "In this sense and in this sense only can these be said to be a convention, but its scope is somewhat limited. It is a convention only as to administrative practice. It does not inhibit legislation or discussion of a bill on a special motion. It operates only within the sphere of questions and other debates and only in relation to matters in respect of which there is, for the time being no ministerial responsibility at Westminster."

4–10   Another example of where the courts have recognised the existence of conventions, in *Attorney-General v. Jonathan Cape Ltd.*[14] Here the case involved the recognition of the important convention of collective ministerial responsibility. Richard Crossman, a Labour Minister from 1964 to 1970 had maintained a daily political diary with a view to publication after his death. Crossman died[15] in 1974 and his executors published the diaries and also extracts from his diaries in *The Sunday Times*. The Attorney-General argued that collective Cabinet responsibility provided a fundamental requirement of Cabinet secrecy which should be enforced through an injunction. Lord Widgery C.J. concluded that a convention could not be enforced in that way if it was[16] "an obligation founded in conscience only" but in general terms the courts might be willing to enforce Cabinet confidences when "the improper publication of such information can be restrained by the court." Redress might therefore be available for a breach of a conventional rule.

4–11   Another example is provided in Canada.The British North American Act 1867 passed by the United Kingdom Parliament left Canada, after the Statute of Westminster 1931, an independent State but with little or no competence to amend the 1867 Act. Amendments had to be through the United Kingdom Parliament, usually at the request of the Canadian Parliament. In 1980 the Federal Canadian Government

---

[12] H. Calvert, *Constitutional Law in Northern Ireland* (1968), pp. 103, 110.
[13] Calvert, *op. cit.* p. 103.
[14] [1976] Q.B. 752.
[15] Crossman, *Diaries of a Cabinet Minister* (London, 1976), Vol. 2.
[16] [1976] Q.B. 752, at p. 765.

decided to end the power of the United Kingdom Parliament to legislate and to incorporate the Charter of Rights as part of its independence. The question arose as to the legal powers of the United Kingdom Government when faced with a desire to change the existing status of the Canadian Constitution arising out of representations made from the Federal Government, when *only* two Canadian Provinces, Ontario and New Brunswick agreed. The remaining Canadian Provinces objected to the Federal Governments' terms.

The Federal Canadian Government claimed that the United King- **4–12** dom Parliament was bound to accede to its request. This raised the question of what the United Kingdom Parliament was required by convention to undertake under the Statute of Westminster 1931. Doubts were expressed as to the existence of such a convention and if one existed should it be enforced? The Foreign Affairs Committee in its report to the House of Commons 1980–81, concluded that there was no binding convention upon the United Kingdom Parliament to accede to the request of the Federal Canadian Government. The matter was put to the Supreme Court of Canada.[17] A majority decision concluded that[18] there was no legal objection to the Federal Government position to petition the Queen for agreement without the consent of the Provinces, but "at least a substantial measure of provincial consent" was required, and as this was not present it was unconstitutional for the Federal Parliament to act. In the end nine Provinces (with the exception of Quebec) did agree and the Canadian Bill 1982 was passed. The Canadian example raised a great deal of discussion about how conventions arose, who decided on their importance and what role the court performed.

A recurring theme in most of the discussion is Dicey's distinction **4–13** between laws and conventions and how this might be observed. Unlike common law rules made by judges, conventions are established by the institution of government. Conventional rules might conflict with formal legal rules and therefore are difficult to enforce. Perhaps the courts' search for conventions, and judicial "recognition" of their existence is, as some writers concluded "enforcing the convention?" Strictly speaking recognition does not mean enforcement in the same way as a statute or by-law. The question of why conventions are obeyed is difficult to answer.

Conventions seem to arise in ordinary day usage and develop over **4–14** a period of time culminating in their general recognition and acceptance. Once a convention is accepted and then followed, it becomes an acceptable form of good practice. Little is known about why conventions are actually obeyed. They do not normally imply any sanction

---

[17] *Reference Re Amendment of the Constitution of Canada* (1982) 125 D.L.R. (3d) 1.
[18] Munro, *Studies in Constitutional Law*, p. 45; P. Hogg, *Constitutional Law of Canada* (1992), p. 795; Heard, *Canadian Constitutional Conventions* (1991).

for their breach and as Turpin has noted, they have a remarkable ability to survive and change[19]:

> "Conventions are always emerging, crystallizing and dissolving, and it is sometimes questionable whether a convention has been broken or has simply changed."

4–15 It is a mistake to confine the discussion of conventions to merely good political practices and thereby beyond constitutional significance. Although unwritten in form and unclear in existence, they offer important guidance over the behaviour of government.

Some significant constitutional conventions may be briefly mentioned. Dicey noted the importance of both ministerial and Cabinet responsibility. The convention that a government that loses the confidence of the House of Commons must resign or advise dissolution has a significance in the constitutional history of the United Kingdom. Brazier[20] notes how such conventions have a certain vagueness and uncertainty about when they apply. When may a government be said to have lost the confidence of the House? How major or significant has a "policy" defeat to be before a principle of confidence is raised? Marshall's conclusion[21] on these matters explains how old or even outmoded conventions may undergo change.[22]

> "In the 1960's and 1970's, in any event, governments seem to have been following a new rule, according to which only votes specifically stated by the Government to be matters of confidence or votes of no confidence by the Opposition are allowed to count. Just conceivably one can imagine amongst recent Prime Ministers those who might have felt it their duties to soldier on in the general interest even in the face of such a vote."

4–16   The most important convention, which Dicey recognised, is collective responsibility of individual Ministers and of the Cabinet. As discussed in the previous chapter, individual ministerial responsibility is traditionally defined to mean that a Minister is responsible for his private conduct and that of his department, including the acts of the civil servants in his department. The latter suggests some degree of responsibility, for civil servant incompetence or negligence.

---

[19] Turpin, *British Government and the Constitution*, p. 99.
[20] R. Brazier, *Constitutional Texts* (Oxford, 1990), pp. 345–389. Also see de Smith, *Constitutional and Administrative Law* (1989), pp. 28–47.
[21] G. Marshall, *op. cit.* p. 346.
[22] *ibid.*

One example is the ministerial resignation of Thomas Dugdale in 1954 following the Crichel Down inquiry which concluded that the Department of Agriculture had acted in an arbitrary manner. Various civil servants were criticised and the Minister, Thomas Dugdale, resigned.[23] This resignation at the time was perceived to be a triumph over the bureaucracy of irresponsible civil servants. More recently, fresh evidence has suggested that ministerial resignation came about because of the government's embarrassment. As Peter Carrington, then joint Parliamentary Secretary, explained[24] in *Reflect on Things Past*, he and Dick Nuggent had offered their resignation to Churchill who agreed they should carry on. In such circumstances Ministers may resign or retain office simply because the Prime Minister concedes it is in the government's interests.

Ministerial resignations since 1960 have appeared to arise from **4–17** differences in policy over government collective decisions such as entering into the European Communities or disputes over government policy. An eclectic assortment of reasons may be offered to support the convention of *resignation* which meets the needs of the government of the day as much as any principle of accountability to Parliament. Nevertheless responsibility of Ministers means that mistakes, blunders or the incompetence of ministers, are issues which may be raised as matters for the debate and scrutiny of the House of Commons where resignation is rarely the sanction. Instead criticism, rebuke or embarrassment may be the stimulus for Ministers to improve. Overall the standing of the government of the day may decline when poor ministerial judgement is exposed to the glare of publicity. Constitutional conventions may give rise to greater political effects than have constitutional significance. This underlines the remarkable feature of the United Kingdom's unwritten Constitution which often leaves political judgement to determine the outcome of constitutional practices. To countries with a written constitution, this appears an unusual characteristic of the United Kingdom's Constitution where much political power resides and determines constitutional practice.[25]

Conventions have invariably attracted a wide spectrum of opinion **4–18** from lawyers and political scientists. Why have conventions and what purpose do they perform? Hood Phillips notes that[26]:

---

[23] Wilson, *Cases and Materials on Constitutional and Administrative Law* (Cambridge, 1976), pp. 155–164, 172.

[24] P. Carrington, *Reflect on Things Past*; P. Cosgrove, *Carrington: A Life and a Policy* (1989), pp. 55, 57.

[25] See the discussion of the Westland Affair in Chap. 3 and also D. Oliver and R. Austin, "Political and Constitutional Aspects of the Westland Affair" (1987) 40 *Parliamentary Affairs* 20. Also see D. Woodhouse, *Ministers and Parliament* (Oxford, 1994).

[26] Hood Phillips, *op. cit.* p. 119; R. Brazier, "Choosing a Prime Minister" [1982] P.L. 395.

"The ultimate object of most conventions is that public affairs should be conducted in accordance with the wishes of the majority of the electors."

Examples supporting this view are: the conventions relating to the choice of government which is formed from the majority party in the Commons; the convention that the Queen should act on the advice of Ministers; or the convention that the Queen will not refuse Royal Assent to a Bill.

4–19   On more mundane matters such as a request by the Leader of the Opposition for the recall of Parliament during recess, the position is regulated by both convention and the Standing Orders of the House of Commons. Standing Order No. 12., allows Ministers to recall Parliament should the Speaker be satisfied by representations that[27] "the public interest does so require." In fact convention seems to indicate that requests by opposition M.P.s to recall Parliament in recent years have been invariably refused. Emergency recall has been rejected on four occasions in the past 20 years. However, since 1945 Parliament has been recalled 14 times. In 1950 to discuss military involvement in Korea, the Suez crisis in 1956, and the Berlin crisis in 1961. More recently recall was granted over the Falklands invasion in 1982 and the Gulf war in 1990. A request for a recall in 1992 on the economy and the sending of British troops to Bosnia was refused.[28]

4–20   Conventions as precedent for past practice may, in the examples shown, not provide much guidance as to future practice. The government may find it easy to make up its mind on the basis of the facts in each case.

Academic writers have discussed[29] the question of whether conventions might be codified. It is suggested that the importance of conventions is such, that they should be collected together into a single code which would attempt to be comprehensive. The attraction of such a code would be to end uncertainty and vagueness associated with knowing whether a particular convention exists or not. The disadvantage is that a code might lead to rigidity; once codified would a convention lose its flexibility to change and so become fixed at one period in time? Are all conventions capable of enforcement by the courts? This might invariably follow once a convention became written and adopted in a code.

4–21   Attempts at the classification of the subject matter of conventions have identified conventions arising in the exercise of prerogative

[27] Standing Order of the House of Commons No. 12 (1948).
[28] The Soviet invasion of Czechoslovakia and the Biafran war in 1968, the imposition of internment in Northern Ireland in 1971 and the collapse of the power-sharing Executive in 1974, all merited the recall of Parliament.
[29] Marshall has discussed codification as has Brazier in de Smith, *Constitutional and Administrative Law* (1985), p. 46 and in new edition (1989), pp. 34–37.

powers, the workings of Cabinet, the proceedings in Parliament and relations between Lords and Commons, and finally, in relations between the United Kingdom and Commonwealth. This list is not exhaustive.

Conventions may be adopted into statute such as the convention of the United Kingdom not legislating for a former dependent territory in the preamble and section 4 of the Statute of Westminster 1931.

The survival of conventions owes much to their general acceptance **4–22** and the requirement of constitutional government with ultimate electoral accountability. When a convention is breached, the convention is usually sufficiently flexible to survive. Even though there may be doubt as to its value once it is discovered that the convention was unable to prevent the breach in the first place. It is ultimately the electorate who will determine the government's worth if there are flagrant breaches of constitutional convention.[30] The courts remain reluctant to enforce conventions. In 1981 Lord Diplock in *R. v. Inland Revenue Commissioners, ex p. National Federation of Self-Employed and Small Businesses Ltd*[31] made clear that while Ministers were responsible to both Parliament and the Courts there was an important distinction. This distinction he explained in terms of law and policy:

"They [Ministers] are accountable to Parliament for what they do so far as regards efficiency and policy; and of that Parliament is the only judge; they are responsible to a court of justice for the lawfulness of what they do and of that the court is the only judge."

Lord Diplock's distinction recognises the differences between Parliament's role to oversee conventions and the courts' authority to determine what is lawful.

Some reflections may be offered on the value of conventions. **4–23** Constitutional lawyers face great difficulty when attempting to understand the different practices of government. Such practices do not easily conform to legal analysis and present problems of ordering, classifying and describing. Constitutional conventions provide a useful organising category, permitting the discussion of government behaviour and activities elevated to constitutional consideration rather than party politics. Loughlin warns that conventions may appear too neatly packaged and therefore may give a distorted[32] analysis:

"It leads too easily to a false ascription of meaning to events and, by trying to generalise from the exceptional cases and ignoring the

---

[30] N. Johnson, *In Search of the Constitution* (1977), pp. 31–33.
[31] [1982] A.C. 617.
[32] M. Loughlin, *Public Law and Political Theory* (Oxford, 1992), p. 53.

common case (in which resignation does not occur) has a distortive effect."

Taking Loughlin's *caveat* seriously, however, there is still value in studying and understanding conventions, although their limitations ought to be admitted. Conventions may appear descriptive, but in fact they are also normative and interpretative. Perhaps too great an expectation is placed on conventions to fill the gaps in the unwritten Constitution.

4-24 Johnson reflects that perhaps the place given to conventions within the United Kingdom's constitutional arrangements is misplaced and over-optimistic? This may arise from the changing nature of social life and the speed and variety of such change. Johnson notes[33] that:

> "there is no longer that degree of commitment to particular procedures, that respect for traditional values and habits, nor that breadth of agreement about how political authority should be exercised and for what purposes, which would justify the belief that convention alone is a sheet anchor on which we can rely for the protection of civil rights or for the survival of a particular form of government."

If in the past conventions appeared to offer predictability in the conduct of government activities it is doubtful if this remains so today. In a general way this reflects on the workings of an unwritten constitution. Johnson warns that the qualities of flexibility and adaptability in the Constitution may become simply a means for executive power to increase.

4-25 Perhaps the most positive opinion about conventions is that of T.R.S. Allan who observes that conventions might provide[34] "a primary source of legal principle". Allan also argues that such principles might inform how the rule of law might develop.[35]

3. The Rule of Law

4-26 Government in the United Kingdom is highly centralised and carried out within a unitary state. Governmental power is not confined by a written constitution or domestically entrenched Bill of Rights. Government is said to be both accountable and responsible. Responsible

---

[33] N. Johnson, *op. cit.*, note 30, p. 33. Jeffrey Jowell, "The Rule of Law Today" in Jowell and Oliver (eds.) *The Changing Constitution* (Oxford, 3rd ed., 1994), pp 58–62.

[34] T. R. S. Allan, *Law, Liberty and Justice* (Oxford University Press. 1993).

[35] Sir N. Browne Wilkinson, "The Independence of the Judiciary in the 1980's" (1988) *Public Law* 44. See: A. Lester, "English Judges as Law Makers" (1993) *Public Law* 269.

government is carried out according to constitutional conventions, international obligations such as the European Convention on Human Rights, obligations through membership of the European Community and the rule of law. Great significance has been given to the rule of law within the United Kingdom's Constitution.

Constitutional lawyers continue to be influenced by Dicey's explan- **4–27** ation of the rule of law contained in his *Introduction to the Law of the Constitution*. The term "rule of law" Dicey acknowledged was not originally his own but taken from the writings of William Hearn (1826–88).[36]

Hearn, in fact, acknowledged[37] that his understanding of the rule of law owed much to his analysis of the ideal of government, according to law, from the debates on English government in the seventeenth century. Hearn suggests that the rule of law is of ancient origin and may be found in the literature on the role of the State in society. One of the earliest writings on the ideal of the authority of the State acting according to pre-existing laws and not arbitrarily, may be found in Plato's[38] *Laws*.

Similar ethical considerations apply in various writings in the **4–28** twelfth and fourteenth centuries of how rulers or the State should apply the law and subordinate their authority to the law. In the thirteenth century in England, there was strong resistance to the idea that the King should be above the law. Considerable ambiguity surrounds the implications of Magna Carta (1215) when conceded by King John. Some of its chapters place the law of the land as paramount. By implication rather than expressly, the King's accept- ance of Magna Carta was also acceptance of the principle of subser- vience to the law.[39]

Sir John Fortescue (1394-1476), an English Judge and early English authority on the rule of law, wrote that the King could not override the law as judges must decide according to law, even when com- manded to do otherwise.[40]

As mentioned above, Hearn's inspiration for his ideas on the rule **4–29** of law lay in the constitutional conflicts of the seventeenth century. James I claimed royal authority over law despite much acknowledged advice to the contrary.[41] The claim against such royal authority lay in

---

[36] W. Hearn, *The Government of England, its Structure and Development* (1867).
[37] H. W. Arndt, "The Origin of Dicey's Concept of the Rule of Law" 1957 Austl.L.J. (31) pp. 117-123.
[38] Plato, *Laws*, p. 715d. Also see Cicero, *De Legibus* Bk.1.12.13. A discussion may be found in J. M. Kelly, *A Short History of Western Legal Theory* (Oxford, 1992), pp. 69–70 and 176–179.
[39] Bracton, *De legibus et consuetudinibus*.
[40] Fortescue, *De Natura legis naturae*, Bk.1.16.
[41] Coke in *Prohibitions Del Roy* (1607) 12 Co. Rep. 63.

its arbitrary nature and even though Monarchy was restored after the Civil Wars royal authority was not. John Locke (1632-1704) articulated the principles which Hearn was later to rely on, namely that government should be exercised according to the law "promulgated and known to the people" as opposed to extraordinary powers dispensed through proclamation. It is noteworthy that Locke's clear analysis of how the governed should be governed, is less clear over how government itself should be subject to law. While accepting the ultimate authority of law, Locke conceded that discretion was a necessary element in rules and that the prerogative may be a required power for the ruler. Since it was impossible to make full provision for all problems, arguably, much discretion may be considered necessary.

4-30   Dicey's own reasoning about the existence of the rule of law, in large part depended on the work of Blackstone, Coke and John Austin. In common with his views on conventions, it was Austin's analysis that had the greatest influence on Dicey, and in particular Austin's views on the ultimate omnipotence of Parliament. Dicey recognised the difficulty of resolving the operation of constitutional conventions and the compatibility of parliamentary sovereignty with the rule of law.

4-31   Parliamentary sovereignty[42] had both a legal and a political dimension. Parliament was susceptible to change through the extension of the franchise and what Dicey perceived as "the working class vote." Dicey, somewhat grudgingly, accepted what he termed "the progress to democracy," but he admitted the potential for conflict between Parliament's sovereignty and reforming legislation which might radically alter the Union or challenge the fundamental characteristics of the Constitution. Dicey believed in the rule of law and the use of conventions as essential mechanisms against abuse, especially of discretionary power. Conventions recognised public "morality" which self-limited the power of Parliament.

4-32   In the absence of any formal doctrine of the separation of powers or a written constitution limiting the powers of the Executive within the State, the rule of law provided a convenient means to express concern over the uncontrolled powers of a newly enfranchised Parliament. Dicey feared the growth in incremental powers to the State. In particular, legislation which might interfere with individual liberty, particularly property rights.

The rule of law is susceptible to a number of different meanings often based on value judgements. In its broadest sense it may be viewed as a general political doctrine. The rule of law is both

---

[42] T.R.S. Allan, "Legislative Supremacy and the Rule of Law: Democracy and Constitutionalism" (1985) 44 Camb.L.J. 111.

descriptive and prescriptive, characteristics it shares with conventions[43] of the Constitution. Dicey found three meanings for the rule of law to be considered as part of the constitutional order of the United Kingdom.

First, Dicey[44] insisted on the predominance of "ordinary law." **4–33** Government power, especially when it affects the citizen, must be accompanied by observance of the correct legal rules and have the authority of law. Secondly, discretionary power however broadly based must not be abused or used in an unrestricted way to circumvent the legislative authority of Parliament. The Executive should be amenable to parliamentary control. Thirdly, Dicey believed that the enforcement of the principles of the rule of law was best achieved through the ordinary courts and not as part of a written constitution or through the setting up of a special system of courts. Dicey assumed that civil liberties were best protected through the system of remedies which had developed historically through the courts.[45] Parliamentary sovereignty, which could at a whim destroy the delicate nature of the rule of law, was instead in Dicey's view, intended to compliment and reinforce the rule of law. Concerns about the potential for the abuse of sovereignty, were offset by Dicey's focus on the elected accountability of Parliament. Craig explains how Dicey attempted to reconcile the apparent contradiction that sovereignty might threaten the rule of law[46]:

"The two main elements of Dicey's rule of law possesses both a descriptive and a normative content. In descriptive terms it was assumed that the regular law predominated, that exercise of broad discretionary power was absent, and that all people were subject to the ordinary law of the realm. Public power resided with Parliament. In normative terms it was assumed that this was indeed a better system than that which existed in France, where special rules and a distinctive regime existed for public law matters."

Dicey's belief in the rule of law assumed fundamental importance **4–34** in his understanding of the Constitution. A jaundiced view might be, that Dicey hoped that the rule of law might be a valuable tool in his attempt to argue against major political changes, to which he was

---

[43] S.E. Finer, "The Individual Responsibility of Ministers" (1956) 34 *Public Administration* 377.

[44] J. F. McEldowney, "Dicey in Historical Perspective-A Review Essay" in McAuslan and McEldowney, *Law, Legitimacy and the Constitution* (Sweet and Maxwell, 1985), pp. 55–60. Also see Dicey, *Law of the Constitution* (1885), pp. 187–196.

[45] *ibid.*

[46] P. Craig, *Public Law and Democracy in the U.K. and U.S.A.* (Oxford, 1990), p. 21. Also see Harlow and Rawlings, *Law and Administration* (1984), pp. 1–6 and pp. 15–19.

personally opposed. Home Rule for Ireland, votes for women and social legislation might be postponed if they offended the rule of law.

How might Dicey's vision of the rule of law apply today? A major misunderstanding in Dicey's belief in the rule of law was the scope of ministerial power and its delegation to a wide variety of other agents. Even in Dicey's time there was a miscellaneous number of administrative institutions outside the ordinary courts; their existence was not fully appreciated by Dicey which greatly weakened the cogency of his arguments about the rule of law and the role of the courts. The nature of the errors in Dicey's misconceptions are explained more fully in Chapter 7. However, this should not detract from the eloquence of Dicey's views on the rule of law and the importance of Dicey's influence on the development of administrative law.

4–35   As remarkable as his description of the rule of law is, Dicey's analytical method, employed in the formulation of legal principles, also deserves mention. Dicey's method involved abstracting basic principles from legal materials. His style was to begin his text with generalised principles, discussed in more detail later in the work. At times the clarity of his original principles became obscured by the later discussion and contradictions may obscure the principle.

4–36   Dicey's critics[47] have identified such weaknesses and some of Dicey's views have been revised and re-examined. The challenge mounted by his critics is to expose Dicey's analytical method and the political values upon which his theory rests. Both parliamentary sovereignty and the rule of law have been subjected to such criticism. Loughlin suggests that Dicey was mistaken in his perception of administrative power[48]:

> "In general public law should ensure that the legal framework within which government operated provided an effective and equitable structure for the implementation of the public good, as expressed in the positive functions of the State. From this perspective delegated legislation and administrative adjudication was not a symptom of despotic power but of the changing role of the state."

It may be concluded that Dicey's perception of the[49] role of central government in 1885 was influenced by the centralising tendencies of government power[50] and his belief that such powers could be

---

[47] W. A. Robson, *Justice and Administrative Law* (London, 1928); Jennings, *Law and the Constitution*, p. 54; Laski, *Studies in the Problem of Sovereignty* (London, 1929); Robson, "Justice and Administrative Law Reconsidered" 32 (1979) C.L.P. 107.
[48] Loughlin, *op. cit.* p. 168.
[49] J. Jowell, "The Rule of Law Today" in Jowell and Oliver, *The Changing Constitution* (1989), pp. 3–23.
[50] *ibid.*

adequately controlled. This depended on his view of the courts enforcing the rule of law as a means of keeping in check the boundaries of parliamentary power.[51] This raises the question of the role of the courts in applying and upholding the rule of law.

The courts adopted different strategies depending on their percep- **4–37** tion of procedural rules, the nature and complexity of the law and remedies and the nature of the issues they were invited to consider, at the time. The emergence in the late seventeenth century of judicial review was largely free from doctrinal development, and reflected the changing nature of parliamentary power. Craig explains[52]:

> "On the one hand, the judiciary began to justify the exercise of jurisdictional control more specifically in terms of ensuring that the authority in question did not usurp or extend the area over which the legislature had granted it jurisdiction. The objective was to ensure that the agency did not assume authority to regulate behaviour or to legislate in areas outside those delegated to it by Parliament. On the other hand, the courts become more aware, in form at least, of the legitimate limits to the exercise of their judicial power."

Craig's thesis is that[53] the courts often adopted conflicting dir- **4–38** ections and interpretations over the nature of legislative powers, the delegation of such powers to inferior bodies and the precise *discretionary* nature of their own judicial powers. A number of cases may be cited in support of this view. A common theme is the question of whether the delegated body has competence to determine its own decisions. Accordingly the power of appeal to a court of law is distinguished from a review. The former examines the correctness of the decision while the latter the legality. This leaves the courts with a less certain role in evaluating the activities of inferior bodies. This gives rise to a perception that the courts powers of review are limited to technical or procedural requirements as distinct from substantive review. Nevertheless there are a number of legal cases where the

---

[51] The extension of the franchise in 1867 broadened the appeal of Parliament. The Commons had undertaken a vast legislative programme of reform extending statutory provision across a range of activities from railways to factories, public health to education, licensing to Company Act companies. Standing behind such reforms was a new intellectual movement for law reform supported by the major Statistical Societies and evidenced by statistical study. Dicey's perception was that public power, through ministerial responsibility and civil service anomynity required even greater protection through the rule of law. See Chap. 9 on administrative powers and Chap. 7 for a discussion of Dicey. See V. Bogdanor, *The People and the Party System: The Referendum and Electoral Reform in British Politics* (Cambridge, 1981).

[52] Craig, *op. cit.* p. 22.

[53] *ibid.*

courts have sought to curtail the unfettered exercise of State power. In *Entick v. Carrington*,[54] Lord Camden in the Court of Common Pleas examined the legal power of the Secretary of State to arrest John Entick, an alleged author of seditious writings, to seize his papers and books and use these as evidence. Entick successfully sued the officers and obtained damages when Lord Camden held that the warrant was illegal and void. The legal reasoning in the case depended on the absence of any legal authority supporting the legal claim that the warrants were lawful. The result was to leave the courts with a power of review but subject to the legislative authority of Parliament. Statutes which expressly confer the rights of arrest or seizure may leave the courts with a minimal role in finding any legal grounds to support the rights of the citizen beyond the narrow scope of the wording of the Act of Parliament.

4–39   There may be a number of limitations on the role of the courts. A number may be mentioned here. The "intention of Parliament" is open to interpretation by the Courts. The courts may be limited in the scope of their interpretation. Acts of Parliament cannot be held to be unconstitutional, severely limiting the extent of judicial intervention. Constraints on judicial activism in reviewing informal bodies often depend on the type of body, and their powers under review.

4–40   Implicit in our current unwritten constitutional arrangements is that there is no hierarchy of rights such that any one of them is more entrenched by the law than any other. This point is explained by Mr Justice Laws in *R. v. Lord Chancellor, ex p. Witham*[55]:

> "The common law does not generally speak in the language of constitutional rights, for the good reason that in the absence of any sovereign text, a written constitution which is logically and legally prior to the power of legislature, executive and judiciary alike there is on the face of it no hierarchy of rights such that anyone of them is more entrenched by the law than any other. And if the concept of a constitutional right is to have any meaning, it must surely sound in the protection which the law affords to it. Where a written constitution guarantees a right there is no conceptual difficulty. The state authorities must give way to it save to the extent that the constitution allows them to deny it."

It may be fair to conclude that in the unwritten constitution where the common law accords legislative supremacy to Parliament the existence of rights for the citizen may be difficult to imagine.[56]

[54] (1765) 19 State T.R. 1030.

[55] See *R. v. Lord Chancellor, ex p. Witham* [1997] 2 All E.R. 779 at 783f–j.

[56] See *Report of an Interdepartmental Working Group Concerning Legislation on Human Rights, with Particular Reference to the European Convention* (1976–77) HL 81. Also see: K.A.P. LeSeur, "The Judges and the Intention of Parliament; is Judicial Review Undemocratic?" (1991) 44 *Parliamentary Affairs* 283. Also see: F. Mount, *The British Constitution Now* (London, Heinemann, 1992), P. Norton, *The Constitution in Flux* (Oxford, 1982).

Local government, is not only an elected element of government **4–41** but possesses wide statutory authority to carry out activities including the promotion of private Bill legislation, the enforcement of criminal sanctions and the expenditure of public money. The courts have held that a local authority[57] acts unreasonably "if no reasonable public body" could have made a decision. The Wednesbury Corporation was empowered to grant licences for Sunday entertainment subject to conditions which it thought fit. The condition that no children under 15 be admitted to a cinema was challenged as unreasonable and *ultra vires;* Lord Greene accepted that the courts could not substitute its policy for that of the local authority – an inherent limit on the jurisdiction of the courts. However the courts may intervene as to the legality of the decision on the basis of applying a test of reasonableness. Within the scope of unreasonableness the courts have a wide discretion as to the legality of the powers under review. In *Associated Picture Houses Ltd v. Wednesbury Corporation*[58] Lord Greene acknowledged both the jurisdiction of review of the courts *and* the jurisdiction of the decision-maker to make decisions.

Dicey's belief in the rule of law paradoxically inhibited the courts **4–42** for many years from developing a coherent system of administrative law. His objection to the French *droit administratif* was more generally[59] interpreted as an objection to administrative law, a view which Dicey later retracted.

Dicey also failed in his analysis of the rule of law to take account of the "body of special rights, prerogatives and immunities." Dicey considered that these no longer existed when in fact government powers include not only the statutory variety discussed above, but prerogative powers and common law rights. We have seen that the courts have developed in recent years, powers of review over the prerogative,[60] but Dicey failed to appreciate the extent of government or State powers exercised through prerogative powers and therefore largely outside the controls implied in the rule of law.[61]

Dicey's understanding of the rule of law has had an important **4–43** effect on the perceptions of many generations of lawyers. In one sense the rule of law may be synonymous with equality before the law and the protection of civil and religious liberty. It also acts as a restraint on power and its abuse. Dicey's analysis was clearly rooted in procedural and technical observance of the law, as a consequence

---

[57] *Associated Provincial Picture Houses Ltd v. Wednesbury Corporation* [1948] 1 K.B. 223.
[58] *ibid.*
[59] See Jennings, "In Praise of Dicey 1885-1935" (1935) 13 *Public Administration* 123; Dicey, "The Development of Administrative Law in England" (1915) 31 L.Q.R. 148.
[60] See Chap. 2.
[61] Loughlin, *op. cit.,* p. 168; Lloyd, *The Idea of Law* (1970), p. 164.

indirectly Dicey helped to promote the idea that law, politics and the outcome of legal rules should be separated from the legal rules themselves. As Sugarman has observed[62]:

"Dicey's rule of law endeavoured to create a new procedural natural law or Bill of Rights which could be used to ensure that legal change was slow paced and conservative."

---

[62] D. Sugarman, "The Legal Boundaries of Liberty: Dicey, Liberalism and Legal Science" (1983) M.L.R. 102, at p. 110.

Chapter 5

An Introduction to Administrative Law

In the preceding chapters the outline, structures and principles of the **5–01** United Kingdom's Constitution have been examined, including the role of central government and the civil service. This chapter is intended to explain the development of administrative law: its nature, purpose and significance within the context of the United Kingdom's constitutional arrangements.

This chapter introduces students to the basic framework of administrative law in outline. In Part III of the book, chapters will be found covering local government, judicial review, remedies and citizens' grievances in more detail. It is hoped that the reader will find the explanation contained in this chapter useful background reading before the more advanced discussion undertaken in Part III.

1. Introduction

Administrative law may be defined as the law relating to the control **5–02** of government power and including the detailed rules which govern the exercise of administrative decision-taking. A wide variety of institutions and bodies are subject to administrative law: the Executive and central government; local authorities; tribunals; inquiries; fringe bodies or non-departmental bodies such as quangos and even inferior courts.

A. V. Dicey was reluctant in his *Law of the Constitution* in 1885, to accept the idea of specialised and specific legal rules governing administrative decision-making. Nevertheless English law has developed administrative law especially through the growth in case law over the last 30 years. Lord Diplock in *R. v. Inland Revenue Commissioners, ex p. National Federation of Self-Employed and Small Businesses Ltd*[1] regarded the development of English administrative

---

[1] [1982] A.C. 617.

law "as having been the greatest achievement of the English Courts in my judicial lifetime."

5–03 In this chapter we examine the historical development of administrative law, the allocation of functions, the role of the courts and the function of tribunals and inquiries. There are noticeable underlying trends in the development of administrative law. First, as noted by Daintith,[2] "text-book writers have tended to see governmental power more as a threat to the individual than as the means of implementing public policy." The cause of this tendency is an emphasis on parliamentary sovereignty and the inspiration for the study of many of the rules of administrative law has been through the study of judicial review. This only represents one "mode" of government activity and usually one that is conflict ridden and problematic. Thus, the temptation is for lawyers not to see administrative law as a means to achieve good administrative decision making, but as power which requires control either through legislation or the courts.

5–04 Secondly, an over-emphasis on case law avoids consideration of the different techniques of decision-taking. Daintith[3] identifies the Government's powers of bargaining and economic regulation, as examples of how implementation of governmental policy may be achieved. This is a recurring theme which is returned to in Part III of the textbook. An understanding of administration as well as administrative law is necessary in the context of how government activities are carried out.

2. Historical Perspectives and Administrative Law

5–05 Modern government has a vast array of State powers which may[4] affect the lives of the ordinary citizen in both domestic and foreign affairs. If the nineteenth century is compared to the present day, the size, shape and functions of government have greatly changed.[5] Public expenditure[6] in the 1870s represented less than 10 per cent of the gross national product.[7] Today it is nearly 50 per cent of the gross

[2] Daintith, "The Executive Power Today: Bargaining and Economic Control," in Jowell and Oliver, *The Changing Constitution* (O.U.P., 1989), p. 194.

[3] *ibid.*

[4] D. L. Keir, *The Constitutional History of Modern Britain* (1938) provides a useful historical overview. Also see Cornish, de N. Clark, *Law and Society in England 1250–1950* (1989).

[5] H. Parris, *Constitutional Bureaucracy* (1969), also D. Roberts, *Victorian Origins of the British Welfare State* (1960).

[6] W. Robson, *Justice and Administrative Law*; Roy Church (ed.), *The Dynamics of Victorian Business* (1980).

[7] O. MacDonagh, *Early Victorian Government* (1977).

domestic product. The size and activities of the civil service, even with restraints and cutbacks, is larger today than in 1900. In 1900 there were 50,000 civil servants, by 1980 this had risen to 548,600. Outside central government today there are about 600,000 local government officials and 100,000 administering the Health Service. Similarly a rapid increase in the legal activities of the State such as in the growth of legislation may also be recognised when compared to the period before and after 1900.[8]

"Thus in 1900 Acts of Parliament covered 198 pages of the Statute Book, in 1935, 1515 pages, in 1975, 2,800 pages. As for regulations these were comparatively few before the first world war; in 1947 statutory instruments covered 2,678 pages; in 1975, 8,442."

Commensurate with the changes in government activities there **5–06** have been changes in the habits, customs and expectations of citizens.[9] Voting at elections before the Great Reform Act of 1832 was a mere 652,000 out of a population of 13.9 million.[10] Today under universal franchise there is an electorate of over 43 million with a turnout at general elections fluctuating between 72 per cent and 84 per cent of the electorate. Party politics from the latter part of the nineteenth century dominate the exercise of political and therefore governmental powers.

What legacy remains from the formative period of administrative **5–07** law in the nineteenth century?

This question deserves close attention, as developments in the nineteenth century provide much of the explanation of how administrative law developed in England. Craig explains that[11]:

"the period between 1830 and 1850 witnessed a considerable expansion in the functions performed by central government. Reform in four main areas provides the basis for this expansion: factory legislation, the Poor Law, railways and public health."

These reforms were as a result of the growing industrialisation in **5–08** Britain. Administrative lawyers consider that administrative law developed on a pragmatic and often sporadic basis. There are a number of points to note. First, administrative law depended very largely on statutory intervention. In addition, regulation of many

---

[8] Justice/All Souls Review 1981, paras. 18–22 and cited in Harlow and Rawlings, *Law and Administration*, pp. 6–7.
[9] M. W. Thomas, "The Origins of Administrative Centralization" [1950] C.L.P. 214.
[10] Craig, *Administrative Law* (2nd ed., 1989), p. 45.
[11] *ibid.* p. 35; also see Lubenow, *The Politics of Government Growth* (1971).

activities was carried on in an informal way sometimes using contract or through procedures avoiding the direct use of legal powers. Major administrative developments were carried out through legislative initiatives or in certain cases, legislative acceptance of rules or existing arrangements. Secondly, there was no single or coherent model which applied uniformly. Different forms of adjudication, fact-finding, decision-taking and policy making were used and made to fit particular circumstances. Debate focused on the nature of the growth in the legislative and judicial powers of the Executive. The categorisation of legal powers was a major preoccupation from the mid-nineteenth century until the 1930s and the setting up of the Donoughmore Committee on Ministers Powers.[12]

5–09   Thirdly, the courts' role in developing different techniques to overview administrative decision-taking was often marginal and limited by technicalities. One example of a technicality, is the difficulty of suing the Crown in tort,[13] which remained problematic until the Crown Proceedings Act 1947. The Crown was allowed certain excepted privileges and this applied to central government ministries, thus precluding the courts' intervention. Crown servants could be sued individually for any wrong, but this did not offer an effective basis for establishing administrative law. Fourthly, most State intervention through legislation directly interfered with private property rights and market forces. This is a legacy which remains today when courts are faced with the task of reconciling newly created public statutory rights of State interests with traditional private rights in contract and property law. In the nineteenth century interpretation of statutory arrangements appeared unfamiliar and restrictive to judges instructed in the art of advocacy and in the technicalities of property law. An additional difficulty, was the recognition of the different forms of State intervention with the growth in local government as a means of delivery of the many services needed for a locality.

5–10   Finally, the nature of legal rights changed remarkably during this period. Dicey described the nature of the change as a gradual shift from "individualism" to "collectivism." Developments in the growth of administration during the nineteenth century were greatly influenced by utilitarian ideology.[14]

---

[12] Cmd. 4060 (1932).
[13] *R. v. Commissioners of Income Tax* (1888) 21 Q.B.D. 313; G. E. Robinson, *Public Authorities and Legal Liability* (1925). See G. S. Robertson, *Civil Proceedings by and against the Crown* (1908).
[14] A. V. Dicey, *Law and Pubic Opinion* (1905).

(a) State Intervention and Legislation

MacDonagh[15] identifies the pattern for the growth in government **5–11** activities in the nineteenth century. He believes it was based on a practical response borne out of identifying problems and suggesting solutions. Beginning with social problems and their amelioration, various legal responses were applied. General legal prohibition or regulation was attempted, followed by the creation of an administrative body charged with improving the efficiency of decision-taking. Gradually the newly formed administrative body adopted strategies to inform, persuade or encourage compliance with its directions. If necessary central government powers were used, and ultimately Ministerial decision-taking might be adopted. Compliance techniques ranged from prosecutions to licensing strategies which might be used to achieve policy implementation and direct compliance. This called for further legislation in order to meet new problems or gaps in the law identified by the new administrative bodies. There was a cycle of formation, growth and demise of administrative bodies.

MacDonagh's analysis is not universally accepted. The main tenets **5–12** of his analysis suggest that administrative developments depend on factual necessity rather than any ideological influences. Critics of MacDonagh argue that he failed to take sufficient account of such influences as Bentham's utilitarian principles. His main critic in this regard is Paris[16] who, as Craig points out, argues that:

"MacDonagh overstresses the anti-collective strain within Benthamism: the application of the principle of utility could lead to laissez-faire or state intervention depending upon the subject matter. For Parris,[17] therefore nineteenth century government development must be seen as a function both of organic change and contemporary political and ideological thought, one of the main currents of which was Benthamism."

The debate between MacDonagh[18] and Parris[19] is largely unre- **5–13** solved. Their contribution to our understanding of administration in the nineteenth century is that pragmatic developments in administrative law may be due to the nature of changing administrative bodies. A number of influences may be involved in that development such as practical necessity, ideological belief and enthusiasm for change.

---

[15] O. MacDonagh, *A Pattern of Government Growth: The Passenger Acts and their Enforcement* 1800–1860 (1961).
[16] H. Parris, *Government and the Railways in Nineteenth Century Britain* (1965).
[17] Craig, *Administrative Law* (2nd ed., 1989), p. 45.
[18] H. Parris, "The Nineteenth Century Revolution in Government: A Reappraisal" (1960) 3 Hist. J. 17.
[19] *ibid.*

5–14   A significant influence on government policy and law reform in mid-Victorian Britain, was the existence of the statistical movement. The collection of official statistics prepared by government departments complemented the activities of various private statistical societies.[20] The first association for the study of statistics, was the statistical section of the British Association formed in Cambridge in 1833. Various statistical societies were formed in other parts of the United Kingdom, with lawyers a dominant influence in the membership. The first, in Manchester in September 1833 was later followed by societies in London, Ulster and Dublin. Building on Brougham's famous law reform speech in 1828, which suggested that Britain's social problems could be identified and remedies proposed, the first meeting of the Association for the Promotion of Social Sciences was held in 1857. The collection of civil and criminal judicial statistics assisted in establishing the operation of laws and practices which had hitherto remained obscure. Similarly finding "facts" on births, deaths and marriages led to greater knowledge about population growth, its distribution and public health.[21]

5–15   Statistical study[22] achieved a factual basis for law reforms to be proposed. "Objective facts" were used to ascertain needs, a major focus of attention was the social, economic and political problems arising from urbanisation. Victorian idealism often lacked coherence. The dogma of benevolence and good works was unsystematic and often counter-productive. Empirical research, achieved through statistical inquiry, informed the work of countless inquiries and Royal Commissions held in the nineteenth century. The activities of organisations such as the statistical societies, were variously described as "volunteer legislators" or outdoor Parliament. Prominent intellectuals, politicians and civil servants were members of the main statistical societies.

The outcome of statistical study may be[23] seen in a large number of legislative initiatives which became the political agenda for the growth in Victorian liberalism. In the administrative law field, the variety and diversity of the different forms such legislative initiative took, may be shortly explained through a number of examples illustrating the use of commissions, boards, inspectors and Ministers.

5–15A   Craig identifies[24] a number of examples illustrating the distinctive nature and the variety of regulatory style adopted. The Poor Law,

---

[20] J. F. McEldowney, "Administration and Law in England in the 18th and 19th Centuries" 8 JEV (1996), pp. 19–36.

[21] *ibid.*

[22] *ibid.*

[23] McEldowney and O'Higgins "The Common Law Tradition and Irish Legal History" in McEldowney & O'Higgins, *The Common Law Tradition* (1991), pp. 13–25.

[24] Craig, *op. cit.* 56.

revised after the Poor Law Report 1834 and influenced by Edwin Chadwick[25] and Nassau Senior, shifted[26] the role Poor Law relief was expected to perform. High costs and the lack of tangible benefits from the input of resources had left the old system of Poor Law relief discredited. Originally, under the jurisdiction of the Justice of the Peace who combined judicial office with administrative functions, the Poor Law Amendment Act 1834 introduced a three-man Commission, independent from Parliament. This model of administration had its earliest origins in the eighteenth century in the creation of Boards, designed to prevent individual excess or corruption and provide checks and balances through its reports and published activities.

Cornish[27] explains how the Boards system was transformed after 1832, when it developed some of its own independence: " . . . it was conceived as a way of conferring semi-autonomous authority for a particular function; this achieved a certain distinction from the immediately political."

In the creation of the Poor Law Commissioners after 1832, a wide **5–16** variety of legal powers accompanied their role. Prosecutions, legal action through *mandamus* and an appointment power of local officers in workhouses were all combined in their functions. It is noticeable that the Poor Law Commissioners neatly linked central government with local government activities. Also noteworthy is that the granting of such powers was couched in general terms with the agreement of a Minister and Parliament in general rule-making. The Commissioners had the ability to make their own rules and regulations as part of their powers.

Experimentation was invariably involved in the choice of administrative body adopted for any particular activity. Cornish notes[28]:

"The Railway Department in the Board of Trade (1840) was to become a 'Board' (still departmental – 1844) and a Commission (independent – 1846) before being re-absorbed *de facto* (1849) and then *de jure* (1851) into the Board of Trade. Between the 1850's and 1906 those boards which constitutionally remained distinct from ministries were all important cases placed under some form of ministerial supervision."

Another model of administrative body was the inspectorates. **5–17** Examples which came under the jurisdiction of the Home Office were factories, prisons, mining and burial inspectors. Inspectorates were

---

[25] S. E. Finer, *Life and Times of Sir Edwin Chadwick* (1952).
[26] Generally, see, G. Sutherland, *Studies in Nineteeth Century Government Growth* (1972).
[27] Cornish, pp. 55–58.
[28] *ibid.* p. 56.

fact finders, investigators and adjudicators. They possessed limited powers to impose fines and prosecutions, but their role of serving notices and enforcing standards relied on voluntary compliance as much as coercive sanctions. Very often their activities involved some form of compromise because of hostility to the use of their powers and a reluctance to comply with the imposition of an external standard. The Factory Inspectors, in particular, adjusted their powers to meet opposition or objections. Inspectors had the status of magistrates, but the Home Office in 1844 directed inspectors not to use their enforcement jurisdiction by introducing a new Factories Act 1844[29] which constrained their powers.[30]

5–18   Public Health was another area of administrative growth and an example of administrative decision-making which directly interfered with property rights. It is also illustrative of the use of private law techniques, such as actions in nuisance, combined with statutory powers. In administrative decision-making findings from various reports and commissions of inquiry had confirmed the existence of disease and poverty among the poor. Health hazards were directly linked to urbanisation and industrialisation. Sanitary improvements were required and introduced on a piecemeal basis; first in 1848, then in 1872 and 1875 various Public Health Acts were passed giving legislative powers to various sanitary authorities to set standards and achieve improvements in living conditions.

5–19   Public health legislation[31] directly interfered with property rights and substantially overlapped with the use of nuisance law in cases where an injury was caused by a neighbour's occupation of land. The role of the courts in applying and developing such remedies was largely a pragmatic one, taking each case on its own particular facts.

As industrialisation spread new processes and industry throughout the country, regulation of these activities was left to individual initiative in the first instance. By 1869 the judges had at last concluded that nuisance from noise, dirt and pollution from railways permitted an occupier of premises affected by the nuisance to seek legal redress.

5–20   Finally, another source of administrative growth was in the development of local government. Local corporations and parishes developed a myriad of legal powers to deliver many of the new responsibilities that gradually became entrusted to local authority control. A major source of income came through the raising of local taxes and rates. Slowly, incremental changes occurred to the various newly established administrative bodies, but eventually they were to

[29] 7 & 8 Vic. c. 15., Cornish, *op. cit.* pp. 516–541.
[30] *ibid.*
[31] W. C. Lubenow, *The Politics of Government Growth* (1971).

come under local authority control. The Poor Law Commissioners shifted from a Board to a Tribunal of Appeal in 1847. In 1868 it could appoint district auditors, who in 1879 became civil servants on the creation of the Local Government Board.

Local authorities gained the administrative function[32] of delivering **5–21** what was termed "public goods." First the Municipal Corporations Act 1835 provided elected local authorities. From 1843 to 1929 local authorities gained responsibility for such "public goods" including water; gas; transport; education; housing and health services.

A distinctive feature of these developments, was the acceptance of local political accountability through local elections and Parliament's willingness to encourage local legislation, to enable local authorities to carry out their tasks. Local authorities developed considerable legal powers[33] through private Bill legislation.

(b) Courts, Lawyers and Legal Techniques

The growth in administrative bodies and their wide diversity, broad- **5–22** ened the scope of legal powers and raised questions about accountability and control. Arthurs[34] notes how a number of constraints were invoked to prevent abuses. Statutes or regulations often required ministerial approval for their implementation. Ministerial responsibility to Parliament constrained administrators from acting without recourse to political authority and observance of legal rules. Government Law Officers restrained and inhibited any internal decision-making since account had to be taken of their legal opinions.

Despite such constraints it is recognised that wide discretionary powers were enjoyed by many officials. Such powers[35] were often resented and when in conflict with the landed interest or the new wealth industrialists, led to conflicts. Self-interest and protection led many administrative bodies to adopt codes of conduct and practice to ease the application of their rules.

The period of Victorian growth[36] in administrative bodies led to **5–23** distrust over the considerable powers enjoyed by administrators. Victorian lawyers seemed deeply suspicious of the new powers possessed by the State. The broad discretionary powers favoured in the new legislation were seen as delegating wide powers to administrators, without obvious checks and balances. Some of these powers

---

[32] S. & B. Webb, *History of the Poor Law* (1929).
[33] S. & B. Webb, *English Local Government: I The Parish and the County* (1906).
[34] H.W. Arthurs, *"Without the Law": Administrative Justice and Legal Pluralism in 19th Century England* (1985).
[35] A retrospective examination is provided by Robson, "The Report of the Committee on Administrative Powers" (1932) 3 *Political Quarterly* 346.
[36] P. S. Atiyah, *The Rise and Fall of Freedom of Contract* (1979).

were necessary, some were the product of legislative draftsmen unaccustomed to the new found administrative bodies and some drafted in the spirit of enthusiasm for the newly found reforms.[37] Perhaps the most important reason for the way legal powers were drafted, was the narrow and limited role performed by lawyers. Lawyers drafted legislation without much experience of how legal powers were exercised. The most eminent lawyers were members of the statistical societies which did most to promote reform and law codification or amendments. Lawyers acted as legal advisers to the government of the day. In 1860, Henry Thring[38] was appointed Counsel to the Home Office and nine years later became head of the new office of Parliamentary Counsel to the Treasury. Eventually this office became responsible for drafting all Government Bills. Lawyers appeared in court, gave legal advice and as judges in the higher courts, adjudicated disputes. A noticeable gap in their lawyerly activities was that they were rarely called upon to *implement* legislation. Their experience of administration was necessarily limited.

5–24   A further consideration was the question of how best to supervise such administrative bodies. Many lawyers believed that this task was best performed by the ordinary courts. The preference for the use of the ordinary courts as opposed to the use of special administrative courts was reinforced by Dicey's scepticism of the benefits of *droit administratif*, the French system of specialised administrative courts. Dicey feared that the formation of administrative courts might encourage the encroachment on the private rights of citizens by governmental powers in the interests of the State, a hangover from the period of the Crown's extensive use of arbitrary powers. Dicey believed that the ordinary courts afforded the best protection against any incremental growth in the powers of government intervention.

5–25   Dicey's analysis has since been subject to criticism but his powerful influence has endured. de Smith described how Dicey's assumptions about the role of the courts may have misled English administrative lawyers into complacency after the nineteenth century[39]:

"Representative and responsible Government was securely founded: political and administrative morality was unusually high; the administration of justice by the ordinary courts was even-handed and uncorrupt; the common law, itself pre-eminently

---

[37] McEldowney, *op. cit.* note 23. See John McEldowney, "Administration and Law in England in the 18th and 19th Centuries" Vol. 8. *Yearbook of Administrative History* (1996) pp. 19–36.

[38] Also see: J. E. Pemberton, *British Official Publications* (1971); Sir C. Ilbert, *Legislative Methods and Forms* (1901); G. Drewry, "Lawyers in the UK Civil Service" (1981) 59 *Public Administration* 15–46.

[39] de Smith, *Judicial Review of Administrative Action* (4th ed., 1980), p. 7.

pragmatic was tenacious but adaptable. Such an environment bred the assumption that England had little to learn from other countries in matters of public law. Moreover the absence of judicial review of the constitutionality of legislation conduced to a lack of informed interests among practising lawyers in the judicial problems of government. And the role assigned to constitutional and administrative law in legal education was conspicuously modest."

Throughout the period of growth in administrative bodies, it is noteworthy that the courts retained exclusive jurisdiction over the criminal law. Government had carefully circumvented any attack on the courts' powers in this area.

The fact that the courts had an unbroken historical past which 5–26 could be traced back to the thirteenth century, further encouraged the government to refrain from interfering with the role of the courts. To the extent that central government perceived the role of the courts, the question of judicial intervention depended on the nature of the body exercising powers. Limited immunity to the Crown preserved Crown activities from judicial supervision. Ministerial accountability to Parliament allowed discretion to be exercised and largely escape judicial scrutiny. Moreover the growth in legislative powers enjoyed by Parliament as law-makers left the courts less facilities to exercise law-making powers of their own. The massive effort towards the enforcement of the new legislation was in the hands of an administrative bureaucracy and occasionally, local magistrates. The superior courts' role in enforcement declined in proportion to the spread of administrative decision-taking. Belief in the rule of law and the jurisdiction of the ordinary courts implied that Ministers, officials and citizens were amenable to the same law. Moving to a new form of administrative law supervision was seen as inconsistent with the supremacy of the law even as late as 1932. The Committee on Ministers' Powers found the proposal for such an administrative court inconsistent with the supervisory jurisdiction of the High Court and a threat to the rule of law. Such reservations over the development of administrative law have remained influential among lawyers in the United Kingdom until more recent times.

In addition to the role of the courts other procedures are note- 5–27 worthy. The various techniques of decision making, adjudication, discretion, fact-finding and inquiries were supplemented by the development of statutory inquiries. Techniques of inquiry and investigation were commonplace in the work of the Royal Commission and even in some of the administrative tasks entrusted to Justices of the Peace, such as wage bargaining in the eighteenth and early nineteenth centuries.

5–28   Statutory inquiries may be found in[40] the 1801 Enclosure Act with ad hoc Commissions of Inquiry appointed. Some explanation may be advanced as to why such procedures were adopted. The use of private Bills or public Acts of Parliament did not always provide the necessary coverage of all the issues to be decided. Wade[41] attributes this fact as a reason for adopting inquiries outside Parliament. The procedures of parliamentary committees, already existing inside Parliament and familiar in the passage of legislation, were conveniently adopted and employed.

5–29   Special law-making procedures were available through provisional orders. The provisional order procedure under an Act of Parliament granted powers to some statutory authorities to make a provisional order once an inquiry had been held and objections considered.

Special procedures were introduced applicable to enclosures to overcome the need for provisional orders. In 1845, the General Enclosure Act[42] required publication of the enclosure scheme and a public meeting "to their objections." Similar procedures were permitted under the Local Government Acts 1858–1933 and various Public Health Acts 1848–1931. Eventually the need to make a provisional order was abandoned, allowing the order to take effect in the absence of any objections or opposition, as in the Statutory Orders (Special Procedure) Act 1945.

Another variation to provisional orders may be found in the Local Government Act 1894 whereby county councils could acquire land under a public inquiry procedure. The Council could make an order followed by a local inquiry if opposition to the order was made in a memorial to the Council.

5–30   The development of tribunals as a means of adjudication is also noteworthy. Railway companies were compelled in 1854 to afford "reasonable facilities and preferences" to particular traders, in an effort to prevent railways achieving a virtual monopoly. Complaints could be made to the Court of Common Pleas but this was unsatisfactory and in 1893 a tribunal of commissioners was appointed. Fifteen years later it was reformulated into a Railing and Canal Commission. Appointment was through the Home Secretary on the recommendation of the President of the Board of Trade. The Chancellor could nominate a High Court Judge. The Commission adjudicated, found facts and achieved decisions on a judicial basis, having many of the formalities of a Court of Law.

Similar techniques[43] were employed in 1897 when workmen's compensation was payable. The use of tribunals developed an

---

[40] Report of the Committee on Administrative Tribunals and Enquiries, Franks Committee 1957, Cmnd. 218 (1957).

[41] H. W. R. Wade, *Administrative Law* (6th ed., Oxford, 1988).

[42] A. J. Taylor, *Laissez-Faire and State Intervention in Nineteenth Century Britain* (1972).

[43] The Exchequer and Audit Departments Act 1866.

importance in the resolution of disputes over workmens compensation. This has remained today.

Finally, a neglected but important element in nineteenth century **5–31** administration, was the use of audit procedures as a check on financial arrangements. Central government audit combined judicial and administrative decision-making. The medieval Court of Exchequer responsible for carrying out the audit of public expenditure, Holdsworth identified as analogous to "an administrative court." The decline of judicial scrutiny over public expenditure began in the sixteenth century when Parliament assumed responsibility for the power of appropriation. The nineteenth century saw the introduction of the modern office of Comptroller and Auditor General with responsibility given to the Public Accounts Committee[44] to oversee public expenditure. Audit techniques included investigation, certification and reporting of accounts.

Local government audit may be traced to the[45] fifteenth century **5–32** with the records of a Commission for the hearing of the accounts of the collectors of money. Audit techniques included investigation, certification and where necessary the power "to charge" on the defaulters where sums were found improperly in their possession.

The development of the Poor Law in the sixteenth century and the consolidation of the Poor Relief Act 1601, provided safeguards in the form of audit undertaken by Justices of the Peace. In the eighteenth century the principles of modern audit procedure in local government evolved. The Poor Relief Act 1743 required church wardens and overseers to keep "a just, true and perfect account in writing fairly entered in a book or books . . ."

The requirements of signed and verified accounts were combined **5–32A** with the rights of rate payers to *inspect* accounts. Over a hundred years later the Poor Law Amendment Act 1844 introduced the office of district auditor with powers to deal with illegality and misconduct. The techniques of certification were supplemented by powers to examine, audit and disallow accounts. In cases where misconduct was identified legal remedies could be provided by the High Court. The role of the Justice of the Peace in these matters of audit was finally ended with the transfer of their functions to the district-auditor. As Jones notes[46]:

"The audit remained judicial in nature; indeed, in comparison with the 1834 provision, the 1844 system was markedly more complete

---

[44] R. Jones, *Local Government Audit Law* (2nd ed., 1985). See Local Government Finance Act 1982, ss.19 and 20.
[45] Cornish, *op. cit.* pp. 59, 462.
[46] Jones, *op. cit.* p. 4, para. 1.12.

in its judicial character by virtue of the procedure for appeal to the High Court. It was also more effective in its precise statutory power to compel restitution and in its provisions for increasing the independence of the auditor."

5–33   Strengthening of the audit system was achieved by the District Auditors[47] Act 1879, which provided for the payment of district auditors, partly out of central funds and partly from fees collected from the audited authorities. Adaptations of the principles of the audit system were continually made as changes were introduced to the system of local government.

In terms of administration and law, the nineteenth century legacy may be shortly stated: the assortment of different agencies, administrative bodies and the variety of institutions ranging from courts, inquiries, tribunals, inspectors, commissions and boards represent the "untidiness of the British Administrative System." The form and substance of judicial scrutiny offered by the courts as fact-finders, combined with adjudicatory and judicial functions, may be found replicated in the wide variety of bodies charged with regulating administrative bodies.

5–34   The role of the courts requires some additional consideration. Two distinctive roles were apparent. First, the courts[48] applied principles of law to the activities of the body under review. Historically, points of law could be raised on the record by the various prerogative writs, most notably certiorari for "error of law on the face of the record." Review in certain circumstances might also include mandamus, applied for by inspectors such as the mines inspectors, to compel the determination of charges made against mine owners and heard before magistrates.

Judicial decision-making established by the superior courts, assisted in the development of the grounds for judicial review. Through the system of remedies,rights were gradually established. These included establishing procedures at hearings, rights of consultation and representation among the parties, knowing the case against the defendant and their right to an unbiased hearing.

5–34A   Second, the courts[49] had an extensive appeal jurisdiction. Since 1857 the Summary Proceedings Act provided an appeal by way of a case stated to the superior courts against errors of law by magistrates. Appeals through the use of the Factories Acts also permitted the courts a role in shaping standards for the performance of individual acts of the inspectors.

[47] ibid.
[48] Memoranda submitted by Government Depts. (HMSO, 6 Vols.) to the Franks Committee (1957).
[49] ibid.

Taken together, both roles, appeal and judicial review, gave rise to **5–35** an expectation that a greater role might be mapped out for the courts. This was slow in developing and only became more significant later in the present century. In the nineteenth century Parliament created statutes with summary jurisdiction, such as the Summary Jurisdiction Act 1848, which made it impossible for the courts to correct errors of law except those which were within the technical question of jurisdiction. After the 1870s the use of certiorari for errors of law on the face of record was rarely obtained. Various technical problems inhibited the development of judicial review by the courts, most notably Dicey's perspective that the existing "rule of law" was adequate to the tasks of the new administrative bodies, when it was clear that it was not.[50]

Lawyers and courts, while providing useful procedures to oversee **5–36** administrative decisions did not necessarily benefit administrators. Lawyers gained influence through drafting laws, representation in Parliament, advising on the law and representing commercial and industrial interests. However, the superior courts were not actively engaged in regulating administrative decisions. Nor were lawyers developing legal principles to make administration effective. Once lawyers' techniques appeared unhelpful or unsatisfactory, they could be circumvented. Higher priority was given to the economic, political and social activities than to the vested interests of lawyers. Legal rules may not be taken as indicative of how administrative bodies make decisions. They may however, act as legitimatising principles which allow administrative decision-making of a broad, discretionary kind, to take place under a veneer of legality.[51]

3. Allocation of Functions

Modern administrative law remains influenced by the legacy of the[52] **5–37** past and the often bewildering development of various institutions, techniques and strategies to carry out administrative decisions. It is convenient to attempt to classify administrative decision-taking in a way which may help identify the relevant legal powers, on whom the powers are granted and how those powers are exercised. Identifying these issues assists in clarifying the procedures and rules which govern the making of decisions, the methods of accountability and the role of the courts, if any.

[50] Craig, *op. cit.* pp. 4–23.
[51] W. R. Wade and C.F. Forsyth, *Administrative Law* (7th ed., 1994).
[52] W. R. Wade, *Towards Administrative Justice* (Michigan, 1963).

5–38   The classification of government institutions and various functions vested in those institutions, is probably easier under a written constitution than under the arrangements in the United Kingdom.[53] Under a written Constitution the citizen may be provided with legally enforceable rights. In the United Kingdom the citizen relies on the availability of remedies depending on the nature of the decision. The citizen may be affected by a decision-maker in different ways – such as whether there is an appeal procedure or whether review may be obtained through the courts or there is a tribunal.[54]

5–39   Decision-making itself involves broad discretion. Fact-finding and applying rules are discretionary elements in decision-making. Officials or administrators exercising their powers operate within a broad discretion in both the interpretation of rules and their application. Value judgements may be required as to the application of rules and how they are to be interpreted. Ganz[55] makes the point that Parliament may make the value judgements and embody these in precise rules in Statutes. The degree of freedom of choice left to the decision-maker may vary according to the type of rule, the context and extent to which discretion may be exercised.

The definition of "discretion" is difficult. It is not a precise word with a clearly defined legal meaning and the context in which it is found may change its meaning. Discretion describes how value judgments, rules and procedures may be combined in the decision-maker.

5–40   In discussing the allocation of functions, consider first the form the relevant legal powers may take. These consist of first, primary legislation and delegated legislation. Second there are prerogative powers, licences and contract.[56] An explanation of each is helpful within the context of administrative decision-making.

(a) Legislation, and Delegated Legislation

5–41 Parliament's law-making[57] powers are exercised through Acts of Parliament which broadly provides the main policy and general details of the law. This leaves Ministers, local authorities, corporations or other bodies to make rules, orders and regulations setting out

---

[53] W. A. Robson, *Justice and Administrative Law* (3rd ed., 1951).

[54] Local Justice Morris, "The Courts and Domestic Tribunals" (1953) 69 L.G.R. 318; J.D.B. Mitchell, "Domestic Tribunals and the Courts" (1956) 2 *British Journal of Administrative Law* 80.

[55] G. Ganz, "Allocation of Decision Making Functions" (Pts. 1 and 2) 1972 P.L. 25 and 299; G. Ganz, *Administrative Procedures* (1974); G. Ganz, *Government and Industry* (1977).

[56] Daintith, *op. cit.* note 2, p. 194.; J. Golding, "The Impact of Statutes on the Royal Prerogative" (1974) 48 A.L.J. 434.

[57] Ganz, *Quasi-Legislation: Recent Developments in Secondary Legislation* (Sweet & Maxwell, 1987).

in greater detail the technical and precise rules. Such delegated rules may take different forms and are known as delegated legislation. The Queen in Council may make Statutory Orders in Council such as under the Emergency Powers Act 1920. Ministers and heads of government departments may make departmental rules or ministerial regulations under Act of Parliament. Similarly, local authorities may have wide powers to make regulations such as under the Local Government Act 1972. Various public bodies or even private bodies have been granted legal powers to carry out their activities. These may take the form of regulations, by-laws or Orders. Examples such as the Gas Act 1986 and the Electricity Act 1989 confer such powers either to the relevant Secretary of State or to the relevant regulator set up by Parliament.[58]

The courts also enjoy a variety of rule-making procedures such as **5–42** the Rules of the Supreme Court under the Supreme Court Act 1981. There is a County Court Rule Committee, under County Courts Act 1984, s.75 which make rules for the County Court.

Powers may be conferred to the Church of England under the Church of England (Assembly) Powers Act 1919, allowing measures in the form of delegated legislation to be enacted. Such measures may amend or repeal the whole or any part of any Act of Parliament. The Northern Ireland Constitution Act 1973 provides under sections 4 and 5, procedures for the passing of measures of the Northern Ireland Assembly to "have the same force and effect as an Act of the Parliament of the United Kingdom." Such measures are presumed, as are relevant subordinate instruments, not to discriminate "against any person or class of persons on the ground of religious belief or political opinion" under section 17 of the Act.

There are a multitude of Special Procedure Orders under the **5–43** Statutory Orders (Special Procedure) Act 1945. A special joint committee of both Houses considers any objections and allows an opportunity for objections to a proposed order to be heard at a local inquiry. This procedure is particularly valuable for water, planning and various other statutory activities.[59]

Delegated legislation might also loosely describe various codes of practice. These have legal effect because of the statutory provisions which permit their introduction. The Health and Safety at Work Act 1974 permits the Health and Safety Commission to approve a Health and Safety at Work Code which is issued under sections 16 and 17 of the Act. Guidance, codes, recommendations, directions and determinations describe the wide variety of types of delegated powers which operate in modern administrative law.

---

[58] Telecommunications Acts 1984, ss.16–19; Gas Act 1986, ss.28–30; Electricity Act 1989, ss.25–38; Water Act 1989, ss.20–22.

[59] T. Prosser, *Nationalised Industries and Public Control* (1986); C. Graham and T. Prosser, *Privatising Nationalised Industries* (1991).

5–44   The rationale for delegated legislation is wide ranging. The Committee on Ministers' Powers[60] 1932, identified six reasons in favour of the "necessity for delegation," while admitting the need for safeguards and with the provision "that the statutory powers are exercised and the statutory functions performed in the right way." The six reasons[61] are: that pressure upon parliamentary time is too great; the subject matter of modern legislation is technical; it is difficult to include all the details in a single Act; constant adaptation may take place without the necessity of amending legislation, thus flexibility is encouraged; experimenting with new ideas is possible and lessons from past experience learnt. Finally, in a modern state, delegated legislation provides a convenient and speedy remedy when there may be either emergency or urgency in the matters covered by the legislation.

5–45   The Deregulation and Contracting Out Act 1994 intended to reduce the burdens on industry by reducing the level of government regulation of industry.[62] A unique feature of the 1994 Act are two powers contained in Chapter 1 of Part 1 of the Act. First, there is a power to amend or repeal by ministerial order any primary legislation that is deemed to impose an unnecessary burden on business.[63] Secondly, there are powers to improve enforcement procedures consistent with fairness and transparency. There are over 600 proposals for action under the 1994 Act involving deregulation orders. The unusual nature of the legislation is that it allows a Minister to use an order to suspend an Act of Parliament, a power that is seldom used in peace-time. This is usually referred to as a Henry VIII clause because there is a wide power in the legislation that gives wide discretion to a Minister.[64]

5–46   A form of delegated legislation which has become more popular in recent years is what Ganz refers to as "quasi-legislation." Unlike statutory instruments or orders, the legal force of much "quasi-legislation" depends on the enabling Act of Parliament. Quasi-legislation[65] may be defined to mean, "codes of conduct guide-lines, circulars and a miscellany of rules." No one is quite sure of the extent and scope of quasi-legislation because it does not always conform to the clearest pattern of organisation. Some examples illustrate the meaning of the term. The Highway Code lays down general guidance and advice to motorists. Breach of any of its guidance does not make

---

[60] Cmnd. 4060 (1932).
[61] *ibid.*
[62] See *The Citizen's Charter First Report* Cm. 2101 (1992) p. 58.
[63] Criticism of this power was voiced by the House of Lords *Delegated Powers Scrutiny Committee* 1993/94 H.L. 60 para. 1.
[64] See Michael Ryle, *The De-regulation and Contracting Out Bill 1994.*
[65] Ganz, *op. cit.,* note 57.

the offender subject to a criminal prosecution. However it may be used in either civil or criminal proceedings as relevant to the consideration before the court.

The Police and Criminal Evidence Act 1984 (PACE) provides the **5–47** police with various codes of conduct. Breach of any of the guidance in the code make the police liable to disciplinary proceedings but not prosecution. Under the Electricity Act 1989 various codes of practice set out the conditions for Public Electricity Suppliers. These may be relevant in[66] the Determinations made by the Director General of Electricity Supply. Additionally, voluntary codes of practice have been agreed by the various electricity companies regarding their disconnection powers and rights of consumers. Such codes operate within the legal framework set by the Electricity Act 1989, but are not directly enforceable by the citizen, though they can form the basis of a dispute which may be determined by the Director General.

As Ganz[67] observed, one of the dangers inherent in quasi- **5–48** legislation is that codes of practice may occupy a wider breadth of activity than originally intended by Parliament. One example is the Code of Practice on Picketing, which limited the number to six pickets. The enabling Act, the Employment Act 1980, did not include such a number but the practice of limiting the number of pickets to six has been accepted by the police and the courts.

Delegated legislation may be considered by the courts as to its legality, under the enabling legislation. Great care must be taken when ministerial circulars or advice are issued because such advice may pre-judge an individual case or a particular issue. Each case must be considered on its merits.

(b) Prerogative Powers, Licences and Contracts

The Prerogative remains an important source of legal powers. As **5–49** noted in Chapter 2, in *Malone v. Metropolitan Police Commissioner*[68] the Vice-Chancellor, Sir Robert Megarry recognised that the Home Secretary had a limited power to authorise telephone tapping. This power was a residue of the power to open articles through the post, said to exist through the prerogative. Such powers have been made statutory under the Interception of Telecommunications Act 1985, but the case is illustrative of the prerogative as a source of legal powers applied in modern circumstances.[69]

---

[66] J. F. McEldowney, *Electricity Law and Practice: The Electricity Industry Handbook* (Chancery, 1992).
[67] Ganz, *op. cit.* note 57.
[68] [1979] Ch. 344.
[69] Hood Phillips, *Constitutional and Administrative Law* (7th ed.), pp. 269–270.

5–50   In the *GCHQ* case, the House of Lords accepted the prerogative as the basis of legal powers to ban trade unions at the Government Communications Headquarters. Judicial review of prerogative powers was also accepted by the majority of their Lordships as justiciable by the courts. Some doubts were expressed in the case as to the nature of the prerogative powers. The exact issue of the legal powers depended on seeing an Order in Council as derived from the authority of the prerogative or under Act of Parliament.

This is a characteristic of prerogative powers. Their exact nature, scope and extent are often difficult to review or define. Occasionally this may give rise to difficulty when there are statutory powers which are incomplete or inadequate and the question arises as to whether the prerogative may supplement these powers.[70]

5–51   In *R. v. Secretary of State for the Home Department, ex p. Northumbrian Police Authority*[71] the Court of Appeal was willing to supplement the Home Secretary's powers under the Police Act 1964 to permit the issuing of a circular providing plastic bullets and C.S. gas to local police forces. Relying on the prerogative power "to keep the peace," the Court of Appeal concluded that this entitled the Home Secretary to all that was[72] "reasonably necessary to preserve the peace of the realm." This entitled the Home Secretary to rely on the prerogative powers even though the statutory arrangements appeared comprehensive and conclusive in the matter. The case has been heavily criticised but it represents an indication of how important it is to clarify the nature of legal powers.

5–52   Sources of legal powers are not restricted to legislation, quasi legislation or prerogative powers. Increasingly public bodies rely on contracts or licences to establish the legal authority and powers necessary to carry out their activities. Such powers operate within a statutory framework but are undeniably private law powers.

In the case of gas, telecommunications, electricity and water, the newly privatised companies require licences issued by the Secretary of State to carry out their activities. Such licences, under the relevant legislation, provide criminal sanctions for anyone attempting to carry out specified activities without a licence. The licence conditions are detailed and technical. They contain legal powers, duties and conditions which must be performed. The licences are amenable to modification by the Director General of the industries.[73] General directions to the industry may be given in the case of Telecommunications under section 47(3) of the Telecommunications Act 1984. Similar powers exist for gas and electricity utilities.

---

[70] *ibid.* H. W. R. Wade, "Procedure and Prerogative in Public Law" (1985) 101 L.Q.R. 180.

[71] [1988] 2 W.L.R. 590.

[72] *ibid.*

[73] Graham and Prosser, *Privatising Nationalised Industries* (1991).

The novelty of the use of licences in the newly privatised indus- 5–53 tries, leaves the prospect of negotiation and modification a matter for political decision-making as well as legal powers. References to the Monopolies and Mergers Commission are possible by any one of the new regulatory agencies set up to regulate utilities such as, gas, electricity, water or telecommunications. Additional responsibility is shared between the Secretary of State and the regulators over how the industry is to be regulated and a division of powers for enforcing licences and their conditions is made. Such a framework requires careful consideration as to the *exact* nature of the legal powers, how they are to be exercised and by whom.

Monitoring the tariff charges of the various utilities also involves the legal powers of the regulators. Careful consideration of the economic and social aspects involved in the price formula is required, to balance the efficiency of the industry with consumer protection.

Contractual powers[74] offer the most demanding and interesting use 5–54 of legal powers in the allocation of functions of public bodies. As a source of power, there is usually some legislative authority permit-ting the use of contract. One example is the contractual powers of local authorities. Recent legislation such as the Local Government Act 1988, requires local authorities to subject a number of services such as street cleaning, vehicle maintenance, schools and welfare catering, refuse collection, and the management of sports and leisure facilities, to competitive tendering. The law requires that private companies be permitted to bid for the work involved. Setting performance stand-ards and competitive tendering are included in the Local Government Act 1992. Such legal powers are intended to encourage contracts and competition and to increase the effectiveness of local authority powers.[75]

Some doubts as to the legal powers to enter financial contracts 5–55 arose in *Hazell v. Hammersmith and Fulham*.[76] The local authority had invested substantial sums in various investments known as "interests rate swaps" in order to finance expenditure, during a period when central government financial support to local authorities had dimin-ished. In order to invest in such activities as interest rate swaps, the local authority relied on section 111(1) of the Local Government Act 1972, which empowered local authorities to borrow according to what was "calculated to facilitate or conducive or incidental to, the discharge of any of their functions". Doubts over the legality of such

---

[74] Daintith, *op. cit.*, note 2; M. Freedland, "Government by Contract and Public Law" [1994] P.L. 86–104.

[75] McEldowney, "Current Issues in Local Government" in Günter Weick (ed.), *National and European Law on the Threshold to the Single Market* (Peter Lang, 1993), Chap. 12, pp. 67–86.

[76] [1990] 2 W.L.R. 1038.

powers were raised by the District Auditor. The House of Lords held that the local authority borrowing powers under section 111(1) were curtailed by Schedule 13 to the 1972 Act. It was concluded that the local authority had no contractual power to enter the swap market.

5–56   In *Crédit Suisse v. Allerdale Borough Council*[77] the Court of Appeal considered the operation of a local authority company and whether the establishment of the company was consistent with Schedule 13 section 111 of the 1972 Act. The local authority wished to establish a leisure pool complex. The setting up of a company for such a purpose was regarded as a means of overcoming statutory borrowing restrictions. The company was formed and borrowed £6 million from *Crédit Suisse*. The recession caused the company to fail and the bank claimed repayment of the loan. In considering the express and implied powers of the local authority the Court of Appeal concluded that the local authority had no powers to set up a company for the purposes of borrowing the requisite finance for the various recreational activities favoured by the local authority. The Court of Appeal followed the approach in *Hazell v. Hammersmith*. It acknowledged that local authorities were empowered under section 19(1) of the Local Government (Miscellaneous Provisions) Act 1976 to provide recreational facilities. Such authorisation, however, does not apply to borrowing. Thus the purported borrowing contract was *ultra vires*.

5–57   The method of statutory construction given by the Court of Appeal to the 1972 Act follows the pattern observed in previous decisions regarding local government. Unless there are clear words the courts will not imply any discretion or general assumptions concerning local authority powers. Indeed the nature of *ultra vires* contracts are such that they cannot be enforced.

In another case, *Crédit Suisse v. Waltham Forest*[78] the same judges considered a claim against a local authority which had guaranteed a bank loan to a company. The Court of Appeal followed the *Allerdale* case and held that the borrowing was *ultra vires*.

5–58   Contractual powers may be the main source[79] of legal powers for a particular activity. This may give rise to questions of the reviewability of the activities in question. In *R. v. Panel on Take-overs and Mergers, ex p. Datafin*[80] the Take-overs Panel, a non-statutory body involved in regulating city take-overs and mergers, was provided with regulatory powers by contract. The courts regarded the take-over panel as an important element in the regulation of take-overs. The Government,

---

[77] *Crédit Suisse v. Allerdale Borough Council* [1996] 4 All E.R. 129.
[78] *Crédit Suisse v. Waltham Forest* [1996] 4 All E.R. 176. Also see: K. Walsh "The role of the Market and the Growth of Competition" in S. Leach *et al.*, (eds.), *Enabling or Disabling Local Government* (Buckingham, Open University, 1996).
[79] [1990] 2 W.L.R. 1038.
[80] [1987] Q.B. 815.

together with the Bank of England approved the appointment of the Chairman, even though no statutory basis existed for the Panel. The Court of Appeal regarded the "authority of the government" as sufficiently relevant to give the Panel a public law dimension. In that way, the Courts were prepared to offer judicial review of the Panels' activities.

Contracts are likely to become an increasingly important source of legal powers. Daintith[81] explains how government has a number of powers available to carry on its activities. These powers divide into two: *imperium* and *dominium*. Under *imperium* the government may prohibit through legislation or promote through existing legal powers, various activities. Under *dominium* it might offer subsidies or purchasing agreements or licensing arrangements favouring one activity or another. The vast range of possibilities makes classification of the legal powers involved an important element in understanding how powers are allocated. **5–59**

(c) Central and Local Government

Identical legal powers may be[82] viewed differently depending on who exercises the power and how the power is exercised. There are a variety of factors relevant in the choice of decision-making bodies. **5–60**

In the context of administrative decision-making, central government may be distinguished[83] from local government even though both share the common feature of being directly elected. Local authorities represent local interests and are accountable to the local electorate. However, since the nineteenth century, the wide range of activities carried out by local authorities for housing, education, police and public health, have required increasing statutory activity. Diversity in size and in politics have given local authorities a great deal of autonomy. However, local authority activities are not the only way to judge the role of local government. Viewed from the perspective of central government, local activities are carried out on behalf of central government policy-making. The sovereignty of Parliament suggests that local authorities' powers are *allocated* by central government.[84] There is no independence or constitutional autonomy given to local authorities other than that presented by Acts of Parliament. Legal powers from Acts of Parliament, give the government of the day authority to lay down policy and prescribe local authority

---

[81] Daintith, *op. cit.* note 2, p. 194.
[82] Ganz, *op. cit*, note 55, p. 47.
[83] See Chap. 3.
[84] M. Loughlin, *Local Government in the Modern State* (London, 1986).

activities. Legal powers may also be found through appeals by laws and circulars.

5–61   Many local authority activities such as in the area of planning, leave the right of appeal to a Minister after a refusal of planning permission by a local authority. Byelaws made by a local authority require ministerial approval. Central government circulars may set policy guidance for local authorities.[85]

In the area of local authority finance, central government had extensive powers to place a legal "cap" on the amount of Community Charge which may be levied by the local authority. Ultimately, powers granted to local authorities may be removed by central government, such as the abolition of the Greater London Council and the Metropolitan counties, under the Local Government Act 1985. The successor to the Community Charge under section 1 of the Local Government Finance Act 1992 came into effect on April 1, 1993. The Secretary of State has powers under section 54 to determine the maximum budgetary requirement of each local authority and to place a "cap" on local authority expenditure.

5–62   Ministerial discretion provides extensive powers for central government decision-taking. Reserve powers are provided in many statutes allowing the Secretary of State authority to make decisions, delegate powers or allocate powers to other bodies. Central government powers, operate within the framework of ministerial responsibility to Parliament; Ministers alone, may raise public expenditure through Act of Parliament. This power of taxation is exclusively controlled by the government of the day on the authority of Parliament.

Allocating functions between central and local government raises important issues about where political and legal power ought to reside.[86]

(d) Types of agencies distinguished

5–63 In public law the names of particular institutions that are hived off from government follows no exact science. The civil service organised around the various departments of central government is undergoing radical change. On April 1, 1996 there were 494,292 permanent civil servants. Since 1988 the Next Steps initiative has been in operation intended to deliver better services within available resources. By April 1, 1996 there were 102 Next Steps agencies in the Home Civil Service. In addition there are agencies within HM Customs and

---

[85] Under the Education Act 1944, as amended. S. H. Bailey, "Central and Local Government and the Courts" [1983] P.L. 8.
[86] Loughlin, op. cit. note 79.

Excise and the Inland Revenue. Taken together this amounts to 71 per cent of the civil service, approximately 350,126 permanent staff.[87] The powers and responsibilities of such agencies fall within the "Framework Documents" setting up the agency. The agency also comes within Treasury guidance and financial control. The increase in the number of agencies has required the re-writing of the Treasury Handbook on *Government Accounting*.[88] The chief executive of the agency has responsibility for the day to day management and decision making of the agency. In theory this leaves ministerial responsibility confined to the overall policy of the agency.

The Next Steps agencies need to be distinguished from other forms **5–64** of agency established independently from the Next Steps arrangements. Such agencies may appear to share some similarities with the Next Steps type of agency. However, unlike Next Steps agencies these are usually set up under statute. For the purposes of convenience they may be given the generic title of fringe organisations.

(e) Fringe Organisations and Statutory Bodies

The allocation of powers may be entrusted to various non- **5–65** governmental organisations (Quangos).[89] Most have a statutory framework such as the Equal Opportunities Commission, the Civil Aviation Authority, the Gaming Board, The Monopolies and Mergers Commission, and the Health and Safety Commission. Many of their activities are directly related to carrying out statutory powers, but their remit outside government departments gives scope for a broader view of their activities.

In 1993 the Cabinet Office[90] listed four types of Non-Departmental **5–66** Public Bodies (NDPs). Annual reports are published by the Cabinet Office. In common usage these bodies are often referred to as fringe organisations or Quangos. Such bodies have a role in the process of national government but are not part of a department and operate at arm's length from Ministers. The first type are Executive Bodies. They employ staff and have their own budget. Some may have the status of a public corporation. In 1979 there were 492 such bodies employing 217,000 staff and spending £6,150 million. In 1993 there were 358 employing 111,300 staff and spending £15,410 million. In 1996 there were 309 with expenditure of £21,420 million. Executive Bodies range

---

[87] See *The Civil Service Yearbook 1997* (Stationery Office, London).
[88] Stationery Office, London, April 1997.
[89] The term "fringe organisations" may apply.
[90] See *Public Bodies 1993* (Cabinet Office, 1993), *Public Bodies 1996* (Cabinet Office, 1996) and also see: *The Governance of Public Bodies* Cm. 3557 Feb. 1997.

in size and diversity such as the Agricultural Training Board to the Higher Education Funding Council for England and Wales with wide statutory powers.

5–67   The second type are Advisory Bodies. This group consists mainly of bodies which are set up by Ministers to advise them and their departments on matters requiring specialist expertise. Included in this category are Royal Commissions. Generally advisory bodies do not employ their own staff or incur their own expenditure. In 1979 there were 1,485 advisory bodies. In 1993 there were 829. In 1996 there were 674.

The third type are Tribunals. In this category are bodies with licensing and appeal functions. Generally they are serviced by staff from the sponsoring department. In 1979 there were 70 and in 1993 there were 68. In 1996 this had increased to 75.

Finally, there are a miscellaneous group of other bodies comprising the boards of visitors to penal establishments in Great Britain and boards of visitors and visiting committees in Northern Ireland.

The four types of NDPs are not an exhaustive list of fringe organisations.

5–68   Privatisation of many nationalised industries has increased the range and scope of specialised statutory bodies. In the case of telecommunications (OFTEL), gas (OFGAS), electricity (OFFER) and water (OFWAT), new regulatory agencies have been created with extensive legal powers to supervise the activities of the newly privatised industries. In some cases, as in gas and telecommunications, the regulator may be described as a surrogate competitor, in order to encourage greater competitiveness in the industry. This is particularly noticeable in the case of gas, where OFGAS are regulating a monopoly, British Gas. The intended privatisation of British Rail and British Coal has created further regulatory bodies. In the case of Railways under the 1993 Railways Act there is the Office of Passenger Rail Franchising (OPRAF) and the Office of the Railway Regulator (ORR).

Some regulatory agencies fall into different categories. For example the Office of Standards in Education (OFSTED) has a staff of 500 and a budget of £56m. It is set up to monitor the four-yearly inspection of schools and advise the Secretary of State for Education on the quality of schools.

5–69   Baldwin and McCrudden[91] have identified reasons for the creation of the wide variety of regulatory agencies. Hiving off government work may be more efficient and reduce the size of the civil service. Particular expertise is sought outside a government ministry. Independence from government may be required to develop the necessary

[91] R. Baldwin and McCrudden, *Regulation and Public Law* (1987).

experience and expertise. Delegation of rule making functions may be required in order to facilitate giving technical detail. Constant updating and adjustment are more suited to such bodies than government departments. Interest groups, industry and policy formulation may be assisted through the creation of such agencies. Funding from outside government sources may be easier to achieve. Treasury interference or inter-departmental rivalries may be more easily resisted through the creation of regulatory agencies.

There are also a wide variety of functions discharged by such agencies. Baldwin and McCrudden[92] identify five different governmental functions present: first, the prevention of undesirable activities; secondly, the provision of techniques to the various parties to reach agreement or compromise; thirdly, the provision and allocation of various benefits such as particular services or ensuring good standards such as competitive and economical industries; fourthly, setting standards through legal mechanism and finally, providing dispute facilities.

Decision-making bodies may be influenced by the need to provide **5–70** some elements of adjudication in the decision-maker. Adjudication may be informal or formal. Informal adjudication may take place without lawyers and be confined to internal procedures. Formal methods of adjudication inevitably involve the use of the courts, tribunals or inquiries. Lawyers tend to become a dominant influence. Jowell[93] described this process as "judicialisation." The choice to be made, is to consider the role of courts and the function of tribunals and inquiries.

4. Courts

(a) The Judiciary and the Administration of Justice

Openness, integrity, impartiality and fairness are some of the charac- **5–71** teristics necessary for a decision-maker to follow when adjudicating disputes. Courts appear to offer such characteristics. Although historically England had a large number of special local courts, these have now been displaced by a centrally organised system of courts: the High Court, Court of Appeal and House of Lords for civil matters.[94]

---

[92] ibid.

[93] Jowell, "Courts and Administration in Britain: Standard, Principles and Rights" (1988) Israel L.R. 409.

[94] Abolition of a miscellaneous number of local courts was carried out by the local Government Act 1972, and the Administration of Justice Act 1977.

The courts gained independence in the 17th century and although proposed in the nineteenth century, a Minister of Justice covering judicial appointments, law reform and the legal profession, was never implemented. The jurisdiction of the High Court has developed as a place where the legality of acts and decisions of public bodies may be challenged.

5–72   It is the adjudicatory nature of the courts' role with its implied independence and appearance of non-political decision-making, that makes the facility of the courts an important model for allocating powers. The value of the court may come from techniques for dealing with law and facts. An illustration of this valuable role, is provided by the employment of High Court judges in chairing inquiries or investigations.

The use of the court's techniques may require adaptation to meet specialised needs. The Restrictive Trade Practices Act 1956 was passed after debate in the House of Commons on the value of a tribunal rather than a court. The former was answerable to the Minister while the latter was not. In the end a tribunal was favoured. The hallmark of courts such as rules of evidence, representation, cross-examination, and oral hearings have been adapted to the way certain tribunals and inquiries may function. Courts are seen in many instances to provide a useful means of protecting civil liberties and citizens' rights.

5–73   In England and Wales[95] the High Court exercises a civil jurisdiction. There are three divisions: Queen's Bench, Chancery and Family. On appeal there is the Court of Appeal, Civil Division. The Supreme Court comprises the High Court, the Court of Appeal and the Crown Court. Appeals lie to the House of Lords, sitting as a court, from the Court of Appeal and in some instances direct from the High Court. There is a limited civil jurisdiction exercised by the county courts and by the magistrates' court. The Lord Chancellor may extend the jurisdiction of county courts under the Courts and Legal Services Act 1990. (See Fig. 1)

5–74   Criminal jurisdiction is provided for summary offences before the magistrates' courts and in jury trials before the crown court. Criminal

---

[95] In Scotland civil jurisdiction may be found in the Court of Session. A wide civil jurisdiction is also exercised by the sheriff court from which appeals may lie to the Inner House of the Court of Session. Appeals from Scotland in civil cases, but not in criminal cases, may be taken to the House of Lords. In Northern Ireland, civil jurisdiction is exercised by the High Court, comprising Queen's Bench, Chancery and Family Divisions, and the Court of Appeal which comprise the Supreme Court of Northern Ireland. In civil and criminal matters there is an appeal to the House of Lords. On constitutional issues there is special provision for an appeal to the Judicial Committee of the Privy Council under section 18 of the Northern Ireland Constitution Act 1973. Previously under the Government of Ireland Act 1920 in force until 1972 under analogous provisions only one reference was made. See *Reference under the Government of Ireland Act 1920* [1936] A.C. 352.

appeals may be taken to the Queen's Bench Divisional Court or to the High Court or to the Court of Appeal, Criminal Division. A further appeal on matters of law may lie to the House of Lords. (See Fig. 2)

The House of Lords when sitting as a court may be composed of **5–75** up to 11 Lords of Appeal in Ordinary. Usually appeals are heard by five judges and in exceptional cases, seven judges may sit. Since 1844 by convention[96] no lay peer should take part in appellate work of the Lords. The hearing of appeals is carried out by an appellate committee sitting as one or two appellate committees of the House. Appeals may be heard irrespective of whether Parliament is sitting or not. Since 1966 the House of Lords is not bound by its previous decisions though it does not depart from former decisions which it regards as normally binding.

Judicial appointments are made by the Executive. There is no **5–76** formal machinery such as an independent commission providing advice independent of the Executive. Appointments to senior judicial positions such as Lord Chief Justice, Master of the Rolls and President of the Family Division are made by the Crown on the advice of the Prime Minister. High Court judges, recorders and circuit judges are appointed by the Crown on the advice of the Lord Chancellor. The Courts and Legal Services Act 1990 has changed the qualifications necessary for judicial appointments. Before 1990 judges of the High Court had to be barristers of at least 10 years standing. After the 1990 Act it is possible for solicitors with rights of audience in the High Court and for circuit court judges to be appointed. Appointment as a Lord Justice of Appeal to the Court of Appeal previously required standing as a barrister of at least 15 years or previous appointment as a High Court judge. After 1990 solicitors with rights of audience in the High Court are eligible and the 15 years has been reduced to 10 years. Non-practising barristers may in certain circumstances be appointed High Court judges, where there is a particular specialism required.[97]

The independence[98] of the judiciary provides important safeguards. **5–77** Judges must be free from political pressures when deciding cases. The terms and conditions of judicial appointments are therefore important in contributing to the independence of the judiciary. Judges have security of tenure. Judges of the High Court, Court of Appeal and Lords of Appeal hold office during good behaviour, subject to the power of removal by the Queen on an address presented to both Houses of Parliament.[99]

---

[96] See the discussion in *O'Connell v. R.* (1844) 11 Cl. & Fin. 155.

[97] The appointment of Brenda Hoggett, after service on the Law Commission is an example of an academic appointment from someone with specialist knowledge and expertise.

[98] See Robert Stevens, *The Independence of the Judiciary* (Oxford, 1993).

[99] Supreme Court Act 1981, s.11(3).

5–78   Judicial appointments are made for life but since 1959 statutory retirement ages have been introduced; 72 for a circuit judge and 75 for a High Court judge. This has been modified in 1993 when the Judicial Pensions and Retirement Act 1993 introduced a new retirement age of 70 which may be extended to 75. Since 1973 there are procedures[1] for determining judicial incapacity and grounds of retirement.[2]

Judicial salaries are charged permanently from the Consolidated Fund, relieving Parliament of the obligation of approving salaries every year. Salaries fall under the review procedure set up by the government for review by the advisory Review Body on Top Salaries. The Lord Chancellor with Prime Ministerial approval may increase salaries[3] in line with the recommendations from the Review Body.

5–79   As noted above the Lord Chancellor is concerned with all judicial appointments, including the magistracy, circuit court judges and High Court judges. The general administration of the Supreme Court is also his responsibility. The Rule Committee consisting of the Lord Chancellor and other judges, together with practising barristers and solicitors provide the Rules of the Supreme Court. The Lord Chancellor[4] is also responsible for the allocation of business between the High Court and county courts. The administration and management of the magistrates' courts was transferred from the Home Secretary to the Lord Chancellor in April 1992. In addition to his judicial functions, the Lord Chancellor is speaker of the House of Lords and is a member of the Cabinet. The Lord Chancellor is also important in promoting law reform and appoints for England and Wales members of the Law Commission. The Law Commission has statutory responsibility to keep under systematic review the law including codification, simplification and where relevant modernisation of the law.

5–80   Judges are often required to preside over royal commissions or inquiries set up under the Tribunals of Inquiry (Evidence) Act 1921. Ad hoc inquiries set up in the public interest are often chaired by a High Court judge. Judicial involvement in such a role is often accompanied by great publicity. The subject matter[5] of many inquiries is often controversial and may indirectly involve judges in political issues of the day. This has its dangers. The public may find it difficult to draw a distinction between the primary judicial function of judges and their role in inquiries set up by the government of the day.

---

[1] See Spencer, *Jackson's Machinery of Justice* (Cambridge, 1989), pp. 411–413.
[2] See Lord Taylor, *The Judiciary in the Nineties* (BBC Education, 1992).
[3] High Court judges are paid about £87,620, the Lord Chief Justice receives £108,940.
[4] The Lord Chancellor also has responsibility for the Public Records Office, the Land Registry and under the Courts and Legal Services Act 1990 for the appointment of the Legal Services Ombudsman.
[5] See Lord Denning's *Report on the Profumo Affair* (1963).

In recent years the public and media attention on the procedures[6] **5–81** and outcome of the Scott inquiry[7] was particular intense. There were a number of reasons for this heightened and at times almost hysterical attention given by the media to the inquiry. First, the nature of the inquiry itself and the undoubted public interest in its contents. Secondly, the public standing of the witnesses including the Attorney-General, senior Government Ministers including the then serving Prime Minister Mr Major, and Mrs Thatcher, the previous Prime Minister. Thirdly, the nature of public cross-examination attracted media attention. The undoubted charisma of Sir Richard Scott and the appointment of a Counsel to the inquiry, Presiley Baxendale Q.C., all added a sense of drama to proceedings. Finally, the political parties seized on every opportunity afforded by the inquiry to embarrass government Ministers about the potential findings of the inquiry. In the end the Government was able to use the charges laid by the opposition parties as a means to deflect criticism. This allowed media attention to diminish once any ministerial resignation was defeated in the House of Commons. All this served to illustrate the delicate nature of judicial independence, public scrutiny and media attention.

Judges often have a difficult task in ensuring that they are **5–82** perceived by the public as independent. The diversity of the tasks entrusted to judges by the government of the day only reinforces the importance of judicial independence. Judges are regularly invited to chair the Security Commission which investigates the workings of British Intelligence.

Judges must observe the convention that they must not become involved in party political activities. They must not engage in conduct which is likely to bring the judiciary into disrepute. Members of the government, and civil servants are constrained by convention not to criticise a judicial decision by attacking the competence or credibility of the judge. Similarly M.P.s exercise self-restraint in their criticism of judges. Parliamentary debate is expected to observe the *sub judice* rule when matters awaiting judicial decision are brought before the courts. At times this may seem an undue fetter on the freedom of the House of Commons to debate, but it is generally accepted as a necessary protection of the judiciary.[8]

Judges are protected at common law from any action for acts done **5–83** or words spoken in their judicial capacity in a court of justice. This

---

[6] The details of the procedures may be found in the Scott report, part K4. Chapter 1.

[7] *Return to an Address of the Honourable House of Commons dated 15th February 1996. Report of the Inquiry into the Export of Defence Equipment and Dual-use Goods to Iraq and Related Prosecutions* The Rt Hon. Sir Richard Scott, The Vice-Chancellor H.C. 115 (HMSO, London, 1996).

[8] See H.C. Deb., Col. 710 (July 13, 1987) on the Spycatcher litigation arising from Peter Wright's book on British Intelligence.

protection appears extensive. It may even cover anything done or said however corrupt, oppressive or malicious.[9] In recent years the protection afforded to superior court judges is increasingly applied to lower courts such as magistrates. The Courts and Legal Services Act 1990 provides that a magistrate will not be liable for any acts done within his jurisdiction nor for any acts outside his jurisdiction unless bad faith may be shown. Judicial incompetence which may result in a wrongful conviction[10] does not render the judge liable in either civil or criminal law. Negligence or poor judgment does not result in disciplinary action. There is at least some extension of judicial immunity to the vast array of inferior tribunals where the duties involve judicial rather than administrative decisions. It may be questioned whether absolute judicial immunity outlined above is entirely defensible.

5–84   Finally, it is important to note that the courts have extensive powers in respect of contempt of court. Contempt of court allows the courts to punish conduct that threatens, obstructs or prejudices the administration of justice. The law has been amended[11] in the Contempt of Court Act 1981. Civil contempt is the failure to obey the order of a superior court that has prescribed conduct for a party to a civil action. Criminal contempt may arise where there is conduct calculated to interfere with proceedings which are in their nature criminal proceedings. However, both civil and criminal courts have jurisdiction over criminal contempt. Obedience to the orders of the court is required against litigants. In the case of the Crown or government departments, the courts may issue injunctions against officers of the court and the contempt jurisdiction of the courts extends to Ministers.[12]

5–85   Contempt proceedings may be invoked for matters that are said to scandalise the court, or where there are threats made in the face of the court. Contempt proceedings may arise from publications that are held to prejudice the course of justice or other acts that interfere with the course of justice.

Securing judicial independence is a continuous process at times involving judicial self-restraint and critical self-analysis. Judges are expected to be active members of society participating in discussion and demonstrating that their independence does not mean isolation. Increased media scrutiny is likely to continue and require judges to observe the etiquette of careful judgment and thoughtful comment.

---

[9] See A. Olowofoyeku, *Suing Judges* (Oxford, 1993); *Sirros v. Moore* [1975] Q.B. 118.
[10] Compensation is payable by the Home Office for wrongful convictions.
[11] For a detailed discussion see C. J. Miller, *Contempt of Court* (2nd ed., 1989, Oxford).
[12] *M. v. Home Office* [1992] Q.B. 270.

(b) The Development of Judicial Review

In the previous chapter, mention was made of Dicey's influential *Law* **5–86**
of the Constitution[13] (1885), in which he suggested that the fundamental safeguard in the United Kingdom's Constitution against abuse of
power, was the doctrine of the rule of law. Rights, for example, to
personal liberty or to hold public meetings arise "as the result of
judicial decisions determining the rights of private persons in particular cases brought before the courts." The rule of law expresses the
idea that the independence of the judiciary is part of a fundamental
legal doctrine that government must be conducted according to law.
Disputed cases require judicial decisions according to detailed rules
in both substance and procedure.

The courts are uniquely placed to consider the relationship between **5–87**
the citizen and the State. Interpretation of statutes, reviewing discretion, sometimes adjudicating between different government departments, or in local and central relations and supervising regulatory
agencies fall within the broad remit of the supervisory jurisdiction of
the High Court.

Before 1977, litigants or "aggrieved citizens"[14] as they are termed,
had to choose which of a number of ancient prerogative writs was
suited to their needs. These included habeas corpus, certiorari,
prohibition and mandamus. Habeas corpus is still referred to as a
writ, all the rest are now orders since the Administration of Justice
(Miscellaneous Provisions) Acts 1933 and 1938. Such orders could not
be "mixed" with other remedies such as declaration, damages or
injunctions. Technical rules of standing (locus standi) applied to each
remedy. Different grounds for seeking each remedy also applied. In
the case of certiorari and prohibition, the availability of the remedy
depended on the body performing the function complained about.

Proposals to reform the procedures and the substantive law of **5–88**
remedies were made by the Law Commission in 1969, which recommended a comprehensive review of administrative law by a Royal
Commission or body of comparable status. Although this advice was
persuasively argued, it was rejected. In 1969 the Law Commission
was instructed to study the law of remedies, which led to recommendations in 1977, contained in Order 53 and now section 31 of the
Supreme Court Act 1981. These procedures, commonly known as
Order 53, provide for the application for judicial review.[15]

---

[13] Hood Phillips *et al.*, "Dicey and the Constitution" [1985] P.L. 583–721.
[14] H. W. R. Wade, *Administrative Law* (1987). Also see E. C. S. Wade, "The Courts and
the Administrative Process" (1947) 63 L.W.R. 164; McEldowney, "Administration
and Law in England in the 18th and 19th Centuries" Vol. 8 JEV (1996) pp. 19–36.
[15] *O'Reilly v. Mackman* [1983] 2 A.C. 237.

Currently, the Crown Office, responsible for the administration of applications for judicial review,[16] has recorded nearly 3,000 applications, of which 20 per cent are planning or statutory procedures. In recent years, 1992–93, there has been an 18 per cent increase in the number of cases on current figures.

5–89   An application for judicial review is made with the leave of the Court. The first stage is to request leave and if this is refused a second application may be made to a Judge in open court. All applications must be made to the Divisional Court of the Queen's Bench Division. Leave is based on the applicant showing grounds which the court considers to be of "sufficient interest." The first stage for leave must be made within three months of the grievance occurring. Once leave is granted, the second stage is a full hearing in the Divisional Court. Usually the first stage is on affidavit evidence and only one party, the applicant, is present. Remedies may be granted at the Court's discretion and remedies may be mixed; damages are available. The decision to grant a remedy is discretionary, depending on the nature of the body under review and the powers reviewed. Normally the application for judicial review is confined to "public law" matters, a term which is difficult to define and is often hard to reconcile with the various decisions made by the courts.[17]

5–90   Judicial review does not always afford the citizen redress. Parliament may entrust certain types of decision-making powers to Ministers and not the courts. In *R. v. Secretary of State for Education and Science, ex p. Avon County Council*,[18] the Court of Appeal reviewing the powers granted to the Minister of Education under the 1988 Education Reform Act, noted that:

"Parliament did not entrust the making of that judgement, the Ministers approval for grant maintained status of a school to the Court but to the Minister who was answerable to Parliament."

The role of the courts may be limited or excluded in the allocation of functions by Parliament.[19] In terms of subject matter, judicial review covers a wide range of activities. Sunkin and research for the *Public Law Project* have identified the average case-load of applications for judicial review to be approximately 2,600 applications per annum. The bulk of the case-load relates to "immigration, housing,

---

[16] Lord Chancellor's Department: Crown Service Annual Report 1991/2 Crown Office List.
[17] Discussed more fully in Chap. 15.
[18] *The Independent*, May 25, 1990; [1991] 1 All E.R. 282.
[19] See M. Sunkin, "What is Happening to Applications for Judicial Review?" (1987) 50 M.L.R. 432. Lee Bridges *et al.*, *Judicial Review in Perspective* (Public Law Project, Cavendish, 2nd ed., 1995).

planning and licensing" cases. Education, homelessness and prisoners' rights are also fairly widely represented in applications.

Historically, grounds for judicial review include review of a tribunal or official where there is an error of law. A description applied to review of such matters is "illegality." This ground has been considerably broadened in recent years to correct mistakes of law made by inferior bodies, where there was not necessarily any right of appeal. Even where there may be an overlap between an appeal and a review, the courts have a discretion to offer review. A second ground for review is where there is "irrationality." This is defined to mean, as Lord Diplock explained, where the decision[20]: **5–91**

"is so outrageous in its defiance of logic or of accepted moral standards that no sensible person who had applied his mind to the question to be decided could have arrived at it."

This ground affords the opportunity to review the exercise of statutory powers or discretion. The test of "reasonableness" leaves considerable judicial flexibility in how to apply for review which even extends to reviewing inferior courts such as the legal powers of magistrates.

The third ground for judicial review identified by Lord Diplock, is[21] "procedural impropriety." On this ground the correct procedure has not been properly followed. A broader interpretation of procedural impropriety is where the rules of natural justice have been broken. There are two rules of natural justice. The first, is to hear both sides of the case, giving an opportunity to hear each side is a fundamental part of the common law principles developed by the courts. The second is that no one should be a judge in his own cause. Decisions must be made in an unbiased way. An open mind and unprejudiced thinking before the case is presented, is required. Both rules of natural justice require fairness of decision-makers and apply to a wide range of public bodies especially when required by the interests of the litigant. If there is a "legitimate expectation" or if rights are affected then the courts have a discretion to apply such rules. **5–92**

The application for judicial review[22] may succeed if any of the grounds for review outlined above are proven to the court. The granting of a remedy and the ultimate success of the application, is nevertheless discretionary.

---

[20] *Council for Civil Service Unions v. Minister for Civil Service* [1985] A.C. 374.
[21] *ibid.*
[22] A. P. Le Sueur, M. Sunkin, "Applications for Judicial Review: The Requirements of Leave" [1992] P.L. 102.

5. Tribunals and Inquiries

5–93 The nineteenth century witnessed the growth[23] in various forms of adjudication. The Railway and Canal Commission set up in 1888, was a good example of the use of a specialised tribunal, sharing some of the characteristics of a court but specialised in its findings and activities. Appointment to the Railway and Canal Commission consisted of two members appointed by the Home Secretary and a High Court judge nominated by the Lord Chancellor. The Commission was judicial in form and the proceedings resembled those of a court.

In the nineteenth century the use of specialised commissions or tribunals was fairly common but not universal. Not all tribunals conformed to a single pattern. Often there were appeals to the courts. Even the county courts were used occasionally to undertake dispute settlement such as workers compensation disputes.

5–94 While the pattern of growth in adjudicating procedures[24] was uneven, the necessity for adjudication became greater as the Welfare State took shape. State contributed funds for unemployment benefit or sickness benefit to workers increased the scale of state expenditure and also the need for fair and reasonable procedures to solve disputes. The National Insurance Act 1911 provided state benefits and adjudication procedures over unemployment pay were deputed to Insurance Officers appointed by the Board of Trade. Appeals lay to a Court of Referees representing employers, employees and a chairman appointed by the Board of Trade. Often the procedures were cumbersome, complicated and bureaucratic with several levels of decision-making.

5–95 Both World Wars had significant consequences in shaping the role of government and responsibilities accepted by the State. State responsibility or involvement covered pensions payable to the disabled and dependents of the dead killed in action. A plethora of local tribunals assisted in the administration of appeals, known as the Pensions Appeal Tribunals.

Reconstruction of the inter-war economy saw the reorganisation of transport, both road and rail and the streamlining of freight to assist in the regulation of trade and industry. Tribunals were commonplace as an effective way to administer such changes. The Second World War further increased the growth in government powers and the need for new tribunals. The reason was not seen as a reactive one, but

---

[23] M. Sunkin, "The Judicial Review Case-load 1987–89" [1992] P.L. 490.
[24] W. A. Robson, "Administrative Justice and Injustice: A Commentary on the Franks Report" [1958] P.L. 12; W. A. Robson, "Justice and Administrative Law" reconsidered (1979) 32 C.L.P. 107.

proactive, as a means of increasing the availability of welfare services based on need. Tribunals could introduce new policies and new regulatory legislation.

Tribunals mirrored government activities, as the Franks Committee **5–96** observed[25]:

"The continuing extension of governmental activity and responsibility for the general well-being of the community has greatly multiplied the occasions on which an individual may be at issue with the administration or with another citizen or body, as to his rights and the post war years have seen a substantial growth in the importance and activities of tribunals."

The introduction of the modern Welfare State after the Second World War increased benefits payable by the State under the National Insurance Acts 1946 and 1948. Tribunals proliferated with the inherent dangers of increasing government powers. Warnings that the State was too powerful were not slow in coming. First in 1928 with W. A. Robson's *Justice and Administrative Law*[26] which warned against the growth of judicial powers exercised by Ministers and tribunals. A year later Lord Hewart C.J., author of *The New Despotism*,[27] and who had held the offices of Attorney-General and Solicitior General in the post-war Liberal Government, warned, for different political reasons to Robson, of the increase in civil service power and influence.

The concern over the use of the civil service in the machinery of **5–97** tribunals was taken up by the Donoughmore Committee on Ministers' Powers 1932.[28] The Committee made recommendations in an attempt to find some rationalisation of the administrative system. Some tribunals were categorised as "specialised courts of law," others were called "ministerial tribunals." While recognising the value of each, the Committee recommended the use of the former rather than the latter, thus preserving the ad hoc development of the English tribunal system. The Committee left unresolved the value and the merits of tribunals as against courts.[29]

The Second World War had incrementally[30] increased the powers **5–98** granted to Ministers to operate the wartime emergency. Tribunals were required to cope with compensation claims for war damages,

---

[25] D. G. T. Williams, "Public Local Inquiries – Formal Administrative Adjudication" (1980) 29 Int. & Comp. L.Q. 701. Franks Committee, Cmd. 218 (1957).

[26] W. A. Robson, *Justice and Administrative Law* (London, 1928), (2nd ed., 1947) (3rd ed., 1951).

[27] See W. A. Robson, "Justice and Administrative Law" reconsidered (1979) 32 C.L.P. 107; G. Hewart, *The New Despotism* (London, 1929).

[28] Cmd. 4060 (1932).

[29] *ibid.*

[30] Criticism of the report was made. See Robson, *Justice and Administrative Law* (3rd ed., 1951), p. 423.

disability and bereaved persons. Arising out of the question of land acquistion, the Crichel Down affair[31] caused the Government embarrassment. The outcome led to the setting up of a Committee of Administrative Tribunals and Enquiries under Sir Oliver Franks (The Franks Committee), only 25 years after the Donoughmore Committee.

5–99   The Franks Committee considered the constitution and the workings of tribunals other than the ordinary courts of law and examined the workings of such administrative procedures for holding inquiries by or on behalf of the Minister. This was the first occasion that the question of allocation was fairly grasped. The committee examined the distinction between Ministers' powers and tribunals. Franks[32] concluded that both decision-making Ministers and tribunals should share characteristics of openness, fairness and impartiality. Tribunals were "not ordinary courts" and not appendages of government departments. Tribunals were set up for adjudication and were not part of the machinery of administration.

5–100   The outcome was the Tribunals and Inquiries Act 1958 which was later amended in 1966 and consolidated in the Tribunals and Inquiries Act 1971, and 1992. Today there are over 2,000 tribunals covering as Ganz explains[33] "such diverse areas as social security, immigration, employment, rents, taxation, rates and the National Health Service." The existence of such an extensive number of tribunals is a practical response to the need for an adjudication system other than the ordinary courts. Their practical advantages are cheapness, they have less formality than courts, and speed of operation. However, procedures vary according to the tribunal in question and the activity to be regulated. Many are chaired by lawyers and legal representation is not uncommon. There is a Council on Tribunals set up to oversee the operation of tribunals and also inquiries. It has been compared to a Departmental Committee, membership is unpaid and part-time. An annual report is published and the Council operates as a watchdog. There are proposals for its reform and expansion to meet the growing needs and changes in the role of tribunals.

5–101   The Franks Committee also included inquiries within its remit. It separated consideration of inquiries from tribunals but this separation is difficult to make in practice and the legislation currently in force covers both tribunals and inquiries.

The purpose of inquiries outlined by Franks is[34]:

---

[31] W. A. Robson "Administrative Law in England 1919–1948" in G. Campion (ed.), *British Government Since 1918* (London, 1950).

[32] G. Ganz, *Understanding Public Law* (1987) Chaps. 3 & 4, pp. 51–53.

[33] *ibid.*

[34] Franks Committee Cmd. 218 (1957).

"to ensure that the interests of the citizens closely affected should be protected by the grant to them of a statutory right to be heard in support of their objections and to ensure that thereby the Minister should be better informed about the facts of the case."

The contrast between tribunals and inquiries is explained by Wade,[35] who offers a distinction between the respective role of each. Wade argues that a tribunal "finds facts and decides the case by applying legal rules laid down by statute or regulation." An inquiry hears evidence, finds facts "but the person conducting it finally makes a recommendation to a Minister as to how the Minister should act in some question of policy."

However plain this distinction may appear,[36] Parliament has **5–102** experimented with many different procedures which share the characteristics of inquiries and those that share the characteristics of tribunals. Thus the distinction may not always be easy to find. Particularly prevalent in recent years has been the use of public local inquiries associated with housing, town and country planning, motorways and the compulsory acquisition of land. D. G. T. Williams has found no less than 105 statutory provisions incorporating mandatory inquiries. Public local inquiries can be seen as large in scale, expensive in outlay and slow in reaching conclusions when major issues are at stake. For example, the third London Airport, the Sizewell B enquiry into nuclear power generation and a variety of large inquiries on motorway planning. Many of the issues at such inquiries have required intervention by the courts to review the procedures at the inquiries, admissibility of evidence and fairness in cross-examination of witnesses. There is also the ultimate question of whether the Minister ought to accept the decision of the inquiry if there are errors in its conduct.

Both inquiries and tribunals provide for the citizen's consultation and participation in the decision making process. This may be seen as supplementary to the decision of Ministers and the role of Parliament.[37]

---

[35] Ganz, *op. cit.* note 57.
[36] Wade, *Administrative Law* (6th ed. 1988).
[37] D. G. T. Williams, "The Council on Tribunal: The First Twenty Five Years" [1984] P.L. 79.

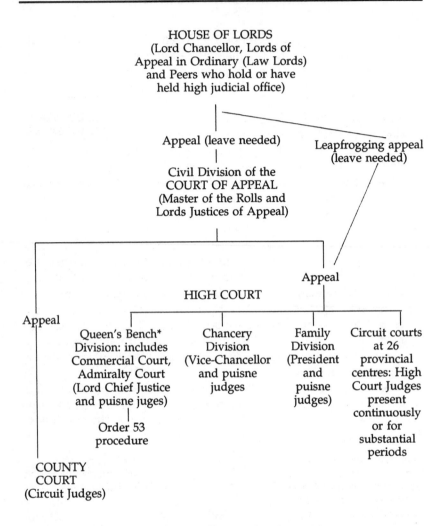

Fig. 1. The civil jurisdiction and appeal structure. (Reproduced from p. 39 Spencer, J.R. (1989) *Jackson's Machinery of Justice* by kind permission of the author and Cambridge University Press. © Cambridge University Press 1989). *Order 53 Procedure.

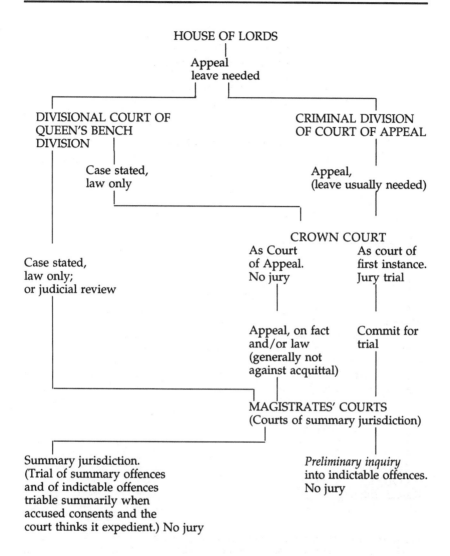

HOUSE OF LORDS
|
Appeal
leave needed

DIVISIONAL COURT OF
QUEEN'S BENCH
DIVISION
|
Case stated,
law only

CRIMINAL DIVISION
OF COURT OF APPEAL
|
Appeal,
(leave usually needed)

CROWN COURT

As Court   As court of
of Appeal.   first instance.
No jury   Jury trial

Case stated,
law only;
or judicial review

Appeal, on fact   Commit for
and/or law   trial
(generally not
against acquittal)

MAGISTRATES' COURTS
(Courts of summary jurisdiction)

Summary jurisdiction.
(Trial of summary offences
and of indictable offences
triable summarily when
accused consents and the
court thinks it expedient.) No jury

Preliminary inquiry
into indictable offences.
No jury

Fig. 2. The criminal jurisdiction and appeal structure. (Reproduced from p. 211 Spencer, J.R. (1989) *Jackson's Machinery of Justice* by kind permission of the author and Cambridge University Press. © Cambridge University Press 1989).

PART II:
Public Law, Politics, Ideas and Influences

Part II of the text book contains three chapters. In Chapter 6 the importance of the electoral system is discussed in terms of representative government. The question of political influences on the institutions of government is examined as part of the overall theme of accountable government. Chapter 7 provides an explanation of the ideas and influences which have shaped the development of public law in the United Kingdom. Chapter 8 explains the European dimension to the United Kingdom's constitutional arrangements including membership of the European Union.

Chapter 6

The Electorate, Politics and The Constitution

1. Introduction

Representative democracy is one of the most important measure- **6–01**
ments to judge the success of an electoral system.[1] In the United
Kingdom the trust that resides in Parliament to hold government to
account also gives rise to the idea that citizens have a right to
participate in the electoral process for the selection of members of the
House of Commons. There is no electoral process for the House of
Lords. The concepts of citizenship and participation depend on an
effective electoral system. As Blackburn[2] has observed:

> "The crucial democratic link between politicians and people — or
> government and the governed — is the electoral system. The
> quality of that electoral system itself determines the quality of our
> democracy."

Yet oddly for many commentators[3] in the United Kingdom supreme
authority has never resided in the people. Over the past few decades
great attention has been given to the question of whether the current
electoral system in the United Kingdom lives up to these high ideals.
No one can doubt that the debate on electoral reform is an important
element in any healthy deomcracy. In the United Kingdom that
debate has been added to by the demand for a referendum for the
introduction of the common currency under the European Monetary
System. There is the recent experience of a referendum for the
introduction of devolution in Scotland and Wales.

---

[1] See Robert Blackburn, *The Electoral System in Britain* (Macmillan, St Martin's Press,
1995).
[2] *ibid.* p. 1.
[3] See C. Turpin, *British Government and the Constitution* Butterworths third edition 1995,
p. 417.

6–02   The purpose of this chapter is to explain the United Kingdom's system of parliamentary elections. The United Kingdom is described as having representative and responsible government within a parliamentary democracy. The nature of that democracy depends on the electoral system. The relative political stability of the United Kingdom is attributed to the electoral system and the development of strong political parties. Strong political choices are evident in the electoral results on May 1, 1997 which provides the new government with a large majority after a large number of electoral defeats since 1979.

6–03   The modern system of parliamentary elections gradually evolved from the nineteenth century. Progress towards universal adult franchise and the elimination of election corruption was gradual. The development of the present electoral system is due more to pragmatism than the adoption of a theoretical ideal system. No pretence is made that present arrangements are ideal, rather that they produce strong government and therefore are seen to leave choice with the electorate.

Elected government raises questions about accountability, the representative nature of government and the powers of government in the House of Commons. Also important are the growth and influence of political parties and the use of the electoral manifesto and public opinion when considering how the policies of government are made. Increasingly relevant are the influences of pressure groups, the media and the press on government policy-making.

6–04   Constitutional lawyers are particularly concerned with the question of how parliamentary accountability and sovereignty are compatible; this raises one of the most difficult issues under the United Kingdom's constitutional arrangements. Johnson, writing[4] in 1975, fears that over the years there has been "a retreat from constitutional ways of thinking in Britain." This makes it more difficult to set limits on the powers of government and uncertainty arises as to the principles which govern many of "the institutions and practices, political habits and modes of behaviour."

6–05   In recent times criticism of the electoral system has focused on two issues. First, what may be termed "institutional" criticism summarised by Ganz[5] to mean: "that the elected part of Parliament, namely the House of Commons, having achieved supremacy over the unelected parts, namely the Queen and the House of Lords have summoned its sovereignty to the government which controls it through the party machine." This represents a profound challenge to the idea of elected and accountable democratic government. Second, criticism is made that the United Kingdom's electoral system of "first

---

[4] See N. Johnson, *In Search of the Constitution* (1977), pp. vii–viii. See table 1, p. 212.
[5] G. Ganz, *Understanding Public Law* (1991).

past the post" has a discriminatory effect against minority parties. The United Kingdom and recently Italy, stand out from other European countries in adopting a first past the post system of elections. This is said to favour strong government with a decisive majority. In fact, coalition governments were not uncommon before the Second World War when governments were formed on a multi-party arrangement.[6] Election results, since the Second World War, show a marked disparity between votes cast and seats gained in the House of Commons. Turpin notes that a party can be put in power with far less than a majority of votes and may govern without having to accommodate its policies to the interests of a majority of voters represented by the other parties in Parliament.

Such alleged unfairness in the voting system[7] has resulted in calls for reform of the present electoral system and the introduction of some form of proportional representation.[8]

2. Parliamentary Democracy, Origins, Ideas and Influences

Different meanings are accorded to the idea of democracy. In **6–06** countries with written constitutions, it is customary to locate the sources of power, the authority of the constitution and the basis of law as resting on the people.[9] This is an aspiration, even an ideal that may be unattainable given the reality of how power is in fact exercised. Such constitutional idealism places individual rights at the centre of the values which are sought to be protected. This creates a constitutional tradition where the political and legal institutions are made to conform to set values and rights. In such a tradition the protection of minorities or diverse groups is made an aspiration as part of the creation of a stable and diverse community. Such a tradition of constitutional idealism is illustrated in countries such as the United States which offer individual rights and constitutional protections as part of their constitutional arrangements. Even countries with one party states may offer constitutional arrangements which appear to give democratic authority to the people as a means of providing some form of legitimacy for government.

---

[6] The dates of governments so formed are : 1915, 1916, 1924, 1929, 1931 and 1940. See G. Marshall and G. Moodie, *Some Problems of the Constitution* (1968), p. 54.

[7] A full discussion is provided in V. Bogdanor, *The People and the Party System* (1981), p. 205; P. Dunleavy and C. T. Husbands, *British Democracy at the Crossroads* (1985).

[8] P. Norton, "Does Britain Need Proportional Representation?" in R. Blackburn, *Constitutional Studies* (Mansell, 1992), p. 136.

[9] See the United States Constitution and the Japanese Constitution drafted on the American model in 1946.

6–07   In the United Kingdom, history and tradition have contributed to a different political tradition[10] than the constitutional idealism discussed above. Solutions are worked out according to experience and institutions are expected to operate flexibly and develop as a response to experience and the needs of the time. The United Kingdom's tradition developed historically and the principles which have influenced its development such as parliamentary sovereignty, conventions and majority government, are a reflection of that political development.

6–08   The evolution of parliamentary democracy and the ideals of democracy fit uneasily within the doctrine of parliamentary sovereignty.[11] This is better understood when two different meanings of sovereignty are compared. First, legal sovereignty, as outlined in earlier chapters, is far removed from the people, as it is vested to the Crown in Parliament. A government with an overall majority is more free than in most other democratic countries to introduce its own legislative programmes with the likelihood of their passage into law. As in theory Parliament is free "to make or unmake any law," this provides considerable scope for government to exercise public power.

Second there is political sovereignty. Political sovereignty emphasises the elected nature and authority of government. Political scientists[12] find it helpful to understand that the legitimacy of government depends on its elected and representative nature. Constitutional lawyers have been greatly influenced by Dicey's attempts to reconcile parliamentary sovereignty with popular franchise.

(a)   Dicey, Parliamentary Sovereignty and Popular Democracy

6–09   Reforms in the electoral franchise in 1832 and 1867 gradually moved the United Kingdom towards a popular franchise. Existing governmental institutions survived but were subtly changed. Effectively the House of Commons became the centre of political power and determined the composition of the government. There was no fixed idea of democratic government and no theoretical model to which political and legal institutions were expected to conform. Instead parliamentary democracy gradually evolved.

6–10   Dicey's[13] vision of constitutional and administrative law in the United Kingdom and how any extension of the franchise might be

---

[10] The common law tradition is an apt description of the U.K.'s approach to constitutional law and is more fully discussed in Chap. 7. See Loughlin, "Tinkering with the Constitution" (1988) 51 M.L.R. 531, 536; P. Norton, The British Polity (1985). Also the discussion in C. McCrudden, "Northern Ireland and the British Constitution" in Jowell and Oliver, The Changing Constitution (Oxford, 1989), pp. 298–299.

[11] See Loughlin, Public Law and Political Theory (1992), pp. 140–156.

[12] See Johnson, op. cit., note 1.

[13] June 13, 1880 Nation. Dicey's influence is discussed in Chaps. 1, 5 and 7. Here we are concerned with the question of how Dicey's influence may be perceived by modern writers on political theory.

accommodated within existing frameworks and institutions, is relevant in understanding how parliamentary sovereignty and popular franchise challenged the established order. Dicey recognised the importance of legal sovereignty but conveniently distinguished legal from political sovereignty. In his essay[14] "Democracy in England in 1880" Dicey outlined his belief that "English democracy depended on love of order, the spirit of ordinary morality as the guide to public life and of constitutional morality" and in Dicey's view secured the sovereignty of the people. The clear implication was that political power must be tempered by obedience to the norms of the constitution – a view advanced out of fear that popular franchise posed a threat to the natural order maintained under the Constitution.

Dicey's attempt to reconcile his vision of democracy with his description of the main constitutional doctrines in the Constitution was fundamentally challenged both by his contemporaries and recent writers. His thesis rested on two premises. First, that the power of Parliament could be used to control government because "the will of the nation" was represented in the House of Commons. Second, that democracy could be "self-correcting" namely, the flexibility inherent in an unwritten constitution allowed change but preserved the sovereignty of Parliament and the rule of law. **6–11**

The challenge to Dicey's views came from contemporary writers of the period and succeeded in convincing Dicey of some errors in his views, which received a belated acknowledgement from Dicey in his later writing.[15] However this did not cause any major re-think of the propositions Dicey advanced. Dicey's attempted reconciliation of the rule of law and sovereignty of Parliament revealed further weaknesses in his own analysis.

A number of conclusions may be deduced from Dicey's formulation of constitutional principles with the experience of democratic, elected and popular government. First, when the rule of law is challenged by Parliament, it is parliamentary sovereignty which remains supreme. Craig[16] observes: **6–12**

"If the majority within Parliament does enact legislation which is detrimental to minority interests, no sanctions can be expected from the Common law. When representative democracy proves incapable of aligning the interests of the elected representatives with the nation as a whole, so that some are constitutionally

---

[14] A. V. Dicey, *13 June 1880 Nation;* J. F. McEldowney, "Dicey in Historical Perspective – A Review Essay" in McEldowney and McAuslan, *Law, Legitimacy and the Constitution* (1985), pp. 47–60.

[15] Loughlin, *op. cit.*

[16] P. Craig, *Public Law and Democracy in the U.K. and USA* (Oxford, 1991).

disadvantaged, the oppressed can but hope for a shift in their political fortune."

6–13   Secondly, the "advance in democracy" whereby the franchise was broadened, hastened the development of party politics. Votes were won rather than bought. The Executive demanded more control over the activities of the Commons as Cabinet Committees proliferated; delegated legislation increased in range and extent and gradually power moved from the Commons to the Executive. These developments put strain on Dicey's vision of the ideal constitution to the extent that it may be questioned whether it destroyed the vision entirely. In Dicey's later writings contained in his lectures[17] on the *Relation between Law and Public Opinion in England during the Nineteenth Century* (1905), Dicey refined and broadened his understanding of democracy as including either a social condition or a form of government. The former he drew from de Tocqueville that democracy created "a state of things under which there exists a general equality of rights and a similarity of conditions of thoughts, of sentiments and of ideals." The latter, influenced by Austin, he defined in its "older sense" to mean "a form of government; namely a constitution under which sovereign power is possessed by the numerical majority of the male citizens."

6–14   Dicey recognised the changes brought about by the extension of the franchise but he found it difficult to assess their significance within the conceptual framework of the constitution. He explained the[18] "advance of democracy" as a fitting description for the transfer of "supreme power" from either a single person or from a privileged and limited class, to the majority of the citizens. Throughout his life and in his writings, Dicey attempted to reconcile both the conflicting nature of the United Kingdom's constitutional arrangements and conflicts in his own thinking. Dicey warned about the dangers of democracy in action. While supporting the extension of the franchise in 1832, he began to doubt its efficiency in 1867 and 1884 when Irish Home Rule[19] and the demands for the franchise for women became part of the political agenda. He warned of the dangers of strict party discipline, and feared the restriction of individual liberty and the growth of administrative bureaucracy.[20]

6–15   Dicey found the referendum mechanism a useful tool to counterbalance the tendency to party politics in government which he feared

[17] P. Craig, "Dicey, Unitary, Self-Correcting Democracy" (Jan., 1990) 106 L.Q.R. 105–143.
[18] A term used by Dicey in his book: A. V. Dicey, *Lectures on the Relation between Law and Public Opinion in England during the Nineteenth Century* (1905).
[19] See J. McEldowney, *op. cit.*, note 11 on pp. 47–49.
[20] *ibid.*

contributed to the decline of Parliament's prestige. A referendum also emphasised the role of the people as part of the political sovereignty of the nation. Dicey's vision of the unity of the United Kingdom provides a link between elections to Parliament and through the House of Commons, the authority of the government of the day. That vision is an uncomplicated vision of a single unitary State wherein change could easily be accommodated through the politics of the day, while guarded against by the morality of the Constitution through the supremacy of the law. Conventions of the Constitution provided "a modern code" but undoubtedly it distracted the balance implicit in Dicey's "self correcting" vision of the Constitution.

Contemporary writers such as Bagehot[21] realised that parliamen-   **6–16** tary democracy did not always entail the "election of just and moderate men." Legislation might distort and change the fundamentals of the Constitution. Instead of representative democracy, policies became party political dominated by a single leader, controlling a Cabinet government. Belatedly, Dicey recognised this threat in the form of Home Rule in Ireland and in the passage of administrative legislation granting wide discretion, largely unsupervised, to administrators.

Craig[22] concludes how Dicey's influence has endured despite much criticism and weakness in his analysis:

> "The realisation that political and social developments had undermined many of the premises upon which Dicey has built his constitutional doctrine was never truly appreciated by the immediate successors to Dicey in the field of constitutional scholarship. They were content to draw upon Dicey's conclusions without ever evaluating the reasoning through which those conclusions were reached."

By the end of the nineteenth century parliamentary democracy   **6–17** brought with it, the recognition that party discipline might curtail the independence of individual M.P.s; that debate in the House of Commons may be curtailed by procedures which favoured the Executive; and that the Cabinet rather than the House of Commons, exercised real political power. This leaves unresolved the question raised by Turpin that "if the people were acknowledged in constitutional theory as the source of political authority debates on these matters would be conducted in different terms." In a similar way Keir writing about parliamentary democracy for the period 1867–1937

---

[21] W. Bagehot, R. S. Crossman (ed.), *The English Constitution* (1867) (London and Glasgow, 1963).

[22] Craig, *op. cit.*

identified the "distinctive characteristics" within the United Kingdom's constitutional arrangements which may influence future developments[23]:

"In the modern state, an extended executive able to make, enforce, and interpret law, has come into being under imperfect parliamentary and judicial control. The principles of the separation of powers have been violated. Considerations of "policy and government" as they would have been called in the seventeenth century, have been accorded a larger place in the constitution than they have held for two hundred years."

The life cycle of politics means that political power is constantly shifting, while the institutions of government remain remarkably static.

6–18   One of the remarkable features of the United Kingdom's political system is the two-party system. Government and a single "official opposition" is mainly a reflection of the electoral system and has a physical manifestation in the architectural design and shape of the House of Commons. Thus adversarial politics are encouraged and seen as part of the political culture of the country. The failure of smaller parties to make any inroads into the power of the Conservative or Labour party is also a feature of the existing state of the political parties. The major parties seem remarkably agile at providing a broad range of options to favour the widest possible appeal. In fact, as Colley has observed[24]:

" . . . since 1885 the Conservatives have been the single dominant party for 85 years. By contrast, in only 18 of these 107 years has a single party other than the Conservatives had a clear Commons majority. In other words, the one party dominance that characterised British politics so often in the 18th and 19th centuries has become if anything still more pronounced in this century."

(b)   Parliamentary Franchise 1832-1948

6–19 The Representation of the People Act 1832, known as the Great Reform Act, represents the starting point for modern[25] elected government. The 1832 Act was intended to broaden the franchise and

---

[23] See Turpin, *British Government and the Constitution* (3rd ed., 1995) pp. 416–473; Keir, *Constitutional History of Modern Britain* (1938), p. 520.

[24] Linda Colley," The Illusion of a Two-Party State" *The Independent*, October 28, 1992.

[25] D. E. Butler, *The Electoral System in Britain since 1918* (2nd ed., 1963); D. Butler, *Governing without a Majority: Dilemmas for Hung Parliaments in Britain* (1983).

introduce a more fair and representative system of elections. Keir described the reforms as introducing[26]:

"organic changes which reflected the increasing ascendancy of the radical thought stimulated by Bentham[27] and reinforced by the democratic impulse received from the doctrine of the French revolution."

The Act maintained the influence of property rights, but property other than land fulfilled the qualification necessary to be included within the franchise.[28] Old boroughs were abolished, and the population shift to the towns was for the first time represented in the franchise. New boroughs were created and this process of reform applied throughout the country. The 40 shilling freeholder was retained but an additional residence qualification was added. New qualifications in terms of copyholders, leaseholders and tenants at will with rent not less than £50, were included.

In counties,[29] tenants at will were retained and this preserved and **6–20** continued the landlord's influence. An entirely new qualification, that of the £10 occupier was created. The outcome of these reforms was to increase the electorate by 50 per cent adding 217,000 to the electoral total of those qualified to vote.

The significance of the 1832 Act was remarkable. In previous chapters we have noted how, in constitutional terms, incremental change accompanied organic growth. Reform of the electorate introduced by the 1832 Act, resulted in a marked shift in political power and influence from the unelected to the elected. This change only became noticeable gradually. In the case of patronage and royal influence the decline in royal power over the Cabinet had been gradual. In 1834 after royal attempts to influence the appointment of the Prime Minister and Ministers through the selection of Sir Robert Peel, Peel failed to obtain a majority at a general election and royal influence was rejected.

The 1832 Act also introduced a new procedure for registration of voters. This began a process of law reform which proved significant in shaping the modern law.

In 1867 the Representation of the People Act introduced the vote **6–21** for many urban workers and extended new categories of eligible

---

[26] D. Keir, *Constitutional History, op. cit.* p. 595.

[27] Bentham, *Introduction to the Principle of Morals and Legislation* (1888).

[28] See Keir, *op. cit.*

[29] Catholic emancipation was granted in 1829 admitting Roman Catholics on a declaration, in lieu of the oath of supremacy, to both Houses of Parliament, all corporate offices and most judicial positions except Lord Chancellor of England, Lord Lieutenant or Lord Chancellor of Ireland. The latter post was filled in 1869 by Thomas O'Hagan.

voters in boroughs to include lodgers and certain occupations. Even after 1867, the electorate was entirely male and this principle had been upheld by the courts.[30] A further extension of the franchise was achieved under the 1884 Representation of the People Act which, by extending the franchise to certain householders in counties, enfranchised agricultural workers.

It is difficult to estimate the effects of both the 1867 Act and the 1884 Representation of the People Act as many qualified voters may have failed to register. It is estimated that apparently only 60 per cent of adult males were on the register before 1914.[31]

6–22   In 1918 a considerable achievement was made in introducing universal adult male suffrage, by sweeping away the old complex property qualification. Instead of property, there was a residence qualification, requiring living in the constituency or adjoining constituency six months before a qualifying date. There was also a business and university qualification. This shift from property to residence as the basis of the qualification significantly broadened the franchise. For the first time a limited franchise for women over 30 was granted and in 1928 for women over 21.

In 1945 the Representation of the People Act joined the local government franchise[32] to that of central government. Three years later the business and university franchise was removed thus introducing the principle of "one man one vote." The 1948 Representation of the People Act also provided that only one member of Parliament should be returned for each constituency. The modern system of popular vote or univeral franchise had been achieved.

3.   The Electorate

(a)   The Franchise

6–23 Since 1948 a number of changes in the franchise have been made in the direction of further refining the principle of universal franchise. First, the voting age was lowered from 21 to 18 in 1969 under the Representation of the People Act 1969. The age period for entitlement to be on the electoral register is based on whether the citizen reaches 18 during the period of the register. As soon as the citizen reaches 18 he or she may vote. Secondly, for the first time under the 1969 Act,

---

[30] *Chorlton v. Lings* (1868–69) 4 L.R.C.P. 374 held women were not entitled to vote.
[31] C. O'Leary, *The Elimination of Corrupt Practices in British Elections 1868–1911* (1961).
[32] See Chap. 12.

merchant seamen may register as if they were resident at a home address or hostel. Thirdly, the Representation of the People Act 1985 introduced overseas voting. Any British citizen resident overseas, provided their residence within the United Kingdom was within the preceding five years, is entitled to vote.[33] The Representation of the People Act 1993 makes additional arrangements for members of the forces and service personnel to facilitate their voting rights.

Qualification for inclusion on the register requires: residence; **6–24** citizenship of the Commonwealth or of the Republic of Ireland; the age qualification discussed above and that the citizen should not be subject to any legal incapacity. Disqualification from the franchise extends to aliens, minors, peers, persons serving prison sentences or unlawfully at large and persons convicted of contempt or illegal election practices. Disenfranchisement of the last two groups is for a period of five years.[34]

Residence for electoral purposes requires "some degree of perma- **6–25** nence;" students at universities are so qualified.[35] Temporary absence from permanent residence does not disqualify. It is possible, there-fore, to be resident at more than one address and be registered in the relevant constituency. However, it is not permissible to vote in more than one constituency at the same parliamentary election. The Regis-tration List of Electors is subject to correction by the courts[36] or the Registration Officer.

Despite the popularity of exercising the franchise, with high turnouts[37] for most parliamentary elections at both general elections and by-elections, failure to register on the electoral register is not confined to a small number. It is estimated that almost 2 million failed to register at the general election in 1992: in England and Wales more than 1.8 million of the 40.4 million people who were of voting age did not register; in Scotland almost 124,000 of the 4 million eligible, did not register.[38] The total electorate is over 43 million.

(b) Constituency Boundaries

Since 1911, section 7 of the Parliament Act 1911, has required the **6–26** maximum duration of Parliament to be five years. Any extension of the five year period may be provided only through Act of Parliament.

---

[33] Representation of the People Act 1985, ss.1–3. See s.59 of the Representation of the People Act 1993.

[34] *ibid.*

[35] *Fox v. Stirk* [1970] 2 Q.B. 463 and see ss.1(4) and 61(2)(a) of the Representation of the People Act 1983.

[36] See *Hipperson v. Newbury Electoral Officer* [1985] Q.B. 1060. In Northern Ireland see *McGrory v. Hendron and Another* [1993] 5 B.N.I.L. 48.

[37] Turnout at elections averages well over 70%. See Turpin, British Government and the Constitution (1990), pp. 524–525. At the 1983 election, 72.7%; in 1987, 75.3%; in 1992, 80.0%.

[38] *The Independent,* November 9, 1992.

The United Kingdom is divided into 651 constituencies each sending one Member of Parliament to the House of Commons. Constituency size is roughly around 65,000 people though there are variations on this. The drawing up of constituency boundaries, a key feature of the reformed electoral arrangements since 1832, is one of the most controversial issues of electoral practice. Electoral boundaries may be *the* most crucial matter when determining electoral results.

6-27   Since 1944, for central government, there are four permanent and independent Boundary Commissions for England, Scotland, Wales and Northern Ireland. The Speaker is chairman of each Commission with a deputy chairman appointed from the High Court. In Scotland it is the Court of Session, the equivalent to the English High Court.

Reports from the Boundary Commission are laid before the House of Commons by the Secretary of State together with a draft Order in Council to give effect to the Commissions' recommendations. The draft order must be approved by resolution of each House[39] before the final order is approved by the Queen in Council.

6-28   This process is not without problems. In 1969 the then Labour government was in receipt of the Commissions' recommendation in April. No action was taken until June, notwithstanding the obligation to take action "as soon as may be" possible to lay a resolution before the House of Commons. When the resolutions were laid, no attendant Orders in Council accompanied the proposals. A Bill intended to implement the proposals and providing the Home Secretary with immunity because of any breach of duty was introduced. The Bill did not pass the House of Lords.

6-29   Mandamus was sought by an elector, Mr McWhirter, to compel[39a] the Home Secretary to lay a draft Order in Council in accordance with the 1949 and 1958 Acts. The Home Secretary duly agreed to comply and the mandamus application was withdrawn. In the event a Bill was introduced with a positive recommendation by the Government to reject it. The Government used its majority and in that event the Bill was rejected. The Government had made use of its majority to influence the outcome, when the spirit of the arrangements was intended to prevent direct political intervention by the government of the day. The ensuing election had to be fought on the old 1954 boundaries and not the new ones. After 1970 when the Conservative Government was returned the new boundaries were implemented.

6-30   The controversial nature of the drawing up of the boundaries was recognised when Parliament set up the Boundary Commission[40] with

---

[39] See H. F. Rawlings, *Law and the Electoral Process* (London, 1988), pp. 24–72.
[39a] Rawlings, pp. 52, 54. *R. v. Home Secretary, ex p. McWhirter, The Times*, October 20, 1969.
[40] *ibid.*

rules contained in the 1949 and 1958 Acts. The events outlined above showed how a cynical use of power could frustrate Parliament's intentions.

There is no exact science in drawing up constituency boundaries and predicting the outcome of any proposed changes is often difficult. An attempt to set out legislative rules for the line drawing of constitutency boundaries was made in 1986. The Parliamentary Constituencies Act 1986 consolidated previous legislation, and in Schedule 2 contains rules for the redistribution of seats. Each Commission must carry out a general review of constituency boundaries in its part of the United Kingdom at intervals of not less than 10 or more than 15 years. Particular areas may be given an interim review. Such an interim report was made in 1989 recommending changes to Milton Keynes in Buckinghamshire because of population growth.

The rules are complex and difficult to interpret. Broadly they are as **6–31** follows, Rule 1 sets the number of seats for each of the four parts of the United Kingdom, Rule 2 requires that only one member may be retained for each constituency. Rule 3 applies to the city of London only. Rules 4-6 sets out how boundaries are to be drawn for each constituency. Rule 7 provides for any variation or departure from the rules set out in Rules 4–6, but there is considerable scope for interpretation of each of the rules.[41]

At present the rules provide that there are a minimum number of **6–32** seats. This means a minimum of not substantially greater or less than 613 seats for England, 71 for Scotland, 35 for Wales and from 16 to 18 seats for Northern Ireland. Controversy surrounds the interpretation of Rule 1, as the rules so interpreted with a minimum number of seats indicated, may appear to give undue preference to Scotland, Wales and Northern Ireland. Calculations if based on the removal of each region's guaranteed minimum would mean reductions: Scotland 12 seats, Northern Ireland 1, Wales 6 and England would gain 19. In 1991 the average electorate in constituencies in England was 69,279, in Wales 58,086 and in Scotland 54,369. Rawlings has pointed out[42]:

"the Commission will clearly be well advised not to allow an excessive growth in Welsh and Scottish constituencies given that the seat minimum set out in rule 1 even if not exceeded, still incorporate a substantial measure of over-representation."

Such imbalance may appear odd in a modern electoral system, but this is a reflection of the historical development of electoral rules. Northern Ireland received additional seats after the demise of the

---

[41] Rawlings, p. 34.
[42] *ibid.*

system of government with its own elected Parliament under the Government of Ireland Act 1920. Adjustments to the seats accorded to the four geographical regions might have to be made if some form of devolution government were to be introduced in Northern Ireland, Scotland or Wales.

6–33   Interpretation of Rules 4 and 5 involves how the boundaries of each seat should be determined. Rule 4 provides principles for local government boundaries. Rule 5 provides the objective for the drawing up of the boundaries, namely the achievement of equal sized constituencies in numerical numbers of electors.

Reconciliation of Rules 4 and 5 is controversial and was the basis of an important challenge in the courts by the Labour Party in 1983. Some explanation of each rule is required.

6–34   Rule 4 involves the Commission determining an electoral boundary for each constituency taking account of local government boundaries. Since 1976 the changes in population growth and in the movement from inner cities to outlying regions caused distortion in the sizes of constituency electorates. This resulted in disparity between constituencies, with nearly 30 per cent over quota in one example of the proposed constituencies of Hornsey and Wood Green and nearly 15 per cent under quota in Hendon South.

Rule 5 involves the Commission setting an electoral quota[43] taking account "as far as is practicable" of the geographical limits set for the local government boundaries. The application of this principle of equal constituencies in terms of number of electors, was rendered almost impossible by the requirements of the local government boundaries set out in Rule 4.

6–35   In 1982 the Commission completed its Review and made proposals to correct imbalances between constituencies taking account of the demographic changes mentioned above. A number of constituencies were removed from the Greater London Council area. In order to keep within the physical limitations of Rule 5, great distortion arose in the constituency size in terms of the number of voters represented. The two examples of Hornsey and Wood Green, and Hendon South showed the disparity. Criticism was made that the Commission's proposals violated the principle of one vote having equal value, in every constituency.[44]

6–36   The Labour party believed the proposals were unfavourable to their electoral prospects. Before the Boundary Commission Report was brought before Parliament, and to avoid exclusion from judicial review by the courts once the Report was approved, the Labour party through its then leader, Mr Foot, sought the remedies of prohibition

---

[43] Quoted in Turpin at p. 420.
[44] *ibid.*

and injunction against the Boundary Commission. Their contention was based on two arguments:

(1) That the Commission had failed to give proper weight to Rule 5 containing the principle of equal representation between constituencies.

(2) The Commission was failing in its duty to propose constituencies which crossed county and London borough boundaries. The point of this argument was to insist that the Commission ought to give primacy to Rule 5 in practice.

Unsuccessful in the Divisional Court, the applicants appealed to the **6–37** Court of Appeal. Sir John Donaldson first asserted the correctness of the courts' powers to check whether Ministers or local authorities or other bodies including the Commission had exercised their powers according to law – "the courts can and will interfere in the defence of the ordinary citizen." He went on to conclude[45] as between Rules 4 and 5:

> "The requirement of electoral equality (Rule 5) is, subject to the second limb of Rule 5, subservient to the requirements that constituencies shall not cross county or London borough boundaries."

The second limb of Rule 5 authorises departure from Rule 4 only where[46] "it is desirable to avoid an excessive disparity between the electorate of any constituency and the electoral quota." However in the argument advanced by the Labour Party it was claimed that the Commission had exercised their *discretion* wrongly. The Court of Appeal concluded that the Commission had exercised such a discretion but it was exercised on sufficient grounds. Any objection based on this argument was rejected by the court.

The Court of Appeal upheld the Commission's proposals and rejected the application, leave was later refused to the House of Lords.

One effect of the courts' interpretation is the primacy and respect **6–38** for local government boundaries (Rule 4) over equal representation between constituencies (Rule 5). However, the Court of Appeal entered a *caveat* in certain circumstances where disparity between electoral boundaries might be unacceptable[47]:

> "the theoretical possibility that in a given instance the disparity between the electorate of a proposed constituency and the electoral

[45] Cornelius O'Leary, *The Elimination of Corrupt Practices in British Elections 1868–1911* (1962).
[46] *R. v. Boundary Commission for England, ex p. Foot* [1983] 1 Q.B. 600 at 603.
[47] *ibid.*

quota might be so grotesquely large as to make it obvious in the figures that no reasonable commission which had paid any attention at all to rule 5 could possibly have made such a proposal."

Leaving open the possibility of reviewing any disparity in the electoral quota which is "grotesquely large" for the future, must cause the Boundary Commission difficulty for the years ahead in the balance needed between Rules 4 and 5. In fact up until the *Foot* case the courts have shown remarkable consistency in self-restraint in this area. This is shown in the judgement of Oliver L.J. in the *Foot* case arguing that judicial intervention is inappropriate in boundary disputes. For the future it might be advisable to reconsider the formula "as near the electoral quota as possible" and substitute precise guidelines to the Boundary Commission in terms of the percentage of divergence which is permissible.

6–39   Such criticisms are not shared by all commentators. As M.P.s are said to be constituency trained they will not favour cross-boundary constituency work which may entail two or more local authorities. Departure from local boundaries adds to the Boundary Commission's task and complexity. Perhaps the most difficult problem at the heart of the matter is how to preserve community participation in electoral activities, when shifts in population change the nature of the community. However, popularity of voting has not been inhibited by boundary changes. Electoral turn-out at central government elections is well over 70 per cent of the electorate so it may be asked, do electoral boundaries really matter? The answer depends largely on party politics. It is rather difficult to find any precise constitutional basis for any objection to the electoral system. There is a sense of constitutional propriety, meaning that government may lose its political authority if it does not pay sufficient attention to the electorate.[48] In theory government is said to be representative, even if in practice the Commission appears to need to be given greater priority to achieve equality between constituencies.

(c)   Elections

6–40   Regulation of the conduct of elections is provided for by a number of statutes. The Representation of the People Acts 1983 and 1985 apply to election campaigns, election expenditure and the conduct of elections.[48a]

Nomination papers must be submitted to a returning officer signed by the proposer, seconder and containing eight other electors. A

[48] See R. Blackburn, *The Electoral System in Britain* (1995).
[48a] Rawlings, *Law and the Electoral Process*, p. 134.

system of deposits is used, these are forfeited if the candidate fails to obtain one-twentieth of the votes cast. The deposit is usually set at £500 though proposals to increase this amount have received a mixed reaction.

A more controversial issue, and one of considerable importance in **6–41** the winning of elections, is the question of election expenditure. Since the end of the nineteenth century, the Corrupt and Illegal Practices Prevention Act 1883 established a limit on election expenses for each candidate.[49] The principle adopted related not to national campaigns but to the limitations set on individual candidates at constituency level. These remain today. Expenditure on national campaigns is not restricted by legal controls over their financial funding. Rawlings attributes the focus on constituency control as a reflection of the role of the House of Commons and individual M.P.s within the constituency[50]:

"This perception of the House as 'a geographical representation of the United Kingdom' or a 'congress of constituencies', inevitably directs attention to the regulation of constituency electioneering, whereas a system providing for a mass poll of the citizens might lend legislators to formulate rules dealing with the national campaigning that would inevitably ensue."

The 1883 Act also limited the number of people a candidate could employ as campaign helpers. It also placed liability for expenditure on the candidate. Arising out of the 1883 legislation, detailed regulatory arrangements were put in place.

These controls based on the 1883 Act exist today but are supple- **6–42** mented by the Representation of the People Act 1983. Personal expenses are permitted and are broadly defined but they are required to be reasonable and must be included in the electoral returns made by the candidate's Parliamentary election agent.[51] Oliver notes that the limits are updated from time to time with no statutory provision for automatic index-linking.[52]

Campaign expenditure is also widely defined and under sections 73–75 of the 1983 Act, any expenditure other than that authorised by the candidate or agent is prohibited. This covers a miscellaneous and

---

[49] The present limit for each candidate is approximately £3,648 plus an additional 4.1p for every registered voter in a County constitution or 3.1p in a Borough constituency.
[50] Rawlings, *Law and the Electoral Process*, p. 141. Also see the Bribery Act 1729.
[51] *ibid.*
[52] D. Oliver, "Fairness and Political Finance: The Case of Election Campaigns" in R. Blackburn, *Constitutional Studies* (Mansell, 1992), p. 120. An estimated £5,000–£6,000 per candidate was spent in the 1987 election.

broadly defined category "on account of or in respect of the conduct or management of the election." This clause has been interpreted by the courts to cover expenditure which is intended to assist the election of the candidate by preventing the election of another candidate. The key words are "promoting or providing the election of a candidate."[53]

6–43   The various controls on elections apply to expenditure before, during and after an election. The main question is whether the expenditure was concerned with the conduct or management of an individual campaign. However, with the advent of modern electoral techniques it is difficult to determine when the election campaign begins and ends. The same point is also relevant to local government elections.[54]

Given the blurring of the lines between the start of formal election campaigning and continuous electoral techniques of persuasion, or promoting the merits of a particular political party, the question arises as to whether a more satisfactory arrangement is required? Rawlings makes the point that[55]:

"it appears to be accepted that expenditure undertaken by a prospective parliamentary candidate will not normally be considered as counting towards election expenses, at least if undertaken before the dissolution of Parliament (or issue of the writ in a by-election."

Further it is also accepted that expenses may be set running, indirectly, long before the declaration of candidacy.

6–44   The present regulation of electoral expenses seems not to accord with current practices, well established and intended to make use of the gaps in the present arrangements. At present the average maximum is about £6,000 per candidate. On average candidates for the three main parties spend under £4,000 each. It appears that the effect of Part II of the 1983 Act does not control expenditure on advertising in the national press during a general election. Figures for the national campaign reveal the extent of the differences in expenditure during elections between the major parties. For example in 1987 taken together the total expenditure was about £15 million. Conservatives

---

[53] Rawlings, *op. cit.* p. 141. Also see R. J. Clayton (ed.) *Parker's Conduct of Parliamentary Elections* (1990). In the *Tronoh Mines* case [1952] 1 All E.R. 697, a company criticised the Labour Party by inserting an advertisement setting out the call for a strong government and arguing against the policy of the Labour Party to introduce a scheme of dividend restraint.

[54] Rawlings, *op. cit.* p. 141.

[55] *ibid.* See *Paying for Politics: the Report of the Hansard Society Commission upon the Financing of Political Parties* (1981).

spent £9 million, Labour £4.2 million and the Alliance roughly £2 million. In the 1992 general election campaign expenditure consisted of £10.1 million for the Conservatives, £7.1 million for Labour and the Liberal democrats spent £2.1 million. There is general concern about the extent of election expenditure.[56] Compared to other countries the amount spent in the United Kingdom is small. In the USA one reason for the large amount spent on elections is the ability of candidates to purchase broadcasting time on T.V. Over $100 million was spent in 1988 on the U.S. Presidential election campaign on T.V. commercials alone.[57] In the 1992 campaign, one of the candidates made history by spending $1 million per day on television advertising.

Unlike the USA, in the United Kingdom expenditure on T.V. is **6–45** precluded, although the parties are entitled to purchase advertising in the press. In the United Kingdom, election broadcasting is regulated by the BBC and ITC, the Independent Television Commission, (the predecessor of the IBA for independent T.V.), for Party Election Broadcasts. Supplementary coverage is provided in news and current affairs programmes, interviews with candidates and general discussion programmes.

Both BBC and ITC seek to establish impartiality in the conduct of election broadcasts and news reports. There is a Committee on Political Broadcasting which is chaired by the Prime Minister and comprises the senior management of the BBC and ITC. Unofficial in status, unpublished in determinations and unknown in terms of reference, the decisions of this Committee find their way into the allocation of "slots" for each political party.[58]

The general test of entitlement to a single electoral broadcast is **6–46** based on the number of candidates fielded at the election – currently 50. Though the question of the allocation of broadcast time between the main parties is more difficult to ascertain. One view is that it is based on the allocation of seats in the House of Commons at the dissolution. Another view is that the allocation should be based on, not only seats won but also on votes obtained.

A number of legal challenges to the criteria have been made. The Communist Party unsuccessfully challenged the BBC in its allocation of broadcasts. It was argued that the BBC assisted the candidates who were permitted broadcasts and that such expenditure for T.V. programmes should count against each individual candidate's election

---

[56] See *Paying for Politics: Report of the Hansard Society Commission upon the Financing of Political Parties* (1981).

[57] Note Rawlings *op. cit.* p. 143; European Assembly election expenditure is £8,000. See L. P. Hitchens, "Media Ownership and Control" A European Approach" (1994) 57 M.L.R. 585.

[58] *R. v. Tronoh Mines Ltd* [1952] 1 All E.R. 697. Unauthorised election expenditure did not extend to general propaganda made by a political party even if it assisted individual candidates.

expenses. Today section 9(4) of the Representation of the People Act 1969 as amended by section 75(1)(c) permits broadcasting authorities to present to the electorate, party figures who happen to be candidates, without incurring the problem of each candidate's expenditure maximum for elections.[59]

6–47   The fact that allocation decisions over election broadcasting are amenable to judicial review provides an important safeguard. However many issues are unresolved. The time schedules of programmes, the content of interviews, the perspective of the interviewer may all contribute to give one party more favourable exposure than another. The major political parties engage in monitoring the major television programmes and make claims of political bias whenever appropriate. Claims are made by the smaller parties that present arrangements favour the two larger parties. Little may be expected to change, as the present arrangements are unlikely to be reformed if they continue to favour the larger parties.[60]

6–48   Newspapers also have a dominant role in the election campaigns of the various political parties. Supervising newspaper coverage is equally problematic. Unlike the BBC and ITC which claim impartiality, newspapers are free to be partisan. The Press Council is the body charged with oversight of the self-regulation of the newspaper industry.[61] Currently an inquiry is being carried out to establish whether there is the need for privacy laws to protect public figures from an intrusive invasion of their personal and private lives. Politicians find the glare of publicity a necessary part of their profession, but recent complaints about press behaviour have raised the issue of whether private and personal affairs of public figures should be kept from public scrutiny in the press.

6–49   Many complaints and criticisms are made of press coverage[62] during elections. The fact that newspapers legally support one political party as against another may lead to gross distortions in the news and unfairness to the other parties. Generally it is accepted that newspapers favourable to the Conservatives outnumber those favourable to Labour. Equally clear is that minority parties may not be represented by the large national newspapers.

---

[59] *Grieve v. Douglas-Home* [1965] S.C. 315.
[60] In N. Ireland see *Lynch v. BBC* (1983) 6 N.I.J.B.; [1983] N.I.L.R. 193. As there is no independent committee on political broadcasting this gives rise to various allegations arising out of the policies adopted over allocation. In the *Lynch* case the Workers' Party was excluded from the election forum broadcast by the BBC. They challenged the decision arguing that the BBC was acting in breach of its duty (implied) to remain unpolitical. *Held:* Hutton J. even if such a duty existed it was open to the BBC's discretion how best it might be satisfied.
[61] D. Butler, D. Kavanagh, *The British General Election of 1983* (1984).
[62] *R. v. Broadcasting Complaints Commission, ex p.* Owen [1985] Q.B. 1153; Rawlings, *op. cit.* p. 207.

Support for each party brings large scale donations. In the case of Conservatives, almost 30 per cent comes from company donations. In the case of the Labour party, almost 55 per cent comes from trade union donations with a political levy. Donations have fallen as trade union membership has diminished.

The law relating to political funding of parties is unsatisfactory and **6–50** there is support for reform and perhaps some system of national funding. In the case of company donations, the assumption, commonly made about their legality comes from the terms of the memorandum of associations in most companies which permit such donations. Shareholders have little direct say in the donation or the amount. Exact details of donations are often difficult to discover and the amounts may vary according to the political allegiances of the directors of the company at the time.

Trade union contributions are covered by the Trade Union Act **6–51** 1984. Political funds may only be established and maintained after balloted approval has been obtained from the membership within the last 10 years. Funds for political objects are affected and the term "political objects" is defined in the 1984 Act as to "relate to activity designed to secure and maintain a candidate in elected office."[63]

It is possible, that once approved under the 1984 Act, the individual trade union member may opt out of the donation. The means to exercise this right must not cause discrimination amongst trade union members.

There is an obvious disparity between the principles applicable to **6–52** trade union funds and those relevant to company donations. Rawlings comments[64]:

"Unless the company voluntarily assumes such a procedure, shareholders neither have the opportunity to vote on the principles of political contributions, nor to opt out of such contributions on an individual basis should the majority adopt a policy that contributions be made."

The question of how to remedy such disparity also arises in connection with the amount of contribution raised. Conservative fund-raising is greater than that of the Labour Party. Additional issues arise when the plight of smaller parties is considered. The disparity between smaller parties and the two larger parties seems more difficult to resolve.

---

[63] K. Ewing, *The Funding of Political Parties in Britain* (1987).
[64] See Rawlings, *op. cit.* p. 207. Trade Union Act 1913, s.3(1)(b); See Report of the Committee on Financial Aid to Political Parties, Cmnd. 6601 (1976); C. Munro, *Elections and Expenditure* [1976] P.L. 300. See *Conservative and Unionist Central Office v. Burrell* [1982] 2 All E.R. 1.

The 1976 Committee on Financial Aid to Political Parties recommended annual grants should be payable from the Exchequer funds to the central organisations of the parties. No immediate action is forthcoming on this proposal.

6-53   In comparison to company and trade union contributions, individual donations are free from much controversy or legal controls. Hidden from public scrutiny are the conditions which may attach to such contributions and the implication of this might well be serious if the information regarding conditions was made public. A particularly sensitive question is the suggestion that there might be a link between political donations by individuals or companies and the granting of personal honours by the Monarch on the advice of the Prime Minister.

Party politics is the life blood of the working Constitution. Political rivalry occupies a central feature of the competition for electoral victory. Fairness ought to be a prominent feature in how parties are funded and how they carry out their activities. Financial advantage to the two larger parties may effectively deprive smaller parties of a fair opportunity to put their case to the electorate.[65]

4. Europe

6-54 In 1979, direct elections to the European Assembly, now called the European Parliament,[66] were first held. Prolonged negotiations had taken place within the community to settle the question of the allocation of seats in each Member State. A group of countries, France, Germany, Italy and the United Kingdom were each allotted 81 seats. Once the allocation of seats was carried out, each Member State was left to introduce the necessary domestic election law and machinery. In the United Kingdom responsibility rested on the Boundary Commission to draw up Assembly boundaries. In Northern Ireland arrangements in place before 1979 had introduced a system of elections for the Northern Ireland assembly and these arrangements were sufficiently flexible to accommodate European Assembly elections. The arrangement of the electoral system in Northern Ireland was changed to meet the needs of the minority Catholic population by the use of proportional representation rather than the first past the post system.

---

[65] See Loughlin, *op. cit.* pp. 138–162.
[66] From July 1, 1987, the Single European Act came into force and changed the name of the European Assembly to European Parliament.

The European Assembly Elections Act 1978, as amended,[67] provides **6–55** the main legal framework for elections. The division of representation is 66 seats for England, 8 for Scotland, 4 from Wales and 3 from Northern Ireland. With the exception of Northern Ireland, elections are held on the British system of first past the post. In Northern Ireland the single transferable vote system is used.[68]

At the Edinburgh summit in December 1992, it was agreed to increase representation to reflect German unification. The European Parliamentary Elections Act 1993 increases the number of representatives for the United Kingdom to be elected to the European Parliament. There are 87 seats, 71 for England, and 5 for Wales. Representation for Scotland and Northern Ireland remains unchanged. The 1993 Act sets up a European Parliamentary Constituencies Committees for each of England and Wales. The work of the Committee is in drawing up constituency boundaries for European Parliamentary Constituencies. Draft recommendations approved by the Secretary of State have to be laid before Parliament for approval.

Doubts about the legality of adopting the British electoral system **6–56** were raised in Scotland in a court case[69] taken by the Social Democratic Party/Liberal Alliance, that the first past the post system was discriminatory, and was in conflict with the spirit of Article 138 of the Treaty, which implied equality of voting procedures throughout the Community. The United Kingdom is alone, among other Member States in not having an electoral system based on some form of proportional representation. The Scottish Court refused the application, as *inter alia* it was doubtful if enforceable rights were created under Article 138. There were additional procedural objections to making a reference under Article 177 which were not in the applicant's favour due to problems with how the pleadings were drafted.

This leaves unresolved the question of whether the United Kingdom's electoral system is a fair one and ultimately, the question of whether, in the period of debate after the drawing up of the Maastricht Treaty, the United Kingdom's electoral system is sufficiently representative. Voter turnout at European Parliament elections was 32.6 per cent in 1979 and 1984, 36.2 per cent in 1989 and 1994. This is relatively low when compared to central government elections.

---

[67] Now referred to as the European Parliament Elections Act 1978 because of s.3(2) of the European Communities (Amendment) Act 1986.
[68] See McCrudden, *op. cit.* note 7.
[69] *Prince v. Secretary of State for Scotland* [1984] 1 C.M.L.R. 723; [1985] S.L.T. 74.

5. Manifesto, Mandate and Pressure Groups

(a) Manifesto and Mandate

6–57 Political parties aspire to become the government. The relationship between the electoral process which influences the selection of the government and the policies of the government once elected, is one of intense and continuous debate. Governments are free to depart from any electoral promise but they do so at the expense of their own popularity. The question of allowing the electorate some influence over the functioning of the government of the day is not easy to address. Dicey,[70] it will be remembered, favoured the use of referendums but in modern times the preferred view is that this device has limitations and should be used sparingly.[71] Matters of great constitutional debate, such as membership of the E.C. or in some countries the changes proposed in the Maastricht Treaty, require a referendum to sanction any change.

6–58 By-elections caused by the death, illness or retirement of M.P.s, give an opportunity for the popularity of the Government's policies to be judged by the electorate. Normally a by-election is held within three months of the vacancy occurring. However successful opposition parties may be in winning by-elections, it is difficult to regard such results as accurate predictions of the outcome of a general election or of government popularity. Opinion polls may help gauge public opinion but are not always reliable.

6–59 The electorate may exercise some influence over the government of the day through the implications of the electoral policies contained in the party manifesto. Is there a mandate to govern? The idea of electoral mandates has its appeal. It stresses the principle of representative government and that an M.P. is somehow a "delegate" of the people. However popular this view may appear it does not accord with historical precedent. Turpin notes the resolution in 1947 of the House of Commons that members of the House of Commons are not delegates[72]:

" . . . the duty of member being to his constituents, and to the country as a whole rather than to any particular section thereof."

6–60 The independence of M.P.s is a zealous guarantee of an individual's right to vote according to conscience but the reality of political

[70] Discussed in more detail in Chap. 7.
[71] The proposals for a referendum on the Maastricht Agreement were made by Mr Tony Benn M.P. but rejected by the Government.
[72] Turpin, *op. cit.* pp. 535–539. (July 15, 1947. H.C. Deb., Vol. 440, col. 365) quoted in Turpin, p. 535.

power seems oddly inconsistent with individual M.P.s voting according to free will. Party government is the modern form of government and M.P.s are expected to conform.

A more realistic view of the practical role attributed to the M.P.'s function is provided by Griffith and Ryle[73]:

> "When a voter at a general election, in that hiatus between Parliaments, puts his cross against the name of a candidate, he is (most often) consciously performing two functions: seeking to return a particular person to the House of Commons as Member for that Constituency; and seeking to return to power as the Government of the country a group of individuals of the same party as that particular person. The voter votes for a representative and a Government."

Griffith and Ryle's[74] analysis places emphasis on representation as **6–61** well as government. Not all M.P.s can be involved in government even if their own Party wins the election. The role an M.P. may adopt may involve membership of a select committee or one of the many backbench committees formed to promote the interests of particular causes. The Conservative Party "1922 Committee," is a good example of the function such a committee may perform. It may warn and criticise. It provides a conduit for party workers in constituencies to make their views known to the government of the day when the Conservative Party is in power. As a critic of the government, an M.P. must be prepared to both maintain the government in power *and* scrutinise its activities.

From the perspective of the M.P., the idea of government possessing a mandate seems strangely inconsistent with his own role and function. From the perspective of the political party, an electoral mandate or manifesto promise may control party members, focus the activities of M.P.s, and help unite the party. From the perspective of the electorate, the manifesto may appear to clarify the policies of each political party and thereby allow choice of support.

The courts may take account of the manifesto in elections. In **6–62** *Bromley*[75] the House of Lords considered the now defunct Greater London Council's manifesto promise to reduce fares on public transport in London. Lord Diplock was clear that the manifesto did not provide a local authority with a mandatory requirement to carry out policies. Members of a local authority must not "treat themselves as irrevocably bound to carry out pre-announced policies" in election

---

[73] Griffith and Ryle, *Parliament: Functions, Practice and Proceedings* (1989), p. 69.
[74] *ibid.*
[75] *Bromley London Borough Council v. Greater London Council* [1983] 1 A.C. 768.

manifestos. However this view is not always consistently followed. In *Tameside*,[76] Lord Wilberforce regarded the electoral policy of the Conservative local authority to retain grammar schools as one which "bound" the authority to carry out its task.

6–63   The current view of the courts is more likely to follow the direction set by *Bromley*.[77] In terms of central and local government relations the view of Lord Templeman[78] in *Nottingham C.C. v. Secretary of State for the Environment*[79] is similar to the strict "allocation of power" analysis made out by Lord Diplock in *Bromley*. The analysis is based on the theory that legal powers should be exercised not according to their political agenda but according to law. The role of the courts is confined to determining the law and not the politics or policy of the law. Policy may only be questioned in Parliament and not the courts[80]:

> "Where Parliament has legislated that the action to be taken by the Secretary of State must, before it is taken be approved by the House of Commons, it is no part of the judges's role to declare that the action proposed is unfair, unless it constitutes an abuse of power the sense of which I have explained; for Parliament has enacted that one of its Houses is responsible. Judicial review is a great weapon in the hands of the judges; but the judges must observe the constitutional limits set by our parliamentary system on their exercise of this beneficient power."

6–64   The distinction between review according to law and review as to policy may be difficult to make, but the implications are clear, party politics set certain boundaries for the courts in determining the extent of their review powers. An example of policy dispute between a local authority and the relevant Minister is found in *R. v. Secretary of State for Education and Science, ex p. Avon County Council*, Lord Justice Ralf Gibson explained[81]:

> " . . . The application was misconceived in so far as it asked the court to intervene in what was analysed, a dispute as to educational policies between Avon [the local authority] and the minister . . ."

In a concurring judgment Lord Justice Nicholls commented:

---

[76] *Secretary of State for Education and Science v. Tameside Metropolitan Borough Council* [1977] A.C. 1014.
[77] *Bromley London Borough Council v. Greater London Council* [1983] 1 A.C. 768
[78] *Nottinghamshire C.C. v. Secretary of State for the Environment* [1986] A.C. 240, 255–1.
[79] *ibid.*
[80] *ibid.* Lord Scarman, pp. 250–251.
[81] *The Independent*, May 25, 1990, C.A.; (1990) 49 L.G.R. 498.

"Given the notice of the subject matter of the decision, it was difficult to see how the Councils' challenge on the ground of 'irrationality' could ever get off the ground."

Both judgments stressed how inappropriate it was to review the Minister's decision in such circumstances.

The courts assume that policy questions are under the doctrine of **6–65** ministerial responsibility, a matter for parliamentary discussion and debate. The formulation of party policy through the manifesto gives electors an opportunity to see the shape of their government's policies. Rarely are such manifesto promises seen as an enforceable mandate in the legal sense, against party policy changes or shifts in government policy.

The influence of party manifestos[82] has perceptibly increased since 1979. The government of the day's adoption of more radical policies such as privatisation and reforms in education, the health service and local government highlights the importance of the manifesto in government policy. Careful drafting of manifesto promises is seen as an important political expedient. The calculating of "keeping pledges" is a way to continue keeping faith with the electorate. The fact that one party has had an uninterrupted period of government since 1979 may partly explain the greater attention to the details of the manifesto.

(b) Pressure Groups

Pressure groups are an important part of the political life of Britain. **6–66** Broadly defined by Grant[83] as "groups that seek to influence public policy," this definition recognises such characteristics as a defined membership, with stated objectives in terms of public policy and paid staff. Pressure groups may create their own social movement, and self-interest in promoting their cause. The question is the extent to which pressure groups contribute to democracy?

The first point to note is that pressure groups are not a modern phenomenon. Patricia Hollis has written that pressure groups in the nineteenth century came from two groupings, those that lobby for an interest and those that adopt a crusade for a cause. The lobby of a vested interest may be seen as "within" the establishment, the crusade for a cause may be perceived as coming from outside the establishment and thus distinct from vested interest.

[82] D. Kavanagh, *Constituency Electioneering in Britain* (1970); B. Jones *et al.*, *Politics U.K.* (Philip Allan, 1991), pp. 257–259.
[83] Wyn Grant, *Pressure Groups, Politics and Democracy in Britain* (Philip Allan, 1989), p. 3; C. Harlow and R. Rawlings, *Pressure Through Law* (London, 1992).

6–67   In the nineteenth century, after the 1832 Reform Act, Parliament became increasingly responsive to public opinion. Claiming to speak for public opinion gave pressure groups a legitimacy. Hollis concludes that pressure groups significantly contributed to the life of the nation.[84]

> "Nineteenth century pressure from without did have some effect on legislation; it had a marked effect on class harmony and social tranquillity; and both enlarged the realm of government and the breadth and base of government."

Hollis[85] makes a number of further observations namely that pressure groups depend on "a sense of political pluralism." Their purpose is to provide an alternative means to express political ideas. There is a belief[86] that this alternative strengthens the existing political institutions and the political health of society. There is also a sense that pressure groups may exert greater flexibility into existing political institutions and therefore provide an important channel of action or alternative political strategy.

6–68   In modern times there are a number of distinctive pressure groups which are easily identifiable and have well-known campaigners prominent among their membership. Groups such as Greenpeace, an environmental group; and Campaign for Nuclear Disarmament (CND), a group campaigning for no nuclear weapons, fit into the category of protest groups and are good examples of their kind. Also important but not seen as a protest group, are the various bodies representing "sectional" interests such as the Law Society, Bar Council, British Medical Association and the like. Grant notes[87] that business alone has over 1,800 associations representing their interests. Added to these, are groups such as the Confederation of British Industry (CBI) and the various trade unions, which all contribute to the activities of persuasion and representation of their interests. Particularly useful by way of analysis are the various farmers' unions representing the agricultural sector. These have been successful in representing their interests in the governments' attitude to the Common Agricultural Policy of the European Union.

6–69   In recent years various consumers' associations and "the consumer" have become a target for pressure groups activation. The National Consumer Council set up in 1975 is partly funded by government but it carries out intensive lobbying activities.

---

[84] P. Hollis, *Pressure from Without* (1975), p. IX.
[85] *ibid.*
[86] Grant, *op. cit.* p. 2.
[87] *ibid.* See D. Wilson, *Pressure: The A to Z of Campaigning in Britain* (Heineman, 1984). Also see M. Olson, *The Logic of Collective Action* (Harvard, 1965); M. Olson, *The Rise and Decline of Nations* (Yale University Press, 1982).

The variety of pressure groups has grown in recent years and the more active and aggressive areas such as Animal Rights have warranted criticism over allegations that some of their members take part in direct action. Wilson[88] believes, that pressure groups contribute to democracy.

The argument in favour rests on a number of assumptions. First, there "is more to democracy than an occasional vote;" pressure groups engage in "participatory democracy." Secondly, pressure groups are specialised to the particular issues and therefore provide more effective opposition than the main opposition party. This permits minority parties or views to be better represented.

Criticism of pressure groups casts doubts on their effectiveness as **6–70** agents of democracy. Brittan[89] has argued that because of the entrenched nature of the various "industrial, economic and political interest groups" this will limit what may be achieved by any form of economic management, new or old, attempted by the government of the day.

Brittan's argument is that democracy should not be seen as[90] "an unprincipled auction to satisfy rival organised groups who can never in the long run be appeased because their demands are mutually incompatible."

There is value in Brittan's observations, not least because of the **6–71** unreliable nature of any accountability over the activities of pressure groups. Grant warns[91] of the damages of allowing pressure groups too much influence. In the competition for public opinion there is no guarantee that pressure groups will not eventually run into political issues and as a consequence either misunderstand or misrepresent the issues. This is often the point of criticism raised by Government Ministers or the main political parties. In that sense pressure groups may be held in check by political parties and their policies.[92]

Grant concludes with a useful analysis of pressure group activities **6–72** and results[93]:

"Pressure group power is limited: it is based on the ability to persuade and to influence, rather than to take decisions or, with certain exceptions, to veto them."

---

[88] Wilson, *op. cit.* S. Brittan, *The Role and Limits of Government* (1987), pp. 74–79.
[89] S. Brittan, "The Economic Contradictions of Democracy" *British Journal of Political Science*, Vol. 5, pp. 129–159.
[90] *ibid.*
[91] Quoted in Grant, *op. cit.* p. 39.
[92] Grant, *op. cit.* p. 163.
[93] Grant, *op. cit.* p. 164. Turpin provides an interesting list of such diverse groups as the Association of British Insurers, the British Medical Association and the War Widows' Association of Great Britain.

The contribution of pressure groups is an eclectic one. Through their activities the government of the day may be influenced and their contributions may improve the quality of policy-making and decision-taking. However there are dangers. Inside groups may achieve unwarranted influence and unduly tip the balance against a more open style of government. Within political parties, pressure groups may operate largely undetected and provide a counterbalance to the public debate outside. In the final analysis pressure groups may be seen as an inevitable result of the close bargaining of party politics. Not everyone may join in and the temptation is to split off and join a group representing only one's interests. Taken to extreme levels the damages of pressure group activity should be recognised, but pressure groups perform a valuable task of ensuring that the distance between government and the governed does not become too great.

6. Electoral Reform

6–73 The United Kingdom until changes introduced in Italy[94] in 1993 was unique among other Member States of the European Union in adopting for central and local government elections, "the first past the post" or "plurality" system. Northern Ireland has had its own separate electoral system with proportional representation on the single transferable vote system for local government elections since 1973, as well as for elections to the Northern Ireland assembly.[95]

6–74   Voting systems are complex and there is no single formula which translates votes into seats. Criticism of the United Kingdom's present electoral arrangement has come from the smaller parties, who point to the electoral results of past general elections to show that their share of the popular vote leads to an unfair representation in terms of the number of seats obtained in the House of Commons. The disproportion of votes to seats is also clear when it is recognised that rarely do the winning party which forms the government, with a majority of seats, win with more than 50 per cent of the total vote. Thus the Conservatives in 1983 had only 42.4 per cent of the vote, and in 1987 42.3 per cent of the vote, in 1992, 41.86 per cent when they won again.

[94] See M. Bull, "Electoral Reform in Italy: When consequences fail to meet expectations" 1996/7 *Representation* 53–67.

[95] Rawlings, *op. cit.* pp. 61–64. European Assembly (Pay and Pensions) Act 1979 provides for salaries, allowances and pensions to be paid to representatives elected to the European Assembly. Northern Ireland's electoral system for the European Parliament is by proportional representation.

Turpin draws attention to the "strikingly demonstrated dispropor- 6–75
tionality" which may result[96]:

"In each of the two 1974 elections the Liberals with over 18 per
cent. of the total vote, won only 2 per cent of the seats, and it was
observed that more than ten times as many votes were needed to
elect a Liberal M.P as to elect a Labour or Conservative M.P."

In 1983, election statistics show that the Liberal/SDP alliance received
25.4 per cent of the vote and only 23 seats while Labour received 27.6
per cent of the vote, but 209 seats. The pattern of disproportion has
continued in the 1987 and 1992 elections.

From time to time a Speaker's Conference on electoral law may be 6–76
convened to secure all party support for any reform proposals. The
conference is usually in private and proceedings are not usually
published. Recommendations, if any, are not binding on the
Government.

The conclusion drawn by many critics is that the "first past the post
system" does discriminate unfairly against smaller parties. Conversely it favours the two major parties.

Proposals for reform have come from the Liberal Democrats, the 6–77
Institute of Public Policy Research, and the Hansard Society Commission on electoral reform. Of the two major parties, the Labour Party is
currently considering the question of an alternative system in the
form of proportional representation, in a wide ranging review of the
electoral system.

In considering the question of electoral reform it is important to
identify the aims and objectives of any electoral system.[97] A number
of different expectations may be said to arise from the electoral
system. These are: that the result produces a legislature reflecting of
the main trends and views of the electorate, that the government is
able to act according to the wishes of the majority of the electorate;
that government is strong and stable and that the representatives
chosen by the electorate are sufficiently competent to perform their
task of governing and legislating.

Many of these expectations will not be met or even agreed to, in 6–78
any single electoral system. Representativeness, good government
and electoral choice may be claimed by a variety of different electoral
systems. It is often difficult to anticipate in advance the effect of a
particular system in terms of the electoral outcome. Thus competing
demands are made, often partisan and inclined to favour one system

[96] R. Blackburn, *The Electoral System in Britain* (Macmillan, St. Martin's press, 1995).
Turpin, p. 440.
[97] J. A. Chandler, "The Plurality Vote: A Reappraisal" (1982) 30 *Political Studies* 87.

as against another, without much evidence to judge or make conclusions as to the most suitable.

6–79		Bogdanor has argued that the United Kingdom's electoral system is no longer justifiable. This view points to the "adversarial" nature of British politics and the arrangement of a two-party system. The first past the post plurality system has favoured strong majority government. This means the electorate make a clear decisive choice and discourages coalition government or compromise politics. Bogdanor[98] points out that election results in Britain do not necessarily reflect the pressure of popular support for or against policies among the electorate. Distortions in the seats gained through the votes cast means that the electorate who do not vote for a winning candidate have little chance to have their votes counted and their opinion is not represented in the overall outcome of the election.

6–80		Bogdanor[99] identifies particular groups such as women and minorities within the United Kingdom as being disadvantaged by the present arrangements. Co-operation between the political parties is handicapped, consensus is difficult to attain and compromise is shunned. However, it may be pointed out that for a lengthy period since the Second World War the electoral system has permitted strong and responsible government. Radical changes in policy, for example privatisation of the nationalised industries, introduced since 1979 would have been more difficult to accommodate under any other electoral system. Thus change and continuity, the hallmark of the United Kingdom's unwritten Constitution may be combined and strengthened under the present electoral arrangements. Nevertheless, criticism of the electoral system has been strengthened by the argument that since 1979, the Government has abandoned consensus policies in favour of strong non-consultative government. Critics of Mrs Thatcher attribute the cause of her "style and intent of government" to the electoral success of a large seat majority.

6–81		The suggestion is made that some form of proportional representation is to be preferred. How far does present dissatisfaction go in terms of popular demand for reform? Stuart Weir,[1] has recently completed empirical research into this question. He concludes that:

> "The survey showed that dissatisfaction with the governing system was at 63 per cent, as high in 1991, as in the crisis torn mid-1970s. Most voters agreed that government power is too centralised (60 per cent to 18 per cent) that rights are too easily

[98] V. Bogdanor, The People and the Party System (1981), p. 205.
[99] ibid.
[1] Stuart Weir, "Waiting for Change: Public Opinion and Electoral Reform" (June 1992) 63 Political Quarterly 197 at 216.

changed (54 per cent to 22 per cent) and that Parliament does not have enough control over government (50 per cent to 23 per cent)."

If these findings are borne out by subsequent research then they **6–82** indicate that there is both popular and intellectual demand for reform of the United Kingdom's electoral system. However, if reform is required what reforms might be adopted?

There is a great lack of clarity, not only in the form of any new arrangements, but also in their expected results. This is hardly surprising given the complex task of divising a new electoral system.

One form of proportional representation is the single transferable **6–83** vote (STV) system, currently in use in Northern Ireland and in the Republic of Ireland. This system is based on redrawing existing constituencies into larger multi-member constituencies. The most likely outcome would be to create five member constituencies based on the electoral quota of about 3,000,000 voters. Voting on the ballot paper is undertaken by indicating an order of preference for each candidate. Winning an election according to this system requires setting an "electoral quota." Broadly this means setting a proportion of votes expressed as a percentage which must be achieved before a member is returned for that constituency. Depending on the number of seats for each constituency the successful candidate will require 16.6 per cent of the vote whereas in a two-member constituency 33.3 per cent of the vote is required. Once a candidate passes the electoral quota, the candidate wins. Passing the electoral quota is determined by the returning officer counting the number of first preference votes. It is possible that often a candidate will achieve a sufficient number of first preference votes. On this basis the number of seats will determine the number of winning candidates. Once a sufficient number of first preference votes are achieved, the returning officer counts all the second preferences recorded by the voters who gave first preference votes. In this way no votes are wasted. Once the second preference votes are counted, the returning officer *transfers* a proportion of the preferences given to each candidate. This may permit another candidate to achieve the electoral quota or better. The process is continued permitting all the candidates who reach the electoral quota to be elected.

In theory the advantage of such a system is to provide a coinci- **6–84** dence between the distribution of votes among parties and the distribution of seats. Variables in such a system will depend on the size of constituencies determined by the number of voters and the number of seats in each constituency. It is assumed that the smaller the number of constituencies, the greater the degree of representativeness possible. If the entire country were treated as a single constituency this would amount to the minimum distortion. Only in Israel and the Netherlands does this arrangement operate.

An alternative to STV is the list system, popular in Western Europe. Votes are cast for parties, seats are distributed according to the parties' proportion of their share of the votes. Candidates are thus elected on the allocation of votes in the order of preference. Modification of these arrangements are usually introduced by a "cut-off point" being applied. If a party fails to reach this barrier it will not be qualified to receive any seats.

6–85   Proportional representation has many advocates. Critics point to the fear that a government elected under such a system may not have a worthy overall majority. Weak government, proliferation of small parties and a constant need to go to the electorate are seen as characteristics of the proportional representation systems in countries such as Italy, Holland and Israel. Critics further argue that there is a high likelihood of a hung parliament. Coalition between the parties are inevitable and there is a greater likelihood for the need for coalition government.

6–86   Proportional representation *does* pose major questions in terms of many of the constitutional conventions, the role of political parties and ultimately *how* Parliament might function. This is not always appreciated. Membership of the Cabinet is currently *de facto*, restricted to the government of the day. Inclusion of opposition nominated M.P.s and members of smaller parties might change the nature and role of the Cabinet. Cabinet secrecy and collective decisions might be more difficult to achieve. M.P.s would be freer from the importance of strict party discipline and the power of the whips which might change the relationship between M.P. and party.

Many of these changes might be seen as beneficial but undoubtedly they may flow from proportional representation. David Butler concludes[2]:

"In these and many other matters the rules of the game of British politics would be transformed if appeals to the people no longer produced single party parliamentary majorities. A change in voting procedures would have fundamental consequences. Electoral systems are not matters of technical detail. They lie at the very heart of a nation's arrangements."

6–87   The likelihood of electoral reform is difficult to assess. The Government is not committed to the introduction of proportional representation and it is suspected that opposition parties are unsure of the exact effects of its introduction, although the Liberal Democrats is most

---

[2] D. Butler, "Electoral Reform" in Jowell & Oliver, *The Changing Constitution* (O.U.P., 1989), p. 383. Dissatisfaction resulted in the Kilbrandon Report into the working of the Constitution.

enthusiastic about its introduction. The debate is likely to continue. The winning party under the first past the post system has a vested interest to perpetuate the system.

Rawlings[3] draws attention to other elected reforms which should **6–88** be considered within the existing plurality system. These include the setting up of an agency on the same basis as the Commission for Racial Equality to keep the law under review, initiate reform and maintain an independent view of the current electoral system. Electoral campaigning laws require scrutiny, especially the expenditure on national campaigns. These areas of detail require attention as part of the ongoing search for improving and modifying the electoral system.[4]

Popular demand for electoral reform will ensure that throughout the 1990s this issue will continue to dominate British politics and debates on the United Kingdom's Constitutional arrangements. It is proposed that elections for the European Parliament in 1999 will take place under proportional representation. This may depend on whether the timetable for such elections may be met.[5]

7. Referendums

Referendums have an important role in any well functioning **6–89** democracy. Dicey in the late nineteenth century was an eventual convert to the value of a referendum.[6] His main ground for seeing the value of the referendum was that it avoided the "evils" of the party system and the conflict between political parties; Dicey regarded party political conflicts as an impediment to the consensus necessary for the effective working of the political system. In the aftermath of the Irish Home Rule debate in 1886 and in 1894 when a new Home Rule Bill was introduced for Ireland, Dicey supported a referendum as a device to avoid "extreme" legislation. At the time the influential *National Review* held a symposium on the merits of the referendum. Dicey believed its role on matters of fundamental constitutional importance was invaluable. There were few converts to this idea. On the whole, the value of a referendum was not seen in terms of a

---

[3] Rawlings, *op. cit.*, pp. 232–241. See "The Plant Report on Proportional Representation" (1992).

[4] See "The Royal Commission on the Constitution 1969–73" (Cmnd. 5460). Jack Lively, *Democracy* (1975).

[5] *The Guardian*, June 22, 1997.

[6] See Richard Cosgrove, *The Rule of Law Albert Venn Dicey, Victorian Jurist* (Macmillan, 1980) pp. 105–110.

generally applicable principle, but it was conceded that on some matters of constitutional importance, a referendum might have a role. This view did not hold sway in the debates on the Parliament Act 1911. Then the opposition were unsuccessful in the demand for a referendum to affirm the changes in the role of the House of Lords.

6–90   In contemporary times in Northern Ireland in the Northern Ireland (Border Poll) Act 1972 referendum was approved to allow the electors of Northern Ireland to vote on whether Northern Ireland should remain part of the United Kingdom or join with the Irish Republic. There is also express provision in the Northern Ireland Constitution Act 1973 for holding a referendum on the status of Northern Ireland.

6–91   The decision to join the European Community in 1972 was taken without a referendum. However, the political controversy about joining has remained a sensitive issue in British politics. The Referendum Act 1975 was seen as an attempt to avoid internal party political disagreements and allowed the electorate to vote on June 5, 1975 on the question of whether the United Kingdom should stay in the European Community. The majority, 67.2 per cent voted for staying in the Community out of an electoral turn-out of 65 per cent. The referendum has not settled the question of membership of the European Community. The signing of the Maastricht Treaty was accompanied by demands for a referendum, although a Bill proposing this course of action failed in the House of Commons. The 1997 general election campaign saw the renewed efforts of the Referendum Party, formed in 1994, to have a referendum to consider membership of the Community. The Referendum Party failed to attract significant electoral support.

6–92   The use of referenda was at the centre of the debate on devolution in 1978. Both the Scotland Act 1978 and the Wales Act 1978 allowed for a referendum on the matter of devolution. The test of agreement was a threshold requirement of 40 per cent of the electorate. If this failed to be achieved, then both the 1978 Acts had to be repealed. While a majority of those that voted in Scotland favoured devolution, this amounted to only 32.9 per cent of the electorate. Devolution failed to be implemented in Scotland. In Wales only 20.2 per cent were in favour, representing only 11.9 per cent of the electorate. Devolution also failed to be implemented in Wales. The referendum may have tested the wishes of the electorate on the form of devolution on offer rather than on the principle of devolution *per se*. The limitations of the referendum are found in the way the question is posed and on the timing of the referendum. These matters may be influential with the electorate. Referendums are not necessarily a good barometer of public opinion rather they may provide politicians with a way forward when party political loyalties are divided. In all the examples mentioned above the referendum has not proved conclusive.

There are at least two matters that may fall to the referendum **6-93** device over the next few years. First, the Government has promised to hold a referendum in 1997 to consider proposals for devolution for Scotland and Wales. Secondly, there may be a referendum in the United Kingdom to consider the introduction of a common currency as part of the development of the European Community. In both examples, the argument in favour of using the referendum device is that some matter of constitutional importance is involved. Determining what is or what is not of constitutional significance is unclear. For example, a proposal to introduce some form of proportional representation is likely to be accompanied by the requirement of a referendum.[7] There is some difficulty in knowing whether a referendum is suitable or approporiate for the issue to be decided. A referendum on the restoration of capital punishment may provide a clear outcome in favour, but leave politicians and the judiciary with uncompromising choices. When a referendum is used it is very often because political parties have to respond to internal disagreements. The referendum may not be wholly satisfactory as party divisions may emerge later and all the referendum has done is provide a brief respite.

There are some limitations in the use of the referendum mechanism as seen with the devolution issue in 1978, determining the ground rules for holding a referendum is itself controversial. The initiative lies with the Government of the day and the outcome of the referendum may be unduly influenced by the way the question is drafted and the rules relating to how the electorate's choice may be counted. There is also a question of how fully informed the electorate may be in determining the choices represented in the referendum. The way information is presented may provide a biased account. The media and advertising may distort the values of the arguments presented by different groups.

In principle there is great merit in the use of the referendum. The idea behind the referendum may appear to be an attractive one, namely that it appeals to the authority of the electorate rather than rely on political choices decided in Parliament. This may be misleading. The nature of the United Kingdom's current constitutional arrangements are that the referendum[8] may disguise where real political power and authority actually reside.

---

[7] Blackburn, p. 427.
[8] See Austin Ranney (ed.), *The Referendum Device* (1981); Michael Gallagher and Pier Vincenzo Uleri, *The Referendum Experience in Europe* (Macmillan, 1996).

General Election Results 1945–1997

Year	Party	% Votes	% Seats
1945	Labour	47.7	61.4
	Conservative	39.7	32.8
	Liberal	9.0	1.9
	Others*	3.6	3.9
1950	Labour	46.1	50.4
	Conservative	43.4	47.4
	Liberal	9.1	1.4
	Others	1.3	0.5
1951	Labour	48.8	47.2
	Conservative	48.0	51.3
	Liberal	2.5	0.9
	Others	0.7	0.5
1955	Labour	46.4	44.0
	Conservative	49.7	54.8
	Liberal	2.7	0.9
	Others	1.2	0.3
1959	Labour	43.8	40.9
	Conservative	49.4	57.9
	Liberal	5.9	0.9
	Others	0.9	0.2
1964	Labour	44.1	50.3
	Conservative	43.4	48.3
	Liberal	11.2	1.4
	Others	1.3	0.0
1966	Labour	48.0	57.8
	Conservative	41.9	40.1
	Liberal	8.5	1.9
	Others	1.5	0.1
1970	Labour	43.1	45.7
	Conservative	46.4	52.4
	Liberal	7.5	0.9
	Others	3.0	1.0
1974 (Feb)	Labour	37.2	47.4
	Conservative	37.9	46.8
	Liberal	19.3	2.2
	Others	5.6	3.6

General Election Results 1945–1997—*continued*

Year	Party	% Votes	% Seats
1974 (Oct)	Labour	39.2	50.2
	Conservative	35.8	43.6
	Liberal	18.3	2.0
	Others	7.7	4.1
1979	Labour	36.9	42.4
	Conservative	43.9	53.4
	Liberal	13.8	1.7
	Others	5.4	2.5
1983	Labour	27.6	32.2
	Conservative	42.4	61.1
	Liberal/SDP	25.4	3.5
	Others*	4.6	3.2
1987	Labour	30.8	35.2
	Conservative	42.3	57.8
	Liberal/SDP	22.6	3.4
	Others	4.3	3.6
1992	Labour	34.4	41.6
	Conservative	41.9	51.6
	Liberal Dem.	17.8	3.1
	Others	5.9	3.7
1997	Labour	43.2	63.4
	Conservative	30.7	25.0
	Liberal	16.8	7.0
	Others	9.3	4.6

*others include Green Party, Plaid Cymru, SNP, N. Irish Parties, Independent Labour, Commonwealth, Independents, etc.

Number of Seats, Electorate Size, Percentage of Electorate Turnout

Year	Total Number of seats	Total electorate	Turnout %
1945	640	33,240,391	72.8
1950	625	34,412,255	83.9
1951	625	34,919,331	82.6
1955	630	34,852,179	76.8
1959	630	35,397,304	78.7
1964	630	35,894,054	77.1
1966	630	35,957,245	75.8
1970	630	39,342,013	72.0
1974 (Feb)	635	39,753,863	78.8
1974 (Oct)	635	40,072,970	72.8
1979	635	41,095,649	76.0
1983	650	42,192,99	72.7
1987	650	43,180,753	75.3
1992	651	43,249,721	77.7
1997	659	44,863,488	71.5

Chapter 7

Public Law and Legal Thought

1. Introduction

As Van Caenegem[1] reminds us: "the concept of public law is itself **7–01** somewhat problematic". He describes how continental jurisprudence developed a system of public law distinguished as a separate field of study from private law. In marked contrast, England, he observed, did not conform to such a separation or distinction[2]:

> "Until the nineteenth century, and even beyond, English doctrine proudly maintained that, unlike the continent, England knew no separate public law or public-law courts; the traditional common law assumed that the law was indivisible in the sense that the same body of rules applied to the government and its agents as well as to private citizens."

It is against this common law inheritance that in the preceding chapters various writers and their ideas, influential in the development of the United Kingdom's constitutional arrangements, have been noted. Albert Venn Dicey (1835–1922), and his contemporaries are perhaps the most influential and their importance endures in understanding the present constitutional[3] arrangements. This chapter is intended to examine the legal and philosophical thinking, influential in the development of public law.

In recent years attention has focused, not only on Dicey and his critics, but also on contemporary legal thought and its influence on public law.

---

[1] R. C. Van Caenegem, *An Historical Introduction to Western Constitutional Law* (Cambridge University Press, 1995) p. 1
[2] *ibid.* p. 3.
[3] See T. R. S. Allan, "Pragmatism and Theory in Public Law" (1988) 104 L.Q.R. 422; also Allan, "Constitutional Rights and Common Law" (1991) 11 O.J.L.S. 453; T. R. S. Allan, *Law, Liberty and Justice* (Oxford, 1993).

7–02   Craig[4] examines the theme of how constitutional and administrative law are inter-related. Craig also explains how the background of political theory assists in understanding both how society and law have developed, and also how the contribution of different commentators on the United Kingdom's constitutional arrangements may be assessed. Loughlin[5] discusses the connection between public law and politics. He explores the development of ideas and influences in public law, specifically addressing an inquiry into the nature and distinctiveness of public law. Such books are among many written by lawyers in recent years which probe the boundaries between law, theory and politics.

7–03   This chapter is an attempt to outline current discussion and debate about public law. Whether as Loughlin believes, there is a crisis in "public law thought" may be open to conjecture, but there is certainly a sustained and important debate concerning the nature of public law, the value of a theoretical approach to the subject and its future development.[6]

It is hoped that the brief introduction to legal thought in this chapter will facilitate the analysis and inquiry undertaken in the remainder of this textbook. Is public law a distinctive subject? What are its boundaries? How do public lawyers differ in their approach to problems or disputes from private lawyers? Discussion of these questions is essential to understand the value and nature of public law.

2. The Common Law Tradition

7–04 Constitutional and administrative law evolved historically, mainly from tradition and the general development of the common law. The common law tradition[7] is the subject of specialist works of legal history such as Milsom's *Historical Foundations of the English Common Law*.[8] Such accounts are instructive in the insights they provide on

---

[4] P. Craig, *Public Law and Democracy in the United Kingdom and the United States of America* (1990). Also see H. Arthurs, *Without the Law* (Toronto, 1985).

[5] M. Loughlin, *Public Law and Political Theory* (1992).

[6] See P. S. Atiyah, *The Rise and Fall of Freedom of Contract* (1979); J. G. A. Pocock, *The Ancient Constitution and the Feudal Law* (1987); Singer, "The Legal Rights Debate in Analytical Jurisprudence from Bentham to Hohfeld" (1982) *Wisconsin Law Review* 975.

[7] A definition of "the common law" is provided by J. R. Spencer, *Jackson's Machinery of Justice* (1989), p. 16; "in a wide sense the expression 'common law' is used to mean the legal system and the habits of legal thought that Englishmen have evolved. In this sense it is contrasted with systems of law derived from Roman law."

[8] F.H. Lawson, *Selected Essays* (1977), (2nd ed., 1981), Vol. 1, p. 207; Gordon, "Historicism in Legal Scholarship" (1981) 90 Yale L.J. 1017.

explanation of the role of lawyers in the development of the common law, particularly in terms of the adoption of legal techniques and methods of analysis. However, rarely are substantive issues of constitutional and administrative law made distinctive, when the emphasis in such works is on the development of the common law in terms of courts and procedures, property law, including both land law and equity, contract and occasionally the criminal law, where legal skills are explained and analysed. Legal methods and techniques developed in the area of property relations *are* relevant to understanding the traditions of the common law. As English law did not develop a separate jurisdiction[9] over matters of constitutional and administrative law, the same common law techniques are helpful in understanding the role of the State and its relationship with the citizen.

General assumptions about the nature of law informed the mind of **7–05** common lawyers. One such assumption was that law is perceived as having universal application. No special status is awarded to the State or to the Constitution and disputes between the citizen and the State are not seen as peculiar or different. Thus, English law failed to recognise any intrinsic differences between disputes arising out of the law of contract between two private citizens and contractual disputes where the contract is between the citizen and the State.

The fact that today courts make a distinction between public and private law has come about in the context where English law in the past failed to draw any such distinction. The absence of any special group of rules or analysis associated with public law in its early development creates difficulties in defining public law[10] and delineating its boundaries with private law. The question of what is the distinctiveness of public law, assuming that it is possible to identify such, is not readily answered.

However, despite such difficulties it is possible to identify some of **7–06** the characteristics found in the common law tradition which are important in understanding public law. Atiyah and Summers[11] identified formal reasoning and pragmatism as major influences in English law.

---

[9] Hearn, *The Theory of Legal Rights and Duties* (1883); Hohfeld, *Fundamental Legal Conceptions as Applied in Judicial Reasoning* (1919); Austin (ed. H. L. A. Hart), *The Province of Jurisprudence Determined* (1954).

[10] Public law is a difficult term to define. Here it is used to refer to constitutional and administrative law. However, it can be used in other senses. A substantive meaning may seek to distinguish between legal rules applicable to public bodies and rules applicable to the private citizen. A procedural meaning comes in *O'Reilly* v. *Mackman* [1982] 3 W.L.R. 604 as a jurisdictional procedure to distinguish remedies against public bodies and private citizens.

[11] Useful background reading may be found in M. A. Eisenberg, *The Nature of Common Law* (1988); Atiyah and Summers, *Form and Substance in Anglo-American Law* (Oxford, 1987).

Formal reasoning contains a number of influences which relate to how[12] law is perceived and developed. Interestingly, both contract and property law provide the most useful analysis and examples of formal reasoning. How might formal reasoning be explained? First, rules are recognised as legally authoritative, that is by their context or status, their validity is accepted. Formal reasoning may place emphasis on[13] certain requirements such as a seal, or registration of title, a signature of a witness or the requirements of writing. Technical correctness is a hallmark of the precision associated with formality and the idea that problems may be reduced to a study of the rules alone.

7–07   Second, formal reasoning places weight on the value of coherence. That the law is a unified body of law lies at the heart of the judges relying on previous decisions and on the authority of the particular court.[14] The creation of legal principles through points of law or legal doctrine further supports the view that law is internally coherent. The influence of *stare decisis* makes clear the distinction between judgments which are binding and those that are merely persuasive. As law reporting developed, the tradition of authoritative decision-making in the higher courts on points of legal technicalities influenced the lower courts in their decisions. Assumptions underlying this unified operation of law is that law provides protection to the individual and that reverence, universality and respect are provided by the legal process.

7–08   Pragmatism[15] is not inconsistent with formalism and when combined, seems influential in helping to develop legal principles. How formalism and pragmatism may be combined[16] is illustrated in the example of administrative law. de Smith, writing in the second edition of his work on *Judicial Review of Administrative Action* observed that as English law originally failed to admit the existence of administrative law, its existence today has been influenced by pragmatic development. His analysis is equally valid if applied to the whole enterprise of public law as he explained[17]:

---

[12] P. Stein, *Legal Evolution* (Cambridge, 1980).

[13] S. F. C. Milsom, "Reason in the Development of the Common Law" in *Studies in the History of the Common Law* (1989).

[14] D. Sugarman, "Legal Theory, the Common Law Mind and the Making of the Textbook Tradition" in W. Twining (ed.), *Legal Theory and Common Law* (Blackwell, 1986), pp. 26–61. There is an excellent explanation of the role of the textbook in P. Birks, *Introduction to the Law of Restitution* (Oxford, 1992), pp. 1–3.

[15] See Brian Simpson, "The Common Law and Legal Theory" in W. Twining (ed.), *Legal Theory and Common Law* (Blackwell, 1986), pp. 8–25. *Stare decisis* in its modern meaning binds courts to agreed legal principles. In historical terms the common law tradition had developed based on customary rules rather than formal law.

[16] Montrose explained in his "Return to Austin's College" (1960) C.L.P., p. 9, "that the task of systematisation both simplifies and idealises."

[17] de Smith, *Judicial Review of Administrative Action* (2nd ed.), p. 4.

" . . . in place of integrated coherence we have an asymmetrical hotch potch, developed pragmatically by legislation and judicial decisions in particular contexts, blending fitfully with private law and magisterial law, alternately blurred and jagged in its outlines, still partly secreted in the interstices of medieval forms of action."

de Smith found that administrative law lacked clear principles and noted that the "dearth of coherent principles of administrative law" is an example of formalism in the quest for certainty, clarity and reason through principle. de Smith's explanation that administrative courts were opposed to the traditions of the English common law in the seventeenth century, is compelling. Suspicion was commonly held that any encroachment by a specialised court in the sphere of public law, might re-kindle the arbitrary powers of the discredited court of Star Chamber and the prerogative courts in medieval times.

The void left by no separate administrative law court was rapidly **7–09** filled by ad hoc developments. The strongly held view was that the ordinary courts may control the Executive and its agents in much the same way as any other legal dispute might be resolved by the courts.

Pragmatism and formalism encapsulates the essential qualities of the common law. How influential have such characteristics been in shaping public law?

Some writers link the formalism, explained above, to "the common **7–10** law frame of mind". This seeks "to dig deep" to find coherent and unified rules amidst the irrational, the chaotic or the exceptional. Generalisations are drawn to create principles with the appearance of objectivity and coherence. Such techniques of analysis are familiar to lawyers and are applied to find great principles or define legal issues and are particularly suited to case law analysis. Lawyers[18] make use of judicial decisions and seek to explain their relevance as a coherent set of rules available to be applied to a new set of problems or facts. The mastery of techniques of case law analysis depends, whenever relevant, on drawing distinctions, recognising exceptions and if necessary special circumstances in order to categorise and create a coherent set of legal rules.

Like any model of analysis it may be readily adapted for different **7–11** purposes. Applied to judicial decisions by lawyers it is also applied by academic lawyers[19] in their textbooks. The influence of the "common law mind" is seen particularly in the development of legal education in the mid-nineteenth century.[20]

The law schools in the major universities became influential not only in the role they began to perform of educating lawyers, but also

---

[18] Sugarman, *op. cit.* pp. 28–29.
[19] *ibid.*
[20] *ibid.*

in the textbooks written by the leading academics of the period. An example of the role of the textbook in the study of public law is Dicey's *Introduction to the Law of the Constitution*. Dicey's lectures which formed the core of the book,were constructed around the idea of analysing, defining, and creating a uniformity of legal rules based on coherent principles. Dicey's achievement, in both the clarity of his style and the presentation of principles in the form of a working constitutional code, all contributed to the influence of the textbook in the development of public law. Textbooks readily filled a gap in the uncodified system of English law. They appeared to bridge the gap between the needs of the practitioner in the courts who required a compendium of relevant cases and precedents, and the academic study of law which required a coherent synthesis of the law. The standing of academic lawyers remained low, and the precedent value of their opinions was not readily accepted before the courts.

7–12   Aside from the influence of textbooks, other characteristics of the common law are striking when the common law tradition is compared to the civil law. English law in the public law area developed a system of remedies rather than rights. Remedies may be traced to the development of legal actions in the early history of the common law. The inheritance of the medieval Constitution focused on Parliament's powers and their development, to supersede the King's powers to make law and influence affairs of State through patronage. Once Parliament's authority was resolved the question of rights was regarded as a residual matter.

7–13   The judges, responsive to the need to develop legal rules, attempted to interpret the needs and problems of society through flexible solutions applied in individual cases. Much of the development of English law depended on the ability of the law to grant a suitable remedy in an individual case. Whilst remedies may have offered solutions to practical problems often these were constructed in narrowly defined ways and limited by procedure and form. No codified set of statutes or codified doctrine existed.

The English common law[21] was particularly influenced by the practitioner's concerns. This may explain how its survival and the haphazard nature of its development was achieved. The common law was remarkably antitheoretical in its approach. Notions of policy, justice and legal doctrine found in the common law were determined by procedure and form rather than through reasoned or theoretical principles. From an impartial view the law had to find an appropriate remedy to solve the case.

---

[21] See Sheldon Amos, *A Systematic View of the Science of Jurisprudence* (London, 1872).

Opposition[22] to codification[23] also marked out the English common **7–14**
law tradition as distinctive. This was particularly striking in the case
of the criminal law in the nineteenth century. Bentham's *Principles of
Penal Law* set out basic principles of law, both in theory and in
substance, and contained a draft criminal code. Generally, codification was not proceeded with even after Brougham, as Lord Chancellor, appointed Criminal Law Commissioners to consider
consolidation of existing common law principles and statutes into one
coherent set of rules. Continental systems[24] of law more easily
adopted codified systems of law influenced by the French Code
Napoléon and the Roman law tradition found in the Corpus Juris
Civilis. In part this may be a reflection[25] of the differing political
developments in England compared with European countries. But
evaluation is difficult because the common law rarely articulated
explanations of its own developments in contrast to scholars proposing and formulating codes.

Another distinctive feature of the common law tradition bearing on **7–15**
the development of public law is the development of statute law.
Parliament's role as a regular source of legal change was bound up
with the theory of the sovereignty of Parliament. The eighteenth
century Constitution emphasised a balance between the Executive
and Parliament freely admitting that parliamentary power might
become governmental power. The nineteenth century Constitution
with an extended franchise made Parliament a major source of law
through legislation.

Statutory law was an important source of formal reasoning, that **7–16**
maintained the sovereignty of Parliament. As Atiyah and Summers[26]
note:

"England has a long tradition of narrow, detailed drafting; the
English draftsman has always (or at any rate for at least two
centuries) tried to produce language which is capable of neutral,
non-purposive interpretation. An English statute has traditionally

---

[22] Dicey admitted that constitutionally guaranteed rights supported by adequate
remedies could be effective. See P. P. Craig, "Bentham, Public Law and Democracy"
[1989] P.L. 407.

[23] In contrast in Germany, Anton Thibaut (1772-1840) a law Professor, Heidelberg,
argued in his essay "On the Necessity for a General Civil Code for Germany."
Reservations about the universal nature of such a code was made by Friedrich Carl
Von Savigny (1779–1861).

[24] R. C. Van Caenegem, *Judges, Legislators and Professors: Chapters in European Legal
History* (1987). I. Loveland, *Constitutional law* (Butterworth, 1996).

[25] See Michael John, *Politics and the Law in Late Nineteenth Century Germany: the Origins
of the Civil Code* (Oxford, 1989). Also see D. P. Kelly, *Historians and the Law in Post-
revolutionary France* (Princeton, 1984).

[26] Atiyah and Summers, *Form and Substance in Anglo-American Law* (1988), p. 323.

been drafted in such detail that it can be said to be a catalogue of rules."

The strong orientation in favour of hard and fast rules contained in the mass of technical statutory law reflects the traditions of English government, based on a single winning party with strong political objectives presented in legislative form and passed by Parliament.[27] There is an equally strong tradition of skilled parliamentary drafting carried out by professional lawyers, with skills developed through the experience of permanent officials over a period of time. Most of this expertise remains confined to the resources of government departments.

7–17   The traditions of parliamentary sovereignty are therefore reinforced by the absence of any judicial power to review the legality of Acts of Parliament and until recently in the context of European Community law, this tradition remains strong. While public lawyers in the United Kingdom require the skills of reading cases and interpreting judicial decisions, equally and perhaps more important are the interpretative skills over complex, technical and precisely drafted statutes. Public law in the United Kingdom is to be found more in a statutory form than in the decisions of decided cases by judges.

7–18   Statutory developments have been so extensive that, it will be appreciated, this has added to the diffuse nature of the subject. Specialisms developed in public law where statutory developments have been extensive, include such subjects as local government, housing, planning law, immigration and the environment. The specialist nature of these subject areas make any generalisations of legal principle difficult. Moreover, any generalisations that attempt to explain the context where government activity takes place, such as housing, immigration or social security law, invariably become entangled in a mass of technical and complex rules that add further difficulty to understanding the nature of public law in the United Kingdom.[28]

7–19   A similar problem arises in the examination of principles of judicial review. Judicial review of administrative decisions lacks any detailed code of general principles.[29] Any attempt to formulate such a code is frustrated by the pragmatic and often sporadic nature of judical review. Arguably, legal principles derived from a small number of legal cases are limited in their general application.

---

[27] See Loughlin, *Public Law and Political Theory* (Oxford, 1992), pp. 244–245; discusses the neglect of the study of legislation.
[28] W. T. Murphy, "The Oldest Social Science? The Epistemic Properties of the Common Law Tradition" (1991) M.L.R. 182–215; Neil MacCormick, "Jurisprudence and the Constitution" [1983] *Current Legal Problems* 13.
[29] P. Cane, *An Introduction to Administrative Law* (2nd ed., 1992), p. 12. (3rd ed., 1996).

The eclectic and diffuse nature of public law, the absence of clearly defined principles and the historical legacy of an unwritten constitution have affected the development of public law. Public lawyers engage in a certain amount of gap filling. This means finding solutions from past experiences which do not always fit the challenges posed by new problems. Hence the attention given to conventions, understandings or practices which explain the working of the Constitution, but which may in reality be little more than the political habits of the government of the day.

The attraction of accomplishing[30] legal changes relatively easily 7–20 within an unwritten constitution compared to a written constitution may be misleading. Equally important is the possibility at least that the flexibility of an unwritten constitution may be adopted to the needs of government anxious to extend public power potentially unlimited or uncontrolled by any *constitutional* brake or device.[31]

The main characteristics of the United Kingdom's common law tradition may be briefly summarised. The unitary and centralised nature of the State, the formality and pragmatism of English law, the continuity offered by an unwritten constitution have their origins in the historical influences of the past and notably in the last century.[32] As McCrudden observed[33]:

"An important theme running through British thought concentrates on history and tradition when evaluating the processes by which political and legal decisions are made. Problems are solved, in this empiricist tradition, on the basis of experience. Solutions are what works and what lasts. Institutions should therefore operate flexibly, learn from the past and develop to suit the conditions of their time. This is the essence of the common law tradition."

[30] G. Marshall, G. C. Moodie, *Some Problems of the Constitution* (London, 1968), p. 19.
[31] N. Johnson, *In Search of the Constitution* (London, 1977) pp. 31–33.
[32] The common law itself was described by Milsom as "the by-product of an administrative triumph, the way in which the Government of England came to be centralised and specialised during the centuries after the conquest." See S. F. C. Milsom, *Historical Foundations of the Common Law* (London, 1981), p. 11. Also see J. H. Baker, *An Introduction to English Legal History* (3rd ed., Butterworth 1990), p. 223 and Henry Maine, *Ancient Law* (1861), p. 24, for a discussion of the fictions of the common law. See P. Birks and N. MacCormick (eds.), *The Legal Mind* (1986). Especially see P. Birks, "Fictions Ancient and Modern" in Birks and MacCormick, (eds.) *op. cit.*, pp. 83–101. For a useful description see J. G. A. Pocock, *Virtue, Commerce and History: Essays on Political Thought and History, Chiefly in the 18th Century* (Cambridge, 1985).
[33] C. McCrudden, "Northern Ireland and the British Constitution" in Jowell and Oliver (eds.), *The Changing Constitution* (2nd ed., 1989), p. 298. (3rd ed., 1994) pp. 323–379.

3. The Historical Legacy

7–21 The question arises as to the influences public law has experienced throughout its development. Arguably, the content of public law which is found in statutes, common law principles, conventions, rules and institutions may only be understood in the broader context of the ideas and influences which a society experiences. Most contemporary legal writers would accept that it is impossible to understand administrative law as a distinct subject without recognising the close inter-relationship between the constitutional arrangements within which administrative law must operate.

7–22 There is no complete congruence between legal theory or the ideas of political scientists or philosophers and public law. Differing assumptions about the role of the State, the exercise of power and the role of law itself make any informed discussion of legal theory and public law difficult to achieve. A further *caveat*, is that traditionally lawyers have reacted against broadening the nature of their inquiry beyond the confines of legally enforceable rights and the study of purely technical legal rules. This is a reflection of an approach confined to the study of court orientated rules. However, the nature of public law is such that many issues are not justiciable before the courts and depend not on legally enforceable rights, but on an understanding of the nature of law and political power under democratic and accountable government.

The task of assessing the influence of legal thinking on pubic law may be facilitated by the division of the discussion into two parts; first, consideration of the historical influences and second an introduction to contemporary discourse on public law. It is not possible to account for the development of all political theory in the nineteenth century. A selection is necessary, of the *influences* confined to explaining some of the main developments in public law.

7–23 The eighteenth century enlightenment is a convenient starting point to begin to trace the influences of legal thinking, theory and philosophy on public law. The United Kingdom had established without revolution, effective change by the end of the seventeenth century, contained in the Bill of Rights (1689), the Act of Settlement (1701) and the Act of Union (1707). Taken to be the framework of modern constitutional arrangements, the shape, function and operating practices of the Constitution remained to be defined and clarified.

7–24 Montesquieu's (1689–1755) influence was remarkable.[34] Influential in the idea that institutions of the State both political and legal might be criticised, he advanced the view that law was linked to the needs

---

[34] Montesquieu, *L'Esprit des Lois* (1748); *Défense de l'Esprit des Lois* (1750).

of society. His studies in England from 1729–31, and particularly the influence of the writings[35] of John Locke (1632–1704) led him to believe that natural law rights determining through constitutional law, the liberty of the individual. Montesquieu found attractive the liberalism of the English Constitution and this promoted the value of the United Kingdom's constitutional arrangements in Europe.

Montesquieu's influence became known in terms of social contract theory which linked the civil state, the laws and constitutions to the general state of society. Montesquieu helped promote belief in the doctrine of separation of powers setting out how government ought to carry out its legislative, executive and judicial functions, each working independently. Undoubtedly these ideas became influential as to *how* government was perceived to act within a framework contained in the eighteenth century Constitution. Building on Locke's thesis of the sovereignty or supremacy of Parliament, Montesquieu identified the various functions of government such as the legislative, executive and judicial. Believing in "checks and balances" Montesquieu also identified the necessary balance between the different elements of government to achieve some degree of self-regulation. **7–25**

Many of the assumptions underlying Montesquieu's analysis found recognition[36] in the works of later writers.[37] Recently contemporary writers such as Robson adopt Montesquieu's analysis when describing the working of the modern Constitution.

The quest for order in society[38] is a familiar theme among constitutional writing in the eighteenth century. This theme was developed in the writings of William Blackstone (1723–80) in his *Commentaries on the Laws of England*. Blackstone asserted the sovereignty of Parliament but this did not prevent him from accepting some natural law ideas as a means of achieving enforcement. Natural law concepts formed part of various social contract theories in an attempt to reconcile Parliament's legislative supremacy and individual justice. At times, there emerges in Blackstone's writing an explanation of constitutional "rights." These are asserted as part of the general protection afforded to the citizen under the law. Arguably such statements appear **7–26**

---

[35] Locke, *Essay Concerning Human Understanding* (1690).

[36] Scottish philosopher David Hume (1757–1838) was also influential. Loughlin draws attention to the much neglected work of John Millar (1735–1801), *An Historical View of the English Government* (1787). See Loughlin, *Public Law and Political Theory* (Oxford, 1992), pp. 6–8. Millar's work was a pioneering first constitutional history of the British Isles, Millar was regarded as an extreme radical and Whig supporter. He was Professor of Law at Glasgow University.

[37] A discussion of such influences may be found in Kelly, *A Short History of Western Legal Theory* (Oxford, 1992). Also see M. J. Horwitz, *The Transformation of American Law 1870-1960* (Oxford, 1992).

[38] See the letter from Dicey to Leo Maxse, September 25, 1909. Quoted in Richard Cosgrove, *The Rule of Law: Albert Venn Dicey, Victorian Jurist* (Macmillan, 1980), p. 62.

idealistic rather than practical and there is no acknowledgement of the difficulty of attempting to put their meaning into practice. We shall see below the importance of Blackstone in the development of the science of law.

7-27   Nevertheless, natural law concepts were significant for many eighteenth century legal writers because a law of nature conveniently fitted the natural reasoning of the period. Certainly in European legal philosophy, natural law concepts helped[39] form international law, and provide a strong tradition for a debate over the role of law in society. Both Montesquieu and Blackstone contributed to the discussion of natural law concepts in England. Blackstone's formal presentation of the law and formidable understanding of legal principles helped make the influence of his *Commentaries* extend beyond a small legal audience, to become part of "the literature of England."

7-28   In the English courts,[40] during the period when codification took root in Germany and France, principles of English law became solidified. The question arises as to what were the influences at work in the decisions of the courts during the seventeenth and eighteenth centuries?

Developments in public law included some early seventeenth century cases that laid the foundations of natural justice and standards of reasonableness as principles of the common law. The explanation for such judicial creativity came from the separate development of "natural rights" from natural law. Political writers in the eighteenth century influenced by Locke's explanation of and justification for the English revolution, developed more sophisticated understandings of rights being created through legal rules. Legal writers such as Coke (1552-1634) had linked property to rights and both Locke and Coke contributed to the views on the rule of law and natural rights which were later influential among French writers prior to the French Revolution. Locke's thinking on the rule of law had an important influence on Blackstone, whose analysis of the royal prerogative included the view that the Crown should not enjoy any immunity from civil liability by virtue of the nature of the prerogative.

7-29   Judicial developments[41] in the eighteenth century were about[42] the relationship between law,[43] the State and moral authority. One of the leading eighteenth century cases of *Entick v. Carrington* (1765)[44]

---

[39] J. M. Kelly (1964) 9 Natural Law Forum 103. See *Boswell's case* (1606) 6 Co. Ref. 48b; *Bagg's case* (1615) 11 Co. Rep. 93b.

[40] Also see *R. v. Venables* (1725) 2 Ld. Rayn 1405; *R. v. Alington* (1726) 2 Str. 678; *Harper v. Carr* (1797) 7 T.R. 270; *R. v. Chancellor of the University of Cambridge* (1723) 1 Str. 557.

[41] F. Pollock (1845–1937), *History of English Law Before Edward I* (1891).

[42] Coke's *Institutes* (1628–44).

[43] On Locke's *Rights of Man* see Friedmann, *Legal Theory*, p. 130.

[44] *Entick v. Carrington* (1765) 19 State Tr. 1030.

applied, in a practical way, the principle of individual rights as a protection against the implementation of a general warrant of arrest against John Wilkes which the courts declared illegal.

It will be apparent that a number of themes, recognisable from the discussion in Part I of the textbook, emerge from the eighteenth century writings on legal theory and political thought. These include the doctrine of the separation of powers, the rule of law and natural rights. Such constitutional principles become relevant in understanding the English Constitution. Particularly important was the influence of the doctrine of separation of powers as a protection against abuse and tyranny. By the end of the eighteenth century the role of the courts in developing common law principles had become articulated in disputes between the King and the judges over taxation and in the legality of arrest, search and seizure. The focus on principles of the common good were identified as an objective of law and good government. These principles became more fully developed at the beginning of the nineteenth century as pertinent to the questions raised about the increasing use of legislation.[45]

(a) The Science of Law

Attempts to systemise English law came from two directions. One 7–30 approach, influenced by Blackstone, attempted to add continental ideas about rights to the reasoning implied in the common law. The other approach dominated by Jeremy Bentham (1748–1832), aimed to provide a codification of principles. Whilst different directions may be detected in both approaches there was common ground. The methodology of science and the reasoning of statistical study were influential in the writings of both Blackstone and Bentham. This ensured that scientific methodology was integral to the analytical methodology and the legal reasoning employed in the development of the common law.

Blackstone encouraged the idea that English law was "a science which distinguished the criterion's of right and wrong".[46] His attempts to reconcile the historical development of the common law with a flexible and rule bound system gave rise to an analytical method. This proved to be very influential especially when later adopted by Dicey in his analysis of the English Constitution.[47] The

---

[45] Rights of Man and the Citizen (1789).
[46] W. Blackstone, Vol. I Commentaries 5–6.
[47] See J. F. McEldowney, "Dicey in Historical perspective — A Review Essay" in McAuslan and McEldowney, Law, Legitimacy and the Constitution (Sweet and Maxwell, 1985).

essential of Blackstone's legacy found that English law could be understood from a deductive system of reasoning incorporating natural law principles. This required a mathematical approach to law through a deductive method of analysis. It favoured the formality of legal rules and the formal reduction to specific points the resolution of any dispute.

7-31   It is not surprising to find that at the end of the eighteenth century many lawyers had become empiricists at a time that scientific discovery and science attracted the attention of the age. Whether this was coincidence or not is difficult to determine. What was remarkable, was that lawyers found that through detailed empirical investigation law was treated as practical and relevant rather than theoretical and abstract.[48] The law on pleading was a clear example of the view that the legal system was a functioning set of rules that provided the tools for the practitioner to fashion remedies for the client. Writers considered "the science of pleading" rooted in the belief that the precision of rules would give rise to the revelation of truth. The system of writs accentuated the idea that correct procedure gave rise to an accurate record and this lay the foundations of law.[49]

7-32   On a broader analysis empirical methodogy lay at the root of deciding cases. The development of case law followed from the efforts to systematise. The idea that English law could be found in decided cases rested on the development of a reliable and comprehensive system of law reports. The system of *stare decisis* and the doctrine of precedent rested on judicial reasoning being applied by analogy to cases with similar facts. Technical and formal rules applied in an analytical and scientific way rooted the common law to the empiricist tradition and the logic of the judges.

Within this tradition lay considerable self-doubt and disenchantment. The desire for a clearly defined set of rules for judges to apply prompted many English lawyers to examine the value of the civil law as a source of principles and jurisprudence. Generally there was considerable reluctance to reconcile the common law with the civil law system in all its forms.

7-33   Bentham's disillusionment with the common law identified in his later writings came from the inadequacy of the procedural rules, the absence of clear principles and the lack of comprehensiveness. His pursuit of universal codification of English law proved a life-time work which ultimately ended in frustration. There is evidence to show that in determing the contents of codes and their application Bentham shared the techniques implied in the scientific method as a means to determine concepts and ideas. Lobban explains[50]:

---

[48] Also influential was the writing of Montesquieu (1689–1755) *De l'esprit des lois* (1748).
[49] See *Mirehouse v. Rennell* (1833) 1 Cl. and F.527 at 546.
[50] M. Lobban, *The Common Law and English Jurisprudence 1760–1850* (Clarendon Press, Oxford, 1991) p. 155.

An Introduction [to the Principles of Morals and legislation] was perceived by Bentham to be a 'metaphysical' work, standing in relation to the substantive law as a treatise of pure mathematics stood to natural philosophy."

Bentham's codification project was ultimately rejected despite many attempts through numerous Royal Commissions and law reform initiatives. Bentham had sought to devise a science of principles derived from the immutable laws of human nature. In his principles of utility may be found the science of law reform. Diagnosing a wide range of social reforms from prisons to the workhouse, from education to the courts and from the substantive criminal law to a codified constitution, Bentham's ambitious aim was that through codification a legislative solution to the problems of society may be found.

The measurement of law against some standard or criterion was **7–34** the dominant theme in Bentham's pioneering work *A Fragment of Government* (1776) followed by his *Introduction to the Principles of Morals and Legislation* (1789). Bentham's task,[51] to develop a science of human action, began with a search for fundamental meaning in defining legal terms. His initial inquiry disputed the basic assumptions underlying Blackstone's *Commentaries* that all law was to be accepted without questioning its utility. Bentham questioned not only how law might be defined but what law should be. Bentham divided law into two categories, the first that of the legislator, he described as "authoritative law", and the second, law that was unauthoritative. By this means he questioned the quality of law according to his theory of utility namely the greatest happiness principle. This became an important theme developed at great length in his book[52] *A Fragment of Government.* Bentham's influence became apparent in the impact of his ideas on how legislation was to be appraised by lawyers in the nineteenth century. Bentham insisted that legislation should encourage the general good and to that end linguistic analysis might be called in aid of statutory interpretation. Weak laws might be avoided by an accurate analysis of legal terminology and an understanding "of the art of legislation."

Bentham's influence was wide-ranging. His philosophy was read **7–35** by a wide range of interested disciplines beyond law. In particular he was influential in fostering the idea that law might create improvements if subjected to an analytical approach and careful appraisal.

---

[51] P. Schofield, "Jeremy Bentham and Nineteenth Century English Jurisprudence" (May 1991) 12, J.L.H. No. 1, 58–88. Also see S. Collini, D. Winch, J. Burrow, *That Noble Science of Politics: A Study in Nineteenth Century Intellectual History* (Cambridge, 1983).

[52] J. M. Burns and H. L. A. Hart, (ed.), *A Comment on the Commentaries and A Fragment on Government* (London, 1977); J. Dinwiddy, "Early Nineteenth Century Reactions to Benthamism," *Transactions of the Royal Historical Society* XXXIV (1984), pp. 47–69.

The full importance of Bentham's work became clear in the nineteenth century as Bentham's legislative principles became influential. One explanation of Bentham's influence was the interpretation given to Bentham's writing by John Austin (1790-1859). Austin's lectures on jurisprudence were first published in *The Province of Jurisprudence Determined* (1832) which were later amended and expanded by a number of editors after his death. In terms of thinking about issues of public law, Austin's influence was probably the most significant in the nineteenth century, partly because his lectures appeared in the style of a textbook and in the absence of a major rival, Austin's views dominated jurisprudence.

7-36   Comparing Austin to Bentham is difficult, but it is generally accepted that Austin's view of law was narrower than Bentham's. It is also suggested that had Bentham published in his lifetime his work *Of Laws in General* this might have established[53] Bentham's pre-eminence over Austin. The narrowness of Austin's analysis[54] is due to the distinction he drew between the analysis of legal terms and reform of the law. Bentham conveniently drew both together, while Austin's desire to strictly interpret the law came from his definition of law to be "a command supported with a sanction." The essential clarity of the conception of law helped later writers, such as Dicey, to distinguish laws from conventions. Austin, along with Bentham, promised an analytical form of jurisprudence. Laws could be considered by jurists through defining their meaning and explaining their terms. Austin was less concerned than Bentham with considering what laws ought to consist of. Nonetheless both were influential in the development of public law in the nineteenth century.

7-37   Both Austin and Bentham belonged to the analytical school of jurisprudence. The analytical jurists classified, defined and expressed laws freed from any normative analysis. An equally significant influence in nineteenth century jurisprudence came from the historical school of jurisprudence. The historical school disputed that all law might be resolved as a command of a sovereign and insisted that custom, history, and opinion might be important sources of law. In contrast to the analytical school, the historical school, founded by Savigny (1779-1861) and influenced by Maine's (1822-88); *Ancient Law* (1861) and *Early Law and Custom* (1883) examined the relationship between law and morality. This inquiry questioned how existing practices and institutions reflected moral ideas and influences.

7-38   Both analytical and historical[55] schools came under various attempts to combine the strengths of each at different times

---

[53] Schofield *loc. cit.* note 43 on p. 62; J. Bowring (ed.), *The Works of Jeremy Bentham* (11 vols). See *The Limits of Jurisprudence Defined* (1945).

[54] Discussed in Schofield *loc. cit.*

[55] See J. M. Kelly, *A Short History of Western Legal Theory* (Oxford, 1992), pp. 312–325.

throughout the nineteenth century but with limited success. Taken generally there emerged a "science of jurisprudence", as an attempt to combine the virtues of both analytical and historical schools. Methodology became an important means to bridge the differences between each of the philosophical schools of thought.

The science of law[56] united both analytical and historical schools in the study of legislation. Denis Caulfield Heron (1825-1881)[57] in his work, *An Introduction to the History of Jurisprudence* (London, 1860) wrote how legislation was a "compromise between history and philosophy." The influence of codification in Europe encouraged consideration of law as a means of setting standards. While codification itself was rejected in England, the search for some reasonable standard to judge law united both the historical method of the historical school, with the analytical style and method of the analytical school.

In the nineteenth century the development of public law came **7–39** under similar influences as other areas of knowledge. Generally, it was commonly assumed that law could be regarded in the same way as other disciplines. In particular the science of law influenced how writers such as Dicey came to consider Parliament's role in developing legislation. Public law was influenced by the popularity of law reform. Law reform became a major catalyst for change and in the late nineteenth century became the forum for debate as to precisely the extent of Parliament's role.[58] The Reform Acts of 1832 and 1867 by extending the franchise, considerably broadened the franchise and the scope for change through an extended scope for Parliament's legislative authority.

As a result, English law resisted the attempt to provide a single **7–40** jurisprudence of rights and remedies. the jurisprudence of Blackstone, Bentham, Austin and Dicey allowed lawyers to conceive law through an analytical jurisprudence rooted in an empirical tradition bearing many characteristics of scientific proof. Strict procedural rules determined the precise point of dispute for deliberation by the court. Judges attempted to discover through deductive reasoning the resolution of the dispute from the material facts presented by the litigants in each case. So much lay outside the control of any single system of

---

[56] L. Goldman, "A Peculiarity of the English? The Social Science Association and the Absence of Sociology in Nineteenth Century Britain" (February 1987) 114, *Past and Present* pp. 133–171. Also see D. M. McKenzie, *Statistics in Britain, 1865–1930: The Social Construction of Scientific Knowledge* (Edinburgh, 1981).

[57] Denis Caulfield Heron (1825–1881), Professor of Jurisprudence and Political Economy, Queen's College, Galway 1849–1859. Q.C. 1860, M.P. for Tipperary 1868–74, Third Sergeant-at-Law 1880, Vice-President, *Social Inquiry and Statistical Society of Ireland* (1871–81).

[58] T. Porter, *The Rise of Statistical Thinking 1820–1900* (Princeton, 1986); John A. Hannigan, *Environmental Sociology* (Routledge, 1995).

rule. The litigant determined the cases that came to court and the facts each case presented. The judges responded to the challenge in a haphazard way drawing on wide range of sources and ideas to find solutions. The jury added to the lack of predictability of outcome. The common law built on the reasoning common to "ordinary men" and the rules of procedure that guided the discourse set the agenda for judges. The absence of a systemised Engish law and a coherent theoretical underpining of the principles of law underlines the importance of the analytical method used in the common law.[59]

(b)   The Statistical Movement

7-41 Schofield noted[60] that the science of law had two parts:

> "the first an analysis and a classification of the general principals which are to be found in advanced systems of law, and the second the discovery of the origin and growth of legal notions."

Public law was greatly influenced by both the methods of analysis and the search for principles in the growth and development of the common law tradition. Equating law and its study with other disciplines was encouraged by the development of the statistical movement in Britain.

Statistical study had its origins in the seventeenth century in the development of a scientific approach in the work of William Petty[61] (1623–87). Petty applied "political arithmetic" to the study of social problems. Collective phenomena could be investigated on the basis of a statistical method which permitted reasoning through the use of numbers. Statistical information could be collected and in 1835 Quételet[62] identified the "average man" in his essay *Sur l'Homme* which related a number of examples to an assessment of what was average.

7-42 This combination of ascertaining "facts" through statistics[63] and quantifying the "average" had wide application. The study of statistical phenomena attracted the formation of various statistical societies. One of the first such associations was the study[64] of statistics

---

[59] See Martin Loughlin, "The Pathways of Public Law Scholarship" in G. P. Wilson, (ed.), *Frontiers of Legal Scholarship* (John Wiley, 1996) pp. 163–188.

[60] Schofield, *loc. cit.*, note 43.

[61] William Petty, *Political Arithmetic* (1691).

[62] L. Quételet (1796–1874), *L'Anthropométrie* (1871).

[63] See Auguste Comte (1798–1857), *Cour de Philosophie Positive* (6 Vols.) (1830–42).

[64] M. Cullen, *The Statistical Movement in Early Victorian Britain* (Hassocks, 1975); David Elesh, "The Manchester Statistical Society: A Case Study of Discontinuity in the History of Empirical Research" (1972) 8 *Journal of the History of Behavioural Sciences* 280.

undertaken by the British Association for the Advancement of Science in Cambridge in 1833. The Manchester Statistical Society first met in September 1833 and soon after, in the 1840s, statistical societies appeared in Bristol, Ulster and in other parts of the United Kingdom.

An important source of statistical study came from official statistics prepared by government departments. The General Register Office and the Board of Trade became a major centre for statistical study in Britain. Parliamentary Committees of Inquiry sat during the nineteenth century, received evidence and collected statistical data.[65]

The attractions of statistical study[66] and its affect on public law **7–43** require explanation. A number of factors are evident from the influence of statistical study. The first is that "statistical facts" offered not only curiosity to the uninformed, but also the basis of knowledge and ultimately power to those with influence.[67] Secondly, official support for statistical study through various official departmental studies created an important database for government to make projections as to the future. Statistics contributed to an estimation of the problems confronting society such as crime, public health, education, literacy and housing. Thirdly, statistical study provided "an era of enthusiasm." A new sense of optimism or enthusiasm for law reform in the hope for future improvement combined with statistical study. Industrial progress could be vindicated by laying the blame for many social problems on other causes such as alcohol abuse, moral degeneration or urban life, linked to crime and destitution.

A recurrent theme of statistical study was the use of "objective **7–44** facts" to provide persuasive evidence to encourage legislative reform. This added to the persuasive authority of Brougham[68] (1778-1868) who founded the Social Science Association in 1857 and favoured law reforms on a large scale. A speech to Parliament in 1828, on law reform led to the investigation of law reform by the Common Law Commissioners. In 1864 this led to the setting up of a Law Amendment Society.[69] Thirty years later new Civil Judicial Statistics were published, the inspiration of that Society and Brougham's influence.

The statistical movement attracted an eclectic group of followers: **7–45** intellectuals, largely middle class but inter-disciplinary, combining the study of mathematics, the natural sciences, economics, law,

---

[65] O. R. McGregor, *Social History and Law Reform* (London, 1981).

[66] T. S. Ashton, *Economic and Social Investigations in Manchester: A Centenary History of the Manchester Statistical Society* (London, 1934).

[67] McEldowney and O'Higgins (eds.), *The Common Law Tradition* (Irish Academic Press, 1990). S. Milin Shannon, *Historical Memoirs* (Dublin, 1970).

[68] Henry Brougham (1778–1868), Founder of the Social Science Association (1857); Brougham, *Life and Times* (3 Vols., 1871). Founder Edinburgh Review 1802).

[69] L. Goldman, "A Peculiarity of the English? The Social Science Association and the Absence of Sociology in Nineteenth century Britain" (February 1987) 114 *Past and Present* 133–171.

philosophy and jurisprudence. The prominent role of the Social Science Association in promoting law reform on a wide variety of issues from education, public health, criminal and penal reform to the poor law, led it to be described as an "outdoor parliament" or "unofficial parliament." Such "volunteer legislators" were influenced by Bentham's principle that social, economic and political problems might be solved through legislation.[70]

7–46   Statistical study greatly contributed to the general development of political thought in mid-Victorian Britain. As a period of liberal influence, a growing professionalism in techniques of analysis and expertise was evident in the use of scientific analysis when applied to social problems. Victorian idealism often lacked coherence. The dogma of benevolence and good works was unsystematic and could easily be counter-productive. Philosophical ideas required a practical output and scientific method appealed to a wide cross-section of the main disciplines of the period. Law received an enhanced reputation when worked up into a practical science. Especially so when the economic laws of production and wealth and the main theories of political economists appeared too abstract to be relevant.[71] Social science, through statistical study appeared to offer a way forward in diagnosing both the cause of social problems as well as solutions through legislation. Statistical study provided lawyers with a new role for Parliament and therefore Public law. A vast variety of welfare legislation from the 1870s to the 1940s came under the influence of the statistical movement. The Statistical movement was aimed at first establishing an empirical basis for reform; such reforms were intended to ameliorate social distress. Such changes were gradual and found favour within government departments and through the influences of law teachers in universities.

(c)   Dicey and his Contemporaries

7–47 The emergence of an influential group of academic lawyers in the late nineteenth century must be set against a background of neglect in legal education. The 1846 Select Committee on legal education[72]

---

[70] Also see P. G. Stein, *Legal Evolution: the Story of an Idea* (Cambridge, 1980); Alexander Henry, *Jurisprudence: or, The Science of Law, Its Objects and Methods. An Introductory Lecture delivered at University College, London* (November 2, 1883), (London 1884); R. Smith, *The Fontana History of the Human Science* (1997).

[71] J. Harris, "Political Thought and the Welfare State 1870–1940: An Intellectual Framework for British Social Policy" (May 1992) 135 *Past and Present* 116–141.

[72] J. H. Baker, "University College and Legal Education 1826–1976" (1977) 30 C.L.P. pp. 1–13. See D. Sugarman in W. L. Twining (ed.), *Legal Theory and the Common Law* (1986), Chap. 3.

described "the lamentable state of legal education" and criticised the teaching of law in the universities of Oxford and Cambridge. Practical training in articles or pupillage was not well regulated or examined. Only gradually did change occur, first in 1852, with the establishment of the Council of Legal Education to regulate education of Bar students. Then in 1877, the Law Society succeeded in establishing solicitors qualifying examinations and eventually in 1903, a School of Law in London.

The Royal Commission Report, in 1856, continued demands for reform and the preference that universities should concentrate on the theoretical and philosophical study of law, leaving the teaching of practical law to the profession.[73]

The creation of new courses and posts in Oxford and Cambridge in **7–48** the latter half of the nineteenth century brought a new intellectual influence. The question was how to establish a role for academic lawyers[74] which numbered Maine (1822-88), Whewell, Professor of International Law in Cambridge, 1887, Bryce (1838-1922) Regius Professor of Civil Law at Oxford (1870-93), Anson (1843-1914) Warden of All Souls, Oxford (1899-1914), Holland (1835-1926) Chichele Professor of International Law and Diplomacy, Oxford 1874-1910, and Dicey (1835-1922) Vinerian Professor of Law, Oxford 1882-1909.

The answer came from analytical jurisprudence; so influential in **7–49** shaping legislation, it also influenced academic law.[75] Academic lawyers faced two pressures. One from within university education where academic respectability required a body of expertise and coherence. The other came from the legal profession which required understanding of legal principle, and practical explanation. As already mentioned above, academic lawyers found that legal textbooks[76] offered a suitable solution. This permitted an exposition of the law as a coherent whole, together with[77] an analysis of legal doctrine consistent with the tasks of legal education[78] and scholarship. In the field of public law, Dicey's writings came to dominate.

It has already been noted that Dicey's lectures at Oxford came to be **7–50** published[79] in 1885 in his *Introduction to the Law of the Constitution*.

---

[73] Philip Schofield, "Jeremy Bentham and Nineteenth Century English Jurisprudence" (May 1991) 12 J.L.H. No. 1 at 58–88.

[74] See Henry Maine, *Ancient Law: its Connection with the Early History of Society and its Relation to Modern Ideas* (London, 1861).

[75] Schofield, *loc. cit.* note 64. Also see M. Berg, *The Machinery Question and the Making of Political Economy* 1815-48 (Cambridge, 1980).

[76] Generally see Brian Abel-Smith and Robert Stevens, *Lawyers and the Courts: A Sociological Study of the English Legal System 1750-1965 (London, 1967)*.

[77] F. H. Lawson, *The Oxford Law School 1850–1965* (Oxford, 1968).

[78] P. Stein, "Legal Theory and the Reform of Legal Education in Mid-nineteenth century England" in A. Guiliani and N. Picarda (ed.) L'Educazione Giuridica II: Profili Storici (Perugia, 1979); MacCormick and Birks, *The Legal Mind* (Oxford, 1986).

[79] J. F. McEldowney, "Dicey in Historical Perspective – A Review Essay" in McAuslan and McEldowney, *Law, Legitimacy and the Constitution* (Sweet and Maxwell, 1985), pp. 39–61.

Influenced by the analytical school of thought, Dicey carefully set out the legal principles which guided the student of the Constitution. Originality of thought was not claimed, but by identifying the guiding principles which underpinned the unwritten constitution he created a legal textbook for lawyers devoid of much historical explanation.

Dicey's contribution to public law and his enduring influence may be examined[80] in two respects. First, Dicey's method of analysis and its significance when interpreting the law of the Constitution. Secondly, Dicey's explanation of the Constitution, especially his description of the legislative sovereignty of Parliament, the rule of law and the role of constitutional conventions, may be noted as to its significance for the study of public law. Throughout this text book various references may be found to the explanation of basic principles provided by Dicey. Even though his ideas remain controversial they are nevertheless influential.

7–51   Dicey's analytical method was based on Austin's analytical approach to legal thinking. The analytical method of inquiry favoured abstracting basic principles from legal material and subjecting constitutional law to scientific study. Dicey presented a vision of constitutional law corresponding to the earlier influences of Blackstone, Bagehot and Montesquieu. The English Constitution when subjected to Dicey's analysis appears as a triumph of achievement. Dicey's formulation of principles have the hallmark of a codified constitution providing uniformity, and formality through the application of Dicey's analytical method. Dicey's achievement was to provide the required exposition, conceptualisation and systematisation of constitutional law in the United Kingdom. In short, Dicey's *Law of the Constitution* filled a gap without encroaching upon law reform or the codification movement.

7–52   The enduring qualities of Dicey's analysis are reflected in his formulation of constitutional principles. It is useful to draw together the main elements in Dicey's thinking which remain influential today. It is readily apparent that Dicey borrowed many of his ideas from the various schools of jurisprudence mentioned above. Here we are concerned with general principles only, the details of many of these principles are discussed in the appropriate part of the textbook.

7–53   Dicey's vision of constitutional and administrative law begins with his analysis of sovereignty, both political and legal. Dicey acknowledged that Parliament could "make or unmake any law" but accepted that political and legal sovereignty could be distinguished.

---

[80] Loughlin, *Public Law and Political Theory* (Oxford, 1992); M. Lobban, *The Common Law and English Jurisprudence 1760–1850* (Oxford, Clarendon Press, 1991).

Political sovereignty placed certain influence with the majority of the electorate but this was to be entirely self-adjusting. Craig noted[81]:

"The absence of constitutional review and the Diceyan conception of sovereignty are therefore firmly embedded within a conception of self-correcting majoritarian democracy."

Dicey's idealism led him to believe that a unitary state embodying elected government might reinforce the rule of law. Paradoxically, the rule of law which later commentators considered the weak element in Dicey's analysis, came to reinforce sovereignty. The assumption is that the Commons might control the government. Dicey's style of analysis at first appears descriptive. His focus on principles and analytical style appears to offer a neutral perspective of the Constitution. Beneath the level of general description there are strong elements of value judgement. Dicey assumed that the English model of the Constitution was a better model than France or Germany or Switzerland, whose Constitutions Dicey had studied in great detail.

Dicey's rule of law adopted ideas from William Hearn (1826– **7–54** 1888)[82] in his work *The Government of England, its Structure and its Development* (London, 1867) and Dicey's understanding of conventions came from Edward Freeman (1823–1892)[83] in his work *Growth of the English Constitution* (London, 1877). The essentials of Dicey's analysis are as follows: The rule of law depended on the absence of broad discretionary power and that all public power resided with Parliament. The courts' power to review legislation was inappropriate when Parliament's role was to keep government under scrutiny. Judicial review did not require a separate or distinct system of courts when the Commons might control the Executive and the direction of all governmental power was through Parliament.

Such assumptions lie behind Dicey's vision of judicial intervention **7–55** being limited only to legislative intention. Even when the development of judicial scrutiny began in areas where the legislature had jurisdiction, Dicey was reluctant to envisage the courts developing beyond a narrow and defined remit, namely to ensure that the authority or power was exercised within its jurisdiction.

---

[81] P. Craig, *Public Law and Democracy in the U.K. and the USA* (Oxford, 1990), pp. 15–16. See M. Loughlin, *Legality and locality* (Clarendon Press, Oxford 1996).

[82] William Edward Hearn (1826–1888). See H. W. Arndt, "The Origin of Dicey's Concept of the Rule of Law" (1957) 31 Austl. L.J. 117-123. Hearn was Professor of Greek at Queen's College, Galway, and the first Dean of the Faculty of Law, University of Melbourne.

[83] Edward Augustus Freeman (1823–1892) an historian, was educated at Trinity College, Oxford. Succeeded William Stubbs as Regius Professor of Modern History. *History of Federal Government* (1863) and *History of the Norman Conquest* (1867-76).

Conventions come under the same tension as the rule of law when threatened by the sovereignty of Parliament. Dicey's reconciliation of conventions to a "modern code of constitutional morality" and thereby representative democracy, linked the power of Parliament to that of democracy. Government was believed to be representative.

7–56 However, democracy was narrowly defined as confined to male citizens. The dangers of popular opinion when it called for trade union reform, Home Rule for Ireland or votes for women were seen as threats to the single unitary model of the Constitution. Dicey's later writing reflected his concerns about the break up of the constituent parts of the United Kingdom through any federal constitutional arrangement.

To summarise, Dicey's skill at linking the historical roots of the common law tradition to constitutional change in the nineteenth century gave coherence to his vision of constitutional law. Adept at combining the influences of both the analytical and historical schools of jurisprudence, Dicey's work on the Constitution became influential. This was due to the combination of Dicey's analytical and expository style and the effect of providing in a codified form, a set of principles to guide discussion of constitutional law. Dicey had recognised a gap in textbook writing in constitutional law and by skilful analysis he provided a legacy for future generations of lawyers.[84]

7–57 Eight editions of the work were published during Dicey's lifetime. None were given substantial revision, though his last edition in 1914 received a revised introduction. By that time the shortcomings in Dicey's analysis had been noted and recognised.

The growth in delegated powers and in party government extended beyond any of Dicey's ideas of representative government. The ability of the Commons to control the Executive was doubted. Dicey also doubted whether the rule of law could survive given the combination of party politics and weak parliamentary control. The growth in legislation, and especially the debate over Irish Home Rule[85] had pointed to a growing tension between Dicey's model of the ideal constitution formulated in 1885 and the reality of the Constitution in 1914.

Such acknowledged defects in Dicey's vision of the constitution, apparent even to Dicey himself, did not lessen the importance of the Law of the Constitution. Paradoxically, the more defective the work was shown to be, the more influence[86] it seemed to hold over lawyers and public law.

---

[84] D. Sugarman, "The Legal Boundaries of Liberty: Dicey, Liberalism and Legal Science" (1983) 46 M.L.R. 102–111.
[85] R. Cosgrove, The Rule of Law, Albert Venn Dicey, Victorian Jurist (1980).
[86] Trowbridge Ford, "Dicey as a Political Journalist" (1970) 18 Political Studies 220–235.

The most glaring weakness[87] in Dicey's analysis was his failure to **7–58**
recognise the development of administrative law and his misunderstanding of French *droit administratif* which he erroneously saw as
equivalent to tyranny and something alien and Continental. English
traditions were seen as superior to French traditions[88] and the
character of English law and its institutions influenced Dicey's vision
of English administrative law.[89] In 1915 Dicey belatedly recognised
administrative law as a branch of English public law. In so doing
Dicey identified a role for the courts in overseeing the exercise of
powers by government departments. Relying on cases such as *Local
Government Board v. Arlidge* and the *Board of Education v. Rice*, Dicey
believed that the courts offered greater guarantees of the rule of law
than ministerial responsibility.[90]

"But any man who will look plain facts in the face will see in a
moment that ministerial liability to the censure not in fact by
Parliament, not even by the House of Commons, but by the party
majority who keep the Government in office, is a very feeble
guarantee indeed against the action which evades the authority of
the law courts."

Despite his earlier reservations about judicial review, Dicey gave **7–59**
the impression that the courts might provide the best protection of
liberties within existing constitutional arrangements.[91] Dicey's death
in 1922 left unanswered in any detail whether this revision of his
earlier views might have altered the fundamental principles of the
constitution he explained in 1885. Dicey's contemporaries at Oxford:
Bryce, Pollock, Holland and Anson, also wrote textbooks setting out
principles in a coherent and lawyerly fashion. However, it is Dicey,
alone among his contemporaries, whose influence became the most
significant.[92]

---

[87] H. Perkin, "Individualism versus Collectivism in Nineteenth Century Britain: A False
Antithesis" (1977) 17 *Journal of British Studies* 105–118.

[88] Craig, *op. cit.* pp. 19–29, 47–55.

[89] H. Arthurs, *Without the Law: Administrative Justice and Legal Pluralism in Nineteenth
Century England* (Toronto, 1985); H. Arthurs, "Rethinking Administrative Law"
(1979) *Osgoode Hall Law Journal* 1–45.

[90] A. V. Dicey, "The Development of Administrative Law in England" (1915) 31 L.Q.R.
148. See F. H. Lawson, "Dicey Revisited', (1959) *Political Quarterly* 109–126.

[91] C. S. Emden, *Principles of British Constitutional Law* (1925).

[92] Sugarman, "The Legal Boundaries of Liberty: Dicey, Liberalism and Legal Science"
(1983) M.L.R. 102–106. Also see M. J. Horwitz, "The Conservative Tradition in the
Writing of American Legal History" (1973) 7 *American Journal of Legal History* 275.

4. Contemporary Writers and Public Law

(a) Robson and Laski

7–60 Over one hundred years have passed since publication of the *Law of the Constitution*. During this period public law has continued to be influenced by Dicey's work. No less an influence came from writers challenging Dicey's vision of the constitution.

The period after the First World War witnessed an enormous growth in the role of both central and local government which had continued from the nineteenth century. Major political developments such as the growth in party politics and coalition government had already put a strain on Dicey's views of the constitution. Legal developments included an extension of governmental powers and functions, and the growth of public health and welfare provisions. This growth in administration had not been accompanied by any re-think of how the rights of the citizen and the role of the State might be held in balance.

7–61 Criticisms of administrative bureaucracy and inefficiencies at the expense of individual freedom were made in the late 1920s and throughout the period leading to the Second World War. William Robson[93] was influential in re-considering the Dicey model of the constitution which he complained lacked an adequate administrative law to meet the demands of an extensive administrative State. A source of major concern was the "acquisition of legislative and judicial functions by the Executive." Shortcomings in the system of tribunals, then in existence, were pointed out. Other writers criticised Dicey's analysis that administrative law was foreign or alien to English law. Particularly forthright in pointing out the errors in Dicey's analysis and understanding of French administrative law, Jennings[94] asserted that administrative law had a valuable role in a country with a highly developed sense of political organisation. Jennings also disputed Dicey's analysis of sovereignty and questioned the value of individual rights contained in the rule of law as outlined by Dicey. In general Jennings favoured a broader more sociological approach to public law. Dicey had analysed public law in terms of applying private law concepts and principles to government, sovereignty and the State. Jennings adopted a different approach, preferring to develop public law concepts in terms of duties, powers and responsibilites by adopting a "sociological method."

---

[93] W. A. Robson, *Justice and Administrative Law* (London 1928). Also see W. A. Robson, "The Report of the Committee on Ministers' Powers" (1932) 3 *Political Quarterly* 346.

[94] I. Jennings, *The Law and the Constitution* (London, 1933). See Jennings, "The Report on Ministers' Powers" (1932) 10 *Public Administration* 333; Jennings, "In praise of Dicey 1885–1935" (1935) 13 *Public Administration* 123.

Jennings defined the role of the lawyer interested in the Constitu- 7–62
tion as different from the practitioner[95]:

> "The sociological process is simply to examine the facts, including
> the ideas of any given society. A jurist or a constitutional lawyer,
> unlike the practising lawyer is not concerned with the set of ideas
> possessed by lawyers alone, but with the ideas of people
> generally."

Broadening the debate as to the relationship between the nature of
law and the State brought more influences in the development of
public law. The most formidable was the work of Harold Laski[96]
(1893–1950), whose influence on the theory of the State called into
question assumptions behind the liberal State and the exercise of
political power. Laski was greatly influenced by American jurists
such as Holmes and Pound. By rejecting high theory he argued for
practical, common sense and realistic assessments to be made of the
reasoning behind judicial decisions and an exposition of assumptions
which lay behind the value judgements contained in policy decisions.

Laski also questioned the single, unitary view of the State favoured 7–63
by Dicey.[97] Far removed from Dicey's idealism of the perfection he
found in the Constitution, Laski sought justification for the consequences of government power and linked economic and social
power to legal authority. Developing these ideas caused Laski to
challenge the liberal theory of the State with the result that his
sociological approach found support in the writings of Jennings and
Robson.

Variations in Laski's reasoning,[98] especially in his later works, have
echoes of the influences of pragmatism which may also be found in
other writers of the period. No single, coherent theme may be
identified from among all of Dicey's critics but the debate about the
nature of public law had changed remarkably from Dicey's influence.
The period 1928–1932 marked an intense debate about public law.

Robson's influential *Justice and Administrative Law* was published in 7–64
1928. A year later the Lord Chief Justice, Lord Hewart had published
The New Despotism[99] and a year after, F. J. Port's *Administrative Law*.[1]
Hewart's warning of "administrative lawlessness" feared that government had become too powerful and in common with Dicey's fears

---

[95] Jennings, *The Law and the Constitution* (London, 1933).
[96] H. Laski, *Studies in the Problem of Sovereignty* (1917); *Authority in the Modern State*
(1919); "The Growth of Administrative Discretion" (1923) 1 *J. of Public Admin.* 92;
Report of the Committee on Ministers' Powers, Cmnd. 4060 (1932) Annex V.
[97] H. Laski, *Studies in the Problem of Sovereignty* (London, 1917).
[98] H. Laski, "Judicial Review of Social Policy in England" (1926) 39 *Harvard L.R.* 839.
[99] G. Hewart, *New Despotism* (1929), pp. 43–44.
[1] F. J. Port, *Administrative Law* (1930).

voiced in 1915, Hewart feared that the rule of law might become meaningless. All these influences came to the fore when in 1929 the Donoughmore[2] Committee was set up inquiring into Ministers' powers, the use of delegated legislation and judicial decision-making. The Report was published in 1932 and Laski was included among the membership of the committee. Hewart's *New Despotism* claimed that the power of government had expanded[3]:

> "The official is anonymous, he is not bound by any course of procedure nor by any rules of evidence, nor is he obliged to give any reasons for his decision. . . . The exercise of arbitrary power is neither law nor justice, administrative or at all."

English administrative law with its distinctive use of administrative tribunals and inquiries was ill co-ordinated and lacked rationality.

7–65 Despite such strictures little was achieved by the Donoughmore Committee in terms of unifying the hotch-potch of administrative tribunals into a coherent whole. After Donoughmore, tribunals grew in an uncontrolled and bureaucratic way with specialised and complex rules accompanying their development.

The rejection of Robson and Laski's analysis which favoured an independent tribunal system may be attributed to[4] *droit administratif* and Dicey's objections. The Committee feared that setting up a uniform and independent tribunal system amounted to a rival form of administrative law to the ordinary courts and especially so if judicial review was excluded. While Dicey's influence still inhibited the growth of administrative law, it was only after the Second World War that the opportunity to break with the past arose. The Franks Committee in 1957, set up after the Crichel Down[5] affair, reported in favour of creating a proper system of tribunals with clearly defined objectives and procedures under the Council of Tribunals. In effect this abandoned Dicey's opposition to such a system.

7–66 Recognition that administrative law had a proper place in English law came slowly. In 1964 Lord Reid observed[6] "We do not have a developed system of administrative law – perhaps because until fairly recently we did not need it." Thereafter doubts about the existence and need for administrative law slowly dispelled. What remained, however, was a fundamental debate about the role of the courts in the future development of administrative law.

---

[2] Report of the Committee on Ministers' Powers, Cmnd. 4060 (1932).
[3] Hewart, *op. cit.* pp. 43–44.
[4] Craig, *Public Law and Democracy in the U.K. and USA* (Oxford, 1990), pp. 20–52.
[5] Discussed in Chaps. 4 and 5.
[6] *Ridge v. Baldwin* [1964] A.C. 40.

Dicey's rule of law asserted that the ordinary law should be supreme and that the ordinary courts should act as the cornerstone of the rule of law. Expanding the role of the courts through increased judicial intervention as the means of developing administrative law seemed to many as supporting Dicey's rule of law. Under this view administrative law came to mean *only* judicial review. Remedies available to the litigant were narrowly and often procedurally defined and restricted to issues which to the courts appeared similar to settling contract or tort liability disputes in the private sector. This comparison of administrative law to actions in the private sector is useful when understanding how judicial review in the early development of administrative law remained restricted and constrained by narrow and technical concerns.

While Laski, Robson and Jennings, had set a new agenda for the **7–67** development of public law, judicial attitudes seemed to reflect Dicey's influence.[7] One reason lay in the historical development of remedies and the narrow confines of statutory intention in terms only of legislative intent. The courts were presented with individual rights and specific remedies with the requirements of a specific *locus standi* rather than any broader inquiry into how powers were exercised. No conceptual framework for administrative law was put in place once administrative law became an established part of English law.

Another reason may be gleaned from the nature of Dicey's inheri- **7–68** tance bequeathed to lawyers. With hindsight Dicey's original principles seem untenable given the nature of political and economic changes since 1885. Later writers had successfully shown contradictions in Dicey's principles and even Dicey's later revisions failed to support his original premise. Despite these flaws and rather like a many-headed hydra, Dicey's influence was not confined to his written text but his *vision* of constitutional arrangements triumphed over past practices and early history. Errors or flaws in Dicey's principles seemed to have been overlooked or distinguished as if they represented old precedents, which allowed Dicey's vision to continue and *Law of the Constitution* to remain a significant textbook for the study of constitutional and administrative law. Dicey's analytical method, which owes much to the empirical tradition in law, has also remained influential in the style of public law scholarship.[8]

---

[7] In particular see H. W. R. Wade, *Administrative Law* and "Law, Opinion and Administration" (1962) 78 L.Q.R. 188 and *Constitutional Fundamentals* (1980).

[8] Discussed in Loughlin, *Public Law and Political Theory* (Oxford, 1992), pp. 190–198; I. Harden, "Review Article: The Constitution and its Discontents", B.J. Pol. S. 21 at pp. 489–510.

(b)   Public Law and Political Change

7–69 Robson and Laski invigorated the study of public law by broadening the terms of inquiry into the nature of power and how power is exercised by the State. Economic, social and political issues became relevant in understanding public law. Further advances in understanding public law came from the influence of philosophy on law, which underwent a remarkable transformation under the influence of H. L. A. Hart.

Dicey, following Austin and Bentham defined law as the command of a sovereign. After the Second World War jurisprudence became influenced by linguistic analysis from the writing of Wittgenstein and Gilbert Ryle.[9] The Oxford lawyer and philosopher H.L.A. Hart questioned[10] the Austin view of sovereignty and law, pointing out inadequacies in the understanding "of all law as a command." This contributed further to the discourse on public law by bringing questions of morality and explicit notions of adjudication in seeking to explain why laws are obeyed. Distinguishing legal from moral rules, Hart argued, depends on how society views the status of a particular rule.[11]

7–70   The diversity of the influences[12] in the development[13] of public law includes contributions from political science, international studies and sociology. The blurring of subject categories as well as legal categories further complicates the question of whether public law is a distinctive subject? Daintith observes that a noticeable trend in writing about public law[14] "is the prevailing descriptive and eclectic mode of writing about the United Kingdom's constitution and public law." The various influences currently at work in public law scholarship may be noted as follows.

7–71   Dicey's influence and analytical method may find familiarity in public law writing today. Some writers see the present development of administrative law as a product of Dicey's influence and the furtherance of the rule of law. Other writers take their point of reference from Laski and Robson and seek to expand the study of public law through an analysis of present day problems supported by detailed empirical investigation. Their focus of study does not adopt

---

[9] Kelly, *A Short History of Western Theory* (Oxford, 1992), pp. 403–447.

[10] H.L.A. Hart, *The Concept of Law* (Oxford, 1961); "Definition and Theory in Jurisprudence" (1954) 70 L.Q.R. 37. See also J. Raz, *The Morality of Freedom.*

[11] W. N. Hohfeld, *Fundamental Legal Conceptions as Applied in Judicial Reasoning and Other Legal Essays,* (W. W. Cooke ed., Newhaven, 1919).

[12] T. R. S. Allen, "Pragmatism and Theory in Public Law" (1988) 104 L.Q.R. 422.

[13] The evolution of legal education to meet the needs of society. See Laswell and MacDougal, "Legal Education and Public Policy" (1943) 52 Yale L.J. 203.

[14] T. Daintith, "Political Programmes and the Content of the Constitution" in Finnie, Himsworth and Walker (eds.), *Edinburgh Essays in Public Law* (1991), pp. 41–55.

any *one* single particular perspective, nor are there distinct schools of thinking with clearly defined theory or analysis. Those that seek to develop public law beyond Dicey's vision come under a number of influences that may be conveniently identified.

There is a continued interest in the historical development of public law.[15] Studies of contemporary issues often include historical analysis. Recent scholarship in particular has sought to identify how administrative law developed the structure of nineteenth century administration and the influences of political science in public law.

Contemporary writing on constitutional and administrative law has also reflected the fast-developing specialisms[16] which may conveniently fit within the broadest definition of public law. These include planning law,[17] environmental law,[18] housing law[19] and welfare law.[20] Such subjects receive separate treatment in specialised texts but the nature of the subject matter raises questions about government powers, administrative decision-taking and the role of the courts. Generalisations made from the study of such specialisms about public law require careful elucidation. **7–72**

Also noticeable is the trend to develop expertise within public law itself. Subjects include privatisation,[21] regulation,[22] European Community Law,[23] local and central government,[24] and public finance.[25] Public law issues are therefore increasingly perceived as not only involving the courts but a range of institutions and bodies, some with quasi-governmental functions. Another significant influence on the development of public law is the increasingly relevant writings **7–73**

---

[15] Craig, *loc. cit.* note 80; J. Mitchell, "The Causes and Effects of the Absence of a System of Public Law in the United Kingdom" [1965] P.L. 95.

[16] On civil liberties see P. Thornton, "Decade of Decline; Civil Liberties in the Thatcher Years" (NCC, 1989); G. Robertson, *Freedom, the Individual and the Law* (6th ed., Penguin Books, 1989) (7th ed., 1992); K. Ewing, C. A. Gearty, *Freedom under Thatcher* (Oxford, 1990); Bailey, Harris and Jones, *Civil Liberties* (4th ed., 1996).

[17] P. McAuslan, *The Ideologies of Planning Law* (Oxford, 1980); M. Grant, *Urban Planning Law.*

[18] John McEldowney and Sharron McEldowney, *Law and the Environment* (Longman, 1996).

[19] See G. Ganz, *Understanding Public Law* (1987), pp. 47–63.

[20] G. Ganz, *Quasi-legislation: Recent Developments in Secondary Legislation* (London, 1987).

[21] C. Crouch and R. Dore, *Corporatism and Accountability* (Oxford, 1990); Vickers and Yarrow, *Privatization, An Economic Analysis* (1988); Mayer *et.al.*, *Privatisation and Regulation* (Oxford, 1986).

[22] T. Prosser, *Nationalized Industries and Public Control* (Oxford, 1986); Graham and Prosser, *The Privatisation of Public Enterprises.* Also see P. Birkinshaw, I. Harden, N. Lewis, *Government by Moonlight* (1990); A. Ogus, *Regulation* (Clarendon Press, Oxford, 1994). T. Prosser, *Law and the Regulators* (Clarendon Press, Oxford, 1997).

[23] Kapteyn and Verloren Van Themaat, *Introduction to the Law of the European Community* (1989).

[24] M. Loughlin, *Local Government in the Modern State* (London, 1986).

[25] J. McEldowney, "The National Audit Office and Privatisation" in Freedman and Power, *Law and Accountancy* (Chapman, 1992), pp. 165–187.

undertaken by political scientists.[26] A good example is N. Johnson's *In Search of the Constitution*, which critically examines the existing constitutional arrangements in the United Kingdom in 1975. Johnson notes[27]:

> "It becomes more and more difficult to set limits to the powers of government; there is growing uncertainty about the terms in which public bodies are expected to act: the authority of those in political life is weakened; and it becomes steadily harder to justify political action by reference to constitutional norms."

Political scientists found common cause[28] with lawyers in the discussion of devolution proposals made in the Kilbrandon Report in 1979. A range of important topics[29] such as the new select committees,[30] electoral reform,[31] reform of the House of Lords,[32] freedom of information,[33] police accountability,[34] central-local relations[35] and emergency powers in Northern Ireland[36] represent major areas where political scientists and lawyers have had a fruitful dialogue. Parliament, its function and role has also attracted multi-disciplinary attention.

7–74   Two areas in particular may be mentioned as coming under intense scrutiny as part of the socio-legal approach and analysis of public law issues. First, in the subject of non-judicial means of dispute, resolution between citizens and administration. Attention is given to tribunals, inquiries, ombudsmen and M.P.s as part of the dispute procedures involved in grievance machinery. Empirical research, case studies and theoretical analysis are often combined in research projects covering a

---

[26] An example G. Drewry, "Foreword from FMI: "The Next Steps" (1988) P.L. 505. See the contributions between lawyers and political scientists in Jowell and Oliver (eds.), *The Changing Constitution* (2nd ed., Oxford, 1989).

[27] N. Johnson, *In Search of the Constitution* (1977), p. viii.

[28] Kilbrandon Report: *Report of the Royal Commission on the Constitution 1969–73* Cmnd. 5460 (1973). A. Lester, "The Constitution: Decline and Renewal" in Jowell and Oliver (eds.), *The Changing Constitution*, (2nd ed., Oxford, 1989, pp. 345–369. See F. F. Ridley, "Defining Constitutional Law in Britain" (1991) 20(2) Anglo-Am. L.J. 101–115.

[29] A review of administrative law literature may be found in R. Rawlings "The Complaints Industry: A Review of Sociological Research on Aspects of Administrative Justice" (E.S.R.C., 1986).

[30] G. Drewry, *The New Select Committees: A Study of the 1979 Reforms* (Oxford, 1989). See Greenwood and Wilson, *Public Administration in Britain Today* (1989).

[31] V. Bogdanor, *The People and the Party System. The Referendum and Electoral Reform in British Politics* (Cambridge, 1981); "Constitutional Law and Politics" [1987] 7 O.J.L.S. 454.

[32] Hood Philips, *Reform of the Constitution* (1970). The debate has included a number of Government proposals: House of Lords Reform, Cmnd. 3799 (1968).

[33] P. Birkinshaw, *Freedom of Information* (1988).

[34] M. McConville, Sanders and Leng, *The Case for the Prosecution* (1991).

[35] M. Goldsmith (ed.), *New Research in Central-Local Relations* (1986).

[36] C. Palley, *The U.K. and Human Rights* (1991).

wide range of institutions. Although the Law Commission declined[37] in 1965 to undertake a detailed analysis of administrative law, the studies carried out over the last 25 years provide an important resource if such a study were to be undertaken in the future.

Secondly, and related to the first, regulation of the newly privatised **7-75** utilities has set a new direction for public lawyers. Hybrid powers involving statutory authorities, licences, contracts and Company Act company agreements, provide the main means for carrying out many of the main activities in provision of telecommunications, water, gas and electricity. Research into these fields involves economists, political scientists and lawyers.

Public lawyers have also been attracted to the analysis of the **7-76** United Kingdom's constitutional arrangements with a view to reform.[38] In the past 25 years, the possible adoption of a Bill of Rights has become a question of intense debate. Human rights literature including work on social, religious or gender discrimination has focused attention on the absence of a written Bill of Rights or written constitution in the United Kingdom. Public lawyers have been instrumental in setting the agenda in this debate.[39]

The "descriptive and eclectic" mode of writing about public law **7-77** has also extended to a more radical critique of the United Kingdom's constitutional arrangements. In the past three years, no fewer than four written constitutional proposals have been advanced, setting out detailed drafts containing these proposals. This is perhaps a symptom of the difficulty diagnosed by many lawyers when writing about the United Kingdom's constitutional arrangements. The problem is to know precisely what "constitutional" or "unconstitutional" may mean.[40]

This difficulty of understanding the term "constitutional" leads to **7-78** the absence of any clear meaning to be attached to the unconstitutional, leaving the word merely as Grant has observed[41] "an expression of unease, a code-word indicating disquiet with a destabilising intervention." In this way any normative, as distinct from the descriptive use of the word "constitutional," leaves lawyers uneasy.

---

[37] *Administrative Justice – Some Necessary Reforms* (1988).

[38] L. Scarman, *English Law – The New Dimension* (London, 1975).

[39] In 1990, published drafts included: Liberal Democrats, Federal Green Paper No. 13 "We the People: Towards a Written Constitution" (1990), Institute for Economic Affairs, Constitutional Reform in the United Kingdom (1990), Tony Benn, M.P., the Commonwealth of Britain Bill (1990–91) H.J.C. 161, and in 1991 Institute for Public Policy Research, The Constitution of the United Kingdom (1991).

[40] Anson expressed the point in 1886: It is well to attempt some limitation or definition of the subject. To define our subject, it is necessary to determine the place of constitutional law in the corpus juris of the courts. Anson, *The Law and Custom of the Constitution* (1886).

[41] M. Grant in Jowell and Oliver, *The Changing Constitution* (2nd ed., 1989), pp. 247–272.

This may mean that the term may have no direct legal significance it invites condemnation as a political[42] rather than a legal judgment. This may state the case too starkly. In fact "unconstitutional" may provide a useful device to allow a more theoretical analysis of the norms and understanding implicit in the working of the Constitution.

7–79   Public lawyers have become increasingly aware of the political origins[43] and nature of the changes in society as reflected in the legislation passed as a result of the policies of the government of the day. As a result a large body of literature attempts to set the boundaries of public law within the framework of theoretical debate.[44] Attempts to provide new criteria or norms to evaluate the "legitimacy" of government action or principle to direct critical analysis of government decision-taking have not been wholly successful. However frustrated such attempts have been there is merit in setting out to improve the analysis of values and techniques intended to provide for more open and accountable government.

7–80   As part of this development of more theoretical based studies there is a growing unease about the futility of the operation. Loughlin's expectation that legal theory helps us to render explicit the styles of public law thought is somewhat blunted by the difficulty of finding a suitable vocabulary to provide public lawyers with a suitable agenda for the future. There is in fact a veritable hotch potch of theories and ideas competing for influence in setting public law on a clear direction for the future. Loughlin summarises his vision for the future[45]:

> "In confronting these important issues concerning the relationship between government and law, the functional logic of modern law must be accepted. This means that any contribution which public law may provide to the development of effective and accountable structures of government should be based on a sociological orientation. Studies need to be rooted in a socially constructed field and, from that perspective, should investigate the interplay of cognitive and normative considerations. The normative structure of law should be recognised. But unlike the normatist approach, the question of laws' normative structure is itself an object of inquiry."

---

[42] P. McAuslan, "Public Law and Public Choice" (1988) 51 M.L.R. 681.

[43] P. McAuslan and J. McEldowney, "Legitimacy and the Constitution: the Dissonance between Theory and Practice" in McAuslan and McEldowney (1985).

[44] Harden and Lewis, *The Noble Lie The British Constitution and the Rule of Law* (London, 1986); Graham & Prosser (eds.), *Waiving the Rule: The Constitution under Thatcherism* (Open University Press, 1988). The critical legal studies tradition incorporates many of these ideas: see Critical Legal Studies Howard Law Review (1983) 561, 592, 607; J. Finnis, "The Critical Studies Movement" in *Oxford Essays in Jurisprudence*, (3rd ser., Oxford, 1987) p. 157. A more realistic approach is found in D. Oliver, *Government in the United Kingdom* (Open University Press, 1991).

[45] Loughlin, *op. cit.* p. 247.

Other writers have sensed the need for new directions but have been reluctant to set out an agenda for the future.

The breadth of the inquiry presently undertaken by public lawyers **7–81** is formidable. As Daintith has observed "the conscientious search for a structure of constitutional obligation might well show that we possess no reliable rules over large areas of public life."

The focus of public law scholarship extends from the legal to the non-legal.[46] Because many of the informal rules or understandings which guide public institutions are important, the task in hand extends beyond the ordinary remit of legal training. Political science, history, sociology and economics have a relevance to the future direction of public law within the United Kingdom even if that relevance requires justification and explanation to fit each task under review.

The future role of public law is likely to be found from the agenda **7–82** of constitutional reform advanced by the new Government. A modern Bill of Rights, devolution for Scotland and Wales, and a possible Freedom of Information Act will reshape the existing constitutional landscape. The old constitution inherited from the past will have to adapt to the constitution in the making. This will amount to a revolution in our constitutional arrangements, and a curiosity about the role of the public law scholar[47] facing the challenges of a new scholarship in the era of reform.

The inquiry is not narrowly confined to the United Kingdom. Comparative evaluation of constitutional arrangements in Canada, Australia and the United States of America have provided useful influences in understanding common law systems and their adaptation. The European Community and the influence of European institutions are important for the future of public law in the United Kingdom and are considered in more detail in the chapter which follows.

---

[46] See Griffiths, "The Political Constitution" (1979) 42 M.L.R. 1; and *The Politics of the Judiciary* (London, 1991). Echoes of Jennings' view are apparent in Loughlin's thesis: See Jennings, *The Law and the Constitution* (1942), p. 300: "The process of explanation is the function of constitutional law (or jurisprudence) or of that part of political science which is concerned with the actual workings of institutes; the process of justification belongs to political theory (or the philosophy of law) or to that part of political science which relates to the theory of institutes."

[47] Loughlin, p. 188.

Chapter 8

The European Union

1. Introduction

8–01 The European Union comprises 15 Member States and now stands on three pillars. The Community pillar governs the operation of the various institutions such as the Commission, Parliament, the Council and the Court of Justice. From the coming into force of the Maastricht Treaty on November 1, 1993 this involves managing the internal market and common polices of the Community.[1]

There are two other pillars of the European Union.[2] Foreign and security policy forms one and the other is formed around asylum and immigration policy, the police and justice. The development of the European Union is set to be further changed by the plan to create economic and monetary union. On January 1, 1999 it is intended that subject to Member States satisfying certain economic criteria and the maintenance of sound financial management there should be a common currency, the Euro, and agreed fixed exchange rates.[3]

8–02 The aim of this chapter is to examine European influences on the United Kingdom's system of public law. As discussed in Chapter 1, the Treaty of European Union signed at Maastricht, created the European Union, ratified and adopted into the United Kingdom by the European Communities (Amendment) Act 1993.

---

[1] See the unsuccessful legal challenge *R. v. Secretary of State for Foreign and Commonwealth Affairs, ex p. Rees-Mogg* [1994] Q.B. 552.

[2] See Neill Nugent, *The Government and Politics of the European Union* (3rd ed., Macmillan 1994); Bernard Rudden and Derrick Wyatt; eds., *Basic Community Laws* (6th ed., Oxford, 1996).

[3] See Neil Walker, "European Constitutionalism and European Integration" (1966) *Public Law* 266–290; Rémy Prud'Homme, *Public Finance with Several Levels of Government* (Brussels, 1990); M. Shackelton, *Financing the European Community* (Pinter Press, London, 1990); Ian Harden, "Budget: Objectives, Norms and Procedures" chapter IV in A. Wildavsky and E. Zapico-Goni (eds) *National Budgeting for Economic and Monetary Union* (Institute of Public Administration, London, 1994).

2. European Ideas and Influences

Since January 1, 1973, when the European Communities Act 1972 **8–03** took effect, the United Kingdom became a member of the European Community (E.C.).[4] The United Kingdom's membership[5] of the E.C. is not static. Change within the E.C. is both evolutionary and pragmatic in the creation of a new European legal order. Intense political debate and controversy very often accompany discussion of the future direction of the E.C. The United Kingdom is an important, albeit at times, reluctant part of a single market, a major economic and social unit which has as its objective, benefits for the economy of the United Kingdom. The development of a true single market among Member States is the ambition of the Single European Act, signed by all Member States in 1986. Membership of the E.C. has raised significant implications for the United Kingdom's existing constitutional arrangements. Many of these issues, such as the impact of membership on the United Kingdom's sovereignty, are still being addressed and are likely to remain prominent for the foreseeable future.

In this chapter it is intended to consider how new directions and **8–04** influences may come from European ideas and influences, in addition to the influences of domestic law. Milsom[6] reminds us that:

"It has happened twice only that the customs of European peoples were worked up into intellectual systems of law; and much of the world today is governed by laws derived from the one or the other."

(a) Historical Influences

Many European countries, with the exception of the United Kingdom, **8–05** adopted a civil law tradition as part of their development. The civil law tradition cast a rich inheritance[7] of law, morality and culture

---

[4] The term European Community and its abbreviation (E.C.) will be used throughout this chapter for convenience. There are in fact four distinct communities namely, the European Coal and Steel Community, the European Economic Community, and the European Atomic Energy Community, it is common to refer to the E.C. Finally there is the Treaty on European Union has created a European Union wider than the Economic Community.

[5] Currently E.C. membership comprises: U.K., France, Germany, Italy, Republic of Ireland, Denmark, Netherlands, Belgium, Luxembourg, Portugal, Greece, Spain, Austria, Finland and Sweden. In Chap. 1 the structures of the E.C. have been shortly outlined. A more comprehensive analysis is provided in P. J. G. Kapteyn and P. Verloren Van Themaat, *Introduction to the Law of the European Communities* (Kluwer, 1990), English edition edited by Laurence Gormley. S. Weatherill and Paul Beaumont, *E.C. Law* (2nd ed., Penguin, 1995). E. Ellis and Takis Tridimas, *Public law of the European Community: Text Materials and Commentary* (Sweet and Maxwell, 1995).

[6] S. F. C. Milsom, *Historical Foundations of the Common Law* (2nd ed., 1981), p. 1.

[7] For contemporary significance see G. Slynn, *Introducing a European Legal Order* (London, 1992), pp. 136–137.

which was also influential in English law but there it did not take root and endure. From early European history it is possible to trace European influences. The growth of European trade in the Middle Ages had encouraged the development of various rules of European law which began to become collected and recognised as part of a legal[8] order[9] which transcended individual states.[10] These influences were particularly significant for trade and commercial dealings.

8–06   Some examples of European influences on law may be identified. The beginnings[11] of modern contract[12] doctrine may be found in a shared origin between common lawyers and civil lawyers based on a "similar doctrinal structure based on similar legal concepts." This shared inheritance owes much to the philosophy of the *Corpus Juris Civilis*, but in the later development of contract, civil and common lawyers separated. Leaving behind their shared inheritance, the outcome of reformulation in the nineteenth century was two distinct systems. The fact that the theoretical and philosophical home of English contract law is derived from the European legal model is often overlooked by English lawyers.

8–07   More closely related to the role of the State was the influence of codification. Relying on inspiration from continental theorists, English law drew ideas from Roman law, especially from the writings of Savigny (1779–1861).[13] Maine's (1822–88) general legal theory about the law and State owed much to the influence of Roman law and this in turn presented codes as part of an evolutionary process in the development of society. As Stein has noted[14] "English law has always

---

[8] The intellectual research and development agenda is considerable. See *E.C. Research Funding* (2nd ed., 1990). During the first decades of the history of the Community, research was concentrated in the key area of community competence: coal, steel and nuclear energy.

[9] G. P. Wilson, *Materials Section 1, English Legal System* (unpublished, 1994). Quoted in Wilson. See J. H. Merryman, *The Civil Law Tradition*, (Stanford University Press, 1985), p. 1. Also see A. Von Mehren, *The Civil Law System* (Little Brown, 1957).

[10] *ibid.* On French law and the code system see R. David, H. P. de Vries, *The French Legal System* (Oceana, 1958).

[11] P. Stein, *Legal Evolution* (Cambridge, 1980); John Austin (1790–1859), Henry Maine (1822–88), Fredrich Carl von Savigny (1779–1861); Albert Bleckman, "Le Droit Européen Commun dans le Domaine du Droit Administratif" in Bruno de Witte and Caroline Forden, *Le Droit Commun de l'Europe et l'Avenir de l'Enseignement Juridique* (Kluwer, 1992); R. C. Van Caenegem, *Judges, Legislators and Professors: Chapters in European Legal History* (Cambridge, 1987); P. S. Atiyah, *Pragmatism and Theory in English Law* (London, 1987); J. M. Kelly, *A Short History of Western Legal Theory* (O.U.P., 1992), pp. 156–157. The Rolls of Oléron were later incorporated into the English Black Book of the Admiralty.

[12] J. Gordley, *The Philosophical Origins of Modern Contract Doctrine* (Oxford, 1991). Also see R. C. Van Caenegem, *The Birth of the English Common Law* (2nd ed., 1988). Also in Europe a *jus commune* was established, namely a European common law influenced by Roman law.

[13] Savigny, *System of Roman Law* (1840–49).

[14] P. Stein, *op. cit.*, p. 123.

been strong on its legal rules, but weak on its legal theory." Nevertheless, English legal theory especially for Austin and Bentham, drew insights from Roman law and the codification favoured by civil lawyers.

Membership of the E.C. injects into English law a European civil **8–08** tradition. Mitchell[15] was one of the few lawyers to foresee the possibility that British and Continental legal systems might combine with significant results. While the majority of United Kingdom lawyers failed to understand this particular consequence of E.C. membership, it is likely that Mitchell's analysis will prove far sighted. Already in one particular instance the influence of the European tradition has been acknowleged as helpful. On the question of the distinction between public law and private law the experience of the civil law where such a distinction has developed has been acknow-ledged as a fruitful source for ideas.[16]

The civil law tradition is more fully developed in defining the **8–09** significance of the distinction between public and private law. Public law is concerned with the interests of the whole community, the preservation of the State and the maintenance of order. Private law is concerned with property rights and the resolution of such disputes. At work in developing such a distinction is the desire to give property ownership and its enjoyment, maximum protection accord-ing to the law. The philosophical tradition found in the jurisprudence of civil law lays the theoretical basis of private and public law. It might be considered that this influence has already helped to draw a distinction between public and private law in recent court[17] cases in the United Kingdom. Still further, it is possible to foresee that the new legal order borne out of the European Community may require a re-interpretation of the United Kingdom's basic understanding of constitutional and administrative law.

On the question of national sovereignty, Mitchell's[18] view, that the **8–10** United Kingdom's sovereignty had been altered on entry into the E.C. and that this would lead inevitably to recognition by the courts of the primacy of E.C. law, has to some extent been realised. The recent *Factortame*[19] case confirms Mitchell's view by ascertaining the supremacy of E.C. law over a United Kingdom Act of Parliament. If

[15] J. D. Mitchell, "The State of Public Law in the UK" (1966) 15 I.C.L.Q. 133. Also see "The Causes and Effects of the Absence of a System of Public Law in the United Kingdom" [1965] P.L. 95.

[16] See Francis Jacobs, "Human Rights in Europe: New Dimensions" (1992) *The King's College Law Journal* 49.

[17] *ibid. O'Reilly v. Mackman* [1983] 2 A.C. 237; *Cocks v. Thanet D.C.* [1983] 2 A.C. 286; *Davy v. Spelthorne B.C.* [1984] A.C. 262; *Wandsworth v. Winder* [1985] A.C. 461.

[18] Mitchell, *op. cit.*

[19] Case C–213/89, *Factortame:* [1990] E.C.R. I–2433, [1990] 3 C.M.L.R. 375; Weatherill and Beaumont, *op. cit.* pp. 318–322. J. Hanna, "Community Rights all at Sea" (1990) L.Q.R. 2.

this aspect of sovereignty has been settled, there remains the question of the future influence E.C. membership might have on the United Kingdom's constitutional and administrative law.

(b) *The European Convention on Human Rights and Fundamental Freedoms*

8–11 Human rights provide an example of the importance of wider European influences not confined simply to membership of the E.C. In 1949, 25 European States, including the 15 currently existing members of the E.C., founded an international organisation known as the Council of Europe.[20] This was an attempt to form a "unified" Europe and address the problem of human rights. The outcome was a treaty known as the European Convention on Human Rights (ECHR). Further, it was hoped that such an organisation might act as a "watchdog" against human rights atrocities and through community action as a deterrent preventing further atrocities from taking place. This primary function of the Council of Europe has gone into abeyance, leaving the ECHR as a means to raise legal issues in the Member States of the co-signatories. Out of the 25 Member States, 23 formed an agreement and put into force, in 1952, the ECHR Czechoslovakia and Hungary are the two members who are not party to the convention.[21]

8–12 The main objectives of the convention are to secure civil and political rights. Other social rights are protected under a separate arrangement known as the European Social Charter signed in 1961. In the United Kingdom the impact of the ECHR is significant, as the debate about a Bill of Rights[22] being introduced into domestic law usually considers the desirability of making the ECHR part of our domestic law in the United Kingdom.

A number of important decisions made by the European Court of Human Rights under the European Convention on Human Rights concern Northern Ireland[23] and the question of interrogation techniques and methods. The Court held that such techniques did not constitute a "practice of ill-treatment," but held that certain techniques disclosed "torture" and other "inhuman treatment."

---

[20] Bailey, Harris and Jones, *Civil Liberties* (1992), pp. 749–845 and P. Van Dijk, F. Van Hoof, *Theory and Practice of the European Convention on Human Rights* (2nd ed., 1990). Also see R. Beddard, *Human Rights and Europe* (2nd ed., 1980), J. E. S. Fawcett, *The Application of the European, Convention on Human Rights* (2nd ed., 1987). D. Feldman, *Civil Liberties and Human Rights* (Oxford, 1993).

[21] The U.K. is a party to various agreements: 1966 International Covenant on Civil and Political Rights, International Covenant on Economic, Social and Cultural Rights and to U.N. agreements.

[22] Michael Zander, "A Bill of Rights?" (1985); Lloyd, "Do we need a Bill of Rights?" (1976) 39 M.L.R. 121; J. Jaconelli, *Enacting a Bill of Rights: The Legal Problems* (1980).

[23] *Ireland v. U.K.* European Court H.R. Series A, Vol. 25, January 18, 1978, 2 E.H.R.R. 25.

While many of the techniques continued to be used after the **8–13** judgment of the Court, nevertheless new procedures were introduced for the interrogation of suspects. Public opinion was greatly influenced by the significance of the findings.

The general expectation is that the existence of the ECHR helps to establish a "new legal order" as part of the desire to deal with domestic problems on a European rather than a State basis.

In the United Kingdom, the convention is not binding[24] on domes- **8–14** tic law because it has not been given effect in an Act of Parliament. Thus the provisions of the ECHR are not enforceable in the courts. In a recent case Lord Donaldson in *R. v. Secretary of State for the Home Department, ex p. Brind*[25] explained that a Treaty obligation could be adopted in a number of ways. First, and this had not happened, it could be given effect in statute law. Second, the Government could "review English common law and statute law" with a view to reconciling it with the ECHR This was the course of action adopted but the results may be regarded as unfortunate. Lord Donaldson admitted[26]:

> "It follows from this that in most cases the English Courts will be wholly unconcerned with the terms of the Convention. Exceptions to this principle, where the United Kingdom's courts may directly interpret the E.C.H.R. depends on statutory interpretation and Parliamentary intent. Only where it may be said that Parliament has legislated in a manner consistent with the Treaty obligation will effect be given to the interpretation of the E.C.H.R."

This restrictive interpretation[27] normally leaves the United Kingdom **8–15** courts free to ignore the existence of the ECHR The possibility of interpreting the ECHR within domestic law depends on statutory construction and this is subject to a further restriction. An interpretation permitting inclusion of the ECHR applies only to primary legislation and not delegated powers or indeed prerogative powers. This further restricts the opportunity to read the ECHR as part of domestic law as a matter of interpretation.

A more constructive view is to see the United Kingdom courts **8–16** pursuing a parallel, even if distinctive approach to that taken by the court of the ECHR. There are strong arguments for adopting the convention and making it part of domestic law.[27a] A reluctance to take

---

[24] See *Re M and H (Minors)* [1988] 1 W.L.R. 462.
[25] [1991] 1 A.C. 696; [1990] 1 All E.R. 469 at p. 477.
[26] *ibid.* p. 477. See Gearty [1993] Camb.L.J. 89–127.
[27] A number of significant decisions have been made considering the effect of the convention. The most notable and useful are in *Attorney-General v. Guardian Newspapers Ltd* [1987] 1 W.L.R. 1248.
[27a] Zander, *op. cit.* note 19.

such a step may come[28] from a desire among English lawyers not to accept the technique and methods adopted in the ECHR. English lawyers have traditionally emphasised remedies rather than rights. Ewing and Gearty explain[29]:

"The British emphasis, as we have seen, is on liberty as the residue, the bit left over after the law has had its say. The European method is exactly the reverse: the right exists unless it has been abridged by a law which, moreover, has to be specifically justified. It [E.C.H.R.] is just the sort of Continental Charter that was despised by Dicey."

8–17   The court of the ECHR has achieved a number of noteworthy cases critical of English law, including, prisoners' rights, terrorism, contempt of court, telephone tapping, and, in Northern Ireland, homosexuality. In such areas the laws of the United Kingdom fall behind European expectations in observing citizens' rights. Successive government's reluctance to incorporate the ECHR into domestic law with directly enforceable rights, implies lack of trust in the judiciary. This leaves United Kingdom citizens with the impression that rights are better protected outside the United Kingdom by reference to the European Court of Justice.[30]

The present Government is expected to favour some form of incorporation.[31] There has been a marked increase in the frequency with which the United Kingdom has been summoned to answer allegations of alleged violations. In 1991 there were 843 files opened and in 1994 this had risen to 946 cases.[32]

(c)   Membership of the E.C.: Aims and Objectives

8–18 The United Kingdom's membership[33] of the E.C. has undergone significant change as the E.C. has adopted[34] new policies and objectives. The original treaty[35] arrangements envisaged four areas where

---

[28] K. Ewing, C. A. Gearty, *Freedom Under Thatcher* (Oxford, 1990), pp. 263–267, 272–274.

[29] *ibid.* p. 14. (1996) *Public law* pp. 226.

[30] See Chap. 20 "The Citizen and Civil Liberties".

[31] Many members of the judiciary are sympathetic to this direction. See S. Sedley, "The Common Law and the Constitution" *London Review of Books* Vol. 19 No. 9 (8 May, 1997); Sir Stephen Sedley, [1995] *Public Law* 386; Sir John Laws [1995] *Public Law* 72; Lord Woolf of Barnes, [1995] *Public Law* 57.

[32] See Sue Farran, *The United Kingdom before the European Court of Human Rights* (Blackstone Press, 1996, p. 391).

[33] Generally see Nigel Foster, *EEC Legislation* (Blackstone, 1990) and Josephine Steiner, *Textbook on EEC Law* (2nd ed., 1990) (4th ed., 1994).

[34] Gordon Slynn, *Introducing a European Legal Order* (Hamlyn Lecture, 1992), pp. 41–62.

[35] Chap. 1 sets out some of the general institutional arrangements and matters of sovereignty. There are now four Treaties: The Treaty on European Union; the European Community Treaty; the European Coal and Steel Community Treaty and the European Atomic Energy Community Treaty.

economic freedoms within a common market might be established. These include goods, persons, services and capital. An important area of policy concerned with fundamental principle is the development of a common agricultural policy[36] which has proved controversial and difficult.[37]

Additional areas of substantive E.C. law include[38] provisions covering competition and harmonisation of laws, provisions relating to social policy, research, technological development and environmental policy. Provisions covering commercial policy are intended to facilitate major political, economic and institutional reform.

In 1986, reforms towards a single market among Member States **8–19** were introduced through the Single European Act 1986. The 1986 Act was intended to remove any remaining barriers as obstacles to a single internal market. The form of the 1986 Act was a Treaty which was later ratified into United Kingdom domestic law by legislation.[39]

The main objective of the 1986 Act is to achieve a single internal market by the end of 1992. Community competence is therefore extended into a wide variety of new areas including environment, energy, regional policy, and a common commercial policy. A significant part of these reforms are institutional and procedural in terms of giving more potential for the European Parliament in certain areas of E.C. law to exert some influence.

An equally[40] important area is the establishment of a new European marketing system leading to harmonisation of economic and monetary policy.

Since 1969 the development of economic and monetary union has **8–20** been considered. Ten years later the European Monetary System (EMS) came into operation with all Member States including the United Kingdom and also latterly Greece, Spain and Portugal joining after they became members of the Community.

Four elements are included[41] in the EMS; membership entitles Member States to participate but not necessarily join each of the elements of the EMS. The four elements are: the exchange rate mechanism, which obliges members to maintain exchange rates within certain limits; the European Currency Unit, which calculates the value of Community currencies and their worth against fixed

---

[36] Francis Snyder, *Law of the Common Agricultural Policy* (1985).
[37] Art. 2 sets out objectives. Art. 3 sets out 11 areas of activity.
[38] European Communities (Amendment) Act 1986.
[39] *ibid*. Competition Policy see Arts. 85 and 86, Commercial Monopolies, Art. 37, Restrictions on State Aids, Arts. 92–94.
[40] Werner Report: Report to the Council and the Commission on the realisation by Stages of Economic and Monetary Union in the Community (1970), E.C. Commission. Bull. E.C. Suppl. 11/70.
[41] Economic and Monetary Union: An Evolutionary Approach. December 1989. Economic Progress Report (Treasury, 1989).

quantities of Community currencies; the European Monetary Co-operation Fund, which regulates the issues of the ECU (European Currency Unit) throughout the Community, and fourthly, to allow short-term credit facilities among Member States.

8–21   In 1989, the Delors Report proposed a three-stage approach to Member States within the Economic Monetary Union (EMU). These proposals have important economic and political implications for Member States.

Stage 1 seeks to achieve a single market among Member States in goods, services and capital. This assumes a strengthening of competition policy, reduction of state aids and a close co-ordination of economic and monetary policies.

Stage 2 is a transitional state, involving setting up the European System of Central Banks, while retaining with Member States, elements of ultimate policy-making responsibility. Stage 3, the most controversial, envisages the removal of the formulation and implementation of monetary policy to the European System of Central Banks to act as a regulator of exchange rate and currency markets.

8–22   The implications of Stage 3 are so wide-ranging that they would involve amendment to the Treaty of Rome. The outcome of Stage 3 implies binding restraints on national budgets and the Community of Member States acting as a single entity in terms of international policy measures. The role of the Central Bank would be critical in the setting of exchange rates, currency market intervention and the management of official reserves. Currently this power has rested with the Bank of England which acts under Treasury control and ministerial influence. The result of adopting the substance of Stage 3 would be a severe curtailment of the national banks of Member States. In the United Kingdom this would mean a sharp break with the past where the Bank of England[42] comes under ultimate ministerial direction and responsibility. The outcome would leave the Bank of England independent from such influences and direction.

8–23   The United Kingdom had agreed to enter the Exchange Rate Mechanism at the first stage. This was intended to enable the United Kingdom to plan implementation on an incremental basis of the next two stages. However, events during September 1992 resulted in an unexpected and dramatic change when the United Kingdom was forced to leave the ERM when the pound came under severe pressure from the financial markets. Similar factors caused other Member States to leave the ERM.

8–24   At the heart of the debate on the EMU is the question of the role of the European System of Central Banks. It appears that there is reluctance in the United Kingdom to vest control in the European Central Bank away from the Bank of England.[43]

---

[42] Discussed in Chap. 11 on "Public Finance".
[43] Economic and Monetary Union (December 1989), loc. cit. note 37.

"The Delors plan [Stages 1–3] would take the control of monetary policy away from National governments while leaving those governments answerable to their electorate for policies over which they would have no control."

As a result,[44] it is likely to be some time before the full implementation of Economic and Monetary Union with the United Kingdom as a leading participant is completed. It is arguable how successful such a union might be, but it is certainly likely to dominate the future shape of the E.C. and the amount of influence national governments and parliaments can expect to exert on future E.C. policy and laws. The fact that the E.C. has its own legal personality and political systems gives it a life of its own. The European Parliament has favoured progress towards European union and this direction is likely to be pursued for the foreseeable future.

There is finally a unique quality to the E.C. No other international **8–25** treaty has been so extensive in delivering a wide variety of social policies, obligations, rights and enforceable laws within the Member States' own courts. The Court of Justice of the E.C. has developed its own jurisprudence and applied a degree of creativity in helping to pursue the general objective and policies of the E.C. As a result of the Treaty on European Union which was signed at Maastricht, there are now four Treaties namely: the Treaty on European Union; the European Community Treaty; the European Coal and Steel Community Treaty (ECSC) and the European Atomic Energy Community Treaty. The Treaties set out the general framework. This leaves the institutions, the Commission, Council and Parliament and the Court of Justice to settle many details through delegated powers.

3. Institutions and Structures

(a) Council and Commission

The Council of the E.C. which was set up in December 1974, is **8–26** comprised of representatives of the governments of the various Member States. As the Council has some control over the various legislative initiatives, the system of representation gives Member States an influence. The Council concludes international agreements on behalf of the E.C. It may also lay down budgetary procedures.

---

[44] *An Evolutionary Approach to Economic and Monetary Union* (H.M. Treasury, 1989).

Usually it acts on the basis of consultation with the Commission. There are rules of procedure and a body known as a Committee of Permanent Representatives, who are ambassadors and head the Permanent Representatives of each of the Member States in the Community.[44a] This body advises, prepares the agenda and sets the co-ordinates of policy.

Various specialised meetings of the Council may take place permitting specialist Ministers to take part. Regular meetings of Finance Ministers take place outside the Council's regular meetings.

8–27   The Single European Act 1986 provides that Heads of State and Foreign Ministers, together with the President of the Commission are to meet at least twice a year. The Commission has initiated[45] major reforms such as direct elections to the European Parliament, the setting up of the European Monetary System (outlined above) and various policies on Value Added Tax. There is a sense that because of the links between the Heads of Government of the different Member States and the Council, there is greater influence and a higher priority given to the Council when compared to the Commission. The council acts as a co-ordinator; settling national policies, administering common policies not settled in the Treaties, and with the Commission and the European Parliament ensuring that the Treaties are observed and implemented and extending the scope and proposing revision of the treaties.

8–28   Voting procedures within the Council of Ministers may vary. Some decisions require a unanimous vote, a qualified majority on proposals from the Commission or a simple majority vote. The latter is extended by the Treaty on European Union into various areas such as environmental protection, consumer affairs and public health. There are six monthly meetings of the Council in the form of European Summit Meetings. The European Council consists of the heads of State or government of the Member States and the President of the Commission. It first met in 1975 and since then has met regularly. This is an example of powers evolving rather than being established by any of the Community Treaties. The chairmanship of the European Council rotates every six months with the presidency of the Council. The European Council submits a report to the European Parliament after each meeting.

8–29   The decision-making procedures have been altered by the Maastricht Treaty. Unanimity is now required only in respect of the two pillars of the Community that cover Common Foreign and

---

[44a] Heads of State and Foreign Ministers: see Art. 2 of the 1986 Single European Act.
[45] P. J. G. Kapteyn and P. Verloren Van Themaat, *Introduction to the Law of the European Communities* (1990), pp. 107–108. Commission's powers, Arts. 155–163. Council's powers Art. 145–154.

Security Policy and Justice and Home Affairs. Unanimity will also apply where the Council wishes to amend a Commission proposal and this is against the Commission's wishes.

Qualified majority voting now applies to most types of decisions covering the main policy issues of the European Union. The voting rules are allocated as follows depending on the size and economic significance of the Member State: 10 votes each are given to France, Germany, Italy and the United Kingdom, Spain has eight votes, Belgium, Greece, the Netherlands and Portugal have five votes each, Austria and Sweden have four votes each, Denmark, Finland and Ireland have three votes each and Luxembourg has two votes. In almost every case there must be at least 62 votes out of 87 for the proposal to be accepted. There remain a few instances where simple majority voting, in which each Member State has one vote each, is used. From February 1994 this includes matters such as anti-dumping and anti-subsidy tariffs within the Common Commercial Policy.

The Council acts in Community matters with the co-operation of **8–30** the Commission whose duty is to serve the general interest of the Community as a whole. Presently the Commission consists of 17 members, who must be nationals of a Member State. The aim of national governments is to ensure that the Commission reflects the balance of European political interests. Members of the Commission serve a term of four years in office, enjoy various privileges and immunities to ensure that their duties are carried out unimpeded. The independence of the Commission is important, and although Commissioners are drawn from Member States, they must not be seen to act in a partisan way.[46]

The Commission acts as an independent body and is not under **8–31** mandatory instruction from the Council of Ministers. Together with the Council it has to perform the task of formulating Community policies[47]:

> "The Commission is a body having its own political responsibility, its own political task and its own accountability to an elected Parliament."

This view of the role of the Commission provides a good summary of its activities.

The Commission has a President, six Vice-Presidents and each member of the Commission has a personal staff, namely his cabinet, and Chefs de Cabinet who meet regularly to discuss the role and objectives of Commission policy. The Commission has a staff of over 15,000, divided into 23 Directorates General.

---

[46] ibid. p. 111. See N. Nugent, The Government and Politics of the European Community (3rd., ed., Macmillan, 1994).
[47] ibid.

8–32　　Collaboration between the Council and the Commission is required. In particular Article 15 of the Merger Treaty provides they must "consult" and "decide by common accord." One view is that recently the Commission has tended to see itself less as[48] "an embryonic European Government" than in earlier times. This marks a shift in the fortunes of the European Parliament which has had direct elections since 1979.

8–33　　Powers[49] granted to the Commission and the Council permit the taking of decisions which become legally binding on Member States and individuals within the E.C. The formulation of such powers gives the initiative to the Council, on a proposal from the Commission and after consultation with the European Parliament, to take appropriate legal measures. In theory there is great scope for the broadening of such powers under Article 235 based on the doctrine of "implied power," namely, that filling a gap in express powers may fit within the generally granted power if it is implied or necessary. There are doubts as to the precise scope and requirements for such powers.

8–34　　The Commission acts as an "overseer" of the interests of the Community and Article 5 obliges it to take appropriate measures to ensure "fulfilment of the obligations" from the Treaty. Extensive investigative[50] powers are granted to the Commission which require Member States and even individuals to provide information allowing the Commission to carry out its task.

A number of specific policy areas fall within the jurisdiction of the Commission such as the competition policy of the E.C. and the implementation of the Common Agricultural Policy. This delegates to specific commissioners wide-ranging powers and activities.

8–35　　The impact[51] of the Single European Act is important in the completion of the internal market outlined above. In order to expedite the completion of the market, arrangements are in place under the 1986 Act to permit the carrying out of legislative measures by a qualified majority in the Council of Ministers. This leaves only certain fiscal[52] matters and employment rights to be adopted by unanimous voting. These arrangements permit decisions to be made against the wishes of a single Member State's national government or parliament.[53]

---

[48] *ibid.* p. 131.

[49] Chiefly see Art. 235 EEC.

[50] Art. 213; Reg. 17/62; Art. 14.

[51] See Chap. 1 for a brief discussion. Voting is awarded weighting on the size of each country. The largest group where 10 votes are allocated comprises U.K., Germany, France and Italy. Spain has eight votes, Portugal, Belgium, Greece and the Netherlands have each five votes. Austria and Sweden have four votes each. Finland, Ireland and Denmark have three votes each.

[52] Some derogation under Art. 100A(4) is permitted for legislation passed by qualified majority.

[53] Arts. 137–144.

(b)   The European Parliament

Directly elected[54] since 1979, the Parliament was originally perceived **8–36**
as having an advisory role. Its formal powers such as dismissal of the
Commission or rejecting the budget for the Community institutions
proposed by the Commission may only be exercised on the basis of a
two-thirds majority. In the 1980s the European Parliament rejected
the budget for five years. The power to dismiss the Commission
exists more in theory than as a practical reality. The Parliament is
required by various articles of the Treaty to be consulted but this is
procedural[55] in many instances. The Parliament meets in plenary
session 12 to 14 times a year. Members sit and vote in political
groupings rather than national allegiance.

Since 1977 various conciliation procedures have existed to promote **8–37**
co-operation between Parliament, Council and Commission. This
allows the Parliament a second opportunity to examine legislation.
Amendments may be proposed and sent to the Commission but even
if rejected by the Commission, the amendments may be adopted by
the Council by a unanimous vote.

The European Parliament may assist in the scrutiny of the Commission, who are required to give answers to questions raised by the
Parliament. The Council sends reports to the Parliament and three
times every year Parliament provides a review of the Council's
activities. Thus the Commission is "superseded" rather than held to
account directly through any political control. There are 639 members
of the European Parliament. The United Kingdom including Northern
Ireland, has 87 seats.

In terms of future developments in the European Community it is **8–38**
likely that the Parliament will perform an increasingly important role.
The European Parliament holds a number of characteristics which
make its existence difficult to reconcile with the traditional United
Kingdom Parliament. For example, it can refer matters to the Court of
Justice[56] if the Council or the Commission infringe E.C. rules. It may
approve fundamental amendments to the Treaty under a limited
revision power.[57] However, although it can determine elections to it,
it does not have any formal right to initiate community legislation.[58]
This does not prevent the Commission promoting legislation on its
behalf. The Treaty on European Union strengthened the powers of
the European Parliament but some weaknesses remain. Parliament

---

[54] See the European Parliamentary Elections Act 1978 and 1993.
[55] Case 138/79, *Roquette Frères SA v. Council* [1980] E.C.R. 3393.
[56] Arts. 175 EEC and 148 Euratom.
[57] Art. 95.
[58] Kapteyn, Verloren and Van Themaat, *op. cit.* p. 143, Weatherill and Beaumont, *op. cit.*
pp. 79–114.

does not have to be consulted by the Council, even in matters connected with proposed Treaty-based legislation. Once consulted by the Council, Parliament does not have the power to block legislation.

(c) The Court of Justice

8–39 The Court of Justice, commonly called the European Court, ensures that the Treaty[59] and its obligations are interpreted.[60] There are 15 judges appointed with the agreement of the Member States. A wide range of matters comes within its remit ranging from social, economic, constitutional and administrative law. The jurisprudence of the court is influenced by the civil law tradition. Its workload has increased. Slynn notes[61]:

> "Not far short of 400 new cases have been arriving at the Court each year, though in 1990/91 the number was down to 355. Allowing for 200 judgments and, on average, 130 withdrawals or summary dismissals, the backlog can only increase, and by September 1991, the "stock" of cases before the Court and the Court of First Instance amounted to 782, of which 614 were before the Court."

Current delays can amount to over 16 months, commensurate with the scope[62] and range of the court's activities which are broader and more linked to the economic, political and social issues than would be commonly found in English judicial decisions.

8–40 The 1986 Single European Act introduced a new Court of First Instance[63] which may be called le Tribunal (its full title is Tribunal de Première Instance). Twelve judges sit, one appointed from each Member State, principally in chambers of three or five judges and its first proceedings began on September 1, 1989. Its primary function is to consider disputes under the E.C.'s competition law and applications for judicial review and changes under the ECSC Treaty. Disputes between the E.C. and its staff also fall under its jurisdiction.

---

[59] Art. 164-168.
[60] Reflections on the Future Development of the Community Judicial System, by the Court of First Instance of the European Community (1991) 16 Vol. 3 E.L. Rev. 175–189. See Weatherill and Beaumont, *op. cit.* pp. 158–164.
[61] Gordon Slynn, *Introducing a European Legal Order* (Hamlyn Lecture 1992), pp. 136–137.
[62] There are 13 judges, one for each Member State assisted by six Advocates-General. Note the style of judgment which differs from the English style of law report. The opinion of the Advocates-General although not binding comes as a recommendation which may be used as a persuasive argument in later cases.
[63] See the statement made by the Court, *loc. cit.* note 56.

It has been argued that the case load of the European Court might be shared with le Tribunal.[64]

The jurisprudence of the European Court has significant effects on **8–41** the United Kingdom's constitutional and administrative law and legal system. The jurisdiction of the European Court is provided under Article 177, which permits the European Court to give preliminary rulings on Community law. A preliminary ruling may be requested by the courts of the Member States. For example at the level of the magistrates' court it is possible for a direct approach to be made to the European Court under Article 177. The European Court is competent to interpret the Treaty, to consider the validity and interpretation of acts of the various Community institutions, noted above, and to consider the constitution of any of the bodies set up by the Council of the Community.

Guidelines were provided for the United Kingdom's courts in **8–42** *Bulmer v. Bollinger*,[65] and although criticised, they provide the general approach adopted by the United Kingdom's courts. In deciding whether to refer to the European court, Lord Denning explained that: (i) the decision must be necessary; (ii) the decision must be conclusive of the case, and if necessary; (iii) the court has to exercise its discretion to determine all the circumstances as the delay involved, difficulty of the issues, the expense involved and the burden on the court. The main area of dispute arising from Lord Denning's three categories was the issue of "conclusive." On a narrow interpretation this might inhibit an English judge from referring a matter if there was doubt as to the suitability of the European Court resolving the dispute before it with sufficient clarity. On a broad interpretation, as Community law is part of domestic law it might be considered that any domestic court of the Member State of the European Community is entitled to receive the opinion of the European Court. Lord Denning explained that the facts should first be established by the English courts before a reference might be made. He added that if the law was clear then it was unnecessary to refer the matter to the European Court. This point is also open to question, as some argue that it is perfectly acceptable to receive an interpretation of a clear point of law just as it is for an unclear one, from[66] the European Court.

---

[64] Appeals for le Tribunal may be made to the European Court.

[65] [1974] Ch. 401. Also see *R. v. Henn* [1981] A.C. 580 and *R. v. Plymouth Justice ex p. Rogers* [1982] Q.B. 863. See McEldowney, *Pigs Marketing Board for Northern Ireland v. Redmond* [1980] N.I.L.Q. 165–172, Case 83/78: [1978] E.C.R. 2347; [1979] 1 C.M.L.R. 177. See [1997] E.C. 1 ECJ.

[66] J. Coppel, A. O'Neill, "The European Court of Justice: Taking Rights Seriously?" (1992) 12(2) L.S. 227–245. See Vittorio Grilli, *The Road to European Financial Integration from Rome to Maastricht and Beyond* (1992). Also note the wide-ranging developments

8–43 Article 177 permits a preliminary reference mode by "any court or tribunal." Another possibility covered in the Article 177 procedure, is where there can never be an appeal. This applies in the case of the House of Lords, because it is the final appellate court within the United Kingdom where the House of Lords is bound to refer such a question to the Court. But the procedure applies to decisions where there are no further domestic remedies available. There is therefore an important role given to the House of Lords. In *Chiron Corporation v. Murex Diagnostics Ltd*,[67] it is regarded as the court against which there is no judicial remedy. Reference will be made where the question is required for the decision in the case. If there is already case law on the matter or where the Court of Justice has already resolved the issue then no reference is required.[68]

8–44 In addition to preliminary rulings it is possible for references to be made directly by the House of Lords. In such cases the requirements are that the principles in dispute or raising matters of Community law, should be set out in the reference. This invariably involves the formulation of specific questions to be taken before the European Court.

In England the first reference for the House of Lords was made in 1981 in the case of *R. v. Henn*[69] which raised the question of whether importing obscene or indecent articles, which was a criminal offence in the United Kingdom, amounted to a restriction of imports within Article 30 and whether this was justifiable under Article 30. The European Court accepted the judgment in terms of Article 36 relating to "public morality, public policy or public security."

8–45 References have to be made by the Employment Appeal Tribunal, the High Court and by the magistrates' court. Criminal law matters often raise issues of European Community law. In Northern Ireland the first reference concerned the prosecution of Redmond, a pig dealer, under the Northern Ireland Movement of Pigs Regulations 1972, enforced by the Pigs Marketing Board, set up under a scheme requiring local pig producers to sell to the Board, bacon produced by pigs in Northern Ireland.

The European Court determined that the prosecution was inconsistent with E.C. law and the Board's powers unlawfully interfered with the Community market in pigmeat. A similar fate awaited other marketing boards, but the reference illustrated the flexibility of the

in environmental law. See P. Sands, "European Community Environmental Law: Legislation, The European Court of Justice and Common-Interest Groups" (1990) 53 M.L.R. 685; Haigh, *EEC Environmental Policy and Britain* (2nd ed., Longman, 1989). Han Somsen, (ed.), *Protecting the European Environment* (Blackstone, 1996).
[67] [1995] All E.R. (EC) 88.
[68] *Srl CILFIT v. Ministry of Health* [1982] E.C.R. 3415.
[69] [1980] A.C. 850.

European Court's procedures. In marked contrast to the formality of English procedure, the European Court greatly assisted the magistrates in the formulation of the issues involving E.C. law raised in the case. This raises the question of how Community law takes effect in the United Kingdom. The E.C. legal order consists of Regulations, Articles, Directives and Decisions and how each takes effect in the United Kingdom requires explanation.

In *Bulmer v. Bollinger*[70] the United Kingdom's courts have acknow- **8–46** ledged, as Lord Denning explained, that "rights or obligations created by the Treaty are to be given legal effect." More recently, Lord Bridge in *Factortame*[71] declared:

> "It has always been clear that it was the duty of a United Kingdom Court, when delivering final judgment, to override any rule of national law found to be in conflict with any directly enforceable rule of Community law."

This raises the question of the concept of "direct effect" and its meaning as to the "rights or obligations" which are enforceable rights by individuals or Member States within the Community? The answer may depend on the interpretation of "direct effect." Ambiguously worded, the term may be found in international law as well as Community law. In international law the term refers to the concept of national courts applying at the suit of individuals" rights and obligations.

Regulations under Article 189, as amended by the Treaty on **8–47** European Union are directly applicable but little further guidance is provided other than the fact that they bind Member States in their entirety without further implementation. Occasionally regulations may be drafted in a conditional or provisional mode, requiring further action for their implementation, but generally they apply with immediate effect. This means that they may create individual rights enforceable before national courts.

Articles of the Treaty[72] are said to have internal effect in the Member States of the E.C. However, doubts exist as to when all Articles of the Treaty would be so treated. Over time the European Court has held many of the Articles of the Treaty to be directly applicable.

Directives are described under Article 189 as being "directly **8–48** applicable." It was once thought that only regulations might have

---

[70] [1974] Ch. 401.

[71] Case C–213/89, *Factortame*: [1990] I–2433 E.C.R.; [1990] 3 C.M.L.R. 375.

[72] See Case 26/62 *Van Gend en Loos v. Nederlandse Administratie der Belastingen*: [1963] E.C.R. 1, C.M.L.R. 105. A good discussion is provided in J. Steiner's *Textbook on EEC Law* (2nd ed.), pp. 20–33, which has facilitated understanding of the complexity of this case.

"direct effect" as distinct from "direct applicability." The latter term was interpreted as to mean that direct effect was not given. However, in a number of Decisions,[73] the European Court took the view that some Directives might have "direct effect." While not all Directives might be said to have "direct effect," in the *Marshall* case[74] it was decided that Directives might be relied upon by individuals within Member States against any part of the "state." The question of direct effect depends on the subject matter and whether the wording is "unconditional and sufficiently precise."[75] Not every national court has accepted the view that Directives may have direct effect. Not all Directives before the courts may fall into the category of direct application because of a further ambiguity caused by the concept of the "state." This term is not precisely defined but may be generally used to mean a public body or agency of the State. It is difficult to put this characteristic of such bodies into categories which give rise to general principles of universal application.[76]

8–49 A broad interpretation was adopted by the House of Lords in *Foster*[77] as to a body[78] "which has been made responsible pursuant to a measure adopted by the State for providing a public service under the control of the state." Such a body might be granted "special powers" which differentiate it from any individual. On such an interpretation the State could be all embracing as to include any entity which had legal powers over individuals and this might cover a Company Act company. On such an interpretation, noticeably broader than in other areas of law, the House of Lords held that the British Gas Corporation[79] under the Gas Act 1972, then a nationalised industry, fell within the definition.

8–50 A further possibility over direct effect has been mooted by the European Court which is to allow a Directive to have an application in domestic law indirectly, as a means to interpret national law as part of Community law.[80] The possibilities of interpretation make this

[73] Case 9/70, *Grad v. Finanzamt Traunstein*: [1970] E.C.R. 825; [1971] C.M.L.R. 1. See Kapteyn and Van Themaat *op. cit.* pp. 339–349. *Van Duyn v. Home Office* [1974] E.C.R. 1337. Also see Case 222/84 *Johnston v. The Chief Constable of the Royal Ulster Constabulary* [1986] E.C.R. 1651; [1986] 3 C.M.L.R. 240.

[74] Case 152/84 *Marshall v. Southampton and South West Hampshire Area Health Authority (Teaching)* [1986] E.C.R. II–723, 748; [1986] 1 C.M.L.R. 688; [1986] 2 All E.R. 584.

[75] See P. Mead, "The Obligation to apply European Law: Is Duke Dead?" (1991) 16 E.L. Rev. 490–499.

[76] Case 14/83, *Von Colson v. Lord Nordrhein—Westfalen* [1984] E.C.R. 1891; [1986] 2 C.M.L.R. 430.

[77] Case C–188/89, *Foster v. British Gas plc* [1991] 1 Q.B. 405. In Case 222/84, *Johnston v. Chief Constable of Royal Ulster Constabulary* [1986] E.C.R. 1651; [1986] 3 C.M.L.R. 240 the Chief Constable was defined as an "emanation of the State".

[78] [1990] 3 All E.R. 897, 922.

[79] Now a Public Act company under the Gas Act 1986.

[80] Known as the *Von Colson* principle (Case 14/83). See Grainne de Burca, "Giving effect to European Commmunity Directives" 1992 M.L.R. 215 and Steiner "Coming to terms with EEC Directives" (1990) 106 L.Q.R. 144.

area of law subject to intense discussion and debate. Particularly so, since many of the E.C.'s most significant social and economic policies are enacted into legislative form through the means of Directives. The United Kingdom courts face a formidable challenge in developing their interpretative skills to overcome the difficulties mentioned above. Not least, is the difficulty that even if a Directive is held to be directly applicable, thereby conferring on an individual various rights against the State, there is not always an available remedy in domestic law open to the court. This leaves a considerable gap in the jurisprudence of the ECJ in the development of the principle that there is a strong obligation on Member States to enforce Directives through domestic courts.[81]

Finally there are decisions of the E.C. which are binding under 8–51 Article 189. This is largely unproblematic as the decision is addressed to a specific issue or problem and may be made to an individual or Member State. The assumption is made that because the decision is made to address an individual or Member State it should be involved and enforced as a binding rule. Lord Denning's reference in *Bulmer v. Bollinger* to "rights or obligations" under Community law raises a different expectation than simply the interpretation and application of Regulations, Decisions or Directives. Perhaps the European Court in interpreting the Treaty and its obligations might create its own jurisprudence of fundamental rights to supplement national courts and constitutions?

In the early years of the[82] Community, the European Court rejected 8–52 the idea that fundamental rights might be protected directly by the Court's interpretation of E.C. law. Instead reliance was placed on national courts and constitutions developing their own jurisprudence of fundamental rights. However, in subsequent years[83] and more recently since 1989 it has been observed:

"that the court was seen openly to take the step of assessing the validity of an act of a Member State on the basis of fundamental rights considerations."

The result of the European Court of Justice's movement towards a "fundamental rights" jurisprudence permits jurisdiction to the European Court to review national law from the perspective of Community

---

[81] de Burca, *op. cit.* p. 216. See N. O'Loan, "U.K. Implementation of the Services Directive 92/50" (1994) 3 *Public Procurement Law Review* 60; the Public Service Contracts Regulations 1993 (S.I. 1993 No. 3228).

[82] J. Coppel and A. O'Neill, "The European Court of Justice: Taking Rights Seriously" (1992) 12 L.S. 227–245. See p. 231.

[83] "A Constitution for Europe" (1989) 26 C.M.L.R. 595. See Case 183/74, *Frontini v. Ministero delle Finanze* [1974] 2 C.M.L.R. 372.

law in terms of whether human rights have been breached.[84] This implies an overlapping jurisdiction with the European Court of Human Rights, as Member States of the E.C. have (with the exception of the United Kingdom) incorporated the European Convention on Human Rights into their domestic constitution. This might suggest the requirement of national courts to apply such rights as part of Community law and therefore extend to any field of activity covered by Community law. The new direction into the field of human rights favoured by the European Court will greatly affect the jurisprudence of human rights within the Community.

8–53　　The activities of the European Court in interpreting and discussing Community law[85] requires national courts to accept the status of Community law. The question of compatibility between the law of the Member State and Community law has been reviewed in a protracted series of cases arising from the *Factortame* case.[86]

The facts of *Factortame* are as follows. In 1988 the Divisional Court requested a preliminary ruling under Article 177 from the European Court to determine the compatibility of the Merchant Shipping Act 1988 and the provisions of the E.C. Treaty. The 1988 Act and subsequent regulations required shipping vessels previously registered under a nineteenth century statute to re-register with new conditions to prevent Spanish fishing vessels entering the register and thereby gaining access to British fishing areas which are under E.C. quota regulation. Registration was thereby conditional on a nationality requirement. Spanish fishing vessel owners sought to challenge[87] the legality of the 1988 Act in terms of the E.C. law and sought an interim injunction by way of judicial review.

8–54　　A secondary issue in the *Factortame* case arose in connection with the grant of interim[88] relief. The Court of Appeal set aside an interim injunction granted by the Divisional Court pending the outcome of the European Court. The House of Lords upheld the Court of Appeal's decision, because it reasoned that English courts could not

[84] *S.P.U.C. v. Grogan* [1990] 1 C.M.L.R. 689. Grogan raised the legality of abortion in Ireland where under a 1983 amendment in the Irish constitution purported to "safeguard the right to life of the unborn" thus making the legalisation of abortion a matter of constitutional dispute. The case was referred to the European Court of Justice for a preliminary judgment under Article 177 of the EEC Treaty.

[85] U.K.'s Sunday Trading laws—trading on Sunday. See Case 145/88, *Torfaen Borough Council v. B and Q plc* [1990] 1 All E.R. 129; [1989] E.C.R. 3851; [1990] 1 C.M.L.R. 337. On disablement benefits under the U.K.'s Social Security Act 1975 see *Thomas v. Adjudication Officer* [1991] 2 Q.B. 164.

[86] [1989] 2 All E.R. 692; [1991] 1 All E.R. 70.

[87] *Garden Cottage Foods Ltd v. Milk Marketing Board* [1984] 3 W.L.R. 143.

[88] See Case C–6/90, C–9/90, *Francovich and Others v. Italian Republic* [1991] E.C.R. I–5357; [1993] 2 C.M.L.R. 66; N. Gravells, "Disapplying an Act of Parliament pending a Preliminary Ruling: Constitutional Enormity or Community Law Right?" [1989] P.L. 568; Barav, (1989) 26 C.M.L. Rev. 369; Churchill, (1989) 14 E.L. Rev. 470.

grant an interim injunction against the Crown. However, this question of whether Community law obliged national courts to grant interim protection of E.C. rights was also referred to the European Court.[89] Pending the outcome of the decision, the European Court gave interim relief and the United Kingdom government introduced an Order in Council amending the relevant section 14 of the 1988 Act.

The ruling of the European Court examined two issues. First, the **8-55** issue of sovereignty, the validity of a United Kingdom statute and subordinate legislation as against E.C. law. Second, the issue of interim relief, in the form of injunctions against the Crown.

On the first question of sovereignty, the European Court reasoned that community law prevailed over United Kingdom law even if the result meant abrogation of the 1988 Act. Because of the extent to which the 1988 Act offended against E.C. law, it was inapplicable and ineffective. This outcome asserts the right of the European Court to disapply national legislation. On the second question, on the availability of interim relief against the Crown, it would appear that interim relief must be available to give full effect to E.C. law. It appears that injunctions and interim injunctions are available against the Crown when an issue of Community law arises.[90]

The *Factortame* decision supports those who view the European **8-56** Communities as creating a new era for the jurisprudence of the United Kingdom This much is acknowledged by the House of Lords and it appears not to be confined to cases involving the application of E.C. law. In the *GCHQ* case, Lord Diplock accepted the concept of proportionality as part of English Administrative Law, which suggests[91] borrowing from the French system of administrative law. More recently Lord Goff discussed the concept of Leichtfertigkeit, or recklessness, in German law in his discussion of the English law on recklessness.[92] The development of human rights jurisprudence and the influence of the European Union is set to continue to find relevance in the United Kingdom's domestic law and institutions.

---

[89] See D. Oliver, "Fishing on the Incoming Tide" [1991] M.L.R. 442–451. An additional action was taken by the Commission to enforce Art. 169 before the European Court. Case 246/89, *Commission v. United Kingdom* [1989] E.C.R. 3125; [1991] 3 C.M.L.R. 706.

[90] See *M. v. Home Office* [1992] Q.B. 270; [1993] 3 W.L.R. 433, the House of Lords held that the courts had jurisdiction to issue injunctions against officers of the Crown.

[91] [1985] A.C. 374. See Sophie Boyion, "Proportionality in English Administrative Law: A Faulty Translation?" (1992) 12 O.J.L.S. 237–264.

[92] *R. v. Reid* [1992] 3 All E.R. 673 at p. 689.

(d) The Court of Auditors

8-57 The Court of Auditors[93] established under the 1975 Treaty amending Certain Financial Provisions of the Treaties[94] became under Article 4 of the Masstricht Treaty an institution of the Community. The Court is based in Luxembourg and it has important functions for ensuring that the finances of the Community are properly accounted for. Each Member State is entitled to one member of the Court appointed by a unanimous vote of the Council of Ministers and in consultation with the European Parliament. Members of the Court must act in a non-partisan way.

The activities of the Court centre around the task of examining the accounts of all revenue and expenditure of the various Community bodies[95] and of the finances of the Community.[96] This covers the general budget of the European Union.[97] The Court also monitors the work of DGXX, the Directorate that is concerned with Financial Control within the Community. Audit arrangements include both internal and external audits. There is also an important initiative over the past five years to combat fraud within the Community.[98] The Court must liaise with the audit arrangements and procedures in Member States. Once Community funds are transferred to Member States[99] the scrutiny of the community money falls under the budget[1] arrangements of the Member States. This means that 15 separate budget[2] systems have to be considered by DGXX and also by the Court.

8-58 Various strategies for the improvement of the accountability of the Community budget in Member States may be considered such as the Commission's Anti-Fraud Strategy and Work Programme. There are further additional measures to consider in order to achieve sound financial management of the Community that emerge from the United Kingdom budgetary system. Many of the main suggestions are usefully summarised in a recent Treasury Report.[3] The main

[93] D. O'Keefe, "The Court of Auditors" in D. Curtin and T. Heukels (eds.), *Institutional Dynamics of European Integration* (Kluwer, London, 1994).

[94] It came into force in 1977.

[95] Ian Harden, Fidelma White, Katy Donnelly. "The Court of Auditors and Financial Control and Accountability in the European Community" (1995) *European Public Law*.

[96] R. Henderson, *European Finance* (McGraw-Hill Book Company, London, 1989).

[97] See Brigid Laffan, *The Finances of the European Union* (Macmillan, 1997).

[98] HM Treasury, *European Community Finances* Cm. 2824, April 1995.

[99] Tim Frazer, "The New Structural Funds, State Aids and Interventions on the Single Market" 20 (1995) *European Law Review* 3.

[1] John Edsberg, "The European Community's Budget: Budget Discipline and Budget Accounting" (1994) *Financial Accountability and Management* 10(1) 1–16.

[2] A. Widavsky and Z. Zapico-Goni (eds.), *National Budgeting for Economic and Monetary Union* (Institute of Public Administration, London, 1994).

[3] HM Treasury, *European Community Finances* Cm. 2824 April 1995 p. 14 para. 50.

principles that may be considered that emerge from an analysis of the report are as follows:

- use of targeting according to risk of fraud;
- setting precise goals and targets in the anti-fraud action programme of the Commission;
- enhanced co-ordination of anti-fraud measures;
- fraud-proofing new legislative proposals;
- periodic review of all budgetary operations;
- all Community expenditure should be subject to principles of sound public finance;
- prior appraisal should precede the commitment of Community money in order to assess economic benefits are in keeping with the resources deployed.

4. Policies and Objectives

(a) The Treaty on European Union

Since accession into the European Community, the United Kingdom's **8–59** foreign trade with the European Community has steadily increased from exports of 30 per cent in 1970 to over 49 per cent in 1987. Imports have a similar pattern, 27 per cent in 1970, to nearly 53 per cent in 1987. Commensurate with membership of the European Community has been a decline in connections with the Empire and Commonwealth nations, and the growing importance of European markets. Economic and social developments in the United Kingdom are more intertwined with the Community than in the past, which makes the Community an important element in the life of the nation.

Future developments within the European Community are difficult **8–60** to predict with certainty. Change is usually rapid and ongoing. The likelihood is that the Community will enlarge with membership drawn from countries in Eastern Europe.[4] Physical size and economic growth are also accompanied by major structural changes within the Community. The Maastricht Agreement, signed by Member States' foreign and finance ministers on February 7, 1992 has received ratification by the national parliaments of the 15 Member States.

The Maastricht Treaty[5] creates the European Union. This may be **8–61** broadly defined in its essentials as including: a common European

---

[4] Committee on the European Communities. Enlargement of the Community 1992/3 (1992/93; H.L. 5). Application is made under Art. 237 of the Treaty.
[5] Maastricht Treaty: A guide to the Treaty on European Union. (February 24, 1992, Brussels). I am grateful to Professor Yves Demeer, Lille University, for advice on the Treaty. See *R. v. Secretary of State for Foreign and Commonwealth Affairs, ex p. Rees-Mogg* [1994] 1 All E.R. 457.

money by 1999 at the latest, new citizenship rights including membership of the Community through European citizenship, increased rights for the European Parliament and an extension of the Community responsibility into major areas of activity such as energy, transport, telecommunications, environmental developments, social policy and co-operation in domestic and commercial policy. The introduction of a common foreign and security policy, broadening the interests of the Community into education, research, public health, increased consumer protection and in the issuing of visas.

8–62   As the Single Market is an evolutionary process involving political as well as legal rights the stages necessary to complete the Single Market arrangements may require more time and effort than originally envisaged.

The Treaty on European Union introduces institutional[6] changes as a necessary part of the European Union proposed in the Treaty. An increased role is envisaged for the Court of Auditors in auditing the European Community. The European System of Central Banks and the European Central Bank are established (Article 4c) and this may be seen as a necessary step towards eventual monetary union envisaged in the third stage of the Delors plan discussed above.

8–63   The European Court of Justice (Articles 164–188) is changed in respect of organisation as is the Court of First Instance (Le Tribunal). The European Court is given additional powers to impose a lump sum or penalty payment on a Member State not complying with the court's judgment.

The European Parliament should be given the same rights as the Council to request the Commission to make proposals. This would considerably expand the role of the European Parliament, especially in the light of other changes proposed such as the right to set up temporary committees of enquiry, the right to appoint an ombudsman, and the opportunity to have intra-Parliamentary conferences between the European Parliament and national parliaments. Article 189B of the Treaty provides for a co-decision procedure allowing a Commission proposal to be made followed by Parliament giving a majority decision and after consultation with various committees, the Council may make the decision according to a qualified majority. The co-decision procedure may at first only apply by a unanimous decision of the Council in the areas of research and culture.

8–64   Changes in the Council are also included in the Treaty. Member States no longer have to be represented on the Council by a member

---

[6] Principles are set out as follows:
  – Common Provision Articles A–F explains the objectives of the European Union.
  – Amendments to the Treaty Articles 2 – 7C.
  – Citizenship proposals are contained in Articles 8 – 8E.

of the central government and recognition is given to the general secretariat in the Treaty.

Changes in the Commission are consistent with broadening the European Parliament's powers. The main innovation is increasing the European Parliament's role in appointing[7] the President and members of the Commission. The term of office has been increased to five years, to run concurrently with the life of the Parliament.

The full implications[8] of the Maastricht Treaty require further **8–65** discussion and elaboration. In the case of the United Kingdom various modifications to the main Treaty were negotiated in particular, extending the Social Charter was accomplished separately from the United Kingdom.

The Treaty adopts the view that whereas Member States had substantial responsibility in areas of environment, industrial strategy, health, education, and consumer affairs, these areas may be more fully treated within the framework of the Community. At first glance this appears to offer a *de facto* shift in decision-making from national governments to the Community. However, as a counter-balance to the centralising tendencies contained in the Treaty towards Brussels, there is also the adoption of the principle of subsidiarity.

Subsidiarity is a difficult concept to define. The new Maastricht **8–66** Treaty contains a definition in Article 3b, namely the principle: "that the Community is to act within the limits of the powers conferred upon it by this Treaty and of the objectives assigned to it therein." In areas which are outside the exclusive competence, the principle of subsidiarity would apply. This means that decisions by parliaments, governments and other authorities must be taken at national level, either local or central government, rather than at higher Community level, unless there are good reasons to the contrary.

Interpretation of subsidiarity is likely to become a vast and complex undertaking according to the view of each of the Member States. One view is that in fact susidiarity represents a form of federalism, denoting the allocation of powers between the centre, namely the European institutions, and local, namely the Member States of the E.C.

---

[7] Nomination of the President first takes place by the Member States in consultation with Parliament. Nomination of other members of the Commission takes place along with the nominee for President. Vote of approval by Parliament is followed by formal appointment by the Member State.

[8] Generally see F. Snyder *et al*, "New Perspectives on European Law" [1990] 53 M.L.R. 573–698, for a discussion of the major issues in the new developments towards a single market.

(b) Towards A European Public Law?

8-67 The constitutional and political complications of the Treaty on European Union[9] may cause the United Kingdom to consider once more the question of its own parliamentary sovereignty. While it is doubtful if the Treaty fundamentally alters the United Kingdom's constitutional relationship with the Community as this has already been established in the Single European Act, it is less clear what effects the Treaty may have on political decision-making.[10]

8-68 In evidence to the House of Commons Select Committee on Foreign Affairs it was argued that greater political power may be transferred from the Government in the United Kingdom to the Community. This may be due to economic and social factors as much as to the Treaty. However, this is likely to rekindle a debate about the nature of political power in the United Kingdom. In evidence to the Commons Foreign Affairs Committee, Paul Taylor explained that:

> "For political reasons, however, members of the executive who are opposed to the development of closer relations with the Community would like it to be believed that the legislation is equally a victim – to conjure up a common enemy is to strengthen an alliance."

Political and constitutional issues are easily intertwined but it is clear that national[11] governments of Member States in the Council of Ministers may veto proposed legislation of which it disapproves. Member States may continue to pursue their own policies within the Community and subsidiarity permits regional differences to be retained.[12]

8-69 Sovereignty, whether political or legal, is not the only issue raised by the proposals for a European Union. Harlow[13] has raised the question of how the Community as a common market has created its own internal political system of "pressure group politics and its attendant

---

[9] Second Report of the Foreign Affairs Select Committee *Europe after Maastricht*, Minutes of Evidence, Vol. II (1991/92; H.C. 223-ii).

[10] Note that new committees are proposed, such as the Committee of the Regions, made up of representatives of sub-regions in Member States and given a consultative role.

[11] D. Morris, "The Scope for Constitutional Challenge of Westminster Legislation" (1991) Stat. L.R. 166–213 discusses the potential for challenge after *Factortame*.

[12] An important report sets out arguments about law-making powers of the Community: Seventeenth Report of the Select Committee on the European Community, Political Union: Law-Making Powers and Procedures (1991/92; H.L. 80).

[13] C. Harlow, "A Community of Interests? Making the Most of European Law" (1992) 55 M.L.R. 331–350. Justin Greeenwood, *Representing Interests in the European Union* (Macmillan, 1997).

professions of lobbyist and public relations expert." Her view is that
the Community's origins as a transnational organisation has produced[14] "the 'wheeler/dealer' style of Brussels politics" borrowed from
the world of diplomacy and the influence of American style business
with its forms of professional lobbyists and interest group politics.

This gives rise to questions about how far "open" government and, **8-70**
among decision-makers, accountability may be found within the
Community? The answers may not easily be found in any institutional changes nor in the policy formulations involved in European
union. Harlow argues that the United Kingdom's parliamentary
system may provide a valuable contribution to how a more open and
democratic community may evolve.[15]

Finally, the question arises as to the possible development of a
European public law? European Community influences on the United
Kingdom's domestic legal system have already been noted. A grow-
ing jurisprudence exists in the European Court of Justice and in the
United Kingdom's adaptation of Community law. Principles of
French or German law may be found, explained and examined in
English courts" decisions at the highest levels.[16] Influences such as the
European Convention on Human Rights are also relevant and
important.

Koopmans has written that common influences may be detectable **8-71**
even amidst differences between Member States. Citizens are more
litigious[17] and perhaps more likely to challenge authority in some
European countries than in others. While different Member States
may adopt Directives of the Community in distinct ways, the European Court may receive an overview of the activities of all the
Member States. His conclusion is[18] that despite differences:

"We are bound to come to one European system. The integration
process cannot be discontinued."

The differences and diversity of the Member States of the European
Union may remain but are there signs that there is newly emerging a
common law of Europe?

The answer to this question may well depend on the development
of future policies and objectives within the European Union.

---

[14] *ibid.* p.344.
[15] T. Koopmans, "European Public Law: Reality and Prospect" [1991] P.L. 53–63.
[16] *Council of Civil Service Unions v. Minister for the Civil Service* [1984] 3 All E.R. 935; *R. v.
Secretary of State for the Home Dept., ex p. Brind* [1991] 1 AC 696; *R. v. Reid* [1992] 3 All
E.R. 673. and in *Kirklees Metropolitan Borough Council v. Wickes Building Supplies Ltd*
[1992] 3 All E.R. 717, on Sunday trading.
[17] Case 222/84, *Johnston v. Chief Constable of the RUC* [1986] E.C.R. V–1651; [1986] 3
C.M.L.R. 240.
[18] Koopmans, *op. cit.*

Part III:
The Public Law of the United Kingdom

The preceding chapters in Parts I and II of the textbook have been primarily concerned with providing an introductory framework of the constitutional and administrative law of the United Kingdom, including the ideas and influences which have shaped its development. Part III of the textbook comprises an examination in more detail of some of the increasingly specialist areas of public law in the United Kingdom. Chapters 9–11 are intended to explain, respectively, how present day government operates within the parliamentary system of accountability, how the civil service is managed and how public finance is scrutinised. Chapter 12 comprises an analysis of local government and its relationship with central government. Chapter 13 outlines some of the new regulatory arrangements after privatisation of the major utilities. Chapters 14–16 provide an explanation of the main remedies available for the redress of citizens' grievances particularly obtaining remedies in administrative law. Chapters 17–21 cover problems of public order, State secrecy, Northern Ireland and the protection of civil liberties.

Chapter 9

Central Government and Accountability

1. Introduction

In previous chapters[1] the respective role of government and Parlia- **9-01** ment has been discussed in outline. In this Chapter it is intended to explain how government may be made accountable. Accountability takes many forms. A wide variety of techniques and institutions are involved in the scrutiny of government, including the work of parliamentary Select Committees and courts. The system of government is essentially one of party government, the political process may exert influences on the style of government and public affairs. Also relevant in how government may be held to account for its actions is the work of the various audit bodies such as the National Audit Office and in the case of local government, the Audit Commission. Reference to their role may be found in Chapters 11 and 12 respectively.

How government may formulate its policies and how it carries out **9-02** the tasks of government may place strain on existing constitutional arrangements. In recent years an increasing trend towards centralisation of government powers has coincided with a period of government with a large working parliamentary majority. The size of the government's parliamentary majority may affect the ability of Parliament to scrutinise effectively the Executive. In fact governments with a large parliamentary majority may raise questions about the effectiveness of constitutional arrangements to hold government to account.

---

[1] See Chaps. 2 and 3 as an introduction to the functions of Parliament and government.

2. Accountability Defined

9–03 To be accountable[2] is to give reasons and explanations for actions or decisions taken. The characteristic of medieval accountability was the direct responsibility of the individual servant to the King.[3] The idea of accountability may be traced back to the earliest form of organised government. Normanton has pointed out how accountability has "an historical connection between administrative secrecy and the hierarchical state." Such a connection may arise where the State is a hierarchy and all accountability is to the head. Accountability as a means of authorisation control may promote secrecy[4]:

> "The ruler must learn what his servants have been doing, so that he can promote or punish; private persons need know nothing of the secrets and errors of administration, and within unitary states they are rarely allowed to do so. Government is an authoritarian mystery."

9–04 The link between secrecy and accountability has not entirely ended with medieval government. Present day government may be described as responsible government, but this does not always give rise to open or adequate accountability. One explanation is that accountability may be both *internal* and *external*. Internal accountability relates to internal guidance within government departments based on rules of conduct that are not statutory and some may not be widely published. A good example,[5] is the use of Treasury Solicitor's Guidance[6] or Treasury Memorandum as a means of checking on government expenditure and accounts. Internal accountability may prove effective, but it is often hidden from external scrutiny and to some extent this may perpetuate secrecy as the nature of internal review involves confidential and sensitive information.

9–05   External accountability relates to the idea that Ministers are "responsible" or "answerable" to Parliament. This covers such matters as appearing before Select Committees or answering parliamentary questions. Information provided through parliamentary debate,

---

[2] See 1st Report Public Service Select Committee (H.C. 234 1996–7) *Ministerial Accountability and Responsibility.*

[3] In medieval times the members of the Exchequer were the King's commissioners for the enforcement of accountability. Normanton defines public accountability: "as consisting in a statutory obligation to provide, for independent and impartial observers holding the right of reporting their findings at the highest levels in the state . . ." E. Normanton, *The Accountability and Audit of Governments* (1966), p. 2.

[4] Normanton, *op. cit.* p. 4; R. Chapman (ed.), *Ethics in Public Service* (Edinburgh, 1993).

[5] See Chap. 11 for an explanation of the Treasury's role in these matters.

[6] In the case of part payment of legal fees relating to the then Chancellor of the Exchequer, Norman Lamont, reliance was placed on a hitherto unpublished Treasury Solicitor's Memorandum: *Defamation of Ministers and Civil Servants* (May, 1990).

and media coverage contributes to the functions of holding Ministers to account and also controlling government. Advice tendered to civil servants as to their duties and responsibilities in attending before Select Committees, sets out lines of responsibility between civil servants and Ministers.[7] However such advice, if invoked, might be considered restrictive of more open government.

Accountability also involves legal redress. The appeal to courts or **9–06** tribunals or the establishment of an inquiry with investigative powers with the right to examine evidence and establish facts provides an external assessment of government actions. As part of the fact-finding process a court, tribunal or inquiry may seek to establish reasons or justifications for action taken. The giving of reasons becomes an important element for establishing the grounds for decision-making. This is aimed at remedying citizens' grievances but it also assists in improving the quality of administration. Well reasoned and considered decisions with recourse to advice and consultation are the hallmark of good government. Recent judicial decisions appear to be in sympathy with those aims. In *Rowling v. Takaro Properties Ltd*[8] the Privy Council considered how Ministers may be liable under a duty of care, in an action for negligence arising out of their public duties as Ministers. In considering whether such a duty may be imposed was a question of[9] "an intensely pragmatic character." In *Lonhro v. Tebbit*[10] the Court of Appeal accepted this point and affirmed the role of the court to consider the issue. In *M. v. Home Office*[11] the House of Lords held that the contempt jurisdiction of the courts extended to Ministers of the Crown.

There are also various forms of accountability involved in **9–07** achieving better administration. In addition to the courts these involve various audits carried out by the Comptroller and Auditor General and the National Audit Office, or the Audit Commission in the case of local government. There are various ombudsmen, namely the Commissioner for Local Administration in the case of local authorities, or the Parliamentary Commissioner for Administration in the case of central government. Ombudsmen perform important investigative functions.

Responsible government also implies parliamentary control as Turpin has noted[12]:

---

[7] *Memorandum of Guidance for Officials Appearing before Select Committees* (Cabinet Office March, 1988 version).

[8] [1988] 1 All E.R. 163 at 172.

[9] *ibid.*

[10] [1992] 4 All E.R. 280.

[11] *M. v. Home Office* [1992] Q.B. 270; [1992] 4 All E.R. 97.

[12] Turpin, "Ministerial Responsibility: Myth or Reality" in Jowell and Oliver, *The Changing Constitution* (1989) (2nd ed., 1994), p. 56.

"The notion of 'responsible government' implies both acceptance of responsibility for things done and 'responsiveness' to influence, persuasion, and pressure for modifications of policy. Activist parliamentarians of our day aim to 'redress the balance' of the constitution in favour of Parliament by strengthening both control and responsibility of the executive, without making a fine discrimination between these concepts."

9–08   There are further attempts to clarify different forms of accountability. Sir Robin Butler seeks to make a distinction between "the duty to give an account" and "the obligation to accept responsibility". This formulation may be found in the booklet produced as guidance to ministers known as *Questions of Procedures for Ministers*.[13] This document has no legal status but it sets out current thinking on such matters.[14] The question arises as to how the distinction made by Sir Robin Butler works in practice. The answer may be found in considering the findings of the Scott inquiry. Clearly Sir Richard Scott accepted the basis of the distinction but then reaches a number of conclusions that find difficulty in drawing any clear line between the duty to give an account and the obligation to accept responsibility.

9–09   If the findings of the Scott inquiry are closely examined it is apparent that the following conclusions are reached. Sir Richard Scott considered that the guidelines on arms sales, known as the Howe Guidelines, were conceived as a statement of policy and that as a result of revising the guidelines this reflected the *actualité* that policy had been changed. Government statements made in 1989 and 1990 about policy on arms exports "consistently failed to discharge the obligations imposed by the constitutional principle of Ministerial responsibility".[15]

Sir Richard Scott also found that the Attorney-General was at fault in not making clear to the court at the trial of the Matrix Churchill directors that Mr Heseltine, then President of the Board of Trade, was reluctant to agree signing the certificate claiming public interest immunity.[16] A second criticism was that the Attorney-General had mistakenly interpreted the law on public interest certificates when he claimed that Ministers were bound to sign such certificates when requested to do so. Criticism was also made of a number of Ministers for the reasons they gave for signing certificates.[17]

---

[13] Cabinet Office May, 1992.
[14] See Fifth Report from the Treasury and Civil Service Select Committee (H.C. 27 1993–4). Peter Hennessy, *The Hidden Wiring* (London, 1995).
[15] See the Scott report D4.63.
[16] See the Scott report G13.69–72.
[17] See the Scott report paras. G117, 125, 54, 67 and 106.

Aside from such criticisms Sir Richard considers that Ministers **9–10** were albeit, perhaps mistakenly, engaged in acting in what they took to be the national and therefore the public interest. Ministers gained no direct benefits from the arms sales and had been influenced by the need to operate within the competitive conditions of the market. The information then available to Ministers at the time was less than the information which is now available with the benefit of hindsight. Ministers and civil servants are to be judged by what they then knew and on the basis of what they believed at that time. At the heart of the ministerial defence on arms exports was the claim that Ministers had applied the spirit of the guidelines of necessity. In short, Ministers could rely on their subjective defence. They may now appear to have been mistaken but at the time they acted in good faith and with the public interest in mind.

While Scott reserves strongest criticism for the failure of Ministers in not publishing the revised guidelines and giving Parliament the opportunity to debate them but stops short of laying blame having found faults in the conduct of government. Could Scott have come to conclusions on the same evidence that would have forced ministerial resignation?

It is possible to read the Scott findings and evidence and apply a **9–11** different standard of blameworthiness than the one applied by Scott. If Ministers knew that they had misled Parliament because the revised guidelines remained concealed from Parliament and the public were they then not to blame? Whether Ministers had the intention to mislead Parliament or not is irrelevant if the course of conduct they adopted led inexorably to the outcome that Parliament and the public believed that the original Howe guidelines were still in place. In the language of strict liability Ministers must be presumed to have sufficient knowledge of the effects of their actions whether they intended those effects or not. On this basis a more blameworthy conclusion might be reached with the requirement that the ultimate sanction of resignation should have been applied. The fact that Scott chose to apply a subjective standard based on what Ministers claimed they believed, left the report devoid of any positive recommendation that resignations of any Minister should follow from the findings in the report.

There are thus several important implications to be drawn from **9–12** Scott's findings on government wrongdoing. Ministers might consider that they have obtained the best "get out" clause possible from ministerial blameworthiness, that their view of events may be accepted as the best judge of establishing the limits of their own responsibility. After all it was a Minister, Mr Alan Clark, who precipitated the discovery that the guidelines had been revised from his frank disclosure at the arms to Iraq trial that the guidelines were regularly bypassed. The Scott report carefully finds blame to be attached to the actions of several Ministers but the question of fault—finding and ultimate resignation is left to the political arena. If there are shortcomings on blame it is Parliament that must act not tribunals of inquiries. For the future it would appear that a Freedom of Information Act might be the only effective way to police ministerial integrity in these matters.

9–13   The publication of a new Civil Service Code[18] appears to confirm the existing orthodoxy.[19] One way forward is proposed by Diane Woodhouse[20]:

> "Moving into the twenty-first century, the convention of ministerial responsibility can be defined loosely as requiring, first, information rather than resignation; secondly, ministerial 'accountability' for everything but 'responsibility' for only some things; thirdly, civil servant 'responsibility' for some things but 'accountability' only when this suits ministerial interests.

The added dimension to parliamentary control is political accountability to the electorate. This raises questions about how party politics influence government.

(a) The Party System

9–14 Political parties engage in policy formulation and in setting the agenda for the period they hope to occupy government. In the case of the Conservative Party, policies are determined through a variety of advisers through the co-ordination of the Conservative Research Department. Included are the Institute of Economic Affairs, the Centre for Policy Studies founded in 1974 by Sir Keith Joseph, and the Adam Smith Institute. The annual party conference rarely sets the scene for the formulation of policy, rather it acts as a fulcrum of support for the party leadership. A key feature of the procedure for the selection of the Leader of the Conservative Party is the role of the influential backbench 1922 Committee whose chairman, not the chairman of the Conservative Party, is responsible for the conduct of all ballots. The time-table for election is within 28 days of the opening of the new session of Parliament.[21] The process of election is by a secret ballot system among all the elected M.P.s holding the party

---

[18] See *Hansard* H.L. Deb. January 9, 1996 W.A. 21 January 1, 1996.
[19] See H.C. Deb. February 12, 1997 cols 273–293.
[20] Diane Woodhouse "Ministerial Responsibility: Something Old, Something New" [1997] *Public Law* 262.
[21] In the case of a new Parliament the "election shall be held not earlier than three months nor later than six months from the date of assembly of that Parliament."

whip and who are members of the Conservative Party. The elected candidate who becomes Leader of the Party and if the party is the government of the day, the Prime Minister, is the one candidate who: "[i] both receives an overall majority of the votes of those entitled to vote and (ii) receives 15 per cent. more of the votes of those entitled to vote than any other candidate." The second ballot is more straightforward with the winner declared on the basis of an outright majority.

Descriptions[22] of the election of Mr Heath in 1965, following the **9–15** resignation of Sir Alex Douglas Home, show how the victory of Mr Heath over other candidates came through careful electioneering, well-managed campaigns and well-focused appeals to backbench loyalties. The leadership election of Mrs Thatcher in 1975 showed similar tactics in winning loyalty from backbench M.P.s.[23] Clearly party leaders who then become Prime Minister have the reality of party support as the basis of exercising power.

On November 19, 1990, the premature resignation of Mrs Thatcher **9–16** as Prime Minister, reinforced the power of party politics and underlined the collective force of Cabinet government. Nigel Lawson in his memoirs[24] explains the consequences of the Prime Minister's political unpopularity:

"It was unprecedented: yet there were good reasons why no fewer than 45 per cent of her parliamentary colleagues felt unable to support their leader of the previous fifteen years and more in the first ballot – and among the 55 per cent who did there were many, particularly among her ministerial colleagues, who had allowed their loyalty to get the better of their judgement in the first ballot but would not have done so in the second. Those reasons essentially boiled down to one: the conviction that Margaret had become an electoral liability and that the Conservative Party could win the coming general election only under a new leader."

Nicholas Ridley[25] attributed Mrs Thatcher's failure to gain sufficient **9–17** votes in the first ballot to win the leadership as down to bad tactics. The first error was the timing of the election to coincide with a period when, the Prime Minister had to be out of the country while attending a conference in Paris. Secondly, there was a clear mistake in deciding "to appoint a weak campaign team."

The team contained five ex-Cabinet Minsters who Ridley believes did "not know large numbers of M.P.s." The team merely canvassed

[22] James Prior, *A Balance of Power* (London, 1986), pp. 98–101.
[23] *ibid.*
[24] Nigel Lawson, *The View From No. 11* (London, 1992), pp. 1000–1001.
[25] Nicholas Ridley, *My Style of Government* (1992), pp. 241–242.

opinion and did not seek to persuade. This example underlines the point already noted of the careful relationship required between the political party and the leadership.

The election of the leader of the Conservative Party following the defeat of Mr John Major at the general election on May 1, 1997 highlighted the problems of the lack of input into the constituency party. The election of Mr William Hague took three ballots, although the canvass of constituency support was in favour of Mr Kenneth Clarke. The constituency associations were not part of the ballot which was confined to Conservative M.P.s.

9–18   In the case of the Labour Party, unlike the Conservative Party, the formulation of policy is partly carried out through the party conference. Thus, "direction and control" of the work of the party is in theory left to the conference. This body provides a wide canvass for Labour Party support. The trade unions and other affiliated groups comprise about 90 per cent of the conference votes. There is a National Executive Committee elected by the party conference which sets out the main developments and direction of policy. There are various sub-committees which carry out the actual work of devising policy. The manifesto is jointly arrived at by the National Executive Committee and the leadership of the parliamentary party comprising the party leader, deputy leader and shadow Cabinet, if out of government. Advice to the Labour Party comes from a wide variety of sources including the Adam Smith Institute, the Institute for Public Policy Research and various trade union-funded advisers.

9–19   Attempts to shift control from the parliamentary party leadership to the National Executive Committee have been unsuccessful. Given the fact that the Labour Party had been unsuccessful in gaining office in the General Elections from 1978 to 1992, the Labour Parliamentary Party has resisted attempts to have the annual conference impose control over its policy. In fact centralising tendencies within the party have adopted a more directed approach to policy than hitherto. This has resulted in policy initiatives largely controlled by the party leadership. The election victory in May 1997 confirmed strict party discipline as an element in election success.

9–20   Nominations for leadership must be supported by 20 per cent of the Commons members of the Parliamentary Labour Party. There are three constituencies entitled to participate in voting. The votes for each nominee in a section are to be calculated as a percentage of the total votes cast in that section and apportioned according to a set percentage. First for the Commons members of the Parliamentary Labour Party, the apportioned vote is 30 per cent. Second, for delegates from affiliated Constituency Labour Parties present at party conference, the apportioned vote is 30 per cent. Third, for delegates from affiliated trade unions, and various related societies and interest groups, the apportioned vote is 40 per cent. There is in addition, once the votes have been apportioned according to the percentage noted above, the requirement that[26]: "the candidate receiving more than half of the votes shall be declared elected and if no candidate reaches this total on the first ballot further ballots should be held on an elimination basis."

The above procedure with its weighting in favour of respectively, **9–21** affiliated labour organisations, the Constituency Labour Party and the Parliamentary Labour Party, makes the question of the manifesto a difficult issue in the development of the policies of any future Labour Government. Attempts by the National Executive Committee to mandate the Parliamentary Labour Party with an election manifesto drawn up by the National Executive Committee would leave any future Labour Government with little discretion over their policies. This would pose a serious question about the propriety of a future Labour Government being bound by the National Executive Committee, a body that is not responsible for the implementation of any policies.

The Social and Liberal Democratic Party has a Federal Party for **9–22** matters of policy common to England, Scotland and Wales. For specific matters within each of the regions, there is a State Party for each region. The Federal Party determines issues which overlap with policies decided in each of the regions. There is a Federal Policy Committee, responsible for research and development. Ultimate authority is found to vest within the Federal Conference which has representatives from the local party. Election of party leader is by the system of a Single Transferable Vote, STV, and by secret ballot. Nominations must be supported by 200 members and the nominee must be a member of the parliamentary party in the House of Commons.

The internal organisation of political parties may well have reper- **9–23** cussions on the government's treatment of various issues and in the organisation of the government itself. Accountability of the government of the day to political parties emphasises the nature of party government. Thus it is likely that the policies created through the political process will also have an effect on the institutions of government itself.[27] In that way different forms of accountability are continually evolving. For example, impeachment of Ministers preceded the development of political accountability to Parliament. The fact that one form of accountability gives way to some new idea is

---

[26] Constitution of the Labour Party. The death of Mr John Smith Q.C. in 1994 resulted in the election of a new leader of the Labour Party adopting the new electoral procedures outlined above for the first time.

[27] Geoffrey Marshall, "The Evolving Practice of Parliamentary Accountability: Writing Down the Rules" (1991) *Parliamentary Affairs* 460–469.

recognised by Marshall who identifies a number of elements in the continuous development of constitutional practice. Marshall identifies "removability," "answerability" and resignation as elements in this process.

Accountability involves the principles of Cabinet and individual responsibility to Parliament. From this perspective the role of Parliament may be examined.

3. The Role of Parliament

9–24 Parliament provides the framework for government accountability but it also provides the government with the means to carry out its policies through legislation. Current concern is that the legislature has become too dominated by the Executive. Some commentators have attributed Parliament's role[28] to merely one of influencing policy. While others believe that there is little need to refer to Parliament when the vast majority of government work is accepted into law.[29]

The increase in the volume of legislation[30] passing through Parliament illustrates the problems of modern government. New legislation is complex and detailed often amending previous Acts of Parliament and seeking to meet every contingency. The problem of increasing governmental powers gives rise to increasing administrative bureaucracy. Reid noted[31]:

> "In 1913 there were 38 new statutes occupying only 301 pages. In 1956, there were 59 new statutes occupying 1,016 pages. In 1988, 55 statutes were passed and in 1989, 46 statutes in 2,489 large pages. Those statutes cover primary legislation."

9–25   In addition, in the last decade it is estimated that over 7,000 Orders in Council had been made through which Ministers may be given power to issue rules and on an annual basis around 1,000 statutory instruments are issued. Most primary legislation emanates from

---

[28] P. Norton, "Independence, Scrutiny and Rationalisation: a Decade of Changes in the House of Commons" in L. Robins (ed.), *Political Institutions in Britain: Development and Change* (Longman, 1986), pp. 58–86.
[29] M. Ryle, "The Commons Today" in S. A. Walkland and M. Ryle, *The Commons Today* (1981), p. 14.
[30] See Lord Renton, "Modern Acts of Parliament" in *The House Magazine*, February 11, 1991, p. 14.
[31] Wiliam K. Reid "Changing Notions of Public Accountability" (1992) *Public Administration* 81–87.

central government while local authority and public corporations bye-laws, departmental rules and regulations or decisions, add to the increase in legal powers and the breadth of their distribution.

Parliamentary accountability offers a wide variety of forms of control over government. One form is in the scrutiny of legislation, another is through the work of the new departmentally-related select committees and a third is through parliamentary debate and ministerial responsibility.

(a) Scrutiny and Passage of Legislation

Parliament's role in the scrutiny of primary legislation involves **9–26** debate at the various stages of the Bill. Scrutiny of legislation provides a good example of both procedural rules and debate used as a means of scrutiny. The first reading is purely formal, the title of the Bill is approved.

The second reading may be referred to a Second Reading Committee which is a Standing Committee, nominated for the consideration of the Bill referred to it. It is intended to save time allowing a number of non-controversial Bills to proceed through the House of Commons with the minimum of time spent in debate in the Chamber of the House. The procedure is open to objection by at least 20 members of the House.[31a] After second reading, the Bill goes to one of the standing committees unless the House disagrees. It is possible for some parts of the Bill to be examined by the standing committee while the remainder is examined by a committee of the entire House. The procedure in committee can be painstaking and involve consideration line by line of each clause of the Bill.

Once through the committee stage the Bill, if amended is reported **9–27** to the House. There then follows the third reading. At this stage the debate is confined to general principles only and verbal amendments may be moved. Once carried by vote, the Bill is then sent to the House of Lords for consideration. There the procedure generally follows the Commons. After the Lords, the Bill is returned. It is then subject to assent by the Commons including any amendments introduced by the Lords.

Parliamentary scrutiny of delegated[31b] legislation is less uniform **9–28** when compared to primary legislation. There is no requirement to

---

[31a] There is a similar procedure for Scottish Bills but this must be supported by at least six members.

[31b] The term delegated legislation is all embracing; it may refer to Statutory Orders in Council made by the Queen in Council. Departmental and ministerial rules regulations, and orders are made by Ministers or departmental heads. The Local Government Act 1972 entitled local authorities to pass by-laws. The Rules Com-

comply with a single standard procedure. The explanation for the lack of standardisation in procedure, lies in the fact that delegated powers are exercised by a very wide variety of bodies and fall within specialised rules according to the nature of the powers involved.

The procedures which may be invoked, according to the nature of the regulations or orders to be enacted are as follows. The first procedure is that of laying the delegated legislation or instrument before Parliament. Invariably this procedure applies to statutory instruments but the requirement of laying does not apply to all such instruments even those that fall within the Statutory Instruments Act 1946.

9–29   Statutory instruments may take effect immediately but are subject to annulment by Order in Council of either House. Section 5 of the 1946 Act prescribes a period of 40 days before laying where an instrument subject to a negative resolution may be annulled. Excluded from the time period are days when Parliament is dissolved, prorogued or adjourned. Statutory instruments may be laid in draft before Parliament and made subject to a resolution that no further proceedings need be taken.

9–30   Statutory instruments may be subject to affirmative parliamentary procedure. These may be laid before Parliament either in draft or completed form, but do not take effect until approved. This requires government time, as normally a Minister must present the instrument and there are no amendments possible. Occasionally an instrument may be laid to have immediate effect but will cease to have this effect unless approved by resolution within a prescribed time period. There are, in uncommon examples, procedures for laying instruments and Parliament is only to be informed of the action to be taken, thus leaving Ministers in control. There is also a lack of clarity over the precise legal requirements of laying instruments. One view is that in the cases of instruments subject to negative resolution and possibly those requiring positive resolution, the requirement is directory and not mandatory. This leaves uncertain a key issue of requiring appropriate sanctions over the government in the exercise of parliamentary control.

9–31   The second procedure involved in the parliamentary supervision of delegated legislation is the use of scrutinising committees. The Select Committee on Statutory Instruments usually meets with a Lords Committee to form a Joint Committee. Its role and function is to bring

---

mittee of the Supreme Court is entitled to make procedural rules for the administration of the courts. See Supreme Court Act 1981, s.86. Special procedures are available for the passage of Statutory Orders (Special Procedures) Act 1945. Various statutory powers enable rules to be made. See: the Electricity Act 1989; the New Roads and Street Works Act 1991 and the Deregulation and Contracting Out Act 1994.

some improvement to the form and content of statutory instruments. A small number of instruments gave rise to a referral to the House. The terms of reference of the Joint Committee were agreed[31c] in 1973 and include consideration of any instrument to decide whether special attention of the House needs to be drawn to any matter coming within any one of eight categories. These are as follows: Does the instrument impose any charge on the public revenues or any fee to a public authority for services or a licence? Does an instrument made in pursuance of an Act of Parliament exclude challenge by the courts? Does the instrument have retrospective effect in circumstances where the parent Act does not confer any such authority? Has there been any unjustifiable delay in the publication of the instruments or in the laying procedure before parliament? Are there unjustifiable delays in informing the Speaker in the case of instruments in operation because of urgency before Parliament was informed? Are there doubts as to the legality of the instrument? Is the drafting in order and not defective? Or could the wording or construction of the instrument require additional explanation?

An important innovation since 1973 has been the power to refer **9–32** instruments to a Standing Committee on Statutory Instruments[32] to question their merits. However it appears that the referral is limited as each committee meets only once and is limited to one and a half hours of debate and cannot reject an instrument or secure a debate in the Commons. Any Order in Council made under the Northern Ireland Act 1974, Sched. 1, paragraph 1 is[33] excluded. The Committee may take evidence only from government officials or HMSO[34] Some commentators[35] claim that the main benefit of the Standing Committee is that the government has made use of their role to save time on the floor of the House. In 1989–90, the Select Committee on Procedure[36] received evidence recommending that; debate in the House of Commons on instruments subject to affirmative resolution should not proceed until the Committee reported on the instrument; the remit of the Committee should extend to include Northern Ireland instruments requiring negative resolution; the Committee should be free to take

---

[31c] Report of the Joint Committee on Delegated Legislation (1971/72; H.L. 184) and (1971/72; H.C. 475) known as the Brooke Report, recommended many of the changes introduced in 1973. See (1991–92; H.C. 271) 1,291 instruments were considered by the Joint Committee but only in 166 instances were there grounds for report to the two Houses. See M. Zander, *The Law Making Process* (1994).

[32] Standing Order No. 124.

[33] Also excluded are measures under the Church of England Assembly (Powers) Act 1919.

[34] Select Committee on Procedure: The Working of the Select Committee System, Memoranda, (1989/90; H.C. 19–1), p. xlvii.

[35] P. Silk, R. Walters, *How Parliament Works* (Longmans, 1987), pp. 15–8.

[36] *ibid.* See Hansard Society Commission on the Legislative Process (1992).

evidence from any source and that codes of practice should be more regularly open to scrutiny. Finally greater regard should be taken of the Committee by other departmental committees.

9–33   An additional check on the procedures for Statutory Instruments is the requirement of publicity. First in 1893 under the Rules Publication Act, and now under the Statutory Instruments Act 1946, there are specific requirements for the printing and publication of statutory instruments, *i.e.* "they should be printed and sold as soon as possible."

The use of statutory instruments extends from rules relating to national insurance contributions, welfare benefits and employment protection procedures affecting the everyday lives of many people. Normally security and taxation matters are outside the remit of statutory instruments, with the exception of Northern Ireland since 1972 where direct rule has been carried out through the use of statutory instruments. This leaves many major issues largely under-debated in the House of Commons and therefore not subject to the normal scrutiny of parliamentary debate.

9–34   A controversial innovation is contained in the Deregulation and Contracting Out Bill introduced in January 1994. If enacted the Bill would allow a Minister to make an order to amend or repeal primary legislation which imposes an unnecessary burden on a trade or business provided necessary protection in the original Act of Parliament is not removed. The Select Committee on Procedure has recommended that there should be a new Scrutiny Committee in each House to allow debate over deregulation proposals.

(b)   Select Committees

9–35 One of the main functions of the House of Commons is to scrutinise the policies of the government of the day. Accountability may therefore be achieved through a number of select committees which carry out this task. Up until May 1997 there were 30[37] such committees, normally appointed under the permanent Standing Orders of the House. The exact number of such committees has not yet been determined since the election in May 1997. Committees have a long

---

[37] In 1989–90 there were three Private Legislation Committees; Court of Referees, Standing Orders, Unopposed Bills. Domestic Committees concerned with the House of Commons domestic matters include Services such as Catering, Accommodation and various matters such as the Library. Other Committees under this category include: Chairmen's Panel, Members' Interests, Privileges, Procedure, Selection and Sound Broadcasting, Scrutiny Committees include Consolidation and Bills, European Legislation, Parliamentary Commissioner for Administration, Public Accounts, Statutory Instruments (meets with the Lords as a Joint Committee).

history that may be traced back almost 400 years. Following[38] consideration of the committees in use in the House of Commons' reforms were introduced and adopted in 1979. The new select committees are directly related to the departments[39] they oversee. The initiative for the formation of the new select committees owed much to the then leader of the House, Norman St John Stevas who pledged support from the government in the operation of the new committee system.[40]

In theory the new select committees are independent from party **9–36** politics. However, in practice the nomination for the selection of backbench M.P.s to serve on a Committee through the Committee of Selection has seen some party political activity. The convention has developed that the members of the two main parties' names go forward, but the party whips are consulted as to who to appoint. Concern[41] has been expressed that party discussion overshadows the selection process to the detriment of the independence of the work of the committees. Each Committee has either nine or 11 members. Normally there is a majority of backbench M.P.s from the government party.

Membership of the select committee endures for the life-time of the Parliament. The chairmanship of committees is shared between the opposition and the government. The procedure allows the committee to elect their own chairman but the party of the chairman has been agreed beforehand. The powers of the committees are to send for papers, persons and records. In their work[42] the committees are department-led.

Michael Ryle has noted[43] some ommisions in the present arrange- **9–37** ments concerning the working of the Select Committees. At present the scrutiny of the work of the Law Officers, notably the Lord Chancellor's Office is excluded from review. The Scottish Office is also not included in any scrutiny. More controversially there was no Select Committee for Northern Ireland Affairs until 1994. After the

---

[38] Select Committee on Procedure 1977–78, H.C. 588.

[39] They include: Agriculture; Defence; Education, Science and Arts; Employment; Energy. This committee was recently abolished in the Summer of 1992 following the abolition of the Department of Energy and the transfer of its functions to the Department of Trade and Industry; Environment; Foreign Affairs; Home Affairs; Scottish Affairs (not always nominated); Social Services; Trade and Industry (now including responsibility for Energy); Transport; Treasury and Civil Service; Welsh Affairs, National Heritage and Health.

[40] (June 25, 1979; H.C. Deb.), Vol. 969, col. 45.

[41] Select Committee on Procedure (1989–90; H.C. 19–1) para. 16 of the Memorandum of the Chairman of the Liaison Committee.

[42] Gavin Drewry, *The New Select Committees* (O.U.P., 2nd ed., 1995); *First Report from the Select Committee on Procedure* (1977–78; H.C. 588–1).

[43] Memorandum by Michael Ryle on *The Select Committee System*, Select Committee on Procedure (1989–90; H.C. 19–II).

election of the new Labour government on May 1, 1997, it is proposed to have a 15-member Select Committee to consider modernisation of the work of the House of Commons.[44]

9–38 The new select committees do not review systematically how Acts of Parliament are in fact operating. Select Committees also have a role in overseeing some aspects of public expenditure but the main work in this area is delegated to the Public Accounts Committee, a specialist scrutiny committee. The view put forward by Ryle is that there is a case for expanding the role of departmental select committees into the questions of choices over public expenditure plans. This expanded role might also lead to a greater contribution to the various debates on Finance Bills and detailed tax proposals.

9–39 The advantages of the new select committees include better information for Members of Parliament, and this informs the quality of scrutiny offered in the Commons debate. Public understanding and knowledge is thereby increased in the work of the Select Committee.[45] The examination of witnesses, especially since the most topical issues when examined by the committee are televised, has increased the public awareness of the work of the committees. This gives expert witnesses and pressure groups an opportunity to be heard. The fact that reports are not normally aired in the House of Commons suggests that the government may not face the full extent of the pressure generated by the Reports of the Select Committee.

9–40 A central question in the role of the committees in providing scrutiny of government policies is the attendance of witnesses before the committees. Gavin Drewry[46] has identified that there are instances "where select committees have faced difficulties in summoning witnesses and compelling disclosure of documents." Some instances of these difficulties may be noted. In 1984, the Government declined to allow the Director of the Government Communications Headquarters to give evidence to the Select Committee on Employment.[47] In the notable Westland Affair, in 1986, officials of the Department of Trade and Industry were refused permission to give evidence to the Defence Committee, although the Head of the Civil Service appeared and gave answers to specified questions.[48]

9–41 More recently, the attendance of witnesses has raised questions about whether the right to silence or the protection against self-

---

[44] For example, reform of the second reading procedure for Public Bills a Law Commission report.

[45] P. Giddings, "What has been achieved?" in Drewry, *The New Select Committees: A Study of the 1979 Reforms* (OUP, 2nd ed., 1995).

[46] *ibid.* Memorandum from Gavin Drewry, *Reform of the Select Committee System submitted on behalf of the study of Parliament Group.* Select Committee on Procedure (1989–90 H.C. 19–II).

[47] First report from the Employment Committee (1983/84; H.C. 238), paras. 6–7.

[48] Fourth Report from the Defence Committee (1985/86; H.C. 519), paras. 225–38.

incrimination might apply. The aftermath of the death of Robert Maxwell, raised such questions over the refusal of his sons to answer the questions put to them by the Select Committee on Social Services.

The attendance of civil servants[49] may be at the committees' compulsion but there is no duty on the part of civil servants to answer questions. The relationship between civil servants and the committee is explained in the Memorandum of Guidance for Officials Appearing before Select Committees. While officials are to be helpful to the work of the committee the principle is that officials appear before the committee "on behalf of Ministers." Ministerial instruction may be given to officials as to how they should conduct their appearance before the committee.

The question arises as to how successful the new select committees **9–42** are in the scrutiny of government and perhaps as important how success may be measured. There are two opposing views of their effectiveness. George Jones argues[50] that the committees have failed to fulfil their terms of reference and therefore they are not worth pursuing. The opposing view appears from much of the evidence received by the Select Committee on Procedure, which is generally praiseworthy of the performance of the committees and only minor adjustments are recommended. In setting out the criteria for evaluation, both opposing views are vague in explaining how the work of the committee may be properly tested.

Philip Norton, in evidence to the committee on procedure provides **9–43** a more comprehensive evaluation and suggests that "select committees are now the essential agents for such scrutiny of Parliament in subjecting government to informed, detailed and continuous scrutiny." The latter point is perhaps one of the most essential elements in any system of accountability. Continuous scrutiny allows past experience to be supplemented. Norton notes how techniques of questioning and cross examination of Ministers have improved and how[51] "there is sufficient evidence to demonstrate changes in public policy, changes that would not have taken place but for the recommendations of the committees."[52]

Norton also draws attention to the value for money offered by the **9–44** select committee system which has meagre resources and financial assistance. The key to the success or failure of the committee system appears to be the development of the political will to make the

[49] *Memorandum of Guidance for Officials Appearing before Select Committees* (Cabinet Office) revised version March 1988.

[50] G. W. Jones, "Send the Watchdogs Packing" *The Times*, November 4, 1989.

[51] P. Norton, *Memorandum to the Select Committee on Procedure* (1989–90; H.C. 19–11) p. 139.

[52] A list of 150 recommendations compiled and accepted by government see (H.C. Deb. 98), cols. 396–446, quoted in Norton, *op. cit.*

system effective. Norton identifies some shortcomings such as: limited interests by members in committee reports; limited time and resources; absence of career development in the select committee structure; finally, the committees do not appear to have a sufficiently strong link with the chamber of the House of Commons. Additional pressure on the select committee system may come from government in terms of the need to pass large volumes of legislation and from the career demands and self interests of the backbench M.P.s who serve on the committees.

9–45   It may be concluded that while the new committees have not radically altered the relationship between Parliament and the Executive, they have provided information and knowledge about the internal workings of government. There is also the contribution made by the committees in keeping a clear focus on the work of backbench M.P.s. The House of Commons maintains a Register of M.P.s interests and the Select Committee on Members' Interests (declaration)[53] sets out the main interests of M.P.s included in the Register. These are specific classes of pecuniary interest or benefit, lobbying activities or advice and consultancy.

The potential for the committees to develop their role rests on political will and sufficient vision of the future that a more informed and critical analysis of government policy will improve the accountability of government.[54]

(c)   Parliamentary Debate and Ministerial Responsibility

9–46 Accountability for the actions and policy of the government of the day involves public debate in the media and in Parliament. The question arises as to how effective parliamentary debate may be in changing the opinion of the government or in forming a separate policy agenda from the government of the day. The answer may depend on the size of the parliamentary majority enjoyed by the government. There are only a small number of examples where the outcome of a *speech* made in a debate has been influential[55] for the course of[56] legislation. The Immigration Rules in 1972, when the government was defeated because of speeches made by several Conservative M.P.s and the failure of the Foreign Secretary to give concessions, lost the vote. In 1986 the Shops Bill was lost in a second

---

[53] (1974–75; H.C. 102).
[54] D. Oliver, *Government in the United Kingdom* (Open University Press, 1991), pp. 42–45.
[55] There are many examples where the government of the day has suffered defeat, rarely is this attributable to speeches which persuade M.P.s as to their voting intentions.
[56] Jones *et alia, Politics U.K.* (1991), p. 331.

reading despite the government's overall majority. Speeches made by many Conservative M.P.s resulted in the unprecedented loss in modern times of a government Bill after second reading.

Such examples serve to show that Parliamentary debate may have limitations in terms of accountability over government policy.

Political opinion and support for the government in office requires **9–47** that the government must take account of its political standing. In constitutional terms, a government that loses the confidence of the House of Commons must either resign or advise dissolution. For example in 1924, under Ramsay Macdonald, and in 1979, under James Callaghan, the Government was defeated in a confidence motion and advised dissolution. Similarly the classic formulation of ministerial responsibility attributes to the entire Ministry responsibility for all official acts performed by individual Ministers. Turpin concludes that accountability of government through ministerial responsibility[57]:

" . . . depends upon procedure and custom, upon intangible understandings and traditions, and upon political circumstances and the government's need for the co-operation of Opposition and backbenchers. Ministerial responsibility, both collective and individual, in large part involves conflicts of interests between the government on the one hand and Parliament and the public on the other."

Brazier, writing in 1990, records that since 1960, there have been 24 **9–48** ministerial resignations on grounds of collective responsibility.[58] In the case of individual responsibility there have been 12.[59] Most recently the resignation of Mr Mellor added to that list based on intensive media coverage of his private and personal life. It is not uncommon for Ministers to resign because of private and personal matters. While Ministers are responsible for their private conduct, the conduct of their department and acts of their civil servants, this does not always give rise to resignation.

In 1982, the then Home Secretary Mr Whitelaw did not resign even though a breach in security allowed an intruder into the Queen's private bedroom. A year later, in 1983, the then Secretary of State for Northern Ireland, Mr Prior, did not resign, because of a break-out at the Maze prison in Northern Ireland due to security lapses. The Hennessey Report into the escape of prisoners concluded that there were no policy mistakes responsible.

The question of ministerial resignation has as much to do with **9–49** damage limitation by the Prime Minister of the day as with accountability to Parliament. In that sense the Prime Minister's judgement of

---

[57] Turpin, "Ministerial Responsibility: Myth or Reality?" in Jowell and Oliver, *The Changing Constitution* (1989), p. 85.
[58] Brazier, *Constitutional Texts* (Oxford, 1990), pp. 359–360.
[59] Brazier, *op. cit.* p. 378.

what may be acceptable to the House of Commons for the survival of the government may depend on parliamentary debate. A reasonably wide latitude appears to be given to Ministers given the pressure of work many endure. In 1971–72, the collapse of the Vehicle and General Insurance Company did not lead to ministerial resignation. There was criticism of civil servants and the acceptance that Ministers may experience a steady turn over of appointments and departments, and that the actual percentage of matters within departments which are referred to Ministers for personal attention is very small. In the case of the Vehicle and General collapse in 1971, less than 1 per cent of the department workload was referred to the Minister; and there had been since 1964, six different Ministers appointed.[60] In the debate, following the inquiry into the collapse of the insurance company, the Home Secretary explained[61]:

> "In my own department we get 1 1/2 million letters a year, any one of which may lead to disaster. It is no minimising of the responsibility of Ministers to Parliament to say that a Minister cannot be blamed for a mistake made if he did not make it himself and if he has not failed to ensure that that sort of mistake ought not to be made."

9–50   One recent example is the dismissal of Derek Lewis as Head of the Prison Service following the report by Sir John Learmont into prison escapes from Parkhurst.[62] The then Home Secretary Michael Howard refused to resign drawing on the distinction between operational and policy matters; he claimed that as the Home Secretary was responsible for policy and no policy had been found to be at fault, he was entitled to rely on this fact and not resign. On this fine distinction, the question of responsibility is confined to the duty to be accountable. Thus it may be argued that ministerial responsibility for the acts of civil servants appears to be non-existent.[63]

9–51   Ministerial responsibility is susceptible to the ebb and flow of political debate. What may appear settled, may on reflection seem less clear. For example the resignation of Thomas Dugdale, over the sale of land at Crichel Down in 1954, was attributed to criticism of his civil servants' behaviour. With the benefit of hindsight and access to

---

[60] (February 16, 1972; 831 H.C. Debs. 419) See Report of the Tribunal of Inquiry into the Cessation of Trading of the Vehicle and General Insurance Co. (1971–72), H.C. 133; H.L. 80, February 15, 1972.

[61] (May 1, 1972; 836 H.C. Deb. 33.) C. Turpin "Ministerial Responsibility" in Jowell and Oliver (eds.), *The Changing Constitution* (3rd ed., 1994).

[62] H.C. Deb. 264 cols. 502–6 18 November 1995.

[63] See G. Mather, "Clarifying Responsibility and Accountability" *Government Accountability* (CIPFA, 1996).

official papers it appears that the civil servants who were blamed were the victims of ministerial indecision and policy changes. Resignation came from backbench pressure and the Prime Minister's political judgement.[64] Ministerial responsibility that leads to resignation may ultimately depend on public opinion and political judgement.

4. Government and the Crown

(a) Ministers and Public Interest Immunity

Accountability, it has been noted from the foregoing discussion, may **9–52** also be linked to secrecy. As Birkinshaw has noted,[65] in historical terms Parliament saw secrecy for its proceedings "as a necessary protection against the Crown's absolutist tendencies". The struggle for information became the centre of the desire for control. This legacy remains. So does the status of the Crown. A great deal of secrecy and mystique still surrounds the Crown, both as to the personal wealth and fortune of members of the Royal family and also as to the relationship and role of the Monarch with the government of the day.

Ministers are chosen by the Prime Minister but appointed by the **9–53** Queen, in constitutional theory they are servants of the Crown. Major public powers remain vested in the Crown or in Ministers who act as servants of the Crown.[66] Civil servants under ministerial direction remain servants of the Crown.[67] The creation of modern government has not dispensed with the various common law powers, privileges and immunities that were ascribed to royal power but today they are exercised by the government of the day with few powers remaining personal to the Queen.[68]

In the appointment of Prime Minister the convention of whether the person to be appointed commands the confidence of the House of Commons, is left to the Queen and her advisers. Normally the leader

---

[64] See the account in P. Carrington, *Reflect on Things Past*, pp. 90–93.

[65] P. Birkinshaw, *Freedom of Information* (London, 1988), p. 63.

[66] *Town Investments Ltd v. Department of Environment* [1978] A.C. 359.

[67] There is considerable scope for debate as to whether the characterisation in law of the Crown as a corporation has much significance. See Geoffrey Marshall, *Constitutional Theory* (1971), pp. 18–19.

[68] Many of the personal powers of the Queen are exercised on the advice of ministers. The Queen may appoint the Prime Minister but choice is based on the convention of the person who may command sufficient support in the Commons to form a government. Advice to the Queen will seem to establish such a person.

of the largest party is selected, but in making a choice the Queen may face difficult judgements when there is no overall majority party and the choice of person is less obvious.

9–54   In the dismissal of Ministers, the Queen's prerogative is exercisable by convention, on the advice of the Prime Minister but the retention of this prerogative maintains the role of the Crown in constitutional matters.[69] Finally in the dissolution of Parliament the normal convention is that in the exercise of the prerogative of dissolution, the Queen acts on the advice of the Prime Minister.

9–55   The Crown's exercise of powers does not readily conform to the normal arrangements for accountability. The Crown has traditionally enjoyed certain Crown privileges. Before the Crown Proceedings Act 1947 claims against the Crown for breach of contract were brought through Petition of Right, thus providing that the Home Secretary's agreement had to be sought before proceedings could begin.[70] In addition in constitutional law, the presumption of statutory construction is that the Crown is not bound by an Act of Parliament. This does not prevent the Crown from benefiting from statutory powers. The Crown Proceedings Act 1947 permits claims formerly made by Petition of Right to be made and enforceable through ordinary civil proceedings instituted in county courts. This does not affect the taking of proceedings against the Queen in her own personal capacity, which remain by way of Petition of Right.[71]

9–56   The Crown retains certain privileges which may be beneficial to the government of the day in the exercise of Crown powers. The remedies of injunction and specific performance were traditionally not available against the Crown. Crown Servants may be sued personally for civil wrongs committed by them even when they are acting in their official capacity at the time. The House of Lords held in *M v. Home Office*[72] that the courts could issue injunctions against Crown officers in judicial review proceedings. Ministers are amenable to the contempt jurisdiction of the courts. The use of prerogative powers is amenable to judicial scrutiny by way of judicial review, but prerogative powers give considerable powers to the government of the day in addition to any statutory authority. In the exercise of Executive powers to allocate licences, approve appointments to public

---

[69] See C. Turpin, *British Government and the Constitution* (2nd ed., 1990), pp. 137–153.

[70] See The Petitions of Right Act 1860 repealed by the Crown Proceedings Act 1947.

[71] In tort liability the Crown Proceedings Act 1947 made the Crown liable in the same manner and form as a private person of full age and capacity for most torts. The Crown is also liable for torts committed by its servants or agents. See *Tamlin v. Hannaford* [1950] K.B. 18.

[72] [1993] 3 W.L.R. 433. See Gould, [1993] P.L. 568. In *McDonald v. Secretary of State for Scotland*, *The Times*, February 2, 1994 the House of Lords decision in *Re M* was not binding in Scotland.

office, engage in contracts, undertake research and development and provide loans and subsidies, the carrying out of government is by nature confidential and often removed from direct accountability. It is in the nature of government that some of its most important activities are free from direct parliamentary scrutiny or control.

Crown immunity or public interest immunities as it is more **9–57** commonly called, provides the government of the day with an important claim in the event of legal proceedings. Crown privilege or immunity[73] may be claimed as the basis for the non-disclosure of documents which are confidential. The Crown may argue that to disclose such documents in legal proceedings may be "injurious to the public interest." Most of the authorities on Crown immunity involve civil proceedings rather than criminal prosecutions.

In the House of Lords in 1942 in *Duncan v. Cammell Laird & Co.* **9–58** *Ltd*,[74] the basis of such a claim was made clear: Crown privilege may be claimed in respect of two alternative grounds. First that the disclosure of the contents of a particular document would injure the public interest such as endangering national security or prejudicing diplomatic relations with other countries. Secondly, that the document comes within a certain category, or "class" of document which by its nature should be withheld to ensure the proper working of the public service. In the first ground the Crown had to satisfy the court of the nature of the contents of the particular document. In the second ground, the category of documents that fitted the particular class of documents for which immunity was sought, was very broad. In seeking to find a balance between freedom of information and protection of the State, the class of documents was reviewed.[75] A statement made by a Minister in the proper form could claim immunity and establish within which of the two categories the document came. The *Duncan* case concerned a civil action undertaken by the widow of one of the sailors drowned when the submarine *Thetis* sank whilst undergoing sea trials. In order to pursue her action in negligence, the plaintiff claimed from the Ministry of Defence documents such as the plans of the submarine. The effect of the *Duncan* case considerably restricted the official documents allowed to be admitted in evidence in legal proceedings giving the Crown a wider discretion to withhold documents than had previously been accepted.

---

[73] The terminology currently used by the courts is public interest immunity. This term is preferred over Crown Privilege. See *Rogers v. Secretary of State for Home Department* [1973] A.C. 388 and also see *Alfred Crompton Amusement Machines Ltd v. Customs and Excise Commissioners No. 2* [1974] A.C. 405.

[74] [1946] A.C. 401. In *Glasgow Corporation v. Central Land Board* (1956) S.C. 1 (H.L.) the House of Lords held that *Duncan v. Cammell Laird* did not apply in Scotland.

[75] 197 H.L. Official Report (5th Series) 741, 237 H.L. Official Report (5th Series) 1191.

9–59   Under section 28 of the Crown Proceedings Act 1947 the courts may make an order for discovery of documents or require the Crown to answer interrogatories. However, this power did not affect an existing rule of law that the Crown may refuse to disclose any documents or answer any questions on the ground that this would be injurious to the public interest.

9–60   In 1968 the House of Lords considered the law in *Conway v. Rimmer*[76] which concerned a number of documents being withheld in a civil action undertaken by a probationary police constable. The Secretary of State objected on the grounds that the reports fell into classes of documents where disclosure would not be in the public interest. The reports related to the conduct of individual officers and investigation into particular crimes. In reaching a conclusion on these matters the House of Lords rejected the approach in *Duncan* as restrictive in admitting documents, preferring instead to assert a judicial power to consider and decide on whether the documents should be excluded. Lord Reid distinguishing *Duncan* asserted the judicial role[77] "to hold the balance between the public interest, as expressed by a Minister, to withhold certain documents or other evidence and the public interest in ensuring the proper administration of justice."

9–61   The House of Lords also accepted the need to give the greatest weight to the Minister's opinions. However the question arises as to whether the courts will always be prepared to exercise their judgement by balancing the interests of the Minister against the interests of disclosure. It appears that certain classes of documents ought never to be disclosed. For example Lord Widgery in *Attorney-General v. Jonathan Cape Ltd*[78] claimed that "no court will compel the production of cabinet papers in the course of discovery in an action." Thus routine or less sensitive documents may be more likely to be admitted in evidence than higher grade or more secret documents.[79]

9–62   Following *Conway* the House of Lords have further considered how to strike the balance of interests between competing claims of the Minister and the need to disclose information. In *Burmah Oil Co. Ltd v. Bank of England*,[80] the Chief Secretary to the Treasury signed a certificate that the production of documents would be "injurious to the public interest." The documents related to negotiations between the Bank of England, Burmah Oil and the Government over the purchase by the Bank of England of stock in British Petroleum owned

[76] [1968] A.C. 910.
[77] *ibid.* at p. 938–939.
[78] [1976] Q.B. 752.
[79] Lord Mackay, "Development of the Law on Public Interest Immunity" (1983) C.J.Q. 337.
[80] [1980] A.C. 1090.

by Burmah at a price per unit of stock of £2.30. Within a year the value of the stock had doubled and Burmah brought an action against the Bank of England with regard to the sale on the ground that it was unreasonable and unconsionable. The sale took place at a time when Burmah experienced financial difficulties and the Government insisted that they could not share in any profit from the resale of the BP shares by the Bank of England. It had originally been intended that some profit in any sale of the shares might be shared between the Bank and Burmah.

The House of Lords concluded that on judicial inspection of the **9–63** documents they did not contain material which was necessary for a fair consideration of the case. The case establishes a number of points:

First, no class of document is entirely excluded from the process of balancing the different interests between the Minister and the need to disclose information.[81] Secondly, that the courts had a power of inspection of documents. This includes deciding the category or class of document to which the documents may belong, whether disclosure is necesssary for a fair trial of the issues in the case and whether the balance of interests criteria, outlined above, has been satisfied to permit disclosure. In these matters it is not always clear at what stage inspection is used. It is not always the case that the court will order inspection. When inspection is required, is it fair to both parties that the judge should examine documents which one of the parties has not seen?

The third point to emerge in *Burmah Oil*, is that the courts are **9–64** unwilling to grant immunity from disclosure simply because the documents contain matters of "candour," though it may be regarded as a factor[82] which might be useful in deciding on the balance of interests criteria. The courts are sensitive to arguments in favour of more open government that may lead to a fishing expedition for information. Speculative claims are unlikely to gain favour with the judges.

When public interest immunity is pleaded the other party faces a **9–65** difficult task to persuade the judge to admit the documents in question. What standard of case must be made out ? In the *Burmah Oil* case the judges differed in their choice of criteria to be satisfied before disclosure is granted. Some judges preferred a real likelihood, others, reasonable probability, and Lord Wilberforce who dissented, suggested that a positive case must be shown before the documents would be admitted. What must be shown is that the documents must be necessary for "fairly disposing the case."[83]

---

[81] This principle has been applied in *Rogers v. Secretary of State for the Home Department* [1972] 2 All E.R. 1057 at 1071 and *Neilson v. Laugharne* [1981] 1 Q.B. 736.

[82] Lord Scarman and Wilberforce (the latter dissented in the case), argued that candour should be considered: [1980] A.C. 1090, 1112.

[83] See *Air Canada v. Secretary of State for Trade (No. 2)* [1983] 2 A.C. 394.

9–66   There are various matters relevant to deciding how the balance of interests is to be calculated. In *D v. National Society for the Prevention of Cruelty to Children*,[84] D's application to have NSPCC documents admitted, was refused because of the nature of the NSPCC, its voluntary status, statutory powers and the receipt of information on a confidential basis, required immunity. In *R. v. Chief Constable, ex p. Wiley*[85] the Court of Appeal held that public interest immunity in police complaints proceedings extended to the use in civil proceedings of information generated through the complaint proceedings. Public interest immunity prohibited the use of the documents or information contained in the police files for any purpose other than that for which they were obtained. They could not be used as the basis for or against the Chief Constable in civil proceedings.

9–67   In *Halford v. Sharples*[86] a claim was made by Alison Halford, Assistant Chief Constable of Merseyside that her promotion within the police was blocked because of sex discrimination. In support of her claim she wished to have access to confidential files but one was refused by the Court of Appeal. The reasoning that there was an overwhelming public interest in maintaining the integrity of police complaints and disciplinary files prevented disclosure of the files to Alison Halford but it also prevented the Chief Constable from relying on information on the files. An important element in the reasoning in this case came from reliance on an earlier Court of Appeal case, *Makanjoula v. Commissioner of Police for the Metropolis*.[87] In *Makanjoula*, statements that had been given to the police by witnesses were withheld from the court, even when the witnesses might have given their consent. Bingham L.J. said[88]:

> "Where a litigant asserts that documents are immune from production or disclosure on public interest grounds he is not (if the claim is well founded) claiming a right but observing a duty. Public interest immunity is not a trump card vouchsafed to certain privileged players to play when and as they wish. It is an exclusionary rule, imposed on parties in certain circumstances even where it is to their disadvantage."

9–68   Interpretation of " observing a duty" in the judgment of Bingham L.J. in *Makanjoula* became the central issue in the recent Matrix Churchill case.[89] Criminal prosecutions taken against certain directors

---

[84] [1978] A.C. 171.
[85] [1994] 1 All E.R. 702.
[86] [1992] 1 W.L.R. 736.
[87] [1992] 3 All E.R. 617.
[88] *ibid.* at 623.
[89] Unreported but see *The Independent*, November 17, 1992. The outcry caused by this case had led to an inquiry under Lord Justice Scott. See Ian Leigh, "Matrix Churchill, Supergun and the Scott Inquiry" [1993] P.L. 630; D. Leigh, *Betrayed: The Real Story of the Matrix Churchill Trial* (1993).

of Matrix Churchill by Customs and Excise, over allegations that the company had broken trade sanctions in the sales of weapons to Iraq, resulted in public interest immunity being claimed by Ministers over confidential documents relating to the government's policy on arms sales. The Ministers concerned claimed that they had "a duty" to sign the certificates and were advised to do so by the Attorney-General.[90] One minister, Michael Heseltine only signed the certificate after he was instructed that he was under a clear duty to do so.

Some support for this view that Ministers are under a duty to sign **9–69** public interest immunity certificates, is taken from what was said by Bingham L.J. in *Makanjoula*. However, a further reading of the judgment of Bingham L.J. reveals further clarification on whether there is a duty in all cases to assert an immunity claim. Bingham L.J. added[91]:

"This does not mean that in any case where a party holds a document in a class prima facie immune he is bound to persist in an assertion of immunity even where it is held that, on any weighing of the public interest, in withholding the document against the public interest in disclosure for the purpose of further-ing the administration of justice, there is a clear balance in favour of the latter."

There is a division of opinion over the interpretation of the **9–70** judgment of Bingham L.J. In the *Matrix Churchill* case Ministers claimed that at the time the certificates were signed they had no choice but to sign the certificates. Some legal opinion takes the view that there is no obligation or duty on Ministers to make a claim. Ministers are free to authorise disclosure to the public of confidential documents and by analogy are free to decide whether to sign certificates or not.

The better view is that Ministers have a discretion as to whether to claim public interest immunity or not. They are not bound to sign a certificate even where there is a prima facie case that the documents may belong to a class where public interest immunity may be sought. The courts decide "where the balance of public interest lies" in such cases.

Since the *Matrix Churchill* trial, the House of Lords have now **9–71** accepted[92] in *ex p. Wiley* a number of propositions about public interest immunity. The view that there is a class of documents which may guarantee exclusion from disclosure is no longer tenable. This

---

[90] This advice was later confirmed in a letter to *The Times* by the Attorney-General.
[91] [1992] 3 All E.R. 617 at 623g–h.
[92] *R. v. Chief Constable of the West Midlands, ex p. Wiley* [1994] 3 All E.R. 420 at 423.

view has been made clear by the Lord Chancellor and the Attorney-General in changes that have been announced to the administration of public interest immunity certificates.[93] Furthermore it is considered that in criminal cases the scales of justice have to be more keenly balanced to protect the accused. The House of Lords in *ex p. Wiley* also rejects the proposition that there is a duty on Ministers to sign public interest immunity certificates. From the above discussion, it may be concluded that the Attorney-General's interpretation is unsound in principle and wrong in its potential effects on the accused.

9–72   A further consideration is whether there is any distinction between civil and criminal cases. In a criminal trial, accused persons may be convicted notwithstanding that there is evidence showing their innocence. This appears inconsistent with the public interest. In criminal litigation the courts have been concerned about the balance of interests and the protection of the accused when public interest immunity is claimed by the prosecution.[94] In *R. v. Governor of Brixton Prison, ex p. Osman*[95] Lord Justice Mann accepted that public interest immunity may be claimed in criminal proceedings but he noted ". . . that the application of the public immunity doctrine in criminal proceedings will involve a different balancing of interest to that in civil proceedings." Relying on a number of authorities including *Marks v. Beyfus*,[96] Lord Justice Mann noted that the privilege of public interest immunity "cannot prevail if the evidence is necessary for the prevention of a miscarriage of justice. No balance is called for. If admission is necessary to prevent miscarriage of justice, balance does not arise."[97] The courts have not always been consistent in their approach. In *R. v. Lewes Justices, ex p. Home Secretary*[98] concerning criminal libel, the House of Lords upheld a claim for crown privilege in respect of police documents relied upon by the Gaming Board. An applicant had been unsuccessful in applying to the Gaming Board for a licence for a Bingo Club. He alleged that the police had sent the Gaming Board a libellous letter and for this reason he had been unsuccessful in his application. Lord Reid reasoned that much of the information came from a letter from the police based on information from sources that must be protected. The nature of the information may disclose the source and this required protection. This case is

---

[93] H.L. Deb. Vol. 576, Col. 1507, and H.C. Deb. Vol. 287, col. 949 (December 18, 1996).
[94] Section 28 of the Crown Proceedings Act 1947 provides for discovery against the Crown in civil proceedings. Rules of the Supreme Court Order 24, rr. 5 and 15 and Order 77, r. 12 provide rules of procedure.
[95] [1992] 1 All E.R. 108.
[96] (1890) 25 Q.B.D. 494.
[97] [1992] 1 All E.R. 108 at p. 118a–b.
[98] [1973] A.C. 388, HL.

open to a narrow interpretation. Although the House of Lords upheld the claim made on public interest immunity to prevent disclosure of documents, the case may be said to have raised special facts. Lord Reid noted that the documents were not intended to deprive the applicant of any legal right. The only reason the documents came into existence was because the applicant "is asking for a privilege and is submitting his character and reputation to scrutiny."[99] It is significant that Lord Reid upheld the important principle that should be observed in public interest immunity cases namely that the "course of justice should not be impeded by the withholding of evidence."[1]

In *Ward*[2] the Court of Appeal observed that there were require- **9–73** ments laid upon the prosecution if they wished to claim public interest immunity. First, notice must be given to the defence if the prosecution wished to rely on immunity and that the prosecution are applying to the court for a ruling. Secondly, the defence must be given some idea of the category of information involved. Thirdly, the defence must be given the opportunity to make representations. Lord Justice Glidewell made clear that it was for the court to make the ultimate decision as to whether evidence is to be disclosed. This does not prevent the Crown Prosecution Service deciding in exceptional cases to volunteer information without obtaining a court order.[3]

The courts have generally[4] been sensitive in criminal prosecutions **9–74** to prevent the claim of public interest immunity from interfering with the rights of the accused. Lord Justice Mann in *ex p. Osman (No. 1)*[5] noted that: "it may be that prosecutions are not initiated where material is not to be exposed, or it may be that the force of the balance is recognised by prosecuting authorities and the immunity is never claimed." In *Neilson v. Laugharne*[6] Lord Justice Oliver said: "If public policy prevents disclosure, it prevents it, in my judgement, in all legal circumstances except to establish innocence in criminal proceedings."

---

[99] *ibid.* Lord Reid at p. 401G-H.
[1] *ibid.*
[2] *R. v. Ward* [1993] 2 All E.R. 577. Also see *R. v. Davis* [1993] 2 All E.R. 643.
[3] See *R. v. Horseferry Road Magistrates' Court, ex p. Bennett (No. 2)* [1994] 1 All E.R. 289.
[4] See Lord Taylor C.J.'s reservations in *R. v. Davis* [1993] 2 All E.R. 643 about notifying the defence about the category of documents subject to the certificate of public interest immunity. See *R. v. Johnson Davis and Rowe* (1993) 97 Cr. App. Rep. 110 and *R. v. Keane*, March 14, 1994 unreported.
[5] [1992] 1 All E.R. 108 at p. 116.
[6] [1981] 1 All E.R. 829 at p. 839h. See Adam Tomkins, "Public Interest Immunity after Matrix Churchill" [1993] P.L. 650. I am grateful for advice from Mr Tomkins on the questions raised by the Scott Inquiry and Public Interest Immunity. See Lord Callaghan's letter to *The Times*, February 24, 1994, stating that "I was never advised by law officers or by civil servants that a class of documents existed which placed a binding duty upon a minister to sign a Public Interest Immunity Certificate irrespective of its contents." Also grateful thanks to Lord Justice Scott for his help with my research in this area of law. *Wallace Smith Trust Co. Ltd [In liq.] v. Deloittle Haskins & Sells (a firm)* [1996] 4 All E.R. 403.

9–75   In the *Matrix Churchill* case, which involved a criminal prosecution, the trial judge allowed the documents to be admitted in the case and this, together with evidence from a former Minister, led to the failure of the prosecution case. The furore caused by the case in Parliament and the broader implications that Ministers may have misled Parliament has led to the setting up of an inquiry under Lord Justice Scott.

9–76   The higher appellate courts had until *ex p. Wiley*[7] been mainly concerned with civil proceedings. The use of public interest immunity certificates in criminal cases has given rise to a clear difference of opinion on the part of the Government's legal advisers and the Scott report on this issue. Sir Richard Scott recommended[8] that class claims should no longer be used in criminal litigation and seldom used[9] in civil litigation.[10] However in the Government's response[11] the view of government advisers remained as follows:

> "The understanding of those advising Government was and is that the general principles of PII [Public Interest Immunity] apply in the same way in criminal proceedings as they do in civil proceedings. In each case both class and contents claims can properly be advanced; and in each case the public interest in non-disclosure falls to be balanced (at the material time, by the court) against the public interest in disclosure for the purposes of the administration of justice. The balance is much more likely to come down in favour of disclosure in criminal proceedings, and procedural differences exist, but the general principles are the same."

However, in *ex p. Wiley* Lord Templeman explained[12]:

> "Prosecution authorities know which documents are relevant to the prosecution but they cannot know for certain which documents will be relevant to the defence. . . . In order to avoid criticism and a miscarriage of justice one way or the other, the police authorities now feel obliged to disclose documents of doubtful relevance and materiality."

---

[7] *R. v. Chief Constable of the West Midlands, ex p. Wiley* [1994] 3 All E.R. 420.

[8] See the authority of *R. v. Governor of Brixton Prison, ex p. Osman* [1991] 1 W.L.R. 281 is discussed in great detail in the Scott report. The case involving an application for *habeas corpus* which for the purposes of the discussion of Public Interest Immunity Certificates were characterised as criminal proceedings.

[9] See *R. v. Chief Constable of the West Midlands, ex p. Wiley* [1994] 3 All E.R. 420.

[10] The Scott Report Vol. III, para. G18.86 at p. 1525.

[11] *Government's Response* para. 3.1, p. 14.

[12] *R. v. Chief Constable of the West Midlands, ex p. Wiley* [1994] 3 All E.R. 420 at 423.

In the light of these differences criminal cases involving public interest immunity[13] claims have to be considered in a different context than cases where civil issues are resolved.

The Criminal Procedure and Investigations Act 1996 contains a **9–77** Code of Practice[14] which lays down the basis for documents relevant to the investigation to become available to the defence. The 1996 Act does not make substantive changes to the case law on public interest immunity. The Act strengthens the view put forward by Scott that in criminal cases the issue of disclosure of information is whether it might be of relevance to the defence. The Act introduces the requirement of defence disclosure. Paradoxically the Act will limit the role of the judge as there will be few occasions when the judge will have to rule on disclosure because the Act will require disclosure of most material.[15]

In summary the following appears to be the current law. As **9–78** already mentioned the view that there is a class of documents which may guarantee exclusion from disclosure is no longer tenable. This view has been made clear by the Lord Chancellor and the Attorney-General in changes that have been announced to the administration of public interest immunity certificates.[16] Furthermore, Ministers will only claim public interest immunity when it is believed that disclosure of a document would cause real damage or harm to the public interest. Contained in the certificate will be an explanation of how disclosure could cause real damage to the public interest. Although these changes apply to the use of public interest immunity certificates claimed by the government it is expected that the changes will have wider application.

(b) Government and Secrecy

The ethos of secrecy is an intrinsic part of government. While Cabinet **9–79** government requires and maintains the confidence of the House of Commons, its deliberations and decisions are bound together through collective Cabinet responsibility. This is intended to ensure confidentiality of decision-making as much as responsibility.

Many of the rules of the Cabinet are confidential. Ministers are not expected to divulge the existence of cabinet committees, or the

---

[13] See T. R. S. Allan, "Public Interest Immunity and Ministers' Responsibilities" (1993) *Criminal Law Review* 660; A. W. Bradley, "Justice, Good Government and Public Interest Immunity" (1992) *Public Law* 514; G. Ganz, "Matrix Churchill and Public Interest Immunity" (1993) 56 *Modern Law Review* 564.

[14] Mike Redmayne, "Process Gains and Process Values: The Criminal Procedure and Investigations Act 1996" (1997) 60 *Modern Law Review* 79.

[15] See sections 3 and 7 of the Criminal Procedure and Investigations Act 1996.

[16] H.L. Deb. Vol. 576 col. 1507, and H.C. Deb. Vol. 287, col. 949 (December 18, 1996).

membership of the committees or the rules under which the committees operate. Such confidentiality appears to favour Prime Ministerial influence, the exchange of information on a need to know basis within government and the protection of the civil servants in giving advice. Confidentiality is also required in the contractual and financial relations undertaken by the government of the day. For example in January 1985 a leak of information on the Government's policy on foreign exchange rates, resulted in a story in *The Sunday Times*.[17] Nigel Lawson, then Chancellor of the Exchequer, recalls in his memoirs[18] how the leak came from Bernard Ingham, then press secretary to the Prime Minister. The leak cost the government a great deal of upheaval in the exchange markets and confidence in the city. This is an illustration of the need for confidentiality within government and this example also underlines the influence of the press and media over the government's economic policies.

9–80   The ethos of secrecy in government is maintained through the use of various restraints on free access to information. The most formidable are the various legal restraints such as section 2 of the Official Secrets Act 1911. The breadth of this section was illustrated in 1984 by the prosecution of Sarah Tisdell, a civil service clerk convicted for leaking the Government's plans for policing and keeping order at Greenham Common, the base intended to receive Cruise Missiles. Clive Ponting, a senior civil servant, was prosecuted under this section for leaking documents relating to the sinking of the Argentinian warship *The General Belgrano* during the Falklands War. Although the jury was instructed that Ponting had no defence because he claimed that he owed a duty to Parliament to provide information, the jury, to his surprise, acquitted.

9–81   In addition to section 2, there are a variety of devices such as "D" notices, available to indicate to the press and media that publication may not be within the law. An official committee of press and broadcasting representatives known as the Defence, Press and Broadcasting Committee acts as a scrutineer of the system.

Conventions[19] that Ministers do not reveal the inner workings of government remain. However, since the *Crossman Diary* case,[20] which permitted the posthumous publication of Richard Crossman's diaries, a number of former Cabinet Ministers have published their diaries, even when the diaries were made contemporaneously with their official duties.

---

[17] *The Sunday Times*, January 6, 1985.
[18] Lawson, *op. cit.* p. 1–469.
[19] Committee of Privy Counsellors on Ministerial Memoirs (Chairman Lord Radcliffe) Cmnd. 6386 (1976).
[20] *Att.-Gen. v. Jonathan Cape Ltd* [1976] Q.B. 752.

Actions for breach of confidence may also be involved to protect **9–82** official secrets such as in the litigation[21] arising out of the *Spycatcher* book. This book contained, the memoirs of Peter Wright, a former member of MI5, revealing details of the inner workings and operations of the security services.

The question arises as to the compatibility of open government with confidentiality. This question is considered in more detail in Chapter 18, but it is apparent that the United Kingdom does not benefit from any general presumption in favour of access to official information. This gives rise to the question of how effective government accountability may be within the restrictions imposed on information.

5. Policy Formulation and Government

The ethos of secrecy pervades the culture of how government **9–83** conducts its business. Limitations on the flow of information available to the public restricts the opportunities for the critical analysis of government policy. This may have a detrimental effect on how effective government and its related agencies may be in making policy decisions. The decision to release more information on Treasury forecasting of the economy in September 1992, was made in an effort to gain greater credibility for government Ministers in managing the economy. This is a good illustration of the obvious benefits to be gained by making more information available allowing more informed judgements.

A step in the direction of greater openness came in 1993 with **9–84** publication of the White Paper on Open Government[22] and a proposed relaxation of the laws prohibiting disclosure of information. There is a *Code of Practice on Access to Government Information.*[23] This Code sets out how a complaint may be made and how there are five commitments to open government. These are to supply the facts and analysis with major policy decisions; to open up internal guidelines about departments' dealings with the public; to supply reasons for administrative decisions; to provide information under the Citizen's Charter about public services; and to respond to requests for information. A formal request may be made for information with a guarantee of a reply within 20 working days.[24]

---

[21] *Att.-Gen. v. Guardian Newspapers Ltd (No. 2)* [1990] 1 A.C. 109; [1988] 3 W.L.R. 776.
[22] Cm. 2290 (1993).
[23] Cabinet Office, Whitehall, London.
[24] *The Civil Service Yearbook 1997* (The Stationery Office, 1997).

9–85   Access to more information and knowledge of government strategy is an important element in the ideal of democratic government. Citizens should be able to clarify information and check its accuracy. For example the Data Protection Act 1984, requires that information must be obtained and processed fairly and lawfully, it must be held only for specific purposes and not used or disclosed in any way incompatible with those purposes. The Data Protection Registrar set up under the Act along with the Data Protection Tribunal, oversees the regulation of information used and classified under the 1984 Act.

Citizens may view access to more information as a means of redressing grievances but also there is the greater opportunity to participate in government decision-making. Government consultation through White Papers, Royal Commissions, and committees of inquiry, all contribute to the provision of more information as well as to the general level of government accountability.

9–86   Some steps in the direction of greater accountability have taken place. The new select committees discussed above have made an important contribution in this area. In 1977 the then Head of the Civil Service issued what has become known as "the Croham" Directive namely that background material on policy matters should be published unless Ministers specifically object. This system has declined in use since 1979 but it is illustrative of how important initiatives may be taken.

The Citizen's Charter[25] which sets out standards for the delivery and quality of a wide range of public services provides expectations and greater openness in the process of government. Equally important for the accountability of government has been the internal reforms introduced in the civil service which are considered in the next chapter.

[25] Cm. 1599 (1991).

Chapter 10

Public Administration and Management

1. Introduction

The civil service, over the last 30 years, has come under detailed **10–01**
scrutiny. The Fulton Report in 1969 examined the lack of effective
management in the civil service that has given rise to concern.
Demands for greater efficiency and effectiveness in the civil service
has become a theme of the relations between the government and the
civil service. Senior civil servants advise Ministers on major policy
issues, take many policy decisions, implement and co-ordinate complex administrative schemes and manage large departments. Such
tasks require, not only high administrative skills, but also managerial
ability. Perceived deficiencies in the structures and management
techniques within the civil service have led to change and a break
with the past traditions of public service.

Also related to change within the civil service has been recognition
that long term or strategic planning was absent from the system of
Cabinet government. Civil servants recognised that seldom were the
impact of government policies fully reviewed, discussed and considered in the light of future policies, by the Cabinet.

In this chapter the changes introduced into the civil service will be **10–02**
discussed, such as the introduction of Next Steps Agencies. These
have challenged some of the principles of the civil service established
since the Northcote-Trevelyan Report in 1853 which may be taken to
be the beginning of the modern development of the civil service.
Since Fulton, the aims, objectives and management of the civil service
has undergone intense scrutiny. The steps taken to introduce management techniques into the civil service will be examined and the
setting up of the "Next Steps" Agencies, by hiving off department
activities is explained in terms of the constitutional implications for
parliamentary accountability. Such fundamental changes to the civil
service have raised questions about the future direction and development of the civil service. Questions about Agency Status have raised

issues about the criteria used to measure their success and the value
of Agencies in the efficiency of service provision.

2. Civil Service – Evolution and Reform

10–03 Since the nineteenth century, the civil service has been the focus of
attempts to reform its role and function. Prior to Mrs Thatcher
becoming Prime Minister in 1979, the civil service had largely
withstood major reforms to its organisation and management. These
comprise Plowden in 1961, Fulton in 1968 and reforms under Mr
Heath in 1970 in hiving off departments.

In 1961 the Plowden Report[1] on the public expenditure process,
introduced the Public Expenditure Survey (PES) which was aimed at
changing the financial procedures involved in planning government
strategy. This involved "regular surveys" of public expenditure as a
whole over a period of years ahead. Decisions "should be taken in
the light of those surveys." The intention to create a continuous
programme of the spending objectives for the medium term, was
intended to allow bilateral discussions in Cabinet at the beginning of
the Autumn. It also encouraged Civil Service efficiency within a
framework directed by Ministers. In reaching policy decisions within
departments the civil service was expected to be more cost effective
and better informed of the economics advice tendered to Ministers.
However the Civil Service proved resistant to any fundamental
changes and the PES ran into major economic problems during
periods of inflation and itself came under considerable change.[2]

10–04   In 1968 the Fulton Report[3] on the civil service made recommendations for major changes. When it reported, the civil service had grown
to 20 times the size of the civil service in 1854. Arguably the increase
in size reflected larger departments and a greater workload with an
increasingly complex system of government.[4] Both its size and the
variety of work expected from civil servants confirmed the need to re-
consider how the civil service was managed. Particularly important
throughout the last two decades has been the need to improve
strategic planning and management of resources.[5]

---

[1] Plowden Report, (1961) Cmnd. 1432, The Control of Public Expenditure.
[2] The details of the system are examined in Chap. 11.
[3] Fulton Report, Cmnd. 3638 (1968).
[4] J. Greenwood and D. Wilson, *Public Administration in Britain Today* (2nd ed., 1989), p.
103. William Plowden, *Ministers and Mandarins* (IPPR, 1994).
[5] Sir Douglas Wass, *Government and the Governed* (1984). Also see Wass, "Checks and
Balances in Public Policy Making" [1987] P.L. 181–201.

Fulton was the first major inquiry into the civil service since the **10–05** Northcote-Trevelyan inquiry in the nineteenth century. The report offered both an analysis of the structure, management and organisation of the civil service and provided recommendations for reform. It recognised a number of defects concerning how the civil service was organised. At one level the nineteenth century had ensured fair and open competition, selection on merit, the ethos of public service, political neutrality and professionalism. At another level the system of classes, clerical, executive and administrative, impeded the work of the civil service. There was a proliferation of specialists within a complex departmental structure. Fulton also recognised that the "generalist" dominated the service, and this may have contributed to the undervalue given to specialist skills. More significantly, Fulton recognised the lack of management skills, the exclusive nature of the service which resulted in the lack of contact between the service and the rest of the community. Poor personal management stifled the most gifted and this led to problems within the complicated class structure.

Fulton made 158 recommendations and this led to the creation of **10–06** the civil service department which stopped the control of the civil service from being the direct responsibility of the Treasury. It is suggested that many of Fulton's other proposals were undermined[6] by senior civil servants who did not desire change. The establishment of a Civil Service College, the recruitment of graduates and the abolition of classes were successfully introduced. However successful these changes were in restructuring the civil service, by 1980 there were still 700,000 civil servants serving over 100 Ministers.

One major omission in the Fulton Report was the absence of a clear answer to the question of the future role of the modern civil service. To a large extent the answer to this question emerged in the late 1980s as a result of a number of developments in the way the civil service carries out its functions.

On becoming Prime Minister, Mrs Thatcher identified a number of **10–07** shortcomings in the existing civil service. Led by private managerial techniques perceived to avoid waste and save money, Mrs Thatcher's Government adopted the strategy of applying private management to the public sector.

The initial stage was to target 100,000 civil service jobs by April 1984, reducing the civil service to 630,000. In 1993 the number of civil servants fell below 600,000. Reducing the size of the civil service was only a first step, the most fundamental development was to build on the reforms of the past and develop an efficiency strategy. The main themes involved in this strategy will be examined below.

---

[6] P. Kellner and Lord Crowther-Hunt, *The Civil Servants: An Inquiry into Britain's Ruling Class* (1980), p. 220.

10–08   The origins of the Efficiency Strategy may be found in the appointment of Sir Derek Rayner in 1974, and later Sir Robin Ibbs as the Prime Minister's Special Adviser on Efficiency. The Rayner efficiency studies had their origins in the work undertaken after Fulton during the 1970s, under Edward Heath's proposals for creating "super" departments and hiving off through the Central Policy Review Staff, major policy decision-taking. A Programme Analysis and Review System designed to enhance the strategy of the decision-making powers of the Cabinet, was introduced.

10–09   Rayner's analysis brought private management skills into government coupled with a series of scrutinies aimed at identifying and eliminating areas of costs, inefficiency, duplication and overlap. Such scrutinies differed from past attempts to reform the civil service because generally the studies were carried out in a spirit of co-operation within the civil service. Department civil servants identified areas of administrative work where gains might be introduced cheaply and efficiently. Once specific areas were identified in reports, the second part of the efficiency strategy was introduced. The second part of the strategy was intended to consolidate and integrate evidence gained from individual scrutiny based on such findings, a major reform initiative was expected to take place with more far-reaching and long-lasting consequences than merely departmental savings.

10–10   Another significant difference in the Rayner studies was that reforms were focused on internal processes rather than external review. Beginning with Rayner as an efficiency adviser, the Prime Minister set up an Efficiency Unit as part of the Prime Minister's Office. This comprised a small unit located in the Cabinet Office. When the Civil Service Department was abolished in November 1981, introduced as one of the Fulton reforms, the responsibility for managing the civil service was divided between the Treasury and a newly-created Management and Personnel Office. The under secretary who headed the Efficiency Unit was responsible for the management and efficiency division of the Management and Personnel Office. Thus the impetus for civil service reform came from within rather than from without.

10–11   The Rayner efficiency programme also accommodated the other policies of the Government. Pledged to provide value for money throughout the public sector, the Government set to work in an ambitious privatisation programme which moved the major nationalised utilities into Public Act Companies in the private sector. Internal reforms within the Civil Service picked up the guiding philosophy of the period, a world[7]:

---

[7] A. Gray and I. Jenkins, "Accountable Management in British Government: Some Reflections on the Financial Management Initiative" (1986) *Financial Accountability and Management* No. 3, 171–87, at 171.

" . . . where bureaucrats (and ministers) are redefined as accountable managers, public sector operatives sub-divided into businesses, and the public seen as the customer."

The period to the end of 1982 saw the first results of the 133 Rayner
Scrutinies and when Sir Derek Rayner relinquished the post, his
successor, Sir Robin Ibbs, continued the process begun by Rayner. An
estimate of the savings accomplised by Rayner and the reforms
recommended for adoption is put at[8]:

"Once and for all savings of £56 million and recurrent savings of
£400 million and 21,000 posts per annum. Firm decisions had been
reached on £29 million once and for all savings, with annual
savings of £180 million and 12,000 posts. The recurrent savings
recommended by October 1985 were £600 million, of which £300
million have actually been achieved. A further £145 million have
been rejected, and the rest are somewhere in the pipeline."

Some mention should be made of the techniques adopted in the **10–12**
Rayner scrutiny. Specific objectives included:

(a) The examination of a specific policy or activity; including the
investigation of all work normally taken for granted.

(b) Recommendations for solutions seeking to achieve savings and
cut costs, thus improving the efficiency and effectiveness of
policies.

(c) Implementation of agreed solutions with a clear knowledge of
the implications of any solution proposed and its cost.

There are five main stages to setting up an efficiency scrutiny. First,
topics for scrutiny are regularly suggested from within departments;
secondly, investigations are carried out by departmental staff according to a set timetable, usually 90 working days are allowed before
reports should be submitted to Ministers; thirdly; action plans setting
out savings to be approved within three months of the report;
fourthly, implementation is the responsibility of the departmental
permanent secretary and finally, action taken, savings made and
achieved are included in a report to be produced within two years of
the start of the scrutiny.

A number of side effects are evident as a result of the Rayner **10–13**
scrutiny. Metcalfe and Richards have noted[9] that scrutineers within

---

[8] Les Metcalfe and Sue Richards, *Improving Public Management* (2nd ed., 1990), p. 10.
[9] *ibid.*

departments continue to carry out their role even after their study has been completed. This has led to some departments instigating their own form of scrutiny. The advantages of continuous monitoring become obvious over a long period of time.

Also noted has been the ability of the Efficiency Unit to make cross-department comparisons. This has helped to highlight difficulties within particular departments and encouraged ministerial kudos for making savings and carrying out waste reduction policies. This has given an increasing management function to the permanent secretary and deputy secretaries in each department.

10–14   The question arises as to whether such changes in the ethos of public service to the better managing of public resources has been accompanied by any cultural change within the civil service.

Throughout the Rayner efficiency studies the dominant theme has been to improve management structure within the civil service. Spearheaded by a Prime Minister committed to saving money was a necessary pre-condition to finding the necessary will to undertake the studies in the first place. However, as Metcalfe and Richards note[10]: "Relying on political clout underestimates the extent to which the obstacles to reform are specifically cultural."

10–15   The reliance on a politically-driven and motivated efficiency system has given rise to some reservations about the lasting impact of Rayner's reforms. Johnson noted that there was a remarkable continuity between existing prescriptions for better management under the Rayner Scrutinies and earlier prescriptions for administrative improvement. It is suggested that the narrow perception of management found in the studies might suggest that all government administration was concerned with "controlling and supervising." The focus on economy, efficiency and effectiveness gives rise to what Metcalfe and Richards refer to as the limited "role of public managers to programmed implementation of predetermined policies. They disregard the problems of adapting policies and organisations to environmental change."

10–16   A comparison between public sector and business management techniques reveals that different management roles are preferred by different layers of management. Top management in the private sector deals with strategy, policy in new opportunities and even areas of uncertainty where a surprise change in the business environment may threaten existing arrangements. In public sector management little adaptation and learning are built into the processes and no clear differentiation is made between layers of management.

10–17   Metcalfe and Richards are sceptical as to whether Whitehall has learnt any lessons from business and little attention is given to

[10] Les Metcalfe and Sue Richards, *Improving Public Management* (1990), p. 15.

questions about the machinery of government. By 1985 a total of 266 reviews were conducted amounting to annual savings of £600m, with an additional £67m as one-off savings. The Public Accounts Committee noted in 1986 that savings of £950m had been made at a cost of only £5m in scrutiny costs. As we shall see, impressive though such savings are, further steps were required in an effort to bring more long-term progress. In terms of civil service management and reform, first Rayner and then Ibbs had dramatically changed the conventional wisdom of how the civil service might perform its role.

3. Management Techniques

The Rayner efficiency studies have encouraged the development of **10–18** management techniques in the civil service. Since 1980 further changes introduced into the civil service have continued the development of new structures and organisation in the civil service. The following is an account of how and why the techniques of managing business have become part of the ethos of the civil service.

In 1980, following the introduction of the Rayner efficiency studies, a more broadly-based initiative began to introduce structural changes within public management inside the Civil Service. This initiative, known as the Management Information System for Ministers (MINIS) identified the need to obtain information as one of the most important elements in exercising control and scrutiny and therefore avoiding waste.

The introduction of MINIS came from the pioneering efforts of **10–19** Michael Heseltine,[11] then Secretary of State at the Department of the Environment. The essential objectives of MINIS were to ascertain departmental economic targets, how they were set and how the department was carrying out its activities. MINIS was intended to remedy the defects in the chain of responsibility and to ascertain the data needed for decision-making. There was also an important role given in MINIS to the Minister, that of manager, assembling information and ensuring that the Minister was fully in charge of the department for which he was responsible. Soon MINIS became a commitment about information systems in public management.

MINIS involves three stages: first, each section head prepares a **10–20** statement of activities with details of staff numbers, achievements and potential for future activities. Secondly, statements agreed within

---

[11] M. Heseltine, *Where There's a Will* (London, 1987), p. 18; "Ministers and Management in Whitehall" (1980) 35 *Management Services in Government* 61–68.

departments are considered by Ministers and management. Section heads are called to give evidence and subject to cross-examination on the policies contained in the statements. Finally, implementation of the second stage is carried out. The three stage process is conducted annually. Each "cycle" of MINIS activity allows annual activites to be monitored.

The potential for MINIS is far-reaching. Staffing and expenditure may be more accurately assessed, expenditure cuts offered and while most audit systems are normally *ex post facto*, MINIS attempts to be proactive and forward thinking. However, MINIS is not entirely innovatory. Many departments had experimented with some system of information retrieval, MINIS is simply more rigorous and stream-lined. Fulton had advocated a MINIS-type initiative with specific cost centres[12] working with allocated budgets. This had proved difficult to implement.

10–21   To civil servants MINIS offers an opportunity to find out exactly the true potential of their departments and despite initial opposition to Heseltine's initiative in 1982 all departments were expected to develop a similar management system.[13]

MINIS and its introduction throughout Whitehall bore some similarities to the Rayner and Ibbs Efficiency Unit mentioned above. The success in introducing MINIS came from the initative of a strong Minister supported politically by the Prime Minister. In its initial stages the political rhetoric about its introduction may have facilitated some civil service resistance to its full effect. MINIS simply defines objectives, gives greater importance and focus to responsibilities and, in theory at least, supports the constitutional position of ministerial responsibility and civil service duty. This last matter has involved some serious questions about the relationship between civil servants and Ministers.

10–22   Three events[14] have served to underline the idea of civil servants owing a duty to the government of the day rather than directly to Parliament. These are the Maze prison breakout in 1983, the Clive Ponting trial in 1985 and the Westland affair in 1985–86, which brought greater attention to the role of civil servants than ever before. In the Maze prison breakout, civil servants were found at fault for a major failure in security at the Maze prison for which the Governor was held responsible. No Minister resigned because the escape was

---

[12] Joubert study divided the Department of Environment into 120 cost centres as a basis of the Financial Management Initiative.

[13] See *Financial Management in Government Departments* (HMSO, 1983), pp. 50–52.

[14] Marshall, "Cabinet Government and the Westland Affair" [1986] P.L. 184; Oliver and Austin, "Political and Constitutional Aspects of the Westland Affair" (1987) 40 *Parliamentary Affairs* 20; *Hennessy Report: Report of an Inquiry by H.M. Chief Inspector of Prisons into the Security Arrangements at H.M. Prison Maze* (1983–84, H.C. 203).

not attributed to any failure of policy but the Governor of the Maze did resign.

In the case of Clive Ponting, a civil servant was prosecuted under **10–23** the Official Secrets Act for releasing the text of a memorandum on the sinking of the Belgrano during the Falklands War. Although acquitted by a jury, the trial judge stated that civil servants owed a duty to Ministers as: "the government of the day" rather than Parliament. In 1985–86 Mr Leon Britton, then Secretary of State for Trade and Industry, resigned after he authorised civil servants to take the improper action of releasing a confidential letter written by the Solicitor General to the Secretary of State for Defence.

As MINIS was developing so was media interest in government and civil service activities. The fact that MINIS appeared to release greater information about government came as a surprise to many commentators and increased interest in how government departments were organised. The civil servants involved in the examples mentioned above received greater publicity about their role in the conduct of government than ever before. The later litigation on the Spycatcher Book containing the memoirs of Peter Wright, a former MI5 officer and the evidence in Australia from the then Head of the Civil Service, Lord Armstrong, maintained at a high level, public interest in the civil service.[15] The civil service has continued to enjoy greater publicity than at any time in their history.

While MINIS kept parliamentary interest engaged in changes in **10–24** attitude to management structures within the Civil Service, it was the introduction of the Financial Management Initiatives (FMI)[16] in 1982 that secured a stronger niche for MINIS itself. The idea behind FMI was to promote a management accounting system within the civil service. This linked the activities of managing the civil service to the question of public expenditure surveys and estimates. These matters are discussed in more detail in the following Chapter on Public Finance.

The aims of the FMI comprised three objectives: First, to set objectives and assess through the measurement of outputs of performance the achievement of the objectives. Secondly, consider how resources are best managed, especially through value for money studies. Third and finally, set out costs, information on training and access to expertise to ensure that objectives are met.

Linking the management of the civil service to wider issues **10–25** involving public expenditure built on the successes found in MINIS and in the early Rayner efficiency studies. It was no accident that

---

[15] *Att.-Gen. v. Guardian Newspapers Ltd (No. 2)* [1988] 3 W.L.R. 776.
[16] Efficiency and Effectiveness (1982), Appendix 3; *Financial Management in Government Departments* (1983).

Rayner pioneered the FMI system before he left in 1983 to return to Marks and Spencer. FMI was co-ordinated by a specially created unit of the Cabinet Office. Along with the Treasury later in 1985 this was replaced by a Treasury Cabinet Office Joint Management Unit.

The significance of MINIS and FMI was that for the first time the techniques of business management adapted to the public sector actually created changes in the structure and management of the civil service. MINIS may be perceived as usefully establishing a more accountable management structure. Clearer delegation of authority and levels of policy decision-making have been introduced. Another perception is that MINIS actually encouraged disclosure of information. More open government was encouraged. Published information provided opportunities for greater accountability for government activities.

10–26   A number of side-effects arising from the introduction of FMI may also be noted. The prevailing tendency towards centralisation of government powers, found that FMI appeared to offer a counter-balancing effect on decision-taking. Delegation and decentralisation were encouraged as part of cost-centre management. This led to the introduction in April 1988 of new running costs imposed on departments with cash limits set on individual civil service managers.

10–27   Any assessment of MINIS must take into consideration the frustrated attempts in earlier years to make management information systems part of the culture of the civil service. But this should be seen as only a first step towards a process which ultimately might lead to greater accountable management within departments. Injecting new ideas and innovatory ways to manage the public sector faces stiff opposition from the continuity fostered by the public service ethos, a legacy of the Victorian past. The Government's own assessment of FMI and further consideration of the steps to be taken for the future awaited a Report from the Government's Efficiency Unit begun in 1986, but not published until 1988 and known as *The Next Steps*.

4. The Next Steps

10–28 The background to the development of the Next Steps Initiative began after Robin Ibbs succeeded Derek Rayner as Head of the Efficiency Unit in 1983. While anxious to maintain the momentum set by Rayner, Ibbs shared the same drive for greater efficiency inside the management structure set within the civil service. The main question was how to assess FMI and how might initiatives to remedy any problems with the FMI system be introduced.

10–29   The period from 1983 to 1986 was dominated by the attempt to implement FMI. In theory FMI, by delegating executive responsibility to managerial decision-makers at a local level, gave more budgeting control to individual civil servants, who would become largely autonomous and removed from the direct oversight of ministerial control. Civil servants, at least in the potential given to them to set and manage their own policy, seemed remarkably freed from the tight hierarchical control favoured within the traditional civil service. No major structural reforms had been introduced to implement the major changes such delegation may produce and not surprisingly difficulties were experienced in the full implementation of FMI.[17]

Many reasons for "this patchy development"[18] of FMI have been **10–30** suggested. A number of institutions had overlapping jurisdictions and the fragmented institutional arrangements within central government led to problems of identifying the respective roles of each element in the management chain. Some departments adjusted more easily to the demands of FMI than others. Progress on some elements in FMI was greater than in other elements. For example, Wilson and Greenwood note[19]:

"Progress was greater, for example, with developing management systems than with defining objectives, decentralization was developed more readily in field offices than in headquarters and policy divisions, and performance measurement applied more easily to inputs than outputs, and to administrative roles rather than programme expenditure."

Nevertheless FMI proved more durable than might have at first been supposed. Although a political initiative taken by a Government agreeable to the introduction of the business management ethos, into the civil service. Inter-government research on FMI surveys has shown that the introduction of FMI has been accepted by the civil service. It is likely therefore, to survive beyond the political views of one particular government. The success in persuading departments that "efficient management" is a necessary prerequisite of the civil service seems accepted by most commentators.

In 1986 the Public Accounts Committee report noted that a new **10–31** momentum was required to speed up implementation of FMI. This touched a sensitive issue. It appears that some reservations among top civil servants and even Government Ministers about Robin Ibbs's views on spending within government departments may have contributed to problems in implementing FMI.

A new initiative, in the form of a scrutiny report, begun in 1986 by Sir Robin Ibbs was published in 1988. The report from the Efficiency

---

[17] *Progress in Financial Management in Government Departments 1984.*
[18] J. Greenwood and David Wilson, *op. cit.* p. 135.
[19] *ibid.* G. Drewry, "Forward from FMI: The Next Steps" [1988] P.L. 505.

Unit: *Improving Management in Government: The Next Steps,* suggested, to the surprise at least of Nigel Lawson, then Chancellor of the Exchequer, that executive functions of government should be hived off into separate executive agencies to be run like businesses by chief executives.

10–32   The evaluation underlying[20] this recommendation was that delegating budgeting, the basis of FMI, was difficult to implement because of many of the traditions of the civil service. One problem identified in the report was the lack of management experience in top civil servants. This appeared to originate from top civil servants supporting policy advice to Ministers in Parliament rather than focusing on managing their departments. In order to change such administrative traditions, Ibbs suggested three main priorities. First, each department should reorganise its activities to ensure that the systems and structure provided for the effective delivery of policies and services. Second, the management of each department must ensure that their staff have the relevant experience, skills and abilities required to undertake tasks that are essential to effective government. Third, each department should have value for money in the delivery of its policies and services. In achieving value for money there should be continuous pressure to secure that objective throughout the department.

10–33   Setting objectives, however well formulated, did not guarantee their success, and Ibbs went one step further than before. The Next Steps scrutiny team in their report recommended that agencies should be established to carry out some of the executive functions of government. Departments could set the general policy and resources but agencies should be developed to carry out the tasks allocated.

The Next Steps agencies, as they were referred to, were to be set up, but as Nigel Lawson noted this left unresolved two major questions[21]:

> "It was clear that Ibbs had not addressed the two principal problems involved in a change of this kind, however sensible the concept may have been. The first was the question of Parliamentary accountability. Members of Parliament would not take kindly to the idea of a Minister being able to shrug off a constituent's complaint as being nothing to do with him since the wrong suffered by the constituent had been inflicted by an autonomous agency, whose head was, according to the original Ibbs blueprint, effectively accountable to no-one."

The second problem identified by Lawson[22] was that of maintaining effective financial control over the agencies' expenditure. Resolution

[20] Nigel Lawson, *The View from No. 11,* pp. 390–392.
[21] Lawson, *op. cit.* p. 392.
[22] *ibid.*

of this problem came through an agreement reached with the Treasury and the appointment of Peter Kemp as manager of the Next Steps project with the status of Second Permanent Secretary.[23]

The Ibbs report implied that once Next Steps agencies were put in **10–34** place the role of the civil service would change. Changes introduced through the development of agencies might include differences in the allocation of resources and greater demands for value for money.[24]

On the question of accountability[25] the creation of Next Steps agencies gave rise to fundamental questions about the relationship between the agencies, the civil service and the role of Ministers.

5. Administrative Agencies

In February 1988 a small cohesive Next Steps Unit was set up under **10–35** Peter Kemp in the Office of the Minister for the Civil Service.[26] By 1991 it was estimated[27] that over 50 executive agencies, comprising 200,000 civil servants had been set up.

The first agency created under Peter Kemp was the Vehicle Inspectorate, responsible to the Department of Transport for heavy goods vehicles and licensees of garages. The model adopted became the standard practice. Responsibility for the day-to-day operations of each agency were delegated to a Chief Executive. The Chief Executive was responsible for management within a framework of policy objectives and resources set by the responsible Minister in consultation with the Treasury.[28] Some other executive agencies were created with Her Majesty's Stationery Office one of the largest, the Central Office of Information, the Land Registry and the Passport Office.

By December 31, 1996 there were 348,529 civil servants working **10–36** in Next Steps Agencies amounting to 129 agencies. In addition, HM Customs and Excise, organised in 24 Executive Units, and the Inland Revenue, organised in 25 Executive Units, brought the total figure of 421,679 civil servants working on Next Steps lines.[29] A further 27 Next Steps Agencies are being planned. Further developments[30]

---

[23] (February 18, 1988); H.C. Deb. Vol. 127, col. 1149. The Prime Minister outlined the system of agencies.
[24] Metcalfe and Richards, *op. cit.* pp. 230–233.
[25] *The Next Steps Initiative*, HMSO (1988). Cm. 1761 (1991). The Government's reply to the Seventh Report from the Treasury and Civil Service Committee, (1990/91; H.C. 496).
[26] Lawson, *op. cit.*, p. 392.
[27] See *The Next Steps Agencies Review 92.* Cm. 2111 (1992).
[28] *ibid.*
[29] *The Civil Service Yearbook*, 1997 p. lxxxvi.
[30] *Next Steps Review* Cabinet Office 1995.

include the appropriate training and development of the civil service on the basis of the White Paper *Development and Training for Civil Servants: A Framework for Action*.[31] This initiative is accompanied by the plan to maintain the standards of the civil service while adapting to change.[32] Managing the civil service in an area of change also has to confront the stereotype as explained by Gillian Peele[33]:

> "The bias at the higher levels towards graduates of Oxford and Cambridge has not, however, been the only concern about the civil service's composition. It was clear from the Cassells Report of 1983 that although almost half of the civil service were women, they formed a much higher proportion of the junior grades than of the senior one. . . . The evidence on recent developments with respect to the role of women in the civil service is somewhat mixed. By 1994 very few of the top 38 posts at permanent secretary rank were held by women. . . .

It remains to be seen whether the Next Steps agencies will break the mould.[34]

10–37   The innovatory nature of the agency arrangements has given rise to a number of initial problems. Prior to the grant of agency status a business plan and corporate identity requires careful consideration. The term Chief Executive carries high expectations of managerial control and business initiative. However, in public sector activities these may appear illusory because detailed financial control may still rest with the Treasury. Thus it took some time before bonus payments based, on group and not individual initiative were accepted. This required protracted negotiation in the Vehicle Inspectorate before it was agreed. Chief Executives are generally drawn from the civil service and this may continue old interests and pressures in the new guise of agency status. Similiarities with business appear inapplicable when it is recognised that ultimately financial failure is not a sanction.

10–38   Lawson notes[35] that "the main practical advantage . . . is that by creating accounts, boards of directors and saleable assets future privatisation may prove less difficult." It may be well within the scope of future governments to provide privatisation of civil service activities as the ultimate reform of the civil service. Therefore the idea

[31] July 1996.

[32] *The Civil Service: Taking Forward Continuity and Change* Cm. 2748.

[33] Gillian Peele, *Governing the United Kingdom* (3rd ed., Blackwell, 1995), p. 137.

[34] See A. Gray and B. Jenkins, "The Management of Central Government Services" In Jones (ed.), *Politics U.K.* (1994) pp. 433–4. Peter Barberis (ed.), *The Civil Service in an Era of Change* (Dartmouth, 1997).

[35] Lawson, *op. cit.* pp. 390–392.

that agency status is "second best to privatisation" may suggest that the Next Steps may be only one step in the progress toward complete privatisation.

Agency status remains in its early stages of development. The Employment Service agency is an example of one of the largest agency arrangements and employs over 34,500 staff. The largest agency created is the Social Security Benefits agency employing over 89,248 staff. The Prison Service employs over 38,936 staff.

It is therefore no exaggeration to claim that[36] "Next Steps is **10–39** radically altering the organisation of the Civil Service." It will also require careful scrutiny to determine if any of the desired changes in the management of civil service activities is actually achieved through agency status.

Initial studies contained in research work by Elizabeth Mellon into **10–40** the working of a number of Executive Agencies, have suggested criteria for evaluating an Agency. Three methods of evaluation may be adopted. First, on examination of performance measures from inside and outside the organisation may determine whether available resources have delivered services more efficiently and effectively. In this assessment an examination of cutting costs, and the performance criteria set out in the originating framework documents may be helpful.[37] Secondly, to test the extent, control has been given to members of staff inside agencies, which may assist in determining how leadership and responsibility within the agency may have changed. Thirdly, the introduction of the concept of "customers" within the civil service may allow feedback from customers, and responsiveness to customer needs may be quantified and tested.[38]

Useful as such criterion may be, there are doubts as to whether agency status in itself may produce significant change to the operating practices of civil servants.[39]

(a) Agencies, Accountability and Control

Agency status has raised questions regarding accountability and **10–41** control. How do agencies fit into the structure of constitutional oversight offered by select committees, ministerial responsibility and

---

[36] Elizabeth Mellon, Memorandum, Appendix 1 in Evidence to the Treasury and Civil Service Committee Seventh Report, *The Next Steps Initiative* (1990/91; H.C. 496).

[37] See P. Dunleavy and A. Francis, *The Development of the Next Steps Programme 1988–90* Appendix 5 in the Eighth Report of Treasury and Civil Service Committee (1989/90; H.C. 481). *Progress in the Next Steps Initiative* (1989/90; H.C. 481).

[38] Efficiency Unit 1988, "Improving Management in Government: the Next Steps" (HMSO, 1988).

[39] Patricia Greer, "The Next Steps Initiative : An Examination of the Agency Framework Documents" (1992) 70 *Public Administration* 80–92.

the existing status of the civil service. The answer to these questions has been raised, not only within the civil service and the government, but also in Parliament. At the forefront of discussion is the Parliamentary Select Committee on the Treasury and Civil Service. Reports since 1987/88 have both monitored and contributed to the information available on the role of agencies. It is now accepted that agencies have a bi-partisan approach from the political parties, that the Committee itself has a role in monitoring arrangements on an annual basis. The Government has continued to provide assistance to the Committee on the subject of agencies.

10–42   In their fourth report 1990/91, the Select Committee on the Treasury and Civil Service noted that while agency status increased, the core departments in central government should continue to exercise "general responsibility for the oversight of the Civil Service."

In allocating agency status, the Chief Executive is required to manage the agency effectively[40] "to achieve the ends dictated by the Minister responsible." The Chief Executive is a civil servant in formal terms. The Chief Executive may appear before select committees responsible directly for the work as head of an agency. Thus the Chief Executive appears to give evidence to select committees like any other civil servant on the Minister's behalf. While this preserves the constitutional continuity between agency and civil service, Select Committees have voiced concern that in effect chief executives are not like any other civil servant because their responsibility as chief executives, laid down in framework documents, differed from ordinary delegated authority given to the civil service by Ministers.

10–43   Parliamentary accountability for agencies appears to[41] continue to rest on the Minister who is responsible to Parliament. Accountability also follows from this, through scrutiny by select committee, and individual M.P.s may ask parliamentary questions about areas within ministerial control.

Parliamentary questions[42] and procedures have proved difficult for agencies to fit into existing practices. Ministers normally reply to questions by promising to write to the M.P. When a parliamentary answer states that an executive agency will write, the letters written are to be sent to the Department of the Library, House of Commons.

---

[40] Cm. 1263 (1990), p. 3; H.C. Deb., Vol. 186, Cols. 270–2W. There is an Office of Public Service and Science (OPSS) established in May 1993. It reports to the Minister of Public Service and Science. Within OPSS there is a Management Development Group, intended to manage the objectives and standards of Next Step Agencies. This group also secures better accountability and clearer lines of communication between departments and Next Step Agencies.

[41] Third Report of the Select Committee on Procedure, Parliamentary Questions, (1990–91; H.C. 178), para. 125.

[42] ibid.

However, on detailed financial policy where the Agency Chief Executive is responsible, Ministers may have little scope for reply. Inconsistency of approach between different Agencies and Departments may arise. One recommendation is that all replies from Chief Executives should be included in the Official Report. In this way access to all replies either from Ministers or chief executives would conform to a common method.

In conclusion, the formulation of how Next Steps Agencies fit **10–44** within the conventional arrangements for ministerial responsibility appear to follow the distinction between operational and policy matters. Chief Executives may answer for operational or day-to-day decisions, while Ministers retain responsibility for policy matters. Even when Ministers may interfere in operational matters, unless there are clear policy issues at stake, Chief Executives shoulder the burden of responsibility.

Undoubtedly one of the benefits attributable to agency status has been a growth in publications concerning the function of the agencies. Detailed accounts, future plans, corporate strategy, reviews of activities over the past financial year, objectives and key performance targets have all been included in a mass of agency annual reports. One criticism raises questions about the variety and lack of standardisation in the way such reports are produced, and the details of information they contain. Such inconsistency may give rise to confusion. Generally publications from agencies have been welcomed as providing additional information to Parliament.

A key factor in determining control over agencies is the question of **10–45** budget management and financial scrutiny. The chief executive of an agency[43] is appointed an Accountancy Officer or Agency Accounting Officer and is therefore accountable to the Committee of Public Accounts for the financial budgets of the agency. The Treasury has issued a note of guidance setting out the obligation for Annual Reports and Accounts. This accountability[44] through the publication of annual reports and accounts is also provided by the work of the National Audit Office.[45]

The financial arrangements for agencies fall under direct vote that is, supply financed by the relevant government department or under trading fund arrangements. Supply financed agencies cover a wide

---

[43] *The Financing and Accountability of Next Steps Agencies* Cm. 914, (December 1989).

[44] Government response to the *First Report of the Select Committee on the Treasury and Civil Service on Next Steps*, Cmnd. 524, p. 9. "In practice where a Committee's interest is confined to the day-to-day operations of an Agency, Ministers will normally regard the Chief Executive as being the person best placed to answer on their behalf. The Chief Executive will be able to give an account to the Committee of how the policies and tasks set out in the framework document have been carried out."

[45] The role of the National Audit Office is discussed in Chap. 11.

spectrum of activities. Some agencies rely entirely on voted expenditure to cover only operating and capital requirements while some agencies may cover all their costs. Supply financed agencies are cash limited in the normal departmental appropriation accounts. In such cases the departmental Accounting Officer remains accountable for all payments to the agency for Votes for which he accounts.

10–46   In the case of trading fund agencies, the Treasury has published a guide to the *Establishment and Operation of Trading Funds*.[46] This guide sets out the criteria for the use of Trading Funds for:

> "certain kinds of operations within Government, particularly those where the outputs of the organisation are financed from related receipts and the demand for output fluctuates, for which cash control based on inputs can inhibit effective management."

Trading funds therefore provide agencies with greater flexibility than the normal restrictions implied in vote finance. In particular the financing framework covers all operating costs, receipts, capital expenditure, borrowing and cash flow. Compared to voted expenditure, trading funds have standing authority to meet outgoings from receipts and do not require advance approval by Parliament of income and expenditure. Such a fund may borrow and create reserves, thus maintaining a higher degree of flexibility than voted expenditure which may have difficulty meeting unexpected demands.

10–47   Agencies set up under the Trading Fund arrangements fall under the detailed requirements of the Government Trading Act 1990, which amends the Government Trading Funds Act 1973. The 1990 Act broadened the statutory criteria for setting up such funds. This necessitates removal from the normal parliamentary supply controls of the funds expenditure and receipts. Before setting up such a fund parliamentary approval by affirmative Order is required, setting overall limits on borrowing.

The statutory tests[47] are that: first, operations to be financed by a trading fund must already be carried out by a government department. Second, revenues of the fund must primarily consist of receipts "in respect of goods or services provided." This means that funds arise from payment for goods, services rendered and not through block grants or taxation. Finally, the funds must be established in the interests of "improved management, efficiency and effectiveness."

10–48   The enabling powers under both the 1973 and 1990 Acts are supplemented under section 2 of the 1973 Act, which provides

---

[46] Appendix 10: Memorandum submitted by H.M. Treasury, *Guide to the Establishment and Operation of Trading Funds*, Seventh Report of the Treasury and Civil Service Committee, The Next Steps Initiative (1990/91; H.C. 496), p. 123.

[47] *ibid.*, Treasury Memorandum, Appendix 10.

administrative suitability for each fund to be worked out with the Treasury and the sponsoring government department responsible. Trading Funds are therefore more likely to provide greater flexibility for agencies than voted accounts.

Accountability is driven both through the *internal* structures and accounting practices of each agency as well as *external* information to parliamentary select committees and published reports. An added incentive is that the *Citizen's Charter*[48] envisages standard setting for the delivery of goods and services. All agencies within the Citizen's Charter remit must comply with the principles of the Charter including complaints procedures, consultation with customers and clients, and compile track records of their activities.

(b) Civil Servants and Ministers

The Armstrong Memorandum in 1985 asserted that the duty of the **10–49** individual civil servant is "first and foremost" to the Minister of the Crown.[49] The new *Civil Service Code* (1996) contains the requirement that civil servants should not deceive or knowingly mislead Parliament or the public.[50] This has given rise to questions concerning the procedures to be adopted in the event of a dispute between a civil servant and a Minister. While the legal position is clear that civil servants do not owe any direct duty to Parliament but absolute loyalty to Ministers, there is concern that the public interest does not always coincide with the law. In effect civil servants may find that they are covering up for ministerial mistakes or bad policy decisions. This raises questions about the role of Parliament in its holding of civil servants to account. No satisfactory solution to this question appears given the convention of ministerial responsibility.

The Treasury and Civil Service Select Committee[51] has received **10–50** detailed evidence on the question of accountability of Next Steps Agencies Chief Executives. One view was that the Chief Executive for an Agency might have some form of parallel responsibility to that of the Minister and thus fit into a separate category of direct accountability to Parliament from the Minister. This view was rejected as inconsistent with the doctrine of ministerial accountability. The example of Derek Lewis, the former Director General of the Prison Service,

---

[48] Citizen's Charter Cm. 1599 (1991), pp. 36–38.
[49] Sir Robert Armstrong, *The Duties and Responsibilities of Civil Servants in Relation to Ministers: Note by the Head of the Home Civil Service* (1985; H.C. Official Report, Vol. 74).
[50] H.L. Deb. January 9, 1996 W.A. 21.
[51] *Minutes of Evidence taken before the Treasury and Civil Service Select Committee 1993–4*, H.C. 27, November 23, 1993.

who resigned following the report by Sir John Learmont into prison escapes from Parkhurst.[52] The then Home Secretary Michael Howard refused to resign, drawing on the distinction between operational and policy matters. He claimed that as the Home Secretary was responsible for policy and no policy had been found to be at fault, he was entitled to rely on this fact and not resign. The Lewis case shows how difficult it would be to "force" Agency Chief Executives to hold Ministers to account.[52a]

10–51   In the case of the Next Steps agency there is greater transparency between administrators and policy-makers and Ministers and Chief Executives. The relationship between Ministers and Chief Executives is contained in the framework documents subject to review every three years. The "quasi-contractual nature" of that relationship may give rise to questions of adequate decision-making and accountability for any policy or management mistakes giving rise to claims in negligence.

(c) Assessing Management in the Civil Service

10–52 The Ibbs Report was broadly titled *Improving Management in Government*. Agencies set up under the Next Step initiative are part of the operational management of government. Assessing their value as agencies requires careful and detailed scrutiny. One source of assessment is to use the various Framework documents used in setting up the agency to judge whether services have been delivered more efficiently. Agency type may make a difference in the performance expected or delivered. In the case of Exchequer funded (direct vote financed) agencies their financial activities are under government influence. This dictates their ability to achieve effectiveness and efficiency. In the case of trading funded agencies, depending on the nature of the activity involved, the agency may very well become self-sufficient and move into the private sector.

10–53   There is also the question of whether[53] the extent and scope of parliamentary scrutiny might inhibit risk-taking in agencies which may be necessary for their future long-term strength. If so, this suggests that the agency arrangement may not necessarily benefit from public scrutiny in its business-like management of its own activities. Public scrutiny and private sector activity, as in the case of the nationalised industries may not easily be combined.[54]

[52] H.C. Deb. 264, Cols. 502–6, November 18, 1995.
[52a] See *Minutes of Evidence taken before the Select Committee on Public Services* H.C. 313 (1995–6), May 22, 1996.
[53] Patricia Greer, "The Next Steps Initiative: An Examination of the Agency Framework Documents" (1992) 70 *Public Administration* 89–98.
[54] *ibid*. R. Butler, "The Evolution of the Civil Service – A Progress Report" (1993) 71 *Public Administration* 395–406.

The agency framework is intended to make civil servants more innovative, pro-active and forward thinking, rather than reactive. The public ethos of service and the politically neutral relationship with Ministers, may have served the United Kingdom well in the evolution of a permanent, professional and respected civil service. In the 1990s such values are openly questioned. Next Steps Agencies allow external appointments to agencies and consultative arrangements over pay and conditions to become a new part of the civil service. The question arises as to the remaining part of the civil service, described as "core departmental" activity not included in the agency arrangements. How will agencies change the way that core departments carry out their work?

As with most changes introduced as a result of radical rethinks **10-54** many of the changes are incremental. It is therefore difficult to predict what the result of the Next Steps will be on core departments.

How radical are the reforms contained in the Ibbs Report in the setting up of the agencies? The Fulton Committee had recommended "hiving off" specific activities to autonomous agencies. The Heath Government had considered similar ideas. The Ibbs Report put into practical operation the ideas canvassed in previous considerations of the role of the civil service. In terms of administrative changes, the reforms have been far-reaching and the expectation is that up to three quarters of the civil service will be engaged in agency activity. The size of the civil service has also been reduced and management studies are now in place.

In constitutional terms[55] the Agency arrangements have been **10-55** adapted to conform as far as possible to existing constitutional means of scrutiny.[56] In that sense no radical or revolutionary break with procedure has occurred. However, the civil service is no longer a single unified coherent unity. It is devolved into separate, specialist agencies, many with their own budgets and management systems for the delivery of services.

In management terms the civil service as a public sector institution **10-56** is going through a creative time, developing new ideas on public management. However, two *caveats* require consideration. First, public management is not necessarily best described as a business because of the added dimension of greater accountability. Such pressures for accountability need to be accommodated within public sector management techniques. As Metcalfe and Richards point out[57]:

> "Pouring new managerial wine into old accountability bottles may have explosive consequences. Part of the future agenda of public management will be designing accountability systems."

[55] Hennessy, "The Last Retreat of Fame: Mrs Thatcher as History" (1991) 54 M.L.R. 492.
[56] G. Drewry, "Forward from FMI; The Next Steps" [1988] P.L. 505.
[57] Metcalfe and Richards, *op. cit.* p. 236.

The second *caveat* is that government itself, by hiving off activities to agencies, remains subject to the question of how best to develop for the future. This may pose the most demanding challenge for the civil service especially as past experience has shown that administrative change has been gradual, piecemeal and incremental.

10–57   The role of the senior civil servant in advising Ministers retains civil service power and influence. Ministers often seek the support of outside advisers as political and specialist support in carrying out their policies. It has been argued that identifying civil servants, often named to the public, with particular government policies impairs the political neutrality of civil servants[58]:

> "Individual senior civil servants are already associated with particular government policies. The present government's recent appointments at senior levels of the Civil Service acknowledge and reflect this political reality by the selection of civil servants committed to the formulation and effective implementation of specific policies consistent with the general framework of government policy. Civil servants have become, in a sense, political advocates, capable of arguing the case for and implementing different sets of policies depending upon the political complexion of the government of the day."

One effect of agencies in the civil service is to allow greater scrutiny to be given to civil service activities as an indirect result of establishing new agencies. In this new environment civil service secrecy and confidentiality comes increasingly under threat. Annual reports from Agencies provide much more information than previously available from within government departments. The business of government and the management of administration are now closely combined with results that are still to be fully determined.

---

[58] Rodney Austin, "Freedom of Information: The Constitutional Impact" in Oliver and Jowell, *The Changing Constitution* (2nd ed., 1989), p. 413.

Chapter 11

Public Finance

1. Introduction

Public finance refers to the government's requirements in relation to **11–01** raising and spending money. The House of Commons performs the important function of authorising public expenditure and taxation. In the management of the economy, government exercises wide powers through economic policy, and controls through its influence on the economy and the Bank of England. Money supply, interest rates and the economic policy of the government of the day are often linked to the various international financial institutions such as the International Monetary Fund and the World Bank.[1] Since 1969 Member States of the European Community have been discussing economic and monetary union. Ten years later the European Monetary System (EMS) came into operation. Membership of the EMS is open to all Member States. The United Kingdom is currently a member. Members of the EMS take part in discussions on the future functioning and development of the system. Membership of the EMS may involve four elements,[2] including membership of the Exchange Rate Mechanism (ERM). The United Kingdom left the ERM in September 1992. Increasingly, issues raised about public finance are linked to the development of economic policy and relations within the European Community.

The purpose of this chapter is to examine the main procedures and **11–02** institutions used to manage, control and hold to account public

---

[1] See The International Financial Institutions in Economic Briefing (September 4, 1992, H.M. Treasury).

[2] The other three are the European Currency Unit (ECU) which provides for a common calculation of the currency values of each Member State within the E.C. The European Monetary Co-operation Fund, consisting of the Governors of the central banks monitoring ECU arrangements. The very short-term financing facility, which allows Members States short-term credit facilities. R. Henderson, *European Finance* (1993).

expenditure.[3] The starting point is to provide an introductory outline first, of the sources of government revenue and second, the structures for the control and planning of public expenditure.

(a) Public Revenue

11–03 Government raises taxes in order to finance public spending. Public expenditure currently runs at about 40 per cent of the entire economy's national income. This amounts to approximately £220 billion. Taxation takes many forms and must be authorised by Act of Parliament. An annual Finance Act sets the limits of the amount payable each year. The courts have been vigilant in ensuring that legal authority has been correctly granted. In *Bowles v. Bank of England*,[4] Bowles was successful in suing the Bank of England for a declaration that income tax could not be deducted by virtue of a budget resolution alone and until such tax had been imposed by Act of Parliament, he was not required to pay it. The case led to the Provisional Collection of Taxes Act 1968 which gives statutory force for a limited time to resolutions of the House of Commons varying taxation levels and soon to be made part of the Finance Act.

11–04 In 1975, in *Congreve v. Home Office*[5] the Court of Appeal held that it was unlawful for the Home Office to make use of its revocation powers under the Wireless Telegraphy Act 1949, to revoke the T.V. licence to prevent licence holders benefitting from an overlapping licence purchased to avoid an increase in the licence fee. Congreve and about 20,000 other licence holders had purchased a second licence, while their existing licence was still valid in anticipation of an increase in the licence fee. Lord Denning claimed that the Bill of Rights 1689 had been infringed as a levying of money without grant of Parliament. There is some doubt on this interpretation. Congreve had sought avoidance of a tax through the purchase of a second licence, clearly not intended by the Wireless Telegraphy Act. However the case illustrates how the judges will adapt statutory interpretation to uphold the principle of authorisation.

11–05 In *Woolwich Building Society v. Inland Revenue Commissioner (No. 2)*,[6] the House of Lords considered the general principle that money paid

---

[3] Generally see A. Likierman, *Public Expenditure* (Penguin, 1988); Hood Phillips, *Constitutional and Administrative Law* (7th ed., 1989), pp. 217–233; Lawson, *The View from No. 11* (1992); Leo Pliatzky, *Getting and Spending* (Blackwell, 1989); *The Treasury Under Mrs Thatcher* (Blackwell, 1989).

[4] [1913] 1 Ch. 57. Also see *British Oxygen v. Board of Trade* [1971] A.C. 610; *Burmah Oil v. Bank of England* [1980] A.C. 1090.

[5] [1976] Q.B. 629.

[6] [1992] 3 All E.R. 737.

to a public authority pursuant to an *ultra vires* demand should be repayable as of right.[7] The case arose out of an Inland Revenue demand for tax from the Woolwich Building Society, which was later declared by the courts to have no lawful basis. It was accepted that the money paid to the revenue was not paid under any mistake of law on the part of the tax payer; but the Woolwich Building Society had no express statutory right to repayment of the money. The House of Lords held that money pursuant to an *ultra vires* demand was prima facie repayable as a common law right of the subject. Lord Goff considered how far the principle might[8]:

" . . . extend to embrace cases in which the tax or other levy has been wrongly exacted by a public authority not because the demand was ultra vires but for other reasons, for example because the authority has misconstrued a relevant statute or regulation."

Lord Goff's views, although *obiter dicta* emphasise the vigour with which the courts may review the taxation powers of the revenue. In the *Woolwich case* the payment of tax amounted to almost £57 million with interest and dividends, an illustration of the role of the courts in revenue matters with an indirect effect on expenditure totals. The government has estimated that the total cost of repaying composite rate tax to all Building Societies which had overpaid amounted to £250 million.[9]

The annual cycle of raising and spending money continues the **11–06** tradition of established constitutional practice. The government, in the name of the Crown demands money, the Commons grant it and the Lords give assent. Central government has the important long-term role of managing the economy. The government receives direct taxes levied on income or capital and indirect taxes levied on spending. The Inland Revenue under the authority, direction and control of the Treasury, collects[10] direct taxes[11] and Her Majesty's Customs and Excise are responsible for collecting customs duties on goods entering the European Community and most excise duties. They also collect value added tax (VAT), which is the most important indirect tax raising over £35 billion in 1991–92.

---

[7] See J. Beatson, "Restitution of Taxes, Levies and Other Imposts: Defining the Extent of the Woolwich Principle" [1993] L.Q.R. 401.

[8] [1992] 3 All E.R. 737 at 764d–e. (See also Lord Slynn at p. 783, for example).

[9] Beatson, *op. cit.* p. 428 Beatson also notes the effect of the decision in *Pepper v. Hart* [1993] 1 All E.R. 86 on the taxation of benefits in kind which may lead to £30m in refunds of tax.

[10] Various Acts of Parliament give the Treasury authority to collect tax such as the Taxes Management Act 1970.

[11] The taxpayer may appeal decisions of the Inland Revenue to an independent tribunal either the General Commissioners of Income Tax or the Special Commissioners of Income Tax.

11–07   In addition to taxation, the government may borrow money to finance its expenditure. This may be achieved through borrowing from the International Monetary Fund or World Bank. The government may also obtain receipts from the sale of assets. For example, receipts from privatisation sales have netted over £30 billion since 1981. An additional source of income has been revenue from the Crown Estates, in return for which the Queen is paid a fixed annual sum called the Civil List.[12] The recent proposals in November 1992 that the Queen will pay income tax on a voluntary basis, will alter the basis of this arrangement.

All public revenue is paid into the Consolidated Fund. In addition the National Loans Acts 1968–73 and extended by the Government Trading Act, 1990, established a National Loans Fund as the central government account for all government borrowing and most domestic lending operations. Loans from the fund require statutory authority.

(b) The Control of Public Expenditure

11–08 The requirement of statutory authority for both the levying of taxes and the expenditure of money has created since Gladstone in the mid-nineteenth century a "circle of control." This is based on an annual cycle of revenue and expenditure. The following description of the present system takes account of the most recent proposals made in March 1992 for Budgetary Reform[13] which were implemented from December 1993.

Past practice up to 1993, was based on a two-stage process, the Chancellor announced the government's spending plans in the November Autumn statement, and in March, before the start of the financial year, presented a full budget to Parliament. The practice of a March Budget developed since the late 1960s. Before then, the Budget was the occasion for presenting both tax and spending proposals to Parliament. Then the details of the Estimates and the basis for public spending contained in the Financial Secretary's memorandum were laid before the Commons at an earlier time.

11–09   From December 1993 there has been one budget statement to Parliament a year, covering both the Government's tax plans for the coming year and the Government's spending plans for the next three

---

[12] The Civil List is currently at £7.9 million inflation indexed. It has risen from £4.6 million in 1988. See Report of the Royal Trustees (1984) H.C. 183; (1990) H.C. 629.

[13] *Budgetary Reform* Cm. 1867 (March 1992). A major part of this chapter is drawn from: J. McEldowney, "The Control of Public Expenditure" in Jowell and Oliver, *The Changing Constitution* (1994), pp. 175–207.

years. The main advantage claimed for the changes since 1993 is to provide a closer link between spending plans and taxation. This is hoped to lead to a better and more informed debate, easier decision-taking on the merits of proposals, and improved presentation to Parliament. The revised timetable for the introduction of the unified budget system with a December budget fits within the existing financial year which runs from April to March, as follows:

December: Budget statement covering tax for one year and spending proposals for the next three years. Also included is the Autumn Statement which contains the forecast of the economy, details of changes in national insurance, social security and an outline of planned expenditure for the year and the Financial Statement. This includes the government's medium term financial strategy, public finance information on revenue and tax reliefs and an analysis of the departmental spending plans for the next three years.

January: Finance Bill and parliamentary consideration of its contents.

February: Departmental Reports as part of the Public Expenditure White Paper.

May: Finance Bill receives Royal Assent.

The new changes since 1993 provide that the choice between **11–10** borrowing and spending should be made together and on decisions taken by the whole Cabinet. There are fears that the Cabinet may become more fragmented over its economic policy than when previously it took direction from the Prime Minister and Chancellor. Cabinet disagreements over public spending are quite common. However convincing the arguments in favour of Cabinet government might appear, there is suspicion that the unified budget system may lessen the Government's overall direction and control over spending. Spending Ministers may find the new arrangements working to their benefit.

The control of public expenditure raises the role of what Elliott describes as various "constitutional actors." These are the Treasury, Parliament, the National Audit Office and the courts. Each may be examined in the context of the techniques, procedures and structures used to control expenditure.

2. The Treasury, Planning and Controlling Public Expenditure

(a) The Treasury

11–11 The Treasury[14] is the main department under the Chancellor of the Exchequer responsible[15] for the management of the economy. The Haldane Report[16] in 1918 identified a number of functions that describe the modern Treasury. In addition to the management of the economy, the Treasury, with the authority of Parliament, imposes and regulates taxation, arranges funds to meet day-to-day demands for public services and manages and controls the national debt. Finally in the control of public expenditure the Treasury supervises and prepares the supply estimates.

11–12 The Treasury combines the work of a government department with the role of exercising internal financial control over government departments. Control is usually *a priori* because the Treasury prepares, monitors, audits, and authorises under parliamentary authority, the expenditure of money. The rules relating to public finance have a miscellany of sources. The Treasury produces a large looseleaf guide to *Government Accounting*[17] which is regularly updated with amendments. Conventions, practices and statutory arrangements are noted and described. In addition, and dating back to 1934, with a revision in 1977, there is a Treasury Handbook: *Supply and other Financial Procedures of the House of Commons.*[18]

11–13 The Treasury may act as a guide to departments in terms of advice and consultation. In preparing legislation, departments are required to keep the Treasury informed of any proposals for legislation with a financial implication.[19] Consultation is expected at an early stage and the amendments to Bills should be included if they affect the financial arrangements. This represents a major influence over how departments consider spending public money.

---

[14] The Treasury from the earliest record dated about 1635, began exercising control through warrants and written orders to the officers of the Exchequer. From about 1660 the Treasury had offices in Whitehall and its own permanent staff from the Exchequer.

[15] An excellent account of the Treasury may be found in Henry Roseveare, *The Treasury* (Penguin, 1969); M. Wright, *Treasury Control of the Civil Service 1854–1974* (Oxford, 1969).

[16] Cmd. 9230 1918.

[17] HMSO 1989 with subsequent revisions: April 1990, January 1991, June 1991, and March 1992, March 1997.

[18] Published by H.M. Treasury. Also see Campion, *An Introduction to the Procedure of the House of Commons* (1958 ed.); Epitome of the Reports from the Committee of Public Accounts, Vol. I (1857–1937) and Vol. II (1938–69) and subsequent reports with Treasury Minutes.

[19] Government Accounting Amendment (No. 4), 1992, paras. 45.8.2–13. Also Amendment (No. 7) 1997.

The key official within departments, who exercises considerable **11–14** responsibilities for public finance is the Accounting Officer. The Accounting Officer is appointed by the Treasury and their responsibilities are contained in detailed Memorandum which they each receive on appointment. Accounting Officers are in effect expected to combine their task of ensuring a high standard of financial management in their department with the duty to serve their Minister. An Accounting Officer is appointed for every vote account in compliance with section 22 of the Exchequer and Audit Departments Act 1866, and section 4(6) of the Government Trading Funds Act 1973 and the Trading Fund Act 1990 provides for the appointment of a departmental Accounting Officer by the Treasury for Trading Accounts.[20] The Accounting Officer is given responsibility for signing accounts and appearing as the principal witness on behalf of the department before the Committee of Public Accounts (PAC).

The Accounting Officer has the crucial role in ensuring that **11–15** Treasury sanction is obtained for expenditure and that funds are applied to the extent and for the purposes authorised by Parliament.[21] The internal network of Treasury control over expenditure depends on his exercise of authority. He is a powerful ally to both Government, Treasury and the PAC in controlling expenditure and ensuring propriety. He provides the link between internal control and the external audit carried out by the Comptroller and Auditor General (C&AG) and the Public Accounts Committee, while maintaining his independent status. It can be appreciated that in practical terms the effectiveness of the C&AG depends on his obtaining the co-operation of Accounting Officers and Government departments. The latter role is of crucial importance to the Treasury system of internal audit. There is a specialised manual for Government Internal Audit.[22] This contains the basic standards for the Treasury's internal audit representing good practice. An internal audit is an independent appraisal within a department as a service to management in measuring and evaluating standards within the department.

Through the system of internal audit the Accounting Officer may **11–16** be assisted in his task. Internal audit is not however seen as a substitute for line management, it is a means to ensure that appraisal within a department is properly carried out. It is usual practice to carry out such appraisal by the appointment of a unit charged with responsibility to the Accounting Officer. As the Accounting Officer is usually the permanent head of the department this "reflects the view

---

[20] See Chap. 10 for the discussion of trading accounts as part of the Next Steps Initiative in setting up agencies.

[21] *ibid.*

[22] *Government Internal Audit Manual*, H.M. Treasury, July 1988.

that finance and policy cannot be considered separately." Thus good management is the key to his function. He must ensure compliance with parliamentary requirements in the control of public expenditure. In his role he is to avoid waste and extravagance and to seek economy, efficiency and effectiveness in the use of all the resources made available to the department.[23]

11–17   It would appear that the Accounting Officer carries out internally as part of his management function, a similar function to the external examinations carried out by the C&AG. Achieving internal audit in these terms means having a clear view of objectives and the use of resources, assigning well defined responsibilities and processing the correct information particularly about costs in the training and expertise required. However the Accounting Officer is also expressly concerned with *policy*. He has responsibility to advise Ministers on all "matters of financial propriety and regularity" and to ensure that departmental expenditure is justified to the PAC. In matters where a Minister may disagree he is free to set out his own advice and the overruling of it by the Minister. He is free to point out to Ministers the possibility of the department receiving criticism by the PAC.

11–18   Procedures exist for an Accounting Officer to notify the Comptroller and Auditor General should his advice be overruled.[24] There are important responsibilities to ensure that appropriate advice is tendered to Ministers "on all matters of financial propriety and regularity and more broadly as to all considerations of prudent and economical administration, efficiency and effectiveness." Thus where the Accounting Officer is unhappy with a course of action he is free to draw the attention of the Minister to his advice. If overruled then "he should ensure that both his advice and the overruling of it are apparent clearly from the papers."[25]

11–19   Controversy surrounding the payment of any money by the Treasury may be raised by the PAC, or the C&AG may inquire into accounts. In 1992, contributions were made out of public funds to the legal expenses of Norman Lamont, the then Chancellor of the Exchequer. The Chancellor's legal expenses arose from the eviction of a tenant from his private residence. The payments caused a furore that resulted in investigation of the payment by the C&AG. It is also possible for departmental led select committees to inquire into such matters. For example the Treasury and Civil Service Committee decided to investigate the Chancellors' legal expenses.

---

[23] *Government Accounting*, paras. 6.1.1.–6.2.8.

[24] *Government Accounting Amendment* 4/1992, para. 6.1.5.13. Amendment 7/1997 (3/97).

[25] *ibid*. paras. 13–15. Para. 6.1.6 adds: "The need for Treasury approval of a course of action involving a payment is a matter of regularity. The procedure in paragraph 13 (noted above) of the memorandum therefore applies if instructions are given by a Minister to proceed in the absence or in breach of Treasury authority, irrespective of the grounds on which the Treasury has withheld approval."

In the course of press coverage of the affair, the Treasury revealed **11–20** hitherto unpublished internal guidance, *Treasury Solicitor's Rules on "Defamation of Ministers and Civil Servants"*[26] relating to the conduct of Ministers in the performance of their official duties. It appears that[27]:

> "if a minister applies to his department for financial assistance in taking [legal] proceedings, assistance may be given to him if the department decided after consultation with its legal advisers that it is in the department's interests that proceedings should be instigated."

In the normal way such payments are authorised by high ranking Treasury officials. In the Lamont case the Permanent Secretary to the Treasury issued an internal Treasury Memorandum authorising the payment on the grounds that it was in the interests of the department that the matter should be dealt with quickly.

(b) Planning and Controlling Public Expenditure

The Treasury's annual Public Expenditure Survey (PES) is the central **11–21** factor in planning and controlling public expenditure. Since 1963, following the Plowden Report[28] which recommended that decisions on public expenditure should be taken "in the light of surveys of public expenditure as a whole over a period of years, and in relation to prospective resources," there has been an annual survey published as the Public Expenditure White Paper. This sets out the aims, and objectives of all government spending, for the forthcoming three financial years for central government departments and local government. The Public Expenditure White Paper published in the 1980s contained two volumes. Volume I contained an outline of the general spending policies of the government and became in 1988–89 merged in an expanded version of the Autumn Statement. There is a supplement containing the statistical information of the aggregate of departmental spending is published along with the Autumn Statement in a Autumn Statement Statistical Supplement. Volume II, which had covered individual departments has been replaced by a series of separate papers published by departments in 1988–89. A further refinement in 1991–92 has been the publication of departmental reports. The Public Expenditure White Paper has now been

---

[26] *The Independent*, December 1, 1992.
[27] *The Guardian*, December 1, 1992. See *Committee of Public Accounts* (1992/93; H.C. 386-ii) *Payments to meet legal expenses incurred by the Chancellor of the Exchequer and other Ministers.*
[28] Plowden Report, Cmnd. 1432 (1961).

effectively replaced by the Autumn Statement Statistical Supplement and Departmental Reports.

11–22   The planning of public expenditure sets the agenda between differing departmental demands for money. Between the end of the PES round in October and the Autumn statement in November, winners and losers in the expenditure debate were settled in the final resort in the event of disagreement in the "Star Chamber." This is a special Cabinet committee with a membership of Senior Ministers which hears the case presented by the Chief Secretary to the Treasury and settles disputes. This allows Treasury influence into the heart of the government's expenditure plans. The Star Chamber sat in 1981, 1983, 1984 and since 1985 on a more regular basis, until 1992 when it did not meet and the system was put in abeyance. Usually chaired by a Senior Cabinet Minister, in the event of further disagreement recourse is made to the full Cabinet. This system appeared to work well under Mrs Thatcher when Prime Minister, but in 1992 for the first time it gave way to a meeting of all spending Ministers in the full Cabinet.

11–23   Driven by the desire to reduce the public sector borrowing requirement the Treasury evolved improved techniques of accounting[29] in the public sector in the control of public expenditure as an essential means to defeat inflation. Since the mid-1970s the introduction of cash limits[30] and the dispensing with volume planned public expenditure in favour of cash planning in 1983, has attempted to avoid incremental budgeting and introduce restraints on the costs of goods and services in the public sector. Since 1979 the Government developed the objectives of limiting the amount of money supply in the economy and cutting public spending and taxation. Greater efficiencies were required,[31] and the government, as we have already noted in the previous chapter, adopted a wide range of techniques within government departments such as the Rayner Efficiency Studies

[29] Generally see John J. Glynn, *Public Sector Financial Control and Accounting* (Basil Blackwell, 1987); Sir G. Downey, "Public Accountability: Fact or Myth" (1986) Public Money, Vol. 6, No. 1 June 1986, 35–39; D. Henley, C. Holtham, A. Likierman, *Public Sector Accounting and Financial Control* (1986). See the Fulton Committee Cmnd. 3638 (1968); M. Elliott, "Cash limits" (1977) 40 M.L.R. 569. Also see M. Elliott, "The Control of Public Expenditure" in J. Jowell and D. Oliver, *The Changing Constitution* (Oxford, 1989), pp. 165–191.

[30] R. G. Bevan, "Cash limits" (1980) 4 *Fiscal Studies;* Colin Thain and Maurice Wright, "The Advent of Cash Planning" (Autumn 1989) 5(3) *Financial Accountability and Management*, 149–162 and C. Thain, "Running Cost Controls and Manpower Planning," The Treasury and Whitehall Working Paper No. 9 (December 1988). A comparative analysis may be found in T. Ward, "Note Cash v. Cost planning of Public Expenditure." Appendix 40 (January 26, 1982) of the Sixth Report of the Treasury and Civil Service Committee (1981/82; H.C. 137), Minute of Evidence pp. 130–131.

[31] Discussed in Chap. 10.

(1979),[32] the Financial Management Initiative[33] (FMI) (1983) and the Next Steps (1988) to achieve this.[34] Such strategies are designed to reduce cost, improve the economy and efficiency of government, avoid waste and provide greater value for money. Accountancy techniques and business practices have been adopted as principles of government policy replacing the traditional Whitehall model in the organisation and management of government departments. This is reflected in the personnel of the Treasury. When Treasury advice may have been inconsistent with government policy outside advisers were sought. In the late 1980s there was concern that the Treasury might loose some of its best talent.[35] Higher salaries and better prospects outside the civil service appeared more attractive. The resignation of Nigel Lawson, as Chancellor of the Exchequer was precipitated by his claim that the Prime Minister's private financial adviser Professor Sir Alan Walters undermined the authority of the Chancellor in matters of economic policy.

Following withdrawal from the ERM in September 1992, the **11–24** Government's Autumn statement[36] introduced a number of changes to the system of public expenditure control through the introduction of a New Control Total. This replaces the planning total and differs from it by excluding the main elements of cyclical social security and privatisation proceeds; it includes local authority self-financed expenditure. Cyclical social security expenditure is excluded as recognition of the fact that this element of spending is very difficult to control. Privatisation proceeds are excluded at a time when proceeds have fallen to less than 3 per cent of the planning total, but they were included in the planning total when proceeds were high and expanding. The inclusion of local government self-financed expenditure reflects the significance of an important area of public finance currently estimated to be £1.4 billion. The intention of the New

---

[32] Headed by Lord Rayner, later by Sir Robin Ibbs and now Sir Angus Fraser. See Andrew Flynn, Andrew Gray and William Jenkins, "The Next Steps and the Management of Government" (1990) 43 *Parliamentary Affairs*, 159–178. Also see the 39th Report of the Committee on Public Accounts (1985–86; H.C. 322). *The Rayner Scrutiny Programmes 1979–83*, *The Financial Management Initiative*, 13th Report (1987/8; H.C. 61); L. Metcalfe and S. Richards, "Raynerism and Efficiency in Government" in A. Hopward and C. Tomkins, *Issues in Public Sector Accounting* (1984), pp. 188–211.

[33] Progress in Financial Management in Government Departments Cmnd. 9297 (1984), L. Metcalfe and S. Richards, *Improving Public Management* (1987). See Helco and Wildavsky, *The Private Government of Public Money* (1981).

[34] Gavin Drewry, "The Next Steps: The Pace Falters" [1990] P.L. 322 and Gavin Drewry "Forward from F.M.I. The Next Steps" [1988] P.L. 505.

[35] *The Economist*, February 21, 1987.

[36] Cm. 2096 (1992) paras. 1.02, 2 C.1–2. Also see The Treasury and Civil Service Committee First report, *The 1992 Autumn Statement and the Conduct of Economic Policy* (HMSO, 1992).

Control Total is to insulate the planning process from fluctuations in the cycle of economic growth and for the government to have a more accurate assessment of expenditure plans. This, it is hoped, will lend greater stability to the planning process over the long-term – a persistent criticism made about the old planning total was that it failed in its objectives of long-term planning.[37]

11–25   The Treasury also performs an important policy function in advising through economic forecasts, the state of the economy and the prospects for inflation, unemployment and growth. Criticism has been made of the accuracy of the Treasury forecasts and the failure to identify in the late 1980s the increase in credit and housing inflation. The Treasury, possibly because of its dual role as both a government department and as an important constitutional control over government expenditure, is itself more scrutinised than most other departments of government. It retains its power and influence and expertly manages confidential and from an economic perspective, sensitive, information.

(c) The Bank of England

11–26 The Bank of England is the United Kingdom's central bank and acts as banker to the government. The accounts held in the Bank of England on the government's behalf are the Consolidated Fund and the National Loans Fund. Also held are the accounts of the Inland Revenue and Customs and Excise (the Revenue Departments), the National Debt Commissioners and the Paymaster General. The Bank of England is also a full member of the clearing system with the other major banks. Various other public sector enterprises have accounts at the Bank but the tendency is for departments to consider carefully whether in situations where there is no statutory duty to make use of the Bank of England, there are any advantages to be gained in using the Bank of England. Since April 1, 1989 departments and public bodies are required to pay "explicit charges" to the Bank of England to cover the costs of holding accounts or undertaking other financial services.

11–27   A list of banks[38] is published by the Treasury and if departments wish to open an account with a bank not on the list then the Treasury

---

[37] R. G. Bevan, "Cash limits" (1980) 4 *Fiscal Studies;* Colin Thain and Maurice Wright, "The Advent of cash planning" 5(3) *Financial Accountability and Management* 149–162, Autumn 1989 and C. Thain, "Running Cost Controls and Manpower Planning." The Treasury and Whitehall Working Paper No. 9, December 1988. A comparative analysis may be found in T. Ward, "Note Cash v. Cost planning of Public Expenditure." Appendix 4 (January 26, 1982) 6th report, *Treasury and Civil Service Committee* (1982–82; H.C. 137) Minute of Evidence, pp. 130–131.

[38] *Government Accounting* 89, paras. 28.2.14.

must be consulted. Banks accredited with the Bank of England are not necessarily good investment institutions, as a number of creditors and local authorities found when a major bank collapsed.

Detailed internal rules exist for the various financial transactions carried out by central government departments including the use of credit cards, debit cards and in the handling of receipts and payments.

The Bank of England is distinctive from the comparable European **11–28** central banking institutions in coming under the direct influence of the government of the day. Monthly meetings between the Treasury and the Bank of England are held under the chairmanship of the Chancellor of the Exchequer. While the Bank may act independently of government, the government through the Treasury exercise influence and in fact the Bank is subordinate to the Treasury,[39] although the exercise of direct statutory intervention in the form of a direction to the Bank has not proved necessary.[40] The Bank of England is not a government department and does exercise independent advice. The Bank and its functions fall within the remit of the Treasury and Civil Service Select Committee. The Governor and his staff may be called to give evidence and be cross-examined before the committee.

Since 1979[41] under the Banking Act 1979, the Bank of England has **11–29** formal powers to supervise[42] banking institutions in the United Kingdom. Formal powers under the 1979 Act to grant or refuse recognition of banking institutions are designed to protect creditors. The 1979 Act distinguished between banks that may be recognised and other "deposit-taking" institutions which it may licence. Four criteria existed to obtain recognition, namely carrying on business for a reasonable time, integrity and prudence in carrying out activities, the business must be effectively directed "by at least two individuals" and the net assets of an amount considered approriate by the Bank of England.

In the case of a licence, a deposit-taking institution must meet two criteria, namely that every director or manager "was a fit and proper person" to hold office and secondly, the business of the institution must be conducted in "a fit and proper" manner with regard to assets

[39] N. Lawson, *The View from No. 11* (1992), p. 83.
[40] T. C. Daintith (1976) 92 L.Q.R. 62.
[41] The White Paper on Banking Supervision published in 1976 (Cmnd. 6584) led to the Banking Act 1979. In addition in 1974, the Committee on Banking Regulations and Supervisory Practices was established known as the Basle Committee.
[42] Prior to 1979, the Bank of England's supervision of financial institutions extended back to the mid-nineteenth century. Section 4(3) of the Bank of England Act 1946 permits the Bank to make recommendations and with the authority of the Treasury to issue directions to be undertaken by the Bankers. This power appears not to be used and it was assumed that direct statutory basis for intervention did not exist until 1979.

and adequate liquidity. Wide powers under section 16 of the 1979 Act related to the obtaining of information and production of documents and under section 17 persons could be appointed to investigate the state, conduct and operation of the Bank.

11–30   Such supervision, introduced under the 1979 Act depended largely on a degree of flexibility in its application. The supervisory powers were welcomed by the Governor[43] as providing flexibility over rigid rules[44]:

> "flexibility is preferable to a system of supervision in which detailed rules and regulations are rigidly codified. We have always believed that the broad, strategic interest of supervisors and supervised in the banking business are as one."

In September 1984 Johnson Mathey Bankers Ltd (JMB), a major commercial Bank and lending institution engaged in gold bullion transactions went into financial difficulties. Investigations into the management of the bank exposed serious difficulties with the monitoring of credit, adequate security and inadequate financial returns to the Bank of England. This led to a committee of inquiry,[45] a Treasury working party and a White Paper[46] and the Banking Act 1987. The 1987 Act repealed almost all of the 1979 Act and introduced new arrangements, while retaining the supervisory role of the Bank of England. While some important parts of the 1979 Act were virtually retained albeit in a new formulation.

11–31   Section 39 of the 1987 Act required an authorised institution to provide information, documents and reports by accountants. Such powers were exercisable where it appeared to the Bank to be required in the interests of depositors. On the same basis under section 41 the Bank could appoint persons to investigate and report to the Bank on[47] "the state of the institution's business or any particular aspect of it, or the ownership or control of the institution."

The 1987 Act set up a Board of Banking Supervision to assist the Bank of England in its supervisory role. The Bank was to report to the Board and in cases of dispute the matter was to be raised with the Chancellor of the Exchequer. The Bank of England was entitled to give authorisation to institutions for the acceptance of deposits otherwise the activity was prohibited. Authorisation status granted from the Bank of England built on the four criteria mentioned above

---

[43] *The Listener*, November 24, 1983.

[44] *ibid.*

[45] The Leigh-Pemberton Report (Cmnd. 9550). Report of the Committee set up to consider the system of Banking supervision.

[46] Cmnd. 9695.

[47] Bingham Report, paras. 1.46–1.65.

under the 1979 Act. Institutions authorised under the 1979 Act remained authorised under the 1987 Act.

Section 11 of the 1987 Act provides the Bank of England with **11–32** powers to revoke an authorisation. These legal powers consisted of either where the Bank was empowered to revoke an authorisation or where it was obliged to do so. In the former, the two criteria are that any of the grounds for authorisation have not been fulfilled or the interests of depositors are threatened by the manner in which the institution is conducting its business. In the latter, the Bank is obliged to revoke an authorisation, where a winding up order was made against the institution or in cases where the institution's place of business is outside the United Kingdom in another Member State of the European Community, the supervisory authority had withdrawn its authorisation. There are powers to restrict institutions activities and detailed procedures for disclosing to the Bank of England under section 38, transactions where risk exposure was very great.

The inquiry by Lord Justice Bingham into the supervision of the **11–33** collapse of the Bank of Credit and Commerce International[48] (BCCI) revealed the extensive powers available to the Bank of England. BCCI's collapse was due to widespread fraud and led to considerable concern about the Bank of England's regulatory and supervisory functions. The power to revoke a licence arose, if it appeared to the Bank[49]:

> "that any of the criteria applicable to the institution in question had not been fulfilled, or if the institution had failed to comply with any obligations imposed by the Act or if the institution had in any other way so conducted its affairs as to threaten the interests of its depositors."

In addition, the Bank could attach conditions to a licence, but this required revocation first. The conditions could be at the discretion of the Bank and were intended to protect creditors.[50] The Bingham Report was critical of the Bank of England's supervisory powers and its failure to warn Treasury officials and Ministers from early 1990 of the serious risk of a collapse of BCCI.[51] Further criticism was made of the failure to invoke revocation powers, outlined above under the

---

[48] Inquiry into the Supervision of the Bank of Credit and Commerce International, October 22, 1992, (HMSO) Chair, Lord Justice Bingham, hereinafter the Bingham inquiry.

[49] Bingham, para. 1.20.

[50] *ibid.* Bingham notes how an appeal against the Bank's decsion to revoke or attach licences could be made to the Chancellor of the Exchequer advised by a specially constituted tribunal and appeal also lay to the courts on a point of law.

[51] Bingham, para. 2.515.

1979 Act, as early as 1986 in order to set conditions on the management of BCCI.[52]

11–34 The Bank of England's supervision of BCCI extended over 19 years but there was no obligation under the 1987 Act to disclose to the Treasury or consult with the Treasury about particular institutions. Lord Justice Bingham found that at fault in the supervision of BCCI appeared to be the need to find a greater responsiveness based on alertness and vigilance. This involved a "greater awareness of context, of the history of an institution and its relation with supervisors."

11–35 This raises questions about whether the Bank of England should continue to act as a banking supervisor. Demands for setting up the Bank as an independent body were rejected in the Bingham Report.[53] The general role of the Bank of England especially in its practice of following government advice on interest rates has concerned economists. Nigel Lawson in his memoirs made public the text of a minute to the Prime Minister of November 25, 1988 arguing for a fully independent Bank. The Lawson proposal rests on a division of responsibility as follows[54]:

> "(a) The bank would assume sole responsibility for the operation of monetary policy, with a statutory duty to protect and maintain the value of the currency. It would thus be responsible for setting short-term interest rates and monetary targets.
>
> (b) The Government would remain responsible for determining the exchange rate framework – for example, whether we were part of any international agreement, of whatever kind, formal or informal. The bank would then be responsible for the conduct of exchange rate policy within that framework."

11–36 The Chancellor of the Exchequer in the new Labour Government formed after the general election on May 1, 1997, announced that the Bank of England would set interest rates on an independent[55] assessment from the Government. A new panel of advisers would be appointed to sit with the Governor of the Bank of England to undertake this task. A further reform was also announced that the Bank of England's Banking supervision department would be hived off under the Deputy Governor to act as an independent regulatory body of the banking sector. This sector has expanded through the

---

[52] *ibid.*, para. 2.64–66.

[53] *ibid.*, para. 3.4–5.

[54] Nigel Lawson, *The View from No. 11* (1992), p. 1060. See *H.C. Treasury and Civil Service Committee* (1993/4; H.C. 98–1) *The Role of the Bank of England.*

[55] See Terence Daintith, "Between Domestic Democracy and an Alien Rule of Law? Some Thoughts on the Independence of the Bank of England" [1995] *Public Law* 118.

creation of new Banks from the old mutual societies, formerly the Building Societies.

(d) The Private Finance Initiative

The Private Finance Initiative (PFI) was launched in 1992. Its aims are **11–37** to improve the quality and quantity of public sector capital projects.[56] The aims of PFI are to secure funding for all public sector procurement. This means that all central government departments and sponsored bodies should screen all capital projects for PFI potential. Areas that are likely to receive sympathetic consideration include roads, prisons, tunnels, light railway systems, health facilities and major equipment and office accommodation. Joint ventures between the public and private sectors are also included.

PFI has implications for the way finances are considered. Flynn explains[57]:

> As well as capital investment projects, the PFI was used as a way of contracting work out to the private sector, while reducing cash outflows in the short term.

The implications of PFI are that it is intended to locate all capital **11–38** projects within a PFI framework. This may give rise to greater expectations than are actually possible. Although there is no equivalent requirement on local authorities to consider PFI, there are new rules since April 1996 to assist local authorities in setting up PFI schemes. Particular emphasis is given to the Public Private Partnerships Programme. There are six objectives namely to promote private investment; to improve value for money; to encourage rationalisation and upgrading of local authority property; to encourage transfer to the private sector of trading assets; to facilitate joint ventures; and to remove unnecessary obstacles to partnership.[58]

The expected scale of PFI activities is currently under review. Also under review are the procedures for application with the intention of simplifying these. Estimates of the success of PFI are difficult to give. It is estimated that at the beginning of the financial year 1996/97 there were over 150 information technology projects under active consideration with a total cost of £3 billion.[59] PFI, therefore, maintains a vast potential for changing the way capital projects may operate

---

[56] Norman Flynn, *Public Sector Management* (3rd ed, 1997) pp. 117–9.
[57] *ibid*. p. 119.
[58] *Private Finance Initiative*, Department of the Environment, February 1997.
[55] Flynn, p. 119.

and moving from the public to the private sector much of the risk as well as the potential for wealth.

3. Parliament

11–39 The basis of parliamentary control over public expenditure has evolved historically. Control is exercised through Parliament's role in planning and monitoring public expenditure, and the means adopted are both procedural and technical. Parliamentary authority is required for both the expenditure of public funds and the raising of finance through taxation. In constitutional terms government is carried out in the name of the Crown and is charged with the management of public revenue. This description is commonly used even though Cabinet government is established dependant on the support of the House of Commons.

11–40 It seems to be generally accepted that due to the general influence of Ministers and where the government has a majority control over the House of Commons, that the House of Commons' power of control is reduced to a right to criticise. This admits the reality that both political power and economic control may really reside in the government of the day. Standing Orders of the House of Commons Nos. 46 and 47 assert that it is the Crown's initiative and sole responsibility for expenditure. This has been interpreted to mean that private members or the Opposition are unable to propose increased charges on public funds or initiate legislation involving expenditure out of public funds.[60]

11–41 The requirement of statutory authority is satisfied through the supply procedure of the House of Commons providing on an annual basis by means of the Consolidated Fund Acts and by an Appropriation Act. The following account is in outline[61]: the supply procedures required to enable the House of Commons to vote, supply and provide the government with funds from the Consolidated Fund. The supply procedures appear technical and formal. In reality little substantial scrutiny is actively involved in such procedures, and the policy objectives on which the money is spent is not determined by the Commons but by the government of the day, but their importance resides in the constitutional authority of Parliament and the internal controls exercised by the Treasury.

---

[60] *Government Accounting*, paras. 1.24–1.2.6.
[61] Details of the rules relating to supply may be found in Supply Procedure, *Government Accounting*, paras. 11.1.1–11.9.1.

Supply estimates provide the House of Commons with the necessary **11–42** information to provide the government with funds from the Consolidated Fund. They must be approved by the date of the budget, currently in November, and this remains so under the unified Budget introduced after 1993. Estimates of departmental expenditure are drawn up and must be approved by resolutions of the Commons for the necessary release of funds from the Consolidated Fund. Since 1986, the supply estimates have been divided into about 20 major categories with detailed sub-clauses within the various votes for each department. The estimates provide the majority, over 70 per cent, of annual public expenditure. There is an annual Appropriation Act[62] enacted by July/ August each year authorising the Bank of England to make payments from the Consolidated Fund. The estimates must conform to Treasury format and approval and must not be altered unless Treasury authority has been granted. The audit carried out by the Comptroller and Auditor General is focused on the estimates which when divided into heads of expenditure appear as "votes."

Departments work on the supply estimates in the Summer or early **11–43** Autumn of each financial year. On or about the time of the budget each year, the estimates are published. If a department's needs exceeds that of the estimates then a supplementary may be passed subject to Treasury and parliamentary approval. The Standing Orders of the Commons provide three opportunities to introduce supplementary estimates with the benefit of a guillotine procedure ensuring their speedy passage: supplementaries for Summer are presented in June, for Winter in November and for Spring in February. At other times of the year but without the benefit of the guillotine procedure, estimates may be submitted.

The following time-table sets out the three periods for Parliament's **11–44** consideration of the estimates. Special supplementary estimates are debated whenever they arise.

> March-July for the main estimates, June-July for the Summer supplementary estimates. Estimate day debates take place in July and at the time of the Appropriation Act.

> November-December for the Winter supplementary estimates followed by any debates and a Consolidated Fund Act.

> February-March for the Spring supplementary estimates followed by any debates on the Consolidated Fund Act.

Since 1982, the Financial Management Initiative insists that good financial management should be part of financial decision making within departments.

---

[62] The Appropriation Act begins life as the Consolidated Fund (Appropriation) Bill.

11–45   The requirement for statutory authority for authorisation of public expenditure is seriously regarded by the Treasury. *The Treasury Handbook* holds to this principle that statutory authority for the payment of expenditure out of moneys provided by Parliament[63] "must be and can only be given year by year by means of votes and the Appropriation Act." A Minister[64] "when exercising functions which may involve the expenditure of money may only do what he does if Parliament votes him the money."

11–46   Since 1982 there have been three specific days to consider the estimates. The Commons may only reduce the estimates but even this is unlikely if the government of the day has an overall majority. Parliament is unable to initiate its own expenditure on its own behalf rather than the government's. During this century the Commons has not rejected an estimate and the scrutiny function appears a limited one. While the presentation of the estimates has become more attractive and readable, little progress has been achieved in restoring earlier practice to modern times of making debate and scrutiny a substantive control of the Commons over the Executive.

11–47   There is a Contingencies Fund which may be used to finance urgent expenditure.[65] The fund is a reserve fund intended to meet unforeseen items of expenditure. In technical terms it is used "to meet payments for urgent services in anticipation of Parliamentary provisions for those services becoming available." Total advances outstanding from the fund should not exceed 2 per cent of the previous year's total estimates provision. Money withdrawn from the Fund must be repaid.[66] The Treasury may authorise payment out of the Fund subject to the limit of 2 per cent set under the Contingencies Fund Act 1974. The use of the Fund is regarded as "exceptional" particularly if the Fund is used for a new service. The instructions contained in *Government Accounting* state[67]:

---

[63] *Treasury Handbook*, paras. 47–49.

[64] *ibid.* The Public Accounts Committee considered in 1932 the question of whether the Appropriation Act is sufficient authority for the expenditure, whether there is or not specific statutory authority for the service concerned. In concluding that the Appropriation Act is sufficient in itself for such authority, known as the 1932 PAC Concordat, the Treasury have accepted that provided the government of the day undertakes to ask Parliament for authorisation services under the Appropriation Act this would come within the PAC Concordat. However it is preferable to seek specific statutory authority.

[65] See McEldowney "The Contingencies fund and the Parliamentary Scrutiny of Public Finance" [1988] P.L. 232–245.

[66] The Contingencies Fund should not be confused with the Contingencies Reserve which falls within the public expenditure plans but is unallocated to any particular expenditure in advance of demands upon the Reserve being made during the year. The reserve is therefore unallocated but authorised funds intended to provide a safety net without upsetting the total expenditure planned by the Budget. Uses of the Reserve may vary from national disaster to providing additional borrowing for the nationalised industry or to provide money to assist in the defence of the currency.

[67] *Government Accounting*, paras. 11.6.4–11.6.5.

"The criterion is not convenience, but urgency in the public interest. If the amount of money involved, or the potentially contentious nature of the proposal is such as to create special difficulty in justifying anticipation of specific Parliamentary approval, it may be necessary to consider the alternative of immediate presentation of a Supplementary Estimate, outside the normal time-table, to be followed by a special Consolidated Fund Bill."

The Contingencies Fund offers an unusual example where the main **11–48** scrutiny of the government's use of the Fund largely depends on effective Treasury control. Legislation giving authority for the expenditure involved must be introduced at the earliest possible time and ought never be postponed. Additional guidance[68] issued in 1992 makes clear that the government of the day must be prepared "to take the responsibility of assuming that legislation being considered by Parliament will pass into law." In 1974 the then Financial Secretary to the Treasury explained that: "The Contingencies Fund cannot be drawn upon for any purpose for which the statutory authority of Parliament is required until legislation seeking that authority has been given a Second Reading."

The Contingencies Fund has been used for a variety of purposes. **11–49** The relief of national disasters, the manufacture of the first Atomic Bomb, victory celebrations and at time of war, for financing urgent supplies. Concern about the use of the Contingencies Fund is focused on the question of Parliamentary accountability. The total expenditure from the Fund, within the resources available to the Fund is considerable. There are no clear statutory conditions for expenditure being advanced from the Fund. Reliance is placed on the system of internal Treasury control and audit. No select committee directly monitors the use of the Fund. In the area of policy there are no satisfactory means to inquire into the policy behind the government's use of the Fund prior to the Fund being used. Any *ex post facto* inquiry is difficult since the money has already been used. The fact that the money is to be repaid hardly seems an adequate safeguard to question the purpose for which the Fund has been used.

Doubts about the legality of the existence of the Fund[69] were **11–50** raised in 1983 but have been seemingly resolved and the Fund is assumed by the Treasury to be legal. The Contingencies Fund is an example of where Parliament has through inactivity, allowed an exception to the principle that Parliament should vote money before

---

[68] *Government Accounting Amendment No. 4* (1992), para, 11.6.6–11.6.7.
[69] See Sixth Report from the Treasury and Civil Service Select Committee, Budgetary Reform (1981/82; H.C. 137), Appendix 20, pp. 167–194.

expenditure is incurred. There is also tacit acceptance that Treasury control may be more effective in this instance than Parliamentary[70] scrutiny.

(a) The Committee of Public Accounts (PAC), the New Select Committees and the Comptroller and Auditor General (C&AG)

11–51 Once expenditure is settled then the question of scrutiny and audit arises. Since 1861 the Committee of Public Accounts (PAC) acts on behalf of Parliament to examine and report on accounts and the regularity and propriety of expenditure which are matters usually covered by the Comptroller and Auditor General's (C&AG) certification audit. In more recent times value for money audit (VFM) examinations have become a major part of the work of the PAC.[71] In that regard the PAC works with the assisstance of the C&AG. The constitutional importance of the PAC is beyond question. It has traditionally been seen as the doyen of all select committees with "its world wide prestige and the reputation of being the terror of the departments. No other select committee had the same authority, clarity of remit and breadth and depth of advice available to it."[72]

11–52 Select committees generally, may exercise *ex post facto* control over public expenditure. The Select Committee on Procedure and the Treasury and Civil Service Committee have been particularly active in assisting in the development of strategies for greater availability of information on public expenditure and its more effective control.[73] The PAC's authority and remit differs from other select committees mentioned in Chapter 9 because of two factors. The first is the non-party political approach it devotes to its task and the fact that it is chaired by a senior opposition M.P. and has no more than 15 members. The second is its inquiries are almost all audit based and it receives expert assistance from the C&AG. In the case of VFM examinations its reports to Parliament carry considerable weight.

11–53 A limitation shared by all select commmittees but not the PAC, is that the giving of evidence by civil servants is determined by the Osmotherly Rules.[74] This means that the government determines what information is given to Parliament. However the PAC may rely on the National Audit Office (NAO) which has a statutory right to

---

[70] This account is drawn from McEldowney, *op cit.*
[71] Generally see G. Drewry (ed.), *The New Select Committees* (2nd ed., 1989).
[72] Ann Robinson, "The Financial Work of the Select Committees" Chap. 17 in G. Drewry, *The New Select Committees* (1984).
[73] See N. Johnson, *The Commons under Scrutiny*, pp. 182–184.
[74] *Memorandum of Guidance for Officials Appearing Before Select Committees* (the Osmotherly rules) Cabinet Office revised March 1988 (subject to revision).

obtain information under the National Audit Act 1983, "reasonably required for the investigations in question." In normal practice such legal powers are seldom relied upon as departments co-operate with the NAO in carrying out their scrutiny.

One criticism of the PAC is that in its scrutiny its *ex post facto* review leaves much to be desired.[75] As Robinson explained, in common with the audit of Government, "in too many cases its structures are like shutting the door after the horse has bolted." The money is spent, the waste has occurred and such are the PAC's findings that call for future changes, inevitably it is difficult to trace and recover money.[76]

An example of the work of the PAC is the investigation carried out **11–54** in 1984 into the use of public money invested in Delorean Cars[77] in Northern Ireland. Over £77m was invested, a large proportion of this was found to have been improperly used. The PAC called for tighter rules on the use of public money for business ventures in private companies. Particularly difficult has been the area of defence contracts where costs may overrun earlier estimates quite easily.[78] In April 1986 the resignation of Michael Heseltine, over the Westland affair, resulted in the appointment of George Younger as Defence Secretary. This made possible the removal of the block grant system for defence spending and its replacement by an expenditure round on an item by item basis supervised by the Treasury. The agreement was in the form of an "unrecorded concordat" between the Ministers and officials.

Another difficulty is that the size of the task under consideration invariably leads to an emphasis on small examples of bureaucratic blunder which are easier to pick up and debate than larger examples of overspending which may have inherent causes in the procedures.[79]

Although the PAC rarely divides on party political lines, it is made **11–55** up of busy M.P.s who may find it difficult to give the complexities of the National Audit Office reports their full attention. By implication matters of importance may be missed in the outlook for the PAC which is targeted to parliamentary debate and acceptability. An added complication is that the new departmental select committees,

---

[75] V. Flegman, "The Public Accounts Committee" (1980) *Parliamentary Affairs* 168. Also see Sheldon, "Public Sector Accounting and the United Kingdom Public Committee" (1984) *The Parliamentarian*, 91–98.

[76] Robinson, *op. cit.* 38 on p. 316. Also N. Johnson, "Financial Accountability to Parliament" Chap. 13 in Smith and Hague, *Dilemma of Accountability in Modern Government* (1971).

[77] J. Redwood, *Going For Broke* (1984), Chap. 2.

[78] PAC Ninth Report on the Chevaline Ministry of Defence Expenditure (1981/82; H.C.). Costs on the chevaline project were not properly disclosed. Treasury Minute Cmd. 8759 (1982).

[79] *ibid.*, Nigel Lawson, *The View from No. 11* (1992), p. 313.

introduced since 1979, have a sufficiently wide remit which invariably brings the reports of the PAC and the C&AG within their jurisdiction.[80] In 1988–89 the House of Commons Select Committee on Procedure recommended and the Government accepted, that departmental select committees should take greater consideration of the analysis of broad expenditure priorities.[81] Unlike the PAC the membership of these committees is such that party politics may intrude in their analysis. At least one commentator has been critical of the way in which the success or failure of the new select committee depends not so much on the institution itself but on the willingness of individual M.P.s to work on complex, technical and intricate detail. Few political rewards are obvious from such time consuming work.[82] The combination of the PAC and the new select committees may pose a fresh challenge for the C&AG. In exercising his independent audit function he must be sensitive to the problem that the PAC should not divide on party lines when discussing his reports. On the other hand, the new select committees, the news media and individual back bench M.P.s are likely to seize every opportunity to take political advantage from a critical report of a department's use of public funds. Parliamentary debate is both a method for publicising the findings of the C&AG and an opportunity for political debate. While the C&AG may rely on both as a sanction against an obdurate government department, he must remain independent.

11–56 Finally it should be recognised that as an external form of audit the independent status of the C&AG means that he relies heavily on cooperation with departments and their Accounting Officers who exercise internal control. The C&AG reports contain findings of facts and opinions in the case of VFM examinations as to how performance is related to objectives set. It is often a delicate calculation as how best to preserve the privileges of access to confidential information with conclusions on the outcome of his examination.

The constitutional protection awarded to the C&AG determines his independence and status. However, it is the C&AG's discretion which determines the scope of his remit for VFM examinations of privatisation sales. These have been developed within the framework of the above analysis of the constitutional role and jurisdiction of the C&AG.

---

[80] Priscilla Baines, "History and Rationale of the 1979 Reforms" Chap. 1 in G. Drewry, *The New Select Committees* (1985).

[81] *The Working of the Select Committee System: Government Response to the Second Report of the House of Commons Select Committee on Procedure*, Cm. 1532 (1989/90).

[82] Robinson, *op. cit.* 61 at p. 318. See recent concerns over millions of pounds in waste and fraud identified in government departments and agencies. Some examples are £56.6 million lost by the Property Services Agency, £55 million in doubtful and incorrect payments by the Dept of Environment, *The Guardian,* January 28, 1994.

4. The National Audit Office

The constitutional status of the Comptroller and Auditor General **11–57** (C&AG) provides that in carrying out his functions he acts on behalf of Parliament. The independence and constitutional status of the C&AG may now be considered.[83] Since the Exchequer and Audit Act 1866, the C&AG is required to examine accounts on behalf of the House of Commons. The 1983 National Audit Act recognised the constitutional implications of this requirement and made the C&AG an Officer of the House of Commons and provided for his appointment. The C&AG is head of the National Audit Office (NAO), which was created under the 1983 Act, and replaced the Exchequer and Audit Department. The C&AG appoints staff, who are no longer civil servants, and subject to the 1983 Act determines grading, pay and conditions. The C&AG is independent from party politics or the political influence of the government of the day.[84]

The NAO is itself independent from the civil service and may **11–58** recruit and train its own staff, usually qualified by the Chartered Institute of Public Finance and Accountancy or the Institute of Chartered Accountants in England and Wales. Recently the NAO has been able to adopt its own in house training scheme (TOPS) for professional Chartered Accountants, on a par with the city commercial accountancy firms. The NAO is free to hire outside experts and consultants as required.[85]

The NAO is itself subject to audit[86] by the Public Accounts Commission, a body appointed for this purpose under section 2 of the 1983 Act which came into existence on January 1, 1984. The Commission comprises nine members of the House of Commons two are *ex-officio* members, one being the Leader of the House of Commons, the other the Chairman of the PAC. None of the members may be Ministers of the Crown.

The purpose of the Public Accounts Commission is threefold. First, **11–59** to appoint a suitable Accounting Officer for the appropriation

---

[83] *The Role of the Comptroller and Auditor General*, Cmnd. 8323. Also see Eleventh Report from the Expenditure Committee Session (1976–77; H.C. 535). First Report from the Select Committee on Procedure Session (1977–78; H.C. 588). Second Special Report from the Committee of Public Accounts (1978–79; H.C. 330). The salary of the C&AG is paid directly from the Consolidated Fund without the annual approval of the Executive or Parliament. The Exchequer and Audit Departments Acts 1866 and 1921 and the National Audit Act 1983 provide that the C&AG is appointed by letters patent on an address from the House of Commons and after agreement with the chair of the Committee of Public Accounts. Funds for the NAO are provided by Parliament through supply grant.

[84] Gordon Downey, "Public Accountability: Fact or Myth?" (1986) 6 *Public Money* 35–38. Also see *Government Accounting*, Chap. 7.

[85] Annual Report of the Comptroller and Auditor General (1989/90).

[86] *Government Accounting* paras. 7.1.41–7.1.42.

accounts of the NAO. Second to appoint auditors, and third, to examine estimates and take advice from the Treasury or the PAC.

The 1983 Act has been criticised for failing to give the C&AG the right to trace "all public money."[87] Excluded from the jurisdiction of the NAO in schedule 4 to the 1983 Act, is the audit of the nationalised industries and other public authorities. Local authorities are separately audited by the Audit Commission which is itself subject to audit[88] by the NAO. The Audit Commission is examined separately in Chapter 12 on local government. Since privatisation the remaining nationalised industries fall under the system of private sector audit since the nationalisation legislation setting up each industry, required that the industry should follow "best accounting practice." Gradually some degree of uniformity of accountancy practice was adopted in 1978 after a government White Paper[89] and in 1981 from guidance issued by the Nationalised Industries Chairmens Group Financial Panel.[90] Each industry developed its own accountancy practices within a common structure but these practices are absent from the Accounting Standards Committee.[91] The NAO undertakes two forms of auditing, Certification Audit and Value For Money Audit.

11–60 In the case of certification audit, the C&AG carries out on behalf of the House of Commons the audit and certification of all government departments and a wide range of public sector bodies. These include appropriation accounts of departments. Receipts for privatisation and expenses are presented to Parliament in the form of a standard government Appropriation Account[92] relevant to the government department responsible for the sale. In such cases the C&AG provides an audit certificate which states his opinion as to whether either (a) the "account properly presents" the expenditure and receipts of the vote and payments of the organisation or (b) the account presents a "true and fair view" where accounts are prepared on an income and expenditure basis.[93]

11–61 This form of audit is "departmental led"[94] that is, it is focused on the department's responsibilities. The C&AG may seek an explanation from the sponsoring department concerned if he is dissatisfied

[87] John Garett, "Developing State Audit in Britain" (1986) 64 *Public Administration* 421–433. Also Public Money, "The National Audit Office: the First Twelve Reports" (September, 1984).

[88] Local Government Finance Act 1982.

[89] The Nationalised Industries, Cmnd. 7131 (1978).

[90] Code of Practice for Current Cost Accounting in the Public Sector Corporations issued by Nationalised Industries Chairmen's Group. See John J. Glynn, *Public Sector Financial Control and Accounting* (1987), p. 243. See Competition Act 1980, s.11.

[91] Accountancy Standards Steering Committee (1975), The Corporate Report, London. It later became known as the Accountancy Standards Committee (ASC). See *Accounting in the Nationalised Industries* (ASC, 1976).

[92] *Government Accountancy*, Chap. 7, para. 7.1.16.

[93] *ibid.*, para. 7.1.15.

[94] See Beauchamp, *op. cit.* p. 57.

with any aspect of the accounts and may qualify his certificate with his reservations.[95] The primary focus of such an audit is to assess whether accounts are accurate or whether they may mislead someone relying on the accounts. In particular, if there is expenditure which requires Treasury authority which has not been given, the matter is reported to the Treasury.[96]

Normally the audit work involved in certification audit is confined to the proper presentation of receipts and expenditure. In common with most of the auditing work of the NAO it is scrutiny *ex post facto* with the implication that any past errors may provide lessons for the future. This is open to the criticism that an *a priori* examination might offer a means of avoiding mistakes and therefore save public money.[97]

In the case of Value For Money (VFM) examinations, these are **11–62** potentially more far-reaching means of accounting.[98] Section 6 of the 1983 Act provides a statutory basis for VFM examinations at the discretion of the C&AG. Included within this jurisdiction are government departments and other public bodies where the C&AG has statutory rights of inspection or where he is the statutory auditor. VFM audit is not extended to the nationalised industries.[99] For many years the Committee of Public Accounts (PAC) encouraged the C&AG to examine expenditure and receipts in departments and to bring to the notice of Parliament weakness in the system which appeared "to involve imprudent, uneconomical or extravagant expenditure or waste."[1] The 1983 Act placed such examinations on a statutory basis. However the Act makes an important proviso that VFM examination shall not be construed as entitling the C&AG to question the merits of the policy objectives of the department or body concerned.

---

[95] Government Accounting, para. 7.1.17–7.1.19.

[96] *ibid.*, para. 7.1.19.

[97] C. Graham and T. Prosser, *Privatizing Public Enterprises* (Oxford, 1991), pp. 59–64.

[98] Generally see P. Anand, "Monitoring and Auditing Value for Money in the UK: The Scope for Quantitative Analysis, Financial Accountability and Management" (Winter 1988), pp. 253–270 and M. Grimwood and C. Tomkins, "Value for Money Auditing—Towards Incorporating a Nationalistic Approach, Financial Accountability and Management (Winter 1986), pp. 251–272. Both articles have led to an intense academic debate: Anand, "Monitoring and Auditing Value for Money in the UK: The scope for Quantitative Analysis—A Reply (1989) Financial Accountability and Management" 191–195; "A comment" by Tomkins 185–189. Generally see Control of Public Expenditure: Plowden Report on the Machinery of Government Cmnd 1432 (London HMSO, 1961); *Report by the Comptroller and Auditor General* (April, 1987).

[99] E. L. Normanton, "Reform in the Field of Public Accountability and Audit: a Progress Report" (1980) 51 *Political Quarterly*, 175–99.

[1] *Government Accountancy*, para. 7.1.20.

11–63   Privatisation sales have gradually become an important source of revenue for the Exchequer.[2] The early sales of shares in Companies such as B.P., Amersham International, Cable and Wireless yielded small amounts in revenue. Later privatisations such as British Telecom, British Gas and the Water Companies have increased the net receipts to the Exchequer to sums in excess of £30 bn.[3]

11–64   Privatisation has posed new challenges for the National Audit Office, to ensure for taxpayers good value for the assets sold.[4] The NAO is the first national audit institution faced with the challenge of privatisation sales of such variety, complexity and undertaken in such a short time.[5] Some of the most important VFM studies have been into the major privatisations and are carried out at the C&AG's discretion. They are subject to the important restraint that the merits of the policy is outside the jurisdiction of the C&AG. Thus the government's decision to privatise an industry cannot be questioned as a matter of policy. This point is explained by Beauchamp[6]:

"Thus the Government's decision to privatise an industry in a particular way and the objective set for that exercise, are not open

[2] Major privatisations include: Department of Trade & Industry: Sale of Government Shareholding in British Telecommunications plc (1984/85; H.C. 495). Department of Energy, Trade & Industry & Transport: Sales of Subsidiary Companies and other assets by Nationalised Industries. (1984/85; H.C. 162). Department of Transport, Trade & Industry & Energy: Monitoring and control of investment by the Nationalised Industries in fixed assets (1984/85; H.C. 284). Report by the C&AG: Ministry of Defence: Incorporation of the Royal Ordnance Factories (1984/85; H.C. 343). Department of Transport: Sale of Government Shareholding in BAA plc (1987/88; H.C. 312). Department of Transport: Sale of Government Shareholding in British Airways plc (1987/88; H.C. 37). Department of the Environment: Disposal of New Town Assets (1986/87; H.C. 76). Department of Energy: Sale of Government Shareholding in British Gas plc (1987/88; H.C. 22). Department of Trade & Industry: Sale of Government Shareholding in Rolls Royce plc (1987/88; H.C. 243). Ministry of Defence: Sale of Royal Ordnance plc (1987/88; H.C. 162). Ministry of Defence: Transfer of the Royal Dockyards to Commercial Management (1987/88; HC 359). Ministry of Defence: Further Examination of the Sale of Royal Ordnance plc (1988/89; H.C. 448). Department of Transport: Sale of the National Bus Companies (1989/90; H.C. 43). Department of Trade & Industry: Sale of Rover Group plc to British Aerospace plc (1990/91; H.C. 9). Department of Energy: Sale of the Twelve Regional Electricity Companies (1991/92; H.C. 10). Department of Energy: Sale of National Power and Power Gen (1991/92; H.C. 46). The sale of the second tranche of shares in British Telecommunications plc (1992/93; H.C. 568) The Office of Telecommunications (1992/93; H.C. 529).

[3] Hansard, H.C. Debs. cols. 357–360, April 27, 1990. The Prime Minister Stated: "Twenty-nine major businesses have been privatised and around 800,000 jobs have been transferred to the private sector. Receipts so far amount to some £27.5 billion with future sales projected at a rate of about £5 billion a year."

[4] J. F. McEldowney, "The National Audit Office and Privatisation" (1991) M.L.R. 933–55.

[5] Chris Beauchamp "National Audit Office: its Role in Privatisation" (1990) Public Money and Management 55–58. Hereinafter Beauchamp. A Framework for Value for Money Audits (National Audit Office).

[6] Beauchamp, op. cit. p. 58.

to question. We, therefore, have to review how sponsor departments implement the agreed policy and consider whether they are successful in achieving the objectives for the sale."

Aside from restraints on policy questions, VFM audit of privatisation **11–65** is restricted by the fact that the NAO does not have a statutory right of access to the papers and documents of the Nationalised Industries. The NAO's VFM examination of a privatisation sale is, in common with the accounting audit, discussed above, departmental led. Thus section 8 of the 1983 Act gives free access to the books of accounts of departments and "other documents relating to the accounts for the purpose of audit."[7] In privatisation sales the C&AG is restricted to the documents provided to the sponsoring Department by the industry due to be privatised. Voluntary co-operation may be given of the newly privatised company to a request for information from the C&AG. In the case of VFM examinations the C&AG's statutory right to access is at all reasonable times "to all documents which he may reasonably require," provided the documents are under the custody or control of the department concerned. The term "documents" includes correspondence and minutes held on files and working papers relevant to VFM examinations. Normally it has not been the practice for the C&AG to be given access to Cabinet or Cabinet committee papers or minutes. A request for access is referred to the Cabinet Office. Beauchamp explains how the NAO carry out their tasks[8]:

"In carrying out VFM examinations of privatisations the NAO's main information comes from our departmental files, investigations have to concentrate on the papers of the sponsoring departments, the information and advice they require and the decisions resulting from that advice.[9]

This raises an important question about how the independence of **11–66** the NAO co-exists with a working relationship with government departments? The NAO provides an external audit of government expenditure and is accountable to Parliament. To provide an effective scrutiny the NAO depends on co-operation between government departments and officials. In fact, before embarking on a major VFM examination the timing and scope of the examination is discussed by the NAO and the staff in the sponsoring departments engaged in the privatisation sales. It is a common procedure that once the examination findings and conclusions are resolved they are normally set out

[7] *Government Accountancy*, para. 7.1.29.
[8] *ibid.* para. 7.1.30.
[9] Beauchamp, *op. cit.* p. 55.

in a draft report. The draft report is sent to the Accounting Officer of the relevant government department to enable him to comment on its accuracy, the finding of the facts and presentation.[10] In that way there is an important link between the internal audit of government carried out by Accounting Officers and the external VFM examination provided by the NAO.[11] In carrying out VFM examinations the C&AG may expect that the Accounting Officer will appear before the PAC covering expenditure and receipts in the votes. The Accounting Officer is expected to furnish the PAC with explanations of any indications of weakness in policy to which the C&AG has pointed out in his report.

11–67 Section 6 of the National Audit Act 1983 provides the statutory authority for the NAO to carry out Value for Money examinations of departmental activities. The 1983 Act simply defines such examinations in terms of "economy, efficiency and effectiveness." As the words are contained in a statute it might be assumed that they carry a precise legal meaning and certainly a court might be called upon to give legal effect to the phrase. In the example of privatisation sales, their size and scale posed a challenge to sponsoring departments and their relationship with the NAO. At least 20 per cent of NAO staff and consultants are engaged in VFM examinations which is a significant proportion of its activity.[12]

11–68 Evaluating efficiency and effectiveness is a common theme in recent years[18] in the development of government policy objectives. It has become commonplace that government borrows techniques, methods and objectives from business or commerce. How to measure efficiency and effectiveness is the key issue and evaluation may be as difficult as setting the objectives in the first place. In 1981 the Treasury and Civil Service Committee in its Report on Efficiency and Effectiveness set out some criteria for evaluating efficiency and effectiveness.[14] The criteria include clarifying the intention of the programme, setting *objectives* which are quantified as targets. Objectives may be assessed in terms of *output*. An *efficient* programme is one where the target is achieved with the least use of resources and instruments for change. An *effective* programme is one where the intention of the programme is being achieved. This means that the

---

[10] *Government Accountancy*, para. 6.1.5.
[11] *Memorandum* note 33 on pp. 12–17.
[12] Annual Report of the Comptroller and Auditor General 1989/90.
[13] See *The Reorganisation of Central Government*, Cmnd. 4506 (1970); *Financial Management in Government Departments*, Cmnd. 9058 (1983) and *Progress in Financial Management in Government Departments*, Cmnd. 9297 (1984).
[14] Report of the Treasury and Civil Service Committee, *Efficiency and Effectiveness in the Civil Service* (H.C. 236). Also see *Helping Managers Manage*, Report of the Cabinet Office Efficiency Unit (1984).

intention is contained in operational objectives which are set as defined targets. Thus the output of the programme is equal to the target set. In this way an effective and efficient programme may be evaluated.

Such criteria are similar to those in use within the NAO in carrying **11-69** out a VFM examination. This is defined to mean economy, efficiency and effectiveness which the NAO explain as follows[15]:

"Economy is concerned with minimising the cost of resources acquired with regard to appropriate quality.

Efficiency is concerned with the relationship between output of goods, services or other results and the resources used.

Effectiveness is concerned with the relationship between intended results and the actual results of targets."

The NAO has developed[16] VFM strategies which emphasise the avoidance of waste, the setting of clearly defined policy objectives and obtaining good value for the tax-payers. There is a duty on government departments to consider the NAO's reports and the PAC recommendations and to provide replies to the House of Commons on matters raised in the reports.[17] VFM examinations would seem to be a blend of conventional auditing skills with management consulting techniques. The former benefits from a degree of independence and objectivity and the ascertaining of facts through the skills of an auditor. The latter draws on the analytical skills of the management consultant.[18] In contrast to ordinary certification auditing, VFM takes the opportunity to understand the effects of policy and whether those effects relate to the intention behind the policy. The NAO's experience has increased given the large number of VFM studies[19] since 1983. Particularly difficult to categorise is the distinction to be drawn between the implementation of policy, a legitimate concern of VFM, and the merits of policy which is outside the jurisdiction of the NAO. A criticism levied at all public sector VFM examinations is that put forward by Butt and Palmer namely[20]:

---

[15] See Report of the National Audit Office, *A Framework for Value for Money Audits*, Minute on the First Four Reports from the Committee of Public Accounts (1985/86) (Cmd. 9755), paras. 21–23; Cmnd. 8413, para. 87.

[16] A. Hopwood, "Accounting and the Pursuit of Efficiency," Chap. 9 in A. Hopwood, C. Tomkins, *Issues in Public Sector Accounting* (1984).

[17] *Government Accounting*, paras. 7.1.38–7.1.40.

[18] See Price Waterhouse, *Value for Money Auditing Manual* (1983).

[19] Prosser and Graham *op. cit.* p. 62; H. Butt and D. Robert Palmer, *Value for Money in the Public Sector* (1985), pp. 19–20. Also see J. Perrin, "Accounting for Public Sector Assets" in Hopwood and Tomkins, *Issues in Public Sector Accounting and Financial Control* (1983). See Criticisms of the NAO, "The National Audit Office: The First Twelve Reports" in 4 *Public Money* 35–39 and G. Downey, "National Audit Office Reports" 6 *Public Money* 10–11.

[20] Butt and Palmer, *op. cit.* pp. 19–20.

"Many barriers must be overcome in order to achieve VFM. These include politics, weak governing bodies, tradition, lack of motivation and lack of education and training programmes. There is conflict that all politicians face; that is, the trade-off between constituency interests and national priorities. These may often not be the same and as, presumably, the politician wishes future re-election, his opinions may, not unnaturally be biased."

Given its present remit it is clearly impossible for the NAO to move so broadly in the direction of assessing the merits of policy even where this may be indicated by their examination. The *ex post facto* nature of this examination has the benefit of hindsight but this may make it difficult to evaluate all the pressures experienced by a sponsoring department.[21] Generally, the NAO has concluded that based on its VFM examination "privatisations have generally been well conducted and that departments have taken due note of lessons learned from earlier sales."[22]

11–70 In carrying out VFM examinations of privatisation sales the NAO's reports have followed a common pattern. Three areas in particular have been highlighted as giving cause for concern to the PAC in their response to the NAO reports. The three areas are: preparation for sale, the methods of sale and pricing and the cost of sales. The approach followed in the VFM examination emphasises the objectives set by the department in arranging a sale and whether those objectives have been achieved. In some instances the NAO admit to having difficulty in making judgments on how arrangements could have been improved.

In their VFM studies the NAO have had difficulties in setting guidance to meet problems such as the difficulty of predicting share price movements, the need to discount shares to encourage investment, and balancing the interests of encouraging a greater amount of share ownership set against the needs of tax payers, to see an adequate return on the sale.

11–71 The NAO reports into VFM examination of privatisation sales have laid the foundation for a number of recommendations from the PAC which have generally been welcomed by the relevant government department and the Treasury. The experience of past privatisations has been a useful learning process. Departments have built into their early preparations for sales the use of external advisers. This has been of assistance in assessing the value of the company to be privatised and the share price to be offered. In cases where there is a risk that land or assets which may subsequently realise a large profit for the

---

[21] *ibid.*
[22] Beauchamp, *op. cit.* p. 57.

seller over the price when they were sold as part of the existing business, departments are aware of the advantage to be gained of using a "claw back agreement" to secure a more adequate return for the tax payers over the privatisation sale.[23]

The introduction of greater competition among underwriters in **11–72** terms of commission charges has also proved a useful way to avoid past mistakes of inflated underwriting costs. Share incentives are given closer scrutiny to ensure that there is an adequate return for the tax-payer, thus avoiding excessive windfall profits.

Despite these achievements there are two areas where the NAO has still to make much impact on the arrangements for privatisation. The first is over the choice of sale method by the department and the second is the problem of after sales increases in share values. In both cases the NAO has given little guidance as to how matters might be improved. Admittedly both problems are difficult to predict in advance of the sale. The rise and fall of the stock market makes a solution difficult especially as there may be some uncertainty over the success of the sales. The main criticism of the NAO is that more detailed analysis contained in the VFM examinations might assist departments as to how best to avoid the obvious pitfalls in preparing for sales.

The general role of the NAO in the development of VFM examina- **11–73** tions of central government departments has received some critical reviews. The most fundamental criticism is that the NAO has failed to set out future directions which should be followed by departments. It is pointed out that in the NAO's role in developing efficiency and effectiveness one handicap has been the basic accounting systems of Government departments. It is said that the NAO may find the data provided by a focus on departmental accounts inadequate to the task of VFM examinations. This criticism has to some extent been over-taken by the changes introduced in the late 1980s with the prepara-tion of departmental spending White Papers[24] at the same time as the departmental estimates submitted before the budget. The introduc-tion of FMI programmes and efficiency studies has alerted depart-ments to the need for more accountable management. But it is clear from the NAO's own reports of the introduction of FMI and Rayner efficiency studies that departments adopt different approaches to the introduction of management initiatives. The Government's efficiency strategy has not exacted a uniform response from government departments which has led to unevenness in the implementation of the procedures for accountable management.[25]

---

[23] Beauchamp, *op. cit.* pp. 57–58.

[24] See Elliott, *op. cit.* pp. 174–175. A. Likierman, *Public Expenditure* (1988), pp. 74–79.

[25] Report of the NAO, *The Financial Management Initiative* 1986 (1985/86; H.C. 588). Also see Thirteenth Report from the PAC, *The Financial Management Initiative* (1986/87; H.C. 61), paras. 20, 43. See Fry, Flynn and others, "Symposium on Improving Management in Government" (1988) 66 *Public Administration* 429–445.

11–74   It is clear, therefore, that the NAO may find it difficult to set down directions for future privatisation when departments adopt differing approaches to the various government efficiency strategies. The NAO's remit is narrowly drawn to exclude interfering in questions of politics or the merits of policy. In the case of the Rayner efficiency studies not all recommendations were accepted by Ministers and some may be in conflict with government policies. Nevertheless the directions which the NAO may prefer departments to adopt for privatisation sales and which might form a future strategy, are far from clear. Graham and Prosser make the criticism that:

> ". . . Scrutiny of [privatisation sales] by the National Audit Office and the Public Accounts Committee has been patchy and has had little effect in producing any long term improvements; for example, no government guide-lines existed on the conduct of private sales at the end of 1989, despite the critical reports referred to above . . . ."[26]

The NAO has issued principles and guidelines in respect of two areas of activity: The Selection and Use of Management Consultants[27] and the Audit of Management Buyouts in the Public Sector.[28] The question arises as to whether the NAO might issue a code of principles or guidelines for departments for future privatisation sales.

11–75   The arguments in favour are, that guidance of the type contained in the two reports, mentioned above, transforms an exclusive *ex post facto* review which the NAO presently offers into an *a priori* review. The sponsoring department confronted with a list of issues to be addressed would in effect be self-regulatory in implementing the guidance compiled by the NAO. This might facilitate the *ex post facto* review undertaken by the NAO once the privatisation sale is completed. It might avoid past mistakes and bring departmental thinking into line with the NAO's preferred strategies. In that way VFM objectives might guarantee better value for the taxpayer.

The arguments against, are that no two privatisations are the same; that it may be impossible to predict the *precise* area of weakness in a department's strategy for the sale until the sale is completed. The wrong signal might be given to the sponsoring department over the role of the NAO. Departmental second guessing of the NAO's own strategy may bring the NAO into conflict with ministerial priorities or policies.

---

[26] Graham and Prosser, *op. cit.*, p. 129.
[27] Report of the NAO, *Selection and Use of Management Consultants* (1989).
[28] Report of the NAO, *Audit and Management Buyouts in the Public Sector* (1991).

On balance it would seem that unless the NAO's constitutional **11–76** remit as explained above were to be broadened beyond the departmental focus, it is difficult to see how guidance over future privatisations might be possible. The NAO's expertise may not extend to the area of the privatisation sale with the obvious limitations this may have on any attempt to set out in a strategy document, guide-lines for the future. The calamity of a department which followed the NAO's guide-lines only to discover that in the end an unsuccessful privatisation sale resulted, would have repercussions on the credibility of the NAO itself. That risk may be too great for the NAO to take.

This last argument raises an issue as to the usefulness of VFM **11–77** examinations. John Glynn has argued that the role of auditors advanced today by some commentators may exceed any realistic expectation of what auditing techniques may achieve. In general terms, he argues that:

> "At present the auditing profession cannot deliver fully on its VFM mandates. This is partially due to the fact that the auditors role is evolving in response to changing public needs and expectations ... The major inhibiting factor ... is the lack of a political will to reform the general framework of financial management, and to define more clearly the scope of programme objectives."[29]

The difficult combination of management techniques and political choices is precisely the challenge facing the NAO in its future direction for VFM examinations. Ministers set policies and define political choices in terms of electoral mandate and party support. Managerial techniques of evaluating economy, efficiency and effectiveness developed by the NAO will always require careful consideration to take account of the political choices set by politicians. This is despite the fact that the NAO may not question the merits of policy decisions. In the final analysis, Ministers are accountable to Parliament and ultimately the electorate for such policies. The present constitutional status and independence of the NAO under the C&AG, acts as a restraint on any policy review which encroaches on ministerial accountability.

In the aftermath of privatisation there remain the new regulatory **11–78** bodies which fall under the remit of the NAO. These include gas, (OFGAS), water (OFWAT), electricity (OFFER), and telecommunications (OFTEL). The C&AG admitted that the NAO's responsibility to audit such bodies poses a fresh challenge:

---

[29] See Glynn, *op. cit.* pp. 119–20.

"How does one address and consider the performance of regulatory agencies? That will be an area that will be carving out new territory. Not much has been done on it."[30]

11–79 In July 1996, the National Audit Office produced one of the most important reviews examining the work of the Directors of Telecommunications, Gas Supply, Water Service and Electricity Supply.[31] The report is well produced and contains impressive details on the work of the regulators. There is a detailed and comprehensive questionnaire, an explanation of their powers and functions and the aims and objectives of regulation over the next five years. There is a useful summary of current issues and future trends. This marks an important beginning in the development of the NAO's role in monitoring the regulators. There are some fundamental issues which arise from the NAO's experience of VFM studies to date. How valuable are VFM examinations in the development of public sector accounting?

11–80 Doubts have been raised about the contribution of VFM examinations. The main criticism is that VFM examinations have concentrated too heavily on "economy and efficiency" rather than effectiveness. The questions raised about "effectiveness" are linked to the ability of auditors to perceive and quantify the link between intentions and outcomes of decisions within government. Given the complexity of decision-making, it is thought that it is often difficult to quantify and assess the intention behind decisions and their outcome. Some scepticism is raised as to the ability of auditors to assess decisions within government as not every decision is the result of explicit planning. Objectives may not always be clearly defined or prioritised. There may be conflicting aims in the objectives set. There is also concern that not all departmental files are available to the NAO. Press coverage has highlighted non-disclosure of information relating to aid from the Overseas Aid Administration to build the Pergau dam scheme in Malaysia.[32]

11–81 Some of the general doubts raised by VFM examinations in the public sector have arisen from the analysis of VFM studies undertaken by the Audit Commission. This is the only other statutory body required to carry out VFM examinations. The Audit Commission was set up under the Local Government Finance Act 1982 and it covers the traditional financial audit of local authorities. Section 15 of the 1982 Act requires the Commission to carry out VFM Audit and

---

[30] Fourth Report of the Public Accounts Committee (1988; H.C., November 4, 1988). See one of the first reports in the work of a regulator set up after privatisation: *The Office of Telecommunications* (1992/93; H.C. 529) (NAO).

[31] National Audit Office (1995/6; H.C. 645). *The Work of the Directors of Telecommunications, Gas Supply, Water Service and Electricity Supply.*

[32] *The Independent,* January 25, 1994.

section 14 requires it to keep under review at five yearly intervals, a code of audit practice. The Audit Commission has had an important and successful impact on the management culture of local authorities.[33] The desire for techniques to control public expenditure has encouraged public sector accounting to grow in significance.

Finally some mention should be made of the Court of Auditors of **11-82** the European Communities. This is a body set up in June 1977, after the implementation of the Treaty of Brussels of July 1975. Independent from other European Community (E.C.) institutions, its remit applies only to E.C. public funds. The Court of Auditors assesses the legality and quality of the management of public funds. The work of the Court emphasises the European and international development of public sector auditing.[34]

5. The Courts

The courts have accepted Parliament's role in the matter of financial **11-83** control. Viscount Haldane in *Auckland Harbour Board v. The King*,[35] a Privy Council case, noted that payments out of the Consolidated Fund without parliamentary authority were illegal. Direct challenges to central government on constitutional issues raised by public expenditure issues are not commonplace. The major disputes involving public finance arise on the supply side involving issues of taxation. However there are cases which do raise issues which may indirectly affect public spending. For example in *Metzger and others v. Department of Health and Social Security*[36] the duty of the Secretary of State for Social Services to carry out reviews of the rates of pension payable under the Social Security Act 1975, was considered and the cost of uprating pension benfits ascertained. The impact on public expenditure was large if the court decided to grant a declaration which it refused.[37] The role of the courts generally in decisions on public expenditure of central government has been minimal. This is in contrast to the audit of local authorities in cases such as *Roberts v.*

---

[33] B. McSweeney, "Accounting for the Audit Commission" (1988) 59 *The Political Quarterly* 28–43, p. 42. See Audit Commission, *Handbook on Economy, Efficiency and Effectiveness* (1983).

[34] D. O'Keefe, "The Court of Auditors" (unpublished, 1992); Price, "The Court of Auditors of the European Communities," (1982) *Yearbook of European Law*, pp. 239–48, 6th Report, House of Lords Select Committee on the European Communities (1986–87; H.L. 102) *Court of Auditors*.

[35] [1925] A.C. 318, 326.

[36] [1977] 3 All E.R. 444.

[37] Elliott calculated the cost to be £500m.

Hopwood[38] or more recently in *Hazell v. Hammersmith*,[39] where the House of Lords considered the investment powers of local authorities in the swop markets.

11–84   In *Bromley v. Greater London Council*[40] the concept of fiduciary duty was developed and extended to apply to the duty owed by a local authority to its ratepayers. The case involved the now defunct Greater London Council and its policy of providing cheap fares for London Transport. Having regard to the term "economic" in sections 1 and 5 of the Transport (London) Act 1969, the House of Lords held that the GLC was not empowered to adopt a fares policy unduly beneficial to transport users at a cost to ratepayers in London. The interpretation of "economic" involved careful judicial consideration of the benefits and costs involved.

11–85   The scope for such judicial intervention, as has been shown with the local authority cases, is very wide. For example in the expression "economy, efficiency and effectiveness" the National Audit Act is silent as to the exact meaning of the terms used in the phrase and to date no court has given a legal definition of the phrase. The result is that although many judicial elements, which were the hallmark of the early history of public audit, remain, there has been little modern judicial creativity in this area. Elliott[41] noted that judicial characteristics may be found in "the proceedings of the Public Accounts Committee and the duties of the Comptroller and Auditor General are judicial in form."[42] But Elliott also noted that[43]:

> "while the courts have been constantly creative in developing techniques and methodologies for submitting claims of a power to tax and the scope of a tax to detailed scrutiny. But on the expenditure side there has been little modern judicial creativity."

The absence of any active judicial intervention in this area leaves the C&AG with the discretion both as to how to carry out VFM examinations and when to embark on such an examination. The law merely defines the broad terms of reference of his inquiries by setting a legal framework. A decision to carry out VFM examinations of privatisation sales is made by the C&AG.

---

[38] [1925] A.C. 578.
[39] [1991] 1 All E.R. 545. But see *Bromley CBC v. GLC* [1983] 1 A.C. 768 on the meaning of "economic." See Loughlin, "Innovative Financing in Local Government: The Limits of Legal Instrumentation – Part I" (1990) P.L. 372–405. Also C. Holtham "Local Government: Internal Control and External Reporting" in D. Henley *et al.* (eds.), *Public Sector Accounting and Financial Control* (1983).
[40] [1982] 1 A.C. 768.
[41] See M. Elliott, "The Control of Public Expenditure" in J. Jowell and D. Oliver, *The Changing Constitution* (Oxford, 1989), pp. 165–191.
[42] *ibid.,* pp. 168–169.
[43] *ibid.,* p. 169.

One of the most significant cases in recent years is *R v. Secretary of* **11–86**
State for Foreign Affairs, ex p. World Development Movement.[44] The
World Development Movement, a well known and internationally
recognised pressure group, sought judicial review to challenge the
decision by the Foreign Secretary to make a payment of aid under the
Overseas Development and Co-operation Act 1980 to the Malaysian
government. The case is an important authority on the law of
standing, but it is also an important case on the question of financial
authority. In granting standing the factors that weighed heavily with
the court were the necessity to uphold the rule of law, the nature of
the breach of the duty complained about and the importance of aid.[45]

The Divisional Court found that the grant of aid for the Pergau
Dam project was economically unsound. It therefore did not satisfy
the criteria set out in section 1 of the 1980 Act and it was therefore
unlawful. A declaration was granted that the grant was unlawful. In
reaching this conclusion Lord Justice Rose considered the proceedings of the Public Accounts Committee and the findings of a National
Audit Office scrutiny. Clearly the case provides a good example of
the range of judicial review today that includes an evaluation of the
economic as distinct from the political and social merits of decisions.
A powerful tool in the hands of the litigant is the work of the various
parliamentary watch-dogs such as the Committee of Public Accounts.

6. New Proposals

Financial reporting to Parliament has undergone intense debate[46] over **11–87**
the past 10 years. Reports from the Committee of Public Accounts[47]
and from the Treasury and Civil Service Committee[48] have resulted in

---

[44] [1995] 1 All E.R. 615.

[45] I am very grateful to George Mézsaros for his help and advice in making available to
me a copy of the bundle of materials used by the applicants in the case.

[46] See Report of the Comptroller and Auditor General, *Financial Reporting to Parliament*
(1985/86 H.C. 576).

[47] There are also various reports from the Committee of Public Accounts: *Financial
Reporting to Parliament* 8th Report (1986/87 H.C. 98); *Financial Reporting to Parliament*
18th Report (1988/89 H.C. 354); *Central Funds and Accountability and the Exchange
Equalisation Account* 8th Report (1989/90 H.C. 267); *Financial Reporting to Parliament:
Changes in the Format of the Supply Estimates* 25th Report (1993/94 H.C. 386); *Resource
Accounting and Budgeting in Government* 15th Report (1994/5 H.C. 407).

[48] There are various Treasury and Civil Service Committee Reports: *The Form of the
Estimates* 6th Report (1980/81 H.C. 325); *Efficiency and Effectiveness in the Civil Service*
3rd Report (1981/82 H.C. 236); *The Structure and Form of Financial Documents
Presented to Parliament* 2nd, 7th and 10th Reports (1984/85 H.C. 110, 322, & 544);
Financial Reporting to Parliament 6th Report (1987/88 H.C. 614); *The Form of the
Estimates: The Government's Response to the Third Report from the Committee* 3rd Report
of (1993/94 H.C. 192); 3rd Special Report (1993/94 H.C. 441); *Simplified Estimates and
Resource Accounting* 4th Report (1994/95 H.C. 212).

a debate about any changes to the presentation of the estimates and the desire to see improvements in the information available to Parliament on the aims and objectives of departmental expenditure.[49] In July 1994 the Treasury published a Green paper[50] *Better Accounting for the Taxpayer's Money: Resource Accounting and Budgeting in Government* which contains far-reaching proposals for the introduction of accrual based resource accounts to supplement current cash based accounts. There are also proposals from the Treasury to revise the format of the estimates[51] as part of the Treasury's on-going Fundamental Expenditure Review. This is intended to provide more effective controls over public expenditure. These proposals have been considered by both the Committee of Public Accounts and the Treasury and Civil Service Committee.[52] Consideration of the most effective means of providing financial information for Parliament is not confined to the United Kingdom. There is also a similar and important comparative analysis being undertaken of the New Zealand system of financial reporting and budgeting.[53]

Against this background, it is necessary to consider resource accounting and the implications of its introduction for the current system of financial reporting to Parliament. The United Kingdom is currently considering the introduction of resource or accrual accounting to replace the current system of cash budgeting. Resource accounting is proposed to take effect from 1999–2000 and is currently under review by Government following the Treasury's paper[54] of July 1994. The recent National Audit Office Report[55] on *Resource Accounting and Budgeting* noted:

"The Government's proposals represent the most important reform of central government accounting and budgeting arrangements since Gladstone's reforms of the mid-19th century."

[49] See Appendix A, NAO Report, *Resource Accounting and Budgeting in Government* (1994/95 H.C. 123).

[50] Cm. 2626.

[51] Memorandum submitted by the Treasury to the Treasury and Civil Service Committee in the Treasury and Civil Service Committee 3rd Report (1993/94 H.C. 192), minutes of evidence pp. 1–2.

[52] See the Treasury and Civil Service Committee 3rd Report (1993/94; H.C. 192); 3rd Special Report (1993/94 H.C. 441), and see the Public Accounts Committee, *Financial Reporting to Parliament: Changes in the Format of the Supply Estimates* 25th Report (1993/94 H.C. 386), *Resource Accounting and Budgeting in Government* 15th Report (1994/5 H.C. 407).

[53] See for example New Zealand Fiscal Responsibility Act 1994 No. 17.

[54] Cm. 2626 *Better Accounting for the Taxpayer's Money* (HMSO, 1994).

[55] NAO Report, *Resource Accounting and Budgeting in Government* (1994/95 H.C. 123) para. 3.

(a)   Resource Accounting

It is necessary to define and explain the context for the introduction **11–88**
of resource or accrual accounting. Initiatives to improve the management of public expenditure have already been noted above. The
Financial Management Initiative in 1982 began a process that has now
included accrual or resource accounting.[56] The 1995 NAO report[57]
usefully defines resource accounting as involving two elements:

- a set of accruals-based techniques for accounting and reporting
  on the expenditure of United Kingdom central government;
  and
- a framework for analysing expenditure by departmental objectives, related to outputs wherever possible.

Currently, cash based accounts provide the main method for
government accounting. Under current arrangements there is no
requirement to match expenditure with revenues for the period to
which they relate. There is no framework for the valuation of assets
and liabilities. Capital spending is made to account wholly in the year
in which the capital purchase or disposal is made. In contrast it is
argued that accruals accounting makes up for these deficiencies. The
NAO report summarises the main benefits of accruals accounting
over the existing cash accounting system:

- accruals accounting records expenditure and income in
  accounting period to which they relate;
- accruals accounting spreads the cost of capital items across
  their useful lives;
- accruals accounting provides a detailed snapshot of the assets,
  liabilities and net worth of an organisation at a given moment
  of time and through a Balance Sheet provides a better picture
  of the true cost of departments' activities;
- accruals accounting is intended to increase information and
  detailed inventories of departmental holdings, deployment and
  stewardship of assets.

Resource accounting based on an accruals accounting system is **11–89**
intended to match more closely resources used to departmental
objectives. The outputs of departmental activities can then be used to

---

[56] See A. Likierman, D. Heald, G. Georgiou and M. Wright, "Resource Accounting and
Budgeting: A Symposium" (1995) Vol 73 (Winter) *Public Administration* pp. 561–70.
[57] NAO Report, *Resource Accounting and Budgeting in Government* (1994/95 H.C. 123)
para. 10.

measure departmental achievements. It is intended that departments will in future provide a schedule showing the true cost of resources consumed and a schedule measuring output performance against each main objective. Introducing such a system will depend on the adoption of the United Kingdom Generally Accepted Accounting Practice[58] supplemented by specific requirements developed for departmental accounts. It is not intended to include non-departmental bodies within resource accounting although account will have to be taken of the Agencies as part of the objectives and inputs from the sponsoring department.

(b) The European and international dimension

11–90 New Zealand is the only country to have recently introduced accruals based or resource budgeting. In many European countries, such as Finland, Spain and Sweden, consideration of adopting an accrual accounting system is underway[59] for the central budget. There are also similar developments in the United States, Australia and Canada. The motives for introducing such a form of accounting Likierman and others have noted comes from a general desire for improvements to the management of the public sector.[60] Linking inputs to outputs which is a common feature of many budgetary systems, including the United Kingdom's is more effectively achieved through an accrual system of accounting than through cash accounting. The International Federation of Accountants in their 1993 report noted that accrual accounting was the most appropriate for reporting on cost efficiencies and cost recoveries and on the resources controlled.[61] The claims for a resource based accounting system include the provision of better information. It is also assumed that this may lead to a more strategic approach to budgeting and therefore the better management of public funds.

(c) Time-table for the introduction of accrual accounting in the United Kingdom

11–91 The time-table for the implementation of resource accounting is set out in the Green Paper as follows:

---

[58] This is defined as the accounting standards required of the Companies Act 1985 and the accounting standards set by the Accounting Standards Board.
[59] See E. Buschor and K. Schedler (eds.), *Perspectives on performance measurement and public sector accounting* (Berne Haupt, 1994). Also K. Luder, *Harmonisation of governmental accounting and financial reporting* (Speyerer Arbeitschefte 85, Speyer, 1989).
[60] Likierman and others, *loc. cit.* fn 37, p. 567.
[61] IFAC, *Elements of the Financial Statements of National Governments Study 2* (IFAC, New York, 1993).

- Implementation in the majority of departments by April 1, 1997 and in all departments by April 1, 1998;
- Resource accounts to be laid before Parliament 1999–2000;
- First survey on a resource basis will be carried out in 2000;
- New estimates based on resource accounting to be presented to Parliament 2001–02.

The introduction of departmental resource accounting has implications for the way financial reporting to Parliament is undertaken. The Green Paper acknowledges that parliamentary approval for a new form of estimates will have to be agreed. It is proposed that departmental resource accounts should include five statements and supporting information:

- three standard financial statements which include information such as operating costs, balance sheet and cash flow statements. The three statements will be known as schedules A–C.
- two supplementary statements. One will contain an objectives analysis of departmental activities to be known as schedule D and the other to contain an output performance analysis to be known as schedule E. Schedule D will be compulsory while schedule E will be optional but desirable.

Such accounts will be audited and it is envisaged that this obligation will be carried out by the Comptroller and Auditor General as Parliament's auditor. It is intended that resource budgeting will also be introduced into the Public Expenditure Survey and play a key role in how public expenditure is planned and controlled.

At the time of writing the implications of resource budgeting for **11–92** financial reporting to Parliament have not been fully considered by the Government, the Treasury or Parliament. What follows is therefore tentative. It is accepted in the NAO report that changes will be required to the legislation relating to Supply procedures and the Estimates and Appropriation Accounts. There are a number of further questions that will require consideration for the future.

Will resource accounting preserve parliamentary control and authority? Current Treasury proposals for simplified Estimates envisage that departments would only need to obtain Treasury approval to *vire* provisions between Estimates at a higher level than at present. Currently virement is required between subheads but under Treasury proposals for simplified Estimates virement would only be necessary at the level of Estimates lines, broadly equivalent to sections in the current Estimates.

Currently there are roughly 130 votes with large departments having more than one vote. Treasury proposals for simplified Estimates are to reduce the number of votes to about 60. This will have the effect of giving departments greater freedom than at present to manage within their voted totals. Treasury proposals for simplified Estimates will relieve departments of the need to seek Treasury approval for virement in many circumstances where current arrangements require such approval. This will have the effect of giving departments greater discretion and contol over the management of their resources.

If the treasury proposals are taken together they might result in Parliament appearing to have less opportunity to exercise authority through a reduced number of votes. Correspondingly, departments will have more authority to manage their own resources and have less need to require Treasury authority over virement powers.

11–93   Will resource accounting preserve the principle that voted sums cannot be exceeded? How will the introduction of resource accounting preserve the principle that there is a set limit to the resources or cash authorised by Parliament? Currently in cases where more expenditure is required the principle that further authority should first be obtained from Parliament is rigidly observed. Thus, departments cannot raise or dispose of large sums without parliamentary authority. How will this principle be addressed under resource accounting?

11–94   Will resource accounting preserve the principle of annuality, namely that the sums authorised by Parliament are only available in the financial year in which they are appropriated? The principle of annuality is to ensure that the sums voted by Parliament are only available in the financial year for which they are voted. The Estimates reflect this principle as they show cash sums that are to be applied in the year to which they relate. Although the principle of annuality has been diluted over the past 10 years, since 1983 the Treasury have approved some schemes for long-term projects that allow departments to carry over under spent money, these arrangements have been considered as part of parliamentary authority to include in subsequent years' Estimates any amount of the money carried over. The question arises as to whether the introduction of resource accounting will allow continuity of the annuality principle?

11–95   Will resource accounting allow parliament greater transparency over departmental accounts? The key issue here is whether resource accounting will improve or diminish parliamentary supervision over departmental spending? In principle it is argued that an accrual system of accounting may provide greater not less transparency. However, Parliament would need to assess this proposition. An additional dimension is that accrual based accounting gives further authority to accountancy techniques rather than to parliamentary means of holding to account. The two may not be mutually exclusive. However, if Parliament becomes more dependent on accountancy principles in order to perform its constitutional role then the supervision of auditors and accountants becomes a crucial part of its function. Recognition of the challenges posed by the introduction of resource accounting is the first step in reappraisal of the financial procedures of the House of Commons.

(d) Conclusions

In the United Kingdom there is considerable debate about how **11–96** effective are the current arrangements for the financial reporting of government expenditure. There is a strong preference for the introduction of a system of resource accounting to replace the present system whereby moneys are brought to account at the time they are paid or received. The recent NAO report on Resource Accounting suggests that:

"The introduction of resource budgeting would provide an opportunity to reappraise the options for financial reporting by departments. One option would be to move to: a departmental plan in February containing a resource budget including the Estimates; and an annual departmental report in October containing the resource account and Appropriation Account."

It is clear that the introduction of resource accounting involves a fundamental reappraisal of the financial procedures of Parliament. In the United Kingdom a number of questions are posed: If resource accounting is introduced will Parliament be provided with better information and the means to carry out its constitutional functions in the scrutiny of government departments? Should Parliament's authority not be codified in a Budget Law that sets out its role and the means to achieve its goals?

In this discussion of the United Kingdom's budgetary system there **11–97** are implications for Europe. Various strategies for the improvement of the accountability of the E.C. budget in Member States may be considered such as the Commission's Anti-Fraud Strategy and Work Programme. There are further additional measures to consider in order to achieve sound financial management that emerge from the United Kingdom budgetary system. Many of the main suggestions are usefully summarised in a recent Treasury Report.[62] The main principles that may be considered that emerge from an analysis of the report are as follows:

- use of targeting according to risk of fraud;

---

[62] H.M. Treasury, *European Community Finances* Cm. 2824 April 1995 p. 14 para. 50.

- setting precise goals and targets in the anti-fraud action programme of the Commission;
- enhanced co-ordination of anti-fraud measures;
- fraud-proofing new legislative proposals;
- periodic review of all budgetary operations;
- all Community expenditure should be subject to principles of sound public finance;
- prior appraisal should precede the commitment of Community money in order to assess economic benefits are in keeping with the resources deployed.

The Sixth Report of the Committee of Public Accounts[63] sets out how the United Kingdom's budgetary system fits within the Community system. This is a glimpse of how future developments are likely to involve closer liaison. The National Audit Office in the United Kingdom has been awarded the contract for the certification of the European Agricultural Guidance and Guarantee Fund with ever closer links with the European Court of Auditors.

---

[63] See (H.C. 1996/97); Sixth Report of the Committee of Public Accounts; *The Audit of European Community Transactions* (November 6, 1996) H.C. 84.

Chapter 12

Local Government

1. Introduction

The United Kingdom is a unitary state. Local government in the **12–01** United Kingdom provides a means to allocate decision-making that is different from central government. Locally elected authorities provide citizens with a large range of services which have a degree of local autonomy. Superficially, local government may appear uncomplicated. Elected local authorities have wide statutory powers including powers of local taxation. They also receive large financial support from central government. As an administrative agency, local government appears similar to other agencies with statutory powers and duties. In law, local authorities are statutory corporations. They are subject to judicial review, and accountable for their expenditure to the Audit Commission,[1] an independent statutory body with a similar role for local government as the National Audit Office provides to Parliament for central government. Local government is also accountable to the Commissioner for Local Administration,[2] with similar functions to the Parliamentary Commissioner for Administration. Local authorities may develop their own politics and policies within the legal powers they possess. Because of their elected nature, local

[1] The Local Government Finance Act 1982 provides for the establishment of the Audit Commission for England and Wales, which appoints auditors for each local authority either as part of the district audit service employed by the Commission or by a private accounting firm. The conduct of local authority business was investigated by the Widdicombe Report (Cmnd. 9797, 1986). This report has led to further legislative changes in how local authority business is conducted. Increased powers were given to the local authority auditors in the Local Government Act 1988 which allow pre-emptive use of the courts to prevent any threatened illegality or wrong doing in respect of local authority finance. Citizens may alert the auditor to any case of financial irregularity. Such changes envisage an increasingly important role for both the District Auditor and the courts.
[2] The Local Government Act 1974 introduced local Commissioners, one for England and one for Wales with powers to investigate maladministration which is similar to the central Government ombudsman.

authorities are accountable to their electorate for their policies and spending plans. This form of electoral accountability may give rise to political and ideological differences with central government. Conflicts between the centre and local authorities are not easily reconciled, and this has increased the centralising tendancies of the legislation passed for local government.

12–02 Local government organisation, management and structure continues to undergo change and critical analysis of its functions. Controversy surrounds its present role and future functions. Major statutory changes introduced to control local government expenditure and re-direct its activities have been prolific and have resulted in legal complexity and difficulty in the interpretation of local authorities' powers and duties.

Undoubtedly the major changes that have taken place in local government finance have led to increased regulation of local authority activities. Since 1979, central government has attempted to reduce public expenditure and has limited resources available to local government. This has posed financial problems for local authorities intent on providing any growth in services or in maintaining existing services. Local authority activities are wide ranging from police, public transport, and social services to planning and education.

12–03 Central government policies have given rise to conflict between local and central government over local government finance, and the role and functions of local authorities within a unitary state.[3] A number of disputes involving financial issues have led to litigation. A significant increase has taken place in the number of applications for judicial review involving local authorities. This includes cases taken against a local authority as well as local authorities seeking judicial redress against central government or other agencies including other local authorities.

There have also been attempts to give the citizen greater opportunities to challenge local authority decisions.[4] The Committee of Inquiry in 1986 under the Chairmanship of David Widdicombe, (hereinafter the Widdicombe Report), recommended that the right of objection to accounts should be extended to all ratepayers and that greater publicity should be given to the auditors' reports. The latter recommendation became law under the Local Government Finance (Publicity for Auditors Reports) Act 1991.

---

[3] Currently the DOE is keeping under review local authority functions. See DOE Consultation Paper, "A New Tax for Local Government" in *Local Government Review*; DOE Consultation Paper, (April, 1991) "The Structure of Local Government in England" in *Local Government Review*; DOE Consultation Paper, (April, 1991) "The Internal Management of Local Authorities in England" (July, 1991), *Local Government Review*.

[4] *Report of The Conduct of local Authority Business* Cmnd. 9797 (1986). Chairman David Widdicombe Q.C., hereinafter the Widdicombe Report.

Changes have taken place in the way local authorities are expected **12–04** to manage their own affairs, including their control of their financial arrangements. Traditionally local authorities have employed the necessary staff to carry out the services for which they are responsible. This includes, for example, social service staff, teachers, and refuse collection. The Local Government Act 1988 requires local authorities to subject a number of services such as street cleaning, vehicle maintenance, schools and welfare catering, refuse collection and the management of sports and leisure facilities to competition. Competition has set new management challenges and has had profound effects on the way local authorities manage themselves. The law requires that private companies must be permitted to bid for the work involved and this element of competition within public service provision sets new directions for the future of local authorities.[5]

Since May 1991 the Secretary of State for the[6] Environment has **12–05** instigated a review of local government and four consultative documents have been published. The Local Government Act 1992 includes proposals for changes to introduce performance standards for local authorities and increased powers for competitive tendering in line with the provisions in the *Citizen's Charter*.[7]

Perceptible changes are evident in the role of local authorities as a **12–06** result of these developments.[8] First, there is a tendency towards centralisation of powers and policy decision-making. Secondly, there is a challenge to the effectiveness of local authorities being accountable to their own electorate. Current government thinking questions the efficiency of local government elections as an adequate means of accountability over local government. Since 1979 the bi-partisan approach of the major political parties to local authority decision-making has been abandoned. Local authorities are perceived as "instruments of social welfare" and therefore seen as acting in opposition to the policies of central government. Thirdly, there is a tendency to envisage local authorities developing management styles more consistent with *regulating* local authority activities rather than delivering the services. Fourthly, there is a perceptible shift in the variety and type of legislation which local authorities are required to follow. The Victorian style of legislation containing broadly drafted

---

[5] Diane Dawson, "Economic Change and the Changing Role of Local Government" in M. Loughlin *et al.*, *Half a Century of Municipal Decline 1935–1985* (London, 1985), pp. 26–99. Also see C. D. Foster, R. Jackman, M. Perlman, *Local Government Finance in a Unitary State* (1980).

[6] See the Local Government Act 1992 setting up the Local Government Review.

[7] *Citizen's Charter*, Cm. 1599 (1991).

[8] See J. P. W. B. McAuslan and J. McEldowney, "Public Challenge and Local Government" (1988) *Coexistence* 89–102. Also see Edward Page, *Localism and Centralism in Europe* (Oxford, 1991).

wide discretion with enabling powers has been replaced with complex, technical and precisely formulated provisions which require enforcement. Legal rules have replaced broad discretion. The courts are expected to enforce such rules even if they conflict with policy objectives of the duly elected local authority.[9]

12–07   This chapter is intended firstly to explain the role and function of local authorities in a period of change.[10] The account is limited to England and Wales, as Scotland has its own system of law applicable to local government, and Northern Ireland's arrangements[11] are distinctive to that region. Secondly, to explain how changes in the structure of local authorities have introduced the use of competitive tendering in local authority services. Thirdly to explain relations between local and central government which has set new challenges for the courts. Finally, to explain the work of the Audit Commission in the accountability of local authorities.

2. The Role and Function of Local Government

(a) Evolution and Change

12–08 The historical background provides an explanation of the development of modern local government. The nineteenth century brought a growth in towns and new laws to deal with problems such as health, housing, sanitation, law and order, and education. The Municipal Corporations Act 1835 created *elected* local authorities, but local authorities' statutory powers developed during the remainder of the century on an ad hoc basis. Diane Dawson explains the considerable growth in local authority responsibilities during the nineteenth century as an important stage in the development of local government in Britain[12]:

"From 1843 to 1929, the assumption of responsibility for water, gas, transport, education, housing and health services was a

---

[9] See Report of the Committee of Enquiry into Local Government Finance, Cmnd. 6453 (1976). (The Layfield Report.)

[10] Currently the DOE is examining in its consultation document the idea of uniting local authorities and providing greater management skills in local authorities' activities. Increasingly local authorities are asked to act as regulators of their services rather than service providers.The full significance of this shift in emphasis remains to be determined.

[11] See Chap. 19 describing the Northern Ireland system of government.

[12] Dawson, *op. cit.* p. 27. C. J. D. Robinson, *Handbook of Local Authority Legal Practice* (Sweet & Maxwell, 1994). M. Loughlin, *Legality and Locality* (Oxford, 1996) pp. 9–72.

perceived response to the inadequacy or inefficiency of private enterprise and voluntary organisations in supplying these services."

By the end of the nineteenth century elected councils were established for counties, county borough, urban and rural districts and most parishes. Local authorities had become as Robson described,[13] "the most effective instrument of social welfare in our national life."

Over the years local authorities have gained wide and extensive **12–09** statutory powers.[14] They may initiate their own private Bill legislation and possess wide secondary law-making powers made in the form of by-laws. They have limited but important powers to raise rates, a form of local taxation. The present structure, organisation and legal framework of local government for local authority activities in England and Wales, is derived from the Local Government Act 1972.[15] The 1972 Act introduced major re-organisations in the size and shape of local government in England and Wales[16] and were put into operation after intense debate in 1974. The report of the Redcliffe – Maud Committee[17] in 1969 favoured 58 unitary authorities but in major conurbations such as Liverpool, Manchester and Birmingham it favoured a two-tier system. The 1972 Act departed from this recommendation and established a two-tier system with a different distribution of functions.[18] London was treated separately under the London Government Act 1963 following a Royal Commission on Local Government in 1960. The 1963 Act created the Greater London Council and 32 larger boroughs and the City of London within the area defined as Greater London. The 1972 Act also defined the boundaries of the metropolitan counties and districts and the non-metropolitan or Shire counties. A local Government Boundary Commission was also established to review electoral arrangements and boundaries.

---

[13] W. A. Robson quoted in Dawson *op. cit.*

[14] Hay, The origins of the Liberal Welfare Reforms 1906–1914 (1975); P. Craig, *Administrative Law* (2nd ed.), p. 94; M. Loughlin, *Local Government in the Modern State* (1986); Rhodes, *Control and Power in Central – Local Government Relations* (1981).

[15] Scotland has its own separate legislation but shares a common framework with England and Wales. Northern Ireland has its own distinctive arrangements which fall outside the remit of this Chapter. It is significant that the British turn-out at local elections averaging between 40–48% is lower than most European local elections.

[16] In 1975 the Scottish system of local government was reformed following the Wheatley commission in 1969, Cmnd. 4150 (1969).

[17] Report of the Royal Commission on Local Government in England, Cmnd. 4040 (1969). [Redcliffe – Maud] See Local Government Acts 1963, 1972 and 1985.

[18] In London specific changes were made on April 1, 1986, to the London and Metropolitan Counties. This tier of local government including the Greater London Council was abolished.

12-10   Altogether there were 514 principal local authorities in Great Britain, Northern Ireland is treated differently and does not fall within this structure. There are 404 authorities in England, 65 in Scotland and 45 in Wales. The two-tier system operates throughout the "shire" areas in England, in all of Wales and on the mainland in Scotland.[19] The two-tier system comprises an upper tier and a lower tier. In England and Wales the upper tier is known as counties where there are 47 counties (38 in England and 9 in Wales), and in Scotland as regions where there are 9 regions. The lower tier authorities are known as districts. There are 53 districts in Scotland, 37 in Wales and 296 in the Shire areas of England.

12-11   In Greater London and the six metropolitan counties of England[20] a different system prevailed. In London, the upper tier comprised the Greater London Council and the lower tier comprised 32 London boroughs and the City of London. In the case of the six Metropolitan Counties of England, the upper tier comprised six County Councils, and the lower tier consisted of 36 district councils. This structure has remained intact, except for the Local Government Act 1985 which from April 1, 1986 abolished the Greater London Council and the six Metropolitan County Councils. The result of these changes left functions distributed to the remaining tier of government and some functions were shared with new single purpose joint authorities. In the case of Inner London a new directly elected education authority was created.

12-12   The movement in favour of unitary local government authorities has gathered momentum. The re-drawing of local government took considerable time to implement. The Local Government (Wales) Act 1994 and the Local Government etc. (Scotland) Act 1994 provided for unitary authorities in Wales and Scotland replacing the dual authority system inherited and re-organised in the 1970s. In Scotland there are now 28 local authorities, 25 of which replaced the nine regional and 53 district councils. The remaining three refer to the Highlands and Islands which remain intact. In Wales 21 unitary authorities now replace (eight county councils and 37 district councils. These arrangements have now been operative from April 1, 1996.

12-13   There has been no equivalent legislation to introduce unitary authorities for England. In England under current arrangements there are 32 boroughs in London and outside the capital there are six metropolitan areas which have 36 district councils. England has 39 counties and 296 district councils and roughly 900 community and town councils. Under the Local Government Act 1992 the Local

---

[19] In the island areas of Scotland there is only one tier of government.
[20] The six metropolitan counties are Greater Manchester, Merseyside, South Yorkshire, Tyne and Wear, West Midlands and West Yorkshire.

Government Commission for England was established with the task of undertaking a review of local government areas. Matters of such party political sensitivity exposed the ground rules of the Commission given in the form of guidance to a great deal of controversy. Section 13(6) of the 1992 Act matters that should guide the Commission included preference to be given to "natural communities" and that account should be taken of peoples' preferences. However, the government insisted in its revised guidance issued in 1993 that the aim of having a unitary system of local authority should be considered. In *R. v. Secretary of State for the Environment, ex p. Lancashire County Council*[21] the guidance that sought to give undue weight to the Government's preference for unitary authorities was unlawful.

The approach taken thereafter was to consider the introduction of **12–14** unitary authorities on a consultation basis. This process, begun in 1992, has proved more time-consuming and complex than was first envisaged. In addition, periodic electoral review is undertaken to rectify electoral imbalances in a local authority area. The Commission completed its review in early 1995. In the end, 50 all purpose unitary authorities were proposed. Since March 1996 over 30 local authorities have been considered and the results of these deliberations will be forthcoming in the form of further consultation papers. The preference for an overwhelming number of unitary local authorities appears to have been held in check.

Turning to examine the role and function of local government **12–15** within the United Kingdom's constitutional arrangements, there are a number of factors to consider. There is no federal arrangement and the sovereignty of the United Kingdom Parliament provides a unitary state. The role and function of local authorities was examined in the Widdicombe Report[22] (1986). The main characteristics of modern local authorities were identified. These include its diversity, the opportunities given for local democracy, the responsiveness to local needs through the delivery of services and finally its contribution to the national political system through its diversity of politics.

Diversity comes about through the geographical size and management style in different local authorities. The size of local authorities varies throughout the country and this includes the geographical areas covered, the size of population, (from as few as 25,000 to over 1.5 million), and the amount of local authority expenditure which varies considerably from less than £1.5 million to the largest, Strathclyde Regional Council of over £1,500 million.[23]

The Widdicombe Report drew attention to the difficult question of **12–16** the role of local authorities. There is intense debate, as to how local

[21] [1994] 4 All E.R. 165.
[22] Widdicombe Report (1986).
[23] *ibid.* para. 2.14.

authorities with such diversity in politics, size, finance and policy priorities may best develop relations with central government. In 1976 the Layfield Report[24] on local government finance identified two opposing views of local authority activities which were relevant to the Widdicombe inquiry.

The "centralist" view is that local authorities act as agents for central government. As custodians of the interests of the local community they mitigate the dangers of remoteness and bureaucratic organisation which would occur if government were entirely centralised. On this view emphasis is placed, not on the elected element in local authority activities, but on the sovereignty of Parliament to direct local authorities to carry out activities on behalf of central government policy-making. On this view local authorities are less free to develop their own distinctive policies which may conflict with central government's general direction and policy-making.

12–17	The opposing view is the "localist" view,[25] that local authorities are decentralised with real political authority and power in respect of the functions which can appropriately be performed at the local level. On this view emphasis is placed on the statutory duties local authorities are expected, and in many cases, required to perform. Local authorities are entitled to develop their own strategies and are free to promote their own distinctive policies even if they might conflict with the policy of the government of the day.

12–18	The Widdicombe Report found this dichotomy of views unhelpful in the sense that the true constitutional status of local authorities was that they derived all their powers, not as autonomous entities with an entrenched constitutional status, but from Parliament. The view of central government and the tendency towards centralism in the past policies of central government left local authorities no option but to accept "as a fact of life" the reality of central government's legal authority. As Grant has argued[26]:

"The constitutional element of the central-local relations debate is potentially empty and barren, and neither of the two approaches [one[27] that gives formal constitutional protection to local government and the other[28] that gives limited protection to local government, providing for a more consensus political arrangement for the distribution of functions between central local relations] has overcome the initial problems. The constitutional debate is not only

[24] Layfield Report.
[25] ibid.
[26] M. Grant, "Central-local Relations: The Balance of Power" in Jowell and Oliver, The Changing Constitution (1989), pp. 251–252.
[27] This view is favoured by Professors Jones and Stewart; see G. Jones and J. Stewart, "Defending Local Government" (1982) Local Government Chronicle 75.
[28] M. Elliott, The Role of Law in Central – Local Relations (1981).

potentially empty in itself because of the tendency inherent in it to attach *a priori* values and attributes to legal institutions and to pursue principles more for their traditional value than their contemporary utility. But also, because of its focus upon the formal relationships between government bodies it threatens to overlook the broader grounds of recent central-local conflict."

Grant's analysis has greater acceptance today in the current **12–19** approaches to local government. We shall see that the differences between centralism and localism have an ideological effect on the cultures of local authorities. Many local authorities are steeped in the idealism of localism which has been partly fostered by the sense that the local authority delivers public services and in that way fits Robson's description of acting as "an instrument of social welfare." Local authorities that adopted the welfare view of their functions found that after 1979 they came into conflict with central government policies. This led to disputes over local authority finance and in some cases litigation between local and central government.[29]

The extent of the re-structuring of local government is noted by **12–20** Loughlin[30]:

"Since the 1930's local government functions have been radically restructured. Local authorities have been stripped of various responsibilities, including trunk roads in 1936, electricity in 1947, gas in 1948, water and sewerage in 1974, public assistance between 1934 and 1948, hospitals in 1946 and the remaining local health services in 1974."

Since 1979, the role of local government has undergone considerable change. In key areas of local authority activities, changes have been introduced which have questioned local authority involvement. Some examples illustrate the extent and the nature of these changes. The Government has introduced extensive provisions which entitle the tenant to the "right to buy" under the provisions of the Housing Act 1980. Local transport was extensively de-regulated in 1985 under the Transport Act 1985. Education is undergoing continuous change, the most recent is discussed in the White Paper *Choice and Diversity*.[31] Currently local authorities, through the relevant local education authority (LEA) have a duty under the Education Act 1944 to ensure that there are sufficient numbers of primary and secondary school

[29] *ibid.*
[30] M. Loughlin, *Local Government in the Modern State* (1986), p. 6.
[31] Report of the Department of Education, *Choice and Diversity A New Framework for Schools* (July, 1992).

places avaliable for children aged between five and 19. In the provision of financial arrangements LEAs are responsible for the recurrent budget of the various primary and secondary schools that they maintain. However the Government have introduced a scheme whereby responsibility is delegated between the LEAs and the schools who are in the scheme. Many see this as further attempt to erode local authority influence over schools.

12–21 The Education Act 1993 contains detailed powers and technical provisions reforming and consolidating education provision in England and Wales. The 1993 Act replaces and amends much of the Education Act 1944 and subsequent amendments. The Education Act 1993 has centralising tendencies. Sections 1 and 2 set out general duties of the Secretary of State to promote education and use regulatory powers to improve standards in schools. LEAs are no longer to be the main administrators for grant-maintained schools. Sections 9 and 10 establish the Funding Agency for Schools in England and the Schools Funding Council for Wales appointed and supervised by the Secretary of State for Education. The new funding authorities take over the responsibility for administering funds for grant-maintained schools and either jointly with the LEA or on their own, have responsibility for ensuring that there are sufficient schools in an area. Section 20 empowers the Secretary of State to determine disputes about the functions to be exercised by the LEAs and the funding authorities. Once a funding authority is in operation in any one particular area the power of the LEA to establish new schools is limited.

12–22 Nevertheless the value of local government is that it provides a useful check on the centralisation of power in central government. Even within the limits of its statutory authority, local government carries out a wide range of activities. The Local Government Commission, set up under the Local Government Act 1992 to review local government activities has provided a comprehensive list and description of the activities and functions of local authorities in England and Wales.[32] Planning, transport, (including highways), environmental protection, environmental health, consumer protection and trading standards, education and related services, libraries and museums, personal social services, housing, police and local courts are the main activities carried out by local authorities. Many of the services are provided by different tiers of local authority. For example Building Control is carried out by the District Councils and the London Borough Councils, whereas Ancient Monuments are the responsibility of County Councils, District Councils and London Borough

---

[32] Report of the DOE "The Functions of Local Authorities in England" in (1992) *Local Government Review*.

Councils. In matters of environmental protection some local authorities are designated waste regulation authorities under the Environmental Protection Act 1990. Such designated authorities are County Councils and Metropolitan District Councils, while in Greater London, Greater Manchester and Mersyside there are specific statutory joint authorities. While the division of responsibilities may appear confusing and complicated, there are additional responsibilities such as consultation with other agencies.[33] In the example of environmental protection, local authority consultation takes place with a number of other bodies such as the Environment Agency under the Environment Act 1995, in matters of pollution control over polluted water caused by the disposal of waste; the Health and Safety Executive, in the matter of issuing a waste management licence and the Nature Conservancy Council for land sites under the Wildlife and Countryside Act 1981. Compared to the other agencies mentioned only the local authority concerned is an elected administrative agency.

Local authorities possess some widely drawn statutory powers in **12–23** addition to specific statutory duties mentioned above. A few examples illustrate how local authorities may be provided with wide statutory powers. Any local authority may exercise under section 111 of the Local Government Act 1972 general powers "to do anything which is calculated to facilitate or is conducive or incidental to, the discharge of any of their functions". Such powers, especially if used to raise money by borrowing or lending money, must also conform to detailed rules regulating these activities.

Section 137 of the Local Government Act 1972 is a general power to **12–24** incur expenditure subject to an annual financial limit. Such a power is intended to be used where there is no other statutory power available. More recently, the Local Government and Housing Act 1989 provides local authorities with a general power to promote economic development and considerable flexibility in carrying out their plans. Regulations assist in setting the limits of the permitted activities which may fall within their powers. The Local Government (Amendment) Act 1993 extends local authority powers to make grants to ethnic minorities by extending their powers under section 11 of the Local Government Act 1966.

---

[33] Examples include links with the Commission for Racial Equality under the Race Relations Act 1976. Under s.97 of the Water Industry Act 1991, local authorities are empowered to carry out certain sewerage functions with sewerage undertakers under the Local Authorities (Goods and Services) Act 1970, local authorities may enter agreements with other local authorities to supply goods and services, and under section 142 of the Local Government Act 1972 as amended by the Local Government and Housing Act 1989, to provide assistance and information to charities and other voluntary bodies.

(b) Elections

12–25 The Local Government Act 1972 provides arrangements for the return of local councillors for each electoral area, that is at county, district or parish level. Electoral areas are designated according to the different levels of local government.[34] There is a Local Government Boundary Commission, established under the 1972 Act[35] for the purposes of keeping under review the "electoral arrangements" of the principal authorities. The Commission may also determine the number of councillors that may be returned for each constituency. The aim in carrying out both functions is the same, namely to provide arrangements "in the interests of effective and convenient local government."

12–26 Part II of the Local Government Act 1992 establishes a Local Government Commission. One of its tasks is to take over the responsibilities of the Local Government Boundary Commission for England in the conduct of periodic reviews of electoral arrangements. Directions or guidance may be given to the Commission by the Secretary of State. The setting up of the Commission is intended to review matters concerning elections, boundaries and the structure of local government without recourse to a Royal Commission or similar inquiry. The general intention in the current thinking of the Government is that whereas a single tier or unitary authority is preferrable to the two-tier system in operation at present.[36]

12–27 Three advantages[37] are claimed from a unitary system of local government. Firstly, a unitary system might promote local democracy by increasing the accountability of local authority communities. Secondly, a unitary system might reduce bureaucracy and administrative costs inherent in the duplication of central management at county and district level. Thirdly, a unitary system offers the opportunity for improved co-ordination and cost-effectiveness in the delivery of local government services.

It is clear that devolution in Scotland[38] and Wales[39] will have implications for local government. In the case of England, the Local Government Commission's task under the Local Government Act 1992 is divided into five tranches for the submission of recommendations to the Secretary of State.[40] Devolution proposals might follow for England once devolution is introduced in Scotland and Wales.

---

[34] For Scotland see the Local Government (Scotland) Act 1973.
[35] See ss.47(1) and 54(1) of the Local Government Act 1972.
[36] See DOE, "The Structure of Local Government in England" (1991) in *Local Government Review*. The Local Government Commission is headed by John Banham.
[37] See *Renewing Local Government in the English Shires* (HMSO, 1993).
[38] Local Government, etc. (Scotland) Act 1994.
[39] Local Government (Wales) Act 1994.
[40] The five are: the Isle of Wight, Derbyshire, Cleveland and County Durham, Avon, Gloucestershire and Somerset, and Humberside, Lincolnshire and North Yorkshire.

Under the 1972 Local Government Act the structure of local **12–28** authorities is as follows: in the case of the County Councils the area is divided into electoral divisions, with one council member returned for each division. Elections must be held every four years with each member retiring simultaneously.

In the case of the Shire district councils, the area is divided into electoral wards with three members normally returned for each ward. All the members of the council retire simultaneously, but it is possible to opt for a system of election based on one third of the council retiring at a time. Voting takes place only in those wards where a member is retiring. In wards where there are only one or two members returned, it is not possible to vote every year.

In the case of the metropolitan district councils, the electoral area is **12–29** divided into wards with three members for each ward.[41] One-third of the members stand for election and elections are commonly held in three years out of four. On the principle that a member retires in each ward at each election, the entire electorate has the opportunity to vote.

In the case of the Parish or Community Council, any number of councillors may be elected. There is no maximum number for the size of the Parish Council, but the minimum is set at five. There are requirements under the Representation of the People Act 1983 that each District Council or London Borough Council must appoint an electoral officer. Responsibility falls on the electoral registration officer to prepare and publish each year an electoral register for both parliamentary and local government elections.

The electoral qualification for local government is similar[42] to **12–30** central government.[43] However disqualification is more widely drawn. Tenure of any office of profit at the disposal of a local authority or any of its committees, is a disqualification for office as a councillor. Also bankruptcy, surcharge by the auditor or conviction for corrupt or illegal practices and incurring imprisonment within five years of an election is also a disqualification.

The electoral registration officer must also publish notice of the election, receive nominations and co-ordinate the arrangements for

---

[41] Under the Local Government Act 1972, the numbers of members to be divisible by three so in theory it might be possible to have wards with three, six or nine members. See T. Byrne, *Local Government in Britain* (Penguin, 1992).

[42] See the Municipal Corporations Act 1835 conferring the vote on every male of age and occupation in premises in a borough for two years preceding registration and who lived within seven miles of the borough and paid rates. Amendments since then have broadened the franchise considerably; see section 43 of the Local Government Act 1894 allowing married women the vote and finally see Local Government Act 1972 for the current law.

[43] See Chap. 6.

polling day.[44] Turnout at local government elections is usually significantly less than at elections for central government; on average 40–50
per cent, compared to 75 per cent at a general election.

12–31　　Research conducted in 1977 showed that[45] "50 per cent. of councillors were over the age of 54, 83 per cent. were male, 76 per cent.
were owner occupiers and less than 25 per cent. had a background in
manual work." Similar findings were made in the research undertaken by the Widdicombe Committee.[46] Some of the findings from
this research suggest that in urban areas local councillors are likely to
be younger.

12–32　　The political dimension to local authority decision-making became
an important question in the conduct of local authority business in
the 1980s. Central government's concerns over the political and
ideological motivation of local authority activities led to the appointment of the inquiry chaired by Mr David Widdicombe Q.C. A strong
perception arose that local government was dominated in the cities
by the extreme political left, and the basis of support rested on
political organisations who were largely inefficient and quite possibly
corrupt. Various Labour-led local authorities such as the GLC (before
its abolition) and Liverpool had clashed publicly and openly with the
policies of central government. In 1985 it took over three months
before Liverpool City Council and Lambeth Borough Council set their
rates (then the local government means of raising tax) because of
disagreement over central government policies and grant.[47] Greater
politicisation and vociferous demands for an increase in local government services challenged the policies of central government.

12–33　　The Widdicombe Committee concentrated on the conduct of local
authority business and not its finance or structure.[48] While accepting
that there was an important role for central government, the report
concentrated on making local government more accountable. To that
end a large number of recommendations have been implemented
including additional powers to the Audit Commission and tighter
scrutiny of the internal management of local authorities.

---

[44] See the Local Government Act 1972, the Representation of the People Acts 1983,
1985, 1989, 1990 and the Local Elections (Principal Areas) Rules 1986, the Local
Elections (Parishes and Communities) Rules 1986.
[45] A. Gray and B. Jenkins, "Administering Local Government" in Jones et al., Politics
U.K. (1991), p. 447. See Byrne, op. cit., pp. 92–132.
[46] Research Volume II, The Conduct of Local Authority Business: The Local Government
Councillor, Cmnd. 9799 (1986).
[47] Lloyd v. McMahon [1987] A.C. 625.
[48] The Widdicombe Committee made 88 recommendations and four large reports.

3. Change and Structure in Local Government

(a) Structure and Organisation

Unlike central government with a clearly defined executive, local **12–34** government does not have any clearly defined executive branch. Similarly local government has no equivalent of ministerial responsibility, leaving a gap in the arrangements for accountability which has been filled by the development of a separate Audit Commission in 1982 and the creation of a local government ombudsman.

Local government may be described as combining an elected **12–35** element, namely the councillors, and an administrative staff, comprising at the most senior level, professional officers. The council chairman is annually elected, decisions are taken by resolutions of the council or through officials acting with delegated authority. The council usually works through a large number of committees. Standing orders and minutes are kept of the conduct of meetings and under the Public Bodies (Admission to Meetings) Act 1960 members of the public are normally admitted.[49] The Chairman has power to exclude the public in cases of disorderly conduct[50] and meetings may be kept confidential and closed to the public where the nature of business or public interest requires.

Following the Widdicombe Committee report legislation was intro- **12–36** duced to bring greater openness into the conduct of local authority business. The Local Government (Access to Information) Act 1985 requires councils to give public notice of meetings, make available certain relevant documents and make the agenda, minutes and relevant reports public. The main *caveat* is that they do not have to be disclosed if confidential information relating to government departments or the like is disclosed. Reports and background papers are open to inspection by members of the public for four years in the case of any background papers and six years for other papers.

Excluded from open access are matters relating to personal infor- **12–37** mation about members of staff in connection with employment and this restriction includes access to information regarding wages and the payment of benefits.[51]

The Widdicombe Committee paid particular attention to the role of the principal officer of a local authority and the committee structure

---

[49] See *R. v. Liverpool City Council, ex p. Liverpool Taxi Fleet Operators Association* [1975] 1 W.L.R. 701, which discusses the rights of the public to attend meetings.

[50] *R. v. Brent Health Authority, ex p. Francis* [1985] Q.B. 869.

[51] S.11 of the Local Government and Housing Act 1989. See *Oliver v. Northampton Borough Council* (1986) 151 J.P. 44, which extended rights under s.17 of the Local Government Finance Act 1982 to access to wages books. S.11 of the 1989 Act restricted this right because it was thought that the *Oliver* case had gone too far.

of local authority decision-making. The aim of the Widdicombe Committee was to strengthen the system of democratic account-ability. For example *R. v. Waltham Forest London Borough Council, ex p. Baxter*[52] illustrated how leading councillors and local political activists met and later attended meetings of the council. The link between ideology and local authority decision-making seemed complete. This link was criticised by the courts.

12–38   The Local Government and Housing Act 1989 provides important changes to the organisation and management of committees ensuring that representation on committees and sub-committees comprises various political groups. There are provisions to prevent officers from serving on more than one local authority and for the non-voting of non-elected and appointed members of committees. Some provision is made for the appointment of political advisers. The changes introduced in 1989 were less than those recommended by the Widdicombe Report.[53]

(b) Competitive Tendering for Local Authority Services

12–38A   The shift in focus from local authorities as[54] "providers of services" to local authorities as "enablers and regulators" is well illustrated by the introduction of competitive tendering. Britain is the only European country in which competitive tendering for certain local authority services is compulsory. The British experience to date has probably represented the most systematic and comprehensive experience of compulsory tendering. The stages adopted in the use of competitive tendering began in the National Health Service prior to 1988 and introduced catering, domestic and laundry services to competitive tendering. Individual health authorities extended various support services such as porters and ground maintenance to competitive tendering. In various central government departments such as the Ministry of Defence and also in the civil service competitive tendering has been extensively used.

In 1980, the Local Government Planning and Land Act 1980 (Part III) required certain local authority construction and maintenance work to be made subject to competitive tendering. Highways and building work were included. Traditionally for such work local authorities operated their own Direct Labour Organisations (DLO).

---

[52] [1988] Q.B. 419.
[53] P. McAuslan, [1987] P.L. 47.
[54] (1989) *Municipal Review*, (April, 1989) p. 9. See Byrne, *op. cit.* Chaps. 9 and 10. Also see *The New Local Authorities: Management and Structure* (the Bains Report) (HMSO 1972).

After 1980 DLOs could continue to carry our their work but on the basis of winning a competitive contract not on an automatic basis.

In 1985 the Government issued a White Paper: Competition in the **12–39** Provision of Local Authority Service[55] (February 1985) which argued for an extension of competitive tendering to a wider range of activities such as catering, refuse collection, building, cleaning schools and welfare catering, sporting and leisure activities. An exemption was granted if the costs to run these activities was small (less than £100,000 in the previous year). Also exempted were police and fire vehicles from cleaning contracts. The Government responded to the White Paper by passing the Local Government Act 1988 which required local authorities to provide competition for the above services. DLOs are permitted to bid for contracts but are not given any preferential treatment. Services subject to contract bids were expected to be subject to competition at six month intervals between August 1, 1989 and January 1, 1992. If a local authority DLO or in the case of services District Services Organisation (DSO) is successful in its bid, separate trading accounts are required in order to prevent any cross subsidy between different accounts.

The extension of competition into local authority activities is set to **12–40** continue. Parallel legislation such as the Education Reform Act 1988 and, the Local Government and Housing Act 1989 have continued to introduce competitive elements into education and local authority companies.

The Local Government Act 1988 has not been the subject of much interpretation before the courts as the legislation is presently being brought into operation. In terms of legal issues the most critical has been drawing up contracts which have to conform with the 1988 Act in terms of "anti competitive behaviour." This is a complicated issue which raises matters relating to the use of tender prices, the packaging of single or multiple contracts, the size of contract and the use of local authority plant or depots.

There are also matters of "non commercial nature" which the 1988 **12–41** Act forbids an authority to take into account in letting contracts. These matters are as follows:

(a) terms and conditions of employment of workers or the composition of, the arrangements for promotion, transfer or training of, or the other opportunities afforded to the workforce;

---

[55] Generally see J. A. Rehmuss, *Contracting Out in Government* (Jossey – Bass, 1989); report of the Audit Commission, *Competitiveness and Contracting Out of Local Authorities' Services* (HMSO, 1987). J. Cubbin, S. Domberger, A. Meadowcraft, "Competitive Tendering and Efficiency: Indentifying the Sources of Efficiency Gains" (1988) 8 *Fiscal Studies*, (No. 3). See Public Service Contracts Regulations 1993 (S.I. 1993 No. 3228).

(b) whether the terms on which contractors contract with their sub-contractors constitute, in the case of contracts with individuals, contracts for the provision by them as self-employed people of their services only (that is labour only contracts);

(c) involvement in irrelevant fields of government policy;

(d) conduct of, or involvement in industrial disputes;

(e) country of origin of supplies, or location of business activities;

(f) political, industrial, sectarian, affiliations;

(g) financial support or lack of support for any institution to or from which the authority gives or withholds support;

(h) use or non-use by contractors of services provided by the authority under the Building Act 1984 or the Building (Scotland) Act 1984.

As the late Kieron Walsh concluded[56]:

"The experience of the Local Government Act 1988 is still limited. There are many areas of uncertainty and differences in interpretation. The meaning of anti-competitive behaviour is not yet fully clear and provides much more room for debate, for example on what are acceptable methods of packaging contracts. The meaning of 'non-commercial' matters is also open to interpretation. In addition there are difficulties over matters relating specifically to contract law, notably what are acceptable forms of default clauses. The role of lawyers in interpreting the legislation has been important because of the difficulties involved."

12–42 The compulsory requirements of competitive tendering have raised issues about the compatibility of competitive tendering and the European Community rules contained in the Acquired Rights Directive 1977. These rules may be found in the Protection of Employments Regulations 1981 which applied generally to the commercial and not the public sector. The European Commission is considering whether the United Kingdom's Government was wrong to exclude the public sector from the benefit of the rules. This has the potential

---

[56] Kieron Walsh, *Competitive Tendency for Local Authority Services* DOE (HMSO, 1989), p. 15, para. 3.13.

of making competitive tendering inconsistent with the E.C. rules which may complicate the future development of competitive tendering.[57] This question involves the transfer of Undertakings (Protection of Employment) Regulations 1981 which implemented the 1977 Directive into United Kingdom law.[58] It is likely that trade union concerns may lead to further litigation on these matters.

Further refinements to the existing system of competitive tendering **12–43** are included in the Local Government Act 1992. Additional procedures for competitive tendering, the further definition of competitive or anti-competitive conduct, and the publicity required for tender specifications are contained in sections 8–11 of the 1992 Act. Compulsory competitive tendering (CCT) continues[59] to be introduced into a wide range of local government activities. The powers to add new areas of activities to the list may be found in the Local Government Act 1988 (Competition) (Defined Activities) Order 1995. CCT requires local authorities to compulsorily contract out many specified activities to the private sector and this has important implications for employment rights.[60] These range from refuse collection to legal services and sport and maintenance.

Some tentative conclusions may be made from the research work **12–44** already undertaken into competition tendering.[61] Major management challenges as a result of competition have had a fundamental effect on the attitudes of both officers and elected members of local authorities. A number of weaknesses have been highlighted such as lack of management and organisation, poor information systems and lack of priorities in local authority administration. Also revealed in the research are the lack of adequate monitoring and inspection. This has led to a greater pressure on work, more demanding timetables for action and greater cost efficiency demanded in carrying out local authority activities. Overall, competitive tendering is likely to shape the future of local authorities for the foreseeable time. Recognition of

---

[57] "Contracting Out", *The Independent*, November 12, 1992. See R. v. *London Borough of Islington, ex p. Building Employers' Confederation* (1989) 45 B.L.R. 45; M. Bowsher, "Prospects for Establishing an Effective Tender Challenge Régime: Enforcing Rights under E.C. Procurement Law in English Courts" (1994) 3 *Public Procurement Law Review*, 30–46. Brian Bercusson, *European Labour Law* (Butterworths, 1996) pp. 234–247.

[58] Case C–382/92 E.C. *Commission v. U.K.* [1994] E.C.R. I–2435.

[59] See *CCT and Local Government*, Annual Report, Department of the Environment (London, 1995).

[60] B. Napier, *CCT, Market Testing and Employment Rights; The Effects of TUPE and the Acquired Rights Directive* (Institute of Employment Rights, London, 1993). Also see the Trade Union Reform and Employment Rights Act 1993.

[61] DOE, *Competition in the Provision of Local Government Services* (1985). See S. Domberger, S. Meadowcraft, D. Thompson, "Competitive Tendering and Efficiency: The Case of Refuse Collection" (1987) 17 *Fiscal Studies* No. 4; K. Hartley, M. Huby, "Contracting Out in Health and Local Authorities" (1985) *Public Money*.

the rôle of local authorities in developing public sector skills and experience may be found in the Local Government (Overseas Assistance) Act 1993. This gives local authorities powers to advise and offer assistance to overseas bodies engaged in activities of local government.

12–45   The Government has taken steps to encourage private finance to be invested in public sector activities. Since November 1992 the Private Finance Initiative (PFI) allows private finance to be used for public sector capital activities including buildings, computer technology, know-how and new management systems. The most notable examples of PFI are in the Channel Tunnel Rail Link and other new construction projects. H.M. Treasury have insisted that their criteria for a PFI project is that "the genuine risk" is transferred to the private sector and the project represents value for money when public sector finance is involved.

PFI has the potential to transform the problems of long-term capital underfunding in local government. In the context of local authorities PFI requires careful supervision because of the restrictive nature of local authority powers (discussed below in more detail). Recently local authorities have been circulated with details of PFI and its potential for local government projects. The outcome of this exercise remains to be seen.

(c)   Devolution and local government

12–46 Devolution for Scotland and Wales is currently being proposed by the government. If such proposals are accepted and introduced into law then there are likely to be profound changes in the way local government will function. Devolution entails the setting up of a regional Parliament with many powers and responsibilities granted by the United Kingdom Parliament. The principles of subsidiarity as stated in the preamble to the Maastricht Treaty on European Union will require that the newly created regional assemblies will have to work closely with local government and community decision making. Various models of the legislation that might be introduced have been published by various groups[62] setting out proposals for reform.[63] A critical element in the success of devolution and its relationship to regional government is the question of finance. A recent financial study[64] has pointed the complexity of local taxation, with devolved

---

[62] See *Key Proposals for Scotland's Parliament: A Report to the Scottish Constitutional Convention from the Executive Committee* (1996).

[63] See The Constitution Unit at the Faculty of Laws, Bentham House, University College, London.

[64] Laura Blow, John Hall and Stephen Smith, "Financing Regional Government in the U.K.: Some Issues" (1996) *Fiscal Studies* Vol. 17 no. 4 p. 99–120.

regional government. It is ironic that the decentralising tendencies that favour devolution might appear to weaken local government and its autonomy and authority.

(d)   The Environment Act 1995 and local government

The Environment Act 1995 has created a new unified Environment **12–47** Agency for England and Wales and for Scotland, the Scottish Environment Protection Agency (SEPA). Both agencies have broadly similar aims and objectives such as the achievement of sustainable development and responsibilities for water pollution and the management of integrated pollution controls. There are some important implications for local authorities. In Scotland local authority responsibilities as enforcing authorities for air pollution control have been transferred to SEPA. However, in England and Wales local authorities remain the air pollution enforcers and the Environment Agency did not receive such powers.

In Scotland SEPA has less enforcement functions for river pollution than the Environment Agency for England and Wales. This continues an historic tradition which makes SEPA a pollution control body in contrast to the Environment Agency's integrated management functions.

The new agencies are given powers to give guidance to local **12–48** authorities on contaminated land. Considerable powers under the Environment Act 1995 provide for waste management responsibilities on producers. There are also powers to provide a National Air Quality Strategy. The agencies may act as consultants to the Secretary of State when drawing up such plans. Similarly there are powers for drawing up a National Waste Strategy for England and Wales. In Scotland SEPA is charged with the responsibility for preparing the waste strategy.

4.   Central-Local Government Relations

Relations between local and central government have proved contro- **12–49** versial, especially in recent years. Central government has sought greater accountability over the provision of public services, especially with regard to local government finance. The introduction of cash limits on each expenditure block at the level of central government has been accompanied by attempts to reduce local government expenditure. As Elliott has noted this approach "was a bipartisan policy," begun in 1975 under a Labour Government. It has been accelerated under the Conservatives since 1979. It is therefore not surprising that the main focus[65] in the relationship between central and local government is finance.

(a) Local Authority Finance

12–50 Currently local authority spending comprises £62 billion. The vast amount of expenditure is taken up with education, housing, and personal social services.[66]

The structures of local government's financial arrangements are complex and have undergone considerable change. In outline the following description is an attempt to explain the main features of the system from the old system of rating valuation to the new system of community charge, in operation until April 1, 1993, and afterwards its replacement by the Council tax.[67]

12–51 Historically local authorities were given wide discretion and a degree of self-regulation over the financial arrangements and accounting practices in use in local government. Local authority expenditure is divided between revenue and capital. Revenue expenditure refers to short-term matters such as salaries and office supplies and is funded out of current income; capital expenditure refers to longer term spending such as buildings and is funded from borrowing.[68] The latter has caused central government to restrict and control the extent of local government borrowing in order to control public spending as part of its long-term policy.

Local authority finance is often complicated and beset by technical and detailed legal rules.[69] Current expenditure is funded from three main sources of income: charges made by local government for services, etc.; central government grants and up until 1990 rates. Of the three, the main sources of local authority income came from rates (now replaced by the Council tax) and grants from central government.

12–52 Rates were based on a property valuation and were levied on both domestic and business occupancy. Their origin may be traced to the

---

[65] M. Elliott, "The Control of Public Expenditure" in Jowell and Oliver, *op cit.* pp. 165–192.

[66] In descending order of expenditure the services provided comprise education (33%), housing (22%), local environmental services (17%), personal social services (9%), police (8%), local transport (7%), fire (2%), libraries (1%) and other Home Office matters (1%).

[67] See The Councillors' Guide to the Local Government Finance Act 1992, available from CIPFA, London.

[68] This includes the money markets explained in more detail below.

[69] C. M. G. Himsworth, "Poll Tax Capping and Judicial Review" [1991] P.L. 76–92. Also see C. M. G. Himsworth and N. C. Walker, "After Rates? The Community Charge in Scotland" [1987] P.L. 586.

earliest development of local authorities. In the Vagabonds Act 1535, churchwardens were responsible for the administration of the poor through relief charged upon each parish. The Poor Relief Act 1597 recognised the growing scale of the amount of relief and introduced a general system of local rating. Compulsory rating, enforced through distress and sale of chattels for non-payment, was accompanied by a system of audit, later through a district auditor under the Poor Law Amendment Act 1866, and proper accounting introduced by the Poor Relief Act 1601. Consolidation of enforcement procedures was further provided in the General Rates Act 1967. The basis of the rating system depended on regular valuation of property values. Property values, which set the basis of the rating system, had not been revalued since April 1973 in England, and any revaluation was seen as problematic, which prompted the Government to consider changes in the rating system of local government finance.

A further complication arose when local authorities increased the **12–53** amount of revenue from the rates by sharply increasing rate levels. By 1974 this had caused a "crisis in local government finance which led to the setting up of the Layfield Committee[70] into local government finance which reported after two years of deliberations in 1976."[71]

An additional complication to the rating system was the need for major financial support from central government through a rate support grant[72] (RSG) under the Local Government Act 1966 and later amended by the Local Government, Planning and Land Act 1980, Pt. VI. In the mid-1970s the extent of central government grants received by local authorities exceeded the amount raised by rates. Over 60 per cent of local authority funding came through central government grant, an indication of the dependency of local authorities on central government. The form of grant, called Rate Support Grant, (RSG), was as a block grant which left local authorities free to determine how spending priorities could be identified within their statutory duties imposed on local authorities. Local authorities could increase the level of their rates to take account of their expenditure.

Central government desired to impose a new financial discipline on **12–54** local authorities and imposed a revision of the RSG system on each local authority. The revision was set out according to the assessment

---

[70] Reports of the Layfield Committee, Cmnd. 6453 (1976).
[71] The Layfield Report left unanswered the basic problems of the directions to take over local government finance. It recognised the need for additional charges to be made for local government services, an increase in income initiatives, and perhaps some form of local income tax.
[72] Originally grants were prescribed for specific purposes but over the years there developed a block grant system leaving the local authority free to determine how best to distribute its funds.

of each local authority spending conducted by central government under the Local Government, Planning and Land Act 1980. Included under the 1980 Act were controls on local government capital expenditure in an effort to reduce local government expenditure and curtail the freedom of local authorities to depart from the financial policies of central government.

The theory behind the 1980 Act was that differences in local authority spending habits might be identified and controls applied to the more prolific spending authorities. Further refinements to the 1980 Act were provided by the Local Government Finance Act 1982 by setting spending targets and penalities on local authorities. The 1982 Act introduced the Audit Commission to improve the financial management of local authorities. The 1982 Act also abolished supplementary rates.

12–55 Local authority ingenuity contrived to avoid the effects of central government's initiatives at control. Setting targets for local authority spending did not prove efffective and in 1984 the Rates Act included powers to the Secretary of State to control the making of rates and the issuing of precepts. This introduced the concept of "rate capping" whereby the Secretary of State could determine the rates of "over spending" authorities and limit their rate levels. This led to further "creative accounting" by local authorities. Central government found that the making of regulations and their enforcement a complex and expensive game of "cat and mouse" between local and central government.

The abolition of the Greater London Council and the six Metropolitan Counties took place in 1985 as a further attempt to curtail the more irritating excesses of local government. However these changes and the adaptation of the rates system to bring it within central government control failed to address the central issue of how to provide a satisfactory system for the finance of local government.

12–56 The Layfield Committee[73] in 1976 in reviewing local government rating, had noted the difficulty of re-valuation of property based on notional rental values. The Layfield Committee recommended that re-valuation should take place on the basis of property sale price. The system of rating remained unchanged, although the government in its election manifestos from 1979 promised to introduce reforms to the rating system. The Department of Environment published in December 1981, a Green Paper entitled Alternatives to Domestic Rates which examined the three options possible for reform: a local sales tax, a local income tax and a poll tax. Although there were considerable doubts about the desirability and cost of the poll tax, not least from

---

[73] Report of the Layfield Committee, Cmnd. 6453 (1976).

the then Chancellor of the Exchequer Nigel Lawson, who "was unequivocal" in his opposition to the Poll Tax, and who noted that the Poll Tax was chosen as the best option for the reform of local government finance. Nigel Lawson in his memoirs stated[74]:

> "The Poll Tax was then given fresh momentum by the removal of Patrick Jenkin as Environment Secretary in the first week of September 1985 and his replacement by Kenneth Baker, who as Minister of State in charge of local government was part-author of the original proposal."

Dissatisfaction with the rating system resulted in its abolition and replacement with the Community Charge, commonly called Poll Tax, under the Local Government Finance Act 1988 and the Local Government and Housing Act 1989. The responsibilities of local authorities included the conduct of a canvass of properties in their areas, allocating between chargepayers the various categories of charge such as the personal[75] or collective community charge, maintaining a register and a public extract, imposing penalties and demanding payments.

The introduction of the Community Charge was intended to **12–57** remove the need for the complex rate capping procedures and the acrimonious relations between local and central government. The tax was essentially on each of the electors in each local authority. All adults were expected to pay the tax and it was first implemented in Scotland in 1989 in advance of England and Wales. Originally in 1988 the charge was estimated at £200 *per capita* but by 1990 when the tax came to be implemented the average tax was around £400.[76] The business rates remained unaffected by the introduction of the Community Charge.

Complications in the implementation of the charge added to the **12–58** general dissatisfaction over the tax. Non-payment of the tax, difficulty of enforcing court orders against defaulters and massive administrative costs of keeping the register up to date made the tax difficult and cumbersome to collect. Anomalies arose in the way the charge was calculated leading to larger than expected charges. Some conservative local authorities, considered to be well run and managed found charges over 30 per cent greater than had been expected. In others the cost was up to 36 per cent greater. As a result the Secretary of State was forced to use his charge capping powers with a formula, which

---

[74] Nigel Lawson, *The View from No. 11* (1992), pp. 561–585. See Butler and others, *Poll Tax* (forthcoming, 1994).
[75] The standard charge was levied on empty properties.
[76] Lawson, *op. cit.* p. 580.

proved controversial, to limit the amount of the charge on certain local authorities. In 1990 21 local authorities were charge capped. Extra assistance from the Treasury only served to reinforce the earlier doubts about the efficacy of the Community Charge. Invariably the Government's popularity diminished which may have contributed to the leadership crisis leading to the resignation of Mrs Thatcher.

12–59   The dissatisfaction with the Community Charge caused the Government to reconsider once more the basis of taxation for local government. A Council Tax took effect from April 1, 1993 under the Local Government Finance Act 1992, involving an element of property valuation, in the setting of the charge. Ironically this has required the valuation of the entire housing stock in order to implement the changes introduced by the new tax. The tax is based on the banded capital value of domestic property, with discounts for the number and status of the adults who are resident in the property. There are provisions for people on low incomes. There is a Valuation Office Agency responsible for the valuation of domestic property for the Council Tax.

12–60   The current law is to be found in the Local Government Finance Act 1992. The council tax may best be described as "a hybrid." It is not wholly a property tax but in part bears some resemblance to the community charge as it has some elements of "a household tax," because of the use of rebates depending on the income of the occupier. The property element comes from the fact that the council tax[77] is based on a valuation of property in which the person lives on April 1, 1991. There are eight property bands with different limits in England, Scotland and Wales to take account of differentials in the property market. In theory the higher band tax payer will pay about three times as much as the lower band payer. The household element comes from a rebate scheme based on income. This element is intended to mitigate the poverty of the household in cases of small or no income. Thus the household will be unaffected by the tax set by the Council if the means of the occupants of the property are such that there is a reduction in tax.[78] There are, in addition, certain groups specifically exempted.[79]

The impact of the council tax has yet to be fully assessed. Early indications are that the regressive nature of the community charge

---

[77] See C. Giles and M. Ridge, "The Impact on Households of the 1993 Budget and the Council Tax" (1993) 14 *Fiscal Studies (No. 3)* 1–20. Also see N. Lawson, "Inside Number 11" (1992), pp. 561–572 and 573–585. J. Hills and N. Sutherland, "The proposed Council Tax" (1991) 12 *Fiscal Studies (No. 4)* 1–21.

[78] S.11 of the Local Government Finance Act 1992.

[79] Sched. 1 to the Local Government Finance Act 1992. Exempted groups are students, mentally impaired and under Sched. 9 there are benefits available to recipients of social security benefits. Non-domestic rates remain and apply to many businesses and property. See Non-Domestic Rating Act 1994 which sets limits on increases in non-domestic rates.

has been solved. The council tax appears with the other budget arrangements to be progressive," but the mitigation is limited" as the poorest households appear disadvantaged.[80]

(b) The Courts and Local Authority Activities

Local authorities are subject to the rules of administrative law in the **12–61** same way as any other administrative decision-maker that has statutory powers. In fact some of the most important principles of administrative law emerged in cases involving local authorities. In *Associated Picture Houses Ltd v. Wednesbury Corporation*[81] the courts tested the condition of a licence, restricting children under 15 to admission to Sunday performances in a cinema according to whether the condition was unreasonable or not. In upholding the condition of the local authority as legal the courts established a test of reasonableness which has been influential in the development of administrative law.[82] The test is known as Wednesbury unreasonableness when the authority has come to a conclusion "so unreasonable that no reasonable authority could ever have come to it."

Judicial review of discretionary powers exercised by local author- **12–62** ities involves ensuring that the purpose, policy and objectives of a statute should not be frustrated in the exercise of statutory powers.[83] Irrelevant considerations should not be taken when making decisions. Ignoring facts or errors of law or fact, may give rise to a ground for challenge.[84]

Judicial review may be seen as an important means to check on the legality of local authority activities. It also provides for the resolution of disputes between the parties especially in the resolution of disputes between central and local government.[85] Increasingly judicial review has been sought. For example for the period 1987–89, there were 134 applications instituted by local councils, over half of which were brought against central government. Sunkin[86] has estimated that "approximately 20 per cent were challenges to decisions of other local authorities."

A sizeable proportion of the applications for judicial review involve **12–63** the local authority in areas such as homeless persons, education

---

[80] See Giles and Ridge, *op. cit.* p. 20.

[81] [1948] 1 K.B. 223.

[82] See *Re Westminster City Council* [1986] A.C. 668 and *Wheeler v. Leicester City Council* [1985] A.C. 1054.

[83] *Padfield v. Minister of Agriculture Fisheries and Food* [1968] A.C. 997.

[84] *Secretary of State for Education and Science v. Tameside MBC* [1977] A.C. 1014.

[85] *Secretary of State for Education and Science v. Tameside Metropolitan B.C.* [1977] A.C. 1014.

[86] M. Sunkin, "The Judicial Review Case-load 1987–89" [1991] P.L. 490 at 498.

disputes, matters involving planning and the environment and the internal affairs of local authorities.[87] Local authorities have also a role in representing the public interest and a limited role in seeking to protect rights narrower but analogous with the Attorney-General's role. Section 222 of the Local Government Act 1972 contains legal powers for the "promotion and protection of the interests of the inhabitants of their area." A Local authority is competent to take proceedings in its own name without the consent of the Attorney-General.[88] Proceedings by local authorities have included action against illegal trading under the Shops Act 1950, the control of noise pollution and trading in breach of controls over sex shops.[89]

12–64   The constitutional importance of judicial review is underlined by the authors of the study as follows[90]:

> "There are lessons to be drawn here about the constitutional significance of judicial review. Judicial review is often depicted as a weapon in the hands of the citizen against the over-mighty powers of central government, and it has certainly performed this role in a number of recent high profile cases. Our data suggests, however, that over the past decade it has been used more often as a weapon to further limit the autonomy of local government rather than as a constraint on the power of the central state."

Public lawyers interested in local government will consider that the recent Court of Appeal decision in *Credit Suisse v. Borough Council of Allerdale*[91] is significant. Allerdale local authority engaged in a joint venture through a number of companies set up by the local authority, technically known as "local government influenced companies", to build and operate a leisure complex. A time-share scheme was envisaged as the best means to operate the complex. Credit Suisse, a leading international banking institution, provided substantial loans repayable over a fixed period. The district auditor queried the legality

---

[87] Examples of such cases are *Bromley LBC v. GLC* [1982] 2 W.L.R. 62; [1983] 1 A.C. 768, over the Greater London Councils "fair fares" policy. Protracted litigation over the rates system of local government finance and its replacement by the Community Charge (commonly called poll tax) has also resulted in litigation. Creative accounting by local authorities has been challenged in the courts by the District Auditor. In *R. v. District Auditor No. 3 district, ex p. West Yorkshire Metropolitan County Council* (1985) 26 R.V.R. 26, the court declared invalid the creation of a trust to carry forward funds raised by the local authority from one year to the next, under the provisions of s.137 of the Local Government Act 1972. This case raised the question of the legality of a local authority using a trust to carry out its financial management.

[88] See *Solihull MBC v. Maxfern Ltd* [1977] 1 W.L.R. 127 also B. Hough "Local Authorities as Guardians of the Public Interest" [1992] P.L. 130.

[89] Hough, *op. cit.* p. 138.

[90] *ibid.* pp. 193–4.

[91] [1996] 4 All E.R. 129. *L.A. LAW* issue 5/96 (June 19, 1996).

of the local authority joint venture companies, the local authority involvement and the investment of Credit Suisse. This arose when the ability of the local authority companies to repay the loans came into doubt. The case involved legal consideration of the powers and duties of the local authority and its relationship to Credit Suisse. The Court of Appeal held that the arrangements with the joint-venture companies was *ultra vires* the powers of the local authority.

The Court of Appeal has therefore adopted a highly restrictive **12–65** approach in the interpretation of local government powers. The result of the case left Credit Suisse largely exposed to debts and liabilities that arise from the *ultra vires* transaction. This will seriously inhibit local government joint ventures with the private sector.

Local authorities possess wide statutory enforcement powers which **12–66** may give rise to litigation. In *Kirklees Metropolitan Borough Council v. Wickes Building Supplies Ltd*[92] the local authority sought an interlocutory injunction under section 222 of the Local Government Act 1972 restraining a Do It Yourself shop from trading contrary to section 47 of the Shops Act 1950. Criminal prosecutions under the Shops Act 1950 had little deterrent effect with large stores prepared to pay fines as a "tax" on Sunday opening. The use of an injunction by the local authority was an attempt to enforce the law when criminal prosecutions were ineffective. The use of injunctions is a common practice for local authorities[93] in a range of circumstances where the criminal law may be of dubious value in terms of its effectiveness. In such cases the question arises as to the making of a cross-undertaking in damages. In the *Kirklees* case the local authority declined, most likely because such an undertaking might result in large liabilities for the local authority should the case be finally resolved in favour of the shops. Lord Goff in the House of Lords accepted that a local authority could be treated in the same way as the Crown and not be required to give an undertaking in damages.[94]

Occasionally major issues of policy are raised involving the precise **12–67** nature and role of the local authority. In *Bromley LBC v. GLC*[95] the House of Lords held unlawful the subsidy of the, now defunct, GLC

---

[92] [1992] 3 All E.R. 717.
[93] See *Portsmouth City Council v. Richards* [1989] 1 C.M.L.R. 673 where the Court of Appeal upheld an interlocutory injunction to restrain the operation of sex shops. Also see *City of London v. Bovis Construction Ltd* [1992] 3 All E.R. 697 where the Court of Appeal upheld the grant of an interlocutory injunction to restrain a breach of the Control of Pollution Act 1974.
[94] Lord Goff explained: But the considerations which persuaded this House to hold that there was a discretion whether or not to require an undertaking in damages from the Crown in a law enforcement action are equally applicable in cases in which some other public authority is charged with the enforcement of the law" *Kirklees B.C. v. Wickes Building Supplies Ltd* [1992] 3 All E.R. 717 at p. 728.
[95] [1983] 1 A.C. 768.

to the London Transport Executive. The majority group in the GLC
had regarded themselves bound by an election manifesto and had
accordingly fettered their discretion unreasonably. The subsidy supported a reduction in fares of 25 per cent and this was regarded by
the House of Lords as an improper exercise of discretion. The
majority in the House of Lords also held that local authorities owed a
general fiduciary duty to their rate payers.

12–68   Local authorities are statutory corporations. They may enter contracts and freely negotiate commercial arrangements. Local authorities are subject to their own statutory powers and the *ultra vires* rule.
This rule means that a local authority should not act outside its
statutory powers. Each local authority has its own legal personality[96]
and may make use of private Bill legislation to enhance its powers.
Private Bills are a regular means for local authority powers to be
extended. Though it is doubtful if a local authority can sue for libel in
respect of its governing or administrative reputation. However this
does not prevent a local authority or[97] "any corporation, whether
trading or non-trading, which can show that it has a corporate
reputation (as distinct from that of its members) which is capable of
being damaged by a defamatory statement, can sue in libel to protect
that reputation, in the same way as can a natural person, although
there will of course be certain types of statement which cannot
defame an artificial person."

12–69   Loughlin has reviewed[98] the increase in the use of legal rules
settling disputes over the functions, structures and financial arrangements of local government. One area, which illustrates this phenomenon are disputes over local government finance, particularly
over the rate support system under the rating system replaced by the
Community Charge and later the Council Tax.

The Secretary of State was obliged to follow complex rules to set
the amount of rate support grant available for the year. A report had
to be prepared and laid before the House of Commons before the
individual local authority grant could be determined. Disputes on the
policy which informed the Secretary of State's view of the aggrega-
tion rules gave use to court cases challenging the application of the
rules. In one such case, however, *R. v. Secretary of State for the
Environment, ex p. Nottinghamshire County Council*[99] the House of

---

[96] In *Derbyshire County Council v. Times Newspapers Ltd, The Independent*, February 21,
1992; [1992] 3 All E.R. 65, the Court of Appeal held that local authorities as non-
trading statutory corporations could not sue for libel in respect of its governing or
administrative reputation, if no actual financial loss was pleaded or alleged. Leave to
appeal to the House of Lords was granted.

[97] *Per* Balcombe L.J. in *Derbyshire C.C. v. Times Newspapers* [1992] 3 All E.R. 65 at 75.

[98] M. Loughlin, "Innovative Financing in Local Government: The Limits of Legal
Instrumentalism" Parts I and II [1990] P.L. 372–407 and [1991] P.L. 568–599.

[99] [1986] 2 W.L.R. 1.

Lords showed reluctance to interfere in the discretion of the Secretary of State who was making a "political judgment." Only in exceptional cases would judicial review be available and only if the Secretary of State had failed to consult or ignored matters expressly listed in the legislation. Local authorities have continued to seek to exploit ambiguities, "loopholes" or uncertainties in the law in order to increase the revenue available to their needs. Often Labour controlled authorities have spearheaded the manipulation of financial rules to meet expenditure programmes. The court's willingness to declare some of the more speculative local authorities schemes as unlawful may be seen in *Stockdale v. Haringey LBC*.[1] The Court of Appeal struck out as unlawful the use of Haringey LBC's loans fund to maintain its expenditure programmes.

Local authorities have continually resorted to new techniques to **12–70** find additional revenue and as these techniques are put in place, so central government rules are introduced to attempt to control prolific spending by local authorities through "innovative financing."[2] Central government's frustrations were not helped by the additional complexity of the rules and the excessive legalism of their application. The growth in litigation and the need for expensive legal opinions before decisions could be reached contributed to the decision to replace local authority rates with the Community Charge.

A particularly difficult area was the power of central government **12–71** to "rate cap" local authorities for excessive spending. The "rate cap" was a fiscal device used by central government to prevent an individual local authority from increasing its revenue by increasing the rates charged to inhabitants within its area. This was a bitterly contested power under the Rates Act 1984 which it was hoped the introduction of the Community Charge would end. In theory the Community Charge was a *per capita tax*, allowing a substantial level of autonomy to local authorities. Local authorities with large expenditure totals would charge their inhabitants more than local authorities with lower expenditure requirements. Central government labelled local authorities who were high spenders as wasteful. It was expected that such local authorities would be electorally unpopular as inhabitants would suffer higher "Poll Tax" Bills. Potentially the "Poll Tax" had the political significance of giving electoral advantage to the Conservative, rather than the Labour controlled local authority. Labour controlled authorities were alleged to need to spend large amounts of public money to provide their services.

The introduction of the Community Charge,[3] first in Scotland, then **12–72** in England, required the Government to introduce "charge capping

---

[1] [1989] R.A. 107.
[2] Loughlin, *op. cit.*
[3] Abolition of Domestic Rates, etc., (Scotland) Act 1987, s.22 and Sched. 3.

powers." These were similar to the rate capping powers abolished with the rates. They were proved necessary because the Government undertook a review of the appropriate level of total standard spending of all local authorities which resulted in an allocation of the appropriate spending needed for each individual local authority. The result of that exercise showed that a number of local authorities' Community Charge Bills exceeded the expections of the central government based on their predictions and calculation of the requirements for each local authority.

12–73   In *Hammersmith and Fulham LBC v. Secretary of State for the Environment*[4] the House of Lords considered the legality and the operation of the poll tax capping rules. Two arguments were made by Hammersmith and Fulham against the Secretary of State's decision to cap the local authority poll tax charge. First, that the Secretary of State should satisfy himself that the authority's budget was excessive and secondly the Secretary of State should consider whether the authority's budget should be designated as requiring the application of the poll tax cap. Both arguments were rejected by Lord Bridge. In upholding the legality of the Secretary of State's powers the House of Lords left the subjective judgement of the Secretary of State intact. The judicial viewpoint was that there was no objective criterion which could be used to determine excessive expenditure. No "procedural impropriety" could be found in the Secretary of State's decision. As a result separate and therefore different levels of expenditure applied in different local authorities. In applying this criterion the Secretary of State admitted that differences based on political considerations might apply. This gave rise to inconsistencies in the level of the "cap" with the political implication that Labour controlled local authorities were not fairly treated. However the courts were unwilling to offer any review of the criteria. The House of Lords concluded that the Secretary of State was the best judge of the differences and was free to set his own principles. There was no obligation to set out the reasons behind the principles.

12–74   The *Hammersmith & Fulham* decision raises important questions about the use of judicial review. The local authority perspective is that the role of the courts is to act as a fetter on the potentially unrestrained powers of central government. Statutory interpretation should be sufficiently creative to allow the courts an opportunity to intervene. From the courts' perspective, however, there is difficulty in finding suitable and acceptable standards which may be used to adjudicate between central and local government. Courts have found this area of the law to be complex. Especially so when the doctrine of

---

[4] [1990] 3 All E.R. 589.

ministerial responsibilty applies in the case of central government Ministers who are accountable to Parliament. As Himsworth commented[5]:

"On the one hand there is the question of whether there is any justification at all for a role for the courts exercising powers of judicial review in reaction to these battles between tiers of government. Secondly, there is the question of the standard of review to be called in aid by the parties and applied by the courts. An understanding of these standards is required because without them tests such as that of procedural impropriety, proportionality, irrationality and even illegality remain, despite their familiarity, meaningless and vague."

The complexity of the legal rules, the vagueness of standards of 12–75 judicial review and the political nature of local authority decision-making, give the courts wide discretion when reviewing the powers of local authorities. The courts are in a sensitive area of having to adjudicate between central and local government over matters involving the fundamental role of local authorities.

Local authority speculation in the swaps market highlights another dimension to judicial review. In *Hazell v. Hammersmith and Fulham LBC*.[6] Hammersmith had invested substantial sums in the swaps market in order to find investment income to finance expenditure. The basic principle of the swaps market is that a borrower at a fixed interest rate contracts with a third party to pay or receive the difference between his interest liability and what it would have been at a variable interest. Many local authorities became active in this lucrative market. Hammersmith had gained up to £37m in interest premiums by the end of 1989. But with the rise in interest rates on local authority borrowings and the loss of confidence in the stock market, it was estimated that Hammersmith might lose between £74m and £186m. A large number of other local authorities had similarly invested. The precise legality of the investments was open to doubt.

The local authority relied on[7] section 111(1) of the Local Govern- 12–76 ment Act 1972 which empowered local authorities certain borrowing powers: "calculated to facilitate, or conducive or incidental to, the

---

[5] Himsworth, *op. cit.* pp. 90–91.
[6] [1990] 2 W.L.R. 1038; [1991] 2 W.L.R. 372.
[7] This section should be read alongside Sched. 13 which limits s.111(1): The terms of Sched. 13 are such that Lord Templeman (at p. 387) stated: "Schedule 13 establishes a comprehensive code which defines and limits the powers of a local authority with regard to its borrowing. The Schedule is in my view inconsistent with any incidental power to enter into swaps transactions."

discharge of any of their functions." The local government auditor challenged the legality of local authority investment in the swaps market as all being unlawful. This court case initiated by the auditor, was opposed by the banks and financial institutions who wished to show the transactions were lawful.

If the transactions were held to be unlawful, the banks would have to bear the burden of the debts because local authority liability could not extend to transactions which were potentially void because of their illegality. In a curiosity of the case, the local authorities who at first argued for the lawfulness of the transactions, found that their best interests would be served if the transactions were declared void. This would leave the local authority free of the bulk of any debt liability.

12–77　The House of Lords concluded that Hammersmith's swap transactions were *ultra vires*. Their reasoning relied on the statutory interpretation of section 111(1). Particular emphasis was placed on Part 1 to Schedule 13 of the 1972 Act which limited the general powers of borrowing given to local authorities under section 111(1). Lord Templeman concluded that the Schedule was "inconsistent with any incidental power to enter into swaps transaction."

The case had far reaching effects. Local authority debts arising out of the swaps market were generally taken up by banks and financial institutions through protracted litigation in an attempt to unravel the nature of many individual swaps transactions. Currently, uncertainty arises as to the liability of financial advisers and lawyers advising local authorities to enter the swap market.

12–78　Loughlin criticises the courts.[8] He argues that in reaching their decisions the Lords adopted a "strict constructionist line" and were affected by their perceptions both of the nature of the swaps market and the reasons for local authority investment in it. This raises the question of how suitable the courts may be in developing "a managerial role" over local authorities. Loughlin questions whether

---

[8] "1. Without prejudice to section III above – (a) a principal council may borrow money for the purpose of lending money to another authority . . .

(b) a local authority . . . may borrow money for any other purpose of class of purpose approved for the purposes of this sub-paragraph by the Secretary of State and in accordance with any conditions subject to which the approval is given . . ."

However this general power is negatived by the provision of para. 7 and is subject to regulation 7.-(1) Where expenditure incurred by a local authority for any purpose is defrayed by borrowing, the local authority shall . . . debit the account from which that expenditure would otherwise fall to be defrayed with a sum equivalent to an instalment of principal and interest combined such that if paid annually it would secure the payment of interest at the due rate on the outstanding principal together with the repayment of the principal not later than the end of the fixed period [of the loan]."

Loughlin, *op. cit.* Also see N. Deakin, "Local Government; Some recent change and future Prospects" [1991] *Parliamentary Affairs* 493–504.

the courts have sufficiently developed techniques to interpret complex regulatory and financial issues. There is also the question of the adjudicative functions performed by courts and their suitablility in enforcing legal rules of such complexity involving financial management.

In this regard the characteristics of legislation affecting local **12–79** authorities in the 1980s deserve mention. Loughlin describes this as "a new style of legislation" namely precise, directive powers setting out a comprehensive regulatory structure. Such legislation gives the courts little opportunity not to apply the exact wording and letter of the law to local authorities. Courts are, in effect required to exercise a regulatory role over local authorities.

Against this criticism there is the counter-balancing argument that the courts are effectively the only fair way to determine what the law is. In the decision of the auditor to seek a judicial remedy lies the question of whether the legal rules were correctly applied by the local authority. Ultimately such legal issues require the courts to clarify the law however inconvenient or overridden with policy issues.

The question of the management of local government sets new **12–80** challenges for the courts. The traditional value of the courts in developing procedural redress on the basis of *Wednesbury* unreasonableness[9] or where local authority councillors may be surcharged as in *Roberts v. Hopwood*[10] is only a starting point. Courts are increasingly required to develop their legal techniques of review and are required to make more exacting judgement on the regulation of decision-making in local authorities. This raises questions about how best local authorities may be managed.

The role of the courts is often problematic. Increasingly called upon to enforce legal controls over local authority activities, the complexities of financial management, social, economic and political issues expose the inadequacies of many legal techniques of analysis. Invariably courts offer *ex post facto* review, limited to highly technical and procedural problems which may not fit the management requirements which the law adopts when used as a regulating mechanism. Techniques of statutory construction in use by the ordinary courts pose the question raised by Loughlin. Do the courts possess "the cognitive conceptual and material resources" to enable them to perform the functions expected?

The challenge for the future development of judicial review is **12–81** reminiscent of the challenge indentified in 1947 by William Robson

---

[9] *Associated Picture Houses Ltd v. Wednesbury Corp.* [1948] 1 K.B. 223. See *CCSU v. Minister for the Civil Services* [1985] A.C. 374.
[10] *Roberts v. Hopwood* [1925] A.C. 578; *Pickwell v. Camden LBC* [1983] Q.B. 962.

which then formed the development of administrative law. Robson explained that administrative law had to respond[11]:

> "to the creation of new types of offences against the community, the growth of a new conception of social rights, an enhanced solicitude for the common good and a lessening of that belief in the divinity of extreme individualistic rights which was envinced in the early 19th century."

Today the courts face a growing belief in the market as a regulator, the preference for individual choice and sceptism about the ability of local government to manage and deliver services as part of their statutory responsibility.

5. Audit Commission and Accountability

12–82 Part III of the Local Government Finance Act 1982 established the Audit Commission for local authorities in England and Wales. The Audit Commission built on the established system of local authority audit with its modern origins in the late nineteenth century.[12] However the earliest origins of auditing may be traced back to the fifthteen century. District Auditors for each local authority are appointed by the Audit Commission. Auditors may be either officers of the Commission or appointed private firms of accountants. The status of the Commission rests on its professionalism and statutory powers. It is not directly responsible to any Minister but makes annual reports to Parliament. The Commisson is itself subject to audit by the National Audit Office. There are provisions in the 1982 Act[13] for co-ordination between the Commission and the National Audit Office. The Commission is not a servant of the Crown and its staff are not Crown servants.[14]

12–83   Radford[15] has pointed out that the Audit Commission was appointed:

> "with the twin objectives of emphasising the independence of the audit process and greater value for money in local authority

---

[11] W. A. Robson, *Justice and Administrative Law* (London, 1947), p. 31. Generally see Dawson, *op. cit.*

[12] Reginald Jones, *Local Government Audit Law* (2nd ed., HMSO, 1985 and supplement to 2nd ed., 1992).

[13] Local Government Finance Act 1982, s.27(2)(4).

[14] Local Government Finance Act 1982, Sched. 3, para 2.

[15] Mike Radford, "Auditing for Change: Local Government and the Audit Commission" [1991] M.L.R. 144.

spending, the government being of the view that 'improving public sector efficiency is still in large measure a matter of improving scrutiny, monitoring and management within the context of existing institutions'."

The Audit Commission is responsible for the drawing up of a code **12–84** of practice for local authorities subject to parliamentary approval.[16] This code has been extended by the National Health Service and Community Care Act 1990 to the National Health Service in England and Wales. The Code contains "what appears to the Commission to be the best professional practice" with respect to the audit responsibilities of the auditors concerned. The Commission may undertake studies for economy, efficiency and effectiveness in local authorities. This power clarified an area where the District Auditor had been active in the past. Powers to report on any matter which came within the notice of the auditors was also clarified. All auditors were given the same powers that the District Auditor had enjoyed namely, the power to make objections to the accounts on the basis of illegality, failure to account or gross misconduct. It must publish an annual report and the Commission publishes the studies it has undertaken.

Auditors appointed by the Audit Commission, must ensure in the **12–85** word of Lord Sumner in *Roberts v. Hopwood*[17] that:

"The purpose of the whole audit is to ensure wise and prudent administration and to recover for the council's funds money that should not have been taken out of them."

The Audit Commission was further strengthened after the review undertaken by the Widdicombe Committeee in 1986. Various powers enjoyed by the Auditors under sections 19 and 20 of the Local Government Finance Act 1982 were transferred to the Audit Commission. Section 19 concerned unlawful items of account and section 20 related to loss due to misconduct, and both sections envisaged procedures which might lead to surcharge or disqualification.

Additional powers were also granted to the Audit Commission. **12–86** The Local Government Act 1988 inserted new sections into the 1982 Act which empowered the auditor to issue a prohibition order preventing a body or officer under audit from carrying out any particular decision or action which might lead to an unlawful account or is likely to cause a loss or deficit. An innovation under the 1989 Act was the power granted to the Audit Commission to seek a judicial review[18] of any decision of a body under review by the Commission.

[16] Local Government Finance Act 1992, s.14.
[17] [1925] A.C. 578.
[18] See *R. v. Wirral MBC, ex p. Milstead* (1989) 87 L.G.R. 611 on an application for judicial review by the auditor,the court made an order for certiorari quashing various factoring agreements entered into by the local authority. Also see *R. v. Secretary of State for Education and Science, ex p. Avon C.C.* [1991] 1 Q.B. 558.

Thus the Audit Commission has been granted statutory *locus standi* to take action in the courts.

(a) The Audit Commission and Local Authority Audit

12–87 In carrying out its tasks as auditors the Commission has followed a similar *modus operandi* to the National Audit Office. The Commission conducts an inspection audit focused on the regularity of accounts where local authority accounts are examined for any defects in accounting, misconduct, illegal payments or unlawful expenditure.

In addition to the regularity audit, the Commission may carry out value for money examinations. Similar considerations apply to the conduct of value for money examinations in central and local government but there are important differences. Local authorities do not operate on the basis of departmental decision-making or under the doctrine of ministerial responsibility to Parliament. Local authorities do, however have various legal duties and responsibilities.

The Audit (Miscellaneous Provisions) Act 1996 provides for an extension of the functions of the Audit Commission and the National Health Service in England and Wales. Amendments under the 1996 Act include powers to undertake collaborative studies of social services and to permit publication of information on performance indicators. All these changes are intended to facilitate greater openness in accounting.

12–88 In 1983 the House of Lords in *Bromley London Borough Council v. Greater London Council*,[19] established that local authorities had a fiduciary duty to their rate payers. Lord Diplock noted that such a duty was "not to spend money thriftlessly" but make full use of the financial resources available. In the context of establishing good guidance for local authorities the Commission has followed this principle and has attempted to apply it to the development of strategies for the future of local authorities.

The Audit Commission may advise on the legality of local authority investments or financial plans. This is an important task and as discussed above, illustrates the watchdog function the Commission performed in the example of *Hazell v. Hammersmith*[20] which was initiated by the District Auditor. In giving advice the Audit Commission is primarily addressing the Auditors under its control, although this does not preclude the advice becoming widely known to the local authority.

12–89 The most controversial investigation recently carried out by the District Auditor is into the policy of Council house sales undertaken

---

[19] [1983] 1 A.C. 768.
[20] [1991] 1 All E.R. 545.

by Westminster City Council. The Auditor's report makes allegations of political bias and illegality in the operation of the right to buy scheme for council housing. If the Auditor's report is upheld then surcharges may be levied on some of the members of the Council engaged in the operation of the scheme.

An equally controversial and difficult area in the giving of legal advice is cross-boundary competitive tendering, where the Commission has considered such arrangements as of dubious legality on the basis that local authorities have no legal powers to enter into municipal trading for a profit.[21] The Audit Commission tends to combine two functions, watching and checking accounts and warning of future problems ahead. In this pro-active role the Commission seeks to influence local authorities into providing greater efficiency and effectiveness as good value for money.

In developing value for money examinations the Audit Commis- **12–90** sion has established its own methodology. First it provides a statistical profile of each local authority; secondly it undertakes on an annual basis a comparative evaluation on a national level of the activities of local authorities leading to various special studies to raise good practices and set out issues for the future. The Commission has sought to change the culture of local authorities and introduce innovations in management.

The Commission has provided its own definition of value for **12–91** money[22] in terms of economy, efficiency and effectiveness. Economy sets the terms under which an authority acquires human and material resources, efficiency sets the relationship between goods or services in terms of inputs needed to produce them and outputs found and measured in the product itself, and effectiveness determines the assessment of how well a programmme achieves its aims and objectives. Some commentators believe[23] that in setting out to provide value for money examinations the Commission has neglected effectiveness, in favour of economy and efficiency. One view[24] is that this is because the Commission is itself attempting to set its own objectives for local authorities rather than accept the objectives determined by the local authorities. In this respect the Audit Commission is

---

[21] Report of the Audit Commission, "Cross Boundary Tendering: Local Authorities doing work for One Another" (London, Audit Commission Technical Release 23/90, 1990).

[22] Report of the Audit Commission: "Improving Economy,Efficiency and Effectiveness in Local Government in England and Wales" (London, 1984), J. Gyford, "Local Authority Audit: An Alternative Tradition" (1989) *Local Government Studies* 9.

[23] A. Neilson, "Value for Money Auditing in Local Government" (1986) 6 *Public Money* 52; Arthur Midwinter, "The Politics of Local Fiscal Reform" (1989) 4 *Public Policy and Administration* 2–9.

[24] B. McSweeney "Accounting for the Audit Commission" (1988) 59 *The Political Quarterly* 28–43.

creating its own form of public sector management with an emphasis on management consultancy and innovative competition in the development of local authorities.

(b) Accountability

12–92 The developing role and function of the local authority as a regulator of services and the demand for better management of public money poses new challenges to the use of law and techniques of legal analysis. The courts, Audit Commission and central government are required to work in a harmonious relationship in the complex task of regulating local government. Ultimately the future shape of local government depends on the success of that relationship. Uniquely, the continuity fostered by the British Constitution may be overwhelmed by change.

12–93   The agenda for change in local government is set to continue for the 1990s. The objectives have been clearly set in the Department of Environment's Review.[25] These are: to promote more effective, speedy and business like decision-making; enhance the structure of decision making; increase the interest taken by the public in local government; and to provide scope for committees to devote more time to their constituency role. Such objectives involve both *internal* and *external* changes to the way local authorities make decisions. In particular in the internal management of local authorities there is concern that the majority of decisions are regularly taken by the whole council or by committees or sub-committees. The Widdicombe report[26] criticised decision making of this kind as time-consuming and cumbersome. Newly streamlined local authorities are demanded to avoid time wasting.

12–94   On the *external management* of local authorities decision-taking, the role of the Audit Commission has been set to develop new strategies in improving performance in terms of efficiency, effectiveness and economy. These strategies are consistent with the approach taken in the *Citizen's Charter* and competition in local authority tendering. In assessing the goods and services undertaken by local authorities, the Audit Commission provides a league table of local authorities and a direction setting performance targets for each financial year.[27]

12–95   The overall structure of local authorities is set to return to the original principle favoured by Redcliffe – Maud of unitary authorities. The key factors in carrying out local authority functions are: a

---

[25] *Local Government Review* (DOE, 1991).
[26] Cmnd 9797 (1986).
[27] Audit Commission, *The Citizens Charter Local Authority Indicators* (1992). Also see *Charting a Course* (HMSO, 1992).

shift to a more open style of competitive contract bidding; increased reliance on the private sector to deliver the various goods and services expected from the local authority; and a greater potential for joint enterprises between the public and private sector. A good example is in the formation of Company Act Companies or joint ventures.

The consultation paper makes explicit how these newly articulated activities are expected to be met[28]:

> "local authorities are undergoing a fundamental transformation from being the main providers of services to having responsibility for servicing their provision. The task of setting standards, specifying the work to be done and monitoring performance is done better if it is fully separated from the job of providing the services."

Local government finance is set to continue to dominate relations **12–96** between local and central government. The Council tax preserves central control over local government expenditure. There is an added dimension to local authority finance in terms of party politics and the contest for political control over local authority activities. A unitary system of local authorities is intended to improve the management of local authorities and the search for further and better ways of accountability and control.

Finally some consideration should be given to the question of how **12–97** influential and long term are the changes to local government outlined above?

Studies into the use of compulsory contract tendering (CCT), have indicated the far-reaching effects of such changes. As Walker has shown[29]:

> "Competition and the economic environment within which it is currently taking place had significantly affected the employment levels and practices of most of the case study DLO's."

Other findings showed that changes had taken place between DLO's and central service departments within local authorities. Even elected members of the various local authority boards involved with DLO's have shifted ideological and political perspectives as a result of the change in culture from the introduction of CCT.

---

[28] Local Government Review: "The Structure of Local Government in England" (April 1991) *Local Government Review* 4, para. 18.

[29] See B. Walker, *Competing for Building Maintenance Direct Labour Organisations and Compulsory Competitive Tendering* (HMSO, 1993) p. 75, para. 9.14.

12–98   A detailed investigation of the changes introduced under the Local Government Act 1988 has shown how contract compliance and competition may combine to produce change[30]:

> "The continuing pressure of competition was leading to enhanced monitoring of services and the way that they are managed, so that this effect is likely to persist."

A further gain was an improvement of the information available to the local authority on the costs of services. Setting targets and using contract compliance to encourage competition are seen as the new managerialism present in local authorities.

12–99   Contract compliance may represent substantial gains. There are questions about whether costs savings may only be as a result of "one off changes" introduced as a radical break from past practice. Indeed the evidence about the long-term effects of competition appears sketchy. Competition may itself result in increasing bureaucracy; vetting and monitoring are time-consuming and resource expensive. As Walsh and Davies note:

> "The introduction of competition has led to massive change in local authorities, and they are still at the stage of learning how to cope with the change. The immediate tasks required by competition have largely been accomplished. Long-term changes, for example, ensuring a coherent link between contracting and policy, are yet to be effectively dealt with."[31]

Despite the obvious experimental nature of many of the changes introduced there are a whole range of activities subject to competition through contract. These include the social services, education, waste management and more recently the police.[32] There are a wide variety of techniques available to promote competition such as management buy-outs, the establishment of trusts, the use of internal local authority companies and partnerships with private organisations and the voluntary sector. The fundamental assumption is that there can be, by analogy with the private sector, "a separation of client and contractor or purchaser and provider".[33] Yet it is unclear whether this assumption is valid or not.

---

[30] Kieron, Walsh and Howard Davis, *Competition and Service: The Impact of the Local Government Act 1988* (HMSO, 1993) p. 165, para. 15.2.

[31] Walsh and Davis, *op. cit.* p. 167, para. 15.11.

[32] See: *The White Paper on Police Reform* (Cm. 2281) and the *Sheehy Report* (HMSO, 1993) on the pay, conditions and status of the police. See McEldowney, "Managing the Police" (1993) *Local Authority Law* pp. 5–6.

[33] Walsh and Davis, *op. cit.* p. 167 para. 15.12.

Future developments are likely to include extending competition to the process of budgetary control, a focus on quality control and the incorporation of management and policy development as part of the process of monitoring. An assurance system, with certification to an agreed standard of quality is also encouraged such as BS 5750[34], is also likely to be high on the agenda of local authorities.

Walsh and Davis admit the fundamental challenge awaiting local authorities:

"So far, local authorities have been learning to manage competition. The next stage is to learn to manage the local authority with competition as one part of a new management system."[35]

Ken Young draws on the parallel of the nineteenth century revolution in government to conclude that the most profound changes are in the way we think about local government.[36]

---

[34] "Guide to Quality Management and Quality Systems Elements." See "Quality Management in Construction – Contractual aspects" *CIRIA* (Special publication) No. 48.

[35] Walsh and Davis, *op. cit.* p. 168 para. 15.16.

[36] See Ken Young, "Reinventing Local Government? Some Evidence Assessed" *Public Administration* Vol. 74, Autumn 1996, pp. 347–367.

Chapter 13

Privatisation and Regulation

1. Introduction

13–01 Privatisation of the major nationalised industries since 1979 has created a number of new regulatory agencies and legal framework to oversee the development of the newly formed Company Act Companies post-privatisation. A wide range of statutory powers, contracts, licenses and conditions provide the main legal mechanisms which govern the relationship between regulator, the company and the consumer. Largely discretionary, but also of great importance to the future of each industry is the role of the relevant Secretary of State and the complex legal powers which are devoted to the relationship between the regulator and the Secretary of State.

13–02 This chapter outlines some of the legal powers of the main regulators such as OFTEL, OFGAS, OFWAT and OFFER who, respectively, regulate the telecommunication, gas, water and electricity industries. Also relevant is the role of the Monopolies and Mergers Commission (MMC) and the Office of Fair Trading (OFT) which combine to investigate anti-competitive practices. The Director-General of Fair Trading may make a monopoly reference to the MMC or a reference covering an anti-competitive practice. Statutory authority for such a reference is included in the legislation relevant to each of the privatised utility industries.

13–03 The quest for further privatisation[1] has continued since the mid-1990s. The Government has sold some of its remaining shareholdings and added new privatisations to its list. Since the first privatisation, remaining shares have been sold in British Telecom and in the electricity industry there has been the sell-off of British Nuclear. New privatisations include British Coal (see the British Coal

---

[1] See M. Bishop, J. Kay and C. Mayer (eds.), *The Regulatory Challenge* (Oxford University Press, 1995); M. Bishop, J. Kay and C. Mayer, (eds.), *Privatization and Economic Performance* (Oxford University press, 1994).

Act 1993), British Rail (see the Railways Act 1993 and privatisation has been completed by 1997), and H.M. Stationery Office.

Privatisation proceeds[2] have significantly fallen to £2,500 million for 1995–96 from a peak in the year 1992–93 of £8,184 million. Taken as a whole for the period from 1979–96 privatisation proceeds are in total in excess of £64 billion. Privatisation has varied in the different forms it may take. Contracting out strategies[3] have been in operation in local and central government and within the National Health Service. There is also the popularity of management buy-outs such as may be found in the examples of parts of British Coal and in the National Freight Corporation.

The encouragement of private sector finance in the public sector is **13–04** part of the Private Finance Initiative.[4] This is a substantial effort to provide private funding of a whole range of activities from roads to bridges, from computer facilities to hospitals. Flynn has estimated that there are 150 information technology projects under consideration in the financial year 1996–97 at a total cost of £3.5 billion.[5]

Regulation[6] is a crucial part of the structures put in place for the **13–05** major utilities after privatisation. This is underlined by the fact that many of the utilities in the United Kingdom remain virtual monopolies. Regulation through a variety of semi-independent regulators is primarily intended to protect the interests of consumers but is, increasingly, required to provide the necessary supervision of competition in the utility industries.[7] To date, the experience of regulation has highlighted uncertainty over the extent of the regulators' powers, and increased sensitivity to the political issues which surround regulatory issues. Safeguarding the interests of the tax-payer, the consumer and the shareholder involves complex and often competing demands. Political choices are involved in setting priorities and providing an agenda for the future development of the utilities. Regulation policy is therefore at the heart of good regulation.

The British experience has been ad hoc; there is no coherent **13–06** policymaking to achieve a consistent approach among regulators, combining accountability with performance indicators. At the outset of privatisation the political dimension of each regulator's role was

---

[2] See *Public Expenditure: Statistical Supplement to the Financial Statement and Budget Report* 1995–96 Cm. 2821 H.M. Treasury, London.

[3] *Competing for Quality* Cm. 1730 (London, HMSO, 1997).

[4] See Norman Flynn, *Public Sector Management* (3rd ed., Prentice Hall, 1997) pp. 117–19.

[5] *ibid.* p. 119.

[6] See John F. McEldowney, "Public utilities: Is the British experience a model for developing countries?" in Julio Faundez (ed.), *Good Government and Law* (Macmillan in association with the British Council, 1997) pp. 147–62.

[7] See Richard Green and Catherine Waddams Price, "Liberalisation and Divestiture in the UK Energy Sector" *Fiscal Studies* (1995) Vol. 16. No. 1 pp. 75–89.

concealed in discussions about ownership, and debates about efficiency and effectiveness of the nationalised industries. It is only now by clarifying the political dimension that full assessment of the privatisation programme will emerge. Changes in the regulatory culture has significance for the way utility companies operate. The choice of individual regulator may also affect market sensitivity to regulation. There are doubts about the effectiveness of government policy towards regulation when conflicting interests such as consumer prices and shareholder dividends are considered. Doubts remain about the effectiveness of privatisation strategies when competition may require re-structuring of the utility industries. Even breaking up natural monopolies may not promise a solution to the problem of competition. The monopoly operator may provide economies of scale not available to smaller operators. A smaller operator may not provide economic efficiency because it may lack expertise or sufficient bargaining power through the contracts it makes with larger units. There may be a tendency to wish to develop and undertake the various contracts on its own. A smaller operator may wish to develop into a larger single unit and through its internal organisation provide more efficient organisation of the external contracts it once entered into.[8] Complexity and confusion emerge from the regulation of the utilities that may cast doubt on the value of the British experience of privatisation as a model for the future.

13–06A   Privatisation has provided an important agenda for developing innovative and creative legislation concerning the regulation and the day-to-day running of the newly privatised enterprises. Privatisation policies are fashionable in Europe,[9] North America and Japan and also among developing and newly-industrialised countries.

2. Nationalisation

13–07   Nationalisation requires some explanation and a brief outline of the attempts by successive governments to provide effective controls and efficient running of the nationalised industries. Thirty years ago,

---

[8] See C. Foster, *Privatisation, Public Ownership and the Regulation of Natural Monopoly* (Oxford, Blackwell, 1992).

[9] See Istvan Pogany, "Privatisation and Regulatory Change in Hungary" in M. Moran and T. Prosser, *Privatization and Regulatory Change in Europe* (Open University Press, 1994). Also see Jacques Pelkmans and Norbert Wagner, *Privatization and Deregulation in Asean and EC* (1990, Institute of Southeast Asia Studies) and L. Gray Cowan, *Privatization in the Developing World* (New York West Port Connecticut, London, Prager, 1990). T. Prosser, *Law and the Regulators* Clarendon Press, Oxford, 1997.

William Robson in the first edition of Nationalised Industries and Public Ownership[10] defined the meaning of nationalised industry in Britain as:

"State intervention of a positive kind in the ownership, operation or regulation of industries and services in a vast movement of world wide dimension."

Robson listed the public undertakings which fell within his defini- **13–08** tion. These included the major utilities such as water, gas, electricity, transport including rail, bus and air. It also covered the British Steel Corporation, the Post Office and the United Kingdom Atomic Energy Authority.

Nationalisation is of unquestionable political, economic and social significance. Constitutional lawyers have recognised that nationalisation has posed questions about the role of law and constitutional questions on the effectiveness of ministerial accountability for the industries.

(a) Nationalisation: Policy and Structures

The legal structure and organisation of the nationalised industries **13–09** requires explanation. Foulkes has noted[11] that nationalisation is a term used to describe various industries brought into:

". . . public or 'national' ownership by being vested in bodies corporate directed by persons appointed by a minister of the Crown, and who have to manage the industry within a statutory framework of obligations to the minister, who in turn is accountable to Parliament for his decisions in relation to them."

Forty years ago the establishment of the main nationalised indus- **13–10** tries was achieved through the creation of public corporations. The characteristics of the public corporation included a wide range of statutory powers granted by Parliament to allow the particular activities to flourish. Statutory powers usually included the grant of a

---

[10] W. Robson, *Nationalised Industry and Public Ownership* (1960) (2nd ed., 1962), p. 17. Also see L. Gordon, *The Public Corporation in Great Britain London* (1938); E. Goodwin, *Forms of Public Control and Ownership* (London, 1951); T. Prosser, *Nationalised Industries and Public Control* (Blackwell, 1986); T. Prosser, M. E. Dimook, *British Public Utilities and National Development* (1983, Chester), p. 3; L. Hannah, *Electricity before Nationalisation* (Electricity Council, 1929); H. Ballin, *The Organisation of Electricity Supply in Great Britain* (1946).

[11] D. Foulkes, *Administrative Law* (7th ed., 1990), p. 23.

monopoly over the supply to the sectors the utilities served and a framework which effectively separated the day-to-day working of the corporation from government intervention. A wide range of statutory formulations existed to achieve these characteristics. Sometimes the government took a major shareholding in an existing company, in other examples regulatory mechanisms were placed through the structure of the corporation itself.[12] As Nigel Lawson summarises in his memoirs,[13] five arguments advanced in favour of nationalisation during the 1940s. These include: the improvement of industrial relations; the promotion of full employment; the gain in productivity from the removal of absentee ownership; the efficient regulation of monopolies; the replacement of short term profit-maximisation by wider national and social priorities. Ideological reasons for public ownership were if anything more important than the desire to remedy defects.

13–11   Labour party thinking emphasised the belief that certain activities were essential to the well-being of the nation and should be run by the State. Industries with a natural monopoly were an obvious target for nationalisation. Accompanying the desire to run the natural monopolies was the idea that excessive profits should not be accumulated by exploiting a monopoly. Added to this there was a strong belief that industry should be working to the benefit of the nation[11] and provide services rather than rely on the market as a regulator.

---

[12] See J. F. McEldowney, *Electricity Industry Handbook* (John Wiley, 1992). In the case of electricity, state ownership provided an entire structure for the generation, supply and distribution of electricity through one uniform system. This replaced a system of electricity generation which in the 19th century had resulted in many failed corporate enterprises. Local government areas had been regarded by entrepreneurs as a convenient size for electricity generation and distribution. Between 1880 and 1882 the number of local authority electricity companies had risen from 14 to 102. Most of the companies attracted share speculators but the financial returns proved disappointing. The quick profit sought by shareholders was rarely achieved. As a result many of the companies ended in disaster with bankruptcy and the shares subsequently became worthless. The Parliamentary supervision of such enterprises was strengthened by the Electric Lighting Act 1882. This Act insisted on a licence period before a local authority could be given the right to purchase any undertaking. Instead of a collection of Private Bills, containing enabling powers for local authorities to run electricity companies the 1882 Act substituted a system of provisional orders allowing companies to be set up with the necessary statutory powers. In effect this was an arrangement based on a bargain, whereby Parliament granted statutory powers in return for closer supervision of the activities of the companies. It also reflected the lack of adequate Company Act provisions to meet the needs of national monopolies. At the end of 1883, 69 provisional orders were issued, with the result that 55 electric companies were set up.

[13] N. Lawson, *The View From No. 11* (1992), pp. 201–202.

[14] For a background study of nationalisation as part of the public economy see: Tomlinson, *Public Policy and the Economy Since 1900* (1990).

(b) Government as a Regulator of the Nationalised Industries

The model adopted for most nationalised industries followed the **13–12** Morrisonian model[15] named after Herbert Morrison whose ideas were the most influential. Thus the public corporation was the chosen form with statutory powers to provide services for the newly nationalised industries. Such arrangements were heavily influenced by ideology[16]:

> "The public corporation must not be a capitalist business . . . It must have a different atmosphere at its boardtable from that of a shareholders meeting; the board and its officers must regard themselves as high custodians of the public interest."

A number of influences could be directed by Ministers upon the **13–13** nationalised industry. Such influences included the power of appointment to the boards of nationalised industries, the issuing of general directions as to policy and specific ministerial approval over financial planning. Also included were ideas about encouraging the buying of British goods, an emphasis on the direction of returns on profits which could be ploughed back into the industry and overall policy objectives on employment conditions such as wage bargaining. The theory of ministerial supervision could in practice allow Ministers to "run the industry." Critics of the nationalised industries feared that such intervention might interfere with the efficiency of the industry itself.

Nationalisation however did not come about as a coherent and well **13–14** considered plan. Initially corporations were given little guidance on the policies they were to follow. There was general uncertainty as to the precise role such industries should play in the economy and confusion over the extent to which government influence should dictate managerial decisions. In general it was considered sufficient to appoint prudent managers to allow the industries to run themselves. The major issue was whether the nationalised industries required more direct intervention. The answer to this question was slow in coming.

The government of the day located the running of the nationalised industries as an important part of the general economy.[17]

Three government White Papers,[18] in 1961, 1967 and 1978 set out **13–15** policy considerations which were influential. The 1961 White Paper

---

[15] H. Morrison, *Socialisation of Transport* (1933).
[16] *ibid.* See J. F. McEldowney, "The Nationalisation Legislation of the 1940s and the Privatisation Legislation of the 1980s: A Constitutional Perspective" in R. Blackburn, *Constitutional Studies* (Mansell, 1992).
[17] R. Molyneux and D. Thompson, "Nationalised Industry Performance: Still Third Rate?" (1987) 18 *Fiscal Studies* (1987), p. 48.
[18] *Financial and Economic Obligations of the Nationalised Industries*, Cmnd. 1337 (1961); *Nationalised Industries: A Review of Economic and Financial Objectives*, Cmnd. 3437 (1967).

set out financial targets to be achieved, specified as a rate of return on assets set by Ministers. The formula used was crudely expressed; each nationalised industry was required to manage their affairs with the requirement of taking one year with notice to be sufficient to meet all items chargeable to revenue account. Thus "targets" were set for the industry to pay its way. Within this framework the industries were remarkably free to develop their own management strategies.

13-16   The 1967 White Paper marked a more significant development in providing detailed guidelines as to how the nationalised industries were to perform. Specific financial targets were set with a requirement on capital investment projects of a certain minimum rate of return fixed for all the industries by the Government. Further requirements included:

(a) The separation of non-commercial responsibilities in accounts with investment based on a social cost-benefit evaluation;

(b) Prices were to be set on the basis of long-run marginal costs. This meant that cross subsidisation between markets was to be avoided;

(c) Investment was to be based on a value of the expected future return on projects.

13-17   The means to monitor the operation of the 1967 White Paper was the Prices and Incomes Board. A weakness in the arrangements was the emphasis on financial instruments and little attention devoted to productive efficiency. A major concern was the potential power of Ministers to intervene, thus causing confusion over the exact boundaries of decision taking between Ministers and the nationalised industries. Thompson and Molyneux concluded[19]:

"In particular, the institutional framework provided for ministerial intervention in decision-making in ways which blurred ultimate responsibility for particular actions. The specification of objectives and accountability of performance against them both emphasised in the business management literature were thus absent."

13-18   A further deficiency was that in the early 1970s Government policy to counter inflation required public corporations to hold down prices at a level which made productivity uneconomic. Compensation for this policy appeared in the form of subsidies, paid to the industry in

---

[19] Molyneux and Thompson, *op. cit.* note 11.

order to mitigate the economic consequences of loss-making activities. Critics regarded the Government's short-term limited objectives based on political choices as inconsistent with the need to develop efficient industries.

The 1978 White Paper[20] went further than the two previous White **13–19** Papers and set the following targets for the nationalised industries in an attempt to provide for the weaknesses in government policy. In effect the targets set were intended to make the nationalised industries more efficient and avoid the problem of recurring losses.

(a) It strengthened financial controls by the Government over public corporations through external financial limits (EFLs) adopted for each industry;

(b) Financial targets became the prime instrument of Government policy requiring each industry to publish performance indicators to assess the efficiency of each industry through the relevant Government departments;

(c) The level of pricing was set to meet the financial targets.

(d) Investment was to be examined on the overall performance of the corporations' investment programme rather than individual projects.

Although the 1978 White Paper was broadly unclear as to how the **13–20** level of financial targets was to be estimated there was ample opportunity for Ministers to intervene on the basis of determining "each industry's target in the light of general policy objectives, including consideration of social, sectoral and counter-inflation policy."

The 1978 White Paper had resulted in a major shift towards auditing the efficiency of the nationalised industries. The 1980 Competition Act allowed the Monopolies and Mergers Commission to undertake efficiency audits at the request of Ministers. Productive efficiency became the basis of the overall financial controls set on each industry. The "non-commercial objective" of the nationalised industries characterised by the Labour Party[21] in its early nationalisation policies were set to one side in favour of greater financial scrutiny

---

[20] *The Nationalised Industries,* Cmnd. 7131 (1978).

[21] Graham and Prosser, "Privatising Nationalised Industries: Constitutional Issues and New Legal Techniques" (1987) 50 M.L.R. 16; T. Prosser, *The Privatisation of Public Enterprises in France and Great Britain; The State, Constitution and Public Policy,* EUR Working Paper No. 88/364 (1988), p. 37.

through efficiency audit. As Paul Craig has observed[22]: "The tension between the exercise of commercial freedom and the utilisation of public corporations as part of a broader governmental strategy is apparent once again."

13–21   Although individual statutory arrangements differed, depending on the particular industry involved, nevertheless some common features may be noted. A degree of day to day autonomy was granted to each industry leaving Ministers overall policy and direction. Ministers could influence the membership of the boards of the industry through individual appointment and the giving of general directions. Financial control, especially over borrowing and in major development programmes, was largely dependant on ministerial discretion and sanction. Generally, the role of the nationalised industries was vague and uncertain and left to the policies of successive governments. Rarely were legal powers invoked or actually used in the relationship between Ministers acting as an "arms length" regulator and responsible to Parliament through ministerial responsibility. Financial target setting after the 1978 White Paper heralded a new breakthrough whereby sponsoring government departments assessed individual efficiency of each government industry through scrutiny of the financial targets of the relevant industry. The question of the annual debt of each nationalised industry and the amount of public expenditure became a key aspect of ministerial policy. Such issues gave rise to relatively few legal disputes and were subordinated to the day to day management of the industry and the government's overall economic policies. A common complaint of nationalisation was the lack of information and knowledge of the working of the industry concerned.

13–22   Studies of the nationalised industries prior to privatisation have indicated that after a long struggle by successive governments the nationalsied industries had become more efficient and well run.[23] It is open to controversy whether this was because of the preparation for privatisation or simply a process of providing better management and targets through the White Papers mentioned above.[24]

(c) Accountability of the Nationalised Industries

13–23   Although the governing bodies of nationalised industries were not directly accountable to Parliament, in theory Ministers were responsible through the relevant department. The main opportunity for

[22] P. Craig, *Administrative Law* (2nd ed., 1989), pp. 84–87.
[23] M. Bishop and J. Kay, *Does Privatisation Work?* (London Business School, 1988); J. Kay, *et al.*, *Privatisation and Regulation – the UK Experience* (Oxford, 1986).
[24] Nigel Lawson is of the opinion that privatisation was the main catalyst for changes in the nationalised industries; N. Lawson, *The View from No. 11* (1992), pp. 239–240.

discussion arose from legislation affecting the industries, the reports of committees such as the Select Committee on Nationalised Industries.[25] It has been argued that a major weakness of such control was the absence of direct control through information becoming available to committees rather than to industry. The Select Committee on Nationalised Industries was set up in 1956 but in 1979, with reforms of the select committee system, it was abolished. It was replaced by provision for ad hoc subcommittees of two or more of the relevant department select committees to look at matters affecting nationalised industries. Elliott believes[26] that if implemented properly departmental committees could be more effective than the old Select Committee on Nationalised Industries could ever be. Since then reports have been prepared into aspects of the nationalised industries. Regret was expressed, that in 1983, in the reforms introduced in the setting up of the National Audit Office, no provision was made for the nationalised industries which remain outside the ambit of the Comptroller and Auditor General. Efforts to have the nationalised industries included was defeated by Government intervention in adopting the private Bill originally introduced by Norman St. John Stevas.

Thus parliamentary control appears to depend very much on ministerial accountability which is seen as a weakness in the existing arrangements. The Treasury may also exercise control and the major influence over the nationalised industries is the use of financial targets. The 1978 White Paper introduced the concept of external financing limits (EFLs) on each industry. This represented the total of public financial support for each corporation and are included in the Public Expenditure White Paper. They are subject to cash limits and in theory would seem to represent a positive statement of the sum that government may make over to the industry. In fact as Elliott has pointed out they were used in the financial year 1983–84 to produce a price increase in the gas and electricity industries because they bound the industry to meet their EFL through their own financial resources rather than additional government grants. **13–24**

Since 1980 the MMC offers a ministerial influence over the nationalised industries through reviews of efficiency. In fact this power has been increasingly used since 1982 as a means of increasing the efficiency of commercial objectives of the industry thereby decreasing the amount of public funds available. In 1983 reports by the MMC into the National Coal Board[27] and the Serpell Committee of Inquiry into Railway Finances together with a memorandum from **13–25**

---

[25] P. Craig, *op. cit.*; T. Prosser, *Nationalised Industries and Public Control* (Blackwell, 1986).
[26] M. J. Elliott, "The Control of Public Expenditure" in J. Jowell and D. Oliver, *The Changing Constitution* (Oxford, 1985), pp. 149–173.
[27] Cmnd. 8920 (1980).

the Comptroller and Auditor General to the Public Accounts Committee on the monitoring and control activities of three Departments sponsoring nationalised industries, complained of the way huge public subsidies were being used inefficiently or for purposes other than those originally intended. The main point of such criticisms was directed to the failure by departments to devise and operate an effective system of control. Although the objects of the MMC inquiry may be determined by Ministers concern that the MMC itself may not exercise a sufficiently independent function in their reports seem to be unfounded. Collins and Wharton concluded in their 1984 study that the MMC reports demonstrated an independent remit. However they admitted that there was no consensus on what basis the reports were made. Thus the follow-up to reports is unclear and the procedures for improvement left a lot to be desired.

13–26   The main focus in achieving accountability over the nationalised industries has been economic considerations as to the best method by which resources are allocated between competing uses and the best use made of them. By the 1980s as the Government[28] began to embark on its privatisation programme both questions remained unsatisfactorily answered. This point was succinctly explained by Maurice Garner when he wrote[29]:

> "The object of all accountability is to increase efficiency. The object of autonomy for the management of nationalised industries is efficiency. In Britain autonomy and accountability have come to be seen as antithetical".

3.   Privatisation, Policy and Objectives

13–27   Craig has identified a number of reasons for privatisation and included are many of the objections to the nationalisation programme of the 1940s[30]:

> "The reasons for privatisation are, like those for nationalisation, eclectic. They include the following; improving efficiency, reducing

---

[28] Both Molyneux and Thompson *op. cit.* in their study of the performance of the nationalised industries called for more reforms in the direction indicated by the 1978 White Paper particularly in respect of increased competition.

[29] M. Garner, "Auditing the Efficiency of Nationalised Industries: Enter the Monopolies and Mergers Commission" (1982) 60 *Public Administration* 409 at p. 426; B. Collins and Bob Wharton, "Investigating Public Industries: How has the Monopolies and Mergers Commission Performed?" (September, 1984) *Public Money*, pp. 15–23.

[30] P. Craig, *loc. cit.* note 16. The MMC powers refer to s. 11 Competition Act 1980.

government involvement in decision-making of industry, ordinary share ownership, encouraging share ownership by employees, alleviating problems of public sector pay determinate, reducing the public sector borrowing requirement and the enhancement of economic freedom."

Doubts about the efficiency of the nationalised industries were part **13–28** of a study undertaken by Richard Pryke in the late 1970s.[31] Such studies proved influential with the government of the day. Nigel Lawson noted how[32]:

"Most damaging of all was the inevitable politicization of nationalised industries. While governments find it hard to exercise strategic control over their industrial empire, the temptation to indulge in short-term interference in everything from prices and salaries to the placing of new plant in marginal constituencies is almost irresistible. The effect on nationalised industry management is equally bad: accommodating government or placating pressure groups becomes more important than commercial results."

Driven by strong ideological beliefs that the nationalised industries required dramatic re-construction, the Government also desired to widen share ownership. This had a political motive as according to Lawson[33] ". . . the more widely the shares were spread the more people who had a personal stake in privatisation, were thus unlikely to support a Labour party committed to renationalisation."

Privatisation may be examined according to its historic develop- **13–29** ment. It is necessary to make a crucial distinction between smaller privatised companies and larger activities. For example smaller companies such as Amersham International, Jaguar, Sealink and British Aerospace operate within a competitive[34] framework and pose little concern to the constitutional lawyer as to how their activities may be regulated. The Government's initial forays[35] into implementing its privatisation policy were based on identifying these smaller activities which were privatised as the first phase of the Government's policy. Stage 1, as it may be referred to made privatisation acceptable and attractive to the public and an electoral winner.

---

[31] See Pryke, *Public Enterprise in Practice* (1973); Pryke, *The Nationalised Industries, Policies and Performance Since 1968* (1981); Pryke, "The Comparative Performance of Public and Private Enterprise" (1982) 3(2) *Fiscal Studies*.
[32] Lawson, *The View from No. 11* (1992), p. 203.
[33] *ibid.* p. 208.
[34] Cento Veljanowski, *Selling the State: Privatisation in Britain* (London, 1988). See John Kay, *et al*, *Privatisation and Regulation the U.K. Experience* (Oxford, 1986).
[35] L. Hancher, M. Moran, *Capitalism, Culture and Economic Regulation* (OUP, 1989).

In contrast the larger privatisations such as British Telecom[36] in 1984 and British Gas[37] in 1985, electricity in 1989 required a regulatory framework which attempts to deal with the larger market to which the newly privatised industry belongs.[38] These larger privatisations were the second stage of the Government's privatisation policy. The regulatory structure adopted to regulate each industry created new controls and agencies in the United Kingdom.

4. Regulation, Structures and Techniques

13–30 The characteristics[39] of the British approach to legal regulation have a long history and evolved gradually on a case by case basis. It is useful to place the newly created regulatory bodies in the context of the approach to regulation adopted in the United Kingdom. Historically[40] the regulation and scrutiny of industry in Britain developed from the nineteenth century. Legal powers were first granted through Private Acts of Parliament in return for statutory responsibilities assumed by the industries – the railways and the electricity companies are two good examples. Also relevant is the experience of the early Poor Law Commission in 1834 which struck a balance between central and local government. This early form of government regulation permitted commissioners to determine the qualification and duties of local Poor Law guardians and they, in turn, appointed paid officers to administer relief, subject to the Poor Law Commission. The establishment of Boards, which acted in a quasi-ministerial manner combined administrative decision-taking and both non-political or semi-independent status. A number of examples such as railways and the factories inspectorate, illustrate the experiment of placing certain activities beyond the direct reach of political intervention. Eventually these activities succumbed to ministerial control but attempts at combining or isolating ministerial intervention with regulation were made. In the example of the railways, the Railway Department in the Board of Trade in 1840 was a department board in 1844, a Commission in 1846 before absorption into the Board of Trade in 1851.

13–31 A wide variety of powers were enjoyed by such regulators, invariably, a statutory framework would set the general shape and

---

[36] M. E. Beesley, *Liberalisation of the Use of the British Telecommunications Network* (London, HMSO 1981).
[37] Deloitte, Haslins and Sells, *British Gas Efficiency Study* (1983).
[38] Vickers and Yarrow, *Privatisation, An Economic Analysis* (1988), p. 248.
[39] See R. Baldwin and C. McCrudden, *Regulation and Public Law* (1987).
[40] W. Cornish, G. de N Clerk, *Law and Society in England 1850–1950* (1989).

scope of the individual Board or inspectorate. Additionally codes of practice, circulars, directions, rules, regulations were all included as part of that legal framework. Occasionally a feature of regulation involved enforcement procedures through adjudication processes which invariably might involve a fine or criminal sanction. For example the early factory inspectorate under the Factories Act 1934 had the status of a magistrate with corresponding legal powers. Inevitably claims of partisanship and bias were made against individuals in carrying out their duties and activities. One of the characteristics of the nineteenth century was a remarkable degree of detail and openness in the reports published by the various Boards, departments and agencies. This characteristic gradually diminished as the nationalisation process took place in the post-Second World War period which was characterised by secrecy and lack of information on the actual performance of each industry.

Overviewing the activities of Boards, inspectors and Ministries the **13–32** courts had a limited but important role. Various devices such as Crown immunity up until 1947 were used to prevent law suits in the case of torts and the amenability to judicial review depended to some extent on the remedy sought. In the case of mandamus, for example a Crown servant could not be compelled to perform a duty solely owed to the Crown. As Cornish[41] has pointed, out a wide array of legal powers were available. For example, the Poor Law Commission were advised to keep within the rules of natural justice and when they acted all their members had to be present. The courts were unpredictable in their application of the rules of natural justice. Technical distinctions were the hallmark of this area of the law. At one time the courts appeared to apply distinctions based on the classification of the bureaucratic function as "judicial" "quasi-judicial," "legislative" or "administrative." In 1964 the House of Lords adopted a more permissive approach in the landmark case of *Ridge v. Baldwin*[42] and thereby abolished the technical distinctions which inhibited the development of judicial review.

In summary, the characteristics of regulation such as judicial **13–33** scrutiny, adjudication of disputes and ministerial accountability were all in place during the lifetime of nationalisation. No coherent system existed to oversee and monitor the system of regulation, as development was ad hoc and pragmatic. The legal controls that there were, seldom became the subject of litigation. Few lawyers were involved apart from internal law advisers over the Company Act provisions and the requirements[43] of the specific statutory authority of each of the nationalised industries.

---

[41] Cornish, *op. cit.*
[42] [1964] A.C. 40.
[43] P. Craig, *Administrative Law* (2nd ed., 1989).

(a) Privatisation of the Utilities

13–34   (i) **British Telecom.**   The privatisation of British Telecom in 1984 and the Telecommunications Act 1984 were the first major reforms of a public utility industry which had been from 1912 until 1981 a State-owned monopoly. In 1981 the first stage, prior to privatisation, took place, when legislation, the British Telecommunications Act 1981, separated telecommunications from postal services thereby establishing British Telecom as a public corporation. The 1981 stage relaxed the restrictions of supply of customers' equipment and allowed licensing of other telelcommunications systems. The 1984 Telecommunications Act created a Director-General of Telecommunications (DGT) with regulatory powers based on guidelines as to how the DGT is expected to perform his duties. The hallmark of this particular privatisation was the need to find a suitable competitor for British Telecom. The Government effectively promoted the creation of a competitive rival, Mercury, which is the only competitor licensed to date to compete with British Telecom. The experience of nationalisation[44] may be seen in the power under the 1984 Act to refer, for example, British Telecom to the Monopolies and Mergers Commission and the matter is one which operates against the public interest.

13–35   The legal structure of the 1984 Act is significant because it sets a model for future privatisation. The characteristics of the 1984 Act are the use of an independent regulator (OFTEL) appointed by the Secretary of State (section 1 of the 1984 Act), the operators of telecommunications systems must possess a licence granted by the Director-General of OFTEL and the Secretary of State. There is a power to refer matters to the Monopolies and Mergers Commission (MMC) to decide if the matter referred, is in the public interest. The Director-General of Fair Trading has powers to supervise and investigate any possible anti-competitive practices or abuses of market power. Included in the regulation is a price formula designed "to cap" the prices charged to consumers for services. Privatisation of water (OFWAT), electricity (OFFER) followed similar principles.

13–36   Another characteristic is the requirement to build a pricing structure into the regulatory arrangements. Currently BT cannot increase prices by more than the Retail Price Index minus 3 per cent. The success of the pricing mechanism is to be gauged on how efficient and cost-effective the industry may be, and this remains to be seen.

---

[44] Heald and Steel, "Privatising Public Enterprise: An Analysis of the Government's Case" in Kay and Thompson *et al.*, *Privatisation and Regulation – the U.K. Experience* (1986). See Blanche Sas, "Regulation and the Privatised Electricity Supply Industry" (1990) (53) M.L.R. 485. See Eugene D. Cross, *Electric Utility Regulation in the European Union* (John Wiley, 1996).

The creation of the Director-General of Telecommunications as a means to secure effective competition, economy, efficiency and growth and development of the telecommunications business in the United Kingdom both national and international depends on how effective the regulatory system might be. Criticism of the 1984 Act focuses on three matters. First, the legislation fails to provide any requirement that adequate information is available to the DGT. Second, there is concern that the resources of the DGT may not be adequate to maintain supervision of the organisation and third that the DGT and Office of Telecommunications (OFTEL) may be perceived as too closely linked with the industry. Thus their independence and impartiality might be questioned if their perceived role became too protective of the industry.[45]

The Goverment's strategy for privatisation also addressed the **13-37** question of the value of the market as a regulator of the newly privatised activity. Rather than simply privatise a monopoly some liberalisation was attempted both before and after privatisation. This policy required legal powers to regulate the market. In the case of telecommunications, competition between Mercury and BT was created when Mercury was set up to provide an element of competition. The duopoly that resulted has itself been subject to criticism and review. OFTEL has been concerned with the terms of Mercury's network connection with BT. After delays and intervention by the courts, OFTEL ruled that the two networks should have full interconnection charges based on BT's costs and a time-scale was set for the implementation of connection arrangements. This applied to both national and international calls. In March 1991 the long awaited White Paper[46] on the duopoly review was published. Its main conclusion, that all applications for new licences to provide new telecommunications systems would be considered, and this would include both national and international services. This may be seen as broadening the possibilities for competition beyond the original framework of the 1984 Act.

The 1984 telecommunications regulatory structure was perceived to **13-38** be weak. Additional powers have been introduced under the Competition and Services (Utilities) Act 1992 intended to set a uniform standard of regulation for the utilities, and in the case of telecommunications, gas and water, greater competition. Thus the 1992 Act

---

[45] In fact few references have been made by the DGT to the Monopolies and Mergers Commission and there is an added difficulty. Legal powers do not exist to prevent British Telecom becoming an owner or participating in industries outside the telecommunications area. The desire to do so may conform with the interests of BT but not necessarily the interests of a competitive telecommunications industry in Britain. In this respect the 1984 Act is defective.
[46] *Competition and Choice: Telecommunications Policy for the 1990s,* Cm. 1461 (1991).

introduces additional powers for the Director of Telecommunications to set standards for levels of performance, provide greater information to the Director on the working of the industry, to determine disputes between the customer and the industry, and to make provisions relating to consumer protection such as disconnection charges. Many of these proposals arise out of the *Citizen's Charter*.[47]

13–39 (ii) **Gas.** The privatisation of the gas industry faced similar regulatory problems as identified in the case of telecommunications. In 1985 the Government decided to privatise British Gas and the question of how competition and efficiency might be achieved was given serious consideration but with limited and disappointing results.

The nationalisation of the British Gas industry in 1948 and its centralisation in 1962 had created a single industry centralised under a public corporation responsible for the activities of 12 area boards who were autonomous over the manufacture and supply of gas. Sole rights to purchase gas from producers had been granted to the corporation in 1982 and pricing had been characteristically low with a resultant lack of investment. This lack of investment has been attributed to poor policy direction by the government of the day.

13–40 Privatisation was undertaken by the Gas Act 1986 which followed the model set by telecommunications in 1984. A regulatory structure was set up under a Director-General of supply (OFGAS) and an OFGAS office.[48] The newly created Company, British Gas, did not have any competition and unlike BT and Mercury none was created by the 1986 Act for the Gas industry. No attempt was made to create a restructuring of the industry in the 1986 Act. The 12 regional boards could have become gas companies with a company to control the distribution system. The strong ideological belief that the timetable of the Government's privatisation strategy should not be altered or slowed down meant that restructuring of the gas industry was avoided. As Craig noted:

---

[47] Citizen's Charter, Cm. 1599 (1991). On telecommunications see NAO, The Office of Telecommunications: Licence Compliance and Consumer Protection (1993; H.C. 529), HMSO; NAO, *The Sale of the Second Tranche of Shares in British Telecommunications plc*, (1993, H.C. 568), HMSO. See Scott, [1993] *Utilities Law Review* 183.

[48] In the case of electricity (OFFER) and gas (OFGAS) the role of the Director-General share a common identity. The Director-General may share functions with their respective Secretary of State, they may act in an advisory capacity before the granting of licences and give general advice and information to the Secretary of State. They are required to each publish an annual report and oversee the promotion of efficiency within their respective industry. Once a licence is issued by the Secretary of State it is the Director-General who invariably may agree changes with the licence and where necessary may make a reference to the MMC. Director-General, exercise adjudicative functions in determining disputes or complaints within the licence conditions. They keep their respective industries under review and each publish a wide variety of useful information about the industry.

"The decision not to reorganise the industry had been termed a response to interest group pressure from management and consumers, in which short term electoral considerations assumed precedence over longer term considerations of economic efficiency."

It is clear that the Gas Act 1986 in practical effect insulates British **13–41** Gas from competition. As no new competitor was created it is difficult not to see the monopoly of British Gas as virtually impregnable by any new entrant to the market.

Finally the 1986 Act provided a complex formula for pricing supervised by the Director-General of Gas Supply (DGGS) and OFGAS. Legal powers similar to OFTEL were provided to OFGAS to promote efficiency to gas suppliers and users. The DGGS may impose conditions upon the grant of authorisation to a public gas supplier and there is a possibility of a referral to the Monopolies and Mergers Commission to specify any modification to the authorisation.[49] Compliance powers granted to the DGGS and investigative powers over conditions granted in the authorisation are all part of the regulatory framework.

The powers of the regulator are considerably less than the powers **13–41A** possessed by British Gas. For example under the 1986 Act it is impossible for the DGGS to alter the legal structure of the gas industry. Some doubts exist as to the powers of the DGGS to provide transparency of pricing and in opening up of the transmission system through supplies to third parties. Vickers and Yarrow make the point which has general application to the privatisation strategies[50] of the Government:

"What has happened is that one of the major deficiencies of the UK control system for nationalised industries – preoccupation with short-term political issues has been duplicated in the policy framework set for the regulated privately owned gas industry."

In the case of gas the Director-General has powers to promote **13–42** competition within the contract market, i.e. over 25,000 therms per annum[51], but lacks a general duty to promote competition overall. In contrast the Director-General of Electricity has such powers which are widely drawn but not easily interpreted with a precise and clear

---

[49] P. Craig, *Administrative Law* (1989), pp. 164–169.

[50] P. Cameron, "Five years of regulating Britain's gas industry" Summer 1991 *Utilities Law Review* 70–77. See: *Gas: The Monopoly and Mergers Commission*, Cm. 500 (1988), and *The Gas Review*, OFT October 1991 (Summary Version).

[51] S.37 of the Competition and Service (Utilities) Act 1992 gives the Director powers to modify this threshold.

meaning. Gas privatisation had resulted in a virtual monopoly for British Gas which unlike the telecommunications industry with Mercury, no competitors were established at the time of privatisation. British Gas was in a strong market position post-privatisation with the resultant effect that the regulator (OFGAS) became a surrogate competitor in its attempts to regulate the gas industry effectively. A major threat to any monopolistic conduct is the use of the Fair Trading Act 1973 (Schedule 8) in requiring the MMC to consider whether such conduct militates against the public interest. A wide range of remedial action is available including adjusting contracts, the formation or winding up of a company and consideration of the division of the business "by the sale of any part of the undertaking or assets or otherwise . . ."

13–43   In the early stages of the newly privatised life of British Gas, it was apparent that a number of grounds for dissatisfaction existed. These included: individual prices were unclear and companies had difficulty estimating future gas costs; a wide variation in prices was experienced between customers with the same or similar levels of requirement; tendering for contracts lasted for only three month periods at a time and future gas costs were difficult to estimate, given the lack of transparency in pricing; British Gas was reluctant to quote prices for interruptible supplies and required in many cases the installation of dual fired equipment which was costly; British Gas were also unwilling to offer supply to certain types of companies which would close down when supplies were interrupted.

13–44   Such complaints were reviewed by the MMC after OFGAS made a reference on the basis of there being a monopoly enjoyed by British Gas. The MMC upheld this view of a monopoly and concluded that greater competition was required. An additional finding was that the only effective means of remedying adverse consequences flowing from the monopoly status of British Gas was direct gas to gas competition. A long list of recommendations relating to the pricing and tendering of gas, third party access to the gas transmission system operated by British Gas and transparency in the system of gas schedules were also made by the MMC.

13–45   Inevitably the MMC findings in 1988 required a reorganisation of the gas market and provided the regulator with increased powers in terms of enhancing his status and in securing compliance with his objectives. Ultimately the Secretary of State's wide powers under Schedule 9 of the Fair Trading Act provide a threat hanging over the industry should the monopolistic practices be continued. As a result British Gas in February 1990 entered into a number of undertakings which included: not to purchase more than 90 per cent of gas on offer, not to require the inclusion of contract terms which could frustrate that objective; to provide common carriage quotations within a four-week period. In addition price schedules were introduced for firm and interruptible contract customers to prevent British

Gas from blocking market entry by a strategy of discriminatory pricing.

In July 1991 the effectiveness of the remedies applied by British Gas **13–46** after the MMC Report (1985) was referred to the OFT for consideration. The result of that review was published in October 1991 and concluded that although British Gas had complied with its undertakings, nevertheless the dominance of British Gas in the market had remained. British Gas, because of its size and market dominance was able to assert its influence. Thus it could cross-subsidise, act in a predatory manner on pipeline competition and set price levels in the indemnities market that a competitor could not match. All these factors led the OFT to conclude that British Gas should consider the following:

(a) British Gas to release a significant proportion of its contracted gas and to reintroduce a revised version of the 90/10 undertaking;

(b) on appropriate undertaking on the tariff monopoly;

(c) the establishment of a separate subsidiary to operate the gas transmission and storage system on a non-discriminatory basis at arms length from the rest of British Gas and agreement to OFGAS regulation of changes.

Taken together the OFT report represents a fundamental recon- **13–47** sideration of the market position of British Gas.[52] In 1993 the MMC published two reports on Gas. Some conclusions may be reached[53] from a reading of the reports. First that competition had been attempted in the gas industry before privatisation but with very limited success. Since the Oil and Gas (Enterprise) Act 1982 initiated competition in gas supply by allowing competing gas suppliers access to British Gas's pipelines. In fact no agreement was ever reached. The 1986 Gas Act as outlined above, preserved the *de facto* monopoly of British Gas. Even though the 1986 Act gave freedom of competition to suppliers to large industrial and commercial customers above 25,000 therms, but this did not remove the monopoly position of British Gas.

Turnover of British Gas is currently about £8.5 billion. There are **13–48** about 18.8 million people, the bulk of the domestic market, at or

[52] See Villiers, "Promoting the efficient use of gas and improved service standards for gas consumers" [1993] *Utilities Law Review* 117. See MMC, *Reports on Gas Industry* (HMSO, 1993).
[53] *MMC Report into the Gas Supply Industry* (London, HMSO, 1993); *MMC Report into British Gas Plc.* london, HMSO, 1993).

under 2,500 therms and therefore falling within price controls. In 1995 the Gas Act gives additional powers to the regulator to allow for a more radical re-structuring of British Gas to provide additional competition for suppliers to domestic customers and for access to the gas pipe-line. This new structure has the following features:

(a) the setting up of Trans Co, British Gas's transportation and storage business with assets inclusive of about £17.4 billion;

(b) from March 1995 separation of Trans Co from British Gas;

(c) the Gas Act 1995 came into force on March 1, 1995.

13–49 The 1995 Act sets up a new structure for the licensing of gas supply. The main features of the 1995 Act are that access is now available to the pipeline owned by British Gas for any licensed supplier. There are licences for the following:

(a) Public Gas Transporter (PGT) for firms that operate a pipeline system and contract with gas shippers;

(b) gas shipper licences for licence holders who contract to provide a public gas transporter to be conveyed through the pipeline of the PGT;

(c) gas supplier licences for companies that sell at the meter which has been delivered through pipelines by a shipper. This includes supply to domestic customers.

The introduction of licensed suppliers into the domestic market is a gradual one.[54] Currently gas suppliers are licensed to supply into the competitive market above 2,500 therms. But for domestic customers below, 2,500 therms, there are 9 licensed suppliers to supply into the market below 2,500 therms in the South West of England.

(a) by the end of January 1998 British Gas monopoly to be removed at the discretion of the regulator

(b) By mid-1997 further two million customers to be given choice of supplier in South West after half a million given choice of supplier from April 1996.

13–50 The above analysis of the British Gas example points to inherent structural problems in the way British Gas was privatised. Splitting

---

[54] See *National Audit Office, The Work of the Directors General of Telecommunications, Gas Supply, Water Services and Electricity Supply* (1995/96; H.C. 645).

up the distribution side from the production of gas supply might have avoided the problems of monopoly mentioned above. The model for such a restructuring may be seen in the Electricity Act 1989 (discussed below) where the transmission grid was separated from the production and distribution system.

Additional powers have been granted to the Director of Gas Supply under the Competition and Service (Utilities) Act 1992. These include the powers to set standards,[55] improve the procedures for complaints by customers and set regulations to determine disputes over the accuracy of bills. An increase in competition in the gas market is intended by reducing the gas monopoly threshold of 15,000 therms to a lower amount or to abolition the threshold altogether.[56] These changes are the result of the introduction of proposals contained in the *Citizen's Charter*.

The Citizen's Charter Report on an annual basis sets out the **13–51** achievements of the Charter.[57] In the Report there is a list of a wide range of achievements including setting up Codes of Practice, setting standards for dealing with complaints and arranging for payments for failure to meet standards. For example in 1994 British Gas paid a total of £2,439,272 in compensation. The bulk of this went to a single domestic user. The Public Electricity Suppliers paid in 1994 £115,000 and the water companies paid £267,900.

In addition to the Citizen's Charter the government has embarked on new procedures to simplify existing regulations and unnecessary rules. The Deregulation and Contracting Out Act 1994 provides that amending orders, called deregulation orders, may be introduced to amend delegated legislation or where necessary primary legislation.[58] This procedure is a novel way to lift the burden of unnecessary regulation from industry.[59]

The British Gas example also shows the flexibility inherent in the **13–52** legal mechanisms used to regulate the industry. The legal basis for referral to the MMC and the resultant modification of the authorisation allowed gradual changes to be introduced. The existing legal framework is also sufficiently flexible to realise the creation of a separate gas transmission subsidiary company. This could be achieved by British Gas voluntarily adopting the recommendations of the OFT. In the event of non-compliance the regulatory structure is

---

[55] See ss.11–15 and 18–19 of the Competition and Service (Utilities) Act 1992.
[56] See s.37 of the Competition and Service (Utilities) Act 1992.
[57] See Citizen's Charter *Improving Service* September 1995, Cm. 2970.
[58] See Michael Ryle. "The Deregulation and Contracting Out Bill 1994 – A Blueprint for reform of the Legislative process?" (1994) 15 *Statute Law Review* pp. 170–181.
[59] The Deregulation and Contracting Out Act 1994 follows the recommendations of the Hansard Society in their report: Hansard Society, *Making the Law* (Hansard Society, 1993).

sufficiently flexible to hold the threat of referral to the MMC. The combination of regulatory supervision by OFGAS, overview by the OFT and MMC combines wide legal powers with oversight by the relevant Secretary of State.

The experience gained from gas and telecommunications privatisations proved to be insufficient to meet the challenge posed by electricity privatisation. The Government's proposals to privatise the electricity supply industry faced a sterner test because the electricity industry was the largest of the United Kingdom's nationalised industries in terms of turnover and capital employed. For example in 1985 revenue was £11 million on a capital stock of £40 billion.

13–53   (iii) **Electricity.** Electricity privatisation also posed some of the most complex legal problems. Electricity is a natural monopoly, involves the use of fuels as diverse as solar power to nuclear energy and is a heavy polluter of the environment. Under nationalisation the generation, supply and transmission of electricity were integrated by the 1957 Electricity Act. The Central Electricity Generating Board (CEGB) was put in charge of both generation and transmission. A national grid was created with 12 Area Boards for distribution purposes. These purposes were left to the autonomy of the boards particularly in respect of financial matters. Consumers' interests in England and Wales were represented by 13 district organisations. There were 12 Area Electricity Consultative Councils, one for each Area Board and an Electricity Consumers' Council.[60]

13–54   The privatisation strategy adopted by the Government was contained in the White Paper Privatising Electricity[61] which set out six objectives to be followed namely: the needs of customers should be considered an important part of the industry; competition is an essential guarantee of customers' interests; regulation was required to promote competition, oversee prices and protect customers' interests; security and safety should be maintained; customers should be given new rights and share ownership should include those who work for the company.

In the case of electricity privatisation the experience of both British Gas and Telecommunications suggested that a different model should be adopted to provide increased competition as part of the legal structure for the newly privatised industry. The electricity supply

---

[60] The Electricity Supply Industry provided for the virtual separation of the generation and transmission of electricity undertaken by the CEGB. Distribution and retailing were undertaken by the Area Boards. Overall direction and the electricity requirements set up by the 1957 Act were required to be met by the CEGB, such as supplying British Rail with electricity: McAuslan and McEldowney, *The Electricity Act 1989 Current Legal Statutes* (1989); Capel, *Reshaping the Electricity Supply Industry in England and Wales* (London, James Capel, February 1990).

[61] Cm. 322 (1988).

industry (ESI) is a key industry in the energy field – especially in promoting energy efficiency and addressing environmental concerns.

Despite objections to the White Paper proposals and the belated **13–55** recognition that the nuclear power side of generation was too much of a high risk in terms of economic cost (partly due to decommissioning costs) the Government pushed ahead with the existing proposals. In October 1989 and after the Electricity Act 1989 had been passed for the privatisation of the industry, the Government reluctantly removed the nuclear side of the industry from privatisation and it will remain in Government control.[62] A separate company called Nuclear Power was set up under Government ownership.[63] A nuclear levy, known as the non-fossil fuel levy acts as a subsidy to nuclear electricity, and is payable by all users of electricity.

The Electricity Act 1989 adopted a combination of licensing, con- **13–56** tractual and statutory powers to regulate and operate the newly created structure under the post-privatisation arrangements. Licensing is a power which combines the work of both Secretary of State[64] and the Director. Wider reserve powers are given to the Secretary of State in the case of electricity than in gas or telecommunications. Such reserve powers given to the Secretary of State (section 96) are for preserving the security of electricity supply, the maintenance and the security of buildings or installations used for the purposes connected with the generation, transmission or supply of electricity. The Secretary of State may set the percentage of electricity required from non-fossil fuel after consultation with the Director-General of electricity and suppliers, such order is subject only to negative resolution in the procedure of laying the order before Parliament.

The Director-General of electricity with the consent of the Secretary **13–57** of State and after consulting public electricity suppliers and affected individuals may set individual and overall standards of performance. The Director-General of electricity is required to publish information

---

[62] It appears that the problems of insurance and the economic viability of nuclear power was widely appreciated in government. Nigel Lawson notes, *op. cit.*, p. 237, ". . . the nuclear power stations had to be removed from the privatization altogether, and the whole of the Government's nuclear power building programme put on ice, as the financial and economic truths which State ownership had successfully concealed from successive Governments were at last exposed in the run-up to privatization."

[63] Generally see: G. Borrie, "The Regulation of Public and Private Power" (1990) P.L. 552. Also see D. Helm and G. Yarrow, "The Regulation of Utilities" *Oxford Review of Economic Policy*, Vol. 14, No. 2, 1988.

[64] It is also possible under s.6 of the 1989 Act to delegate the licensing power to the DGES. Even here the Secretary of State may direct the DGES not to make modifications to a licence. See C. Foster, *Privatization, Public Ownership and the Regulation of Natural Monopoly* (Oxford, 1993).

which is expedient to provide information for customers of public electricity supplies.

This wide range of statutory powers is also reinforced by licensing conditions such as the avoidance of cross subsidisation and the separation of accounts between different businesses.

The 1989 Act follows the pattern in the privatisation of British Gas which allows the DGES a discretion to make a reference to the Monopolies and Mergers Commission (MMC). But the Secretary of State for Energy can direct the MMC not to proceed with the reference. Once a report is prepared the Secretary of State may prohibit publication of "any matter" if it appears to him that it would be against the public or commercial interest of "any person."

13–58　　The Secretary of State possesses wide powers to keep a register of information on licences, modifications and the like. Effectively placing the Secretary of State as the electricity supply industry's licensing authority, the 1989 Act, allows intervention in the work of the DGES as a regulator that challenges any sense of independence or freedom from political influence which the DGES may want to develop. While the DGES has a duty to review the "carrying on" of electricity generation, transmission and supply the Secretary of State may give the DGES directions as to the priorities or matters which form the DGES's remit.

The Secretary of State's powers extend to the day to day operations of the Electricity Supply Industry. The constitution of generating stations and the consents required may be supervised by the Secretary of State, under section 36 of the Act. The use of fuel stocks, the requirement that electricity is available from non-fossil fuel sources are all part of the wide powers possessed by the Secretary of State.

13–59　　The management functions of the person operating the generating station could be directed by the Secretary of State as well as the "specified objectives" which may be given to the National Grid Company to operate the transmission system. It is clear that the legal powers contained in the 1989 Act provide the Secretary of State with the means to take over the operational management of the industry. Finally, wide emergency powers are included in Part III of the 1989 Act which provide the Secretary of State with extensive powers to give directions to the industry. The term "civil emergency" is widely defined in subjective terms in section 96 of the 1989 Act. It includes any national disaster or other emergency which in the opinion of the Secretary of State is against the interest of national security or commercial interests. The power to give directions does not contain any requirement of laying the direction before Parliament. The 1989 Act provides the Secretary of State unparalleled powers in the history of the electricity supply industry to intervene in the day to day running of the industry.[65]

The electricity privatisation provided more extensive regulatory **13–60** powers than previous privatisations. The few changes introduced by the Competition and Service (Utilities) Act 1992, include standards of performance, complaints and disputes, the level of achievement of each public electricity supplier, and the power for the Director to make determinations regarding the accuracy of bills.[66]

The Electricity industry is undergoing further changes. Currently the industry comprises the following:

(a) 14 Public Electricity Suppliers (PES) (12 regional electricity companies) Scottish Power and Scottish Hydro electric;

(b) 32 Second tier supply licensees. Supply to customers above 100kw in England (22 in Scotland). This also includes 14 PES as above which have second tier licensee outside their geographical area;

(c) 3 Transmission licensees: National Grid Company; Scottish Power and Scottish Hydro-electric. Note National Grid is throughout England and Wales;

(d) 36 generation licensees: Includes National Power, PowerGen Nuclear Electric Scottish Power, Scottish Hydro-electric, Scottish nuclear, the Pumped storage Business of First Hydro.

The current value of the industry in sales is £16.7 billion (1994–5). **13–61** There are 25 million electricity customers in England, Wales and Scotland. The future likely to include the introduction of further competition within the industry. At privatisation there were the following companies:

(a) The National Grid Company owned by the Regional Electricity Companies including the bulk supply of electricity and two pumped storage power stations;

(b) 3 generating companies: National Power Plc, PowerGen plc, and Nuclear Power – the latter in the public sector;

---

[65] Also see David Heald, *Public Expenditure* (Blackwell, 1987). The need for an inter-regulatory agency becomes apparent as more of the privatisated industries engage in activities outside their original remit. For example, British Gas owns shares in BT or in electricity companies.

[66] See ss.20, 21, 22, 23, 24 and Sched. 1 of the Competition and Service (Utilities) Act 1992.

(c) 12 regional electricity companies (RECs) for the supply and distribution of electricity.

Since privatisation and the developments in the market there have been a number of takeover bids for many of the RECs, including a takeover bid by National Power for Southern Electric and by PowerGen for Midland Electricity Board. Both takeovers were rejected by the Secretary of State and referred to the Monopolies and Mergers Commission. In addition there has been the privatisation of the nuclear generation industry.

13-62   All these changes have maintained a virtual monopoly in respect of domestic customers who are deprived of any real choice of supplier. The 14 PES retained their supply monopoly. Only customers over 1MW were allowed to seek a competitive supply and in April 1994 this limit was reduced to 100KW. This secured an increase in customers from 5,000 to 50,000 who could freely contract for their supply of electricity outside their area. It is intended from April 1998 that all customers will be able to buy electricity from suppliers other than their local PES.

In generation of electricity again there are signs that competition has been limited. The electricity pool was established in order to favour competition within the generation industry in England and Wales but not Scotland. In fact new entrants have only taken 7 per cent share. In the area of transmission the National Grid Company has a virtual monopoly over transmission competition and is unlikely to have any major competition in this area for the foreseeable future.

Political controversy has surrounded the generation of electricity which has led to an inquiry into energy policy and the question of the viability of the coal industry.[67]

13-63   In March 1995 the electricity regulator had to reconsider the RPI-X formula used in pricing, in the light of new information on the profits available to the regional electricity companies.[68] This information only became available after there was a threatened takeover of a major electricity company. The consequences of the regulator's decision were particularly price-sensitive. Share prices in the electricity sector fell sharply, a take-over bid by Trafalgar House for Northern Electric was abandoned, the Government were embarrassed when the timing of the regulator's announcement coincided with the sale of further

---

[67] A review of the use of gas in electricity generation and the economics of gas-generated electricity has taken place by the regulator of electricity, Prof. Stephen Littlechild. See OFFER, *Statement on Independent Assessor's Reports on Plant Closures* (1993). Also Stern, "The UK Energy White Paper: Poor Prospects for Coal, Good Prospects for Gas" [1993] *Utilities Law Review* 114.

[68] See Leader article, "Have the utility regulators run out of control?" *The Independent*, March 12, 1995.

government shares in National Power and PowerGen, and, finally, at the time doubts arose over the intended stock market flotation of National Grid Holdings.

(iv) **Water.** The privatisation of water also proved a greater **13–64** problem than gas or telecommunications. Water privatisation had to address one of the most complex[69] legal arrangements for water services. In the case of water 10 public water authorities and 29 private water companies comprised the water industry before privatisation. The Water Act 1989 had to address the problem of not only the new structure under privatisation but the question of merger and investment in the water industry, also included major health and evironmental issues. In the run up to privatisation concern among the water authorities was expressed because of the fear of predatory take-overs by French Water Companies.

Privatisation was carried out under the Water Act 1989 which **13–65** created a new public body, the National Rivers Authorities (NRA) now subsumed under the Environment Agency under the Environment Act 1995 with the rights and liabilities of the existing water authorities divided between the NRA and successor companies. The 29 statutory water companies are retained as water undertakers for their areas. The successor companies inherit the responsibilities of sewerage and water subject to the terms of the instruments of appointment. The various commercial companies as water and sewerage undertakers have received powers under the Water Industry Act 1991. The duty to maintain and develop an efficient and economical water supply and sewerage system falls under sections 37 and 94 of the 1991 Act. The supply of water for domestic purposes[70] must be wholesome and of adequate quality. There is a Water Services Office with a Director-General of Water Services.

NRA, within the Environment Agency has responsibilities for the control of river and coastal water pollution, water resource management, land drainage, fisheries, navigation and flood defence. A major feature of the legislation is a complex pricing formula, detailed environmental protection arrangements, and a new regulatory body under the Director-General of Water Services. The latter is required in effect to balance the protection of the consumer from monopoly exploitation and the efficient running of the utility.

The Water Act 1989 (section 230 (3)) gives the Monopolies and **13–66** Mergers Commission (MMC) power to consider whether any proposed merger might prejudice the Director-General of Water Services'

---

[69] See MacRory, *The Water Act 1989 Current Law Statutes* (1989); Byatt, "The Office of Water Services: Structure and Policy" [1990] *Utilities Law Review* 85–90.

[70] Ss.68 and 69, impose a duty to provide wholesome water for domestic purposes. (S.I. 1989 No. 1147 and S.I. 1989 No. 1384). E.C. requirements are provided under Directive 80/778. See the Water Industries Act 1991; the Water Resources Act 1991.

ability to regulate the industry and whether the proposed merger was against the public interest.

A merger must fulfill the requirements that:

(a) either it must not reduce the number of companies under independent control; or

(b) the merger must achieve some other benefit of greater significance.

The latter may be achieved by a substantial benefit to customers. Nevertheless a large number of the existing water companies had received French investment before the Act was in force thus the regulatory protection appeared too late to be effective.

13–67   The Water Act 1989, however, broadly follows some of the legal characteristics of the post-privatisation arrangements of the other main utilities. The main regulatory instrument is the licence which contains a regulatory mechanism which "caps" the price companies may charge their customer. The annual increase is restricted to the "RPI plus an additional factor K allocated to the companies on an individual basis for each of the next 10 years." This is designed according to Director-General of Water, Ian Byatt "to off-set the significant investment programmes which have been necessary to achieve the higher standards which we all seek."

13–68   In the case of water, reference to the MMC may be made by the Secretary of State for Trade and Industry following advice from the OFT. The water companies may appeal to the MMC if they wish to contest the action of the Director-General of Water Services in respect of determining the "K" factor in the price cap, amendments to their licences and accounting guidelines.

The actual management of the industry is, subject to the legal framework identified above, left to the individual water companies to develop. Within OFWAT's remit is a periodic review every 10 years of the company, investment programme, management plan, efficiency standards and the regulatory regime in general.

13–69   Additional powers and responsibilities were added under the Competition and Services (Utilities) Act 1992. Section 39 of the 1992 Act makes changes to the mergers procedures, under the Water Industry Act 1991, as to the matters which the MMC must take into account such as the number of companies in separate ownership, in considering water mergers referred to the MMC. In addition the 1992 Act provides[71] the giving of greater information on research, consumer views and an improved complaints system for customers[72] as part of the proposals contained in the *Citizen's Charter*.

---

[71] See ss.26–33, 39, 40–47, 50, 52 and 53(2)–(4) of the Competition and Services (Utilities) Act 1992.

[72] Sched. 2 to the Competition and Services (Utilities) Act 1992.

Clearly the water privatisation plans present yet another example of problems in terms of efficiency and accountability. The present statutory formulation would seem to do little to achieve competition between the different parts of the industry. Concern is expressed by critics of the legislation that competition will be ineffective and the costs required to provide environmental protection will prove expensive to the consumer.[73]

(b) The Regulatory Structure

Post-privatisation experience is that more information is available and **13–70** greater openness is given to practices and understandings which were hitherto confidential and kept within the culture of the particular industry. Although there is a tendency for both government and industry to prefer secrecy and confidentiality, the legal powers of the Director-General coupled with referral powers to the Monopolies and Mergers Commission, may provide for greater information on matters such as pricing.

There are variations in the legal powers available to the respective **13–71** Secretary of State of each industry. In the case of electricity it is noticeable how wide powers have been granted to the Secretary of State, not only in the power to licence generators, transmitters and suppliers, but also in the use of non-fossil fuel. Directions as to the fuel stocks at generating stations, the construction, operation and financial organisation of generating stations all fall directly within the Secretary of State's powers. Compared to the powers granted to the Secretary of State under nationalisation these powers post-privatisation are wider and more extensive. Generally the powers of the four regulators, for telecommunications, gas, electricity and water, have been brought into line by the Competition and Service (Utilities) Act 1992.

There is also the question of the extent to which the Secretary of **13–72** State may intervene in the work of the regulator? Once a licence has been issued the Secretary of State has no power to amend the licence, such power rests with the respective regulator. There is therefore a separation of the responsibilities between the Secretary of State and the regulator. However in a number of ways the Secretary of State may influence the regulator. There is informal discussion and agreement. A variety of techniques are available depending on the legal powers involved. The Secretary of State has reserve powers in the case of electricity, to stop a proposed licence modification. In the case

---

[73] See [1992] 3 *Utilities Law Review* 21 and [1993] 2 *Utilities Law Review* 72. On Water pricing see OFWAT, *Paying for Quality: The Political Perspective* (1993).

of gas, such modification proposals may be referred to the Mono-polies and Mergers Commission. The close relationships between the relevant government department and the industry is therefore neces-sary and may give rise in future years to questions of the openness and accountability involved in such contacts. In the case of telecom-munications, the Secretary of State may give general directions to the regulator, as to matters that should be taken into account in consider-ing aspects of the telecommunication industry which are subject to review. There is no absolute requirement to publish such directions. In the cases of gas and electricity, where similar powers exist for each respective Director-General, such directions should be published. The requirement of publication appears to apply only to formal directions and there is no bar against informal discussion or agreement remain-ing private.

13–73   The question of enforcing licence conditions lies with the respective Directors-General. Power to amend the licence may be with the agreement of the licensee or through a reference to the Monopolies and Mergers Commission. The Director-General also enjoys a number of other powers for supervision of their respective industries which removes any potential in the legal sense for the Secretary of State to intervene in the direct general running of each industry.

13–74   In addition to the regulatory agencies put in place post-privatisation, mention should also be made of the various "quasi-governmental agencies" or non-departmental public bodies. There is a wide range and a large number of such bodies ranging from the Gaming Board, the Advisory Conciliation and Arbitration Service, Health and Safety at Work, Civil Aviation Authority, the Office of Fair Trading, the Monopolies and Mergers Commission, the Commis-sion for Racial Equality and the Equal Opportunities Commission. Their diversity and size is reflected in their ad hoc development. For example new areas of legal regulation such as Data Protection often necessitate new regulatory bodies. The Data Protection Act 1984 created a new Data Protection Registrar to regulate the operation of the legislation. Similarly, the creation of new licensing arrangements by the creation of the Independent Television Commission replacing the Cable Authority and the Independent Broadcasting Authority.[74]

13–75   The newly created Independent Television Commission from Janu-ary 1, 1991 allocated 16 of the new Channel 3 licences during 1991/92. The power to licence and effectively to relicence television companies carries formidable effects for the companies who have been unsuc-cessful. This is a good illustration of the legal powers and scope such administrative agencies may exercise.

---

[74] See the Television Act 1954 as amended by the Broadcasting Act 1981. Also see *R. v. Secretary of State for the Home Department, ex p. Brind* [1991] 1 All E.R. 721 on directives issued by the Home Secretary to the broadcasting authorities.

Agencies may be set up under statutory authority as in the examples given and exercise statutory powers, or may simply perform within a statutory framework, activities which rarely involve the exercise of their legal powers as in the case of the Countryside Commission. Innovatory procedures and specialisms give rise to new agencies such as the Human Fertilisation and Embryology Authority under the Human Fertilisation and Embryology Act 1990. Regulating professional standards of various occupations may require statutory interventions. The Osteopaths Act 1993 establishes a new body known as the General Osteopathic Council. This Council will regulate the professional education and conduct of around 2000 persons in the United Kingdom in the delivery of osteopathic treatment.

The reasons for creating such agencies and the likelihood that they **13–76** will continue to be favoured as a means of exercising administrative powers are varied. Studies undertaken as to why fringe bodies are created have identified[75] a number of reasons. Fringe organisations may protect certain activities from direct political intervention. As they are outside the departmental system of government they may provide access to expertise and greater independence in decision-making. They may permit and encourage new initiatives away from the restrictions of both civil service and ministerial direction. Fringe organisations appear to lessen the grip of a single bureaucracy and allow greater diversity in decision making. All the advantages claimed for such bodies make them attractive to successive governments as a means of spreading patronage in the appointment and selection of the management of such bodies.

Fringe organisations give rise to questions about accountability and **13–77** patronage as well as concerns about their effectiveness. Accountability may vary with the organisation concerned. It may be to a Minister or to a Select Committee of Parliament. Occasionally there is accountability to the courts, although the exact outcome of judicial review may depend on the statutory arrangements setting out the relationship between Ministers and the agency.[76]

---

[75] Hague, McKenzie and Barker (eds.), *Public Policy and Private Interests: The Institutions of Compromise* (1975).

[76] See *Laker Airways Ltd v. Department of Trade* [1977] Q.B. 643. This case provides a good case study of the complexity in the legal arrangements which provide for the giving of directions and guidance to the Civil Aviation Authority, CAA, under the Civil Aviation Act 1971. The Court of Appeal held that the Secretary of State's guidance was *ultra vires* because it apeared that the policy guidance given to the CAA contradicted the precise objectives set out in the 1971 Act. It was unclear how the contradiction was made out. The effect of the decision was to permit Mr Laker to run his Skytrain service to the United States of America. Subsequently Laker Airlines went bankrupt, the Civil Aviation legislation was amended by the Civil Aviation Act 1982.

5. Future Directions

13–78 Privatisation has provided public lawyers with new challenges in extending their knowledge of regulation into areas of contract and licensing, which involve private law techiques in drafting and understanding legal rules. Privatisation sales since 1979 have gained net receipts to the Exchequer[77] of sums in excess of £64.029 billion.

It is perhaps significant, with the value of hindsight to find that the steps taken since 1978 to provide a framework for a coherent nationalised industry policy seemed on an economic analysis to be working. Both Molyneux and Thompson found[78]:

> "The upturn in performance since 1978 points to the success of the various institutional reforms that have been implemented. . . . We suggest that the type of reform indicated by our analysis is one that would place emphasis on increased competition, a proposal substantially at variance with current initiatives involving the privatisation of the State Monopolies."

13–79 In the case of telecommunications and gas, a weak regulatory framework has little impact on the essential requirement of competition. Constitutional lawyers can sense that the regulatory bodies constructed under both major privatisations lack clearly-defined objectives and the means to achieve them. The privatisation of electricity has provided in the Electricity Act 1989, a stronger framework for direct political intervention in the industry than under nationalisation.

This raises the question in constitutional terms of accountability. Constitutional lawyers may seek to find the answer in a number of institutions. First the various regulators, (including the MMC) who should be seen to have adequate powers to oversee the industry. Secondly, the courts and the power of judicial review, and finally the Secretary of State in terms of ministerial responsibility to Parliament.

13–80 There is also the question of the precise techniques available to public lawyers when regulating privatised industries and seeking to achieve a balance of interests between consumers, the market, the industry, and the role of government. A number of issues arise involving: first, reliance on the use of licences and contracts has

---

[77] J. McEldowney, "The National Audit Office and Privatisation" (1991) 54 M.L.R. 933–956. See F. Woolf and S. McCue, "Who regulates the regulator? The Great Debate" [1993] 4 *Utilities Law Review* 199; C. Foster, "The Future of Regulation" [1993] 4 *Utilities Law Review* 110.

[78] Molyneux and Thompson, *op. cit.* T. Prosser, *Law and the Regulators* (Clarendon Press, Oxford, 1997).

involved legal drafting in the technical side of formally operating the industry. Complex and detailed licences have required skilled inter-pretation and careful drafting. In the case of electricity they run to many hundreds of pages and provide in formal legal language the mechanisms of running the industry. This has given rise to a number of determinations made by the Director-General over the interpreta-tion of various licence conditions and statutory powers.

Secondly, the use of a specialised regulatory agency for each utility **13–81** has opened up the industry to greater transparency in the dealings with customers and competitors. This preserves a day to day opera-tional autonomy in each industry according to the best management of each company. At the same time the statutory duties shared between OFT and the individual utility regulator combine to ensure a greater observance of the regulator's wishes than the legislative powers might have otherwise permitted. The sanction of a referral to the MMC has been effective in bringing about changes in British Gas. This combination of ministerial supervision, independent regulatory agency and the enforcement of statutory powers is familiar to the nineteenth century evolution of regulation and its development in inspectors and Boards. Curiously the degree of openness in the publication of reports and evidence of modern regulations is strangely reminiscent of the nineteenth century experience of Boards and their reports.[79] This is in contrast to the marked reticence of the nationalised industries to reveal their activities. In the energy indus-try is there a case for combining some of the functions of the gas and electricity regulators into a single energy regulator?

Thirdly, the courts have not had a major role in developing and **13–82** interpreting the newly privatised regulatory structures. It is fair to say as Graham and Prosser[80] state "the role of the courts has been purely technical in the few cases where they have been called upon." Nevertheless their potential for intervention remains. In the unre-ported decision of the divisional court: *R. v. Director-General of Gas Supply and Another, ex p. Smith and Another*,[81] Mr Justice Pill applied the rules of national justice to the investigative powers of the Director-General of Gas Supply in his role in determining whether British Gas was justified in using its disconnection powers where it suspected an offence was committed. Relying on the main legal

---

[79] General discussion of the Monopolies and Mergers Commission see: B. Collins and B. Wharton, "Nationalised Industries: Responses to the Monopolies & Mergers Commission," *Public Money*, Vol. 4. (1984–85) 30–32, M. Garner, "The White Papers on the Nationalised Industries" (1979) 57 *Public Administration* 7.

[80] Graham and Prosser, *op. cit.*

[81] CO/1398/88. See: J. McEldowney "Theft and meter tampering and the gas and electricity utilities" (Autumn 1991) *Utilities Law Review* 122-126. Also see *R. v. British Coal Corporation and the Secretary of State for Trade, ex p. Vardy* [1993] IRLR 104.

authorities such as *O'Reilly v. Mackman*[82] the courts have developed
the potential for intervention to review the decision of regulators or
Ministers where it is thought unreasonable, procedurely unconve-
nient or on some grounds of unfairness.[83] The danger of the courts
substituting its view for that of the designated authority who have
been given that authority by Parliament was recognised by Lord
Justice Watkins in *R. v. Secretary of State for Trade and Industry, ex p.
Lonrho*.[83a] The boundary of the courts jurisdiction would seem to be
that the courts should not "arrogate to themselves executive or
administrative decisions." Interpretation of this phrase is difficult to
predict and open to narrow or broad interpretations. Courts are
expensive and time consuming; the outcome is often unpredictable
and very often broad policy objectives are difficult to find communicated in legal decisions. The outcome is too often based on the
principle of "the winner takes all" which may not assist in reaching
compromise and negotiation. The courts in the United Kingdom have
to date only performed a limited role, indicative of the preference for
self-regulation and the expense and uncertainty of any potential
litigation. Despite such reservations about the shortcomings of using
the courts, it is likely that litigation will provide an important element
in the future of the various utilities. Courts may offer an alternative to
the use of the Monopolies and Mergers Commission if their role is
expanded.

13–83   Fourthly, in the area of competition law the characteristics of the
British system are a broad discretion within ministerial control and a
limited role given to individuals or the courts. The MMC, OFT and
the Secretary of State for Trade and Industry combine with the
relevant regulators to oversee anti-competitive practices. Largely left
to ministerial discretion the courts have shown reluctance to challenge a refusal by the Secretary of State to make a non-referral even
when no reasons are given as in the *Lonrho* case above.

13–84   Taken together the British system of law and regulation post-
privatisation presents the following characteristics. Political policy
and broad discretion are combined in ministerial decision-taking.
Adjudicative and investigative functions are combined in the work of
the relevant regulatory agency which offers an independent dimension to overseeing the activities of the newly privatised enterprises.
Enforcement procedures are largely self-regulatory and negotiated
between regulator and privatised utility but subject to supervision by
the tough regularity powers of the MMC. This referral power to the
MMC may act as a sufficient incentive to encouraging voluntary

[82] [1983] 2 A.C. 237.
[83] See *R. v. Panel on Takeovers and Mergers, ex p. Datafin plc* [1987] 1 Q.B. 815.
[83a] [1989] 1 W.L.R. 525.

compliance and negotiated compromises. To date the courts have provided a limited role in developing the regulation of the utilities.

The remaining question to be addressed is the likely future **13–85** direction of legal techniques of regulation in Britain. An obvious influence is likely to be the application of E.C. law in the fast developing area of environment (environmental impact assessment), energy policy and regulation of competition practices. A recent example is *Foster v. British Gas plc European Court*.[84] Here the European Court interpreted a dispute concerning the implementation of an E.C. Directive 76/207 (February 9, 1976) on equal treatment for men and women as regards access to employment working conditions and promotion. The case has implications for anybody that engages in supply services such as privatised industries, quangos and civil servants. Under the principle of the *Marshall* case,[85] if the British Gas Corporation were a public body then the corporation were in breach of the Directive. British Gas plc as successors would have to accept liability for the unfair dismissal. More important was the question of how E.C. law becomes applied by the national courts as E.C. Directives cannot be directly applied by national courts and tribunals. But where a private individual has a complaint against a state body a Directive will be directly enforceable. The judgement of the European Court has left to the national courts their ideas of public service and the application of criteria laid down by the courts. This leaves a degree of uncertainty for the future as to the precise nature of the criteria and the likely result. There is confusion in the courts as to how directly and indirectly effective Directives may be applied.

A number of possibilities for the future are worth considering. **13–86** Gordon Borrie[86] argues for a Director of Civil Proceedings able to take proceedings at the instance of members of the public to redress complaints. Perhaps the role of the MMC and the different ultimate regulations requires an intra-regulatory agency to ensure consistency and long-term planning as part of its strategic functions? Borrie also suggests that private actions may be adopted as an alternative to official action in the courts against abuse of monopoly power. The comparison between the Monopolies and Mergers Commission and the courts, is difficult to make. Each offers its own distinctive form of adjudication with inherent advantages and disadvantages. It is not that one is intrinsically better than the other, more that the tendency to make greater use of the courts may come from two directions.

---

[84] Case C–188/89, *Foster v. British Gas*: [1990] 1 E.C.R. 3313, [1990] 2 C.M.L.R. 833.

[85] Case 152/84, *Marshall*: [1986] E.C.R. 723; [1986] 1 C.M.L.R. 688. R. Nobles, "Application of E.C. Law to Supply Services" (1990) *Utilities Law Review* 127–129, B. Fitzpatrick, "Direct Effect of Directives" (1991) *Utilities Law Review* 34–38.

[86] Borrie, "The Regulation of Public and Private Power" (1989) P.L. 552. See Deregulation and Contracting Out Bill 1994.

First, the interpretation of E.C. law and implementation may be led by the Court of Justice. Secondly, there is a desire for legal[87] finality which may make courts attractive.

13–87 In comparison to courts, the MMC offers a more inquisitorial and investigative procedure. Various oral hearings may be held and its own staff may carry out investigative and technical analysis. The MMC may form its own conclusion as to "the public interest" and proceed to adopt long term policy approaches to ongoing problems. The MMC may be able to formulate policy considerations within its broad discretion. Implementation of its proposals, however, depends on ministerial agreement and this may leave ministerial discretion with an influence over the ultimate decision. The MMC is itself subject to review by the courts and it must carry out its task in accordance with natural justice and fairness.

13–88 Taken together the requirements of public information, overview of privatised companies, and the prevention of monopolistic abuses suggest that regulators are likely to look to a greater reliance on the courts to develop legal techniques to supervise the privatised industries. A good start would be in a code of good administration for regulators and privatised industry alike. The *Citizen's Charter* may encourage a greater sense of individual consumer rights with the necessary requirements for a more proactive role for regulators in supporting consumer rights. The British system of law and regulation, inherited from the nineteenth century has yet to undergo a radical transformation as the whim of government policy may change and litigation is likely to develop in importance. The various regulatory agencies have yet to fully determine their future style and the use they may have for the legal techniques available. Perhaps a Royal Commission is required to oversee the work of the various regulators. This might encourage common policies and long term planning.

13–89 The question of accountability and efficiency raised by the nationalised industries in their relationship with the government of the day led to a wide range of techniques introduced to allow competitive industries to become consistent with political ideology. As Prosser[88] pointed out:

"Thus the nationalisation process was seen as almost exclusively a matter of transferring property rights whilst issues of control and accountability were treated as determined by ownership and so of little interest in their own right."

---

[87] See *R. v. National Joint Council for the Draft of Dental Technicians (Disputes Committee),* *ex p. Neate* [1953] 1 Q.B. 704.
[88] C. Graham and T. Prosser, *Privatising Public Enterprises* (Oxford, 1991), p. 272; C. Graham, "The Regulation of Privatised Enterprises" [1991] P.L. 15.

Changes are possible to the role of regulatory bodies and the development of inter-regulation agencies in the style of the United States Federal Administrative Procedure Act. Setting up such procedures might provide a more satisfactory solution to the problems posed above allowing data, analysis and rules to be co-related.[89]

The Government is seriously considering the idea of replacing the **13–90** individual nature of the way the regulator's powers are exercised by the adoption of an inter-regulatory body that takes account of cross-sectional regulatory problems that apply for all the utilities. This may take the form of a Regulatory Commission or panel of experts. The advantage of such a scheme is that it might provide some uniformity of approach and the cult of the individual regulator is avoided. Recently[90] the Government has commenced a Department of Trade inquiry as part of a cross-ministry review of the main utility regulators. The review will consider the interests of consumers, shareholders and the industry. Included within the terms of reference are the pricing formula and the question of profit-sharing between the different interest groups. A major incentive for such a review is the Government's decision to introduce a windfall levy on the utilities.[91] This has provoked a considerable discussion about the general quality of regulation. Claims that the utility companies were sold off too cheaply and that monopoly powers of some of the utility companies have been exploited have added pressure for a full scale review of regulation.

---

[89] Graham and Prosser, *op. cit.* Lewis and Harden, "Privatisation, De-Regulation and Constitutionality Some Anglo-American Comparisons" (1983) 34 N.I.L.Q. 207–21. Cento Veljanovski, *Privatisation and Competition* (Institute of Economic Affairs, 1989).
[90] *The Guardian*, July 1, 1997.
[91] See Lucy Chennells, *Labour's Windfall Levy* Institute of Fiscal Studies (1997).

Chapter 14

Citizens' Grievances

1. Introduction

14–01 The purpose of this chapter is to consider the opportunities for the citizen either individually or collectively to make complaints about public bodies and seek redress. The focus of the chapter is on the means to resolve disputes other than recourse to the courts. The courts and judicial review are examined in detail in subsequent chapters.[1]

14–02 Administrative law should have the means to hold the administration accountable. Responsible government is also accountable government. This analysis is summarised in the Canadian Law Reform Commission's report,[2] that public administration constantly produces and applies rules[3] which, even though they are not legislation, nonetheless govern the activities of administrators[4]: The Canadian Law Reform Commission also noted the variety of complaints procedures available to the citizen:

> "Control of administrative action is a function that can be shared among many institutions or types of decision-makers. Law and bodies entrusted with law application and creation are primary candidates for organizing control. However a plurality of independent modes, bodies and procedural regimes that reflect the diverse

---

[1] See Chaps. 15 and 16 on "Judicial Review and Remedies."

[2] *Towards a Modern Federal Administrative Law* (Law Reform Commission of Canada, 1987), p. 23. Also see Working Paper 51, *Policy Implementation, Compliance and Administrative Law* (Law Reform Commission of Canada, 1986).

[3] Such rules appear as guidelines, instructions, manuals circulars, or internal procedures which may not create legally enforceable rights, nonetheless as these rules affect the public they should be included in considering the scope of administrative law. See G. Ganz, *Quasi Legislation* (1989). Also see Baldwin and Houghton, "Circular Arguments" [1986] P.L. 239.

[4] *Towards a Modern Administrative Law* (Law Reform Commission of Canada, 1987), pp. 23–24.

nature of the control function, is called for. For instance, legal control can address jurisdiction only, or questions of law; control through an appeal can reach facts and the merits of a decision. Non-legal control bears not upon the legality of a decision, but upon its regularity, expediency or financial soundness. A legal dispute may involve several parties, or simply an individual and a decision-maker. This we call a contentious procedure. It implies adversariness which is treated by following a trial-type procedure. The suitability of that model for all legal controls is questionable."

The vast array of grievance mechanisms include adversarial as well as inquisitorial methods. This may involve some form of investigatory function, for example under the jurisdiction of the ombudsman. Inquisitorial procedures are also highlighted in the discussion in the chapter of the Scott inquiry[5] noted below.

This does not deny the importance for the citizen of the oppor- **14–03** tunities to seek legal redress in the courts. In a recent House of Lords decision in *Woolwich Building Society v. IRC (No. 2)*[6] concerning the recovery of payments made from an invalid government demand, the House of Lords by a majority of three to two, held that there was a common law right to recover such payments where the demand was based on a regulation which was held to be invalid. The litigation arose from the payments made by the Woolwich Building Society representing tax paid to depositors. Through judicial review the validity of the regulations was successfully challenged.[7] The revenue returned the capital sum but refused to repay the interest on the money during the period that it held the money.[8] The case is a good illustration of the advantages of the courts in offering settlement of a dispute involving a considerable sum of money. However the citizen may be less able than a Building Society to initiate complex and costly litigation.

There are a range of formal investigative powers entrusted to **14–04** specific bodies to deal with the citizen's complaints. Such bodies have "specialist grievance" procedures for dealing with complaints arising out of particular areas of activity. Some examples are as follows. In the case of complaints arising out of the various public utilities such as gas, water, electricity, telecommunications, complaints may be

---

[5] *Return to an Address of the Honourable House of Commons dated 15th February 1966. Report of the Inquiry into the Export of defence Equipment and Dual-use Goods to Iraq and Related Prosecutions* The Rt Hon. Sir Richard Scott, The Vice-Chancellor H.C. 115 (HMSO, London, 1996).

[6] *Woolwich Building Society v. I.R.C. (No. 2)* [1992] 3 All E.R. 737.

[7] *R. v. IRC, ex p. Woolwich Building Society* [1990] 1 W.L.R. 1400.

[8] The amount held involved the sum of £6,730,000. See Arrowsmith, "Recovery of Unlawful Taxes" [1992] New L.J. 1726.

made to the particular regulator concerned. In the case of Data Protection under the Data Protection Act 1984, a complaint may be made to the Data Protection Registrar. In the case of the police, a complaint may be made to the the the Police Complaints Authority which has a duty to supervise the complaint and it may invite an officer from another constabulary other than the one under investigation to carry out an investigation into the complaint.[9]

14-05 The chapter is focused on alternatives to the courts and the importance of informal and internal means to redress disputes involving the administration. This includes the use of tribunals, inquiries and ombudsmen. The Justice-All Souls review[10] in 1988 recognised the problem that there is no single institution within the United Kingdom[11] "to keep under constant review all the procedures and institutions whereby the individual may challenge administrative action." This deficiency led to their recommendation that there should be an independent body separate from the Executive charged with the responsibility of reviewing all aspects of administrative law. This proposal might take the form of a standing Royal Commission or even an extended role for the Council on Tribunals discussed below.

2. Informal Mechanisms of Complaint and M.P.s

14-06 An aggrieved citizen may find that the first avenue of redress concerning a public body is to make a formal complaint to the body concerned. In fact the citizen may find that the help of their constituency M.P. is a necessary first step in making any complaint because of the complexity of complaining. Many M.P.s feel that they play a significant role in "trouble shooting" on behalf of their constituents. Accurate estimates of the extent that M.P.s engage in this watch-dog function are difficult to make. Norton[12] has estimated that approximately 10,000 letters a month are written to Ministers by M.P.s on behalf of their constituents. Corresponding with Ministers is an efficient way to have matters raised and may solicit an effective remedy. Letters are usually kept private away from the glare of publicity, often invite some form of response from the Minister and allow departments to be alerted to particular problems and diffi-culties before any public action needs to be taken. Birkinshaw notes that[13]:

---

[9] See Cmnd. 9072 (1983).
[10] Justice All Souls Review: *Administrative Justice: Some Necessary Reforms* (Oxford, 1988).
[11] *ibid.* Chap. 4, pp. 75–84.
[12] P. Norton, *The Constitution in Flux* (1982). The importance of MP-to-Minister Correspondence" (1982) 35(1) *Parliamentary Affairs* 59–72. Also A. Mitchell, *Westminster Man* (1982).
[13] P. Birkinshaw, *Grievances Remedies and the State* (2nd ed., London, 1985), pp. 24–25.

"In 1981, the Department of Employment received in the region of 8,000 letters from M.P.s dealing with constituent's complaints. The D.H.S.S. stated their average to be 22,000–25,000 per annum and the Home Office 22,500 letters from M.P.'s in 1981, though some of these were requests for information and concerned bodies other than central departments."

M.P.s may also take advantage of various contacts they may have **14–07** on select committees, within government departments and among Cabinet Ministers. If a letter from an M.P. fails to provoke a satisfactory response then an M.P. may raise the issue in a parliamentary question[14] or during a debate in the House of Commons or during a half hour adjournment debate.

An M.P. may make use of an Early Day Motion,[15] as a means to raise a complaint from a constituent. This acts as an accurate "notice board" for any grievances raised by M.P.s especially when there is a common cause of complaint affecting many constituents or involving several constituencies. If the matter is very contentious the debate may be accompanied by the collection of a large number of signatures supporting the debate. Topics included in Early Day Motions are very broad and through debate grievances may be aired on a regular basis during each parliamentary session.

Enthusiasm for the M.P. system as a form of redress should be **14–08** tempered by the problem that many citizens may not know their M.P., may fail to understand the role of an M.P. and may not have confidence in the M.P.'s abilities to remedy any grievance. Disputes may fall outside the remit of the M.P. when there are legal proceedings imminent or where the matter may be more properly dealt with by an alternative means of redress. Various studies have suggested that the work of M.P.s may be obscure to the average constituent.[16] The inadequacy of the M.P. as an effective watch-dog was partly acknowledged in the setting up of the central government Parliamentary Commissioner for Administration.

In terms of informal means to redress grievances there are a wide **14–09** number of pressure groups or trade unions who may act as a watchdog for the citizen. There are about 850 local Citizens Advice Bureaux, mostly staffed with volunteers who provide information and advice on access to both formal and informal means to redress grievances. Since the opening of the first Law Centre in 1970 there has

---

[14] House of Commons Standing Order No. 17(1)–(7), there is also a procedure for an emergency debate under House of Commons Standing Order No. 20, but in practice not many are allowed in any one Parliamentary year.

[15] Usually restricted to about 250 words and on average about 1,000 are tabled each session.

[16] See Morrell (1977), quoted in Birkinshaw *op. cit.*

been a steady development in their work and activities, although recently their funding and support has been put in doubt. Law Centres provide legal advice and may specialise on specific problem areas which require specialist advice such as housing and immigration problems. Some times the matter complained about involves some form of consumer redress such as a housing problem which may fit in the category of a private law problem between the landlord and tenant, or if there is a public body involved local authority and tenant. The hybrid nature of such problems makes a knowledge of both public and private law essential.

14-10 Citizens grievances in the public law arena may benefit from newspaper or media coverage to force officials to take account of the citizens grievance. This may involve "in depth" investigative journalism or simply drawing attention to the nature of the disputes.

The first report of the Government's Citizens' Charter initiative[17] announced the intention of setting up a Complaints Task Force to examine and advise on setting up and improving complaints systems in the public sector. Guidance issued to the Task Force by the Council on Tribunals from June 1993 includes advice on complaints investigation procedures. There are also some important developments in open government under the Code of Practice on Access to Government Information.[18] This includes the intention in the future to provide some statutory rights[19] to information, perhaps on the same basis as the Local Government (Access to Information) Act 1985. The current Government appears to be well disposed to a Freedom of Information Act some time in the next five years.

3. Tribunals and Inquiries

(a) Tribunals

14-11 In considering alternatives to the courts in the adjudication of disputes importance must be given to the work of tribunals. Tribunals[20] were commonly in use in the nineteenth century.[21] Today

---

[17] Cm. 2101 (1992). See Guidance on the Conduct of Complaints Hearings (June, 1993).
[18] See the Cabinet Office, Open Government 70, Whitehall, London, SW1A 2AS.
[19] See Access to Personal Files Act 1987 and some examples such as Access to Medical Reports Act 1988, Access to Health Records Act 1990.
[20] See, generally, Katherine Bell, "Social Security Tribunals–A General Perspective" (1982) 38 *Northern Ireland Legal Quarterly* 132.
[21] See Chap. 5 for a discussion of some of the background reasons for the creation of tribunals. Generally see D. Foulkes, *Administrative Law* (7th ed., 1990), Chap. 5.

they perform a wide variety of functions and may take a number of forms for redressing the citizens' grievances. The Employment Appeals Tribunal is a superior Court of Record. The Local Valuation Courts set up under section 88 of the General Rate Act 1967, hears appeals on land drainage, and before the Community Charge and Council Tax, valuation courts heard a whole range of rating matters with appeals to the Land Tribunal,[22] valuation courts appear to have all the formalities of a court of law.

Franks[23] regarded tribunals as part of the machinery provided by **14–12** Parliament for the purposes of adjudication rather than as part of the machinery of the administration. A wide variety of bodies and institutions rely on the work of tribunals. The Franks Committee[24] in 1957 recommended the creation of the Council of Tribunals[25] to keep under review the working and the constitution of tribunals. The work of the Council closely monitors the development of the system of administrative tribunals "to provide some consistent principles" to guide the work of tribunals. Since the Tribunal and Inquiries Act 1958 following the recommendations of the Franks Committee, the number of tribunals which fall within the jurisdiction of the Council on Tribunals[26] exceeds 50.

It is impossible to provide any coherent organising principles to **14–13** group the work of tribunals. However on the basis of the jurisdiction of the Council on Tribunals the following examples give an indication of the activities covered by tribunals.[27] Schedule 1 of the Tribunals and Inquiries Act 1992 contains a list of the Tribunals falling under the direct supervision of the Council on Tribunals.

Various disciplinary bodies may take the form of a tribunal. For **14–14** example, the General Dental Council,[28] the Central Council for Nursing, Midwifery and Health Visiting,[29] the General Medical Council[30] and the Architects Registration Council for the United Kingdom[31] exercise a variety of disciplinary powers within a statutory framework. Licensing also forms an important function of the work of

---

[22] Part II of the Lands Tribunal Rules 1975 (S.I. 1975 No. 299).

[23] Franks Report, *op. cit.*, paras. 37 and 40.

[24] *Report of the Committee on Administrative Tribunals and Enquiries*, Cmnd. 218, (1957).

[25] There are in fact two standing councils one for England and Wales, the other for Scotland.

[26] *The Functions of the Council on Tribunals*, Cmnd. 7805 (1980).

[27] A comprehensive list is provided in the encylopaedia by John Bowers (ed.), *Tribunals Practice and Procedure* (1985).

[28] Dentists Act 1984, s.27.

[29] The Nurses, Midwives and Health Visitors (Professional Conduct) Rules 1983 (S.I. 1983 No. 887). Also see the Nurses, Midwives and Health Visitors Act 1979.

[30] Legislation dates back to the Medical Act 1858 and consolidated by the Medical Act 1983.

[31] The Architects (Registration Act) 1931.

tribunals such as the Civil Aviation Authority,[32] or the Consumer Credit Licensing Hearings.[33] As Hendry has noted[34]:

> ". . . a multiplicity of tribunals each operating within the bounds of a confined jurisdiction and each directed toward disposing of claims and arguments arising out of a particular statutory scheme."

14–15 Specialised and comprehensive rules are now provided in Part III of the Trade Union Reform and Employment Rights Act 1993 for the constitution of industrial tribunals. The 1993 Act established for the first time in primary legislation the basic constitution of industrial tribunals.

Taxation in its various forms has also created the need for a number of tribunals. For example the General and Special Commissioners of Income Tax through the various Income Tax Acts dating back to 1816 hears appeals against assessments to tax, reliefs against tax and oversees the administration of the taxation system in the United Kingdom. In the case of value added tax an appeal jurisdiction exists with the various Value Added Tax Tribunals set up under the Finance Act 1972 and subsequent amendments.[35]

14–16 There is also the introduction in 1993 of the Revenue Adjudicator, entrusted to investigate complaints about the Inland Revenue. This jurisdiction was expanded in 1995 to include Customs and Excise and the Contributions Agency. The idea of an Adjudicator is also adopted in respect of prisons, and Companies House.[36] Adjudicators build on the experience of a variety of different tribunals by filling any perceived "gaps" in the system. Dissatisfaction in existing methods of redress for taxation matters favoured what Morris has described as[37]:

> "In short there was a pressing need for a speedy, user-friendly, cheap but independent complaints mechanism whereby tax payers could ventilate grievances regarding the *manner* in which the revenue has exercised its powers, and an Adjudicator scheme was seized upon as the ideal solution."

14–17 Some areas of tribunal activity have come under particular scrutiny by the courts, partly because of the nature of the work involved. For

---

[32] Civil Aviation Act 1982, s.7(3).
[33] Consumer Credit Act 1974.
[34] K. H. Hendry, "The Tasks of Tribunals: Some Thoughts" (1982) 1 C.J.Q. 253.
[35] A consolidation has taken place under the Value Added Tax Act 1983. See the VAT Tribunals Rules 1972 (S.I. 1972 No. 1344).
[36] See P. E. Morris, "The Revenue Adjudicator – The First Two Years" [1996] *Public Law* 309–22.
[37] *ibid.* p. 311.

example the Prison Board of Visitors[38] with its origins in the Prison Act 1898 appears to have developed into a tribunal in all but name when performing a wide adjudicative function on charges of offences under the Prison Act 1952 and amendments.[39] The disciplinary function can be vast as over 81,000 disciplinary offences were punished in the year 1989.[40] Such disciplinary proceedings are subject to judicial review by the courts. There is concern that legal representation should be available at such hearings as the powers of the Board of Visitors have been compared to the jurisdiction of the magistrates' courts. In *R. v. Board of Visitors of H.M. Prison, the Maze, ex p. Hone*[41] Lord Goff noted the observations made on behalf of the appellant:

"a hearing before a board of visitors is a sophisticated hearing. In particular, he [counsel for the appellant] submitted there is an oral hearing; a formal plea is entered; cross-examination is allowed and witnesses are called; the onus and standard of proof are the same as in a criminal trial; free legal aid is available; punishments are imposed; a plea in mitigation can be entered, and the board has greater powers of punishment than those exercised by magistrate's courts."[42]

The House of Lords rejected the submission that those appearing before the Prison Board had a right to legal representation by a lawyer.[43] The courts have consistently upheld the principle that the rules of natural justice apply to the Board of Prison Visitors in making their adjudications.

Immigration appeals also fall under the work of a tribunal, the **14–18** Immigration Appeal Tribunal[44] which has considerable discretionary powers. Section 16 of the Immigration Act 1971 provides rights of appeal to an adjudicator against directions for the removal of illegal immigrants but in the case of deportation there is no statutory right of appeal.[45] Further provisions on the appointment of adjudicators are

---

[38] Judicial review of the Board was the subject of the House of Lords decision in *O'Reilly v. Mackman* [1983] 2 A.C. 237.

[39] See the Prison (Amendment) Rules 1989 (S.I. 1989 No. 330).

[40] *Statistics of Offences Against Prison Discipline and Punishments England and Wales 1989,* Cm. 1236, (1990).

[41] [1988] A.C. 379; [1988] 2 W.L.R. 177; *Hone v. Maze Prison Visitors* [1988] 1 All E.R. 321.

[42] The submission relied on the authority of *R. v. St Mary Abbotts, Kensington Assessment Committee* [1891] 1 Q.B. 378 for the authority for the proposition that the appellant had a common law right to appoint a lawyer as his agent. This view was rejected by Lord Roskill.

[43] The rules of natural justice do apply to the Prison Board and this may give rise to a judicial review. See *R. v. Blundeston Prison Board of Visitors, ex p. Fox-Taylor* [1982] 1 All E.R. 646.

[44] Immigration Act 1971, s.12.

[45] See *R. v. Secretary of State for Home Affairs, ex p. Honsenball* [1977] 3 All E.R. 452.

contained in Schedule 5 of the Act. Procedures for adjudicators are provided in detailed rules[46] made under section 22 of the 1971 Act including written notices of all decisions for which an appeal may lie.[47]

14–19 Social welfare rights created a number of statutory bodies which have the designation of a tribunal. This is a vast area where adjudication lies at the heart of the many social welfare provisions introduced since the setting up of the modern Welfare State.[48] Social Security Appeal Tribunals[49] hear a whole range of matters relating to social welfare benefits. In outline the system depends first on civil servants appointed as local adjudication officers working in the local offices of the Department of Health and Social Services. Their tasks are to adjudicate claims affecting the payments of a wide range of benefits, collecting evidence on claims, and acting independently of the Department in their interpretation and application of the law. There are various Chief Adjudication Officers entrusted to advise adjudication officers.[50] A Single Appeals Tribunal introduced under the 1983 Social Security Adjudications Act[51] provides an appeal procedure. There is a President of the Social Security Appeal Tribunals who must be a lawyer of at least 10 years standing, appointed by the Lord Chancellor. Thus the Social Security Tribunal System is based on a presidential system in common with the Pensions Appeal Tribunal and the Lands Tribunal. This is claimed to have a number of advantages[52]: independence from government departments as a President may assist in the administration of the system instead of relying on the government department concerned. Also a presidential system allows a degree of monitoring over the performance of individual tribunals, and co-ordination of the work of tribunals. In addition setting the focus and the aims of the system may be greatly facilitated by having a President in overall oversight.

14–20 The Social Security Appeal Tribunals are normally chaired by a lawyer of not less than five years standing and two persons selected from a panel made up of representatives from employers and

---

[46] See the Immigration Appeals Regulations 1984 (S.I. 1984 No. 2041).

[47] See the Immigration Appeals (Notices) Regulations 1984 (S.I. 1984 No. 2040).

[48] The earliest poor law provisions date back to the 16th century. The National Insurance Act 1911 introduced unemployment benefit, but the modern system of social security dates from the 1940s.

[49] See the Health and Social Services and Social Security Adjudication Act 1983. Regulations made thereunder include the Social Security (Adjudication) Regulations 1984 (S.I. 1984 No. 451).

[50] See L. N. Brown, "The British Social Security Tribunals: A New Unified System" [1986] Camb. L.J. 40.

[51] Previously there was a system of local tribunals, and a system of Supplementary Benefit Appeals Tribunals.

[52] Annual Report of the Council on Tribunals for 1982/83, (1984/84; H.C. 129).

employed persons. There may be a further appeal to the Social Security Commissioners. In 1980 the Social Security Act introduced for the first time an appeal on a point of law from the decision of Commissioners to the High Court.

The Social Security Act 1986 introduced a replacement for the **14–21** system of supplementary benefits, consisting of "income support and family credits for regular payments." In the case of special needs a Social Fund[53] was created. An aggrieved claimant could have his case reviewed by the Social Fund Officer, in effect the person who made the decision in the first place, then followed by a more senior officer in the same office. However the Government rejected the idea[54] that there should be an independent right of appeal to some tribunal preferring instead to have the matter determined within the administrative system without recourse to an independent source external to the adjudication.

This represents a serious shift in the determination of benefits. As a **14–22** result the Council on Tribunals complained in 1986 in a special report[55] that this might possibly deprive a number of claimants of their rights. Significantly the Council pointed out that 25 per cent of appeals involving single payment claimants heard by Social Security Tribunals were upheld and that in any one year there were over 35,000 appeals regarding single payments. The government's response was to offer a review of decisions of Social Fund officers by setting up a system of Social Fund inspectors. This would appear barely adequate to meet the concerns raised by the Council although recent research has pointed to the objective way inspectors have considered their work.[56] The Council has continued to argue for an independent tribunal and concern exists that the question of the financial cost of tribunals may make their future uncertain.

The Council on Tribunals has fought hard for an increased role and **14–23** additional powers to carry out its role. The original legislation, the Tribunals and Inquiries Act 1958, subsequently modified and later consolidated in 1992.[57] The 1958 Act set up the Council and its composition combines practising lawyers, and academic lawyers with non-lawyers who are in the majority. All members are appointed by the Lord Chancellor or the Lord Advocate for Scotland. The Council has presently no jurisdiction in Northern Ireland.

---

[53] *Reform of Social Security* (1985) Cmnd. 9517.

[54] Social Security Act 1986.

[55] Social Security-Abolition of Independent Appeals Under the Proposed Social Fund, Cm. 9722 (1986).

[56] R. Drabble and T. Lynes, "The Social Fund–Discretion or Control" [1989] P.L. 297.

[57] See the Tribunals and Inquiries Act 1966 and the consolidation contained in the Tribunals and Inquiries Acts 1972 and 1992. See the Child Support Act 1991 for appeals against assessments of child support maintenance.

14-24 An important function of the Council on Tribunals is providing detailed consideration of draft rules and procedures of individual tribunals. Foulkes has noted[58] how a limited but important role is performed by the Council in considering areas of dispute settlement in the recent privatisation legislation for electricity and water, where the legislation gave the respective Directors-General a role in the determination of disputes. The Council has a role in overseeing the rules laid down for the procedures in the conduct of determinations made by the regulators. In 1991 the Council published a Report on Model Rules of Procedure for Tribunals.[59] The report contained guidance in setting up adjudication procedures. In general such guidance is to ensure that there are fair procedures and reasons for decisions are made known as part of those procedures.

14-25 The Council has been active in setting the standards of how rights and procedures might be efficiently combined into the operation of the tribunal system. This includes the rules of evidence, the award of costs, the rights of appearance of witnesses, the rules relating to the disclosure of confidential information and the time-limits for appeals and such matters. During the course of its work a number of issues have been raised by the Council, most notably the need to avoid the proliferation and expansion of the number of tribunals without careful consideration. This has led to the suggestion that tribunals might be consolidated to give greater efficiency[59a] to the system overall.

14-26 In 1980 in a special report the Council considered the functions of the Council and how best to develop them for the future.[60] The Council argued for an advisory role over "the whole area of administrative adjudication." There is currently no obligation on Ministers to consult with the Council at any stage when Bills are being prepared which may establish new tribunals or affect existing ones. The Council considered that this deficiency should be remedied. The Government's response[61] considered that it would be inappropriate to lay a statutory duty on Ministers to consult the Council on Tribunals on the legislation that they were considering. While consultation on an ad hoc basis might be encouraged and subsequently a Code of Practice[62] was formulated by the Council for the guidance of officials

---

[58] D. Foulkes, "The Council on Tribunals and the Utilities" [1990] *Utilities Law Review* 145.
[59] Cm. 1434 (1991).
[59a] Annual Report 1975/76, paras. 94–97.
[60] *The Functions of the Council on Tribunals: Special Report*, Cmnd. 7805 (1980).
[61] See 419 H.L. Debs. 5th series, col. 1118. See D. G. T. Williams, "The Tribunal System– Its Future Control and Supervision" (1990) 9 C.J.Q. 27.
[62] See Appendix C to the *Annual Report of the Council on Tribunals 1986/87* (1987/88; H.C. 234). See *Annual Report of the Council on Tribunals 1992/93* (1992/93; H.C. 78).

involved in drafting legislation when to consult with the Council. However the Code has not been given any statutory endorsement. The Council has noted that despite the Code being reissued in 1986 it is not always followed by every government department.[63]

The Council has also raised a further shortcoming in its arrange- **14–27** ments for dealing with any complaints which may be made to it about the working of tribunals. The Council has not got the statutory powers to deal with major complaints even though they may raise fundamental issues.[64] While the Council historically believes its role is to consider "openness, fairness and impartiality" in the tribunal system, it also has to meet new demands for "efficiency, effectiveness, and economy."[65] Settling the inevitable tensions between the differing standards expected of the Council is a challenge for the future. While the Council has embarked on providing a research register[66] of those interested in tribunals and inquiries through the appointment of a part-time research co-ordinator in 1987, it admits that its largest deficiency is the lack of manpower and the resources to provide a detailed knowledge of the working of the system of tribunals.[67]

The Council has commented[68] on the attempts made by the **14–28** Government to set up new tribunals by subordinate legislation rather than Act of Parliament. One example is Service Committees of Family Health Service Authorities. Another is the Special Educational Needs Tribunal. The Council is critical in its annual report of the use of regulations establishing tribunals rather than Act of Parliament. The Council would prefer regulations to be confined to detailed rules rather than their use in establishing tribunals.

Tribunals are often compared to courts and may appear to perform the work of departments in adjudications. However, the Franks Report was clear[69]: "tribunals . . . are not ordinary courts, but neither are they appendages of Government Departments . . ."

Defining the role and objectives of tribunals presents formidable **14–29** problems given the great diversity of their work and the lack of uniformity in their functions. All tribunals which deal with disputes between the citizen and the government are concerned with administrative power and how it may properly be exercised. The Justice All Souls review noted[70]:

---

[63] *Annual Report of the Council on Tribunals 1986/87* (1987/88; H.C. 234).
[64] Cmnd. 7805 (1980).
[65] *Annual Report of the Council on Tribunals 1985/86* (1986/87; H.C. 42).
[66] The Council on Tribunals publishes a Research Bulletin.
[67] In the case of inquiries discussed below the Council also wishes to have a statutory right to advise on the system of procedures involving statutory inquiries.
[68] *Annual Report of the Council on Tribunals 1992/93* (1992/93; H.C. 78).
[69] Franks, *op. cit.* para. 40.
[70] Justice All Souls Review, p. 212.

"... that the true role of the courts is restricted to a review of legality and the judges are not concerned with the merits in the sense of the rightness (or wrongness) of the decision. Tribunals on the other hand, are given a different role. Very commonly they are concerned with the merits of the decision and typically they will be given the task of deciding, as between citizen and the state, whether an official has dealt correctly with a claim or application."

Tribunals may also exercise similar decision-making functions as Ministers. Franks expressed a preference for tribunals over the largely discretionary powers of Ministers and preferred courts over tribunals. In the allocation of functions it appears quite difficult to decide the advantages of one over the other. However it is possible to set out some of the reasons for creating independent statutory tribunals.

14-30   The main reasons and by implication the advantages claimed for a system of tribunals are the following. Tribunals provide access to expert and specialist knowledge of complex areas of law and practice. The forum of a tribunal allows a wider degree of expertise than would normally be possible with the courts. In addition tribunals are claimed to provide cheap, reasonably speedy and efficient means for the resolution of disputes. The procedures may claim to be less formal than courts though as pointed out above, some tribunals appear to have inherited all the procedures almost identical to the courts. Another claimed advantage is that tribunals are not bound by very complex and legalistic rules of evidence and the decisions reached at tribunals may cover more widely developed considerations than the courts.

14-31   This raises the broader question of whether tribunals may offer a distinctive system of adjudication that is not orientated to the adversarial process in the way that the courts are? Lord Denning in *R. v. National Insurance Commr, ex p. Viscusi*[71] suggested that tribunals were "more in the nature of an inquiry before an investigating body charged with the task of finding out what happened." However, with the question of representation at tribunals, almost all tribunals permit legal representation,[72] and the desirability of legal aid for all tribunals,[73] advocated by the Lord Chancellor's Advisory Committee,[74] there is a temptation to see tribunals moving under the influences of lawyers[75] into an adversarial role. Investigating the characteristics of

---

[71] [1974] 1 W.L.R. 646.
[72] The Service Committee of Family Practitioners Committees appears one of the few exceptions. Also see the Board of Prison Visitors mentioned above.
[73] Recommended in 1945 by the Rushcliffe Committee (Cmnd. 6641), but not introduced in the original Legal Aid and Advice Act 1949.
[74] *Lord Chancellor's Advisory Committee 24th Annual Report* (1973/74; H.C. 20).
[75] See the *Royal Commission on Legal Services*, Cmnd. 7648 (1979), para. 15(12).

tribunal procedures and whether they represent a distinctly inquisitorial system is an important issue in the light of recent doubts about miscarriages of justice in the criminal courts.[76]

Tribunals fall under the jurisdiction of the courts. Sections 10–12 of **14–32** the Tribunals and Inquiries Act 1992 provides that tribunals must "furnish a statement either written or oral, of the reasons for the decision." Under section 13 of the Tribunals and Inquiries Act 1971, now section 11 of the 1992 Act, a party dissatisfied on a point of law with a decision of the tribunal may appeal or make a case stated to the High Court if the tribunal falls in the category of a Schedule 1 tribunal listed in the Act.

Great difficulty is experienced in identifying with any clarity the meaning of "a point of law" which has to be settled by the courts. Errors of law may include the misinterpretation of a statute,[77] taking irrelevant considerations into account, or an abuse of discretion.[78] But distinguishing a point of law from one of fact appears to be made on the basis of each case. Craig suggests that[79]:

"Two questions can arise which are not always properly distinguished. The first is whether the error alleged involves any question of law at all. Presuming an affirmative answer to this first question, the second is by what standard will the courts determine whether there has been an erroneous construction of this legal term?"

The problem may also be seen in terms of the latitude the courts **14–33** are willing to allow the decision-maker and the extent to which intervention by the courts substitutes judicial decision-making for the tribunal.[80] Wade distinguishes[81] between two rival approaches followed by the courts on the distinction between facts and law. One approach suggests that matters of fact may be confined to the primary facts of the case. Once such facts are established the question of whether they satisfy some legal definition must be a question of law. "The facts themselves not being in dispute, the conclusion is a matter of legal inference." The other approach proceeds on the assumption that the "meaning of an ordinary word in the English language is not a question of law" unless the interpretation given to it by the tribunal is unreasonable. Wade shows that the courts have not

---

[76] See M. McConville et al., *The Case for the Prosecution* (Routledge, 1992).

[77] *R. v. Northumberland Compensation Tribunal, ex p. Shaw* [1952] 1 K.B. 338.

[78] *Att.-Gen. v. Fulham Corp.* [1921] 1 Ch. 440.

[79] P. Craig, *Administrative Law* (1989), p. 124.

[80] See *Edwards v. Bristow* [1956] A.C. 14 for the discussion of the principles involved in facts and law distinctions.

[81] Wade, *Administrative Law* (6th ed., 1988), pp. 940–943.

been consistent in their approach and this leaves considerable[82] discretion in the interpretation of this complex issue.

14–34   Tribunals in reaching their decisions must keep within their legal powers. The Court of Appeal declined to allow a review of the validity of income support regulations through the statutory appeal system. The Social Security Commissioner had held on an appeal from a Social Security Tribunal that its decision was *ultra vires* and contrary to law.[83] The Court held that such a finding is inconsistent with the role of the Commissioner. The House of Lords has reversed the decision of the Court of Appeal and held that a Commissioner has jurisdiction to determine any challenge to the *vires* of a provision in regulations when considering if a decision order appeal was an error in law. This raises the possibility of appeals raising identical issues to that of review. The scope for development in this area requires further consideration by the courts. A distinction[84] should be drawn between an appellate and a judicial review jurisdiction. Normally the courts will not permit *vires* to be raised on appeal, though this may depend on the nature of the body involved as there are some decided cases which do accept this possibility.[85]

(b)   Inquiries

14–35   Aggrieved citizens may find that the forum which allows their view point or objections to be most clearly expressed and openly considered is through the use of inquiries. Compared to tribunals, where there is a need to adjudicate disputes between the citizen and the State, inquiries developed historically as an alternative to the Private Bill procedure where proposals for powers by government in matters involving public authority were investigated through parliamentary committees. Inquiries, developed from different considerations than the tribunal system. Wade notes[86]:

> "The typical tribunal finds facts and decides the case by applying legal rules laid down by statute or regulation. The typical inquiry hears evidence and finds facts, but the person conducting it finally

---

[82] See *Ransom v. Higgs* [1974] 1 W.L.R. 1594 compared to *Edwards v. Bairstow* [1956] A.C. 14.

[83] See *Chief Adjudication Officer v. Foster* [1992] Q.B. 31; [1993] 1 All E.R. 705.

[84] In *R. v. Secretary of State for Social Services, ex p. Child Poverty Action Group* [1990] 2 Q.B. 540, the Court of Appeal declined to intervene in the administrative arrangements under ss.98 and 99 of the Social Security Act 1975 in the delays caused by problems in the staffing and organisation of the adjudication system under the supplementary Benefits System.

[85] See *R. v. Inland Revenue Commmissioner, ex p. Preston* [1985] A.C. 835.

[86] Wade, *op. cit.* p. 900.

makes a recommendation to a minister as to how the minister should act on some question of policy, eg, whether he should grant planning permission for some development scheme."

In essence inquiries allow the citizen the right to a hearing before **14–36** an important administrative decision may be made. This means that inquiries allow more public participation than would otherwise be possible especially in the planning law area where there is controversy over the siting of an airport, a power station or a major motorway.

Traditionally inquiries are limited to an investigative role, usually through the provision of evidential material to allow a Minister to reach an ultimate decision. Rarely do they make the actual decision. Inquiries have developed in an ad hoc way. As a valuable technique in administrative law, the basic elements of independent investigation, presentation of evidence and the making of recommendations allow for great flexibility. Inquiries also have the potential to cross the boundary between public law and private law issues. For example the Department of Trade enjoy wide powers to appoint inspectors to investigate companies,[87] which include under section 177(1) of the Financial Services Act 1986, the power to appoint inspectors if it appears to the Secretary of State that there is a breach of the Company Securities (Insider Dealing) Act 1985.

Inquiries into accidents may be set up under various statutory **14–37** powers. Section 466 of the Merchant Shipping Act 1894 gives powers to hold an inquiry into a collision of a ship at sea, there are various statutory powers to hold inquiries into railway accidents, gas explosions, or nuclear installations. The normal formulation of the terms of reference of such inquiries includes questions of why did the accident occur, and what lessons may be gained from past mistakes? In some instances the basis of the inquiry may give rise to criminal prosecutions or disciplinary procedures. Civil liability may therefore be largely dependent on the outcome of an accident inquiry and this raises questions about the confidentiality of evidence and the rights of witnesses who give evidence and afterwards find that criminal prosecutions are taken. In that respect account needs to be taken of the possibility, now accepted but at one time doubted, that in English criminal law a corporation could be convicted of manslaughter. In *P & O European Ferries Ltd*[88] Mr Justice Turner held that an indictment for manslaughter might lie against P&O Ferries after the Zeebrugge disaster. The evidence which may form the basis of any criminal prosecution,[89] may come from the evidence obtained as part of the

---

[87] See the Companies Act 1985.
[88] [1991] Crim. L.R. 695.
[89] *R. v. Coroner for Kent, ex p. Spooner* (1989) 88 Cr.App.R. 10.

findings of the inquiry into the disaster.[90] The Sheen Report[91] found that from the Board of Directors[92] "through the managers of the marine department down to the Junior Superintendents" fault could be established. The conclusion reached in the report was that: "From top to bottom the body corporate was infected with the disease of sloppiness."

14-38   Inquiries may also have an important role in establishing facts arising from social problems such as child abuse. Such inquiries may come under section 26 of the Child Care Act 1980 or inquiries undertaken by review panels appointed by local authorities or local agencies. The standing of the person appointed to hold the inquiry and the nature of the recommendation may prove influential with the government of the day even though there is no obligation to accept any of the recommendations made in the report prepared by the inquiry. Not everyone favours the inquiry as an investigative technique in such cases. In 1981 the Annual General Meeting of the British Association of Social Workers rejected the use of committees of inquiry in such cases. Dissatisfaction of the Association has focused on the show piece nature of the inquiry and the feeling that those under investigation are perceived by the media as "on trial."[93]

14-39   The principles identified by Franks that ought to apply to inquiries such as openness, fairness and impartiality, have been recognised in the Tribunals and Inquiries Acts 1958 and in section 11 of the 1971 Act and their consolidation in 1992. This legislation permits the Lord Chancellor to make various procedural rules for the conduct of inquiries. An example of these rules may be found in the Town and Country Planning (Inquiries Procedure) Rules 1988.[94] In drawing up such rules the Council on Tribunals may be consulted, such rules are advisory only.

14-40   In addition to the above procedures there are a miscellaneous number of statutory provisions which permit the holding of inquiries.[95] Formal powers for the investigation of improper official behaviour of officials in 1921 were enacted under the Tribunals of Inquiry (Evidence) Act 1921. The 1921 Act is sparingly used for such matters of "urgent public importance." It has been estimated that these powers have only been used in less than 20 occasions in the

---

[90] The Report was carried out by Mr Justice Sheen, with assessors and published in July 1987. Also see J. McEldowney, "Public Inquiry into the Piper Alpha Disaster" [1991] *Utilities Law Review* 2.

[91] *ibid.*

[92] The Sheen report, *op. cit.* para. 14.1.

[93] *Child Abuse Inquiries* (Council of the British Association of Social Workers, 1982).

[94] S.I. 1988 No. 944. Also see the Town and Country Planning Appeals (Determination by Inspectors) (Inquiry Procedure) Rules 1988 (S.I. 1988 No. 945).

[95] The National Health Service Act 1977, the Education Act 1979, and various provisions under the Child Care Act 1990 as amended.

past. There are also a variety of non-statutory inquiries where it is desired to carry out an investigation and a statutory inquiry is not required. The most well known example of this is the Crichel Down inquiry,[96] and the Stansted inquiry into the siting of London's third airport.[97] Inquiries may be set up where there are public concerns about the role of Ministers. In 1963 Lord Denning's inquiry into the Profumo affair[98] was set up informally and had no statutory powers. The Salmon Commission later recommended that such inquiries should not normally be used in matters of such public concern.[99] However, there have been instances where inquiries without statutory powers have been used. The Bingham report into the collapse of BCCI, discussed in Chapter 11, is one such example. The collapse of the trial of three former executives of the machine tool company Matrix Churchill charged with deception in obtaining export licences led to the setting up of an inquiry chaired by Lord Justice Scott. At the trial the prosecution had alleged that the intended use of the machine tools supplied to Iraq was for weapons. The defence claimed that the government was fully aware of the use of the machine tools which had been subject to a licence application. Evidence given by Alan Clark, the former Minister of State at the Department of Trade and Industry confirmed that there was no deception as the Government were aware of the intended use of the machine tools. The judge quashed public interest immunity certificates served by the prosecution to prevent disclosure of intelligence information. The documents released at the trial revealed how high level departmental and ministerial contact had taken place over the licence application. Controversy surrounds the use of public interest immunity certificates and the role of government Ministers in signing the certificates. Also of significance is the question of the legal advice tendered by the Attorney-General that Ministers were under a duty to sign the certificates. The role of Customs and Excise in bringing the prosecutions is also questioned.

The terms of reference of the Scott inquiry were announced by the **14–41** Prime Minister[1] "to examine and report on decisions taken by the prosecuting authority and those signing public interest immunity certificates in *R. v. Henderson*[2] and any other similar cases that he considers relevant to the inquiry; and to make recommendations."

---

[96] *Report of the Public Inquiry into the Disposal of Land at Crichel Down*, Cmnd. 9176 (1954) See Chap. 3 for a fuller discussion.

[97] *Report of the Commission on the Third London Airport* (1971).

[98] Cmnd. 2152 (1963).

[99] Cmnd. 3121 (1966).

[1] H.C. Deb. Vol. 214, col. 74 (November 16, 1992).

[2] *R. v. Henderson*, November, 1992, unreported. Also see D. Leigh, *Betrayed: The Real Story of the Matrix Churchill Trial* (London, 1993).

The Chairman of the inquiry appointed an independent counsel to the inquiry who in practice took the main burden of asking questions of witnesses. The inquiry has heard evidence in public and the evidence is available from the Public Records Office.

14–42   The inquiry was not set up under the Tribunals and Inquiry (Evidence) Act 1921 and thus it did not have statutory powers to subpoena witnesses. The Prime Minister gave assurances that civil servants and ministers would be required to give evidence. Former ministers accepted invitations to attend including Lady Thatcher, the former Prime Minister. John Major also gave evidence as serving Prime Minister. Witnesses had been given immunity from prosecution for their evidence given at the inquiry.

14–43   As an ad hoc inquiry with no express statutory powers, this gave Sir Richard Scott the freedom to determine the procedures to be adopted at the inquiry itself. The procedures adopted at the Scott inquiry proved as controversial as the subject of the inquiry itself. The starting point is to consider the six cardinal principles adopted by Lord Salmon as guidance for inquiries laid down by the Royal Commission 1966 under the chairmanship of Lord Salmon. The six Salmon principles are as follows:

1. Before any person becomes involved in an inquiry the Tribunal must be satisfied that there are circumstances which affect him and which the tribunal proposes to investigate.

2. Before any person who is involved in an inquiry is called as a witness he should be informed of any allegations which are made against him and the substance of the evidence in support of them.

3. He should be given an adequate opportunity of preparing his case and of being advised by legal advisers; his legal expenses should normally be met out of public funds.

4. He should have the opportunity of being examined by his own solicitor or counsel and of stating his case in public at the inquiry.

5. Any material witnesses he wishes called at the inquiry should, if reasonably practicable be heard.

6. He should have the opportunity of testing by cross-examination conducted by his own solicitor or counsel any evidence which may affect him.

14–44   It is important to remember that the six principles, outlined above, are not rules of law but guidance which might be followed. The

Salmon principles were intended to provide the basis for Tribunals operating under the Tribunals of Inquiries Act 1921. While many commentators see the principles as fundamental ones,[3] the Scott inquiry was free to depart from them. The approach taken by Scott was to acknowledge that as far as possible the principles should be applied and followed. However, the nature of the Scott inquiry required both adversarial and inquisitorial techniques. In the end the procedures that were adopted of necessity reflected the inquisitorial approach taken by the inquiry. Scott rapidly discovered that if the inquiry adopted all of the six Salmon principles it might take a considerable time to complete. The principle that caused most controversy relates to the question of cross-examination and legal representation at the inquiry. In the past, notable inquiries such as Lord Justice Crom-Johnson into the Crown Agents affair took considerable time and were subject to extensive delay. Cross-examination by lawyers at the inquiry was held largely responsible for that delay.

The question of whether Scott was correct in adopting an **14–45** inquisitorial approach remains highly debated. Criticism focused on the argument that the inquisitive nature of the procedures were inappropriate when conducted in public hearings, left witnesses unprotected and put due process in jeopardy. Scott's response to such criticisms, notably from Lord Howe[4] was to point to the increasingly large amount of written submissions received throughout the entire period of the inquiry, the fact that oral proceedings were only a small fraction of the inquiry's work and that witnesses were granted legal advice at considerable cost to the tax-payer though admittedly not cross-examination. This last point, the absence of cross-examination rights remains a contentious issue. In its recent consideration of the Scott procedures, the Council on Tribunals broadly favoured the Scott approach whenever inquisitorial procedures were involved. There remains some lurking doubts that perhaps the procedures were in some way defective because the key element of cross-examination by lawyers was absent. There was also the sheer scale of the work generated by the inquiry. Lord Howe makes the following observations:

"My own case may be seen as a useful illustration. Unrepresented as I was until very near the end (only my closing submissions were prepared by counsel and solicitors rather than myself), I struggled to keep abreast of the mountains of transcripts that filled the months before and after I gave evidence, and over the years during which I was obliged to comment on several distinct batches of

---

[3] Lord Howe, "Procedure at the Scott Inquiry" [1996] *Public Law* 445–460.
[4] Lord Howe of Aberavon, "Procedure at the Scott Inquiry" [1996] *Public Law* 445.

preliminary conclusions. I estimate that I spent at least 30 unre-
warding (and unrewarded) days, testifying to or preparing the
increasingly prolix questionnaires, which they had to inflict upon
others as well as themselves. By contrast with this prolonged
ordeal, Lord Justice Edmund Davis's Aberfan report was published within nine months of the disaster. So too was Lord Justice
Bingham's Report on the collapse of BCCI."

14–46 Following on from Lord Howe's strong reservations about the Scott
inquiry procedures, the Council on Tribunals[5] has considered the way
forward. In general terms the key objectives of an inquiry are
effectiveness, fairness, speed and economy. No single constitution or
model set of rules are possible to achieve these goals. However, the
Council did recommend "that inquiry reports of any length should
provide   for   an   executive   summary   of   the   findings   and
recommendations".

14–47 More commonly used are powers under the compulsory acquisi-
tions of land legislation to hold a public local inquiry. The Acquisition
of Land Act 1981 provides an opportunity for objectors to make their
case heard in the case of the compulsory purchase of land. However
the role of the inquiry is not confined to this objective alone, as the
effect of such inquiries is to provide administrators with a sense of
the public interest. The courts have upheld this view of the inquiry as
a means of providing authorisation for the use of land for public use.[6]
In this sense the inquiry procedure legitimates and informs government decision-making in addition to providing the citizen with a
means of redress.

14–48 Planning appeals require that the Secretary of State should allow
the appellant and the local planning authority an opportunity of
putting their case. Invariably, though not necessarily, this may mean
holding an inquiry under powers granted to the Secretary of State
under the Local Government Act 1972 to direct[7] that a local inquiry
should be held. Planning appeals arise when planning permission has
been refused or is granted subject to conditions. Public local inquiries
have recognisable[8] characteristics. They are held in the locality where
the proposed schemes are situated. The inspector is normally
appointed by the Minister with the relevant statutory authority.

---

[5] *Advice to the Lord Chancellor on the procedural issues arising in the conduct of public
inquiries set up by Ministers* Council on Tribunals, July 1996.
[6] Lord Diplock in *Bushell v. Secretary of State for the Environment* [1981] A.C. 75.
[7] The Local Government Act 1972, s.250 confers powers to order inquiries authorised
under Town and Country Planning Act 1971, s.282(1).
[8] See Wraith and Lamb, *Public Inquiries as an Instrument of Government* (1971), Chap. 2
contains a history of inquiries. Also see A.R. Mowbray, "Public Inquiries and
Government Policy" (1987) 137 New L.J. 418.

Currently the Department of the Environment has a corp of nearly 400 inspectors responsible for over 3,000 inquiries each year. The subject matter of the inquiry relates to the objections to the proposed scheme received by the Minister from private parties or local authorities. The purpose of the inquiry is to provide the relevant Minister with the necessary information to allow the Minister to consider the scheme in light of the public benefit to be derived from the scheme if implemented. Weighing up all the material factors is greatly assisted by the inquiry process. However this does not preclude taking other matters into consideration, including the policy of the government, advice from experts or departmental considerations.[9]

A particularly controversial area of planning are highways **14-49** inquiries into large motorway projects.[10] Detailed rules exist as to the conduct of these inquiries[11] and efforts are made to improve the information available to objectors.[12]

Distinct from planning appeals the planning system adopts inquiries as a means to allow public participation in the planning process. Local plan inquiries allow objectors to raise issues surrounding the publication of local plans or structure plans prepared under Part II of the Town and Country Planning Act 1971. The Town and Country Planning (Costs of Inquiries etc.) Act 1995 authorises the Secretary of State to recover from local planning authorities the costs borne by the Secretary of State in relation to the appointment of inspectors to hold local public inquiries.[13] The 1995 Act provides express powers for the defrayment of such expenses.

The inquiry procedure is a key issue for planning and administra- **14-50** tive lawyers. Inquiries may resemble a court where the trial of the issues involves the presentation of the appellant's case after the inspector makes introductory comments. The appellant has a right of final reply, and often the legal representation at inquiries ensures that the proceedings are formal and may appear over-legalistic. The adversarial nature of the proceedings is characterised by the cross-examination of witnesses who may be experts in their field. Witnesses who give evidence are protected from actions for defamation because they enjoy absolute privilege.[14] However, the inspector has the right

---

[9] See Lord Greene in B. *Johnson & Co. (Builders) Ltd. v. Minister of Health* [1947] 2 All E.R. 395 at p. 399.

[10] S. Tromans, "Roads to Prosperity or Roads to Ruin? Transport in the Environment in England and Wales" (1991) 3 J.P.L. 1.

[11] See the Highways (Inquiry Procedure) Rules 1976 (S.I. 1976 No. 721).

[12] *Report of the Review of Highway Procedures*, Cmnd. 7133 (1978).

[13] See *R. v. Richmond-upon-Thames London Borough Council, ex p. McCarthy & Stone (Developments)* [1992] 2 A.C. 48 held that there was no expresss power to levy a charge for such services. The 1995 Act attempts to overcome the absence of statutory powers.

[14] *Trapp v. Mackie* [1979] 1 W.L.R. 377; [1979] 1 All E.R. 489.

to intervene, ask questions, and re-examine witnesses. The extent that an inspector adopts an inquisitorial style may be due to the style and personality of the inspector. An inquiry may attract news media and unlike a court does not have contempt powers, thus the issues tested at an inquiry may well be simultaneously examined in the media. The inspector is at a disadvantage compared to the courts in controlling outbursts of anger or strong feelings among the participants. The Planning Inquiries (Attendance of Public) Act 1976 provides that in principle oral evidence should be given in public and that documentary evidence should be open to inspection.

14–51   Inquiries may be seen as a safety valve for the views of the community and local opinion is often organised to put their case. In theory, at the discretion of the inspector, anyone may attend an inquiry, while certain groups are entitled to appear such as the National Park Committee where the land is situated in a National Park. However the giving of evidence is left to the discretion of the inspector.

The nature of the discretion exercised by the inquiry inspector is subject to statutory rules such as the Town and Country Planning (Inquiries Procedure) Rules 1988.[15] Evidence may be taken on oath and may require the attendance of persons and documents. A timetable for the inquiry may be drawn up with a pre-inquiry meeting to ensure that the inquiry is held efficiently and expeditiously. This allows the Secretary of State to serve notice of the issues which are likely to be relevant and to be considered. The date fixed for the inquiry must be within eight weeks of the conclusion of a pre-inquiry meeting and not later than 22 weeks after the date of notification of the holding of an inquiry. The 1988 rules also allow the Secretary of State an influence in the appointment of assessors and to indicate the weight to be attached to their opinion.

14–52   After the inquiry is held and the inspector's report is made to the Secretary of State, rule 16(4) provides the basis for the resolution of any disagreement between the inspector's report and the Secretary of State. Generally, the Secretary of State is free, provided the procedures are correctly followed and due weight is attached to the inspector's findings, to make his own conclusion. Then the Secretary of State must notify all the parties to the inquiry of his decision and his reasons under rule 16(5) of the 1988 rules. The applicant may make further representations within 21 days, and if necessary the Secretary of State may re-open the inquiry.

---

[15] S.I. 1988 No. 944 and No. 945. See S.I. 1990 No. 512 on planning appeals and S.I. 1987 No. 701.

The courts have exercised vigilance over the conduct of inquiries, the findings of fact[16] made by the inspector and the observance of natural justice throughout the inquiry[17] proceedings.

The Franks Committee envisaged that inquiries would be informal, **14–53** accessible and open. Legal representation gives rise to the question about legal aid and advice. Legal advice and assistance but not legal aid is normally available at inquiries on the same basis as tribunals. Section 250 of the Local Government Act 1972 empowers the award of costs in connection with statutory public inquiries. There is little guidance in the section as to how this power may be exercised. There is considerable debate about how this wide discretion may be exercised,[18] though restrictive in the present exercise of this discretion, some argue that the rules should be permissive to permit the speedier resolution of matters when one party delays or acts inefficiently. Examples of where it may be used include where one party refuses to discuss the matter or provide information or has been unable to support their decision by the necessary evidence.

In contrast to the use of inquiries at a local level, inquiries into **14–54** large-scale developments place greater stress and strain on the system of inquiries. The model of the public local inquiry seems ill-suited to dealing with these major issues. For example the inquiry concerned with the Greater London Development Plan in 1970 took 240 days. The inquiry into the Sizewell B Power station[19] lasted 340 days. In the case of the Third London Airport inquiry chaired by Lord Roskill, a non-statutory inquiry was set up with 11 Commissioners with both investigative and adjudicative powers. These procedures offered an alternative to a planning application with a site chosen and a public local inquiry focused on the suitability of the site. Instead a more wide-ranging investigation could be undertaken reviewing a whole range of possibilities and hearing local evidence about the site in anticipation of any decision. The inquiry was able to carry out its own evaluation of air patterns and regional transport planning. Evaluating all this information and any objections provided an invaluable source of information for the Secretary of State.

However as Grant has observed[20]: **14–55**

"But the crucial question which in fact subsequently determined that action taken by the government, was excluded from the

[16] See, *e.g. Luke v. Minister of Housing and Local Government* [1968] 1 Q.B. 172.
[17] See *Miller (T.A.) Ltd v. Minister of Housing and Local Government* [1968] 1 W.L.R. 992; [1968] 2 All E.R. 633.
[18] See Circular 73/65 and the guidelines offered by the Council on Tribunals, *Report of the Council on Tribunals on the Award of Costs at Statutory Inquiries*, Cmnd. 2471 (1964).
[19] T. O'Riordan, R. Kemp, and M. Purdue, *Sizewell B: An Anatomy of the Inquiry* (1988). The inquiry was chaired by Sir Frank Layfield.
[20] M. Grant, *Urban Planning Law* (1982), p. 603.

Commission's terms of reference. It was the question of the need for the airport at all."

This suggests that there are serious weaknesses in such a format of inquiry if the main issue does not come under the terms of reference of the inquiry. However as to the procedures, public participation is an important goal of the inquiry system and the use of large inquiries gives opportunities for the public to object, hear evidence and find out more information on complex issues. At the same time as the Roskill inquiry, the government introduced procedures for a Planning Inquiry Commission in the Town and Country Planning Act 1968.[21] The arrangements consists of a two-stage process. The first stage is analogous to a Royal Commission and consists of a general investigation and only at the second stage do objections come to be considered.

The Planning Inquiry Commission procedure has not been implemented, partly because it was considered unfair that having taken part in the first stage, to hear objections in the second stage might not appear to offer objectors a fair hearing.

14–56   The Sizewell B inquiry, already mentioned above, was carried out under the Electric Lighting Act 1909 into the Central Electricity Generating Board's (CEGB) proposal to build a nuclear generating station at Sizewell, Suffolk. The investigation examined the merits of different types of nuclear generating stations, and assessed the British designed steam generated heavy water reactors compared to the more popular American designed Pressurised Water Reactor (PWR). The decision to recommend the building of the PWR followed after the Layfield inquiry. The Sizewell B inquiry was the longest public inquiry ever held, surprisingly the full costs of nuclear electricity only became apparent when the Government later embarked on its electricity privatisation scheme. As Nigel Lawson, for a time Energy Secretary, noted in his memoirs[22]:

> "It turned out that for years the CEGB, wittingly or unwittingly, had been making a deceptive case in favour of the economics of nuclear power that had taken in even Frank Layfield and was not finally exposed until the government was in the final stages of the privatization of the industry in 1989, and a detailed prospectus had to be drafted."

14–57   The scale of the deception appears staggering, as the CEGB had in 1989 estimated decommissioning costs at £3.7 billion whereas in 1990

---

[21] See incorporation under s.48(2) of the Town and Country Planning Act 1971 which contains the main legislation. Also see ss.47–49 of the 1971 Act.
[22] N. Lawson, *The View from No. 11* (1992).

the costs were estimated to be in excess of £15 billion. The virtues of the inquiry had quickly turned into shortcomings as ministerial suspicion over the true cost of decommissioning were not satisfied until the Layfield inquiry was completed and then the decision to go ahead with the building of Sizewell B was taken without the matter being given a satisfactory analysis.

Such shortcomings in the inquiry system may be because the ultimate decision depends on political and ministerial discretion which is outside the control of any inquiry. Inquiries may be regarded as providing important techniques in the administrative system of decision-making. O'Riordan has identified some procedural techniques in use at the Layfield inquiry. The investigative nature of the proceedings was supported by the appointment of a counsel to the inquiry. This enabled evidence to be sifted on behalf of the inspector and its presentation made more ordered. There was also a pre-inquiry stage to allow for the strategic planning of the inquiry. Since Sizewell, a Code of Practice has been published containing details of how a pre-inquiry meeting is to be held, should the Secretary of State require one. **14–58**

The use of inquiries albeit with some of the shortcomings mentioned above, is seen as an important element in allowing public participation in the administrative process. The findings of inquiries do not have to be followed as in the Vale of Belvoir inquiry where the Energy Secretary rejected the inspector's report. Doubts about inquiries have focused on the delay,[23] expense and the postponement of decisions because of the need to consult and the requirements of inquiries. Frustration over the inquiry process may have led the government to support a hybrid Bill which became the Channel Tunnel Act 1987, to allow the building of the Channel Tunnel construction project between Britain and France. No inquiry was therefore necessary and the tunnel could be constructed without delays in the planning process. This procedure, although criticised, was more speedy and efficient than the procedures under a public inquiry but at the expense of public participation. **14–58A**

(c) Inspectorates

Finally in the general context of tribunals and inquiries an additional technique adopted in administrative law for the examination of a complaint is through the use of inspection powers. Inspectorates have a history extending back into the nineteenth century such as the **14–59**

---

[23] See *Speeding Planning Appeals* (HMSO, 1986).

development of factory inspectors. A modern example is the use of inspectors to provide information on prisons through the report of the H.M. Chief Inspector of Prisons,[24] or since 1987, the formation of H.M. Inspectorate of Pollution, which although independent from government,[25] incorporates the industrial Air Pollution Inspectorate and the Radiochemical and Hazardous Waste Inspectorate from the Department of the Environment. Powers granted to the H.M. Inspectorate of Pollution under the Environmental Protection Act 1990, (now under the Environment Agency) are comprehensive, including the power to make examinations and investigations, take samples, test articles and substances found on premises and require information. Inspection along with licensing powers may provide greater sanctions for the enforcement of standards than the traditional role of fact-finding and distributing blame from the use of an inquiry.

4. Ombudsmen: Local and Central

(a) Central Government

14–60 The system for citizens' complaints about the administration was considered in 1961 in an influential report by Justice.[26] Many complaints do not warrant the full-scale use of an inquiry, or indeed give rise to an action in the courts. The expense, uncertainty and the difficulty in always establishing facts may leave the ordinary citizen aggrieved and without a satisfactory remedy. An illustration of the deficiency in the system for citizens' grievances came in the *Crichel Down* case, which highlighted the difficulty of finding a suitable means of redress. Even the use of Members of Parliament may be unsatisfactory as a means of investigating and finding the facts needed to establish redress. *Crichel Down* also illustrated the sheer impossibility in many cases of establishing the exact nature of the mistake or the basis for the policy where the decision is politically sensitive and where access to information is impossible for the ordinary citizen.

14–61   The 1961 Justice report recommended the introduction of the Scandinavian idea of an officer or commissioner with investigative powers known as an ombudsman. The technique depends on the

---

[24] See *Report of H.M. Inspector of Prisons* (1989–90; H.C. 598).
[25] See Cm. 1200 (1990) with proposals at p. 232 for making the H.M. Inspectorate of Pollution independent from the DOE.
[26] Justice, *The Citizen and the Administration* (1961).

receipt of a complaint by the ombudsman who may enter government departments and inspect correspondence, discuss matters with officials and ascertain what has taken place and why.

The Parliamentary Commissioner Act 1967 established a Parliamentary Commissioner for Administration or ombudsman. Soon after further commissioners were established[27] including a Commissioner for Local Government, discussed below. The exact nature and jurisdiction of the ombudsman for central government may be considered.

The Parliamentary Commissioner for Administration (PCA) must **14–62** be considered, not as a replacement of the parliamentary system and ministerial accountability, but as a supplement. Thus the PCA receives complaints through M.P.s and appears before the House of Commons Select Committee on the Parliamentary Commissioner. The Chairman of that Select Committee may be consulted on the appointment of the PCA who holds office under the Crown. The PCA holds office during good behaviour,[28] but he may be removed by the Crown following addresses by both Houses of Parliament. The PCA is an *ex officio* member of the Council on Tribunals. The PCA is assisted by a staff of about 90, appointed with the approval of the Civil Service Department. Unlike the Comptroller and Auditor General, the PCA is not an officer of the House of Commons.

The PCA is likened to an agency of Parliament; the holders of the **14–63** office to date have been lawyers or ex-civil servants. The appointment of a civil servant carries the advantage of someone who may understand the system from within, but the disadvantage of being perceived as too close to the body that is being investigated. The appointment of a lawyer has the advantage of bringing independent legal analysis and techniques to bear on the complainants case and the disadvantage of an over-formalistic and legalistic approach to complaints.

The 1967 Act gave the PCA jurisdiction over central government **14–64** departments. There is a list, contained in Schedule 2 to the Act, which sets out the various departments and bodies which fall within the PCA's jurisdiction. It is noteworthy that ministers fall within the PCA's jurisdiction. Government departments include the Home Office, the Treasury, Department of Transport and Environment, Ministry of Defence, and the Foreign Office, etc. This list did not

---

[27] The Health Service Commissioners were established in 1972 for Scotland under the National Health Service Reorganisation Act 1972, and for England and Wales under the National Health Service Reorganisation Act 1973. The Parliamentary Commissioner (Northern Ireland) Act 1969 established a Commissioner and the Commissioner for Complaints, under the Commissioner for Complaints (Northern Ireland) Act 1969, a Commissioner for Local Government; both offices are held by the same person.

[28] He may be removed due to incapacity through mental illness (s.11(8) of the Supreme Court Act 1981) and may be removed by the Crown as a consequence of addresses from both Houses of Parliament.

include various governmental quangos[29] but in 1987 under the Parliamentary and Health Service Commissioners Act 1987, over 50 such bodies were included within the PCA's jurisdiction. These additions include the Arts Council, the various research councils and Tourist Boards. The list may be amended by Order in Council. But there are restrictions on the scope of such an Order in Council. An entry to the schedule may be inserted provided it relates to a government department whose functions are exercised by the crown, or if it relates to a body established by a minister, and all or some of its members are appointed by the Crown and at least half the revenue is provided by Parliament. Excluded are bodies which act in a predominantly commercial manner or a corporation carrying on an industrial undertaking under public ownership.

14–65 Complaints have been rejected as not falling within the jurisdiction of the PCA such as against the Parole Board, local authorities, the courts, the police and nationalised industries. There is a Schedule 3 list of excluded matters outside the PCA's remit of investigation. Exclusions included in the list cover matters of foreign affairs, the commencement or conduct of civil or criminal proceedings and the prerogative of mercy. Contractual and commercial relations and personnel matters are excluded as are the grant or award of honours, awards, privileges or charters. Despite criticism of the exclusion of government contractual matters from the remit of the PCA, the government has maintained opposition to their inclusion.[30] The main argument for their inclusion rests on the absence of practical remedies or adequate ways to investigate an individual's grievance as opposed to the departmental scrutiny offered by the National Audit Office.

14–66 The hospital service was excluded under the 1967 Act from the jurisdiction of the PCA mainly because it was organised by local authorities. Separate provision was made under the National Health Service Reorganisation Act 1973 for the appointment of Health Service Commissioners.[31] Direct access is allowed for complaints to the Service Commissioners whose office is held by the PCA. The complaint must be made by the person aggrieved or in certain circumstance where he is unable to make a complaint by a member of the same family, or representative appointed for the purpose. Health Service Commissioners may investigate any alleged failure in a service provided by the authority, or a failure in a service provided on its behalf or other action

---

[29] Quasi-autonomous non-governmental organisations.
[30] *Fourth Report from the Select Committee on the Parliamentary Commissioner for Administration*, 1979/80 and *the Observations of the Government*, Cmnd. 8274 (1981).
[31] There is one appointed for England and one for Wales. In Scotland there is separate legislation under the National Health Service (Scotland) Act 1972. It is usual for the three Commissioners and the PCA to be held by the same person.

it may have taken. The complainant must show that injustice or hardship resulted from any alleged failure in the service taken by the authority or taken on its behalf. In respect of any other action taken by the authority maladministration must be shown. The precise meaning of this term is discussed below. Finally, the National Health Service Commissioner reports to the Secretary of State, rather than to Parliament as is the case with the PCA. The Health Service Commissioners Act 1993 is a consolidation of the law relating to the Health Service Commissioners. The Act is intended to facilitate consultation between the Health Service Commissioners and other Commissioners including the Local Commissioners for Administration. The Health Service Commissioners remain empowered to examine complaints made directly to them. Complaints that may be considered are those that relate to maladministration, failure in the provision of a service to be provided by a health service body. The complaints may relate to delays in admission to hospital, a failure to indicate that patients may refuse to be examined in front of medical students and inadequate or illegible medical notes. However there remains no jurisdiction to investigate matters solely from the exercise of clinical judgement.

Provided the body to be investigated falls within the PCA's **14–67** jurisdiction then an investigation may be undertaken but it is assumed that the investigation may only concern the administrative functions[32] of the department. This appears to exclude the department's legislative role, although the interpretation of legislation falls within the remit of an administrative function. Also excluded might be any judicial function of a department, as tribunals[33] and courts are outside the jurisdiction of the PCA. However, after considerable debate section 110 of the Courts and Legal Services Act 1990 provides that administrative functions undertaken by staff of courts or tribunals appointed by the Lord Chancellor, shall be deemed to fall within the remit of the Lord Chancellor's department and therefore fall within the jurisdiction of the PCA. Remaining outside the PCA's jurisdiction will be action taken under the direction or authority of a person acting in a judicial capacity.

The PCA is not a substitute for legal action in the courts, or the **14–68** remedies available through a tribunal. Where the complainant has a right of appeal or remedy in law it is not normal for the PCA to investigate. However a proviso to the 1967 Act in section 5(2) may permit an investigation if the PCA is satisfied that in the particular circumstances it is not reasonable to expect the right or remedy to be

---

[32] s.5(1) of the 1967 Act.
[33] Note that Social Fund officers and inspectors remain outside the jurisdiction of the PCA as the Department of Social Security refuses to accept that they act within the agency of the Secretary of State.

investigated or invoked. It is possible therefore to see the PCA as an alternative to the courts but it may be the case that an overlapping jurisdiction is required. In *Congreve v. Home Office*[34] a complaint to the PCA was accompanied by legal redress through the courts which eventually was granted by the Court of Appeal in the matter of overlapping television licences. This appears an unusual case as the PCA may have doubted, until the Court of Appeal decision was made, that the complainant had a legal remedy and had this been clear in the first instance may not have felt able to offer an investigation.

14–69   A complainant must have "sustained injustice in consequence of maladministration." The term maladministration is not defined in the 1967 Act but in the debate on the second reading of the 1967 Bill Richard Crossman[35] explained that maladministration "might include bias, neglect, inattention, delay, incompetence, ineptitude, perversity, turpitude, arbitrariness and so on." The word injustice was used in the legislation in preference to "loss or damage" which might be construed with legal overtones too restrictive to the spirit of the legislation.

14–70   The PCA is not entitled to question the merits of the policy of a "decision taken without maladministration" under section 12(3) of the 1967 Act. This is a difficult section to interpret, and at one time was given a restrictive meaning that the quality of discretionary decisions could not be questioned even when it was shown that they contained bias or perversity. However after prompting from the Select Committee[36] the PCA was willing to criticise decisions which were bad on their merits.

Studies[37] of the meaning given to the term maladministration have indicated that drawing any useful distinction between merits and maladministration is pointless. The lack of merits is surely grounds for maladministration? Reform proposals made in 1977 by Justice said that[38] "maladministration" might be replaced by "unreasonable, unjust, or oppressive action" by government departments. This proposal was rejected by the Select Committee on the PCA[39] and later in 1988 the Justice All Souls report declined[40] to make any recommendation for change.

14–71   Complaints received by the PCA each year are on average[41] approximately 700, though there was a significant increase in 1991

[34] [1976] Q.B. 629.
[35] 734 H.C. Deb, Ser. 5, col. 42.
[36] (1967/68; H.C. 350), para. 36.
[37] G. Marshall, "Maladministration" [1973] P.L. 32.
[38] *Our Fettered Ombudsman* (1977).
[39] *Review of Access and Jurisdiction* (1977–78; H.C. 615).
[40] Justice All Souls Review, *op. cit.*, Chap. 5.
[41] Allen and Thompson, *Cases and Materials on Constitutional and Administrative Law* (2nd ed., 1992), p. 495 point out that in 1988 the collapse of Barlow Clowes gave rise to several hundred complaints and these have been dealt with as a single investigation. See *First Report of the Parliamentary Commissioner for Administration Session 1989/90; The Barlow Clowes Affair.*

bringing the total for that year to over 800. The procedure of referring the complaint through a Member of Parliament, a requirement of the current law,[42] has been subject to much debate and criticism. In theory the addition of this requirement keeps in place the principle of ministerial responsibility to Parliament by linking the investigation of complaints to the role of the M.P. The number of M.P.s who refer complaints each year stands at around 400. The PCA receives just as many direct complaints as from M.P.s. In practice the complainant may be referred back to his or her M.P. by the PCA and the complaint is then correctly made through the M.P. Nevertheless the use of the M.P. filter is seen as a curtailment in the role of the PCA and perhaps the office is unduly inhibited from developing its full potential.[43] On the other hand the concern is that the removal of the M.P. filter might cause the PCA's workload to expand to an unacceptable high level.

The debate on access raises fundamental questions about the role of **14-72** the PCA. The procedures[44] adopted by the PCA are investigative and targeted on individual case files and this is costly and time-consuming. Presently it is estimated that the average time taken by the PCA is over 15 months to complete an investigation.[45] Is such an investigative system capable of handling very large numbers of complaints? How far could an expanded role be met by the necessary expertise and resources? Only when both these questions are satisfactorily answered will the role of the PCA be adequately considered.

There is no rule that the complainant must be a British citizen but **14-73** there is under section 6(4) of the 1967 Act a requirement of residence. There is also a time limit. Section 6(3) provides that the PCA must be informed of the complaint within 12 months from the date when the citizen had notice of the matter complained of. Special circumstance may permit an extension of time.

The PCA in carrying out its investigation may hold formal hearings and allow legal representation in the course of the investigation. Section 8 of the 1967 Act allows access to official documents and papers and the PCA's powers are analogous to those of the High Court. A limitation is provided under section 8(4) which permits the issuing of a certificate of immunity in respect of Cabinet papers issued by the Secretary to the Cabinet.[46]

The remedies available to the PCA are first under section 10 of the **14-74** 1967 Act to make a report which is normally sent to the M.P. who

---

[42] S.6(3) of the 1967 Act.

[43] G. Drewry and C. Harlow, "A Cutting Edge? The Parliamentary Commissioner and M.P.s" [1990] 53 M.L.R. 745.

[44] C. Harlow, "Ombudsman in Search of a Role" (1978) 41 M.L.R. 446.

[45] Annual Report 1989, para. 10. See: "First and Second Reports of Select Committee on the Parliamentary Commission for Administration 1993–4", H.C. 33–1; H.C. 33–2.

[46] This procedure is rarely used but it was invoked in the *Court Line* case, see Gregory, (1977) *Parliamentary Affairs* 269.

raised the complaint. A copy of the report is sent to the principal officer of the department concerned. An annual report is prepared by the PCA and laid before Parliament. That report details the PCA's activities for the year. In detailing his findings, departments are subject to scrutiny by Parliament and this provides a major source of the PCA's influence. Departments may conform to his recommendations under threat of an adverse report. Under section 10(3) of the 1967 Act, the PCA may lay a special report before Parliament giving details of the complaint, attempts to resolve it and the outcome. Secondly, the PCA operates through negotiation and conciliation. There are no formal powers to enforce the PCA's decision. Thus a department in the legal sense cannot be compelled to pay money, to take action or to refrain from a particular practice. However departments may make administrative changes as a result of the findings of the PCA; the Driving and Vehicle Licensing Centre introduced changes to deal with delays for applicants for driving licences.[47]

14-75   The co-operation necessary for the PCA to gain access and a working relationship with the department concerned may make it difficult to give the PCA sanctions with an enforcement power. The PCA depends on negotiation and following the exposure of maladministration it is hoped will give rise to a remedy. The PCA has succeeded in gaining financial settlements for the citizen in a variety of tax cases[48] where repayment was made by the department concerned. In the Sachsenhausen case the PCA criticised decisions made by Ministers not to allow compensation to be payable to the victims of Nazi atrocities applying the rules laid down by the then Foreign secretary R.A. Butler, that compensation was only payable to those detained in concentration camps or equivalent conditions.[49] This led to compensation payable as a result of the PCA's intervention.[50] The Barlow Clowes Affair investigation in 1988 conducted by the Ombudsman did lead "99 per cent. of investors to receive at least 85 per cent. of their capital" and came about through the findings of the PCA's investigation.[51]

14-76   However there are grounds for concern that perhaps such examples reflect an increasing problem of finding maladministration. In the first few years after 1967 only 10 per cent of cases investigated

---

[47] See Gregory, "The Select Committee on the Parliamentary Commissioner for Administration 1967–80" [1982] P.L. 49–88.

[48] The PCA was influential in obtaining changes to the 1974 and 1975 Finance Acts for the repayment of interest for delayed tax repayments.

[49] *Third Report of the Parliamentary Commissioner 1967–68*. The report was debated February 5, 1968; H.C. Deb. ser. 5, col. 108, (February 5, 1968).

[50] In the *Court Line* case, criticism of ministers was rejected over the collapse of a travel company; 897 H.C. Deb. ser. 5, col. 575.

[51] *PCA Annual Report for 1989* (1989–90; H.C. 353) See: Gregory and Dewey, "Barlow Clowes and the Ombudsman" [1991] P.L. 192 and 408.

resulted in such a finding being made. In the 1970s this increased to about 30 per cent and in the 1980s 40 per cent. In the mid-1980s about 75 complaints annually are found to show maladministration.[52] The main departments concerned are Social Security and the Inland Revenue.

An important development in the PCA's role is the growth in **14–77** recent years of case studies containing advice on administrative practices. Potentially this may create the most significant contribution of the Ombudsman system.[53] Through this means the individual complainant receives the benefit of the PCA's interpretation of the rules, and the existence of principles within government departments. This provides a blend of external scrutiny and internal review; fact-finding through investigation combined with administrative guidance. Following the White Paper on Open Government[54] the PCA may receive written complaints concerning compliance with a Code for greater openness in government information. The code is expected to come into force from April 1994. This code will enhance the role of the PCA.

The attraction of using the PCA for the citizen is that the costs are **14–78** borne by the PCA and not the complainant and the investigative role of the PCA may be crucial where there are no other remedies available for redress. An assessment of the effectiveness of the PCA is a mixed one. While the PCA has shortcomings there are sufficient successes to suggest that the PCA has made a worthwhile contribution in providing citizens redress where before none existed. The techniques of the PCA have proved valuable and have been copied in a wide variety of areas in the private sector including insurance, newspapers, building societies and banking. A more difficult question is the value of the investigative techniques employed by the PCA. As a contrast to the adversarial style of courts are the PCA's inquisitorial[55] powers more effective in finding facts and evaluating behaviour? Has the PCA encouraged good administration and affected the existing culture within government departments?

---

[52] These figures are taken from Greenwood and Wilson, *Public Administration in Britain Today* (1989), p. 315.

[53] Alastair Mowbray, "A Right to Official Advice: The Parliamentary Commissioner's Perspective" [1990] P.L. 68.

[54] Cm. 2290 (1993).

[55] See M. McConville *et al.*, *The Case for the Prosecution* (1992) at p. 207. McConville argues in his case study of the police that: accountability, if it is to have any relevance to police-work practices, must be both prospective and able to penetrate the control networks which the police utilise to perpetuate police values and ideologies and screen out external inspection mechanisms. Does the same practice occur with government departments?

The PCA is susceptible to judicial review.[56] However the courts are reluctant to intervene when the PCA acts in accordance with his own discretion whether to initiate, continue or discontinue an investigation (section 5(5) of the 1967 Act) or decide the procedures to be adopted in any investigation (section 7(2) of the 1967 Act).

(b) Local Commissioners for Administration

14–79 Redress of citizens grievances in local government is provided by the appointment of Local Commissioners for Administration under the Local Government Act 1974 following the influential Justice report in 1969 on the creation of a local government ombudsman. There are three Local Commissioners for Administration for England and one for Wales under two separate Commissions; one for England and the other for Wales. The Local Government Commissioner (LGC) does not act under the same constitutional relationship as the PCA does for central government, who is acting through ministerial responsibility and complaints through the complainant's M.P.

14–80 The jurisdiction of the LGC is similar to the 1967 Act and the PCA, and the powers of investigation are the same as the PCA.[57] The LGC may investigate complaints where a member of the public has "sustained injustice in consequence as maladministration." The number of complaints has steadily increased over the years. In 1983/84 there were approximately 3,000 complaints but in 1990/91 the number had increased to over 9,000. Originally there was a councillor filter equivalent to the M.P. filter for the PCA discussed above. The Widdicombe Report[58] recommended and the Government accepted the desirability of allowing direct access and this was granted under the Local Government Act 1988. In terms of jurisdiction, in common with the PCA the LGC may not inquire into contractual or commercial matters. The Widdicombe Committee recommended reform to allow these areas to be investigated but this was not implemented by the government. The Widdicombe Report also favoured the LGC to be given powers to iniate investigations on their own behalf but this was also rejected. The government was concerned that if such powers were given the LGC might have problems in their relations with local authorities. However, under procedures introduced by the Local

---

[56] R. v. Parliamentary Comr. ex p. Dyer [1994] 1 All E.R. 375. N. Marsh, "The Extent and Depth of Judicial Review of the Decisions of the Parliamentary Commissioner for Administration" (1994) Public Law 347–50.

[57] S.184 of the Local Government, Planning and Land Act 1980 cures the interpretation in Re A Complaint Against Liverpool City Council [1977] 2 All E.R. 650 of s.32(3) of the Local Government Act 1974.

[58] Cm. 9797 (1986).

Government and Housing Act 1989, the LGC may issue codes of practice on good administrative procedures for local authorities. In particular, section 31 of the 1989 Act allows the Secretary of State to publish a code to be laid and approved by a resolution of each House of Parliament.[59]

Maladministration is interpreted by the LGC in a similar way to the **14–81** PCA. In *R. v. Local Commissioner for Administration for the North and East Area of England, ex p. Bradford Metropolitan City Council,*[60] Lord Denning considered that the LGC is concerned in matters of maladministration with the manner in which decisions are reached and the manner in which they may or may not be implemented. The nature, quality and reasonableness of the decision are not part of the LGC remit. The subject matter of investigations conducted by the LGC covers a wide cross-section of local authority activities; housing, planning and education comprise a large proportion of the case-load of the LGC. Sections 266–269 and Sched. 16 of the 1993 Education Act extend the LGC's remit to appeal committees in grant-maintained schools. Complaints are made within twelve months from the day the complainant has notice of the matter complained of, although there is a discretion to investigate complaints out of time.

A Commission may not investigate a complaint which affects all or nearly all of the inhabitants of a local authority. Complaints about public passenger transport and the internal management of local authority schools are also excluded from this jurisdiction.

The remedies offered by the LGC comprise, first, a report of the **14–82** investigation showing maladministration is made available for public inspection for three weeks. If the local authority fails to take account of the report the LGC may make a further report. Secondly, the LGC, having made a report and attempted to persuade the local authority to comply with the terms of the report, the local authority is under section 26 of the Local Government and Housing Act 1989, under a duty to consider the LGC's report and must within three months respond to it. A further report may be made by the LGC and if the local authority does not take satisfactory action, the report may be published in a local newspaper with the local authorities reasons for not implementing the report. The LGC is unable to take any further action to enforce its report. Unlike the PCA who has recourse to the House of Commons, there is no satisfactory equivalent for the LGC, although under section 5 of the Local Government and Housing Act 1989, a local authority must appoint a monitoring officer to report on findings of maladministration.

---

[59] To be known as the National Code of Local Government Conduct.
[60] [1979] Q.B. 287.

14–83   Despite strong advice to the Widdicombe Committee in favour[61] of giving the LGC power to seek judicial review this was not favoured by the Committee in its report. Instead the Widdicombe Report recommended that following an adverse report in favour of the complainant, the complainant should be able to go to the County Court for a remedy.

Compared to the Audit Commission, the LGC has less pro-active powers to seek enforcement for its findings. This may indicate that the role of the LGC is a more difficult one as the experience of non-enforcement of the LGC reports by some local authorities may indicate. Legal powers to enforce the LGC findings may be counter-productive and give rise to disputes between local authorities and the LGC in the courts.

14–84   The possibility for judicial review of the LGC's findings was envisaged when the 1974 Act was debated in the House of Commons. A number of challenges to the jurisdiction of the LGC have resulted in judicial scrutiny of the powers of the LGC.[62] Two decisions have recently focused on the role of the LGC. The first is *R. v. Local Commissioner for Administration for the South, ex p. Eastleigh B.C.*[63] After a complaint to the LGC, from a householder that Eastleigh B.C. failed to properly inspect sewers in accordance with the Building Regulations 1976, the LGC found maladministration and that the householder had suffered maladministration. However the LGC accepted that even if the inspection of the sewers had been carried out diligently it was unclear that the defects would have been spotted. Consequently Eastleigh should pay only part of the costs of any remedial action. Eastleigh B.C. sought judicial review.[64] Lord Donaldson in the Court of Appeal reinforced the earlier observations of Lord Denning[65] when he distinguished between the merits or reasonableness of a decision of a local authority and the means adopted by the local authority. The Court of Appeal accepted the legality of the LGC's report but granted Eastleigh B.C. a declaration on the basis that the LGC's report did not justify his findings.

14–85   Lord Donaldson considered judicial review of the LGC's reports as unusual and "unlikely to succeed." Soon after Eastleigh, Woolf L.J. in

---

[61] In Northern Ireland the Commissioner for Complaints Act (Northern Ireland) 1969 permits the complainant to apply to the County Court after a finding of injustice caused by maladministration. The County Court may award damages, injunctions or other specific relief.

[62] *Re A Complaint Against Liverpool Council* [1977] 2 All E.R. 650 the LGC power to produce documents was reviewed.

[63] [1988] Q.B. 855.

[64] The grounds were that the LGC had questioned a discretionary decision under s.34(3) of the Local Government Act 1974, and that the LGC had made a report where the maladaministartion did not show that the householder had suffered an injustice; the High Court upheld the Council's submission.

[65] [1979] Q.B. 287.

the High Court found that a report made in 1986 by the LGC in *R. v. Commissioner for Local Administration, ex p. Croydon LBC*[66] was *ultra vires*. The case arose out of an unsuccessful appeal by parents against the decision of Croydon LBC as to the school their daughter should attend. The appeal was heard by the Education Appeal Committee established by Croydon. The LGC investigated a complaint by the parents about the outcome of the appeal. The LGC found maladministration in the way the Appeal Committee gave weight to Croydon's policy on education. The Council sought judicial review of the LGC's investigation. In holding that the LGC acted *ultra vires*, several grounds for review were considered. First, that the possibility of legal action by the parents should have been considered by the LGC throughout his investigation, and this might have resulted in the LGC declining jurisdiction in the matter. Secondly, the Appeal Committee had evaluated the evidence and based its decision on the merits of the case. The LGC had no grounds for finding maladministration in such circumstances.

One of the difficult issues raised in the case is the suitability of **14–86** using the courts compared to the LGC. Lord Justice Woolf concluded that the courts were more appropriate in cases such as the Croydon case where the issues demanded an understanding of the relevant law and legal obligations. The preference for using the courts for legal disputes is important in clarifying the jurisdiction of the LGC, even though it is unclear where the boundaries may be set. Maladministration will rarely offer Judicial Review as a form of redress. One possible solution[67] is for the LGC or the PCA to refer matters to the High Court when legal issues arise in the course of their investigation.

The *Croydon* case firmly establishes the principle that the LGC's **14–87** reports are subject to judicial review. In both cases of *Eastleigh* and *Croydon* the courts appear to deal with the review of the LGC's powers rather than reviewing the exercise of the LGC's discretion. However in *ex parte Dyer* in the Divisional Court, Lord Justice Simon Brown concluded that judicial review is available to review the LGCs discretion. This result may not be entirely satisfactory. The threat of judicial review, however rare, may inhibit the working of the LGC when confronted by local authorities prepared to use the courts to challenge the LGC's decisions. This may have the unfortunate consequence of damaging the standing and investigative functions of the LGC and the citizen may be less certain of having a grievance remedied. The likelihood of many cases being challenged in the

[66] [1989] 1 All E.R. 1033.
[67] Himsworth, "Parliamentary Teeth for Local Ombudsmen" [1986] P.L. 546. See *R. v. Parliamentary Comr. for Administration, ex p. Dyer* [1994] 1 All E.R. 375.

courts is small, nevertheless, the LGC must take account of the possibility of judicial review when writing their reports.

14–88   An assessment of the value of the LGC has been conducted in a number of studies[68] with favourable results. The quality and scope of investigations are of a high standard. The investigations are based on individual complaints and to what extent can local authorities learn from the various case studies of individual complaints? The question arises as to whether the reports of the LGCs may lead to better administration within local authorities? There is a question of co-ordinating complaints mechanisms within local authorities. The Widdicombe Committee heard evidence of the extensive system of internal complaints procedures within local authorities. Is there a case for greater co-ordination of the work of the LGC with the internal system of complaints resolution within local authorities?

(c) The European Ombudsman

14–89 The European Parliament may appoint an Ombudsman to receive complaints of instances of maladministration against the activities of the Community institutions or bodies. The European Ombudsman[69] was established in July 1995 and has an establishment of 16 including five legal officers. Although based in Strasbourg there is an office in Brussels from February 1997. Since its inception there have been over 1,000 complaints. There has been a large number arising out of the French nuclear tests in the Pacific. The limitations on the remit of the European Ombudsman is that his jurisdiction does not extend to allegations against national governments of the Member States. However, it is possible for him to initiate complaints himself and he may gain the co-operation of Community institutions in pursuing his investigations.

5. The Citizen's Charter

14–90 Citizens with specific grievances arising out of public services may find that the *Citizen's Charter*[70] provides redress for complaints. The *Citizen's Charter* is focused on how public services are delivered and

---

[68] Lewis, Seneviratne and Cracknell, *Complaints Procedures in Local Government* (Sheffield, 1987).

[69] The current post holder is Jakob Soderman from Finland. The author is grateful to Professor Ian Harden, the European Ombudsman's Principal Officer, for all his help and advice and for much of the information on the European Ombudsman. Views expressed are the author's.

[70] Cm. 1599 (1991).

managed. In that sense the aim is to provide such economy, efficiency and effectiveness in the high quality of services that complaints will become a means to ensure standards[71] as well as dealing with the grievances of the citizen. This approach is consumer-orientated, and extends complaints mechanisms and the right to redress when services fall below certain targets. It also raises expectations and by suggesting "rights" rather than remedies reverses the tradition in English law which focuses on remedies.

The *Citizen's Charter* sets high expectations and provides well **14–91** publicised complaints procedures, some based entirely on contractual rights, others enforced through standards set by legislation such as the Competition and Service (Utilities) Act 1992 in respect of the main utilities such as water, gas, electricity and telecommunications. Support for quality standards comes through the award of performance related targets for each service. Accreditation through the standard of the British Standards Institute is common as many local authorities require accreditation to BS 5750 as a contract condition. Competitive tendering is another element in ensuring contract compliance with the standards expected from the Charter. Compensation paid to the customer when the quality of a service falls below a certain standard, is another means to ensure better standards.

The aim of the *Citizen's Charter* is "to give more power to the **14–92** people." Information, accessibility, openness and standards are involved in the *Charter's* techniques to provide the citizen with a benchmark to gauge the quality of the services provided. Potentially the *Citizen's Charter* may have far reaching effects on the public's perception about complaints and their resolution. This remains to be seen. Incrementally the *Citizen's Charter* may have a wider effect on the procedures for the resolution of grievances within the United Kingdom, than was envisaged or perhaps originally intended. In the current run up to enactment of a modern Bill of Rights, the Citizen's Charter is a first step in a direction for change that will re-write the map of citizens' rights in the United Kingdom.

---

[71] See Barron and Scott, "The Citizen's Charter Programme" [1992] 55 M.L.R. 526.

Chapter 15

Judicial Review

1. Introduction

(a) The Scope of Judicial Review

15–01 The focus of this chapter is on the development of judicial review where an aggrieved citizen may seek redress through the courts. Judicial review[1] may also arise where there are inter-governmental disputes. This is where, for example disputes arise between different government departments or between local and central government. This list is not exhaustive as administrative decisions cover a variety of powers and duties that are susceptible to judicial review.

15–02 It is necessary to consider the role of the courts in the context of the administrative process. In the previous chapter we have seen that since the Franks Report[2] the redress of citizens' grievances,[3] involving the administrative process, may be made through a wide range of institutions and procedures from informal mechanisms to tribunals, inquiries and ombudsmen. An underlying assumption which informed the discussion of administrative law was that in the 1960s and 70s administrative discretion and any potential for its abuse was mainly to be found in an obdurate official such as a civil servant or a Minister. Grievances were identified as arising from the growth in the role of the State[4] in its development both as a regulator and as a service provider. The growth in State powers has been significant.

---

[1] A detailed analysis of judicial review is provided in de Smith, *Judicial Review of Administrative Action* (4th edition, 1980). Also see Foulkes, *Administrative Law* (7th ed., 1990); P. Cane, *Administrative Law* (2nd ed., 1992).

[2] Cmnd. 218 (1957).

[3] Justice, *The Citizen and the Administration* (1961). Also see Justice, *The Citizen and his Council – Ombudsman for Local Government* (1969); *A British Bill of Rights* (IPPR, 1991).

[4] See *Towards a Modern Federal Administrative Law* (Law Reform Commission of Canada, 1987). Note: Scotland does not have the prerogative orders as part of Scots law. See C. Himsworth, Chap. 19 in the Superstone and Goudie (eds.), *Judicial Review* (1991). de Smith, Jowell and Woolf, *Judicial Review of Administrative Action* (1995).

Since the mid-nineteenth century and commensurate with the growth in administrative activities, the franchise was broadened and the system of party government became fully established. The role of the State as a regulator was recognised in the development of public health, the commercial regulation of the economy through the development of competition policy and the regulation of banking and insurance. As a provider of services, the State delivered a wide range of activities; railways, public utilities, education and the system of welfare provision. The scale and size of the machinery of government encouraged the increase in the use of law to regulate activities which were in the public ownership of the state.[5] Nationalisation policy in the 1940s was concerned with the transfer from private to State ownership with monopoly powers through legislation. Privatisation in the 1980s has significantly affected the role of the State.[6] This shift of public ownership to the creation of Company Act companies has created a new range of regulatory agencies entrusted with a wide variety of legal powers.

It is clear that regulating the utilities involves complex licensing, **15–03** contractual and statutory powers. The British system of regulation depends on the ability of the regulator to gain the confidence of a wide range of interested groups from consumers, and shareholders, to the industry and the government. Regulatory decisions are not clearly articulated and regulatory policy appears to be vague. Regulation of this kind has implications for the value of shares of regulated companies. Possessing such market sensitive information and decision making in this area requires sound judgment and good communication skills. A more open culture of regulation in Britain is not well developed. In addition there is considerable uncertainty as to how future governments may change regulatory policy.

The vast array of statutory power is supplemented by a bewilder- **15–04** ing assortment of administrative rules such as licences, codes of practice, guide-lines, regulations and contractual conditions. Administrative discretion and the potential for its abuse[7] is not the sole preserve of civil servants and Ministers but may occur in the exercise of administrative powers by various regulators, agencies and in the activities of Company Act companies.

---

[5] Constitution Paper No. 1. *Report of the Committee on Administrative Tribunals and Enquiries* (The Franks Report) Cmnd. 218, (1957).

[6] John F. McEldowney, "Law and Regulation: Current Issues and Future Direction" in Bishop, Kay, Mayer and Thompson, *Privatisation and Regulation* (O.U.P. 2nd ed., 1994). David Marsh, "Privatisation under Mrs Thatcher: A Review of the Literature" *Public Administration* 69. (Winter 1991) 459–480.

[7] Carol Harlow, "The Justice/All Souls Review: Don Quixote to the Rescue" (1990) 10, O.J.L.S., (No. 1), 85–93. Also see T. Prosser, "Towards a Critical Theory of Public Law" (1982) *A British Journal of Law and Society* 1.

15–05 The changing nature of administrative powers and their impact on the citizen are important in examining the role of the courts in the context of the allocation of decision-making[8] by an expanding and miscellaneous variety of public bodies and agencies. Traditionally courts offer an external check on the legality of legal powers. The courts may determine the nature of legal powers and how powers may be exercised. The focus is usually directed at resolving a dispute between the individual and the administration. In the United Kingdom the litigant seeks a remedy in order to create rights. Judicial review may thus appear limited and offer a formal, technical and narrowly focused form of accountability. Too often this may appear negative in form in setting out what may or may not be done within the law. Thus judicial review may appear pragmatic and unsystematic. Normally courts offer *ex post facto* rather than *a priori* review, limited to remedies for wrongful actions rather than providing a prescription for the future conduct of administration. Establishing administrative efficiency and securing objectives of good administration is not easily accomplished through the courts.

15–06 In March 1987 the Cabinet Office Management and Personnel office published a pamphlet for administrators, entitled the *Judge Over Your Shoulder*.[9] Prepared by the Treasury Solicitor's Department it gave advice to administrators at all levels on the principles of administrative law and judicial review. The existence of such a document proved highly controversial but it was practical and commonsensical in its approach. Its aim was to give guidance on the principles involved and to highlight the danger areas where Ministers may be at risk to a challenge in the courts. The pamphlet marked acceptance of the reality of the expansion in the role of the courts over the last 25 years and the likely impact of judicial review on government decision making. In local government, the Local Government Ombudsman has promoted a *Guidance on Good Practice on Good Administration*[10] intended to aid decision makers in axioms of good administration.

15–07 Judicial review has continued to expand during the 1990s. This is marked by a perceptible growth in judicial self-confidence in their

---

[8] *Towards a Modern Federal Administrative Law, op. cit.* note 4. In particular see pp. 2–3 "We should approach the study of administrative law mindful of the functions of the state's administrative apparatus. . . . Legal regimes do not exist in isolation from society, legal structures and rules have profound economic and sociological effects which must be studied; as well, criteria must be developed for assessing the desirability of proposed alternatives in administrative law. The analytic tools of related disciplines such as political science, economics, sociology and public administration can be used to improve our understanding of administrative law."

[9] A new edition of the pamphlet was issued in 1994 to civil servants (*The Times*, December 6, 1994). See A. Bradley, "Protecting Government Decisions from Legal Challenge" (1988) *Public Law* 1.

[10] The Commission for Local Administration, *Guidance on Good Practice on Good Administration*, August, 1993.

role and increased visibility in a number of headline cases[11] that have attracted public comment and media attention.[12] The judges have exposed new areas of governmental power to judicial review. Some senior judges support a modern Bill of Rights[13] and the influence of the Court of Justice of the European Union has strengthened the role of judicial review and the authority of the courts. The influence of the civil law tradition is evident in the way the United Kingdom judges now perceive their role and this influence is likely to shape the future development of the common law.[14]

Despite limitations, the courts have an important and fundamental **15–08** role in establishing the legality of decisions. Invariably judicial review is *ex post facto* and limited to the particular dispute in question and primarily on the issues before the court rather than the broader policy objectives. In the United Kingdom the courts are limited in expanding their role because of parliamentary sovereignty and the theory of ministerial responsibility. Recent research undertaken by the Public Law Project has found that only a small number of solicitors firms have any experience of judicial review.[15]

Judicial review is not confined to the needs of the individual **15–09** citizen. Government bodies may engage in judicial review as a means of establishing the basis of their relationship with the citizen, or with another public body. In the chapter on local government, it was noted how relations between local and central government were considered by the courts. Inter-governmental disputes may well form the basis of judicial review as much as the individual citizen seeking redress.

Judicial review must also be considered within the overall constitu- **15–10** tional context of accountability of public bodies. Earlier chapters have outlined the structure of central and local government and the civil service. In theory, in the common law tradition many public bodies[16] are accountable to Ministers who are held accountable to Parliament through the doctrine of ministerial responsibility. However as the Law Reform Commission of Canada have noted there are reasons to be concerned about the effectiveness of the doctrine of ministerial

---

[11] On the work of pressure groups see for example: *R. v. Secretary of State for Foreign Affairs, ex p. World Development Movement Ltd* [1995] 1 All E.R. 611. *R. v. Inspectorate of Pollution, ex p. Greenpeace Ltd* (No. 2) [1994] 4 All E.R. 321.

[12] *R. v. Secretary of State for Foreign Affairs, ex p. World Development Movement Ltd* [1995] 1 All E.R. 611.

[13] See Sir N. Browne-Wilkinson, "The Independence of the Judiciary in the 1980's" (1988) *Public Law* 44. Also see: A. Lester, "English Judges as Law Makers" (1993) *Public Law* 269.

[14] John F. McEldowney, "Contract Compliance and Public Audit as Regulatory Strategies in the Public Sector" Chapter 4 in C. Willet, (ed.) *The Citizen's Charter* (Blackstone Press, 1997).

[15] *Judicial Review in Perspective* (London, Public Law Project, 1993).

[16] See "Non-Departmental Public Bodies: A Guide for Departments" (1985, Cabinet Office and H.M. Treasury).

responsibility even when accepting the centrality of that doctrine in the constitutional arrangements in the United Kingdom. This raises the question about the role of the courts in reviewing administrative action. Controlling administrative decisions is further complicated if the forms of political accountability appear weak and the role of the courts appears expanding. Are the courts able to respond to an expanded role in carrying out their functions? Such a role might lead to greater scrutiny of the judiciary and may bring judges more closely within the agenda of political debate.

(b) The Classification of Administrative Decision-Making

15–11 The making of administrative decisions effects the lives of many citizens. In the context of the body making a decision, it is necessary to consider the various ways decision-making may be classified. A discretion whether or not to make a decision or pursue a course of action may be classified as a power to make the appropriate decision, whereas an obligation to take action may be classified as a duty to act or make a decision. There is a working presumption that provided the action is not prohibited by law, there is freedom to do anything. Determining what falls within the law involves careful consideration of the nature of the body making the decision, the nature of the legal powers involved, and the question of whether the correct procedures have been applied. The answer to these questions generally involves statutory interpretation as many legal powers have a statutory basis. In previous chapters we have noted how many governmental powers are derived from the prerogative which are reviewable by the courts. Contract or licenses may also form the basis of legal powers. Disputes may involve civil action in tort or contract rather than judicial review. The courts may be confronted with a hybrid of powers some statutory, contractual or prerogative.

15–12 Powers and duties provided by statute may be interpreted by the courts. The courts' role in interpreting statutory enactments depends on resolving ambiguities through the interpretation of the meaning of words in the statute and giving account to parliamentary intention. There are differences in the style of drafting statutory provisions. The Victorian style was to encapsulate the common law position within a statutory framework. Modern statutory drafting may be more technical and detailed with narrowly defined powers and duties leaving little room for any creative statutory interpretation by the judges. There is also a judicial role in "filling in gaps," or seeking to give effect to Parliament's intentions through techniques of statutory interpretation. Government White Papers and official reports may be useful in construing parliamentary intention.

Recently the House of Lords accepted in *Pepper (Inspector of Taxes)* **15–13**
v. Hart[17] that the rule prohibiting courts from reading parliamentary
material as an aid to statutory construction, should be relaxed. Where
the legislation was ambiguous or obscure or the literal meaning led to
an absurdity then it might be helpful to examine the relevant
parliamentary materials, subject to questions regarding parliamentary
privilege. This might include statements by a Minister or other
promoter of the Bill which led to the enactment of the legislation, and
other material which might be necessary to understand such statements provided the statements were clear. However the relaxation of
the rule is confined to Ministers or promoters of the Bill which might
exclude full parliamentary debates. Lord Browne-Wilkinson
explained how the courts in construing statutory instruments had
regard to the statements made by Ministers who may have initiated
the debate on regulations.[18] Expanding this principle to primary
legislation would enable the courts to understand the nature of the
issues raised by the legislation.

Earlier cases had accepted that the courts might consider *Hansard* in **15–14**
ascertaining whether a statutory power had been used for an
improper purpose. The House of Lords in *R. v. Secretary of State for the
Home Department, ex p. Brind*[19] attached importance to what the
Minister had said in Parliament as an aid to interpretation. Indeed, in
general matters of statutory interpretation beyond the ministerial
remit, the courts may be called upon to draw a line between political
and legal material that has to be interpreted by a regulatory agency.
In *Regina v. Radio Authority, ex p. Bull and another*,[20] the Court of
Appeal examined the decision of the Radio Authority to regard
Amnesty International's campaign for human rights as mainly of a
political nature. Under section 92(2)(a)(i) of the Broadcasting Act 1990
advertising of a political nature was banned from the radio. Interpretation of the political nature of human rights and the restrictions
imposed by the 1990 Act required the Court of Appeal to make a
careful value judgment of Amnesty's campaign, even though Lord
Woolf accepted that such a campaign was "commendable".

The House of Lords relaxation of the rules regarding statutory **15–15**
interpretation is probably acceptance of practices that have been
developing over the last 30 years. Does this make it more likely for
the courts to question the merits of a decision? Traditionally the
courts have refrained from overtly considering the merits of the case
and judicial review may fall short of substituting[21] judicial decision-

[17] [1993] 1 All E.R. 42.
[18] See *Pickstone v. Freemans plc* [1988] 2 All E.R. 803.
[19] [1991] 1 A.C. 696.
[20] *The Times Law Reports* January 21, 1997.
[21] See Griffiths, *The Politics of the Judiciary* (3rd ed., 1985), pp. 129–149.

making for that of the decision-maker entrusted by Parliament. The limits of judicial review were acknowledged by Lord Justice Watkins in *R. v. Secretary of State for Trade and Industry, ex p. Lonrho.*[22] When he suggested that the courts' role would not take on the responsibility of making "executive or administrative decisions." The dangers of an excessively interventionist approach by the courts were pointed out by Lord Scarman in *Nottingham C.C. v. Secretary of State for the Environment*[23]:

> "Judicial review is a great weapon in the hands of the judges; but the judges must observe the constitutional limits set by our parliamentary system upon the exercise of this beneficent power."

The courts in the United Kingdom cannot review the legality of a United Kingdom Act of Parliament in matters of strictly domestic law that does not involve matters of European Community law.

(c)　Statutory Appeals

15–16 The citizen may have available a right of appeal. Appeals provide the courts with an opportunity to rule on the legality of particular decisions and are as important as judicial review when considering the role of the courts and the procedures open to the citizen. Unlike judicial review which developed from common law origins, appeals are statutory in origin. The statutory formulation includes express provision usually setting out the grounds for appeal and the appellate jurisdiction of the courts. It is difficult to generalise any principles involved in appeals provided by statute. Parliamentary developments in creating appeals have been on a case by case basis depending on the nature of the issues expected to be raised on appeal. The Franks Committee noted "the desirability of some form of appeal," but there is no universal principle setting out a minimum standard of *when* an appeal should be provided, nor the scope of an appeal once conferred by statute.

15–17　　The existence of an appeal procedure raises the question of whether under an appeal procedure the legality of action may be challenged? The Law Commission has noted that many judicial review applications were initiated as desperate and ill-disguised attempts to appeal against the decision in question. Conversely, appeals may be widely interpreted to include matters that could be reviewed. Occasionally the courts have accepted a wider remit to the

---

[22] [1989] 1 W.L.R. 525.
[23] [1986] A.C. 240, 250–251.

appeal system even where it may overlap with the application for judicial review. An appeal against the decision of the district auditor under the Local Government Finance Act 1982 raised questions of the legality and fairness of the auditor's decision. Such matters the Court of Appeal acknowledged could also be the subject of an application for judicial review. In *Lloyd v. McMahon*[24] the Court of Appeal was content to allow the appeal in that instance, to include issues of the legality of the auditor's decision. In the House of Lords, Lord Bridge accepted the overlapping jurisdiction of an application for judicial review and appeals under the 1982 Act, but preferred the wider grounds of an appeal to raise the legality of the auditor's report.

In *Foster v. Chief Adjudication Officer*[25] the House of Lords allowed a **15–18** social security claimant an appeal to a tribunal when a benefit claim was rejected but based on consideration of whether the regulations were *ultra vires*. The Commissioner's were given jurisdiction to consider the question of *vires*, thus indicating a trend in favour of plaintiffs raising through private law claims in ordinary civil proceedings issues[26] of legality.

Appeals are not normally provided against discretionary decisions **15–19** involving Ministers or policy matters involving the allocation of resources or the implementation of Cabinet decisions. The absence of an appeal structure may be due to the political nature of the policy where the appropriate forum is in Parliament. However, this may not be a satisfactory reason to cover all cases where there is no appeal. In the previous chapter, criticisms made by the Council on Tribunals of the lack of a proper appeals system following the replacement of supplementary benefit payments by payments from the social fund made by social fund officers under the Social Security Act 1986, were noted. The absence of an appeal procedure was perceived as creating unfairness. The Council on Tribunals view judicial review as an inappropriate means of appeal from tribunal decisions. For example, instead of judicial review of immigration cases the Council on Tribunals favoured the introduction of an appeal on a point of law from the Immigration Appeal Tribunal, now to be found under the Asylum and Immigration Appeals Act 1993.

Statutory appeals may be used as an alternative to an application for judicial review which is subject to a three month time-limit whereas some appeals are restricted to six weeks. For example the Acquisition of Land Act 1981 forbids any challenge to a compulsory purchase order other than under its section 23 appeal procedure to the High Court on matters of law.[27]

---

[24] [1987] A.C. 625.
[25] [1993] 1 All E.R. 705; *The Independent*, January 28, 1993.
[26] C. Emery, "Tribunals, Courts and Powers" (1993) New L.J. 177.
[27] See: *R. v. Secretary of State for Transport, ex p. de Rothschild* [1989] 1 All E.R. 933. On appeals under the Asylum and Immigration Appeals Act 1993 see: *T. v. Secretary of State for the Home Dept.*, [1996] 2 All E.R. 865.

15–20 Appeals may consist of an appeal on questions of fact or on the merits of a decision. Usually the right of appeal is confined to "persons aggrieved." The grounds of appeal may vary according to the content of the statute. Lack of evidence and the failure[28] to give adequate reasons,[29] may amount to an error of law which may be considered on appeal. A decision may be reversed on appeal to the courts on a point of law. The leading case of *Edwards v. Bairstow*[30] concluded that a decision of the Inland Revenue Commissioners might be reversed by the courts where the facts did not justify the inference or conclusion of the Commissioners. In such instances the courts are willing to consider issues of fact giving rise to questions of law when no reasonable interpretation would support the finding of facts disputed in an appeal.

There is at present no satisfactory arrangement for standardising the grounds for an appeal, the availability of an appeal or the way appeals are considered by the courts. Lord Justice Woolf, as he then was, has suggested[31] that a more coherent appeals system might replace the present random and chaotic system.

2. Public and Private Law

(a) Defining the distinction

15–21 The availability of judicial review allows a decision or action to be challenged in the courts on the basis of remedies available in public law. This means that the grounds for challenge depend on rules developed by the courts as grounds for review in public law. The distinction between public law[32] and private law becomes critical when considering the procedures known as the application for judicial review. In Chapter 5 judicial review was examined in outline. Here it is necessary to consider in greater detail, how the courts have developed an exclusive jurisdiction for the application of judicial review for public law matters. This is central to an understanding of the position of the litigant who wishes to obtain remedies in public law.

---

[28] *Mount View Court Properties Ltd v. Devlin and Others* [1971] J.P.L. 113 D.C.
[29] See *Crake v. Supplementary Benefits Commission* [1982] 1 All E.R. 498, concerning the Supplementary Benefit (Appeal Tribunal) Rules 1971, the court was reluctant to quash the tribunal's failure to give adequate reasons.
[30] [1956] A.C. 14.
[31] H. Woolf, "A Hotchpotch of Appeals – The Need for a Blender" (1988) 7 C.J.Q. 44.
[32] P. Cane's definition provides a good starting point. P. Cane, *Administrative Law* (1992), p. 12.

The development of the application for judicial review may be **15–22** traced back to the work of the Law Commission. In 1969, despite demands from the Law Commission[33] for a Royal Commission on administrative law, all that was achieved was a study of the existing law of remedies for the judicial control of administrative action. No review of the whole system of administrative law was undertaken. Following the Law Commission's[34] recommendation on the law of remedies it was left to the Rules Committee of the Supreme Court to implement modest proposals for reforms in the application for judicial review under Order 53 of the Rules of the Supreme Court.[35] This reform received statutory modification in section 31 of the Supreme Court Act 1981.

Order 53 streamlined the procedures for obtaining remedies by **15–23** permitting an applicant to seek any one or more of five remedies which includes mandamus, certiorari, prohibition, declaration or injunction. At the same time interlocutory procedures such as discovery and interrogatories are theoretically available. In addition the court may award damages if claimed by the applicant and if they could have been awarded in an action at the same time.[36] The inclusion of declaration and injunction alongside the prerogative orders of mandamus, certiorari and prohibition was innovatory. For the first time traditionally private law remedies, that is remedies also available by ordinary writ, might be obtained alongside the traditional public law remedies of the prerogative orders of mandamus, certiorari and prohibition, under the application for judicial review.[37]

The first step in the application for judicial review is obtaining the leave of the court based on whether there is an arguable case. The aggrieved citizen has to overcome this hurdle in order to pursue his claim. Normally this first stage is heard by a single judge on affidavit evidence.[38] Applications must be made without "undue delay" and this falls under section 31(7) of the 1981 Act, and is subject to a three month time-limit.

The "exclusive nature of the application for judicial review" was **15–24** expressed by Lord Diplock in the House of Lords in *O'Reilly v.*

---

[33] The Law Commission No. 20, Cmnd. 4059 (1969). Also see Law Commission Working Paper No. 13, July 1967. Appendix A to Law Commission No. 20.

[34] The Law Commission No. 73, *Report on Remedies in Administration Law*, Cmnd. 6407 (1976). Also see: A Report by Justice, *Administration Under Law* (Keith Goodfellow, Q.C. Chairman) (London, 1971). See also R.S.C. (Amendment) 1993 (S.I. 1993 No. 2133 (L20)): leave to appeal to CA required from the High Court in judicial review cases not involving homelessness.

[35] See R. Baldwin, J. Houghton, "Circular arguments: the status and legitimacy of administrative rules" 1986 P.L. 239–84; J. A. G. Griffith, "Judicial Decision-Making in Public Law" [1985] P.L. 564–582.

[36] *R. v. South Glamorgan Health Authority ex p. Phillips*, *The Times*, November 21, 1986.

[37] See Chap. 16 for a discussion of the law on remedies.

[38] See S. Sedley, "Now you see it, Now you Don't: Judicial Discretion and Judicial Review" (August 1988) (*Warwick Law Working Papers*) (No. 48).

Mackman,[39] where the distinction between public and private law was drawn and rigidly imposed. The House of Lords considered actions brought by writ in the case of four plaintiffs who were prisoners in Hull Prison charged with various disciplinary offences arising out of riots in December 1976 and in 1979. The plaintiff claimed that the Board of Visitors, in the exercise of their disciplinary functions had breached the rules of natural justice. Lord Diplock held that the prisoners' challenge to the legality of the Boards decisions could not be made by ordinary writ but should have been made through the application for judicial review under Order 53, now amended by section 31 of the Supreme Court Act 1981 (hereinafter referred to as Order 53).

15–25   The reasoning in the case rested on the assumption that the prisoners' legitimate expectation of the rules of natural justice rested in public law, not private law. Lord Diplock established a general rule that an applicant seeking to establish rights recognised in public law was required to make use of Order 53 procedure. His reasoning for this rule rested on a number of assumptions. First, that Order 53 contains certain safeguards such as the requirement of standing, the use of affidavits at the first stage in the application, and the time limit of three months set a restriction on the period which permitted a legal challenge to be mounted. Second, that Order 53 provides a speedy resolution of the issues. In theory these procedures offer, in the public interest, safeguards to public bodies and third parties.

15–26   The question of distinguishing between public and private law came to be considered in a number of cases following *O'Reilly v. Mackman*. In *Cocks v. Thanet*,[40] the House of Lords considered whether a declaration and injunction sought by the plaintiff, *Cocks*, in the county court claiming that a local authority had breached its duty under the Housing (Homeless Persons) Act 1977, should have been brought under the Order 53 procedure for judicial review. The House of Lords, in a decision given on the same day as *O'Reilly v. Mackman*, concluded that the issues raised by the plaintiff were public law matters. The local authority had a duty to inquire if the plaintiff might be made homeless and whether he was legally entitled to temporary or permanent accommodation. Such public law rights needed to be determined before any private rights such as the plaintiff may have could be established. Ironically once the local authority established that the plaintiff was entitled to be housed then private law rights existed. The court appeared to classify the decision-making function of the local authority as a public law matter when concerned with the question of whether the criteria in the 1977 Act

[39] [1983] 2 A.C. 237.
[40] [1983] 2 A.C. 286.

were satisfied. Once the criteria were satisfied by the applicant and the local authority acted in its executive capacity in considering the rights of the applicant, this gave rise to an action in private law.

In *Davy v. Spelthorne B.C.*[41] the plaintiff owned premises used to **15–27** make precast concrete. The plaintiff entered an agreement with the local planning authority not to appeal to the Secretary of State against an enforcement notice in respect of the use of the premises on condition that the authority would not seek to enforce the notice for three years. Two years after the notice was served and the time for an appeal had lapsed, the plaintiff brought an action in the Chancery division, claiming that the agreement was *ultra vires* and damages in respect of negligent advice given to him by the local authority. The local authority applied to strike out the proceedings on the basis of the rule in *O'Reilly v. Mackman*. The Court of Appeal followed *O'Reilly v. Mackman* and struck out the plaintiff's claim for an injunction restraining the local authority from implementing the enforcement notice and an order that the enforcement notice should be set aside. However, the claim in damages could stand as a private law matter as it was based on a common law duty of care. The local authority appealed to the House of Lords on the basis that the claim for damages should also be struck out.

The argument that the claim for damages was linked to the exercise **15–28** of a statutory duty and therefore a public law matter was considered alongside the opposing argument that the plaintiff's common law rights had been infringed. The House of Lords decided that no public law issues were involved in the plaintiff's claim for damages for negligence. In reaching the decision in *Davy*, the House of Lords distinguished the decision in *Cocks*. In *Cocks* the challenge depended on public law rights under the 1977 Act being declared *before* any private law rights existed. In *Davy* public law rights were not being exercised by the plaintiff, although the failure of the local authority to enforce the notice may have been a breach of its discretion. The plaintiff was claiming damages for negligent advice on the part of the local authority which resulted in his losing the opportunity to appeal the enforcement order. Thus, because the plaintiff did not seek to impugn the enforcement order it did not give rise to public law rights and it was not an abuse of process to proceed in negligence against the local authority.

Does the approach of the House of Lords in *Davy* show some **15–29** relaxation to the rule in *O'Reilly v. Mackman*? The most difficult analyses relate to cases raising a combination of public law and private law issues. The decision in *Davy* shows the reluctance of the

---

[41] [1984] A.C. 262.

courts to interfere with the award of damages in an action in negligence by imposing Order 53 procedures on ordinary litigation. A similar approach appears evident in *Roy v. Kensington and Chelsea and Westminster Family Practitioner Committee*.[42]

15–30 In *Roy* a general medical practitioner engaged in private consultancy work in addition to his National Health duties, was considered by the Family Practitioner Committee to have spent an insufficient amount of his time on his National Health duties and his remuneration was accordingly reduced by 20 per cent. Roy brought an action against the decision of the Committee and the Committee applied to strike the action out because it breached the exclusivity rule in *O'Reilly v. Mackman*. The House of Lords refused to strike out the claim. Lord Bridge explained that the case involved the litigant asserting his rights in private law. Lord Lowry agreed but considered that there were two approaches[43] to the interpretation of *O'Reilly v. Mackman*:

> "The 'broad approach' was that the 'rule in *O'Reilly* v. *Mackman*' did not apply generally against bringing actions to vindicate private rights in all circumstances in which those actions involved a challenge to a public law act or decision, but that it merely required the aggrieved person to proceed by judicial review only when private law rights were not at stake. The 'narrow approach' assumed that the rule applied generally to *all* proceedings in which public law acts or decisions were challenged, subject to some exceptions when private law rights were involved."

15–31 Choosing between these approaches is not always possible and Lord Lowry acknowledged that it might be preferable for the matters to be heard rather than conduct an analysis over procedure. Difficulty in choosing how to apply the rule in *O'Reilly v. Mackman* arises because in many cases litigants have,[44] "a bundle of rights." In *Roy's* case these included:

> "his private law rights against the committee, arising from the statute and regulations and including the very important private law right to be paid for the work he has done."

15–32 A welcome signal that the House of Lords is prepared to adopt a flexible approach[45] to *O'Reilly* may be found in *Mercury Communications Ltd v. Director General of Telecommunications*.[46] Lord Slynn delivered a unanimous view of the House. The case arose, not through

---

42 [1992] 1 All E.R. 705.
43 [1992] 1 All E.R. 705, at p. 728.
44 [1992] 1 All E.R. 705, at p. 725H.
45 Anthony Tanney, "Procedural Exclusivity in Administrative Law" (1994) *Public Law* 31.
46 [1996] 1 All E.R. 575.

Order 53 procedures, but in the Queen's Bench Division (Commercial Court) by originating summons seeking a declaration. The issue arose out of a licensing dispute between Mercury and British Telecommunications and the Director General of Telecommunications under the Telecommunications Act 1984. Both the respondents, Mercury and British Telecommunications claimed that the Director General had misconstrued the licence and therefore raised matters of public law which should not properly fall under the originating summons procedure but instead should be taken under Order 53. The Director General sought to enforce the licence under the originating summons as raising enforceable licence matters that came within the jurisdiction of the summons. The question that required consideration was whether a public law matter was involved and if this was the case then the matter would have to be taken under Order 53 through new proceedings for judicial review.

Lord Slynn was practical and to some extent pragmatic in his **15–33** approach. He was not attracted to the view that it was a misuse of process to allow the originating summons to deal with questions of public law. In examining the role and functions of the Director it was clear that there were disputes that might fall outside the realms of administrative law just as government departments may enter contractual or tortious disputes. The appellants were successful in having the matter determined under the originating summons. While the case does not end the application of the *O 'Reilly* rule, it marks a significant step in confirming that the courts have moved to a flexible and pragmatic interpretation of the rule on a case by case basis.[47]

A further difficulty in deciding between private and public law **15–34** arises from some general exceptions to the rule established in *O'Reilly v. Mackman*. Lord Diplock, while accepting that the application of the rule was to be determined on a case by case basis, envisaged two possible exceptions. First, where the parties agreed to use the ordinary writ procedure or summons to obtain a declaration or injunction then they might waive the rule in *O'Reilly v. Mackman* and proceed with their case. Second, an exception to *O'Reilly v. Mackman* might arise where the challenge is collateral. This might arise where in the course of some other claim involving private law, an issue of public law arises.

The exact nature of the collateral exception has been considered in **15–35** a number of subsequent decisions. In *Wandsworth London Borough Council v. Winder*[48] Wandsworth Borough Council was the landlord of a flat occupied by Winder. Winder had a contractual right to occupy the flat on standard conditions including the condition that the rent

[47] *British Steel plc v. Customs and Excise Comrs.* [1996] 1 All E.R. 1002.
[48] [1985] A.C. 461.

would be paid. The local authority increased the rent charged under its statutory powers under the Housing Act 1957. Winder refused to pay the increase but continued to pay rent and only such increase that appeared reasonable. The local authority took proceedings in the county court for arrears of rent. The question of a collateral issue arose when Winder sought to defend his refusal to pay the rent increases by arguing that the increases were *ultra vires* and void. He counterclaimed for a declaration that the only rent payable was the old rent. In the House of Lords, the authority argued that Winder's counter claim should only be by way of judicial review. In fact Winder had applied for judicial review but it had been refused because he was outside the time limit of three months.

15–36 Did Winder's counter-claim come within the collateral exception to the rule in *O'Reilly v. Mackman*? Lord Fraser in the House of Lords distinguished *Cock's* case and *O'Reilly v. Mackman*. *Winder's* case was distinctive from both cases. *Winder's* case was based on private law rights, based on contract. Winder had not initiated litigation, but merely sought to defend the legal action taken against him. Lord Fraser considered that *Winder's* case did not fall into Lord Diplock's exception of a collateral matter to the rule in *O'Reilly v. Mackman*. The House of Lords found in Winder's favour and allowed the *ultra vires* question to be considered even though it was not under the Order 53 procedure. In the event Winder's defence later proved unsuccessful.[49]

15–37 Since *Winder* there have been a number of cases where the courts have sought to distinguish *Winder*.[50] One example serves to show the pragmatic nature of judicial discretion in this area. In *Waverley Borough Council v. Hilden*[51] a defendant sought to question the local authority's powers under section 222 of the Local Government Act 1972 where the challenge should have been by the Order 53 procedure. Occasionally the courts will allow the issue of legality to be raised in criminal cases rather than require the use of the Order 53 procedure.[52]

15–38 The courts have adopted a case by case approach in settling on whether to allow ordinary civil actions[53] to raise matters of public law. In delineating between public and private law for the purposes of the rule in *O'Reilly v. Mackman*, clear principles are hard to determine. The nature of the body must be considered alongside the

---

[49] *Wandsworth London Borough Council v. Winder (No. 2)* (1987) 19 H.L.R. 204.
[50] See *Avon County Council v. Buscott* [1988] Q.B. 656.
[40] [1988] 1 W.L.R. 246.
[52] See *R. v. Jenner* [1983] 1 W.L.R. 873 but also see *Plymouth City Council v. Quietlynn Ltd* [1988] Q.B. 154 and *R. v. Reading Crown Court, ex p. Hutchinson* [1988] Q.B. 384.
[53] See *An Bord Bainne Co-Operatives Ltd (Irish Dairy Board) v. Milk Marketing Board* [1984] 1 C.M.L.R. 519 allowing rights arising out of E.C. law to be enforced in a similar way to ordinary statutory rights.

activities the body performs. In the case of Walsh, who was employed by the East Berkshire Health Authority, even though the regulations of his employment were statutory, he was refused leave to challenge his dismissal through judicial review. The Court of Appeal in *R. v. East Berkshire Health Authority, ex p. Walsh*[54] decided that mere employment by a public authority does not make the matter one of public law and therefore justiciable, mistakenly bound by a policy or previous practice may likewise be regarded.[55]

This permits a court to consider if the case is suitable or not[56] or **15–39** where it might be inconvenient or inappropriate for judicial review to apply. It is noticeable, however that there are areas where the courts seem unwilling to offer review. In *ex p. Puhlofer*[57] the House of Lords restricted access to judicial review to cases under the Housing (Homeless Persons) Act 1977. Similarly in *ex p. Swati*[58] the discretion to refuse leave is operated when there are alternative remedies. In immigration cases there is adjudication by the Immigration Appeal Tribunal and appeal to the courts from that Tribunal under the Asylum and Immigration Appeals Act 1993.

Some guidance might usefully come from the common sense **15–40** approach of Henry J., in *Doyle v. Northumbria Probation Committee*[59] which posed the question of raising matters of public law as a defence in a civil action by writ. The facts concerned probation officers who took action for breach of contract against their employers, a probation authority, a body corporate with statutory powers. The dispute raised matters of contract and the matter came to court within the time limit set for an action in contract, namely six years. The defence argued that the case raised a fundamental question about the legal powers of the probation authority that should have been raised by judicial review. Henry J. considered that the plaintiff's claim was entirely based on private law rights and to decide otherwise left the plaintiffs out of time for judicial review.[60] He concluded that there were three operating principles from the legal authorities. First, for cases which fall within the *O'Reilly v. Mackman*

---

[54] [1985] Q.B. 152. Also see *R. v. Lord Chancellors Dept., ex p. Nangle* [1991] I.R.L.R. 343; *Roy v. Kensington and Chelsea and Westminister Family Practitioner Committee, The Independent*, February 11, 1992; [1992] 1 All E.R. 705. Lord Bridge allowed private law rights exercised through the writ procedure to raise public law issue incidentally. Lord Lowry regarded the litigant as having a "bundle of rights," which permitted the case to be heard.

[55] See *ex p. Benwell* [1985] 1 Q.B. 152.

[56] *Air Canada v. Secretary of State for Trade (No. 2)* [1983] 2 A.C. 394.

[57] [1986] A.C. 484; *ex p. Benwell* [1985] 1 Q.B. 152. See *ex p. Dew* [1987] 1 W.L.R. 881.

[58] [1986] 1 All E.R. 717.

[59] [1991] 4 All E.R. 294.

[60] Mr Justice Henry noted that there were at least eight cases, five had been taken to the House of Lords on the issue.

rule, the courts must "be astute" to see that there is no evasion of the protections afforded by Order 53 in cases which are unmeritorious. Secondly, there is no "overriding objection" to public law issues being litigated in writ actions. Thirdly, that in principle, Order 53 should not be used for the litigation of private law claims. A further qualification important to note is that where the parties agree this will permit an ordinary action to raise matters of public law.[61]

15–41 Drawing together some conclusions from the case law is difficult. Some examples serve to show how judicial decision-making is influenced very much on the facts of each case, the nature of the dispute involved and the application of the three operating principles noted by Henry J., in the *Doyle* case. In *Gillick*[62] an ordinary action challenging the health authority's guidance to medical practitioners on contraceptive advice, was permitted to proceed even though an application for judicial review was possible. In *ex p. Noble*[63] a deputy police surgeon sought to challenge his dismissal by way of judicial review and this was dismissed on the grounds that a private action was more appropriate. Similarly this line of reasoning was applied in *McLaren v. Home Office*[64] that an ordinary writ was appropriate for a declaration of a prison officer's employment conditions.

15–42 The exact nature of the distinction between public and private law is problematic and leaves the need for law reform to be greater than perhaps in 1969 when a Royal Commission was proposed but rejected. However, in 1988 an unofficial Royal Commission namely the Justice All Souls Review Committee[65] reported after a 10 year study of administrative law. The report does not have the status of an official inquiry and its findings focus on setting out principles of good administration. The Justice report recommended reform of the rule in *O'Reilly v. Mackman* and that the House of Lords should re-consider their decision. The report criticised the imprecision of the term "public law" and suggested that Parliament might wish to consider the circumstances where an applicant might be obliged to use Order 53 and be barred from proceeding by action or originating summons.[66]

15–42A As matters now stand the procedural rules are in favour of litigants who think that they have a public law matter to proceed by Order 53.

---

[61] See the discussion in *Gillick v. West Norfolk and Wisbech Area Heath Authority* [1986] A.C. 112.

[62] *ibid.*

[63] *R. v. Derbyshire C.C., ex p. Noble* [1990] I.C.R. 808.

[64] [1990] I.C.R. 824.

[65] *Administrative Justice: Some Necessary Reforms* (O.U.P., 1988). Hereinafter, The Justice Report. See S. Fredman and G. Morris, "The Costs of Exclusivity: Public and Private Re-examined" (1994) *Public Law* 69.

[66] *ibid.*, paras. 6.15–6.19.

If it later appears that this was the wrong procedure then Order 53, rule 9(5) permits matters to continue as if the procedure had been by ordinary writ. This is only permitted if the applicant has sought an injunction, declaration or damages. However a litigant who commences an ordinary writ and then raises public law matters, may only do so if the court exercises a *discretion* to proceed as if the issue had been raised by Order 53. That discretion is rarely exercised and would only be exercised if it would not be unfair to the respondent and where the court would be prepared to waive the safeguards included in the Order 53 procedure.

It may be concluded that on the basis of procedural rules the **15–43** distinction between public and private law is important to litigants. The signs are that the courts are beginning to recognise the problems in making such a distinction in cases, as in *Roy*, where the litigant has a "parcel of rights." Careful consideration is required of the question whether any great disdavantage seems to come from allowing the ordinary writ procedure to raise some matters of public law. However, great uncertainty surrounds the principles as to when the courts regard such cases as acceptable. One possible way forward is to consider clarifying the protections afforded under Order 53 to public bodies and consider extending these to the ordinary writ procedure.

(b) Directions for the future: Lord Woolf and public law

As Cane has recognised the present law leaves litigants with[67] "a **15–44** procedural minefield". There are suggestions that repealing Order 53 and introducing a single procedure for all High Court actions may be found helpful. The Law Commission[68] has rejected this approach in favour of retaining Order 53 and introducing greater flexibility in "transferring out" and "transferring into" cases that have wrongly been commenced in the wrong court. There are also useful ideas for streamlining[69] the law. However, as Cane points out[70]:

> . . . this recommendation only relates to actions begun in the High Court or the County Court. It does not consider how to deal with collateral challenges or with direct challenges before forums other than the High Court of the County Court."

---

[67] Peter Cane, *An Introduction to Administrative Law* (3rd ed. Oxford, Clarendon Law Series, 1996) p. 104.
[68] Law Com. No. 226 H.C. 669, October 1994.
[69] SS Sir Konrad Schiemann [1996] *Public Law* 240.
[70] *ibid.* p. 105.

15–45   Consideration has also been given to the public law jurisdiction of the High Court in the review carried out by Lord Woolf.[71] The main aims of the review[72] are to provide uniformity of procedure in civil litigation and to make the system more responsive to the needs of citizens. Within the public law area a need to distinguish between the availability of appeals that allow grievances to be examined and the use of judicial review as a last resort. There are a number of proposals put forward by Lord Woolf. In outline these include the following which have been carefully summarised in Blake's analysis of the Woolf recommendations[73]:

"(a) To ensure uniformity and fairness in the procedure adopted in Crown cases. This objective is complementary to the efficient management of cases;

(b) To ensure that Crown Office procedures are similar to those available in private law cases;

(c) To provide greater flexibility in switching between public and private law procedures;

(d) To increase the number of nominated judges by bringing judges from other divisions;

(e) To allow the disposal of some judicial review cases by judges on Circuit. This might apply in cases where the issues involved do not involve local or central government;

(f) To encourage the use of advisory declarations where appropriate in the public interest;

(g) To retain the preliminary leave stage with a new test for leave "whether there is a realistic prospect of success". The leave stage should be renamed "preliminary consideration". This test will also be used to strike out applications in private law cases;

(h) To provide a broad test of public interest standing and in suitable cases for costs to be paid from public funds. The courts might be given a discretion over third party interventions;"

---

[71] Generally see *Access to Justice*, Interim Report (June 1995).
[72] See Lord Woolf, *Access to Justice, Final Report* (July 1996, HMSO).
[73] See Charles Blake, "Access to Justice: the Public Law Element" (1997) *Public Law* 215–22 at p. 216.

(i) To continue the approach to streamlining and the careful management of cases that has already begun[74] setting firm constraints on any wasted court time.

The Woolf proposals are a welcome consideration of the pro- **15–46** cedures for judicial review. In the most part they are clear and sensible proposals which will do much to streamline procedures and provide a better system of case management. There remains the question of whether such ideas will work in the absence of some form of organisation such as a Director of Civil Procedure. If judicial review becomes the focus of the debate on the Bill of Rights, then it is inevitable that such an official might have a key role in the protection of the public interest.[75]

3. Grounds for Review

Deciding the procedural route to take action in the courts depends on **15–47** the nature of the dispute and the grounds for complaint. It is also necessary for the grounds for review applied by the superior courts to be considered. It is significant that there has not been any consolidation into statutory form of the different grounds available for review. This area has been left to develop on a case by case basis. Lord Diplock acknowledged the achievements of the courts in developing judicial review[76] in 1984 in *Council of Civil Service Unions v. Minister for Civil Service*[77] when he suggested that "the English law relating to judicial control of administrative action has been developed upon a case by case basis which has virtually transformed it over the last three decades". In the same speech Lord Diplock referred to the grounds for judicial review as consisting of three "heads" upon which administrative law is subject to control. These have been considered in outline in Chapter 5 and are as follows: "Illegality" meaning the decision-maker must understand the law and give effect to it[78]; "irrationality" by which a decision which is unreasonable or so outrageous in its defiance of logic or of accepted moral standards that "no sensible person who applied his mind to

---

[74] For example see: Practice Note (judicial review: documents to be lodged) [1997] 1 All E.R. 128. Also see *R. v. Horsham D.C., ex p. Wenman* [1994] 4 All E.R. 681.

[75] For a useful analysis of judicial review and its future in administrative law see: Carol Harlow, "Back to Basics: Reinventing Administrative Law" [1997] *Public Law* 245.

[76] [1984] 3 All E.R. 935.

[77] [1985] A.C. 374.

[78] See J. Jowell and D. Oliver, *New Directions in Administrative Law* (Oxford, 1988).

the question to be decided could have arrived at it"; and finally there is" procedural impropriety" by which there is a failure to observe basic rules of natural justice or to fail to act with procedural fairness towards the person who will be affected by the decision. A further possibility, that of proportionality was also mentioned. Here the courts have to balance the appropriateness of the various objectives set out in law, the adverse affects which its decision may have on the rights, the liberties or interests of the persons and purposes it pursues. Proportionality, while recognised fully in French, German and E.C. law has only become understood in its "application in English Administrative law in recent years" although it is a concept which has historical roots in much earlier cases. The above developments must be understood in the context of the absence of any codified system of administrative law.

The grounds for review may now be considered in further detail bearing in mind that Lord Diplock's classification is not exhaustive.

(a) Ultra Vires and Excess of Jurisdiction

15–48 Lord Diplock's classification of illegality comprises a number of categories. Some categories may overlap and the classification is not exhaustive. As a general principle public bodies are expected to act within their legal powers. When a power is vested in a public body and the public body acts in excess of that power, its acts are invalid and *ultra vires*. The task of the courts, through judicial review is to consider the legal powers of public bodies at common law, statute or under the royal prerogative[79] and determine whether the public body has acted within its powers. Determining whether or not a public body is within its powers depends on statutory interpretation. The breadth of the powers contained in the statute will influence the courts powers to intervene. Even broadly drafted powers are not immune to review. In *Hazell v. Hammersmith*, noted[80] in the chapters on local government and in the work of the Audit Commission, the House of Lords found that swap transactions were not authorised under Schedule 13 to the Local Government Act 1972. This was notwithstanding a broadly drafted power contained in section 111 of the 1972 Act namely that a local authority ". . . shall have power to do anything (whether or not involving the expenditure, borrowing or lending of money or the acquisition or disposal of any property or

---

[79] The inclusion of the prerogative arises through the application of Lord Diplock's speech in *Council of Civil Service Unions v. Minister for the Civil Service* [1985] A.C. 374. See *R. v. Wandsworth London B.C. ex p. Beckwith* [1996] 1 All E.R. 129.
[80] [1991] 2 W.L.R. 372.

rights) which is calculated to facilitate, or is conducive or incidental, to the discharge of any of their functions."

The House of Lords viewed the swap transactions as speculative **15–49** and therefore outside the remit of local authority powers. The extensive nature of section 111 has been increasingly narrowed by the courts in an attempt to keep local authorities within their legal powers.[81] On the same approach to the interpretation of local government powers following the House of Lords in *Hazell* is the Court of Appeal in *Crédit Suisse v. Allerdale B.C.*[82] Allerdale local authority engaged in a joint venture through a number of companies set up by the local authority, technically known as "local government influenced companies", to build and operate a leisure complex. A time-share scheme was envisaged as the best means to operate the complex. Crédit Suisse, a leading international banking institution, provided substantial loans repayable over a fixed period. The district auditor queried the legality of the local authority joint venture companies, the local authority involvement and the investment of Crédit Suisse. This arose when the ability of the local authority companies to repay the loans came into doubt. The case involved legal consideration of the powers and duties of the local authority and its relationship to Crédit Suisse. The Court of Appeal held that the arrangements with the joint-venture companies were *ultra vires* the powers of the local authority. The result of the case left Crédit Suisse largely exposed to debts and liabilities that arise from the *ultra vires* transaction. This will seriously inhibit[83] local government joint ventures with the private sector.[84]

Powers granted for one purpose cannot be assumed to provide **15–50** powers for another purpose, even if closely related. In *Att.-Gen. v. Fulham Corporation*[85] Fulham Corporation had statutory powers under the Baths and Wash-houses Acts 1846–78 to establish baths and wash-houses. The question arose as to whether facilities for washing and drying clothes which included the operation of drying equipment by employees of the corporation, came within the powers of the legislation. The court held that the statutory powers only permitted the carrying out of clothes washing by customers themselves, and did not extend to operating a laundry service.

The review of statutory powers also extends to their exercise by **15–50A** Ministers. The Court of Appeal in *Laker Airways*, held that the

---

[81] See: *R. v. Richmond upon Thames London Borough Council, ex p. McCarthy and Stone (Developments) Ltd* [1991] 3 W.L.R. 941.

[82] [1996] 4 All E.R. 129.

[83] Also see *Westdeutsche Landesbank Girozentrale v. Islington London B.C.* [1996] 2 All E.R. 961 on restitution matters arising from the *Hazell v. Hammersmith* decision of the House of Lords.

[84] Also see *Crédit Suisse v. Waltham Forest London B.C.* [1996] 4 All E.R. 176.

[85] [1921] 1 Ch. 440.

Secretary of State had acted *ultra vires*. Guidance under the Civil Aviation Act 1971, subsequently amended, to the Civil Aviation Authority to the effect that British Airways should be the sole carrier on the Stanstead to New York route, resulted in Laker Airways having their licence withdrawn. The guidance had been approved by both Houses of Parliament. The Court of Appeal regarded the guidance as effectively a directive power. The guidance was also contrary to the objectives given to the Civil Aviation Authority. Also the guidance was intended to explain and amplify the meaning of the objectives and not to replace them. The Court of Appeal considered that Laker Airways should be entitled to fly the New York route.

15–51   Local government provides another example of the power of the courts to review statutory powers. The courts may appear quite innovative in construing statutes when local authority powers are involved. In *Bromley*,[86] the House of Lords was asked to consider the "fair fares" policy of the GLC (now abolished). "Ordinary business principles" were applied to the reduction of fares and as the policy did not operate on those principles the proposed reduction in fares was *ultra vires*. Although the GLC had powers to make grants "for any purpose" to the London Transport Executive (LTE) the grant involving a supplementary rate was quashed because the purposes for which it was intended were *ultra vires*. There was "a fiduciary duty" on the GLC as a local authority, and the fares policy failed to live up to that standard which was owed to ratepayers. The Courts had to balance the GLC's duty owed to ratepayers against its wider power to provide reasonable transport facilities for transport users. The fact that a "fair fares" policy had been a manifesto condition in the election of the ruling party in the GLC was not relevant to the courts' powers of review, as such a condition was "not binding" on the local authority.

15–52   The application of any legal principles in this area of the law is always difficult. The courts may construe the statute as providing incidental powers within the jurisdiction of the body concerned provided the act is not expressly forbidden. In *Att.-Gen. v. Crayford UDC*[87] the general powers of management of local authority housing under section 111(1) of the Housing Act 1957 were considered by the court in respect of a local authority decision to issue insurance policies to its tenants. Did such a scheme fall within "prudent management" by the local authority of its housing. The court held that the scheme was within the local authority's powers. The question of whether the scheme was *ultra vires* or not depended on whether it "may fairly be regarded as incidental to, or consequential upon" the powers granted to the authority under the 1957 Act.

[86] [1983] 1 A.C. 768.
[87] [1962] 1 Ch. 575.

A public authority must direct itself according to law and must not **15–53** purport to exercise powers it does not have nor the powers that someone else may have.[88] Statutes invariably provide that powers may only be exercised by a specific body or person or that the powers must operate within certain safeguards which must be obeyed. The *ultra vires* doctrine will apply where the delegation of powers is improper. Effectively the courts wish to ensure that discretion is properly exercised, free from pressure and unfettered in its application.

Some examples serve to illustrate the courts' review of the exercise **15–54** of the delegation of discretion. In *ex p. Brunyate*,[89] the Court held that a local education authority may not use its powers to dismiss and appoint governors as a means of changing the educational policy of the Education Act 1944. The Court of Appeal in *R. v. Monopolies and Mergers Commission, ex p. Argyll Group PLC*[90] noted that the Monopolies and Mergers Commission, rather than its chairman should have decided whether to proceed with a reference made to it by the Secretary of State in the case of a take-over bid. The fact that the delegation of power to the chairman was *ultra vires* did not prevent the court from refusing to quash the chairman's decision.

In *R. v. Waltham Forest LBC, ex p Waltham Forest Ratepayers Action Group*[91] the courts struck down a decision of Waltham Forest councillors which was based on instructions from a pressure group known as the Local Government Group.

Over-reliance on rules,[92] exercising a discretion when fettered by **15–55** contract or pre-existing rules[93] have all been regarded by the courts as examples of a failure to exercise discretionary powers correctly. Some latitude may be given to the correct[94] delegation of ministerial powers to officials. In *Carltona*,[95] a wartime case arose when a factory owner challenged the Commissioners of Works over the exercise of requisition powers granted by statute. In fact the Commissioners never met and their powers were carried out by officials acting on their behalf. The Court of Appeal broadly interpreted delegation and upheld the legality of the procedures. Some official self-restraint must be taken not to extend the *Carltona* principle too broadly. More recently, in *ex p. Oladehinde*[96] the House of Lords upheld the lawfulness of the Home

---

[88] See *R. v. The Mayor, Aldermen and the Councillors of Stepney* [1902] 1 K.B. 317.

[89] *R. v. Inner London Education Authority, ex p. Brunyate* [1989] 1 W.L.R. 542.

[90] [1986] 1 W.L.R. 763.

[91] *Ex p. Baxter and others* [1987] 3 All E.R. 671; [1988] Q.B. 419.

[92] See *R. v. Police Complaints Board, ex p. Madden* [1983] 1 W.L.R. 447.

[93] See *Lavender (H.) & Son Ltd v. Minister of Housing and Local Government* [1970] 1 W.L.R. 1231.

[94] See *Local Government Board v. Arlidge* [1915] A.C. 120.

[95] *Carltona v. Commissioners of Works* [1943] 2 All E.R. 560.

[96] *R. v. Secretary of State for the Home Department, ex p. Oladehinde* [1991] 2 A.C. 254.

Secretary's common practice to delegate to senior officials, namely immigration officers, his powers under the Immigration Act 1971 to serve notices of deportation. In such instances of delegation the House of Lords noted that care should be taken not to widen the delegation of powers unduly. Some caution must be exercised to establish that the officials are sufficiently senior and that they possess the necessary experience to carry out the statutory duties under the 1971 Act. The *Carltona* principle is applied to central government departments and the devolution of functions to civil servants.

15–56   In local government section 101 of the Local Government Act 1972 permits the delegation of wide powers to officials to carry out specific functions of the local authority. The nature of any delegated power must be given close scrutiny. If the power rests with an officer who may consult with members of the council, it is wrong for the powers to be actually exercised by the councillor rather than the officer.[97]

15–57   A discretion which is mistakenly bound by a policy or previous practice may likewise be regarded as an abuse of discretion and subject to possible review by the courts. In *Bromley*,[98] discussed above, the local authority mistakenly felt bound by its election manifesto. The House of Lords held that this was an abuse of power. A contract to bind a public body and its successors to exercise its powers in a particular way is likely to be declared void by the courts.[99] In such cases the courts will consider the nature of the powers being exercised. A commercial body that enters a commercial undertaking not to increase its statutory charges was considered to be making an acceptable exercise of power by virtue of its status as a commercial undertaking.[1]

15–58   The exercise of discretionary powers may be influenced by the doctrine of estoppel. Estoppel has been developed as part of private law, it is relevant in public law as creating narrow and strictly defined exceptions to the strict application of the doctrine of *ultra vires*. The basis of estoppel was succinctly explained by Wade[2]:

"a person who by some statement or representation of fact causes another to act to his detriment in reliance on the truth of it is not allowed to deny it later, even though it is wrong."

In private law, particularly in the law of contract, estoppel may prevent the enforcement of contractual rights where there was some

---

[97] See *R. v. Port Talbot Borough Council, ex p. Jones* [1988] 2 All E.R. 207.
[98] [1983] 1 A.C. 768.
[99] See *Ayr Harbour Trustees v. Oswald* (1883) 8 App.Cas. 623.
[1] See in contrast to *Ayr* the decision of the House of Lords in *Birkdale Electric Supply Company v. Southport Corp.* [1926] A.C. 355.
[2] Wade, *Administrative Law* (1988), p. 261.

undertaking not to enforce those rights in law. In the area of public law estoppel may arise where a citizen may be misled by advice from an official or public body and suffer detriment. However as a general principle estoppel cannot be used to give a public body powers which it would otherwise not have.[3] In *Maritime Electric Company*[4] an electricity authority misread a customer's electricity meter and consequently undercharged the customer for two years. The authority had a statutory duty to collect the full amount and could not use the doctrine of estoppel to accept the lesser amount because it lacked the statutory powers to do so.

The question arises as to whether there are situations where the **15–59** courts might be willing to enforce an *ultra vires* decision. Estoppel might assist an applicant when relying on advice. In *Western Fish Products*[5] where the power to make a decision was incorrectly delegated but where the plaintiff assumed it to be correctly delegated, then provided the courts are satisfied about the nature of the incorrect assumption, the plaintiff may in certain circumstances rely on the estoppel principle as an exception to what would otherwise be an *ultra vires* decision. The Court of Appeal asserted that estoppel could not prevent a statutory body from exercising its discretion or performing its duty.

Considerable difficulty surrounds defining the nature of the **15–60** assumption made by the plaintiff that might be sufficient to satisfy the estoppel principle in public law cases. Two possibilities emerge from the *Western Fish Products* decision. First, estoppel may only operate when it reasonably appears to the plaintiff that the authority to make a decision has been correctly delegated to the relevant officer or body and where "there is some evidence" justifying the plaintiff in believing that the officer or body was binding the authority. Secondly, depending on the construction of the statute, Lord Justice Megaw explained that estoppel may arise where there is a procedural requirement in the statute waived by the statutory body in the exercise of its powers. For example," . . . if a planning authority waives a procedural requirement relating to any application made to it for the exercise of its statutory powers, it may be estopped from relying on lack of formality."

In an earlier case, that of *Robertson v. Minister of Pensions*,[6] where a **15–61** citizen relied to his detriment on an assurance he was given that he was entitled to a military pension by someone who had no power to make the assurance. Denning J., advanced a wide interpretation that

---

[3] See *Minister of Agriculture and Fisheries v. Matthews* [1950] 1 K.B. 148.
[4] *Maritime Electric Company v. General Dairies Ltd* [1937] A.C. 610.
[5] *Western Fish Products Ltd v. Penwith D.C.* [1981] 2 All E.R. 204.
[6] [1949] 1 K.B. 227.

the plaintiff is entitled to rely upon a government department "having the authority which it assumes. He does not know and cannot be expected to know, the limits of that authority."

However this wide interpretation was rejected in *Western Fish Products* and also by the House of Lords in *Howell v. Falmouth Boat Construction Co. Ltd*[7] which considered that Denning's interpretation of the estoppel principle did not seem consistent with the principle that legal authority cannot be delegated.

15–62   Estoppel may arise when a change of policy occurs and the result is to the detriment of the plaintiff. For example in *Lever Finance*[8] a planning officer, when asked by Lever Finance as to whether fresh planning permission was required in respect of their decision to alter the original plans of a housing scheme, concluded that no fresh application was required. Lever Finance began construction but after neighbours objected they were then advised that planning permission was required. Lever Finance applied for planning permission which was then refused. The Court of Appeal accepted that the planning officer had followed common practice, that Lever Finance relied on the planning officer's advice, and therefore the planning officer had authority to bind the council.

15–63   There has been criticism of the approach in *Lever Finance*. In *Western Fish Products Ltd* the Court of Appeal restricted the use of estoppel in planning matters as estoppel could not prevent a statutory body from exercising its discretion or duty.

The law relating to estoppel in public law is unsatisfactory. This may be due to the difficulty of importing estoppel's private law characteristics into public law and of reconciling the principles of estoppel with the overriding obligations found in statutes. Even creative interpretations of statutory duties, discretions and procedural rules may result in hard cases where there is no legal remedy. One solution favoured by Wade[9] in seeking to find compatibility between the application of the *ultra vires* doctrine and fairness to the plaintiff, is to compensate the plaintiff when the law must be enforced but injustice results. Compensation provides the means of ensuring fairness while retaining the doctrine of *ultra vires*. However compensation has been found to be equally difficult to apply in public law.[10]

15–64   Cane[11] considers a different solution. Instead of adhering to the strict application of the doctrine of *ultra vires*, consider whether

---

[7] [1951] A.C. 837.

[8] *Lever Finance Ltd v. Westminster (City) London Borough Council* [1971] 1 Q.B. 222.

[9] Wade, *Administrative Law* (1988), p. 385.

[10] See *R. v. Knowsley B.C., ex p. Maguire and others* [1992] 142 New L.J. 1375 Schiemann J., considers the problems of compensation in cases of judicial review caused by breach of statutory duty.

[11] Cane, *op. cit.* pp. 225–256.

balancing the different interests between the parties might provide a more acceptable solution. This approach provides a more fundamental evaluation of the true function of *ultra vires*. Thus a decision taken by a public body might be enforceable even if it were *ultra vires* where the injury to the plaintiff was such that the public interest would not be served by enforcing the decision. Invariably such an approach invites considerable judicial discretion in setting the principles to be applied in such cases. Also it might be considered inappropriate to re-consider the doctrine of *ultra vires* in this way as the doctrine performs an important function of keeping a check on the discretion of public bodies.

The *ultra vires* doctrine may apply where there are certain procedural **15–65** requirements contained in the statute. Procedural requirements or conditions may be imposed before specific statutory powers may be exercised. Procedural requirements may be merely discretionary or mandatory. The latter is likely to lead to a decision being quashed. In certain examples it may be helpful to classify the type of error or mistake made by the public body. Some are minor and may not affect the jurisdiction of the body making the decision. The courts' powers of supervision are usually intended to allow public bodies to make decisions within their jurisdiction. Thus in finding on the merits of a case the public body should be allowed to make mistakes that are not so fundamental that the jurisidiction of the body is impugned. Defining whether a mistake goes to jurisdiction or not is largely dependent on the role of the courts and the nature of the procedural rules.

In *Anisminic*[11a] the United Kingdom Government received payment **15–66** from the Egyptian Government of a sum of money intended to compensate for loss of British property sequestered. The Foreign Compensation Commission, on behalf of the United Kingdom Government, had the task of determining claims made against the money available. An Order in Council set out the conditions required before any payments could be made. The Commission concluded that Anisminic had not made out its case. The Commission's interpretation of the Order in Council required that Anisminic should be British and a "successor in title." Anisminic could fulfill the former but not the latter condition and challenged the Commission's interpretation of the Order in Council in the courts despite the ouster clause contained in section 4(4) of the Foreign Compensation Act 1950 namely that the Commission's determination "should not be questioned in any court of law." The House of Lords concluded that the Commission had erred in law in holding that Anisminic should be a "successor in title." The ouster clause was held not to protect "purported" determinations only real determinations.

[11a] *Anisminic Ltd v. Foreign Compensation Commission* [1969] 2 AC 147.

15–67   The question arises as to the nature of the error that is regarded as a jurisdictional error and therefore open to review by the courts. Are all errors jurisdictional? In *Anisminic*, the Foreign Compensation Commission had correctly interpreted its powers to consider Anisminic's application and inquire into the facts of the application. If the Commission had considered matters extraneous to its powers its determination would have been a nullity. Lord Roskill considered:

> "There are many cases where although the tribunal had jurisdiction to enter on the inquiry, it has done or failed to do something in the course of the inquiry which is of such a nature that its decision is a nullity."

Lord Reid identified those errors which may be considered as going to jurisdiction. These are: acting in bad faith, making decisions without the requisite powers, breaching the requirements of natural justice; failing to take into account relevant considerations; or taking into account irrelevant considerations. The list is not exhaustive, but it is based on the assumption that there is a distinction between those errors which do and those that do not go to jurisdiction.

15–68   The courts have considered the nature of such a distinction. In *Pearlman v. Keepers and Governors of Harrow School*,[12] Lord Denning explained that any such distinction between errors which are jurisdictional and those that are not are so fine that the distinction may be discarded. Pearlman was a tenant who had installed central heating. He applied to the county court for a declaration that it constituted a "structural alteration" of the premises. The county court decided that it did not and Pearlman sought certiorari to quash this decision in the High Court, notwithstanding the fact that the county court decision was by statute "final and conclusive."

15–69   Lord Denning's attempts to render obsolete the distinction between errors within jurisdiction and those that were outside jurisdiction was rejected in the Privy Council case of *South East Asia Fire Bricks*[13] by Lord Fraser. Lord Diplock[14] in *O'Reilly v. Mackman* believed that there was still an important distinction to be drawn between those bodies where error of law within jurisdiction remained relevant and bodies where it had become an unnecessary distinction. Inferior courts fell within the category of review such as tribunals and administrative agencies, while the ordinary courts such as the County Court in *Pearlman* were entitled to rely on the distinction between errors within jurisdiction which are not reviewable and errors outside jurisdiction which are subject to review.[15]

---

[12] [1979] Q.B. 56. See *Williams v. Bedwelty Justices* [1996] 3 All E.R. 737.

[13] *South East Asia Firebricks Sdn. Bhd. v. Non-Metallic Mineral Products* [1981] A.C. 363.

[14] See *Re Racal Communications Ltd* [1981] A.C. 374. Lord Diplock drew a distinction between different bodies such as commissions and tribunals on the one hand and courts on the other. The former were open to review while the latter could rely on the principle of errors which are within jurisdiction as free from review.

[15] See *R. v. Greater Manchester Coroner, ex p. Tal* [1985] Q.B. 67.

It may be concluded that such a distinction between errors that are within jurisdiction and those that are not is necessary to safeguard the decision-maker and allow freedom to make the decision freed from over-rigid intervention by the courts. The courts are in turn allowed some discretion in setting the limits of their own jurisdiction.

(b) Abuse of Discretion

Discretion exercised by a public body must not be exercised wrongly. **15–70** Abuse of discretion may arise where the power has been exercised for a purpose not intended or expressed in the statute when the powers were conferred. The use of powers for improper purposes may result in the powers being declared *ultra vires* by the courts. For example, compulsory purchase powers should not be used for an ulterior or improper purpose.[16] In *Sydney Municipal Council v. Campbell*[17] compulsory purchase powers "to carry out improvements in remodelling any portion of the city" under the Sydney Corporation Amendment Act 1905 could not be used to secure a benefit of an increase in land values.

In construing a statute the courts may look at the "policy and **15–71** objects" of the statute in order to consider whether the motivation for a decision and its outcome are within the powers conferred by Parliament. In *Padfield*[18] mandamus was granted by the House of Lords in favour of milk producers who had complained that the differential element, based on geographical areas, in the price fixed for their milk purchased by the Milk Marketing Board was too low. The Agricultural Marketing Act 1958 provided two methods of grievance resolution, arbitration and procedures under section 19 involving the setting up of a committee of investigation. The first was accepted as unsuitable for the type of complaint. The second, the Minister declined to do. Padfield sought an order of mandamus. The House of Lords concluded that the Minister had misunderstood his powers and therefore frustrated the purpose of the Act. The terms of the Minister's powers to refer the matter to a committee of investigation were if the Minister "in any case so directs." Lord Reid noted that this showed that the Minister had some discretion, but such a discretion must be in accordance with the intention of the statute. The courts, in considering whether discretion[19] has been exercised reasonably, may consider reasons for the decision or in the absence of reasons may infer whether the decision is a reasonable one or not.

[16] See *Marquess of Clanricarde v. Congested Districts Board for Ireland* (1914) 79 J.P. 481.
[17] [1925] A.C. 338.
[18] [1968] A.C. 997.
[19] See *R. v. Secretary of State for Trade and Industry, ex p. Lonhro plc* [1989] 2 All E.R. 609.

In the event, after the House of Lords decision in *Padfield*, the Minister was compelled under the Agricultural Marketing Act 1958 to set up an enquiry in the form of a committee of investigation. This was duly convened and reported in favour of the complainants but the Minister's ultimate discretion allowed him to take no action.

15–72   In the exercise of discretion it is possible to take into account irrelevant considerations or fail to take account of relevant considerations. Abuse of discretion on these grounds may occur for the most altruistic reasons but may not conform to the relevant statutory requirements. In *Roberts v. Hopwood*[20] Poplar Borough Council introduced a "minimum wage" for its employees. The power to set wages under section 62 of the Metropolis Management Act 1855 contained the power to pay "such salaries and wages as . . . [the council] may think fit." This conferred a broad discretion on the local authority but the district auditor questioned the validity of the setting of a minimum wage and accordingly surcharged the local councillors. The House of Lords noted that the national average wage for similar workers was substantially less than the minimum wage set by the Council. The rationale for the minimum wage was based on an election mandate which the councillors felt bound to follow. However, the payment of the minimum wage was made without due regard for the interests of the ratepayers. The House of Lords viewed the minimum wage payments as amounting in effect to gifts to the workers which was an improper purpose and not intended by the legislation. The Council had not taken account of the wages paid to other workers and the result was that the minimum wage was unlawful. The House of Lords reached its conclusion by balancing the interests of the ratepayers with the statutory powers exercised by the local authority as to what is reasonable and a proper exercise of discretion.

15–73   A similar approach is evident in the Bromley[21] decision. The House of Lords held that the "fair fares" policy of the Greater London Council was *ultra vires* on the basis that the decision had not taken account of the fiduciary duty owed by the council to the rate payers. In balancing the different interests of ratepayers, transport users and the duties of the local authority, the House of Lords concluded that the Council had acted unreasonably.

15–74   Unreasonableness is also a ground for holding that a discretion has been abused. In *Wednesbury Corporation*[22] Lord Greene M.R. considered the meaning of the term "unreasonable" and concluded that where an authority's decision "was so unreasonable that no reasonable authority" could ever come to the decision then it could be

[20] [1925] A.C. 578.
[21] [1983] 1 A.C. 768.
[22] *Associated Provincial Picture Houses Ltd v. Wednesbury Corporation* [1948] 1 K.B. 223.

impugned by the courts. The courts are left with considerable discretion as to how to apply this direction. The question is whether a reasonable authority "could" ever come to the decision. What is the standard of the reasonable authority? On a narrow construction of the test, the courts should rarely intervene. As Lord Diplock recognised in the GCHQ case[23] the decision would have to be so outrageous or in defiance of logic that no sensible person could come to such a decision. On this view, unreasonableness is unlikely to result in the courts intervening with the exercise of discretion. This appears to give decision-makers considerable latitude before offending against the criteria set by Lord Diplock. Unreasonableness will therefore provide a justification for upholding the exercise of discretion on the one hand but imposing self-restraint on the courts on the other. In *Nottingham County Council*[24] the view of Lord Scarman was that the decision must be so absurd that the decision-maker "must have taken leave of his senses."

15–75 An alternative to the narrow interpretation of *Wednesbury* unreasonableness is that the courts are prepared to seek more active intervention on the grounds of unreasonableness defined in terms of review in discretion where it is found to be illogical or against good sense.[25] The courts are free to consider as in *Padfield* whether the policy and objects of the statute have been frustrated. In *Wheeler v. Leicester City Council*[26] Lord Roskill considered whether the local authority's decision to terminate the agreement with the Leicester Rugby Football Club to make use of the council's recreation ground was "unreasonable." The Council had responded to the Club's decision to take part in a rugby tour of South Africa. Lord Roskill concluded that the Council had used an unfair means to achieve its objectives. Although the judges had failed in the lower courts to classify the decision of the local authority as *Wednesbury* unreasonableness, Lord Roskill was prepared to hold that the local authority had acted unreasonably.

15–76 Unreasonableness may be used to impugn a bye-law or delegated rule-making function.[27] Statutory interpretation provides the main basis for adopting the test of unreasonableness, though it may be the basis of a tort action in negligence against a public body. In addition to unreasonableness, vagueness or a lack of fair hearing such as is implied in the rules of natural justice may result in the courts holding that discretion has been abused.

---

[23] *Council of Civil Service Unions v. Minister for the Civil Service* [1985] A.C. 374 at p. 410.
[24] *Nottingham County Council v. Secretary of State for the Environment* [1986] A.C. 240 at p. 247.
[25] See *West Glamorgan County Council v. Rafferty* [1987] 1 W.L.R. 457, discussed by R. Ward [1987] C.L.J. 374.
[26] [1985] A.C. 1054.
[27] *Kruse v. Johnson* [1898] 2 Q.B. 91.

The concept of "unreasonableness" is difficult to categorise satisfactorily. The courts are reluctant to review decisions on their merits and the policy behind decisions very often falls outside the courts remit. One way forward is to see the role of the courts as providing a more systematic guide to the development of principles of good administration. Avoiding arbitrariness or inconsistency and ensuring that fair decision-making takes place might be further assisted if "unreasonableness" were focused on what constitutes good administration.

15–77   There have been a number of cases that have provided further elaboration of the *Wednesbury* principle. There are three cases where the breadth and possible objective standards implied in the *Wednesbury* test are discussed. In *R. v. Chief Constable of the Devon and Cornwall Constabulary, ex p. Hay,*[28] Mr Justice Sedley granted certiorari and mandamus directing the Chief Constable to hear and determine disciplinary charges. Some irrelevant and extraneous matters had been taken into account but "it was in the public interest" that where there was unfairness the disciplinary proceedings should be reinstated. In *R. v. Secretary of State for the Home Department, ex p. Onibiyo,*[29] the use of general *Wednesbury* principles was deployed in respect of an application for asylum. Sir Thomas Bingham noted that[30] ". . . the decision whether an asylum-seeker is a refugee is a question to be determined by the Secretary of State and the immigration appellate authorities whose determinations are susceptible to challenge only on *Wednesbury* principles."

15–78   In discussing *Wednesbury* principles Sir Thomas Bingham noted that[31] "on any *Wednesbury* ground of which irrationality is only one. . ." This is a useful reminder that strict categorisation of the grounds of review into self-contained compartments is to be avoided. *Wednesbury* principles may provide a "hard look" doctrine for the courts to discover if there is objectively any grounds for upholding a review. This approach favouring the overturning of any perverse decision making may be found in *R. v. Wandsworth London B.C., ex p. Mansor,*[32] a case on homeless persons.

15–79   Finally, in addition to the grounds of review already discussed consideration should be given to Lord Diplock's suggestion[33] that proportionality might be adopted as a ground for review in English law. The principle of proportionality provides the courts with the opportunity to consider whether the harmful effects of a particular

---

[28] [1996] 2 All E.R. 711.
[29] [1996] 2 All E.R. 901.
[30] at p. 912 c–d.
[31] at p. 912 f.
[32] [1996] 3 All E.R. 913.
[33] See *Council of Civil Service Unions v. Minister for the Civil Service* [1985] A.C. 374.

exercise of power are disproportionate to any benefits which may occur. Support for the adoption of such a doctrine into English administrative law[34] focuses on the opportunity it may provide the courts in evaluating what is fair. In *ex p. Brind*[35] the Home Secretary under the Broadcasting Act 1981 and under the powers under the BBC's licence agreements issued an order prohibiting the broadcasting of words spoken by members of certain proscribed organisations or their supporters. The applicants sought judicial review of the ban and argued that the effects of the ban might produce greater harm than any good that might result. The House of Lords considered the concept of proportionality but refused to recognise proportionality as a distinct principle from *Wednesbury* unreasonableness. The outcome of the case was that the ban was upheld. However, the reticence of the House of Lords to develop more fully a doctrine of proportionality seems well placed given the nature of French administrative law which has helped develop the concept of proportionality. Differences between the French and English legal systems as to standard of proof, method of legal reasoning and the constitutional role of the courts, require more careful consideration before the concept may be assessed as to its value in English administrative law.[36]

As matters stand it appears that under the principles of *Wednesbury* **15–80** unreasonableness the courts might consider the reasonable relationship between the objective which is sought to be achieved and the means used to achieve it. Proportionality, as a principle of European Community law is therefore part of the law of the United Kingdom. It is unlikely that this concept will be expanded into a separate heading for review. It is more likely to infiltrate the thinking and approach of judges when confronted with cases where it is felt that it is disproportionate to grant judicial review.[37]

(c) Natural Justice

Natural justice in administrative law is usually defined to include two **15–81** rules. First the requirement to hear the other side of the case or give a fair hearing otherwise known as *audi alteram partem*. Secondly to avoid bias in the hearing or on the part of the decision maker, known as *nemo judex in sua causa*. Both rules provide the basis for procedural

---

[34] See Jowell and Lester, "Beyond *Wednesbury*: Substantive Principles of Administrative Law" [1987] P.L. 368.

[35] [1991] 1 A.C. 696.

[36] See S. Boyron, "Proportionality in English Administrative Law: A Faulty Translation?" [1992] O.J.L.S. 237. Proportionality is found in many countries such as Germany, France, USA and Canada.

[37] I.D. Loveland, *Constitutional Law A Critical Introduction* Butterworths, 1996.

standards to be applied by the courts in the supervision of public bodies. Lord Diplock in the *GCHQ*[38] case referred to the rules of natural justice as procedural impropriety. In that case procedural mistakes in not giving the Unions any consultation on the decision to ban Union membership at GCHQ, were regarded as a breach of a legitimate expectation to be consulted, and was amenable to judicial review. However, considerations of national security outweighed such legitimate expectations and the courts declined relief.

15–82   The sources of such rules of procedure vary according to the type of body and the relationship between the plaintiff and the decision-maker. In applying the rules of natural justice it is first necessary to inquire does natural justice apply? The answer often depends on the nature of the body involved. Natural justice may be provided in a statutory form, or under contractual relations or through licences or even from a legitimate expectation that such rights may exist through the rather nebulous concept of private rights such as fiduciary relationships or quasi-contract. As Tucker L.J. explained[39]:

> "The requirements of natural justice must depend on the circumstances of the case, the nature of the inquiry, the rules under which the tribunal is acting, the subject-matter that is being dealt with and so forth"

Natural justice is important in disciplinary hearings, employment disputes and in the rules of various regulatory authorities for sporting bodies.

15–83   In the early development of natural justice the courts developed principles on the basis of the common law. It was relatively easy to develop such principles when there was little statutory intervention. Gap-filling of this kind, however is less common today. Statutory developments have became more comprehensive and often provide detailed rules relating to the conduct of hearings and the rights of parties.

15–84   The role of the courts has adapted to comprehensive statutory definitions setting out the principles of natural justice. This adaptation has been marked by a shift in focus from the rules of natural justice to the development by the courts of "the duty to act fairly." In *Re H(K) an infant*[40] Lord Parker considered the decision of an immigration officer meet the requirements of having to act fairly when refusing entry to K who was entitled to enter the United Kingdom provided he satisfied the immigration officer that he was under 16. The

---

[38] See note 4, above.
[39] *Russell v. Duke of Norfolk* [1949] 1 All E.R. 109.
[40] [1967] 2 Q.B. 617. Also see *Re Pergamon Press Ltd* [1971] Ch. 388.

immigration officer relied on medical evidence that K was at least 16 but Lord Parker considered that K was entitled to know what had determined the matter in the mind of the immigration officer so that K would have the opportunity to answer the evidence. In fact the court found that the immigration officer had acted fairly.

The "duty to act fairly" may mark a shift in direction in judicial review.

At times the courts have considered the duty to act fairly as a **15–85** substitute for the rules of natural justice. Lord Diplock in *GCHQ* considered that natural justice was replaced[41] by the duty to act fairly. At other times, such as in *ex p. Hosenball*[42] the courts continue to discuss the rules of natural justice.

The question arises as to whether the use of the duty to act fairly represents a substantive change in the approach by the courts to applying principles of natural justice. Fairness[43] appears a broader and more flexible concept than the rules of natural justice. It might appear to offer the courts the opportunity to look behind procedural rules and consider whether the outcome is fair. An alternative interpretation is to deny any difference between natural justice and the duty to act fairly. It is unclear whether the courts will adopt the duty to act fairly as a general expression of natural justice and the terms will be interchangeable.

The right to a hearing is one of the rules of natural justice. This may **15–86** take a number of forms: the right to put ones own side of the case, the right to be consulted, the right to make representations, or to submit reasoned arguments rebutting any allegations are all considered as elements in the duty imposed upon all decision-makers to act in good faith and listen fairly to each side of the case.

In *Ridge v. Baldwin*[44] Ridge, a Chief Constable was subject to disciplinary action by the Watch Committee after he was acquitted of conspiracy to corrupt the course of justice. Remarks made by the trial judge critical of Ridge's conduct became the ground for disciplinary action. The Watch Committee decided to dismiss Ridge acting under section 191(4) of the Municipal Corporations Act 1882 without granting him a hearing. Ridge's solicitor requested and was granted a hearing and was permitted to appear before a later meeting of the Watch Committee. Ridge exercised his right of appeal to the Home Secretary but his appeal failed. He applied to the courts arguing that he had been given no opportunity to be heard and was not allowed to

---

[41] See *Bushell v. Secretary of State for the Environment* [1981] A.C. 75 and also *Re Pergamon Press Ltd* [1971] Ch. 388.
[42] [1977] 3 All E.R. 452.
[43] See Mullan (1975) 25 U.T.L.J. 281.
[44] [1964] A.C. 40.

make representations. The House of Lords found in his favour and granted him a declaration that the decision of the Watch Committee was void and breached the rules of natural justice.

15–87 In disciplinary hearings for students, doctors, dentists and prisoners the rules of natural justice have been applied. Natural justice may arise because the plaintiff's rights have been affected or because there is some legitimate expectation that consultation might take place.[45]

Particularly problematic has been a long established reticence on the part of the courts to review the internal disciplinary rules of sporting bodies. Examples of such bodies vary from the administration of boxing clubs by the British Board of Boxing Control, to the Jockey Club, and the Football Association.[46] The courts' reluctance may stem from the rules themselves conforming to a certain minimum standard of natural justice and partly a concern that a large amount of litigation may result from active judicial intervention.

15–88 Even where it may be established that natural justice applies it does not follow that this includes the right to legal representation. The question of representations may arise because of the nature of the proceedings. For example in *ex p. Hone*[47] the House of Lords considered whether legal representation was an absolute right. Lord Goff declined to accept that such a right existed in every case. The facts of *Hone* involved disciplinary charges against prisoners heard by the Board of Prison Visitors.[48] The House of Lords accepted that there were circumstances where the need for legal representation might not be required. Matters which might be relevant in determining when to permit legal representation were outlined in *ex p. Tarrant*[49] cited in opinion by Lord Goff. The list includes the serious nature of the charge, the question of whether any points of law are raised, the ability of the prisoner to make out his or her case, procedural questions of the difficulty of the rules, the need for reasonable efficiency in decision-making and finally fairness between prisoners. However while legal representation may be open to such considerations, the courts[50] have maintained the view that cross-examination is an important element in a fair trial. Thus the plaintiff is nearly always entitled to this right.

---

[45] See *R. v. Liverpool Corporation, ex p. Liverpool Taxi Fleet Operator's Association* [1972] 2 Q.B. 299.

[46] E. Grayson, *Sport and the Law* (1988).

[47] *R. v. Board of Visitors of H.M. Prison the Maze, ex p. Hone* [1988] 1 A.C. 379.

[48] See *Fraser v. Mudge* [1975] 1 W.L.R. 1132.

[49] *R. v. Secretary of State for the Home Department, ex p. Tarrant* [1985] Q.B. 251. *R. v. Secretary of State for the Environment, ex p. Kirkstall Valley Campaign Ltd* [1996] 3 All E.R. 304.

[50] *Bushell v. Secretary of State for the Environment* [1981] A.C. 75.

The giving of reasons is also an important aspect of natural justice. **15–89**
The courts have been reluctant to provide a general duty to give
reasons, but have considered that there must be sufficient reasons for
the parties to know the nature of the case that has been considered. In
*R. v. Higher Education Funding Council, ex p. Institute of Dental
Surgery*,[51] Mr Justice Sedley considered whether the University Funding Council, as it then was should be required to give reasons when
making evaluations of the assessment of the quality of institutional
research. He concluded that there was no general duty to give
reasons but there are classes of case where a duty might arise. One
example of such a class is where the subject matter is so highly
regarded by the law, such as personal liberty that reasons might be
given as of right. Another class of case is where the decision appears
aberrant. In the interests of fairness reasons may be required so that
the recipient may know whether the aberration is in the legal sense
real. In the case in question, a clear exercise of academic judgement
does not fall within a decision which is challengeable only by
reference to the reasons given for it.

An example, where the House of Lords was prepared to require **15–90**
reasons is *Doody v. Secretary of State for the Home Department*.[52]
Prisoners convicted of murder and mandatorily sentenced to life
imprisonment were entitled to be told by the Home Secretary what
period or periods had been recommended by the judiciary to serve
their sentence. The requirement to give reasons must therefore
depend on the class of case involved and the role of the decision-
maker under review.

The second rule of natural justice is the rule against bias. Pecuniary **15–91**
interests[53] may disqualify a person from considering the case put
before them. The courts have articulated this rule[54] in the test of
whether there is "a real likelihood of bias?" Direct pecuniary advantage extends to other forms of bias. Prejudice or direct involvement
with one party as against another may amount to sufficient interest to
be regarded as a breach of natural justice. A judge must not be the
accuser or the prosecutor. In *Franklin*[55] the Minister appeared at a
public meeting after he had prepared a draft order under the New
Towns Act 1946 which designated Stevenage as a new town, and
after he had decided to hold a public inquiry. At the meeting, amid
strong objections from those who attended he said "It is no good
your jeering: it is going to be done." This raised a challenge to the

---

[51] [1994] 1 All E.R. 651.
[52] [1993] 3 All E.R. 92.
[53] *Dimes v. Grand Junction Canal* (1852) 3 H.L.Cas. 759.
[54] *Metropolitan Properties v. Lannon* [1969] 1 Q.B. 577.
[55] *Franklin v. Minister of Town and Country Planning* [1948] A.C. 87.

fairness of the Minister's judgement. The House of Lords accepted that there was no evidence that the Minister had not made a genuine consideration of the matters put before him and they upheld the legality of the Minister's approval of the order. Thus it is possible for the courts to accept that Ministers may follow a certain policy but in making their mind up as to the particular application of the policy a genuine consideration must be given to any objections.

15–92   Difficulty in establishing a satisfactory test for bias may stem from the question of the perspective to take when judging bias. The assumption behind the "real likelihood of bias" test is that the matter is to be judged by the standards of the reasonable man. However it may be necessary to consider a more subjective viewpoint. The perception of the plaintiff or others involved in the dispute may differ from the objective and balanced view of the hypothetical reasonable man. This may appear to be an equally valid perspective on the issue as the reasonable man. It may therefore appear necessary to consider both subjective and objective grounds as to whether there is bias or not.

15–93   Great care must be directed at providing in the membership of any disciplinary committee clear distinctions between the different levels of decision-making when disciplinary hearings are involved. The complainant should not be part of the adjudication committee and the appeal committee should not be tainted by the membership of the first instance committee. A separation between each function is important[56] in such cases, especially involving closely knit groups within employment or in educational establishments. Most universities have well established internal rules to adjudicate disciplinary matters with representation for students and if necessary legal representation.

(d) Excluding Judicial Review

15–94   The High Court's supervisory role in the development of judicial review is derived from its common law powers of supervising "inferior bodies." In some examples there may be reasons for attempting to exclude the courts from interfering with the exercise of power or the application of the discretion of an inferior court or public body. While there is a presumption at common law in favour of the supervisory role of the courts, there are occasions when the courts may decline jurisdiction.

Judicial self-restraint or self-limitation may mean the courts do not intervene in reviewing the legal powers or the exercise of discretion

---

[56] *Hannam v. Bradford Corporation* [1970] 1 W.L.R. 937. See *R. v. Secretary of State for Wales, ex p. Emery* [1996] 4 All E.R. 1; [1996] 3 All E.R. 304.

of a public body. The courts' recognition of ministerial accountability to Parliament, may result in not intervening in ministerial discretion. Similarly, invoking national security or the interests of the State will usually exclude the courts.

The courts may regard the existence of an appeal or other griev- **15–95** ance mechanism adequate to the needs of the plaintiff. This may arise, for example when the jurisdiction to consider grievances is given to a tribunal or a special body entrusted with particular responsibility. In *Page v. Hull University Visitor*[57] the House of Lords declined to exercise review over the jurisdiction of the Visitor in determining disputes arising under the domestic law of Hull University. The Visitor's jurisdiction included questions of fact or law and provided such powers were exercised within jurisdiction that the adjudication of disputes fell within the University rules, then the courts would refrain from intervening. If the Visitor acted outside his jurisdiction and acted in a manner incompatible with his judicial role or in breach of the rules of natural justice, then the courts might intervene. Lord Browne-Wilkinson explained[58]:

"It is not only modern universities which have visitors: there are a substantial number of other long-established educational, ecclesiastical and eleemosynary bodies which have visitors. The advantages of having an informal system which produces a speedy, cheap and final answer to internal disputes has been repeatedly emphasised in the authorities . . .."

However as an illustration of an exception to the courts not **15–96** reviewing such bodies, in *ex p. Calder*[59] the Court of Appeal explained that judicial review was available against the disciplinary Tribunal of the Inns of Court. Judicial review jurisdiction also applied to the visitors to the Inns of Court. In *Calder's* case the Visitors had misapprehended their role, and sat not as an appellate body but as a reviewing body.

The courts may decline to review on the basis that the right **15–97** involves private law rights which are not suceptible to judicial review. In *R. v. Disciplinary Committee of the Jockey Club, ex p. Aga Khan*[60] the Court of Appeal considered the role of the Jockey Club, incorporated by Royal Charter since 1970. The issue was whether a decision by the Jockey Club disqualifying a steward from chairmanship of a local panel was susceptible to review. The Court of Appeal

---

[57] [1993] 1 All E.R. 102.
[58] *ibid.* at p. 109. See *Patel v. University of Bradford Senate* [1978] 3 All E.R. 841 and *Thomas v. University of Bradford* [1987] 1 All E.R. 834 at p. 850.
[59] *R. v. Visitors to the Inns of Court, ex p. Calder; ex p. Persaud* [1993] 2 All E.R. 876; *The Independent*, January 29, 1993.
[60] [1993] 2 All E.R. 853; *The Independent*, December 22, 1992.

held that the Rules were based on contractual agreement between the parties and owed their existence to private law rights. Thus they were not susceptible to review by the courts on the basis of judicial review. Undoubtedly if the Jockey Club had not provided such rules then Parliament would have had to intervene. This did not bring the matter within the category of a public body. Classification[61] between public and private bodies provides a useful categorisation for the courts to decide whether the body is susceptible to review. However this does not always lead to consistency in approach. In *Datafin*[62] the takeover panel was susceptible to review notwithstanding that it was not created by statute or prerogative but because there was evidence that its powers would have been granted to the Department of Trade and Industry through legislation rather than through the informal rules set by the takeover panel. In this context there are similarities between the Jockey Club and the takeover panel. The former is not susceptible to review while the latter is.

15–98   Various techniques may be invoked to make judicial review either difficult or excluded altogether. The exclusion of the courts may occur when the wording of the statute contains such widely phrased powers that are couched in subjective terms that make review impossible. The form of words adopted may vary, such as "as the minister thinks fit," or "the minister's decision shall be conclusive" or the powers may be exercised "in such circumstances as the minister may believe." Faced with the prospect of subjective wording and unlimited discretion conferred on a Minister or public body, the courts require that the decision is made in good faith and that the powers are exercised fairly.[63] Even faced with very wide discretionary powers, the courts may consider there is scope to intervene. In *Tameside*,[64] the Secretary of State for Education directed a local authority under section 68 of the Education Act 1944 to implement a 1975 scheme for the introduction of comprehensive education. Following a change in the political power of the local authority from Labour to Conservative the direction under section 68 of the 1944 Act, was intended to prevent the Conservative controlled local authority from implementing a selection process and retain a number of grammar schools. The terms of section 68 of the 1944 Act were expressed in subjective terms namely " If the Secretary of State is satisfied . . ." and ". . . give such directions as appear to him to be expedient. . . ." The House of Lords concluded that there were

---

[61] Also see *R. v. Disciplinary Committee of the Jockey Club, ex p. Massingberd-Mundy, The Independent*, December 29, 1989.

[62] *R. v. Panel on Take-overs and Mergers, ex p. Datafin* [1987] Q.B. 815.

[63] See *Robinson v. Minister of Town and Country Planning* [1947] K.B. 702 and also *Liversidge v. Anderson* [1942] A.C. 206 at p. 233.

[64] *Secretary of State for Education v. Tameside M.B.C.* [1977] A.C. 1014.

matters which the Secretary of State had to address his mind to, before the powers under section 68 could be invoked. Lord Salmon interpreted the section to mean that the Secretary of State had to ask could "any reasonable local authority act in the way, in which this authority have acted or is proposing to act?" The Secretary of State had failed to ask the right questions and therefore the decision was reviewable by the courts and the House of Lords held that the Secretary of State had acted unlawfully.

A further technique of avoiding the jurisdiction of the courts is to **15–99** attempt to oust their jurisdiction. The most clear attempt to use an ouster clause may occur with the words: "shall not be called in question" in any court of law. In *Anisminic*,[65] already discussed above, the nature of the ouster clause was that under section 4(4) of the Foreign Compensation Act, the Commission's determinations "should not be questioned in any court of law whatsoever." The House of Lords considered that the ouster clause only protected "real" determinations. The error of law made by the Commission in requiring Anisminic to be "a successor in title" resulted in the Commission's determination becoming a nullity and therefore the ouster clause was inoperative. Lord Reid regarded the purported determination of the Commission as in the eyes of the law one that had no existence. The courts had power to consider whether the determination made by the Commission was correct in law, notwithstanding the presence of an "ouster clause."

The success of ouster clauses may appear to be heavily qualified by **15–100** the discretion of the courts in reviewing errors that go to the jurisdiction of the tribunal concerned. In *Johnston v. Chief Constable of the Royal Ulster Constabulary*[66] it was noted that statutory ouster clauses could not be used to oust the jurisdiction of the courts in matters of E.C. law. In *Johnston*, a reserve police officer claimed sex discrimination by the failure of the RUC to renew her contract of employment. The reason given was that the RUC had a policy that women police constables should not carry firearms and there were sufficient full-time RUC officers to carry out all the jobs designated to women officers. The Secretary of State issued a certificate "that was conclusive" that she had been dismissed in the interests of national security. The European Court of Justice ruled that the order was inconsistent with E.C. law.

An alternative formulation to ousting the jurisdiction of the courts **15–101** may be attempted. Instead of expressly stating that the courts are excluded a more subtle form of exclusion is used. Techniques of exclusion may vary but one method is to adopt the formula that a

---

[65] *Anisminic Ltd v. Foreign Compensation Commission* [1969] 2 A.C. 147.
[66] [1987] Q.B. 129.

regulation or order "shall have effect as it enacted in this Act." A clause may provide that the confirmation of an order by a Minister is "conclusive evidence" of the requirements[67] of the Act.

15–102　　A widely used procedure is to limit the opportunity which allows a decision to be challenged in the courts. This may be achieved by specifying time limits for taking legal action. One example of the use of time-limits is discussed in *Smith v. East Elloe RDC*[68] A person aggrieved with a compulsory purchase order made under the Acquisition of Land Act 1981, may apply to the High Court "within six weeks" for it to be quashed. Thereafter, the order could "not be questioned in any legal proceedings whatsoever." In the case of *Smith* the order was made five years before Smith decided to sue the Council claiming that the order was made in bad faith and therefore invalid. The House of Lords was divided on the matter, but the majority held that the time limit effectively left the courts unable to review the order. Some of the judges advanced the view that had the proceedings been taken within the time limit of six weeks and even if bad faith were proven, the courts could not intervene.

15–103　　Reconciling the principles in *Smith* and *Anisminic* has been complicated by the lack of clarity in the *Smith* decision. In *ex p. Ostler*[69] which held that the authority of *Smith* had not been diminished by *Anisminic*.[70] The *Ostler* case effectively distinguished the *Anisminic* case, the former raised the question of a time limit, while the latter was an ouster clause. The true interpretation of both the *Ostler* case and *Smith v. East Elloe* rests on what is served by the public interest. Thus time limits may retain their value as a protection in the public interest for some degree of finality to the judicial process. This leaves public bodies with some degree of certainty that projects once commenced may be safe from later review.[70a]

4.　University Procedures and Discipline

15–104　A good example of situations where alternatives to the courts may be sought and may be regarded as preferable in some circumstances, is in the area of student discipline. The foundation document in this

---

[67] See *Minister of Health v. R., ex p. Yaffe* [1931] A.C. 494.

[68] [1956] A.C. 736.

[69] *R. v. Secretary of State for the Environment, ex p. Ostler* [1976] 3 All E.R. 90.

[70] *Ex p. Ostler* has also been followed in a number of cases upholding the principles that time-limit clauses may be effective. See *R. v. Secretary of State for the Environment, ex p. Kent* (1988) 57 P. & C.R. 431.

[70a] See Lord Irvine [1996] *Public Law* 59.

area is the Report of the Task Force on Student Disciplinary Procedures chaired by Professor Graham Zellick.[71] The general principles involved in the use of university disciplinary proceedings are considered in the Zellick report. There are however cases where it might be inappropriate to adopt internal disciplinary proceedings. Rape is given as an example of a serious offence where it might be considered that only in exceptional circumstances should university disciplinary proceedings be adopted. The Zellick report offers the following advice[72]:

> The police, Crown Prosecution Service or Procurator Fiscal Service may decide not to prosecute. Then the University may decide whether to proceed internally. However, it should do so only exceptionally and only where it is clear that the police or CPS decision is based on some special factor which has nothing to do with the quality of the evidence.

The prosecution authorities have a discretion to prosecute. In considering how to exercise their discretion two questions are are normally relevant.[73] First, is there sufficient evidence to produce a "realistic prospect of a conviction". Secondly, on the basis that there is sufficient evidence, is it in the public interest that a prosecution should be taken? The Zellick report clearly sees the importance of keeping distinct the role of criminal prosecution and the use of disciplinary proceedings. Line drawing of this sort is an important judgement to be made on the merits of each case.

Concerns about the expense and complexity of judicial review are **15–105** evident in the quest for many universities and colleges to seek internal procedures that permit student appeals and staff disputes to be resolved without recourse to the courts. In many instances it may be impossible to exclude the courts altogether. Another incentive for considering the question of appeals and disputes arises out of Lord Nolan's work on setting standards in public life.

Alternatives that might be considered, include the use of arbitration **15–106** or a panel of independent persons to review cases on their merits.[74] The following sets out some of the criteria which might be relevant in considering a system of complaints and appeals.

---

[71] *Final Report of the Task Force on Student Disciplinary Procedures* chaired by Professor Graham Zellick, CVCP, December 1994.

[72] At para. 15 on p. 9 of the Zellick report.

[73] See *Annex: The Code for Crown Prosecutors* Annual Report of the Crown Prosecution Service, 1994–5, Cm. 472, HMSO, 1995.

[74] See *The Independent Review of Student Appeals and Staff Disputes* CVCP, January 27, 1997. The author is very grateful for assistance from the Registrar, the Deputy Registrar and the Academic Registrar together with many members of the Registry of the University of Warwick. Also to Professor Judith Masson for her ideas about conciliation principles. Opinions expressed here are the author's.

(a) Complaints procedures should provide a clear, simple and easy to operate system of handling complaints that is as far as possible transparent within the confines of confidentiality. It is recognised that there is a minimum cost required to ensure that procedures are fair and are not weighted against the interests of any party. It is equally important that cost should not interfere with the attainment of justice. The aims of the complaints procedure ought to ensure that the financial burdens should not involve excessive expenditure through incurring legal fees or over-rigid formality.

(b) The system of complaints must be fair and impartial and meet all the requirements of natural justice.

(c) The system of complaints must command widespread support and respect throughout the university and avoid over-legalistic or procedural technicalities.

(d) The system of complaints should be capable of drawing on past university experience and should be flexible enough to accomodate changes in the culture of a modern university.

(e) The complaints system should have specific safeguards against abuse. Time-limits may be used at each stage of the deliberations.

(f) The administrative costs of the complaints procedures should be kept under review on an annual basis.

(g) There should be a link between the knowledge about administration gained through the complaints process and improvements in university administration.

The main principles that should govern the handling of complaints are:

(a) Complaints must be handled efficiently and within a reasonable time;

(b) The parties must be given an opportunity to give their side of the case and an opportunity to respond;

(c) Conciliation must be available at every stage of the complaints process;

(d) An annual report should be laid before the university setting out the lessons to be gained from the past experience of handling complaints. Any recommendations made in the report should be taken up for consideration by the relevant university committee and the various departments concerned;

(e) The complaints procedures cannot affect any legal rights of the complainant to go to court or seek judicial review. However, it is expected that if the complaints system meets all the criteria set out above recourse to the courts will be avoided.

5. Future Directions

Sunkin[75] in his research on the case-load of applications for judicial **15–107** review has noted how judicial review has developed into an important and essential means for the citizen to seek redress as well as for the courts to oversee the work of administrative decision-making. His research findings underline the breadth, diversity and range of issues which come before the courts. Significantly, he notes that "there were very few applications brought explicitly by interest or pressure groups; only 19 applications were known to have fallen within this category and eight of these were applications instituted during 1989 by the Friends of the Earth challenging water authorities over pollution control."

The statistical evidence in Sunkin's studies also shows the use of **15–108** judicial review by local authorities against central government. A major proportion of judicial review cases come from litigation involving prisoners, housing disputes including homeless persons, planning and licensing disputes. Immigration cases are also significant over the refusal of entry or challenging asylum decisions.[76] In two areas in particular, immigration and homelessness, judicial review has grown in size. In other areas judicial review has been used sparingly. Judicial review is used to challenge local government but its use in challenging the new generation of non-departmental public bodies is uncertain at present.

Many of the conclusions to be drawn from Sunkin's study under- **15–109** line the variables present in determining whether to seek judicial review. Variables include matters such as the availability of legal aid,

---

[75] M. Sunkin, "The Judicial Review Case-load 1987–1989" [1991] P.L. 490–499. Also see M. Sunkin, "What is Happening to Applications for Judicial Review?" (1987) 50 M.L.R. 432.
[76] Sunkin [1991] P.L.490. See Sunkin, Bridges and Mészáros, *Judicial Review in Perspective* (Public Law Project, 2nd ed., June 1993).

the existence of alternative remedies, the ability of complainants to identify legal problems and lawyers to decide within the three month time limit to seek an application for judicial review. The availability of evidence, its preparation and the willingness to litigate are all hidden factors in the availability of judicial review.

15–110   An additional question in using the courts is whether the adversarial nature of the English judicial system provides an adequate basis to lay down normative principles for the solution of administrative mistakes, inefficiencies or even in providing a grievance resolution for citizens. There is also the issue of how far formal legal rules may not only constrain officials but also condition or determine their behaviour. For example, recent studies on police reactions to critical scrutiny of their behaviour show that much of police behaviour may be made to fit within legal rules because the rules are sufficiently flexible to facilitate the situations where the police need to find a rule to cover their activities. Judicial review of administrative action seldom questions how legal rules are understood or applied by administrative decision-makers. There is a danger that the apparent observance of court orientated rules may hide or obscure bad decision-making.

15–111   There have been significant developments in the availability of judicial review. There is an increasing awareness among public authorities and judges of the principles of judicial review. In *R. v. Panel on Take-overs and Mergers*[77] the Court of Appeal held that the self-regulatory City Take-overs Panel was subject to judicial review. The Take-over Panel was not set up by statute or under any of the prerogative powers. A point which found favour with the court was that if such a body had not been set up on a voluntary and informal basis then the likelihood was that Parliament would have intervened with statutory powers. This raises the possibility that a wide range of domestic bodies or tribunals might fall under the review powers of the court. For example, committal proceedings are amenable to judicial review where there is a really substantial error which might lead to an injustice.[78] In deciding whether or not to extend the scope of judicial reviews there is a lack of consistency in the approach adopted by the courts.

15–112   Traditionally in the area of central government, policy-making is often outside the remit of the courts review powers. Ministerial responsibility provides the courts with an alternative to exercising their own powers of review. For example In *Re Findlay*,[79] the courts were not prepared to review parole policy. In *Bushell v. Secretary of*

---

[77] [1987] Q.B. 815.
[78] See *Neill v. North Antrim Magistrates' Court and another* [1992] 4 All E.R. 846.
[79] [1985] A.C. 318.

State for the Environment[80] public inquiries into highway policy were excluded. In *Nottinghamshire C.C. v. Secretary of State for the Environment*[81] Lord Scarman refused to review the rate capping powers of the Secretary of State, pointing out that such powers required parliamentary approval, which provided an acceptable substitute to judicial review, as a means of scrutiny over the powers of the Secretary of State.

In contrast, the courts, when reviewing local government powers **15–113** have been more willing to extend review even to the extent of policy considerations, where there is a political dimension. Relations between central and local government have raised important issues regarding the value of judicial review as a means of requiring local government to conform to central government policies. The fact that local government is elected and represents a second tier of government decision-making adds to the complexity of the problems facing the courts. The absence of any principle of ministerial responsibility in local government appears to allow the courts greater discretion. The courts may appear as a significant regulator of local authority discretion.

The courts have developed considerable techniques to intervene **15–114** whenever necessary. The well known dicta in *Wednesbury*[82] of "unreasonableness" might permit the courts to review the policy or motive behind a decision taken by a local authority. In the case of *Roberts v. Hopwood*[83] the House of Lords held that the Council acted unlawfully when it attempted to introduce a minimum wage. The district auditor surcharged the councillors for payments which were contrary to law. The courts upheld the surcharge and rejected the policy arguments advanced by the Council.

The courts may be seen as a means of achieving enforcement **15–115** powers. For example as noted in Chapter 12, the Auditor under the Local Government Act 1988 may take action in the courts through a prohibition order if he has reason to believe that the body, or one of its officers whose accounts he is charged with auditing, is about to make or has made a decision which would involve the body incurring unlawful expenditure or engaging in an action which would be unlawful or is about to enter an item of account the entry of which is unlawful. The Auditor's power[84] to take legal proceedings also applies where the item of account is unlawful.[85]

---

[80] [1981] A.C. 75.

[81] [1986] A.C. 240.

[82] *Associated Picture Houses Ltd v. Wednesbury Corporation* [1948] 1 K.B. 223.

[83] [1925] A.C. 578; *Pickwell v. Camden L.B.C.* [1983] Q.B. 962.

[84] See *Hazell v. Hammersmith* [1990] 2 W.L.R. 17, M. Loughlin, "Innovative Financing in Local Government: The Limits of Legal Instrumentalism – Part I" [1990] P.L. 372, Part II [1991] P.L. 568.

[85] M. Radford, "Auditing for Change: Local Government and the Audit Commission" (1991) M.L.R. 912–932.

15–116   It is difficult to gauge the effect of judicial review on administration. In recent years within government departments a pamphlet prepared by the Treasury Solicitors was circulated entitled "The Judge over your Shoulder" with the clear implication that potential judicial intervention might be considered as part of the decision-making process. Judicial review features as an element in the training of civil servants. It may well be that the threat of review has a greater significance than the reality where its use is confined to specific areas of litigation and it is not uniformly applied. The effectiveness of judicial review requires further research and analysis.

15–117   Judicial review has both a limited[86] and potentially far-reaching role. An example of the far-reaching potential of judicial review may be seen in *Hazell v. Hammersmith*,[87] a case involving vast sums of money, and affecting the outcome, was the financial status of many local authorities. In *Lonrho v. Tebbit*[88] Sir Nicolas Browne-Wilkinson accepted that the Secretary of State could be sued in negligence in his exercise of statutory powers. The case arose out of the long running dispute involving Lonrho and its frustrated attempts to acquire a majority shareholding in House of Fraser shares. It is also an example of a public law issue being raised as part of a collateral matter in an ordinary action – one of the excepted categories from the principles laid down in *O'Reilly v. Mackman*.[89] The question which was answered in the negative was "whether the courts would not be going beyond their proper role if they sought to attach private liabilities to the discharge of such public functions." The case is on appeal but recognises a remarkable extension of judicial supervision over Ministers.

15–118   The courts have insisted that regulators should apply the rules of natural justice when their investigative powers are used.[90] In *R. v. D.G. of Gas Supply and another, ex p. Smith and another*.[91] Mr Justice Pill applied the rules of natural justice when OFGAS investigated the use of disconnection powers by British Gas in a case where a meter offence had been committed.

The courts have also considered a related number of diverse regulatory issues. The focus is on the role of the courts in securing different evaluations of the decision-making process.[92] The fairness of

---

[86] *Ex p. Benwell* [1985] 1 Q.B. 152. Also see Carol Harlow, "Public and Private Law: Definition without Distinction" (1980) 43 M.L.R. 241.

[87] [1990] 2 W.L.R. 17.

[88] *The Independent*, September 26, 1991. Ministers may be sued for libel or negligence.

[89] [1983] 2 A.C. 237. See *ex p. Lovelle* [1983] 1 W.L.R. 23.

[90] Co. 1398/88. See John F. McEldowney, "Theft and meter tampering and the gas and electricity utilities" [1991] 2(3) *Utilities Law Review* 121.

[91] C.O. 1398/88.

[92] P. Craig, *Administrative Law* (2nd ed., 1989), pp. 147–164.

procedures or the reasonableness of the decision are common grounds for seeking redress. For example in *Regina v. Independent T.V. Commission, ex p. TSW Broadcasting Ltd,*[93] one of the T.V. Companies, TSW applied for judicial review of the Independent T.V. Commission in seeking to grant licences for T.V. service. Although the application for judicial review was unsuccessful, the Court of Appeal considered the fair procedures applicable to the award of T.V. licences under Broadcasting Act 1990.

Another example of the diversity of judicial review is *Regina v.* **15–119** *Secretary of State of the Environment and another, ex p. British Telecommunications*[94] Mr Justice Auld dismissed British Telecom's application for judicial review of the 1989 Order setting the rateable values of BT's hereditaments. However the Divisional Court considered the policy and objects of the enabling legislation in order to consider the legality of the 1989 Telecommunications Industry (Rateable Values) Order.[95]

The system of overview of administrative[96] regulation is further complicated by the fact that the regulators are themselves subject to audit by the National Audit Office (NAO) under[97] the direction of the Comptroller and Auditor General. This is an entirely new area which poses new challenges for the scrutiny of regulatory functions by the[98] NAO. The performance of regulators in terms of value for money audit is also part of the remit of the NAO security.

In *R. v. Secretary of State for Foreign and Commonwealth Affairs, ex p.* **15–120** *World Development Movement,*[99] the World Development Movement, an international pressure group, successfully challenged the provision out of the foreign aid budget to build a dam in Malaysia. The pressure group were able to rely on the NAO report and other accounts to claim that the dam was uneconomic in terms of its building costs and its use. This is a good illustration of how judicial review may be used by a pressure group to establish its own case which relies to a large part on information available for a different purpose than judicial review namely, parliamentary accountability.

---

[93] *The Independent*, February 2, 1992. Also see *Luby v. Newcastle under Lyme Corporation* (1964) 2 Q.B. 64. Lord Justice Diplock explained "it is not for the court to substitute its own view of what is a desirable policy in relation to the subject-matter of the discretion so conferred. It is only if it is exercised in a manner which no reasonable man could consider justifiable that the court is entitled to interfere".

[94] *The Independent*, September 5, 1991.

[95] S.I. 1989 No. 2478.

[96] See J. Vickers and G. Yarrow, "Regulation of Privatised firms in Britain" in J. Richardson (ed.) *Privatisation and Deregulation in Britain and Canada* (1990) pp. 221–228.

[97] J. F. McEldowney, "The National Audit Office and Privatisation" 1991 M.L.R. 933.

[98] *ibid.*

[99] [1995] 1 W.L.R. 115.

15–121 The characteristics of administrative decision-making range from the judicial scrutiny of determinations by regulators to the widest policy questions shared between Secretary of State and regulator. Issues of policy are intertwined with statutory duties and powers. The overview of the administrative process requires careful adjustment of the wide variety of agencies and techniques available.[1]

An important conclusion is that achieving administrative justice sets complex objectives across a great variety of agencies, institutions, tribunals, ombudsmen and courts. Invariably most regulatory agencies are set up by Act of Parliament. This may combine some form of political accountability through ministerial responsibility with policy objectives. But this only highlights the diffuse nature of our regulatory agencies. Techniques of accountability may be both *external* and internal, legal and non-legal.

The fact that judicial review has come of age[2] and found in the judiciary a robust self-confidence about its future, marks out the period of development of judicial review over the past 25 years. There remains considerable uncertainty about the values that inform judicial decision making. This places the judiciary in the spotlight of speculation about the future.[3]

---

[1] *ibid.*

[2] The latest Crown Office figures show that up until December 1996 there were 3,901 applications for leave to apply for judicial review. The Author is grateful to George Mészaros for this information.

[3] See R. Mallender "Judicial Review and the Rule of Law" (1996) 112 *Law Quarterly Review* 182–4.

Chapter 16

Remedies

1. Introduction

English law with its distinctive constitutional tradition, has developed **16–01** a system of remedies rather than a system of positive rights. Rights do in fact arise in English law through the development of the common law and in express statutory enactments. Significant rights developed in the common law tradition are often expressed as negative rights to be protected in a particular way. The value of positive rights as a basis for the enforcement of remedies and in particular asserting the grounds for judicial review by the courts, has received attention in recent years in the discussion of a Bill of Rights or through consideration of the *Citizen's Charter*.[1] It is at the least arguable that rights are worthwhile only if there are adequate remedies for their enforcement. Conversely the difficulty of enforcing remedies is that unless rights are well known and enforceable the adequacy of remedies may be open to doubt.

An important factor in assessing the remedies that are available to **16–02** the citizen is the question of expense. Legal aid and its availability is often overlooked in the discussion of remedies. As Bridges and others[2] have explained:

> "Although the availability of legal aid to pursue judicial reviews did not appear to be problematic for the generality of applicants, our data point to at least two worrying aspects of the legal aid decision-making process. First, there were very wide variations between the 13 Legal Aid Area offices in their grant/refusal rates for such applications. . . . The second issue arising from our research concerns the way in which the criteria for the general

---

[1] Cmnd. 1599 (1991).
[2] Lee Bridges *et al.*, *Judicial Review In Perspective* The Public Law Project (Cavendish Press, 1995), pp. 105–6.

reasonableness test for deciding legal aid applications fail to relate to the purposes of judicial review in an important, yet numerically small, group of cases."

It is proposed by the Law Commission[3] that amendments should be made to the Civil Legal Aid (General) Regulations 1989 to enable considerations to be given to the wider public interest in having a judicial review case heard. In effect this might allow the development of an important "public interest test" to be applied to judicial review applications. This might assist in managing the work load of judicial review and testing whether the benefits of a particular application may have general application.

16–03 The focus on remedies in English administrative law underlines the procedural nature of how many rules in administrative law developed. For example the Law Commission recently has noted[4]:

"Rules about judicial review procedures and its remedies are influenced by considerations of the balance between the interests of the individuals affected by a decision and public interests."

In assessing competing interests when considering the availability of remedies, there is a balance to be struck between individual grievances and their remedy through the courts and the use of public interest litigation intended to remedy grievances in the interest of the public. Striking such a balance involves the discretion of the courts and the rules of standing. Speed, certainty and upholding the rule of law are all relevant in deciding how such a balance may be struck.

There are also questions about the effects of judicial review on the system of administration. How far can the existing law of remedies provide principles to guide administrative decision-making and at the same time provide a satisfactory remedy to an aggrieved citizen?

16–04 In the previous chapter the application for judicial review under Order 53 was discussed in terms of the distinction between public and private law. In considering remedies available to the litigant the distinction between remedies available in public law and those available in private law is also important. This chapter is focused on the role of the courts in the development of remedies. First, consideration is given to public law remedies and secondly, on remedies available in private law.

---

[3] Law Commission Report No. 226.
[4] The Law Commission Consultation Paper No. 126, *Administrative Law: Judicial Review and Statutory Appeals* (HMSO, 1993).

2. Forms of Relief

Remedies may be statutory or non-statutory. In the case of statutory **16–05** remedies, commonly this may take the form of an appeal to the High Court or the form of an application to a single judge of the High Court to quash or make an order depending on the terms of the statute. For example in the case of compulsory purchase orders there is an appeal to the High Court that the order may be *ultra vires*. Supervision by the courts[5] of the planning process is an important and significant influence over how the planning system operates. Such rights of appeal originated in the 1947 Town and Country Planning Act and have been maintained under the 1971 Town and Country planning legislation. Thus the validity of development plans and various other planning orders may be challenged in the High Court within a six week period. In such cases the rights of appeal are usually available to "any person aggrieved" by the plan or its amendment.

The provision of remedies through the system of appeals allows for **16–06** the quashing of the decision at first instance. Generally appeals may be by rehearing, or on a point of law or by case stated. There are a number of procedural routes that may be taken to achieve an appeal. Many are derived from statutory provision or from the Rules of the Supreme Court.[6] Appeals by way of rehearing under Order 55 give the appellate court powers to reverse the decision of the lower court. Appeals by way of case stated[7] are usually from the magistrates' court[8] to the High Court or specialist tribunals or the Crown Court[9] to the High Court.[*]

The Law Commission has considered the case for the rationalisation of the system of appeals. This would require careful and detailed consideration of the procedures and suitability of appeals on a uniform basis. In particular the work of the Crown Office requires study to ascertain the most effective way forward.[10]

In the case of non-statutory remedies, the development of the **16–07** various remedies available in administrative law may now be considered. In 1969 the Law Commission considered the law relating to the

---

[5] M. Grant, *Urban Planning Law* (Sweet and Maxwell, 1986), pp. 610–629.

[6] See R.S.C., Ord. 55, in particular r. 7.

[7] See R.S.C., Ord. 56.

[8] See R.S.C., Ord. 56, rr. 5 and 6; rr. 76–81 Magistrates' Court Rules 1981, an appeal jurisdiction of the magistrates' courts under section 111 of the Magistrates' Court Act 1980.

[9] See R.S.C., Ord. 56, rr. 1–4a; s.28 of the Supreme Court Act 1981.

[*] See figs. 1 and 2 on the Courts in England and Wales.

[10] See Law Commission Consultation Paper No. 126, note 2, above, pp. 95–115. A more detailed scrutiny of this important issue is provided in the Law Commission Paper.

remedies available "for the judicial control of administrative acts or omissions with a view to evolving a simpler and more effective procedure." Following their report,[11] in 1977 the Order 53 procedure was introduced and took effect[12] in 1978. The importance of this reform, and afterwards in 1981 its modification by section 31 of the Supreme Court Act 1981, was that the application for judicial review became the exclusive procedure for obtaining the prerogative writs. It was noted in the previous chapter that Order 53, r. 9(5) empowers the court to order the transfer out of Order 53 in an appropriate case. However there is no provision for transfer into judicial review. The Law Commission are considering whether there ought to be a power to transfer a case which only raises issues of public law rights into the Queen's Bench Divisional Court. Also considered is whether there should be a power to join the two forms of proceedings so that all issues could be properly determined and the remedies provided in one court.

16–08   Prerogative remedies have a long history in English law. Certiorari according[13] to Lord Atkin in *R. v. Electricity Commissioners, ex p. London Electricity Joint Committee*[14] is available "whenever any body of persons having legal authority to determine questions affecting the rights of subjects, and having the duty to act judicially, act in excess of their jurisdiction." Certiorari is available to quash a decision in breach of the rules of natural justice or which is *ultra vires*. Prohibition is available to prevent action or the continuation of action which breaches the rules of natural justice or is in excess of jurisdiction. Mandamus compels the performance of a public duty. The prerogative remedies were first known as writs brought by the King against the offending official to compel the legal exercise of their powers. The Crown could ensure the performance of public duties and responsibilities by public authorities and inferior bodies kept within their jurisdiction. In 1933 the Administration of Justice (Miscellaneous Provisions) Act 1933 introduced a system whereby an *ex parte* motion had to be made to the High Court asking first for leave to apply for the remedy. The *ex parte* nature of the application resulted in only the applicant being represented and the other parties were not represented or given notice of the case. Rules of the Supreme Court[15] laid down a time limit of six months for seeking certiorari subject to the Court's discretion. The prerogative writs were subject to further

[11] *Report on Remedies in Administrative Law* (Law Commission Paper No. 73) Cmnd. 6407.
[12] January 11, 1978 (S.I. 1977 No. 1955 later amended by S.I. 1980 No. 2000). See s.31 of the Supreme Court Act 1981.
[13] See de Smith, "The Prerogative Writs" (1951) 11 C.L.J. 40.
[14] [1924] 1 K.B. 171, 205.
[15] R.S.C. 1965, Ord. 3, r. 5.

change under section 7 of the Administration of Justice (Miscellaneous Provisions) Act 1938, which provided that the prerogative writs should be known as prerogative orders. Their development is part of the inherent supervisory jurisdiction of the High Court to review inferior bodies. Finally, there is also *habeas corpus* as a means of questioning the legality of detention exercised by administrative authorities and tribunals. The role of *habeas corpus* has diminished in use in recent years, but it still provides an important element of supervision over the detention powers of the executive.

In addition to the prerogative orders the citizen may seek a **16–09** declaration and injunction. Declarations set out the rights of the parties and could settle the legality of a particular cause or action, but it could not review cases where there was error of law on the face of the record. Injunctions provide the main remedy in private law prohibiting the commission of an unlawful act such as a breach of contract or a tort. It is a discretionary remedy and in origin owes its earlier existence to the Court of Chancery. The popularity[16] of both declaration[17] and injunction came to rival the use of the prerogative orders particulary certiorari, traditionally regarded as the main order for keeping public bodies within their legal powers. Litigants found a number of procedural drawbacks with the prerogative orders which may, in part, account for this development. First, that the prerogative orders did not provide for any interrogatories, normally available in any private action. Interrogatories included the lack of discovery of documents. Secondly, it was not possible to "mix" remedies. This means it was impossible to seek a certiorari along with damages or an injunction or declaration. Thirdly, the rules of standing varied according to the remedy sought and the circumstances differed where one remedy was available and another was unavailable.

Declaration provided the basis for establishing some of the most **16–10** important developments in administrative law and helped to shape and change the substantive law of judicial review.[18] Declaration offered the litigant certain advantages. These included the absence of requirement of leave and the absence of a short time limit for action such as the six month time limit for certiorari. Litigants' solicitors may have found the declaration a more attractive remedy because of its common use in many private law matters, whereas *certiorari* provided greater complexity concerning the nature of the decision that may be reviewed.

The Justice All Souls Review identified the problems that existed[19] **16–11** before the introduction of the Order 53 reforms as follows:

---

[16] See *Congreve v. Home Office* [1976] Q.B. 629.

[17] See de Smith, *Judicial Review of Administrative Action* (4th ed., 1980), Chap. 10.

[18] See *Ridge v. Baldwin* [1964] A.C. 40 and *Anisminic Ltd v. Foreign Compensation Commission* [1969] 2 A.C. 147.

[19] *Administrative Justice Report of the Committee of the Justice – All Souls Review of Administrative Law in the United Kingdom* (Oxford, 1988), p. 143.

"The applicant, however, could not get sight of the relevant files of the authority nor could he cross-examine its witnesses. The general rule was that discovery of documents and interrogatories were not available and that evidence was confined to affidavit material. Different time-limits applied in relation to each remedy. If the applicant applied for the wrong remedy the whole proceedings would fail and he would have to start again (if still in time). The court had no power to award the right remedy.

In addition to declaration and injunction there is also an action for damages arising out of a public authority's liability in tort or contract. Such remedies are discretionary and subject to rules relating to *locus standi*.

16–12   Order 53 introduced significant reforms to the system of remedies. In public law matters an application for judicial review for mandamus, prohibition or certiorari, or declaration or injunction may be made to the High Court. Discovery may be ordered. Damages may be joined to the application for judicial review at the discretion of the court. Before considering each of the remedies in more detail it is first necessary to explain the law of Standing.

A majority of judges in the House of Lords have held that a declaration may be given in judicial review proceedings brought by a plaintiff with sufficient *locus standi* even though the court cannot in the circumstances of the case, grant a prerogative order.[20]

3. The Law of Standing

16–13 The law relating to standing, *locus standi*, is important in both private law actions and in the application for judicial review. The rules of standing set out the entitlement of the aggrieved citizen to seek redress in the courts for the particular remedy sought. The rules of standing have a "gate keeping" function as providing the means to exclude vexatious litigants or unworthy cases. Standing may appear as a procedural requirement but procedural rules in this instance are linked to substantive issues.

16–14   The arguments in favour of liberal rules of standing appear persuasive. Access to the courts should be open to the citizen as a means of complaint. Wide rules of standing permit the courts a large discretion in remedying the abuse of public power. Traditionally this

---

[20] *EOC v. Secretary of State for Employment* [1994] 1 All E.R. 910.

fits Dicey's view that the rule of law requires that disputes as to the legality of acts of the government ought to be decided by judges independent of the executive. This implies that illegal conduct should be prevented or stopped which is a necessary corollary of enforcing the law. Flouting of the law may occur where the procedures for redress are inadequate. If illegality is not checked then the law may be diminished in status.

What is the purpose of having rules of standing? One view is that **16–15** standing rules provide administrators some protection against vexatious litigants and this protects the conduct of government business to be carried on unrestricted from outside interference. Setting limits on who may litigate prevents government from an over-cautious and over-legalistic approach to problem solving. Interest groups and organisations may be prevented from waging a political struggle by adopting legalistic techniques in order to challenge existing rules. There is a fear that politically motivated litigation may involve the courts in political struggles and the courts may regard such a use of judicial review as an unacceptable abuse of the courts proper role. However, distinguishing acceptable from unacceptable motives in seeking litigation may not be easy and the need for flexible rules of standing may permit the courts a much needed discretion.

Standing may also permit public institutions to enforce the law. In **16–16** the case of the Audit Commission, it is envisaged that under section 25(d) of the local Government Finance Act 1982 provided by section 30 and Schedule 4 of the Local Government Act 1988, that the auditor appointed in relation to the audit of accounts may apply for judicial review. This may arise where there is a failure by the body audited to act arising out of any decision where it might reasonably be considered that it would have an effect on the accounts of the local authority. Such powers to seek judicial review include the power to take action in anticipation of any breach of the law.[21] In 1990 a Code of Audit Practice was published to facilitate the use of the auditor's legal powers and provides for consultation with the body under audit.

Local authorities under section 222(1) of the Local Government Act **16–17** 1972 have in respect of civil proceedings and where "it is expedient for the promotion or protection of the interests of their inhabitants," the right to institute proceedings. The use of injunctions in the case of the Sunday Trading laws is an example of this power.[22] In many instances such rights of standing have been used to enforce the law in respect of nuisance through stop-notices. In criminal matters local

---

[21] See *R. v. Secretary of State for Education and Science, ex p. Avon C.C.* [1991] 1 Q.B. 558.
[22] *Kirklees MBC v. Wickes Building Supplies Ltd, The Times,* June 29, 1992; [1992] 3 All E.R. 717.

authorities are given wide powers to institute prosecutions for specific breaches of the criminal law that fall within their jurisdiction.

16–18   The Attorney-General occupies a unique role in terms of standing. As the guardian of the public interest, he has a special duty to enforce the law. The Attorney-General may agree to lend his name to the actions of a private citizen in seeking redress in the courts. When a private individual is unable to establish sufficient standing for the institution of a private action, which may involve public rights, the Attorney-General may permit the action to proceed as a "relator" action. Today the occasions to do this are rare as *locus standi* has been sufficiently broadened to permit the citizen direct access to the courts.[23] The use of the Attorney-General has expanded the role of injunction and declaration as providing a protection arising from private law for many public law grievances.

16–19   The case for having a flexible approach to standing appears well made. However, permissive rules of standing may give rise to serious administrative problems in the organisation of the courts. The courts may become overburdened with the flow of cases and delays in having cases heard may lead to injustice. Currently, there is a delay of at least 15 months before an application for judicial review may be heard by a single judge. There are also questions about the cost of administering the system. In many instances the opportunities for litigation may depend on the availability of legal aid which is paid out of public funds. The cost of legal aid may become a consideration in the expense of operating the system of judicial review and pressure to reduce costs may require adjustments to the present arrangements.

(a)   Standing in Private Law

16–20   The rules of standing may be considered with respect to private actions. The use of remedies available in private law for public law wrongs requires there to be standing. In general in private law the entitlement to a remedy and the right to apply for the remedy are treated together. The most common remedies are the action for an injunction or declaration. In *Boyce v. Paddington Corporation*[24] the plaintiff brought an action to restrain the council from constructing a hoarding adjacent to a building site, which would obstruct the plaintiffs right to light. The right to sue was accepted in respect of a public wrong where the plaintiff suffered damage to his private rights. This is capable of both narrow or broad interpretations depending on the nature of the issue.

---

[23] Sir Harry Woolf, *Protection of the Public – A New Challenge* (Hamlyn Lecture, 1990). See *Gouriet v. Union of Post Office Workers* [1978] A.C. 435.
[24] [1903] 1 Ch. 109.

In the case of a private action against a public authority in *Steeples* **16–21**
v. Derbyshire County Council[25] it was held that the plaintiff's action
based on private propriety rights could provide sufficient *locus standi*
when affected by the exercise of public law powers. The plaintiff was
granted sufficient standing to challenge the grant of planning permission over two leisure complexes. The plaintiff claimed that his private
rights such as enjoyment of his property as against nuisance caused
by noise, or enjoyment of the use of a lane and the risk of vandals or
litter were infringed. He also claimed that there was a breach of
natural justice in the granting of the planning permission. The
grounds for standing arising out of both private rights were equivalent to those available to him to make an application for judicial
review if necessary.

The courts may wish to restrict the availability of private law **16–22**
remedies only to those directly affected rather than to any citizen's
sense of public spirit. In cases where the private person may lack the
necessary standing, the Attorney-General[26] may be requested to give
his permission to a relator action. In *Gouriet*[27] Lord Wilberforce
explained how a relator action, which allowed the Attorney-General
at the suit of individuals to bring an action or assert a public right,
might be used in a private action for an injunction to restrain a
threatened breach of the criminal law by a trade union. However,
such a relator action was at the discretion of the Attorney-General
and the courts were unwilling to review such a discretion.

Similarly the courts are sensitive to the need to restrict the **16–23**
availability of remedies so as to exclude busybodies or unmeritorious
cases. Invariably standing may be sought by ratepayers, tax payers or
"aggrieved citizens." Applying *Boyce v. Paddington*[28] such citizens
may sue in their own name where a public right causes special
damage. In *Barrs v. Bethell*[29] some ratepayers from Camden sought an
injunction against the local authority alleging that there had been
various abuses of the discretion given to councillors and requiring
that cuts should be made in services. It was decided that they could
not sue in their own name but could seek a relator action through the
Attorney-General.

(b) Standing in Public Law

The application for judicial review under Order 53 requires consid- **16–24**
eration of the applicant's standing. It will be remembered that the
procedure under Order 53 is a two-stage process. At the first stage

---

[25] [1985] 1 W.L.R. 256.
[26] *Att.-Gen. v. Crayford Urban District Council* [1962] Ch. 575.
[27] *Gouriet v. Union of Post Office Workers* [1978] A.C. 435.
[28] [1903] 1 Ch. 109.
[29] [1982] Ch. 294.

there is a leave requirement. Obtaining leave requires that an arguable case is made out and if this is not found leave may be refused. In practice this sets a low threshold but it may be seen as a procedural sieve or hurdle to be surmounted before the full hearing of the issues is considered at the second stage.

The Law Commission has noted[30]:

"In 1980 there were 525 applications for leave to move for judicial review, in 1984 there were 918, and in 1991 there were 2089 such applications. This trend was maintained in 1992: in the first ten months there were 2034 applications for leave, compared with 1708 for the same period in 1991. In 1992 there were at any one time, on average two Divisional Courts and two (occasionally three) judges dealing with Crown office business, *i.e.:* with statutory appeals as well as judicial review."

There is no such leave requirement in ordinary civil actions and the leave requirement has been criticised as wrong in principle.[31] However the requirement of leave may be justified as an important way to exclude vexatious litigants[32] or busy bodies. The leave requirement acts as a means to filter out hopeless or unmeritorious cases. In *ex p. Doorga*[33] it was noted that leave should be granted where there are prima facie reasons for granting judicial review, but refused either when there is no prima facie case and where the case is wholly unarguable. In practical terms there are cases where the issues clearly appear arguable and those that require more detailed consideration to determine whether they are worth further consideration. In the former leave will always be granted while the latter require more careful scrutiny.

16–25 At the first stage an application for leave normally is made *ex parte* to a single judge,[34] usually on affidavits and subject to amendment at the discretion of the judge. The *ex parte* nature of the proceedings results in the absence of any representation from the defendant and this requires that the courts take time to ensure the accuracy of the affidavits. All relevant matters must be disclosed and there is a presumption of good faith on the part of the applicant. Thus if

---

[30] Law Commission Consultation Paper No. 126, *Administrative Law: Judicial Review and Statutory Appeals* (HMSO, 1993), p. 8.

[31] Justice All Souls: Administrative Justice: Some Necessary Reforms (1988) pp. 152-155 Also see A. P. Le Sueur and M. Sunkin, "Application for Judicial Review: The Requirement of Leave" [1992] P.L. 102.

[32] See Sir Harry Woolf, *Protection of the Public – A New Challenge* (1990), pp. 19–23.

[33] *R. v. Secretary of State for the Home Department, ex p. Doorga* [1990] C.O.D. 109.

[34] It is possible to make an application to the Divisional Court before a single judge sitting in open court.

material facts are suppressed or withheld the court may dismiss the application without reference to the merits of the case.[35] In cases where the judge is uncertain of whether an arguable case is made out, it is possible for the judge to invite the defendant to appear in person and make representations on the nature of the case. An application may be made under the general jurisidiction[36] of the court to set aside leave which has been granted. The criteria is whether the judge is satisfied that the case has no reasonable prospect of success.[37]

The Law Commission has considered whether the leave require- **16–26** ment is required in the application for judicial review. Various suggestions might be considered such as an oral hearing from both sides with more comprehensive grounds stated as to why leave is refused. Where both parties agree that there is a serious issue to be tried leave might be dispensed with.

Refusal to grant leave for an application for judicial review may result in a renewal application made without a hearing to the Divisional Court[38] in matters relating to criminal causes. In civil cases a refusal of leave may be renewed, but not appealed, the renewal may be made either before a single judge or to the Divisional Court. In cases where the refusal was made by the Divisional Court after an oral hearing, then the application may be renewed in the Court of Appeal. The right of access to the Court of Appeal is without leave and attempts to restrict this right in 1985 were defeated after intense debate in the House of Lords.[39] There is no jurisdiction for the House of Lords to hear an appeal against the refusal of a renewed application for leave.

The Order 53 procedure permits applying in a single application, **16–27** for the prerogative remedies of certiorari, mandamus and prohibition, together with declaration, damages or injunction. The requirement of standing is now part of the leave requirement for the application for judicial review and is contained in section 31(3) of the Supreme Court Act 1981, "that the applicant has a sufficient interest in the matter to which the application relates."

Originally the Law Commission had envisaged that the standing **16–28** rule should be part of the consideration of whether to grant any of the remedies sought. However as matters presently stand the question of standing may be raised as to the grant of leave to apply for judicial review under section 31(3) of the 1981 Act but there remains

---

[35] See *O'Reilly v. Mackman* [1983] 2 A.C. 237.
[36] R.S.C., Ord. 32, r. 6.
[37] See *R. v. Governor of Pentonville Prison, ex p. Herbage (No. 2)* [1987] Q.B. 1077; [1987] 2 W.L.R. 226.
[38] R.S.C., Ord. 53, r. 3(4)(a).
[39] H.L. Deb. Vol. 461 cols. 443–464 (March 19, 1985) and H.L. Deb. Vol. 459, cols 939–954 (February 5, 1985).

the possibility that standing may be considered also at the second stage when there is a substantive hearing of the case. This possibility emerges from consideration given to the law of standing by the House of Lords in *R. v. Inland Revenue Commissioners, ex p. National Federation of Self-Employed and Small Businesses*,[40] which may be conveniently referred to as the *Fleet Street Casuals* case. An application for judicial review was made by an association of tax payers who objected to the Inland Revenue waiving the arrears of income tax for 6,000 workers in the printing industry in Fleet Street. The association objected to preferential treatment which it viewed as condoning illegality in newspaper practices in hiring casual labour for the printing industry in Fleet Street.

16–29   This case raises important issues over the interpretation of the existing law of standing but the decision unfortunately leaves uncertainty as to the precise legal principles which may apply. The case favoured a flexible and liberal approach to standing but failed to set out clear principles, preferring to leave a large measure of judicial discretion and policy-making.

The law of standing before the introduction of Order 53 varied according to the particular remedy sought. After the *Fleet Street Casuals* case there is still some doubt as to whether there is a single test for standing under the new procedures under Order 53. Thus it may still remain relevant to consider the nature of the particular remedy that is sought. However, it is generally accepted that in the *Fleet Street Casuals* case the general preference in judicial opinion was in favour of a uniform test for standing freed from any undue procedural or technical differences depending on the remedy sought. This preference emerges from the following opinions.

16–30   Lords Diplock, Scarman and Wilberforce agreed that standing had to be considered not in isolation but as part of the legal and factual context of the application. Lord Fraser dissented on this point but it was commonly agreed that the applicants had failed to show any breach of the duty of the Inland Revenue and that the Revenue had wide managerial powers which allowed them to make special agreements of this kind. Consequently the association according to Lord Scarman had failed to show sufficient interest to justify any further proceedings.

On the general matter of standing, Lords Diplock, Scarman and Roskill agreed that the law on standing was the same for all remedies. Lords Diplock and Scarman considered that mandamus was not stricter than certiorari and that injunction and declaration are available where certiorari would lie. The consensus of opinion in favour of

---

[40] [1982] A.C. 617; [1981] 2 All E.R. 93.

liberal rules of standing raises the question about the nature of the rules that should apply to determine standing.

The judges refer to standing being determined as a question of **16-31** "mixed law and fact." Statutory interpretation and the general context of the application are relevant to determine the nature of the applicant's interest in the case. Legal principles are expected to be applied to determine standing rather than general discretion, though Lord Diplock admitted that he regarded the judges as having an unfettered discretion to decide what sufficient interest may mean in a particular case. Searching for legal principles from the *Fleet Street Casuals* case, it emerges that every person who has a good case, has standing. This might be interpreted to mean that standing no longer forms a distinct category as every good case will fulfil the standing requirement on its merits. Standing only becomes a relevant issue for those cases where there is doubt about the merits of the decision. However this view does not find universal acceptance and the matter remains uncertain.

The *Fleet Street Casuals* case, by joining the issue of the applicant's status and interest to the merits of the case, appears to move in favour of presuming that citizen's have the right of legal redress. However, this does not always guarantee that citizen's action is approved of by the courts. Consistent principles in this area of the law are difficult to formulate. Factors that contribute to uncertainty include the use of the discretion of the courts and the fact that in some cases the Crown will waive any consideration of standing when issues arise that the Crown considers require adjudication by the courts.

In *Covent Garden Community Association Ltd v. Greater London* **16-32** *Council*,[41] the Covent Garden Community Association was a company formed to protect the rights and interests of Covent Garden residents. Woolf J. accepted that this gave the Association sufficient interest and therefore *locus standi* to challenge planning permission, but certiorari was refused on the merits of the case. A similar approach was evident in *R. v. Hammersmith and Fulham Borough Council, ex p. People Before Profit*[42] where a company limited by guarantee sought leave to object to the planning policy committee of the local borough's decision to grant planning permission after a planning report following a public inquiry had favoured objectors. *Locus standi* was established on the "legitimate" bona fide reason that any person was entitled to object to a planning matter. The status of a company did not provide sufficient ground to prevent standing. However the application was refused because the case was not a reasonable one.

[41] [1981] J.P.L. 183.
[42] (1981) 80 L.G.R. 322.

16–33   A more fundamental objection to citizens challenging decisions appears from *R. v. Secretary of State for the Environment, ex p. Rose Theatre Trust Co.*[43] Schiemann J., considered the standing of a trust formed from local residents, well known and renowned archaeological experts and leading actors, who applied for judicial review to preserve the remains of a site in London which was claimed to be the remains of the Rose Theatre and of great historical interest.

The case raised the fundamental question of the role of a pressure group and the law of standing. Leave was granted to apply for judicial review but the question of standing became a central issue at the full hearing of the application. Schiemann J. considered whether standing was established. He observed, that even after leave was granted the court which hears the application ought to consider whether the applicant has sufficient interest. Whether an applicant has sufficient interest is not purely a matter for the court's discretion. Not every member of the public can complain of every breach of statutory duty. The fact that "some thousands of people join together and assert that they have an interest does not create an interest if the individuals did not have an interest." A company which has a particular power within its memorandum to pursue a particular objective does not create for a company an interest in the case. It remains to be seen whether this restrictive view of public interest litigation will be followed by the courts in future cases[44]

16–34   The *Rose Theatre* case adopts an approach which emphasises the importance of establishing a sufficient interest even if the effect is to allow unchallenged the legality of the Secretary of State's powers. In deciding that the applicants failed to meet the standing requirement the question of who might have sufficient standing was also considered and it was concluded that "no individual has the standing to move for judicial review." This reasoning appears unduly protective of the powers of the Secretary of State, but it may arise from an unwillingness by the courts to become involved as an instrument of pressure group activity. This interpretation may arise from the particular statutory arrangements under section 1 of the Ancient Monuments and Archaeological Areas Act 1979 which did not envisage any appeal or review. However there is also an apparent reluctance from the case to develop public interest litigation. Two reasons may contribute to this reluctance. First, administrative pressures on the courts to cope with the increased volume of judicial

---

[43] [1990] 1 Q.B. 504; see also *R. v. Darlington B.C., ex p. Association of Darlington Taxi Owners, The Times,* January 21, 1994 Auld J. held that an unincorporated association did not have the capacity to apply for judicial review.

[44] See *R. v. Tower Hamlets London Borough Council, ex p. Thrasyvoulou* (1990) 23 H.L.R. 30. See C. Harlow and R. Rawlings, *Pressure Through Law* (1992).

review. Secondly, a concern that policy formulation is best left to parliamentary supervision rather than judicial review.

Is the law of standing[45] in a satisfactory state? The answer depends **16–35** on the earlier discussion[46] about the precise role of the rules of standing. Galligan distinguishes standing which concerns an individual's capacity to seek judicial review where his private interest is some way affected, from the position where a person seeks to challenge simply on the basis of the public interest in not allowing official power to be used improperly.

The current state of the law allows great flexibility in the courts and even though there are doubts about public interest challenge, such challenges have been allowed by the courts albeit on a restrictive basis. It is useful, for example to contrast the use of public challenge to local authority decisions when compared to the use of public challenge to matters involving central government. The former was expressly approved by the Widdicombe report[47] as a means to control local authority activities.

The importance of pressure groups at both the national and **16–36** international level includes such well known groups as Friends of the Earth, Greenpeace and the World Development Movement. They have been active campaigners and have been active in the lobbying process for better protection of the environment and in challenging government policy. In *R v. Secretary of State for Foreign and Commonwealth Affairs, ex p. World Development Movement*[48] the World Development Movement successfully challenged the payments from the overseas aid budget to build a dam in Malaysia.

Greenpeace has been particularly active in monitoring radioactive waste, Mr Justice Otton in *R. v. Pollution Inspectorate, ex p. Greenpeace*[49] described how the organisation had nearly 5 million supporters world-wide with 400,000 supporters in the United Kingdom and about 2,500 of them lived in the Cumbria region where the British Nuclear Fuels plant was situated.

The role of pressure group or lobby group is often controversial. In **16–37** recent years their importance has become more significant in the area of legal challenge. The Law Commission, in their recent report on administrative law[50] acknowledged that interest groups may have good grounds for having standing, in the public interest, to make an

---

[45] See P. Cane, "Statutes, Standing and Representation" [1990] P.L. 303.
[46] See Craig, *Administrative Law* (Oxford, 1989), pp. 349–378; J. Vining, *Legal Identity: The Coming of Age of Public Law* (Yale University Press, 1978); D. J. Galligan, *Discretionary Powers* (Oxford, 1986), pp. 379–382.
[47] *The Conduct of Local Authority Business*, Cmd. 9797 (1986).
[48] [1995] 1 All E.R. 615.
[49] [1994] 4 All E.R. 321 at 349.
[50] Law Commission No. 226.

application for judicial review. This might apply in cases where the pressure group feels that the public are adversely affected by an administrative decision of a government agency or government itself. Clearly there is evident flexibility in permitting pressure groups a role in bringing in the public interest matters before the courts.

16–38 The Law Commission has considered the use of standing in administrative law. Suggestions for reform include expressly linking public interest to the applicant's link with the case, as a basis for standing. Also considered might be the possibility of setting up a Director of Civil Proceedings[51] as an alternative to individual public interest litigation.

16–39 Concern arises out of the *Rose Theatre* case, if interpreted to mean that the ordinary citizen in the absence of an express statutory right is debarred from challenging decisions, even where it appears that there may be a public interest served by such a challenge. This may leave a gap in the arrangements for public challenge. There may be a role for the Attorney-General in such cases. But as Galligan notes the traditional role of the Attorney-General may be inappropriate to the needs of public interest litigation and therefore some means must be found for individuals to make a challenge.[52]

> "There is, however a serious flaw in the apparent symmetry between the object of review and the standing rules; the object of review is to ensure that officials act within their powers, while the point of standing is to determine who may bring an action. These are two different issues and the determination of the legality question is not linked in any logical way to the decision about who brings the action."

An important dimension to the law of standing in the United Kingdom, is the development of European Community Law.[53] Article 173 of the EEC Treaty provides standing for individuals or one who is directly concerned by a decision, to challenge decisions made by Community institutions. National rules set down by Member States of the Community may not be used to inhibit the enforcement of a community right.

16–40 The extension of this right has been recognised in *Factortame* and in *Francovich*[54] where the European Court has created a remedy under Community law enforceable by individuals in their national courts against defaulting Member States. Thus any obstacle such as a

---

[51] Sir Harry Woolf, "A Possible Programme for Reform" [1992] P.L. 221.
[52] Galligan, *op. cit.* p. 380.
[53] See Ross, "Beyond Francovich" 1993 M.L.R. 55.
[54] *Francovich and Bonifaci v. Italy* [1992] I.R.L.R. 84; [1993] 2 C.M.L.R. 66.

restrictive view of standing may be placed to one side by the European Court in cases concerning Community law. In a particular context, for example European environmental law[55] where Community environmental rights may be wider than domestic rights, the law on *locus standi* of the United Kingdom may be more restrictive than that available under the law of the European Community. Inevitably reconciling domestic and European Community law may take some time, but in this particular example where the activities of pressure groups is high, there will be inevitable pressure to expand the rules of *locus standi* in favour of public interest litigation.

It is also inevitable that greater account will have to be taken of the provisions of European Community law in the interpretation of Order 53 and section 31 of the Supreme Court Act 1981 in cases involving rights conferred by Community law.[56]

4. Public Law Remedies

(a) Procedural Matters

In the previous chapter, attention was given to the exclusivity **16–41** principle, namely that after *O'Reilly v. Mackman* the courts have required the Order 53 procedure to be exclusively confined to public law matters. Linked to this principle is the requirement of a time limit in English law in which to make the application.[57] Before Order 53 was introduced certiorari was the only prerogative remedy which required a time limit, namely six months. While the courts had a limited discretion to review the six month period this was rarely exercised. In the case of civil proceedings for declarations and injunction time limits did not apply.

The law on time limits for all applications for judicial review is **16–42** contained in Order 53 rule 4 and also sections 31(6) and (7) of the Supreme Court Act 1981. Currently the time limit is three months though there is a complexity in reconciling[58] the terms of rule 4 with

---

[55] See Cameron, "Environmental Public Interest Litigation" in Environmental and Planning Law (Butterworths, 1991); A. Geddes, "*Locus standi* and EEC Environmental Measures" (1992) Vol. 4, No. 1 *Journal of Environmental Law*, pp. 29–39.

[56] See *EOC v. Secretary of State for Employment* [1994] 1 All E.R. 910. The Equal Opportunities Commission had "sufficient interest" to take judicial review proceedings arising out of the case of part-time workers and their legal right under E.C. law.

[57] In Northern Ireland R.S.C. (N.I.) Ord. 53, r. 4 states that where leave to apply has not been sought within three months, the court may not grant leave or relief unless it is satisfied that this would not cause hardship or unfairly prejudice the rights of any person. See Hadfield, (1991) 42 N.I.L.Q. 332 and (1988) 7 C.J.Q. 189.

[58] *R. v. Dairy Produce Tribunal, ex p. Caswell* [1990] 2 A.C. 738.

section 31(6). Rule 4 applies only to applications for leave to apply for judicial review whereas section 31(6) applies to both applications for leave and to applications for substantive relief. This adds to the complexity of the issue when it is also considered that rule 4 is concerned with good reasons for extending the three month time limit whereas section 31(6) is confined to the effects of dealing with grounds for refusing relief either at the substantive stage or at the application stage.

The present law is unsatisfactory for two reasons. First, the law attempts to enforce a rigid rule of three months but if the application is not made promptly, even if made within the three months the application may be refused.[59] Secondly, the date from which the time limit may run is unclear. The circumstances where the court might exercise its discretion is unspecified.

16–43 The crucial issue is "promptness." In *ex p. Caswell*[60] the House of Lords affirmed the view that the three month time limit was not an entitlement. In cases where there is undue delay even within the three month period reasons must be given. Even where an extension of time is given at the first stage, that is, the application for leave, this may be considered at the full hearing after representations from both parties are heard. In *ex p. Caswell*[61] the applicants conceded that there had been undue delay. The House of Lords then had to consider whether the granting of relief would be likely to cause hardship or prejudice or would be detrimental to good administration. The answer to this question depended on the effect of whether after the lapse of time, the Dairy Produce Quota tribunal's decision had been made in 1985, it would be detrimental to good administration to grant relief. The House of Lords concluded that it would and dismissed the appeal.

16–44 Time limits under Order 53 and section 31 of the Supreme Court Act 1981, appear too short and the ground of the courts discretion too vague. The Law Commission[62] is considering whether clearer criteria might be adopted in formulating the law. The question of whether it is desirable to retain a three month time limit or in general whether time limits are needed is also under consideration.[63]

---

[59] See *R. v. Independent Television Commission, ex p. TV NI Ltd, The Times,* December 30, 1991.

[60] *R. v. Dairy Produce Tribunal, ex p. Caswell* [1989] 1 W.L.R. 1089.

[61] *ibid.* The applicants applied in 1987 two years after the tribunal decision.

[62] Law Commission Consultation Paper No. 126.

[63] On European Community law, see Case 209/83, *Ferriera Valsabbia* Case [1984] E.C.R. 3089.

(b) The Discretionary Nature of Remedies

All the remedies available under the application for judicial review **16–45** fall under the discretionary jurisdiction of the Divisional Court. There are no simple criteria on which this discretion is based. Generally the court will consider the availability of any alternative remedies such as appeals or the existence of a specialised tribunal before granting judicial review. As a general rule it is expected that the applicant will have attempted to make use of any available alternative remedies before coming to the court. In *ex p. Calveley*,[64] Sir John Donaldson suggested that the courts would only rarely exercise their jurisdiction to grant judicial review in cases such as this one when there was available an alternative appeal remedy. Only in "exceptional circumstances" would review be accepted in preference to appeals available to the applicant. In *ex p. Calveley*, in the case of police officers subject to disciplinary proceedings, certiorari was granted notwithstanding the existence of rights of appeal under the Police (Appeal) Rules[65] 1977. This was a case where departure from the disciplinary procedures was such that on the merits the courts would intervene by way of judicial review. But this exercise of judicial discretion is not always a predictable one. For example in *Puhlhoffer*[66] a local authority's decision that a person is not entitled to accommodation under the Housing (Homeless Persons) Act 1977 was not open to appeal. The House of Lords was clear that judicial review should be confined to only exceptional cases. In *ex p. Swati*[67] a person refused leave to enter the United Kingdom was refused leave to apply for judicial review. The applicant would have to rely on his appeal rights only. However the circumstances which determined whether judicial review might be available appeared unquantifiable and appeared to "defy definition" in the case.

Considerations which may guide the exercise of the courts' discre- **16–46** tion are very wide. It may be that there is concern for the work-load generated by judicial review in certain areas such as immigration cases or homeless persons. The courts preference for seeking alternative remedies is in part recognition of the degree of specialist advice available to appeal tribunals. It is also recognition of the nature of many of the disputes which cover multi-disciplinary issues that the courts may wish to confine their jurisdiction and not usurp the jurisdiction of appellate bodies.[68]

---

[64] R. v. Chief Constable of the Merseyside Police, ex p. Calveley [1986] Q.B. 424.
[65] S.I. 1977 No. 759.
[66] Puhlhoffer v. Hillingdon London Borough Council [1986] A.C. 484; [1986] 1 All E.R. 467.
[67] R. v. Secretary of State for the Home Department, ex p. Swati [1986] 1 W.L.R. 477.
[68] See R. v. Epping and Harlow General Commissioners, ex p. Goldstraw [1983] 3 All E.R. 257.

16–47   Another approach is to consider the balance of convenience. This is
where the courts regard proceedings taken by judicial review as an
acceptable means to resolve the dispute because "in all the circumstances" it is the most cost-effective. Lord Justice Glidewell took this
view in a number of cases[69] following from the *Royco Homes case*[70] in
1974. Lord Widgery explained that while a planning condition could
be challenged on the basis of the statutory appeal structure, certiorari
might lie where it was more efficient and effectual.

16–48   In exercising their discretion,[71] the courts may also consider matters
of delay and the *locus standi* of the applicants. Both these matters may
be considered at the full hearing stage as well as at the initial
application for leave procedure. Indeed the entire boundary between
public law and private law rights, invites consideration of a whole
range of questions which also admit the discretion of the court. This
may include the subject matter of the dispute, the nature of the
remedy sought and the implications for administrative decision
making. In this area of judicial discretion the courts find it difficult to
explain why discretion is exercised in one case and not another.
Consistency of approach should be important as well as the merits of
the specific case, but courts are not always predictable.

16–49   There is an increasing judicial awareness of the cost benefit analysis
of judicial review. This may mean considering the question of
whether good administration is encouraged by the outcome of the
decision. In *ex p. Argyll Group*[72] the courts reluctance to quash the
decision of the Chairman of the Monopolies and Mergers Commission even though it was found to be illegal, was based on the needs of
public administration. In assessing whether to exercise the courts
discretion it was noted that third parties had already acted on the
decision and that the Commission would have made the same
decision as its chairman. Lord Donaldson explained[73] how the courts'
discretion may be influenced by the following factors, though not
intended to be a complete catalogue they emphasise the importance
of substance over form. These factors include: a proper consideration
of the public interest; of the legitimate expectations of the individual
citizens; of the financial interest involved and finally decisiveness and
finality in decision-making. The speed of decision-making is also
relevant. Decisiveness and finality are important virtues in the
process of good administrative decisions.

16–50   A final issue for consideration is the grant of legal aid. Section 18(4)
of the Legal Aid Act 1988 provides that the respondent must establish

---

[69] See *ex p. Waldron* [1986] Q.B. 824 and *ex p. Cowan* [1984] 1 All E.R. 58.
[70] *R. v. Hillingdon London Borough Council, ex p. Royco Homes Ltd* [1974] 1 Q.B. 720.
[71] See Bingham, "Should Public Law Remedies be Discretionary?" [1991] P.L. 64.
[72] *R. v. Monopolies and Mergers Commission, ex p. Argyll Group plc* [1986] 1 W.L.R. 763;
[1986] 2 All E.R. 257.
[73] [1986] 2 All E.R. 257 at p. 266d–h.

"severe financial hardship" unless an order is made. In matters involving judicial review there is consideration by both the courts when granting leave and the Legal Aid Board when considering legal aid, of the "appropriateness" of bringing the application.[74] Two questions arise, first whether public bodies when they are involved in litigation should be able to receive legal aid, when presently they may not because they do not fall under the heading of "severe financial hardship?" Secondly, whether the merits test as regards granting by the courts should be the same as the Legal Aid Board when granting legal aid? It is quite possible for the two different bodies to come to different conclusions when purporting to follow the same test. The Law Commission is presently considering both questions.

(c) Void and Voidable Administrative Action

A related and important question when considering remedies and the **16–51** grounds for challenge either through judicial review or appeal is the question of the effect of an *ultra vires* decision. This question arises in connection with the effects of two types of error of law. One is jurisdictional and the other is non-jurisdictional. The former may render the decision void and having no legal effect. When the court decides to quash the decision it does so in a retrospective way. The latter may have had some legal effect but because of some mistake in the law, it does not remain valid once the court decides to exercise its discretion and quash the decision. This is described as a voidable as opposed to a void decision. The court when quashing a voidable decision does so prospectively, because the decision is valid until the time comes for the court to quash the decision.

While there remains some doubt as to whether there is a distinction **16–52** between jurisdisctional errors which render a decision void and not voidable, the concept of void and voidable is an additional element in judicial discretion. While it is not always easy to know whether an act is void or voidable, the categorisation may also have a direct result on a number of related issues. For example, the exercise of a right of appeal will not always cure the defect of a void act and the courts may wish not to consider an appeal against a void decision.[75] A void act may be ignored by the person affected whereas a voidable act may not. If an act is potentially voidable, the courts may still regard the act as valid until it is declared invalid.

There are a variety of views[76] as to the importance of the void and **16–53** voidable distinction and there is a lack of consistency in the use of

---

[74] See *R. v. Legal Aid Board, ex p. Hughes* (1992) 142 New L.J. 1304.
[75] *Metropolitan Properties Co. v. Lannon* [1969] 1 Q.B. 577.
[76] Wade (1967) 83 L.Q.R. 499; Taggart, "Rival Theories of Invalidity in Administrative Law" in Taggart (ed.) *Judicial Review of Administrative Action in the 1980s* (1986); P. Craig, *Administrative Law* (2nd ed., 1989), pp. 323-328.

language when describing how void and voidable may apply to a decision. Judicial application of the distinction may not always be consistently applied. In *Anisminic*[77] the House of Lords accepted that an *ultra vires* act was void and a breach of natural justice was similarly void.[78]

For the reasons outlined above, the void and voidable distinction appears important when considering the legal position of the parties and may affect the outcome of the decision.[79]

(d)　Certiorari, Prohibition and Mandamus

16–54 The main public law remedies may be briefly mentioned. Certiorari[80] has the effect of quashing a decision which may be done by an excess or abuse of power, whereas prohibition is intended to restrain a body from acting unlawfully in the future or preventing an excess or abuse of power. Certiorari and prohibition are similar and both are available as remedies in public law. The criteria for deciding which acts and decisions are subject to certiorari and prohibition was expressed by Lord Atkin in the *Electricity Commissioners* case[81]:

" . . . Wherever any body of persons having legal authority to determine questions affecting the rights of subjects, and having the duty to act judicially, act in excess of their legal authority they are subject to the controlling jurisdiction of the King's Bench Division."

The interpretation of the duty to act judicially has been widened considerably since the case was decided. Since *Ridge v. Baldwin*[82] the courts have interpreted the phrase to include those bodies that have the power to decide and determine matters which affect the citizen. This means that certiorari generally may be available to review all administrative acts. This includes such variety of examples as a valuation officer,[83] the grant of planning permission,[84] the Criminal

---

[77] *Anisminic Ltd v. Foreign Compensation Commission* [1969] 2 A.C. 147.
[78] Also see *Ridge v. Baldwin* [1964] A.C. 40 for differences in judicial opinion.
[79] See, *e.g. Hazell v. Hammersmith and Fulham London Borough Council* [1990] 2 Q.B. 722; [1992] 2 A.C. 1.
[80] Craig, *op. cit.* (2nd ed., 1989), p. 381. Craig explains how the origins of certiorari may be traced back to the Royal demand for information. See Rubinstein, *Jurisdiction and Illegality* (1965).
[81] *R. v. Electricity Commissioners, ex p. London Electricity Joint Committee Co. (1920) Ltd* [1924] 1 K.B. 171.
[82] [1964] A.C. 40.
[83] *R. v. Paddington Valuation Officer, ex p. Peachey Property Corporation Ltd* [1966] 1 Q.B. 380.
[84] *R. v. Hillingdon London Borough Council, ex p. Royco Homes Ltd* [1974] Q.B. 720.

Injuries Compensation Board set up under the prerogative,[85] and mandatory grants to students.[86] However certiorari was not available to quash a provisional order made by the Secretary of State for the compulsory purchase of land by the Hastings Board of Health.[87]

The formulation of acting judicially commonly used today is that **16–55** favoured by Lord Diplock in *O'Reilly v. Mackman*[88] that it is enough to show that the body or person has legal authority to determine questions affecting the common law or statutory rights of other persons. Historically it was assumed that certiorari would not be available for contractual matters[89] or purely domestic disputes.

Certiorari is available to quash decisions that are *ultra vires*, in **16–56** breach of natural justice or where traditionally there has been an error of law on the face of the record. This includes most forms of *ultra vires* discussed in Chapter 15. As Lord Slynn suggested in *Page v. Hull University Visitor*,[90] the scope of certiorari may be interpreted widely:

"If it is accepted, as I believe it should be accepted, that certiorari goes not only for such an excess or abuse of power but also for a breach of the rules of natural justice."

Prohibition shares a similar scope to certiorari but it lies to restrain such action[91] rather than quash it. It is important to emphasise that both certiorari and prohibition are discretionary remedies. While the law on *locus standi* has been discussed above with respect to the changes introduced by Order 53 it is worthwhile mentioning the law before Order 53 was introduced, as there is still the possibility that the courts may wish to consider the old law. *Locus standi* for certiorari distinguished between "persons aggrieved" and strangers. This distinction was left to the courts to define. A person aggrieved was explained by Lord Denning in *ex p. Liverpool Taxi*[92] as including any "person whose interests may be prejudicially affected." Strangers included busy bodies, interfering in matters which did not concern them.

Mandamus[93] is a court order which commands the performance of **16–57** a public duty. Public duty has been described as[94] a concept which is

---

[85] R. v. *Criminal Injuries Compensation Board, ex p. Lain* [1967] 2 Q.B. 864.

[86] *ex p. Nilish Shah* [1983] 2 A.C. 309.

[87] R. v. *Hastings Board of Health* (1865) 6 B. & S. 401.

[88] [1983] 2 A.C. 237.

[89] R. v. *National Joint Council for the Craft of Dental Technicians, ex p. Neate* [1953] 1 Q.B. 704.

[90] [1993] 1 All E.R. 97, at p. 114b.

[91] See *Dimes v. Grand Junction Canal Co.* (1852) 3 H.L. Cas. 759; 10 E.R. 301.

[92] R. v. *Liverpool Corporation, ex p. Liverpool Taxi Fleet Operators' Association* [1972] 2 Q.B. 299.

[93] See A. J. Harding, *Public Duties and Public Law* (Oxford, 1989).

[94] *ibid*. p. 1.

"important but elusive." The courts have drawn attention to the distinction between a duty or a power. The former is enforced by mandamus while the latter is not. The question of what constitutes a duty is inconclusively defined by the courts. Statutory interpretation may depend on the purpose for which duties are to be exercised. Invariably the public character of the duty is crucial in the courts discretion to make mandamus available. The source of a public duty may arise from the common law, prerogative or statute. It may also arise in respect of licences or contracts or from legal powers through charters or customs. The bodies amenable to mandamus include, local authorities,[95] the Metropolitan Police Commissioner[96] and ministers.[97]

16–58   Mandamus may lie where there is a breach of procedural jurisdiction or even where there is a discretion that involves public duties. In *Padfield*[98] the Minister was said by Lord Reid "to have a duty to act" even though such a duty was expressed in discretionary language "if the minister in any case so directs." If such a power is used for an improper purpose or irrelevant considerations are taken into account, the courts may decide to grant mandamus to correct the misuse of power. Mandamus is a powerful remedy because it commands the performance of set obligations or responsibilities. Failure to obey the terms of mandamus may result in proceedings for contempt of court.

16–59   Mandamus usually required a strict rule of standing before Order 53 was introduced. In *R. v. Lewisham Union*[99] standing required there to be a "legal specific right." The case raised particular facts relating to the attempt to compel the guardians of the poor to undertake compulsory vaccination to prevent outbreaks of smallpox. A less strict view was favoured in *ex p. Blackburn*[1] which favoured a public interest aspect to the enforcement of public rights created by the criminal law. This liberal trend has been further advanced by the House of Lords in the *Fleet Street Casuals* case[2] discussed above.

16–60   Mandamus may not lie against[3] the Crown. This is a rule that has also been interpreted to include servants of the Crown.[4] The rationale behind this rule owes its origins historically to the role of the courts in not commanding the Sovereign to command her own performance of any duty. Crown immunity, however does not appear to prevent mandamus taken against the activities of the Crown, for example the

---

[95] See *R. v. Camden London Borough Council, ex p. Gillan* (1988) 21 H.L.R. 114.
[96] *R. v. Metropolitan Police Commissioner, ex p. Blackburn* [1968] 2 Q.B. 118.
[97] *Padfield v. Minister of Agriculture* [1968] A.C. 997.
[98] *ibid.*
[99] [1897] 1 Q.B. 498.
[1] [1968] 2 Q.B. 118.
[2] [1982] A.C. 617.
[3] See *R. v. Customs and excise Commissioners, ex p. Cook* [1970] 1 W.L.R. 450.
[4] See Harding, *op. cit.* pp. 85–95; *R. v. Treasury Lords Commissioners* (1872) L.R. 7 Q.B. 387.

Income Tax Commissioners in their function of revenue collection. The development of the declaration has limited the restrictions such a rule might appear to hold. Mandamus will also be refused where there are circumstances that suggest that all steps that could be taken have been taken and thus the courts intervention would be inappropriate.

(e) Habeas Corpus

Habeas corpus is an ancient remedy[5] which allows a person detained **16–61** to challenge the legality of detention. The law relating to habeas corpus has been kept outside the reforms introduced under Order 53 and consequently the remedy has been given less attention in recent years compared to its historical importance. Application is made to a Divisional Court of the Queen's Bench Division. The remedy is technical and narrow in scope as invariably other remedies have been developed to allow the detention of the applicant to be tested, such as the right of appeal or appearance before a magistrate. However there are circumstances where habeas corpus is the only remedy available to an applicant. In *X v. United Kingdom*[6] the European Court of Human Rights expressed dissatisfaction about the procedures open to mental health patients to challenge their detention. The European Convention was not satisfied by the limited scope of the habeas corpus application. Habeas corpus also appears to be useful in immigration cases. In *Khawaja*[7] the House of Lords considered that common principles might be applied to habeas corpus and judicial review but failed to clarify the scope of the courts inquiry.

The Law Commission has considered the restrictive nature of **16–62** habeas corpus applications which are confined to the facts on which the detention is based. As Lord Donaldson noted in *Muboyai*,[8] the application for judicial review afforded a wider opportunity for challenging and administrative decision and this favoured using judicial review as opposed to habeas corpus. Perhaps the time has come to rationalise the relationship and set out the exact role that habeas corpus is expected to fulfill when reviewing powers of detention. One suggestion is to allow interim relief at the leave stage to allow the legality of detention to be questioned.

---

[5] See Sharpe, *The Law of Habeas Corpus* (2nd ed., 1990).

[6] (1981) 4 E.H.R.R. 188.

[7] *R. v. Secretary of State for the Home Department, ex p. Khawaja* [1984] A.C. 74.

[8] *R. v. Secretary of State for the Home Department, ex p. Muboyai* [1992] Q.B. 244. A similar approach is evident in: *R. v. Oldham Justices, ex p. Crawley* [1996] 1 All E.R. 464.

5. Private Law Remedies

16–63 Remedies such as declaration, injunction and damages are available in ordinary civil proceedings. Order 53 provides that such remedies are added to the prerogative remedies of certiorari, prohibition and mandamus, and are available under the application for judicial review procedures in public law matters. In effect this gave the potential for an overlapping jurisdiction between the power to seek declaration and injunction in civil proceedings and under the application for judicial review. The limitations set by *O'Reilly v. Mackman* have been considered in Chapter 15. It is important to consider in this section not only the remedies of declaration and injunction but also the special position of the Crown and the availability of tort and restitution remedies against public authorities.

(a) Declaration and Injunction

16–64 A declaration or as it is sometimes referred to a declaratory judgment is an order of the court. The procedure by way of originating summons is under R.S.C. 1965 Order 5, r. 2, or under Order 15, r. 16 and it is also available under Order 53 on the application for judicial review for public law matters as defined in *O'Reilly v. Mackman*. The preferred means of obtaining a declaration raising a public law matter is under the Order 53 procedure. In the case of an originating summons there is no power to grant an interim declaration of rights but some broadening of this rule has occurred under Order 5, r. 4. Such a limitation does not arise under the Order 53 procedure.

16–65 Declaration is a wide ranging remedy. In *Dyson*[9] the applicant challenged the Inland Revenue's decision to require him under penalty to supply them with information. There was no cause of action and little authority for the use of the procedure under the then existing procedure, Order 25, r. 5 which has since been amended by Order 15, r. 16. The aim of providing a speedy and simple procedure in part underlines the reasons behind the *Dyson* decision. As a declaration is available against the Crown, this underlines the usefulness of this remedy.

16–66 The courts have not provided a complete list of situations or categories where a declaration may lie. In declaring rights there is the added implication that illegality will be established. This is useful in setting out the scope of a public bodies duties, liabilities and lawfulness of decisions. In *Gillick*[10] advice on contraception for girls

---

[9] *Dyson v. Att.-Gen.* [1911] 1 K.B. 410.
[10] *Gillick v. West Norfolk and Wisbech Area Health Authority* [1986] A.C. 112.

under 16 was considered as to its legality and the House of Lords upheld the advice as legal. Thus declaration may be useful for settling many doubtful matters relating to the exercise of legal powers. Planning permission, the work of the Boundary Commission, reports of public inquiries and the like are typical examples of the versatility of a declaration.

Despite the potential width and scope of a declaration there are **16–67** limitations to its availability. In general terms a declaration will not be granted where the court considers that the statute retains an exclusive jurisdiction to the tribunal or other body provided in the statute. In *Barraclough v. Brown*[11] the House of Lords held that the plaintiff's claim for declaration was one which arose under a statute and the statute had provided a procedure for grievances. The courts were confined by the procedures laid down in the statute and therefore declaration was not available. In contrast, in *Pyx Granite*,[12] the House of Lords distinguished *Barraclough*. A declaration might be available notwithstanding any statutory rights where there remained common law rights. These may be enforced through a declaration.

A declaration will not be granted by the courts if its effect is to **16–68** usurp the authority of the body under review. A declaration is not based on a speculative or hypothetical basis, it only issues as a ground of relief where relief is real[13] and is needed. Unlike some countries where a written constitution permits a form of judicial preview, English law has historically been reluctant to take abstract or moot points as part of the remit of the courts. A declaration is available to the Equal Opportunities Commission for the purposes of determining whether the relevant provisions of the Employment Protection (Consolidation) Act 1978 are compatible with Community law.[14]

The question of whether a declaration is available for an error of **16–69** law is problematic. Such an error is usually regarded as resulting in a voidable and not a void decision. This means that the decision remains valid until action is taken to control or remedy the error. As a declaration merely declares what the rights of the parties may be and does not alter their position, this suggests[15] that declaration would not be a useful means to control such an error of law. However this limitation may be less[16] important with the availability of certiorari under the Order 53 procedure.

---

[11] [1897] A.C. 614.
[12] *Pyx Granite Ltd v. Ministry of Housing and Local Government and Another* [1960] A.C. 260.
[13] See *Blackburn v. Att.-Gen.* [1971] 1 W.L.R. 1037; [1971] 2 All E.R. 1380.
[14] *EOC v. Secretary of State for Employment* [1994] 1 All E.R. 910 at p. 926.
[15] See *Punton v. Ministry of Pensions and National Insurance (No. 2)* [1964] 1 W.L.R. 226.
[16] Craig, *Administrative Law* (2nd ed., 1989), p. 397.

16–70   Injunctions are of equitable origin and may restrain a person or body from illegal action. The equitable nature of the remedy makes the injunction a discretionary remedy in common with the prerogative remedies. Thus an injunction may be refused if there are alternative remedies available or where the court regards the granting of the injunction[17] unnecessary. Injunctions may be prohibitory, or mandatory and may be expressed in terms of positive obligations or in the form of negative prohibition. Injunctions may be interim or interlocutory, that is, pending the outcome of the full hearing of an action, an injunction may be granted to preserve existing arrangements. This form of interim relief is important as for example under Order 53 the applicant seeks an order of mandamus or declaration the main form of relief is through an interim injunction. When granted in the form of an interim injunction, the plaintiff is normally required to give an undertaking to indemnify the defendant for any loss he suffers as a result of the interim order. This practice does not always apply in the case of the Crown seeking an injunction.

16–71   The test applicable when interim relief is sought is based on principles developed in the decision of the House of Lords in *American Cyanamid Co. v. Ethicon Ltd.*[18] The test is to decide if the applicant has a good arguable case and, if he has to take into account the balance of convenience when considering the duties owed by the public body and the interests of the public. An addition to this criteria[19] is the inclusion of a *prima facie* case needed to justify the granting of relief when the court is exercising its discretion.

A good arguable case means one with a real chance of success, not necessarily a 51 per cent chance. The balance of convenience may take into account the interest of the public.

Injunctions may be perpetual and granted at the end of the action. Injunctions are available to one who has an arguable case, that is not frivolous or vexatious and that there is at least an arguable case which is likely to succeed.[20] When considering such matters as the likelihood of success the court may take account of the balance of convenience and the interests of the public.

16–72   The availability of injunctions may be by judicial review under Order 53 or in the following circumstances where an injunction may lie at the suit of a private individual. In a private action injunctions are available on the same basis of *locus standi* as a declaration where, some private right appears to be affected or where special damage

---

[17] See *Glynn v. Keele University* [1971] 2 All E.R. 89; *Bradbury v. Enfield London Borough* [1967] 3 All E.R. 434.

[18] [1975] A.C. 396.

[19] *Factortame (No. 2)* [1991] 1 A.C. 603; Case C–213/89, [1990] E.C.R. I–2433; [1990] 3 C.M.L.R. 1.

[20] Lord Diplock in *American Cyanamid v. Ethicon Ltd* [1975] 1 All E.R. 504.

peculiar to the private individual arises from an interference with a public right.

Injunctions are also available at the suit of the Attorney-General on behalf of the Crown. This may arise where the protection of public rights or the interests of the public require the Attorney-General to take action to restrain breaches of the criminal law. Where a public body may be acting *ultra vires* the Attorney-General may intervene to prevent a threatened or immediate breach of the law.

The Attorney-General may take a relator action. Such action may **16–73** arise where the Attorney-General allows at the suit of a private individual, his name to be joined to the action on the basis that he believes such action should be taken. The reponsibility of the relator is to ensure that when the Attorney-General is satisified[21] that such an action should be taken. In *Gouriet v. Union of Post Office Workers*[22] the House of Lords considered the refusal of the Attorney-General to agree to a relator action to enforce an injunction restraining a threatened breach of the criminal law. It is considered unlikely that the courts may wish to review the discretion of the Attorney-General in such matters.

The value of the relator action is less certain, since the general liberalisation of the rules of standing under Order 53, as the necessary standing may be given to the private individual in cases of judicial review. In the *Rose Theatre*[23] case the Attorney-General did not agree to a relator action and so recourse to judicial review was necessary.

(b) The Crown

One of the often discussed limitations on the use of the injunction is **16–74** that it is not traditionally available against the Crown. This rule has a long historical development. Section 21(1) of the Crown Proceedings Act 1947 expressly provides that the court shall not grant an injunction against the Crown. It had been generally accepted that this prohibition also applied to servants of the Crown. The reforms introduced under section 31(2) and Order 53, r. 3(10) had possibly given the courts powers to grant injunctions, including interim injunctions, against Officers of the Crown and against government Ministers acting under statutory powers in their own names. However in protracted litigation concerning the question of the award of interim relief against the Crown the House of Lords[24]

---

[21] See *Att.-Gen. (ex rel. McWhirter) v. IBA* [1973] Q.B. 629.
[22] [1978] A.C. 435.
[23] [1990] 1 Q.B. 504.
[24] *R. v. Secretray of State for Transport, ex p. Factortame Ltd (No. 1)* [1990] 2 A.C. 85.

disagreed with this possibility and held that the court had no power to grant relief against a Minister of the Crown. Subsequently the question of interim relief, when the applicant is seeking to enforce rights recognised under European Community law arose in a decision of the European Court of Justice.[25] The Law Commission noted[26]:

> "The position now therefore is that there is a two tier system regarding interim injunctive relief against the Crown and Crown officers. Where Community rights are involved (even only putative rights), the courts have jurisdiction to grant an interim injunction against the Crown and also to disapply an Act of Parliament. But in domestic law *Factortame (No. 1)* rules out any such interim injunction."

The House of Lords in *Re M.* have, since *Factortame*, considered the availability of injunctions against the Crown. Injunctions are generally available against departments or Ministers. Although it was conceded that the use of injunctions against government departments would be rare.[27]

16–75 While the current position is anomalous[28] it is clearly open to the House of Lords or preferably Parliament, to reconsider the law relating to the Crown. The Law Commission favours reform which would eliminate the anomalies between the Crown and other public bodies.

Ministers of the Crown may be subject to the power of the courts to grant a stay of proceedings against a decision made by the Minister. One view is that such a procedure avoids the difficulty of the interim injunction being available against a Minister. In *Avon*[29] it was accepted that such a stay could be granted against a Minister, and this extended to an officer making a decision under the Minister. The Privy Council[30] have since doubted this decision, but it remains a possibility open to the courts.

(c) Discovery, Damages and Restitution

16–76 Discovery[31] of documents forms an important pre-trial preliminary in ordinary civil proceedings. The availability of discovery in public law matters under Order 53 allows for the cross-examination and

---

[25] *R. v. Secretary of State for Transport, ex p. Factortame Ltd (No. 2)* [1991] 1 A.C. 603.
[26] Law Commission Consultation Paper No. 126, para 6.6, p. 39.
[27] See *Re M.* [1993] 3 All E.R. 537.
[28] See Lord Donaldson in *M. v. Home Office* [1992] Q.B. 270 p. 306, now see [1993] 3 All E.R. 537. In *McDonald v. Secretary of State for Scotland, The Times*, February 2, 1994 the Second Division of the Inner House of the Court of Session held that in *Re M* did not apply to Scotland.
[29] *R. v. Secretary of State for Education and Science, ex p. Avon County Council* [1991] 1 Q.B. 558.
[30] *Minister of Foreign Affairs v. Vehicle and Supplies Ltd* [1991] 1 W.L.R. 550.
[31] See R.S.C., Ord. 24, r. 13(1).

appearance of affidavits. This is regarded as an important inclusion under the application for judicial review procedures. Since *O'Reilly v. Mackman*[32] the courts have generally adopted a common approach to the granting of discovery but in judicial review applications the courts have favoured[33] a more restrictive approach and the careful exercise of discretion on the merits of each case. Not all documents will be relevant to the judicial review and those that are not will not normally be included in the granting of discovery. An additional issue is that the Crown is able to claim public interest immunity arising out of certain documents[34] or indeed rely on the confidential nature of the papers as a means to prevent disclosure.

The Law Commission is considering whether the arrangements for **16–77** discovery in judicial review proceedings require reform.

Under Order 53 claims for damages may be joined to the application for judicial review. In England and Wales there is no provision for restitution proceedings. In *Woolwich Building Society v. I.R.C. (No. 2)*[35] the House of Lords considered the question of restitution proceedings after an application for judicial review had established that the regulations on which the Revenue based its demand for tax payment against the Woolwich Building Society were illegal. The approach adopted by the House of Lords established the right of the citizen to recover money paid by the citizen under regulations[36] which are *ultra vires*. The Law Commission is considering whether the application for judicial review should include proceedings for restitution.

(d) Tort and Contract Liability of Public Authorities

A public body that acts *ultra vires* may be liable in tort in the same **16–78** way as a private citizen, provided a cause of action is established. Section 2 of the Crown Proceedings Act 1947 permits the Crown to be sued on the same basis as private individuals. Although the courts have a discretion whether to award damages or not, especially when policy issues may be concerned in the question of liability. Statutory interpretation is often difficult when it comes to the question of the application of tort principles to public bodies. When comparing public bodies to private individuals, the former usually possess wide statutory powers whereas the latter do not.

---

[32] [1983] 2 A.C. 237.
[33] See *R. v. Secretary of State for the Environment, ex p. Islington London Borough Council, The Independent*, September 6, 1991.
[34] *Air Canada v. Secretary of State for Trade* [1983] 2 A.C. 394.
[35] [1992] 3 All E.R. 737.
[36] Lords Keith and Jauncey dissented.

16–79   As a general principle public bodies may be liable for the negligent exercise of their powers. The courts in their discretion have attempted to apply similar principles to the liability of public officials and authorities as apply to private persons. In the interpretation of statutory duties the courts may hold public bodies liable in damages for breach of their duty. For example a breach of a duty to provide housing for homeless people under the housing legislation may give rise to liability in damages.[37] However it is a good defence to argue that the alleged tort is carried out according to express or implied statutory powers. In *Geddis*[38] the court accepted that even if the Act was authorised by the legislature if carried out negligently it may give rise to liability. It is not easy to categorise how the courts will respond in each individual case. The courts have not found it easy to lay down clear principles when decisions amount to *ultra vires* and when decisions are to be regarded as negligent policy decisions to be reviewed by the courts, there is often uncertainty.

16–80   Principles of liability on the basis of *Anns v. Merton LBC*[39] were established by the the House of Lords. The Council had statutory responsibility to regulate building regulations and requirements for the proper construction of property. The House of Lords accepted that the Council was liable in negligence for the cost of repairing buildings when the foundations had been improperly inspected or the inspector had negligently carried out inspections. Since *Anns* a more restrictive view of the extent of liability for economic loss has been accepted in *Murphy v. Brentwood*[40] which distinguished *Anns* on the basis that there can be no liability in tort for the cost of repairing defective premises in anticipation of any personal injury or property liability.

16–81   Public bodies may be liable for nuisance but there is a presumption that statutory powers are not intended to be exercised so as to cause nuisance. However, the question of whether a nuisance may be condoned in the exercise of statutory powers depends on the nature of the powers[41] and their interpretation by the courts. In *Burgoin SA v. Ministry of Agriculture*[42] the question arose out of the entitlement of a trader in a claim alleging liability because of a breach of European Community regulations against the Ministry of Agriculture. The courts were divided on the matter and decided in that instance that there was no liability, this is likely to become an important issue for the future.

---

[37] *Thornton v. Kirklees MBC* [1979] Q.B. 626.
[38] *Geddis v. Bann Reservoir Proprietors* (1878) 3 App. Cas. 430.
[39] [1978] A.C. 728. See the development by the courts of foreseen damage in *Cambridge Water Co. Ltd v. Eastern Counties Leather plc* [1994] 1 All E.R. 53.
[40] [1991] 1 A.C. 398.
[41] See *Metropolitan Asylum District v. Hill* (1881) 6 App. Cas. 193, HL.
[42] [1985] 3 All E.R. 585.

Powers to engage in contracts are an important element in the **16–82** activities of both central and local government. Such powers may be statutory or through the development of the European Community subject to public procurement[43] directives.[44] Increasingly such contracting powers are a means to enforce standards and this may provide remedies for the citizen. The financial controls over public bodies in their role of entering contractual relations are an important element of scrutiny. Local government powers to undertake competitive contracting are carefully proscribed under Part 2 of the Local Government Act 1992.

The courts rarely intervene through judicial review over the terms **16–83** of contracts but the legal powers to enter contracts are carefully scrutinised.[45] This may be achieved in two ways. First, has the public body the requisite legal authority to enter into the contract? If the court finds that the body has acted *ultra vires* the contract is void. Second, where there are sufficient legal powers to enter into a contract and the contract is *ultra vires*, the question then falls to be determined under principles of ordinary contract law that the public body may be liable for any breach of contract.

---

[43] The Public Supply Contracts Regulations 1991 (S.I. 1991 No. 2679), the Public Works Contracts Regulations 1991 (S.I. 1991 No. 2680). See Kapteyn and Verloren Van Themaat, *Introduction to the Law of the European Communities* (Kluwer, 1990), p. 466–468.

[44] See Directives 77/62 and 71/305 and Article 169.

[45] C. Turpin, *Government Procurement and Contracts* (1989).

Chapter 17

Public Order

1. Introduction

17-01 The focus of this chapter is first, on how the law regulates public meetings, processions or demonstrations. A second focus is to consider emergency powers in the context of civil disturbance. Historically the development of popular protest gained important constitutional rights such as the broadening of the franchise, the right to vote for women, and in industrial relations the rights of trades unions. Many rights gained through popular movements have endured. In a democratic and accountable society that is open to change the freedoms enjoyed by any particular group or the majority are dependent on how the law treats such protests in the context of public order. A wide variety of political causes or beliefs may attract public protest which may take the form of public meeting, demonstration or protest. A responsibility rests on the police to fulfil their general function of keeping the peace. Their responsibility applies to a wide variety of public order problems as wide ranging and as diverse as pop festivals, and football crowds to political demonstrations.

17-02 As Lord Denning recognised in *Hubbard v. Pitt*[1] "the right to demonstrate and the right to protest on matters of public concern . . . are often the only means by which grievances can be brought to the knowledge of those in authority." Detecting that the liberty of the individual to assemble is a hallmark of an open society, Lord Scarman noted that while peaceful assembly is a fundamental right[2]:

> "A balance has to be struck, a compromise found that will accommodate the exercise of the right to protest within a framework of public order which enables ordinary citizens who are not

---

[1] [1976] 1 Q.B. 142.
[2] *The Red Lion Square Disorders of 15 June 1974: Report of the Inquiry by the Rt. Hon. Lord Scarman O.B.E.* Cmnd. 5919 (1975).

protesting to go about their business and pleasure without obstruction or inconvenience."

In this area of law[3] one of the most important questions is how police powers to maintain public order, may be balanced in the interests of society to ensure freedom of assembly and association. Discussion of the freedom to protest, assemble or demonstrate within the context of the discussion of public order has undoubtedly facilitated more extensive powers to uphold public order. This fact reinforces the need to balance discussion of public order and the effect of those laws upon freedom of expression.

In recent years, one of the most notable periods for intense debate **17-03** about public demonstrations was in the 1980s and the development of the peace movement as part of the Campaign for Nuclear Disarmament (CND). Another notable occasion for public protest which raised a number of public order issues came from an industrial conflict. A period of one year from March 1984 to 1985 when coal miners embarked on industrial action involved widespread picketing and protests at collieries throughout the country. The mobilisation of the police and the national co-ordination of police resources based on the National Reporting Centre at New Scotland Yard in London raised questions about policing in the 1980s. Subsequent prosecutions of the strikers were accompanied by the use of binding over orders and bail requirements to contain the activities of striking miners.

The Public Order Act 1986 has been strengthened by the Criminal **17-04** Justice and Public Order Act 1994. The background to the 1994 Act arose out of the recommendations of the Royal Commission on Criminal Justice[4] but many of the ideas and changes in the law which considerably strengthen the powers of the police came from the Home Secretary following his October 1993 political party conference. The main focus of the 1994 Act is on acts of trespass and the disruption of lawful activities. These changes in the law have proved controversial and the passage of the Bill through Parliament was beset with amendments and debate.[5]

---

[3] See D. G. T. Williams, *Keeping the Peace* (1967); R. Card, *Public Order The New Law* (Butterworths, 1987); A. T. H. Smith, *Offences Against Public Order* (1987).

[4] Cm. 2263 (July, 1993).

[5] See Francesca Klug, Keir Starmer and Stuart Weir, *The Three Pillars of Liberty* (Routledge, 1996) pp. 83–90.

2. Historical Perspectives

17-05 The setting up of Sir Robert Peel's new police force in the nineteenth century was greatly advanced by the need to regulate popular protest. The historical[6] role of policing identified by Cornish[7] as covering a wide selection of popular issues and demands; "strikes, elections, political demands and periods of poor trade each contributed to spasmodic unrest" also represented a significant opposition to military intervention in the internal maintenance of order in England.[8] The lessons of policing developed through experience. Past mistakes were quickly overcome by a delicate mixture of Royal Commission and judicial oversight. The first attempt to provide comprehensive police powers to control public protest emerged in the Public Order Act 1936 which spearheaded the legal prohibition of "quasi-military organizations." The Act was passed at a period of high activity[9] for the British Union of Fascists.

17-06   The importance of popular protest as providing pressure for reform had succeeded in gaining the vote for women, and greater trade union rights. Political authority gained from addressing the hustings and delivering directly to the electorate, party political promises to gain election victory has become an important feature of English democracy. Special arrangements are provided[10] for policing the Metropolis with specific attention given to the rights of Parliament[11] to sit unimpeded. Policing is inextricably linked to public order. Public order requires high levels of intelligence and surveillance activities.

17-07   Maintaining public order may involve the State in the use of extreme powers at times of emergency or civil unrest. The benefits of Empire and the colonial experience informed English constitutional writing on martial law and states of emergency. Townshend noted[12]:

---

[6] See C. Emsley and B. Weinberger, (eds.), *Policing Western Europe Politics, Professionalism and Public Order, 1850–1940* (Greenwood Press, 1991).

[7] W. R. Cornish, *Law and Society in England 1750–1850* (London, 1989); J. Stevenson and R. Qinault (ed.), *Popular Protest and Public Order* (1974).

[8] See C. Townshend, *Political Violence in Ireland* (Oxford, 1983) on the use of military in Ireland.

[9] See s.2 of the Public Order Act 1936.

[10] s.52 of the Metropolitan Police Act 1839 directions under the Act may be given by the Commissioner for the regulation of "carriages and persons, and for preventing obstruction of the streets during public processions etc., or in the neighbourhood of public buildings, etc."

[11] Both Houses of Parliament prior to the commencement of each session of parliament may direct the Metropolitan Police Commissioner to keep the streets of Parliament open. S.23 of the Seditious Meetings Act 1817 for meetings of more than 50 people to be held within one mile of Westminster Hall during the sitting of Parliament now repealed under the Public Order Act 1986.

[12] C. Townshend, "Martial Law and Civil Emergency" (1982) *The Historical Journal*, 167–195 at pp. 174–175.

"The whole drift of thinking about martial law, or emergency powers in general, was concerned with the problem of legality, and of ethical or political acceptability, not with that of practicality . . ."

Martial law may be defined as the common law duty of the executive to repel force with force. The courts, after the event could, determine what was justified on the basis of what was reasonable. Set against this extreme, some doubted if martial law meaning a state of seige,[13] and the partial transfer of powers to the military, might exist within English domestic law. Doubts about the effectiveness and acceptability of the use of the army in peacetime to control civil disorder on mainland Britain remain[14] and the onus is on the police as the primary agency to keep the peace.

Currently the law of public order is contained in the Public Order **17–08** Act 1936 and detailed powers granted to the police in the Public Order Act 1986 and the Criminal Justice and Public Order Act 1994. Other measures such as the Highways Act 1980 and Police Act 1964 are also relevant. Common law powers such as breach of the peace have also survived.

3. Police Powers

(a) Public Meetings and Assemblies

Various freedoms such as the right to take part in public meetings, **17–09** processions and demonstrations or to engage in political activities by joining trade unions or political clubs or associations may be discussed in the context of the powers the police have to preserve public order. For example the freedom to assemble and to engage in peaceful protest may be generally accepted as among[15] "our fundamental freedoms: they are numbered the touchstones which distinguish a free society from a totalitarian one . . ." However, the freedom to assemble is not unfettered. The law may regulate both the conduct and location of public assemblies. The policing of popular demonstrations and protests is often carried on in the glare of publicity with wide media coverage and reporting of meetings and demonstrations.

---

[13] *Notrecht*, or state of seige is not recognised in English law but it may be found in the French Constitution Arts. 36 and 16.
[14] See Chap. 19 on Northern Ireland.
[15] *Review of Public Order Law*, Cmnd. 9510 (1985).

17–10   The various powers granted to the police to *anticipate* problems arising from organisations and associations are both common law and statutory. The Public Order Act 1936 provides a number of relevant powers. Section 1 prohibits the wearing of a uniform which has political objectives, introduced to prohibit the increasing use of uniforms by political groups in the 1930s, with the rise of Fascists. In addition, section 2 of the 1936 Act prohibits the rise in quasi-military organisations by banning their organisation and association.[16] Vigilante groups may fall within the category of proscribed organisation.[17] In the absence of express statutory prohibition there is also the possibility of conspiracy offences arising out of an organisation set up to carry out illegal activities. The *caveat* to any prosecution is that the illegality must be capable of being committed by a single individual.[18]

17–11   In the case of using the highway there are both statutory and common law offences regulating the conduct involved. Section 137 of the Highways Act 1980 provides[19] that "a person, without lawful authority or excuse, [who] in any way wilfully obstructs the free passage along the highway" is guilty of a criminal offence. The question of what constitutes a lawful excuse may be considered by the courts. In *Hirst and Agu v. Chief Constable of West Yorkshire*,[20] animal rights supporters were convicted after they protested outside shops selling furs in Bradford city centre. Mr Justice Glidewell in the Divisional Court considered their appeal against conviction. In the earlier decision of *Nagy v. Weston*,[21] Lord Parker considered the obstruction of the highway by a hot dog vendor. The question of whether it was a reasonable use:

> "depends upon all the circumstances, including the length of time the obstruction continues, the place where it occurs, the purpose for which it is done and of course whether it does in fact cause an actual obstruction as opposed to a potential obstruction."

17–12   Applying Lord Parker's dicta to the facts in *Hirst and Agu*, Glidewell L.J., considered three questions to be posed in such cases and quashed the convictions on the basis that the issues were not properly considered in the Crown Court. First was there an obstruction? Any stopping on the highway could amount to an obstruction

---

[16] See Chap. 19 for a discussion of the relevant powers in Northern Ireland. The Prevention of Terrorism (Temporary Provisions) Act 1989, has wide restrictions on membership of illegal terrorist organisations.

[17] See *R. v. Jordan and Tyndall* [1963] Crim.L.R. 124.

[18] See the Criminal Law Act 1977.

[19] Previously see s.121 of the Highways Act 1959.

[20] (1987) 85 Cr.App.R. 143.

[21] [1965] 1 All E.R. 78.

whether it is on the footpath or carriageway. Secondly was the obstruction wilful? If the stopping was deliberate this could amount to wilful obstruction. Thirdly was the activity complained about lawful? Lawful excuse requires the court to consider that "lawful excuse embraces activities otherwise lawful in themselves which may or may not be reasonable in all the circumstances." This leaves unclear the exact balance to be struck between activity such as obstructing the highway when a group of friends meet to discuss their holidays for 20 minutes or so, which is lawful, and that which is not. In the case of distributors advertising material or free periodicals outside major rail stations, this may raise issues of legality because it may appear to be unreasonable.[22] The courts may regard conduct which is ancillary to the use of the highway as acceptable and reasonable, and that which is not as unreasonable.

The obstruction of the highway may constitute a public nuisance **17–13** and it may also involve private nuisance and trespass. In the case of public nuisance, at common law this is a misdemeanour triable in either the Crown Court or before magistrates. The exact terms of the common law offence are broadly described[23] as Smith and Hogan note[24] to include obstructing the highway and:

">. . . it also includes a wide variety of other interferences with the public; for example the carrying on of an offensive trade which impregnates the air 'with noisome offensive and stinking smoke' to the common nuisance of the public passing along the highway, polluting a river with gas so as to destroy the fish and render the water unfit for drinking . . ."

The interference in such cases must be substantial and unreasonable. The courts appear to have a discretion[25] to decide where the limits lie between what is "reasonably incidental" to the right of passage on the highway and what is inconvenient. The degree of obstruction or inconvenience may determine the legality of what is permissible.

While it is not necessary to show that the defendant intended to **17–14** create a nuisance, it is necessary to show that his actions constituted a nuisance. In criminal cases the defendant may be intentional or reckless in his actions. This may be more widely construed in the light of the *Caldwell*[26] criteria for recklessness which implies some

[22] *Waite v. Taylor* (1985) 149 J.P. 551 a Busker found guilty of obstruction because his purpose was not ancillary to the use of the highway.

[23] Stephen, *Digest* 184.

[24] Smith and Hogan, *Criminal Law* (1992) p. 762.

[25] See *Hubbard v. Pitt* [1976] 1 Q.B. 142.

[26] *Metropolitan Police Commissioner v. Caldwell* [1982] A.C. 341.

degree of criminal liability for acts which are not foreseen by the defendant to involve risk but are foreseen to the reasonable man. This may in effect provide for criminal negligence as a basis for liability. In criminal cases of nuisance the prosecution must prove beyond a reasonable doubt whereas in civil cases involving nuisance proof on a balance of probabilities is sufficient.

17–15   A public nuisance may be actionable in civil law, usually at the instance of the Attorney-General or a private citizen who must show special loss that is particular to the individual and not the public at large. It is necessary to distinguish civil cases from criminal cases although there has been considerable overlap arising from the grounds of nuisance liability. In *Southport Corporation v. Esso Petroleum*[27] Lord Denning observed how in a civil action once nuisance was proved and the defendant shown to have caused the act or omission constituting the nuisance, the legal burden shifts onto the defendant to justify or excuse his action.

A private nuisance is actionable at the instance of the private citizen who suffers a wilful interference with the enjoyment of land or rights over or in connection with the land.

17–16   Part V of the Criminal Justice and Public Order Act 1994 gives additional and wide powers for the police to deal with squatters, large-scale trespass and those participants in raves or connected with hunt saboteurs. There is a new offence of aggravated trespass. This applies with trespass on land in the open air by those who seek to obstruct or disrupt those that are engaged in lawful activity. There are powers to direct people to leave the land should the police have reasonable belief that the trespassers will disrupt a lawful activity. An offence is committed if a trespasser fails to obey a police direction. There are powers to prevent people attending raves or other events by stopping people and directing them to disperse. Failure to disperse is a criminal offence.

17–17   The police have powers to regulate what is called a "trespassery assembly". This is an assembly of 20 or more people on land to which the public has no right of access. There are powers to remove trespassers with six or more vehicles on land. Failure to comply with the directions of a police officer is a criminal offence.

17–18   There are extensive remedies available under the Act which permits owners or occupiers to go to the County Court to require the squatter to leave the occupation of the land within 24 hours. The police are empowered to enforce this order. Finally, local authorities are given powers to direct unauthorised campers to leave the land. Failure to comply with this request is a criminal offence. An enforcement order may be obtained from the magistrates and the police may

---

[27] [1954] 2 Q.B. 182 at 197.

take reasonable steps to enforce the order including entering on the land and removing any vehicles. Obstructing the police in carrying out their duties is an offence.

Injunctions may be sought to prevent any threatened illegal assem- **17–19** bly or picket. This is a common remedy used to enforce employment law and the rules about picketing.[28]

The carrying on of a meeting or demonstration may be the subject of legal restrictions as to *where* the meeting may be held. It is a common law trespass to hold meetings on highways or public places. Restrictions on holding meetings in open spaces such as parks or recreation areas may depend on the geographical location and therefore the jurisdiction such open space comes under. By-laws empower local authorities to regulate such open spaces according to whether there is conduct amounting to a nuisance or the use of specific statutory powers for the good government of the area.[29] In addition to these powers conditions may be imposed on such meetings by the police under the Public Order Act 1986 discussed below.

Part IV of the Criminal Justice and Public Order Act 1994 gives the **17–20** police extended powers to stop and search for offensive weapons or dangerous instruments. This power is constrained to a particular area for a specific and limited time provided a senior police officer reasonably believes that violence may break out.

Parliamentary candidates at elections have specific protection afforded to the traditional meetings carried out during the election period.[30] Similar provisions apply to the carrying on of local government elections.[31]

The law also facilitates the carrying on of election meetings in **17–21** public halls.[32] The freedom of political discussion is an important responsibility which the governing bodies of Universities and Colleges of Further Education are expected to uphold[33] and take reasonable steps in order to ensure that there is freedom of speech afforded to visitors and members of the institution concerned.[34] Interpretation of this provision can be extremely difficult when the University

---

[28] See *Thomas v. National Union of Mineworkers (South Wales Area)* [1985] 2 All E.R. 1, *Newsgroup Newspapers Ltd v. Society of Graphical and Allied Trades '82 (No. 2)* [1987] I.C.R. 181.

[29] See, *e.g.* Open Spaces Act 1906, s.15 the various Public Health Acts 1875 and s.235 of the Local Government Act 1972, the Parks Regulations Act 1872. In London see the Trafalgar Square Regulations 1952 S.I. 1952 No. 776.

[30] See s.95 of the Representation of the People Act 1983.

[31] See s.96 of the Representation of the People Act 1983 as amended by Sched. 4 para. 38 of the Representation of the People Act 1985.

[32] See s.96 of the Representation of the People Act 1983.

[33] See s.43 of the Education (No. 2) Act 1986.

[34] See E. Barendt, "Free speech in the Universities" [1987] P.L. 344.

authorities are considering the likelihood of violence on the campus. In *ex p. Caesar-Gordon*[35] the University of Liverpool granted permission to the student Conservative Association to hold a meeting. Restrictions were issued on the confidential nature of the organisational details of the meeting. The University considered that there was a threat of disorder because of the nature of the meeting and public feeling outside the University. These fears of disorder were in part because the University had little control over members of the public having access to University premises. Previously there had been widespread disorder in Toxteth, an area of Liverpool not far from the University. The Divisional Court granted a declaration and held that the University was not entitled to take account of the threat of disorder other than on the University campus. This did not however invalidate the conditions imposed by the University. Each University is expected to publicise its own rules of conduct as codes of practice for public meetings within its own premises.

17–22   Extensive powers are provided under the Public Order Act 1936 to control public processions. Section 3 permits a chief officer of police who reasonably apprehends that a procession may "occasion serious public disorder" to apply in London to the Home Secretary for a banning order, or elsewhere, to a local authority, the order may be for a period up to three months. This power has been supplemented by Part 1 of the Public Order Act 1986. The 1986 Act provides under section 11 for advance notice[36] and section 12 regulates advance notice for processions. The Act includes the circumstances where there may be conditions attached to the permission to hold a procession, and under section 14 for the imposition of conditions on assemblies. Hitherto, the 1936 Public Order Act was silent as to the regulation of an assembly which is stationary and not engaged in a procession.

17–23   Imposing conditions on processions and assemblies arises out of the experience of past years. During the 1960s and 70s an increase in political agitation led to a greater number of public demonstrations with their opposing counter-demonstrations. Popular causes have included the Vietnam war, apartheid, and the activities of the Campaign for Nuclear Disarmament. The National Front has also been active contesting a number of parliamentary by-elections. Balancing the needs of each group to present its viewpoint requires careful judgement on the part of the police and the prosecuting authorities.

17–24   The police have at their disposal a wide range of possibilities. Rerouting processions away from counter-demonstrations may be

---

[35] *R. v. University of Liverpool, ex p. Caesar-Gordon* [1990] 3 All E.R. 821.
[36] See The Brixton Disorders Cmnd. 8427 (1981).

adopted. Conditions on the route of the procession may include a ban on using certain streets or thoroughfares. Matters which may be considered in regulating processions or meetings include the question of whether there might be serious damage to property, serious disruption to the life of the community and intimidation.[37] In making any tactical judgement on these matters there is an added consideration which is the cost of policing, the manpower involved and the question of the most effective deployment of police resources. Public meetings may distract the police from other activities, engage a large amount of police overtime and increase the workload on the courts in any prosecutions taken as a result of disorder.

There are a number of offences which may be committed by those **17–25** who take part in or are engaged in the disruption of a public meeting or in certain circumstances carrying out a protest arising from a trade dispute. These include obstructing the police in the execution of their duty,[38] criminal damage,[39] the possession of offensive weapons,[40] the use of threatening violence to enter premises,[41] trespassing on premises and failure to leave at the request of a displaced occupier, trespassing with an offensive weapon, and obstructing the court officers in the execution of their duty.

During the Miners' Strike in 1984, the police made use of powers under the Road Traffic Act 1972 to stop vehicles. This was used to ascertain whether the occupants were engaged in picket duties. Failure to comply with a request by the police to re-route their journey and return home ran the risk of prosecution under section 51(3) of the Police Act 1964, namely obstructing a police officer in the execution of his duty.

The action taken by the police is usually left to their discretion. **17–26** Even though the courts may review that discretion, there is a reluctance to overturn police tactical decision-making. This reluctance may be traced back to cases decided at an earlier period though the courts may occasionally interpret the law to protect demonstrators. In *Beatty v. Gillbanks*[42] members of the Salvation Army were subject to a binding over by magistrates not to assemble and hold a meeting. The binding over was the result of a police direction that the assembly might cause a breach of the peace because a rival and opposing organisation, the Skeleton Army intended to counter demonstrate against the Salvation Army. The Salvation Army appealed to the Divisional Court against the magistrates' order. Field J. concluded

---

[37] See the White Paper on Public Order 1987.
[38] s.51 of the Police Act 1964.
[39] s.1 of the Criminal Damage Act 1971.
[40] s.1 of the Prevention of Crime Act 1953.
[41] ss.6–10 of the Criminal Law Act 1977.
[42] (1882) 15 Cox C.C. 138.

that the Salvation Army were wrongly bound over. There were no grounds for saying that the Salvation Army were holding an illegal protest. Any disturbance that was caused in the past had come from the Skeleton Army, and the Salvation Army did not incite or intentionally provoke a breach of the peace.

17–27   The case may be regarded as establishing an important principle that an assembly that is legal does not become illegal merely because it causes a counter-demonstration or when others threaten illegality. However, in practice how far might this principle be applied? It was possible for the court in *Beatty v. Gillbanks* to clearly distinguish the motives or good faith of the Salvation Army from the Skeleton Army, but where this is not possible the principle may not easily be upheld. There is also in Field J.'s formulation of the law, that if the natural and probable consequences[43] of the action of the lawful assembly is to create a disturbance then there could legally be a binding over. It is hardly convincing that the Salavation Army did not share some element of responsibility. If their meeting were not held it is at least arguable that there would be no counter-demonstration.[44]

17–28   Counter-demonstrations or protests were considered in *Wise v. Dunning*.[45] A Protestant pastor George Wise, made provocative comments about Catholics in Liverpool and the majority of his meetings were held in Catholic areas of the city. He was bound over to keep the peace by magistrates and challenged the legality of the binding over. As breaches of the peace were likely to be the natural consequence of his meetings, the binding over[46] was held by the Divisional Court to be legal.

17–29   In *Duncan v. Jones*[47] Mrs Duncan, a communist, was about to make a speech at a public meeting in a quiet cul-de-sac in Deptford near the entrance to an unemployment centre. Duncan was convicted by magistrates of obstructing a police officer in the execution of his duty when she stepped on a box which she had placed on the road to deliver her speech. In a previous meeting held by Mrs. Duncan fourteen months previously, there had been some disturbances. The Divisional Court upheld her conviction at Quarter Sessions.[48] The case raises the possibility that because the police may fear a breach of the peace, even if none occurs, a peaceful meeting may be amenable to prosecution for the offence of obstructing the police in the execution

---

[43] See *Wise v. Dunning* [1902] 1 K.B. 167 which distinguished *Beatty v. Gillbanks*.

[44] See *O'Kelly v. Harvey* (1883) 15 Cox C.C. 435 doubting the principles in *Beatty v. Gillbanks*.

[45] [1902] 1 K.B. 167.

[46] Today it is likely that he would be prosecuted under the Public Order Act 1986.

[47] [1936] 1 K.B. 218.

[48] The case has been heavily criticised by Daintith [1966] P.L. 248 and Williams, *Textbook of Criminal Law* (1983) p. 203. See *Piddington v. Bates* [1960] 3 All E.R. 660.

of their duty. The far reaching potential of *Duncan v. Jones* means that the police may make use of the obstruction offence to regulate and control the activities of lawful pickets involved in trade disputes. The courts have been reluctant to challenge the day to day operational decision of the police in these matters. Thus there appears to be little requirement on the police to prove that a threat to the peace is apprehended.

The role of the courts has proved problematic. On the one hand the **17–30** courts may be invited to consider the legality of police powers, especially the powers to seek a ban on a public demonstration.[49] On the other hand, the courts have not provided much oversight of police operational practices,[50] such as deciding how many demonstrators to allow to attend a meeting or how many pickets to permit at the place of work of the strikers.[51] A code of practice exists[52] for industrial disputes, stating that in general the number of pickets should not "exceed six at any entrance to a workplace; frequently a smaller number will be appropriate."

In recent years an additional concern has been the policing of **17–31** sports fixtures. The Sporting Events (Control of Alcohol, etc.) Act 1985 regulates the sale of alcohol inside sports grounds and at the entry to stadiums. Following the Hillsborough football disaster,[53] the Football Spectators Act 1989 was passed enabling the courts to make restriction orders preventing supporters from attending football matches if they have been involved in hooligan activity. The Football Offences Act 1991 further strengthens the law regulating crowds at football matches. Offences such as throwing missiles, chanting indecent and racial abuse, running onto the pitch without any reasonable excuse and selling tickets on the day of the match without the express authority of the Home Club, are intended to provide preventative powers as well as enabling the police to respond to incidents at football matches.

(b) Breach of the Peace

The police have common law powers of arrest for breach of the peace. **17–32** If the police reasonably apprehend that the holding of a meeting or a demonstration will give rise to a breach of the peace, then such

---

[49] See *Kent v. Metropolitan Police Commissioner, The Times*, May 15, 1981, C.A.
[50] *E.g.* see *Arrowsmith v. Jenkins* [1963] 2 Q.B. 561.
[51] See *Moss v. McLachlan* [1985] I.R.L.R. 76; *Thomas v. National Union of Mineworkers (South Wales Area)* [1985] 2 All E.R. 1.
[52] s.15 of the Trade Union and Labour Relations Act 1974 as amended by s.16(1) of the Employment Act 1980. Code of Practice on Picketing see s.3(8) of the Employment Act 1980.
[53] *Report on the Hillsborough Disaster*, Cm. 962 (1990).

powers may be invoked. In *R. v. Howell*[54] the Court of Appeal attempted to classify such powers, which have been distinctive in their breadth. Watkins L.J. held that there is a power of arrest for breach of the peace:

> "(1) where a breach of the peace is committed in the presence of the person making the arrest, or (2) the arrestor reasonably believes that such a breach of the peace will be committed in the immediate future by the person arrested although he has not yet committed any breach or (3) where a breach has been committed and it is reasonably believed that a renewal of it is threatened."

17–33   Relying on Halsbury[55] the Court of Appeal considered that a breach of the peace might be defined:

> ". . . where there is an actual assault, or where a public alarm and excitement are caused by a person's wrongful act. Mere annoyance and disturbance or insult to a person or abusive language or great heat and fury without personal violence are not generally sufficient."

17–34   This leaves unanswered the exact nature of the arrest powers available to the police because of the difficulty in defining breach of the peace. The elusive nature of any satisfactory definition of breach of the peace has received criticism.[56] Peaceful behaviour in a public place may fall within the remit of a breach of the peace if the nature of the activity commands public attention and therefore a larger attendance of the public than if it were ignored. Lord Denning in *ex p. Central Electricity Generating Board*[57] considered that a breach of the peace might arise if someone, who is lawfully carrying out his work, is unlawfully and physically prevented from doing so, illustrating the potential for a wide police discretion in terms of arrest powers.

It was also accepted by the court that a person making an arrest is entitled to rely on what he reasonably believes. This raises the question of whether that belief relates to an actual breach of the peace or an apprehended breach of the peace. In *Howell* the possibility that an *apprehended* breach of the peace is sufficient considerably widens the arrest powers of the police.[58]

17–35   In *ex p. Central Electricity Generating Board*[59] the Court of Appeal refused an application for mandamus requested by the Central

---

[54] [1982] Q.B. 416. See *Colhoun v. Friel* 1996 SSCR 497.

[55] See *Halsbury's Laws of England* (4th ed., 1976), Vol. 11, para. 108.

[56] See Ewing and Gearty, *Freedom under Thatcher* (Oxford, 1990) p. 90.

[57] [1982] Q.B. 458.

[58] See G. Williams, "Dealing with Breaches of the Peace" (1982) 146 J.P.N. 199.

[59] *R. v. Chief Constable of the Devon and Cornwall Constabulary, ex p. Central Electricity Generating Board* [1982] Q.B. 458.

Electricity Generating Board (CEGB), to require the Chief Constable to remove protesters encamped on private land with the intention of preventing the CEGB from carrying out a survey of the land for a nuclear power station. The question of the powers of the police in respect of a breach of the peace was considered, but as no breach of the peace had actually occurred the discussion was largely an academic one. The police appeared to have sufficient powers to intervene[60] but the court was unwilling to substitute its judgement for that of the operational decision of the police hence the decision not to grant mandamus. The Court of Appeal approved the test of whether an apprehended breach of the peace existed as this would be sufficient to constitute arrest powers as discussed in *Howell*. However at most this opinion is *obiter dicta* and the question of whether *Howell* will be followed remains unclear.

At common law the power of arrest for breach of the peace appears **17–36** to extend to private property. This point has been indirectly accepted in *McConnell v. Chief Constable of the Greater Manchester Police*[61] and Glidewell L.J. rejected the idea that a breach of the peace on private premises had to have an external effect on public property before there could be an offence.

In addition to arrest powers for a breach of the peace, the police have powers of arrest under sections 24–26 of the Police and Criminal Evidence Act 1984 (PACE) which did not abolish the common law powers of arrest for breach of the peace, although it generally codified other arrest powers. Section 26 allows an arrest for causing unlawful obstruction of the highway provided the arrest is necessary to prevent the unlawful obstruction continuing. Miscellaneous arrest powers are provided under section 25 of PACE arising out of offences under section 28 of the Town Police Clauses Act 1847.

The scope of breach of the peace is also relevant in defining the **17–37** basis of the powers of magistrates[62] to bind over persons to keep the peace. This is a power of historical importance to the development of the magistracy.[63] The power to bind over is that the person remains of good behaviour. Binding over may be used where there is a reasonable apprehension that a breach of the peace may occur. It has been accepted that a binding over power may be used where it is considered that there is no threat to peace but that public morality or

---

[60] Possible options open to the police included: to prevent an unlawful assembly under the common law, but since repealed by the Public Order Act 1986; to prevent obstruction under s.3 of the Criminal Law Act 1967; to deal with any actual breach of the peace or possibly apprehended breach of the peace.

[61] [1990] 1 W.L.R. 364.

[62] Justices of the Peace Act 1968, s.1(7), and Sched. 5 of the Administration of Justice Act 1973.

[63] See Justices of the Peace Act 1361.

"a good way of life" is threatened.[64] The person who is bound over must enter a recognisance to be of good behaviour. The recognisance is forfeited on a breach in the conditions of the binding over. Such an order is both subject to an appeal[65] and to review by the courts under Order 53.[66] Binding over[67] is a frequently used power to attempt to restrict the movement of potential trouble-makers. An additional power vested in magistrates is to set conditions on the grant of bail. Such bail conditions[68] may set limits on the movements of the individual.

17–38   In addition to the above powers there is also the offence of threatening behaviour under section 5 of the Public Order Act 1936. Section 5 has been replaced later by section 4 of the Public Order Act 1986. This was the main public order offence commonly used by the police for 50 years in preference to charges of riot, unlawful assembly and affray.[69] Section 5 of the Public Order Act 1936 covered any person who in a public place or at any public meeting used threatening, abusive or insulting words or behaviour or distributed or displayed any writing, sign or other visible representation which was threatening, abusive or insulting. For a criminal offence to be proven, the conduct was required to be intended to be a breach of the peace or to be of such a nature that such a breach of the peace was threatened. This section has now been replaced by section 4 of the Public Order Act 1986 discussed below.

17–39   The powers of the police to enter private property are also related to the idea of preserving the peace. In *Thomas v. Sawkins*[70] Lord Hewart thought that the power of the police to enter and if necessary remain on private property arose when the police officer had "reasonable ground for believing that an offence is imminent or is likely to be committed." Such generalised powers appear to be too widely expressed.[71] The powers are vague as to when the police must have grounds for belief or the nature of the offence which falls within the police powers. If widely interpreted an extension of police powers in this way seems beyond the proper remit of judicial discretion. The powers of the police to enter on land to deal with nuisance or

---

[64] See *Hughes v. Holley* (1987) 151 J.P. 233.
[65] See Crown Court (Magistrates' Court Appeals from Binding Over Orders) Act 1956. The appeal is normally by way of rehearing see; *Shaw v. Hamilton* [1982] 1 W.L.R. 1308.
[66] *R. v. Londonderry Justices* (1891) 28 L.R. I.r. 440.
[67] See Law Commission Working Paper No. 130, "Criminal Law–Binding Over: The Issues".
[68] See s.117 of the Magistrates' Courts Act 1980 and s.47(8)(*b*) of the Police and Criminal Evidence Act 1984.
[69] Now amended by the Public Order Act 1986.
[70] [1935] 2 K.B. 249.
[71] See Goodhart (1936) 6 Camb.L.J. 22.

collective trespass have been strengthened under Part V of the Criminal Justice and Public Order Act 1994.

(c) Offences under the Public Order Act 1986

The experience gained from the Miners Strike in 1984 and the **17–40** policing of the peace movement led to consideration of the law on public order. The Public Order Act 1986 is largely based on the recommendations of the Law Commission.[72] The law was believed to be too complex and fragmented. This fact led to consideration of a single statute providing for greater clarity. The 1986 Act creates new statutory offences and abolishes the common law offences of riot, unlawful assembly and affray, and the offence[73] under section 5 of the Public Order Act 1936. In fact the 1986 Act appears to add more powers to the police while retaining the miscellaneous powers outlined above and fails to clarify the concept of breach of the peace which remains largely dependent on judicial developments.

Each of the four new offences may be examined namely; riot, **17–41** violent disorder, affray, and causing fear or provocation of violence. At common law, riot consisted of three or more persons, together with a common purpose, with an intent to help one another by force if necessary against anyone who opposed their common purpose and such force or violence is displayed in such a manner as to cause alarm in at least one person of reasonable firmness and courage. Riot is one of the most serious offences and section 1 of the Public Order Act 1986 defines the offence[74] in similar terms to the common law offence but with the requirement of 12 or more persons and not three. If 12 or more persons threaten violence through an unlawful purpose but only one person uses violence then there is a riot but only one rioter. The offence is indictable and punishable with 10 years' imprisonment.

Riot may be committed where the 12 assemble without any pre-arranged plan or by chance. Once they form together all that is required is that they have a common purpose and at some point unlawful violence is used or there is a threat of violence. The common purpose may be inferred from conduct and need not be an unlawful one.

---

[72] Law Commission No. 123.

[73] s.5 of the Public Order Act 1936 is concerned with the use of threatening, abusive or insulting words or behaviour to threaten a breach of the peace.

[74] s.1(1). Where 12 or more persons who are present use or threaten unlawful violence for a common purpose and the conduct of them (taken together) is such as would cause a person of reasonable firmness present at the scene to fear for his personal safety, each of the persons using violence for the common purpose is guilty of riot. (2) It is immaterial whether or not the 12 or more use or threaten unlawful violence simultaneously. (3) The common purpose may be inferred from conduct.

17–42   Violence is generally defined in section 8 of the 1986 Act to include, except in the context of affray, "Violent conduct towards property as well as violent conduct towards persons." Violence is not restricted to conduct causing or intended to cause injury or damage but includes any other violent conduct (for example throwing at or towards a person a missile of a kind capable of causing injury which does not hit or falls short). But the threat of violence or the use of violence must be unlawful, and this appears to allow the excuse of violence used in self-defence. The courts may have a difficult task in establishing whether such force is believed to constitute self-defence when the force is used against the police.[75] It has been held that when the police use force lawfully and that force is reasonable in the circumstances, in the prevention of crime or in the apprehension of suspects, then self-defence is not available against such force.[76] But if the defendant uses force because he suspects that the police are terrorists or criminals, the defence might be available, even where the police might act lawfully.

17–43   The offence of riot is intended to provide for serious disorder where there has been widespread civil unrest and the authorities are required to arrest large numbers of people. There remains considerable difficulty in obtaining convictions. This appears to stem from the mental element of the offence requiring proof of common purpose. It must be proved that the defendant intended to use violence or was aware that his conduct might be violent, being aware of whether one's conduct is violent or not, appears a difficult concept to prove.[77] This would appear to give the police evidential problems in proving the commission of the offence.

17–44   Compensation for riot under the Riot (Damages) Act 1886 is now construed under the definition of riot under the Public Order Act 1986. The majority of cases involving riot raise issues associated with claims for compensation under the 1986 Act. Compensation is payable under the 1986 Act and regard is given to the conduct of the claimant. Relevant considerations are whether adequate precautions were taken by the claimant or whether he participated in the riot. In such circumstance compensation may be reduced.

17–45   Violent disorder under section 2 of the Public Order Act 1986 replaces the common law offence of unlawful assembly, and is punishable on indictment[78] or on summary conviction.[79] This offence is commonly charged and used more frequently than the common law offence of unlawful assembly as a means to regulate crowd

---

[75] See *Devlin v. Armstrong* [1971] N.I. 13.
[76] *R. v. Browne* [1973] N.I. 96.
[77] See s.6(5) and (6) of the 1986 Act relating to intoxicated defendants.
[78] Five years imprisonment or an unlimited fine or both.
[79] Six months imprisonment or the statutory maximum fine or both.

behaviour. For the offence to be proved there is a requirement that there is an assembly of three or more with a common purpose to commit a crime of violence or to achieve some other object whether lawful or not in such a way as to cause reasonable men to apprehend a breach of the peace. There need not be a common purpose as each of the three or more persons may have a different purpose or no purpose. The defendant must be proved to have threatened violence or must have been aware that his conduct might be violent and threaten violence. In *Mahroof*[80] three defendants were charged jointly on one indictment with violent disorder. Mahroof alone was convicted and appealed with the result that his conviction was quashed but a conviction on an alternative offence under section 4 was substituted.[81] It was assumed that if three defendants to a violent disorder are involved and one of the three is acquitted, the others invariably but not necessarily must be acquitted. Invariably the acquittal of one may cause the jury to re-consider the evidence and may lead to the acquittal of the others.

Section 3 of the Public Order Act 1986 replaces the common law **17–46** offence of affray with a new statutory equivalent. Affray under section 3 is triable either[82] on indictment or on summary trial.[83] The offence of affray requires three persons: the person using or threatening unlawful violence; a person towards whom the violence is directed and a person of reasonable firmness who need not be, or be likely to be at the scene. The use of affray is common in prosecutions of fights. The overlap in charging between sections 2 and 3 gives the police discretion in terms of differentiating pre-meditated violence charged under section 2 and spontaneous violence under section 3. It is also possible to charge defendants with a wide range of offences under the Offences Against the Person Act 1861, arising out of the same incident such as assault or causing grievous bodily harm.

Section 4 of the Public Order Act 1986 contains the offence of using **17–47** fear or provocation of violence. The purpose of section 4 was to replace the offence under section 5 of the Public Order Act 1936, noted above concerning using threatening behaviour. The new offence covers both private and public places, and is not confined to where a third party may be likely to be provoked into violence but where a third party fears violence. There is no requirement of proving that there is or has been a breach of the peace.

The phrase "threatening, abusive or insulting" is a component of the new offence which has been retained from the old offence under

---

[80] [1989] Crim. L.R. 72.
[81] See s.7(3) of the Public Order Act 1986 allowing the substitution to be made of s.4 for s.2.
[82] On indictment, three years imprisonment or an unlimited fine or both.
[83] On summary conviction with six months imprisonment or the statutory maximum fine or both.

section 5 of the Public Order Act 1936. The ordinary meaning of English words is employed by the courts when seeking to interpret their meaning and apply them to the facts of a particular incident. However, the addition of the words "uses towards another person" did not appear in the old law and could be interpreted to narrow the offence.

17–48   In addition to the four offences noted above, section 5 of the Public Order Act 1986 creates a summary[84] offence of harassment, alarm or distress. This section was intended to deal with minor acts of hooliganism causing rowdy behaviour, shouting abuse or obscenities. The width of the offence is due to the unspecific nature of the activity which may fall under its ambit. A wide range of fairly innocuous behaviour, including noisy behaviour and high spirits, may come within its scope. This may be committed where a person uses abusive, threatening or insulting words or behaviour, or displays any writing sign or other visible representation which is threatening, abusive or insulting. The person who may be affected by the conduct, could be a policeman or bystander, and therefore to be harassed or alarmed must have the act performed within hearing or sight. It must be proved that the defendant intended his conduct to be threatening, abusive or insulting or disorderly and must be aware that it might be so construed. When drawing up any prosecutions under the Act the purpose of the Public Order Act must be considered when framing charges and the courts have been reluctant to accept charges under the Act for acts which are not intended to be covered by the legislation.[85]

17–49   The width of section 5 allows the prosecution of a wide variety of activities including the wearing of tee-shirts with particular slogans, the distribution of posters with unusual captions or emotive words. All such activities may fall under the criminal law. This raises the question of whether it is satisfactory to use the criminal law in this way. There is a power of arrest which accompanies the use of section 5 after a warning has been given, which extends police powers quite considerably in this area. The Public Order (Amendment) Act 1996 amends section 5(4) of the Public Order Act 1986. This permits a constable the power to arrest without warrant if he engages in conduct which the constable warns him to stop. The offensive conduct is set out in the Public Order Act 1986.

17–50   One of the striking features of the 1986 Act is that it does not set out rights for demonstrators or protestors. In terms of preventative powers for the purposes of controlling meetings or demonstrations, the new Act builds on the old law. Under section 11 of the Public

---

[84] Summary conviction a fine not exceeding level 3 on the standard scale.
[85] See *Parkin v. Norman* [1982] 2 All E.R. 583.

Order Act 1986, the police, subject to few exceptions, must be given written notice of all public processions at least six days before they are due to take place. Reflecting the increase in the carrying out of public processions and meetings, the new law is intended to give the police advance warning and information about organisers, the type of procession, the date, time, route and destination of the march.

Section 12 of the 1986 Act provides the police with powers to **17-51** impose conditions on public assemblies, processions or meetings. The nature of the restrictions comes into operation once there is an assembly of 20 or more in a public place. The power to make conditions is a police power and not vested in magistrates, reflecting an emphasis on the operational control by the police of public meetings or assemblies. The grounds for imposing restrictions are much wider than the apprehension of a serious breach of the peace or public disorder. If the police reasonably believe that serious damage to property or serious disruption to the life of the community may occur then restrictions may be lawfully imposed by the police. Also if the police fear that intimidation of others may occur this may mean that restrictions may be imposed. The intimidation provision is intended to allow police to distinguish between marches which are intended to persuade rather than intimidate.

This distinction may not be at once apparent and thus the police **17-52** have to make their own judgement in such matters. Intimidation may appear to follow from the size of the gathering rather than from the motive of those involved. In trades disputes picketing may seek to persuade but it may also have the effect of intimidating those that are a minority and are fearful of the results of refusing to strike. Line-drawing in these matters is exceptionally difficult. The police are in effect exercising a dual role. Facilitating processions may not be consistent with the maintenance of good order.

The Act also includes powers of arrest and it is a criminal offence **17-53** to disregard the instructions of a police officer acting under the powers contained in the Act. Conditions may be imposed at the scene of the meeting or procession that extend even to a fairly junior police officer as powers are conferred on "the senior police officer" present at the scene, and such a junior officer may be the most senior officer present. Conditions may be such as appear to the police officer to be necessary "to prevent such disorder, damage, disruption or intimidation, including conditions as to the route of the procession."

The need for such powers may be justified in terms of the variety of **17-54** public meetings and demonstrations the police are expected to regulate. The presumption built into the police powers under the Act is that disruption of the normal day to day lives of ordinary people should not be interfered with by public demonstrations. Thus there is an assumption that the police may need to regulate various forms of protest in favour of the more orthodox behaviour in society. Invariably this will mean that the unusual or unorthodox will receive little real protection under the law and are only free to demonstrate within the police tolerance of what is reasonable. Thus inconvenience will be tolerated only marginally subject to the availability of resources and the disposition of police policy.

17–55　　One example of where the police have regarded the inconvenience factor of public meetings as too great and have sought to use their powers is in the annual ritual meeting of the Druids at Stonehenge. A ban under the Public Order Act 1986 was imposed on meetings and assemblies during a period in June to coincide with the Summer solstice. The aim being to avoid disruption when travelling people descended on the area to take part in ceremonies at Stonehenge.

(d)　Police Organisation and Accountability

17–56 The importance[86] of the police[87] in the control of public protest and their extensive powers[88] of arrest, search, seizure and entry requires some consideration to be given to the nature of the police in the United Kingdom. At common law, the police have analogous powers to the ordinary citizen's powers of arrest. However, wide statutory powers such as those under the Public Order Act 1986 have resulted in the police acquiring a special status in terms of both organisation and resources. Traditionally the role of prosecution vested with the private citizen. Gradually the police acquired the prosecution of offences as part of their investigation of crime and the interrogation of suspects. The private citizen rarely prosecuted while the police for over 150 years dominated the prosecution of offences.[89] In terms of prosecution, the Prosecution of Offences Act 1985 created the Crown Prosecution Service headed by the Director of Public Prosecutions and organised into 31 areas, each under a Chief Crown Prosecutor. The powers of the ordinary citizen to prosecute are still retained but according to published guidelines, prosecutions are undertaken by the Crown Prosecution Service.[90]

17–57　　In historical terms the absence of any centralised and controlled national police force, the police have traditionally built up a large degree of local autonomy within fairly clear structures of account-ability. This doctrine of "constabulary independence" governs the operational independence of the police in their day to day functions.

---

[86] A number of police forces exist outside the remit of the Police Act 1964, such as the British Transport Police under ss.69–71 of the Transport Act 1962 and the Ministry of Defence Police under the Ministry of Defence Police Act 1987.

[87] L. Lustgarten, *The Governance of the Police* (1986).

[88] See Chap. 20.

[89] Hay and Snyder, *Policing and Prosecution in Britain 1750–1850* (Oxford, 1989).

[90] Code for Crown Prosecutors.

As noted above the doctrine has been implicity accepted in the way the courts have shown a reluctance to interfere with police judgement arising out of the exercise of their discretion over crowd control and public order powers. In London the Metropolitan Police are uniquely accountable to the Home Secretary while other police forces are organised on a local authority basis and accountable to their respective Police Authority.

The authority of the constable is that he is a public officer. The **17–58** theory of maintaining public order and the Queen's peace gives the police constable wide discretion under the command of a Chief Constable. In reality many of the decisions at the scene of public disturbances are made by fairly junior officers who are under the command of more senior officers. Police officers may be sued or prosecuted as any other citizen. In the cases of negligence claims, the principle of vicarious liability attaches to the Chief Constable who may be indemnified out of public funds.

The office of Chief Constable is an onerous responsibility with **17–59** considerble discretionary powers. However in legal terms the powers of the Chief Constable are often unclear and poorly defined. Reforms to the organisation and structure of the police under the Police Act 1964 leave questions about how the Chief Constable may be directed or made accountable. Outside London there is a local police authority. Each local police authority is composed of two-thirds local councillors, one-third are lay magistrates. The police authority appoints a chief constable, a deputy chief constable and assistant chief constables, which are subject to the agreement of the Home Secretary. The police authority has the power to require the retirement of those senior officers in the interests of efficiency of the police force. An inquiry may be commissioned by the Home Secretary when such powers are adopted to investigate a compulsory retirement. The officer must be given the right to a hearing and the investigation must conform to the rules of natural justice. Powers under the Police Act 1964, permit the Home Secretary to require an authority to retire a Chief Constable. In 1985 this power was used to require the retirement of the Chief Constable of Derbyshire in the interests of efficiency.[91]

The Chief Constable may exercise disciplinary powers over senior **17–60** officers, and has the power of promotion and the appointment of other ranks of officers in his force. Failure to give fair employment opportunities to women or ethnic minorities may result in legal action against the Chief Constable. A failure to promote the assistant Chief

---

[91] See Chap. 20 for discussion of police organisation and management.

Constable of Merseyside, Alison Halford, gave rise to allegations of unlawful discrimination.[92]

17–61   While the Home Secretary is answerable for the activities of the Metropolitan Police to Parliament this does not extend to operational matters for that police force which are in the hands of the Commissioner of the Metropolitan Police. There is no Ministry of Justice in the United Kingdom on the basis of a continental model and the Home Office is not directly accountable for local police forces. However, increasing powers of the Home Office have raised the question of whether local authority accountability should remain a viable organisational basis for the police. The Home Secretary has powers in relation to regulations[93] covering pensions, training, duties and equipment, including the decision to issue CS gas, baton rounds or matters of policy in the deployment of such equipment. In *R. v. Secretary of State for the Home Department, ex p. Northumbria Police Authority*,[94] the Police Authority was opposed to the issuing of CS gas and plastic bullets and applied for judicial review to require withdrawal by the Home Secretary from issuing guidance in the form of a circular to Chief Constables on the availability of such equipment. The Court of Appeal refused the Police Authority's application and upheld the Home Office powers as part of a general power under section 41 of the Police Act 1964 to provide police colleges and forensic evidence for the police. In addition the Court of Appeal recognised a prerogative power to keep the peace which might allow the Home Office to supply such equipment.

17–62   The contribution of the Home Office to expenditure of police forces may represent 50 per cent of the net expenditure. The Home Secretary is advised by a Chief Inspector of Constabulary, who makes an annual report to him on matters such as the efficiency and effectiveness of the police force. If the Home Secretary is dissatisfied, he may withhold grants to the police authority. If necessary through a system of investigations and inquiries the Home Secretary has the potential to widen the remit of parliamentary accountability for the police. A widely drawn power under section 28 of the Police Act 1964 allows the Home Secretary to ensure that powers that ". . . to such an extent as appears to him to be best calculated to promote the efficiency of the police." This power has been used sparingly as the traditional wisdom of Home Secretaries has been to allow police forces autonomy. However, there are signs that this attitude may

---

[92] See *Halford v. Sharples* [1992] 3 All E.R. 624 the allegations of unlawful discrimination were made against the Chief Constable of Merseyside, the Northamptonshire Police Authority, H.M. Inspector of Constabulary, and the Home Secretary.

[93] See Police (Discipline) Regulations 1985 (S.I. 1985 No. 518).

[94] [1988] 2 W.L.R. 590.

change. Chief Constables come under considerable pressure from government controls over their expenditure. Increasingly seen like any other public sector body rather than a special case, police forces are becoming subject to more stringent financial controls. These may directly change the role of the police in their operational activities.

Such concerns about the efficiency of public expenditure on the **17–63** police and the perceived increase in crime but reduction in detection and prosecution rates have resulted in the Home Secretary considering whether reform of the structure of the police is required. Criticism of the police in the interrogation of suspects led to the setting up of a Royal Commission on Criminal Justice and an internal review of the organisation and structure of the police. It is likely that each police force may be required to publish efficiency studies of crime detection and "clear up rates." On the principle that centralisation may be adopted in order to reform, it is likely that pressure for a national police force may grow. The setting up of the National Reporting Centre in Scotland Yard in 1972 to co-ordinate the disposition of the police at times of crisis may be a model for future developments. The counter-intelligence tasks of the police have since 1992 been delegated to MI5 and this is intended to lead to better co-ordination of intelligence against terrorists.[95]

The Criminal Justice and Public Order Act 1994 gives the police **17–64** additional powers for cross-border co-operation between the police in Scotland and England and Wales. The police have in common with many other public bodies come under immense pressure to conform to the new style of public management. Two White Papers[96] in 1993 set out the basis for the Police and Magistrates' Courts Act 1994. The aims of the 1994 Act were to set performance standards for the police and instil a "business management" culture within policing. There are some examples of this new ethos in the Act such as provision for fixed term contracts for the rank of superintendent and above. A movement in favour of free-standing police authorities removed from the necessity of local and elected control is finally consolidated in the new Police Act 1996. This 1996 Act consolidates the earlier law and introduces new statutory provisions for free-standing police authorities outside London. It maintains the distinction that metropolitan police forces are separately treated.

There was intense debate over the proposals for the composition of the new police authorities. Sched. 2, para. 1(1) provides that nine members are to be drawn from the relevant councils, five are to be independent members, and three are to be justices of the peace.

---

[95] See McConville, Sanders, and Leng, *The Case for the Prosecution* (1992).
[96] See *Police Reform: The Government's Proposals for the Police service in England and Wales* Cm. 2281 (1993) and *A New Framework for Local Justice* Cm. 1829 (1993).

Independent members are to be chosen from a short-list prepared by the Secretary of State and after nomination the candidates are submitted to the Secretary of State.

17–65 It appears from research studies that in the area of public order[97] "the police put up with disorderliness only if it ceases on their arrival." Further research has shown that police presence is usually effective, few arrests are made out of many of the disturbances attended by the police,[98] but in periods of mass demonstrations such as the Miners' Strike, the powers of arrest are widely used. One important aspect of police powers is the desire to see that the police have their own authority accepted by the public. While most police officers may seek to avoid confrontations, when the police feel that their authority may be challenged it is more likely that they will wish to intervene even if there is a risk of physical violence. Aggressive police tactics may therefore be seen as a legitimate way to exert police authority and therefore respect for the law.

4. The Intelligence Services' Functions and Policing

17–65A There have been notable improvements in the way the intelligence services are organised and how they might be made accountable. The Security Services Act 1989 placed the activities of MI5 on a statutory basis. The Intelligence Services Act 1994 similarly places the Secret Intelligence Service MI6 and the Government Communications Headquarters (GCHQ) on a statutory basis. The security services are placed under the scrutiny of a tribunal, a Commissioner and a parliamentary committee, the Intelligence and Security Committee which may not compel the attendance of witnesses and may not review operational matters. Policy is under the control of the Secretary of State. The Intelligence and Security Committee is required to make an annual report, but this is subject to vetting by the Prime Minister. There are powers for the Prime Minister to order a report from the committee and to exclude matters either from Parliament or from publication under section 10(7) of the 1994 Act.

17–65B The link between the security services in the collection of information and intelligence and policing is made in the important Security Service Act 1996. This Act amends the Security Services Act 1989 and provides statutory authority for the security services including "the function of acting in support of the prevention and detection of

---

[97] *ibid.*, p. 25.
[98] McCabe *et al. Police, Public Order and Civil Liberties* (1988).

serious crime". This is interpreted to mean "organised crime" involving serious criminal offences. However, there is no definition of what serious crime is and the role of the security services is only generally outlined. This leaves the impression that the detail will not be made clear and will be left to the discretion of the police and the security services. As a result, the Act leaves little guidance on any checks or balances that may be in place to prevent abuse.

The 1996 Act is broadly drafted in another respect which gives a large discretion to the issuing of executive warrants. This is in principle contrary to the constitutional protection articulated in *Entick v. Carrington.*[99] The general nature of the discretions contained in the Act may provide scope for its challenge as incompatible with the European Convention on Human Rights.[1]

5. Military Powers and States of Emergency

Public protest may give rise to a complete breakdown in law and order. With the exception of Northern Ireland,[2] the experience has been rare and mainly confined to particular periods in history, when military power has been required to aid the civil power and restore order. Although the police are mainly unarmed, there is an increasing requirement for armed police to be involved where there is an emergency involving political terrorists. Terrorism poses a major threat to the lives of ordinary citizens and this factor may weigh heavily in the granting of additional powers to the police to maintain civil order.   **17–66**

The use of military assistance during periods of industrial disputes may involve troops in agricultural duties or in preserving public order as part of a general assistance to aid the civil power in preserving public order.[3] The Emergency Powers Acts 1920 and 1964 permit the proclamation of a state of emergency where events have occurred or are likely to occur that are calculated to deprive the community, or a substantial part of the community, of the essentials of life by interference with the supply and distribution of food, water, fuel, or light, or the means of locomotion.   **17–67**

Industrial action in 1921, 1924 and 1926 at the time of the General Strike resulted in the proclamation of states of emergency. In more   **17–68**

---

[99] (1765) 19 St. Tr. 1030.

[1] See Paul O'Higgins annotated comments *Current Law Statutes.* 1996.

[2] See Chap. 19 for a more detailed analysis of the special problems arising from emergency powers in Northern Ireland.

[3] See Reserve Forces Act 1980, s.23 and also the Emergency Powers Act 1964.

recent times, during the Heath Government in the 1970s, regulations were issued covering emergency supplies[4] of electricity and powers to control the dock strike to ensure the essential supply of goods and services. During widespread violence and disruption during the Miners' Strike in 1984–85, the police were utilised to the full and as already noted this brought to bear a wide variety of arrest powers which were later to prove controversial, especially the use of breach of the peace as the basis for stopping and re-directing strikers. The authorities appear reluctant to countenance the use of military powers for the purposes of industrial strikes. Largely this may be because the appearance of the use of the military is an emotive issue and may lose the government of the day much needed popular support.

17–69   Increasingly there is a preference for making use of the ordinary police to cope with civil disturbance and emergency. This is evidenced through the better training given to the police and the issuing of various riot control equipment. On the whole the police may prefer to take this responsibility as part of their general involvement in maintaining public order. However, the model of an unarmed civilian police force may become less credible if the police are required to make increasing use of their powers to control riots and civil disturbances.

In cases where there are serious breaches in the law and rioting becomes widespread and uncontrolled, resort may be had to the use of the military. Both the police and military may rely on the legal right to make use of force under section 3 of the Criminal Law Act 1967. This permits the use of reasonable force in all circumstances in the prevention of crime.[5]

17–70   The judgement between when to make use of force by the police and when to consider the use of the army calls for careful consideration of the level of violence and its likely duration. A Chief Constable may then invite the Home Secretary, in consultation with the Prime Minister and Secretary of State for Defence, to consider the use of military aid to the civil power. Once the military are invited to restore order, then some form of martial law may be said to exist. Lord Diplock in *Attorney-General for Northern Ireland's Reference*[6] explained that at common law:

"There is little authority in English law concerning the rights and duties of a member of the armed forces of the Crown when acting

---

[4] See Emergency Powers Act 1964 and S.I. 1974 No. 350. Also see G. Morris, *Strikes in Essential Services* (1986).

[5] See Chap. 19 for a discussion of the interpretation of these words. See *Attorney-General for Northern Ireland's Reference (No. 1 of 1975)* [1977] A.C. 105.

[6] *Attorney-General for Northern Ireland's Reference (No. 1 of 1975)* [1977] A.C. 105 at 136.

in aid of the civil power; and what little authority there is relates almost entirely to the duties of soldiers when troops are called on to assist in controlling a riotous assembly."

While there is a duty on the private citizen to assist in the maintenance of order, this becomes very difficult to put into practice when the nature of that duty is ill-defined and the citizen is acting under military command.

Martial law is in one sense the suspension of the ordinary law and **17–71** the use of military command over the civil authorities. The term is therefore broad enough to cover the complete suspension of democratic government and its substitution by military orders. In the extreme example of the overthrow of the civilian authorities and the removal of democratic government, martial law may refer to the use of military law. This refers to the body of law under which military rules are administered by military officers through courts-martial. Such courts have military law powers and are subject to review and appeal to the ordinary courts. However, when courts-martial exercise martial law jurisdiction, they are not perceived of as "ordinary courts" but simply a form of military justice administered through a tribunal which may at a future date be subject to oversight by the ordinary courts. This may normally occur once civilian government has been restored.[7]

The Armed Forces Act 1996 makes substantial changes to the **17–72** military justice system. In general terms this is an attempt to modernise the military system, and improve the standards and quality of courts-martial procedures and the general powers of military investigation. The changes introduced under the 1996 Act occur partly because of the case of *Alexander Findlay v. The United Kingdom*[8] considered by the European Commission of Human Rights. It decided that Findlay had not received a fair hearing and this questioned the procedures of military discipline and courts-martial. Similarly, a major revision of the law relating to reserve forces is contained in the Reserve Forces Act 1996. Taken together these changes provide an important modernisation of law and practice for the armed services.

However, in civil emergencies, martial law may be used more **17–73** generally to mean the state of affairs requiring the presence of the military under the direction of the civil authorities. This use of martial law has historical more than contemporary relevance. Given the extremely wide nature of emergency powers under the Emergency Powers Act 1920 and 1964, it is unnecessary for martial law to be

---

[7] See *Re Clifford and O'Sullivan* [1921] 2 A.C. 570.
[8] Application No. 22107/93. (1996) 21 EHRR CD7.

resorted to in those circumstances. In addition, wide powers, under the Prevention of Terrorism (Temporary Provisions) Act 1989 subject to annual renewal, provide comprehensive powers to deal with most emergencies from any acts of terrorism.

17–74 The legal authorities on the existence of martial law and its review by the ordinary courts appear confined to the period during the Irish rebellion in 1916 and its aftermath in the creating of the Irish Republic. It appears to be settled law that the courts may at a later date determine that martial law based on the facts of the case, existed. The question of martial law may settle the legality of the jurisdiction of the military and the question of whether necessity is established justifying recourse to martial law. An important question is whether the civil or military authorities are liable in civil law for their actions. Thus it is often the experience of emergency powers that there is some form of Act of Indemnity[9] restricting civil and even criminal liability for acts done during war or civil emergency.

17–75 There is a presumption in favour of the ordinary courts, while still sitting to have the jurisdiction to determine whether a state of war or martial law is in existence. It is normal for the courts to wait for the cessation of hostilities before determining any proceedings brought by citizens who wish to determine their rights and the liability of the authorities. Military law is therefore seen as a last resort and not to be utilised when the ordinary civilian government is able to function.

17–76 War may require that the authorities exercise both prerogative and statutory powers. The declaration of war and the conduct of the war is subject to the prerogative powers of the Crown and international law. Various powers for requisitioning supplies, ships, vehicles and material are provided in legislation[10] passed during wartime. Such powers may be found in the Emergency Powers (Defence) Acts 1939 and 1940. The trial of civilians by special military courts may also be authorised by statute.[11]

The Import, Export and Customs Powers (Defence) Act 1939 and The Import Export Control Act 1990 provides the government of the day with powers to regulate through the issue of licences for manufactured goods for export. Powers under both Acts were the subject of inquiry in the Matrix Churchill affair under Sir Richard Scott.

17–77 Wartime powers to requisition property may be subject to claims for compensation. Such claims may be subject to legislation which may deprive the citizen of any right of payment, as in the example of the War Damage Act 1965.[12] Many of the major powers given to the

---

[9] The Indemnity Act 1920.
[10] Also see the Defence of the Realm Act 1914–15.
[11] See The Emergency Powers (Defence) (No. 2) Act 1940.
[12] See *Burmah Oil Co. v. Lord Advocate* [1965] A.C. 75.

authorities to protect the State may also be subject to judicial review by the courts. However, the courts[13] have been reluctant to interfere with executive discretion when the interests of the State and national security are pre-eminent. In a number of wartime cases the courts have refused to review the exercise of executive powers.[14] The role of the courts and national security is examined in the next chapter.

[13] See *Liversidge v. Anderson* [1942] A.C. 206, also R.F.V. Heuston "Liversidge v. Anderson in Retrospect" (1970) 86 L.Q.R. 33.

[14] *R. v. Home Secretary, ex p. Lees* [1941] 1 K.B. 72. In more recent times this reluctance of the courts to intervene has continued see *McEldowney v. Forde* [1971] A.C. 632.

Chapter 18

Secrecy and the State

1. Introduction

18–01 Governmental secrecy and the national interests of the State are considered in this chapter in the context of freedom of information. In previous chapters the principles of accountable government have been considered in the context of Parliament and ministerial accountability. Access to information has a crucial role in government accountability. Information is required in the effective use of parliamentary questions and debate in the performance of select committees and in the work of pressure groups. Information is also an essential element in government decision-making and especially in the area of policy formulation.

18–02 The Labour Government elected in May 1997 has promised a Freedom of Information Act. The Scott inquiry produced evidence in favour of such an Act. However, at the time of writing there are no details of this proposal or the form it might take. The pressure for greater openness comes from the widely available access to the international media through the internet. Territorial protection of confidential information is increasingly difficult. Attempts in the United Kingdom to make government more open have resulted in the creation of a *Code of Practice on Access to Government Information*.[1] There is also within the European Union the recommendations of a high-level group of experts set up in May 1995 to examine the necessary changes that come about through an information society. There is the Commission's Information Society Project Office[2] providing information about the Community. There is a strong desire in the Community to provide better information about decision making.

---

[1] Cabinet Office December 1996. Also see Cabinet Office 20, *Good Practice Guide: Guidance for all public service complaints handling systems.*
[2] Access: http//www.ispo.cec.be

The focus of this chapter is on the restrictions and inhibitions which are placed on the freedom of expression and on the access to information which permits the State to retain secrecy.

2. Open Government and Official Secrets

Openness[3] is a necessary pre-requisite to accountable and responsible government. An open style of government permits Parliament, pressure groups and interested members of the public to participate in policy decision-making. A government that is more open is likely to be better informed than a government that is restrictive. A consequence of openness in government is that the quality of decision-making may be improved. Participation in the democratic process should not end with an election vote, but should continue to allow citizens the opportunity to contribute to the system of government decision-making. **18-03**

There is a variety of legal rules and techniques relevant to the secrecy of government. In the absence of a written Constitution and Bill of Rights in the United Kingdom, it is difficult to establish any legally enforceable right to information. But it would be misleading to attribute the culture of secrecy as due to that single cause. Successive United Kingdom governments have maintained secrecy as the hallmark of government decision-making. There are a number of factors which may contribute to this culture. **18-04**

First, the civil service developed, during the Victorian era, the ethos of public service. Hierarchical in structure, disciplined through promotion and advancement through public service, civil servants were kept hidden from public view and their contribution to government preserved under secrecy and the responsibility of Ministers to Parliament. The civil service sought to achieve influence but maintain political neutrality. As a result civil servants have contributed to the high degree of secrecy evident in government. Advice given to Ministers must remain confidential sometimes, because of the nature of the advice itself but also to protect the anonymity of the advice giver.

Secondly, the doctrine of collective Cabinet responsibility, intended to provide collective decision-making and collective deliberations, ensures that the climate of secrecy becomes built into every structure of government. There is in fact a secretive character to the political **18-05**

[3] See P. Birkinshaw, *Freedom of Information* (1988).

culture of the United Kingdom. This is reinforced by the use of Cabinet collective decision-making,[4] which binds the civil service and Ministers to confidentiality. The ethos of secrecy is also underlined by the way information is disseminated to the media. Official leaks of information concerning government policy may quite legally be given to newspapers through the process known as "the lobby system." Ministers may be self-authorising in releasing to the press details of government policy that may affect their department. The lobby system is an arrangement where an accredited group of journalists may be given confidential information in anonymous briefings about government policy on condition that they observe various prescribed limits on what they write.[5]

18–06   Thirdly, individual ministerial responsibility serves to preserve the secrecy of government deparmental decision-making. Ministers are accountable to Parliament and not civil servants. Thus civil servants and Ministers may find secrecy the most effective buffer against outside intrusion or unwanted publicity.

Fourthly, governments are major providers of contracts. In the government's relationship with the private sector there is a high degree of secrecy in contractual relationships. Relations between commercial enterprises seek to preserve confidentiality and protection against competitors through patenting industrial processes or copyright which also contributes to the need to preserve price sensitive and commercially valuable information.

18–07   In addition to the factors mentioned there is also the absence of any freedom of information legislation in the United Kingdom.[6] The absence of any legally enforceable right to information, has resulted in widely drafted laws and judicial statements preventing the disclosure of confidential information. Indeed freedom of discussion in the United Kingdom is no more than[7]:

> "the freedom to write or say anything which is not a violation of the law as interpreted by the courts sometimes with, sometimes without, the aid of a jury."

Thus freedom of speech in the United Kingdom rests on the assumption that freedom may exist outside any area prohibited by

---

[4] The Head of the Civil Service acts as secretary to the Cabinet, draws up the Cabinet minutes and in consultation with the Prime Minister provides the agenda for Cabinet discussion.

[5] See Hugo Young, *One of Us* (Macmillan, 1989), p. 510.

[6] Freedom of information leglislation may be found in many other countries including, the United States of America and within Europe, in Denmark, Finland, Greece, Norway, Sweden and the Netherlands.

[7] P. O'Higgins, *Censorship in Britain* (1972) p. 16. See D. Feldman, *Civil Liberties and Human Rights* (1993), Chap. 14.

law. The list of offences and proscriptions are ill-defined and wide. This leaves considerable uncertainty as to where the boundaries of freedom to information may be drawn, as the extent of proscription may also depend on how rigorously the law is to be enforced.

There is excessive regulation and unnecessary protection. This is recognised in the Deregulation and Contracting Out Act 1994 intended to reduce the burden of regulation on business.

Birkinshaw has noted the historical origins of government secrecy **18–08** which may be traced back before the introduction of the first Official Secrets Act was passed in 1889. Medieval secrecy was provided on oaths of loyalty between the King and his advisers. Bound by loyalty, the enforcement of confidences was provided by widely interpreted treason laws. By the end of the seventeenth century with the restoration of the monarchy in 1660, Parliament had successfully limited prerogative powers of taxation such as ship-money impositions and other taxes. With the achievement of political and legal sovereignty Parliament had gained authority but not control over the central Executive which remained with the Crown. The decline of royal control over Ministers was gradual and ad hoc and even in the eighteenth century, the influence of the monarch over government endured during the period of Walpole's ministry which marked the birth of the office of modern Prime Minister. The secrecy of government was bound up with its mystique. Attempts to invigorate the system of government in the nineteenth century had to tread carefully around the controls over access to official papers.

The adoption of Royal Commissions of Inquiry and the greater use **18–09** of select committees by both the House of Commons and the House of Lords provides a fascinating account of how modern government developed in the Victorian era. Reports from inspectors and the setting up of various inspectorates also increased access to the workings of government. Such developments did not prove successful against the culture of secrecy. Inspectors were subject to ministerial responsibility and confidentiality was retained. The Treasury through the issuing of treasury minutes and memoranda influenced civil service attitudes to secrecy by preventing the disclosure of any official information without proper authority. The Victorian preoccupation[8] with confidential information provides a culture which was receptive to instructions requiring non-disclosure. Equally clear is that attempts to circumvent legal controls were made and often were successful.[9]

The Victorian legacy remains today. As there is no public right to **18–10** information various restrictions remain on the disclsoure of information about the past activities of government. Public records in the

---

[8] See C. Roberts, *The Growth of Responsible Government in Stuart England* (1966).
[9] See William Cobbet and his pamphlets ensuring a constant flow of information on state trials and prosecutions.

Public Records Office are only available for inspection after a period of 30 years has elapsed. Section 5(1) of the Public Records Act 1958 as amended by the Public Records Act 1967, provides that the Lord Chancellor may also proscribe different time periods for the disclosure of documents at the request of the Minister "or other person." Certain categories of papers may be subject to a longer time-scale. These are[10]: "exceptionally sensitive papers, the disclosure of which would be contrary to the public interest whether on security or other grounds", documents which contain information "supplied in confidence" the disclosure of which would or might constitute a breach of good faith and documents containing information about individuals, "the disclosure of which would cause distress or danger to living persons or their immediate descendants."

18–11 In fact it is possible to prevent the disclosure of many documents by the simple expedient of "weeding" out those documents which may be too sensitive to publish and their destruction amounts to the permanent removal from the records of government. Estimates as to the amount of weeding carried out are difficult to make[11] with any degree of accuracy but it is also possible for papers to be destroyed at departmental level before they are ever put into the hands of the staff of the Public Records Office. The responsibility for the Public Records Office is with the Lord Chancellor who is a member of the Cabinet and at present is not answerable to Parliament through any Departmental Select Committee. The assessment of the value of official papers in terms of their historical content is not included in the legislation. Thus it is possible and legal for government Ministers to order the destruction of official papers in the public interest. It is difficult to prevent the destruction of official papers. Would a longer time-limit beyond 30 years result in a different attitude towards publication? A longer time-limit may make the destruction of papers less likely but this may be at the expense of depriving the present generation of information about the activities of the government during their lifetime. Is this a price worth paying in the interests of preserving historical records? There is no guarantee that a longer time-limit would help to preserve official papers without some legal requirement of preservation.

18–12 Whilst the 30-year rule is still in place the *Code of Practice on Access to Government Information* has provided a more liberal attitude to opening up files. Recent examples of such an approach may be found in the release of files on the German occupation of the Channel Islands and the release of the Rudolf Hess and Roger Casement papers. However, there have been surprises such as the revelation

[10] See Wilson Report: *Modern Public Records: Selection and Access*, Cmnd. 8204 (1981).
[11] Government response to the Wilson Report see Cmnd. 8531 (1982) paras. 26–27.

that in 1957 there had been a government decision to keep the details of an accident at the Windscale nuclear plant secret. This was revealed in papers released in January 1988.

An important source of information are ministerial memoirs. Pre- **18–13** vious Prime Ministers and Cabinet Ministers often write biographies and memoirs of their period in office. Such publications usually obeyed certain conventions about confidential information. The advice tendered to the government of the day by the civil service usually fell into this category. However the memoirs of the late Richard Crossman who had been a Cabinet Minister in the Wilson Government 10 years previously[12] created concerns about the revelation of official information. The text of the diaries contained detailed information about the deliberations of the Cabinet. Officials were identified as were the names and views of Ministers. Particularly significant was the advice given to Ministers by civil servants which was also given in great detail. The Attorney-General in 1976 attempted to prevent the publication of the diaries. The arguments made to prevent publication included the confidential nature of Cabinet information, that the public interest requires that publication should be restrained and that the courts had a duty to restrain publication. Lord Widgery took the unusual step of reading the diaries and concluded, that publication 10 years after the event would not inhibit Cabinet discussion and that publication would not harm the public interest. The result of the decision allowed publication of the Crossman Diaries and since then many ex-Cabinet Ministers have provided details of their period in office in a relatively short period after they left office. Such memoirs can often become an indispensable guide to the workings of government and the way in which modern government develops. Following the Crossman case, Lord Radcliffe's committee of privy counsellors considered the advice tendered to Ministers about publication[13] of their memoirs. In general the committee took a restrictive perspective on the publication of information which might put in jeopardy the "confidential relationships" between Ministers within the government. The committee concluded that the opinions or advice of civil servants or ministerial colleagues should not be revealed, nor should the advice of advisers, furthermore that criticism of policy or competence should not be made public. Such guidelines are much stricter than the *Crossman* case accepted. However, enforcement is left to the individual responsibility of each Minister and not through the courts. There is little sign that the Radcliffe view is being followed by Ministers today and it

---

[12] *Att.-Gen. v. Johnathan Cape Ltd* [1976] Q.B. 752.
[13] See Lord Radcliffe, Committee of Privy Counsellors on Ministerial Memoirs, Cmnd. 6386 (1976).

seems more commonly accepted that ministerial memoirs will be forthcoming and that their value as a means of understanding the work of government remains undiminished.[14] The normal convention is that former Ministers or civil servants who wish to publish their memoirs should submit a full text to the Cabinet secretary in advance for clearance. Upon refusal of publication there is an appeal to the Prime Minister who has the final decision in the matter. There is a tacit acceptance that after a period of 15 years, as the Government may no longer be in office, a fairly wide latitude may be shown to former Ministers.

18–14   Attempts have been made in recent years to encourage a more public disclosure of information. In 1977 the then Prime Minister James Callaghan introduced an initiative to make available to the public, background studies and analytical information used when reaching key policy decisions. The text of this initiative became more generally known as the Croham Directive[15] which favoured a more open approach to giving information to the public. This view of greater openness was also espoused by Mrs Thatcher in 1981 when she accepted the Croham Directive and suggested that more information might be available.

18–15   Governments new to office are often enthusiastic supporters of more information being made publicly available but soon the experience of government may dull this enthusiasm. Although Mrs Thatcher was the first Prime Minister to publicly acknowledge the existence of MI5, her government took a strong line on leaks of information including the prosecution of Clive Ponting[16] for leaking secret information to M.P.s about the sinking of the Argentinian battleship General Belgrano, during the Falklands War in 1982.

The published memoirs of a former intelligence officer Peter Wright resulted in protracted litigation[17] attempting to prevent the publication of his memoirs written in order to provide him with compensation and to settle a grievance he had with his former employer the British Government over his pension rights.

18–16   More recent attempts to provide greater public information have come from the initiative under the *Citizen's Charter*.[18] Indirectly as a result of privatisation the public have been made more aware of the standards expected of the various public utility industries such as water, gas, electricity, and telecommunications industries. Charter

---

[14] See B. Castle, *The Castle Diaries* (1980) and N. Ridley, *My Style of Government* (1992).
[15] See 936 H.C. Deb., Cols. 699–700 (October 26, 1977). On July 6, 1977 the then Head of the Civil Service issued a letter to all heads of Government Departments the text of the presumption which favoured publication.
[16] *R. v. Ponting* [1985] Crim.L.R. 318.
[17] *Att.-Gen. v. Guardian Newspapers Ltd (No. 2)* [1990] 1 A.C. 109.
[18] Cm. 1599 (1991). See A. Barron and C. Scott (1992) 55 M.L.R. 526.

Rights enable performance indicators to be published to allow the citizen to see the standards of service to be expected and the likely compensation payable should those standards not be met within a stipulated period and range of conditions. Such an approach has highlighted how many public services may be improved through greater access to information. The Citizen's Charter has an important significance in the way public bodies may provide the public with information. The Next Step agencies also have a more open approach to providing information than was previously available.

In 1993 the Government approved greater openness in a White Paper on Open Government. There is a Minister with responsibility for Open Government and the Citizen's Charter.[19] This policy was implemented in the *Code of Practice on Access to Government Information* first published in 1994 and later revised in 1996.

Another initiative has come through the need for financial markets **18–17** to obtain government confidence after the decision of the Government in Summer 1992 to leave the European Monetary System of fixed exchange rates. As a result the Treasury have decided to give greater attention to publishing some of the working material which is used in government forecasting. In addition a group of leading economists has been appointed to advise the Chancellor of the Exchequer on economic policy. The names and views of these economists and their general advice are made public. In this example the Government believed it to be in its own interests to take these steps in order to encourage a more open style of decision-making and encourage greater confidence in the Government's intentions to manage the economy. There is also less latitude allowed to a government with a small majority compared to a government with a large majority. The former requires greater attention to the views of backbench M.Ps. while the latter may encourage a degree of arrogance about how much information is really needed outside the government.

In contrast to various developments in favour of more open **18–18** government there are some indications that government may from time to time prefer a more closed style of government. In the 1970s and 1980s experiments in government decision-making involving local government, notably the introduction of the Community Charge; in education reform, and in changes in the way schools are governed, have all been introduced in the absence of any Royal Commission or independent investigation or inquiry. This tendency has been viewed by some commentators as giving rise to "an authoritarian approach to law-making" and in some instances has led

[19] Cm. 2290 (1993) White Paper on Open Government.

to major policy reversals for the Government.[20] A more open style of government may have avoided some of the more controversial mistakes in government policy.

18–19 It is often the more mundane and less sensationalist aspects of secrecy that may matter. In recent years a number of safety related matters made public as a result of official reports are an illustration of the problems with excessive secrecy. For example the secrecy of fire brigade reports at British Rail stations was revealed in 1987 after Desmond Fennel Q.C. in his report on the King's Cross fire in 1987, revealed how public safety would have greatly benefitted from the publication of such reports. Fire brigade inspections at London Underground stations are made public but British Rail has not made such reports public.

Tests conducted on the safety of British cars undertaken by the Department of Transport's Vehicle Certification Agency on the basis of European Community safety and environmental standards are kept secret. If the information was made public this would allow the public to make choices based on safety and the effectiveness of different cars depending on the model range.

18–20 Such examples have given rise to demands for greater freedom of information and in 1984 a Campaign for Freedom of Information was launched with support from some major political groups. The Campaign attempts to distinguish between information that is related to official secrets involving national security and information which might be properly available to the public. This confidential information, relating to secret organisations and national security or defence, information relating to commercial contracts or market sensitive financial information, or revelations of confidential advice, would not come within the focus of freedom of information. Even this limited form of right of access has been denied by the Government and the campaign's objectives have not been realised. The introduction of private Members' Bills in pursuit of more open government has failed. Such attempts to reform the law have been unsuccessful in achieving more open government. Progress in the United Kingdom has lagged behind developments in other countries, most notably the United States of America. Ironically information about the United Kingdom Government revealed under the Freedom of Information legislation in the United States is greater than under domestic United Kingdom law. Thus a major initiative to improve the United Kingdom's freedom of information is encouraged by the knowledge that the United Kingdom's Government cannot effectively prevent some information becoming available under the United State's laws. This

---

[20] See V. Bogdanor, "Government of the People by the People" *The Guardian*, August 8, 1992.

may be counter-productive as the amount of information revealed under Freedom of Information legislation may be significantly greater than the Government[21] may wish to accept in this country. This may act as an incentive towards more open government but equally it may also act as a deterrent against any future liberalisation of the law.

(a) Official Secrets Legislation

Various laws and legal restrictions exist against the publication or **18–21** dissemination of official information. At common law various offences such as blasphemy, sedition and conspiracy provided a structure for the prosecution of offences which were intended to limit the variety and content of published material available to the public. The criminal law exercised a crude form of censorship aimed at controlling booksellers, publishers and printers as well as authors. The nineteenth century legacy of secrecy resulted in the passage of the Official Secrets Act 1889 which made it an offence to "improperly divulge official information" was widely drawn but the requirement of proof of the mental elements of the crime made successful prosecutions difficult to achieve. At the end of the nineteenth century legal controls[22] were ineffective whereby many breaches of the law went unpunished under the growing power and influence of newspapers. The need to tighten the law was recognised by the Official Secrets Act 1911. This Act was further refined and reformed by the Official Secrets Act 1920 and again reformed by the Official Secrets Act 1939.

Section 1(1) of the 1911 Act makes it an offence for any person for **18–22** any purpose prejudicial "to the safety or interests of the state" to engage in a number of activities. Those which are covered by the 1911 Act include: approaching or entering a prohibited place; making a sketch or plan calculated or intended to be useful to an enemy; obtaining, publishing, communicating such information; sketch, document or information which is calculated to or is intended to be useful to an enemy.

The purpose which is prejudicial to the interests of the State may be **18–23** inferred from the circumstances. The purpose which is prejudicial refers to the intention of the accused and will be judged not on the actual effect but on what the accused indended. Thus in *Chandler v. DPP*[23] demonstrators for the Campaign for Nuclear Disarmament

---

[22] See J. Michael, *The Politics of Secrecy, The Case for a Freedom of Information Law* (NCCL, 1979).
[22] See *Prince Albert v. Strange* (1849) 1 Mac. and G. 25.
[23] [1964] A.C. 763.

who approached a military airfield were convicted under section 1 of the 1911 Act when it was proved that their intention was to disable the airfield. The House of Lords regarded a "prohibited place" as not confined to specific sites so designated by the Ministry of Defence but applied to places where information would be useful to an enemy. Thus the law, which was intended to cover acts during wartime, had a peacetime operational focus which included protestors, as well as spies, saboteurs or agitators. This broad construction of the Act seems perfectly consistent with the breadth of the language used in the legislation. However, was it correct to have brought such a prosecution under a section which was aimed at spies and saboteurs rather than protestors and demonstrators? This highlights one of the problems with broadly drafted and interpreted laws. Prosecutorial discretion seems to depend on whether the statute is broad enough to catch the undesirable activity, which in this case it was, rather than on whether the Official Secrets Act should be used for such a prosecution.

18–24   The defence in *Chandler* had argued that the purpose of the demonstrators was not to prejudice the interests of the State but to draw attention to the use of nuclear weapons and thereby disarm the aircraft. Such direct action was unjustified and the courts rejected the defendants' arguments. Obstructing the lawful purpose of the armed services was held as prejudicial to the State even when the demonstrators held strongly their conviction that they were acting in the State's interests. The decision has been strongly criticised but the legal interpretation of the legislation is consistent with the words of the statute.

18–25   Section 2 of the 1911 Act is intended to prevent the misuse of any sketch plan or model, document or information. The section is aimed first at the holders of official information and makes it an offence to communicate this information except to a person authorised to receive the communication. A person who receives such information is also guilty of an offence if he has reasonable cause to believe that the information is in contravention of the Act. In *Crisp and Homewood*[24] the scope of the section applied to a clerk in the War Office who handed to the director of a firm of tailors a copy of the clothing contract for the army. The clerk was not directly employed by the War Office but worked under the direction of the office-holder and this was sufficient.[25]

---

[24] (1919) 83 J.P. 121.

[25] See *Loat v. Andrews* [1985] I.C.R. 679, the Act was held by the Divisional court to apply to a civilian who operates the police computer after he passed information from the computer about the location of recent burglaries to a company representative specialising in burglar alarms.

Section 2(1) of the 1911 Act was used to prosecute Sarah Tisdell, a **18–26** civil service clerk in 1984 for leaking to a newspaper a memorandum setting out the plans drawn up by the Government for maintaining public order when cruise missiles arrived at Greenham Common. Tisdell was sentenced to six months imprisonment. Section 2(1) was used in a prosecution against Clive Ponting, an assistant secretary in the Ministry of Defence, after he leaked a memorandum relating to the sinking of the Argentine battleship General Belgrano. Ponting admitted leaking the document but claimed that he owed a duty to the House of Commons, in their constitutional role to hold government accountable. The document contained highly embarrassing revelations which questioned the complete accuracy of the Prime Minister's account of the sinking to the House of Commons. Ponting was acquitted after the jury were able to see the documents and the jury's verdict[26] was a surprise to many after the judges summing up pointed in favour of a conviction. Ponting had not been authorised to leak the documents. The trial judge explicitly rejected Ponting's argument that he was justified in leaking the documents as he could not be said to owe a duty to the House of Commons, such a duty was the duty of Ministers and not civil servants. This direction appears correct in constitutional law. Ponting had breached the confidential nature of his relationship with Ministers and, however altruistic his motives, this was not a breach that could be authorised in law. Some commentators have welcomed the outcome of the case,[27] but it has left unresolved the duty of a civil servant in Ponting's position. One view, later favoured by the Armstrong Memorandum[28] issued to civil servants soon after Ponting's acquittal is that civil servants may use the Head of the Civil Service as a form of appeal court to resort to after exhausting departmental means to remedy any conflict between the civil servant's duties and responsibilities and those of the Minister. However, another view is that Ponting exposed both the failure of the civil service to exercise sufficient control over Ministers in such cases of dispute and that civil servants ought to be able to appeal directly to Parliament as a means to hold Ministers to account. The latter is objected to because of the nature of the Minister's responsibility to Parliament. Undoubtedly Ponting's leak had the effect of breaching an important confidence between a civil servant and his Minister.[29]

---

[26] See C. Ponting, *The Right to Know* (1986).

[27] A range of opinions may be found in Drewry, [1985] P.L. 203; P. Birkinshaw, *Freedom of Information* (1988); R. Norton-Taylor, *The Ponting Affair* (1985).

[28] Sir Robert Armstrong, *The Duties and Responsibilities of Civil Servants in relation to Ministers: Note by the Head of the Home Civil Service* 1985 H.C. Official Report Vol. 74 1984–85 (HMSO, 1985).

[29] See 57 H.C. Deb., Col. 138 (March 27, 1984).

18–27   Ponting's acquittal also highlighted patent defects in the Official
Secrets Acts and this led to the Government's consideration of reform
in preference to various private members' initiatives. Criticism of
section 2 had been of long standing with the Franks Committee
(1972)[30] having recommended its abolition. The broadly drafted
legislation with its "catch-all" quality became so heavily criticised
that it was seldom used. This Draconian law[31] however was said to
have a preventative effect and therefore was perceived as valuable.
About one-third of prosecutions under the Act related to the use of
police information improperly disclosed to journalists or private
detectives.[32] The Franks Committee made comprehensive proposals
for replacing section 2 with a more modern and focused Act. Thus the
use of criminal sanctions would be restricted to areas of major
significance such as wrongful disclosure of information relating to the
defence, security, foreign relations and reserves, Cabinet documents
and the use of official information for private gain or information
supplied about particular individuals. This reform proposal was
accompanied by proposals to regularise the classification of documents, long regarded as the product of an over-protective civil
service. Top secret would be restricted to defence, security foreign
relations and reserves. Prosecution would require a certificate from
the responsible Minister and there would be some form of advisory
committee advising on matters of classification. The Franks proposals
received belated attention in the aftermath of the Ponting trial and
consideration given to implementing some part of them in a White
Paper.[33] The result was the introduction of the Official Secrets Act
1989.

18–28   The 1989 Act replaced section 2 of the 1911 Act[34] and narrowed the
protection of official information considerably. The use of the criminal
law under the Act is restricted to various categories of information.
While all Cabinet documents are not automatically protected under
the Act, documents or information which falls under the following
categories are subject to the criminal law.

It is an offence for a Crown servant or government contractor to
disclose information which falls under any one of the following
categories. The categories under sections 1–4 of the 1989 Act are:
security and intelligence, defence, international relations, information
obtained in confidence from other states or international organisations, information obtained by special investigations authorised by

---

[30] Departmental Committee on s.2 of the Official Secrets Act 1911 (1972) Cmnd. 5104.
[31] It was estimated that s.2 created over two thousand separate offences. See Brazier,
    Constitutional and Administrative Law (Penguin, 1989), p. 494.
[32] See Bailey, Harris and Jones, *Civil Liberties Cases and Materials* (3rd ed., 1991).
[33] Cm. 408 (1988) and the debates at 137 H.C. Deb. 1412–81 (July 22, 1988).
[34] S. Palmer [1988] P.L. 523.

warrant. In the cases of security and intelligence information or where information is obtained by special investigations authorised by warrant, no damage need be proven for the offence to have been committed if the disclosure is made by an officer of the security and intelligence services. In cases where disclosure is made by a Crown servant or government contractor, damage must be proven for there to be an offence. However in the remaining categories covering defence and international relations, damage must be proven to have occurred where disclosure is made by someone other than a member of the security and intelligence services.

The 1989 Act also makes it a criminal offence for any person to **18–29** make without authority a damaging disclosure of information protected under the Act that has come into his possession following an unauthorised disclosure of information by a current Crown servant or government contractor. This applies to information which is made available in breach of a requirement of confidentiality or in breach of section 1 of the 1911 Official Secrets Act. While mere receipt of information is no longer an offence, it is an offence to make disclosure of information relating to security and intelligence, defence and international relations when the information is communicated in confidence by the United Kingdom to another State or international organisation.

Section 8 of the 1989 Act makes it an offence to retain or fail to take care of protected documents and articles or disclose information which may facilitate access to protected material.

In its effect, the 1989 Act means that there is a general prohibition **18–30** against disclosure of information by members of the security services or disclosure of information received from any authorised use of telephone tapping, irrespective of any damage proven. In such cases there is no public interest defence and no defence of prior publication. Raising a defence requires the burden of proof to rest on the accused and this may make a defence to such offences difficult to prove. The 1989 Act does not permit the disclosure of information even where it may reveal any unlawful behaviour. There is no general defence that disclosure was in the public interest thus excluding the type of defence argued by Ponting in his trial, but then rejected by the trial judge. Various defences under the 1989 Act are that in general it is a defence for the accused to prove that he did not know that any of the information fell into a prohibited category or, in certain circumstances indicated above where damage must be shown in relation to the disclosure, that damage did not occur.[35]

---

[35] See J. Mayhew and P. O'Higgins, The Official Secrets Act 1989 *Current Law Statutes Annotated* 1989.

18–31   The scope of the 1989 Act applies generally within the civil service[36] and to some outside bodies. The 1989 Act appears to move in a more liberal direction to official secrets compared to section 2 of the 1911 Act which it replaced. However, the 1989 Act falls short of providing access to information and its scope is supplemented by an increasing reliance on legal devices and techniques other than the criminal law, to prevent disclosures. Very often such techniques involve the use of the civil law.

18–32   In the case of civil servants, the Civil Service Pay and Conditions of Service Code[37] has been revised to take account of the provisions of the 1989 Act and the details of the Armstrong Memorandum mentioned above. Thus civil servants are explicitly required under the terms and conditions of their employment as owing the Crown a duty of confidentiality. This duty applies even after the civil servant leaves his employment. In addition there is an obligation not to frustrate the policies or decisions of Ministers by the use or disclosure of information to which civil servants have access. Such requirements are intended to prevent leaks of information from civil servants who wish to disagree with the government's policy.

Civil servants who prove to be unreliable and untrustworthy are subject to disciplinary procedures which may result in dismissal[38] from the Service. Promotion prospects are severely restricted when civil servants engage in activities incompatible with their duty of confidence to Ministers.

18–33   Recourse to the civil law either on the basis of breach of confidence or through the use of injunctions to protect copyright ownership avoids some of the difficulties encountered with the application of the criminal law. The disadvantages of using criminal prosecutions to punish leaks of information may be attributable to the unpredictable nature of jury trials for serious breaches of the Official Secrets Act and the publicity of court proceedings even when the proceedings may be held in camera or where disclosure is a contempt of court. The scope of contempt laws allows for restrictions on the access to information available to the court. Documents obtained by a solicitor and read out in open court in the course of litigation could not be used for any collateral or ancillary purpose. In *Home Office v. Harman*[39] Harman, a

---

[36] The Official Secrets Act 1989 (Prescription) Order 1990 S.I. 1990 No. 200. The Act applies to members and employees of British Nuclear Fuels plc and Urenco Ltd. The staff of the National Audit Office, the Comptroller and Auditor General, the Parliamentary Commissioner for Administration, the Health Service Commissioner, and to the Northern Ireland equivalents.

[37] 1989–90 H.C. paras. 39–43.

[38] Such dismissal may not come within the terms of the protections offered under the Employment Protection (Consolidation Act) 1978 when dismissal is in the national interest and under Sched. 9 a certificate may be issued by the relevant Minister as evidence for that purpose.

[39] [1983] 1 A.C. 280.

solicitor for one of the parties in a civil action obtained documents by way of discovery which she later revealed to newspapers was held by the House of Lords to have been in contempt of court for so doing in breach of the undertaking given for the disclosure of the documents to the court.

Civil proceedings have other advantages over criminal prosecutions. The burden of proof in criminal cases is higher than in civil cases which rests not on the standard of beyond a reasonable doubt but on the balance of probabilities. In civil cases the judiciary and not the jury, performs the fact-finding role and this may facilitate the proof of the case against the defendant. Normally criminal proceedings are only used after the leak has occurred and the suspect detected. Civil proceedings can be activated in anticipation of any publication and offers prior restraint through the use of injunctions over any proposed publication. The *ex parte* nature of the interim injunction procedures means that the law may be readily applied and take effect as soon as the leak becomes apparent to the government. **18–34**

However it is a mistake to assume that civil proceedings are a complete panacea when the government wishes to retain confidential information which has become available on a world-wide basis outside the United Kingdom and the jurisdiction of the United Kingdom's courts. The long running *Spycatcher* litigation exposed limitations in the use of law to enforce secrecy. The case is an example of the use of litigation to enforce the doctrine of breach of confidence. This doctrine owed its origins to private law and the enforcement of personal rights, including the enforcement of trade secrets and marital secrets. The potential for its use in public law owes its origins to the *obiter dicta* of Lord Widgery in the *Crossman Diaries* case[40] discussed above. Then it was suggested that a breach of confidence might occur when government information was made public. The opportunity to apply this doctrine to its full potential, as an alternative to the use of the criminal law, arose in the *Spycatcher* case. **18–35**

The saga began in 1985 when the Attorney-General commenced proceedings in Australia against Peter Wright and his publisher seeking an injunction to prevent publication of Wright's memoirs detailing the activities of the security services during the period when Wright was a member of MI5. In the United Kingdom *ex parte* injunctions were granted restraining the publication of extracts from the memoirs in *The Guardian* and *The Observer*. After the trial of the issues in the Australian court, the Attorney-General's action was dismissed and Wright's memoirs allowed to be published. Publication **18–36**

---

[40] [1976] Q.B. 752.

also took place in the United States from May 1987 after extracts from the book were published in the Washington Post. The Attorney-General continued to attempt to prevent publication in the United Kingdom and was granted further interim injunctions against *The Sunday Times* and *The Independent*, the *Evening Standard* and the *London Daily News*.

18–37   In the meantime an appeal against permission to publish was heard in the New South Wales Court of Appeal where the Attorney-General was unsuccessful. Finally after *The Independent*, *The Sunday Times* and *The News on Sunday* were fined £50,000 each for contempt of court, the House of Lords in 1990 decided that no injunction would lie against the newspapers against any further serialisation of the book, nor would the newspapers be liable for any financial account of profits to the Government as the information contained in the *Spycatcher* book was now in the public domain and thus could not be restrained.

18–38   The House of Lords' decision to permit publication indicated the ineffectiveness of the law when attempting to restrain publication of information which has entered the international arena. The case also highlights a number of further possibilities open to the government interested in preventing publication. First the House of Lords accepted that neither the publishers nor the author had copyright in the book as copyright vested with the Crown. This gives rise to the possibility that the Crown might seek damages and an account of profits to base its claim. In the future this is likely to be a useful remedy. It could be argued that if a claim had been based on this ground, the Government's attempts to prevent publication might have been more effective. It is unlikely that any publisher would be willing to take such a risk of publication if the profits from publication are put in jeopardy.

18–39   Secondly, the House of Lords considered whether reliance could be placed on Wright's main defence that it was in the public interest to publish. The book was claimed to establish wrongdoing and lack of accountability on the part of the security services. Claims which if proven might give rise to serious public concern about the operational controls over the security services. In particular allegations were made that MI5 may had engaged in activities to destabilise the government when Harold Wilson was Prime Minister. In the House of Lords, Lord Griffiths was prepared to concede that in an extreme case the confidential nature of the trust between security service operatives and the security services might be lifted so that the dangers of a serious abuse might be made public.[41] However, such a

---

[41] [1988] 3 All E.R. 545 at 650.

justification did not appear to arise in the *Spycatcher* case. The House of Lords appeared to accept that once the book was available in the public domain, publication could not be prevented by an injunction. Such an injunction would be "futile," as personal copies of the book had been purchased or received by many United Kingdom citizens abroad and were imported into the United Kingdom. Despite the fact that Wright had a life-long duty of confidence, the reality was that such a duty was in practical terms unenforceable. This gave rise to the surprising result that Wright might be free to return to the United Kingdom and publish his memoirs without any prior restraint. The reality was that he would be prosecuted under the Official Secrets Act.

The effects of the *Spycatcher* litigation were far-reaching. The **18–40** Government was seriously embarrassed by the revelations in the book and attempts to restrict its publication had been unsuccessful. In the earlier consideration of an interim injunction, Lord Bridge in the House of Lords pointed to the absence of any Bill of Rights in the United Kingdom when compared to many other countries. He indicated that the European Convention would most likely result in the unenforceable nature of any ban. As a result the Government resolved to consider the regulation of the security services. This is a welcome approach to providing a statutory framework for the intelligence services.

(b) The Security Services

The unwelcome glare of publicity resulting from the *Spycatcher* affair **18–41** exposed many of the previously held secret activities of the security services. In particular the often quoted comment that[42] Peter Wright and others "bugged and burgled our way across London at the State's behest, while pompous, bowler-hatted civil servants in White-hall pretended to look the other way." In addition allegations made by Cathy Massiter that the phones of prominent CND activists[43] and trade unionists were bugged confirmed the suspicion of many commentators that the security services were not under complete control.

The question of control over the security services is itself often **18–42** shrouded in secrecy. In the 1940s a system of positive vetting developed[44] which was aimed at preventing persons with a commun-ist interest or affiliation from joining the civil service or the security

[42] P. Wright, *Spycatcher* (1987), p. 54.
[43] *R. v. Secretary of State for the Home Department ex p. Ruddock* [1987] 1 W.L.R. 1482.
[44] See 448 H.C. Deb., cols. 1703–4 (March 14, 1948).

services. This procedure applied to personnel mainly charged with handling sensitive information. It also applied to contractors engaged in work which may be similarly regarded as involving sensitive material.

18–42   The system of positive vetting developed as a means to purge the public service and contractors of any communists or sympathisers. Revisions to the system have been continuous since it was introduced[45] in 1952. In 1990 it was revised once more and a written statement made by the Prime Minister defended the operation of the system.[46] The increasing use of positive vetting reflects the increasing complexity and sensitivity of government decision-making. Also the series of leaks by civil servants may cause a wider drawing of the boundaries as to who should or should not be included. The main focus of positive vetting is directed against anyone who might be involved in any activities which threaten national security, such as espionage, terrorism, sabotage, or actions "intended to overthrow or undermine Parliamentary democracy by political, industrial or violent means." Different levels of clearance are necessary for the various categories of secret information ranging from top secret to merely confidential information.

18–43   Judicial review for someone who is refused positive vetting clearance, is limited[47] as the courts have shown reluctance to engage in any substantial examination of what is in the national interest, but there is an appeal procedure to the three advisers constituted to hear cases where there are allegations against a public servant. There is a procedure[48] which relies on the use of three advisers who may take account of the representations of the person affected. The recommendations of the three advisers are made to the Minister who may consider further evidence in the matter including representations from the person concerned. Government contractors may also make use of the three advisers procedure[49] since 1956.

18–44   In the aftermath of the *Spycatcher* case the Government responded. The outcome was first to establish a staff counsellor for the security services to deal with matters relating to concerns of officers about the nature of their work and if necessary the counsellor could have access to the Head of the Civil Service in order to allay fears. Setting up some form of internal grievance mechanism in order to deal with

---

[45] See P. Hennessy and G. Brownfield, "Britain's Cold War Security purge: The Origins of Positive Vetting" (1982) 4 *The Historical Journal* 25 965–973.

[46] 177 H.C. Deb., Col. 159–161 (July 24, 1990).

[47] *R. v. Director of Government Communications Headquarters, ex p. Hodges, The Times,* July 26, 1988, DC

[48] See Statement of the procedure to be followed when the reliability of a public servant is thought to be in doubt on security grounds. Cabinet Office 1985.

[49] Cmd. 9715 (1956).

legitimate concerns about the operational responsibilities of the security services was partly intended to restore morale to the service and also to re-build public confidence in the work of the service. The remit of the Staff Counsellor was later extended to include staff who were former members of the service. Dissatisfied members of the service could have recourse to the departmental Minister or the Prime Minister.

It is doubtful if such arrangements would be effective if they had **18–45** been available to Peter Wright. In fact many of his allegations especially that the one-time Head of MI5 was a double agent had been considered but rejected by his superior officers. It is hard to envisage that an aggrieved officer would be satisfied by a polite refusal internally to take no further action. Thus the creation of a staff counsellor appears to have limited potential for effectiveness. However, the creation of this office further served to strengthen the secrecy binding all members of the security services. This culture of secrecy is further reinforced by the Official Secrets Act 1989.

In addition to the creation of a staff counsellor, the Government **18–46** introduced a new Act. The Security Services Act 1989 to put the security services on a statutory basis. The new legislation[50] marked an important departure in official recognition of MI5 under section 1 of the Act. However this Act did not include any of the other elements in the security services such as MI6, responsible for overseas intelligence activity in liaison with the Foreign Office. There is no mention of the Government Communications Headquarters (GCHQ) at Cheltenham nor any statutory basis for its existence in the legislation. Plans to put the Intelligence Service and GCHQ on a statutory basis are contained in the Intelligence Services Act 1994. The remit covering the activities of the security services is widely drawn. It includes under section 1(2) of the 1989 Act:

> "... the protection of national security and in particular, its protection against threats from espionage, terrorism, sabotage, from the activities of agents of foreign powers and from actions intended to overthrow or undermine parliamentary democracy by political, industrial or violent means."

In addition under section 1(3) the function of the security services **18–47** includes "the economic well-being of the United Kingdom against threats posed by the actions or intentions of persons outside the British Islands." This is so broadly drafted that it might include any industrial commercial activity of foreign or international companies,

[50] See Leigh and Lustgarten (1989) 52 M.L.R. 801; see also Cm. 2523 (1994).

in fact almost anything may be connected to this function. Criticism of this section has focused on the widely drawn nature of the section.

There is provision under the Act for the appointment of a Director-General by the Secretary of State. The statutory responsibility of the Director includes, "the proper discharge of the functions of the service, for the purpose of preventing or detecting serious crime." The Director has to ensure that under section 2(2)b, the "service does not take any action to further the interests of any political party." The legislation, however, is vague on the arrangements for ministerial responsibility. The Government is presently agreed that some form of committee should be set up composed of Privy Councillors to oversee the work of the security services. There is little guidance in the legislation as to when Ministers ought be consulted or the relationship between the Minister and the Director. The implication is that the Director should have broad discretion in carrying out the various duties under the Act.

18–48   Prior to the passage of the Act it was common practice for the security services to operate alongside the Special Branch officers designated for that purpose by each police force. In 1992 the Government announced that the main responsibility for detecting terrorists would be devolved to MI5 away from the Special Branch and the Anti-terrorist branch of the Metropolitan Police. The supremacy of the intelligence officers over the police may be in part a refocusing of their activities in the aftermath of the collapse of the Soviet Union and a perceived end to the military threat of the Soviet Union.

18–49   The Security Services Act 1989 also contains considerable legal powers for the security services to carry out their activities. Prior to 1989, doubt was expressed about the legal powers of the security services to engage in covert activities. Section 3 of the Act remedies such gaps which may have existed in the law by the use of warrants issued by the Home Secretary. A warrant may authorise entry onto property and the "taking of such action" as is specified in the warrant and thought to be necessary. The power to issue a warrant in such circumstances depends on whether the value of the information is likely "to be of substantial value in assisting the Service to discharge its functions" and "cannot reasonably be obtained by other means." This gives extremely wide powers first to the Home Secretary to authorise warrants and second to the security services to carry on their activities. Information obtained under a warrant may not be disclosed as the Security Services Act 1989 makes disclosures a criminal offence.

18–50   It is noteworthy that the powers are Executive-based and there is no recourse to a judicial element[51] which is customary in the granting

---

[51] In contrast see the Canadian Security Intelligence Service Act 1984 where there is a judicial element in the application for warrants and with the approval of the Solicitor-General.

of warrants for example under PACE 1984. This leaves judicial review as the main means to challenge the decision of the Home Secretary or the activities of the security services. Judicial review is limited in such cases because historically judges have been reluctant to look behind the "national interest"[52] and the opportunities for challenge will usually be confined to challenges[53] after the warrants have been issued.

The procedure for granting warrants, which makes use of the **18–51** Home Secretary's powers, is likened to any other delegated authority without any special procedure for obtaining the Home Secretary's permission. There is no requirement to check the nature of the information, its source, reliability, the period for which the warrant may be issued and the places or people that may be effected. Critics of the Act have pointed to the systems in operation in both Canada[54] and Australia[55] which have greater accountability built into the system of granting of authority to the security services.[56]

Although the statutory authority for warrants is very extensive, there is the question of whether prerogative powers may co-exist with statutory authority. The scope of the prerogative is unclear and the question of whether prerogative powers remain after the statute is open to conjecture.[57]

The Security Services Act 1989 also provides procedures for com- **18–52** plaints. A Tribunal for the investigation of complaints against the security services is created with the Security Services Commissioner to undertake investigations with a duty on every member of the security services and every official of the Home Office to "disclose or give to the Commissioner such documents or information" as he may require for the purpose of enabling him to discharge his functions. Reports, including an annual report may be made to the Prime Minister and the Prime Minister is under a duty to lay the annual report before Parliament.

The Intelligence Services Act 1994 performs similar functions for **18–53** the Secret Intelligence Service (MI6) and the Government Communications Headquaters (GCHQ) as outlined[58] under the Security Service

---

[52] *Council of Civil Service Unions v. Minister for the Civil Service* [1985] A.C. 374.
[53] In *Entick v. Carrington* (1765) 19 State Tr. 1029 the courts generally disapproved of common law powers to provide general warrants but in the case of statutory powers the courts may have to accept the nature of the powers as providing a very broad discretion to the executive.
[54] D. Cayley Chung (1985) 26 Harvard Int. L.J. 234 and J.Ll.J. Edwards (1985) O.J.L.S. 143.
[55] H.P. Lee (1989) 38 I.C.L.O. 890.
[56] See Ewing and Gearty, *Freedom under Thatcher* (1990), pp. 130–136.
[57] *R. v. Secretary of State for the Home Department, ex p. Northumbria Police Authority* [1988] 1 All E.R. 556.
[58] See L. Lustgarten and I. Leigh, *In from the Cold: National Security and Parliamentary Democracy* (Clarendon Press, Oxford, 1994).

Act 1989 for MI5. The 1994 Act attempts to strike a balance between more openness and the protection of the national interest. Sections 1(1) and 3(1) are very widely drawn setting out the remit of the operations of MI5 and their functions. Little information can be gained from the definition contained in the Act except its vagueness. For example one function is to protect the "economic well-being of the United Kingdom" and this finds its place alongside the function of "support of the prevention or detection of serious crime".

18–54   The Act establishes a committee composed of M.P.s and members of the House of Lords to examine the administration, expenditure and policy of the three services MI5, MI6 and GCHQ. The committee is called the Intelligence and Security Committee. However, its function is not to review operational matters and it may not summon witnesses. In addition there is a tribunal for the purpose of investigating complaints against any one of the three services. The tribunal has no powers to compel the attendance of witnesses, its reasoning is kept confidential and its decisions are not open to challenge in the courts. Section 9(4) of the 1994 Act stipulates that the decisions of the Tribunal and the Commissioner "shall not be subject to appeal or liable to be questioned in any court".

The Intelligence and Security Committee is intended to supplement the appointment of a Commissioner under the 1989 Act. The Commissioner's reports are delivered to the Prime Minister who acts as a filter before the release of the report to Parliament. This allows the Prime Minister of the day to censor the contents of reports and clearly this provides an inadequate parliamentary check on the activities of the security services. Taken together the Security Services Act 1989 and the Intelligence Services Act 1994 provide a statutory framework for the security services.

18–55   The Security Service Act 1996 adds a further dimension to the law. The 1996 Act gives freedom to the security services to become involved in the "prevention and detection of serious crime". This inclusion of policing functions brings the activities of the security services into line with what many regarded as present day practice. As part of the programme to encourage a National Crime Squad the 1996 Act amends the Security Service Act 1989 and the Intelligence Services Act 1994. The Secretary of State may issue in certain specified circumstances general warrants to enter property or to interfere with wireless telegraphy in circumstances that would otherwise be unlawful. This represents a considerable extension of the legal powers of the security service but in a realistic way it may only reflect the reality of how powers were exercised in the past.

18–56   Reform of the law on surveillance such as telephone tapping and the interception of letters was introduced under the Interception of

Communication Act 1985. The *Malone* case[59] established that telephone tapping was in violation of Article 8 of the European Convention on Human Rights. The case drew attention to the regulation of such practices carried out in the United Kingdom through administrative practices. There was no direct statutory authority for phone tapping. It was argued that section 80 of the Post Office Act 1969 *required* the Post Office to make available to the police; information gained through metering phone calls for the detection of criminal activity.

The 1985 Act creates a new offence of unlawful interception of **18–57** communications by post or by means of a public telecommunications system. The offence is widely drawn and may be committed by journalists, newspapers or others in both the public or private sector. The assumption underlying the Act is that the Home Secretary will continue to make use of warrants authorising the interception of communications. Section 2 of the Act authorises such warrants for the purposes of, the interests of national security, preventing or detecting serious crime or for the purposes of safeguarding the economic well-being of the United Kingdom. Although attempts were made in Parliament to restrict the scope of the issuing of warrants to specific purposes such as the defence of the realm or to prevent subversions of terrorism or espionage, this was rejected in favour of the catch-all quality of the legislation. One troublesome concept is "national security" a phrase that is ideally suited to exclude much judicial scrutiny of the discretion of the executive.

Also noteworthy is that the issuing of warrants remains vested in **18–58** the relevant Secretary of State. There is no judicial or independent element in the decision whether or not to issue a warrant and this has been objected to on the basis that it would be more desirable to subject such a power to judicial control.[60] Since 1966 the Prime Minister has given assurances that the telephones of M.P.s were immune from interception.[61] The issuing of warrants and the coverage of information obtained in the warrants leaves many critics of the system uneasy. The scope of the warrant may specify a single individual or organisation, but this would not prevent the tapping of many 'phones over a protracted period of time without any further need to re-apply for a warrant. Bailey, Harris and Jones have noted that there were on average over 500 warrants, the majority for the interception of telephones[62]:

---

[59] *Malone v. U.K.* Eur. Court H.R., Series A, No. Vol. 82 (August 2, 1984): (1985) 7 E.H.R.R. 14.

[60] See P. J. Duffy and P. Mulchlinski (1980) 130 New L.J. 999. There is some doubt as to whether this part of the Act is consistent with the European Convention on Human Rights. See Baily, Harris and Jones *op. cit.* p. 804.

[61] H.C. Deb., Vol. 736, Col. 639 (November 17, 1966) and H.C. Deb., Vol. 803, Col. 1723 (July 16, 1970).

[62] Bailey, Harris and Jones, p. 517.

"Most warrants concerned 'serious crime'. 60% of the warrants requested by the police related to the importation or distribution of drugs. 'Just under 50% of all warrants issued at the request of the police have resulted directly or indirectly in arrests and in some cases in the recovery of property.' "

18–59   A Commissioner appointed by the Prime Minister together with a quasi-judicial Tribunal provide the main complaints procedures. The decision of the Tribunal is final and may not be reviewed by the courts though this may still leave open consideration by the European Convention on Human Rights. The membership of the Tribunal is for a limited fixed period of five years. The Tribunal has powers to determine whether a warrant to intercept information is properly issued under the Act. This refers to the question of whether there are adequate grounds for issuing the warrant and that statutory procedures are complied with. The means adopted to test the validity of the warrant procedure is akin to a court of law when exercising judicial review powers. This leaves considerable latitude with the security services as the courts are reluctant to apply more than a cursory consideration of national security matters. Indeed, on the basis of the *Wednesbury* criteria[63] of unreasonableness, in most cases ministerial discretion will be presumed to conform with the law unless it is so unreasonable that no reasonable Minister could have taken such a decision. To date the Commission has only found errors in the issuing of warrants of a minor and insubstantial nature. There has not been a finding that a warrant has been issued without cause.

18–60   The Commissioner must report to the Prime Minister on an annual basis. It appears that the remit of the 1985 Act does not cover electronic bugging devices. This leaves open the questions of what controls may exist and should such devices be used by the authorities? The Commissioner has three functions and responsibilities under the 1985 Act. First, to keep under review the various functions carried out by the Home Secretary conferred by the Act. Secondly, to keep under review the arrangements for restricting the use of information obtained under the intercepted material. Thirdly, to give assistance to the Tribunal to carry out its statutory functions.

3. Press and Media

18–61 The Press and media are subject to a wide variety of legal controls over what they may publish or broadcast. Newspapers are subject to the Defence Press and Broadcasting Committee. This Committee is

---

[63] [1948] 1 K.B. 223.

generally referred to as "the D notice system." D notices may be addressed to both radio, television and national and provincial editors of newspapers. In essence the system advises that publication or broadcasting of information would not be in the public interest. The composition of the D notice Committee is based on four government representatives, permanent civil servants, and 11 other representatives of the Press, both national and provincial, and the broadcasting agencies. In practice the minority representatives from the Government were mainly influential in the work of the Committee. A tacit agreement up until 1967, provided that newspapers that accepted and implemented the advice of the Committee were provided with immunity from any prosecution under the Official Secrets Acts. Although in fact there is no direct relationship between the D notice system and the Official Secrets Act. Editors cannot claim that because an item of news was cleared before the Committee that this absolved them of their statutory duties under the Official Secrets Acts.

In 1979–80 the system of D notices was reviewed[64] by the Defence **18–62** Select Committee and evidence given which indicated that the system was not working effectively. Chapman Pincher, a journalist had revealed in 1978 that the D notice system was dependent on the Secretary of State indicating whether the story was covered by a D notice and if not then the journalist would not be prosecuted if the story was published. This had gained some press confidence in the system but once the Secretary of State declined to make any implied undertaking the system became virtually unused. As indicated in the discussion of the *Spycatcher* story, the international press makes it more difficult to retain stories within the national boundaries of the United Kingdom.

The Select Committee divided on the issue of whether the D notice **18–63** system should be reformed. It agreed that some forms of secrecy required control over the Press or Broadcasting authorities. The Committee concluded that the essence of the D notice should be published as common practice was not to mention the use of the D notice system. After consideration of the Committee's report, the Government[65] decided to retain the D Notice Committee but its operation may be revised at some future date. A general introduction to the work of the Committee was published and the Government have promised that the composition of the Committee might be reviewed in the future.[66]

---

[64] Third Report of the House of Commons Defence Committee.
[65] *The D Notice System: Observations Presented by the Secretary of State for Defence* Cmnd. 8129 (1981).
[66] Fourth Report of the Defence Committee (1982–83): Previous Recommendations of the Committee (1982–83; H.C. 55).

18–64　　The advantage of the present system is that it allows representatives of the media to consider the matter in a reponsible manner. The disadvantage is that there is little openness in how the system actually works and the criteria used is far from clear. A more fundamental weakness of the system was revealed when the BBC attempted to broadcast a programme on the *Spycatcher* book.[67] The programme had received clearance from the secretary to the D Notice Committee on the basis that it did not provide any material which was a threat to national security. However the Government sought and obtained injunctions to prevent the broadcast of interviews being held about the programme on the basis that there was a breach of confidence in the disclosure made in the programme. The explanation for the apparent disparity is that the Attorney-General based his injunction on breach of confidence whereas the secretary to the D Notice Committee based his clearance on the basis of national security. There is therefore some doubt about the effectiveness of the D Notice Committee when the Government is actively pursuing greater use of civil remedies rather than the use of the criminal law.

18–65　　There appears to be a case for maintaining some form of D Notice Committee. For the purposes of wartime expediency it would appear to offer a reasonably effective means to preserve some balance between freedom of the press to publish information and the protection of the public interest. But in peacetime it would appear to have become an anachronism, although it is influential with many newspapers and their reporters but in fact largely ignored when the availability of news on an international basis facilitates the dissemination of information so easily available instantaneously on Fax machines.

18–66　　This raises the important question of the extent to which the right to privacy[68] may exist in English law and how this right may be protected by the courts. The Calcutt Committee in 1990 concluded[69] that the most appropriate definition of privacy might cover:

> "The right of the individual to be protected against intrusion into his personal life or affairs, or those of his family, by direct physical means or by publication of information."

Following the recommendations of the Calcutt report the Press Complaints Commission was established in 1991, replacing the Press

---

[67] The programme *My Country Right or Wrong*, see Oliver and Kingsford-Smith (eds.), *Economical with the Truth* (1990).

[68] Justice Report on *Privacy and the Law* (1970); The Younger Committee Report, *Report of the Committee on Privacy* Cmnd. 5012 (1972).

[69] Report of the Committee on Privacy and Related Matters, Cm. 1102 (1990).

Council established in 1953. The Commission is a non-statutory body comprising a chairman and 15 members, one-third of whom are not associated with the press. Any person may complain to the press and the Commission may investigate and return findings such as an adverse adjudication which must be published by the newspapers in question. There is no legal obligation to publish and the criticism about the Commission is that it lacks sufficient legal powers and sanctions.

Further reforms of the law have been considered by a second **18–67** report carried out by the Calcutt[70] Committee. The second report went much further than previous reports by recommending a statutory tribunal to replace the Press Commission. This favoured a move away from voluntary self-regulation in favour of statutory and legal regulation. The tribunal might be presided over by a senior judge appointed by the Lord Chancellor with powers to fine and place injunctions on newspapers. In addition Calcutt recommended that electronic eaves-dropping and long range photography on private property should be prohibited.

The press reacted unfavourably to proposals for tighter regulation. **18–68** In that light the National Heritage Select Committee[71] recommended that there should be a strengthening of the law both civil and criminal on privacy.[72] The Committee favoured the retention of some form of Press Complaints Commission but replacing the existing Press Complaints Commission with a Press Commission to uphold press freedom. The new commission should have powers to order fines and to order publication of apologies and in suitable cases the award of compensation. An appointed ombudsman to be appointed by the Lord Chancellor and funded by the Treasury to supervise adjudications of disputes, with the statutory power to compel newspapers to print apologies in a particular way, including the power of fines, is intended to strengthen supervision of the press. The Government has rejected the idea of Calcutt's statutory tribunal but is considering the best way forward in the light of the proposals. Recent newspaper articles on certain Government Ministers, and the private lives of the Royal Family and other public figures has drawn attention to the need to increase regulation of the press.

The press and media may come under considerable government **18–69** influence in matters of national security. In the case of broadcasting, fear of prosecution under the Official Secrets Acts may result in television or radio programmes being withdrawn. In the same period

[70] Calcutt Committee, Second Report (January 1993).
[71] Report of the National Heritage Committee, *Privacy and Media Intrusion* (HMSO March 1993).
[72] See Chap. 20 for a discussion of the law on privacy.

as the Ponting trial, Channel 4 withdrew one of its television programmes 20/20 Vision which contained detailed allegations made by Cathy Massiter about the use of MI5 but after a period of delay the programme was eventually shown.

18–70   The media is also subject to various search and seizure powers either under the Official Secrets Acts and under the ordinary law. For example there is a power for the police to search with a warrant under section 9 of the Official Secrets Act 1911 and this may be applied to discover journalists' information. In 1986, the BBC had commissioned a film series entitled Secret Society under the direction of Duncan Campbell, a journalist working in the intelligence field. The programme revealed the cost and extent of a secret Defence Ministry project to put a spy satellite into orbit. The programme was banned and an injunction obtained banning Campbell from publishing the story. A search of Campbell's home and offices, and also the Glasgow offices of the BBC, allowed the police to remove substantial numbers of documents. In Scotland, powers under section 9 of the Official Secrets Act 1911 were used while in England, a warrant was issued under PACE 1984.

Little of substance was achieved in the use of these powers. Campbell had already published the story in the *New Statesman* before the injunction[73] had been granted. The BBC eventually broadcasted an agreed version of the programme.

18–71   The media is also subject to ordinary civil action in the form of actions for libel and defamation.[74] In *Joyce v. Sengupta*[75] the Court of Appeal accepted that a plaintiff could establish more than one cause of action against a defendant and this might include both a claim for defamation and a claim for malicious falsehood. The latter gave rise to the possibility of legal aid, while the former did not. The plaintiff's claim arose out of a newspaper article which asserted that the plaintiff, then in the employment of the royal household had stolen certain letters of an intimate character and had handed them to the national press. In such a case the plaintiff's intention in pursuing a claim in the courts was not dependent on the award of damages but the main means open to a plaintiff to clear her name.

18–72   Broadcasting in the United Kingdom is also the focus of State influence. Preserving independence for broadcasters is equally important as preserving the freedom of the press. In the case of the British Broadcasting Corporation (BBC), since 1926 it has been constituted by Royal Charter. The BBC provides public broadcasting on a non-commercial basis, funded through a licence fee payable by the

[73] *New Statesman*, January 23, 1987.
[74] See the Defamation Act 1952, s.3.
[75] *The Independent*, August 11, 1992.

public who have television sets. The BBC operates under its Charter,[76] its Licence and Agreement[77] and where appropriate it receives directions under the relevant authority of the Charter or its licence from the Home Secretary. Failure to comply with such a direction might result in the withdrawal of the BBC's licence. The BBC is expected and required to act in a politically impartial manner and its programmes must be consistent with good taste and public opinion. The courts may be invited to consider whether the broadcasting authorities have complied with the standards of good taste.[78]

The use of the Home Secretary's directions is rare. In 1927 in the **18–73** early life of the BBC the corporation was forbidden to broadcast matters involving any religious, political or industrial controversy. There is a convention that the BBC should not derogate from the authority of Parliament in matters of public record. In recent years the televising of both Houses of Parliament has greatly assisted public information on the workings of Parliament and the broadcast of debates and the hearings of select committees is said to educate the public on the workings of democracy and this has been regarded as beneficial to the role of broadcasters.

In 1988 the Home Secretary announced a ban on the BBC and the **18–74** independent broadcasting companies from broadcasting the spoken words of members of the IRA or its supporters including Sein Fein.[79] This ban is intended to prevent public support or sympathy for the IRA or like organisations.

The Government has been active in opposing programmes that in any way are regarded as promoting the cause of terrorism. Programmes which may be critical of the security services may indirectly appear supportive of the terrorist cause and the drawing of boundaries in such cases as to what is or is not permissible is often controversial.[80] The Government has removed the ban on the broadcasting of Sein Fein in an effort to expedite the peace process. The ban was seen as counter-productive, as the television authorities interpreted the ban as allowing actors' voices to replace the words of Sein Fein spokesmen while broadcasting interviews.

In recent years the focus of attention on the BBC is on the role of **18–75** the Board of Governors. There is a full-time Chairman and a Deputy-Chairman with part-time members of the Board meeting usually at

---

[76] Cmnd. 8313.

[77] Cmnd. 8233.

[78] For example, *Att.-Gen., ex rel. McWhirter v. IBA* [1973] Q.B. 629.

[79] Also banned are members of the Ulster Defence Association. *R. v. Secretary of State for the Home Deparment, ex p. Brind* [1991] 2 W.L.R. 588.

[80] See the 1985 film *Real Lives* objected to by the Home Secretary, but later shown in an amended form after journalists took industrial action in a one day strike of protest against the Board of Governors' decision not to show the film.

least once a month. Discussion has focused on the role of the Governor in the day to day affairs of the BBC, in particular in the question of operational decisions and the policy of the BBC. Political parties from all shades of opinion have from time to time alleged bias in reporting and presentation of political views. Particularly when the government of the day is loud in such accusations, the BBC has been placed on the defensive. The style and direction of the BBC is under pressure to provide greater accountability for the expenditure of public money. Quality assurance, better management style and greater attention to business principles have been encouraged in the run up to the period for the renewal of the BBC's Charter.

18–76   In January 1993 the BBC Chairman and Deputy-Chairman were criticised for allowing the appointment of John Birt as a new Managing Director of the BBC to make his salary payable not under the PAYE scheme but to a company set up for this purpose. Resolution of this problem has called into question the organisation and structure of the management of the BBC.

In the case of commercial broadcasting, regulation is provided on a statutory basis. The Broadcasting Act 1990, replaced the old Independent Broadcasting Authority and for cable television the Cable Authority. A single authority, the Independent Television Commission (ITC) regulates and licences, with the exception of the BBC, all television, and cable and satellite services. The process of franchising television licences depends on bids being made from commercial organisations to carry out the terms of the licence. The ITC is under a duty to consider whether the licence holder "is a fit and proper person to hold" a licence. There are restrictions on certain groups with political or religious connotations from holding a licence.

18–77   Section 10 of the Broadcasting Act 1990 grants the relevant Minister or the Secretary of State, powers to direct licence holders to include announcements or to make a notice to licence holders directing that certain specified matters may not be included in programmes. There is also a Programme Code[81] setting out the standards of broadcasting and the balance required in programming. This is in addition to the Broadcasting Standards Council established as a consumer watchdog in 1988 to oversee broadcasters' activities in respect of violence, sex, taste and decency, and given statutory recognition under section 152 of the Broadcasting Act 1990.

18–78   In common with the BBC, commercial television has found controversy in its desire to broadcast investigative programmes involving terrorist activities and the security services. In 1988, Thames Television[82] broadcast Death on the Rock, an investigative programme into

---

[81] February 1991.
[82] Note this is before the passage of the 1990 Broadcasting Act.

the shooting of three members of the IRA by members of the SAS in Gibralter. The programme received criticism from the then Prime Minister and renewed debate began over whether there had been a shoot-to-kill policy on the part of the security forces. The criticism of the programme resulted in an inquiry into the objectivity and the factual basis of the progamme.[83]

Broadcasters face a climate of opinion which may favour further restrictions on reporting of terrorist activities especially when they involve the activities of the security services. The ban on broadcasting the spoken words of terrorist groups and Sein Fein, has contributed to a greater degree of "self-censorship" within broadcasting. In fact this has probably led to a more effective system of control than would have been possible through the passage of legislation prohibiting the broadcasting of a wide range of investigative programmes.

4. Freedom of Expression

Freedom of expression is commonly acknowledged to be a funda- **18–79** mental attribute of many Western-style democracies. Because of the absence of any written constitutional protection of this fundamental concept, its existence may depend on the interpretation of various laws designed to protect the public in terms of blasphemy, defamation, obscenity[84] and contempt of court. Street summarised the distinctive qualities of civil liberties in the United Kingdom[85]:

"Civil liberties in Britain have been shown to be a patchwork. Some of them rest on the chance that citizens have sued each other and given the opportunity to declare some isolated legal rule. Some rest on sporadic legislation, often passed to meet some specific emergency real or imaginery. The extent of inroads on certain freedoms rests on the subtleties of ministerial responsibility and the muted insistence of Whitehall to be allowed to govern unhindered."

Secrecy and confidentiality discussed above operate in a society **18–80** which is accustomed to legal controls over information in the form of censorship. In that context the criminal law and in certain circumstances the civil law, has developed an extensive jurisdiction over the

---

[83] Windlesham Report, "Death on the Rock" (1989).
[84] See Chap. 20 for a discussion of the obscenity laws.
[85] H. Street, *Freedom, Individual and the Law* (1982), p. 307.

citizen's freedom to see, hear and read matter which is deemed unsuitable.[86] Such freedoms are constrained on the basis of providing legal restraints justified in the public interest. A difficult balance must be struck in such cases between providing a remedy for the citizen to protect his or her rights and the right of freedom of information for the public.

A few examples of such controls are an indication of the scope and breadth of the law. For example, as noted above actions for breach of copyright or breach of confidence may also form the basis of civil actions which allow for the use of injunctions to restrain publication[87] of the information and for damages by way of compensation.

(a) Blasphemy and Defamation

18–81 At common law it is an offence to publish blasphemous matter whether orally or in writing. The definition of blasphemous is to deny the Christian religion, the Bible or the Book of Common Prayer. In *Whitehouse v. Gay News Ltd and Lemmon*[88] the House of Lords held that it is a blasphemous publication if it is said to be indecent or offensive and is likely to outrage the general body of Christian believers. This was the first prosecution for 60 years and the material in question was a poem which was accompanied by an illustration vilifying Christ in his life and crucifixion. While offensive to many people the material in question did not lead to a breach of the peace and there was no evidence that it was likely to provoke violence or civil disorder. Nevertheless a prosecution could be successful once it was shown that the general body of Christian believers might be shocked. The only mental requirements of the crime was proof that the defendants intended to publish the offending words.

18–82 More recently the question of applying the blasphemy laws to religions other than Christian ones, was considered in *ex p. Choudhury*.[89] The material in question was the book *The Satanic Verses* by the author Salman Rushdie. The court held that the law only applied to the Christian religion. The Law Commission's recommendation that the law could be abolished,[90] reflects a growing awareness that in a multi-national and religious society, it is unfair to protect one religious group to the exclusion of any other.

Defamatory statements are ones which ridicule, or cause hatred or contempt of the subject. Defamatory words published in the course of

---

[86] See Chap. 20 for a discussion of the law on obscenity and press censorship.
[87] Copyright, Designs and Patents Act 1988.
[88] [1979] A.C. 617.
[89] *R. v. Chief Metropolitan Stipendiary Magistrate, ex p. Choudhury* [1991] 1 Q.B. 429.
[90] Law Commission No. 145 (1985), *Offences Against Religion and Public Worship*.

a performance of a play amount to a criminal libel under sections 4 and 6 of the Theatres Act 1968. Defamatory matter usually consists of spoken words but when written it is libel and when accompanied by gestures is slander. Libel is writing which tends to vilify a person and bring them into hatred or contempt or ridicule.

Under section 5 of the Libel Act 1843, publication of a libel is a **18–83** common law misdemeanour[91] but it is rarely prosecuted. Normally criminal libel is focused only on serious matters. However sometimes, but not always, this may involve the question of whether a breach of the peace is involved. The use of the civil law is more frequent. The remedy usually lies in damages but the use of an interlocutory injunction may be more effective[92] to prevent the dissemination of the offending material. It is a defence to show that the material published was true or was a fair comment or published in the public interest. Privileged statements such as the proceedings of the House of Commons will not allow for a civil action to be taken, but may well involve investigation by the Committee of privileges should there be any abuse of the privileges of the House of Commons. Absolute privilege attaches to the judicial proceedings and communication between Officers of State. Qualified privilege attaches to the communications between members of the public and M.P.s, M.P.s and Ministers, in the proceedings of public meetings of local councils and in the administration of tribunals and inquiries.

(b) Contempt of Court

Contempt of court provides protection for the administration of **18–84** justice to ensure that it is free from interference and obstruction.[93] The fear of contempt proceedings may cause newspapers or the media not to publish or broadcast the details of their stories and this may interefere with the freedom of expression. A distinction is drawn by the English courts[94] between civil and criminal contempt. In the case of civil contempt, this may arise in disobedience of a court order such as an injunction. Criminal contempt may arise where there are publications prejudicial to a fair trial or civil proceedings, publications which interfere with the course of justice, contempt in the face of the court or acts which interfere with the course of justice. Newspapers may often find that contempt proceedings are used

---

[91] Punishable by no more than one year's imprisonment.
[92] *Corelli v. Wall* (1906) 22 T.L.R. 532.
[93] C. J. Miller, *Contempt of Court* (2nd ed. 1989).
[94] This does not apply in Scotland. The law on contempt in Scotland is subject to procedural differences for the law in England and Wales.

against them. In *Att.-Gen. v. Times Newspapers Ltd*,[95] the House of Lords considered contempt proceedings arising out of the publication by *The Sunday Times* of a series of investigative articles relating to the drug Thalidomide. The House of Lords held that the Attorney-General was the proper person to institute contempt proceedings and that injunctions could be granted to restrain publication of any articles which may be prejudicial to a fair hearing of the case.

18–85   The law of contempt may severely inhibit the freedom of the press to publish articles. Some reform but not codification of the common law rules of contempt was provided in the Contempt of Court Act 1981. This followed recommendations for reform of the law, after the Phillimore Committee Report[96] in 1974 and after the *Thalidomide* case was considered by the European Court of Human Rights,[97] where the court held that Article 10 of the Convention which concerns the right to freedom of expression had been infringed[98] and the restrictions imposed by the injunction were not necessary in a democratic society.[99]

18–86   Newspapers may attempt to protect their sources of information. In the case of Sarah Tisdell, the civil servant who copied documents relating to the defence arrangements for the reception of cruise missiles at R.A.F. Greenham Common, and leaked the information to *The Guardian* newspaper, the identification of Tisdell followed after an investigation of the leak. The Government instituted proceedings for the return of the documents used by the newspaper. Section 10 of the Contempt of Court Act 1981 provides that the court may not require disclosure of information "unless it be established to the satisfaction of the court that disclosure is necessary in the interests of justice or national security or for the prevention of disorder or crime." The Court of Appeal required the newspaper to return the documents which enabled the identity of Sarah Tisdell to be known and she was later successfully prosecuted. Later on the basis of the legal principles involved, the newspaper appealed to the House of Lords.[1] Lord Diplock pointed out that section 10 did not contain any reference to "the public interest." A majority of 3:2 concluded that the need to find the identity of the person who leaked the documents was in the national interest. The claim of national security appears sufficiently strong to provide justification for the courts to require disclosure of

---

[95] [1974] A.C. 273.
[96] Cmnd. 5794 (1974).
[97] *Sunday Times v. U.K.* [1979] 2 E.H.R.R. 245.
[98] The Commission had concluded by 8 votes to 5 that the injunction had breached Art. 10. The decision of the court was by the slimmest margin of 11 votes to 9.
[99] The case illustrated the different balance between the approach at common law and the approach where rights are to be directly protected.
[1] *Secretary of State for Defence v. Guardian Newspapers Ltd* [1985] A.C. 339.

information by the press. In the *Tisdell* case national security was accepted by the courts on the basis of an affidavit sworn by the Ministry of Defence establishment officer that national security required the return of the leaked documents.

The courts have accepted that on general principle a liberal **18–87** interpretation should be given to section 10. However Lord Bridge in *X v. Morgan-Grampian Publishers Ltd*[2] noted that in the balance to be struck between non-disclosure and disclosure, the courts would consider whether the information was obtained legitimately "this will enhance the importance of protecting the source" whereas if the information is obtained illegally, this will diminish "the importance of protecting the source," unless there are counter-balancing factors such as "a clear public interest in the publication of the information, as in the classic case where the source has acted for the purpose of exposing iniquity."

In this area the courts focus their attention on the legality and the motives behind the giving of information to newspapers. The question of the content of the material, its reliability and whether on the merits of the information contained in the material disclosure of the source of information is in the public interest appears a secondary consideration.[3]

Contempt of court protects the deliberations of jurors,[4] the inter- **18–88** ference with witnesses and the course of justice. All are protected by the courts as part of their role in preventing any intentional contempt. In the case of jury deliberations, contempt of court proceedings were instituted[5] after the publication in *The New Statesman*, of an interview carried out with a member of the jury in the trial of Jeremy Thorpe and others. Publications prejudicial to a criminal trial[6] or civil proceedings are likely to fall within the remit of contempt.[7] There is some doubt as to whether contempt may apply to proceedings of a tribunal. The wording of section 19 of the Contempt of Court Act 1981 defines court as "any tribunal or body exercising the judicial power of the state." This has been narrowly interpreted by the courts[8] in relation to a Mental Health Review Tribunal, the Divisional Court held that the Tribunal was not a court for the purposes of the Contempt of Court Act.

The climate of secrecy dominates the British approach to govern- **18–89** ment. This is against a background of what many perceive to be a

---

[2] [1991] 1 A.C. 1.
[3] See T.R.S. Allan, "Disclosure of Journalists' Sources, Civil Disobedience and the Rule of Law" (1991) C.L.J. 131.
[4] Contempt of Court Act 1981, s.8.
[5] *Att.-Gen. v. New Statesman* [1981] Q.B. 1.
[6] Contempt of Court Act 1981, ss.2, 32 and Sched. 1.
[7] *Att.-Gen. v. News Groups Newspapers plc* [1989] Q.B. 110.
[8] *Att.-Gen. v. Associated Newspapers Group plc* [1989] 1 All E.R. 604.

remarkably open and free society. This apparent contradiction appears to come from the fact that the United Kingdom has much less formal protection of fundamental rights and freedoms when compared to international standards.[9] It is clear that access to information is a key element in any democratic system. The government's promise of a Freedom of Information Act in the near future is likely to make a radical change to the culture of secrecy in the United Kingdom.

---

[9] Francesca Klug, Keir Starmer and Stuart Weir, *The Three Pillars of Liberty* (Routledge, 1996), pp. 304–7.

Chapter 19

Northern Ireland

1. Introduction

Northern Ireland's constitutional arrangements and the use of emer- **19–01** gency powers in response to serious civil disturbance are considered in this chapter. Experience in Northern Ireland has tested many institutions and constitutional innovations inherited from the link with Britain. Northern Ireland provides an insight into systems of devolution such as that contained in the Government of Ireland Act 1920. The 1920 Act has been replaced by the Northern Ireland Constitution Act 1973 which also offers a modern model of devolution, even though its provisions have not been implemented because of the lack of agreement over the future of Northern Ireland among politicians in the Province. Northern Ireland, as a case study of conflict offers important lessons. The rich literature about its history and current problems provides constitutional scholars with a study of the limitations of law as well as access to debates about constitutional innovation and change.[1]

In the nineteenth century, the Act of Union 1800, united Britain and **19–02** Ireland. Under the Union, laws were passed at Westminster for Ireland. Ireland's constitutional arrangements were unique within the United Kingdom. Irish government was centred in Dublin Castle which contained the main offices of administration, centralised and well organised with a professional civil service having administrative control over the local administration of law and government. At its head was an appointed Lord Lieutenant and General Governor of Ireland who represented the main link between the British Cabinet and Irish administration. He was assisted by an appointed Chief Secretary as adviser and assistant who directed the administration of justice aided by the Lord Chancellor of Ireland, and various law

---

[1] See John Morrison and Stephen Livingstone, *Reshaping Public Power: Northern Ireland and the British Constitutional Crisis* (Sweet and Maxwell, 1995).

officers. Irish law continued to hold its own distinctiveness. Irish courts and judiciary were separate from the courts and judiciary of England and Wales.

19–03   The events leading to the setting up of Northern Ireland in 1922 form an important chapter in the constitutional history of the United Kingdom. The creation of Northern Ireland may be conveniently examined in two phases. The first is from 1920 to 1973 and comprises the Government of Ireland Act 1920 which created a Parliament for Northern Ireland with a Prime Minister and Cabinet, modelled on Westminster. The government of Northern Ireland had extensive legislative and executive powers under a devolved system of government, which maintained the sovereignty of the United Kingdom Parliament. The second phase, under the Northern Ireland Constitution Act 1973, consisted of first the suspension and later the abolition of the Northern Ireland Government under the Government of Ireland Act 1920 and a period of direct rule from Westminster which presently endures. In 1985 the Anglo-Irish Agreement was signed between the two Governments of Britain and Ireland and provides for the Government of the Republic of Ireland to have an influence over policy matters for Northern Ireland. The 1985 Anglo Irish Agreement is examined as to its constitutional significance for the future of Northern Ireland.

19–04   Amidst further sectarian violence in Northern Ireland, of escalating ferocity, further constitutional initiatives have been attempted. On December 15, 1993, the British Prime Minister and the Taoiseach made a Joint Declaration. The declaration sets out constitutional principles and political realities for the future of Northern Ireland. The Joint Declaration makes a direct challenge to terrorists in Northern Ireland to stop violence and enter into a framework for peace. Both Governments enter a commitment that "following a cessation of violence," democratically mandated parties which establish a commitment to exclusively peaceful methods "are free to participate in discussion between both Governments and the political parties on the way ahead." Significantly the Joint Declaration clarifies that the British Government have "no selfish strategic or economic interest in Northern Ireland." However, Unionists are assured that unification between North and South in a united Ireland can only be by agreement the two parts respectively. How such an agreement might be achieved or once achieved, tested in a constitutional sense is left unclear. The Irish government accepts that it would be wrong to impose a united Ireland. They undertake to examine "any elements in the democratic life and organisation of the Irish state" which are feared by Unionists. Here there are hints that areas of controversy such as constitutional sovereignty claimed by Ireland over Northern Ireland might be examined.

19–05   The Joint Declaration moves matters in Northern Ireland a further step in the direction of inter-governmental agreement between Britain and Ireland. Future initiatives on the government of Northern Ireland are likely to reflect this dimension as part of any agreement. The Joint Declaration is intended to encourage political dialogue. This is controversial when dialogue involves terrorist organisations, even if and when they renounce violence.

The IRA declared a "complete cessation of violence" on August 31, 1994. Since then attempts to continue the peace process have included questions of decommissioning of terrorist weapons, and the setting up of all-party talks with the inclusion of Sinn Fein subject to agreements about the end to violence and the complete renunciation of terrorist activities. There are some relevant statutory provisions. The Northern Ireland (Entry to Negotiations, etc.) Act 1996 provided for elections in Northern Ireland to allow all-party negotiations. The decommisssioning of arms has been the subject of a report under the United States Senator George Mitchell on January 22, 1996 and the Northern Ireland Arms Decommissioning Act 1997 provides a statutory framework for arms decommissioning.

Since 1968 serious terrorist violence has necessitated emergency **19–06** powers, including the abolition of jury trial for specific scheduled offences. Extensive emergency powers allow wide powers of arrest, search, seizure and the right to silence is suspended for terrorist offences. Such powers raise the question of how compatible emergency powers may be with the protection of civil liberties?

Northern Ireland has been compared[2] to a:

"laboratory in which to assess the strengths and weaknesses of two approaches to the Constitution: a pragmatic empiricist approach which is traditionally British, and a constitutional idealist approach, more prevalent for example in the United States and Canada."

It is also unique in having, within the United Kingdom's tradition **19–07** of an unwritten Constitution, a written Constitution which addresses the question of protecting minorities. Northern Ireland's current emergency has raised the question of a Bill of Rights specifically drafted for the requirements of protecting minorities. The Government has rejected the introduction of such a Bill of Rights in Northern Ireland but a Bill of Rights may be considered in the future of Northern Ireland's constitutional arrangements.

---

[2] C. McCrudden, "Northern Ireland and the British Constitution" in Jowell and Oliver (eds.), *The Changing Constitution* (2nd ed., 1989), pp. 297–342 (3rd ed., 1994).

2. Political, Economic and Social Background

(a) Historical Developments in the Formation of Northern Ireland

19–08 A brief account of Northern Ireland's past history[3] may assist in explaining its present day constitutional status and government. In the nineteenth century the Act of Union created for the whole of Ireland a single "United Kingdom of Great Britain and Ireland." Ireland's own Parliament modelled on the English model was abolished and replaced with a legislative union with Britain. Thereafter Westminster legislation applied to Ireland, while taking account of Irish differences.

19–09 In the eighteenth century, attempts to remedy Irish discontent caused the passage of various measures to ameliorate legal disadvantages among the Catholic population.[4] This process continued and by 1829 Catholic emancipation was granted. Catholics were entitled to hold land and vote at elections. Throughout the century Irish discontent continued as the newly enfranchised population asserted rights translated into a demand for Home Rule. Famine and economic distress were at their height in severity in the 1840s. The population in 1851 estimated to be 6.5 million had increased to 8.3 million in 1841, but between 1841 and 1911 it fell by almost half to less than 4.4 million. Emigration and famine combined to cause such dramatic decline.

19–10 The quarter century after the famine years saw the build-up of resistance to English rule in Ireland. This manifested itself in the formation of local tenant societies set up in 1847 to agitate for improvement in the law on landholding.[5] These claims were translated into demands for fair rent, fixity of tenure and free sale. The Land League appeared in 1850 to co-ordinate agitation for land reform, with a wider political agenda in national politics. Sectarian

---

[3] Useful historical accounts may be found in: R. F. Foster, *Modern Ireland 1600–1972* (Penguin, 1988); K. Theodore Hoppen, *Ireland since 1800* (Longman, 1992); P. Buckland, *A History of Northern Ireland* (1981); H. Calvert, *Constitutional Law in Northern Ireland* (1968); S. Wichert, *Northern Ireland since 1945* (1992), Andy Pollack, *A Citizens' Inquiry: The Opsahli Report on Northern Ireland* (Dublin, 1993).

[4] K. Boyle and T. Hadden, *Ireland: A Positive Proposal* (1985); C. Palley, "Ways Forward; The Constitutional Options" in D. Watts (ed.) *The Constitutional of Northern Ireland* (1981); C. Palley, *The Evolution, Disintegration and Possible Reconstruction of the Northern Ireland Constitution* (1972); *Anglo American Law Review* 368; C. Palley, "Constitutional Solutions to the Irish Problem" (1980) 33 C.L.P. 121; C. Palley, *The United Kingdom and Human Rights* (London, 1991).

[5] P. Bew, "The Land League Ideal: Achievements and Contradictions" in P. J. Drudy (ed.), "Ireland: Land, Politics and People (1982) *Irish Studies* 77–92; D. Bowen, *The Protestant Crusade in Ireland, 1800–70: A Study of Protestant – Catholic Relations between the Act of Union and Disestablishment* (Dublin, 1978).

differences between the majority Catholic population and a Protestant ascendancy made the Irish land question a dominant issue. The granting of the franchise to some Catholics in 1829 after considerable pressure only heightened distrust of English law. Protestant resistance increased and Orange lodges feared the end to Protestant ascendancy and land ownership. Seen from the perspective of the[6] British authorities, Protestant influence permeated the minds of magistrates and jurors, while Catholic tenants organised in secret societies and often neutralised the power of the landlord magistrates by intimidating jurors and witnesses.[7] Prosecutions of crimes linked to political, religious or sectarian issues were often problematical.[8]

The term "agrarian outrage," commonly[9] used to describe offences **19–11** arising out of disputes as to the occupation of land or arising out of political or religious antagonisms was endemic in Ireland and affected almost every aspect of the administration of justice. The fact that crimes were motivated by political and religious allegiance meant that the idea of impartial justice received little support in Ireland.

The authorities in Dublin Castle struggled to find policies and laws to respond to widespread economic distress and agrarian outrage. Coercive powers enacted during the nineteenth century by special legislation included restrictions on movement, the possession of arms, suppression of organisations, meetings, publications and often the suspension of habeas corpus. Examples of coercive legislation varied but included in certain circumstances the suspension of jury trials in a proclaimed area.

Contemporaneous with coercive legislation, law reforms were **19–12** introduced, intended to reduce violence and create economic and social stability.[10] The attempt to govern Ireland at this time has been variously described as adopting a policy of coercion and conciliation.[11] In 1881 Gladstone's major initiative, the Land Act 1881, granted

---

[6] See J. F. McEldowney, "Crown Prosecutions in Nineteenth – Century Ireland" in Hay and Snyder, *Policing and Prosecution in Britain 1750 – 1850* (Oxford, 1989), p. 432. Also see M. R. Beames, "The Ribbon Societies: Lower Class Nationalism in Pre-famine Ireland" (1982) 47 *Past and Present* 131–132.

[7] C. Townshend, *Political Violence in Ireland* (Oxford, 1983).

[8] M. Beames, *Peasants and Power: The Whiteboy Movements and their Control in Pre-Famine Ireland* (Brighton, 1983).

[9] *Select Committee of the House of Lords on Irish Jury Laws*, pp. 1881, XI, Parl. Pap. i, para. 3141. See G. E. Christianson, "Secret Societies and Agrarian Violence in Ireland 1790–1840", *Agricultural History* (1972) 46, 369–384.

[10] J. Wyle, *Irish Land Law* (London, 1975), pp. 29–30 Extensive powers included: the Land Law (Ireland) Act 1881, the Purchase of land (Ireland) Act 1885, and Land Purchase Acts 1891–1899. The culmination of such legislative intervention may be found in the Irish Land Act 1903.

[11] P. Bew, *Conflict and Conciliation in Ireland 1890–1910: Parnelites and Radical Agrarians* (Oxford, 1982). K. Boyle and T. Hadden, *Northern Ireland: The Choice* (1994).

fair rent, fixity of tenure and free sale of land. More ambitious reforms soon followed, building on the basis of the earlier 1870 Land Act to enable tenants to purchase land. One of the most innovative and far-reaching State interventions into the rights of private property was attempted with the formation of the Irish Land Commission. Interference with property rights on behalf of a once disenfranchised population was an unprecedented use of law in Ireland.

19–13 The Land Commission acted on behalf of tenants and helped to underwrite their financial arrangements to purchase land and in 1881 received additional powers to provide almost three-quarters of the purchase price of land for the Irish tenants.

Land purchase schemes from 1881 to the end of the century provided tenants with ownership and property rights. Extensive legal powers and financial sources were provided to assist with purchase arrangements. Such initiatives, although surrounded with good will failed to provide an enduring solution to the political question raised by tenant agitation which questioned the existence of the State and English governance. A strong Home Rule movement in Ireland, from its early origins in the 1850s gained widespread support and public acceptance. Home Rule, meaning a local parliament with independent powers from Westminster became a vociferous demand from Irish nationalists, mainly Catholic and mainly tenant farmers. By the 1880s Home Rule had gained acceptance in the highest authorities within the British Cabinet including the British Prime Minister, William Gladstone.[12]

19–14 Gladstone[13] took the initiative in 1886 and introduced the first Home Rule Bill. Opposition from the mainly Protestant ascendancy helped secure the defeat of the Bill but a significant constitutional innovation had been attempted which went far beyond the attempt to make English law in Ireland more acceptable. The form of the 1886 Bill revealed important constitutional, technical, administrative and financial complexity in finding workable arrangements to meet Irish demands and maintain English support. The 1886 Bill drew on the experience gained in the drafting of federal and colonial constitutional laws. In that sense Ireland was compared to other colonial problems of the period.

19–15 The main innovation in the Bill was an Irish legislature in Dublin with extensive executive powers and responsibilities.[14] Aside from

[12] See J. Vincent, "Gladstone and Ireland" (1977) lxiii *Proceedings of the British Academy* pp. 193-238.

[13] Introduced by Gladstone in April 1886. In the election held in July 1886 Gladstone's Liberal Government lost office and there followed nearly two decades of conservative government.

[14] An account is provided in B. Hadfield, *The Constitution of Northern Ireland* (Belfast SLS, 1989), pp. 5–31. See K. Boyle and T. Hadden, *Northern Ireland: The Choice* (1994) and also *Frameworks for the Future* (1995).

excluded matters such as foreign affairs, defence and trade, the legislature in Dublin gained powers of taxation. The existing police forces, the Dublin Metropolitan Police and Royal Irish Constabulary remained[15] but powers in the Bill allowed reorganisation and control under local authorities.

Irish representation at Westminster was to cease but the Lord Lieutenant was retained and the police force remained subject to that authority. The 1886 Bill was perceived as creating a shift in the sovereignty of the United Kingdom's Parliament to an Irish Parliament with extensive legal powers. Doubts were raised at the extent to which, if the Bill was passed, residual sovereignty might reside with the Westminster Parliament.[16]

The degree of autonomy contained in the Bill and the perception **19–16** that Catholic domination might follow caused Irish Protestants to resist any form of Home Rule. Little relief came when the Bill was defeated. The success of Gladstone's conversion to Home Rule brought bitter disappointment to Unionist aspirations. In January 1886 the Ulster Loyalist Anti-Repeal Union was formed and this organisation linked the Orange Order and Protestant Churches in a unified opposition to Home Rule. It was particularly active in Ulster, one of four provinces in Ireland comprising nine counties situated in the North East of Ireland. In the same month as the formation of the Anti-Repeal Union, Ulster Unionist M.P.s formed themselves into a distinct parliamentary group at Westminster.

Gladstone's second Home Rule Bill in 1893 faced the same pros- **19–17** pects of defeat as the failed attempts to introduce Home Rule in 1886. The 1893 Bill passed the House of Commons but was defeated in the House of Lords. The 1893 Bill clarified the issue of sovereignty by expressly stating that the Westminster Parliament created an Irish legislation "without impairing or restricting the supreme authority of Parliament." Irish representation was to be maintained at Westminster, including Irish peers in the House of Lords. The cornerstone of the Bill was the creation of an Irish legislature to legislate "for the peace order and good government of Ireland." More extensive financial powers retained greater autonomy to the Irish Exchequer and Consolidated Fund while customs duties were to be paid into the United Kingdom's Exchequer.

Appeals to the Judicial Committee of the Privy Council were **19–18** substituted for Irish appeals to the House of Lords which would cease once the Bill came into effect. References arising out of the legal

---

[15] *ibid.* The Act of Union provided that Ireland should have representation of 100 seats at Westminster, later this increased to 105.

[16] *ibid.* Colm Campbell, *Emergency Law in Ireland 1918–1925* (Clarendon Press, Oxford, 1994).

powers of the Irish legislature could be made by the Lord Lieutenant direct to the Judicial Committee. In common with previous attempts to introduce some form of local legislature, the attempt to introduce the terms of the 1893 Bill failed, a clear illustration of the strength and effectiveness of Unionist opposition. The opportunity to attempt a third Home Rule Bill in 1912 was made. This attempt was bound to be successful because the Parliament Act 1911 assured the authority of the House of Commons over the Lords. As the Lords' powers were reduced to the power of postponement, ultimatly once the Bill had passed the Commons it would become law.

19–19   In 1912, Asquith introduced the Government of Ireland Bill modelled on the 1893 Bill which the Lords had rejected. The proposed Irish legislature was given the title of Irish Parliament. It was bicameral in composition, to be elected under proportional representation and empowered to make laws "for peace order and good government." Extensive powers to regulate the police were to be transferred to the Irish Parliament after six years. The 1912 Bill also contained clauses intended to prevent religious inequality. Sovereignty was to be reserved to Westminster but the Irish legislative to be set up under the 1912 Bill would have commanded wide powers and autonomy. Opposition to the contents of the Bill moved outside Westminster into the public arena as the Bill's passage into law seemed inevitable. A voluntary military force was set up in Ulster to resist the imposition of Home Rule in Ireland. Separation was deemed possible with the setting up of a "Provisional Government" in 1913 to take control of Ulster should Home Rule become a reality. Delays caused by Unionist opposition to the 1912 Bill resulted in the final passage of the Bill in September 1914. The 1914 Act received the Royal Assent but did not come into effect immediately. Implementation of the 1914 Act was delayed by the commencement of the First World War.

19–20   The protracted period of delays and frustrations caused by intense opposition to the legislation had its effect on the popularity of Home Rule. In Ireland doubts as to the worth of Home Rule were caused by the lack of success in its implementation. Thus increased Nationalist demand for complete independence gained support. Protestant resistance to Home Rule had solidified into direct action which in the eyes of Irish nationalists had proved effective. English law was distrusted and paramilitary groups developed as part of the rising cycle of agrarian disorder. The culmination of frustrated political ambitions and resistance led to the armed uprising in 1916 on Easter Monday. At first it lacked popular support and was unsuccessful in its ambition to defeat the British presence in Ireland. The execution of the uprising's ringleaders, resulted in Nationalists finding common cause with the ambitions of the rising, even though they were doubtful in giving it much support in 1916.

The attempt to find a constitutional settlement was resumed. The **19–21**
1914 Government of Ireland Act[17] was restored to life as constitutional compromise was sought. Nationalists, finding common cause
with the uprising in 1916 demanded nothing less than full independence. Unionists in Ulster would not accept any Irish national rule
that denied the link with Britain. Negotiation for a settlement was
attempted; an Irish Convention met for nine months from July 1916 to
April 1917 but unionist aspirations were difficult to reconcile with
nationalist independence. The end of the First World War brought the
dormant 1914 Government of Ireland Act into contention and inevitable implementation. Faced with the irreconcilable[18] differences
between Unionists and Nationalists a new Home Rule Bill was
introduced[19] in 1920. The Government of Ireland Bill 1920 attempted a
constitutional compromise between Nationalists and Unionists. It
sought to achieve, not the single Irish Parliament contained in the
1914 legislative proposals, but two Parliaments, one for Northern
Ireland and the other for the remainder of Ireland. Northern Ireland
was formed out of the ancient Province of Ulster but retained only six
counties out of the nine. The remaining 26 counties in Ireland came
under the jurisdiction of Southern Ireland. The 1920 Bill envisaged a
Parliament for Northern Ireland which was proposed to sit in Belfast
and a Parliament for Southern Ireland in Dublin.

Some elements of the 1914 Act were retained without change. **19–22**
Ultimate sovereignty for both Southern and Northern Ireland Parlia-
ments was retained at Westminster. Ireland remained within the
United Kingdom with a common High Court of Appeal for both
Northern and Southern Ireland with final appeal to the House of
Lords. It was ultimately intended that there should be a single
Parliament for Ireland and to work towards that end a Council of
Ireland was established with representatives from both Northern and
Southern Ireland.

On December 23, 1920 the Royal Assent was granted[20] to the **19–23**
Government of Ireland Act 1920. As a constitutional innovation for

---

[17] The Government of Ireland Act 1914 became law on September 18, 1914 but there
followed a Suspensory Act delaying its implementation.

[18] One of the constant frustrations of developing an Irish policy was summed up in
October 1881 by Edward Hamilton, (1847–1908) Gladstone's Private Secretary: "The
fact is, the misgovernment of Ireland can be summed up in two words – 'Too late'.
Every act of redress, every message of peace has only come after it was too late to be
of use . . ." Dudley W. R. Bahlman, *The Diary of Sir Edward Walter Hamilton (1880–
1885)* (Oxford, 1972), p. 65.

[19] The electoral success of Sinn Fein (Nationalists) at the 1918 general election added
pressure for independence while the success of Unionists in Ulster strengthened the
argument for the maintenance of the Union in Ulster alone.

[20] The 1914 Government of Ireland Act was repealed. See O. MacDonagh, *Ireland: The
Union and its Aftermath* (London, 1977); MacDonagh, *States of Mind: A Study of Anglo-
Irish Conflict 1780–1980* (London, 1983).

Ireland the 1920 Act effectively partitioned Ireland but failed to remove the Nationalists' aspirations of independence. Unionist aspirations for union with Britain were admittedly protected, but this only served to make the 1920 Act divisive with Nationalists. As Theodore Hoppen concluded[21]:

> "If partition represented the least bad and perhaps the only practical policy in the circumstances of the early 1920s it also ensured that many wounds would continue to be available for vituperative display by those in Ireland dedicated to rejecting the proposition that half a loaf is better than no bread."

The 1920 Act contained constitutional arrangements that satisfied no Irish aspiration entirely. In the South of Ireland division of opinion between Irish Nationalists and the British Government and inside the Nationalist movement itself led to violence and unrest. A provisional government set up in Dublin negotiated an Anglo-Irish Treaty[22] in December 1921 which created the Irish Free State as a self-governing dominion. Northern Ireland accepted the constitutional arrangements under the Government of Ireland Act 1920 and this was formally accepted in December 1922 by the Northern Ireland Parliament.

19–24   This aftermath of the 1920 Act saw the birth of Northern Ireland united with Britain, and the status of an independent Ireland, later ratified by Act of Parliament. Northern Ireland's existence secured Unionist support while Nationalist aspirations sought unity of Ireland and independent status. Part of the 1921 Treaty Agreement envisaged[23] the operation of a Boundary Commission to set boundary lines on the border between North and South. The expectation that the Boundary Commission would impugn the 1922 composition of the six counties forming Northern Ireland was widely held by Nationalists. In the event the Boundary Commission broke down in 1924 and its powers were transferred to the Council of Ireland which never met. Northern Ireland was thus confirmed as comprising six counties with the Government of Ireland Act 1920 establishing a constitutional arrangement for the Northern Ireland Parliament with powers to make legislation for "the good government of Northern Ireland."

---

[21] K. Theodore Hoppen, *loc. cit.* p. 173.
[22] Legislation accepting satisfaction is contained in: Irish Free State (Agreement) Act 1922; the Irish Free State (Constitution) Act 1922; Irish Free State (Consequential Provisions) Act 1922.
[23] *ibid.*

(b) The Government of Northern Ireland 1920–72

The creation of the State of Northern Ireland and its[24] Government **19–25** under the Government of Ireland Act 1920 until the abolition of the Northern Ireland Parliament in 1972, may be examined in some detail. The 1920 Act is significant because it attempted to provide a workable parliamentary system adapted from the Westminster experience of government for Northern Ireland. The contents of the 1920 Act provide a useful case-study of the allocation of legislative, executive and judicial powers under a written constitution with a devolved system of government. Devolution on the basis of the 1920 Act provided Northern Ireland with a model of devolution that included legislative, executive and administrative powers. Sovereignty was ultimately retained by the Westminster Parliament. In this context[25] the term devolution refers to the system whereby government powers are transferred from the Imperial Parliament to a subordinate but generally autonomous legislature.

Under the Government of Ireland Act 1920 Northern Ireland **19–26** possessed a Parliament consisting of the Sovereign, represented by a Governor-General as Head of State, an elected House of Commons and a Senate comprising 24 senators elected by the Members of the House of Commons of Northern Ireland according to a proportional representation system. While the Government of Northern Ireland followed many of the procedures and practices of Cabinet and prime ministerial government in England, the Northern Ireland arrangements were nevertheless distinctive. Effectively the Northern Ireland Parliament had extensive powers subject to certain specified limitations.

In constitutional terms the Northern Ireland Parliament had powers to make laws for "the peace, order and good government of Northern Ireland." This grant of power was similar to many colonial arrangements, but it also laid down excepted or reserved matters outside the powers of the Northern Ireland Parliament and vested in the Imperial Parliament at Westminster.

Excepted matters ranged from those that were envisaged to be **19–27** transferred to an all-Ireland Parliament and the making of laws which interfered with religious liberty which were illegal and outside the powers of the Northern Ireland Parliament. The taking of property without compensation was prohibited, although after 1962 the interpretation of this exception was doubted.[26] The most significant

---

[24] Claire Palley, "The Evolution, Disintegration and Possible Reconstruction of the Northern Ireland Constitution" (1972) *Anglo-Am.* 368–476 at 388–389. Devolution as defined by Hood Phillips (p. 780) "the delegation of central government powers without relinquishment of supremacy." See H. Calvert (ed.), *Devolution* (1975).

[25] See the Wales Act 1978 and the Scotland Act 1978, although passed into law both failed to become ratified in practice.

[26] Government of Ireland Act 1920, s.5 amended by the Northern Ireland Act 1962.

restrictions were that the Northern Ireland Parliament could not make laws which encroached upon Acts of the United Kingdom Parliament and as the Sovereign Parliament, United Kingdom Acts of Parliament[27] could prevail over Northern Ireland Acts, even if the area was one which came within the legal competence of the Northern Ireland Parliament. Section 75 of the Government of Ireland Act 1920 asserted "the supreme authority of the Parliament of the United Kingdom shall remain unaffected and undiminished over all persons and things in Ireland and every part thereof."

19–28 Aside from such restrictions, and also that Acts of the Parliament of Northern Ireland were prohibited from having extra-territorial effect, the Northern Ireland Parliament enjoyed considerable autonomy. Claire Palley explained that the powers of the Northern Ireland Parliament were extensive[28]:

> "Put positively, the Northern Ireland Parliament may legislate on matters relating to law and order, to the police, to courts other than the Supreme Court, to civil and criminal law, to local government, to health and social services, to education, to planning and development, to commerce and industrial development and internal trade, to agriculture and to finance."

19–29 Northern Ireland's constitutional status could by analogy be compared to that of a Dominion Parliament before the Statute of Westminster, and there was early judicial acceptance of the idea that Northern Ireland's Parliament could exercise[29] its own powers according to its own wishes[30] within the powers conferred upon it. In addition to extensive parliamentary powers within Northern Ireland's own Parliament, Northern Ireland was entitled to representation at Westminster. Twelve members of Parliament represented Northern Ireland and were directly elected to their Westminster seats through constituency boundaries drawn up in Northern Ireland.

Viewed from the perspective of the United Kingdom's constitutional arrangement, Northern Ireland affairs seemed distant, remote and within the competence of Northern Ireland's own Parliament. A constitutional convention arose that Parliament at Westminster would not legislate in respect of matters transferred to the competence of the Parliament of Northern Ireland without the consent of the Government of Northern Ireland.[31]

---

[27] Originally 13 members of Parliament were reduced in 1948 to 12 after the abolition of University representation.

[28] Palley, *op. cit.* p. 389.

[29] See *Att.-Gen. for Ontario v. Att.-Gen. for Canada* [1912] A.C. 571 at p. 581.

[30] *Att.-Gen. v. Jaffé* [1935] *Northern Ireland* 97.

[31] H. Calvert, *Constitutional Law in Northern Ireland* (Belfast, 1968), pp. 94-110. Conventions arose concerning the non-discussion of Northern Ireland affairs at Westminster. See H.C. Debs., 5s., cols. 1623–1625 (1935).

In matters of finance,[32] Northern Ireland had its own exchequer but **19–30** a complicated arrangement of taxation prevented Northern Ireland's autonomy in such matters. Major powers of taxation were vested in the Imperial Parliament and Northern Ireland received a share of reserved taxes after deductions of an "imperial contribution" and other necessary adjustments. Northern Ireland was given only limited entitlement to levy taxes on estate duty, licence fees, property rates, etc. Such financial dependency on the United Kingdom was misleading in terms of constitutional power being freely exercised by the Northern Ireland government but in accordance with the general economic direction and policy of the United Kingdom.

The strength of the constitutional arrangements set in place by the **19–31** Government of Ireland Act 1920 appeared proven. As Palley noted[33]:

"Observers of the Northern Ireland constitutional scene had in general evaluated the 1920 Act and its operation favourably, seeing it as providing for speedy action to settle regional problems, for ready access by citizens to a locally based administration and for opportunities to adapt central government legislation to local needs. The Act was seen as a firm basis for the continuation of government in Northern Ireland, subject possibly to some minor modifications to secure greater efficiency in the government machine. Notes of disquiet had only been sounded in two important books. The Irish and Ulster Questions were generally seen by British statesmen as having been solved by the 1920 Act and the 1921 Treaty."

In political terms, and with the value of hindsight, the practice of **19–32** Government in Northern Ireland was not in conformity with the Westminster model with its implication of democracy and a two-party system of government allowing alternative political policies to be adapted. In fact the sophistication of party politics allowing for different factions and interests groups to be represented failed to make significant impact in Northern Ireland. Party politics appeared sectarian in perspective. No comparable political divide between socialist and conservative politics enjoyed much success in Ireland when compared to politics within the United Kingdom in England, Wales or Scotland.

The first Northern Irish Parliament met in June 1921 and consisted **19–33** of 40 Unionists, six Nationalists. Sinn Fein delegates failed to attend.

---

[32] Lawrence, *The Government of Northern Ireland: Public Finance and Public Services* (1965).
[33] Palley, *op. cit.* p. 406. The two books are: Mansergh, *The Government of Northern Ireland* (1936) and, D. P. Barritt and C. F. Carter, *The Northern Ireland Problem: A Study in Group Relations* (1962).

Intermittent periods of abstention by Nationalist Members of Parliament was also accompanied by periodic but sustained periods of violence. Well organised and supported, extreme Nationalists did not recognise the State and sought its downfall. Equally intent in maintaining the Union, Protestant paramilitary organisations sought to defend and justify violence to maintain the State.

19–34   Throughout its history the Northern Ireland Parliament was dominated by Unionist representation. This may fairly be said to have represented the majority of the population, with a population of 1.5 million roughly one-third were Catholics and the remaining two-thirds were Protestants. However such representation appeared one-sided when it retained influence over the major economic, social and political institutions in Northern Ireland. Justifications for the exclusion of[34] Catholics from jobs, housing, and from positions of influence appeared reasonable in the absence of full Catholic participation in the State and the perception that Catholic Nationalists were prepared to destroy the State and seek independence with Ireland. Allegiances in Ireland were linked to religious, social and political habits, formed in the earlier centuries in Irish history but preserved in the folklore of popular history.

19–35   Religious affiliation offered simple and readily recognisable labels which translated into action in terms of allegiance or non-allegiance with the State. The realities of political belief or religious understanding appeared far removed from the instincts of those brought up and educated in two separate cultures, one largely Catholic and Nationalist, the other largely Protestant and Unionist. An additional factor forever present in the minds of Unionists was the presence in the same island of another State, Ireland. The 1973 Act, does not make any provision as to the course of action to be taken should consent for change be expressed in a border poll. Mostrelationship with the Republic of Ireland. In political terms,[35] the Government of the Irish Republic was remarkably insensitive to Unionist concerns especially over issues such as divorce, contraception and abortion where the Catholic influences over the State were pervasive. The Republic of Ireland's Constitution also asserted sovereignty over Northern Ireland.[36]

---

[34] P. Bew and M. Paterson, *The British State and the Ulster Crisis* (1985). Northern Ireland experienced several periods of extreme violence. Between 1920 and 1922, nearly 300 people were killed. See P. Buckland, *The Factory of Grievances: Devolved Government in Northern Ireland 1921–39* (Dublin, 1979).

[35] Arts. 2 and 3 of the Irish Constitution 1937 for a discussion. See James Casey, *Constitutional Law in Ireland* (London, 1987). Art. 2 provides territorial claims over "the whole . . . of Ireland" and Art. 5 "pending the re-interrogation of the national territory."

[36] Irish Constitution 1937, Arts. 2 and 3; Re Article 26 and the Criminal Law (Jurisdiction) Bill 1975 [1977] I.R. 129.

The sense of identity fostered by Unionism appears remarkably **19–36** narrow and isolated. The political and constitutional aspirations of Nationalists and Unionists[37] were mutually exclusive. Reconciliation of both identities and the hope of political compromise remained ultimately impossible given the continuation of violent unrest and substantial economic hardship as unemployment fluctuated between 20 per cent and 35 per cent.

The events leading up to the abolition of the Parliament of Northern Ireland and the introduction of direct rule cover the period from 1968 to 1972. Various explanations are offered for the failure of the Government of Ireland Act 1920.

The most immediate cause, that of escalating violence in Northern Ireland, shocked both the Government in Northern Ireland and in the United Kingdom, out of the complacency assumed from the appearance of a constitutional settlement in 1920. Civil unrest was not simply the outcry of a disaffected nationalism, its roots went deeply into the way the Catholic minority perceived its grievances had been treated by the Unionist majority.

The Report of the Cameron Commission[38] into civil disturbances **19–37** testified to a "widespread sense of political and social grievances for long unaudited and therefore ignored by successive Governments of Northern Ireland": If such grievances appeared legitimate to the majority of Catholics, the justice of the cause offered an opportunity for exploitation among hardened Nationalists. The blurring of distinctions between political objectives to improve the conditions of Catholics within Northern Ireland and the complete overthrow of the State left room for violent means to become accepted. The illegal Irish Republican Army divided into "official" and "provisional" groups allowing the extreme "provisional" to take a dominant influence.

The catalogue of constitutional and political deficiencies within the **19–38** Northern Ireland Government identified in 1969 by the Cameron Report laid bare the unresolved matters left unanswered by the 1920 Act. Palley[39] notes:

> ". . . The result of continuous one-party government from 1920 to 1968: an opposition never able to become a government tending to lose its sense of responsibility and a party in power never able to be turned out tending to complacency, insensitivity to criticism and refusal to accept change or reform."

---

[37] J. H. Whyte, "Interpretation of the Northern Ireland Problem: An Appraisal" (1978) *Economic and Social Review* IX 257–82.
[38] The Cameron Report, *Disturbances in Northern Ireland* (HMSO Belfast, Cmd. 532, (1969)).
[39] Palley, *op. cit.* p. 407.

An added dimension, also identified in the Cameron Report was the problem of policing. Extensive police powers were granted to the Royal Ulster Constabulary (RUC) under the Civil Authorities (Special Powers) Act (Northern Ireland) 1922–43. Heavily armed, and in appearance para-military, the RUC were supported by auxiliary units known as "B" Specials. Although Catholics were encouraged to join the RUC and an allocation of places made to secure representation from the Catholic population, Catholic participation was small. The result was that the RUC appeared to identify with the Unionist rather than the Nationalist cause, the powers of the police were directed mainly against the Catholic population.

19–39   Civil disturbance, public protest and street demonstrations placed the RUC under extreme pressure. In the Summer of 1969 events moved exceedingly quickly. Catholic areas were attacked by Protestant mobs, demonstrations and unrest appeared out of control. On August 14, 1969 British troops were used to support the civil authorities. In effect law and order was no longer in the hands of the police directed by the Northern Ireland Government but under the responsibility of the British military under control from the British Cabinet. The General Officer commanding the army in Northern Ireland took operational control of the police over security matters in Northern Ireland.

Attempts were made to restore normality to policing in Northern Ireland and these included the reorganisation of the RUC after a report in October 1969 into the organisation of the structure of the police.[40]

19–40   Events leading to the demise of the Northern Ireland government came about during the period 1969 to 1972. The most significant constitutional change was direct involvement in Northern Ireland affairs by the British Cabinet. Encouraged to introduce wide-ranging reforms, the Government of Northern Ireland pledged support to "the views of Her Majesty's Government in the United Kingdom" which necessitated following a more open policy on encouraging the Catholic population to support the Government and police.

The scale of changes introduced by the Government of Northern Ireland were impressive and extensive.[41] Reform of the electoral law in Northern Ireland brought Northern Ireland electoral practices and arrangements into line with those prevailing in the United Kingdom. Boundary changes were introduced to favour the principle of giving all citizens equal rights. A Boundary Commission was set up to keep

---

[40] The Hunt Report, *Report of the Advisory Committee on Police in Northern Ireland*, Cmd. 535, (1969).
[41] Electoral Law Act (N.I.) 1969. Electoral Law (N.I.) Order 1972 and the Local Government Act (N.I.) 1969.

under review, representation in the House of Commons from Northern Ireland.

Local government reforms[42] were initiated which introduced a **19–41** restructured system, more streamlined and efficient, but with extensive powers delegated back to Central Government in Belfast from the party politics of local interests groups. Eventually in 1972 reforms were introduced to local government organisation following the Macrory Report[43] that involved the abolition of urban and rural district councils in municipalities and county borough councils. A more streamlined and compact system of local government was introduced. Altogether 26 new district councils were set up for Northern Ireland. In effect many activities of local government were transferred to central government departments or agencies.

Reforms dealing with citizens' grievances included the introduction **19–42** of the office of Commissioner for Complaints in November 1969, with independent powers of investigation and bringing within its remit local government and public bodies and boards not subject to the newly established Parliamentary Commission for Administration (ombudsman). The office of ombudsman was established in Northern Ireland in 1969 closely modelled on the English equivalent set up in 1967.

The law was strengthened on incitement to hatred and a Community Relations Commission was established in 1969 which took proactive steps to encourage humane relations between the two communities. A number of additional bodies were established to oversee public activities which were contentious and had caused political controversy, the most notable was the setting up of the Northern Ireland Housing Executive in 1971. This body, separated from ministerial intervention, set out to provide an impartial and objective system of public housing allocation on a points system of allocation based on need.

While innovation and responsiveness were the hallmark of the **19–43** reforms outlined above, without doubt the passage of these reforms were in favour of the Catholic minority, but this only further alienated Unionist opinion. The Unionist party, while historically cohesive, began to fragment into different groups. Nationalist politics were also fragmented but the formation of a new political group, the Social Democratic and Labour Party (SDLP), represented a new style of opposition politics. Prepared to work within existing institutions the SDLP became an articulate voice for moderate Catholic opinion. The SDLP ended the disparate and incoherent policies of the past and

---

[42] Local Government Act (N.I.) 1972.
[43] Report of the Review Body on Local Government in Northern Ireland, Cmnd. 517 (HMSO, Belfast 1967, 1969, 1970).

encouraged active constitutional participation. However, fragmentation of nationalist allegiance into support for the IRA, especially the more active Provisional IRA, created an efficient and well organised terrorist organisation which took offensive action against the security forces. Northern Ireland suffered a major setback when 13 citizens were shot in January 1972 by members of the British Army.

19–44   Within three months of this incident the British Government asserted sovereignty over Northern Ireland and introduced direct rule in March 1972. The Government of Ireland Act 1920 had failed and the experiment in devolved government in Northern Ireland ended.

McCrudden attributes this situation to the failure of "the pragmatic empiricist tradition of constitutional developments," and thereby the failure of the common law tradition with its emphasis on flexibility, learning from past mistakes and developing solutions to meet future needs. After 1972 the opportunity to experiment with new constitutional arrangements for Northern Ireland came when it was probably least expected and most required.

3.   Constitutional Status

(a) Northern Ireland Constitution Act 1973

19–45 Since 1972, Northern Ireland's Government has been carried out under "direct rule." Orders in Council are prepared and, subject to affirmative resolution, are issued for Northern Ireland. These affirmative resolution procedures are open to criticism and McCrudden has written[44] of the disadvantages of the procedure:

> "The disadvantage of this mode is that Orders are not subject to amendment and are usually debated for a maximum of two and a half hours after 10pm. Government ministers available for Northern Ireland affairs in Parliament do not represent Northern Ireland constituencies."

19–46   Northern Ireland's representation at Westminster was increased to 17 M.P.s. To substitute for the loss of the domestic Parliament Northern Ireland's M.P.s have little direct influence in the government of Northern Ireland, given that no Parliament exists in Northern

---

[44] McCrudden, *loc. cit.* pp. 314–315.

Ireland at present and Westminster matters often overshadow discussion of Northern Ireland affairs. There is also the criticism that in the absence of a specific departmental select committee, Northern Ireland Ministers are not accountable for their actions in the same way as a comparable United Kingdom government department. This criticism also applied to civil servants in Northern Ireland who are not answerable to a specialised committee primarily concerned with Northern Ireland matters. In 1994 a Select Committee for Northern Ireland was set up.

The first period of direct rule[45] covered the years 1972–74. During **19–47** this time future constitutional innovations and adjustments were attempted amidst increasing violence in Northern Ireland. Originally direct rule was conceived as a stop-gap measure but over time it became an accepted policy which soon appeared blighted with many of the shortcomings discussed above in connection with the earlier Home Rule debate.

In March 1973, a referendum[46] was held on the issue of the Border between North and South, and the result confirmed the majority population in favour of the union. Only 58.7 per cent of the electorate cast their votes, Nationalists and their supporters did not vote.

Attempts to fill the vacuum left by the suspension of the Northern **19–48** Ireland Parliament gave rise to a degree of "constitutional tinkering," a term which reflects the difficulty of proceeding with long-term initiatives. Events have always seemed to take the initiative in Northern Ireland and government policy has always lagged behind. However the fundamentals have remained largely unchanged. A majority favour union within the United Kingdom with a sizeable minority in favour of some form of United Ireland. A number of White Papers published at this time from 1972–74 attempted to set out Government thinking. Briefly, this involved consideration of (a) issues of security; (b) attempts to solve economic and social problems within Northern Ireland and finally; (c) attempts to pursue a scheme of devolution whereby some form of government might be formed in Northern Ireland capable of achieving widespread community support. Broadly speaking these remain the current concerns of the attempts to find some solution in Northern Ireland.

Constitutional lawyers interested in the different forms of devolu- **19–49** tion will find the Northern Ireland Constitution Act 1973 and the Northern Ireland Assembly Act 1973 useful models of modern devolved government. The 1973 Act envisaged an Assembly with legislative powers elected by proportional representation and an

---

[45] Northern Ireland (Temporary Provisions) Act 1972 abolished the office of Government and substituted a Secretary of State for Ireland to act as Chief Executive.
[46] The referendum was carried out under Northern Ireland (Border Poll) Act 1972.

Executive drawn from parties representative of both communities. Within the framework of a link with the United Kingdom, Catholics were offered the opportunity to participate in power in a meaningful way for the first time. In return for Catholic acceptance of the Union, Unionists were expected to offer a power-sharing arrangement, a major departure from the idea of majority government. Guarantees of a regular series of border polls were built into these arrangements under the Northern Ireland Constitution Act 1973 in an effort to encourage dialogue but with a guarantee to maintain the Union as long as the majority so desired. As Catholics are ultimately expected to form a majority of the population within Northern Ireland, a period of power sharing seemed inevitable and necessary in an attempt to reach compromise and consensus. It was envisaged that once a power-sharing government became firmly established legal powers devolved to the government of Northern Ireland might increase. The potential for further legal powers appeared unlimited and extended to a large measure of local autonomy.

19–50 The status of Northern Ireland expressed in section 1 of the 1973 Act contained a "constitutional guarantee, that in no event will Northern Ireland or any part of it cease to be part of Her Majesty's dominions and of the United Kingdom without the consent of the majority of the people of Northern Ireland voting in a poll held for the purposes of this section." Section 2 of the 1973 Act was intended to replace the terms of section 1(2) of the Ireland Act 1949 which provides that "in no event will Northern Ireland . . . any part thereof cease to be part of Her Majesty's dominion and of the United Kingdom without the consent of the Parliament of Northern Ireland." The abolition of the Northern Ireland Parliament effectively left this guarantee as inoperative. Its replacement with the "consent of the majority of the people of Northern Ireland" transfers this aspect of political sovereignty from an institution and politicians to a referendum. This may in practice give less security to the unionist majority especially as the geographical reality of political power may mean that large parts of the North West which are nationalist, may wish to sever the link with the United Kingdom.

19–51 The question also arises as to the worth of this guarantee in terms of the constitutional status of Northern Ireland. The 1973 Act, does not make any provision as to the course of action to be taken should consent for change be expressed in a border poll. Most Unionists correctly maintain the 1800 Act of Union as the basis of the Union between Great Britain and Ireland. This would indicate that even if Northern Ireland no longer remains a constitutional jurisdiction claimed by the Constitution of the Republic of Ireland, any future United Kingdom Parliament is free to alter both the terms of the guarantee and cede Northern Ireland to the Irish Republic. Unionists fears are that the current status of Northern Ireland is in fact no more than a leasehold arrangement rather than a freehold permanently protected within the United Kingdom. Parliament is not bound to follow the 1800 Act, as an unalterable statement of legislative intent. This point becomes crucial later when evaluating the status and policy behind the Anglo-Irish Agreement between Dublin and London in 1985.

The Assembly set up under the 1973 Act was elected under **19-52** proportional representation and duly formed a Government, the first of its kind comprising both Catholics and Protestants in a Cabinet of power-sharing Ministers. Unionist opposition to this form of government resulted in civil disturbance and in May 1974, the power-sharing Executive fell, after a General Strike by Protestant workers. Direct rule was resumed under the Northern Ireland Act 1974 and remains in place.

Further attempts to provide a foundation for civil liberties come with the Fair Employment (Northern Ireland) Act 1976. The Act made discrimination on religious and poitical grounds unlawful in the public and private sector. The Act created the Fair Employment Agency to advise, monitor and investigate complaints.[47]

A further attempt for a broadly based power-sharing government **19-53** was attempted under the Northern Ireland Act 1982. This new scheme, referred to as "rolling devolution," provided a detailed committee structure to scrutinise the work of Northern Ireland departments. The Northern Ireland Assembly was granted powers to bring forward proposals for devolved government based on agreements between Unionists and Nationalists. In effect, the more agreement between the representatives of the two traditions, the more power was devolved. The Assembly failed to reach agreement beyond setting up a few committees to scrutinise legislation and in June 1986 it was dissolved by Order in Council. For the future, an Order in Council would be sufficient to revive it and bring it into operation depending on whether agreement could be reached.

Direct rule under the present constitutional arrangements consists **19-54** of a Secretary of State for Northern Ireland together with a Minister of State and four parliamentary Under-Secretaries of State operating under direct rule. Orders in Council or primary Acts of the United Kingdom Parliament may be used to legislate for Northern Ireland. Although United Kingdom government departments are not directly responsible for Northern Ireland, departments' select committees include matters within the remit of the Northern Ireland Secretary of State.

Direct rule for Northern Ireland is likely to continue, given recent **19-55** failure of inter-governmental talks in Northern Ireland between

---

[47] See 3rd Annual Report of the Fair Employment Commission (HMSO, 1993).

Unionists, the Government of the Irish Republic, the United Kingdom Government and the members of the other main constitutional parties in Northern Ireland such as the mainly Nationalist Social Democratic and Labour Party (SDLP). The talks ended in November 1992 with no indication of major agreement between the representatives. It is likely that further talks will be attempted in the foreseeable future.

(b) The Anglo-Irish Agreement

19–56 Northern Ireland's capacity to stimulate new initiatives brought a major departure in 1985 from past attempts to solve Northern Ireland's status and constitutional arrangements through the Anglo-Irish Agreement. Following an inter-governmental meeting[48] at Hillsborough Castle, Belfast on November 15, 1985 the Anglo-Irish Agreement was signed by the Governments of the United Kingdom and the Irish Republic. Unionists politicians were effectively excluded from the inter-governmental talks. The Agreement set out the status of Northern Ireland and recognised for the first time in an international Treaty the legitimacy of the competing aspirations of both Unionists and Nationalists.

19–57 Under the Agreement any change in the status of Northern Ireland would come about only with the consent of a majority within Northern Ireland. This reiterates the status of Northern Ireland set out in the 1973 Act. However for the future, if a majority of the people of Northern Ireland "wish for and formally consent to the establishment of a United Ireland," then legislation would be introduced to give effect to those wishes. The Agreement also recognised that the majority of people in Northern Ireland desired no change in the status of Northern Ireland.

19–58 While the Agreement appeared to offer reassurance to Unionists in Northern Ireland of the position of Northern Ireland within the United Kingdom, it also recognised the legitimacy of Catholics to aspire to a United Ireland. Another part of the Agreement wished to encourage inter-governmental co-operation between the North and South through an Inter-Governmental Conference consisting of British and Irish Ministers. In this forum, Irish Ministers assisted by a permanent secretariat in Northern Ireland could put forward views on political, security and legal matters. This device intended to bring Catholics into a closer recognition of the governmental process in Northern Ireland where in the past they had felt alienated. It also re-

---

[48] The Agreement was signed and later approved by both Parliaments in the United Kingdom and in the Republic of Ireland. Later it was lodged at the United Nations (November 1985).

created the original idea of a Council of Ireland contained in the Government of Ireland Act 1920.

The Agreement also set out to encourage the introduction of some **19–59** form of devolved government. The sphere of influence of Irish Ministers would be curtailed where matters to be discussed were the responsibility of a devolved administration in Northern Ireland. The intention behind this arrangement was to encourage Unionists to accept devolution as a preferable policy to that of including Irish Ministers in discussions on Northern Ireland's domestic affairs. Thus the Agreement might stimulate greater realism and responsibility between Unionists and Nationalists in the political compromises needed to form a power-sharing administration.

Since the Agreement was signed, Unionists' opposition to the Agreement has been unrelenting. The inclusion of Irish Ministers and a secretariat in discussion of Northern Ireland's domestic affairs is seen as another step towards unification and a shift away from the Union with the United Kingdom. The Agreement itself was criticised by Unionists because they were excluded from the earlier discussions about its content.

The Agreement also contained a wide range of inter-governmental **19–60** matters such as policing and security where it was hoped that greater co-operation might make for an effective security policy. Security problems are recognised as not being confined to geographical or political boundaries. The Agreement rests on the assumption that increased security might alleviate any Unionist discomfort from the terms of the Agreement. However, the level of violence has not returned to the 1972 period[49] where it was at its worst, but has maintained on average about 80 deaths and over 1,500 shootings per annum. It is estimated that Britain contributes an average of nearly £2bn per annum to the running of the Northern Ireland economy between 1983 and 1993.

The hope of an end to violence has not been realised and Unionist **19–61** objection to the Agreement has remained constant. Nationalists aspirations have been more fully expressed in the Agreement than at any time since the 1920 Act and the formation of Northern Ireland. Nevertheless, the hope that this might secure a shift to support for the Agreement and away from the terrorist IRA has not been fully realised among the Catholic population.

The question arises as to what significance should be attached to the Agreement when it has not achieved its avowed intentions of reducing tension between the two communities. From a constitutional perspective the Agreement has a number of important ramifications.

---

[49] Estimates are that 467 killed, 10,628 shooting incidents, 1,853 bomb explosions or related incidents. See Brice Dickson, "Northern Ireland's Emergency Legislation – the Wrong Medicine" [1993] P.L. 592.

19–62 First, the Government of the Irish Republic has been given a direct influence over the domestic affairs of Northern Ireland. This remains, under the Agreement, a fact of life until there is some devolved government in Northern Ireland. There is in effect a partnership agreement between the two Governments, external to Northern Ireland, to work together in its day to day running.

Secondly, that when Catholics in[50] Northern Ireland form a sufficient majority in favour of a United Ireland there is a promise that the two Governments will secure legislation to put a United Ireland into effect. This in effect gives a time period to the Unionist population to come to terms with Nationalists. Estimates vary as to the exact length of that time limit, but at present the Catholic population has grown to at least 40 per cent and it is assumed in the next 40 years they may make up the deficit.

19–63 Thirdly, the Agreement has had some noticeable effects on many domestic issues in Northern Ireland such as industrial co-operation but it remains largely untested as to the full scope of its potential.

The Agreement was reviewed by the courts[51] in both England and the Republic of Ireland, in challenges made to its constitutionality. Both cases upheld the Agreement as legal and effective.

19–64 Divisions within Northern Ireland Society[52] seem to remain as divided as the period leading up to the creation of Northern Ireland itself. The experience of Northern Ireland's various attempts at constitutional change suggests that constitutional schemes are marginal. As Palley has pointed out[53]:

> "They may facilitate change or by their non-constructive nature provide safety valves for the expression of grievances. But they must by and large be in accordance with the facts of power, or in the currently fashionable phrases must 'be in accordance with political reality and must conform to the patterns established by institutionalized and non institutionalized force.' No constitution will be effective unless there is political will by the major power holders to work it."

---

[50] "Catholics to be the Majority in Ulster," *The Independent*, November 1, 1992. See P. Compton letters to the editor, *The Independent*, November 4, 1992. Compton asserts the time scale is 70 years.

[51] *Ex p. Molyneaux and Others* [1986] 1 W.L.R. 331. The court refused leave to apply as an International Conference under the Agreement did not contravene any statute or rule of common law or constitutional convention. See *McGimpsey* the unreported case in the courts of the Irish Republic.

[52] Hadfield, (1986) 37 N.I.L.Q. 1.

[53] Palley, *op. cit.* p. 450.

Security problems are an intrinsic part of Northern Ireland's **19–65** unresolved political social and economic problems. Dickson has noted[54] that:

"from 1971 to 1977 an average of 252 persons were killed and 3,269 shootings have occurred each year; for the years 1978 to 1981 the averages have fallen, respectively, to 82 and 1, 574."

Terrorist violence and an increasing sophistication in the means available to terrorists including international support has tested Northern Ireland's emergency powers and posed difficult questions about the use of force by the state and the compatibility of emergency powers with civil liberties. Northern Ireland has provided an important case study in the use of emergency powers. How is the rule of law to be upheld while measures to defeat terrorism are pursued?

(c) Joint Declaration December, 1993

The Joint Declaration agreed between the British and Irish govern- **19–66** ments is contained in a text consisting of 12 points.[55]

The declaration seeks to reinforce the Anglo-Irish Agreement but it goes much further. The document actively seeks the cessation of terrorist violence and offers the opportunity for dialogue following the cessation of violence. For the first time, the British Government asserts that it has "no selfish, strategic or economic interest" in Northern Ireland. A number of commitments follow. First, that the British government is neutral to the ultimate political outcome of Northern Ireland's constitutional arrangements. Secondly, that if the people of Northern Ireland agree to a United Ireland, then the British government will introduce the necessary legislation to implement that agreement. Thirdly, that the primary interest of the British government is to see peace, stability and reconciliation in Northern Ireland.

The Joint Declaration also provides a number of commitments from **19–67** the Irish Government. First, that the Irish Government will examine "any elements in the democratic life and organisation of the Irish

---

[54] B. Dickson, "Northern Ireland's Emergency Legislation – The Wrong Medicine?" [1993] P.L. 592. I acknowledge a debt of gratitude to Professor Dickson for useful information and advice on emergency powers.

[55] Seven of the points contained in the declaration contain points of agreement between both the British and Irish governments. The British government uphold the democratic wish of "a greater number of the people of Northern Ireland on the issue of whether they prefer to support the Union or a Sovereign United Ireland." The declaration contains four points of direct concern to the Irish government.

State" that can be represented to the Irish government as "not being fully consistent with a modern, democratic and pluralist society." Secondly, that the Irish Government accepts that "it would be wrong to attempt to impose a united Ireland, in the absence of the freely given consent of a majority of the people of Northern Ireland." There is also a strong commitment from the Joint Declaration that civil and religious liberties of both communities in Northern Ireland require respect. There is an implication that in any future political and constitutional arrangement the respect of the liberties of both communities will be protected. This may be an indication that adopting a Bill of Rights for Northern Ireland will be considered.

Future discussion of the value of the Joint Declaration will focus on whether the IRA will find the document sufficiently attractive to end violence. The question of whether constitutional change and political debate will result in an end to conflict in Northern Ireland is uncertain.

4   An Overview of Emergency Powers

(a)   The historical legacy

19–68   In 1922, with the creation of the State of Northern Ireland, emergency powers were deemed to be necessary and were immediately brought into operation. Historically emergency powers have formed an intrinsic part of the Government of Ireland. The Act of Union 1800 had been passed in the aftermath of the 1796 rebellion and the Government of Ireland Act 1920 had been passed after the Rebellion in 1916. Constitutional change and emergency powers were and remain inexorably linked.[56]

In the nineteenth century the form of coercive powers, as they were referred to, varied. Suspension of the Habeas Corpus Acts 1781–82 was accompanied by a variety of miscellaneous powers including at times trial without jury for specified offences, extensive powers for search, arrest and seizure of goods. Deportation and internment without trial were also adopted with varying degrees of success.[57]

19–69   Agrarian crime, endemic in the nineteenth century put the ordinary courts and the administration of criminal justice under considerable

---

[56] Charles Townsend, *Political Violence in Ireland* (1983); G. Hogan and C. Walker, *Political Violence and the Law in Ireland*; J. McGarry and B. O'Leary (eds.) *The Future of Northern Ireland* (1990), pp. 318–341.

[57] See R. Clutterbuck (ed.), *The Future of Political Violence* (1980); C. Gearty *Terrorism* (1991); C. Walker, *The Prevention of Terrorism in British Law* (Manchester, 1986).

strain. Ireland, in common with Scotland but unlike England and Wales, developed a public Crown Prosecution system where prosecutions were taken on behalf of victims of crime by Sessional Crown Solicitors. The criminal law with its English origins depended on the lay magistrate and jury trial but under the extremes of Irish violence, required adjustment.[58]

Stipendiary magistrates, legally qualified, were used to supplement the ineffective and often criticised lay magistrates.[59] By 1884, stipendiary magistrates numbered 77, many with a military or police background, some with property or professional qualifications. At times of intense violence, magistrates received additional powers which allowed for the proclamation of districts, the suspension of habeas corpus and the arrest and detention of suspects.

At Dublin Castle, the judicial division, one of three divisions in the **19–70** Irish civil service, recorded the date, time and action taken against political and organised agitation. Spies, informers and undercover agents communicated information to Dublin Castle and assisted in the collection of evidence against suspects. Particularly difficult periods of agrarian unrest and agitation resulted in disturbed parts of Ireland to be proclaimed and stipendiary magistrates received additional powers. For example in 1881 under the[60] Protection of Persons and Property Act 1881, suspension of habeas corpus, arrest and detention of suspects was permitted.

The Crimes Act 1887 allowed[61] resident magistrates the power to admit into evidence the accused's evidence even if it involved self-incrimination. This principle had been first introduced by section 16 of the Prevention of Crimes Act 1882.

Difficulties in obtaining convictions before Irish juries resulted in **19–71** the 1881 Select Committee of the House of Lords[62] recommending that jury trial might be suspended. The Prevention of Crimes Act 1882 in theory substituted trial by three judges for trial by jury but in practice this section of the legislation was not implemented after a resolution was passed by the Irish judiciary opposed to the abolition of jury trial. However, many indictable crimes were made summary offences[63] under the Act which endured until 1898.

---

[58] J. F. McEldowney, "Crown Prosecutions in 19th Century Ireland"; Hay and Snyder (eds.), *Policing and Prosecution in Britain 1750–1850* (Oxford, 1989), pp. 427–457 (legislation included 44 & 45 Vict., c.4; 50 and 51 Vict., c.20, 45 and 46 Vict., c.25). See P. Hunt and B. Dickson, "Northern Ireland's Emergency Laws and International Human Rights" (1993) 2 N.Q.H.R. 173.

[59] See D. S. Greer, "The impact of the Troubles on the law and legal system of Northern Ireland" in A. Ward (ed.), *Northern Ireland: Living with the Crisis* (1987).

[60] 44 and 45 Vict., c.4.

[61] Criminal Law and Procedure Act 1887 (50 and 51 Vict., c.20).

[62] Parl. Pap. 1881 XI. 1.

[63] I. S. Leadam "Substitutes for Trial by Jury in Ireland" (May, 1882) 31 *Fortnightly Review* 547–563.

The Crimes Act 1887 was more permanent and provided special jury trials for disturbed areas when unrest resulted in the area being proclaimed. Proclaimed areas were subject to stronger legal powers. The experience of this Act encouraged the listing of "dangerous associations" which were made illegal.

19–72 The outbreak of war on August 4, 1914 was followed by the Defence of the Realm Act 1914. The 1914 Act represented a shift in emphasis from emergency legislation confined to Ireland to legislation generally applicable throughout the United Kingdom and Ireland. Regulations made under the Act provided extensive powers for serving the public safety and "defence of the realm." This included martial law and trial by court martial of serious offences.

(b) Emergency powers since 1922

19–73 It is necessary to trace the development of emergency powers in Northern Ireland from the period of the inception of the State. Recently the law in Northern Ireland on emergency powers has been codified by the Northern Ireland (Emergency Provisions) Act 1996. This Act substantially re-enacts the Northern Ireland (Emergency Provisions) Act 1991. However, one part of the 1991 Act has not been re-enacted in the 1996 Act. That is matters relating to the confiscation of proceeds of terrorists related activities. This will be the subject of a separate enactment. There is also the Prevention of Terrorism (Additional Powers) Act 1996 which relates to the law in areas where the police impose cordons in connection with the prevention of acts of terrorism following the bomb at South Quay in London in February 1996.

19–74 The Parliament of Northern Ireland shortly after the State was set up, enacted the Civil Authorities (Special Powers) Act 1922. Modelled on the Defence of the Realm Consolidation Act 1914 which only applied to making regulations during war, the Special Powers Act gave extensive regulation making powers for dealing with powers of arrest, search, detention, and seizure. The civil authority under the 1922 Act was widely defined to include a Northern Ireland Minister of Home Affairs, or any Parliamentary secretary or officer of the Royal Ulster Constabulary. In effect, the 1922 Act was so extensive that the powers conferred under the Act were considered as applicable to the army as well as the police in Northern Ireland.[64]

19–75 This point was successfully challenged in the Northern Ireland courts in 1972 in R. v. Londonderry J.J., ex. p. Hume[65] when the then

---

[64]3 See E. Graham, "Religious and Educational – the Constitutional Problem" (1982) N.I.L.Q. 20–52.

[65] [1972] N.I. 91. See Northern Ireland Act 1972, s.1; C. Walker (1989) 40 N.I.L.Q. 1; O'Higgins (1972) 35 M.L.R. 295; Re. McElduff [1972] N.I. 1.

Lord Chief Justice, Lord Lowry declared *ultra vires* regulations purporting to give powers to the armed forces. The United Kingdom Parliament was forced, in an all night sitting, to pass the Northern Ireland Act 1972 retrospectively giving the army the powers which it was assumed they had always possessed. Although the Special Powers Act was intended to be of limited duration, its powers were added to and the life of the Act extended for the duration of the Northern Ireland Parliament until 1972. Since then there have been a number of emergency powers Acts, under the titles of the Northern Ireland (Emergency Provisions Act) 1973 and the Prevention of Terrorism Act 1974. The former replaced the 1922 Special Powers Act, the latter introduced in 1974, after the Birmingham bombing in November 1974. The Prevention of Terrorism (Temporary Provisions) Act 1974 was also passed.

Powers under both these Acts included a power to make regulation **19–76** for detention without trial, power to detain for up to seven days and powers to exclude persons moving from Great Britain to Northern Ireland and vice versa. The most extensive power is internment without trial.

The arguments in favour of internment rest on two assumptions. First, if properly pursued it may act as an efficient means of identifying and rounding up suspects who would remain at large in the community because of the lack of evidence for their arrest. Secondly, internment allows undercover intelligence to work in advance of the internment power and gives supremacy to intelligence gathering over the routine of the police collecting evidence to put before the courts. Thus internment provides a strong military option and its widespread use may curtail terrorist organisations. Both assumptions stress the necessity of internment because of difficulties in using the ordinary courts.

The arguments against internment may similarly rest on two **19–77** assumptions. First, internment may cause public outcry and distrust of law and the legal authority of the Government. This may act as a catalyst for support of terrorist groups and deepen the sense of alienation in the local community. Secondly, internment has a finite existence and arrangements ending internment may become a major constraint on political activity. While this may appear a bargaining chip, it is usually heavily weighted in favour of the terrorist.

Opposition to internment involves arguments concerning the pro- **19–78** tection of individual liberty and against abuse of power. Any one-sided application of internment or the internment of suspects who are later believed innocent may make internment an unreliable and therefore an unjustified risk. In Northern Ireland, before the introduction of direct rule, internment powers were used extensively in August 1971. The outcome of internment at that time was far from satisfactory. Alienation throughout the Catholic community was generally felt and a large number of allegations of torture and brutality were made, arising out of the interrogation techniques adopted by some members of the security forces. Violence increased and great disturbance arose out of the use of the internment power which was perceived as directed only against Catholic violence.

19–79   Internment powers, once used may later be regarded as unjustified if there is no direct reduction in violence. In Northern Ireland internment powers were found difficult to justify in terms of any cessation of violence and this led to a review of emergency powers, specifically the question of how internment might be replaced by some form of trial system. The review was carried out under the chairmanship of Lord Diplock. The Diplock Report[66] marked an important shift from internment by the Executive to judicial trial. Lord Diplock recommended that special courts (popularly named "Diplock courts") should be set up to deal with terrorist offences. The Diplock courts involve trial without jury before a single judge under the Northern Ireland (Emergency Provisions) Act 1973. Since 1973 Diplock courts have heard cases relating to terrorist offences without juries. Internment powers have not been used since 1971.

19–80   Scheduled offences triable before the Diplock courts include crimes commonly committed by terrorists. These include murder, manslaughter, riot, kidnapping, false imprisonment, assault occasioning actual bodily harm, robbery involving weapons, theft, burglary or obtaining by deception and various firearms and explosives offences.[67]

The schedule of offences that may be tried before the non-jury Diplock courts have been extended under the Northern Ireland (Emergency Provisions) Act 1991. A new Part IV to Schedule I includes any non-summary offence which an RUC officer[68] above the rank of superintendent certifies has been charged as a result of an investigation into terrorist funds. This power to schedule an offence as a terrorist one is subject to the Attorney-General's discretion to order an offence not to be treated as scheduled. The width of the scheduling power as it includes most offences involving dishonesty or deception, gives the police a wide discretion in the matter. Where an accused is charged with both a scheduled and non-scheduled offence, the mode of trial is determined by the more serious offence and it is therefore tried as a scheduled offence.[69]

19–81   The powers to hold Diplock courts have now been amended by sections 10 and 11 of the Northern Ireland (Emergency Provisions)

---

[66] Cmnd. 5185 (1972).
[67] See Northern Ireland (Emergency Provisions) Act 1991, Prevention of Terrorism (Temporary Provisions) Act 1989.
[68] Police officers in Northern Ireland are members of the Royal Ulster Constabulary.
[69] See Doran and Jackson, "Diplock and the Presumption Against Jury Trial: a critique", [1992] Crim.L.R. 755.

Act 1996. The 1996 Act substantially re-enacts the Northern Ireland (Emergency Provisions) Act 1991 and the 1996 Act is explained in more detail below. Some points to note are as follows: in respect of the Diplock courts system, section 11 makes the requirement that the trial judge in a Diplock court must give full reasons for the conviction of an accused and subsection 6 of section 11 gives an unfettered right of appeal from the verdict of the trial judge.

Concern about the low acquittal rates arising out of trials heard before the Diplock courts, which depending on the calculation used may vary from between 7.55 or 10.4 per cent, is focused on the question of the fairness of a criminal justice system where there is no jury. There is, however an automatic right of appeal from the decision of the single judge but this has not prevented general unease about the system. Specifically there is concern about some degree of case hardening of the judges in the Diplock courts, though this is not accepted by the periodic review carried out into the operation of the Diplock courts.

One of the major issues arising from any criminal trial, including **19–82** the Diplock courts is the admissibility of confession evidence. Following allegations of ill treatment, various inquiries investigated the use of effective policing methods and their compatibility with "the preservation of civil liberties and human rights." In 1975 Lord Gardiner's report[70] was clear in recommending that the continued "existence of emergency powers should be limited both in scope and duration." Certain methods of interrogation were outlawed after the Compton Report[71] and the Parker Committee[72] in 1972. The Gardiner report was equally sure that however effective security measures might be, Northern Ireland required a solution based "in political terms" and "must include further measures to promote social justice between classes and communities." A further set of recommendations contained in the Bennett Committee Report[73] tightened up procedures for interrogation by using tape recordings or even wider use of video evidence of suspects in custody under cross-examination. The use of Diplock courts has brought into question the rules of evidence available at the trial of suspected terrorists.

On interrogation procedures, the Bennett inquiry[74] in 1979, led to **19–83** stricter controls over police interrogation procedures. The judiciary

---

[70] *Report of a Committee to consider in the context of civil liberties and human rights, measures to deal with terrorism in Northern Ireland*, Cmnd. 5847 (1975). See C. Gearty, *Terrorism* (1991).

[71] Compton Report, Cmnd. 4823 (1971).

[72] Parker Committee, Cmnd. 4901 (1972).

[73] Bennett Committee Report, Cmnd. 7497 (1979).

[74] *ibid*. See also S. Livingstone, "The House of Lords and the Northern Ireland Conflict" [1994] M.L.R. 333.

set tighter controls over the use of confession statements made by the accused. Judicial restrictions on the use of informants and scepticism about the value of such evidence in the absence of any corroboration has undoubtedly limited the effectiveness of informants and the use of confessions in obtaining convictions.

Regular reviews of emergency powers have been carried out and this led to replacing much of the 1978 and 1987 Acts by two new statutes, currently in force in Northern Ireland. The Northern Ireland (Emergency Provisions) Act 1991 and the Prevention of Terrorism (Temporary Provisions) Act 1989 consolidated reforms introduced in 1987. The law has been recently amended by the Northern Ireland (Emergency Provisions) Act 1996.

19–84   The emergency powers in Northern Ireland are an attempt to provide a greater balance between the security requirements of effective and widely drafted legal powers, and the need to provide suspects with acceptable standards of rights. The need to address the question of the rights of suspects has come from a number of inquiries including the decisions of the Court of Human Rights at Strasbourg and judicial decisions in the courts in Northern Ireland.

The various powers granted under the current legislation in force in Northern Ireland may be conveniently examined under three categories; police powers; trial and evidence, and the rule of law.

19–85   In terms of emergency powers two preliminary points may be noted. First, the Prevention of Terrorism (Temporary Provisions Act) 1989 is a major consolidation of emergency powers in use in the United Kingdom and requires annual renewal to remain in force.[75] Part 1 and section 15(1) do not extend to Northern Ireland, section 15(10) extends to England and Wales only, while Schedule 7, Part I extends only to England, Wales and Northern Ireland. Secondly, the Northern Ireland (Emergency Provisions) Act 1991 consolidates much of the 1987 Act noted above and the earlier Emergency Provisions Act 1973. This 1991 Act incorporates many of the provisions of the Prevention of Terrorism Act 1989 but applies only in Northern Ireland. It requires annual renewal and will expire after five years.

(c)   The current law: The Northern Ireland (Emergency Provisions) Act 1996

19–86 It is useful to provide an overview of the Northern Ireland (Emergency Provisions) Act 1996 which consolidates and amends earlier legislation. The 1996 Act repeals the Northern Ireland (Emergency

---

[75] Previous versions of this Act may be found in 1974, 1976 and 1984.

Provisions) Act 1991 and came into force on August 25, 1996 and it expires on August 24, 1998. It applies only to Northern Ireiand and the main lay-out of the legislation is as follows: Part I of the 1996 Act sets out the scheduled offences for the so-called Diplock courts. Powers of arrest, stop and search and questioning are contained in Part II of the Act. There are a general powers of entry contained in section 26.

Part III contains a number of offences. Section 29 makes it an offence to direct terrorism, section 30 to belong to or solicit support for a proscribed organisation; Schedule 2 contains a list of proscribed organisations. This list may be added to by Order in Council by the Secretary of State. Sections 31–35 set out details of offences for displaying support for a terrorist organisation, collecting information or being engaged in training or activities connected with an unlawful organisation. Section 47 deals with access to legal advice. Section 48 concerns fingerprinting. Sections 52–54 allows codes of practice to be issued by the Secretary of State in connection with the detention and questioning of suspects including video recording and evidence of interviews.

In addition, in Northern Ireland, the ordinary criminal law and **19–87** procedures have undergone considerable change in terms of the powers of the police and the rights of suspects. These powers have been consolidated under the Police and Criminal Evidence (Northern Ireland) Order 1989.

5. Emergency Powers and the Protection of Civil Liberties

(a) Police Powers

Police powers to arrest,[76] search and seize are provided under the **19–88** emergency powers in force in Northern Ireland. These powers are intended to supplement the ordinary criminal law. There are occasions when the ordinary law is sufficiently wide to facilitate most emergency situations. For example under Articles 42–45 of the Police and Criminal Evidence (Northern Ireland) Order 1989, detention is possible for up to 96 hours with at least two appearances before magistrates.

Section 11 of the Northern Ireland (Emergency Provisions) Act 1978 **19–89** conferred powers to arrest on any constable "without warrant any

---

[76] See Bailey, Harris and Jones, *Civil Liberties Cases and Materials* (3rd ed., 1992), pp. 239–297. See also D. Bonner, *Emergency Powers in Peacetime* (1985).

person whom he suspects of being a terrorist." This arrest power was intended to be used as a means to begin procedures leading to detention without trial. As such the police had an extended time to detain suspects for questioning. Standard police procedures made use of section 11 powers notwithstanding the existence of arrest powers also under section 13 of the 1978 Act now replaced by section 17 of the 1991 Act or under section 2 of the Criminal Law Act (Northern Ireland) 1967 where detention powers were more heavily constrained.

19–90   Section 11 of the 1978 Act has now been repealed by the Northern Ireland (Emergency Provisions) Act 1987. This leaves the police in Northern Ireland with arrest powers under section 14 of the Prevention of Terrorism (Temporary Provisions) Act 1989. This is the main arrest power in force in Northern Ireland and is also available throughout the United Kingdom. In Northern Ireland, it is used more frequently than in England and Wales. The police in Northern Ireland may also have recourse to powers under section 17 of the Northern Ireland (Emergency Provisions) Act 1991 now re-enacted under s.18 of the Northern Ireland (Emergency Provisions) Act 1996 where the constable's general power of arrest is provided on reasonable grounds.[77] It is noteworthy that section 17 arrest powers appear to be identical to the powers given to the police in Northern Ireland under the Police and Criminal Evidence (Northern Ireland) Order 1989 and it is odd that this overlap should have remained. Arguably the 1989 Order provides sufficient powers of arrest for serious offences such as conspiring, attempting or procuring arrestable offences. The army in Northern Ireland have powers under section 18 of the 1991 Act of arrest and detention up to four hours re-enacted by s.19 of the Northern Ireland (Emergency Provisions) Act 1996. Section 19(2) avoids the need to give the "ground of arrest" if the army states that the arrest is effected as a member of Her Majesty's forces. Thus in effect the army have the power to arrest merely for interrogation purposes. Section 19 also has the requirement that a contemporaneous account of the record of the search of premises must be made and supplied as soon as is practicable to the occupier of the premises searched. In *Murray v. Ministry of Defence*[78] the House of Lords accepted that the giving of information concerning the reasons for the arrest could be delayed. While accepting there was no power to search for incriminating evidence, the House of Lords held that it "is a proper exercise of the power of search to" search every room for other occupants of the house in case there may be those who are disposed to resist arrest. However, this power was limited to arrest

---

[77] This power overlaps with the powers conferred on the police under the Police and Criminal Evidence (Northern Ireland) Order 1989 (S.I. 1989 No. 1341 (N.I. 12)).
[78] [1988] 1 W.L.R. 692.

only and could not be used to carry out a search for incriminating evidence under section 14. It seems in practice that the army use their powers of arrest but within four hours all persons arrested are handed over to the police who may then re-arrest and give the appropriate reasons for the arrest.[79]

The question of the reasonableness required to effect a lawful arrest **19–91** has arisen in a number of cases. In *McKee v. Chief Constable of Northern Ireland*[80] the Court of Appeal in Northern Ireland as approved in the House of Lords, accepted that instructions given to a constable from a superior officer or an officer of equal status might be sufficient to entitle the officer to rely on the suspicion contained in his instructions. Since then it has been accepted that an officer giving the instruction should not necessarily have to be called as a witness in an action for false imprisonment.

The Northern Ireland Court of Appeal in the *McKee*[81] case also considered whether suspicion that a person was a member of a proscribed organisation was sufficient grounds to believe that the person was a terrorist as defined now under section 66 of the 1991 Act. The Court held, that it required real suspicion of the commission or attempted commission of an act of terrorism or of directly organising or training of persons for terrorism. Thus suspicion of membership of a proscribed organisation did not satisfy that criterion.

In *O'Hara v. Chief Constable of the Royal Ulster Constabulary*[82] the **19–92** House of Lords considered the arrest of a suspect under section 12(1)(b) of the Prevention of Terrorism (Temporary Provisions) Act 1984. The Court of Appeal in Northern Ireland had accepted, as had the trial judge that the basis for the officer's reasonable suspicion was a briefing held by his superior officer. This satisfied the requirement of suspicion for the purposes of the Act. In fact the suspect was arrested based on the evidence of the briefing, but released two weeks later without being charged. He brought an action against the Chief Constable for wrongful arrest. A point of law of public importance was raised in an appeal to the House of Lords.

The House of Lords held that neither the trial judge nor the Court of Appeal in Northern Ireland had misdirected itself in construing the requirements of the Act. Lords Steyn and Hope concluded that:

(i) The court was not required to look beyond what was in the arresting officer's mind. The grounds which were in the mind of the arresting officer at the time of the arrest were important;

---

[79] Dickson, *op. cit.*
[80] [1983] 11 N.I.J.B.
[81] *ibid.* See *Oscar v. Chief Constable, RUC* [1993] 2 B.N.I.L. 52 on the award of damages for any unlawful detention or arrest.
[82] [1997] 1 All E.R. 129.

(ii) The officer's suspicion need not be based on his own observations but on the information he received from his briefing or anonymously. It was not necessary for him to prove what was known to his informant;

(iii) The question of whether the information supplied at the briefing was a basis for reasonable grounds depended on its source and context and had to be viewed in the light of all the surrounding circumstances.

The case is important because many arrest powers commonly found in statutes have similar provisions that require reasonable suspicion. The case provides a useful analysis of this important arrest power.

19–93 Doubts surround the use of the above arrest powers for the purpose of gathering intelligence. A general power of intelligence gathering by arresting at random any person within a particular locality was not included in the legislation. Such "screening powers" of suspects are often advocated by military commentators but do not have legal authority under the emergency powers.

Section 23 of the Northern Ireland (Emergency Provisions) Act 1991 re-enacted by s.25 of the Northern Ireland (Emergency Provisions) Act 1996 gives the police and army powers to stop and question any person about their identity, movements and what they may know about recent incidents such as explosions or injury to persons or killings. The breadth of interpretation of such powers may be of concern if there was a widespread practice to saturate areas for stop and search powers to be used indiscriminately.

19–94 Wide powers to proscribe terrorist organisations are contained in section 28 of the Northern Ireland (Emergency Provisions) Act 1991, re-enacted by s.29 of the Northern Ireland (Emergency Provisions) Act 1996 and the list of proscribed organisations includes the Irish Republican Army, and recently added, the Ulster Volunteer Force. Withholding information about acts of terrorism is an offence under section 18 of the Prevention of Terrorism (Temporary Provisions) Act 1989. Wide powers to examine any person on arrival or departure from Great Britain or Northern Ireland, by ship or aircraft, in travelling by land between Northern Ireland and the Republic, are contained in section 16, Schedule 5 of the 1989 Act. Additional powers of investigation for the search of terrorist materials modelled on the Drugs Trafficking Offences Act 1986 are combined in section 17, Schedule 7 of the 1989 Act.

19–95 Additional powers of entry and search of premises for the purposes of arresting terrorists are contained in section 16 of the Northern Ireland (Emergency Provisions) Act 1991, for searching for monitors, radio transmitters and scanning receivers under section 19 and to search for persons unlawfully detained under section 21 of the 1991

Act. These powers have been re-enacted under sections 17–21 of the Northern Ireland (Emergency Provisions) Act 1996.

Section 27 of the 1991 Act, now section 29 of the Northern Ireland (Emergency Provisions) Act 1996, creates one of the most widely drawn offences. The section makes it a criminal offence, a scheduled offence, for:

> "Any person who directs, at any level, the activities of an organisa-tion which is concerned in the commission of acts of terrorism is guilty of an offence and liable on conviction on indictment to imprisonment for life."

The section is aimed at those who direct the activities of terrorism, **19–96** but the section is capable of a broader interpretation to include those who appear to the security forces to have various tools or documents which may be useful to the commission of terrorist acts. This makes it difficult in law to distinguish degrees of support for terrorist organ-isations. On a wide interpretation of the section the link between a terrorist organisation and the activities sufficient to come within the Act need only be very slight. In fact any suspicious objects or activities may fall within the above classification giving wide discre-tion to the security forces. It is an offence under section 18(1)(b) of the Prevention of Terrorism (Temporary Provisions) Act 1989 to have information which a person knows might be of material assistance in securing the apprehension of any person involved in the Commis-sion, preparation or instigation of an act of terrorism and fail to disclose it to the police.

Section 31 of the 1991 Act now section 33 of the Northern Ireland **19–97** (Emergency Provisions) Act 1996 makes it a criminal offence to collect any information about police officers, soldiers, judges and court officials. The burden of proof shifts to the defendant showing lawful authority or reasonable excuse for the possession of such information.

Finally, internment powers are retained but are not in use under Part IV and Schedule 3 of the 1991 Act. These may be brought into force by the Secretary of State through the laying of a statutory instrument. Detailed detention orders may be made under Part IV of the Northern Ireland (Emergency Provisions) Act 1996.

Exceptional powers are provided to outlaw terrorist funds. Sections 9–13 of the Prevention of Terrorist (Temporary Provisions) Act 1989 applies to a wide number of proscribed organisations. Assisting in the retention or control of terrorist funds is a new offence and banks are required to disclose a suspicion that money may have a terrorist source. Forfeiture of money or property is also provided in the legislation.[83]

---

[83] ss. 36–44 of the Criminal Justice Act 1993 apply to Northern Ireland and amend the Northern Ireland (Emergency Provisions) Act 1991 relating to the financing of terrorism.

19–98   Controversial powers to prevent terrorists using the media are provided in section 18 of the 1989 Act. Those who support terrorism and are political organisations may be banned from transmitting "spoken words" in interviews. On October 19, 1988 a notice was issued by the Home Secretary under the Licence and Agreement section and section 29(3) of the Broadcasting Act 1981 preventing the BBC and the IBA from broadcasting such words spoken by spokespersons for any terrorist group named in the ban, most notably the IRA or any political supporter of terrorism. The ban included any words spoken "in the course of proceedings in Parliament or in support of a candidate at a Parliamentary or local or European election." The breadth of this ban covers situations where the individual's words may "support or solicit or invite support."

19–99   The ban is difficult to justify in its present form given the common practice of both BBC and IBA photographing interviews and having actors "voice over" the words spoken by the interviewee. A further difficulty is that there is often a thin line, if at all, distinguishing political from terrorist objectives. There is a desire to encourage political dialogue, not with terrorists, but with those who might give tacit support to the ends – but not the *means* adopted by the terrorist. The ban fails to recognise the importance of political dialogue even though the views of supporters of the objectives set by terrorists may be unpalatable to many. In December 1993 the British Government released correspondence revealing secret talks it has held with Sinn Fein, the political wing of the IRA. The Irish government recently removed its ban on broadcasting interviews.

    The above emergency powers represents a comprehensive and detailed list of wide powers required to deal with terrorist activities. Police powers also involve the question of the use of force in carrying out an arrest or in responding to a threat or act of violence.

(b)   The use of force

19–100 In a number of important cases the courts have interpreted section 3(1) of the Criminal Law Act (Northern Ireland) 1967 which is the Northern Ireland equivalent of the United Kingdom's section 3(1) of the Criminal Law Act 1967 relating to the use of force. This section authorises the use of reasonable force in making an arrest and the use of reasonable force to resist an unlawful arrest. The force authorised by law is "reasonable force." Reasonable force may mean that the minimum force necessary may be exceeded if it is reasonable. On this point the law in Northern Ireland appears to be the same as the rest of the United Kingdom.

19–101 In 1983 in London two policemen shot Stephen Waldorf in the belief, which later turned out to be mistaken, that he was a dangerous escaped prisoner. One officer was tried with attempted murder and wounding with intent to cause grievous bodily harm and the other officer who assaulted Waldorf with his pistol after he had been shot, was charged in addition with causing grievous bodily harm with intent. The officers were acquitted after it was accepted that the policemen believed that Waldorf was a dangerous criminal. Such a belief was honestly held, albeit it was later discovered to have been a mistaken belief. Waldorf's shooting was a case of mistaken identity but this was not apparent to the police officers at the time. The case raised some important issues of legal principle. There is authority for the proposition that the defendant is to be judged on the facts as he believed them to be; *Gladstone Williams*[84] in the Court of Appeal has been approved by the Privy Council in *Beckford v. R.*[85] The *Waldorf* case[86] allowed this defence to be used by the police officers and they were acquitted.

The defence of honest mistake is often joined to the defence of self   **19–102** defence. On self-defence, the view put forward by Lowry L.C.J. in *Browne*[87] is that where a police officer acts lawfully and uses only reasonable force in effecting the lawful arrest of a suspect or an offender, then self-defence is not available to the defendant. This would appear to rule out the mistaken belief, that the defendant is entitled to raise self-defence, if for example he thought the police officer was a gunman. Lord Lowry explained[88]:

"The need to act must not have been created by the conduct of the accused in the immediate context of the incident which was likely to give rise to that need."

Perhaps the question of self-defence is too widely excluded in the *Browne* case. A mistaken belief as to self defence is similar to a mistaken belief that the police officers raised in the *Waldorf* case.

The question of reasonable and honest mistake was raised in the   **19–103** *Attorney-General for Northern Ireland's Reference (No. 1 of 1975).*[89] The House of Lords examined two matters raised by the Court of Criminal Appeal in Northern Ireland. A soldier on patrol killed an unarmed man when he ran away after being challenged. A judge, without a jury, acquitted the soldier of murder as the prosecutor had failed to prove that the soldier either intended to kill or seriously

---

[84] (1984) 78 Cr.App.R. 276. See *Morgan* [1976] A.C. 182 and Smith & Hogan, *Criminal Law* (7th ed., 1992), pp. 252–261.
[85] [1988] 3 A.C. 130.
[86] *The Times*, October 13–20, 1983.
[87] [1973] N.I. 96 at 107.
[88] [1973] N.I. 96 at 107.
[89] [1976] 3 W.L.R. 235.

injure. The killing was justifiable. The House of Lords held, first that whether the force used was reasonable was a matter of fact and whether the intention to kill was satisfied therefore did not arise.

The standard of reasonableness must take account of all the circumstances which gave rise to the use of force. In *R. v. Mac-Naughton*[90] Lowry L.C.J. considered the facts surrounding the use of force. The fact of an explosion before the shooting, a danger of booby-traps and other suspected terrorists could be examined to consider whether the shooting was lawful.

19–104   Even where the arrest is lawful, are the security forces entitled to shoot to kill? Reconstructing the facts leading up to fatal shootings gives rise to many disputes over exactly how the fatality occurred.[91] However in Northern Ireland, arising out of a series of incidents involving the police and the shooting of a number of terrorists, it was alleged that there was a shoot-to-kill policy. Allegations of a shoot-to-kill policy were first investigated by John Stalker[92] and later by Colin Sampson and it was concluded that there was no evidence of a shoot-to-kill policy. However, the number of incidents and the prosecution of a number of members of the security forces for killings using firearms, have given rise to the suspicion among members of the nationalist community, that those engaged in covert operations had a clear understanding that lethal force might be used, but it was never proven that a shoot-to-kill policy was operated in Northern Ireland.

19–105   Two analyses may be drawn from the state of the law in this area. First, clearer guide-lines are needed to set out the general circumstances where lethal force may be used. Currently, members of the security forces have "yellow card" guide-lines on the use of force, but the details of the guide-lines are not published and they do not have the force of law. The need to clarify section 3 of the 1967 Act is apparent when it is realised that the section states a rule of both civil and criminal law. The justification of force on the basis of "reasonable in the circumstances" removes the possibility of a successful civil action or the prosecution of the defendant in criminal proceedings.

19–106   Secondly, the Criminal Law Act 1967 is unclear as to the use of force in self-defence or against an unjustifiable attack. Such a defence exists in common law, and there is a question of whether self-defence is governed by section 3. It is most likely the case, that section 3 governs the law of self-defence, this should be made more clear.[93]

---

[90] [1976] 2 All E.R. 937; [1975] N.I. 203.

[91] [1975] N.I. 203.

[92] *Farrell v. Secretary of State for Defence* [1980] 1 All E.R. 166; *Farrell v. United Kingdom* (1983) 5 E.H.R.R. 466. See also *Magill v. Ministry of Defence* [1987] N.I. 194; *R. v. Hegarty* [1986] N.I. 343; *Lynch v. Ministry of Defence* [1983] N.I. 216; *McGuigan v. Ministry of Defence* [1982] 19 N.I.J.B. Q.B.D (N.I.).

[93] No evidence of a shoot-to-kill policy: see H.C. Deb., Vol. 126, cols. 21–35 (January 25, 1983), J. Stalker, *Stalker* (1988). See also Jennings (ed.), *Justice under Fire* (1990); D. Murphy, *The Stalker Affair and the Press* (1991). Mr John Stalker, Deputy Chief Constable of West Yorkshire, who completed the inquiry into shoot-to-kill.

There is also a remarkable difference between[94] civil and criminal liability in terms of evidential burden. Hutton J. in *McGuigan v. Ministry of Defence*[95] noted that in criminal trials, once the accused raises a defence of reasonable force, the prosecution have the onus to prove beyond a reasonable doubt that the force used was unreasonable. In a civil case the defence have to rely on establishing on the balance of probabilities that a defence of reasonable force is proved.

It is particularly difficult to apply such rules in connection with the **19–107** use of plastic baton rounds or CS gas. Serious injury, even death has been caused by the use of such devices which are primarily intended to avoid the use of lethal force. In the case of using excessive force it is the criminal and civil liability of the individual policeman or soldier that is involved. There is no direct authority clearly stating the principle of where the borderline between superior orders and individual responsibility may lie. It is thought that it is no defence to a criminal charge to plead a duty to obey the commands of a superior where the orders are so manifestly illegal that the soldier must have recognised they are unlawful. Only when the orders are legal may the individual responsible hope to plead superior orders.

Controversy surrounding the use of force came to the fore in the **19–108** case of *R. v. Clegg and Aindow*.[96] Over 350 deaths have been caused by the security forces in the course of their duties in Northern Ireland.[97] This has caused enormous controversy. The *Clegg* case highlights the problems for the prosecution authorities if there are grounds to consider that the use of force is unreasonable. The defendants were members of the British Army manning a road check point. The victims were teenage joyriders in a stolen car. Police evidence was given which challenged the army's version of the shooting incident arising out of the failure of the stolen car to stop at an army check point. At the trial the judge held that the army was justified in firing shots at the car when speeding towards them but not justified in shooting after the car had passed the patrol. Two soldiers were convicted of murder. The Court of Appeal dismissed one defendant, Clegg's appeal, but in the case of Aindow, the other defendant, substituted a conviction for malicious wounding for that of murder. The case went on appeal[98] to the House of Lords which dismissed the appeal. The controversy following has led to the release of Corporal Clegg on licence in July 1995.

---

[94] The 1987 Act was subject to annual review on the basis of Reports undertaken by Viscount Colville of Culross Q.C. See Review of the Northern Ireland (Emergency Provisions) Acts 1978 and 1987.

[95] [1982] 19 N.I.J.B.

[96] June 4, 1993, [1995] 1 AC 482.

[97] Amnesty International, *Political Killings in Northern Ireland* (1994).

[98] [1995] 1 All E.R. 334.

(c) Trial and Evidence

19–109 The Diplock courts[99] allow for the trial of scheduled offences before a single judge without a jury. The principle of using the judiciary in terrorist offences is seen as an attempt to provide a substitute for internment. The operation of the Diplock courts has been criticised because of the absence of jury trial and the resultant changes in the law of evidence.[1] Fears that a single judge might become case hardened[2] have been raised, and some evidence, though not conclusive, has been used to argue that low acquittal rates may be used as a means of testing judicial independence. Although comparisons of acquittal rates are not always valid, the fact that judges need to be alert to the possibility of becoming case hardened is a first step towards preventing this from happening.

19–110 Suggestions for reform of the Diplock courts[3] have ranged from using two or three judges or a judge with assessors or resident magistrates. Demands for return to jury trial have to date not been recommended in the reviews carried out into the operation of Diplock courts. Arguments in favour of restoring jury trial and providing protection for juries have been met with the argument that it is unsafe for jurors to perform their duty in Northern Ireland. A civil jury system is still maintained in Northern Ireland for personal injury cases.

19–111 A number of evidential rules have been altered to meet the requirements of emergency powers in Northern Ireland. In 1988 the Criminal Evidence (Northern Ireland) Order 1988 abolished the defendants' privilege against self-incrimination.[4] Under the Criminal Evidence Act 1898 defendants were first given the right to testify under oath. Section 1(b) prohibited the prosecution from commenting upon the failure of the accused to testify. After 1988 the courts in Northern Ireland can consider whatever weight they wish to the fact that a suspect refused to answer questions or refused to testify. As a result adverse inferences may be drawn from the accused's failure to mention a relevant fact during police questioning or when charged or giving evidence at trial. Inferences may also be drawn from his failure to account for his presence when found by a constable at a place at or

---

[99] *ibid.*

[1] See J. Jackson, "Curtailing the Right of Silence: Lessons from Northern Ireland" [1991] Crim.L.R. 404 and Jackson, "Inferences from Silence: From the Common Law to Common Sense" (1993) 44 N.I.L.Q. 103.

[2] Note also that s.34 Sched. 3 of the Northern Ireland (Emergency Provisions) Act 1991 contains powers of detention without trial.

[3] Greer (1980) 31 N.I.L.Q. 205 and Boyle, *Current Law Statutes Annotated* (1987) and Boyle, Hadden, Hillyard, *Law and State* (1975).

[4] S. Greer and A. White, *Abolishing the Diplock Courts* (Cobden Trust, 1986); Hogan and Walker, *op. cit.*; A. Jennings, D. Wolchover (1984) 134 New L.J. 659, 687.

about the time of the offence for which he was arrested was alleged to have been committed.

The most significant evidential rule in a criminal trial is the rule **19–112** regarding confessions. The detention and interrogation of suspects has given rise to allegations of coercion to obtain confessions. The law has to balance the interests of justice with the rights of the defendant. Section 11 of the Northern Ireland (Emergency Provisions) Act 1991 re-enacts section 8 of the 1987 Northern Ireland (Emergency Provisions) Act. The 1987 Act broadened the range of conduct which makes confessions inadmissible. Section 12 of the Northern Ireland (Emergency Provisions) Act 1996 provides that there are two important safeguards against the accused's self-incrimination under questioning. First, that admissions or confessions are excluded by the court where there is evidence that the accused was subjected "to torture, to inhuman or degrading treatment or to any violence or threat of violence (whether or not amounting to torture), in order to induce him to make a statement". Second, there is a judicial discretion to exclude rule. Violence or the threat of violence is a sufficient ground for the exclusion of a statement where the defendant is able to adduce prima facie evidence that he was subjected to such treatment. This is in addition to the exclusion of a confession obtained by any hope of advantage or fear of prejudice held out by a person in authority. Thus a confession obtained through the use of violence is almost always precluded as section 12 of the 1996 Act precludes confessions obtained through "torture or inhuman or degrading treatment."

Once a prima facie case has been raised that the defendant has **19–113** been subjected to improper treatment, the Crown has the onus of proof beyond reasonable doubt that admissions were not obtained as a result of such treatment. However, two questions remain unclear. First, does section 12 preclude psychological or mental pressure as distinct from threats of violence? Second, the judges in Northern Ireland have accepted the need to have interrogation arrangements designed to obtain information from unwilling suspects. If members of terrorist organisations are to be effectively questioned how may their rights be best protected? How far do such arrangements offend against the test of oppression, *i.e.*: torture, inhuman or degrading treatment and the use or threat of violence.

The House of Lords in *Murray v. DPP for N.I.*[5] considered the **19–114** interpretation of Art. 4 of the 1988 Order relating to inferences which may be drawn from the consequences of not giving evidence. The House of Lords held that the court must not only call upon the

---

[5] [1993] 7 B.N.I.L. 44. See *R. v. Dillon* [1984] N.I. 292.

accused to give evidence but must tell him beforehand and explain the effect of failing to give evidence. The inferences that may be drawn from the accused are not confined to specific facts of the case but in a proper case may include drawing the inference that the accused is guilty of the events with which he is charged. The basis used to adduce guilt must be derived from the circumstances which justify such a finding. This includes the adequacy of the explanation or the failure of the accused to give an explanation.

19–115   Finally on admissibility of evidence it should be noted that section 12(2) of the 1996 Act which states that there is a judicial discretion to exclude statements "if it appears to the court that it is appropriate to do so in order to avoid unfairness to the accused or otherwise in the interests of justice." The origins of subsection (3) may be found in section 8 of the 1978 Northern Ireland (Emergency Provisions) Act and section 8 was based on an earlier section 6 of the Northern Ireland (Emergency Provisions) Act 1973 as a re-statement of the common law discretion to exclude rule. Under s.12(3) of the 1996 Act there is some potential for the courts to exclude statements. Statements obtained by means falling short of torture, inhuman or degrading treatment and therefore admissible may be excluded. The application of this subsection (3) will be on a case by case basis. The view of Lowry L.C.J. in *O'Halloran*[6] was that the concept of voluntary confession at common law "is not by itself" a reason for the use of the discretion to exclude power.

19–116   In addition to rules of evidence on voluntary statements contained in the Emergency legislation in Northern Ireland, the PACE (Northern Ireland) Order 1989 introduces the requirements of the PACE 1984 into Northern Ireland.

Sections 61 and 62 of the Emergency Provisions Act (Northern Ireland) 1991 now sections 52–54 of the 1996 Act provide that the Secretary of State must issue codes of practice in respect of detention, treatment, questioning and the identification of persons detained under the 1991 Act. Similarly, codes of practice must be issued on the powers of the police to stop, question, arrest, enter, search, seize and to close roads. Codes may be specifically issued to the army in Northern Ireland. The standing of such codes is such that breach of one of the provisions of the code may result in disciplinary proceedings against members of the army or police. This falls short of criminal prosecution.

---

[6] [1979] N.I. 45., Jackson, "Diplock and the Presumption Against Jury Trial: A Critique" (1992) Crim.L.R. 755. I am grateful to Mr Jackson for advice on a number of points regarding the criminal justice system in Northern Ireland, see Jackson [1991] Crim.L.R. 404 Jackson, (1989) 40 N.I.L.Q. 105 – recent House of Lords decision in *R. v. Murray*; [1993] 3 B.N.I.L. See *R. v. Latimer and Others* [1993] 3 B.N.I.L. 45.

(d)   Ordinary police powers and emergency powers: a comparative analysis

One of the most important and informative reviews of the legislation **19–117**
against terrorism is provided by the recent inquiry undertaken by
Lord Lloyd.[7] The inquiry began with an assumption that the peace
process in Northern Ireland would continue. In volume 2 of the
inquiry report is a report into the present and future threat to the
United Kingdom from international and domestic terrorism.[8] A key
element of the inquiry is the crucial comparison between ordinary
police powers under the Police and Criminal Evidence Act 1984 and
the special powers found in the Prevention of Terrorism (Temporary
Provisions) Act 1984 and the Northern Ireland (Emergency Provisions) Act 1996.

The findings of the Lloyd inquiry[9] are as follows. First there is a **19–118**
need for anti-terrorist legislation even if there is a lasting peace in
Northern Ireland. A new definition of terrorism might include:

> "the use of serious violence against persons or property, or the
> threat to use such violence, to intimidate or coerce a government,
> the public or any section of the public, in order to promote
> political, social or ideological objectives."

There is a need at some time in the future to replace the existing
emergency laws with measures that might appear in a new Act
designed to supplement the ordinary criminal law. A number of
powers require retention: the power to proscribe terrorist organisations; membership of such organisations to remain a criminal offence;
arrest powers will be required with detention of up to 48 hours;
powers to stop and search will be maintained; the power to examine
people at ports will remain in force; and the powers to control and
investigate terrorist funding are required.

New powers should include powers to enable the arrest and
prosecution of those that conspire to commit terrorist acts abroad; the
proposal that if a terrorist gives evidence in court "he should be
entitled to receive a statutory discount of between one-third and two-
thirds on the sentence which the court would otherwise have
imposed". In the case of a charge of murder with a mandatory life

---

[7] The Rt Hon. Lord Lloyd of Berwick, *Inquiry into Legislation against Terrorism* Cm. 3420
(October 1996) in two volumes.
[8] Paul Wilkinson, *Report of an investigation into the current and future threat to the UK
from international and domestic terrorism (other than that connected with the affairs of
Northern Ireland) and the contribution which legislation can make to measures to counter
that threat. Appendix F to the Lloyd Report Vol. II* Cm. 3420 (October 1996).
[9] See Conor Gearty and John Kimbell, *Terrorism and the Rule of Law* (1996) and Clive
Walker, *The Prevention of terrorism in British Law* (1996).

sentence the discount could be reflected in the minimum period recommended to be served.

19–119   Safeguards for the accused include the need for a special regime for the supervision of the detention of terrorist suspects. Included within these arrangements are the tape-recording of suspect interviews and access to solicitors. The power to examine people at ports should be the subject of a code of practice with specific needs set out such as targeting individual criminals or suspects. Examinations should be limited to a maximum of six hours rather than 24 at present.

The main justification for maintaining emergency powers in place is the problem of response time to states of emergency. Pre-planned legislation is therefore essential even if it may not be possible to maintain permanent legislation in place.

19–120   A number of key elements appear in Lord Lloyd's analysis. Once a lasting peace is established in Northern Ireland the existing system of Diplock courts for terrorist cases might be replaced. Transitional arrangements might be possible such as building into the process some element of flexibility by permitting some cases to be "certified out" from the Diplock court system into trial by jury.

The Lloyd inquiry provides an important context in which to discuss terrorism. Northern Ireland is examined within the context of international terrorism. In responding with legislation to deal with terrorism four important guiding principles are identified[10]:

   (i) Legislation against terrorism should approximate as closely as possible to the ordinary criminal law and procedure;

  (ii) Additional statutory offences and powers may be justified, but only if they are necessary to meet the anticipated threat. They must then strike the right balance between the needs of security and the rights and liberties of the individual;

 (iii) The need for additional safeguards should be considered alongside any additional powers;

 (iv) The law should comply with the United Kingdom's obligations in international law.

(e) The Rule of Law

19–121 The emergency in Northern Ireland has raised fundamental questions about the role of constitutional law in attempting to provide solutions to a wide number of social, economic, religious and political problems. Specifically emergency powers are intended to protect society

---

[10] Lloyd, *op. cit.* p. 9 para. 3.1.

from terrorist activities, while at the same time providing support for law and order. Northern Ireland has witnessed widespread violence, civil unrest and destruction on a scale not seen or experienced in peacetime.

As McCrudden[11] has observed Northern Ireland has provided a **19–122** case-study of the limits of constitutional thinking. Would a more "rights"-orientated approach to civil liberties have resulted in a different perception about law? Or are there severe limitations in the role of law in dealing with civil emergencies in peacetime? Hadden[12] argues that instead of regarding emergency powers as a departure from the norm they should be seen as an integral part of modern constitutional law:

> "The analysis of the rule of law in national systems and of human rights under international law is incomplete without a detailed consideration of the nature and extent of emergency powers and of the related derogations from human rights commitments, for it is precisely in these circumstances that the rule of law and the protection of individual human rights are most at risk."

In 1972 the then Lord Chief Justice, Lord MacDermott[13] warned of **19–123** the dangers of the decline in the rule of law. His focus of concern was on Dicey's valuable strictures against "wide, arbitrary, or discretionary powers of constraint." One example of this decline and the potential for widespread abuse, is the problem of evidence obtained from "supergrasses." The use of "supergrasses" or paid informants, often as undercover agents, came to the attention of the courts in Northern Ireland in the 1980s. Such evidence was often uncorroborated and this led to a number of Northern Ireland Court of Appeal decisions which quashed confessions based on such uncorroborated testimony. After 1986 it seems unlikely that any prosecutions would be taken using supergrass informants. In terms of judicial independence, cases such as *R. v. Gibney*,[14] *R v. Crumley*[15] and *R. v. Graham*[16] on supergrass trials, illustrate how judicial discretion becomes important in setting the dividing line between acceptable and unacceptable police behaviour. Critics of judicial supervision[17] of emergency powers in Northern Ireland have argued that a more

---

[11] McCrudden, *op. cit.*

[12] T. Hadden (1990) 41 N.I.L.G. 391 quoted in Bailey *et al.*, p. 244.

[13] Lord MacDermott, "The Decline in the Rule of Law" [1972] N.I.L.Q. 475 and MacDermott "Law and Order. Times of Emergency" (1972) 17 *Jur.Rev.* 1–21.

[14] *R. v. Graham* [1983] 7 N.I.J.B., *R. v. Gibney* [1986] 4 N.I.J.B. and *R. v. Crumley* [1987] 3 B.N.I.L.

[15] [1987] 3 B.N.I.L.

[16] [1984] 18 N.I.J.B. 23. See also *R. v. O'Halloran* [1979] N.I. 45.

[17] T. Gifford, *Supergrasses: The Use of Accomplice Evidence in Northern Ireland* (1984).

interventionist perspective is required and that a written Bill of Rights might strengthen judicial willingness to protect civil liberties.

19–124   There is an added and more incipient problem raised by the use of emergency powers in Northern Ireland. Both emergency powers legislation and legislation for the prevention of terrorism, have blurred the lines between the specific and temporary powers required to meet an existing emergency and the need for permanent powers to meet any perceived threat for the future. There is also a concern that the effect of such wide powers has also blurred the distinction between the ordinary law and emergency powers. The full extent of the effect of the emergency in Northern Ireland has still to be measured in how ordinary legal powers and police practices may become conditioned by exceptional measures.

6. Future Developments

19–125 Northern Ireland's constitutional and political difficulties are accompanied by severe economic depression. Long term unemployment is endemic. Within the European Communities, Northern Ireland is an Objective 1 region eligible for a variety of funding.[18] Northern Ireland's future seems linked to major economic and financial assistance both from the United Kingdom and from the European Community. It is a small region of 14,000 sq kms in area with a population of approximately 1.5 million. It shares similar traditions with the Irish Republic but it has no direct land link to any other Member States of the European Union and therefore remoteness and peripherality pose important issues in the future policy agenda for Northern Ireland.[19]

Currently the United Kingdom provides a block budget of £5 billion per annum which is planned for three years ahead and is subject to annual review in the United Kingdom's public expenditure survey.

19–126   Although Northern Ireland[20] is linked to the economic aid provided both by the E.C. and the United Kingdom there is a constitutional vacuum left unfilled since the ending of the Northern Ireland

---

[18] Funding comes from a number of separate funds such as the European Regional Development Fund, the European Social Fund, the European Agricultures Guidance and Guarantee Fund and the European Investment Bank.

[19] J. Loughlin "Administering Policy in Northern Ireland" (1991) *Ulster Papers in Public Policy and Management* No. 11 (University of Ulster). See Northern Ireland (Remission of Sentences) Act 1995 as an attempt to liberalise existing sentencing policy.

[20] R. I. D. Harris, C. W. Jefferson, J. E. Spencer (eds.), *The Northern Ireland Economy: A Comparative Study in the Economic Development of a Peripheral Region* (London, 1990).

Parliament. At present, 17 locally elected politicians have seats in the United Kingdom's Parliament at Westminster but have limited influence.

There is now a Select Committee on Northern Ireland affairs which has provided an important element in accountability. However, this has limitations and is not a substitute for a locally elected assembly. One view is that this lack of political accountability for decisions has allowed the local civil service administration to develop their own style and policy which has developed in terms of longer term planning than would otherwise be possible. But this has been at the expense of direct political accountability. Generally Northern Ireland's economic policy has followed the United Kingdom's[21] but Northern Ireland has one of the largest public sectors within the United Kingdom. Northern Ireland has the highest rate of unemployment of all United Kingdom regions, a higher proportion of male unemployment is long-term and there is a high evidence of low income families reflecting the combination of lower earnings, family size and dependence on social security. Northern Ireland's future is shaped by the implementation of government policy such as privatisation. Electricity and some transport industries are privatised.

These economic factors[22] will effect Northern Ireland's future **19–127** constitutional and political development especially in a period of recession in the world economy. Northern Ireland is still dependent on agriculture which accounts for 89 per cent of total employment compared to the rest of the United Kingdom of an average 2.3 per cent. Diversification is limited because of climate, topography and peripherality.

Current E.C. funding has therefore been widely applied and has the potential to have an important impact on regional development in Northern Ireland. Considerable attempts have been made to improve the infrastructure, industrial development and physical planning in Northern Ireland and on an ongoing basis to provide the potential for long-term rather than short-term change. Also evident is the mixture of public funding and private enterprise seen in the policies adopted by the Government to encourage small businesses in Northern Ireland. Northern Ireland has unique experience of public funds mixed with private funds in an attempt to create jobs and improve the economic standing of the community.

---

[21] J. J. McEldowney "Northern Ireland in a European Context," unpublished paper on Programming of Regional Development Activities in European Regions (National Board for Industrial and Technical Development, Stockholm, Sweden, June, 1992). See Criminal Justice and Public Order Bill 1993 on the use of contract out provisions in the prison service in Northern Ireland.

[22] A. Foley and M. Mulearny (eds.), *The Single European Market and the Irish Economy* (1990).

19–128   Some tentative conclusions may be drawn from the Northern Ireland experience. The question of the effectiveness of constitutional innovation and attempts to respond to violence in Northern Ireland have raised important issues about the role of legal and constitutional devices in solving complex political, social and economic problems. The need to resolve the Northern Ireland problem by constitutional means may be frustrated by the failure of a political consensus. McCrudden has questioned whether the British constitutional tradition has been found wanting. In the circumstance of Northern Ireland he suggests that a rebirth of constitutional law is required to concern itself "not only with the distribution of power between the individual and the institutions of the State and between different State institutions, but also with the regulation of power relations between citizens."

19–129   There are also questions about the long-term interests of the British and Irish[23] Governments. Will the Anglo-Irish agreement continue despite Unionist opposition? Can devolution be successfully negotiated for Northern Ireland? Can the peace process be restored and made to work? The answers to these questions[24] are likely to maintain Northern Ireland as an important case study for constitutional innovation and change.

---

[23] K. Boyle and T. Hadden, *Ireland, A Positive Proposal* (Penguin, 1985).
[24] McCrudden, *op. cit.* p. 342.

Chapter 20

The Citizen and Civil Liberties

1. Introduction

The subject of this chapter is the citizen and civil liberties. In previous **20–01** chapters the United Kingdom's arrangements for the protection of civil liberties have been shown to be[1] "a patchwork." Civil liberties are not generally defined in the United Kingdom as matters of principle.[2] Freedoms are perceived in terms of remedies that are enforceable through the courts or as a specific protection granted to a minority or are focused on specific problem areas[3] with specialised legislation passed as a remedy. There is also a perception that civil liberties may be better protected through the development of institutions rather than the development of written fundamental rights. Institutions such as Parliament and the courts are more likely to protect the liberty of the citizen than written documents which may be worthless if they are not supported by the institutions of the Constitution. In a broader sense there is acknowledgement that[4] "political and social pressures" may be more effective in protecting liberty[5] than purely legal rights.

Currently, the present Government has agreed to publish a White **20–02** Paper and then a Bill setting out the way forward towards the incorporation of the European Convention on Human Rights. The main issues in such proposals are how to preserve the future sovereignty of the United Kingdom Parliament and how to continue to develop the rich jurisprudence of the English common law which

---

[1] Harry Street, *Freedom, The Individual and the Law* (1982), p. 306. Also see a wide range of literature in Bailey, Harris, and Jones, *Civil Liberties, Cases and Materials* (Butterworths, 1991 3rd ed., 1995). D. Feldman, *Civil Liberties and Human Rights* (Oxford, 1993).

[2] See P. O'Higgins, *Cases and Materials on Civil Liberties* (1980).

[3] *e.g.* Race Relations Act 1965.

[4] See Abel-Smith and Stevens, *Lawyers and the Courts* (1971).

[5] F.A. Hayek, *The Construction of Liberty* (Routledge, 1960).

provides for a number of bodies set up to deal with specific areas of civil liberties, for example the Commission for Racial Equality? If the Government's proposals become law it will radically change both the legal culture and also the approach taken to civil liberties in Britain.

The United Kingdom was the first Government among the member countries of the Council of Europe to ratify the European Convention on Human Rights in 1951. In 1966 the Government accepted the right of individual petition under the European Convention.[6] Various rights granted since then have included equality of treatment without discrimination in a number of areas such as colour, race,[7] gender,[8] religious belief and political opinion.

20–03 Despite such developments, up until the present Government was elected in May 1997, successive governments have not favoured incorporation of the European Convention into the United Kingdom's domestic law. In June 1976 a discussion document was published setting out arguments for and against incorporation.[9] The House of Lords Select Committee on a Bill of Rights in 1978 also recommended in favour of incorporation.[10] A year earlier the Standing Advisory Commission on Human Rights recommended a Bill of Rights for Northern Ireland.[11] Support for a Bill of Rights has emerged through a variety of different groups and prominent individuals.[12] Currently the Conservative Party appears opposed to a Bill of Rights,[13] the Liberal Democrats[14] are in favour as is the Institute for Public Policy Research.[15] The debate on a Bill of Rights has also been considered in relation to the development of a written constitution for the United Kingdom and reform of the electoral process. Within that larger

---

[6] In 1976 the Wilson Government ratified the UN International Covenant on Civil and Political Rights and the UN International Covenant on Economic, Social and Cultural Rights.

[7] Race Relations Acts 1965, 1968, 1976.

[8] Sex Discrimination Act 1975.

[9] Legislation on Human Rights with Particular Reference to the European Convention: A Discussion Document (HMSO, 1976). See Lester et al., A British Bill of Rights Constitution Paper No. 1 (1990, Institute of Public Policy Research), pp. 16–18.

[10] Report of the House of Lords Select Committee on a Bill of Rights (1978).

[11] The Protection of Human Rights by Law in Northern Ireland. Standing Advisory Commission on Human Rights Cmnd. 7009 (1977).

[12] See Wallington and McBride, Civil Liberties and a Bill of Rights (1976); Scarman, English Law – the New Dimension (1974) and Bill of Rights (3rd ed., 1985) provide arguments for and against. The political struggle to obtain a Bill of Rights has been taken up by Charter 88. Lord Hailsham supported the introduction of a Bill of Rights when Lord Wade attempted to introduce such a Bill in 1979 (H.L. Deb., Vol. 402, Col. 1063 (November 8, 1979)) but has also expressed reservations about such a Bill being adopted.

[13] Brief of the Conservative Research Department, Civil Liberties (1990).

[14] Liberal Democrats' Federal Green Paper No. 13, We the people . . . Towards a Written Constitution (1990).

[15] Report of the Institute of Public Policy Research, The Constitution of the United Kingdom (1991).

context, drafts of a written constitution for the United Kingdom have been written with a Bill of Rights as an integral part.[16]

The debate has also centred on the creation of different types of **20-04** rights such as in the area of environmental protection, or economic and social rights through the European Communities. The *Citizen's Charter* has shown how consumer demands for increased efficiency and standard setting in the delivery of the services of the public utilities may be assisted by the development of specific and enforceable rights.

A strong body of academic opinion believes[17] that the United **20-05** Kingdom has made a major contribution to the development of human rights, the rights of the individual and the protection and independence of the judiciary. An equally strong counter-argument is held by commentators who point to the absence of written fundamental rights within the United Kingdom and the tendency of government to adopt wide powers which amount to a "crisis" facing civil liberties in the United Kingdom.[18]

2. Judicial Approaches to Civil Liberties

There is some evidence that suggests there is a tendency among some **20-06** members[19] of the judiciary to favour a robust approach to civil liberties. This point has been noted in earlier chapters covering judicial review. There is a perception amoung some judges that[20] "judicial review has grown and is continuing to grow at a pace with which the present structure cannot cope".

Judicial review has expanded during a period that has coincided with the election of avowedly radical governments drawn from the same political party between 1979 to 1997. Despite its conservative traditions, government policy has noticeably changed the relationship

---

[16] *ibid.*

[17] Hood Phillips and Jackson, *O. Hood Phillips' Constitutional and Administrative Law* (Sweet and Maxwell, 1987), p. 423; G. Robertson, *Freedom, Individual and the Law* (New Ed., Penguin, 1993).

[18] Ewing and Gearty, *Freedom Under Thatcher: Civil Liberties in Modern Britain* (Oxford, 1990), p. 255.

[19] There is some reluctance to expand existing legal doctrine such as *Wednesbury* unreasonableness into a canon of statutory interpretation. See Lord Irvine, "Judges and Decision-Makers: The Theory and Practice of *Wednesbury* review" (1996) *Public Law* 59.

[20] H. Woolf, Administrative Bar Association Annual Lecture, November 4, 1991, quoted in Sunkin, Bridges and Meszaros, *Judicial Review in Perspective* (Public Law Project, June 1993) p. ix.

between the citizen and the State. Individual choice and responsibility has been broadened through the creation of a management culture[21] in the public sector.[22] Contracting out and privatisation have altered the way public bodies provide goods and services. For example, local government is increasingly required to regulate services rather than engage in service provision.[23] The development of judicial review has been encouraged by a large number of factors. There is an increased awareness on the part of litigants and their advisers of the potential use of judicial review to challenge government decisions. Rights are more commonly complained about and remedies sought in the courts.[24]

20–07   The courts have extended the availability of legal remedies and replaced rigid rules of standing with a greater flexibility. This has enabled "arguable cases" to be considered by the courts when in the past rules of standing may have prevented the case being heard.[25] There is also the availability of legal aid which has opened the possibility of challenge in the courts. Pressure groups[26] are willing to make use of the courts to articulate their cause. In addition, Parliament has provided an elaborate appeals system which provides the courts with jurisdiction over the legality of decisions. Finally, the development of European Community law has encouraged the use of the courts to develop Community law.

There is also an important question about the responsiveness of judges to the political agenda. Accompanying many governmental changes has been a growth in the number of new quasi-governmental bodies.[27] This has led to concerns about the relationship between the

---

[21] See John F. McEldowney, "Contract Compliance and Public Audit as Regulatory Strategies in the Public Sector" chapter 4 in C. Willet (ed.) *the Citizen's Charter* (Edward Elgar, 1995).

[22] John Stewart, "The Limitations of Government by Contract" (1993) *Public Money and Management* July–September pp. 7–9. Mike Radford, "Auditing for Change: Local Government and the Audit Commission" in J. Freedman and M. Power (eds.), *Law and Accountancy – Conflict and Co-operation in the 1990's* (Paul Chapman, 1992) pp. 144–64.

[23] See M. Freedland, "Government by Contract and Public Law"]1993] *Public Law* 86.

[24] This may in part come from a more critical response from consumers about the role of government and the activities of various public utility companies. Dawn Oliver, "What is Happening to Relationships Between the Individual and the State?" in D. Oliver and J. Jowell (eds.), *The Changing Constitution* (Oxford University Press, 1994) pp. 441–61.

[25] This is not to suggest that the present arrangements are unproblematical. See *O'Reilly v. Mackman* [1983] 2 A.C. 237 and the *Rose Theatre Case* [1990] 1 Q.B. 504.

[26] On the work of pressure groups see for example: *R. v. Secretary of State for Foreign Affairs, ex p. World Development Movement Ltd* [1995] 1 All E.R. 611. *R. v. Inspectorate of Pollution, ex p. Greenpeace Ltd (No. 2)* [1994] 4 All E.R. 329.

[27] A provocative account is provided in: P. Birkenshaw, I. Harden and N. Lewis, *Government by Moonlight: the Hybrid Parts of the State* (London, 1990). Also see R. Baldwin, "The Next Steps: Ministerial Responsibility and Government by Agency" (1988) 51 *Modern Law Review* 57.

government of the day and appointments to key non-governmental organisations. The shape of party politics has changed in recent years. The life cycle from opposition to government has changed. A period of strong government with a large majority in the 1970s and 80s has gradually given way to a government with a small working majority. The election of a Labour government in May 1997 has a large majority. European issues have caused much internal government anxiety.

In many ways judicial expertise appears to offer some level of **20–08** predictability and stability in the face of radical change. Dependability is seen as a strong element in judicial independence.[28] Judicial self-confidence about the developing role of judicial review has increased.[29] Judges have exposed new areas of governmental power to the discipline of the courts. In the European context there is a greater awareness among judges of European Community law and an acceptance by many senior judges of the wisdom of a modern Bill of Rights modelled on the European Convention on Human Rights. Judges in their extra-judicial capacity have gained much knowledge about the internal workings of government and financial institutions.[30] Judges have recognised that radical governmental change may also promote judicial activism. Although judicial review is by its nature pragmatic and spasmodic,[31] it offers continuity through legal principles amidst changes in the nature and scale of the public sector.

---

[28] See Sir N. Browne-Wilkinson, "The Independence of the Judiciary in the 1980's" (1988) *Public Law* 44. See A. Lester, "English Judges as Law Makers" (1993) *Public Law* 269.

[29] See Lord Devlin, "The Common Law, Public Policy and the Executive" (1959) 9 *Current Legal Problems* 1; Sir T. Bingham, "Should Public Law Remedies be Discretionary" (1991) *Public Law* 64; Sir John Laws, "Is the High Court the Guardian of Fundamental Constitutional Rights" (1993) *Public Law* 63; Sir John Laws, "Judicial Remedies and the Constitution" (1994) 57 *Modern Law Review* 213; Sir S. Sedley, "The Sound of Silence: Constitutional Lawyers without a Constitution" (1994) 110 *Law Quarterly Review* 270; Lord Taylor, *Richard Dimbleby Lecture: The Judiciary in the Nineties* (BBC Education, 1992); Sir H. Woolf, *Protection of the Public – A New Challenge* (London, Stevens, 1992); Sir H. Woolf, "Judicial review: A possible programme for reform" (1992) *Public Law* 221; Sir K. Schiemann, "Locus Standi" (1990) *Public Law* 342; Lord Scarman, "The Development of Administrative Law: Obstacles and Opportunities" (1990) *Public Law* 490. Also the useful discussion in: G. Drewry, "Judicial Independence in Britain: Challenging Real and Threats Imagined" in P. Norton (ed.), *New Directions in British Politics* (Edward Elgar, 1991) pp. 37–57.

[30] The Denning Report into the Profumo Affair, the Report of Lord Justice Croom Johnson into the Crown Agents, the Bingham Report into BCCI, the Woolf Report into Prisons, the Taylor Report into the management of football, the Scott Inquiry into Arms to Iraq and the Nolan Inquiry into standards in public life are a few examples. Lord Woolf's civil justice review is another example of judicial experience that may be gained from examining the management of the civil justice system.

[31] See John F. McEldowney, 9 *Lesotho Law Journal* (1993) "The Courts and good administration," 1–24.

20–09   The role of the courts in the development[32] of judicial review has not gone unnoticed by successive governments. In March 1987 the Cabinet Office Management and Personnel Office published a pamphlet for administrators, entitled the *Judge Over Your Shoulder*.[33] Prepared by the Treasury Solicitor's Department it gave advice to administrators at all levels on the principles of administrative law and judicial review. The existence of such a document proved highly controversial but it was practical and commonsensical in its approach. Its aim was to give guidance on the principles involved and to highlight the danger areas where Ministers may be at risk to a challenge in the courts. The pamphlet marked acceptance of the reality of the expansion in the role of the courts over the last 25 years and the likely impact of judicial review on government decision making.

3.   A Bill of Rights

20–10 A Bill of Rights may be considered as containing the basic rights of the citizen in both their public and private lives protected in a special law which elevates the status of such rights to a special and protected position within the Constitution.[34] The question of whether a Bill of Rights is a satisfactory solution to the gaps in the United Kingdom's constitutional arrangements may be considered. Even though the present Government has promised to introduce a Bill incorporating the European Convention on Human Rights,[35] it is important to set out the arguments for and against such a Bill of Rights. This provides an introduction to one of the most fascinating and long drawn out debates on constitutional arrangements in Britain. The arguments in favour and those against have been well rehearsed in the literature.[36] The presence in most modern constitutions of some form of Bill of Rights is used to support the argument that the United Kingdom should fall into line with such arrangements. The main substance of the arguments in favour of enacting a Bill of Rights are that there is a

---

[32] See Michael Beloff, "Judicial Review – 2001: A Prophetic Odyssey" (1995) 58 *Modern Law Review* 143.

[33] A new edition of the pamphlet was recently issued to civil servants (*The Times*, December 6, 1994). See A. Bradley, "Protecting Government Decisions from Legal Challenge" (1988) *Public Law* 1.

[34] See Report of The Institute of Public Policy Research, *Constitution of the United Kingdom* (1991).

[35] See J. Croppel and A. O'Neill, "The European Court of Justice: Taking Rights Seriously?" (1992) 12(2) *Legal Studies* 227.

[36] See D. Feldman, *Civil Liberties and Human Rights* (Oxford, 1993), pp. 75–88.

need to make express provision to prevent excess or abuse of powers. There is the need to provide a national standard for human rights and to encourage the United Kingdom legislature to fall into line with the European Convention on Human Rights.

Those that argue for a Bill of Rights point to the fact that the United **20–11** Kingdom has been found guilty of a number of breaches of the European Convention. As the Institute for Public Policy Research notes[37]:

> "The findings of violations include telephone tapping by the police, and covert MI5 surveillance operations against civil liberties campaigners, outside the rule of law; unnecessary interferences with the freedom of speech of newspapers and their readers; insufficient safeguards of the right to respect for private and family life; inadequate protection of parental rights as regards children taken into care; unsatisfactory safeguards for detained mental patients; and the re-detention of life sentence prisoners by the Home Secretary without proper judicial control; inhuman and degrading treatment of suspected terrorists during interrogation in Northern Ireland; degrading punishment through the birching of juveniles in the Isle of Man; excessive periods of detention in police custody; unfair discrimination in the operation of immigration controls, both on the grounds of sex (the "foreign husbands" rule) and on racial grounds (the British Asian passport-holders' case); unreasonable interferences with prisoners' correspondence and obstruction of prisoners' access to the courts."

Membership of the European Union also helps to reinforce support **20–12** for a Bill of Rights. The United Kingdom might be able to develop its own contribution to the perspectives of other European countries in developing human rights. In the face of such strong and persuasive arguments the question arises as to why have successive governments been reluctant to introduce a modern Bill of Rights in the United Kingdom? Palley[38] has noted that a Bill of Rights would not "displace the need . . . for legislation in Northern Ireland" to provide emergency powers and for comprehensive emergency powers legislation for the United Kingdom. Specialised and detailed laws are required for the security services, the regulation of data protection and for the invasion of privacy. A Bill of Rights would not substantially remove the need for such legislation. For example a Bill of Rights might not be as effective as a strong Freedom of Information Act or the strengthening of the laws on immigration, the rights of

---

[37] See note 19, pp. 8–9.
[38] C. Palley, *The United Kingdom and Human Rights* (Hamlyn Trust, 1991).

suspects and the equality of the citizen. Thus a Bill of Rights lacks claim as a panacea of all ills.

20–13   There are other arguments against such a Bill of Rights. First, that a Bill is contrary to the tradition of developing pragmatically; thereby combining continuity and change in the United Kingdom's political and constitutional arrangements. Hailsham makes this point in his recent memoirs when discussing his approach to constitutional change[39]:

> "I believe in change which is cautious, continuous, evolutionary, and carefully thought out, but in its consequence radical."

This may reflect a consensus among politicians of widely different politics and philosophies. Secondly, a further argument is that a Bill of Rights is unnecessary because of the development of piecemeal legislation focused on particular problems within existing constitutional arrangements. Thirdly, aside from the question of the adequacy or not of existing arrangements, one of the most fundamental objections arises in connection with the role of the judiciary within the United Kingdom called on to interpret such a Bill once enacted. Palley notes[40] how successive governments in the United Kingdom have been steadfastly reluctant to trust the judiciary with a Bill of Rights. Such a show of no confidence in the judicial development of rights crosses party politics and even opposition parties when not in government have only latterly adopted policies vaguely supportive of a Bill of Rights, but with no timetable for implementation of such a commitment.

20–14   Palley also notes that[41] the main objection by opponents of a Bill of Rights is that "the judiciary is undemocratic, unaccountable and unqualified." Such criticism is strongly held and difficult to counter. Reservations about the judiciary have canvassed a wide section of legal opinion, suggesting that the judges may be too narrowly drawn in terms of their appointment and too narrow in their training to do justice to the rights they are entrusted to enforce. Many of these concerns are based on political concerns about the accountability of the judiciary, their mode of appointment and the question of relying on judicial authority which is appointed, to adjudicate many of the major social, economic and political issues of the day. Ewing and Gearty have noted that the non-elected and appointed status of the judiciary is ultimately in the hands of the Prime Minister of the day[42]:

---

[39] Lord Hailsham, *On the Constitution* (1992), p. 1.
[40] C. Palley, *op. cit.* p. 154.
[41] *ibid.*
[42] Ewing and Gearty, *Freedom under Thatcher* (1990), p. 268.

"Judges are thus given the power to disrupt decisions and adjustments made by the process of persuasion, compromise and agreement in the political arena. Difficult ethical, social and political questions would be subject to judicial preference rather than the shared or compromised community morality."

A further concern is that a Bill of Rights might give rise to **20–15** increased litigation with no clear objectives as to how general principles might emerge and policies be interpreted. This might cause general uncertainty over the exact outcome of policy issues. Most Bills of Rights are drafted in a general and at times loose way. This may give rise to uncertainty over interpretation of many of the concepts in the Bill of Rights. Undoubtedly such a Bill of Rights might refocus the political agenda to one of legal interpretation over the contents of the Bill. This might result in an over-reliance on legal opinion and a legal understanding of issues. This might deprive Parliament of a considerable amount of real power and mark a shift from the political decision-making process to a legally orientated one.

Objections to the enactment of a Bill of Rights also include the **20–16** question of parliamentary sovereignty and its reconciliation with an entrenched or protected Bill of Rights. The doctrine of parliamentary sovereignty is one which has been discussed in previous chapters. We have encountered the difficulty over membership of the European Community. It means that one Act of Parliament cannot bind future Parliaments. If an Act of Parliament is impliedly inconsistent with an earlier one, the courts will give effect to the later Act of Parliament. Such a doctrine, if applied to a Bill of Rights in the United Kingdom such as through the incorporation of the European Convention on Human Rights, would leave future Parliaments and government free to depart from the terms of the Bill of Rights. The duty of the courts to uphold the legislation would mean that effectively the Government could circumvent a Bill of Rights.

Solutions to this problem must be set in perspective. Many com- **20–17** monwealth countries which have inherited many of the ideas of sovereignty from the United Kingdom have found that it is perfectly acceptable to "entrench" or protect a Bill of Rights in a particular way. For example in Canada[43] the introduction of a Federal Bill of Rights in 1960 preceded the Charter of Rights[44] by 22 years. The Supreme Court of Canada held that legislation passed after the introduction of the Bill of Rights would be ignored to the extent that there was any inconsistency.

---

[43] *R. v. Drybones* [1970] S.C.R. 282.
[44] Introduced in 1982. See Leon Trakman, *Reasoning with the Charter (1991)*. A. C. Hutchinson, *Waiting for Coraf: A critique of Law of Rights* (Toronto University Press, 1995).

The enactment of a Bill of Rights as an ordinary statute, in effect as an interpretation Act may accommodate[45] the principles of sovereignty and the protection of the Bill of Rights against any implied repeal. The Bill of Rights becomes a guide to interpretation over any subsequent legislation. This approach is favoured by the House of Lords Select Committee on the Bill of Rights[46]:

". . . there is no way in which a Bill of Rights could be made immune altogether from amendment or repeal by a subsequent Act. This follows from the principle of sovereignty of parliament which is the central feature of our Constitution . . ."

20–18 A possibility rejected by the House of Lords Committee is to enact a Bill of Rights capable of overriding all other statutes and existing or subsequent law. Techniques of entrenchment may involve the use of referendum, providing a special majority for any Act that might amend or repeal the Bill of Rights. The focus of such techniques is to provide a "manner and form" formula to prevent amendment or repeal of the Bill. There are differing academic views[47] as to the effectiveness of "manner and form" legislation. The source of the rule that Parliament cannot bind itself as to the manner and form of legislation is undoubtedly the common law. Wade argues that as a common law rule has been developed by the judges it may be subjected to further judicial interpretation and may be changed.[48] To encourage such a change, judicial minds require retuning. As part of the Bill of Rights there may be a clause which requires the judges to uphold its values in judicial interpretation or judicial oath of allegiance to the Bill of Rights may make it more acceptable to adjust the common law rule in favour of the Bill of Rights. A referendum prior to the enactment of the Bill of Rights may further facilitate recognition of the Bill within judicial interpretation. There are a sufficient number of Commonwealth cases[49] that illustrate the effectiveness of a referendum as a device to entrench such a Bill of Rights.

20–19 Many of the objections to a Bill of Rights on the basis of the difficulty of entrenchment, owe their origins to the period before membership of the European Community. Over the past 21 years since 1972 the United Kingdom's experience of membership may lead to a more realistic understanding of legal sovereignty in the context

---

[45] Also see *Liyanage v. R.* [1967] 1 A.C. 259.
[46] Report of the Select Committee on a Bill of Rights (1977–78) H.L. 176.
[47] See H.W.R. Wade, [1955] C.L.J. 172, who doubted if it could be achieved and R. F. V. Heuston, *Essays in Constitutional Law* (2nd ed., 1964) who argued that entrenchment might be possible.
[48] H.W.R. Wade, *Constitutional Fundamentals* (New revised edition, 1989), p. 47.
[49] *Att.-Gen. v. Trethowan* [1932] A.C. 526 (P.C.).

of social and political change. Bradley takes the view that much may be gained from the experience of membership of the European Community. He concludes[50]:

"As we saw with Community law, no sovereignty problems arose out of the enactment that Community law should prevail over existing legislation; but difficulties arise if the same statement is made about all subsequent legislation. The notion that a sovereign Parliament may not bind its successors is no obstacle to enacting that certain human rights prevail over earlier Acts, even though this requires the courts to make broad value-judgements in reconciling the existing statute-book with the new Bill of Rights."

By analogy with Community law, it is possible to envisage a new **20–20** broader approach in the courts' attitude to the possible entrenchment of a Bill of Rights. This possibility may admit that the United Kingdom may be capable of enacting and protecting a Bill of Rights and that may make the passage of such a measure a worthwhile expedient.

(a) European Convention on Human Rights

The most favoured formulation of a Bill of Rights to be incorporated **20–21** into the United Kingdom's domestic law is the European Convention on Human Rights (ECHR). This is in part due to the fact that the United Kingdom is currently bound by the Convention as part of international law and adaptation into domestic law follows logically from this fact. The ECHR would remain available to citizens irrespective of any possible development of a Bill of Rights in the domestic law of the United Kingdom.

Commentators[51] have pointed out that incorporation may be only one way forward as it may be necessary to produce a Bill of Rights for the United Kingdom, with some provision covering in more detail racial discrimination which the Convention only covers in part. There is also the different style of legislative drafting. A European drafted law may provide broadly drafted and vaguely worded provisions while the United Kingdom may favour a more technical approach, leaving room for less judicial creativity and a greater focus on particular areas of difficulty. There is also the question of whether the same Bill of Rights would be appropriate for all parts of the United

---

[50] A. W. Bradley, "The Sovereignty of Parliament" in Jowell and Oliver, *The Changing Constitution* (2nd ed., 1989), Chap. 2, p. 45.
[51] M. Zander, *A Bill of Rights?* (3rd ed., 1985).

Kingdom. Northern Ireland may require special treatment given the intensity of religious and political animosity.

20–22 The content of the ECHR specifies basic rights and liberties agreed in the early 1950s. The ECHR was signed at Rome in 1950, ratified by the United Kingdom in 1951 and came into force in the states that ratified the Convention in 1953. The ECHR is an international treaty and has the force of international law. Read in that light, the ECHR appears enthusiastic and idealistic representing expectations about rights which may not always result in practical realities given high unemployment or economic depression. Nevertheless such rights provide a rich jurisprudence arising from the ECHR. Article 1 provides for the citizen the peaceful enjoyment of his possessions and Articles 2 and 3 respectively respect the right to education[52] and to take part in free elections. Such rights are broadly expressed and cover[53]: the right to life; freedom from torture or degrading treatment, or punishment; freedom from slavery or forced labour; the right to liberty and security of the person; the right to a fair trial; the prohibition of retrospective laws; the right to respect for family life, home and correspondence; freedom of thought and religion; freedom of expression and freedom to join a trade union and to engage in peaceful assembly and finally the right to marry and found a family. The ECHR omits general economic and social rights which may cause political controversy.

20–23 There are specific provisions permitting the derogation from such provisions at times of emergency such as in Northern Ireland. Though it is not possible to derogate from freedom from torture, or inhuman or degrading treatment. In addition to the main articles of the ECHR, there are a number of protocols signed by the Member States which allow Member States to enter a reservation. For example under the Education Acts in force in the United Kingdom there is a reservation to Article 2 of the First Protocol to the Convention[54] as to the right to education. This stipulates so far as it is "compatible with the provision of efficient instruction and training and the avoidance of unreasonable public expenditure." Many of the rights are qualified by provisos or exceptions and are subject to judicial interpretation.

20–24 The procedures are complex and time-consuming. To some extent the ECHR is a victim of its own success as the world's most important human rights court.[55] The time-factor has now become

[52] Also included is that the State must respect the parents' rights to educate their children in conformity with their religious belief and philosophical convictions.
[53] See Art. 2–12.
[54] Cmd. 9221 (1952). Also see Fourth Protocol to the Convention Cmnd. 2309 (1963), Sixth Protocol to the Convention 1983 (1983) 5 E.H.R.R. 167, Seventh protocol to the Convention 1984 (1984) 7 E.H.R.R. 1.
[55] A. Drzemczewski, "The Need for a Radical Overhaul for Human Rights" (1993) N.L.J. 126.

quite acute. It is estimated that it may take over six years from commencing proceedings to completion of the case after it has been considered by the court. The popularity of individual petitions has led to a back-log of over 2,500 applications.[56] This may lead to abuse being uncorrected and the delay in hearing cases may cause remedies to be too delayed to be effective.

A case may be taken by one State party as against another under **20–25** Article 24 or in the case of the United Kingdom since 1966, at the petition of an individual against his own State under Article 25. There is a European Commission of Human Rights[57] which consists of one national elected by the Committee of Ministers of the Council of Europe, from each of the Member States who acts not on behalf of the Member State but on behalf of the Commission. The Commission may only deal with matters after all domestic remedies have been exhausted. The Commission must first decide whether the petition is admissible and investigate the case with the representatives of the parties to establish if there is a prima facie case and attempt to reach a compromise. Only after the Commission has failed to come to an agreement will the case be referred to the Court of Justice which sits at Strasbourg. The Commission may make visits to the national State to examine conditions and inspect arrangements relevant to the hearing of the case. In 1992 the Commission was composed of 25 individual members elected by the Committee of Ministers but acting independently.

The question of whether the petition is admissible depends on the **20–26** exhaustion of domestic remedies, the petition must be presented within six months of the particular decision and any petition which is ill-founded or an abuse of the rights of the petitioner will be rejected.[58] The petition must not under Article 27 be incompatible with the ECHR and must raise a violation as a matter of law. There are over 5,500 individual applications each year with about 1,600 registered and approximately 200 considered admissible.[59] Currently less than 300 applications are made from the United Kingdom each year. To date approximately 300 petitions, have succeeded after the Commission has attempted reconciliation and made a report to the Committee of Ministers which may decide whether or not there is a breach; the decision may be made by a two-thirds majority of the Committee.

The Court of Justice at Strasbourg is comprised of 21 judges. The **20–27** title of the Court is the European Court of Human Rights at

---

[56] Drzemczewski, *op. cit.* p. 126. It is estimated that over 1,500 applications have not been examined by the Commission. See C. Gearty (ed.), *European Civil Liberties and the European Convention on Human Rights* (1997, Kluwer).

[57] See F. A. Mann, "Britain's Bill of Rights" (1978) 94 L.Q.R. 512.

[58] See Art. 26 and 27.

[59] Drzemczewski, *op. cit.* p. 126.

Strasbourg (hereinafter referred to as the Court). Usually the Court is composed of seven judges when hearing cases. Their jurisdiction depends on the correct procedures being first followed by the applicant; the State must accept the compulsory jurisdiction of the Court, which the United Kingdom has been prepared to agree over five-yearly periods, and the matter has been referred to the Court by the Commission or the State. There is no direct access to the Court for an individual without first going through the Commission. Since 1983 an individual has the right to be represented in proceedings before the Court. A recent amendment to Article 48 under the Ninth Protocol allows applicants a limited right to refer cases to the Court. An individual may not bring an action against a party unless under Article 25 the party has accepted the right of individual petition.

20–28   The ninth Protocol came into force on October 1, 1994 for the 13 states (excluding the United Kingdom) which agreed to it. However, in May 1994 a new Protocol 11 was formally agreed for signature. Protocol 11 has the potential for far-reaching effects if it is implemented. It re-casts various Articles of the Convention, Articles 19–56, and a new permanent Court is established. It would sit as a general Court. The number of judges will be equal to the High Contracting Parties, appointed by the Parliamentary Assembly from a list of candidates drawn from the nominating state. The present Commission and Court would thereby be abolished. Under Protocol 11 there will continue to be an admissibility stage but decided by a panel of three judges on an unanimous basis. It is also intended that individuals might be able to take their case directly to the Court.

20–29   The powers of the Court include the power to award compensation and make just satisfaction. The decision of the Court is final. There are no coercive powers to compel a State to enforce its rulings but the State as a party to the proceedings does undertake to abide by the rulings of the Court. Thus the Court cannot annul Acts but its judgements are sent to the Committee of Ministers which supervises the execution of its judgements. The force of international law and inter-state relations means that in practice Member States do tend to follow the findings of the Court. Changes introduced in the United Kingdom as a result of decisions of the Court include, the Contempt of Court Act 1981, the Interception of Communications Act 1985 and in Northern Ireland, the Homosexual Offences (Northern Ireland) Order 1982.

20–30   There have been a number of cases taken against the United Kingdom alleging a breach of the ECHR. In over a dozen cases the Court has ruled against the United Kingdom government.

The first cast against the United Kingdom from an individual petition was *Golder*[60] where a former prisoner claimed under Article 8,

---

[60] *Golder v. United Kingdom* (1975) 1 E.H.R.R. 524.

the right to privacy for his private correspondence and under Article 6, a fair hearing. Golder had been refused access to a solicitor under the Prison Rules and denied the opportunity to bring an action against a police officer. The Court held that the Prison Rules were inconsistent with the ECHR and later this resulted in a change in the Prison Rules. The Court has also held that the censorship by the prison authorities of prisoners' correspondence was in breach of Article 8 in *Silver v. United Kingdom*[61] and that there was a lack of an effective remedy under national law. The procedures for the hearing of charges made against prisoners by the Prison Boards of Visitors was found to be in breach of Article 6 relating to the right to a fair trial in *Campbell and Fell v. United Kingdom*.[62]

The use of birching in the Isle of Man was held in *Tyrer*[63] to be a **20–31** degrading punishment under Article 3. Since 1976 when the United Kingdom's declaration under Article 25 was renewed, the Isle of Man was excluded from individual petitions although under Article 63 the ECHR may still apply to the Isle of Man. The United Kingdom has brought the *Tyrer* judgement to the attention of the Isle of Man authorities thus satisfying the United Kingdom's obligations under the judgement but no law preventing judicial corporal punishment of juveniles[64] has been enacted.

The Court has considered the use of corporal punishment in **20–32** schools in the cases of *Campbell and Cosans*.[65] While the Court could not find any breach of Article 3 on inhuman and degrading treatment, they were prepared to hold that there was a breach of Article 2 of the First Protocol, which requires the State to "respect the rights of parents to ensure such education and teaching in conformity with their own religious and philosophical convictions." Since 1986, corporal punishment[66] in State Schools has been abolished[67] in England, Wales and Scotland. This applies to publicly-funded pupils of independent schools but not to the independent schools sector as a whole.[68]

Individual rights such as under Article 8, the right to privacy and **20–33** family life, have been the subject of individual petition. In *Dudgeon*[69]

---

[61] (1983) 5 E.H.R.R. 347.
[62] (1985) 7 E.H.R.R. 165.
[63] *Tyrer v. United Kingdom* (1978) 2 E.H.R.R. 1.
[64] See *Teare v. O'Callaghan* (1982) 4 E.H.R.R. 232. The Isle of Man High Court quashed the decision of Magistrates over corporal punishment in line with the ECHR.
[65] (1982) 4 E.H.R.R. 293.
[66] See *X. v. U.K.* (1981) 24 E.H.R.R. 403 where *ex gratis* payments were made in respect of corporal punishment.
[67] The Education (No. 2) Act 1986, s.47; Education (Scotland) Act 1980, s.48A.
[68] One exception arises from the provisions of s.60 of the Children Act 1989 to boarding pupils of schools with less than 50 boarding students. Recent attempts to include the entire private sector as falling under the prohibition against corporal punishment have failed by the slimmest majority.
[69] *Dudgeon v. United Kingdom* (1981) 4 E.H.R.R. 149.

the Court held that various laws in Northern Ireland making homosexual practices illegal between consenting males was a breach of his privacy[70] and the law in Northern Ireland was subsequently changed to fall into line with the decision of the Court. The *Dudgeon* case has been applied by the courts in their interpretation of the law in the Irish Republic.[71]

In *Gaskin v. United Kingdom*[72] the release of confidential records for the period the applicant was in care were refused. The Court accepted that this refusal was a breach of Article 8 because there was inadequate provision for an independent review of what should or should not be disclosed.

20–34   The Court has also considered the law of contempt in *The Sunday Times v. United Kingdom*.[73] This case arose out of the House of Lords decision in *Attorney-General v. Times Newspapers Ltd*[74] over the legality of *The Sunday Times* publication of articles relating to the drug thalidomide. The Commission had held by a majority that the injunction granted by the House of Lords against *The Sunday Times* was in breach of Article 10, the right to freedom of information. The Court ruled by a majority of 11 votes to 9 that the injunction was inconsistent with the ECHR. This was the first time that the Court had to consider consistency between a common law rule of contempt of Court and the ECHR. The difference in approach in the case taken by the House of Lords and the Court of Justice represents a marked contrast in the jurisprudence of each. While the House of Lords attempted to balance the differing interests between the parties, the Court of Justice focused on the application of freedom of expression to the issues raised in the case.

20–35   The Court has not refrained from considering the question of pornography in the context of freedom of expression under Article 20. In *Handyside*[75] the Court considered the legality of the English courts order to destroy copies of the *Little Red Schoolbook* under the Obscene Publications Act. The book, aimed at children, contained explicit sexual information which had led to the conviction of the applicant under the Obscene Publications Act. The Court held that the conviction was not a breach of Article 10, on freedom of speech.

The procedure for the release of mental patients under section 66(3) of the Mental Health Act 1959 was held to be a breach of Article 5 of

---

[70] See Homosexual Offences (Northern Ireland) Order 1982. However the Court declared inadmissible an application made by a soldier against discharge under s.66 of the Army Act.
[71] *Norris v. Ireland* (1991) 13 E.H.R.R. 186.
[72] (1989) 12 E.H.R.R. 36.
[73] (1979) 2 E.H.R.R. 245.
[74] [1973] 3 All E.R. 54.
[75] *Handyside v. United Kingdom* (1976) 1 E.H.R.R. 737.

the ECHR in *X v. United Kingdom*.[76] The case was notable because the Court had viewed habeas corpus available in the English courts as not a sufficient remedy. Recourse to the Mental Health Review Tribunal was also regarded as inadequate because the tribunal had powers only to make a recommendation. The Mental Health (Amendment) Act 1982 brought English law into line with the judgement of the Court.

The Court considered the provisions of the Trade Union and   **20–36** Labour Relations Act 1974 and their compatibility with Article 11 of the ECHR in the *Young James and Webster* cases.[77] Three British Rail employees refused to become members of a closed shop agreement entered into by British Rail and the Unions in 1975. The closed shop agreement was held to violate the freedom of association protected under Article 11. Since the case was decided, the law relating to trade unions has been substantially altered. In the case[78] of the Government Communications Headquarters[79] where 7,000 civil servants were deprived of their rights to join a trade union, the Commission ruled the application inadmissible.[80]

In *Malone v. United Kingdom*,[81] telephone tapping was held by the   **20–37** Court to be a violation of Article 8 on the right to privacy. Since then the law has been changed to take account of the Court's decision which revealed how the regulation of telephone tapping was carried out through administrative guidance rather than a statutory basis.

In *McCann, Farrell and Savage v. United Kingdom*[82] the shooting of IRA suspects in Gibraltar was not disproportionate to the aim of defending life and protecting property from unlawful violence. However, it was accepted by a majority of 10 to 9 that the killing of the IRA members breached the victims' Article 2 rights to life. The majority held that the inefficient organisation of the undercover operation made their deaths likely, though avoidable. However, the compensation that was payable was only confined to the costs of the applicants.

Aside from the use of the individual petition procedure it is   **20–38** possible for action to be taken by another State against the United Kingdom. The first such case was the *Republic of Ireland v. United Kingdom*.[83] In 1971, Ireland lodged complaints[84] with the Commission

---

[76] (1981) 4 E.H.R.R. 188.

[77] (1982) 4 E.H.R.R. 38.

[78] *Council of Civil Service Unions v. United Kingdom* (1988) 10 E.H.R.R. 269.

[79] See *Council for Civil Service Unions v. Minister for the Civil Service* [1985] A.C. 374.

[80] (1988) 10 E.H.R.R. 269.

[81] (1985) 7 E.H.R.R. 14.

[82] Application 1894/91.

[83] (1978) 2 E.H.R.R. 25.

[84] K. Boyle and H. Hannum, "Ireland in Strasbourg" (1976) *Irish Jurist* 243.

alleging that there had been a failure by the security forces to protect
life under Article 2 over deaths which arose in Londonderry in 1972,
that detained suspects were subject to treatment which amounted to
torture, inhuman and degrading treatment contrary to Article 3, and
that internment without trial violated Articles 5 and 6, and in its
operation it violated Article 14. Finally the allegation was made that
the United Kingdom Government had failed to honour the rights and
freedoms contained in Article 1 of the ECHR.

20–39   The Court upheld complaints relating to interrogation methods as a
breach of Article 3. In addition the Court rejected discrimination
contrary to Articles 4 and 5 by accepting that the focus of internment
was justifiable against Republican terrorists because of the level of
violence from that element in the community. As a result of the
Court's decision, the United Kingdom Government sought to incorporate the substance of Article 3 into the domestic law in Northern
Ireland and enacted section 5 of the Northern Ireland (Emergency
Provisions) Act 1987 which allows the courts in Northern Ireland to
exclude evidence where there is prima facie evidence that the accused
was subject to "torture, to inhuman or degrading treatment, or to any
violence or threat of violence."

20–40   Northern Ireland has continued to prove a problem for the United
Kingdom's emergency laws and their compatibility with the ECHR. A
wide variety of individual applications have been received by the
Commission. McCrudden notes[85]:

> "A wide variety of issues has been raised, ranging from allegations
> of breach of fair trial protections, to torture, from interference with
> correspondence, to internment, from arrest and detention under
> the PTA [Prevention of Terrorism Act] to the law on reasonable
> force, from discrimination to the voting system."

20–41   In *Brogan*[86] the Court considered Article 5 which protects the
freedom of the person in respect of arrests, questioning and detention
for up to seven days under the Prevention of Terrorism (Temporary
Provisions) Act 1984. The question of the length of detention was
considered by the Court. While accepting the availability of habeas
corpus as a remedy, the Court considered that in respect of applicants
detained for more than five days the ECHR's had been infringed. For
applicants detained for up to four or five days, the Court regarded
their detention as not an infringement of the ECHR. The outcome of
the *Brogan* decision proved difficult for the United Kingdom Government and the operational decisions of the police in Northern Ireland.

---

[85] C. McCrudden, "Northern Ireland and the British Constitution" in Jowell and Oliver,
The Changing Constitution (2nd ed., 1989), pp. 320–321.
[86] *Brogan v. United Kingdom* (1989) 11 E.H.R.R. 117.

Taking such matters as general security into account, the United Kingdom Government decided to derogate under Article 15 from its obligations under the ECHR.[87] The requirements under Article 5 that the accused should be charged "promptly" resulted in the Court holding that Article 5 was infringed by the Prevention of Terrorism (Temporary provisions) Act 1984.[88]

Any assessment of the impact of the ECHRs must take account of **20–42** the pattern of civil liberties protection within the United Kingdom. The Court has considerably greater latitude in the interpretation of citizens' rights when the ECHR is focused primarily on the interpretation of rights and fundamental freedoms. In contrast it appears that courts in the United Kingdom face a more difficult task when confronted by legislation which is not focused on citizens' rights. Palley notes how different legal systems may address different priorities[89]:

> "Every legal system that recognises rights, whether in some form of Bill of Rights or in ordinary law, has to decide what rights to accord, how to adjust competing rights, whether to give particular rights priority, and whether to treat some as absolute."

Historically, United Kingdom courts have been reluctant to take **20–43** account of international treaties[90] or conventions when not required to do so.[91] There is also a reluctance, as in *Malone v. Metropolitan Police Commissioner,*[92] for the courts to use the ECHR to legislate in new areas through judicial interpretation. However there are some signs that the judiciary are more willing to include consideration of the ECHR to interpret the law and show a greater sympathy and understanding of the nature of the ECHRs and its usefulness as an aid to interpretation. References to the ECHR are to be found in many law reports[93] and this has increased the awareness among

---

[87] The U.K.'s derogation from certain provisions in the Case of Northern Ireland was upheld. See *Brannigan and Another v. U.K., European Court of Human Rights, The Times,* May 28, 1993; [1993] 4 B.N.I.L. 78.

[88] See H. Hannum and K. Boyle, (1972) 7 *Irish Jurist* (n.s) 329. Also see M. O'Boyle, (1977) 71 A.J.I.L. 674.

[89] C. Palley, *op. cit.* p. 159.

[90] The United Kingdom is party to the 1966 International Covenant on Civil and Political Rights Cmnd. 6702, The United Nations Treaty Series 3, the 1966 International Covenant on Economic, Social and Cultural Rights.

[91] See *Council for Civil Service Unions v. Minister for the Civil Service* [1985] A.C. 374 for failure to take account of various International Labour Conventions and also *British Airways Board v. Laker Airways Ltd.* [1985] A.C. 58.

[92] [1979] 2 All E.R. 620 at p. 642.

[93] See, *e.g.* Lord Scarman in *Ahmad v. Inner London Education Authority* [1978] 1 All E.R. 574, concerning a Muslim employed as a full-time teacher by the Inner London

judges[94] and the academic community of the significance of the ECHR. Judicial notice of the ECHR falls short of ever overturning a United Kingdom statute that may appear in conflict to the ECHR. In *ex. p Brind*[95] Lord Bridge in the House of Lords acknowledged:

". . . it is already well settled that, in construing any provision in domestic legislation which is ambiguous in the sense that it is capable of a meaning which either conforms to or conflicts with the Convention, the courts will presume that Parliament intended to legislate in conformity with the convention, not in conflict with it."

The willingness to allow interpretations of the ECHR to influence the interpretation of domestic law is an important response in the direction of accepting the rights focus of the ECHR.

20–44   How effective has the ECHR been in providing the United Kingdom with additional rights? How might effectiveness be measured or assessed? Conor Gearty neatly sums up the achievements to 1995 to be as follows[96]:

"At the end of 1995, 30 of these 37 decisions [these are cases won in the European Court up to the end of 1995], had been the subject of resolutions of the Committee of Ministers under Article 54. In eight of these cases, it had been decided that no changes in United Kingdom law were required, either because the issue had already been dealt with by the legislature, or because on the facts all that was required was an assurance that no violation would occur, or because it was considered that the payment of compenstion in accordance with the Court's ruling was a sufficient compliance with it."

Gearty goes on to explain that a number of important legislative[97] changes have come about as a result of the ECHR.

Education Authority. His devotion to his religious beliefs required him to make visits to pray at his Mosque on Fridays. His work was disrupted and after his colleagues objected he was forced to resign. His appeal to the Court of Appeal against an Industrial Tribunal's ruling that he was not unfairly dismissed relied on the provisions of s.30 of the Education Act 1944. Lord Scarman was prepared to read into the common law the ECHR's provisions under Art. 9. The appellant lost his case and the European Commission dismissed his case at the admissibility stage. *Ahmad v. UK* (1982) 4 E.H.R.R. 126.

[94] See *R. v. Miah* [1981] A.C. 303 on the interpretation of the Immigration Act 1971 and whether its criminal sanctions were retrospective or not: *R. v. Secretary of State for the Home Department, ex p. Bhajan Singh* [1976] Q.B. 198 on the interpretation of Art. 12 of the ECHR and its application to illegal immigrants.

[95] *R. v. Secretary of State for the Home Department, ex p. Brind* [1991] 1 All E.R. 720.

[96] Conor Gearty (ed.), *European Civil Liberties and the European Convention on Human Rights* (Kluwer, 1995).

[97] Contempt of Court Act 1981, the Interception of Communications Act 1985, Mental Health Act 1983, the Criminal Justice Act 1991 and the Education (No 2) Act 1986.

In addition a similar approach of reading into E.C. Regulations and **20-45** Directives has already been noted.[98] It may be only a matter of time for the ECHR to be recognised as part of E.C. law.

In *R. v. Human Fertilisation and Embryology Authority, ex p. Blood*[99] the Court of Appeal held that the widow could seek medical treatment under Arts. 59 and 60 of the E.C. Treaty which gave her directly enforceable rights. The facts of the case arose when the widow had requested sperm samples to be taken from her seriously ill husband who was in a coma so that at a later date the sperm could be used by her in treatment for artificial insemination. The husband was unable to give consent and later died. The Embryology Authority in the United Kingdom refused to allow the treatment to be carried out as they claimed it infringed the 1990 Human Fertilisation and Embryology Act.

(b) Canadian Charter of Rights and Freedoms

Consideration of any proposed Bill of Rights for the United **20-46** Kingdom may involve drawing on the experience of Canada.[1] The opportunity to consider the better protection of human rights was taken in 1982 when a new Canadian Constitution was passed. The new Canadian Constitution was accepted by the Federal Parliament after approval of all eight provinces except Quebec, and after the proposals were debated and approved at Westminster. The Charter is contained in Schedule B to the Canada Act 1982 as part of the Canadian Constitution. Section 38 of the Constitution Act 1982 provides that any amendment to the Constitution or to the Charter must be approved by the Federal Canadian Parliament and by the legislatures of two-thirds of the provinces with at least 50 per cent of the population of all the provinces.

The Charter has effectively brought new life to Civil Liberties in **20-47** Canada and effectively a new role for the judiciary. The entrenchment of the new Constitution and the Charter gives the judiciary an extended role in their powers and in their role of interpreting statute law. A number of examples illustrate how judicial interpretation of Charter rights has given rise to a more pro-active style of review with at times, dramatic consequences.

---

[98] See Chap. 8. Cases where such rights have been acknowledged include Case 222/84, *Johnston v. Chief Constable of the Royal Ulster Constabulary* [1987] Q.B. 129; [1986] E.C.R. 1651; [1986] 3 C.M.L.R. 240.

[99] [1997] 2 All E.R. 687.

[1] See The British North American Act 1867 and the Statute of Westminster 1931. On the Canadian Bill of Rights see P. W. Hogg, *Constitutional Law of Canada* (Carswell, 1992), pp. 780–88.

The Charter has been construed as redressing individual rights and preventing government from interfering with private rights. On the Canadian equivalent of the Sunday trading laws, the Lord's Day Act 1906, infringed individual liberty to require everyone to observe the Sunday day of rest. The question facing the Supreme Court in *Big M. Drug Mart Ltd*[2] was whether such a right to Sunday rest was "of sufficient importance to warrant overriding a constitutionally protected freedom." The Court struck down the Federal Act as inconsistent with the Charter's guarantees of religious liberty and freedom of conscience.

20–48   The Supreme Court in the case of *Morgentaler*[3] has also struck down various provisions of the federal law on abortion. Section 251 of the Criminal Code required that abortions were to be performed only when the continuation of the pregnancy could or would be likely to endanger the life or health of the mother and approved by a Therapeutic Abortion Committee. The effect of the provisions was that they tended to limit and delay access to abortions even when necessary for health reasons. Doctors charged under the criminal code claimed that the code infringed the right to life, liberty and security of persons under section 7 of the Charter. The Supreme Court held that such provisions were a denial of the right of the pregnant woman to security of person. Section 7 protects "life, liberty and security of the person." The judges argued that[4]:

"liberty in a free and democratic society does not require the State to approve of the personal decisions made by its citizens"

Security of the person must include the right of access to medical treatment. As a result Canada has no longer any legal restrictions on abortion.

20–49   The Supreme Court have struck down[5] a British Columbia statutory provision imposing a mandatory prison sentence for the offence of driving while suspended. This was a strict liability offence and such a sentence was contrary to the Charter provisions guaranteeing life, liberty and the security of the person.

In *R. v. Keegstra*[6] the Supreme Court overruled the Alberta Court of Appeal and held that section 319 of the Criminal Code of Canada was saved by section 1 of the Charter, in making it a criminal offence to

---

[2] *R. v. Big M Drug Mart Ltd* [1985] 1 S.C.R. 295; 18 D.L.R. (4th) 321.
[3] *R. v. Morgentaler (No. 2)* [1988] 1 S.C.R. 30. See Peter Russell, "The first three years in Charterland" (1985) 28 *Candian Public Administration* 367.
[4] At p. 167.
[5] *Reference Re s.94(2) of the Motor Vehicle Act* (1985) 24 D.L.R. (4th) 503.
[6] (1990) 61 C.C.C. (3d) 1. Also see *McKinney v. Bd. of Governors of the University of Guelph* (1990) 76 D.L.R. (4th) 545; *R. v. Zundel* (1987) 58 O.R. (2d) 129.

promote racial hatred. Article 1 of the Charter provides that the Charter shall guarantee "the rights and freedoms set out in it subject only to such reasonable limits prescribed by law as can be demonstrably justified in a free and democratic society."

The majority of the cases under the Charter involve police powers **20–50** and seldom do the courts have to deal with matters that impugn legislation. The development of rights under the Canadian Charter has not always been problem free. Canadian judges face considerable challenges for the future in the development of the Charter. Already this has given rise to criticism in respect of the Supreme Court holding that the Charter does not apply to picketing as this area of law developed from the common law, as part of private law.[7] This raises one of the most difficult issues[8] in the interpretation of the Charter namely whether the Charter applies to both private and governmental spheres. The Supreme Court is inclined to make a distinction between governmental related activities and those confined to the private sector. The Canadian Charter appears to be restricted to the former, while the latter are excluded from the application of the Charter if there is insufficient governmental involvement in their activities. This approach has led to a division of opinion among academics[9] debating the value of the Supreme Court's approach. It appears that if the relevant law is a rule of the Common law, the Charter does not apply; if the relevant law is statutory, the Charter does apply.

In the future development of the Canadian Charter the application **20–51** of rights under the Charter may create difficulties as the courts attempt to delineate the jurisdiction of Charter Rights. Ultimately this may challenge the political neutrality and the role of the judges[10] and inevitably question the interpretation employed by judges:

"However neutral and objective judges claim to be, they cannot arrive at decisions in a social vacuum. They cannot pretend that an

---

[7] See *Retail Wholesale and Department Store Union Local 580 v. Dolphin Delivery Ltd* (1986) 33 D.L.R. (4th) 174. See P. W. Hogg, "The Dolphin Delivery Case: The Application of the Charter to Private Action" (1987) 51 *Saskatchewan Law Review* 273.

[8] D. Gibson, "The Charter of Rights and the Private Sector" (1982) 12 *Manitoba Law Journal* 213. Also see *McKinney v. University of Guelph* (1990) 3 S.C.R. 229 where a University was regarded as not sufficiently a governmental body for the Charter to apply.

[9] P. W. Hogg, *Constitutional Law of Canada* (3rd ed. 1992) broadly supports the Supreme Court's approach. J. D. Whyte, Is the Private Sector Affected by the Charter?" In L. Smith (ed.) *Righting the Balance: Canada's New Equality Rights* (Canadian Human Rights Reporter, 1986), p. 145. Also see D. Gibson, "Distinguishing the Governors from the Governed: the Meaning of 'Government' under s.32(1) of the Charter" (1983) 13 *Manitoba Law Journal* 505 who argues against any such divide.

[10] L. Trakman, *Reasoning with the Charter* (1991), pp. 200–201. D. Beatty (ed.), *Human Rights and Judicial Review: A Comparative Perspective* (Dordneht, Martines Nijhoff, 1994).

imperfect process of social discourse evolves that excludes them. Nor can they render that discourse principled without reconstructing it. For judges to devise an aloof juridical science that somehow excludes political and moral discourse, is not only for them to pretend. It is for them to hide that discourse *within* the very rules and principles which they employ to exclude it."

20–52 The question arises as to whether English judges are prepared to develop strategies that will intellectually meet the challenges of a Bill of Rights within the United Kingdom? The educative function of a Bill of Rights may be the catalyst for changes in judicial attitudes. High hopes are raised in the expectation that a Bill of Rights might provide for judges and administrators, a new dimension to the development of the law and the protection of the citizen.

Doubts remain as to whether a Bill of Rights meets the needs in what is described as[11] "the crisis facing civil liberties in Britain." More fundamental adjustments are considered necessary to the "balance of political power" and attention is directed to reforms in favour of freedom of information, devolution, an elected second chamber and reform of the judiciary itself.[12] Before consideration is given to these issues in the final chapter, it is necessary to examine how the citizens' rights are considered in terms of various freedoms effected by domestic law in the United Kingdom.

The Canadian Charter provides an important model for examination and scrutiny in the context of the United Kingdom's possible incorporation of the ECHR. The debate within Canada also provides an informative literature on the subject.[13]

4. Citizens' Rights and Citizenship

20–53 Citizens' rights may involve consideration of some of the freedoms identified under the ECHR such as the freedom of expression, the right to privacy, the freedom of religion and freedom from racial discrimination or the freedom of movement involving immigration and deportation.

The freedom of expression has already been mentioned in the context of secrecy and the press.[14] The citizen's freedom of expression

[11] Ewing and Gearty, *op. cit.* p. 275.
[12] Consideration is given to these issues in Chap. 21.
[13] See Gavin Anderson, "Filling the 'Charter Gap'?: Human Rights Codes in the Private Sector" (1995) 33(4) *Osgoode Hall Law Journal* 749. Also see David Beatty, *Constitutional Law in Theory and Practice* (Toronto, University of Toronto Press, 1995), and A. Hutchinson, *Waiting for CORAF: A Critique of Law and Rights* (1995).
[14] For a useful analysis see E. Barendt, *Freedom of Speech* (Oxford, 1985).

also raises questions of censorship and obscenity. In outline the various laws that regulate and seek to control obscenity may be considered.

Attempts to regulate and control obscene publications since the **20–54** eighteenth century moved the jurisdiction over obscene materials from the ecclesiastical, to the common law courts. At Common law, an offence punishable by the Common law courts was the publication of obscene material. It was an offence to publish a book that tended to corrupt public morals and was against the King's peace. The Obscene Publications Act 1959[15] creates the statutory offence of publishing an obscene matter. The test of obscene[16] is "if taken as a whole, such as to tend to deprave and corrupt persons who are likely, having regard to all relevant circumstances, to read, see or hear the matter contained or embodied in it." The question of what is obscene is subject to judicial interpretation[17] and originated in the common law. The issue of what is obscene is a matter for the jury properly instructed on the law. The legal meaning of obscene must be distinguished from the meaning given to the word by the ordinary layman. In the *Oz* case[18] the judge left the jury with the impression that obscene could be equated with repulsive, lewd, or filthy material. The crucial question is not only whether a publication fulfils any of these conditions but whether it "has a tendency to deprave and corrupt." An article which is so filthy that causes revulsion, may paradoxically not "deprave and corrupt." The conviction was quashed because the judge failed to make clear to the jury the requirement that the article must deprave and corrupt while making clear it may have been lewd. It is possible that an article may be deemed obscene if it had a tendency to deprave and corrupt but was not lewd.

The use of the Obscene Publications Act 1959 in not confined to **20–55** sexual activities. The publication of *Cain's Book* which highlighted the favourable effects of drug-taking fell within the scope of "deprave and corrupt."[19] Smith and Hogan[20] note:

> "The difficulty about extending the notion of obscenity beyond sexual morality is that it is not now apparent where the law is to stop. It seems obvious that an article with a tendency to induce violence is now obscene, and if taking drugs is depravity, why not drinking, or, if evidence of its harmful effects accumulates, smoking?"

[15] Also see the Obscene Publications Act 1857; G. Robertson, *Obscenity* (1979); *R. v. Hicklin* (1868) L.R. 3 Q.B. 360.
[16] Obscene Publications Act 1959, s.1(1). The Act does not apply to Scotland.
[17] See Smith and Hogan, *Criminal Law* (4th ed., 1992), p. 730.
[18] *R. v. Anderson* and *R. v. Oz* [1972] 1 Q.B. 304.
[19] *Calder (John) Publications Ltd v. Powell* [1965] 1 Q.B. 509.
[20] Smith and Hogan, *op. cit.* p. 731.

20–56   The scope of the 1959 Act also applies to a wide range of literature where readers may engage in their own sexual fantasies without involving any overt sexual activity of any kind. It is possible that an article may be deemed obscene even when directed only to persons already depraved.[21]

The Obscene Publications Act 1959 as amended by section 1(2) of the Obscene Publications Act 1964 also makes it an offence to publish an article for gain or not. The terms "publication for gain" shall mean "any publication with a view to gain, whether the gain is to accrue by way of consideration for the publication or any other way."

20–57   Despite the scope of the legislation, the 1959 and 1964 Acts preserve the common law of conspiracy to corrupt public morals or outrage public decency.[22] Scope for this offence is considerable given the vague nature of the crime of conspiracy and the potential for overlap with the Obscene Publications Acts.[23] Assurances have been given that the use of conspiracy charges will not be used to circumvent the protections[24] available under the Obscene Publications Acts. Such protections under the Obscene Publications Acts include the following. The defendant had not examined the article and had no reasonable cause to suspect that it was obscene and that publication of it would be an offence under section 2 of the Acts. There is also a defence of public good. Once the jury have determined that the article or book is obscene, the defendant may show that publication of the article in question "is in the interests of science, literature, art or learning, or of other objects of general concern."

20–58   There is considerable debate as to the application of the Obscene Publications Acts to works of literature or art. The line to be drawn between what is acceptable and what is not is based not on the intention of the author, but whether the article or book is obscene. The article or book "must be taken as a whole" and considered by the jury after direction by the judge. Very often the jury may find the judge's direction influential as to the outcome of the case.[25]

20–59   The Obscene Publications Act 1857 provided that on summary procedure obscene articles may be forfeited. Section 3 of the Obscene Publications Act 1959 provides that on an oath made before a magistrate a warrant may be issued authorising search and seizure of goods which may be obscene and are intended to be published for gain. The owner may appear and present his case as to why the offending article should not be forfeited with a right of appeal to the

---

[21] *DPP v. Whyte* [1972] 3 All E.R. 12.

[22] See *Knuller v. DPP* [1973] A.C. 435.

[23] See H.C. Deb., Vol. 695, col. 1212 (June 3, 1964) and H.C. Deb., Vol. 698, cols. 315–316 (July 7, 1864).

[24] Right to jury, time limit for prosecution which runs from the publication.

[25] See *Martin Secker and Warburg* [1954] 2 All E.R. 683.

Crown Court. This may give rise to inconsistencies between different attitudes among different magistrates. There is no national or uniform standard, although the advice of the police and the Director of Public Prosecutions may be taken when considering whether to forfeit articles.

There are a range of offences connected with posting indecent or **20–60** obscene material.[26] The test is objective namely offending against recognised standards of propriety[27] and includes sending unsolicited matter describing human sexual techniques.[28] It is possible to interpret indecent and obscene in this context to extend beyond the sexual area. Section 49 of the Customs and Excise Management Act 1979 permits customs officers to seize and destroy "indecent or obscene books" and other articles imported into the United Kingdom. The test is whether an article offends current standards of propriety.

Reform of the Obscene Publications Acts has been recommended **20–61** by the Williams Committee in 1979.[29] A clear distinction should be drawn between material which should be prohibited and denied access to by anyone who wishes to see it. Restricted material should be available to those who wished to see it but not available to the general public. The committee stressed the need to protect young people and therefore restrict the material that is available. The Williams Committee would effectively remove the categorisation of obscene, indecent or violent in favour of a clearer distinction based on access to material.

Protecting the public from obscene material also extends to videos[30] **20–62** and the cinema. The Cinemas Act 1985 provides for the licensing of premises for film exhibitions. There is a British Board of Film Censors founded in 1912 and given statutory powers to act on behalf of local authorities in setting standards and the censorship of films. The Board, renamed the British Board of Film Classification, has led to an age group category[31] awarded to every film and the extension of this system to videos was made in 1984 under the Video Recordings Act 1984 and amended by the Video Recordings Act 1993. Videos are controlled as to the content and the classification of the material. In 1988 the enforcement of the 1984 Act was vested in the Weights and Measures Authorities[32] at local level. Local authorities are responsible

[26] Post Office Act 1953, s.11.
[27] *Stanley* [1965] 2 Q.B. 327.
[28] Unsolicited Goods and Services Act 1971, s.4. It is also a summary offence to make improper use of a public telecommunication system. It is an offence to display indecent matter under the Indecent Displays (Control) Act 1981.
[29] Cmnd. 7772 (1979).
[30] Video Recordings Act 1984.
[31] *U* universal for children, *PG* parental guidance; *12* passed for children of 12 years and over; *15* passed for children of 15 and over; *18* passed only for 18 or over, *R18* restricted distribution through specially licensed shops or cinemas.
[32] Criminal Justice Act 1988, s.162.

for licensing sex establishments in their locality under the Local
Government (Miscellaneous Provisions) Act 1982.[33] Indecent photo-
graphs of children under 16 are prohibited under the Protection of
Children Act 1978.

20–63　　Under the Theatres Act 1968[34] it is an offence to present or direct
the performance of a play which is obscene. The term obscene is
taken from the Obscene Publications Act 1959 which applies. This
means that the work if taken as a whole its effect was such as to
deprave and corrupt persons in all the circumstances likely to attend
it.

(a) Religion and Race

20–64　The freedom of religion involves both the freedom to practice[35]
religion, freedom of discrimination between religions and equal
treatment of different religions. In the United Kingdom older laws
failed to grant religious toleration but many disabilities have now
been removed[36] within the framework of a State-recognised established Church. The question of religious belief and the legal recognition of a religion[37] may arise in connection with charitable status with
the Charity Commissioners and under the Places or Worship Registration Act 1855 for purposes of celebrating marriages, taxation
arrangements and charitable status.

20–64A　　Various fringe religious groups or factions have attempted and
sometimes succeeded in securing charitable status. The law may find
it difficult to categorise such groups and distinguish religious cults[38]
from a recognised religion. The value judgements inherent in such a
distinction are difficult to make.

　　The existence of an established religion, the Church of England, has
ensured through successive statutes that the Sovereign is "the
Supreme Governor of the Realm in all spiritual and ecclesiastical
causes as well as temporal". It is therefore required that the Sovereign
is a member of the Church of England and marriage to a Roman
Catholic is grounds for disqualification.[39]

---

[33] These powers include detailed regulatory powers over licensing and control of such
establishments. See also D. Cooper, *Sexing the City* (1994)
[34] The 1968 Act repealed the Theatres Act 1843 which left censorship under the control
of the Lord Chamberlain. The 1968 Act also applies to Scotland.
[35] St. J. Robilliard, *Religion and the Law* (1984).
[36] Lord Chancellor (Tenure of Office and Discharge of Ecclesiastical Functions) Act 1974
allowing the Office of Lord Chancellor to be held by a Roman Catholic.
[37] *Re South Place Ethical Society: Barralet v. Attorney-General* [1980] 3 All E.R. 918. See *ex
p. Segerdal* [1970] 2 Q.B. 697.
[38] For example the Unification Church known as the "Moonies" which has charitable
status but has caused questions to be raised about its activities and suitability, see
H.C. Deb., Vol. 926, cols. 1597–1598 (February 23, 1977).
[39] The Act of Settlement, s.2 and also see s.3.

A major issue is the teaching of religion in schools, compulsory **20–65** under the National Curriculum under section 2(1)(a) and (8) of the Education Reform Act 1988, and the designation of religious schools. Recognition of religious affiliation is contained in sections 6 and 7 of the Education Reform Act 1988. Schools may be divided into county and voluntary schools. In the case of county schools under section 9(1) of the Education Act 1944 county schools are state schools owned and maintained by local education authorities. Maintained schools as they are commonly referred to, are required to have a daily act of worship under section 7(1) of the Education Reform Act 1988, "wholly or mainly of a broadly Christian character." Exemptions to reflect a particular form of worship may be obtained.[40] Generally the law permits a child's religion and education to be matters for parents until the age of discretion.[41]

Voluntary schools are either controlled, aided, or special agreement **20–66** schools, each with their own specialised sets of rules. Most of the voluntary schools have a religious affiliation such as Church of England, Roman Catholic, Methodist or Jewish. The daily act of worship will therefore be denominational. There are powers under section 13 of the Education Act 1980 to approve schools within the voluntary status such as Muslim Schools. This is a delicate issue. The freedom of Muslims to participate in their own schools has to be balanced against the need to have a racially balanced education system free from sectarian differences which may be exacerbated by the separation of education on the basis of religion. A voluntary-aided school may adopt a religious admission policy by giving account to section 6(3)(a) of the Education Act 1980. This applies where the school is over-subscribed. The House of Lords ruled that the parental wishes of some parents could be defeated on the basis of the School's own admission policy.[42] In effect this may protect the religious preferences of some parents at the expense of others. The parents of two girls one a Hindu, the other a Muslim were unsuccessful in their application to enter a Roman Catholic School which favoured Roman Catholic and other Christian girls as part of the school's admission policy.

---

[40] This applies to a county school who may apply to the local Standing Advisory Council on Religious Education (SACRE).

[41] See ss.2–4 of the Children Act 1989. The courts must have regard to the welfare of the child.

[42] R. v. Governors of Bishop Challenor Roman Catholic School ex p. C and another, The Independent, June 18, 1992.

20–67   The protection of the Christian religion is acknowledged in the law of blasphemy[43] and in various statutes protecting Sunday.[44] Acceptance of religious belief is also recognised in laws which exempt Sikhs from wearing crash helmets on motorcycles and on construction sites.[45] Such arrangements are minor exceptions to the general assumptions that the law is mainly concerned with the Christian or Jewish religions.

20–68   Euthanasia has largely been opposed by religious groups and this opposition has been upheld by the courts. The question of the use of pain-killing drugs by doctors raises religious and ethical issues. In *Adams*[46] Devlin J. expressed a traditional, but not exclusively Christian position that doctors should not prescribe drugs which would shorten life. In *Airedale NHS Trust v. Bland,*[47] the House of Lords was still opposed to euthanasia but held that in the case of an insensate patient with no hope of recovery when it was known that stopping medical treatment would result in death, there was no criminal act provided it was in the patient's best interests not to prolong his life. The courts would provide guidance in the form of a declaratory judgement to doctors in cases of withholding life-prolonging treatment. A minority of judges considered that it was important that Parliament should consider the moral, social and legal issues involved in such cases.

20–69   Freedom of religious belief may be considered in the context of the criminal law. In *Blaue*[48] the victim of a stabbing was a member of the Jehovah's witnesses. She was told that unless she received a blood transfusion, which was the recommended standard medical treatment, she would die. She refused the treatment on religious grounds and her assailant was found guilty of her manslaughter. Lawton L.J. recognised that the religious belief of the victim, whether reasonable or not had to be accepted as part of the principle that the defendant had to take the victim as he found her. The victim included physical attributes such as an "egg shell skull," but also the religious beliefs of the victim.

However, in *R. v. Senior*[49] in the case of a child in need of medical treatment, it was held that to withhold medical treatment from the

---

[43] *Ex p. Choudhury* [1991] 1 All E.R. 306. The Law Commission has recommended by a majority that the crime of blasphemy should be abolished: *Law Commission Report* No. 145.
[44] The Sunday Observance Act 1780, the Sunday Entertainments Act 1932, the Sunday Theatre Act 1972 and section 9 of the Cinema Act 1985. Now see the proposals contained in the Shops Bill permitting Sunday trading.
[45] Motorcycle Crash-helmets (Religious Exemption) Act 1976 and section 1 of the Employment Act 1988.
[46] [1957] Crim.L.R. 365.
[47] [1993] 1 All E.R. 821.
[48] [1975] 1 W.L.R. 1411; [1975] 3 All E.R. 446; .
[49] [1899] 1 Q.B. 283.

child on the grounds of religious belief was manslaughter. Religious belief may be expressly recognised in a statute such as section 4 of the Abortion Act 1967 which recognises religious belief not to participate in an abortion on the ground of conscientious objection.

Religious discrimination is expressly prohibited in Northern Ire- **20–70** land, on the grounds of employment, education and the provision of services to the public.[50] Similar provisions do not apply in other parts of the United Kingdom.

Freedom from racial discrimination is an example of piecemeal **20–71** reform to meet particular problems. Since the 1950s and 60s the number of immigrants from India, Pakistan and the West Indies seeking employment in the United Kingdom focused attention on the multi-racial and ethnical nature of the United Kingdom. Three Acts of Parliament[51] have been extended to cover race relations while immigration policy has been tightened and reviewed.[52]

The current legislation[53] is the Race Relations Act 1976 which strengthens and extends legislation passed in 1965 and 1968. The first attempt at legislation in 1965 made it illegal to discriminate against a person on the grounds of race in certain places of public access such as hotels, restaurants, theatres, sports grounds, places of entertainment, pubs and dance halls, and under section 5, in the disposal of tenancies and also in the creation of the offence of racial discrimination. The difficulty of proving intent to stir up racial hatred made this part of the Act largely ineffective. The Act created a new conciliatory procedure operated by the Race Relations Board (RRB) which made an annual report to Parliament. Failure to achieve a satisfactory settlement of a dispute might result in action by the Attorney-General who could take action in the High Court or County Court through an injunction.

Following criticism[53a] of the 1965 Act, the Race Relations Act 1968 **20–72** was enacted. The Act allowed the RRB to take cases to court rather than having to rely on the Attorney-General. The Act also extended the application of the law to a wider range of activities such as goods, facilities and services, employment, housing and advertisements. The Act also extended to the Crown and the Police.

Interpretation of the Act by the courts gave rise to a number of **20–73** difficulties. Certain private social or political clubs which operated a

---

[50] Fair Employment (Northern Ireland) Act 1976. See Northern Ireland Constitution Act 1973.
[51] The Race Relations Act 1976 repeals the Race Relations Acts of 1968 and the remnants of the Race Relations Act 1965.
[52] See below for a discussion of citizenship.
[53] L. Lustgarten, *Legal Control of Racial Discrimination* (1980).
[53a] Harry Street, Geoffrey Howe and Geoffrey Bindman, *Report on Discrimination Legislation* (1967).

bar on the basis of race were held to escape the provisions of the legislation.[53b] Discrimination against a person on the grounds of a person's nationality as distinct from national origins was not contrary to the Act. The RRB could take action on its own initiative to investigate suspected cases of discrimination. Working on informal techniques of compromise the RRB could attempt to find a solution. The 1968 Act had failed to be effective and after a White Paper[53c] a new Act was passed in 1976. Building on the experience of the previous legislation, the 1976 Act set out to remedy some of the shortcomings mentioned above. The 1976 Act extended the scope of the 1968 Act to cover partnerships and clubs, contract workers and discrimination on the grounds of nationality rather than national origins. Direct and indirect discrimination[53d] and discriminatory practices such as victimisation[53e] are also included within the scope of the Act. Such practices are illegal if they fall within employment, education, goods and services, housing, clubs, or advertisements.[53f]

20–74   The definition of discrimination remains the same, namely a person discriminates if on racial grounds he treats another less favourably than he treats or would treat other persons. It is an offence to incite, instruct or induce someone to act in a discriminatory way. The courts appear to have developed a relatively[54] simple test; would the complainant have received the same treatment from the defendant but for his or her racial background?

The 1976 Act allows direct access to the individual who feels that there is a grievance. Assistance is then given by the Commission for Racial Equality (CRE) which replaced the Race Relations Board and the Community Relations Commission. The CRE may give advice or assistance and if necessary instigate proceedings in the County Court by seeking an injunction. It has considerable powers to require the furnishing of information and the production of documents and if necessary seek court orders to enforce the production of documents. The CRE is appointed by the Home Secretary and it makes an annual

---

[53b] *Race Relations Board v. Carter* [1973] A.C. 868.
[53c] *Racial Discrimination*, Cmnd. 6234 (1975). See Lester and Bindman, *Race and Law* (1972); B. Hepple and S. Fredman, *Labour Law and Industrial Relations in Great Britain* (Kluwer, 1992), pp. 179–99.
[53d] See *Orphanos v. Queen Mary College* [1985] A.C. 761.
[53e] But see, *Kirby v. Manpower Services Commission* [1980] I.C.R. 420. A victim of alleged discrimination reported the matter to a Community Relations Council, this resulted in his transfer to less desirable work. He was held not to have been victimised. The reasoning in the case was that he was treated as any other employee who disclosed confidential information.
[53f] See *R. v. Ford* [1989] Q.B. 868 showing that the composition of a jury must be randomly selected. Defendants are not entitled to representatives with a similar ethnic background.
[54] See a similar approach in the case of sex discrimination, *James v. Eastleigh Borough Council* [1990] 2 A.C. 751.

report to the Home Secretary which is laid before Parliament. It has 15 members and is independent from government.

Discrimination is unlawful in employment except where there is a **20–75** particular racial group where this is a specified qualification for a specific job such as the theatre. Employment in a private household is not included under the Act.

In the case of employment where there are allegations of discrimination, the complainant must complain to an industrial tribunal. The burden lies on the complainant, and if successful the complainant may achieve compensation, or reversal of the policy or act of discrimination. Enforcement in the field of employment depends on the victim of discrimination complaining to an industrial tribunal with an appeal on a point of law to the Employment Appeal Tribunal.

As a result of the difficulty of proving intention under the 1965 Act **20–76** for the offence of inciting racial hatred, the 1976 Act replaced the requirement of intention with an objective test. The defendant's conduct, if judged to stir up racial hatred was guilty of the offence irrespective of whether he intended to do so or not. Further refinement to the law was achieved under Part III of the Public Order Act 1986 which added seven further offences[55] to the offence of stirring up racial hatred.[56]

In the field of racial discrimination some advocate a different **20–77** approach than that outlined in the 1976 Act. Positive discrimination or reverse discrimination is intended to encourage affirmative action[57] to provide positive steps to redress any racial discrimination in society. For example in employment or education one possibility is to allocate places on the basis of race or ethnic origin thus ensuring that there is a fair balance to the opportunities available to ethnic groups. The definition of discrimination under section 1 of the Race Relations Act makes affirmative action illegal. There are some exceptions such as sections 35–38 which may permit a particular group to be granted education, training and special needs. Introduction into the United

---

[55] The offences are to be found in ss.17–23 of the Public Order Act 1986. They include threatening or abusive or insulting words or behaviour, publishing or distributing written material, presenting or publishing a public performance of a play, distributing or showing or playing a recording of visual images or sounds, or directing a programme service involving threatening or abusive language.

[56] There are also a number of defences available such as s.19; the defendant proving that he was not aware of the content of material and did not suspect or have reason to suspect that it was threatening, or s.20 he did not know or suspect that the offending words or behaviour were threatening, abusive or insulting. Similar defences apply to written material, or the content of a recording.

[57] Cmnd. 6234 (1975) the Government sets out reasons against such affirmative action. The Scarman report on the Brixton Disorders April 10–12, 1981 (Cmnd. 8427 1981) also considered programmes to encourage ethnic mix in opportunities available in society.

Kingdom of a full programme of affirmative action requires careful consideration and research.[58]

(b) Privacy

20–78 It suffices to mention here that the right to privacy is numbered an important civil liberty. The subject has been considered in detail in Chapter 18. There is in English law no general right to privacy and there is currently active consideration being given to remedying this omission[59] following the second report (the *Calcutt* Committee[60]) by Sir David Calcutt Q.C., and consideration of the law by the National Heritage Select Committee.[61] The *Calcutt* Committee in its first report[62] in 1990 rejected a general law of right to privacy[63] preferring some form of self-regulation. The operation of press self-regulation was reviewed in the second of *Calcutt's* reports. In his second report *Calcutt* concluded that the Press Complaints Commission "has not proved itself to be an effective regulator" and recommended that the Government should introduce a statutory regime which *inter alia* might impose fines, award costs, give guidance, and require the printing of an apology, correction or reply. The Committee recommended a new Press Complaints Commission modelled on the Broadcasting Complaints Commission allowing more effective redress against the press. Complaints made to the Commission could be investigated where there were allegations of unjust or unfair treatment by newspapers or periodicals. The Commission would be given new powers to recommend the nature and form of the right to reply. The newspaper industry is expected to finance the Commission. In addition *Calcutt* recommended criminal offences in the cases of physical intrusion such as using surveillance devices on private property, the tort of infringement of privacy, and the tightening up of laws under the Data Protection Act 1984, the interception of telecommunications, and legal restrictions on press reporting empowering any court to restrict the publication of the name and address of any person by whom an offence has been alleged to have been committed. The Government's response has not been in favour of a

---

[58] A full discussion of the civil liberties aspects of racial discrimination may be found in Bailey Harris and Jones *op. cit.* p. 563. See also Race Relations (Remedies) Act 1994.

[59] See the Younger Committee Report. *Report of the Committee on Privacy,* Cmnd. 5012 (1972).

[60] Review of Press Self-Regulation, Cm. 2135 (1993). See Geoffrey Robertson and Andrew Nicol, *Media Law* (3rd ed., 1992).

[61] (HMSO, 1993).

[62] *The Report of the Committee on Privacy and Related Matter,* Cm. 1102 (1990).

[63] Strengthening the basis for self regualtion was the thrust of the recommendations from the first report (Cm. 1102 1990).

statutory tribunal, but consideration is being given to the other recommendations of the *Calcutt* Report.

The National Heritage Committee recommended a Protection of **20–79** Privacy Bill including both civil and criminal liability. In the case of civil liability, the Committee recommended the introduction of a tort of infringement of privacy. The criminal law might be applied to offences resulting from the unauthorised use of invasive technology and harassment. The need for such laws arguably rests on the degree of press and media intrusion into the private lives of public figures. In its general discussion of privacy laws the Select Committee also advocated the introduction of a more liberal Freedom of Information Bill. The Committee regarded both as a necessary balance between the two. The Select Committee also considered the question of a Code of Practice for journalists and a statutory ombudsman to adjudicate and publish his findings.

A general right of privacy arose in the case of *Kaye v. Robertson*.[64] A **20–80** popular television personality underwent extensive surgery as a result of a serious accident. Photographs taken of the personality in hospital were taken by a leading newspaper and an injunction obtained by the personality seeking to restrain the newspaper from publishing the photographs. The Court of Appeal considered that there was no right to privacy in English law but conceded that an injunction should be granted on the basis of a malicious falsehood.

The absence of a general right of privacy in English law leaves various bodies such as the Press Complaints Commission and the Data Protection Registrar to fill gaps by setting standards and adjudicating disputes. Few believe that this provides a satisfactory alternative to the right to privacy.

(c) Work

The United Kingdom enacted specific laws to oppose sex discrimina- **20–81** tion. There are two statutes relevant to sex discrimination, first the Equal Pay Act 1970 and secondly the Sex Discrimination Act 1975. The Equal Pay Act is intended to provide women with equal pay when undertaking equal work, or where a job evaluation scheme has been carried out and the work is rated as equivalent to a man's work. In the case of a collective bargain agreement between employer and trade union, that provides different rates for men and women, the collective agreement may be referred to an Industrial Arbitration Board for the removal of any clause which is unfair or discriminatory.

---

[64] [1991] F.S.R. 62.

20–82   Women who believe that they are not getting equal pay may refer their claim to an industrial tribunal. The onus of proof is that she has to show that her work is similar to that of a man's. Once this element of proof has been discharged the onus is then on the employer to show that there are material differences between the man's work and the woman's work. Compensation is payable of up to two years arrears of pay.[65] The Equal Pay Act has also a more general application to a woman's terms and conditions of employment including sickness pay and holiday bonuses. For example Lloyd's Bank Ltd operated a pension scheme which in *Worringham and Humphreys v. Lloyd's Bank Ltd (No. 2)*[66] was held by the European Court of Justice to be a violation of Article 19. Male employees over 25 were expected to contribute 5 per cent of their salary to the pension fund while female employees of the same age were not required to make any contribution. The male employees over 55 received extra salary to compensate them and if they left before 25 they received a full refund.

20–83   The Sex Discrimination Act 1975 bears similarity to the scope of the provisions of the Race Relations Act 1976. In the case of sex discrimination, Part II of the 1975 Act prohibits discrimination in employment and applies to the arrangements for the terms and conditions of employment, access to training, promotion and benefits and to dismissal. This includes job advertisements and includes that a refusal or deliberate omission to offer employment because of a person's sex is unlawful.

There are a number of exceptions to the Act such as employment in private households,[67] and genuine examples where the job may only be performed by someone of a certain sex.

20–84   The Equal Opportunities Commission has powers to bring proceedings in the County Court and extensive powers to carry out formal investigations into employers' policies and practices. In cases where it establishes that there is discrimination or contravention of the equal pay provisions, it may issue a non-discrimination notice. Codes of Practice may be issued or inquiries may be carried out into a specific complaint provided the Commission is satisfied that there has been a breach of the statute before embarking on the inquiry.[68]

---

[65] See the Equal Pay (Amendment) Regulations 1983 (S.I. 1983 No. 1794) after the European Court of Justice in the Case 61/81, *European Commission v. U.K.* [1982] E.C.R. 2601, [1982] 3 C.M.L.R. 284, held that the United Kingdom had failed to apply the principle of equal pay for work of equal value for which no system of proper job classification had existed.

[66] [1982] 3 All E.R. 373.

[67] See the Sex Discrimination Act 1986 which followed *E.C. Commission v. United Kingdom* [1984] 1 All E.R. 353, and repealed earlier provision and exempts employment where work is to be done in a private house which involves a degree of contact with the employer which involves objections to a worker of a particular sex.

[68] Similar powers may be used by the Commission for Racial Equality.

5. Immigration, Citizenship and Extradition

(a) Citizenship

The Treaty on European Union provides for the first time in the **20–85** context of the Community, the formulation of rights for the Citizen of the European Union. The first of the rights pertaining to European citizenship conferred by the new Treaty is the right to move and reside freely throughout the territory of the Member States. The concept of citizenship is an important one for the bestowal of rights and the ascertainment of responsibilities. Race relations in the United Kingdom are not exclusively determined by the Race Relations Acts. An important aspect of immigration policy has been the question of the rights of immigrants to enter and remain within the United Kingdom. Restrictions may be imposed on British subjects.

At common law a British subject was synonomous with allegiance **20–86** to the Crown within His Majesty's dominions. Aliens owed a temporary allegiance. Historical reasons influenced the categorisation of British subjects to be defined as including the United Kingdom and Colonies. The status of British subject became the basis of citizenship and this was recognised under the British Nationality Act 1948. Historical reasons also combined with economic factors to influence restrictions on the freedom of Commonwealth citizens to enter and live in the United Kingdom. For example after a period of growth in emigration from India, Pakistan and the West Indies in the 1950s, there followed a period of restriction. First under the Commonwealth Immigrants Act 1962 and secondly, under the Immigration Act 1971. Thus holding citizenship does not qualify one for living within the United Kingdom.

A major change in the law took place under the British Nationality **20–87** Act 1981 which came into force in 1983. At the end of 1982 anyone who was a citizen of the United Kingdom and Colonies under the 1971 Act and had the right to abode in the United Kingdom became a British Citizen.[69] Those that did not have a right of abode but had

---

[69] A person had a right to abode if he were born, adopted, naturalised or registered in the United Kingdom, the Channel Islands or the Isle of Man or if his parent had citizenship at the time of his birth or adoption, provided that the parent had either acquired citizenship in the United Kingdom or the islands or been born to or adopted by a citizen parent with citizenship acquired in the United Kingdom or islands. Alternatively, anyone who settled at any time in the United Kingdom and was ordinarily resident for the last five years or more or if not a citizen of the United Kingdom and colonies, was a Commonwealth citizen born to or adopted by a parent who had citizenship of the United Kingdom or colonies by birth in the United Kingdom or islands or if married to someone having the right of abode obtained registration as a citizen.

some connection with a British dependent territory became British dependent territories citizens. Those who did not qualify as either British citizens or British dependent territories citizenship become British overseas citizens. So although the 1981 Act introduces the requirement of citizenship as the basis of immigration control, the concept of citizenship is defined to include all those who had the right of abode prior to the 1981 Act. The right to abode is specified in detailed provisions of the 1981 Act. From 1983 onwards birth in the United Kingdom ceased to be a qualification for British citizenship. At the time of birth, if either parent is either a British citizen or ordinarily resident, *i.e.* "settled" in the United Kingdom, then British citizenship is acquired. A minor who is adopted becomes a British citizen if the order is made by a United Kingdom court and either adoptive parent is a British citizen on the date of the Order of adoption. In other cases those born in the United Kingdom acquire British citizenship through registration if they have spent the first 10 years of their life in the United Kingdom.[70] British citizenship may be gained through a system of naturalisation.[71] The Home Secretary has a discretion to naturalise certain categories of applicant but there is no appeal against his refusal. Those married[72] to a British citizen or with a five years residence in the United Kingdom may be included as naturalised citizens.

20–88   The question raised under the Immigration Act 1971 and the British Nationality Act 1981, in force since 1983, together with a variety of immigration rules and regulations[73] is whether a person has a right of abode in the United Kingdom? This question will determine whether the person is subject to immigration control. Those who are subject to control, that is they do not have the right to abode may be classified as those who are expected to be permitted to enter and remain and those that have no such expectation. Determination of such a category depends on the application of immigration rules under section 3(2) of the Immigration Act 1971. This section provides that either House of Parliament may disapprove of a statement of rules within 40 days of such resolution. Section 39(2) of the 1981 Act provides that all British citizens have a right of abode. Commonwealth citizens before 1981 have a right of abode satisfied on the production of a certificate of

---

[70] If a parent subsequently becomes a citizen or is ordinarily resident here while the child is still a minor the child is a citizen of the U.K. A child adopted through a United Kingdom court order becomes a British citizen if the adopter is a British citizen.

[71] See Blake (1982) 45 M.L.R. 179.

[72] The Immigration Act 1988 restricts the possibility of several wives of polygamous marriages qualifying under English law to the right of abode.

[73] See the statement of changes in Immigration Rules 1990 (May 1, 1990) (1989–90; H.C. 251); (1989–90; H.C. 454); Cm. 1220 (1991) and (1990–91; H.C. 160).

entitlement. The right of abode also extends to citizens of the European Community. Two countries where immigration have proved problematic are the Falklands and Hong Kong. First, the case of the Falklands. After the Falklands War the Government passed the British Nationality (Falklands Islands) Act 1983. Those born in the Falklands to parents who were settled there have become British citizens. Secondly the case of Hong Kong where the potential for large-scale immigration into the United Kingdom has increased after the period of British rule and the handing over of the colony to China. The Hong Kong Act 1985 provides a unique category of "British Nationals (Overseas)," after July 1997. This category carries no rights to United Kingdom residence. However a small category of Hong Kong citizens have been granted British citizenship with entry rights intended to encourage them to remain in Hong Kong with the knowledge that they may leave Hong Kong and live in the United Kingdom as an assurance against unfavourable treatment by the Chinese.

Administration of the immigration rules represents an important **20–89** example of administrative discretion. Section 19 of the Immigration Act 1971 provides for an appeal to lie to an adjudicator or to the Immigration Appeal tribunal or both. The immigration Rules are in effect given the force of law and may form the basis or a legal challenge in the High Court on the basis that the rules have been incorrectly interpreted or applied. The question of judicial review is related to the question of whether there are available alternative remedies.[74] The immigration rules are also supplemented by instructions issued from time to time by the Home Office.

Nationals of the European Community once free to enter[75] are free **20–90** from any restrictions on employment or occupation and no work permit is required for prospective workers.[76] Community nationals and their families enjoy generous rights within Member States subject to refusal on the grounds of personal unacceptability such as public security or public health.[77]

---

[74] See *ex p. Swati* [1986] 1 All E.R. 717. Any entitlement that may be derived from the Immigration Rules is only enforceable through appeals or exceptionally through judicial review.

[75] See the Immigration Rules 1990. From 1993 the entitlement to admission or to seek employment does not apply to national of Portugal or Spain. See Council Regulations 1612/68; 1251/70; Council Directives 64/221; 68/360; 72/194; 73/148; 75/34; 75/35; Council Declaration 1451/68.

[76] Rights of their dependants to accompany them are wider than those with respect to others who are not British citizens.

[77] See Case 41/74, *Van Duyn v. Home Office (No. 2)* [1974] E.C.R. 1337. [1975] Ch. 358.

Citizens of the Republic of Ireland are part of a Common Travel Area permitting[78] immigration free travel within the specified area but subject to the provisions applying to emergency powers. New legislation passed in 1987, the Immigration (Carriers' Liability) Act 1987, makes it a criminal offence for the owner of a ship, aircraft or a carrier to allow any person who requires leave to enter the United Kingdom to arrive in the United Kingdom without any necessary passport and visa. The provisions of the 1987 Act make it difficult for asylum seekers as claims for asylum are made on arrival in the country of destination, and not prior to departure. Carriers may in certain circumstances have the penalty under the 1987 Act waived in cases where asylum is granted.

20–91   The Immigration Rules 1994, the Asylum and Immigration Appeals Act 1993, and the Asylum and Immigration Act 1996 provide special considerations which apply where a person seeking entry claims asylum.[79] Asylum may refer to political refugees that is those "owing to a well-founded fear of being prosecuted for reasons of race, religion, nationality, membership of a particular group or political opinion." Making a judgement as to the presence of any of these factors in any particular case requires the discretion of the Secretary of State. Factors which may be considered are facts and information which the Secretary of State is aware of, even if such factors are unknown to the applicant. The question is whether there is "a real likelihood" of persecution which may be based on "substantial grounds" or on a "serious possibility" of persecution.[80] The House of Lords upheld the decision of the Secretary of State to refuse the asylum applications of the six applicants who were Tamils from Sri Lanka, but on appeal to the adjudicator the Tamils were successful on the basis of the findings of the adjudicator made from the evidence before him.

20–92   The Asylum and Immigration Appeals Act 1993 is intended to accelerate the process of immigration control to cope with the growth in the numbers of asylum seekers and problems of blatant abuse. The rights of appeal of asylum-seekers are also covered in the Act. New measures include powers under section 3 to undertake fingerprinting together with arrest powers granted to immigration officers. Section 8

---

[78] The exception to this permission is under the various emergency powers, under the Prevention of Terrorism (Temporary Provisions) Act 1984 which may be used to prohibit or remove citizens of the Republic of Ireland or Northern Ireland. Also see s.9(4), (6) of the Immigration Act 1971 for powers to exclude.

[79] Rule 75 of the Immigration Rules 1990. These Rules are based on the 1951 Geneva Convention on refugees; see Cmd. 9171 (1954), U.K. Treaty Series, No. 39. See A. Dummett and A. Nicoll, *Subjects, citizens, aliens and others: Nationality and Immigration Law* (1990).

[80] See *ex p. Sivakumaran* [1988] A.C. 958; [1988] 1 All E.R. 193.

of the 1993 Act provides a right of appeal in cases where a claim for asylum has been refused. This is now subject to the terms of the Asylum and Immigration Act 1996 discussed below. In certain cases the Secretary of State may certify that in his opinion the asylum seeker's claim is without foundation. Special time-limits will apply in such cases. If the special adjudicator agrees with the Secretary of State's assessment there can be no further appeal to the Immigration Appeal Tribunal. Section 9 provides for a right of appeal on a point of law to the Court of Appeal or in Scotland, the Court of Sessions, from a final determination of the Immigration Appeal Tribunal. The introduction of an appeal represents an important improvement, as hitherto an applicaion for judicial review was the only way in which decisions of the Tribunals could be challenged. The right of appeal does not preclude judicial review. However the 1993 Act does remove long-established rights of appeal from would-be visitors and certain categories of students and their dependents. This means that judicial review may become overburdened with applications from visitors or certain categories of students deprived of the right of appeal under the Act. In addition to the above, the 1993 Act introduces changes to the Immigration Rules dated July 5, 1993. Member States are comparatively free to provide their own restrictive arrangements. At the time of adoption of the Single European Act, Member States adopted a General Declaration retaining the power of the Member States as regards the control of immigration from Third World countries and attempting to control the illicit traffic in drugs and the illegal market in antiques and art.[81] There is also a Dublin Convention signed in June 1990 for asylum seekers suggesting a common approach to restricting asylum seekers throughout the Community, though it is doubtful if once asylum is granted by one Member State there is any free movement within the Community between Member States.[82]

The Immigration Rules 1994 have been added to by the Asylum **20–93** Appeals (Procedure) Rules 1996[83] and the Asylum and Immigration Act 1996. The 1996 Act considerably strengthens the existing law. The 1996 Act has three aims namely[84]: to deal with any bogus claims for asylum expeditiously; to combat immigration racketeering through stronger powers and new offences and higher penalties; and finally to reduce the economic incentives which attract people to come to Britain in breach of the law.

---

[81] COM (88) 640 (European Commission, December 1988) (Commission Report on the Abolition of Controls of Persons at Intra Community Borders).

[82] Dublin Convention on the State responsible for examining applications for Asylum of 15 June 1990. See Briefing Report, *Refugee* (1992). "Council,—The Maastricht Treaty as it concerns asylum issues".

[83] S.I. 1996 No. 2070.

[84] See Hansard H.C. Debs. Col. 699 (December 11, 1995).

20–94   The Act achieves these aims in several ways as follows: It excludes cases from appeals to the Immigration and Appeals Tribunal and substitutes appeals to a special adjudicator.[85] There is a system of certification by the Secretary of State. The special adjudicator may conclude that the appellant does have a well-founded fear of prosecution and allow appeal against removal; or dismiss the appeal[86] on the grounds that the special adjudicator is not satisfied that the appellant has a well-grounded fear of persecution at the date of the hearing. In the latter case the special adjudicator is free to accept or reject the certificate of the Secretary of State. Under these procedures there is no longer the possibility of making a reference back to the Secretary of State. There are changes to the law on removal to "safe third countries" certified as such by the Secretary of State. There is an appeal to a special adjudicator in such cases. There are new immigration offences of obtaining leave by deception under section 4 of the 1996 Act and assisting asylum claimants to obtain leave by deception. There are increased penalties and additional powers of arrest and search under section 7 of the 1996 Act. There is a draconian rule under section 9 that a person subject to immigration control is not eligible for a council tenancy introduced after a number of cases struck down the attempt to impose this rule by statutory instrument.[87] There are also provisions covering social security and child benefit.

(b)   Deportation

20–95 Deportation of all who are not British Citizens is currently regulated under the Immigration Act 1971 as amended by the British Nationality Act 1981 and the Immigration Act 1988 and the[88] Immigration Rules 1990. Anyone who is not a British Citizen with certain specified exceptions, is subject to deportation.[89] There are generally four grounds: first if the Home Secretary deems it "conducive to the public good"; secondly on the recommendation by a court[90] on conviction of a person over 17 for an offence which is punishable by

[85] See R. v. Secretary of State, ex p. Mehari and Others [1994] Q.B. 474.
[86] Ravichandaran v. Secretary of State for the Home Department [1996] Imm. A.R. 97.
[87] R. v. Kensington Borough Council, ex p. Kihara, The Times, July 10, 1996.
[88] See rr.162–171 of the Immigration Rules 1990.
[89] Continuous residence within the United Kingdom amounting to 10 or more years may be considered prima facie evidence for allowing a person to remain. See Gyeabour v. SSHD [1989] Imm.A.R. 94.
[90] See R. v. Nazari [1980] 3 All E.R. 880. Such a recommendation should be made only after the court has inquired into all the circumstances of the case. Normally such a recommendation is made for those that have overstayed their period of time permitted in their entry into the country in their visa. See Zellick, [1973] Crim.L.R. 612.

imprisonment; thirdly, where a person breaks any entry conditions or overstays the period of entry permitted by the immigration officer; fourthly, he or she is the infant child or wife of a person against whom a deportation order is made.

A deportation order may be used for a mixture of motives. In *ex. p* **20–96** *Soblen*[91] the deportation order was used to comply with a request from the United States for Soblen's return. This in effect amounted to extradition, in circumstances where extradition was not possible because Soblen's alleged crimes involved espionage and extradition was not available for such offences. The Court of Appeal upheld the deportation order even though it was apparent that the motives of the Secretary of State were not confined to deportation grounds and that extradition was acheived through the facility of deportation.

The breadth of the Secretary of State's discretion is also indicated **20–97** by the phrase "conducive to public good" which is commonly used in respect of convicted offenders. This may occur even where the court does not recommend deportation but where the Secretary of State is convinced the presence of the individual is not conducive to the public good. Less easy to justify is the use of deportation powers where no cirminal prosecution has been taken and no conviction gained. In cases where the question of political activities of the individual arise, deportation on the basis of objections to such activities is open to criticism. For example the deportation of Rudi Deutschke to West Germany in 1969 and the deportation of journalists Agee and Hosenball[92] on national security grounds raises questions about the use of deportation powers.

There is an appeal system under sections 13–17 of the Immigration **20–98** Act 1971 as amended by the British Nationality Act 1981 against refusal of entry, refusal of certificates of entitlement and refusal of entry, refusal of cetificates of entitlement and refusal of entry clearances. The procedure for appeal lies against the decision of the immigration officer to an adjudicator and then with leave to an independent Immigration Appeal Tribunal. Section 16 of the 1971 Act provides an appeal to an adjudicator against directions for removal of illegal entrants but such appeal may normally only take place after removel[93] from the United Kingdom. There is a presumption that appeals rights should be exhausted before judicial review[94] is resorted

---

[91] R. v. Brixton Prison Governor, ex p. Soblen [1963] 2 Q.B. 243.

[92] See ex p. Hosenball [1977] 3 All E.R. 452.

[93] Unless removal is a result of the entrant having entered in breach of a deportation order and the ground of appeal is the person is not correctly named in the order. The only ground of appeal is confined to the legal question of whether there was in law no power to give the directions on the ground on which they were given.

[94] Harlow and Rawlings, Law and Administration (1984), pp. 501–577. See ex p. Swati [1986] 1 W.L.R. 477.

to by the applicant. The grounds of appeal are limited under rules 369–395 of the Immigration Rules 1994. In a number of circumstances it is no longer possible to appeal against the merits of a deportation decision and appeal is thereby confined to matters of law. Further restrictions have received judicial approval by the House of Lords in *Oladehinde v. Secretary of State of the Home Department*[95] where an adjudicator was not entitled to question the propriety of the Secretary of State's decision to make a deportation order. The adjudication officer is confined to questions of the legal powers to make the order. Similar restrictions apply to both the adjudication officer and the Immigration Appeal Tribunal to review the correctness of the immigration officer's discretion to grant entry clearance to immigrants. The appeal against the entry officer's discretion is confined to the facts of the case known to the officer at the time. Fresh evidence may not be adduced at the appeal procedure.[96]

20–99   There are a number of circumstances where there are no rights of appeal. There are no rights of appeal against decisions relating to work permits or the issue of a special voucher status available to British Overseas Citizens, against the refusal to issue a passport or to withdraw a passport. The ordinary right of appeal is also excluded in cases where a decision to deport or refuse leave to remain is taken for reasons of public good and in cases where there are reasons based on grounds such as the "public good," "national security" or "reasons of a political nature" or diplomatic nature. However there is a right of appeal[97] where the reasons are based on suspicion of involvement in serious crime or there is a long criminal record or other anti-social behaviour.

20–100   In deportation cases where there are no rights of appeal, the Government conceded a system of *ex gratia* appeal to three advisers as a concession during the passage of the 1971 Act. The basis of the procedure[98] was described in the Memorandum as follows:

> ". . . the person will be notified that he can make representations to the three advisers and will be given time to decide whether or not to do so. The advisers will then take account of any representations made by the person concerned. They will allow him to appear before them, if he wishes. He will not be entitled to legal representation, but he may be assisted by a friend to such extent as the advisers sanction. As well as speaking for himself, he may arrange for a third party to testify on his behalf. Neither the

---

[95] [1990] 3 All E.R. 393.
[96] See *ex p. Bastiampillai* [1983] 2 All E.R. 844.
[97] See *ex p. Cheblak* [1991] 2 All E.R. 319 at p. 328.
[98] Written answer, 819 H.C. Deb., Col. 376 (June 15, 1971).

sources of evidence nor evidence that might lead to the disclosure of sources can be revealed to the person concerned, but the advisers will ensure that the person is able to make his points effectively, and the procedure will give him the best possible opportunity to make the points he wishes to bring to their notice."

Criticism of the *ex gratia* procedure concerned the lack of rights recognised by the procedure when compared by analogy to various tribunals which appear to offer greater protection to the individual.

In 1991 the Gulf War resulted in the detention of over 160 Iraqis **20–101** and Palestinians on the recommendation of the Home Office in the interests of national security and pending their deportation. The list of detained persons was drawn up with the advice from the Police, MI5, Special Branch and the Home Office. The accuracy of the information was open to question and the procedures for vetting the information appeared inadequate. The detainees appeared before the three advisers, with the appointment of a further two advisers to cope with the workload. A small number of detainees were released on the advice of the advisers, but the basis of this advice was never made public.

In *ex Cheblak*[99] a challenge on the basis of an application for habeas **20–102** corpus that the Secretary of State had not given reasons for the detention was rejected. This leaves the role of the courts limited in such cases, as Lord Donaldson noted[1]:

"Nevertheless the exercise of the jurisdiction of the courts in cases involving national security is necessarily restricted, not by any unwillingness to act in the protection of the rights of individuals or any lack of independence from the executive, but by the nature of the subject matter."

The courts are also able to review the decisions of the three **20–103** advisers on the basis of whether it acted unfairly. The Home Secretary is accountable to Parliament for his decisions. Both the courts and parliamentary supervision in this area are often sporadic and unpredictable. Harlow and Rawlings usefully summarise the characteristics of decision-making which may be at work in the area of immigration law[2]:

"The Immigration Rules, which supposedly set out the practice to be followed, are not in the form of statutory instruments and their

[99] [1991] 2 All E.R. 319.
[1] *ibid.* at p. 330.
[2] Harlow and Rawlings, *op. cit.* pp. 503–504.

precise legal status remains elusive. Important elements of control, *e.g.* work permits and special vouchers for British Overseas Citizens, lie outside the rules; they are administrative schemes where rule making is conducted in varying degrees of secrecy."

20–104   Complexity arises when consideration is given to the different layers of discretion exercised by different officials administering the system. Administrative practice may determine the outcome of many cases where appeals only perform a limited function and little recourse is made to precedent or legal rules. Harlow and Rawlings helpfully represent decision-making in this area as comprising two elements. First an "inner core" where the applicant is entitled through statutory and other rules to certain rights. Secondly an outer core which is shrouded in discretion and where entitlement is hard to set in tangible criteria. Moving applicants from one set of rules to another is often accompanied by the minimum of formal rules and in the structures of administrative discretion.

Harlow and Rawlings also question whether judicial decisions have a practical outcome in terms of any changes to administrative practice.[3]

6. Personal Freedom

20–105 The citizen's personal liberty and freedom are often guaranteed in a written constitution where a Bill of Rights forms an integral part. Minimum safeguards are often provided for the arrest, detention and trial of an accused on criminal charges. For example there may be the requirement that there should within a reasonable period of time be a trial before a court and a fair hearing. The rules of evidence at a criminal trial entitle a person accused to know the evidence against him, entitlement to some form of legal representation is also required and assistance in the form of legal aid in the preparation of his case.

20–106   Although the United Kingdom's constitutional arrangements lack both a written constitution and a Bill of Rights, the law has developed recognition of many of the principles to be found in countries where a Bill of Rights has been enacted. However, the results of organic growth and piecemeal statutory intervention has provided an untidy and complicated area of law setting out the powers of arrest,

---

[3] The example is taken of *Khawaya v. Secretary of State for the Home Department* [1983] 1 All E.R. 765 where the authors question if there has been any change in the management of illegal immigrants.

questioning of suspects and their rights. The scope of the citizen's freedom is often dependant on the exercise of police powers and in individual cases how the police officer exercises his discretion. The courts have not always followed a consistent approach of how to determine the exact scope of police powers. Judicial intervention has therefore been sporadic.

(a) The Police and Personal Freedom

The Police Act 1996 consolidates the previous legislation which **20–107** includes repeal of most of the Police Act 1964 and drawing together the relevant parts of the Police and Criminal Evidence Act 1984 and the Police and Magistrates' Courts Act 1994. The 1996 Act builds on the structures set by the Police Act 1964 but the 1996 Act establishes new free-standing police authorities. It retains the distinction between the metropolitan forces and the provincial police forces. The 1996 Act introduces greater managerial controls over policing, including tight financial and administrative management. There are clear implications in the Act that a more centralised oversight of the police is required which stops short of creating a national police force.

The Police Act 1964, as amended, contained the main legal frame- **20–108** work for the organisation of the police system in England and Wales.[4] A police force is maintained for every county in England and Wales, for the Northumbria police area and for certain areas constituted under an amalgamation scheme. Each police force comes under the jurisdiction of a police authority with the duty to secure the maintenance of an adequate and efficient system of policing for that area. The police authority, subject to the approval of the Home Secretary, appoints the Chief Constable and Deputy or Assistant Chief Constables. Provision for the equipment and the premises for the use of the police force is also provided by the police authority. The police authority acts as a paymaster for local police expenditure but is subject to Home Office guidance.

Since 1829 the Metropolitan Police[5] has been regulated by the **20–109** Metropolitan Police Acts and some of the provisions of the Police Act

---

[4] There are similar powers contained in the Police (Scotland) Act 1967. Police areas are defined under the Local Government (Scotland) Act 1973 as regions and combined areas. Scottish police authorities are not required to include a proportion of non-elected members of the judiciary.

[5] There is also the City of London Police with a Chief Officer appointd by the Court of Common Council as the police authority for the force. The appointment of Chief Officer is subject to Home Office approval. In addition there are a number of public bodies entitled to maintain a police force such as the Atomic Energy Authority, the British Railways Board, and the British Airports Authority. See the Aviation Security Act 1982 for local police responsibility over airports.

1964. The Commissioner of the Police for the Metropolis is the chief officer of police. The Home Secretary appoints the Commissioner and various Assistant Commissioners. The Commissioner appoints constables and has disciplinary powers to regulate the Metropolitan Police.

A police force is under the direction and control of the Chief Constable. The Chief Constable takes operational decisions and may be accountable to the police authority for general policy questions. The police authority is not in control of the day-to-day working of the police force under its jurisdiction. The police authority with the approval of the Home Secretary has power to require a Chief Constable and deputy or assistant constable to retire in the interests of efficiency. The Home Secretary may institute such action through representations to the police authority. The Chief Constable may make representations to the police authority and the Home Secretary. The rules of natural justice apply in any disciplinary proceedings which may be instituted by the police authority against a Chief Constable.

20–110   Chief Constables exercise disciplinary powers[6] over their police force and are accountable[7] through annual reports to the Home Secretary and the police authority. Also the Home Secretary may require Chief Constables to make special reports and to assist in the collection of statistical information. The Home Secretary may set up a local inquiry into any matter connected with the policing of an area. Additional powers to his statutory ones, include the powers at common law and under the prerogative to secure the protection of the public from public disorder. The Home Secretary has wide regulatory powers over the organisation, administration and management of the police. In financial matters central exchequer funds are made available to the police force in the form of a grant which is now 51 per cent of approved expenses. Section 28 of the Police Act 1964 gave the Home Secretary powers "as appears to him to be best calculated to promote the efficiency of the police force." This leaves matters to the Home Secretary to set criteria for the evaluation of the efficiency of a police force.

20–111   The functions of the Secretary of State are now contained under sections 36 to 39 of the Police Act 1996. There are powers to give directions to police authorities after adverse reports are made under section 40 of the 1996 Act. Additional powers are granted to the

---

[6] In Scotland such disciplinary powers are expressed very firmly in s.17(3) of the Police (Scotland) Act 1967.

[7] S.38 of the Police Act 1964 provides that Her Majesty's Inspectors of Constabulary may make reports on the maintenance and efficiency of the police force. Such reports may be made to the Home Secretary and may include a recommendation to withhold a certificate of efficiency from the police force.

Secretary of State to require a police authority to retire the chief constable. Reports may be required from the police authority on the discharge of their functions.

The police authority for a non-metropolitan force is formed as a **20–112** police committee of the county council. Currently two-thirds of the committee are councillors, appointed by the council and one-third are magistrates appointed by the Magistrates' Courts Committee. There are proposals contained in the White Paper on Police Reform[8] and the report of the Sheehy Inquiry into Police Responsibilities and Rewards[9] to change the composition of police authorities and the management structure of the police. There was intense debate over the proposals for the composition of the new police authorities. Sched. 2, para. 1(1) provides that nine members are to be drawn from the relevant councils, five are to be independent members, and three are to be justices of the peace. Independent members are to be chosen from a short-list prepared by the Secretary of State and after nomination the candidates are submitted to the Secretary of State.

Accountability for the actions of the police to the police authority **20–113** varies considerably. To some extent accountability depends on the relationship between the authority and chief constable. In practice a local police force is more accountable for standards to the Home Secretary than to its police committee. A police authority is expected to keep itself informed about any complaints made against its police force. A police authority may request information from the Chief Constable but this is subject to a proviso. If the Home Secretary and Chief Constable consider that it is not in the public interest to make information available then it may be withheld. It is clear that a police authority has limited powers. A police authority may not instruct the police to carry out certain operational functions. Aside from receiving information and reports and asking the Chief Constable questions, there are in reality limits to what it may do.

The police are accountable to the Police Complaints Authority **20–114** discussed below. Some accountability over the police may arise through questions asked in Parliament by M.P.s on behalf of their constituents. One difficulty faced by M.P.s is that there is no direct ministerial responsibility for the acts of the police or the decisions of police authorities. London is exceptional because the Home Secretary has wide responsibility for the Metropolitan Police. Even here the Home Secretary is unlikely to give detailed answers on the work of the police. One convention is that operational decisions are left to the police and outside the remit of Parliamentary scrutiny. Where there is public disquiet, the Home Secretary may order a public inquiry. The

[8] Cm. 2281 (1993).
[9] The Sheehy Report (HMSO, 1993).

setting up of the Royal Commission on Criminal Justice[10] arose out of concern for the role of the police in investigating crime. Specifically the Commission was asked to consider "the conduct and supervision of police investigations." The Commission considered the role of the police in the investigation and detection of crime. Various proposals have been made including establishing a Criminal Case Review Authority to take over from the Home Office the function of investigating and reviewing any potential miscarriages of justice and referring them to the Court of Appeal.

20–115　The courts may exercise some oversight over the police. The courts have shown a willingness to uphold the clear legal duty which the police owe[11] to enforce the law. However the courts refrain from stating how the police ought to perform any legal duties that they must observe. The courts are unwilling to find the police liable in damages for any negligence in enforcing the law. In *Hill v. Chief Constable of West Yorkshire*[12] the court accepted that in terms of public policy it was undesirable to impose civil liability on the police arising out of any negligence. The case arose out of the claim by the mother of a victim of the Yorkshire Ripper, Peter Sutcliffe, that the police failed to catch Sutcliffe because of negligence in the way the investigation was carried out.

In an action for negligence alleging that the police had failed to take adequate precautions when a burglar alarm was activated, the Court of Appeal held[13] that finding any liability against the police ". . . would not promote the observance of a higher standard of care by the police, but would result in a significant diversion of resources from the suppression of crime."

20–116　Personal freedoms are subject to questions about the role and function of the police.[14] The last 20 years have witnessed considerable changes in the role of the police and the public's perception of their functions.[15] In 1981 the Royal Commission on Criminal Procedure[16] noted how difficult the task had become to identify the protection of individual rights and balance their efficiency in terms of effective prosecution:

> "On the one hand there are those who see the fight to bring criminals to justice as being of paramount necessity in today's

[10] Royal Commission on Criminal Justice Cm. 2263 (1993), chaired by Lord Runciman.
[11] See *R. v. Metropolitan Police Commissioner, ex p. Blackburn* [1968] 2 Q.B. 118.
[12] [1989] A.C. 53.
[13] *Alexandrou v. Oxford* [1993] 4 All E.R. 328. Also see *Ancell and Another v. McDermott and others* [1993] 4 All E.R. 355.
[14] L. Lustgarten, *The Governance of the Police* (1986); R. Reiner, *The Politics of the Police* (1992).
[15] See Ewing and Gearty, *op. cit.* pp. 18–19. "Between May 1979, when the Conservatives came into office, and January 1988 their strength in England and Wales had risen from 109,998 to 122,131, an increase of 11 per cent. . . ."
[16] *Royal Commission on Criminal Procedure*, Cmnd. 8092 (1981).

society. They tend to see the police as struggling against increasing crime, shackled by laws and procedures which, during their investigations, their questioning of suspects, and finally at the trial favour the criminal. On the other side are those who believe that the cards are in practice stacked against suspects and defendants, that the individual has insufficient legal protection against police power, and that the safeguards against abuse and oppression are inadequate. The majority of public and professional opinion is inevitably between the two. But where can a balance be found which will secure the confidence of the public?"

The outcome of the Royal Commission's deliberations[17] is the Police **20–117** and Criminal Evidence Act 1984 intended to transform many of the common law principles into a single coherent statute. At the same time, the Prosecution of Offences Act 1985 created the Crown Prosecution Service (CPS) headed by the Director of Public Prosecutions, organised on the basis of 31 areas, each headed by a Chief Crown Prosecutor covering at least one or two police forces for that area. The power of the private citizen to prosecute is retained but the bulk of prosecutions are taken by the CPS and the CPS may take over any private prosecution when it is regarded as in the public interest.[18]

The Police and Criminal Evidence Act 1984, hereinafter referred to **20–118** as PACE, generally extended police powers on the basis of additional statutory powers but introduced a number of requirements in the form of codes of practice made by the Home Secretary under section 66 of PACE and intended to act as safeguards for the accused. These safeguards include, that those under the exercise of police powers should be informed of the reasons for the exercise of those powers, that reasons be recorded contemporaneously, and that senior officers should undertake a review of the use of powers and that various codes of conduct and practices should be set up to administer the exercise of police powers. There are also extensive provisions under section 58 which confer rights on suspects, such as access to legal advice at police stations.

The arrangements under PACE have recently been extended to Northern Ireland[19] and research into the operation of arrangements under PACE has been undertaken. Questions concerning the efficacy of the safeguards under PACE have been raised.[20] Following a

---

[17] See McConville and Baldwin, 10 *International Journal of the Sociology of Law* 287; M. Zander, *The Police and Criminal Evidence Act 1984* (2nd ed., 1990).

[18] Prosecution of Offences Act 1985, s.23.

[19] See Police and Criminal Evidence (Northern Ireland) Order 1989 (S.I. 1989 No. 1341) (N.I. 12).

[20] McConville *et al.*, *The Case for the Prosecution* (1992).

number of miscarriages of justice,[21] the Government set up a Royal Commission on Criminal Justice and reported in the Summer of 1993.

(b) Arrest

20–119 The police have no general powers to detain suspects for questioning unless they are arrested. Unlawful detention and arrest may amount to false imprisonment which may be actionable as well as a criminal offence. The exercise of arrest powers involves an element of compulsion, and requires that the person arrested is informed that he is under arrest. In effecting an arrest no more physical force must be used than is reasonably required. Unreasonable use of force becomes an actionable assault. The person arrested must be made aware of the fact of his arrest as soon as it is practicable, except where the arrest is by a private citizen and the ground of arrest is obvious.[22] There are stop and search powers available under a number of statutes. Under section 23 of the Misuse of Drugs Act 1971 a constable may search and detain a suspect who he has reasonable grounds to believe to be in unlawful possession of a controlled drug. Section 163 of the Road Traffic Act 1988, provides that a uniformed constable may require a driver of a motor vehicle or a cyclist to stop. Additional powers exist to require the production of insurance or motor licence.

20–120   Powers of arrest under PACE fall into two categories; either without a warrant or with a warrant. Arrest without warrant is provided under section 24. The Royal Commission on Criminal Procedure envisaged that the police should be able to arrest an individual without a warrant if the crime suspected was an imprisonable offence rather than a fine. An additional safeguard was that arrest should be linked to one that is necessary. Necessary conditions may be found in the general arrest conditions in PACE. This is intended to be the main power for arrest without warrant.[23] Any member of the public may arrest without warrant anyone who is in the act of committing an arrestable offence or where there are reasonable grounds for suspecting to be committing an arrestable offence.[24] In addition, a constable may arrest without warrant, anyone

---

[21] See A. Sanders, "Constructing the Case for the Prosecution" (1987) 14 *Journal of Law and Society* 229. *The Royal Commission on Civil Justice* Cm. 2263 (1993) Chaired by Lord Runciman.

[22] See s.28 of PACE 1984.

[23] PACE 1984, s.26 there is a general repeal pf powers other than under s.24 of PACE, arrest without warrant, but note that this section is deceptive as under Sched. 2 there are 42 provisions retained which provide arrest without warrant.

[24] Also note this applies to a person for whom he reasonably suspects to be guilty of an arrestable offence where such an offence has been committed. See *Walters v. W H Smith and Son Ltd* [1949] 1 K.B. 595. An arrestable offence includes all offences where the sentence is fixed by law such as life imprisonment in the case of murder, all offences where a first offender over 21 may be sentenced to 5 years' imprisonment or more.

whom he has reasonable grounds for suspecting committed an arrestable offence, even though no such crime has been committed, anyone who is about to commit an arrestable offence or he has reasonable grounds to believe is about to commit such a crime. A constable, with reasonable grounds may arrest any person whom he suspects is being or has committed or attempted, an offence which is not an arrestable offence, provided that service of the summons is impracticable or inappropriate because certain general arrest conditions are satisfied.[25]

The question of what is an arrestable offence is clarified in section **20–121** 24 such as murder, treason, and other crimes imprisonable for five years or more. However there are a number of offences which do not fit this category, such as offences relating to crimes against property and sexual offences, which are also made arrestable even though they may not carry prison sentences of five years or more. In fact, Schedule 2 of PACE contains 42 provisions retained under section 26 of PACE and granting the power to arrest without warrant.[26] Also various inchoate offences such as conspiring, or attempting to commit or incite or procure the commission of any arrestable offence is also arrestable. The common law power to arrest for breach of the peace is also included.[27]

It may be concluded that the police have very wide powers to **20–122** arrest without a warrant. The requirements of arrest procedures are to be informed of the arrest and of the ground of arrest. In *Abbassy v. Metropolitan Police Commissioner*,[28] a civil case, the Court of Appeal accepted that an arrest for "unlawful possession" was sufficient as a reason to arrest for theft. Even when the arrest is unlawful initially, if the police failed to inform the suspect of the ground of arrest, the police may make a lawful arrest once they comply with this requirement. Arrest with a warrant[29] as provided by statute, empowers the

---

[25] The arrest conditions include: 1. that the suspected person's name in unknown and cannot be readily identified; 2. that the constable has reasonable grounds for doubting whether the name given by the suspect is correct. 3. that the address provided is unsatisfactory for the service of a summons; 4. the constable has reasonable grounds for believing that he may cause physical harm to himself or another or he may suffer physical injury or cause loss or damage to property or commit an offence against public decency or an unlawful obstruction of the highway; or 5. that the constable has reasonable grounds for believing that an arrest is necessary to protect a child or other vulnerable person from the suspected person. See s.25 of PACE 1984.

[26] *e.g.*, Street Offences Act 1959, s.7(3), Immigration Act 1971, s.1(3). Since PACE there have been additions to the list such as: Sporting Events (Control of Alcohol etc.) Act 1985, Public Order Act 1986, s.3(6).

[27] See *R. v. Howell* [1982] Q.B. 416.

[28] [1990] 1 W.L.R. 385; [1990] 1 All E.R. 193.

[29] See s.1 of the Magistrates' Courts Act 1980 and s.125 of the Magistrates' Courts Act 1980 as amended by the Magistrates' Courts Act 1984. See Constables' Protection Act 1750 protecting Constables' from liability in executing a valid arrest warrant.

justice to either issue a summons requiring that person to appear before a magistrates' court of issue a warrant to arrest the person to appear before the court. A warrant is obtained from a magistrate after information is made in writing and substantiated on oath. An arrest warrant may be executed through the use of reasonable force to enter and search premises. A warrant protects the police from liability for the search.

20–123   Aside from the powers of arrest, PACE[30] provides powers of detention after arrest[31] and before charge. Prior to PACE there was considerable doubt as to the legality of detention powers. Once the police decide that there is sufficient evidence to charge a person he must be charged otherwise he must be released. PACE leaves considerable latitude to the police as to how this power may be interpreted. The maximum permitted period of detention is 96 hours but there is a vague expression as a rider to this such as "a person must normally be brought before a magistrates' court as soon as practicable." The time limit is taken from the moment the person arrives at the police station. This leaves the police time to interrogate before arrival at the police station. In *Parchment*,[32] although the police may have broken various rules in their interrogation of a suspect if carried out at the police station, because the interrogation was carried out in the period before arrival at the police station, the court held that the police had not acted illegally.

20–124   In cases of serious arrestable offences a superintendent or above, may authorise detention for up to 36 hours. A magistrates' court may grant a further 36 hours provided the total time does not exceed 96 hours.

Safeguards are provided under various codes of practice[33] which require that certain powers may be exercised only by senior officers or a designated custody officer, defined as being independent from the investigation. The custody officer has various responsibilities under PACE including informing suspects of their rights, keeping detailed custody records, authorising and releasing from detention and deciding whether suspects should be charged or not. Considerable variation appears to exist in how the rules are interpreted and the practices of different police stations throughout the country.[34]

---

[30] Part IV.
[31] Detention powers may also be found in the s.14 of the Prevention of Terrorism Act 1989. See s.30 of PACE 1984.
[32] [1989] Crim.L.R. 290.
[33] Code of Practice for the detention, Treatment and Questioning of Persons by Police Officers (Code C).
[34] See D. Brown, *Detention at the Police Station under the Police and Criminal Evidence Act 1984* (H.O. Research Study 104, 1989). Wide variations were reported in the practices in detention without charge.

(c) Search and Seizure

Powers of search and seizure are often provided on the basis of a **20–125** valid arrest. Following an arrest, a police constable has the power to search a suspect to determine if he believes that he may present a danger to himself or others or has evidence relating to suspected offences or has anything which might assist his escape. Section 1 of PACE and additions provided by sections 139 and 140 of the Criminal Justice Act 1988 provide powers to stop and search for any offensive weapon, stolen goods or for equipment used in offences such as a burglary. Extensive stop and search powers are also available under the Misuse of Drugs Act 1971 as well as a plethora of other legislative enactments.[35] Powers exercised under PACE must comply with a Code of Practice.[36] The suspect must be informed of the grounds[37] for the search and that such "reasonable grounds" must be made out before and not after the stop and search powers are exercised. It is accepted that such stop and search powers are controversial and require tact, forbearance and understanding on the part of the police when exercising their powers in multi-ethnical or multi-racial societies.

Searching premises and seizing goods may arise under search **20–126** warrant powers under section 8 and 9 of PACE. At common law the police had no general power to obtain warrants and warrants could not be generally authorising of police powers to search and seize goods. Such restrictions have been largely removed by Part II of PACE which consists of general powers to enter premises and search after an arrest, a general power of seizure, and general powers of entry. In addition a number of statutes provide quite specific powers for the police to search premises for example in the areas of theft or drugs[38] related crimes.

Search without a warrant may arise following an arrest (section 32 of PACE), or ancillary to arrest powers there is a power to search premises and finally the power to search without a warrant the home of the arrested person (section 18 of PACE).

(d) Interrogation of Suspects

A large part of the safeguards to be found in PACE for the **20–127** interrogation of suspects in custody depend on the actions of the custody officer. The arrival of the suspect at the police station under

---

[35] See, e.g. the Firearms Act 1968, Metropolitan Police Act 1839, s.66.
[36] Code of Practice for the Exercise by Police Officers of Statutory Powers of Stop and Search (Code A).
[37] See R. v. Fenneley [1989] Crim.L.R. 142.
[38] See ss.27–29 of the Drug Trafficking Offences Act 1986, and the powers under s.26 of the Theft Act 1968.

arrest or when he is arrested, results in the custody officer informing the suspect of his right to have someone informed of his arrest; the right to consult privately with a solicitor and the availability of free legal advice. There are detailed rules for the detention of suspects, including the conditions of cells and rooms. A search of the suspect may be carried out and any property may be retained by the custody officer. The right to consult a solicitor is stated in categorical terms under section 58(1) of PACE "to consult a solicitor privately at any time," however the remaining subsections provide a number of caveats restricting this right. These allow for consultation to be "as soon as practicable." An officer of or above the rank of superintendent may delay access where the suspect is suspected of a serious arrestable offence and where the officer believes that one of four situations may arise: interference with or harm to evidence connected with a serious arrestable offence; interference with or physical injury to other persons; alerting other persons suspected of having committed such an offence but who have not been arrested for it; the hindering of the recovery of any property obtained as a result of such an offence.

20–128   While access to legal advice may only be delayed for up to 36 hours, the scope of the delay provisions is sufficiently wide to enable the police to restrict the suspects' rights to consult a solicitor. Further, the term "serious arrestable offence" is sufficiently broad to encourage this category to be expanded and come within the terms of the delay power. The extent of police discretion relies on judicial supervision by the courts. In *Samuel*[39] the defendant's request to see a solicitor was denied, and the police found incriminating evidence in various searches of his house. He was kept in the police station overnight and after an in-depth interrogation he later confessed to the offences of burglary and after he was charged, his solicitor's attempts to interview him were frustrated by the police. The Court of Appeal was critical of the police handling of the case and held that a suspect should always be able to see a solicitor after being charged. The confession obtained by the police was excluded by the court and the defendant's convicition quashed.

20–129   Some qualification to the principles in *Samuel* came in *Alladice*.[40] The Court of Appeal accepted that a confession obtained by the police after refusal of access to a solicitor did not render the confession inadmissible. These cases illustrate some of the difficulties of oversight by the courts. Attempting to balance the interests of the police with those of the accused in the face of statutory provisions which are capable of wide and diffuse interpretation is difficult. Since

[39] *R. v. Samuel* [1988] Q.B. 615.
[40] *R. v. Alladice* (1988) 87 Cr.App.R. 380.

Alladice the Divisional Court in *Robinson*[41] accepted that a solicitor's clerk may be refused access if the police believe that the clerk is unsuitable to give advice based on the capacity of the clerk in the view of the police to perform that function.

An important element in police practice is the requirement that the **20–130** person arrested and charged must be brought before a magistrates' court. Release on bail may be granted by a police sergeant following the arrest without warrant, by the magistrate or by a High Court judge.[42] Conditions of bail may include the accused being asked to enter his own recognisance to keep the peace. A general power remains, that magistrates may make it a condition of bail that the accused does not breach the peace[43] and such bail conditions are open to rigourous enforcement by the courts.[44] The practice of setting particularly restrictive bail conditions on striking miners in 1984 came to be regarded as "usual conditions." This power led to the criticism that the courts were exercising a system of group justice. There appears to be no direct appeal against such orders of the court and the restrictions imposed as bail conditions may be used to inhibit political agitation.[45]

The outcome of the interrogation process is often a statement which **20–131** has some damaging effect on the accused. This may be through the provision of information which may assist the police in the gathering of intelligence or the obtaining of additional evidence. In fact the possibility exists that the police may find it convenient to use such information to create a factual basis for the conclusions they may wish a court to reach. PACE covers the admission of confession evidence under sections 50–60 and 76–78 of the 1984 Act and the various codes of practice. There is a revised Code of Practice C (1995) for interviewing suspects. The courts have a general discretion at common law and under section 78 of PACE to exclude evidence, generally to ensure that the accused was not induced to incriminate himself by deception.[46] Section 78 has been used to exclude identification evidence in breach of the code of practice[47] and to exclude the evidence of precious convictions of persons other than the accused. However, it is unclear the extent to which this power may be used to exclude illegally obtained evidence.

---

[41] (1989) 139 N.L.J. 186.
[42] See s.117(3) of the Magistrates' Courts Act 1980 as amended by s.47(8)(*b*) of PACE 1984.
[43] Justices of the Peace Act 1361.
[44] *R. v. Mansfield Justices, ex p. Sharkey* [1985] Q.B. 613.
[45] See the Magistrates Courts Appeals from Binding over Orders Act 1956 as amended by the Courts Act 1971. Such orders may be quashed on judicial review.
[46] See *R. v. Sang* [1980] A.C. 402.
[47] The Code of Practice for the Interrogation of Persons.

20–132   Section 76 covers the admissibility of confessions where the confession may have been obtained, "by oppression of the person who made it, in consequence of anything said or done which was likely in the circumstances existing at the time, to render unreliable any confession which might be made by him in consequence thereof." Oppression is defined under section 76(8) of PACE as including "torture, inhuman or degrading treatment and the use or threat of violence." Lord Lane in *Fulling*[48] explained that the word should be given its ordinary meaning such as the "exercise of authority or power in a burdensome, harsh, or wrongful manner; unjust or cruel treatment of subjects, inferiors etc. the imposition of unreasonable or unjust burdens."

20–133   Oppression is not satisfied merely by breaches of the law or the codes of practice under PACE, which do not necessarily amount to oppression.[49] Unrealibility of a confession is used more often than the claim of oppression. Breaches of PACE, improperly conducted interviews, and improper inducement may lead to exclusion on the basis that the confession is unreliable.[50]

20–134   The right of the suspect to be silent in the face of police interrogation is a central principle of English law and is of long standing. The right to silence provides that no person may be required to give information to the police in the course of a criminal prosecution. This means that the suspect may decline to answer questions during interrogation. It also means that a person charged with a criminal offence cannot be required to give evidence in court at any stage of the trial. In the past no adverse inferences may be drawn from an accused's silence at an interview or failure to give evidence in court. In recent years the future of the right to silence has been the subject of intense debate,[51] resulting in its removal in 1994.

20–135   The existence of the right to silence does not prevent the police interrogating the accused but it is argued that a number of suspects may avoid being charged by remaining silent. Objection to the right to silence appears to take many forms. At one level[52] it is suggested that guilty people only have something to hide, that the natural instinct is to defend oneself against any allegation. The claim is also made that criminals may escape conviction by remaining silent and not disclosing their defence to the police, and ambushing the court by

---

[48] [1987] 2 All E.R. 65.
[49] See *R. v. Fulling* [1987] 2 All E.R. 65.
[50] See *R. v. Goldenberg* (1988) Cr.App.R. 285; *R. v. Mason* [1988] 1 W.L.R. 139.
[51] See Research Study No. 10 of the Royal Commission on Criminal Justice by R. Leng, *The Right to Silence in Police Interrogation: A Study of some of the Issues underlying the Debate* (1993). See s.34 of the Criminal Justice and Public Order Act 1994 containing powers to remove the suspects' right to silence.
[52] G. Williams, "The Tactic of Silence" (1987) 137 N.L.J 1107.

producing a new defence unsuspected by the police which is difficult to refute. Recent research for the Royal Commission on Criminal Procedure has tended to doubt the main thrust of the arguments relied upon by those who seek to curtail the right to silence. Surprisingly, perhaps, the research has cast doubt on the frequency with which the right to silence is in fact exercised[53]:

> "The picture which emerges suggests that the right to silence is rarely exercised and that about half of those who exercise it are convicted. For cases which fail, there is little evidence to suggest that the prospects for conviction would be enhanced by inducing the suspect to speak or by treating his silence as evidence against him. In particular, the supposed benefits of interrogation — the opportunity to break down the suspect's defence or refute it by further investigation accrue in only a small minority of cases."

In particular the research found that "true ambush defences are **20–136** very rare and may not always succeed when raised." These findings may seek to allay fears that there is conclusive evidence to show that the right to silence may be abused. Following the discovery of a number of miscarriages of justice[54] in the *Confait, Birmingham Six* and *Guildford Four* cases, concern about police practices and the trial of criminal cases have led to discussion of the adversarial system at a criminal trial. Recent research has pointed to the inadequacy of accountability over the police and questioned the effectiveness of the adversarial system of trial. Even more worrying is the conclusion that "internal, legalistic reforms would leave untouched the class, gender and race biases of the system." The search for a suitable reform of the system of criminal justice is problematical. The same researchers conclude that the desire for greater accountability has little meaning as it is directed at providing after the fact explanations which can be simply self-serving to the police to construct the facts to meet the criteria of accountability. The research concludes[55]:

> "Accountability, if it is to have any relevance to police-work practices, must be both prospective and able to penetrate the control networks which the police utilize to perpetuate police values and ideologies and screen out external inspection mechanisms."

(e) Complaints Against the Police

The citizen may seek redress against the police through judicial **20–137** review or in the defence of a criminal charge, or may seek to show that the police acted unlawfully. In the event of the acquittal of

---

[53] Leng, *op. cit.* p. 79.
[54] S. Stockdale and S. Casale, *Criminal Justice Under Stress* (1992).
[55] McConville, *et al., op. cit.* pp. 207–208.

criminal charges because of evidence which shows police doing wrong, this may result in civil action against the police, the most common basis for such action is for assault or wrongful arrest. Extensive provisions contained in section 49 of the Police Act 1964 and sections 83–100 and 105 of PACE establishing a Police Complaints Authority (PCA) are now to be found in Part IV of the Police Act 1996. The regulations that apply to complaints are provided in detail in the Police (Complaints) (General) Regulations 1985.[56] A number of disciplinary offences such as abuse of authority, neglect of duty or using unnecessary violence are available against police officers. Informal resolution of complaint is favoured. The process of complaining involves the Chief Constable deciding whether it should be formally investigated. The PCA supervises the complaint and may appoint an officer from another force to investigate the complaint. The PCA report goes to the Chief Constable who may decide to refer the report to the Director of Public Prosecutions (DPP) with a view to prosecution. The PCA has the power to direct the Chief Constable to refer their report to the DPP. Disciplinary charges may be taken against the police officer involved. In such cases a fair hearing must be given to the officers concerned.

20–138   Criticism of the system of complaints is that the system relies too heavily on the police to investigate complaints against themselves. The PCA is concerned with delays in action being taken by the police and the tendency to retire officers early on ill health where there may be a case for disciplinary action. The rise in the number of civil actions against the police may test public confidence in the ability of the PCA to act efficiently.

20–139   Statements used in police disciplinary hearings are the subject of public interest immunity.[57] This may prevent disclosure of information in civil or criminal proceedings. Documents generated under the police complaints procedures under section 49 of the Police Act 1964, now Part IV of the Police Act 1996, are similarly regarded. Grievance procedures available through an application before an industrial tribunal on the grounds of racial and sexual victimisation may be treated differently. The police officer complained of sexual discrimination and the Employment Appeal Tribunal distinguished grievance procedures for police officers from disciplinary proceedings. While in the former, the applicant was entitled to receive documents, in the latter she was not.[58]

[56] S.I. 1985 No. 520.
[57] See *Makanjoulou v. Commissioner of Police of the Metropolis* [1992] 3 All E.R. 617.
[58] *Commissioner of Police of the Metropolis v. Locker, The Independent*, March 19, 1993. Also see *Neilson v. Laugherne* [1981] 1 Q.B. 736. Confidentiality appears to be accorded to material seized by the Serious Fraud Office set up under the Criminal Justice Act 1987 when exercising powers under the Police and Criminal Evidence Act 1984. See *Morris and Others v. Director of the Serious Fraud Office and Others, The Independent*, September 11, 1992.

The police have a pivotal role in the personal freedoms of the **20–140** citizen. The accountability of the police becomes a significant factor in protecting citizens' rights. More effective accountability may be found, not through greater political control as advocated by some writers,[59] but through effective complaints procedures, and a wider discussion of police practice and culture. The United Kingdom's constitutional arrangements for the protection of civil liberties provides prohibitions and restrictions as well as freedoms and rights. Civil liberties are said[60] to be facing a crisis; not readily cured by the enactment of a Bill of Rights nor easily amenable to any particular legislative reform. In the life cycle of political and constitutional affairs it may be that the most important protection afforded to civil liberties is that the political culture and institutions are continually questioned as to their efficacy in providing the citizen with an adequate enjoyment of civil liberties.

---

[59] Lustgarten, *op. cit.* See G. Marshall, "The Police: Independence and Accountability" in Jowell and Oliver, *The Changing Constitution* (2nd ed., 1989), p. 273.

[60] Ewing and Gearty, *op. cit.* p. 275. Different view are expressed by Palley, *op. cit.*

Chapter 21

Constitutional Reform

1. Introduction

21–01 Continuity and change are characteristics of constitutional arrangements within the United Kingdom. Each century may be seen to have contributed to changes in public administration and in the constitution. The seventeenth century curtailed growth in the Royal Prerogative and developed an administrative system separate from the Judiciary and episcopal influence. The eighteenth century reduced corruption amongst office holders and sought greater efficiency in the system of public administration. The nineteenth century, under the influence of the Northcote Trevelyan reforms, introduced into the civil service greater professionalism and selection on merit. It also began a system of financial control for the accounting and authorisation of expenditure by Parliament that has endured.[1] The first half of the present century had continued trends apparent in the last century. These included broadening the electoral franchise, expanding the role of local government and providing State intervention in the delivery of a range of new services, through the growth in the Welfare State. The growth in legislation, containing comprehensive and detailed drafting often with assorted codes of practice and circulars is also a hallmark of the present century.[2] This requires public lawyers to undertake a great deal of statutory interpretation.

21–02 Membership of the European Community has significantly affected many domestic institutions and challenged traditional assumptions about sovereignty and decision-making in the United Kingdom. In the 1970s and 1980s privatisation of many nationalised industries has marked a significant shift in the role of the State. Legislation has

---

[1] See E. L. Normanton, *The Accountability and Audit of Government* (1966), pp. 424–6; D. L. Keir, *The Constitutional History of Modern Britain 1485–1937* (London, 1938).

[2] See D. Miers, "Legislation, Linguistic Adequacy and Public Policy" (1986) *Statute Law Review* 90. M. Loughlin, "The pathways of Public Law Scholarship" in G. P. Wilson (ed.), *Frontiers of Legal Scholarship* (John Wiley, 1995), pp. 163–188.

continued to grow in size and extent. Newly created regulatory agencies and reliance on contracts and licences set new challenges for public lawyers in developing legal analysis and techniques. Since the mid-1960s the development of judicial review has marked a significant development in the role of the judiciary in the supervision of many public bodies, agencies, government departments and local authorities.

In recent years it is apparent[3] that the Constitution is under strain. **21–03** The machinery of government and the parliamentary system of scrutiny is said to be too antiquated to fulfil the functions required of modern government. An increasingly critical analysis of existing laws and institutions and weaknesses in the present constitutional arrangements has highlighted a number of specific areas of concern.

This chapter can do no more than highlight some of the questions raised when considering constitutional reform in the United Kingdom.

There is concern that parliamentary control over government has **21–04** been considerably weakened with the growth in, and the strength of party government. Modern government, if endowed with a large majority, is said to have become insensitive to constitutional proprieties and resilient to criticism that is not weighted in parliamentary votes. Questions about the meaning and effectiveness of accountability over government have become an important theme in recent constitutional writing.[4] One concern is that "The Next Steps" reforms in the civil service has moved institutions under democratic accountability to services commercially accountable to managers. It is questioned whether public services can be made commercially accountable. Is this form of accountability adequate? In theory, it is one that localises agency responsibility but in practice may weaken ministerial accountability because of its isolation from responsibility for any particular agency. There is also the broader issue of whether government should be treated as a business? This tendency to emphasise the corporate image of government may enhance management accountability but this may lessen the importance of parliamentary scrutiny and political decision-making.

There are concerns about the fairness of the electoral process and **21–05** thereby how representative government is and suggestions for electoral reform have been forthcoming. Doubts have also been raised about the adequacy of the existing unwritten Constitution. Proposals for a written constitution with a Bill of Rights, a central element, have been advanced. Some doubt the direction and desirability of increased judicial involvement in constitutional decisions.

---

[3] Lord Hailsham, *On the Constitution* (1992), p. 7. Also see N. Johnson, *In Search of the Constitution* (1977); G. Ganz, *Understanding Public Law* (2nd ed., 1995).
[4] See D. Oliver, *Government in the United Kingdom* (OUP 1991).

Devolution proposals made in response to the Royal Commission on the Constitution in 1973 and contained in the Scotland Act 1978 and the Wales Act 1978 came to nothing. Fresh proposals for some form of administrative devolution for Scotland were advanced in the Government's White Paper[5] of March 1993. Various forms of devolution are offered in the proposals advanced by the Institute of Public Policy Research in their draft constitution and in recent White Papers on Scotland and Wales.[5a]

21–06   In Northern Ireland constitutional solutions proposed and applied have failed to achieve a satisfactory settlement. The question of how to combine effective emergency powers with protection under the rule of law is not easily answered. The multi-national and multi-ethnical composition of the United Kingdom has required protection against racial discrimination. The protection of civil liberties, in the absence of a domestic Bill of Rights, has relied on principles derived from the European Convention of Human Rights. Sexual equality and the rights of workers have involved consideration of the law and jurisprudence of the European Community. Membership of the European Community has also required adaptation within the United Kingdom's domestic law and institutions. The long tradition of parliamentary sovereignty has not easily been accommodated within the European Community. Such developments have challenged Dicey's analysis of parliamentary sovereignty and the equality of the law found in Dicey's rule of law has proved more theoretical than real.

21–07   Developments in judicial review by the courts in the last 20 years have raised questions about the role of the judges and the distinction between public and private law enunciated in the much criticised decision of *O'Reilly v. Mackman*. Reform of the system of administrative law and statutory appeals after consideration by the Law Commission awaits government decision making. Coincidentally this is during a period of intense debate about the future organisation of the legal profession. Miscarriages of justice led to the appointment of a Royal Commission on Criminal Procedure under the chairmanship of Lord Runciman.[6] Miscarriages of justice remain a stigma attached to the criminal justice system.

Relations between central and local government have created a crisis in the management of local authority activities. A fundamental reappraisal of local authorities has involved creating a more corporate

---

[5] Scotland in the Union, Cm. 2225 (1993).

[5a] Referendums (Scotland and Wales) Act 1997.

[6] *Royal Commission on Criminal Justice, Report*, Cm. 2263 (1993); Bridges and McConville [1994] M.L.R. 75; and see McConville and Bridges, (eds.) *Criminal Justice in Crisis* (Edward Elgan, 1994).

image for local authority functions. Local authorities are undergoing a transformation from the Redcliffe-Maud[7] model of *providers* of services to becoming *enablers* in the task of setting standards, specifying how certain activities are to be performed and monitoring performance. Market testing and in some cases the requirement to contract out certain services is aimed at securing the best services at least cost. Judicial review involving central and local government has become prevalent as litigation is used to enforce statutory enactments and regulate local authority activities. Doubts remain among financial institutions about the financial credibility of local authority schemes and proposals involving private finance.

Privatisation policy has spawned a new range of regulatory bodies **21–08** and legal controls. As noted above this results in the increasing use of contracts and licences in the public law sphere. The effectiveness of regulation is an important element in the future development of the various public utilities such as gas, telecommunications, electricity, water, rail, and coal.

This chapter is intended to consider constitutional reform in the **21–09** context of an on-going debate on the adequacy of existing constitutional arrangements within the United Kingdom. Three themes dominate discussion of current constitutional arrangements and their reform. First, a perception that increased accountability over government and its agents are a desirable objective. Concern about government accountability is not restricted to domestic matters as the question of the future direction of the European Community raise questions about how political power and authority are exercised. Secondly, that judicial scrutiny may have an increased role in our constitutional arrangements through the scope for interpretation of a Bill of Rights or some form of written constitution. Already there is a perception that judicial review has grown in scale and importance with an increase in the applications for judicial review. Some recent research[8] has challenged the belief that judicial review is widely used by the citizen for the redress of grievances. The research shows that judicial review is more narrowly confined and directed to specific areas of government activity such as homelessness and immigration. Currently there is debate over whether any increased role for the judges is to be welcomed. Some commentators regard this as a necessary and worthwhile development while others doubt the advisability and capacity of an increased judicial role. Thirdly, there is a recurring theme that improving the *performance* of the public

---

[7] Report of the Royal Commission on Local Government in England Cmnd. 4040 (1969), para. 28.
[8] See M. Sunkin, Lee Bridges and George Mészáros, *Judicial Review in Perspective* (Public Law Project, June 1993) (2nd ed., 1995).

sector may improve the effectiveness and efficiency of government. How public sector services are delivered is given greater emphasis, rather than any re-thinking of the role of existing institutions. New challenges have come from the plethora of new regulators, created since privatisation, with extensive statutory powers in granting contracts and licences. There is a general interest in value for money studies intended to provide a quality assurance over the standards of services provided by the public sector. For example, *The Citizen's Charter* creates consumer rights which may be found in improved standards in carrying out various public sector activities. The consumer becomes in effect a regulator of the public sector. This raises the interesting question of the use of contract and licences in the relationship between government and the delivery of public services.

2. A Written Constitution?

21–10 Historically the introduction of a written constitution has usually arisen out of crisis; some form of political upheaval or an attempt by newly independent countries to establish independence through international recognition of the government and institutions. Any apparent crisis[9] in the United Kingdom's Constitution would appear to fall short of the criteria offered by any historical examples. Few countries appear to reform existing constitutional arrangements through a thoughtful reflection on its shortcomings and a peaceful introduction of reforms to placate any discontent.

21–11 Demands for a written constitution have come from the Liberal Democrats,[10] the Institute of Public Policy Research[11] and from[12]

---

[9] The assertion that there may be a crisis in existing constitutional arrangements has been advanced in P. McAuslan and J. McEldowney, *Law, Legitimacy and the Constitution* (1985), but equally cogent arguments have been advanced questioning whether "crisis" is not too strong a perception. See a balanced review in T. Daintith, "Political Programmes and the Content of the Constitution" in Finnie, Himsworth and Walker (eds.), *Edinburgh Essays in Public Law* (1991), pp. 41–55.

[10] *"We the people . . ."–Towards a Written Constitution* (1990); F. Mount, *The British Constitution Now* (1992).

[11] Institute of Public Policy Research, *The Constitution of the United Kingdom,* (1991). Also see R. Blackburn (ed.), *Constitutional Studies* (1992).

[12] Charter 88 had obtained over 25,000 signatories by May 1991. Various human rights centres have flourished such as Chapter 19, The Human Rights Centre at Essex University currently undertaking a five year Audit of British Democracy funded by the Joseph Rowntree Charitable Trust, and the Civil Liberties Group at King's College London under Dr Conor Gearty. In Northern Ireland, the important work of Simon Lee to analyse and undertake porposals for the future of Northern Ireland also deserves mention as does the work of LIBERTY.

Charter 88. Prominent constitutional lawyers have called for a written constitution, most notably Lord Scarman[13] and Lord Hailsham,[14] though the latter has been less enthusiastic in recent years. In recent years an increasing body of intellectual opinion has favoured constitutional reform from political thinkers on both the left and the right in politics. However, contemporary writing of the 1980s and 90s is reminiscent of writing in the 1970s and even past diagnosis of the post-war period. Oliver has identified[15] a number of factors which may have created pressure for reform and may be summarised as follows.

The post-war consensus over the range of activities carried out by **21–12** the public sector has come under the strain. Polarisation of the two major political parties has contributed to marked differences in attitudes to the public sector. The election of Mrs Thatcher's Government in 1979 and four successive Conservative Party election victories thereafter have allowed many fundamental changes to be introduced into the delivery of public services. Privatisation is also relevant in the trend away from State ownership in favour of Public Company Act companies for the delivery of public services. Market forces and the consumer are perceived as satisfactory regulators of public services with the minimum of direct State intervention.

Changes in policy perceptions in the early 1980s about the role of **21–13** local government have created tensions in the relationship between central and local government. The trend in favour of more centralised power has encouraged stronger central government as preferable to weak local authorities. Centralisation has a number of motives behind it. A desire to change existing institutions and cultures in line with a greater reliance on market enterprise is more readily accommodated with central control. Strong political ideologies in the 1980s facilitated more central control. Popular causes such as privatisations and council house sales to tenants are seen as attainable only from a strong executive government and carry favour with those who see strong government as a virtue of the United Kingdom's political system. At the same time discontent over the United Kingdom's constitutional arrangements argue for reform and some go as far as to include a written constitution.

Supporters of constitutional reform highlight the weaknesses in **21–14** parliamentary control over the Executive as evidenced by the accretion of centralised governmental power. In the aftermath of a period

---

[13] See R. Holme and M. Elliott (eds.), *1688–1988: Time for a New Constitution* (London, 1988); Lord Scarman, "Bill of Rights and Law Reform" in Holme and Elliott *op. cit.* pp. 103–111. See *The Constitution Unit*, 1995–1997 (UCL London).

[14] Compare recent doubts about a written constitution in Lord Hailsham, *On the Constitution* (1992), pp. 105–106 to his much earlier writing in favour of some form of written constitution: Hailsham, *The Dilemma of Democracy* (1978) and his *Elective Dictatorship* (1976).

[15] D. Oliver, *Government in the United Kingdom* (1991), pp. 3–40.

of strong government with large overall majorities, electoral reform is favoured, linked to the need for a fairer balance in the composition of the House of Commons.

21–15   There is also criticism on how the Cabinet form of government decision-making operates. This relates to the view that the Cabinet is not able to make longer term strategic plans. The Thatcher inheritance suggested that the Cabinet system had developed into a presidential style of government. However, Mrs Thatcher's resignation suggested to some commentators that Cabinet government had been restored. Currently there is concern that political divisions under a more collective style of government may make the government appear weak; in office but not able to exercise authority. It is argued that the Cabinet system of government needs reform. Oliver noted[16]:

> "Neither the Cabinet as a whole nor ministers individually have the support of staff that could enable them to take a strategic view of government policy, or indeed of the policy in their own departments."

During the life cycle of party politics the style and perception of government may differ, very often according to the personality of the Prime Minister. However, to some commentators, weaknesses in the institutions of the government[17] such as the Cabinet system are apparent and suggest that reforms should be introduced.

21–16   The ethos of governmental secrecy is also perceived as a major weakness in the system of parliamentary accountability.[18] This is said to limit the amount of information available on the administration of government and allows government too much flexibility in deciding on the ground rules which apply to its decisions. The temptation is to see secrecy, as supported by the law, as self-serving the interests of government in its political objectives rather than serving the interests of Parliament. The quality of government decision-making is said to suffer from the lack of transparency in government consultation and discussion. When government chooses to be more open, such as the recent appointment of seven advisers to the Chancellor of the Exchequer and the Treasury's publication of a *Monthly Monetary Report* together with the Bank of England's Inflation Report, such steps are welcomed and said to improve government decision-making, and increase parliamentary accountability.[19] Following the

---

[16] Oliver *op. cit.* p. 209.

[17] See P. Hennessy, *Whitehall* (1989); Sir John Hoskyns, "Whitehall and Westminster: An Outsider's View (1983) 36 *Parliamentary Affairs* 137–147.

[18] See Leigh, and Lustgarten, "The Security Service Act 1989" (1989) 50 *Modern Law Review* 801–840.

[19] See the useful discussion in the Fourth Report of the Treasury and Civil Service Committee, *The March 1993 Budget* (1992–93; H.C. 578).

election of the present Government in May 1997, the Chancellor of the Exchequer devolved to the Bank of England an independent role in the setting of interest rates. This in turn may increase government credibility in the money markets and with financial institutions. Demanding greater openness in government may not necessarily increase Parliament's role in holding government to account for its actions.

Centralisation is said to cause pressure on the efficiency and **21–17** effectiveness of government because the system of Cabinet decision-making suffers from "overload." This phenomenon is not confined to the government but may be found in the various parliamentary methods of accountability such as select committees, debates on the passage of Bills and the scrutiny of government legislation. The tendency is that back-bench M.P.s, may become overworked and inefficient. It appears impossible for any single M.P. to undertake a broad oversight of the entire working of government. The technical detail and complexities make this impossible as well as the scale of the enterprise for which individual M.P.s are lacking in resources. Instead the approach undertaken by many is to concentrate on a few specialist areas in which to develop their own expertise. Doubts about the present institutional resources of Parliament to scrutinise the Executive have a long history of reluctance on the part of the government of the day to accept criticism or make amendments to Bills in response to back-bench concerns.[20]

The case for reform of the House of Lords is also made out by the **21–18** desire to improve accountability, effectiveness and improve the representative[21] nature of the upper chamber. Reform of the House of Lords, while acceptable as a means of improving democratic account-ability, is limited to the extent that it may not alter the historical political balance in favour of the Conservative Party and is in any event difficult to achieve. Proposals for reforming the House of Lords have a long history and have been considered by the major political parties. The use of the second chamber as a more representative body of different interests such as trade unions, academics, or business is intended to improve the existing strengths, even acknowledged by critics of the House of Lords. These strengths are the quality and range of the expertise shown in debate, the combination of experience

---

[20] A useful discussion is provided in John Griffith and Michael Ryle, *Parliament* (1989). Also see David Judge, "Parliament in the 1980s" (1989) 60 *The Political Quarterly* No. 4. pp. 400–412.

[21] See N. Fishman, "Extending the Scope of Representative Democracy" (1980) 60 *Political Quarterly* 442–455; J. P. Morgan, *The House of Lords and the Labour Government 1964–70* (1975). See proposals for reforms contained in Cmd. 7390, (1948), Cmd. 3799, (1968). The Parliament Bill (No. 2) 1968, see P. A. Bromhead, *The House of Lords and Comtemporary Politics 1911–1957* (1958).

and political judgement not so tightly controlled on the basis of party politics, which makes the House of Lords an important constitutional watchdog. Hereditary peers and the creation of peers might be removed from the patronage of the Prime Minister and given to a committee formed to scrutinise appointments to the House of Lords. A part or all of the Lords might be formed from elections to represent local interests and provide a more representative chamber. Any reform has to be carefully calculated to preserve the virtues of specialist knowledge and expertise with a democratic system of appointment.

21–19   The case for the introduction of some form of devolution is also taken to justify a written constitution. Devolution, as a response to nationalism in Scotland and Wales in the late 1970s, may also be seen as a means to decentralise central government powers. In election manifestos, both in 1987 and in 1992, the Labour Party and the Liberal/SDP Party contained proposals for devolution. In Labour's case for Scotland only.[22] More recently in its White Paper on Scotland in the Union,[23] the government has identified administrative tasks which may be reallocated and better organised within a form of administrative devolution in Scotland through the Scottish Office. Reallocation of civil servants, improved administration and management of the government in Scotland are intended to locate more decision-making at the point of delivery of the various public sector services. Such proposals fall short of legislative devolution and financial power devolved to an elected local assembly. More radical proposals may be found in the IPPR draft constitution. These include Assemblies for Scotland, Wales, Northern Ireland and the regions of England. The latter is problematic because of the size, diversity and traditions which need to be recognised in any proposal. These proposals follow the minority report of the Royal Commission on the Constitution which favoured the creation of elected regional authorities to take over responsibilities of central government. Proposals for devolution are expected to be implemented in the first years of office following the election of the Labour Government in May 1997.

21–20   The interest and attention given to a written constitution also arises through concern that a Bill of Rights might best be delivered through the mechanism of a Constitution setting out the allocation of functions between the legislature, the Executive and the judiciary. The diagnosis that existing arrangements for the protection of the citizen are weak and ineffectual are a reflection of factors that may contribute to weakness in our Constitution. Government is entitled to use its

---

[22] See (The Labour Party) *Meet the Challenge Make the Change* (1989).
[23] Cm. 2225 (1993).

parliamentary majority to enact laws but those laws may infringe individual rights. There is little opportunity in such circumstances for the courts to do anything other than give effect to Parliament's authority.

The arguments against a Bill of Rights such as mistrust of judicial power, concern over the doctrine of parliamentary sovereignty, and the question of how adequately to entrench the enactment of a Bill of Rights against possible revocation, may be answered by the adoption of a written constitution.

The arguments against adopting a written constitution emphasise **21–21** the flexibility inherent in existing arrangements. The tradition of an unwritten constitution has reinforced the supremacy of Parliament in both the narrow legal sense, and in the broader sense of political majoritarian government. Change may be accomplished without any general rethink of the constitutional arrangements. Adaptation may be seen as part of an organic growth unhindered by the restraint of a constitutional requirement to give the judiciary a final say in any change. The virtues of the present system must not be overlooked even if it is desirable to consider reforms. It is often conceded that many of the reforms mentioned above may be enacted without a written constitution. The strengths of a flexible unwritten constitution may be found in the primacy given to the political process. This may be weakened by entrenching in a written constitution those matters currently governed by convention or political choices. A written constitution might mark a shift from political decision-making to judicial scrutiny which may be too narrow and restrictive of the political choices on offer to the electorate.

Enacting a written constitution may not be a panacea for all **21–22** constitutional law problems. The debate over whether a written constitution might be adopted or not[24] is a useful opportunity for students of the Constitution to analyse and critically examine existing arrangements which will undoubtedly contribute to a deeper understanding of the working of the United Kingdom's Constitution. However, in addition to the general debate on a written constitution, the question of constitutional reform arises in the context of specific areas of concern. Some of the major areas where individual reforming initiatives are continuing may be considered.

---

[24] Popular support for a written constitution may be open to doubt after the last election and the doubts cast upon constitutional reform. See Shell, "The British Constitution 1991–92" (1993) *Parliamentary Affairs* 13. Andrew Gray and Bill Jenkins "Public Administration and Government 1995–96" (1997) *Parliamentary Affairs* 191–211.

3. Local and Central Government

21-23 Debate about local government reform continues as part of an on-
going debate about its role and function. Party political differences
between the central government and local authorities ensure continuous tensions in relations between central and local government.
Local government activities continue to undergo radical change. This
may be attributed to central government's desire for tighter controls
over public expenditure with the inclusion of local government as
part of the cash planning process in the public expenditure survey.
Recently the introduction of the New Control Total has included local
authority self-financed expenditure. Central government has also
developed an ideological preference in favour of a more corporate
culture for local authorities.

21-24   The future direction of local government is difficult to predict in a
period of uncertainty about its role and also because of the way
reform proposals are made. In the absence of a Royal Commission or
inquiry, research into the most effective structures for local authorities appears haphazard with no clear role identified for local authorities. The weighing up of the cost and benefits of change and
comparing the various options has proved difficult.

21-25   Currently proposals for the structure of local authorities in
England[25] may come from the newly created Local Government
Commission set up under the Local Government Act 1992. The Local
Government Commission is currently considering the boundaries and
structures of local authorities in England. Originally the Government
favoured unitary authorities but this has not been universally
applied. The Commission have published preliminary recommendations on local authorities' boundaries in various geographical areas.
Such recommendations mark a shift away from the trend envisaged
by the Department of Environment in favour of a unitary structure
for local authorities replacing the two-tier system in order to reduce
bureaucracy and costs. In Scotland and Wales legislation has been
passed to introduce unitary authorities.[26]

21-26   The Government have provided policy guidance to the Commission[27] to focus on the costs of departmental administration and to

---

[25] Separate proposals have been made in consultation papers for Wales: Consultation
Paper of The Welsh Office, *The Structure of Local Government in Wales* (July 1991) and
Scotland, Consultation Paper of the Scottish Office, *The Structure of Local Government
in Scotland*, (July 1991).

[26] See The Local Government (Wales) Act 1994 and the Local Government (Scotland)
Act 1994.

[27] See DOE, *Local Government Review: Assessing the costs and benefits of Change* (February
1992).

enhance the local identity of the authority. There appears to be greater acceptance that in some cases two-tier authorities may be more desirable than the single tier originally favoured by the Government.

The Local Government Review is in favour of an increase in the corporate identity of local authorities, and a shift in their role from *providers* of services to *enablers* directly involved in regulating and promoting competitive tendering and contracting out of services.[28] In addition it is envisaged that various areas of activity may be placed outside local authority control,[29] such as highways, police, fire, probation service and magistrates' courts. The changing role of local education authorities is reflected in the shift to more grant-maintained schools and removing schools from local authority control.[30] Similarly the trend in favour of National Health Service Trusts, which are expected to consume in excess of 70 per cent of the budget for hospital and community services, is intended to further strengthen competition in the health service market away from local authority controls.

The consultation paper on *The Internal Management of Local Author-* **21–27** *ities in England*[31] invites consideration of how local authority decision-making may be improved. This includes discussion of the suitability of a Cabinet system modelled on central government, appointed council managers with councillors not involved in any day to day management of councils and directly elected chief executives and mayors. There is also considerable support for maintaining existing arrangements. The debate on the corporate responsibility of local authorities involves the setting of standards, awarding contracts, monitoring performance, specifying requirements and taking action to discover how performance may have fallen short of the required levels. As elected bodies, and an important tier of government local authorities are likely to develop new techniques in their role as enablers in the regulation of public sector services. The future reform of local government looks set to continue as more activities are shifted to the private sector and managerial techniques of business continue to be applied.

Changes in the culture of local authorities have been an outcome of **21–28** the continuous work of monitoring carried out by the Audit Commission in the general financial overview of local authority activities which may include value for money audit.

---

[28] See Kieron Walsh, *Competitive Tendering for Local Authority Services* (HMSO, 1989); S. Cubbin, A. Domberger and A. Meadowcraft, "Competitive Tendering and Efficiency: Identifying the Sources of Efficiency Gains (1988) 8 *Fiscal Studies* (No. 3).

[29] DOE, *Competing for Quality: Competition in the Provision of Local Services* (November 1991).

[30] See Cm. 2021 (1992); The Education Act 1993.

[31] DOE *op. cit.* (1991).

The courts may be invited by the Audit Commission to exercise their powers of review and this may provide legal controls over local authority activities.[32] Judicial review of local authority activities may arise through action taken by central government or another local authority. The effect[33] of judicial review may be far-reaching as in the example of *Hazell v. Hammersmith*[34] where over 130 local authorities were involved in the swop markets declared *ultra vires* by the House of Lords. This led to severe financial burdens on the various banks who invested by lending to the local authorities. The courts have continued to approach the financial investments of local authorities with a strict interpretation of the powers of the local authority. This approach is evident in the case of *Crédit Suisse v. Allerdale*.[35]

21–29   Loughlin questions[36] whether the courts in giving reasons for their review of complex technical and financial issues, in an area such as local authority expenditure controls, have sufficient "cognitive, conceptual and material resources" to enable them to perform the functions expected. This is an important issue, as the growth in directive legislation affecting local government provides greater challenges to the role of the courts than hitherto. Such legislation, with precise legal requirements is intended to provide a comprehensive legislative regulation over local authority activities. This is in contrast to the wider more opened textured discretion which is a hallmark of the earlier Victorian legislation which was the foundation of many local authority powers. Very often the permissive legislation of the nineteenth century has been overridden by legislation reflecting a heavy political bias in favour of greater managerial control over local authorities.

21–30   The absence of any principle of ministerial responsibility in terms of local government accountability, appears to offer the courts greater scope for review over local authority discretionary powers than over central government. Some examples serve to reinforce the point. In *Bromley*[37] the House of Lords was asked to consider the "fair fares" policy of the GLC (now abolished). Although the GLC had powers to make grants "for any purpose" to the London Transport Executive (LTE) the grant involved a supplementary rate which was quashed because the purposes for which it was intended were *ultra vires*.

---

[32] M. Loughlin, "Innovative Financing in Local Government: The Limits of Legal Instrumentalism–Part I [1990] P.L. 372.

[33] The courts in *R. v. Knowsley B.C., ex p. Maguire and others* [1992] N.L.J. 1375 held that a local authority is under no liability for administrative conduct amounting to maladministration even when it causes loss or damage to a private person adversely effected by the maladministration.

[34] *Hazell v. Hammersmith* [1990] 2 W.L.R. 17.

[35] [1996] 4 All E.R. 129.

[36] M. Loughlin, Part II [1991] P.L. 568 at 595–597.

[37] [1983] A.C. 768.

There was "a fiduciary duty" on the GLC as a local authority, and the fares policy failed to live up to that standard which was owed to ratepayers. The courts had to balance the GLC's duty owed to ratepayers against its wider power to provide reasonable transport facilities to transport users. The fact that a "fair fares" policy had been a manifesto condition in the election of the ruling party in the GLC was not relevant to the courts powers of review, as such a condition was "not binding" on the local authority.

In *R. v. Waltham Forest LBC, ex p. Waltham Forest Rate-payers Action* **21–31** *Group*[38] the courts struck down a decision of Waltham Forest councillors which was based on instructions from a pressure group known as the Local Government Group. The courts have developed considerable techniques to intervene whenever necessary. The well known dicta in *Wednesbury*[39] of "unreasonableness" might permit the courts to review the policy or motive behind a decision taken by a local authority.[40]

Recent research[41] into the use of judicial review involving local **21–32** authorities either as respondent or as plaintiff concluded:

"Our data suggest, however, that over the past decade it [judicial review] has been used more often as a weapon to limit the autonomy of local government rather than as a constraint on the power of the central state. Moreover, we have yet to see whether judicial review will become a remedy for those seeking to challenge or regulate the powers of the new generation of non-departmental public bodies."

The research also found that local government was[42] "a relatively frequent initiator of judicial review litigation throughout the 1980s." A large number, 36 per cent, were against the Department of the Environment while 18 per cent were against other local authorities. After the introduction of the Education Reform Act 1988 there was an increase in the number of education related cases, a sign of the judicialisation of this area of activity.

A number of trends in the development of judicial review in the **21–33** area of local government are noted in the research. First, that local government is a more frequent respondent to judicial review than

---

[38] [1987] 3 All E.R. 671; [1988] Q.B. 419.
[39] *Associated Picture Houses Ltd v. Wednesbury Corporation* [1948] 1 K.B. 223.
[40] *Roberts v. Hopwood* [1925] A.C. 578 also *Pickwell v. Camden LBC* [1983] Q.B. 962. M. Radford "Auditing for Change: Local Government and the Audit Commission" (1991) M.L.R. 912–932.
[41] M. Sunkin, Lee Bridges, and George Mészáros, *Judicial Review in Perspective* (Public Law Project, 1993), p. 101, hereinafter Sunkin, Bridges and Mészáros.
[42] *ibid.* p. 21.

central government. Secondly, applications for judicial review may be taken by central government but in numerical terms the most significant number of cases concern applicants who are homeless which amount to 35 per cent of cases. The remainder consist of applications covering the general field of local authority activities.[43]

The role of the judges in their scrutiny of local government, an area of increasing judicial activism, raises questions about the future reform of administrative law which may be considered below.

4. Administrative Law

(a) Patterns in the Development of Judicial Review

21-34 Harry Arthurs posed the question[44]:

> "What are our concerns about administrative law today? We want to be assured that the vast machinery of administration which is characteristic of all modern government is performing its appointed tasks effectively."

21-35 We have noted in previous chapters that judicial review is the principal method[45] for allowing the courts[46] to supervise public bodies. The judiciary have laid claims to achievements in the development of judicial review and the flexibility of the reforms under Order 53 introduced since 1977. The expansion in any judicial role over public bodies is a question of considerable constitutional importance. Questions about how judges are appointed, their training and education may arise if there is to be a greater expansion in the judicial role, through the enactment of a Bill of Rights or written constitution. Here we are concerned with reform of administrative law.

21-36 Significant developments in the availability of judicial review include, after *R. v. Panel on Take-Overs and Mergers, ex p. Datafin,*[47] the

---

[43] *ibid.* pp. 26–27. The research data shows that the subject matter of applications include: "other (that is excluding the cases of homelessness) housing 11%, town and country planning 9.5%, education 7%, licensing 6%, and family matters 4%. The period of the research date is 1987–1st quarter of 1991.

[44] H. Arthurs, *Without the Law* (1985), p. 196. Also *Report of the Constitutional Reform Centre, Regulatory Agencies in the United Kingdom* (1991).

[45] There are also opportunities through the system of statutory appeals.

[46] In *Bugg v. DPP* [1993] 2 All E.R. 815, the Divisional Court considered whether the legality of by-laws could be considered as part of criminal proceedings. The Court held that in criminal proceedings the court had jurisdiction to determine the issue of substantive invalidity where the defendant sought to challenge the validity by way of a defence.

[47] [1987] Q.B. 815.

possibility that a wide range of domestic bodies or tribunals might fall under the review powers of the court. In *Datafin* the Court of Appeal held that the self-regulatory City Take-Overs Panel was subject to judicial review despite the fact that the Take-Over Panel was not set up by statute or under any of the prerogative powers. In considering whether to exercise their discretion in favour of review the court considers that the nature of the body must be considered alongside the activities the body performs.[48]

It is also noteworthy that there are areas where the courts seem less **21–37** willing to offer review. In *ex p. Puhlhoffer*[49] the House of Lords restricted access to judicial review to cases under the Housing (Homeless Persons) Act 1977. One of the justifications advanced for restrictions on judicial review is that the use of judicial review in that area of homelessness had become "prolific." Sunkin, however showed that in any one year prior to *Puhlhoffer* there had only been 75 cases with 66 in the year prior to the decision.[50]

Similarly arguments about the prolific use of the courts were made in *ex p. Swati*[51] concerning immigration cases. The court held that the discretion to refuse leave is operated when there are alternative remedies. For example, in appeals in immigration cases which may fall to be adjudicated by the Immigration Appeal Tribunal. The effectiveness of the *Puhlhoffer* decision in reducing the caseload in the area of homelessness[52] was noted by Sunkin in his research.[53]

Ministerial responsibility also provides the courts with an alterna- **21–38** tive to exercising their own powers of review. For example *In Re Findlay*,[54] the courts were not prepared to review parole policy. In *Bushell v. Secretary of State for the Environment*[55] public inquiries into highway policy are excluded. In *Notts. C.C. v. Secretary of State for the*

---

[48] R. v. East Berkshire Health Authority, ex p. Walsh [1985] Q.B. 152. Also see R. v. Lord Chancellor's Department, ex p. Nangle [1991] 1 I.C.R. 743; [1992] 1 All E.R. 897; Roy v. Kensington and Chelsea and Westminister Family Practitioner Committee [1992] 1 A.C. 624; The Independent, February 11, 1992. Lord Bridge allowed private law rights exercised through the writ procedure to raise public law issues incidentally. Lord Lowry regarded the litigant as having a "bundle of rights," which permitted the case to be held. Also see [1986] A.C. 484, Ex p. Benwell [1985] 1 Q.B. 152. See Ex p. Dew [1987] 1 W.L.R. 881.

[49] [1986] 1 All E.R. 467.

[50] Sunkin, Bridges and Mészáros, op. cit. p. 3.

[51] [1986] 1 All E.R. 717.

[52] Sunkin, Bridges and Mészáros, op. cit. p. 3. "The Puhlhoffer decision had two immediate effects on the case-load. First it reduced the known number of homelessness judicial review applications. These fell from 66 in 1985 to 32 in 1986. The second was to increase the failure rate at the leave stage, from less than 10 per cent to over 30 per cent."

[53] M. Sunkin, "The Judicial Review Case-load 1987–1989" [1991] P.L. 490–499, hereinafter Sunkin.

[54] [1985] A.C. 318.

[55] [1981] A.C. 75.

Environment[56] Lord Scarman refused to review the rate capping powers of the Secretary of State, pointing out that such powers required parliamentary approval, which provided an acceptable substitute to judicial review, as a means of scrutiny over the powers of the Secretary of State.

21–39   While judicial review may be by its nature unpredictable, there is the expectation that the ordinary citizen may find beneficial the new procedures for judicial review. One caveat may be considered. The courts have been reluctant to see the citizen's grievance as a useful means for pressure group activity. Though some academic opinion may find this a suitable outlet for public pressure, the courts have expressed a reluctance to become involved in such disputes[57] as Mr Justice Shiemann explained in the *Rose Theatre*[58] case:

> "the decision not to schedule [protected the Rose Theatre site as a protected site] is one of those governmental decisions in respect of which the ordinary citizen does not have a sufficient interest to entitle him to obtain leave to move for judicial review."

Indeed Sunkin[59] in some early research in 1991 found that:

> "there were very few applications brought explicitly by interest or pressure groups; only 19 applications were known to have fallen within this category and eight of these were applications instituted during 1989 by the Friends of the Earth challenging water authorities over pollution control."

21–40   These findings have been confirmed by more recent research which shows that only to a limited extent have applications for judicial review penetrated the practices of solicitors in private practice and into law centres. Pressure groups are infrequently involved in judicial review. The patterns of activity for judicial review are complex but the research data indicates that[60]:

> "All the evidence suggest that any "explosion" in the use of judicial review has been limited to two fields of activity in particular, immigration and homelessness."

---

[56] [1986] A.C. 240.
[57] *Inland Commissioner, ex p. National Federation of Self-Employed and Small Businesses Ltd* [1982] A.C. 617; *Gouriet* [1977] Q.B. 729; [1978] A.C. 435. Also *Gillick* [1986] A.C. 112.
[58] Mr Justice Schiemann in *R. v. Secretary of State, ex p. Rose Theatre Co.* [1990] 1 All E.R. 754. See C. Harlow and R.Rawlings, *Pressure Through Law* (1992).
[59] Sunkin, *op. cit.* Also see M. Sunkin, "What is Happening to Applications for Judicial Review?" (1987) 50 M.L.R. 432, hereinafter Sunkin (1987).
[60] Sunkin, Bridges, Mészáros, *op. cit.* p. 100.

Another finding of the research is that other than the areas of **21–41** immigration, homelessness and crime, the growth in the number of applications "has either been non-existent or relatively modest at different stages in the past decade." It is important to distinguish these findings which relate to *applications* and the final hearing of judicial review cases. In comparison to the number of applications, only a small minority reach a final hearing.

The pattern of judicial review applications identified in the research study reveals that apart from the high concentration of homeless and immigration cases, there are applications from prisoners, housing disputes other than homeless persons, planning and licensing disputes. Immigration cases tend to be over the refusal of entry or challenging asylum decisions.[61]

The research underlines the variables present in determining **21–42** whether to seek judicial review. Variables include matters such as the availability of legal aid, the existence of alternative remedies, the ability of complainants to identify legal problems and lawyers to decide within the three month time limit to seek an application for judicial review. The availability of evidence, its preparation and the willingness to litigate are all hidden factors in the availability of judicial review. The authors conclude that[62]:

"The evidence on representation, for example, shows that judicial review and the use of the courts to challenge the actions of government has yet to become a standard element in the culture of most solicitors or other legal services outlets."

The outcome of this research must seriously question the role of the **21–43** courts in developing remedies and rights for the ordinary citizen beyond the special categories of immigration and homeless cases. The research indicates that far from there being a growth in judicial review, when immigration, homelessness or crime are excluded, there remains a relatively small number of cases. In more general terms the question arises as to what is the effectiveness of judicial review when confined to a numerically small number of cases. This question requires further research.

(b) Procedural Exclusivity and the Rule in O'Reilly v. Mackman

Since the reforms introduced under Order 53, various criticisms and **21–44** concerns have been made concerning the procedures under the application for judicial review. Concern from the judiciary has

---

[61] Sunkin, 1987 *op. cit.* p. 497.
[62] Sunkin, Bridges, Mészáros, *op. cit.* p. 101.

focused on the perception that there is an overload caused by an increase in the number of applications. The recent research study has shown, however, that there is a marked distinction between the increase in applications which have risen rapidly in the last decade and only a more modest increase in the number of cases reaching a final hearing. The research suggests that far from being over used there is great potential for greater use of the judicial review procedure. This includes areas such as health, environment and related areas where judicial review has only rarely been used.[63] The scope for increasing the potential for judicial review appear to be surprisingly high.

21–45   Major criticisms,[64] currently the subject of attention by the Law Commission, largely focus on the doctrine of exclusivity drawn between public and private law by the House of Lords in *O'Reilly v. Mackman*.[65] In favour of maintaining this distinction are arguments that the case-load of applications for judicial review requires that the distinction is retained.[66] The retention of the public law distinction is seen as a discretionary power in the hands of the judges to provide an important control over the direction of such cases. In practice the judges under the application procedure have a discretion whether to allow discovery. This avoids considerable cost to government departments and public bodies. Similarly the requirement of standing and the discretion of whether to allow leave also provide a protection to public bodies. If the distinction between public and private law were abandoned the citizen would be able to use the ordinary writ procedure where the court would not have a discretion in the same way as it presently does under the Order 53 procedure.

21–46   Equally persuasive arguments appear to be advanced advocating reform of the distinction between public and private law. There are at least five proposed options which might be considered in reforming the law. First, to go back to the situation before Order 53 in 1977. While there were difficulties and anomalies there was no fundamental problem equivalent to the public and private law distinction. Admittedly a return to the pre-1977 situation would restore the problem of mixing remedies namely, the prerogative orders with private law remedies. The courts might encourage the granting of

---

[63] Sunkin, Bridges, Mészáros, *op. cit.* p. 8.

[64] See Carol Harlow, "Public and Private Law: Definition without Distinction" (1980) 43 M.L.R. 241.

[65] [1983] 2 A.C. 237. Also see *Council of Civil Service Unions v. Minister for the Civil Service* [1985] A.C. 374; *R. v. Monopolies and Mergers Commission, ex p. Argyll Group plc* [1986] 1 W.L.R. 763.

[66] Arguments put forward on *Procedural Exclusivity* by Mr Justice Laws, *Conference on the Law Commission's Consultation Paper No. 126 Administrative Law: Judicial Review and Statutory Appeals*, (Robinson College, University of Cambridge, May 1993).

declarations which they had done in the 1960s. The disadvantage with this option is that it accepts the return to a special procedure for the prerogative orders and this appears less attractive today when the tendency should be in the direction of removing procedural problems. The second option is to adopt the approach advocated by Wade[67] that there should be a unified procedure. This would permit judicial review to be sought as part of the ordinary procedure involved in private law cases. The advantage is that it removes the need for any jurisprudential or case by case decision on the criteria to be adopted between public and private law. Thus no case could be lost on the apparent technicality that the wrong procedure has been used. The disadvantage might be the necessity of having to give the county court jurisdiction over cases involving judicial review. This may assist if there is any increase in the number of applications.

The third option is to mitigate the rigours of the rule in *O'Reilly* v. **21–47** *Mackman* by liberalising the strict rule that the exclusive procedure is Order 53 for matters of public law. As in the recent House of Lords decision of *Roy*.[68] This option appears to offer the best that might be achieved through the use of judicial discretion. It falls short of any legislative reform or overhaul of the system which may be a preferred option. Broadly this appears to fit the approach taken by the House of Lords in *Mercury Communications*.[69]

The fourth option, is to allow the courts to switch one case from private law to public law. Currently Order 53 does allow a case to be transferred from public law to private law but not vice versa. This option mitigates the rigours of the distinction between public and private law. It allows the courts greater discretion than at present. The question of leave requirements, time limits and the court of trial could be easily resolved if this proposal were implemented.

The fifth option, and one also considered by Wade, is to follow the **21–48** example of the Scots system. The requirement to find a distinction between public and private law does not exist in Scots law.[70] This system appears remarkably uncomplicated and free from procedural problems. Judicial review is available whenever a power of decision-making is conferred on some body whether by statute, contract or through any other means. If the anomalies in the pre-1977 law were removed then the system in Scotland appears appropriate.

Currently there is no consensus on the future direction for reform **21–49** of administrative law. The advantages and disadvantages of each of the options discussed above may begin a process of reform consultation favoured by the Law Commission in their working paper.

[67] Wade, *Administrative Law* (6th ed., 1988), p. 680.
[68] [1992] 1 All E.R. 705.
[69] [1996] 1 All E.R. 575.
[70] *West v. Secretary of State for Scotland* (1992) S.L.T. 636.

Criticisms of the Order 53 procedures have also pointed to the question of the leave requirement. Some writers regard this as "objectionable in principle," and by analogy with other jurisdictions with similar special procedures for judicial review, England, Wales and Northern Ireland insist on this requirement.[71]

21–50   The features of the requirements for leave are intended to protect the process of judicial review and public bodies from exploitation by busy bodies and unmeritorious cases. In theory the leave procedure was intended to be by affidavits to provide a convenient, efficient and easy means to pursue an application. An alternative is to opt for oral hearing. In practice the recent research study has found[72]:

> "Our data indicate that the written procedure has suffered declining popularity among applicants, despite supposedly being quicker, cheaper and more convenient. Part of the reason for this may be the consistent evidence that table [through the use of affidavit] applications are less successful in obtaining leave at first instance than those that proceed immediately to an oral hearing."

The research study also found that while the affidavit procedure was still being maintained there were concerns about good applications not being successful. This may arise when there is insufficient information available at the time to put to the judge, or the case is poorly prepared. There is also evidence that refusal rates have risen and the criteria for granting leave may have been tightened up. A more significant finding is the impact of judicial discretion. Increasingly the leave filter is used as a means of limiting case-load pressure on the system. Thus administrative efficiency is an important factor to take into account when deciding to grant leave or not. In addition there are[73]:

> "... very wide variations between the grant/refusal rates of individual judges. These differences cannot as yet be explained by such factors as the type of procedure (table or oral procedure) or subject matter of the application."

21–51   The question of the leave requirement in judicial review is one of the most contentious issues in the question of reform of the system of administrative law. The need for greater transparency in the reasons given for refusal and more consistency in judicial approach, might

---

[71] Wade, *op. cit.* p. 5. Note that there are no leave requirements in Australia, Canada, New Zealand and Scotland.
[72] Sunkin, Bridges and Mészáros, *op. cit.* p. 72.
[73] Sunkin, Bridges and Mészáros, *op. cit.*

improve the leave system as it presently operates. As most leave applications are *ex parte* there is a question of whether more *inter partes* procedures might encourage case settlement and resolution of the leave procedure in a more fair and open way.

Finally, in the area of procedural reform there is the question of **21–52** time limits. In common with the leave requirement, the existing three month time limit is intended to provide public bodies with an additional protection. It is also intended to encourage good administration by having matters settled as promptly as possible. One possible solution is to revert to a six month time limit which appeared to work reasonably well before 1977 when applied to certiorari. The question of time limits raises a more general question of how much protection should be afforded to public bodies? One solution might be to vest the courts with a discretion which may allow the extension of any time limit in worthy cases.

(c) *Non-departmental Public Bodies and Regulatory Agencies*

Non-departmental public bodies, more popularly known as quangos, **21–53** make an important contribution to administrative decision-making. They vary in size, scope and activity. Currently they account for about one-fifth of public expenditure.[74] Quangos are not directly accountable under ministerial responsibility, though the use of parliamentary questions may be effective in finding out information about their management. The importance of quangos, as reflected in their share of public expenditure is also part of general trends in setting up Next Step Agencies which are steadily taking over the work of the civil service.

McCrudden and Baldwin explain how regulation by agency has **21–54** developed in importance and offers numerous advantages over the use of the courts[75]:

> "The advantages agencies are said to have over traditional courts are numerous. The sheer volume of decisions may call for a separate structure. Economy, speed in decision-making, ability to adapt quickly to changing conditions, and freedom from technicality in procedures are other commonly cited advantages.

---

[74] *Public Bodies* (Cabinet office, 1993). The number of quangos has fallen from 2,167 in 1979 to 1,412 in 1992. The number of staff employed has also contracted from 217,000 to 114,000. The budget allocated has increased from £6,150 million in 1973 to £13,750 million in 1992.

[75] C. McCrudden and R. Baldwin, *Regulation and Public Law* (1987), p. 5. Also see C. Graham and T. Prosser, *Privatising Public Enterprises* (Oxford, 1991). See J. F. McEldowney, *Electricity Industry Handbook* (1992), Chap. 1.

Agencies are also thought to be able to relax the formal rules of evidence when appropriate, to avoid an over-reliance on adversarial techniques, and to avoid strict adherence to their own precedents. Administrative agencies are thought not to be as restricted to formulating policy on a case-by-case basis as are the courts."

21–55　The plethora of agencies ranging from the Gaming Board, Civil Aviation Authority, Health and Safety at Work Executive to the Office of Fair Trading and the Monopolies and Mergers Commission, indicates the diversity, scale and size of regulating agencies in their work and activities. An additional development has been brought about by the privatisation process, with the creation of regulatory agencies for the main utilities, water, gas, electricty and telecommunications.

It may be argued that while judicial review appears to have numerically little impact on regulatory agencies this may be deceptive. In qualitative terms the courts have provided general principles which may apply to such administrative agencies.

21–56　Judicial review has both a limited[76] and potentially far-reaching role. The far-reaching potential of judicial review may be seen in *Lonrho v. Tebbit*.[77] For example in *Regina v. Independent T.V. Commission, ex p. TSW Broadcasting Ltd*,[78] one of the TV Companies, TSW applied for judicial review of the Independent TV Commission in seeking to grant licences for TV service. Although the application for judicial review was unsuccessful, the Court of Appeal considered the fair procedures applicable to the award of TV licences under the Broadcasting Act 1990.

The characteristics of administrative decision-making range from the judicial scrutiny of determinations by regulators to the widest policy questions shared between the Secretary of State and regulator. Issues of policy are intertwined with statutory duties and powers. The overview of the administrative processes requires careful adjustment of the wide variety of agencies and techniques available.[79]

---

[76] *Ex p. Benwell* [1985] Q.B. 554; *R. v. Secretary of State for Trade and Industry, ex p. Lonrho* [1989] 1 W.L.R. 525; [1989] 2 All E.R. 609.

[77] *The Independent*, September 26, 1991; [1992] 4 All E.R. 280.

[78] *The Independent*, February 6, 1992. Also see *Luby v. Newcastle-upon-Lyme Corporation* (1964) 2 Q.B. 64. Lord Justice Diplock explained "it is not for the court to substitute its own view of what is a desirable policy in relation to the subject-matter of the discretion so conferred. It is only if it is exercised in a manner which no reasonable man could consider justificable that the court is entitled to interfere."

[79] See note 78, above.

(d) The Citizen's Charter

Constitutional and administrative reform may appear in a number of **21–57**
guises. The Citizen's Charter may offer the potential for new developments in setting standards and promoting good administration in
public administration. The Citizen's Charter seeks to provide the
citizen with standards, more effective complaints procedures, published performance targets and therefore greater consumer choice.[80]
The Charter has the far reaching potential of seeking to make all
public services such as government departments, agencies, public
utilities, the remaining nationalised industries and local authorities,
the courts, police and emergency services conform to a standard of
quality and service.[81]

The Charter adopts a number of techniques, for example it seeks to **21–58**
use contract compliance as a means to achieve quality control across a
wide range of services and activities. There is a major question as to
how quality might be enforced and how it might be ascertained.
Kieron Walsh, argues that[82]:

> "as the contracting, market-based approach begins to be extended
> to more complicated professional services, such as medicare, law,
> finance or social services, it will be necessary to develop more
> sophisticated approaches to quality specification. The problem is
> not simply one of complexity, but of coping with the fact that
> public services involve value choices. . ."

The Citizen's Charter has attempted to provide a coherent **21–59**
approach to such problems but the mechanisms for improving the
administration process are vague and largely based on political
objectives rather than clear-sighted administrative improvements.[83]
The difficulty of establishing standards involves questions of pri-
oritising and setting sufficiently clear indicators to establish the
financial implications of any new quality standards. In a period
where the public sector borrowing requirement has grown in deficit,
the volume of public expenditure which may be allocated to such
objectives is limited. Consistent with the Citizen's Charter have been
various efficiency strategies set by central government to achieve a
reduction in waste, greater efficiency in management and value for
money. These strategies will have an effect on administrative

---

[80] *The Citizen's Charter* Cm. 1599 (1991).
[81] *ibid.*
[82] Kieran Walsh, "Quality and Public Services" (1991) 69 *Public Administration* No. 4.,
503–514 at 513.
[83] See note 82, above.

decision-making but with precisely what outcome is difficult to predict. As Metcalfe and Richards explain[84]:

"Improving public management is frontier territory – an area of genuine innovation where civil servants will have to develop and apply new concepts to fit the tasks and political contraints of government. This is a challenge which await solution."

(e) Principles of Good Administration

21–60 The Justice All Souls Review of Administrative Law recommended in 1988 the adoption of principles of good administration.[85] The objective is to examine decision-making from the perspective of setting principles for good administration rather than depending on remedies for bad administration. Good administration principles includes both substantive and procedural rights set out in a code which, on a non-statutory basis are intended to encourage all administrators to undertake decision-taking in accordance with principles of fairness. The publication and formulation of such principles is recommended to be part of the work of the Parliamentary Ombudsman.

21–61 The approach of the Justice Review[86] has common themes with the work of the Committee of Ministers of the Council of Europe, the Recommendations of the Administrative Conference of the United States[87] and work undertaken by the Canadian Law Reform Commission[88] and the Administrative Review Council in Australia.[89] However, the point that has been broadly acknowledged by the consultation paper: *Towards a Modern Federal Administrative Law*[90] is that good administration may be achieved through the work of a number of participants with a whole range of techniques.

"Control of Administrative action is a function that can be shared among many institutions or types of decision-makers. Law and

---

[84] L. Metcalfe and S. Richards, *Improving Public Management* (1990). Also see J. F. McEldowney, "Administrative Justice" in R. Blackburn (ed.), *Rights of Citizenship* (1993).

[85] Justice All Souls Review, *op. cit.*

[86] *ibid.*

[87] Also see Patrick McAuslan, "Administrative Law, Collective Consumption and Judicial Policy" (1983) M.L.R. 1; J. F. McEldowney, "Current Privatisation and Regulation Issues in the U.K.: A Case Study of the Proposed Electricity Privatisation (*Law Reform Commission of Canada*, 1988).

[88] Canadian Law Reform Commission W.P. 51: "Policy Implementation, Compliance and Administrative Law" (1986).

[89] M. Partington, "The Reform of Public Law in Britain" in P. McAuslan and J. McEldowney, *Law, Legitimacy and the Constitution* (1985), pp. 191–211.

[90] Law Reform Commission of Canada, *op. cit.* p. 23.

bodies entrusted with law application and creation are primary candidates for organising control. However, a plurality of interdependent modes, bodies and procedural regimes that reflect the diverse nature of the control function is called for."

This view acknowledges the importance of internal as well as **21–62** external controls, non-legal as well as legal which goes beyond the prospectus chosen by the Justice Review. It is the combination of internal and external controls which may ultimately assist in establishing improvements leading to good administration.

Have the courts any role in the development of principles of good administration? Judicial review is pragmatic and unsystematic. As the recent research study into applications for judicial review has shown, large areas of activity do not appear to be the subject matter of judicial review. Its focus is primarily on the issues before the court rather than the broader policy objectives. Courts offer *ex post facto* rather than *a priori* review and this is limited to remedies for wrongful actions rather than a prescription for the future conduct of administration.

An additional question in using the courts is whether the adver- **21–63** sarial nature of the English judicial system provides an adequate basis to lay down normative principles for the solution of administrative mistakes, inefficiencies or even in providing a grievance resolution for citizens. There is also the issue of how far formal legal rules may not only constrain officials but also condition or determine their behaviour. For example, recent studies on police reactions to critical scrutiny of their behaviour show that much of police behaviour may be made to fit within legal rules because the rules are sufficiently flexible to facilitate the situations where the police need to find a rule to cover their activities. Judicial review of administrative action seldom questions how legal rules are understood or applied by administrative decision-makers. There is a danger that the apparent observance of court orientated rules may hide or obscure bad decision-making.

It is difficult to gauge the effect of judicial review on administra- **21–64** tion. In recent years within government departments a pamphlet prepared by the Treasury Solicitors was circulated entitled "The Judge over your Shoulder" with the clear implication that potential judicial intervention might be considered as part of the decision-making process. Judicial review features as an element in the training of civil servants. It may well be that the threat of review has a greater significance than the reality where its use is confined to specific areas of litigation and it is not uniformly applied. The effectiveness of judicial review requires further research and analysis.

One conclusion is that achieving administrative justice sets complex **21–65** objectives across a great variety of agencies, institutions, tribunal, ombudsmen and courts. Invariably most regulatory agencies are set up by Act of Parliament. This may combine some form of political accountability through ministerial responsibility with policy objectives. But this only highlights the diffuse nature of our regulatory agencies. Techniques of accountability may be both *external* and *internal*, legal and non-legal. The privatised industries are particularly good examples of new challenges to existing techniques. Recent developments such as the Citizen's Charter may lead to a new agenda setting economic as well as legal appraisal indicators. There is also an important element of fine-tuning, *i.e.* establishing the necessary expertise to fit the requirements of the activity to be regulated.

21–66   Privatised industries[91] have also broadened horizons as to the nature of regulatory structures. Competition policy, consumer choice, share ownership, environmental efficiency, European Community law, market share and profitability have to be considered together. Carefully balanced judgments have to be taken within a complex legal formulation of the legal powers and duties of regulators. The background political agenda, the use of select committees and parliamentary debate and the policy of the government of the day are all relevant considerations in setting out to assess administrative justice. One suggestion, of setting up a Select Committee on Regulated Industries to replace the defunct Select Committee on Nationalised Industries, might help to co-ordinate the parliamentary oversight of regulatory agencies.

21–67   Another conclusion is that the question of how judicial review may contribute to the development of administrative justice is also related to the diverse nature of the various agencies and regulating bodies. Doubts exist as to the appropriateness of the adversarial system of courts, the *ex post facto* nature of the proceedings and the narrow issues often confronting the courts which may suggest that courts are not ideally suited to providing the formulation of administrative justice. In *R. v. Civil Service Appeal Board*[92] Lord Donaldson suggested how a partnership between regulators and courts might be formed:

> ". . . we had now reached the position in the development of judicial review at which public law bodies and the courts should be regarded as being in partnership in a common endeavour to maintain the highest standards of public administration, including, I would add the administration of justice."

---

[91] See Lord Scarman at RIPA Conference, University of Aston, *The Shifting State: Public Administration in a Time of Change* (Keynote Address, September 14, 1984). Author's own copy. I am grateful to Lord Scarman for sending me his Keynote Address; J. F. McEldowney, "British Public Law and Legal History" Universidad de Malaga (1993). Also M. Loughlin "Tinkering with the Constitution" [1988] 51 M.L.R. 531.
[92] [1991] 4 All E.R. 310 at p. 315.

This aspirational view of the role of the courts is a departure from **21–68** the grievance or remedy orientated approach which historically has been influential in this area. However this raises the question of whether the courts, as Loughlin[93] has asked, "possess the cognitive, conceptual and material resources to enable them to perform the functions expected?" While doubts may exist as to the technical or conceptual techniques that are available to the courts, it is essential that these issues are addressed as the new challenge facing administrative lawyers in the 1990s. As the Canadian Law Reform Commission concluded[94]:

"Overall contentious procedure in judicial review has many gaps. For example, the multiplicity of remedial avenues and the absence of distinctions between public law and private law are sources of confusion, frustration and inequity. We must explore new solutions, especially the unification of crucial remedies and the clarification of their fields of application in administrative law."

There is also the wider question of whether principles of good **21–69** administration may achieve all that is desired? There is a danger that far from constraining bad administration the rules themselves may condition or determine behaviour. This may provide a veneer of legality to what is otherwise objectionable behaviour.[95] The rules or principles of good administration may still permit undesirable practices but make it insulated from scrutiny and therefore outside the sanctions which should apply. It is therefore suggested that reforms favouring good administration are more difficult to implement than the Justice Review considered. The instrumental effect of rules has to be studied in the context of the expected behaviour of the main administrative decision-makers.

Finally, it may be concluded that administrative justice requires that reform of administrative law should take account of the changing nature of our administrative state. Approaches to administrative law must combine the practical with the theoretical, the legal with the multi-disciplinary, the external with the internal rules of good administration.

---

[93] Loughlin, *op. cit.*

[94] Canadian Law Reform Commission, "Towards a Modern Federal Administrative Law," p. 24. Also see Sir Harry Woolf, "Public Law – Private Law: Why the Divide? A Personal View" [1986] P.L. 200; T.R.S. Allan, "Pragmatism and Theory in Public Law" (1988) L.Q.R. 422 at 446. Also see proposal for reform in Constitutional Reform Centre, Politics Briefing No. 11 "Regulatory Agencies in the United Kingdom" (1991).

[95] This point is admirably made by McConville *et al., The Case for the Prosecution* (1981). Generally, see P. S. Atiyah, *Pragmatism and Theory in English Law* (1987), pp. 181–183. Also Lord Goff, "The Search for Principle" (1983) LXIX *Proc. Br. Acad.* 169.

5. The European Union

21-70 Reform of the United Kingdom's constitutional arrangements may be precipitated by developments within the European Union. The importance of the European Convention on Human Rights (ECHR) has already been noted. There is considerable judicial interest[96] in the question of whether incorporation of the ECHR into domestic law may take place through the development of the common law without the need for legislative change. Two propositions are advanced. First, that the ECHR might be interpreted to provide a series of propositions, largely representing the legal norms or values which may be integrated into the United Kingdom's domestic law. The second proposition is to incorporate the ECHR through judicial interpretation giving effect to the text of the ECHR. The second proposition appears an unlikely direction given the views of the judiciary rejecting this way forward.[97] The first proposition might be sustained by the development of greater protection for the citizen through a more dynamic adoption of existing principles through growth in the common law. As one senior judge explained[98]:

> "We should apply differential standards of judicial review according to the subject-matter, and to do so deploy the tool of proportionality, not the bludgeon of *Wednesbury*. A function of this is to recognise that decision-makers whose decisions affect fundamenal rights must inevitably justify what they do by giving goods reasons; and the judges should not construe statutes which are said to confer power with such rights any more favourably than they would view a clause to oust their jurisdiction."

21-71 Avoiding the need to incorporate the ECHR may appear attractive but this is surely only to recognise the fact that successive governments have failed to trust the judiciary with an extended role through the incorporation of the ECHR. Reforms such as incorporating the ECHR should be fully considered and the implications for judicial power and influence debated before judicial influence is expanded. What is to be welcomed and encouraged is a broader understanding and acknowledgment of human rights values[99] within existing constitutional arrangements.

---

[96] See Lord Browne-Wilkinson, "The Infiltration of a Bill of Rights" [1992] P.L. 397 and Sir John Laws, "Is the High Court the Guardian of Fundamental Constitutional Rights?" [1993] P.L. 59.

[97] *The Sunday Times* [1979] 2 E.C.H.R. 245. See Ferdinand Mount, *The British Constitution Now* (1991).

[98] Sir John Laws, "Is the High Court the Guardian of Fundamental Constitutional Rights?" (1993) P.L. 59.

[99] See Claire Palley, *The United Kingdom and Human Rights* (1991) for a reasoned account of the U.K.'s development of human rights.

The European Community is an important source for ideas and **21–72** directions in the reform of the United Kingdom's constitutional arrangements. Community law creates extensive legal, social, economic and political rights for individuals within Member States. Membership of the Community has developed through the combination of the direct effect and the supremacy of Community law. This combination creates rights enforceable in national courts which may override any conflicting national law. Invariably Member States have to act on behalf of the Community to implement Community law very often through domestic law. The importance of the *Factortame*[1] litigation has highlighted the process of defining the relationship between Community law and the domestic law of the Member States by the European Court. National courts are under a duty to construe national law in such a way as to give effect to Community law.[2] Still further, through a series of cases decided by the European Court,[3] on the use of Directives, legal rights became more easily enforceable. Even where the Directive has been wrongly implemented it may nonetheless create directly effective rights which private citizens may enforce against a Member State. The obligation imposed on national courts to give effect to Community law so far as it is possible requires national courts to interpret Directives consistent with national law and the effectiveness of Community law.[4] In the landmark decision of *Francovich*[5] the European Court considered the right to damages where a Member State may fail to implement a Directive. This decision is potentially far-reaching in its effects. On a narrow interpretation, there is liability in damages where an action in damages is brought against a Member State because of a failure to implement a provision of Community law which may include a Directive. On a broader interpretation, there may be some general right to compensation where an individual suffers loss caused by a breach of Community law. This may be stated as a general principle in terms of a general right to damages where the Member State fails to implement a Directive or give direct effect and supremacy to Communtiy law.

---

[1] Case C–213/89, *Factortame and Others* [1990] 2 A.C. 85; [1990] E.C.R. I–2433; [1990] 3 C.M.L.R. 1; *Factortame (No. 2)* [1991] 1 A.C. 603; [1991] 3 C.M.L.R. 589 and also more recently Case C–48/93, *The Queen v. Secretary of State for Transport, ex p. Factortame.*

[2] Case 14/83, *Von Colson and Kaman v. Land Nordrhein-Westfalen* [1984] E.C.R. 1891; [1986] 2 C.M.L.R. 430.

[3] *Marleasing* [1990] E.C.R. 4135, Case, *Van Duyn v. Home Office* [1974] E.C.R. 1337. See the discussion in C. Lewis, S. Moore, "Duties, Directives and Damages in European Community Law" [1993] P.L. 151.

[4] For example see *Webb v. EMO Air Cargo (U.K.) Ltd* [1992] 4 All E.R. 929.

[5] Case C–6/90, *Francovich v. Italian State*; [1992] E.C.R. I–5357; [1992] 2 C.M.L.R. 66; Case C–9/90, *Bonifaci v. Belgian State* [1992] I.R.L.R. 84; [1992] E.C.R. I–5357, [1992] 2 C.M.L.R. 66. See J. Steiner, "From Direct Effects to Francovich: Shifting Means of Enforcement of Community Law" (1993) E.L.Rev. 3.

21–73   The *Francovich* decision may represent another example of gap-filling provided by Community law. The potential for reform is to re-invigorate the tort of breach of a statutory duty, as a useful means to allow an action for damages to lie where the Member State has failed to implement a Directive or give effect to Community law. This has the potential of widening State liability in damages over a wide variety of public duties on Member States arising out of membership of the Community where the Community obligations are capable of a clear construction. This sets a further stimulus for the shaping and development of attitudes to Community law within the United Kingdom. In the post-Maastricht period of debate over the future of the Community, the traditional doctrine of parliamentary sovereignty, the independence of the Bank of England and the future direction of economic policy are intertwined in the future development of Europe. There is a welcome appraisal of the importance of national Parliaments for the future of the European Union as discussions proceed on the developments towards a single currency.[6]

6. Public Law Scholarship

21–74 Public law scholarship has reflected the range and diversity of many recent developments in the changing shape of constitutional and administrative law. It is impossible to provide an exhaustive analysis of the formidable literature relevant to the subject and the student of the constitution is referred to the select bibliography for further references and additional reading. Many specialisms, often outside the traditional confines of law, are now required reading to understand some of the basics of public law. Here, it is possible only to note future directions and to encourage students towards a deeper understanding of the subject.

21–75   Diversity in public law scholarship is partly a reflection of the unwritten constitution and the difficulties posed by the subject matter. The way forward is not easy to locate. The introduction of a Bill of Rights incorporating the European Convention will alter profoundly the legal and political culture of the United Kingdom and thus the role of constitutional law. The reports of the Nolan Committee into the standards in public life are likely to propose the use of

---

[6] See *Twenty-eighth Report of the House of Commons Select Committee on European Legislation*, The Role of National Parliaments in the European Union 1995–96, H.C. 51–xxviii (July 19, 1996), *Twenty-seventh Report of the House of Commons Select Committee on European Legislation*, The Scrutiny of European Business 1995–96, H.C. 51–xxvii (July 18, 1996).

criminal offences for corruption in public office. This proposal will apply to both local and central government. A growing body of public law literature moves from the traditional and often historical concerns of constitutional law to question the theoretical development of the subject and seek explanations rooted in legal theory.[7] There is little convergence as to how best to achieve this ambitious task. Craig has considered some of the approaches which are open to the future study of public law[8] and favours an approach which allows the lawyer to:

> "identify and assess the relevant background theory, consider the public law implications of it, and the political and social and economic background conditions within which it subsists."

While this methodology might not always find favour[9] it represents **21–76** a growing interest among public lawyers of the wider social and political ramifications of how laws work, how they might be applied and whether the legal arrangements are relevant when other factors may be relevant to how decisions are taken. There is some caution in considering whether lawyers do in fact have much, if anything to offer. Writing on the area of discretion and law, Lacey[10] points out limitations in legal methodology and the potential for turning a broadening and enlightening development "into a piece of intellectual and practical imperialism in which lawyers merely incorporate ever more inappropriate areas of activity into their own analytic and political framework." The dangers of what Lacey calls[11] "the legal paradigm" is that legal methodology may tend to operate using generalisation, it tends to "pigeonhole" solutions, operates dichotomies or opposites with either/or decisions, and may tend to assume that there are "right" answers found in some form of objectivity or truth.[12] Furthermore, legal method may assume belief in

---

[7] Loughlin, *Public Law and Political Theory* (1992); P. Craig, *Public Law and Democracy in the United Kingdom and the United States of America* (1990); Harden and Lewis, *The Noble Lie: The British Constitution and the Rule of Law* (1986); Birkinshaw, Harden and Lewis, *Government by Moonlight: The Hybrid Parts of the State* (1990).

[8] See Craig, "What Should Public Lawyers Do? A Reply" (1992) 12 O.J.L.S. (No. 4) 565–577 at 565.

[9] Criticism may be found in O'Leary's review of Craig's *Public Law and Democracy*. See (1992) 12 O.J.L.S. p. 404.

[10] N. Lacey, "The Jurisprudence of Discretion" in K. Hawkins (ed.), *The Uses of Discretion* (1992), 361–388 at 362–363.

[11] The legal paradigm questioned by Lacey is described by her as follows (pp. 362–363): "Problems are typically seen as arising from ambiguities or 'gaps' in the rules, calling for clearer interpretations or further legislative or quasi-legislative action. Disputes are seen as calling for resolution on the basis of the given rules and according to the standards of due process. This approach is closely associated with the ideal of the "rule of law' and hence with liberalism as a doctrine of political morality."

[12] The legal world is classified as presenting "a monolithic, black and white view of the world, and sets this view up, moreover as "objective reality' or "truth.'"

its own self-importance and overestimate the value of the courts and the temptation to bring disputes within "a legal umbrella." Lacey's analysis calls for a pluralistic approach of pooling resources to problems. In the example of her study of discretion this means[13]:

> "The need to integrate empirical, interpretative and normative questions in an attempt to understand discretion and ultimately, to ensure the legitimacy and effectiveness of the exercise of social powers in particular contexts. Discretion must be taken, then primarily as a political question, and one whose centrality in contemporary society calls for the concerted attention of a number of related and interdependent disciplines.".

21–77 Having established some form of methodology or approach public lawyers are often uncertain as to how to establish principles rooted in constitutional law or theory. This problem is particularly acute when legislation is considered as to its policy and philosophy.

Assessing how to evaluate legislation may require consideration of the political issues underlying the law. In the last decade or so this has given rise to much public law literature concerning some of the changes introduced since Mrs Thatcher became Prime Minister. The division between legal and non-legal opinion becomes difficult to draw as public lawyers examine the writings of political scientists and related disciplines. The burgeoning literature that reflects interest in the political as well as theoretical issues underlying constitutional change is also the result of political scientists finding legal analysis helpful.

21–78 Daintith has pointed out that public lawyers may have difficulty in finding a suitably clear constitutional principle or criteria to judge whether political changes have a constitutional impact. This difficulty is compounded by a[14]: "prevailing descriptive and eclectic mode of writing about the United Kingdom constitution and public law." Further difficulties arise because[15]:

> "we have not formulated the twentieth- as opposed to nineteenth-century principles with which the recent legislation comes into conflict or which it purports to displace or modify."

Responses to the problems identified by Daintith have varied. Some have taken a critical view of the Constitution and sought to find

---

[13] Lacey, *op. cit.* p. 388.
[14] Daintith, "Political Programmes and the Constitution" in Finnie, Himsworth and Walker (eds.), *Edinburgh Essays in Public Law* (1991), p. 43.
[15] *ibid.*, p. 46.

expression[16] through the value of "critique," and the need for reforms through the testing of the adequacy of existing arrangements.[17] The political policies and ideology underlying law has also come under scrutiny, sometimes quite openly and directed at the ideology itself[18] which is at the centre of government policy.[19]

There has also been a notable growth in various specialist studies **21–79** designed to highlight particular areas or problems traditionally not within the confines of public law. Innovative work in the area of discretion,[20] regulation[21] and on administration[22] more generally sets new boundaries between the work of a public lawyers and other related disciplines.

There appears to be common ground that the lawyers task is not merely to understand legal doctrine but the wider context of its use, including the ideologies that underpin it and the variety of social forces that exert pressure for legal change. One concern is that because of a long established normatist style, lawyers may believe that solutions are to be found in the refocusing and defining of the common law. Cotterrell notes[23]:

"Treating law and politics as distinct, normatism puts faith in ordinary common law methods of the courts in controlling government, views legislation as potentially an object of suspicion, has ambivalent views on democracy, and tends to assume an atomistic relationship between the individual and the state."

In contrast a functionalist style[24] of public law literature is dissent- **21–80** ing of the normative tradition. It refocuses attention on the use of law as a policy instrument and treats legislation as an embodiment of democratic power as influential and the highest form of law. Suspicious of the ability of the courts to supervise administrative bodies, the functionalist style of public law treats law as progressive evolutionary change and often reflects a positivist attitude to how law may achieve administrative forms.

---

[16] T. Prosser, "Towards a Critical Public Law" (1982) 9 *Journal of Law and Society* 19.
[17] Immanent critique is advanced as one possible way forward by Harden and Lewis, *The Noble Lie* (1986). Immanent critique seeks to remove the restrictions imposed by positivist approaches to law. It seeks to compare and contrast expectations about the role of the constitution through analysis of claims and realities made about the constitution.
[18] P. McAuslan, "Public Law and Public Choice" (1988) 51 M.L.R. 681.
[19] Also take account of the critical legal studies movement. See P. Fitzpatrick and A. Hunt, *Critical Legal Studies* (1987).
[20] K. Davis, *Discretionary Justice* (1969) and more recently K. Hawkins (ed.), *The Uses of Discretion* (1992).
[21] Baldwin and McCrudden, *Regulation and Pubilc Law* (1987).
[22] Harlow and Rawlings, *Law and Administration* (1984).
[23] *The Times Higher Educational Supplement* (June 1993). Also see R. Cotterrell, *The Sociology of Law* (1992).
[24] See M. Loughlin, *Public Law and Political Theory* (1992).

The functionalist style lacks attention to many of the normatist characteristics of law. In fact, as the Daintith analysis has identified, there is a demand greater than ever before to find principles where the policy driven character of law makes such principles more difficult to find. The normative response for greater principle is to assert a more liberal approach[25] in an attempt to find laws which will achieve better systems of control and accountability.

21–81 The merits of both liberal normatism and the functionalist style may leave unanswered Daintith's[26] concerns and the task of the public lawyer:

> "the task of developing a vocabulary and system of talking about our constitution in normative terms – in terms of constitutional obligation. It seems essential to try and find out what the constitution is, and to express that knowledge in the form of principles, rules and exceptions to rules. . ."

An example of how this task might be taken forward is in the formulation of the principles of good administration, or the building up of principles containing the working practices of the Parliamentary Commissioner for Administration. The recurrent themes of accountability, control and scrutiny found in much public law literature require evaluation of different style and techniques beyond a purely legal and court-orientated approach. For example, this may include scrutiny of the work of the national Audit Office and the Audit Commission.

21–82 This may suggest an agenda[27] for further research into public law, such as that outlined by the Canadian Law Reform Commission, *Towards a Modern Federal Administrative Law*.[28] This may include consideration of the control and regulatory functions of government, investigating the dispute-resolving functions of government, and an examination of the legal implications and limitations of the delegation of government functions to private sector actors.[29]

21–83 The future development of public law will benefit from the continuation of empirical studies into judicial review such as those undertaken by Bridges and Sunkin.[30] From this model further

---

[25] See R. Dworkin, *A Bill of Rights for Britain* (1990).

[26] Daintith, *op. cit.* p. 50.

[27] See R. Rawlings, "The Complaints Industry: A Review of Sociolegal Research on Aspects of Adminstrative Justice" (1986) E.S.R.C.

[28] (Ottaway, Canada, 1987).

[29] Long term research also includes; court procedures, internal systems of government decision-making, the structure and nature of internal administrative remedies, access to information and openness, the evidentiary practices in administrative decision-making and the use of procurement cntracts as part of implementing government policy..

[30] Sunkin, Bridges and Mészáros, *op. cit.*

research might be undertaken on the effects of judicial review on public bodies and the potential impact of a code of guidance on good administration examined. In devising future strategies it is essential that the impact of a Bill of Rights is carefully monitored. Similarly the introduction of devolution will impact on the role of the United Kingdom Parliament and on the future of local government within the devolved regions. A research register on public law might be a good starting point representing the diversity of interest in public law. Integrating empirical, interpretative and normative questions will set the future challenge for public law. As the end of the present century is in sight, the future development of public law is likely to reflect its inherent pragmatic qualities; continuous change and steady growth with unpredictable results.

APPENDIX

Further Reading and Select Bibliography

Students of constitutional and administrative law face a bewildering array of writing, both legal and non-legal. The literature relevant to their studies includes primary and secondary sources. A broader view of the subject, resulting from the abandonment of an exclusively court orientated approach to the study of constitutional and administrative law, has led to public law scholarship expanding rapidly. The focus in many textbooks of a mainly descriptive approach setting out the legal rules has given way to a more critical and analytical style. General treatises are more difficult to write as the specialist nature of many topics require detailed examination.

In law schools the content of courses in public law have widened. For example, courses on planning, housing, immigration, civil liberties or environmental law cover materials that provide important knowledge for lawyers interested in constitutional law and public administration. The study of public law includes consideration of the work of constitutional historians, political scientists, economists and philosophers. Students face a daunting task of how to evaluate such widely drawn sources and materials.

Any selection of the literature cannot be exhaustive. It is intended to provide a guide to offer students suggestions for further reading as an aid to understanding the subject. There is not available in published form any specialist bibliography dedicated to constitutional and administrative law. There are a number of general reference works which are helpful: *Index to Legal Periodicals*, New York, Vol. 1 (1960–61)—in progress; *Index to Foreign Legal Periodicals*, (General Editor: W.A. Steiner) (London), Vol. 1, 1960—in progress; *International Political Science Abstracts*, (Paris), Vol. 1, 1951—in progress; *Harvard Law School: Annual Legal Bibliography* (Boston, Mass.), Vol. 1, 1961—in progress. *Halsbury's Laws of England* (1986—in progress; provides useful references to cases and statutes relevant to both constitutional and administrative law. Catalogues available in the Squire Law Library, University of Cambridge and the Bodleian Law Library, University of Oxford are also useful for public lawyers.

The Bristol Centre for the Study of Administrative Justice has published in 1996 *Administrative Justice: A Working Bibliography Working Paper Series No. 1* available from Professor Martin Partington, Department of Law, University of Bristol BS8 1RJ. There is also a vast amount of literature available from the Cabinet Office, and under the White Paper on Open Government Cm. 2290, there is a Code of Practice on Access to Government Information. Information about government is available from: Open Government, Room 417b, Office of Public Service and Science, 70, Whitehall, London, SW1A 2AS. The Internet allows access to a wide variety of materials about the Government, the Royal Family, the Treasury and government departments. Access the following: http://www.open.gov.uk also examine http://www.tagish.co.uk/tagish/links/centgov.htm and also http://www.tagish.co.uk/tagish/links/offices.htm, and also http://www.tagish.co.uk/tagish/links/oss.htm. Finally on local government see: http://www.tagish.co.uk/tagish/links/localgov.htm.

Sources and Materials

A wide range of primary sources may provide useful material for an understanding of the development of constitutional and administrative law.

In the Public Records Office, Kew Gardens, London, there are the minutes and reports of the Poor Law Commissioners, (1830s); the General Board of Health (1840s); the Railway Commission and the Railway Department of the Board of Trade; the Opinion of Law Officers (1840s) and the Cabinet Papers.

Parliamentary Papers and Hansard Parliamentary Debates from the nineteenth century to the present time provide useful information. Access the following: http://www.parliament.the-stationary-office.co.uk/pa/cm/cmhansrd.htm. Government published reports are also relevant and the following are particularly useful:

The Northcote-Trevelyan Report on the Civil Service (1854 Parl. Pap. XXVII 1); the Report of the War Cabinet (Cd. 9005, 1917); The Report of the Committee on the Machinery of Government (Cd. 9230, 1918); The Report of the Committee on Ministers' Powers (Cmd. 4060, 1932); Royal Commission on Justices of the Peace (Cmd. 7463, 1948); Report of the Committee on the Political Activities of Civil Servants (Cmd. 7718, 1949); Report of the Public Inquiry into the Disposal of Land at Crichel Down (Cmd. 9176, 1954); Report of the Royal Commission on the Civil Service (Cmd. 9613, 1953–5); Report of the Committee on Administrative Tribunals and Inquiries (Cmnd. 218, 1957); Report of the Committee into the Working of the Monetary System (Cmnd. 827, 1959); The Control of Public Expenditure (Cmnd. 1432, 1961); Report of the Committee on Security Procedures in the Public Service (Cmnd. 1681, 1962); Report by Lord Denning into the Profumo Affair (Cmnd. 2152, 1963); Report of the Royal Commission on Tribunals of Inquiry (Cmnd. 3121, 1966); Report of the Committee on Management in Local Government (1967); Report of the Committee on the Civil Service 1966–68 (Cmnd. 3638); Report of the Committee on Participation and Planning (Cmnd. 7468, 1969); Report of Royal Commission on Local Government in England 1966–9 (Cmnd. 4040, 1969); Local

Government Reform in England (Cmnd. 4276, 1970); Report of the Tribunal appointed to inquire into Certain Issues Related to the Circumstances Leading up to the Cessation of Trading by the Vehicle and General Insurance Co. Ltd., HL 80, HC 133; Report of the Committee on Legal Procedures to Deal with Terrorist Activities in Northern Ireland. (Cmnd. 5185, 1973); Royal Commission on the Constitution 1969–73 (Cmnd. 5460, 1973); The Red Lion Square Disorders of 15 June 1974; Report of Inquiry by the Rt. Hon. Lord Scarman OBE (Cmnd. 5919, 1975); Report of a Committee to Consider, in the Context of Civil Liberties and Human Rights, Measures to Deal with Terrorism in Northern Ireland (Cmnd. 5487, 1975); Report of the Committee on the Preparation of Legislation (Cmnd. 6053, 1975); Local Government Finance: Report of the Committee of Enquiry (Cmnd. 6453, 1976); Local Government Finance (Cmnd. 6823, 1977); Observations on the Fourth Report of the Select Committee on the Parliamentary Commissioner for Administration (Cmnd. 7057, 1979); Report of Council on Tribunals; The Functions of the Council on Tribunal (1980, Cmnd. 7846); The Royal Commission on Criminal Procedure (Cmnd. 8092, 1981); Efficiency in the Civil Service (Cmnd. 8293, 1981); Falkland Islands Review (Cmnd. 8787, 1983); Financial Management in Government Departments (Cmnd. 9058, 1983); The Review of Public Order Law (Cmnd. 8510, 1985); The Conduct of Local Authority Business (Cmnd. 9797, 1986); Report of the Review Body on Civil Justice (Cm. 394, 1988); The Financing and Accountability of Next Step Agencies (Cm. 914, 1989); Report of the Committee on Privacy and Related Matters (Cm. 1102, 1990); Competition and Choice: Telecommunications Policy for the 1990s (Cm. 1461, 1991); The Working of the Select Committee System (Cm. 1532, 1991); The Citizen's Charter (Cm. 1599, 1991); Budgetary Reform (Cm. 1867, 1992); Review of Press Self-Regulation (Cm. 2135, 1993); Scotland in the Union (Cm. 2225, 1993); Inquiry into Police Responsibilities and Rewards Report, (Cm. 2280, 1993); Royal Commission on Criminal Justice Report (Cm. 2263, 1993); *Better Accounting for the Taxpayer's Money: Resource Accounting and Budgeting in Government* (Cm. 2626, 1994); *European Community Finances* (Cm. 2824, 1995); *The Civil Service: Taking Forward Continuity and Change* (Cm. 2748, 1995); *The Citizen's Charter The Facts and Figures* September 1995 (Cm. 2970 1995); *The Government's Response to the First Report from the Committee on Standards in Public Life* (Cm. 2931, 1995); *Inquiry into Legislation Against Terrorism* (Cm. 3420, 1996); *Spending Public Money: Governance and Audit Issues* (Cm. 3179, 1996); *Next Steps Agencies in Government: Review 1995* (Cm. 3164, 1996). Particular attention should be given to: *Return to an Address of the Honourable House of Commons dated 15th February 1996. Report of the Inquiry into the Export of defence Equipment and Dual-use Goods to Iraq and Related Prosecutions* The Rt Hon. Sir Richard Scott, The Vice-Chancellor HC 115 (HMSO, London, 1996).

.e publications of the various departmental select committees .ve since 1979 led to greater information and transparency in the working of government. Departmental publications which are not normally published through HMSO should not be overlooked, particularly publications from the Cabinet Office, the Treasury, the Home Office, for example, Legislation on Human Rights (Home Office, 1976) and the Department of Environment. Listings of both departmental publications and HMSO publications may be found in the Monthly List published by HMSO.

The Treasury has prepared a useful guide on accounting and financial procedures for the use of government departments, in the form of a loose-leaf: *Government Accounting* (1989) available from HMSO. The guide is regularly updated and covers important matters of constitutional propriety such as the 1932 Concordat between the Public Accounts Committee and the Treasury. In addition the various internal treasury rules for the use within departments in the discharge of their responsibilities to Parliament in the conduct of financial matters, are contained in *Supply and other Financial Procedure of the House of Commons*, (1977) available in the Treasury. This is a handbook for official use within departments. The cabinet office may be the source of important information, for example: *Select Committees: Memorandum of Guidance for Officials* (the Osmotherly Rules) (HMSO, 1980).

Various specialist Select Committees deserve mention such as the House of Lords Select Committee on the European Communities, the Public Accounts Committee, and the Select Committee on Procedure. Some House of Commons Papers that are particularly relevant to constitutional and administrative law are: First Report of the Parliamentary Commissioner 1967–8, H.C. 6; Report from the Select Committee on Members' Interests (Declaration) 1969–70, H.C. 57; Liaison Committee 1982–3: The Select Committee System, H.C. 92; Seventh Report from the Treasury and Civil Service Committee 1985–6: Ministers and Civil Servants: Duties and Responsibilities, H.C. 92; Eighth Report from the Treasury and Civil Service Committee 1987–8: Civil Service Management Reform: The Next Steps, H.C. 494; Third Report from the select Committee on Members' Interests 1989–90, H.C. 561.

An account of the procedures of Parliament is usefully provided by J. Griffith and M. Ryle, *Parliament* (1989); T. Erskine May, *Parliamentary Practice* (20th ed., 1983). An account of British elections results are collated by D. Butler, D. Kavanagh, *The British General Election of 1979, 1983, 1987, 1992* (published in 1980, 1984, 1988, 1993 and 1997).

The various regulatory agencies such as the National Audit Office, the Audit Commission, and the Office of Fair Trading are useful sources of information on the working of government departments.

The reports of the Parliamentary Commissioner for Administration, the Select Committee on European Community Legislation are also helpful. Students of regulation will find the annual reports of each of the Directors General of telecommunications, gas, water, electricity useful in their role of reviewing the utilities. There is also useful information to be gained from the various annual reports, for example, the Crown Prosecution Service, or the Criminal Injuries Compensation Board. The Judicial Statistics for 1975 onwards are also useful. In administrative law the various reports of the Law Commission, are important such as: "Report on Remedies in Administrative Law", Law Com. No. 73, 1976; "Criminal Law: Offences Relating to Public Order", Law Com. No. 123, 1983; "Administrative Law: Judicial Review and Statutory Appeals", Law Com. No. 126, 1993. There is also the "Justice/All Souls Report, Administrative Justice: Some Necessary Reforms" (1988). Various reports from pressure groups or specialist societies such as the Hansard Society, see their "Report of the Commission on Electoral Reform" (1976), *Making the Law: The Report of the Hansard Society Commission on the Legislative Process* (Chair Lord Rippon) in 1993 and a recent report by the Hansard Society *Report on the Regulated Industries* (1996) are very useful. *The Constitution Unit*, which has undertaken an independent inquiry into the implementation of Constitutional Reform at the Faculty of Laws, University College, London up until June 1997, provides some important research papers and briefing reports on a whole range of public law issues. (E-mail: constitution@ucl.ac.uk). The Institute For Fiscal Studies provides important research on a broad range of fiscal matters including public spending (E-mail: mailbox@ifs.org.uk). The Public Law Project continues to collect data and information on judicial statistics with particular reference to judicial review. The Centre for the Study of Regulated Industries (CRI) established in 1991, is an independent research centre of the Chartered Institute of Public Finance and Accountancy. It provides interdisciplinary research into how companies and regulation are working. The European Commission, 8 Storey's Gate, London, SW1P 3A is also an important source of information. European Union information is now available on the Internet. Access http:// www.cec.org.uk.

Many public law issues involve related specialist subject areas. For example in the case of the environment see: ENDS, Directory of Information on Environmental Information, Finsbury Business Centre, 40 Bowling Green Lane, London EC1R ONE. The National Institute of Economic and Social Research, 2 Dean Trench Street, Smith Square, London SW1P 3HE provides useful analysis on a whole range of public sector economic and European issues. Many newspapers provide information on the Internet. For example *The*

dian operated an election network during May 1997 (see: http://
.ction.guardian.co.uk). There are a number of helpful documents
available from government departments. For example *The Lord Chancellor and His Department* (September, 1995) provides a useful up-date
on how the Lord Chancellor's office fits within the constitutional
framwork of the administration of justice. Also useful is the *Strategic
Plan 1996/97 and 1998/99 A Programme for the Future* (Lord Chancellor's Office, 1996).

Diaries of cabinet ministers, or ex-civil servants may be of historical
and contemporary importance and are also a useful source for
students of the constitution such as: R. Crossman, *The Diaries of a
Cabinet Minister,* Vol. 1 (1975); Vol. 2 (1976) and Vol. 3 (1977); B.
Castle, *The Castle Diaries 1964–70* (1984) and 1974–76 (1989); Nigel
Lawson, *The View from No. 11* (1992); M. Thatcher, *The Downing Street
Years* (1993); Alan Clark, *Diaries* (1993). Geoffrey Howe, *Conflict of
Loyalty* (Macmillan, 1994); Peter Walker, *Staying Power* (Bloomsbury,
1995); Jim Prior, *A Balance of Power* (Hamish Hamilton, 1995), Mar-
garet Thatcher, *The Collected Speeches of Margaret Thatcher* (Harper
Collins, 1997). Biographies of major judges may also illuminate
judicial attitudes and issues of policy, see for example: R.F.V.
Heuston, *The Lives of the Lord Chancellors* (1964), or J.L. Jowell and J.P.
McAuslan (eds.), *Lord Denning: The Judge and the Law* (1984), also
useful are the various writings partly anecdotal and partly biographi-
cal of judges, for example, Lord Hailsham, *Elective Dictatorship* (1976);
On the Constitution (1992). Also useful are the biographies of major
legal figures, for example, Richard Cosgrove, *The Rule of Law: Albert
Venn Dicey, Victorian Jurist* (1985); Cecil Fifoot, *Judge and Jurist in the
Reign of Victoria* (1959) and Cecil Fifoot, *Frederic William Maitland: A
Life* (1971); Roy Jenkins, *Gladstone* (Macmillan, 1995).

The private papers of Prime Ministers, ministers and senior civil
servants provide an important historical source, for example the
Gladstone Papers or the Peel Papers in the British Library. Gladstone,
in particular, is easily accessible in J. Brooke and M. Sorensen, eds.,
*The Prime Minister's Papers: W.E. Gladstone i. Autobiographical, Memo-
randa* (1971). Law journals and the main journals of political science,
legal history, economics and social administration all provide useful
sources of materials. Newspapers and periodicals also provide
sources for the study of the constitution set against the background of
the day to day life of the political parties.

Cases and materials books have rapidly expanded to meet the
growth in legal literature. Useful historical material may be found in
Keir and Lawson, *Cases in Constitutional Law* (5th ed., 1967). A useful
starting point in terms of approach to the study of public law may be
found in G. Wilson, *Cases and Materials on Constitutional and Administrative Law* (2nd ed., 1976). A rich collection of materials has been

collected in C. Turpin, *British Government and the Constitution* (3rd ed., 1995). Also useful sources for materials are provided in P. O'Higgins, *Cases and Materials on Civil Liberties* (1988); S.H. Bailey, D.J. Harris, and B.L. Jones, *Civil Liberties Cases and Materials* (4th ed., 1995); S.H. Bailey, B.L. Jones and A.R. Mowbray, *Cases and Materials on Administrative Law* (2nd ed., 1992); M. Allen, B. Thompson and B. Walsh, *Cases and Materials on Constitutional and Administrative Law* (4th ed., 1996); D. Pollard and D. Hughes, *Constitutional and Administrative Law* (2nd ed., 1996) and K. Ewing and C. Gearty, *Cases and Materials on Civil Liberties* (Oxford University Press, 1994). Selected documents are usefully provided in extracts in R. Brazier, *Constitutional Practice* (1994); R. Brazier, *Constitutional Reform: Re-shaping the British Political System* (Oxford University press, 1991); Andrew Le Sueur and Maurice Sunkin, *Public Law* (Longman, 1997); Helen Fenwick and Gavin Pillipson, *Sourcebook on Public Law* (Cavendish Publishing Ltd, 1997). A general description of the English Legal System is provided in: J.R. Spencer, *Jackson's Machinery of Justice* (1989).

Constitutional and administrative Law Textbooks

There are a number of useful textbooks. Rodney Brazier and Stanley de Smith's, *Constitutional and Administrative Law* (6th ed., 1989); E.C.S. Wade and A.W. Bradley, *Constitutional and Administrative Law* (12th ed. by Bradley and Ewing, 1997); Paul Jackson, O. Hood Phillips', *Constitutional and Administrative Law* (7th ed., 1987); B. Thompson, *Textbook on Constitutional and Administrative Law* (Blackstone, 1993). Introductory textbooks include: G. Ganz, *Understanding Public Law* (1987); Peter Cane, *An Introduction to Administrative Law* (3rd ed., 1996); Ian Loveland, *Constitutional Law A Critical Introduction* (Butterworths, 1996); Wade and Forsyth, *Administrative Law* (7th ed., 1994); de Smith, Woolf and Jowell, *Judicial Review of Administrative Action* (London, Sweet and Maxwell, 1995).

Administrative law is the subject of a number of specialist textbooks such as: P.P. Craig, *Administrative Law* (3rd ed., 1994), D. Foulkes, *Administrative Law* (7th ed., 1991); Beatson and Matthews, *Administrative Law: Cases and Materials* (2nd ed., 1988); H.W.R. Wade, *Administrative Law* (6th ed., 1988); Wade and Forsyth, *Administrative Law* (Oxford, 1994). Some thought provoking essays are contained in: J. Jowell and D. Oliver, *New Directions in Judicial Review* (1988).

Contemporary Constitutional Issues

A wide selection of writers, including lawyers, have focused on contemporary issues. As a background study much is to be gained from: N. Johnson, *In Search of the Constitution* (1977). A more contemporary perspective may be found in: H.W.R. Wade, *Constitutional Fundamentals* (London, 1980); P. Norton, *The Constitution in Flux* (1982); P. McAuslan and J. McEldowney, (eds.) *Law, Legitimacy and the Constitution* (1985); Carlow Harlow (ed.) *Public Law and Politics* (1986); I. Harden and N. Lewis, *The Noble Lie: The British Constitution and the Rule of Law* (1986); R. Holme and M. Elliott, (eds.), *1688–1988: Time for a New Constitution* (1988); Cosmo Graham and Tony Prosser, (eds.), *Waiving the Rules: The Constitution Under Thatcherism* (1988); J. Jowell and D. Oliver (eds.), *The Changing Constitution* (2nd ed., 1989, 3rd ed., 1994); P. Birkinshaw, I.J. Harden and N. Lewis, *Government by Moonlight: The Hybrid Parts of the State* (London, 1990); N. Lewis, (ed.), *Happy and Glorious: The Constitution in Transition* (1990); C. Munro, *Studies in Constitutional Law* (1987); K. Ewing and C. Gearty, *Freedom Under Thatcher* (1990); R. Brazier, *Constitutional Reform: Re-shaping the Britiish Political System* (1991); D. Oliver, *Government in the United Kingdom: The Search for Accountability, Effectiveness and Citizenship* (1991); D. Galligan, *Discretionary Powers: A Legal Study of Official Discretion* (1986); P. Birkinshaw, *Grievances, Remedies and the State* (1985). Also see: D. Woodhouse, *Ministers and Parliament* (Oxford, 1994); M. Loughlin, *Legality and Locality* (Oxford, Clarendon Press, 1996); R. Blackburn, *The Electoral System in Britain* (Macmillan, St Martin's Press, 1995).

Civil Liberties

Some recent textbooks on civil liberties deserve particular mention. D. Feldman, *Civil Liberties and Human Rights in England and Wales* (Oxford, 1993); Richard Stone, *Civil Liberties* (Blackstone, 1993); D.J. Harris, M. O'Boyle and C. Warbrick, *Law of the European Convention on Human Rights* (Butterworths, 1995); K.D. Ewing and C.A. Gearty (eds.), *Human Rights and Labour Law; Essays in Honour of Paul O'Higgins* (Mansell, 1994); Sue Farran, *The U.K. Before the European Court of Human Rights* (Blackstone, 1996); Francesca Klug, Keir Starmr and Stuart Weir, *The Three Pillars of Liberty, Political Rights and Freedoms in the United Kingdom* (Routledge, 1966); C.A. Gearty (ed.) *European Civil Liberties and the European Convention on Human Rights International Studies in Human Rights* (Martinus Nijhoff Publishers, Kluwer, 1997).

Public Law, Ideas and Influences

Current discussion of the future direction and influences in the development of public law scholarship are hotly contested. Some helpful background is provided in J.G.A. Pocock, *Virtue, Commerce and History: Essays on Political Thought and History* (1985), and, Quentin Skinner, *The Foundations of Modern Political Thought* (1978, 2 Vols.).

Constitutional and political theory is examined in N. Lewis, *The Noble Lie: The British Constitution and the Rule of Law* (1986), Cosmo Graham and Tony Prosser (eds.), *Waiving the Rules: The Constitution Under Thatcher* (1988); M. Foley, *The Silence of Constitutions* (1989); P. Craig, *Public Law and Democracy in the United Kingdom and the United States of America* (1990); M. Loughlin, *Public Law and Political Theory* (1992); T.R.S. Allan, *Law, Liberty and Justice* (Oxford, 1993). Reviews of some of the above books have indicated the divergence of views. See: I. Harden, "Review article: The Constitution and Its Discontents" B.J. Political Science 21, 489–510; T. Daintith, "Political Programmes and the Content of the Constitution" in Finnie, Himsworth and Walker (eds.), *Edinburgh Essays in Public Law* (1991), pps. 41–55. Also for an informative discussion of the future of public law see: B. O'Leary, "What should Public Lawyers Do?" (1992) O.J.L.S. Vol. 12, No. 3, 404–418; P.P. Craig, "What Should Public Lawyers Do? A Reply" (1992) O.J.L.S. Vol. 12, No. 4, 564–577. M. Loughlin, "Tinkering with the Constitution" (1988) 51 M.L.R. 531–48 and reply from Harden and Lewis (1988) 51 M.L.R. 812–16. R.C. Van Caenegem, *An Historical Introduction to Western Constitutional Law* (Cambridge University Press, 1995); G.P. Wilson (ed.), *Frontiers of Legal Scholarship* (John Wiley, 1995); Norman Lewis, *Choice and the Legal Order* (Butterworths, 1996); Joseph A. Camilleri and Jim Falk, *The End of Sovereignty?* (Edward Elgar, 1992); David C. Wilson, *A Strategy of Change* (Routledge, 1992); Cass R. Sunstein, *The Partial Constitution* (Harvard University Press, 1994); Christopher Pierson, *The Modern State* (Routledge, 1996); Robert Baldwin; (ed.), *Law and Uncertainty Risks and Legal Processes* (Kluwer, 1997); Chris Willett (ed.), *Public Sector Reform and the Citizen's Charter* (Blackstone Press, 1966).

European Community
The European Community has become an important subject of study for lawyers and the following sources are of particular use: P.J.G. Kapetyn and P. Verloren Van Themaat, *Introduction to the Law of the European Communities* (2nd ed. with Lawrence Gormley, 1989); Josephine Steiner, *Textbook on EEC Law (1988); Francis Snyder, New Directions in European Communities Law* (1990); Nigel Foster, *EEC Legislation* (1990); Stephen Weatherill and Paul Beaumont, *EC Law* (Penguin, 1993); Evelyn Ellis and Takis Tridimas, *Public Law of the European Community; Text and Materials* (Sweet and Maxwell, 1995); Brian Bercusson, *European Labour Law* (Butterworths, 1996); Eugene D. Cross, *Electric Utility Regulation in the European Union,* (John Wiley, 1966); Ian Ward, *A Critical Introduction to European Law* (Butterworths, 1996); Michael Gallagher and Pier Vincenzo Uleri, *The Referendum Experience in Europe* (Macmillan, 1996); Justin Greenwood, *Representing Interests in the European Union* (Macmillan, 1997); John

Arrowsmith and Christopher Taylor, *Unresolved Issues on the Way to a Single Currency* Occasional Papers 49, (Copyright National Institute of Economic and Social Research, 1996). I am grateful to Duncan Matthews, Jean Monet lecturer at the University of Warwick for this information.

Specialist Studies

The growth in specialisms within public law demonstrates the vitality of the subject and its breadth. Here it is only possible to mention some of the more readily available sources which students may need to consult on some areas of public law.

On constitutional history see: D.L. Keir, *The Constitutional History of Modern Britain 1485–1937* (1938); H. Arthurs, *"Without the Law", Administrative Justice and Legal Pluralism in Nineteenth-century England* (1985); J.Ll.J. Edwards, *The Law Officers of the Crown: A Study of the Offices of Attorney-General and Solicitor General of England with an Account of the Office of the Director of Public Prosecutions of England* (1964); A.V. Dicey, *Lectures on the Relation Between Law and Public Opinion in England During the Nineteenth Century* (2nd ed., 1914), and *Introduction to the Study of the Law of the Constitution* (10th ed., 1965); Sir Ivor Jennings, *The Law and the Constitution* (5th ed., 1959); John P. Dawson, *A History of Lay Judges* (1960); R.F.V. Heuston, *Essays in Constitutional Law* (2nd ed., 1964); R.C. Van Caenegem, *An Historical Introduction to Western Constitutional Law* (Cambridge University Press, 1995); W. Lobban, *The Common Law and English Jurisprudence 1760–1850* (Clarendon Press, Oxford, 1991); Eric J. Evans, *The Forging of the Modern State 1783–1870* (Longman, 2nd ed., 1996); G.R. Rubin, *Private Property, Government Requisition and the Constitution 1914–1927* (Hambledon Press, 1994); Colm Campbell, *Emergency Law in Ireland 1918–1925* (Clarendon Press, Oxford, 1994); Michael Lobban, "Was there a nineteenth century English School of Jurisprudence"? *Journal of Legal History* (1995) Vol. 16, No. 1 34–62.

On contemporary politics and administration see: P. Self, *Political Theories of Modern Government* (1985); John Greenwood and David Wilson, *Public Administration in Britain Today* (2nd ed., 1989); P. Hennessy, *Whitehall* (1989); Vernon Bogdanor, *Multi-Party Politics and the Constitution* (1983); Douglas Wass, *Government and the Governed* (1984); Max Beloff and Gillian Peele, *The Government of the United Kingdom* (1980); B. Jones, *et al, Politics UK* (1991); Les Metcalfe and Sue Richards, *Improving Public Management* (2nd ed., 1990); Wyn Grant, *Pressure Groups, Politics and Democracy in Britain* (1989); R. Blackburn, ed., *Constitutional Studies* (1992); J. Freedman and M. Power, *Law and Accountancy* (1992); R. Blackburn, ed., *Citizenship and the Law* (1993).

On planning law, see: M. Grant, *Urban Planning Law* (1986 with supplement); *The Encyclopedia of Planning Law and Practice in Progress;*

P. McAuslan, *Land Law and Planning* (1975); and *The Ideologies of Planning Law* (1980).

On housing and environmental law, see: R. Burridge and D. Ormandy, (eds.), *Unhealthy Housing Research, Remedies and Reforms* (1993); D. Hughes, *Environmental Law* (2nd ed., 1992); Ann Stewart, *Rethinking Housing Law* (Sweet and Maxwell, 1996); John F. McEldowney and Sharron McEldowney, *Environment and the Law* (Longman, 1996); Simon Ball and Stuart Bell, *Environmental Law (2nd ed., 1993); David Hughes, Environmental Law* (Butterworths, 2nd ed., 1992); Owen Lomas and John McEldowney (eds.) *Frontiers of Environmental Law* (Chancery Law Publishing, 1991); Churchill, Gibson and Warren, *Law, Policy and the Environment* (Journal of Law and Society, 1991); Jane Holder, Pauline Lane, Sally Eden, *et al.* (eds.), *Perspectives on the Environment* (Avebury, 1993); Rosalind Malcolm, *A Guidebook to the Environmental Law* (Sweet and Maxwell, 1994); Martin Polden and Simon Jackson, *The Environment and the Law* (Longman, 1994); William Birtles and Richard Stein, *Planning and Environmental Law;* (Longman, 1994); Colin Reid, *Nature Conservation Law* (Sweet and Maxwell, 1994). International environmental law is examined in Birnie and Boyle, *International Law and the Environment* (Oxford, 1992) and on European Community Law see: A. Kiss and D. Shelton, *Manual of European Environmental Law* (Cambridge, Grotius Publishers, 1993); Sue Elworthy and Jane Holder, *Environmental Protection Text and Materials* (Butterworths, 1997).

On local government see: M. Loughlin, *Local Government in the Modern State* (1986); Tony Byrne, *Local Government in Britain* (6th ed., 1994); Charles Cross and Stephen Bailey, *Cross on Local Government Law* (7th ed., 1986); Reginald Jones, *Local Government Audit Law* (2nd ed. with supplement, 1992); M. Loughlin, *Legality and Locality* (Oxford, Clarendon Press, 1996).

On tribunals and inquiries see: the loose-leaf service provided in *Tribunals Practice and Procedure* (ed. Bowers) 1986—in progress; R.E. Wraith and P.G. Hutchesson, *Administrative Tribunals* (1973).

On Northern Ireland see: H. Calvert, *Constitutional Law in Northern Ireland: A Study in Regional Government* (1986); Kevin Boyle, Tom Hadden and Paddy Hillyard, *Law and State: The Case of Northern Ireland* (1975); Kevin Boyle and Tom Hadden, *Ireland: A Positive Proposal* (1985); B. Hadfield, *The Constitution of Northern Ireland* (1985); C. Townshend, *Political Violence in Ireland* (1985); J. Darby, *Conflict in Northern Ireland: The Development of a Polarised Community* (1976); C. Palley, *The Evolution, Disintegration and Possible Reconstruction of the Northern Ireland Constitution* (1972); G. Hogan and Walker, *Political Violence and the Law in Ireland* (1989); Colm Campbell, *Emergency Powers in Ireland 1918–1925* (Oxford Clarendon Press, 1994); John Morison and Stephen Livingstone, *Reshaping Public Power; Northern*

Ireland and the British Constitutional Crisis (Sweet and Maxwell, 1995); S.C. Greer, *Supergrasses: Anti-terrorist Law Enforcement in Northern Ireland* (1994); K. Boyle and T. Hadden, *Northern Ireland: The Choice* (1994) and *Frameworks for the Future* (1995).

On the European Convention on Human Rights see: Andrew Z. Drezemczewski, *European Human Rights Convention in Domestic Law: A Comparative Study* (1983); J.E.S. Fawcett, *The Application of the European Convention on Human Rights* (1987).

On emergency powers see: D. Bonner, *Emergency Powers in Peacetime* (1984); Earl Jellicoe, *Review of the Operation of the Prevention of Terrorism (Temporary Provisions) Act 1976;* (Cmnd. 8803) H.M.S.O., 1983. J.B. Bell, *A Time of Terror: How Democratic Societies Respond to Revolutionary Violence* (1978).

On freedom of speech, see: E. Barendt, *Freedom of Speech* (1985); G. Robertson, *Freedom, the Individual and the Law* (6th ed., 1989).

On policing see: R. Reiner, *The Politics of the Police* (1992) and L. Lustgarten, *The Governance of the Police* (1986); S. McCabe and P. Wallington, *The Police, Public Order, and Civil Liberties: Legacies of the Miners' Strike* (1988).

On police and the prosecution system see: M. McConville, A. Sanders and Roger Leng, *The Case for the Prosecution* (1991); D. Hay and F. Snyder, (eds.), *Policing and Prosecution in Britain 1750–1850* (1989).

On anti–discrimination laws see: D. Pannick, *Sex Discrimination Law* (Oxford, 1985); L. Lustgarten, *Legal Control of Racial Discrimination* (1980).

On regulation and public law see: R. Baldwin and C. McCrudden, *Regulation and Public Law* (1987) and on privatisation see: Kay, Mayer and Thompson, *Privatisation and Regulation—the UK Experience* (1986); M. Bishop, John Kay and Colin Mayer (eds.) *Privatization and Economic Performance* (Oxford University Press, 1994); M. Bishop, John Kay and Colin Mayer (eds.) *The Regulatory Challenge* (Oxford University Press, 1995); A. Barker, (ed.), *Quangos in Britain* (1982).

On specialisms within privatisation there is a vast literature, for example, see: the select bibliography in J. McEldowney, *The Electricity Industry Handbook: A Guide to Law Practice and Procedure* (John Wiley, Chancery, 1992), also see Cento Veljanovski, *Privatisation and Competition* (1989).

On public expenditure and its control see: A. Likierman, *Public Expenditure* (1988); H. Heclo and A. Wildavsky, *The Private Government of Public Money* (1981); A. Robinson, *Parliament and Public Spending* (1978); Colin Thain and Maurice Wright, *The Treasury and Whitehall* (Clardendon Press, 1995).

Select Bibliography

ACKERMAN, B., *Social Justice in the Liberal State* (Yale University Press, New Haven, 1980).

ALDER, J., *Constitutional and Administrative Law* (Butterworths, 1994).

ALLAN, T.R.S., "Legislative Supremacy and the Rule of Law: Democracy and Constitutionalism" (1985) 44 Camb. L.J. 111.

— "Dicey and Dworkin: the Rule of Law as Integrity" (1988) 8 O.J.L.S. 266.

— "Pragmatism and Theory in Public Law" (1988) 104 L.Q.R. 422.

— "Constitutional Rights and Common Law" (1991) 11 O.J.L.S. 453.

— *Law, Liberty and Justice* (Oxford, 1993).

— "Equality and Moral independence: public law and private morality" in I. Loveland (ed.), *A Special Relationship* (Clarendon Press, Oxford, 1995).

ALLEN, C.K., *Law in the Making* (London, 1927).

— *Democracy and the Individual* (London, 1943).

— "Administrative Jurisdiction" [1956] P.L. 13.

ALLEN, M., THOMPSON, B. AND WALSH, B., *Cases and Materials on Constitutional and Administrative Law* (4th ed., 1996).

AMERY, L.S., *Thoughts on the Constitution* (Oxford University Press, 1947) (2nd ed., 1953).

ANDREWS, J.A., (ed.), *Welsh Studies in Public Law* (1970).

ANSON, W.R., *The Law and Custom of the Constitution* (Oxford, 1886; 4th ed., 1909).

ARMSTRONG, W., (ed.), *Budgetary Reform in the United Kingdom* (1980).

ARNDT, H.W., "The Origins of Dicey's Concept of the Rule of Law" (1957) 31 Australian Law Journal 117.

ARTHURS, H., *"Without the Law": Administrative Justice and Legal Pluralism in Nineteenth Century England* (Toronto, 1985).

ATIYAH, P.S., *The Rise and Fall of Freedom of Contract* (Oxford, 1979).

— *From Principles of Pragmatism: Changes in the Function of the Judicial Process and the Law* (Oxford, 1978).

AUSTIN, J., *The Province of Jurisprudence Determined* (1832) (H.L.A. Hart (ed.), London, 1954).

AUSTIN, Rodney, "Freedom of Information: The Legal Impact" in J. Jowell and D. Oliver, *The Changing Constitution* (2nd ed., 1989, Oxford, Clarendon Press) pp. 409–50 (3rd ed., 1994).

BAGEHOT, W., *The English Constitution* (Introduction R.H.S. Crossman) (1963).

BAILEY, S.H., HARRIS, D.J., and JONES, B.L., *Civil Liberties Cases and Materials* (1991) (4th ed., 1996).

BAILEY, S.H., JONES, B.L., and MOWBRAY, A.R., *Cases and Materials on Administrative Law* (2nd ed., London, 1992).

BALDWIN, R., "The Next Steps: Ministerial Responsibility and Government by Agency" (1988) 51 M.L.R. 622.

BALDWIN, R., and HAWKINS, K., "Discretionary Justice: Davis Reconsidered" [1985] P.L. 570.

BALDWIN, R., and McCRUDDEN, C., *Regulation and Public Law* (London, Weidenfeld and Nicholson, 1987).

BARBERIS, P. (ed.), *The Civil Service in an Era of Change* (Dartmouth, 1997).

BARENDT, E., *Freedom of Speech* (Oxford, 1985).

BARKER, A., (ed.), *Quangos in Britain* (1982).

BARKER, E., *Political Thought in England 1848–1914* (London, 1915).

BARNETT, J., *Inside the Treasury* (1982).

BARRON, A., and SCOTT, C., "The Citizen's Charter Programme" [1992] 55 M.L.R. 526.

BATES T. St.J.N., *Devolution to Scotland: The Legal Aspects* (Edinburgh, 1997).

BATES, T., St.J.N., *et alia*, (ed.), *In Memoriam J.D.B. Mitchell* (London, 1983).

BEATSON J., and MATTHEWS, *Administrative Law: Cases and Materials* (2nd ed., 1988).

BEESLEY, M., *Liberalisation of the Use of British Telecommunication's Network* (London, 1981).

BEER, S., *Modern British Politics* (3rd ed., 1982).

BEER, S.H., *Treasury Control* (2nd ed., 1957).

BELL, J., *Policy Arguments in Judicial Decisions* (Oxford University Press, 1983).

BELL, J., and BRADLEY, A.W., (eds.), *Government Liability: A Comparative Study* (1991).

BELL, J.B., *A Time of Terror: How Democratic Societies Respond to Revolutionary Violence* (1978).

BELL, K., *Research Study on Supplemetary Benefit Appeal Tribunals* (London, HMSO, 1975).

BENNION, F., *Statutory Interpretation* (2nd ed., 1992).

BENTHAM, J., *The Works of Jeremy Bentham* (J.L. Bowring (ed.), 1843), Vol. III, *A Fragment on Government and An Introduction to the Principles of Morals and Legislation* (W. Harrison (ed.)) (Oxford, 1948).

BEW, P., *Conflict and Conciliation in Ireland 1890–1910* (Oxford, 1982)

BEW, P., and PATERSON, M., *The British State and the Ulster Crisis* (1985).

BIRCH, A.H., *Representative and Responsible Government* (1964).

— "The Theory and Practice of Modern British Democracy" in J. Jowell and D. Oliver (eds.), *The Changing Constitution* (1989), pp. 87–111.

BIRKINSHAW, P., *Freedom of Information: The Law, the Practice and the Ideal* (London, 1988) (2nd ed., 1996).

— *Reforming the Secret State* (Open University, 1990).

— *Government and Information* (Butterworths, 1990).

BIRKINSHAW, P., HARDEN, I., and LEWIS, N., *Government by Moonlight: The Hybrid Parts of the State* (London, 1990).

BIRKS, P., *An Introduction to the Law of Restitution* (Oxford, 1985).

BISHOP, M., and KAY, J., *Does Privatisation Work?* (London, 1988).

BISHOP, M., KAY, J., and MAYER C., (eds.), *The Regulatory Challenge* (Oxford University Press, 1995).

— *Privatization and Economic Performance* (Oxford University Press, 1994).

BLACKBURN, R., (ed.), *Rights of Citizenship* (Mansell, 1993).

— *Constitutional Studies* (Mansell, 1992).

BLACKBURN, R., *The Meeting of Parliament* (1990).

— "Parliamentary Opinion on a new Bill of Rights" (1989) 60 Political Quarterly 469–80.

— *The Electoral System in Britain* (Macmillan, 1995).

BLACKSTONE, W., *Commentaries on the Laws of England* (1765–9) (London, 15th ed., 1809), 4 Vols.

BLOM-COOPER, L., "The New Face of judicial review: Administrative changes in Order 53" [1982] P.L. 250.

BLOM-COOPER, L., and DREWRY, G., *Final Appeal: A Study of the House of Lords in its Judicial Capacity* (Oxford University Press, 1972).

BLOW, L., HALL, J., and SMITH, S., "Financing Regional Government in the UK: Some Issues" (1996) Fiscal Studies, Vol. 17, No. 4, pp. 99–120.

BOGDANOR, V., *Devolution* (Oxford University Press, 1979).

— *The People and the Party System. The Referendum and Electoral Reform in British Politics* (Cambridge, 1981).

— *Multi-Party Politics and the Constitution* (1983).

— "Constitutional Law and Politics" (1987) 7 O.J.L.S. 454.

— *The Monarchy and the Constitution* (Clarendon Press, Oxford, 1995).

BONNER, D., *Emergency Powers in Peacetime* (London, 1985).

BORRIE, SIR GORDON, "Merger Policy: Current Policy Concerns", in J.A. Fairburn and J. Kay (eds.), *Mergers and Merger Policy* (Oxford, 1989).

BOYLE, K., and HADDEN, T., and HILLYARD P., *Law and State: The Case of Northern Ireland* (1975).

BOYLE, K., and HADDEN, T., *Ireland: A Positive Proposal* (1985).

BRADLEY, A.W., "Applications for Judicial Review—the Scottish Model" [1987] P.L. 313.

BRADLEY, A.W., "The Sovereignty of Parliament—In Perpetuity?", in J. Jowell and D. Oliver, *The Changing Constitution*, (2nd ed., Oxford, 1989), pp. 25–52 (3rd ed., 1994).

—   "Justice, Good Government and Public Interest Immunity" [1992] P.L. 514.

BRAZIER, R., *Constitutional Practice* (Oxford, 1988).

—   *Constitutional Texts* (Oxford Clarendon Press, 1990).

—   *Constitutional Reform: Re-shaping the British Political System* (1991).

BRIDGES, L., MESZAROS, G, & SUNKIN M., *Judicial Review in Perspective* (2nd ed., 1995).

BROOKE, J. and SORENSEN, M., (eds.), *The Prime Minister's Papers: W.E. Gladstone, i. Autobiographical Memoranda* (1971).

BROWNING, P., *The Treasury and Economic Policy 1964–1985* (Longmans, 1986).

BUCKLAND, P., *The Factory of Grievances* (1979).

—   *A History of Northern Ireland* (New York, 1981).

BUCKLAND, R., and DAVIS, R. (1984), "Privatisation Techniques and the PSBR", *Fiscal Studies*, 5:47–60.

BUSCHOR, E., and SCHEDLER, K., (eds.), *Perspectives on performance measurement and public sector accounting* (Berne Haupt, 1994).

BUTLER, D., *Governing Without a Majority: Dilemmas for Hung Parliaments in Britain* (1983).

BUTLER, R., "The Evolution of the Civil Service—A Progress Report" (1993) 71 Public Administration 395–406.

BYRNE, Tony, *Local Government in Britain* (6th ed., Penguin, 1994).

CABINET OFFICE, *Public Bodies* (London, HMSO, annual publication, 1997).

—   *The Civil Service Yearbook 1997*, Stationery Office, London.

CLAVERT, H., *Constitutional Law in Northern Ireland* (Belfast, 1968).

—   (ed.), Devolution (1975).

CAMPION, *An Introduction to the Procedure of the House of Commons* (1958).

CANE, P., *An Introduction to Administrative Law* (3rd ed., 1996).

CARD, R., *Public Order: The New Law* (1989).

CARR, C.T., *Delegated Legislation. Three Lectures* (Cambridge, 1921).

CARRINGTON, P., *Reflect on Things Past* (1985).

CASTLE, B., *The Castle Diaries 1964–70* (1984) *and 1974–76* (1989).

CHANDLER, J.A., "The Plurality Vote: A Reappraisal" (1982) 30 Political Studies 87–91.

CHENNELLS, L., *Labour's Windfall Levy*, Institute of Fiscal Studies (1997).

CHESTER, D.N., *The Nationalization of British Industry 1945–51* (1975).

CHRIMES, S.B., *English Constitutional Ideas in the 15th Century* (1966).

CHUBB, B., *The Control of Public Expenditure* (1952).

CLARK, A., *Diaries* (1993).

COCKS, R.C.J., *Sir Henry Maine: A Study in Victorian Jurisprudence* (Cambridge, 1988).

CONSTITUTIONAL REFORM CENTRE, *Company Donations to Political Parties: A Suggested Code of Practice* (1985).

CORNISH, W.R., and CLARKE, de N., *Law and Society in England and Wales 1750–1950* (London, 1989).

COSGROVE, R., *The Rule of Law: Albert Venn Dicey Victorian Jurist* (1985).

CRAIG, P.P., *Administrative Law* (London, 3rd ed., 1995).

— *Public Law and Democracy in the United Kingdom and the United States of America* (Oxford, 1990).

— "The Monopolies and Mergers Commission: Competition and Administrative Rationality", in Baldwin and McCrudden, *Regulation and Public Law* (1987).

CRAIG, P.P. & De BURCA, G., *EC LAW: Text, Cases and Materials* (1995).

CRICK, B., "The Sovereignty of Parliament and the Irish Question" in D. Rea (ed.), *Political Co-operation in Divided Societies* (London, 1983), 229.

CRICK, B., *The Reform of Parliament* (Revised 2nd ed., Weidenfeld and Nicholson, 1964).

CROSSMAN, R.H.S., *Inside View* (1972).

— *Diaries of a Cabinet Minister,* Vol. 2 (London, 1976).

CULLEN, M., *The Statistical Movement in Early Victorian Britain* (Hassocks, 1975).

DAHRENDORF, R., "Citizenship and the Modern Social Conflict" in R. Holme and M. Elliott (eds.), *1688–1988: Time for a New Constitution* (London, 1988), chap. 7.

DAINTITH, T., "Public Law and Economic Policy" [1974] J.B.L. 9.

— "The Functions of Law in the Field of Short-term Economic Policy" (1976) 92 L.Q.R. 62.

— "Regulation by Contract: The New Prerogative", in Lord Lloyd, R. Rideout, and S. Guest (eds.), *Current Legal Problems 1979* (London, 1979).

— (ed.), *Law as an Instrument of Economic Policy: Comparative and Critical Approaches* (Berlin, 1988).

— "Political Programmes and the Content of the Constitution" in W. Finnie, C., Himsworth, and N. Walker (eds.), *Edinburgh Essays in Public Law* (Edinburgh, 1991).

— "Between Domestic Democracy and an Alien Rule of Law? Some Thoughts on the Independence of the Bank of England" [1995] Public Law 118.

de SMITH, S.A., *The Lawyers and the Constitution* (Inaugural Lecture, London School of Economics, May 10, 1960).

— *Constitutional and Administrative Law* (Harmondsworth, 1971; 7th ed., 1994 by R. Brazier).

— "The Boundaries between Parliament and the Courts" (1955) 18 M.L.R. 281.

DARBY, J., *Conflict in Northern Ireland: The Development of a Polarised Community* (1976).

DAVIS, K.C., *Discretionary Justice* (1969).

DENNING, A., *Freedom Under Law* (London, 1949).

Department of the Environment, "Consultation Paper: A New Tax for Local Government" (London, 1991).

— "Consultation Paper: The Structure of Local Government" (London, 1991).

— "Consultation Paper: The Internal Management of Local Authorities in England" (London, 1991).

DEVLIN, P., "The Common Law, Public Policy and the Executive" (1956) Current Legal Problems 1.

DICEY, A.V., *Introduction to the Study of the Law of the Constitution* (London, 1885; 8th ed., 1915; 10th ed., 1959 with intro. by E.C.S. Wade).

— "Droit Administratif in Modern French Law" (1901) 17 L.Q.R. 302.

— *Lectures on the Relation between Law and Public Opinion in England During the Nineteenth Century* (London, 1905).

— "The Development of Administrative Law in England" (1915) 31 L.Q.R. 148.

DIPLOCK, Lord, "Administrative Law: Judicial Review Reviewed" (1975) Cambridge Law Journal 233.

DONALDSON, P., and FARQUHAR, J., *Understanding the British Economy* (1988).

DONOHGUE, B., *The Prime Minister: The Conduct of Policy under Harold Wilson and James Callaghan* (London, Cape, 1987).

DREWRY, G., *The New Select Committees* (Oxford, 1985) (2nd ed., 1989).

DREWRY, G., "Forward from FMI: The Next Steps" [1988] P.L. 505.

DREWRY, G., and BUTCHER, T., *The Civil Service Today* (Oxford, Blackwells, 1988).

DRZEMCZEWSKI, A., *European Human Rights Convention in Domestic Law* (1983).

DWORKIN, R., *Taking Rights Seriously* (Cambridge, Mass., 1977).

— *A Matter of Principle* (Cambridge, Mass., and London, 1985).

— *Law's Empire* (London, 1986).

— *A Bill of Rights for Britain* (London, 1990).

EDWARDS, J.Ll.J., *The Attorney-General, Politics and the Public Interest* (1984).

EFFICIENCY UNIT, *Improving Management in Government: The Next Steps* (London, 1988).

— *Making the Most of Next Steps: The Management of Ministers' Departments and their Executive Agencies* (London, 1991).

EMSLEY, C., and WEINBERGER, B., (eds.), *Policing Western Europe, Politics, Professionalism and Public Order, 1850–1940* (Greenwood Press, 1991).

ERSKINE MAY, *Parliamentary Practice* (ed. Sir C. Gordon, 21st ed., 1989).

EWING, K., *The Funding of Political Parties* (Cambridge, 1987).
— *A Bill of Rights for Britain?* (London, Institute of Employment Rights, 1990).

EWING, K., and GEARTY, C.A., *Democracy or a Bill of Rights* (London, Society of Labour Lawyers, 1991).

FARRAN, Sue, *The UK Before the European Court of Human Rights* (Blackstone, 1996).

FAUNDEZ, J., (ed.), *Good Government and Law* (Macmillan in conjunction with the British Council, 1997).

FELDMAN, D., *Civil Liberties and Human Rights* (Oxford, 1993).

FIFOOT, C., *Judge and Jurist in the Reign of Victoria* (1959).
— *Frederic William Maitland: A Life* (1971).

FINER, S.E., "The Individual Responsibility of Ministers" (1956) 34 Public Administration 377.

FLYNN, N., *Public Sector Management* (Prentice Hall, 3rd ed., 1997), pp. 117–19.

FOLEY, M., *The Silence of Constitutions* (1989).

FORSYTH, C.F., "Beyond *O'Reilly v. Mackman*: the Foundations and Nature of Procedural Exclusivity" (1985) 44 Camb. L.J. 415. "The Provenance and Protection of Legitimate Expectations", (1988) 47 Camb. L.J. 238.

FOSTER, C., *Privatisation, Public Ownership and the Regulation of Natural Monopoly* (Oxford, Blackwell, 1992).

FOSTER, N., *EEC Legislation* (Blackstone Press, 1990).

FOULKES, D., *Administrative Law* (7th ed., 1991).

GALLAGHER, M., and VINCENZO ULERI, P., *The Referendum Experience in Europe* (Macmillan, 1996).

GALLIGAN, D.J., *Discretionary Powers* (Clarendon Press, Oxford, 1986).
— "Judicial Review and the Textbook Writers" (1982) 2 O.J.L.S. 257.

GANZ, G., *Administrative Procedures* (London, 1974).
— *Quasi-Legislation* (London, 1987).
— *Understanding Public Law* (London, 1987) (2nd ed., 1995).

GARNER, J.F., *Garner's Administrative Law* (ed. B.L. Jones) (7th ed., 1991).

GEARTY, C., *Terror* (1991).

GLYNN, John, J., *Public Sector Financial Control and Accounting* (Blackwell, 1987).

GORDLEY, G., *The Philosophical Origins of Modern Contract Doctrine* (Oxford, 1991).

GRAHAM, C., and PROSSER, T., "Privatising Nationalised Industries: Constitutional Issues and New Legal Techniques", (1987) 50 M.L.R. 16–51.

— (eds.), *Waiving the Rules: The Constitution under Thatcherism* (1988).

— *Privatising Public Enterprises: Consistutions, the State and Regulation in Comparative Persepective* (Oxford, 1991).

GRANT, M., *Urban Planning Law* (London, 1986).

— *Rate Capping and the Law* (2nd ed. 1986).

GRANT, Wyn, *Pressure Groups Politics and Democracy in Britain* (1989).

GREEN, T.H., "Liberal legislation and freedom of contract" (1880) in Works, Vol. 3, p. 365.

— *Lectures on the Principles of Political Obligation* (London, 1907).

GREENWOOD, J., and WILSON, D., *Public Administration in Britain Today* (2nd ed., 1989).

GRIFFITH, J.A.G., *Central Departments and Local Authorities* (London, 1966).

— *Parliamentary Scrutiny of Government Bills* (London, 1974).

— *The Politics of the Judiciary* (London: 4th ed., 1991).

— "Administrative discretion and the courts—the better part of valour?" (1955) 18 M.L.R. 159.

— "Judges in Politics: England" (1968) 3 Govt. and Oppos. 485.

— "Whose Bill of Rights?" New Statesman November 14, 1975.

— "Standing Committees in the House of Commons" in S.A. Walkland and M. Ryle (eds.), *The Commons in the Seventies* (London, 1977).

— "The Political Constitution" (1979) 42 M.L.R. 1.

— *Administrative Law and the Judges* D.N. Pritt Memorial Lecture (London, 1978).

— "Justice and Administrative Law Revisited" in J.A.G. Griffith (ed.), *From Policy to Administration: Essays in Honour of William A. Robson* (London, 1976).

— "Constitutional and Administrative Law" in P. Archer and A. Martin (eds.), *More Law Reform Now* (Chichester, 1983).

— "Judicial Decision-Making in Public Law" [1985] P.L. 564.

— (ed.), *From Policy to Administration: Essays in Honour of William A. Robson* (London, 1976).

GRIFFITH, J.A.G., and RYLE, M., *Parliament* (1989).

HADFIELD, B., *The Constitution of Northern Ireland* (1989).

HADFIELD, B., (ed.), *Northern Ireland: Politics and the Constitution* (1992).

H.M. Government, *Civil Service Management Reform: The Next Steps. The Government Reply to the Eight Report*, Cm. 542 (1988).

HAILSHAM, *The Dilemma of Democracy* (London, 1977).

— "Elective Dictatorship" (The Richard Dimbleby Lecture, 1976), *The Listener*, October 21, 1976, p. 496.

— On the Constitution (1992).

HALEVY, E., *A History of the English People in the Nineteenth Century* (London, 1961).

HALLAM, H., *Middle Ages* (London, 12th ed., 1818), Vol. 2.

HAMSON, C.J., *Executive Discretion and Judicial Control* (London, 1954).

HANCHER, L., and MORAN, M. (eds.), *Capitalism, Culture and Economic Regulation* (Oxford, 1989).

HANSARD SOCIETY, *Report of the Commission on Electoral Reform* (London, Hansard Society, 1976).

— *Politics and Industry—The Great Mismatch* (London, 1979).

— *Paying for Politics: Report of the Hansard Society Commission upon the Financing of Political Parties* (1981).

HANSON, A.H., and WALLES, M., *Governing Britain* (4th ed., 1984).

HARDEN, I., "Corporatism without Labour: The British Version", in C. Graham and T. Prosser (eds.), *Waving the Rules: The Constitution under Thatcherism* (Milton Keynes, (1988)).

HARDEN, I. and LEWIS, N., *The Noble Lie: The British Constitution and the Rule of Law* (London, 1986).

HARDING, A.J., *Public Duties and Public Law* (Oxford, 1989).

HARLOW, C.R. and RAWLINGS, R.W., *Law and Administration* (London, 1984).

HARLOW, C., (ed.), *Public Law and Politics* (1986).

HARLOW, C., and RAWLINGS, R., *Pressure Through Law* (London, 1992).

HARRISON, A.J., *The Control of Public Expenditure, 1979–1989* (1989).

HART, H.L.A., *The Concept of Law* (Oxford, 1961).

— "Definition and Theory in Jurisprudence" (1954) 70 L.Q.R. 37.

— "Positivism and the Separation of Law and Morals" (1958) 71 Harv.L.Rev. 593.

HAY, D., and SNYDER, F., (eds.), *Policing and Prosecution in Britain 1750–1850* (Oxford University Press, 1989).

HAYEK, F.A., *The Road to Serfdom* (London, 1944).

— *The Political Ideal of the Rule of Law* (Cairo, 1955).

— *The Constitution of Liberty* (Chicago, 1960).

— *Studies in Philosophy, Politics and Economics* (London, 1967).

— *Law, Legislation and Liberty*; Vol. 1: *Rules and Order* (London, 1973); Vol. 2: *The Mirage of Social Justice* (London,

1976); Vol. 3: *The Political Order of a Free People* (London, 1979).

— Knowledge, Evolution and Society (London, 1984).

HEALD, D., *Public Expenditure: Its Defence and Reform* (Oxford, 1983).

— , and STEEL, D., "Privatizing Public Enterprises: An Analysis of the Government's Case", (1982) Political Quarterly, 53:333–49.

HECLO, H., and WILDAVSKY, A., *The Private Government of Public Money* (1981).

HELM, D., 'A Regulatory Rule: RPI Minus X', in C. Whitehead (ed.), *Reshaping the Nationalised Industries* (Oxford, 1988).

— (ed.), *The Economic Borders of the State* (Oxford, Clarendon Press, 1990).

HENLEY, D., et al., *Public Sector Accounting and Financial Control* (1984).

HENDERSON, R., *European Finance* (1993).

HENNESSY, P., *Cabinet* (1986).

— *Whitehall* (London, 1989, revised edition, 1990).

— *The Hidden Wiring* (London, 1995).

HESELTINE, M., *Where There's a Will* (London, 1987).

HEUSTON, R.F.V., *Essays in Constitutional Law* (London, 1964).

— *Lives of the Lord Chancellors* (1989).

HEWART, G., *The New Despotism* (London, 1929).

HOGG, P.W., *Constitutional Law of Canada* (2nd ed., 1985) (3rd ed., 1992).

HOGAN, G., and WALKER, C., *Political Violence and the Law in Ireland* (1989).

HOLDSWORTH, W.S., *History of English Law* (A.C. Goodhart and H.S. Hanbury (eds.)) (London, 1956), Vol. 5.

— "The conventions of the Eighteenth Century Constitution" (1932) 17 Iowa Law Review 161.

HOLLIS, P., *Pressure from Without* (1975).

HOLMES, O.W., *The Common Law* (Boston, 1881).

HOLME, R., and ELLIOTT, M. (eds.), *1688–1988: Time for a New Constitution* (1988).

HOOD PHILLIPS, O. and JACKSON, P., *Constitutional and Administrative Law* (7th ed., 1989).

HOPPEN, T., *Ireland Since 1800* (Longmans, 1992).

HORWITZ, M.J., *The Transformation of American Law 1780–1860* (Harvard, 1977) *and 1870–1960* (Oxford University Press, 1992).

HOWE, G. (1981), Privatization, Conservative Central Office Press Release 533/81 (London).

INSTITUTE FOR PUBLIC POLICY RESEARCH, *A British Bill of Rights* (London, 1990).

— *The Constitution of the United Kingdom* (London, 1991).

JACKSON, R.M., *The Machinery of Justice in England* (Cambridge, 8th ed., E.J.R. Spencer 1990).
JACONELLI, J., *Enacting a Bill of Rights, the Legal Problems* (1980).
JAFFE, L., and HENDERSON, E.G., "Judicial review and the Rule of Law: Historical Origins" (1956) 72 L.Q.R. 393.
JENNINGS, W.I., *The Law and the Constitution* (London, 1933).
— *Parliament* (2nd ed., 1957).
— *Cabinet Government* (3rd ed., 1959).
— "The Report on Ministers' Powers" (1932) 10 Public Admin. 333.
— "In praise of Dicey 1885–1935" (1935) 13 Public Admin. 123.
JOHNSON, N., *In Search of the Constitution* (London, 1977).
— "Constitutional Reform: Some Dilemmas for a Conservative Philosophy" in Z. Layton-Henry (ed.), *Conservative Party Politics* (London, 1980).
JONES, H., *The Principles of Citizenship* (London, 1919).
JONES, REGINALD, *Local Government Audit Law* (HMSO, 2nd ed., 1985 with supplement, 1992).
JONES, T., *Whitehall Diary*, Vol. 3, (edited R.K. Middlemas) (1971).
JOSEPH, K., *Freedom Under Law* (London, 1975).
JOWELL, J., and McAUSLAN, J.P., *Lord Denning: The Judge and the Law* (London, Sweet and Maxwell, 1984).
— and LESTER, A., "Beyond Wednesbury: Substantive Principles of Administrative Law" [1987] P.L. 368.
— "Proportionality: Neither Novel Nor Dangerous" in J. Jowell and D. Oliver (eds.), *New Directions in Judicial Review* (London, 1988).
— "Courts and Administration in Britain: Standards, Principles and Rights" (1988) Israel L.R. 409.
— "The Rule of Law Today" in J. Jowell and D. Oliver (eds.), *The Changing Constitution* (1989).
— and OLIVER, D. (eds.), *New Directions in Judicial Review* (1988).
— *The Changing Constitution* (Oxford, 2nd ed., 1989) (3rd ed., 1994).
JOWELL and WOOLF, *de Smith's Judicial Review & Administrative Action* (5th ed., 1995).
JUSTICE, *The Citizen and the Administration* (London, 1977).
— *The Local Ombudsman: A Review of the First Five Years* (London, 1980).
— *The Administration of the Courts* (London, Justice, 1986).
— *All Souls, Review of Administrative Law in the United Kingdom* (London, 1988).

KAPETYN, P.J.G., and VERLOREN VAN THEMAAT, *Introduction to the Law of the European Communities* (2nd ed. with Lawrence Gormley, 1989).

KAY, J., and SILBERSTROM, Z. (1984), "The New Industrial Policy: Privatisation and Competition", Midland Bank Review (Spring), 8–16.

KAY, J., and THOMPSON, D., "Privatisation: A Policy in Search of a Rationale", (1986) Economic Journal, 96: 18–32.

KAY, J., MAYER, C., and THOMPSON, D., *Privatisation and Regulation—the UK Experience* (Oxford, 1986, 2nd edition, 1994).

KAY, R., "Substance and Structure as Constitutional Protections", [1989] P.L. 428–39.

KEIR, D., and LAWSON, F.H., *Cases in Constitutional Law* (5th ed., Oxford University Press, 1967).

KELLNER, P., and CROWTHER-HUNT, LORD, *The Civil Servants* (1980).

KELLY, J.M., *A Short History of Western Legal Theory* (Oxford University Press, 1992).

KING, A., *The British Prime Minister* (2nd ed., Macmillan, 1985).

KISS, A., and Shelton, D., *Manual of European Environmental Law* (Grotius, Cambridge, 1993).

LASKI, H.J., *Studies in the Problem of Sovereignty* (London, 1917).
— *Authority in the Modern State* (New Haven, Conn., 1919).
— *The Foundations of Sovereignty and Other Essays* (London, 1921).
— *A Grammar of Politics* (1925: London, 5th ed., 1967).
— "The Growth of Administrative Discretion" (1923) 1 Journal of Public Admin. 92.
— "Judicial Review of Social Policy in England" (1926) 39 Harv. L.Rev. 839.
— "Report of the Committee on Ministers' Powers" Cmd. 4060, Annex V. 'Note by Prof. Laski on the judicial interpretation of statutes'.

LAW COMMISSION, *Administrative Law: Judicial Review and Statutory Appeals*, Consultation Paper No. 126 (HMSO, 1993).

LAW REFORM COMMISSION OF CANADA, *Towards a Modern Federal Administrative Law Consultation Paper* (Ottawa, 1987).
— *Policy Implementation, Compliance and Administrative Law*, Working Paper No. 51 (Ottawa, 1986).

LAWRENCE, R.J., *The Government of Northern Ireland: Public Finance and Public Services* (1965).

LAWSON, NIGEL, *The View from No. 11* (1992).

LEE, S., "Understanding Judicial Review as a Game of Chess" (1986) 102 L.Q.R. 493.

LEIGH, D., *Betrayed, The Real Story of the Matrix Churchill Trial* (London, 1993).

LEIGH, D., and VULLIAMY, Ed., *Sleaze* (Fourth Estate, 1997).

LEIGH, I., and LUSTGARTEN, L., "The Security Service Act 1989" (1989) 52 M.L.R. 801–40.

—   *In From the Cold: The Intelligence Services and National Security* (Oxford, 1994).

LESTER, A., *Democracy and Individual Rights* (London 1968).

—   "The Constitution: Decline and Renewal" in J. Jowell and D. Oliver (eds.), *The Changing Constitution* (Oxford, 1985), Chap. 12.

—   *et al.*, *A British Bill of Rights* (London, Institute of Public Policy Research, Consultation Paper No. 1, 1990).

LEWIS, N., and HARDEN, I. (1983), "Privatisation, De-Regulation and Constitutionality: Some Anglo-American Comparisons", Northern Ireland Legal Quarterly, 34: 207–21.

LEWIS, N., (ed), *Happy and Glorious: The Constitution in Transition* (London, 1990).

LEYLAND, P., WOODS, T., HARDEN, J., *Textbook on Administrative Law* (Blackstone, 1994).

LIEBERMAN, D., *The Province of Legislation Determined* (Cambridge, 1989).

LIKIERMAN, A., *Public Expenditure* (London, Penguin Books, 1988).

LIVELY, J., *Democracy* (1975).

LOBBAN, M., *The Common Law and English Jurisprudence 1760–1850* (Clarendon Press, Oxford, 1991).

LOCKE, J., *Two Treatises of Government* (1690) (P. Laslett ed., Cambridge, 1960).

LOUGHLIN, M., *Local Government in the Modern State* (London, 1986).

—   "Law, Ideologies and the Political-Administrative System" (1989) 16 Journal of Law & Society 21.

—   "Innovative Financing in Local Government: The Limits of Legal Instrumentalism" [1990] P.L. 372 (Pt. I); [1991] P.L. 568 (Pt. II).

—   *Public Law and Political Theory* (Oxford, 1992).

—   "The Pathways of Public Law Scholarship" in G.P. Wilson, (ed.), *Frontiers of Legal Scholarship* (John Wiley, 1996) pp. 163–188.

—   *Legality and Locality: The Role of Law in Central – Local Government Relations*, (Oxford) 1996.

LOVELAND, I., *Constitutional Law: A Critical Introduction* (Butterworths, 1996).

LUSTGARTEN, L., *Legal Control of Racial Discrimination* (Macmillan, 1980).

—   *The Governance of the Police* (London, Sweet and Maxwell, 1986).

MacCORMICK, N., "The Interest of the State and the Rule of Law", in P. Wallington and R. Merkin (eds.), *Essays in Memory of Professor F.H. Lawson* (London, 1986).

MacDONAGH, O., *Early Victorian Government* (1977).

—   *States of Mind: A Study of Anglo-Irish Conflict 1780–1980* (London, 1983).

McAUSLAN, P., *The Ideologies of Planning Law* (Oxford, 1980).

—   "The Plan, the Planners and the Lawyers" [1971] P.L. 247.

—   "Administrative Law, Collective Consumption and Judicial Policy" (1983) 46 M.L.R. 1.

—   "Dicey and his influence on public law" [1985] P.L. 721.

—   "Public Law and Public Choice" (1988) 51 M.L.R. 681.

—   and McELDOWNEY, J.F. (eds.), *Law, Legitimacy and the Constitution* (London, 1985).

—   "Legitimacy and the Constitution: the Dissonance between Theory and Practice" in McAuslan and McELDOWNEY (eds.), *Law, Legitimacy and the Constitution* (London, 1985).

McCABE, S., and WALLINGTON, P., *The Police, Public Order and Civil Liberties: Legacies of the Miners' Strike* (1988).

McCONVILLE, M., SANDERS, A., LENG, Roger, *The Case for the Prosecution* (Routledge, 1991).

McELDOWNEY, J.F., "The Contingencies Fund and the Parliamentary Scrutiny of Public Finance" [1988] P.L. 232–245.

—   "The National Audit Office and Privatisation" (1991) M.L.R. 933–955.

—   *The Electricity Industry Handbook* (John Wiley, Chancery, 1992).

—   "The Nationalisation Legislation of the 1940s and the Privatisation Legislation of the 1980s: A Constitutional Perspective", in R. Blackburn (ed.), *Constitutional Studies* (1992) pp. 42–64.

—   "Administrative Justice" in R. Blackburn (ed.), *Rights of Citizenship* (Mansell, 1993) Chap. 8, pp. 156–78.

—   "The Control of Public Expenditure" in Jowell and Oliver, (eds.), *The Changing Constitution* (3rd ed., 1994) pp. 175–207.

—   "Criminal Law and the development of Labour relations in Nineteenth-Century Ireland" in Hepple, Ewing and Gearty, *Feschrift in honour of Paul O'Higgins* (Mansell, 1994), chapter 12, pp. 267–93.

—   "Public utilities: Is the British experience a model for developing countries?" in Julio Faundez, (ed.), *Good Government and Law* (Macmillan in association with the British Council, 1997), pp. 147–62.

McELDOWNEY, J., and McELDOWNEY, S., *Environment and the Law* (Longman, 1996).

McELDOWNEY, J.F., and O'HIGGINS, P., (eds.), *The Common Law Tradition: Essays in Irish Legal History* (1990).

McCRUDDEN, C., and CHAMBERS, G., (eds.), *Individual Rights and the Law in Britain* (1993).

McCRUDDEN, C., "Northern Ireland and the British Constitution" in J. Jowell and D. Oliver (eds.), *The Changing Constitution* (2nd ed., 1989), pp. 297–344.

MACKINTOSH, John, P., *The British Cabinet* (3rd ed., 1977).

MAINE, H.S., *Ancient Law* (London, 1861).

— *Popular Government* (London, 1885).

MAITLAND, F.W., *The Constitutional History of England* (Cambridge, 1908).

— *Introduction to O. Von Gierke, Political Theories of the Middle Ages* (Cambridge, 1900).

— "The Body Politic" in H.A.L. Fisher (ed.), *The Collected Papers of Frederic William Maitland* (Cambridge, 1911), Vol. III.

MANSERGH, N., *The Government of Northern Ireland: A Study in Devolution* (1936).

— *The Irish Question 1840–1921* (1965).

MARRIOTT, J., *The Mechanism of the Modern State* (Oxford, 1927).

— *English Political Institutions* (Oxford, 4th ed., 1948).

MARSHALL, G., *Constitutional Conventions. The Rules and Forms of Political Accountability* (Oxford, 1984).

— (ed.), *Ministerial Responsibility* (Oxford University Press, 1989).

— and MOODIE, G.C., *Some Problems of the Constitution* (5th ed., 1971).

MATHER, G., "Clarifying Responsibility and Accountability; *Government Accountability* (CIPFA, 1996).

MAYER, C., and MEADOWCRAFT, S., "Selling Public Assets: Techniques and Financial Implications", in J. Kay, C. Mayer, and D. THOMPSON, *Privatisation and Regulation: The UK Experience* (Oxford, 1986).

MAYER, C., "Public Ownership: Concepts and Applications" (1987) Centre for Economic Policy Research Working Paper, Vol. 182.

METCALFE, Les and RICHARDS, S., *Improving Public Management* (2nd ed., 1990).

MICHAEL, J., *The Politics of Secrecy* (1982).

MIERS, D., and PAGE, A., *Legislation* (2nd ed., 1990).

MILIBAND, R., *Parliamentary Socialism* (London, 1961).

— *The State in Capitalist Society* (London, 1969).

— *Marxism and Politics* (Oxford, 1978).

— *Capitalist Democracy in Britain* (Oxford, 1982).

MILL, J.S., *On Liberty* (1859) (G. Himmelfarb (ed.), Harmondsworth, 1974).

—   *Auguste Comte and Positivism* (1865: Ann Arbor, Mich., 1961).

—   "Chapters on Socialism" (1879) 25 Fortnightly Review 226.

MILLER, C.J., *Contempt of Court* (2nd ed., 1989).

MILSOM, S.F.C., *Historical Foundations of the Common Law* (2nd ed., Butterworths, 1980).

MINOGUE, K., "What is Wrong with Rights" in C. Harlow (ed.), *Public Law and Politics* (London, 1986), Chap. 11.

MITCHELL, J.D., *Constitutional Law* (Edinburgh, 2nd ed., 1968).

—   "Reflections on Law and Orders" [1958] J.R. 19.

—   "The Flexible Constitution" [1960] P.L. 332.

—   "The Ombudsman Fallacy" [1962] P.L. 24.

—   "The causes and effects of the absence of a system of public law in the United Kingdom" [1965] P.L. 95.

—   "The irrelevance of the Ombudsman proposals" in D.C. Rowat (ed.), *The Ombudsman* (London, 1965).

—   "The state of public law in the United Kingdom" [1966] 15 I.C.L.Q. 133.

—   "The constitutional implications of judicial control of the administration in the United Kingdom" (1967) Camb. L.J. 46.

—   "Why European Institutions?" in L.J. Brinkhorst and J.D.B. Mitchell, *European Law and Institutions* (Edinburgh, 1969).

—   "The sovereignty of parliament and community law: the stumbling block that isn't there" (1979) Int. Affairs 33.

—   "What happened to the constitution on 1st January 1973?" (1980) Cambrian Law Rev. 69.

—   "Administrative Law and Policy Effectiveness" in J.A. Griffith (ed.), *From Policy to Administration: Essays in Honour of William A. Robson* (London, 1976).

MOORE, J., "Why Privatise?", in J. Kay, C. Mayer, and D. Thompson, *Privatisation and Regulation: The UK Experience* (Oxford, 1983).

MORRIS, G.S., *Strikes in Essential Services* (1986).

MOUNT, F., *The British Constitution Now* (1992).

MUNRO, C., *Studies in Constitutional Law* (Butterworths, 1987).

NATIONAL AUDIT OFFICE, *Resource Accounting and Budgeting in Government* 1994–5 H.C. 123.

NATIONAL AUDIT OFFICE, *The Work of the Directors of Telecommunications, Gas Supply, Water Service and Electricity Supply* 1995–6 H.C. 645.

NICOLSON, I.F., *The Mystery of Crichel Down* (1986).

NOLAN, LORD, *First Report of the Committee on Standards in Public Life* Cm. 2850, *Second Report of the Committee on Standards in Public Life* Cm. 3270–1.

NORMANTON, E.L., *The Accountability and Audit of Governments* (Manchester University Press, 1966).
NORTON, P., *The Constitution in Flux* (1982).

O'HIGGINS, P., *Cases and Materials on Civil Liberties* (London, 1988).
— *Censorship in Britain* (1972).
O'KEFFE, D., "The court of Auditors" in D. Curtin and T. Heukels (eds.) *Institutional Dynamics of European Integration* (Kluwer, London, 1994).
O'LEARY, B., "What should Public Lawyers Do?" (1992) 12 O.J.L.S. No. 3, pp. 304–18.
O'RIORDAN, T., KEMP, R., and PURDUE, M., *Sizewell B: An Anatomy of an Inquiry* (1988).
OLIVER, D., *Government in the United Kingdom* (Open University Press, 1991).
— and AUSTIN, R., "Political and Constitutional Aspects of the Westland Affair" (1987) 40 Parliamentary Affairs 20–40.
OLOWOFOYEKU, A., *Suing Judges* (Oxford, 1993).

PALLEY, C., *The Constitutional History and Law of Southern Rhodesia 1888–1965* (Oxford, 1979).
— *The Evolution, Disintegration and Possible Reconstruction of the Northern Ireland Constitution* (Barry Rose Publishers, 1972).
— *The United Kingdom and Human Rights* (Sweet and Maxwell, 1991).
PANNICK, D., *Sex Discrimination Law* (Oxford University Press, 1985).
PARRIS, H., *Constitutional Bureaucracy* (1969).
PEACOCK, A.T., and WISEMAN, J., *The Growth of Public Expenditure in the United Kingdom* (1961).
PEELE, G., *Governing the United Kingdom* (3rd ed., Blackwell, 1995).
PLANT, R., *The Plant Report* (1990).
PLIATZKY, L., *The Treasury under Mrs Thatcher* (Blackwell, 1989).
— *Getting and Spending* (Blackwell, revised edition, 1984).
POCOCK, J.G.A., *The Machiavellian Movement: Florentine Political Thought and the Atlantic Republican Tradition* (Princeton University Press, 1975).
POGANY, Istvan, "Privatisation and Regulatory Change in Hungary" in M. Moran, and T. Prosser, *Privatization and Regulatory Change in Europe* (Open University Press, 1994).
POLLACK, A., *A Citizen's Inquiry: The Opsahl Report on Northern Ireland* (Dublin, 1993).
POLLARD, D., and HUGHES, D., *Constitutional and Administrative Law* (Butterworths, 1990).

PORTER, Theodore, *The Rise of Statistical Thinking 1820–1900* (Princeton, 1986).

POUND, R., "Liberty of Contract" (1908–9) 18 Yale L.J. 454.

— "Law in Books and Law in Action" (1910) 44 American Law Rev. 12.

— "The Scope and Purpose of Sociological Jurisprudence" (1911) 24 Harv.L.Rev. 591; (1911) 25 Harv.L.Rev. 140; (1912) 25 Harv.L.Rev. 489.

— "The Call for a Realist Jurisprudence" (1931) 44 Harv.L.Rev. 697.

PRIEST, G.L., "The Common Law Process and the Selection of Efficient Rules" (1977) 6 Journal of Legal Studies 65.

PRIME MINISTER'S EFFICIENCY UNIT, *Improving Management in Government: the Next Steps* (London, 1988) (Ibbs Report).

PRIOR, J., *A Balance of Power* (London, 1986).

PROSSER, T., "Towards a Critical Public Law", Journal of Law and Society, (1982) 9: 1–19.

— *Nationalised Industries and Public Control* (Oxford, 1986).

RAWLINGS, H.F., *Law and the Electoral Process* (Sweet and Maxwell, 1988).

RAWLS, J., *A Theory of Justice* (Oxford, 1972).

— "Justice as Fairness: Political not Metaphysical" (1985) 14 Philosophy and Public Affairs 223.

— "The Idea of an Overlapping Consensus" (1987) 7 O.J.L.S. 1.

REDLICH, J. and HIRST, F., *A History of Local Government in England* (London, 1958).

REID, G., *The Politics of Financial Control* (1966).

REINER, R.

The Politics of the Police (2nd ed., 1992).

REPORTS., *Report of the Committee on Ministers' Powers* Cmd. 4060 (1932) (Donoughmore Report).

— *Report of the Committee on Tribunals and Enquiries* (1957) (Franks Report).

— *Report of the Royal Commission on Legal Services* (1980) Cmnd. 7448.

— *Report to the Scottish People by the Scottish Constitutional Convention, Towards Scotland's Parliament* (Edinburgh, 1990).

RIDLEY, N., "My Style of Government" (Fontana, 1992).

ROBERTS, D., *Victorian Origins of the British Welfare State* (1960).

ROBERTSON, G., *Freedom, the Individual and the Law* (7th ed., 1993).

ROBINSON, A., *Parliament and Public Spending—The Expenditure Committee 1970–76* (1978).

ROBSON, W.A., *Justice and Administrative Law* (London, 1928); (2nd ed., 1947); (3rd ed., 1951).
— *Public Administration Today* (London, 1948).
— "The Report of the Committee on Ministers' Powers" (1932) 3 Political Quarterly 346.
— "Administrative Law in England 1919–1948" in G. Campion (ed.), *British Government Since 1918* (London, 1950).
— "Administrative Justice and Injustice: A Commentary on the Franks Report" [1958] P.L. 12.
— "Administrative Law" in M. Ginsberg (ed.), *Law and Opinion in England in the Twentieth Century* (London, 1959).
— "Justice and Administrative Law reconsidered" (1979) 32 Current Legal Problems 107.
ROSE, R., *The Problem of Party Government* (1974).
ROSEVEARE, H., *The Treasury* (1969).
RUDDEN, B., WYATT, D., (eds.), *Basic Community Laws* (Oxford, 6th ed., 1996).

SAS, B., "Regulation of the Privatised Electricity Supply Industry" (1990) 53 M.L.R. 485.
SCARMAN, L., *English Law—The New Dimension* (London, 1975).
SCHERMERS, H.G., and WAELBROECK, D., *Judicial Protection in the European Communities* (5th ed., 1992).
SCHWARTZ, L.B., and WADE, H., *Legal Control of Government* (Oxford, 1972).
SCOTT Report: *Return to an Address of the Honourable House of Commons dated 15th February 1996. Report of the Inquiry into the Export of Defence Equipment and Dual-use Goods to Iraq and Related Prosecutions* The Rt Hon. Sir Richard Scott, The Vice-Chancellor H.C. 115 (HMSO, London, 1996).
SEDLEY, S., "Now you see it, Now you don't: Judicial Discretion and Judicial Review" Warwick Law Working Papers, August 1987, Vol. 8, No. 4.
SELF, P., *Political Theories of Modern Government* (1985).
SHARPE, R.J., *The Law of Habeas Corpus* (2nd ed., 1989).
SHELL, D., *The House of Lords* (2nd ed., 1992).
SHELL, D., and BEAMISH, D., *The House of Lords at Work* (Oxford, 1993).
SKIDELSKY, R., *Politicians and the Slump: the Labour Government of 1929–31* (London, 1967).
— *John Maynard Keynes* (London, 1983).
SKINNER, Q., *The Foundation of Modern Political Thought* (2 Vols., Cambridge University Press, 1982).
SMITH, L.B., "Accountability and Independence in the Contract State", in B. Smith, and D. Hague (eds.), *The Dilema of Accountability in Modern Government* (London, 1971).

SNYDER, F., *New Directions in European Communities Law* (1990).

STEIN, P., and SHAND, J., *Legal Values in Western Society* (Edinburgh University Press, 1974).

STEINER, J., "Direct Applicability in EEC Law: A Chameleon Concept", (1982) L.Q.R. 98, 229–48.

— "How to Make the Action Suit the Case" (1987) 12 E.L.Rev. 102–22.

— *Textbook on EEC Law* (Blackstone Press, 1988).

STEVENS, R., *The Independence of the Judiciary* (Oxford, 1993).

STEWART, A., *Rethinking Housing Law* (Sweet and Maxwell, 1996).

STONE, R., *Textbook on Civil Liberties* (1993).

SUGARMAN, D., "Legal Theory, the Common Law Mind and the Making of the Textbook Tradition" in W. Twining (ed.), *Legal Theory and Common Law* (Oxford, 1986), Chap. 3.

— "The Legal Boundaries of Liberty: Dicey, Liberalism and Legal Science" (1983) M.L.R. 102.

SUMMERS, R.S., *Instrumentalism and American Legal Theory* (Ithaca, 1982).

SUNKIN, M., "What is happening to applications for judicial review?" (1987) 50 M.L.R. 432.

SUNKIN, M., and Bridges, Lee, & Meszaros, G., *Judicial Review* (The Public Law Project, 1993).

SUPPERSTONE, M., and GOUDIE, J., (ed.), *Judicial Review* (1991).

THAIN, C., "The Education of the Treasury: The Medium Term Financial Strategy, 1980–84", (1985) 63 Public Administration, 261–85.

— and Wright, M., "Planning and Controlling Public Expenditure in the United Kingdom (Part 1). The Treasury's Public Expenditure Survey" (1992) 70 Public Admin. 3–24; and part II, (1992) 70 Public Admin. 193–224.

THATCHER, M., *The Downing Street Years* (1993).

THIO, S.M., *Locus Standi and Judicial Review* (1971).

THOMPSON, B., *Textbook on Constitutional and Administrative Law* (1993).

THOMPSON, E.P., *Whigs and Hunters* (Harmondsworth, 1975).

— *Writing By Candlelight* (London, 1980).

THORNHILL, W., (ed.), *The Modernisation of British Government* (1975).

TOMKINS, A., "Public Interest Immunity after Matrix Churchill" [1993] P.L. 650.

TOMKINS, C., *Issues in Public Sector Accounting* (1984).

TOMLINSON, J., *Public Policy and the Economy Since 1900* (Oxford, 1900).

TOWNSHEND, C., *Political Violence in Ireland* (Oxford, 1985).

TREASURY AND CIVIL SERVICE COMMITTEE, Eighth Report, Session 1987–88, *Civil Service Management Reform: The Next Steps*, H.C. 494.

TURPIN, C., *Government Contracts* (London, 1972).
— "Public Contracts in the EEC" [1972] C.M.L.R. 9: 411.
TURPIN, C., *British Government and the Constitution* (London, 1995).
— *Government Procurement and Contracts* (1989).

VAN CAENEGEM, R.C., *An Historical Introduction to Western Constitutional Law* (Cambridge University Press, 1995).
VELJANOVSKI, C., *Selling the State* (London, 1987).
— (ed.), *Privatisation and Competition* (London, 1989).
VIBERT, F. (ed.), *Britain's Constitutional Future* (London, Institute of Economic Affairs, 1991).
VICKERS, J., and YARROW, G., *Privatisation and the Natural Monopolies* (London, 1985).
— *Privatisation: An Economic Analysis* (Boston, 1988).
VILE, M.J.C., *Constitutionalism and the Separation of Power* (Oxford, 1967).

WADE, E.C.S. and PHILLIPS, G.G., *Constitutional and Administrative Law* (London, 1931; 11th ed., 1993 by A.W. Bradley and K. Ewing).
WADE, H.W.R., *Administrative Law* (Oxford, 6th ed., 1988).
— *Constitutional Fundamentals* (London, 1980).
WADE, H.W.R., "The Concept of Legal Certainty. A Preliminary Sketch" (1940–1) 4 M.L.R. 183.
— "Quasi-judicial and its background" (1949) 10 Camb. L.J. 216.
— "The Twilight of Natural Justice" (1951) 67 L.Q.R. 103.
— "The Basis of Legal Sovereignty" (1955) Camb. L.J. 172.
— "Law, Opinion and Administration" (1962) 78 L.Q.R. 188.
— "Unlawful administrative action—void or voidable" (1967) 83 L.Q.R. 499 (Pt. I); (1968) 84 L.Q.R. 95 (Pt. II).
— "Sovereignty and the European Communities" (1972) 88 L.Q.R. 1.
— "Procedure and Prerogative in Public Law" (1985) 101 L.Q.R. 180.
— "What has happened to the Sovereignty of Parliament?" (1991) 107 L.Q.R. 1.
WALKER, C., *The Prevention of Terrorism in British Law* (2nd ed., 1992).
WALKER, D.M., *The Scottish Legal System* (5th ed., 1981) (6th ed., 1992).
WALLER, R., "The 1983 Boundary Commission: Policies and Effects" (1983) Vol. 4 Electoral Studies, 195.
WALSH, K., *Competitive Tendering for Local Authority Services* (HMSO, 1989).
WASS, D., *Government and the Governed* (1984).
WEATHERILL, S., and BEAUMONT, P., *EC Law* (Penguin, 1993).

WEBB, S. & B., *History of the Pool Law* (1929).
— *English Local Government* (1906).
WHEARE, K.C., *Modern Constitutions* (2nd ed., 1966).
WHISH, R., *Competition Law* (London, 1989).
WICHERT, S., *Northern Ireland Since 1945* (London, 1992).
WILDAVSKY, A., and ZAPICO-GONI, E., (eds.) *National Budgeting for Economic and Monetary Union* (Institute of Public Administration, London, 1994).
WILLIAMS, D.G.T., *Not in the Public Interest* (1965).
— *Keeping the Peace* (1967).
— "Public local inquiries-formal administrative adjudication" (1980) 29 Int. & Comp. L.Q. 701.
— "The Donoughmore Report in Retrospect" (1982) 60 Public Admin. 273.
— "The Council on Tribunals: the first twenty five years" [1984] P.L. 79.
WILLSON, F.M.G., *The Organization of British Central Government, 1914–1964* (2nd ed., 1968).
WILSON, G.P., *Cases and Materials on Constitutional and Administrative Law* (Cambridge, 1978).
WILSON, J., "The Rise of the Bureaucratic State" (1975) 41 Pub. Int. 77.
WINCH, D., and BURROW, J., *That Noble Science of Politics: A Study in Nineteenth Century Intellectural History* (Cambridge, 1983).
WOODHOUSE, D., "Ministerial Responsibility: Something Old, Something New [1997] *Public Law* 262.
WOOLF, H., "Public law-private law: Why the divide?" [1986] P.L. 220.
— *Protection of the Public—A New Challenge?* (London, Stevens, 1990).
WRAITH, R.E., and LAMB, G.B., *Public Inquiries as an Instrument of Government* (1971).
WRIGHT, M., *Treasury Control of the Civil Service 1854–1974* (Oxford, 1969).
WYATT, D., and DASHWOOD, A., *The Substantive Law of the EEC* (3rd ed., 1993).

YOUNG, H., *One of Us* (Macmillan, 1991).

ZANDER, M., *A Bill of Rights?* (London, 3rd ed., 1985).
— *The Police and Criminal Evidence Act 1984* (2nd ed., 1984).
ZELLICK, G., *Final Report of the Task Force on Student Disciplinary Procedures* chaired by Professor Graham Zellick, CVCP, December 1994.

INDEX

WITHDRAWN

PUBLIC LAW